Ernst H Kantorowicz.

SELECTED STUDIES

by

ERNST H. KANTOROWICZ

J. J. AUGUSTIN PUBLISHER · LOCUST VALLEY, NEW YORK

1965

Distributed by
J. J. Augustin, Publisher
Locust Valley, New York

Library of Congress Catalog Card Number 65–25431
Printed in Germany *at* J. J. Augustin, Glückstadt

D. M.

ERNESTI H. KANTOROWICZ

MAGISTRORUM MAGISTRI
DISCIPULORUM DISCIPULI
AMICORUM AMICI

VITAM AMAVIT MORTEM NON TIMUIT

EDITORIAL REMARKS

Some months before Ernst H. Kantorowicz died (September, 1963), he was persuaded by friends to plan a volume comprising reprints of some of his essays and articles. The selection which he made for this purpose has been kept in this volume, and the publication has been carried out by the generosity of the Institute for Advanced Study. Our first thanks go to the director of the Institute, Dr. Robert Oppenheimer, for his support and counsel.

Had Professor Kantorowicz himself seen this volume through the press, many essays would have been revised or augmented by the addition of new material; but, as it is, while the phrasing has been changed here and there and small errors—in a name, for example, or a date—have been corrected, no alterations of the original arguments have been made. Still, the simple fact of typographical re-setting has introduced new pagination and sometimes also new numbers for footnotes or figures; and, since these things can be troublesome to readers who come to this volume with references to the pages, notes, or figures of the original imprints, we offer these principles of correspondence of our text with the earlier publications:

The *pagination of the original imprint* has been supplied at the top of our pages: the italicized numbers in brackets indicate where the first word on our page occurred in the original imprint.

The *style of footnotes* has been standardized. This has entailed considerable change in the manner of citation originally used in some essays, but the consistency which has been achieved should obviate the confusion which would have resulted from putting between the covers of this book the mélange of styles which were employed by the different journals in which the essays first appeared. The use of standard abbreviations should bring some advantage also (see p. xv).

The *numbering of footnotes* is the same, with the exception of essays where originally the notes were numbered anew on each page; these numbers have now been made consecutive throughout the essay. Since the original pagination has been roughly provided, the original references to page and note should not be difficult to locate.

The *illustrations* are life-size for those objects which it would seem possible to represent in full dimension (*viz.*: coins and medals, amulets, gems and tessera, manuscript illuminations and book illustrations), unless they are found labeled enlarged or reduced. See also the heading of the Indexed List of Illustrations (page 409) for further remarks.

The illustrations in the present volume are markedly superior to those in the original imprints. Original photographs were gathered for most of the 160-odd figures, and the collotype rendition by the Meriden Gravure Company excels the original publications in most instances and is inferior in none.

The Providentia-Medusa coin decorating the title page was Kantorowicz's *Ex-Libris*. It is an *aureus* of Septimius Severus, and our reproduction (in half-tone process) has been enlarged to half again the actual size. The specimen illustrated is the one formerly in the Collection Belfort, published in the catalogue of the sale of the *Montague Collection* (Paris: April, 1896), Pl. XVI, No. 483.

The colleagues of Professor Kantorowicz in the Institute for Advanced Study and many of his friends in Europe and America helped to procure the illustrative material or gave advice on technical aspects of preparing this book. We are particularly indebted to the following: to Professor Erwin Panofsky, who composed the dedicatory inscription; to Professors Andreas Alföldi, Henri Seyrig, and Kurt Weitzmann, who provided many photographs or informed us about the present-day location of many objects, and doubly to the last-named for his expert advice on the make-up of the plates; to Professors Felix Gilbert and Ihor Ševčenko, who read the proof of the essays written in German, and again to the latter for reviewing the passages in Greek and conferring with us on many problems. Finally, we extend our special thanks to Professor Harold Cherniss, whose initiative and judicious opinions helped shape this volume.

Michael Cherniavsky
Ralph E. Giesey

TABLE OF CONTENTS

ERNST H. KANTOROWICZ

BIBLIOGRAPHY OF WRITINGS

The author drew up this bibliography not long before his death. He did not include occasional writings, such as newspaper articles, but some of these are mentioned by Yakov Malkiel, "Ernst H. Kantorowicz," *Romance Philology*, XVIII (1964), 1–15.

Starred items (*) are reprinted in this book.

1. *Das Wesen der muslimischen Handwerkerverbände.* Dissertation (typescript); Heidelberg, 1921.

2. *Kaiser Friedrich der Zweite.* Berlin: Georg Bondi, 1927. 651 pp. [Known as Vol. I, and the *Ergänzungsband*, below, No. 7, as Vol. II.]

3. ——. English translation by E. O. Lorimer: *Frederick the Second.* London: Constable, 1931. [*Ergänzungsband* not included.]

4. ——. Italian translation by Maria Offergeld Merlo; *Federico II di Svevia.* Milano: Garzanti, 1939. 2 vols. [*Ergänzungsband* not included.]

5. Review of Antonio de Stefano, *L'Idea imperiale di Federico II* (Florence, 1927), in *Historische Zeitschrift*, CXL (1929), 449–450.

6. "Mythenschau," *Historische Zeitschrift*, CXLI (1930), 457–471.

7. *Kaiser Friedrich der Zweite: Ergänzungsband.* Berlin: Georg Bondi, 1931. 336 pp. [Cf. Nos. 2–4.]

8. "Deutsches Papsttum," in *Vom Schicksal des deutschen Geistes* (Berlin: Verlag Die Runde, 1935) 42–57; cf. *Castrum Peregrini*, XI (1953), 7–24.

*9. "Petrus de Vinea in England," *Mitteilungen des Österreichischen Instituts für Geschichtsforschung*, LI (1937), 43–88.

*10. *Die Wiederkehr gelehrter Anachorese im Mittelalter.* Stuttgart: Kohlhammer, 1937. 13 pp.

*11. "The Este Portrait by Roger van der Weyden," *Journal of the Warburg and Courtauld Institutes*, III (1939–40), 165–180.

12. "A Norman Finale of the Exultet and the Rite of Sarum," *Harvard Theological Review*, XXXIV (1941), 129–143.

*13. "Plato in the Middle Ages," *The Philosophical Review*, LI (1942), 312–323. [A review of Raymund Klibansky, *The Continuity of the Platonic Tradition during the Middle Ages* (London, 1939), and *PLATO LATINUS*, Vol. I: *Meno interprete Henrico Aristippo*, ed. Victor Kordeuter (London, 1940).]

14. "Ivories and Litanies," *Journal of the Warburg and Courtauld Institutes*, V (1942), 56–81.

*15. "*Anonymi 'Aurea Gemma'*," *Medievalia et Humanistica*, I (1943), 41–57.

*16. "An 'Autobiography' of Guido Faba," *Medieval and Renaissance Studies*, I (1943), 253–280.

17. "A Diplomatic Mission of Francis Accursius and his Oration before Pope Nicholas III," *English Historical Review*, LVIII (1943), 424–447. [Together with George L. Haskins.]

*18. "The Problem of Medieval World Unity," *American Historical Association, Annual Report for 1942*, III (Washington, 1944), 31–37.

*19. "The 'King's Advent' and the Enigmatic Panels in the Doors of Santa Sabina," *Art Bulletin*, XXVI (1944), 207–231.

20. *Laudes Regiae: A Study in Liturgical Acclamations and Mediaeval Ruler Worship*. (University of California Publications in History, XXXIII.) Berkeley and Los Angeles: University of California Press, 1946. 292 pp.

21. ——. *Notes on the* Christus vincit *Legend on Coins*. Berkeley and Los Angeles: University of California Press, 1946. [Reprint of Chapter 1 (pp. 1–12) and Appendix II (pp. 222–230) of *Laudes Regiae*.]

22. "How the Pre-Hitler German Universities Were Run," *Western College Association: Addresses of 1945* (Fall Meeting, November 10, 1945, Mills College, California), 3–7.

*23. "The Quinity of Winchester," *Art Bulletin*, XXIX (1947), 73–85.

24. Review of Eleanor Shipley Duckett, *Anglo-Saxon Saints and Scholars* (New York, 1947), in *Classical Philology*, XLIII (1948), 265–266.

25. "Christus-Fiscus," in *Synopsis: Festgabe für Alfred Weber* (Heidelberg, 1948), 223–235.

26. Review of Reto R. Bezzola, *Les origines et la formation de la littérature courtoise en Occident: 500–1200* (Paris, 1944), in *Comparative Literature*, I (1949), 84–87.

27. Introduction to Luis Weckmann, *Las Bulas Alejandrinas de 1493 y la Teoría Política del Papado Medieval* (Mexico City, 1949), 7–11.

28. *The Fundamental Issue: Documents and Marginal Notes on the University of California Loyalty Oath*. San Francisco: Parker Printing Co., 1950. 40 pp.

*29. "*Pro patria mori* in Medieval Political Thought," *American Historical Review*, LVI (1951), 472–492.

30.   Review of Leonardo Olschki, *The Myth of Felt* (Berkeley and Los Angeles, 1949), in *Romance Philology*, IV (1951), 281–284.

*31. "Dante's 'Two Suns'," in *Semitic and Oriental Studies Presented to William Popper* (University of California Publications in Semitic Philology, XI; Berkeley and Los Angeles, 1951), 217–231.

32.   Review of Eudes de Deuil, *La Croisade de Louis VII, Roi de France*, ed. Henry Waquet (Paris, 1949), in *Romance Philology*, V (1952), 321–322.

33.   "Der Gastfreund," in *Albrecht Bernstorff zum Gedächtnis* (Munich, 1952), 53–56.

34.   Review of *Martini episcopi Bracarensis opera omnia*, ed. Claude W. Barlow (Papers and Monographs of the American Academy in Rome, XII; New Haven, 1950), in *American Journal of Archaeology*, LVI (1952), 229–230.

*35. "Kaiser Friedrich II und das Königsbild des Hellenismus," in *Varia Variorum: Festgabe für Karl Reinhardt* (Münster-Köln, 1952), 169–193.

*36. "*Deus per naturam, deus per gratiam:* A Note on Mediaeval Political Theology," *Harvard Theological Review*, XLV (1952), 253–277.

*37. "ΣΥΝΘΡΟΝΟΣ ΔΙΚΗΙ," *American Journal of Archaeology*, LVII (1953), 65–70.

*38. "Inalienability: A Note on Canonical Practice and the English Coronation Oath in the Thirteenth Century," *Speculum*, XXIX (1954), 488–502.

*39. "Mysteries of State: An Absolutist Concept and its Late Mediaeval Origins," *Harvard Theological Review*, XLVIII (1955), 65–91.

40.   ——. Spanish Translation by Rodriguez Aranda: "Secretos de Estado," *Revista de Estudios Politicos*, LXV (1959), 37–70.

41.   "*Invocatio Nominis Imperatoris:* On vv. 21–25 of Cielo d'Alcamo's *Contrasto*," *Bollettino del Centro di Studi filologici e linguistici Siciliani*, III (1955), 35–50.

42.   (Co-editor) *Late Classical and Mediaeval Studies in Honor of Albert Mathias Friend, Jr.*, ed. Kurt Weitzmann *et al.* Princeton: Princeton University Press, 1955.

*43. "The Carolingian King in the Bible of San Paola fuori le mura," *Late Classical and Mediaeval Studies* (see No. 42), 287–300.

44.   Review of Johan Huizinga, *Geschichte und Kultur: Gesammelte Aufsätze*, ed. Kurt Köster (Stuttgart, 1954), in *American Historical Review*, LX (1955), 853–855.

45.   "The Baptism of the Apostles," *Dumbarton Oaks Papers*, IX–X (1956), 204–251.

46.   "Feudalism in the Byzantine Empire," in *Feudalism in History*, ed. Rushton Coulborn (Princeton, 1956), 151–166.

*47. "Zu den Rechtsgrundlagen der Kaisersage," *Deutsches Archiv*, XIII (1957), 115–150.

*48. "The Prologue to Fleta and the School of Petrus de Vinea," *Speculum*, XXXII (1957), 231–249.

*49. "On Transformations of Apolline Ethics," in *CHARITES: Studien zur Altertums-wissenschaft* [Festschrift Ernst Langlotz], ed. Konrad Schauenburg (Bonn, 1957), 265–274.

50. *The King's Two Bodies: A Study in Mediaeval Political Theology.* Princeton: Princeton University Press, 1957. 568 pp.

51. Review of Charles Till Davis, *Dante and the Idea of Rome* (Oxford, 1957), in *Speculum,* XXXIV (1959), 103–109.

*52. "The Archer in the Ruthwell Cross," *Art Bulletin,* XLII (1960), 57–59.

53. "On the Golden Marriage Belt and the Marriage Rings of the Dumbarton Oaks Collection," *Dumbarton Oaks Papers,* XIV (1960), 2–16.

*54. "Kingship under the Impact of Scientific Jurisprudence," in *Twelfth-Century Europe and the Foundations of Modern Society,* ed. M. Clagett, G. Post, and R. Reynolds (Madison, Wisconsin, 1961), 89–111.

*55. "The Sovereignty of the Artist: A Note on Legal Maxims and Renaissance Theories of Art," in *De Artibus Opuscula XL: Essays in Honor of Erwin Panofsky,* ed. Millard Meiss (New York, 1961), 267–279.

*56. "Gods in Uniform," *Proceedings of the American Philosophical Society,* CV (1961), 368–393.

*57. "*Puer exoriens:* On the Hypapante in the Mosaics of S. Maria Maggiore," in *Perennitas: P. Thomas Michels OSB zum 70. Geburtstag,* ed. Hugo Rahner SJ and Emmanuel von Severus OSB (Beiträge zur Geschichte des Alten Mönchtums und des Benediktinerordens, Supplementband 2; Münster, 1963), 118–135.

58. "*Oriens Augusti — Lever du Roi,*" *Dumbarton Oaks Papers,* XVII (1963), 119–177.

59. "*Constantinus Strator:* Marginalien zum Constitutum Constantini," in *Mullus: Festschrift Theodor Klauser,* ed. Alfred Streiber and Alfred Hermann (Jahrbuch für Antike und Christentum, Ergänzungsband 1; Münster, 1964), 181–189.

60. Review of Walter Ullmann, *Principles of Government and Politics in the Middle Ages* (New York, 1961), in *Speculum,* XXXIX (1964), 344–351.

ABBREVIATIONS

AHR	*American Historical Review.*
BF	Böhmer, *Regesta Imperii* V, 1–2. Hrsg. v. J. Ficker, Innsbruck, 1881–82.
BFW	Böhmer, *Regesta Imperii* V, 3–5. Hrsg. v. J. Ficker und E. Winkelmann, Innsbruck, 1892–1901.
BZ	*Byzantinische Zeitschrift.*
CIL	*Corpus Inscriptionum Latinarum.*
Clm.	Codices latines monachensis (Munich, Staatsbibl. MSS).
CSEL	*Corpus Scriptorum Ecclesiasticorum Latinorum.*
DA	*Deutsches Archiv für Erforschung* [formerly: *Geschichte*] *des Mittelalters.*
DACL	*Dictionnaire d'archéologie chrétienne et de liturgie.*
EHR	*English Historical Review.*
H-B	Huillard-Bréholles, *Historia diplomatica Friderici Secundi.*
HZ	*Historische Zeitschrift.*
MGH	*Monumenta Germaniae Historica*, various series.
MÖIG	*Mitteilungen des Österreichischen Instituts für Geschichtsforschung.*
NA	*Neues Archiv.*
PdV	Petrus de Vinea, *Epistolarum . . . libri VI*, ed. Basel, 1740, 2 vols.
PG	Migne, *Patrologia Graeca.*
PL	Migne, *Patrologia Latina.*
P	Potthast, *Regesta Pontificum Romanorum.*
QF[i]AB	*Quellen und Forschungen aus italienischen Archiven und Bibliotheken.*
RAC	*Reallexikon für Antike and Christentum.*
RE	Pauly, Wissowa, *et al.*, *Realencyclopädie der classischen Altertumswissenschaft.*

ΣΥΝΘΡΟΝΟΣ ΔΙΚΗΙ

JULIANUS, Prefect of Egypt under Justinian I, addressed one of his very many poems to Tetianus, a high official of the empire. Tetianus had refused to accept the governorship of some distressed areas which the emperor had offered to him, and the poet praised that decision. Tetianus (said he) wished to enjoy his inherited fortune and increase it righteously, and he wished no more. For, "Justice, enthroned beside you, knows (σύνθρονος οἶδε Δίκη) that you loathe to touch wealth won from those that you rule."[1] In Didyma several inscriptions were dedicated to the Proconsul Festus who, in or around A.D. 263, had accomplished some public works. One of his improvements by which he obliged the citizens was the new setting of a fountain which Apollo, miraculously, had caused to gush forth when Gothic barbarians were besieging the city while the town people were parched with thirst. The waters had been sacred to the god; "now, however, (expounds an epigram) this has become the fountain of Festus, throne-sharer of golden Dike" (τὰ νῦν δὲ Φήστου συνθρόνου χρυσῆς Δίκης).[2] A related idea is expressed in an epigram in which a Pretorian Prefect under Justin II is styled "coachman of the throne of Dike" (Δίκης θρόνον ἡνιοχεύων).[3] There is a shift within the metaphor when another governor is called "son of the gold-crowned and right-minded Dike" (τῆς χρυσοστεφάνοιο νοήμονος υἱέα Δίκης).[4] Nevertheless, that, too, forms part of the large number of epigrams for Roman provincial governors which acclaim the justice of the governing official and which have been recently collected and brilliantly discussed by Louis Robert.[5]

Throne-sharing with Dike, of course, was not a new feature. Dike, a daughter of Zeus, sat at the side of the father of gods and men, at whose other side we often find Themis.[6] The two goddesses became also the natural throne-companions of kings, especially when the Hellenistic political philosophies conceived of the king as μιμητής of the supreme god.[7] Dio of Prusa, for example, calls Kingship "the child of Zeus the King" (Διὸς βασιλέως

Reprinted, with permission, from *American Journal of Archaeology*, LVII (1953), 65–70.

[1] *Greek Anthology* 9.445, ed. and trsl. W. R. Paton, III, 249.

[2] *Supplementum epigraphicum graecum*, red. J. J. E. Hondius, IV (1929), No. 467.

[3] *Greek Anthology* 9.779, Paton, III, 421, who forgot to translate these words.

[4] *P. Berlin*, 10580, line 30; *Berliner Klassikertexte*, V (1907), 118.

[5] Louis Robert, *Hellenica*, IV (Paris, 1948), dedicates practically the whole volume to governor inscriptions, disclosing thereby one of the most fruitful sources for the knowledge of political thought. Practically all the epigrams quoted in the present short paper have been discussed by him; for those quoted above, see 25f, 68f, 74f, 98, n. 2.

[6] Thalheim, "Dike," *RE*, 5.574; Rudolf Hirzel, *Themis, Dike und Verwandtes* (Leipzig, 1907).

[7] Erwin R. Goodenough, "The Political Philosophy of Hellenistic Kingship," *Yale Classical Studies*, I (1928), 55–102; Louis Delatte, *Les traités de la royauté d'Ecphante, Diotogène et Sthénidas* (Liège, 1942), Index, *s.v.* "imitation"; Norman H. Baynes, "Eusebius and the Christian Empire," *Mélanges Bidez* (Annuaire de l'Institut de Philologie et d'Histoire orientales et Slaves, 2; 1934), 13–18.

ἔκγονος), and at her sides there were seated Dike and Eirene as well as Eunomia, while Nomos as chief adviser and counsellor was standing nearest to her throne.[8] Occasionally a philosopher might claim that "Zeus himself *was* Dike and Themis and the oldest and ultimate Law," and might therefore accord a similar absolutistic character also to the king. However, more moderate doctrines prevailed: one understood Dike and other Virtues as the king's throne-sharing companions though admitting the king's identity with the Law as νόμος ἔμψυχος.[9] Finally, what applied to the king applied also to the governors, especially when Diocletian's separation of civil and military administrations turned the governors primarily into judges *qui iustitiam vestram (sc. imperatoris) iudices aemulantur.*[10] Hence, it was only after the middle of the third century of our era that epigrams began to praise governors as σύνθρονοι Δίκη (or Δίκης).[11]

The word σύνθρονος, a relatively rare word in classical Greek, appears more often in Hellenistic, late Roman, and Christian times. That gods were said to share their thrones with other gods and demigods, or with kings, heroes, and philosophers, was not only a peculiarity of the pagan ages. Christ as Man became the σύνθρονος of the Father, the Holy Spirit that of Father and Son; Adam was created σύνθρονος of God; the Apostles became throne-sharers of the Redeemer, and the Redeemed were expected to share with Christ the Throne of Eternity.[12] "Throne-sharing" there was also in a less cultual and more figurative or moral sense. Philo, for example, considered Dikaiosyne and Phronesis together with the other Virtues the σύνθρονοι of the Soul, and Origen called the same Virtues "throne-sharers" of Eusebeia who herself had her abode in the soul of the pious who turned towards God.[13]

Do we have to understand the governors' throne-sharing with Dike, as divulged by the epigrams, in a figurative and moral sense, or do we have to take into consideration some cultual substratum? The cultual meaning seems to be favored by W. Vollgraff. He refers to a number of epigram inscriptions mentioning a "Temple of Dike," and like others before him he takes those expressions (τέμενος, πρόθυρα Δίκης, also ἀγχίθυρος ... Δίκης, and others) to mean real shrines of the goddess Dike in front of which "the Greeks

---

[8] Dio Chrysostom, *Oratio* 1.73ff; cf. V. Valdenberg, "La théorie monarchique de Dion Chrysostome," *Revue des études grecques*, XL (1927), 159; cf. 148f, for the imitation of Zeus. For other examples as well as for the whole problem, see Arnold Ehrhardt, "The Political Philosophy of Neo-Platonism," *Studi in onore di Vincenzo Arangio-Ruiz* (Naples, 1952), I, 457–482, whose interesting study came too late to be utilized here.

[9] See Plutarch, *Alexander* 52.4, and *Ad princ. inerud.* 4 (*Moralia*, 781B), for the theories of Anaxarchos; also Themistios, *Oratio* 9.123a, Dindorf, 147,4 (to Valentinian II); further, A. Steinwenter, "ΝΟΜΟΣ ΕΜΨΥΧΟΣ: Zur Geschichte einer politischen Theorie," *Anzeiger der Akademie der Wissenschaften in Wien*, No. 19 (1946), 250–268.

[10] *Paneg. lat.* 2 (10), 3, Baehrens, p. 265, 15f; see Robert, 107ff, in his brief but comprehensive résumé. The phrase *vice sacra iudicans*, frequently found in inscriptions of that time, has the same meaning; cf. Glanville Downey, "Personifications of Abstract Ideas in the Antioch Mosaics," *Trans. Amer. Philol. Ass.*, LXIX (1938), 349–363.

[11] For the alternative construction σύνθρονος τῷδε ⟨καὶ⟩ τοῦδε, see *Scholia in Dionysii Thracis artem grammaticam*, ed. Alfred Hilgard (Leipzig, 1901), p. 389, n. 2 (marginal note on the *Scholia Marciana*).

[12] I shall discuss the material in detail, including the theological aspects, in a forthcoming study: "Σύνθρονος: God and King as Throne-Sharers." For a related subject, see Arthur D. Nock, "Σύνναος θεός," *Harvard Studies in Classical Philology*, XLI (1930), 1–62.

[13] Philo, *Legum allegoriae* 3.247, c. 88, Cohn-Wendland, I, 168: δικαιοσύνη καὶ φρόνησις καὶ οἱ σύνθρονοι ταύτης [τῆς ψυχῆς] ἀρεταί. A similar idea is found in Cicero, *ad Q. fratrem* 1.1.31: "tuas virtutes consecratas et in deorum numero collocatas vides," quoted by Nock, *op.cit.*, 58, note. Origen, *Cels.* 3.50, Koetschau, I, 246, 19: τὰς συνθρόνους ταύτης [τῆς εὐσεβείας] ἀρετάς. Figuratively the word is used also in the *Greek Anthology*, 12.257.8: σύνθρονος ἵδρυμαι τέρμασιν εὐμαθίας. A related meaning seems to be indicated by the enumeration of virtues in inscriptions; cf. Downey, *op.cit.*, 352ff.

of the fourth century had the custom to erect statues of the proconsuls whom they intended to honor."[14] Special sanctuaries of Dike were practically unknown in classical times, and their very existence has been inferred chiefly from the late epigrams of the fourth century and thereafter.[15] However, we may reasonably have our doubts whether in Christian times, as late as the latter half of the sixth century, for example, a statue for Justin II ἐν προθύροισι Δίκης, or for his Empress Sophia Δίκης προπάροιθε θυράων, should really suggest the existence of genuine temples of Dike consisting in (as Vollgraff assumed) "un édifice rond de dimensions modestes."[16] Although Vollgraff does not enlarge specifically on the subject of throne-sharing, we may nevertheless deduce that the person whose statue was placed in front of these alleged temples of Dike could be styled with some justification, and with reference to the temple, a σύνναος or σύνθρονος Δίκης.

Louis Robert, who has inspected the inscriptions for governors more thoroughly than any other scholar, arrives at a slightly different result. While rejecting the thesis of those little round sanctuaries of Dike, he makes it quite plausible that τέμενος Δίκης and similar expressions refer simply to the *praetorium* or to the basilica where the governor sat in court and rendered justice: "C'est là que siège le gouverneur, σύνθρονος Δίκης." He admits, of course, that the statues of governors were erected in front of the sanctuary of Dike, since this fact is attested to by very many inscriptions; but the sanctuary itself, according to Robert, was simply the *praetorium*.[17] Other inscriptions, however, prompt him to claim that the governor was "throne-sharer of Dike" mainly in a figurative sense as a man giving right judgment (ἀνὴρ ἰθύδικος) and sitting on a tribunal from which right judgment emanated (βῆμα ἰθύδικον).[18] In other words, the governor appeared a throne-sharer of Dike through his just decisions and righteous judgments. This interpretation, to be sure, comes very close to a purely figurative or "moral" meaning of the literary image, even though Robert still combines the idea of throne-sharing with the actual duties of the governor-judge.

With regard to Vollgraff's thesis it may be said that it appears highly improbable that τέμενος Δίκης and related expressions entitle us to think of architectural temple constructions any more than when we read in Justinians's *Codex* (1, 17, 1, 5) about the *sanctissimum templum iustitiae* or even about (1, 17, 2, 20) *iustitiae Romanae templum*. This is not *factum de marmore templum*, which Ovid (*Pont.* 3.6.25f.) mentions, but one *mentis in aede suae*. In this sense, a governor of Crete could be styled "temple of Justice" (νηὸς Εὐδικίης).[19] Louis Robert, it seems to me, is perfectly correct when denying the existence of shrines proper of Dike so far as they are evidenced only by the epigrams. He was, however, perhaps not quite specific enough when interpreting σύνθρονος Δίκη chiefly in a figurative sense.

[14] W. Vollgraff, "Argos dans la dépendance de Corinthe au IVᵉ siècle," *Antiquité classique*, XIV (1945), 5ff.

[15] *RE*, 5.574.

[16] *Greek Anthology* 9.812, 813; Vollgraff, 9.

[17] Robert, p. 139. The *praetorium* as a "shrine" is perhaps paralleled, as Professor Downey kindly pointed out to me, by Themistius, *Or.* 4.52c ff., Dindorf, 63, who speaks of Constantinople as the shrine (νεώς) of the emperor.

[18] Robert, 12ff, 17ff, *passim*, for these and similar expressions.

[19] Inscription from Gortyn; Robert, 103. For εὐδικία as the king's throne-sharer, see Themistius, *Or.* 15.189b, Dindorf, p. 233.

1*

There is, I think, some evidence that the governor was throne-sharer of Dike not only figuratively, but also as a *figura*. The Syriac "Life of St. Basil" is falsely ascribed to Amphilochius of Iconium, a friend of the great Cappadocians of the fourth century. To the same author there is ascribed also a Greek biography of Basil which, however, is not identical with the Syriac version. The latter may actually go back to the sixth century.[20] The Syriac version, easily accessible in a German translation, begins with an interesting passage which has some relevance to governors as throne-sharers of Dike.

> The municipal authorities (writes the author) do not deny recognition to governors, even to incapable persons whose administration has been but brief, by erecting images in their honor. In fact, they represent them as just and righteous officers by means of symbolic figures which they place on the right and left sides of the statues. Although the cities may despise the unjust administration of those men they nevertheless exalt them with pompous names. Thus, so as to have at least one pleasure of those men's sins, they preserve in the people's memory the images of the officers rather than their power which has disappeared from the city in which they had been active for a short time only.

The author then mentions the bronze statues put up for the victors in the circus and in the games before he starts to discuss his proper subject, the *monumentum aere perennius* which he ventures to place before the minds of his readers by writing the Life of Saint Basil.

It is evident that the author, when describing the statues or images of governors with the flanking personifications, alludes to something that must have been common practice in the cities of the late empire. We know the "pompous titles" by which the cities extolled the governors, for those eulogizing words, mentioned also by Gregory Nazianzen,[21] have been repeated over and over again in the epigrams. But do we know also the monuments, or can we imagine what they were like?

We are told that the symbolic figures were supposed to represent the governor as just and righteous. In other words, personifications of Dike, Themis, Eunomia, or other civic virtues must have been placed on either side of the governor's statue or image. In the company of those figures the governor would actually appear as "throne-sharer of Dike" or of any other of the personified political virtues (ἰθυντὴρ Εὐνομίης, Σοφίης ταμίης) which the epigrams adduce in his praise and which so ably have been put into focus by

[20] K. von Zetterstéen, "Eine Homilie des Amphilochius von Iconium über Basilius von Caesarea," *Festschrift Eduard Sachau zum siebzigsten Geburtstag*, edited by Gotthold Weil (Berlin, 1915), 223ff, reproduces the Syriac text which had been previously edited by Paolo Bedjan, *Acta Martyrum et Sanctorum* (Paris, 1896), VI, 297ff; cf. A. Baumstark, in *Oriens Christianus*, Ser. 2, vol. 5 (1915), 328f. For a German translation, upon which I have to rely, see Zetterstéen, in *Oriens Christianus*, Ser. 3, vol. 8 (1933), 67ff. There is also a Greek text of a "Life of Basil" attributed to Amphilochius of Iconium, which was published by Combefis, *Amphilochii Iconensis, Methodii Patarensis et Andreae Cretensis opera graeco-latina* (Paris, 1644),

155ff (not accessible to me); see also Karl Holl, *Amphilochius von Ikonium in seinem Verhältnis zu den grossen Kappadoziern* (Tübingen and Leipzig, 1904), 59. The Greek text differs from the Syriac; see, for the date of the latter, A. Baumstark, *Geschichte der syrischen Literatur* (Bonn, 1922), 262, with the note on p. 353.

[21] Gregory Naz., *Carmina* 2.7.7ff; *PG*, XXXVII, 1551; Robert, p. 17. It is not unlikely that the unknown author of the Syriac Pseudo-Amphilochian "Life of Basil" was inspired by Gregory Nazianzen and drew upon the verses *Ad Nemesium*, but the investigation of the Syriac text has to be left to others.

Louis Robert.[22] Such allegorical *synthronismoi* of princes with political or civic virtues are found not only in epigrams but also in the political literature. Dio of Prusa, Themistios, Aulus Gellius, and others offer famous examples of those personified virtues surrounding the throne, and their ideas lingered on throughout the Middle Ages: Placentinus, the great jurist of the twelfth century, outlines in one of his tractates an impressive visionary image of such a *templum iustitiae* in which Justice thrones with Reason and Equity and other virtues.[23]

Similar personifications are just as common in art. The miniatures, for example, of the Paris Psalter abound in personifications of all kinds. David as a harper appears in the company of Melodia and Echo; David slaying the lion is assisted by Ischys; in his fight against Goliath he is protected by Dynamis, and when he prostrates himself to do penance Metanoia is present.[24] More striking, however, and more relevant to the subject discussed here is the formal ceremonious ruler portrait in the same Codex: David with Sophia on his right side and Prophetia on his left. The Psalter in his left hand is, as it were, *his* lawbook which is inspired by the Spirit perched in the shape of a dove on the halo that surrounds his head and crown.[25] Similarly we find the Emperor Nikephoros Botaniates (1078–1081) in the company of Dikaiosyne and Aletheia.[26] The pattern was familiar also in the West where, in the Gospel Book of Monte Cassino, the official state image shows the Emperor Henry II with Justitia and Pietas, Sapientia and Prudentia, Lex and Jus, while Ratio in the shape of the dove of the Holy Spirit, descending from above, indicates the divine inspiration.[27]

The late date of those miniatures (tenth and eleventh centuries) does not abate their importance because the painters were still working within the antique tradition. This has become perfectly clear from the paintings at Touna el Gebel, near Hermopolis, which prove strikingly that the personifications of human affections and emotions, which interpreted the state of mind or the actions of the one portrayed, derived from Hellenistic models.[28] Moreover, in the Vienna Dioscurides (around A.D. 512) we find perhaps the

[22] Robert, pp. 13ff, 86ff, 91ff, 94ff. For the personifications in general, see Downey (above, n. 10).

[23] Above, notes 8, 9; Gellius, *Noctes Att.* 14.4. For the "Temple of Justice" of Placentinus, see Hermann Kantorowicz, *Studies in the Glossators of the Roman Law* (Cambridge, 1938), 183ff.

[24] Hugo Buchthal, *The Miniatures of the Paris Psalter* (London, 1938), Pls. 1, 2, 4, 8. That μετάνοια has the meaning of "prostration" has been stressed by Milton V. Anastos, "Pletho's Calendar and Liturgy," *Dumbarton Oaks Papers*, IV (1948), 261, n. 403.

[25] Buchthal, pl. VII. For σοφία in the epigrams, see Robert, 107, n. 1. A replica of the image of David is found in a 12th-century Psalter of the National Library in Athens (MS 9, fol. 1); cf. Paul Buberl, *Die Miniaturhandschriften der Nationalbibliothek in Athen* (Denkschriften der Wiener Akademie, 60:2, 1917), p. 14, pl. XVII, fig. 38; for other MSS influenced by the Paris Psalter, see Buchthal, p. 26, nos. 3, 4, who adduces also a few parallels (figs. 48–50). That the master of the Paris Psalter was not the one who introduced the type is perfectly evident.

[26] Paris, B.N. MS Coislin 79, fol. 2; Henri Omont, *Facsimilés des miniatures des plus anciens MSS. grecs de la Bibl. Nat.* (Paris, 1902), pl. LXIII. For other representations of Dikaiosyne, see Downey, 349, n. 1 (Coptic, 4th–5th cent.), and 355, n. 13 (Syrian, Euteknia flanked by Philosophia and Dikaiosyne).

[27] The literature on that MS (Vat. Ottob. lat. 74, fol. 193ᵛ) has been conveniently summed up by Herbert Bloch, "Monte Cassino, Byzantium, and the West in the Earlier Middle Ages," *Dumbarton Oaks Papers*, III (1946), 181, n. 53; see fig. 221 for a reproduction. For the Middle Ages in general, see Adolf Katzenellenbogen, *Allegories of the Virtues and Vices in Mediaeval Art* (Studies of the Warburg Institute, 10; London, 1939.)

[28] Sami Gabra, "Caractères de l'art copte: ses rapports avec l'art égyptien et l'art hellénistique," *Bulletin de la société d'archéologie copte*, I (1935), 37–41. For the indication of this article as well as for many another hint I am greatly indebted to Professor André Grabar; it has not been utilized in the excellent, if brief, outline of the history of personifications offered by Doro Levi, *Antioch Mosaic Pavements* (Princeton, 1947), I, 253ff, and *passim*.

most accurate example of those *synthronismoi* which the contemporary epigrams allude to: Anicia Juliana, the noble patroness of arts and learning, seated on her *sella curulis* and flanked by Megalopsychia and Phronesis.[29]

That the governor memorials often consisted of paintings with epigrams added to the picture is shown by Gregory Nazianzen's poem to Nemesius and by many epigrams of the Greek Anthology.[30] On the other hand, there is no doubt that usually the governors would receive statues. Groups such as those described by Pseudo-Amphilochius do not seem to have been preserved. This, however, does not imply that they have not existed. In the so-called "House of Megalopsychia" at Antioch on the Orontes, reliably dated middle of the fifth century, we find in the topographical border (section c) of the great mosaic, between a group of dicing men and the front of a portico of seven columns, a group of three statues.[31] They are standing obviously in the *piazza* in the middle of the town[32] in front of some official building; and although that section of the mosaic border is badly damaged we yet recognize in the center a figure with short tunic and paludamentum — probably a prince or pretorian prefect — flanked by two men whose high rank is suggested by the long chlamys they wear and by the long staffs they hold near their shoulders.[33] We may assume that the governors with their companions of personified virtues were represented in a similar fashion. Statues of Justitia are known to have existed.[34] If represented together with that goddess, the governor would appear in fact as the "throne-sharer of Dike." At any rate, the text of Pseudo-Amphilochius makes it more than likely that the expression σύνθρονος Δίκη had also a more realistic meaning than has hitherto been recognized.

---

[29] *Dioscurides: Codex Aniciae Julianae picturis illustratus ... phototypice editus*, moderante Josepho de Karabacek (Leyden, 1906), fol. 6ᵛ. Perhaps the diptych of Constantius III (?), of A.D. 417 (Richard Delbrück, *Die Konsulardiptychen* [Berlin and Leipzig, 1929], pl. ɪɪ and [text] p. 89), should be mentioned in this connection, too, because the personifications—not of virtues, but of cities: Rome and Constantinople—are found sitting together with the emperors on one throne bench. The two cities, which here are haloed, appear often standing on either side of the chair of the consul (e.g., Delbrück, Pls. 16, 22–25, 32, 35). Only in the Constantius diptych, however, are they genuine throne-sharers after the pattern of the personified Commagene on Nemrud Dagh. See further Katzenellenbogen, *Allegories*, pl. xɪv, fig. 27, for Vergil between two Muses (cf. pl. xv, fig. 29), and for a kindred subject, pl. xvɪ, fig. 31 (Christ between Eleemosyne and Dikaiosyne).

[30] *PG*, XXXVII, 1552 (*Ad Nemesium*, verse 13), where both paintings and sculptures are mentioned. In the Greek Anthology there are many epigrams connected with icons; see also the scholion to *Anthol. Planud.* (*Anth. Graeca* 16), 380, ed. Dübner, II, 640, quoted by A. A. Vasiliev, "The Monument of Porphyrius in the Hippodrome at Constantinople," *Dumbarton Oaks Papers*, IV (1948), 40, n. 29, where an epigram belongs to the paintings in the προκύπτιον (the imperial box) in the hippodrome.

[31] Doro Levi, *Antioch*, II, pl. ʟxxɪxc, to which Professor Sirarpie Der Nersessian kindly called my attention.

[32] *Ibid.*, I, 331. See also Gregory Naz. *Ad Nemesium* 14f, *PG*, XXXVII, 1552: ἐν μεσάτῃσι στήσαντες πτολίεσσιν. Cf. Robert, 17, n. 2.

[33] Doro Levi, *Antioch*, I, 331.

[34] A. Milchhoefer, "Dike," *Jahrb. d. deutschen Arch. Inst.*, VII (1892), 203–208. Justitia in imagery is very common, of course; see above, notes 26, 29.

GODS IN UNIFORM

A PRELIMINARY remark will be needed on what is meant by the term "uniform" in the following pages.

A person carrying arms is not necessarily a uniformed person. Gods as well as goddesses are frequently armed. Athene is practically always helmeted and carries a lance. But she is dressed in a peplos or himation, and not in a uniform. Ares would, *ex officio*, be represented in arms, carrying a spear and a shield and wearing a helmet. But his costume is that of heroic or divine nudity, or of nudity loosely draped (pl. 1, fig. 1*a*), that is, a costume not practical for human warfare. It is, however, a different matter when the same god appears in a cuirass worn over a tunic (pl. 1, fig. 1*b*). For in this case he has donned an armor similar to, or even identical with, the standard army cuirass which the mercenaries in the Hellenistic monarchies received from the royal arsenals, or which the Roman legionaries purchased from the surplus depot of their outfit. The uniformlike attire might even be accentuated by the addition of certain badges or insignia of rank —an officer's sash, a torque, or a fibula.[1]

* * *

A sestertius, issued during the reign of Hadrian by the mint of Alexandria, shows the Dioscuri, the heavenly Twins Castor and Pollux, in military attire. They are clad in a Roman "body" or "muscled" cuirass to which there are attached, at the lower end, a row of metal lappets, the *pteryges*, with long leather tabs dangling down kilt-like and with similar leather flaps protecting the shoulders (pl. 1, fig. 2). The twin gods obviously sported the uniform of Roman legionaries or Roman officers.[2] This is an unusual feature. In classical times the Dioscuri were usually, though not always, naked except for their conical felt caps and their short cloaks or capes fluttering in the wind, as seen on the

Reprinted, with permission, from *Proceedings of the American Philosophical Society*, CV (1961), 368–393. The original has this prefatory note:

Paper read on November 10, 1960. The author wishes to express his gratitude to Professors Andreas Alföldi, Sirarpie Der Nersessian, Otto Neugebauer, Henri Seyrig, James F. Gilliam, and to the Rev. P. Paul Grosjean, S.J., for valuable information and various courtesies; to Professor Ihor Ševčenko, Dr. George Stamires, and Professor Kurt Weitzmann for their efforts to obtain photographs for me; and to the German Archaeological Institute, in Rome, the Dumbarton Oaks Research Library and Collection, and the Musée du Louvre for their readiness to provide me with photographs.

[1] For armed goddesses, see Denyse Le Lasseur, *Les Déesses armées dans l'art classique grec et leurs origines orientales* (Paris, 1919). The two coins of Ares, nude and cuirassed, are both from the mint of Alexandria and both issued under Antoninus Pius; see G. Dattari, *Numi Augg. Alexandrini – Monete imperiali greche* (Cairo, 1901), pl. IX, nos. 2464 and 2460. See below, n. 51f for the rise of uniformed soldiery.

[2] Dattari, *Numi Augg. Alexandrini*, pl. XII, fig. 1681; Reginald Stuart Poole, *Catalogue of the Coins of Alexandria and the Nomes* (London, 1892), 84 and pl. V, fig. 708; Fernand Chapouthier, *Les Dioscures au service d'une déesse* (Paris, 1935), 63 and pl. XI, fig. 54.

reverse side of so many coins of the Roman Republic.[3] They were always conceived of as adolescents or ephebes, and they were the patrons of the Roman youth of equestrian nobility who prided themselves on going to battle with arms but without armor.[4] There are, it is true, Alexandrian coins, of the same Hadrianic period, on which the Dioscuri appear according to the classical tradition: nude, facing each other, armed with their long lances, and holding their horses by the bridle (pl. 1, fig. 3). But the fact remains that a considerable number of issues of the Alexandrian mint depict the Twins in military dress (pl. 1, fig. 4), and it may be mentioned that with almost negligible exceptions all our evidence for the Dioscuri in uniform derives from Egypt and not earlier than the second century of our era.[5]

This is not simply a matter of chance. It is a well-known fact that the Egyptians, especially in Roman times, had a predilection for representing their own Graeco-Egyptian gods in military guise, a custom which almost certainly goes back to the Hellenistic-Ptolemaic era.[6] If we accept the view of Michael Rostovtzeff, the first Egyptian god who (as he puts it) "was enlisted in the regular army" was Heron, an equestrian god of foreign origin, but Egyptianized in Ptolemaic times. He appears indeed in Hellenistic rather than in Roman military dress: a cuirass made of plates or scales and decorated with the gorgoneion (pl. 1, fig. 5).[7] This Hellenistic armor is still worn by Heron in Roman times as seen in a painting from the Fayyûm, now in Paris (pl. 1, fig. 6), where the figure on the right represents that god.[8] A warning, however, should be sounded. The Hellenistic cuirass was still quite common in Roman times and is found with earlier Roman armor statues as well.[9] Therefore, a Hellenistic type of cuirass all by itself cannot be used without qualification as an evidence proving the pre-Roman date of a monument.

However that may be, Egyptian gods in uniform are numerous. Horus, the son of Isis and Osiris, is very often represented not simply armed, but in military garb. A bronze

---

[3] It is true that heavily armed Dioscuri are found, though rarely, in very ancient vase paintings of the 6th century B.C.; see, e.g., Chapouthier, *op. cit.*, 199, fig. 23; but the meaning is held to be agonistic, and not military (*ibid.*, 202 ff).

[4] Andreas Alföldi, *Der frührömische Reiteradel und seine Ehrenabzeichen* (Baden-Baden, 1952), 46ff, 49; W. Helbig, "Die Castores als Schutzgötter der römischen Equitatus," *Hermes*, XL (1905), 101ff. A similar relationship may have existed between the Dioscuri and the Greek ephebes whose badge, the *petasos*, a broad-rimmed flat hat, was worn sometimes by the Twin Gods; cf. Chapouthier, *op. cit.*, 133, fig. 7.

[5] See Dattari, *op. cit.*, pl. XII, fig. 2485 (for the Dioscuri in the nude), and pl. XXIV, fig. 2863 (for another specimen of the uniformed gods). See also Chapouthier, *op. cit.*, 48ff, fig. 26, for the wall-painting from Theadelphia; cf. Evaristo Breccia, *Teadelfia e il tempio di Pneferôs* (Monuments de l'Égypte gréco-romaine, I; Bergamo, 1926), 124ff and pl. LXI, fig. 1. Non-Egyptian is a relief from Telmessos (Pisidia), now in Vienna, where the Twin Gods are seen on horseback in the uniform of legionaries; see Chapouthier, 23ff and pl. I, fig. 2.

[6] Whereas R. Paribeni, "Divinità straniere in abito militare romano," *Bulletin de la société archéologique d'Alexandrie*, XIII (1910), 177ff, and others rendered the *communis opinio* according to which no gods were pictured in military attire in pre-Roman times, Michael Rostovtzeff, "Kleinasiatische und syrische Götter im römischen Ägypten," *Aegyptus*, XIII (1933), 510f, refutes this opinion by calling attention to the Hellenistic uniforms of gods in Palmyra and Dura.

[7] Rostovtzeff, *op. cit.*, 510f. E. Breccia, *Teadelfia*, 110ff, and pls. LVII, LVIII.

[8] F. Cumont, "Un dieu supposé syrien, associé à Hérôn en Égypte," *Mélanges syriens offerts à Monsieur René Dussaud* (Paris, 1939), I, pl. I, facing p. 2.

[9] Cf. Cornelius C. Vermeule III, "Hellenistic and Roman Cuirassed Statues," *Berytus*, XIII:1 (1959), 5 and 40, who (p. 18) styles the statue of M. Holconius Rufus of the Augustan period (pl. IV, fig. 13) the first complete statue that may be called Roman without being based on Hellenistic tradition. In the classicistic atmosphere of the second century A.D., the Hellenistic armor was occasionally revived; see, e.g., Vermeule, *op. cit.*, 5, 57, 60, 61 (Nos. 225–249).

statuette of the second century A.D., now in the Louvre (pl. 1, fig. 7), shows the god with the sparrow hawk's head as a Roman officer, despite some non-Roman features.[10] His cuirass is scaled; he wears around his waist the officer's sash with fringed or tasseled ends, tied in a simple slip-knot, and not yet in the fashion characteristic of later statues of emperors and officers which displayed the so-called Hercules-knot with the ends tucked away.[11] Although his headgear, the white crown of Lower Egypt and the pendants of cloth, is Egyptian he is, nevertheless, decorated with the Graeco-Roman crown of laurel; and his head is surrounded by sun-rays suggesting the fusion of Horus and the sun-god. Another hawk-headed Horus in military attire is in the British Museum. The type is quite frequent.[12] The same type, for example, has been worked into a terracotta bust where the decorated cuirass may suggest officer's rank (pl. 2, fig. 8).[13] How common it was to represent also the youthful Horus, in his hypostasis as Harpocrates, in military dress may be gathered from a figurine in the collection of Arthur D. Nock. The terracotta of Horus putting his hand to his mouth is doubtless mass fabrication; but even so it displays essentially, if in shorthand, the customary features: the armor with the leather tabs, the sash, and a baldric running from the left shoulder to the right hip (pl. 2, fig. 9).[14]

One more statuette of Horus, in the Collection Sinadino in Alexandria, (pl. 2, fig. 10), should be mentioned here on account of the posture; the right arm, so often broken away, is raised and one finger lifted. This hand, perhaps, held originally a spear, unless it was meant to be a gesture of imperatorial greeting. At any rate, the military dress is very accurately that of a Roman officer: the muscled cuirass, the *pteryges* with the leather tabs, and the sash around the waist.[15] Other Egyptian gods display a similar attitude. Of those therianthropic deities the god Apis, with his head of a bull, is among the best known. He appears likewise in full uniform; his right hand is open and raised in a gesture known from Roman emperors when addressing their legions, and the editor of this little bronze statuette, Baron von Bissing, gave it the title of *Apis Imperator* in the attitude of the *allocutio* (pl. 2, fig. 11).[16] We cannot tell whether the dog-headed Anubis of the National Museum in Athens had the same attitude, since the right hand is broken away from this bronze statuette; but he, too, appears in uniform with two rows of lappets covering the

[10] Victor Chapot, "L'Horus garde-frontière du Nome Sethroïthe." *Mélanges Maspéro* (Mémoires...de l'Institut français d'archéologie orientale du Caire, LXVII; 1935–1937), II, 225ff, pls. I–II.

[11] For the sash tied in a Hercules-knot, see Richard Delbrück, *Die Consulardyptichen* (Berlin und Leipzig, 1929), 41; Karl Keyssner, art. "Nodus," *RE*, XVII:1 (1936), 807f, on the *nodus Herculaneus*.

[12] See Chapot, *op. cit.*, pl. II, left figure, for a Horus in the British Museum. Ch. Clermont-Ganneau, "Horus et Saint Georges," *Revue archéologique*, XXXIII (1877), 24, mentions two other statuettes of Horus in military dress in the British Museum; cf. Chapot, *op. cit.*, 228.

[13] P. Perdrizet, *Les terres cuites grecques d'Égypte de la Collection Fouquet* (Nancy, Paris, and Strasbourg, 1921), II, pl. LI.

[14] I am very much obliged to Professor Arthur D. Nock

for calling my attention to, and providing me with a photo of, his interesting terracotta.

[15] Von Bissing, in: *Expedition Ernst Sieglin*, I: "Die Nekropole von Kôm-esch-Schukâfa" (Leipzig, 1908), 149, fig. 93.

[16] Von Bissing, "Eine Apisfigur in der Haltung der *Adlocutio*," *Oriental Studies dedicated to Paul Haupt*, edd. Cyrus Adler and Aaron Ember (Baltimore and Leipzig, 1926), 295–299. The same, or a similar, figure is discussed by B. Breccia, "Osiris-Apis in abito militare romano," *Bulletin de la Société archéologique d'Alexandrie*, XVII (1919–1920), 184. The interesting article by Alfred Hermann, "Der letzte Apisstier," *Jahrbuch für Antike und Christentum*, III (1960), 34–50, reached me only after I had returned the proofs; see it, however, esp. 40f, for the Apis in military attire, and n. 53 for a correction of von Bissing.

tunic of which the lower edge becomes visible.[17] Another Anubis, in the Museo Nazionale in Rome, wearing decorated armor, suggests that the god held in his right hand a spear or a staff scepter (pl. 3, fig. 12).[18] Yet another god, perhaps Oupwaut-Makedon, also therianthropic, is represented in uniform and shown with his right arm raised.[19]

The general appearance of all those Egyptian gods is closely related to a small bronze statuette from the Delta, now in the Louvre (pl. 3, fig. 13).[20] It displays a person in military attire: cuirass with *pteryges*, and leather tabs, the sash with its characteristic knotting, and shoulder tabs. The rays of the sun-god surround the head. The person represented is Alexander or rather Alexander-Helios, that is, Alexander as a god. It is true, the statuette is of Roman times but it may be a replica of an earlier work of art of that type. The attitude should perhaps be compared with that of a Ptolemaic bronze statuette showing Alexander in the aegis of Zeus, normally an attribute of Zeus' daughter Athene, but here given to Alexander the god who was venerated in Alexandria (pl. 3, fig. 14).[21] It has been assumed that the attitude of Alexander in the aegis may go back to a statue by Lysippus which, if this be true, would have influenced also the statuettes of so many of the therianthropic gods previously discussed. Probably the Horus in the Louvre (pl. 1, fig. 7) had also the right hand raised and thus would resemble, with his crown of sun rays, the Alexander statuette (pl. 3, fig. 13) in more than one detail. It would, indeed, be very tempting to draw the straight-forward conclusion that Alexander was the first "god in uniform" and that he, general and god at the same time—as depicted also in a decadrachm of the mint of Babylon[22]—started the Egyptian-Alexandrian tradition of representing not only the native gods in military attire but also the Graeco-Roman gods who in classical times were preferably represented in the nude or loosely draped. But it does not seem likely that this simple and plausible hypothesis can be proved. Nevertheless, the similarity of gesture and attitude displayed by the statuettes of Horus, Apis and Anubis, and by that of Alexander may suggest that they all followed some common model which may have been as famous as Lysippus' statue of Alexander; more likely, however, we have to take into account some radiations of the canonical Doryphoros pose.

It should be added, if only in parenthesis, that in Egypt also other deities were represented in military garb, and that representations following that pattern are found even in so small works of art as amulets. One amulet shows without doubt Anubis in the

[17] Von Bissing, *Ägyptische Kultbilder der Ptolomaier- und Römerzeit* (Der alte Orient, XXXIV:1–2; Leipzig, 1936), 17ff, fig. 16a.

[18] Cf. Paribeni (above, n. 6), pls. VI–VII. My thanks go to the German Archaeological Institute, in Rome, for providing me with a photo of this statuette (Photo No. 60.1199).

[19] Von Bissing, in *Expedition Ernst Sieglin*, I, 143, fig. 89, from the Collection Sinadino, in Alexandria.

[20] Theodor Schreiber, *Studien über das Bildnis Alexander des Grossen* (Abhandlungen d. Sächsischen Gesellschaft d. Wissensch., XXI:3; Leipzig, 1903), 72f, 140, and pl. VII, fig. P. Von Bissing, "Eine Apisfigur" (above, n. 16), 296, has connected the Apis-Adlocutio statuette with the Alexander in the Louvre, but did not follow up his obser-

vation. I owe the Giraudon photo to the kindness of Professor Sirarpie Der Nersessian, in Dumbarton Oaks. For Alexander as a moon-god, with a crescent and three stars, see Cumont, *Recherches sur le symbolisme funéraire des Romains* (Paris, 1942), pl. XVI, fig. 1, and p. 208.

[21] Paul Perdrizet, "Un type inédit de la plastique grecque: Alexandre à l'égide," *Monuments Piot*, XXI (1913), 59–72, pls. IV–V. See pp. 70f for the hypothesis linking this statuette to Lysippus' sculpture of Alexander.

[22] Professor Alfred R. Bellinger obligingly called my attention to this decadrachm which shows Alexander wearing the cuirass and holding in his right, extended, hand the thunderbolt; his head-dress is Persian. Cf. G. F. Hill, *Catalogue of the Greek Coins of Arabia, Mesopotamia, and Persia* (London, 1922), 191, No. 61, and pl. XXII, fig. 18.

dress of a soldier (pl. 3, fig. 15),[23] the same god who in a necropole at Alexandria is shown as anguipede, cuirassed and decorated with the *paludamentum* (pl. 4, fig. 16).[24] Such snake-legged deities are not rare on amulets either, where we find, for example, a lion-headed god in military dress (pl. 4, fig. 17).[25] In Egypt, however, also a Greek goddess, such as Nemesis or the Roman *Dea Roma* (pl. 4, fig. 18), was occasionally represented as a military person,[26] apparently for no other reason than to accommodate to a taste which certainly had gained its full strength in Roman times.

This does not imply that the custom of picturing the gods in officers' uniform developed under the Roman domination only. On the contrary, the findings in Palmyra, Dura-Europos, and Hatra make it perfectly clear that the tradition of providing gods with military trappings was pre-Roman and went back to Hellenistic times. A Palmyrene relief in the Louvre of the first half of the first century after Christ (pl. 4, fig. 19) shows a triad of gods.[27] We recognize in the center a bearded deity, identified as Bēl, wearing a *kalathos* on his head and a diadem with fringed ends. The armor is made of small rectangular scales; the shoulder straps are fastened with rings. Where we normally would find the *pteryges* we see rows of pearls and a meander pattern decorating the lower edge of the cuirass —an Oriental tendency to a certain enrichment of the costume.[28] Dangling down from the armor are two rows of fringed leather flaps. The tight trousers are visible under the edge of a tunic which has long sleeves, a *tunica manicata*. The officer's belt is likewise fringed. The god wears a *paludamentum* which is held by a plaque or fibula on, or just below, the right shoulder. The same uniform (though without the Parthian trousers but enriched by a torque, a necklace usually of twisted gold) is worn by the gods to the right and left: the one to the right is Jarhibol, the sun-god of Palmyra; to the left is Aglibol, the moon-god, identifiable by the crescent in his halo of sun rays.

The emblem of the crescent, however, does not always identify the deity with certainty as the moon-god. There is, for example, the bust of a cuirassed god whom the description, despite the crescent, calls plainly *Helios Theos megistos* (pl. 4, fig. 20); the date is known accurately in this case: A.D. 30.[29] This representation must have been rather popular; for

[23] Campbell Bonner, *Studies in Magical Amulets, chiefly Graeco-Egyptian* (Ann Arbor, 1950), pl. II, fig. 38, and p. 259. Another amulet shows not Anubis, but Seth, likewise in armor; cf. J. Gwyn Griffiths, "Seth or Anubis?," *Journal of the Warburg and Courtauld Institutes*, XXII (1959), 367ff, and pl. 38,a.

[24] Von Bissing, *Ägyptische Kultbilder*, fig. 14a; *Expedition Ernst Sieglin*, I, 142f. The present reproduction was made after a line drawing from the portfolio *Les basreliefs de Kom-el-Chougafa*, ed. F. W. von Bissing and Gilleron (Munich, 1901), pl. XIII, by courtesy of the Dumbarton Oaks Library.

[25] Campbell Bonner, *Magical Amulets*, pl. V, 99–101; pl. VIII, 172. Cf. Martin P. Nilsson, "The Anguipede of the Magical Amulets," *Harvard Theological Review*, XLIV (1951), 61ff.

[26] P. Perdrizet, "Némésis," *Bulletin de Correspondance Hellenique*, XXXVI (1912), 263ff, fig. 1. For the *Dea Roma* on Alexandrian coins, see Dattari, *Numi Augg. Alex.*, pl. XXI, No. 4994; also R. S. Poole, *Coins of Alexan-*

dria, pl. XXIII, fig. 240. Seyrig, in *Syria*, XIII (1932), 263, considers "the case [of the Alexandrian Roma] exceptional." See, in general, Vermeule, *The Goddess Roma in Ancient Art* (Cambridge, Mass., 1959), who, however, does not discuss the Alexandrian coin nor the Roma type represented by it.

[27] Seyrig, *Antiquités Syriennes*, IV (1953), 31, pl. II; Mary Morehart, "Early Sculpture at Palmyra," *Berytus*, XII (1956–1957), 60f and fig. 11, also figs. 12, 13. The number of Palmyrene gods in military dress is excessively great and no effort has been made here to assemble the material completely. For the triad of Bēl, Jarhibol, and Aglibol, see also Otto Eissfeldt, *Tempel und Kulte syrischer Städte in hellenistisch-römischer Zeit* (Der alte Orient, XL; 1941), 83ff.

[28] See, for that tendency, Vermeule, "Cuirassed Statues," 25f.

[29] Seyrig, "Antiquités syriennes, § 72: Bas-relief palmyrénien dédié au soleil," *Syria*, XXXVI (1959), 58ff and pl. XI, 5.

the same design is seen on a *tessera* from Palmyra (pl. 4, fig. 21) where the image of the cuirassed bust of the god decorates the small terracotta token serving its bearer to secure a meal on the feasts of the god.[30] At a later period, the Hellenistic cuirass was replaced by Roman armor. An *aedicula* in the Palazzo dei Conservatori, Rome, dated A.D. 235, shows Aglibol with the crescent in a simple Roman body-cuirass, extending his hand to Malakbēl (pl. 4, fig. 22).[31] It is surprising to find how consistently Palmyrene gods were represented in uniform. Shadrafa, for example, a god whose name is said to be derived from Satrap, the title of the ancient Persian provincial governors, wears a Hellenistic plate armor with sash as well as the long-sleeved tunic and the Parthian trousers (pl. 5, fig. 23).[32] The blending of Hellenistic and Parthian elements characterizes not only the military attire of the Palmyrene gods, but also frequently that of the gods of Dura-Europos.[33] A bas-relief of a local god of Dura, Aphlad, son of Hadad, which belongs to the middle of the first century, shows the god in Parthian trousers and in a long-sleeved tunic over which he wears armor decorated with stars. We notice the sash, and also the torque around his neck (pl. 5, fig. 24).[34] Again, at a later period, the gods of Dura would be dressed in a garb of more Roman appearance, as, for example, the statue of Jarhibol, the sun-god, in a wall drawing of the Artemis temple, annexed to the Praetorium (pl. 5, fig. 25);[35] or the statues of three haloed gods in a fresco dedicated by the Tribune Terentius (pl. 6, fig. 26).[36] The gods wear the golden cuirasses of a full-dress uniform; their silver sashes, however, are more richly decorated than those of Roman officers, nor are they knotted in the same way.

Rather impressive is the recently excavated marble statue of Assur-Bēl of Hatra (south of Mosul), of the first century after Christ (pl. 6, fig. 27).[37] The cuirass differs from most Hellenistic and Roman patterns. The *pteryges* are absent; hence, the two rows of leather tabs dangle down from the cuirass directly; and instead of one row of leather flaps there are three. Moreover, the cuirass is decorated with a bust of Helios whose relief is found

[30] Seyrig, *Antiquités syriennes*, II (Paris, 1938), 116, fig. 50. For the purpose of the *tesserae*, see Seyrig, *ibid.*, and in *Syria*, XVI (1935), 394f; also his study "Les tessères palmyréniennes et le banquet rituel," *Mémorial [M.-J.] Lagrange* (Paris, 1940), 51–58. Cf. Cumont, *Recherches* (above, n. 20), 208.

[31] Seyrig, *Antiquités syriennes*, II, 100, pl. XXXI; also in *Syria*, XVIII (1937), 203, pl. XXXI. I owe the photo to the courtesy of the German Archaeological Institute, in Rome (No. 1936.1108). For Malakbēl in his relation to Aglibol, see Eissfeldt, *Tempel und Kulte*, 89f.

[32] Seyrig, "Note sur les plus anciennes sculptures palmyréniennes," *Berytus*, III (1936), 137, pl. XXX; cf. *Annales archéologiques de Syrie*, VII (1957), pl. VIII, fig. 2; Mary Morehart, in *Berytus*, XII (1956–1957), 63, and figs. 14 and 15. For Shadrafa, see Seyrig, *Antiquités syriennes*, II (1938), 23, n. 4; Eissfeldt, *Tempel und Kulte*, 102f.

[33] Clark Hopkins, "Aspects of Parthian Art in the Light of Discoveries from Dura-Europos," *Berytus*, III (1936), pl. III, fig. 1, facing p. 6 ([Aphlad] "clothed in the dress of a Hellenistic officer"). Cf. C. Hopkins, in: *The Excavations at Dura-Europos: Preliminary Report*, V (1934),

107ff and pl. XIII. Rostovtzeff, "Dura and the Problem of Parthian Art," *Yale Classical Studies*, V (1935), figs. 36 and 38; see *ibid.*, 160ff, and *Dura-Europos and its Art* (Oxford, 1938), for the blending of Parthian and Hellenistic elements; Seyrig, *Antiquités syriennes*, II (1938), 45–73.

[34] Clark Hopkins, in *Berytus*, III (1936), pl. III, fig. 1, facing p. 6. Cf. Rostovtzeff, *Dura-Europos and its Art*, p. 87: "wears a Hellenistic military dress with some Iranian features," and p. 65 for the god himself. For Aphlad, son of Hadad, see Eissfeldt, *Tempel und Kulte*, 139f.

[35] Rostovtzeff, in *Yale Classical Studies*, V (1935), fig. 57, and p. 249; Hopkins, in *Dura Report*, V, 153ff, and pl. XXXVI, figs. 1–2.

[36] Seyrig, *Antiquités syriennes*, I (1934), pl. XLIII; see, for a colored plate, F. Cumont, *Fouilles de Doura-Europos* (Paris, 1926), pls. L and LI, fig. 1. For the golden armor worn by Roman emperors, see Delbrück, *Die Consulardyptichen*, 41; also Vermeule, "Cuirassed Statues," 43, No. 76.

[37] *Illustrated London News*, Dec. 18, 1954, p. 116, figs. 5–6; Heinrich Lenzen, "Ausgrabungen in Hatra," *Archäologischer Anzeiger*, LXX (1955), 339–342, figs. 2 and 3. I am much obliged to Sir Ronald Syme for having called my attention to the monuments of Hatra.

occasionally also on imperial armor.[38] The sash is broader than usual, but knotted in the customary way. This god wears also a torque around his neck. Crouched at his feet, between two eagles, is the Tyche of Hatra. The back of the monument does not repeat the military armor, but displays instead the aegis with the head of Gorgon; it reminds us of the aegis statue of Alexander the Great (pl. 3, fig. 14). Also at Hatra there is a bust of the sun-god in military attire (pl. 6, fig. 28), similar to the busts of Aglibol at Palmyra, but lacking the crescent. The inscription styles the god "The Lord of Offering," and the editor suggests, though without evidence, that the armored god may be Mithras.[39] The shoulder clasps of his cuirass are decorated with eagles, and on a military standard flanked by the eagles of Hatra, the bust of the god is seen once more as a plaque.[40] Here then the image of the cuirassed sun-god has become an object of applied art just as the image of Roman emperors were attached to insignia or displayed on *phalerae* and other military paraphernalia.[41]

There were, of course, many more gods in Syria and Asia Minor who were represented in uniform. Strangely enough the soldier-god *par excellence*, Mithras, appears, it seems, only once in military dress, on a coin of Tarsus (pl. 6, fig. 29), and nowhere else.[42] But another god who was venerated in the military camps, *Juppiter Dolichenus*, is practically always represented in the officer's garb.[43] Swinging in his right hand the double-axe, he is often seen in simple Roman muscled armor (pl. 6, fig. 30),[44] though he too may wear the trousers of the Oriental gods.[45] But as in Egypt so in Syria some definitely Greek gods were represented in armor. Asklepios repeatedly appears in uniform in Syrian monuments, for example on an altar in Hauran where he is seen in a Roman muscled cuirass (pl. 6, fig. 31).[46]

It will be unnecessary for our purpose to give a fuller catalogue of representations of gods in military dress, since the material cited here will suffice to pose a few questions regarding some principles involved.

* * *

[38] The cuirass resembles one in the Olympia Museum; cf. Vermeule, "Cuirassed Statues," pl. XIX, fig. 58, and p. 61, No. 232. For Helios on imperial breastplates, see, e.g., Otto Brendel, "Der Schild des Achilles," *Die Antike*, XII (1936), 272ff, esp. 276f (figs. 3–4), and 278 (fig. 5); Gioacchino Mancini, "Le statue loricate imperiali," *Bullettino della Commissione archeologica communale di Roma*, L (1923), 181 (Nos. 17, 18) and 183 (No. 29), for *Sol* on imperial armor.

[39] *Illustrated London News*, Nov. 17, 1951, p. 806f, fig. 8. For Mithras, see below, n. 42.

[40] *Illustrated London News*, loc. cit., fig. 9.

[41] For *phalerae*, see Alföldi, *Der frührömische Reiteradel und seine Ehrenabzeichen* (Baden-Baden, 1952), 17ff; and his "Zu den römischen Reiterscheiben," *Germania*, XXX (1952), 187–190. Probably the Caracalla plaque, reproduced by Brendel, in *Die Antike*, XII, 175, fig. 2, served also as an insignia.

[42] G. F. Hill, *Catalogue of Greek Coins of Lycaonia, Isauria, and Cilicia* (London, 1900), 213, No. 258, and

pl. XXXVII, fig. 4. Cf. Ern. Will, *Le relief cultuel*, 259, n. 2, who emphasizes the absence of Mithras representations in military attire. For a full bibliography, see Maarten J. Vermaseren, *Corpus inscriptionum et monumentorum religionis Mithriacae* (Haag, 1956), 52, fig. 27, and pl. I, fig. 4.

[43] A. H. Kan, *Juppiter Dolichenus* (Leiden, 1943). The latest study, by P. Merlat, *Jupiter Dolichenus: Essai d'interprétation et de synthèse* (Paris, 1960), has not yet been accessible to me.

[44] See, e.g., the relief found in Rome (Antiquarium in Berlin) and discussed by Seyrig, *Syria*, XIV (1933), pl. XXXVIII, fig. 2; cf. Kan, *op. cit.*, 117f and pl. XIII, fig. 21.

[45] The Renaissance drawing by Pirro Ligorio (16th century) of the Berlin relief shows that the god wore the Oriental trousers; Seyrig, *op. cit.*, p. 370, fig. 1; Kan, *op. cit.*, 117ff.

[46] Louis Jalabert, *Inscriptions grecques et latines de Syrie* (Beirut, 1906), 157ff and pl. II; W. W. Graf Baudissin, *Adonis und Esmun* (Leipzig, 1911), 299 and pl. IX, fig. 1.

The appearance of so many, and especially Oriental, gods in uniform is difficult to explain. The hypothesis according to which these gods should be considered "soldier-gods," who in this capacity donned military attire, has been abandoned long ago.[47] And another suggestion advancing the theory that those gods were considered commanders-in-chief of their religious followers who thus formed a kind of *militia dei* or *deorum*, is not sound either, because it carries later Christian metaphors as realities into the pagan past.[48] The problem should perhaps be attacked in a less straightforward and more circumstantial way.

Treacherous though it is to start from a modern parallel, we should, nevertheless, recall the fact that the custom of European monarchs to appear almost perpetually in some regimental uniform, or in that of a general of the army, was a very late one. It began in the eighteenth century, and became the general habit apparently only by the time of the Napoleonic wars and thereafter. That is to say, it began when the continental nations asserted themselves as military monarchies, with a prevalence of the military at large.

Something similar must have happened in the military monarchies of the Hellenistic world. To demonstrate this, here are six arguments.

1) There were, in classical times, citizens bearing arms and providing their own armor, but there was not a uniformed soldiery.[49] Alexander's *Argyráspides*, however, his *corps d'élite* of "silver-shielded" guards, were a uniformed unit which survived the death of their king. The *Argyráspides* were continued by some of the Diadochs, notably by the Seleucid rulers of Syria.[50] Moreover, in the Hellenistic monarchies the mercenaries received their arms and armor from the royal arsenals instead of themselves providing for their armature as private citizens.[51] The same became true in Rome. From the time of Marius onward the legions carried standardized arms and armor, even though the individual legionary had to pay for his equipment; its value was gradually deducted from his pay in monthly instalments.[52] At any rate, from the Hellenistic period onward we may talk about "uniformed" soldiers.

2) We have to consider the cuirassed statues of kings and generals, and recall their history. In his very thorough study of this subject, Professor Cornelius C. Vermeule has pointed out that cuirassed statues began to make their appearance sporadically in Hellenistic times, whereas in classical times generals and princes would have been represented preferably in divine or heroic guise, that is, more or less naked or draped.[53] The earlier

---

[47] This was, more or less, the current opinion recently refuted by Ern. Will, *Le relief cultuel*, 259f.

[48] Von Bissing, *Ägyptische Kultbilder* (1936), 22f; against his hypothesis, see Will, *op. cit.*, 206f.

[49] The military costume had no roots in the national traditions of the East. "Ceci pour la bonne raison qu'il n'existait pas d'uniform à haute époque; le guerrier se distinguait du civil non par son accoutrement...mais par les armes qu'il tenait à la main." Cf. Will, *op. cit.*, 264.

[50] Cf. H. Droysen, "Argyraspides," *RE*, II:1 (1895), 800f; also his *Heerwesen und Kriegsführung der Griechen* (Freiburg, 1889), 155. For the red cloaks of the Spartans, *ibid.*, 24 and 155, n. 2; Plutarch, *Philopoimen*, ii.

[51] Alfred von Domaszewski, "Bewaffnung," *RE*, III (1897), 376, lines 60ff.

[52] Domaszewski, *op. cit.*, 377, lines 52ff. Ramsay MacMullen, "Inscriptions on Armor and the Supply of Arms in the Roman Empire," *American Journal of Archaeology*, LXIV (1960), 23ff.

[53] Vermeule, "Cuirassed Statues," (see above, n. 9), 7. Anton Hekler, "Beiträge zur Geschichte der antiken Panzerstatuen," *Jahreshefte des österreichischen archäologischen Instituts*, XIX–XX (1919), 192f, emphasizes very strongly that, with the exception of a coin for Themistocles, generals were not represented in armor during the classical period.

Roman cuirassed statues still displayed the influence of Hellenistic armor; thereafter Rome used the "muscled" or "body" cuirass which often was richly decorated, especially the ceremonial armor of emperors, princes, and generals. The statue of Augustus from Prima Porta demonstrates this decorated cuirass, while the barefootedness of the emperor still seems to suggest the nudity of the gods. The high tide of imperial cuirassed statues, however, falls in the second century after Christ when, according to Professor Vermeule, "one senses that the emperors systematically populated the cities of North Africa and Asia Minor with their cuirassed statues."[54] And in another connection he stresses the fact that "the Trajanic and Hadrianic periods produced the greatest number of [cuirassed] statues."[55]

3) Together with the history of cuirassed statues, that of the Roman trophies should be considered, that is, of the cuirassed mannequins with armor placed on a pole. In his illuminating study on the Roman trophy, Professor Gilbert Charles Picard has pointed out that this ritual monument of victory does not antedate, in Greek art and literature, the late sixth or even early fifth century, and that, when it achieved greater popularity in Hellenistic times as an expression of Greek triumphal art, the trophies celebrated mainly the *Tyche* or *Eutychia* of the victorious general, his luck or good fortune.[56] In the Hellenistic monarchies, however, it referred also to the *Arete* of the king. In this sense, the trophy was inherited by Rome where its meaning still was that of the *Felicitas* of the victor, though it was linked under Augustus also to the Genius of the general, to the *genius Augusti*.[57] By the second century of our era, the theology of *Eutychia*, or Latin *Felicitas*, was gradually eclipsed by that of the *Virtus* of the general, that is, of the emperor whose *Virtus perpetua* was the ultimate cause of victory. Hence, the cuirass-trophies became monuments for, or symbols of, the victories of the emperor exclusively and of his *Virtus invicta*—one of the axioms of the late-imperial theology of victory.[58] Perhaps it may be said that the cuirassed statues of emperors, which became so overabundant in the Trajanic and Hadrianic period, made the armored ruler himself, as it were, a τρόπαιον ἔμψυχον, a living trophy glorifying the emperor's *Virtus perpetua*, his perpetual prowess and moral excellence.

4) There is reason to consult the evidence of the coins as well. Professor A. Alföldi has demonstrated strikingly that the Roman emperors in the time of the Principate were not supposed, or even not allowed, to wear the uniform and insignia of an *imperator* within the *pomerium* of Rome—except on the occasion of a *profectio* or some other strictly military event.[59] Normally they wore the toga, that is, civilian clothes. Hence, it was only another indication of the final prevalence of the military over the civilian (the latter represented by the Senate) that eventually, as has been aptly remarked, the *façade civile* gave way to the *réalité militaire*.[60] By the end of the first century the emperor wore almost always, even

[54] Vermeule, *op. cit.*, 7. See also George M. A. Hanfmann, "A New Trajan," *American Journal of Archaeology*, LXI (1957), 228f, and 226, n. 18, for the barefootedness of Augustus.

[55] Vermeule, *op. cit.*, 5.

[56] Gilbert Charles-Picard, *Les trophées romains: Contribution à l'histoire de la Religion et de l'Art triomphal de Rome* (Paris, 1957), 36ff.

[57] Picard, *op. cit.*, 168, 268ff.

[58] Picard, *op. cit.*, 371ff; see 466ff for the imperial theology of victory.

[59] A. Alföldi, "Insignien und Tracht der römischen Kaiser," *Deutsches archäologisches Institut: Römische Mitteilungen*, L (1935), 9ff, 43ff, 47f.

[60] *Ibid.*, 43.

within the *pomerium* of Rome, military attire with the attributes and insignia of his rank, exepting only the occasions when he performed religious functions or met the Senate.

The coins illustrate this development with all the clarity that we could desire. The obverse side of Roman coins displays as a rule the portrait head of the emperor. Of the Julian-Claudian house there is, with the exception of one sestertius of Nero, not a single coin which shows the emperor other than naked, that is, bare-necked.[61] Cuirassed portraits on coins remain extremely rare until the end of the first century. Then, under the emperors-by-adoption, the cuirassed image is found more frequently; it begins to prevail in the second half of the second century. In the third, the naked bust becomes almost obsolete and a real rarity, though it is still occasionally found under Septimius Severus, Caracalla, and Geta, and later under Gordian III, Gallienus, and Probus. The naked bust, however, is regularly found on coins commemorating the consecrated rulers; it becomes a privilege of the *Divi*.[62] The last pieces showing the emperor naked, that is, bare-necked, are a few beautiful medallions of Constantine the Great, one of which shows on the reverse, significantly, the emperor in uniform carrying a trophy over his left shoulder, with the inscription: VIRTUS CONSTANTINI AUG. (pl. 6, fig. 32).[63] Thereafter, in Christian times, all coins show the emperor either draped or, preferably, cuirassed and armed and often helmeted. The military *virtus* of the emperor and the military costume have conquered heroic or divine nudity.

5) The evidence of the coins supports the observations of Professor Vermeule who remarks that the earlier imperial cult statues portrayed emperors and princes in divine and heroic guise rather than in armor.[64] In other words, there originally was an *imitatio deorum* on the part of the emperors and, before their time, on the part of the Hellenistic kings. The armored statues of so many gods seem to indicate the reverse current: an *imitatio imperatorum* on the part of the gods.

An *aureus* of Septimius Severus may illustrate this fact and lead on to some further observations (pl. 7, fig. 33).[65] The coin shows the sun-god stepping on his chariot, the steeds ready to climb the sky which is indicated by cumuli of clouds arching over a *Tellus* who with her cornucopia rests comfortably reclined as though in an age of plenty and peace. The god, naked except for his fluttering shoulder cape is, however, not Apollo, but an Apollo sporting a pointed beard, that is, an Apollo having the features of Septimius Severus. The message of the coin is obvious. When the emperor rises (and his rise, *Oriens Augusti*, is a daily event like the rise of the sun),[66] Earth, *Tellus*, is in a state of grace,

---

[61] Cf. Mattingly, I, p. CLXXI, and pl. XLI, fig. 1 (p. 215, No. 111). For Galba, see I, p. LXIV, and pl. LII, fig. 6 (p. 310, No. 13). This refers only to the portrait on the obverse side of the coins; for on the reverse the emperor was shown even at an earlier date wearing the cuirass; see Alföldi, *op. cit.*, 47f, with fig. 5.

[62] R. Delbrück, *Die Münzbildnisse von Maximinus bis Carinus* (Berlin, 1940), 27ff, 100f, 128f, who emphasizes that the bare-necked portraits (less rare after 260 A.D.) referred above all to deified emperors.

[63] For specimens of these medallions, see Alfred R. Bellinger, "Roman and Byzantine medallions in the Dumbarton Oaks Collection," *Dumbarton Oaks Papers*, XII (1958), 125ff, and figs. 7–11, 13–14; see also figs. 20 and 28 for Constantine's sons, and p. 132 for the description of the *Virtus* medallion (fig. 7).

[64] Vermeule, "Cuirassed Statues," 7.

[65] Mattingly, *Coins of the Roman Empire in the British Museum*, V, 57, No. 226, pl. X, fig. 19 (A.D. 197). To this *aureus* in the British Museum Professor Andreas Alföldi obligingly called my attention, providing me at the same time with a photo.

[66] For this problem, see my forthcoming study *Oriens Augusti*.

Fig. 1 *a-b*. Alexandria mint, bronzes: Ares.

3.

2. 4.

Figs. 2, 3, 4. Alexandria mint, bronzes: Dioscuri.

Fig. 5. Theadelphia, temple of Pneferôs: Heron.

Fig. 6. Panel from the Fayyûm: Heron (right).

Fig. 7. Paris, Louvre, bronze statuette: Horus.

Pl. 2   GODS IN UNIFORM

Fig. 8. Former Coll. Fouquet,
terracotta: Horus.

Fig. 9. Cambridge (Mass.), Coll. A. D.
Nock, terracotta: Harpocrates.

Fig. 10. Former Coll. Sinadino, bronze
statuette: Horus.

Fig. 11. Former Coll. Bissing, bronze
statuette: Apis.

Fig. 12. Rome, Museo Nazionale,
bronze statuette: Anubis.

Fig. 13. Paris, Louvre, bronze statuette: Alexander.

Fig. 15. New York, Metropolitan Museum,
magical amulet: Anubis (enlarged).

Fig. 14. Former Coll. Fouquet,
bronze: Alexander with Aegis.

Pl. 4   GODS IN UNIFORM

Fig. 16. Alexandria, Kom-el Shugafa,
relief: Anubis anguipede.

Fig. 19. Paris, Louvre, relief from Palmyra: triad of gods.

Fig. 17. Univ. of Michigan, magical
amulet: lion-headed god.

Fig. 21. Damascus, Museum,
pottery tessera from
Palmyra: Aglibol.

Fig. 22. Rome, Palazzo dei Conservatori,
aedicula: Aglibol with Malakbêl.

Fig. 18. Alexandria
mint, billon:
Dea Roma.

Fig. 20. Damascus, Museum, relief from
Palmyra: Helios Theos Megistos.

Fig. 23. London, Brit. Mus., relief from
Palmyra: Shadrafa.

Fig. 24. New Haven, Yale University, relief from
Dura-Europos: Aphlad.

Fig. 25. New Haven, Yale University, wall drawing from Dura-Europos: sacrifice to Jarhibol.

Pl. 6   GODS IN UNIFORM

Fig. 26. Dura-Europos, wall painting: three gods.

Fig. 27. Baghdad, Iraq Museum, marble statue from Hatra: Assur-Bēl.

Fig. 28. Baghdad, Iraq Museum, relief from Hatra: sun-god.

Fig. 29. Tarsus mint, bronze: Mithras.

Fig. 32. Washington, Dumbarton Oaks, gold medallion: *Virtus Constantini*.

Fig. 31. Paris, Louvre, altar fragment from Hauran: Asklepios.

Fig. 30. Berlin, Staatl. Museen, relief: Dolichenus.

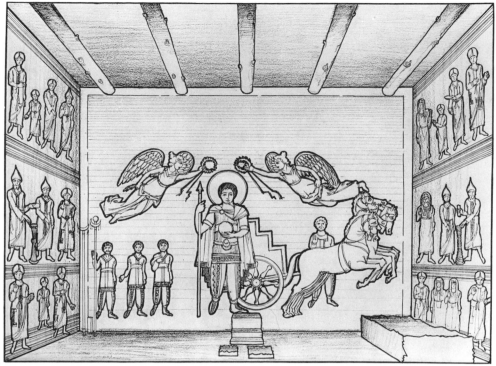

Fig. 35. Dura–Europos, wall painting: Zeus Theos.

Fig. 36. Leyden, Rijksmuseum, stele: Apollo and Artemis.

Fig. 33. London, Brit. Mus., aureus of Septimius Severus: Emperor rising on chariot of *Sol* (enlarged).

Fig. 34. Vatican, *phalera: Sol Invictus Augustus.*

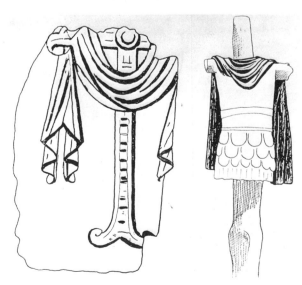

Fig. 37. North Africa: *tropaeum Crucis* and trophy.

Pl. 8   GODS IN UNIFORM

Fig. 38. Stuttgart Psalter, fol. 107ᵛ: Psalm XC, 13.

Fig. 39. Visé, shrine of St.
Hadeline: Psalm XC, 13.

Fig. 40. Ravenna, Archiepiscopal Chapel,
mosaic: Psalm XC, 13.

Fig. 41. Ravenna, San Vitale, mosaic: Justinian.   Fig. 42. Istanbul, Kariye Camii, wall painting: St. George.

Fig. 43 *a-b*. Venice, San Marco, relief: (*a*) St. George, (*b*) St. Demetrius.

Pl. 10　　　　　　　　　　　GODS IN UNIFORM

Fig. 44. Rietz im Oberinntal, Antoniuskirche,
statue: St. Anthony of Padua.

Fig. 45. Postal card (1914): Admiral
St. Anthony and the Tyrol Kaiserjäger.

Figs. 46, 47. Athens, Benaki Museum, fragments of late Roman pottery dishes: Horsemen.

Fig. 1. Rome, S. Maria Maggiore, mosaic: Hypapante.

Fig. 2. Paris, Bibl. Nat. MS gr. 74, fol. 167: St. John (reduced).

Pl. 12   *PUER EXORIENS*

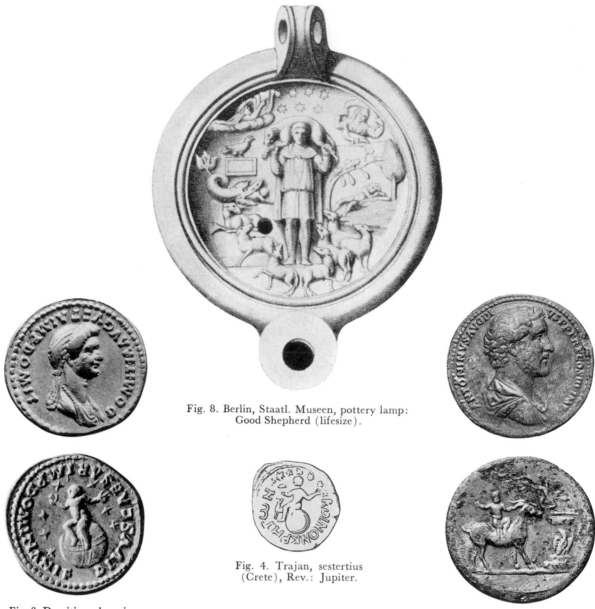

Fig. 8. Berlin, Staatl. Museen, pottery lamp:
Good Shepherd (lifesize).

Fig. 4. Trajan, sestertius
(Crete), Rev.: Jupiter.

Fig. 3. Domitian, denarius:
Rev., Jupiter.

Fig. 5. Antoninus Pius, bronze
medallion: Rev., Jupiter.

Fig. 6. Gallienus, antoninianus:
Rev., IOVI CRESCENTI.

Fig. 7. Gallienus, sestertius:
Rev., IOVI EXORIENTI.

of peace, and of comfort, in the state of a new felicity of a dawning Golden Age—*Tuus iam regnat Apollo* as visualized by Virgil in the Fourth Eclogue. Septimius Severus did not introduce the design. It is found on a *phalera*, a plaque serving as a decoration on the trappings of horses or of armor, now in the Vatican (pl. 7, fig. 34), and ascribed to the second century after Christ.[67] It is further found on a bronze medallion of Antoninus Pius,[68] and on two of Commodus.[69] While one of the Commodus issues clearly shows the youthful sun-god, the other one shows the deity bearded like Commodus. The emperors in their nakedness thus indulged in an *imitatio deorum*. But the opposite trend, closely connected with the militarization of the imperial appearance, made itself felt as well. A relief from Ephesus of the time of Marcus Aurelius shows approximately the same scene.[70] Here, however, the person stepping onto the chariot is clearly the emperor wearing imperial uniform—the cuirass with metal *pteryges* and sash. The chariot is seen also in a wall painting at Dura, in the shrine of Zeus Theos (pl. 7, fig. 35).[71] Here, however, the god, holding lance and globe, is not naked. He is dressed in Hellenistic-Parthian costume, the *paludamentum* held by a golden fibula on his shoulder. Actually, the sun-god himself appears in full imperial dress, though not in military attire, for example, on a stele from Asia Minor, now in the Museum at Leyden (pl. 7, fig. 36).[72]

We notice that the *imitatio deorum* on the part of the emperors was supplemented by an *imitatio imperatorum* on the part of the gods. This principle of mutual imitation was actually carried so far that after the model of the imperial apotheosis (the emperor's ascent on an eagle) the gods in Egypt were "apotheosized" after the same fashion although as gods they were not in need of an apotheosis.[73] But the same idea is found in Syria as well, where a tetradrachm of the third century shows the same design.[74] That is to say, the gods were treated as though they were emperors, and the emperors as though they were gods.

6) There is yet another argument which has been advanced to explain the military costume of so many gods in Egypt and the Near East, and this has to be considered seriously. It has been suggested that the military attire may have rendered many of the foreign gods, the *dii peregrini*, more acceptable[75] to the Romans who, as we know, often

---

[67] Margherita Guarducci, "Sol invictus augustus," *Rendiconti della Pont. Accad. Romana di archeologia*, Ser. III, vol. XXX–XXXI (1957–59), 161ff, tentatively dated the *phalera* second century. The inscription in the exergue reads: *Inventori lucis Soli invicto augusto*. See also F. Cumont, *Textes et monuments*, II, 108, No. 89. I am again greatly indebted to my colleague Andreas Alföldi for a photo of this placque.

[68] F. Gnecchi, *I medaglioni romani* (Milan, 1912), pl. L, fig. 6; cf. p. 16, No. 67. See also Jocelyn M. C. Toynbee, *The Hadrianic School* (Cambridge, 1934), pl. XIX, fig. 8, and p. 141, n. 5.

[69] Gnecchi, *op. cit.* (supra, n. 68), pl. LXXVIII, figs. 3–4, and p. 52, Nos. 3–4; Toynbee, *op. cit.*, pl. XIX, fig. 9.

[70] R. Heberdey, in *Jahreshefte des österreichischen archäologischen Instituts*, VII (1904), Beiblatt 55f; S. Reinach, *Répertoire de reliefs grecs et romains* (Paris, 1909), I, 144, fig. 3; Mrs. Arthur Strong, in *Journal of Roman Studies*, I (1911), 39f, pl. XII, and her *Roman Sculpture from Augustus*

to Constantine (London, 1907), 295; Toynbee, *op. cit.*, 141 and pl. XXXII, fig. 3.

[71] Rostovtzeff, *Dura-Europos and its Art*, pl. XIII, facing p. 74; cf. André Grabar, *Martyrium* (Paris, 1943), II, 140f.

[72] Rijksmuseum van Oudheden, Leiden, to which I am much obliged for providing me with a photo. The stele, as Professor F. K. Dörner kindly informed me, has been published by F. Cumont, in *Comptes-rendus de l'Académie des inscriptions et belles-lettres*, 1915, p. 270ff; cf. Stig Wikander, *Feuerpriester in Kleinasien und Iran* (Lund, 1946), 4f.

[73] J. Vogt, *Die alexandrinischen Münzen* (Stuttgart, 1924), 73f, calls attention to this apotheosis of gods; see also F. Cumont, in *Revue d'histoire des religions*, LXII (1910), 138f.

[74] See, e.g., Alfred Bellinger, *The Syrian Tetradrachms of Caracalla and Macrinus* (Numismatic Studies, III; New York, 1940), pl. IX, fig. 2.

[75] Ern. Will, *Le relief cultuel*, 270f: "pour les rendre acceptables."

equated the foreign gods with their own, at least in name, though not always in substance. Hence, while the gods of the Roman Capitol were always represented as gods and not as officers, if we except Mars who professionally was often shown in military guise;[76] and while it would not have occurred to the Romans to put their own Jupiter into a uniform, it was different with the foreign gods. The *dii peregrini* were assimilated or romanized by means of their uniform, no matter whether the impulse may have come from the Orientals or from the Romans.

*   *   *

If we now review our arguments—(1) the late appearance of uniform military equipment; (2) the development of the cuirassed statues; (3) the development of the armored trophies; (4) the development of the cuirassed coin portraits of Roman emperors replacing the bare-necked portraits; (5) the interrelation of *imitatio deorum* on the part of the emperors and *imitatio imperatorum* on the part of the gods; (6) the tendency to romanize the *dii peregrini* by means of displaying them in military attire—we have a considerable number of clues at our disposal suggesting how it came about that so many gods of Egypt and the Near East were represented in uniform. Nor will it be really surprising to find that also the last of the Oriental and foreign gods penetrating, and finally conquering, the Roman empire fell in with this general militarization and im-perialization of the deities. Christ was repeatedly represented with the imperial purple chlamys around his shoulders, as, for example, in the ceiling-painting of the Roman tomb of Clodius Hermes, *ca.* A.D. 230[77]—that is, at a time when also the expression *Christus Imperator* had become relatively common.[78] Even the victorious cross, taking the place of the pagan trophy, was sometimes decorated with the imperial *paludamentum*, which is found also as a special decoration of the pagan victory trophy the crossbeam of which, supporting the cuirass, may have produced some similarity with the *tropaeum Crucis* (pl. 7, fig. 37).[79]

Christ in military attire, however, is rather rare. A terracotta funerary plaque of early Merovingian times is too worn and its photographic reproduction too indistinct to control its editor's contention according to which Christ was represented in the costume of a Roman general holding a globe in his hand and stepping on the lion and the dragon.[80] It is quite likely, however, that the editor was correct. For in connection with Psalm 90,

[76] See, e.g., Vermeule, "Cuirassed Statues," pl. VII, fig. 24, for Mars Ultor in the Capitoline Museum, in Rome. On coins, of course, he is also very often in strictly military attire; see, e.g., Dattari *Numi Augg. Alexandrini*, pl. IX, where Ares appears both in the nude (no. 2464) and cuirassed (no. 2460) in the times of Antoninus Pius (see our pl. 1, fig. 1 *a–b*).

[77] Fritz Wirth, *Römische Wandmalerei vom Untergang Pompejis bis ans Ende des dritten Jahrhunderts* (Berlin, 1934), 190 and pl. 50: tomb of Clodius Hermes (ca. 230 A.D.), painting in the ceiling of one of the niches.

[78] See Erik Peterson, "Christus als Imperator," in his *Theologische Traktate* (Munich, 1951), 151ff; also J.

Kollwitz, "Christus," *Reallexikon für Antike und Christen-tum*, II (1954), 1257ff.

[79] See J. Baradez and M. Leglay, "La croix-trophée et le reliquiaire d'Aïoun-Berich," *Cahiers archéologiques*, IX (1957), 77, figs. 2–3; for the problem in general, see Gilbert Charles-Picard, *Les trophées romains* (Paris, 1957), 494ff, and André Grabar, *L'empereur dans l'art byzantin* (Strasbourg and Paris, 1936), 239ff.

[80] Raymond Lantier, "Plaque funéraire de terre-cuite mérovingienne," *Jahrbuch des Römisch-Germanischen Zentralmuseums*, I (1954), 237f, a study to which Miss Mary Morehart obligingly called my attention.

13: "Thou shalt tread upon the adder and the basilisk, the lion and the dragon shalt thou trample under feet," St. Augustine, in his *Enarrations on the Psalms*, felt inclined to style Christ the *imperator;* and his commentary, through the agency of the ordinary Psalter gloss, remained influential throughout the Middle Ages.[81] This then may be the reason for the somewhat perplexing fact that the rare medieval representations of Christ as a warrior—*Christus miles* or *Christus belliger*—serve mostly, though not exclusively, as an illustration of this Psalm versicle. Christ in medieval armor is found, for example, in the ninth-century Stuttgart Psalter (pl. 8, fig. 38),[82] and also on the right end of the Hadelinus Casket in Visé, of the late eleventh century (pl. 8, fig. 39).[83] In both cases the warrior Christ wears the purple chlamys, and holds in his left hand the book, in his right a lance or a staff; in the Psalter miniature he even wears the imperial shoes leaving the toes free.

The general pattern of these representations has its history. In the Archiepiscopal Chapel at Ravenna we find a mosaic picturing Christ, holding the book in his left hand and shouldering the cross-staff with his right in exactly the fashion in which Constantine (see pl. 6, fig. 32) carries the trophy. He stands on lion and dragon—not as *Christus miles*, but in the full and authentic uniform of a Roman *imperator* (pl. 8, fig. 40).[84] Over a long-sleeved tunic, he wears a golden cuirass with one row of small *pteryges* from which the leather flaps dangle, fringed at the ends. His shoulders are protected by similar leather tabs. His sash is hardly visible because most of his cuirass is covered by the purple *paludamentum*. The purple itself is fastened at the right shoulder by a round fibula framed by a circle of pearls or stones. From the fibula there dangle three long pendants composed of stiff golden pins ending in a large pearl each.

The fibula with three pendants of pearls is one of the foremost imperial insignia reserved for the emperors exclusively.[85] We know this insignia from the Madrid silver *missorium* of Theodosius I, where the emperor as well as his two sons and co-caesars displays the fibula with the three pendants,[86] and from the mosaic of Justinian in San Vitale at Ravenna (pl. 9, fig. 41).[87] Contrariwise, the imperial governor of Hermopolis, Aphrodisius, seen

[81] Augustine, *Enarrationes in Psalmos*, XC, 5; Migne, *PL*, XXXVII, 1163; cf. E. H. Kantorowicz, *The King's Two Bodies* (Princeton, 1957), 71f, n. 69, for some later radiations.

[82] Stuttgart, Württembergische Landesbibliothek: Psalter; ed. Ernest T. DeWald, *The Stuttgart Psalter* (Princeton, 1930), fol. 107ᵛ.

[83] Alice Baird, "The Shrine of S. Hadeline, Visé," *Burlington Magazine*, XXXI (1917), 20 and pls. I–II; J. Helbig, *Art Mosan* (Bruxelles, 1906), I, pl. facing p. 44.

[84] J. Wilpert, *Die römischen Mosaiken und Malereien* (Freiburg, 1917), I, pl. 89 and p. 47 (the lower part of the mosaic is restored, which, however, does not affect the present argument). See also André Grabar, *L'empereur dans l'art byzantin*, 237ff, and Marion Lawrence, *The Sarcophagi of Ravenna* (Monographs on Archaeology and Fine Arts, II; 1945), 26, n. 130, for additional bibliography. See further E. Weigand, "Zum Denkmälerkreis des Christogramm-nimbus," *Byzantinische Zeitschrift*, XXXII (1932), 73ff.

[85] For the fibula, see Richard Delbrück, *Die Consulardiptychen und verwandte Denkmäler* (Berlin, 1926–1929), text p. 40; Josef Déer, *Der Kaiserornat Friedrichs II* (Bern,

1952), 48ff, with full bibliography, and "Ein Doppelbildnis Karls des Grossen," *Forschungen zur Kunstgeschichte und christlichen Archäologie*, II (1953), 111; see also Kantorowicz, *The King's Two Bodies*, 416, n. 341, for the later development.

[86] Grabar, *op. cit.* (supra, n. 84), pl. XVI; also, for the bibliography, Delbrück, *Consulardiptychen*, 235ff., No. 62. For a better reproduction, see Déer, *Kaiserornat Friedrichs II*, pl. XXIV, figs. 4–5, who (p. 49) for good reasons believes that the new type of the fibula with three pendants does not antedate Constantine the Great (ca. A.D. 315).

[87] The mosaic has been reproduced very often; see, e.g., Grabar, *op. cit.*, pl. XX, fig. 1; Otto G. von Simson, *Sacred Fortress* (Chicago, 1948), pl. III; see also pl. XXVII, for the mosaic in Sant'Apollinare in Classe, where only the ruling emperor, Constantine IV Pogonatus, has the fibula with the three pendants, but not his sons Heraclius and Tiberius, although they, too, are haloed. For the third mosaic (of either Theodoric or Justinian), see Fr. von Lorentz, "Theodorich — nicht Justinian," *Römische Mitteilungen*, L (1935), 333ff, pl. LXIV.

in the mosaic of the arch in Santa Maria Maggiore, in Rome, displays a fibula with no more than two pendants.[88] That is to say, Christ is represented in the correct uniform of a Roman general, or rather an emperor, including the correct insignia.

The Ravenna mosaic of Christ triumphant over lion and dragon is the last representation of what may be called a god in uniform. It is true that certain saints, especially in Byzantine art, were uniformed even in later centuries and their tunics sometimes reveal that they were enlisted in cadres of the imperial guards.[89] The two Saints Theodore (Stratelates and Tiro), Saint George, Saint Demetrius, Saint Procopius, and Saint Mercurius still appear in the late thirteenth-century frescoes of Kariye Camii, at Istanbul, in their traditional late Roman uniform (pl. 9, fig. 42),[90] and even in relatively modern (seventeenth- and eighteenth-century) Russian icons these saints are represented quite often in their quasi-classical military attire. Admittedly, their costume no longer is quite accurate and tends to become fantastic. But Saints George and Demetrius, in their relief icons of the west façade of San Marco in Venice (pl. 9, 43 *a–b*), still show the correct armor of late antiquity and display the officer's sash tied in the Hercules knot.[91]

In the West, some saints were not only awarded knighthood, but received real army commissions, even in quite modern times. It was a paramilitary distinction when Saint Andrew of Amalfi was made a knight of the Golden Fleece by Philip III of Spain, a decoration which the saint actually wears when on his feast-day his statue is carried in procession through the streets of Amalfi. But it is far more startling when we hear that Saint Anthony of Padua, who died in 1231, was appointed in 1731, by Philip V of Spain, an admiral of the Spanish Navy with an admiral's salary, and that the King himself decorated the saint's statue with the plumed hat of an admiral, with the bemedaled sash, and with a sword and a marshal's baton (pl. 10, fig. 44),[92] uniform insignia which the saint wore over his Franciscan cowl. A few years before that event, in 1710, Saint Anthony, a native of Portugal, had been appointed a general of the Portuguese army in the field.[93] In a way, he shared this high military rank with Saint Sebastian, who was a general of the Portuguese army in garrison.[94]

What was good for the mother country, was good for the colony, Brazil, where military honors were conferred upon Saint Anthony. By letters patent of 1751, Saint Anthony was commissioned a captain of infantry in the Brazilian army, captaincy of

---

[88] Wilpert, *Die römischen Mosaiken*, 489 and pls. 66–68.

[89] R. Delbrück, "Der spätantike Kaiserornat," *Die Antike*, VIII (1932), 20, indicates that the military saints wore torques and that the trimmings of their tunics disclosed their attachment to various guard regiments; see also Otto Treitinger, *Die oströmische Kaiser- und Reichsidee* (Jena, 1938), 51.

[90] H. Delehaye, *Les légendes grecques des saints militaires* (Paris, 1909), 2ff; Paul A. Underwood, "Fourth Preliminary Report on the Restoration of the Frescoes in the Kariye Camii at Istanbul by the Byzantine Institute," *Dumbarton Oaks Papers*, XIII (1959), 189, 192f, 195, 197f, 207, figs. 3, 4, 8, 10–14.

[91] Otto Demus, *The Church of San Marco in Venice*

(Dumbarton Oaks Studies, VI; Washington, D.C., 1960), figs. 40–41.

[92] Beda Kleinschmidt, *Antonius von Padua* (Forschungen zur Volkskunde, 6–8; Düsseldorf, 1931), 358, and fig. 344 (p. 360). This study was most obligingly called to my attention by the Rev. P. Paul Grosjean, S.J., in Brussels, who readily provided me with additional information. [Editors' note: Kantorowicz's pl. 10, fig. 44 showed the statue of St. Anthony in the same attire as in pl. 10, fig. 45; our pl. 10, fig. 44 (a new photograph taken on the Feast of St. Anthony, June 13, 1964) reveals the figure somewhat differently arrayed.]

[93] Kleinschmidt, *Antonius*, 359.

[94] *Ibid.*, 360.

Rio de Janeiro.[95] This rank he held, with monthly pay of 4,000 cruzados and back pay of 540,000 cruzados, until 1810, when, by letters patent of October 25 of that year, he was commissioned a major in the Brazilian army with monthly pay of 36,000 cruzados. And finally, on July 26, 1814, he was promoted to the rank of lieutenant-colonel of the Brazilian Infantry. His salary of 80,000 cruzados monthly (*ca.* $40) was actually paid to him—that is, to a Franciscan convent in Rio de Janeiro—until 1911, when the Brazilian government revised all payments made to churches and monasteries. But the military rank of Saint Anthony was not forgotten. In 1914 the Austrian crack regiment, His Apostolic Majesty's Own Tyrol Rifle Regiment (*Tiroler Kaiserjäger*), went to war protected by Saint Anthony in the uniform of a Spanish Admiral, who had his cultual center in the Tyrol, in and around Innsbruck (pl. 10, fig. 45).[96]

What was possible with regard to saints, both Eastern and Western, was not possible with regard to the Christian God. *Christus belliger* or *miles*, as has been demonstrated, was represented occasionally in the Middle Ages; but he wore individual armor, and not a uniform—simply because there were no uniforms in the Western Middle Ages. And when in the late seventeenth century uniforms again made their appearance—the Coldstream Guards for example, date back to King Charles II, and the papal Swiss Guard to the pontificate of Pope Julius II, while the design of their uniform is ascribed to Michelangelo—it no longer was possible or befitting to bestow upon the Christian God the rank of an honorary colonel of the Coldstream or Grenadier Guards or of the Irish Guards. Hence, the late-classical idea of representing gods in the correct military attire with the insignia of rank ended in the Ravenna mosaic of Christ defeating the lion and the dragon.

How are we to explain the idea itself of picturing the gods in the uniform of officers or generals? It is difficult, of course, to give a satisfactory answer which would fit all circumstances. This much, however, may be safely said, that the cuirassed statues of Hellenistic kings and Roman emperors, the cuirassed portraits on coins, and also the display of arms and armor *per se* in the form of trophies shouldered by the emperor or serving as a decoration, all are features indicative of the prowess, the *virtus* of the person so represented or so honored. In a similar sense the cuirass, the military attire of the gods, may have served to indicate their prowess, their *virtus*. It was the *virtus* of the Dioscuri, the *virtus* of Horus, the *virtus* of Asklepius or of the Oriental sun-gods which, just as the *virtus* of the emperors, was to be made manifest by the uniform or armor—and it culminated finally with the *virtus Christi imperatoris* defeating lion and dragon.[97]

Therewith this rapid survey contributes, if from an admittedly narrow angle, to a far broader problem; that is, to the problem of the survival and the continuity of pagan iconography in Christian garb, or to the problem of the transition from pagan Antiquity to the Christian Middle Ages. And this survival by transference is really all that this paper intended to demonstrate.

[95] *Ibid.*, 360f, for the various promotions.

[96] *Ibid.*, 356, fig. 341.

[97] G. C. Picard, *Les trophées romains*, 511f.

APPENDIX

Two fragments of *terra sigillata* from the Benaki Museum in Athens came to the author's attention only after the manuscript was ready for the printer.[98] Whether they are relevant to the problem discussed in the preceding pages will be difficult to decide. But since the two pieces are as yet unpublished they may be edited here, whatever their value may be for the present argument.

The fragments (pl. 10, figs. 46 and 47) form the upper and upper right sections respectively of rectangular dishes of quite fine pottery characteristic of late Roman ware.[99] The dishes have a relatively high rim which on the top is broad enough for the display of ornamental figures produced by stamps.[100] Dishes of this kind are well known. They usually were imitations of silver dishes presented to, or by, the high officers of the Roman Empire, cheap copies fabricated *en masse* for and purchased by the ordinary citizen—paperbacks, as it were, as compared to *de luxe* editions.[101] Those dishes could be round when modeled upon silver *missoria*, or rectangular when copied after a rectangular dish.[102] Roman law mentions both and even discloses their technical name: *lanx quadrata vel rutunda*.[103]

The fragments of the Benaki Museum thus belonged to the type of *lances quadratae* made of pottery, and the similarity of their decorated rims as well as the identity of the design of the central pieces of which actually a third specimen is known,[104] make it clear that we are dealing with objects of mass production. The design of the center *emblema* shows two horsemen facing each other and holding their horses by the bridle, using for this purpose their far hands, that is, the right figure the right hand and the left one his left. In their other hands they hold spears with a broad blade, the right figure carrying the weapon upright, the left one carrying it horizontally. These horsemen in counterposition suggest the Dioscuri who were represented over and over again in this attitude. The costume of the horsemen is richly decorated or embroidered, their sleeved tunics as well as their *paludamenta*. The trappings of their mounts, visible especially in the smaller fragment (pl. 10, fig. 47), are likewise quite rich, an unusual feature in representations of the Dioscuri even when displayed in uniform. More startling, however, are the Phrygian caps which both riders wear. We might be inclined to interpret this headgear as a misunderstood *pileus*, the felt cap normally worn by the divine twins, and accordingly to identify the two horsemen as militarily overdressed Dioscuri.[105]

---

[98] I am greatly indebted to Professor Howard Comfort, of Haverford College, who first called my attention to the larger fragment; to Professor M. Chatzidakis, Director of the Benaki Museum in Athens, for sending me a photograph not only of the larger fragment, but also of the smaller fragment hitherto unknown to me; and to Professor A. Alföldi, my colleague at the Institute for Advanced Study, for patiently giving me advice concerning many essential items.

[99] For the dishes of that kind, see Alan J. B. Wace, "Late Roman pottery and plates," *Bulletin de la société royale d'archéologie d'Alexandrie*, XXXVII (1948), 47–56, a study to which Professor Homer A. Thompson kindly called my attention.

[100] See Wace, 52.

[101] Wace, 54f; cf. H. Fuhrmann, "Studien zu den Consulardyptichen verwandten Denkmälern," *Römische Mitteilungen*, LV (1940), 92–99.

[102] Wace, pl. III, reproduces such a dish. Fuhrmann, 93, mentions that he intended to deal with these rectangular dishes on a later occasion, but he died before publishing that study.

[103] *Digest*, 6,1,6; cf. Delbrück, *Consulardyptichen*, 70, n. 250.

[104] See below, n. 106.

[105] For the Dioscuri in military attire, see above, notes 2 and 5, and pl. 1, figs. 2 and 4.

This identification, however, is defeated by the inscription running in two lines above the heads of the figures. It reads:

ORATIONIBUS SANTORUM PE

RDUCET DOMINUS.

The inscription is the same in both fragments, and it was the same also in a third specimen, found in 1860 by a French farmer in Algiers, of which we have a good description but which no longer exists: "en l'absence du colon Nicollet, ses enfants ont cassé le plat," ends the report of the finding rather disappointingly.[106] The lettering itself is almost identical in both pieces if we except the 'S' in DOMINUS (pl. 10, fig. 47) which apparently was not properly rendered by the stamp and which has been added in a somewhat clumsy and crude fashion. The inscription is obviously incomplete, and we would expect some continuation in the lower section of the pictures; for to the beholder it should be revealed whom and whither *perducet Dominus* on the strength of the prayers of the saints. The whole phrase has a "liturgical" ring, and in fact there are numerous passages in the earliest Western sacramentary, the *Leonianum*, which might serve to supplement the inscription; for example: "...sanctorum deprecatione placatus [Deus] ... [populum] ad sanctorum gaudia sempiterna perducat";[107] or "...nos ad caelestia regna perducens";[108] or "...ad misericordiam perducat aeternam."[109] It would seem most likely that some place of destination similar to those quoted was found in the lower section of the central image. Curiously, the continuation of the inscription was lacking also in the Algerian specimen,[110] and later editors of the inscription added: *nos ad regna caelorum*, with a question mark.[111]

However that may be, it is obvious that the two horsemen are not the Dioscuri, but Christian saints. Who are they? We do not know equestrian saints represented after the fashion of the twin gods. It is true that in the *Pistis Sophia*, a Gnostic tractate of the third century, mention is made quite often of the "Twin Redeemers" (σωτῆρες), but they are identified with the "Child of the Child" which obviously does not fit.[112] Other identifications of the Dioscuri with twin saints are either unconvincing or do not fit the image of the *sigillata* fragments.[113] Unfortunately, the pictures on the rim of the dishes do not offer a clue either. In the frieze of the larger fragment (pl. 10, fig. 46) we recognize in the center an *aedicula* (not upright, but lying on its left side) harboring a person. To the

[106] See *Revue africaine*, VI (1862), 463f. The finder gave a reasonably good description of his *trouvaille* to a local newspaper. His report was reprinted by the editor of the *Revue africaine* whence it was passed on to scholarly works of epigraphy. See *Corpus inscriptionum latinarum*, VIII, 9285, where also the report is reprinted. See further Paul Monceaux, "Enquête sur l'épigraphie chrétienne d'Afrique," *Mémoires présentés par divers savants à l'Académie des Inscriptions et Belles-Lettres de France*, XII: 1 (1908), 308, No. 321; Ernst Diehl, *Inscriptiones latinae christianae veteres* (Berlin, 1925), II, 487, No. 2499.

[107] *Sacramentarium Veronese*, ed. L. C. Mohlberg, Leo Eizenhöfer, and Petrus Siffrin, 12, 16f, No. 87.

[108] *Ibid.*, 72, 2, No. 551.

[109] *Ibid.*, 155, 10, No. 1218.

[110] *Revue africaine*, VI, 463f: "Où le Seigneur conduira-

t-il? Probablement à la gloire, au combat, à la victoire." The finder thought that the two warriors were North-African Arians at war against the orthodox Christians.

[111] So Monceaux, followed by Diehl (above, n. 9).

[112] *Pistis Sophia*, ed. Carl Schmidt, *Koptisch-gnostische Schriften* (Leipzig, 1905), I, 147ff, and passim (see Index, *s.v.* "Zwillingserlöser").

[113] J. Rendel Harris, *The Dioscuri in the Christian Legends* (London, 1903), is brilliant but evasive. Henri Grégoire, *Saints jumeaux et dieux cavaliers* (Bibliothèque hagiographique orientale, IX; Paris, 1905), deals with triplets and not with twins. W. Kraus, "Dioskuren," *Reallexikon für Antike und Christentum*, III (1957), 1134ff, mentions Saints Peter and Paul, Cosmas and Damian as Dioscuri by transference, but these saints cannot be identified with the horsemen of the fragments.

right and left of the *aedicula* are lions running in opposite directions, similar to those found in pottery *missoria* at Madrid and elsewhere.[114] They are purely decorative, just as the amphora (also lying) to the right of the right lion. It would be tempting to interpret the lions as indicative of a *venatio* and the two horsemen as *venatores*.[115] But this meaning would not be supported by the pictures of the third specimen, the dish from Algiers. According to the report of the finder of that dish, there were three male figures on each of the four sides of the rim; the finder first thought they represented the twelve apostles, but gave up the idea because all twelve figures were made of the same stamp. Moreover, in the center of the upper rim there was the figure of a child "holding in its hand an emblem in the form of a 'Y',"[116] that is, the *littera Pythagorae*.[117] Hence, for the interpretation of the horsemen the picture-friezes on the rims of the dishes do not yield a clue either.

There is one more item which demands our attention. Between the two horses is a stand or a table—the Algerian report says "an urn"—on the top of which something that looks like two leaves is plainly visible. Professor Alföldi suggested that the stand might be an agonal table on which the prizes are laid out, the rewards given as a symbol of victory. Among those prizes were not only crowns, but often also individual leaves made of gold or a few gold coins or medals.[118] Similar tables are quite often displayed on coins, especially of Nero.[119] We usually find on them a crown and an urn, whereas under the top of the table we recognize figures such as two sphinxes facing each other or two gryphons. On one specimen, however, there are apparently two horsemen, in this case the twins, who face each other.[120] If indeed there should be in the images of the *sigillatae* an allusion to victory, it might be advisable to supplement the inscription accordingly and add perhaps the words *ad victoriam sempiternam*.[121] The whole inscription, in that case, would read:

> ORATIONIBUS SANTORUM PE
> RDUCET DOMINUS
> [AD VICTORIAM SEMPITERNAM].

It would mean that the orations of the military saints prompted the Lord to lead the faithful to sempiternal victory. Unless, however, an undamaged dish turns up in some other collection or museum it will be impossible to supplement the inscription correctly or even to understand the meaning of the pottery centers. The date of the *sigillatae* may be fourth century or early fifth. They seem to be characteristic of the age of transition from pagan antiquity to the medieval Christian world, and the equestrian saints in military costume, if saints they are, would be exponents of the same evolution.

---

[114] See, for the pottery *missorium* of the Museo arqueologico, in Madrid, Fuhrmann, in *Römische Mitteilungen*, LV (1940), pl. XII.

[115] In the *missorium* of Madrid is indeed one horseman, a *venator*; but his costume is very different from that of the fragments from the Benaki Museum. For the "moral" aspects of the *venatio*, see André Grabar, *L'empereur dans l'art byzantin*, 57ff, 133ff.

[116] *Revue africaine*, VI, 463: "Un enfant, placé au milieu du rebord supérieur, tient à la main un emblême en forme d'Y."

[117] For the literature on the Pythagorean letter, see Theodor E. Mommsen, in *Journal of the Warburg and Courtauld Institutes*, XVI (1953), 184, n. 1; see also his *Mediaeval and Renaissance Studies* (Ithaca, 1959), 184, n. 26.

[118] Delbrück, *Consulardyptichen*, 70ff, § 4.

[119] Harold Mattingly, *Coins of the Roman Empire in the British Museum* (London, 1923), I, pl. 45, figs. 3, 5–8, and p. 250ff, Nos. 259, 264ff.

[120] Paris, Bibliothèque Nationale, Cabinet des médailles, No. 10708, a photograph of which was kindly placed at my disposal by Professor A. Alföldi.

[121] *Sacramentarium Veronese*, 50, 4, No. 366.

PUER EXORIENS

ON THE HYPAPANTE IN THE MOSAICS OF S. MARIA MAGGIORE

In a brilliant chapter of iconographic sleuthing, Professor A. Grabar, efficiently seconded by Professor J. Gagé, has unriddled the meaning of one of the mosaics in the arch of S. Maria Maggiore, in Rome, displaying the Presentation of Christ in the Temple.[1] The feast is now known, in the West, as that of Candlemas or of the Purification of the Virgin Mary, that is, a Marian feast celebrating, in accordance with Ex. 13 and Lev. 12, the purification of the Mother of God on the fortieth day after having given birth to her son.[2] Originally, however, the day marked, both in the East and in the early Western Church, not a feast of St. Mary, but a feast of the Lord, *Hypapante*, or, in Latin, *Occursus Domini*, celebrating the meeting of the aged Simeon with the new-born Saviour of the World.[3]

The earliest-known representation of the *Hypapante*, the one in the arch of S. Maria Maggiore of the second quarter of the fifth century (pl. 11, fig. 1), is at the same time the most cryptic one, for it is unique in every respect.[4] One very strange feature is the separation of Simeon from the Child, carried in the arms of St. Mary before being passed to the arms of Simeon. In the Roman mosaic the two protagonists—the Child and St. Simeon—are separated from each other by a group of three persons: St. Joseph and the

Reprinted, with permission, from *Perennitas. Beiträge zur christlichen Archäologie und Kunst, zur Geschichte der Literatur, der Liturgie und des Mönchtums sowie zur Philosophie des Rechts und zur politischen Philosophie. P. Thomas Michels OSB zum 70. Geburtstag.* Edd. Hugo Rahner, SJ, and Emmanuel von Severus, OSB (Beiträge zur Geschichte des alten Mönchtums und des Benediktinerordens, Supplementband, 2; Aschendorffschen Verlagsbuchhandlung, Münster/Westf., 1963), 118–135.

[1] A. Grabar, *L'empereur dans l'art byzantin* (Paris, 1936), 216–225; J. Gagé, "Le templum Urbis et les origines de l'idée de Renovatio," *Annuaire de l'Institut de Philologie et d'Histoire Orientales et Slaves: Mélanges Franz Cumont*, IV (1936), 151–187, and his study "Saeculum novum" in *Transactions of the International Numismatic Congress in London, June 30–July 3, 1936* (London, 1938), 182ff. Cf. O. Casel, *Archiv für Liturgiewissenschaft*, I (1950), 250, No. 199.

[2] E. Lucius, *Die Anfänge des Heiligenkults in der christlichen Kirche* (Tübingen, 1904), 483f; L. Eisenhofer, *Handbuch der katholischen Liturgik* (Freiburg, 1932), I, 582f.

[3] The *occursus* belongs, as its name suggests (*Hypapante*, ἀπάντησις), to the more general *adventus* or "epiphany" ceremonial; see E. H. Kantorowicz, "The 'King's Advent' and the Enigmatic Panels in the Doors of Santa Sabina," *Art Bulletin*, XXVI (1944), 218, n. 73; 227, n. 123. See also M. Higgins, "Note on the Purification (and Date of Nativity) in Constantinople in 602," *Archiv für Liturgiewissenschaft*, II (1952), 81–83, for the date of the Feast (Febr. 2 or 14) and for the shift from a celebration in which "originally the Saviour was uppermost" to a feast emphasizing the role of St. Mary. Also Eisenhofer, *loc. cit.*

[4] D. C. Shorr, "The Iconographic Development of the Presentation in the Temple," *Art Bulletin*, XXVIII (1946), 17–32, especially 19f, for the representation in S. Maria Maggiore. The author of this in many respects satisfactory and methodical study was unfortunately not acquainted with the results of the works of Grabar and Gagé, nor with the iconographic study of A. Xyngopoulos, Ὑπαπαντή (Ἐπετηρὶς Ἑταιρείας Βυζαντινῶν Σπουδῶν, VI [1929], 328–339), which would have yielded some clues for at least one iconographic type: the Child held over the altar. Nor did she consider sufficiently the liturgical aspects in connection with Is. 6, 6–7, which is of paramount importance for the understanding of the content and iconography of the feast. See below, n. 27.

prophetess Anna, representing the New and Old Testaments respectively, and an angel acting as the unifier of the couple, or their *pronubus*—a scene deriving iconographically, as Grabar pointed out, from the *Concordia* coins and from sarcophagi of imperial Rome.[5] Coin images also served as the key by which Grabar unlocked the riddle of a far more puzzling scene. The *occursus* itself is staged in front of a temple from which St. Simeon steps forth to meet the Child. The building, however, is not the Temple of Jerusalem as the beholder would be entitled to expect on the basis of Lk. 2, 25, but the pagan *templum Urbis* in Rome, the temple of the goddess Roma which for many centuries had symbolized the idea of *Roma aeterna*. This fact has been emphasized most powerfully by the artist himself, since he placed in the pediment of the temple the statue of the *Dea Roma*.[6] For the cult of this goddess a noble college of twelve priests had been instituted in imperial Rome, whose members were of senatorial rank (*duodecemviri Urbis Romae*) and were headed by the emperor as *sacerdos Urbis*.[7] From this temple of the *Roma aeterna* there hastens, in the mosaic, the pious Simeon, frequently designated as a "priest" or even the "high priest" *(sacerdos magnus)* of the Temple of Jerusalem.[8] The mosaicist represented the old man with a short white beard, that is, unmistakably in the guise of St. Peter, "Prince of Apostles," who is followed by the college of *Dea Roma* priests, evidently representing the Apostles.[9]

In this pagan-Roman and Christian syncretism in which all cyphers appear to be exchangeable, the *templum Urbis* signifies an idea of specific importance. Grabar, and especially Gagé, have traced the numismatic history of that temple, founded as the *templum Romae et Veneris* by Hadrian in 121 A.D. and consecrated in 136/37 A.D.[10] In 248, the Roma temple became the centre of the millenary celebrations of the founding of Rome when coins were issued by the Emperor Philippus showing the front of the shrine with the inscription *miliarium saeculum* and *saeculum novum*.[11] During the latter half of the third century, the *templum Urbis* remained the outstanding symbol of the very broad idea of the *Renovatio Romanorum* and, connected with it, of the *Aiōn* implying Rome's *aeternitas*

---

[5] Grabar 217ff; cf. E. H. Kantorowicz, "On the Golden Marriage Belt and the Marriage Rings of the Dumbarton Oaks Collection," *Dumbarton Oaks Papers*, XIV (1960), 3–16, esp. 9, n. 40.

[6] See, in addition to Grabar and Gagé, also C. C. Vermeule, *The Goddess Roma in the Art of the Roman Empire* (Cambridge, Mass., 1959), 95f.

[7] Gagé, "Templum Urbis," 158f; Grabar, 224, n. 1; K. Latte, *Römische Religionsgeschichte* (Munich, 1960), 317.

[8] Not only the *Evangelium Nicodemi*, II, 1 (c. XVII), ed. C. Tischendorf, *Evangelia apocrypha* (Leipzig, 1853), 368, to which Grabar, 224, n. 4 called attention, designates Simeon a priest. The expression is found over and over again. Cf., e. g., Ephraem Syrus, *Sermo de Domino nostro*, c. 48, ed. T. J. Lamy (Mecheln, 1882), I, 258: *Simeon autem sacerdos;* c. 50, p. 264: *bracchia Simeonis sacerdotis;* c. 51, pp. 264, 266, is more or less devoted to Simeon's *sacerdotium;* see also Ephraem's *Hymnus de Simeone sene* (= *Hymni de Beata Maria*, xx), c. 21, ed. Lamy, II, 636: *puerulum quem in ulnis portat sacerdos.* Cf. Sophronius, *Anacreontica IV: In occursum Domini*, lines 44 and 63, where

Simeon is called ἱερεύς (*PG*, LXXXVII: 3, 3752f, with n. 38). Further, *Menaia*, February 2 (editio Romana, 1896), III, 478 (Germanus or Joannes Monachus), 480 (Cosmas), where he is also called ἱερεύς. In the rubric of the *Menologion* of Basilius, Simeon is called πρεσβύτης; cf. *Byzantinon Heortologion*, ed. Manuel I. Gedeon (Constantinople, 1899), 68.

[9] C. Cecchelli, *I mosaici della Basilica di S. Maria Maggiore* (Turin, 1956), pls. LIIIff, 219ff, who does not consider the studies of Grabar and Gagé, calls attention to the fact that the men forming the cortège of Simeon wore the same long white tunics with *clavi* which, in another mosaic of S. Maria Maggiore (pl. xxx, 149ff), was displayed by the priest of Midian, Raguel (Jethro), when he married off his daughter Zipporah to Moses.

[10] For the date, see P. L. Strack, *Untersuchungen zur römischen Reichsprägung des zweiten Jahrhunderts* (Stuttgart, 1931/37), II, 174; Gagé, "Templum Urbis," 154 thinks of 128 A.D.

[11] Gagé, 170, and pl. I (facing p. 160), figs. 7–9, also his "Saeculum novum," pl. xiv, 4–5.

and her eternal rejuvenation.[12] In other words, the image of the *templum Romae* appeared as the iconographic type indicating the ideas of Roman renewal; and in this symbolic meaning the image outlasted not only pagan times—as evidenced, for example, by the *Contorniates*[13]—but also the sack of Rome at the hands of Alaric in 410. Shortly before or after that disaster, the usurper Priscus Attalus, anti-emperor opposing Honorius, issued once more a coin displaying the temple of Rome with the legend INVICTA ROMA AETERNA.[14] And in those very years the poet Rutilius Namatianus, prefect of Rome probably in 414, praised his city in the famous lines:

> *Illud te reparat, quod cetera regna resolvit:*
> *Ordo renascendi est, crescere posse malis....*[15]

It was this mood of a great *quand même* after the catastrophe, which dominated Rome in the age of the invasions and gave nourishment to thoughts of Roman rebirth and Rome's eternity despite all the adversities which had befallen her. Only some twenty years after Alaric's conquest of Rome the rebuilding of the shrine of S. Maria Maggiore was started, and in its mosaic decorations the image of the *templum Romae* served once more to express in symbolic shorthand the ideas of rejuvenation and renovation, of the *saeculum novum*, the *saeculum miliarium*, and of the *temporum felicitas*. All those blessings, so often promised and hoped for, were now to come true for mankind—and therewith also for Rome, the mistress of the world—through the Incarnation of the Son of God.[16] That it to say, the old mottoes of the imperial past remained valid, though valid in a new sense, the Christian sense. A *saeculum novum* there was, but it was identical with the advent of Christ whom a Petrus-like St. Simeon hastens to meet; and it was Simeon who by his *occursus* made visible the oneness and concord of Jerusalem's temple and the *templum Urbis*, of Jerusalem and Rome, of himself and St. Peter, of Christian and Roman priests, New and Old Testaments, old age and new age.[17] The language of symbols and of iconography is in this case unambiguous, and Grabar and Gagé have admirably unravelled the threads of a highly involved texture.

There remains one question that should be raised although it may seem insignificant;

---

[12] Gagé, "Templum Urbis," 161–165, 176ff. See, for the actually slow development of the political notion *aeternitas*, H. U. Instinsky, "Kaiser und Ewigkeit," *Hermes*, LXXVII (1942), 313–355, esp. 320ff for the eternity of Rome, and 333 for the Roman goddess *Aeternitas* who had the attributes of the Graeco-Egyptian *Aiōn*; see also Strack, *op. cit.*, I, 186f.

[13] A. Alföldi, "Die Kontorniaten," *Festschrift der Ungarischen Numismatischen Gesellschaft zur Feier ihres vierzigjährigen Bestehens* (Leipzig, 1942/43), pl. XXIII, figs. 9–11 (*Urbs Roma heterna*), and p. 114, pieces which Alföldi dates before 394 A.D. (cf. pp. 16f).

[14] Grabar, 222; Cohen, *Description des médailles impériales* (Paris, 1892), VIII, 204f, Nos. 3; 5; 6. For Attalus, see O. Seeck, art. "*Priscus Attalos*," *RE*, Neue Bearbeitung, II: 2 (1896), 2177ff. See, for the *Renovatio* idea after the *Sacco di Roma*, G. B. Ladner, *The Idea of Reform* (Cambridge, Mass., 1959), esp. 250ff.

[15] Rutilius Namatianus, *De reditu suo*, I, 133f, ed. J. Vessereau (Paris, 1904), 9; cf. p. 173, for the date of his office of *praefectus urbi*.

[16] For the (from St. Augustine's point of view erroneous) expectations of many Christians in some perpetual progress, see Th. E. Mommsen, "St. Augustine and the Christian Idea of Progress," *Journal of the History of Ideas*, XII (1951), 346–374; also in his *Medieval and Renaissance Studies*, ed. E. F. Rice, Jr. (Ithaca, N. Y., 1959), 265–298.

[17] The tendency to transfer "Jerusalem" to Rome (see, however, the cautious words of Grabar, 224, n. 2) is suggested, for example, by the assimilation of Peter to Moses; see C. A. Kneller, "Moses und Petrus," *Stimmen aus Maria Laach*, LX (1901), 237–257; G. A. van den Bergh van Eysinga, "St. Pierre, second Moïse," *Congrès d'histoire du Christianisme: Jubilé Alfred Loisy* (Paris and Amsterdam, 1928), II, 181–191.

but the answer to it may serve to brace the whole problem and tie some loose ends together. How did it occur to the artist to connect the elaborate ideology of the *templum Urbis* and the *saeculum novum* with the feast of Purification, of the meeting of the aged Simeon with the forty-day-old Saviour? The feast, though it concludes the Christmas cycle of the liturgical year and therefore is still related to Christ's epiphany in the flesh, does not all by itself suggest that interpretation. It is true, the *saeculum novum* coins display sometimes the meeting of two emperors in front of the temple of Roma; but the *occursus* of Simeon to meet the Lord in front of that temple is not really a parallel. On the other hand, the meeting of Simeon, the old age ready to go, with the new age ready to come as represented by the Infant Christ, who in Pseudo-Matthew is called the *redemptio saeculi*,[18] is certainly not an image wanting symbolic strength. But is the meeting of old age and infancy sufficient to explain how it happened that the feast of *Hypapante* was deemed appropriate to illustrate the ideas of *novum saeculum*, of *renovatio*, and of rejuvenation in general? These ideas would hinge exclusively on the contrast of the *senex* Simeon and the *infans* Jesus and obscure perhaps what may be the chief issue.

The prayers and chants by which the Eastern Church celebrates February 2nd, the feast of *Hypapante*, send us in another direction. For when we examine in the *Menaia* the office of that day, we find that the versicles call forth very definitely the vision of world or *god* rejuvenation, and that they repeat incessantly one leading idea, which is:

> Today the Ancient of Days, he that once gave the law on Mount Sinai to Moses, is seen as a babe....[19]

> Today he that of yore gave to Moses the law on Mount Sinai, stoops under the precepts of the law, he that for our sake became the one merciful towards us. Now the pure God as a holy Child opened the chaste womb....[20]

> The Ancient of Days has become a babe in the flesh, and has been brought by his Virgin Mother to the temple....[21]

> For my sake the Ancient of Days has become a babe....[22]

It would be easy to argue that these *stichera*, ascribed to Anatolius, Germanus, Johannes Monachus, and others, are perhaps of a more recent date and not as old as the fifth century.[23] That is true. Sermons, however, of an earlier date reflect similar ideas,[24] and

---

[18] Grabar, 224, n. 4; Gagé "Templum Urbis," 172.

[19] *Menaia* (editio Romana, 1896), III, 478 (Anatolius): Ὁ παλαιὸς ἡμερῶν ὁ καὶ τὸν νόμον πάλαι ἐν Σινᾷ δοὺς τῷ Μωσεῖ σήμερον βρέφος ὁρᾶται.

[20] *Menaia, loc. cit.* (Joannes Monachus): Σήμερον ὁ πάλαι τῷ Μωσεῖ ἐν Σινᾷ νόμον ἐπιδοὺς τοῖς νομικοῖς ὑποκύπτει θεσμοῖς, δι᾽ ἡμᾶς ὡς εὔσπλαγχνος καθ᾽ ἡμᾶς γεγονώς. Νῦν ὁ καθαρὸς Θεὸς ὡς παιδίον ἅγιον μήτραν διανοῖξαν ἁγνὴν κτλ.

[21] *Menaia* III, 479 (Germanus or Anatolius): Ὁ παλαιὸς ἡμερῶν νηπιάσας σαρκὶ κτλ.

[22] *Menaia* III, 481: Νηπιάζει δι᾽ ἐμὲ ὁ Παλαιὸς τῶν ἡμερῶν.

[23] Joannes Monachus, of course, lived in the fifth century. But was he really the composer of all the hymns attributed to him?

[24] Sophronius, *Oratio* III: *De Hypapante* (*PG*, LXXXVII, 3, 3287ff—the Latin version only; the Greek text, published by H. Usener, *Programm Bonn* [1889] was not accessible to me), esp. § 10 col. 3294: *Lex autem vetus et senex et infirma, viso Christo... et ab infirmitate ad salutem [Simeon] reducebatur; et vetustate... convenienter novitati renovata exime-*

these ideas seem to go back to Ephraem the Syrian, who died in 373 A.D. In his *Hymnus de Simeone sene*, Ephraem stresses several times that the aged Simeon testified to it that "the Infant truly was the Ancient of Days," and that he knew that "the child he carried in the Temple on his arms, was the Ancient of Days."[25] From Ephraem there derives also the *topos*, which was so often repeated later on, in both the East and the West, saying that "the aged man was younger than the infant," and that the babe "was older than sun and man."[26] That is to say, Ephraem produced in his Hymn practically all the images and metaphors which were repeated, and elaborated on, by later poets; and it would be difficult to overestimate the influence of Ephraem's poetry, or of the poems ascribed to him.

What is the meaning of those metaphors and images? The frequent references to Moses receiving the law on Mount Sinai are easily explained. St. Mary fulfilled the law—repeated in Lk. 2, 23—according to which "every male that openeth the womb shall be called holy to the Lord" (Ex. 13, 2), and fulfilled also the other law, recorded in Lev. 12, concerning the purification of women on the fortieth day. The Old Testament Lessons on February 2nd are therefore, in the Greek rite as well as in the modern Western Breviary, Ex. 13, and Lev. 12, in addition to the Gospel taken from St. Luke. The Prophetic Lesson from Is. 6 has a different function with which we are not concerned here.[27] On the other hand, "the Ancient of Days again a babe," is a strange image, though its meaning is clear: the One who gave the law on Mount Sinai is identical with the babe presented in the temple. The lawgiver, however, who appeared to Moses on Mount Sinai, is not called "God" or "the Highest," but (with Dan. 7, 9. 13. 22) the "Ancient of Days" who, according to Apoc. 1, 14–20, had in his hand the Seven Stars, whose hairs were white like wool, whose countenance was as the sun shineth in his strength, and who said of himself: *Ego sum primus et ultimus.*[28]

In order to understand the full impact of the liturgical images as well as their con-

batur: lumen enim veterem Israel omni vetustate liberans... oculis cernebatur... Existens novus e veteri... Christum, lumen, [*Simeon*] *aspexit.* See also § 12 col. 3296: *Nos pulchri renovati Christique praesentia in altum sublati... cantemus Domino canticum novum. Renovati etenim sumus, novique facti e veteribus, jussique canticum novum canere Deo ac Patri, qui Christi nos praesentia et innovavit universos et populum illius novum esse demonstravit. Cantemus Domino canticum novum: quia mirabilia fecit atque per Christi quidem praesentiam mirabilius, per quam omnia innovantur... atque in Deum sublata in primam iuventutem transferuntur.* The whole sermon of Sophronius is pervaded by the idea of *renovatio,* although it is rather the rejuvenation brought to others than the rejuvenation of God which is discussed. To Cyril of Jerusalem, *Homilia in Occursum Domini* XI (*PG*, XXXIII, 1200 A) Christ is "the father of the future *Aiōn* (πατὴρ τοῦ μέλλοντος αἰῶνος)." In the *Oratio in occursum Domini* of Amphilochius of Iconium (*PG*, XXXIX, 52f, c. VI) related ideas are expressed, but not that of the rejuvenation of the Ancient of Days.

[25] Ephraem, *Hymnus de Simeone sene,* ed. Lamy, II, 628ff. See especially § 28, p. 638: *Inclinat se senex coram parvulo et senectus testimonium reddit infanti ipsum vere esse*

Antiquum Dierum, and § 29: *Senex sapiens... considerabat eum, et sciens illum esse Antiquum Dierum, deprecabatur.* See also § 13, p. 632, and *Sermo de Domino nostro* § 51, ed. Lamy, I, 266.

[26] Ephraem, *Hymnus de Simeone sene,* § 22, p. 636: *Nisi senex puerulo iunior esset, supplices ei non offeret preces,* and § 23: *...ratus etiam erat illum infantem sole ac homine esse antiquiorem.* A similar idea is expressed in the *Magnificat* Antiphon of the Roman Breviary (February 2): *Senex puerum portabat, Puer autem senem regebat.* In the Mass of that day the versicle forms the core of the Alleluia; the antiphon is found already in the *Liber responsalis* of the 9th century (*PL*, LXXVIII, 746 D) and may well be of a considerably earlier date.

[27] The "live Coal" (ἄνθραξ) held in the tongs (λαβίδες) by the Cherub to cleanse the mouth of Isaiah was commonly understood as a prefiguration of the Child held in the hands of St. Mary and Simeon. See my forthcoming study on *Roma and the Coal.*

[28] For the Ancient of Days, see G. Millet, "La dalmatique du Vatican," *Bibl. de l'École des Hautes Études,* LX (Paris, 1956), 42ff. Cf. H. Gressmann, *Der Messias* (Göttingen, 1929), 403ff.

nection with the *templum Romae aeternae* and with the *renovatio* idea of the *novum saeculum* it will be rewarding to make a detour and inspect certain groups of Roman imperial coins which are relevant to the general problem of the rejuvenation of gods.

* * *

A handsome *denarius*, issued by the emperor Domitian in 82 or 83 A.D., displays, on the obverse, the features of *Domitia Augusta*, the empress. On the reverse side, a babe is shown, a boy seated on the quartered globe, lifting his hands and trying to grab the Seven Stars that surround him. The inscription identifies the child: DIVUS CAESAR IMPERATORIS DOMITIANI FILIUS (pl. 12, fig. 3).[29] To understand the idea of the coin image an epigram of Martial (VI, 3, 1f) on the expected birth of Domitian's offspring has proved to be helpful.[30] Martial greeted the child to be born with words which echoed Virgil's *Fourth Eclogue:* "Be born ..., true scion of gods; be born, illustrious boy"— *Nascere...* | *Vera deum suboles, nascere, magne puer* (*Epig.* VI, 3, 1f). Martial thus assimilated the *vera deum suboles*, offspring of Domitian,[31] to the messianic child and future kosmokrator foretold by Virgil (line 49): *cara deum suboles, magnum Iovis incrementum.* The fact that the babe, on the reverse of the *denarius*, is seated on the quartered globe implies that he is the lord of the earth. The Seven Stars, however, signifying either the planets, or the seven component stars of the Lesser or Greater Bear, manifest him also as the lord of the heavens.[32] That is, the child is designated as the lord of the universe. We should recall

---

[29] H. Mattingly and E. A. Sydenham, *The Roman Imperial Coinage* (London, 1923), II, 180, No. 213, and pl. v, fig. 3, shows an *aureus* of this type; our pl. 12, fig. 3, is a *denarius* (see *ibid.*, but not illustrated), from the collection of Münzen und Medaillen, A.G. (Basel), and the photograph of it was provided by Prof. A. Alföldi. Cf. H. Mattingly, "Virgil's Fourth Eclogue," *Journal of the Warburg and Courtauld Institutes*, X (1947), pl. 10 (facing p. 17). A. Dieudonné, "Une monnaie de l'impératrice Domitia," in his *Mélanges numismatiques*, Ire Sér. [Paris 1909], 1–9) thinks rather of a consecration coin.

[30] Cf. Mattingly, "Virgil's Fourth Eclogue," 18.

[31] That the emperors should appear as sires of gods was a not uncommon idea. See Virgil, *Aeneis* IX 642: *dis genite et geniture deos*; Seneca, *Consolatio ad Marcum* XV, 1: *Caesares qui dis geniti deosque genituri dicuntur.* Also the inscription *CIL*, III, 710 (Diocletian and Maximian): *diis geniti et deorum creatores.* See, for additional places, Alföldi, "Insignien und Tracht der römischen Kaiser," *Röm. Mitt.*, L (1935), 84, n. 2. It is not devoid of some logic that the French kings in the 13th century were styled *reges sancti... cum generent sanctos reges.* See E. H. Kantorowicz, *The King's Two Bodies* (Princeton, 1957), 253, n. 185.

[32] It is not at all easy to identify the "Seven Stars." We would be inclined to think, in the first place, of the seven planets, and this is in fact the interpretation favored by R. Reitzenstein, *Poimandres* (Leipzig, 1904), 111ff. A terracotta lamp, however, shows Christ as *Kriophóros* or "Good Shepherd" with the Seven Stars above his head (pl. 12, fig. 8), but with sun and moon as well; cf. R. Garrucci, *Storia della arte cristiana* (Prato, 1873/81), vol. VI. pl. 474, fig. 2; also L. Perret, *Catacombes de Rome* (Paris, 1851), IV, pl. 17, fig. 3. Since sun

and moon belonged to the planets, the Seven Stars could not easily have been the seven planets, but rather one of the Bears, the Lesser or the Greater. F. Boll, "Aus der Offenbarung Johannis," *Stoicheia*, I (Leipzig, 1914), 21f, 53f, believes that the Seven Stars in the hand of the Ancient of Days indicated the Lesser Bear. This constellation ruling the pole was of some importance with regard to Augustus, because according to Suetonius, *Augustus* 80, there were seven moles found on the child's body at the time of his birth, arranged *in modum et ordinem ac numerum stellarum caelestis ursae.* E. Norden, *Die Geburt des Kindes* (Leipzig-Berlin, 1924), 159f, n. 4, interprets the *caelestis ursa* without qualification as the Lesser Bear. Contrariwise, there are quite a number of Cretan coins showing Augustus (either his head only, or enthroned, or riding a chariot drawn by elephants) surrounded by seven stars, which J.-N. Svoronos, *Numismatique de la Crète ancienne* (Macon, 1890), I, pl. xxxii, figs. 2, 3, 4, always identifies as *les sept étoiles de la Grande Ourse* (see also pp. 334, 348). Both Boll and Norden refer in this connection to the great magical papyrus in Paris, ed. K. Preisendanz, *Papyri graecae magicae* (Leipzig-Berlin, 1928), I, 96 (P. IV, 675ff), where the seven "pole-rulers of the heaven" (πολοκράτορες τοῦ οὐρανοῦ) might be identified with the stars of the Lesser Bear. The divine lord, however, whose epiphany is described in the papyrus (695ff), holds in his hand the golden foreleg of an ox which is called the constellation of the Bear which "turns the heaven and brings it back, ascending and descending according to the hours." This golden foreleg of an ox, studded with seven stars, is well known from pictures in Egyptian astronomical texts, and the distribution of the stars leaves no doubt that the Big Dipper was meant; see O. Neugebauer and R. A.

that the visionary of Patmos, who wrote shortly after Domitian, described the Ancient of Days as one holding in his right hand the Seven Stars (Apoc. 1, 16), an attribute or insignia of him, god or emperor, that rules the pole (πολοκράτωρ).[33] In other words, the babe on the globe is not simply a new-born prince; but he is, as has been convincingly demonstrated by Mattingly,[34] identical with the baby Jupiter. The messianic child, in Virgil's words, was to be *magnum Iovis incrementum,* the "new great scion of the stock of Jupiter," or rather, as emphasized by A. Alföldi,[35] Jupiter himself, rejuvenated and now incarnated in the new-born imperial prince. This interpretation is supported by a coin from Crete, issued under Trajan (pl. 12, fig. 4).[36] Once more we recognize the baby god sitting on the globe and lifting his hands towards the Seven Stars; but an important feature has been added: at the child's right we recognize a goat, the goat Amalthea which had given milk to the new-born Zeus on Mount Ida.[37] This addition makes it clear that in the Cretan coin-image the baby on the globe and lifting his hands to the Seven Stars was meant to be the youthful or rejuvenated Jupiter. And therewith we understand better the coin-image of Domitian's son. It says that the *Divus Caesar Imperatoris Domitiani Filius* is identical, in Virgil's language, with the *magnum Iovis incrementum,* the "great scion of Jupiter's stock," or with old Jupiter himself incarnate as a baby again.[38]

Virgil's messianic eclogue was certainly hovering over imperial Rome until almost the end of the Western empire.[39] A bronze medallion of Antoninus Pius brings further

---

Parker, *Egyptian Astronomical Texts* (London, 1960), I, 28, and pls. 4, 6, 8, 9, and *passim.* The god holding the seven stars of the Greater Bear in his right hand has been identified (not beyond doubt) with Mithras; see A. Dieterich, *Eine Mithrasliturgie,* 3rd ed., publ. by O. Weinreich (Leipzig-Berlin, 1923), 70ff, also 78ff, and against him (*ibid.,* pp. 234ff) Cumont and others; see also M. P. Nilsson, "Die Religion in den griechischen Zauberpapyri," *Bulletin de la Société des Lettres de Lund,* II (1947/48), II, 62, n. 1. But whoever the god holding in his right hand the seven stars set in the golden foreleg of an ox may have been, the parallel with the Ancient of Days holding the Seven Stars in his right hand is obvious. He is the "Lord of the constellation of the Bear," who actually is mentioned (ὁ τῆς ἄρκτου ... κύριος) though not named, in the same magical papyrus, ed. Preisendanz, I, 116 (P. IV, 1291), in which we find inserted also two prayers to the "all-effecting power of the constellation of the Bear" (P. IV, 1275; 1331). Finally, the Seven Stars have been identified with the Pleiades; see below, n. 33. Professor O. Neugebauer, to whom I am much obliged for information on many points, suggested that probably both meanings (i. e. Planets and one of the Bears) were intertwined and therefore both possible whenever the "Lord of the Seven Stars" was alluded to.

[33] As a royal or divine attribute the Seven Stars have, as Professor Neugebauer kindly informed me, a very respectable history which can be traced back to the second millennium B. C. See H. Frankfort, *Cylinder Seals* (London, 1939), p. 251 with fig. 81, and the numerous representations of the ninth century B.C. and thereafter on pl. XXXIII, figs. b, c, g, k; pl. XXXIV, figs. h, i; pl. XXXVI, fig. e. The stars are often accompanied by sun and moon, and Frankfort, 195 and 217, interprets the Seven Stars as

the Pleiades, not as the Planets, nor as one of the Bear constellations which, according to Dr. Neugebauer, were not of great significance in the Mesopotamian orbit, whereas they were of importance in Egypt. See Boll, *op. cit.,* 21f, 53, for him "that rules the pole," and Preisendanz, I, 96 (P. IV, 700f) for the expression πολοκράτωρ. Among those *polokratores* and lords of the Seven Stars we thus have found the Mesopotamian kings, Mithras (?), Augustus, the infant Zeus and imperial princes, the Ancient of Days and Christ.

[34] Mattingly, "Virgil's Fourth Eclogue," 19.

[35] A. Alföldi, "The Numbering of the Victories of the Emperor Gallienus," *Numismatic Chronicle,* 5th Ser., vol. IX (1929), 267ff, esp. 277f.

[36] J.-N. Svoronos, *Numismatique de la Crète ancienne* (Mâcon, 1890), I, pl. XXXV, fig. 1; A. B. Cook, *Zeus* (Cambridge, 1914), I, 51f, fig. 28.

[37] The goat in connection with Jupiter is very frequent on coins of the Roman Republic; see, e. g., H. A. Grueber, *Coins of the Roman Republic in the British Museum* (London, 1910), I, 322, Nos. 2476–2483, pl. XXXVIII, figs. 11–14 and *passim.* But this subject is not under consideration here. See, in general, Cook, *Zeus,* I, 706ff. See also A. Alföldi, "The Main Aspects of Political Propaganda on the Coinage of the Roman Republic," in *Essays in Roman Coinage Presented to Harold Mattingly* (Oxford, 1956), 88f.

[38] See Alföldi, "The Numbering" (above, n. 35), 278, for *vetus* and *novus Iuppiter.*

[39] This has been shown in some detail by Mattingly, "Virgil's Fourth Eclogue," esp. 19, who traces the influence of the Eclogue to a bronze coin of the emperor Gratian holding the Christian standard while the inscription reads: GLORIA NOVI SAECULI, a clear reference to the age of Christ as the *novum saeculum.*

elucidation. On the reverse side, the baby is seen riding sidewise on the goat Amalthea towards an altar beneath a tree (pl. 12, fig. 5). Since the altar is adorned with an eagle, Jupiter's bird, we have to conclude that this picture too demonstrates the rejuvenated Jupiter riding as a baby on his loyal animal.[40] We may pass over a set of bronze coins issued under Commodus, displaying the inscription IOVI IUVENI and implying that the youthful "god of the early days of victory over the Titans was represented in the young ruler of the Roman world," Commodus.[41] Instead we concentrate briefly on a large set of silver coins of the Emperor Gallienus, convincingly interpreted by Alföldi,[42] which suggest related ideas. On these coins the baby Jupiter appears once more reincarnated in a young imperial prince, Valerian II, Gallienus' son. The boy Caesar is represented as the rejuvenated god riding on the goat Amalthea (pl. 12, fig. 6). This idea is borne out by the inscription expounding the intention very distinctly: IOVI CRESCENTI, to the waxing Jupiter. That is, the image alludes to Jupiter who has become an infant again and therefore now is growing. He is both old and young at the same time; and the young one waxes and gathers strength for the government of the world, a *restitutor generis humani* and beginner of a new era, a *saeculum novum*.[43] Another issue of coins of Gallienus for Valerian II, or for his younger son Saloninus,[44] opens up a new perspective. The obverse shows the profile head of the youth with the inscription PIETAS SAECULI; and while the image on the reverse remains practically unchanged, showing the child riding on the goat, from right to left, the legend differs; it now reads: IOVI EXORIENTI, "To the rising Jupiter" (pl. 12, fig. 7).[45]

In this case, the infant Jupiter has been interpreted in solar terms. Young Jupiter "rises" as the Sun rises, and this metaphor suggests yet another aspect of the *saeculum novum* motif. For, the "rising child," *puer exoriens*, ὁ νήπιος ὁ ἀνατέλλων would normally refer to Helios or Sol, the sun-god.[46] "He that gives light to the day, the rising child" is an invocation found, for example, in the famous Paris magical papyrus.[47] Plutarch mentions that the Egyptians considered the rising Sun a child, and the pictures of the

[40] Cook, *Zeus*, I, 713, fig. 528; cf. p. 52; F. Gnecchi, *I medaglioni romani* (Milan, 1912), II, 16, Nos. 60f and pl. L, fig. 4; Alföldi, "The Numbering" (above, n. 35), 268, fig. 1. See, for a similar issue, though without the altar, P. L. Strack, *Untersuchungen zur römischen Reichsprägung des zweiten Jahrhunderts* (Stuttgart, 1937), III, 161, and pl. IV, fig. 658a.

[41] Mattingly, *Coins of the Roman Empire in the British Museum*, IV (London, 1940), Nos. 593*, 623, 633, 635, pp. 810, 819, 821ff, and pl. CVIII, figs. 4 and 9; cf. Introduction, p. CLXIV.

[42] Alföldi, "The Numbering" (above, n. 35), pl. XX, figs. 10, 12–16 gives several examples, and our pl. 12, fig. 6, is yet another specimen (the photograph kindly provided by Prof. Alföldi) from the Kunsthistorische Museum in Vienna; also Cook, *Zeus*, I, 714, fig. 530; also Ph. V. Hill, "Aspects of Jupiter on Coins of the Roman Mint, A.D. 65–318," *Numismatic Chronicle*, Sixth Ser., XX (1960), pl. VIII, fig. 18.

[43] Alföldi, "The Numbering," (above, n. 35), 270; see esp. 278, nos. 92–93.

[44] For the coin for Saloninus, see Alföldi, "The

Numbering," 273; Mattingly, "Virgil's Fourth Eclogue," 18, and cf. 15; Cook, *Zeus*, I, 714, fig. 531; also Hill, *op. cit.*, 122f ("a rare sestertius").

[45] Alföldi, "The Numbering," 271, and pl. XX, fig. 6. That the reign of a *novus Juppiter* ushers in some kind of golden age is a belief which has a long history. See, e. g., Timotheus of Milet (ca. 398 B.C.), frag. 12 (Bergk, *Poetae lyrici graeci* [Leipzig, 1914], III, 624): νέος ὁ Ζεὺς βασιλεύει, / τὸ πάλαι δ'ἦν Κρόνος ἄρχων / ἀπίτω μοῦσα παλαιά. See also Statius, *Silvae* I 6, 39–43, ed. Klotz, 34: *I, nunc saecula compara, Vetustas, / Antiqui Jovis aureumque tempus*, which by implication makes Domitian the *novus Juppiter*: see F. Sauter, *Der römische Kaiserkult bei Martial und Statius* (Stuttgart-Berlin, 1934), 21.

[46] F. Boll, *Griechische Kalender*, Sitzungsber. Heidelb. Akad., I, Abh. 16 (1910), 42f, n. 35. Cook, *Zeus*, I, 714, did not fail to recognize the solar character of the *Iovi exorienti* coin.

[47] Preisendanz, I, 38 (P. III, 154f): ὁ τὴν ἡμέραν φωτίζων ... ὁ νήπιος ὁ ἀνατέλλων; see also Preisendanz, I, 28 (P. II, 120), where the phrase is repeated almost verbatim.

infant Sun sitting on the lotus are common enough.[48] A hymn to the Egyptian Sun-God announces that "he [the Sun] is Ptah, the oldest of all gods. He waxes old and rejuvenates in the revolving course of eternal time."[49] Nor is there any dearth of similar statements.[50] That is to say, Jupiter was not the only god to appear as an old man who, at the beginning of a new *saeculum*, became an infant again. For the same transformation was attributed also to Sol-Helios. His rejuvenation was linked, in the first place, to the daily cycle of morning and evening: a child in the morning, a man at noon, and an old man in the evening. But the image of the sun-god as a baby was likewise valid with regard to the larger cycle of the year. "As an infant *(parvulus)* he appears at the winter solstice," and "he grows old during the year to appear again as a *parvus et infans* on the shortest day," writes Macrobius,[51] and similar statements are found frequently. That is, the rejuvenation of the solar deity is clearly bound to the natural cycles of day and year, and, we may add, of the *saeculum* as well.

*   *   *

It stands to reason that the *Hypapante* chants rendering the message that "today the Ancient of Days has become a babe" have to be viewed against the background of the pre-Christian ideas of rejuvenated gods. An encaustic icon of the sixth or early seventh century in the monastery of St. Catherine on Mount Sinai displays the Emmanuel, the incarnate Christ, on the knees of the Virgin as a *puer-senex* or παιδαριογέρων, that is, with features old out of proportion to the infant's age.[52] An eleventh-century Gospelbook, now in Paris,[53] actually shows (pl. 11, fig. 2) Christ in three different ages: in the central medallion we recognize the Ancient of Days (Παλαιὸς τῶν ἡμερῶν); the medallion to the left, inscribed Χριστός, shows a mature man; and the one to the right, inscribed Ἐμμα-

[48] Plutarch, *De Pythiae oraculis* 400 A (c. 12): Αἰγυπτίους ... ὡς ἀρχὴν ἀνατολῆς παιδίον νεογνὸν γράφοντας ἐπὶ λωτῷ καθεζόμενον; see also *De Iside et Osiride* 355 C (c. 11). For the image of the infant Sun sitting on the lotus, see, e. g., P. Berlin 5026, line 107, ed Preisendanz, I, 26; and, for representations, C. Bonner, *Studies in Magical Amulets* (Ann Arbor, 1950), 140ff and figs. 189–208.

[49] R. Reitzenstein, *Poimandres* (Leipzig, 1904), 235f; cf. P. Friedländer, *Johann von Gaza und Paulus Silentiarius* (Leipzig, 1912), 170, who has collected a number of passages relevant to the infant Sun.

[50] See, e. g. the prayer to the Sun in a magical papyrus at Oslo, ed. Preisendanz, II, 170 (P. XXXVI, 219): ὁ καθ'ἡμέραν γεννώμενος νέος καὶ γέρων δύνων. Further Martianus Capella, *De nuptiis* I 76, ed. Dick, 35: *facie autem mox ingressus est pueri renidentis, in incessu medio iuvenis anheli, in fine senis apparebit occidui, licet duodecim nonnullis formas converteret crederetur.* See, for the twelve changing forms of the Sun (in argreement with the twelve hours of the day or with the Zodiac), Reitzenstein, *Poimandres*, 256ff. Firmicus Maternus, *De errore* VII 7, ed. K. Ziegler, 22, 20: *quis vidit puerum Solem.* John of Gaza, 55ff, ed. Friedländer, 138, describes the Sun as a child and an old man, while mentioning maturity last—characteristic of

the Greek predilection of polarity (beginning—end—middle); cf. F. Boll, "Die Lebensalter," *Neue Jahrbücher für das klassische Altertum*, XXXI (1913), 95; R.-D. Keil, "Anfang, Ende und Mitte," *Antike und Abendland*, VI (1957), 145ff.

[51] Macrobius, *Saturnalia* I 18, 9; cf. Boll, *Griechische Kalender*, 42; Norden, *Die Geburt des Kindes*, 25, n. 3.

[52] I owe the knowledge of this icon to the kindness of Professor Kurt Weitzmann who will publish the icons of St. Catherine's together with other results of the Sinai Expeditions sponsored by the University of Michigan, Princeton University, and the University of Alexandria, Egypt. For the topic *puer senex*, see E. R. Curtius, *Europäische Literatur und lateinisches Mittelalter* (Bern, 1948), 106ff, esp. 109, n. 1, for Jesus as *puer senex*. See also below, n. 57. The Greek technical term was quite popular ever since the fourth century; cf. Curtius, 108 (*PG*, LXVII, 1069 A).

[53] Paris, Bibl. Nat., Ms. gr. 74, fol. 167 (St. John); cf. H. Omont, *Évangiles avec peintures byzantines du XIᵉ siècle* (Paris, n. y.), II, pl. 142. The pictures of the other evangelists follow a similar pattern; see I, pl. 1 (Matthew); pl. 57 (Mark); II, pl. 92 (Luke).

νουήλ, renders Christ as a youth.[54] That Christ was πολύμορφος, was stated occasionally and suggested even more often by implication[55]—just as the *Aiōn* was called παντόμορφος, ποικιλόμορφος, one in whom there is "no earlier nor later, no older nor younger" (οὐδὲ πρεσβύτερον οὐδὲ νεώτερον).[56] "Child, old man, born before the ages, coeval with the Father," explains a verse in the *Greek Anthology*.[57] On the other hand, in the *Vita Abercii*, three persons—actually three blind old women—visualize Christ in three different ages: one experiences him as πρεσβύτης, the second as a beardless young man (νεανίσκος ἀγένειος), and the third one as a small child (παιδάριον μικρόν),[58] because Past, Present, and Future have no meaning in view of the αἰὼν ἑστώς, the immovable *Aiōn*.[59] The same phenomenon came true, according to Marco Polo, when the Three Magi paid their respects to the Holy Child: the youngest of the Wise Men found the Child seemingly of his own age; the middle one found the Child in the age of a mature man; and the eldest one saw Him as an old man.[60] The connections of that triple appearance of the Lord of the Universe with the Sassanian doctrines concerning Zervan, the deified Time and its three consubstantial manifestations expressing the three stages of life, have been pertinently investigated by L. Olschki[61] and are not in need of being re-considered here. But the three mimetic manifestations of the incarnate God who is perceived by every person according to his own stage of maturity, has its parallel in the Third Vision of the *Shepherd of Hermas*. For Hermas, when meeting the *Kyria* dispensing revelation to him (that is, the Church), finds her an old woman; when meeting her a second time she appeared to him much younger and gayer though her body and hair were still that of an old woman; the third time, he found her quite young and very handsome and gay, and only her hair

---

[54] In the Gospels of John Alexander, Czar of the Bulgarians (1331–1371), we find the same scheme, but all three medallions have the same inscription (ΙΗΣΟΥΣ ΧΡΙΣΤΟΣ). See Brit. Mus., Add. Ms. 39627, fol. 213; ed. B. D. Filov, *Les miniatures de l'Évangile du Roi Jean Alexandre à Londres* (Sofia, 1934), pl. cxxxix (an excellent colour reproduction). The miniatures of this Ms. depend throughout on Ms. gr. 74 of the Bibliothèque Nationale.

[55] See E. Peterson, "Einige Bemerkungen zum Hamburger Papyrus-Fragment der Acta Pauli," *Vigilae Christianae*, III (1949), 142–162, esp. 158, where he mentions πολύμορφος; cf. *Vita Abercii*, c. 16 (below n. 58), where the expression πολυώνυμος is found. The related expression πολυπρόσωπος occurs, as Mrs. E. de'Negri kindly called to my attention, in the *Acta Joannis*, c. 91, ed. R. A. Lipsius and M. Bonnet, *Acta Apostolorum apocrypha* (Leipzig, 1898), II: 1, 196. Cf. *Actus Petri cum Simone*, c. 21, ed. Lipsius-Bonnet, I, 69, 18f: *quomodo [viduae] alias et alias dominum viderint*. For the image of Jesus in apocryphal writings, see W. Bauer, *Das Leben Jesu im Zeitalter der neutestamentlichen Apokryphen* (Tübingen, 1909), 313f.

[56] For *Aiōn* in general, see D. Levi, "*Aiōn*," *Hesperia*, XIII (1944), 269–314; 274 n. 9 for bibliography. For *Aiōn* as παντόμορφος θεός, see A. Alföldi, "Der neue Weltherrscher der Vierten Ekloge Vergils," *Hermes*, LXV (1930), 377; for Αἰὼν ποικιλόμορφος, see Nonnos, *Dionysiaca*, VII, 22f; Levi, 276, n. 13. For *Aiōn* being neither older nor younger, see Plutarch, *De E apud Delphos* c. 20; *Moralia* 393 A (ed. F. C. Babbitt, Loeb

Classical Library, V, 244); cf. Levi, 279. For a related idea, see the Leiden Papyrus published by Preisendanz, II, 90 (P. XIII, 70f): ὁ μεταμορφούμενος εἰς πάντας, ἀόρατος εἶ Αἰὼν Αἰῶνος. Cf. *Actus Petri cum Simone* c. 20, ed. Lipsius-Bonnet, I, 68, 14: *hic est omnia*.

[57] *Anthologia Palatina*, I, 21: Παῖ, γέρον, αἰώνων προγενέστερε πατρὸς ὁμῆλιξ. See also I, 20: παλαιγενές, υἱὲ νεογνέ.

[58] *S. Abercii vita*, c. 29, ed. Th. Nissen (Leipzig, 1912), 22, 13ff; cf. Peterson, *op. cit.*, 158. The same story is found in *Actus Petri cum Simone*, c. 21, ed. Lipsius-Bonnet (Leipzig, 1891), I, 68f (the Latin text of the Vercelli Acts). See also *Abercii vita*, c. 16, ed. Nissen, 14, 6ff: ... τὸν εὔμορφον τοῖς νοοῦσιν καὶ ἄμορφον τοῖς ἀγνόουσιν, τὸν παλαιὸν καὶ νεώτερον, τὸν χρόνῳ φαινόμενον καὶ ἀεὶ ὄντα. This description again is found in the *Actus Petri cum Simone*, c. 20, ed. Lipsius-Bonnet, I, 68.

[59] Tatian, *Oratio ad Graecos* 26, ed. E. Schwartz (Texte und Untersuchungen zur Geschichte der altchristlichen Literatur, IV: 1; Leipzig, 1888), 27, line 27. Peterson, *loc. cit.*

[60] Marco Polo, trsl. by H. Yule, *The Book of Ser Marco Polo*³ (London, 1921), I, 79.

[61] L. Olschki, "The Wise Men of the East in Oriental Tradition," in *Semitic and Oriental Studies Presented to William Popper*, ed. W. J. Fischel (Berkeley-Los Angeles, 1951), 375–395, esp. 381ff, who indicates also the belief of the followers of the Old Man of the Mountain in whom "childhood, maturity, and old age were only one condition."

was that of old age. The reason for that ἀνανέωσις of the woman was, according to the information obtained by Hermas, that he, Hermas, himself had changed by reaching successively stages of greater faith, perfection and insight.[62] The forms of appearance are mimetic and vary depending upon the beholder.[63] The decisive feature, however, is that, owing to the Eternity of the godhead, its manifestions of "old" or "young" represent in fact only one condition; and therefore "the Ancient of Days, who once gave the law on Mount Sinai to Moses, is now seen as a babe." He is rejuvenated and, by his incarnation, he introduces a new era; but he is still the same that he was on Mount Sinai, for *Aetatem et sexum non habet haec soboles*, as Paulinus of Nola puts it, and, referring to the Virgin, he explains: *Hac genetrice senex aeque generatur ut infans*.[64]. Or, as Dionysius Areopagita pointed out half a century later, the antithesis of the παλαιός and the νέος implies that the ancient one indicates him who was ἀπ' ἀρχῆς, from the beginning, whereas the young one is ἀγήρως, not aging.[65]

Attention should be called to yet another item which seems relevant to *magnum Iovis incrementum*. In the Canticle of Zacharias (Lk. 1, 78) Christ is referred to as Ἀνατολὴ ἐξ ὕψους, *Oriens ex Alto*, conventionally translated by "dayspring from on high" (*King James*) or "Orient from on high" *(Douay Bible)*. Zacharias, the father of John the Baptist, here harked back to the Prophet Zacharias (3, 8; 6, 12) where the coming of the Messiah is announced, whose name is given as Ἀνατολή, *Oriens*. Perhaps *ortus* would have been a more adequate translation. For the Hebrew word *Zemah*, which Luther uses in his German version without translating it, means the "shoot," the "offspring," in the sense in which Horace (*Carm.* IV 5) addresses Augustus *Divis orte bonis*, "Offspring of the good gods." The *King James* version therefore renders the Hebrew word by "the Branch," just as in Jer. 23, 5, the Hebrew word *Zemah*, or Greek ἀνατολή, is rendered correctly by *germen* in the Latin Vulgate. That is to say, the Messiah is likewise a *magnum incrementum* of the highest God, especially if the underlying meaning of the Canticle of Zacharias is taken to be *Oriens ex altissimo*, ἀνατολὴ ἐξ ὑψίστου, a "scion of the Most High." On the other hand, the messianic epithet Ἀνατολή, *Oriens*, was customarily connected with the Malachian *Sol Iustitiae*, so that two different strands of thought are here interlaced with one another.[66]

After our circumstantial lucubration it will be easier to understand how it happened that the designer of the mosaics in S. Maria Maggiore placed the events of the *Hypapante*, the meeting of Christ and the aged Simeon, in the unexpected surroundings of Rome and chose the *templum Romae* as an appropriate background to interpret the holy scene. The

[62] *Pastor Hermae*, Visio III, cc. 11–13, ed. R. Joly, *Hermas: Le Pasteur* (Sources chrétiennes, 53; Paris, 1958), 129ff [=cc. 19–21.]

[63] See also the *Acta Joannis* cc. 88–89, ed. Lipsius-Bonnet, II, 1, 194.

[64] Paulinus of Nola, *Carmina* XXV, 175f, ed. Hartel (*CSEL*, XXX, 243). See Curtius, *op. cit.*, 109, for the birth legend of a Buddhist saint who had a long white beard when his mother gave birth to him.

[65] Dionysius Areopagita, *De divinis nominibus* X 2 (*PG*, III, 937); also 945/6 for the paraphrase of Pachymeres,

and IV, 385/6, for the scholia of S. Maximus. I am indebted to Professor A. Grabar for calling my attention to this passage.

[66] For the rather involved problem, see A. Jacoby, "Ἀνατολὴ ἐξ ὕψους," *Zeitschrift für die neutestamentliche Wissenschaft*, XX (1921), 205–214, who points out (p. 207) that ὕψος has the meaning of "God" (δύναμις ὑψίστου = δύναμις ἐξ ὕψους). The solar meaning is definitely overstressed in the *New English Bible* (Oxford-Cambridge, 1961), 96: "The morning sun from heaven will rise upon us."

tertium quid should not be sought in the tension between the age-old Simeon and the infant Jesus, but rather in Christ himself who is babe and Ancient of Days at the same time, who is at once old and young as *Roma aeterna* herself. Hence, by the display of the shrine suggesting Roma's eternal rejuvenation as well as by the shrine's symbolic value of the *saeculum novum*, the leading idea of the feast indicating that the Ancient of Days has become a babe again was intensified. The Roman beholder of the mosaic would have been at liberty to interpret the *puer exoriens* of Christian mythology as one next of kin to Virgil's *magnum Iovis incrementum*, or to understand the Christian *Sol Iustiae* as a Ἥλιος ἀνατέλλων, a new rising and youthful Sun who ushers in the new *Aiōn*, the *saeculum novum*,[67] provided that this hypothetical Roman remained aware of one important point. The rejuvenation according to natural cycles into which the Graeco-Roman gods were bound, as well as the plurality of rejuvenations on the part of Jupiter, had drawn to an end. According to the Christian faith no more than one rejuvenation, or renewal, of the world was possible, and this *renovatio* was the consequential result of the Incarnation of the Son of God, the event that made the Ancient of Days to be a child again, a *puer exoriens*. Of the Christian *novum saeculum* there could be no repetition because the incarnate God, though older than the world and older than St. Simeon, was ἀτρέπτως νηπιάσας, "being a babe immutably," or ἀγήρως, "not aging," as Pseudo-Dionysius explained by applying the famous epithet of the Olympian gods to the new-born Saviour.[68] And also the Christian Helios, once he had risen, remained a φῶς ἀνέσπερον and ἄδυτον, a light without evening, a light without setting.[69]

The chants of Ephraem and of the Greek service on the day of *Hypapante* heralded the infant Christ as the reborn and rejuvenated Ancient of Days. These chants have served us here as the indispensable medium to recognize that the syncretistic iconography of the *Occursus* in S. Maria Maggiore in front of the symbol of the *saeculum novum*, the Roma temple, was caused not merely by the confrontation of old age and new age as represented by Simeon and the baby God, but also by the other leading idea which consisted of the doubling of old age and infancy in the incarnate God himself. It is true, of course, that the Incarnation was a singular event which could not be repeated, nor could every new-born imperial prince be visualized as a rejuvenation of the Ancient of Days. But the *mythologumena*, both imperial and divine, of the pre-Christian days, were carried over to the Christian age and, like Jupiter or *Aiōn*, the new Lord of the Seven Stars was at once the *primus et novissimus* (Apoc. 1, 17), since by the Virgin Mother, as Paulinus of Nola put it, *senex aeque generatur ut infans*.[70] For these reasons the *Hypapante* could signify the dawn of the *saeculum novum*.

---

[67] Christ as Ἥλιος ἀνατέλλων is one of the most frequent metaphors; in the chants of the Eastern Church it is found time and time again; see, for the service on *Hypapante*, *Menaia* III, 480. See also my forthcoming study on *Oriens Augusti*.

[68] *Menaia* III 482, 483. See, for Dionysius Areopagita, above n. 65.

[69] *Menaia* III 478, 483.

[70] See, for Paulinus of Nola, above n. 64.

THE "KING'S ADVENT"
AND THE ENIGMATIC PANELS IN THE DOORS
OF SANTA SABINA

1. BENEDICTUS QUI VENIT...

T HE *Rituale Romanum* includes a collection of prayers known as the *Ordo commendationis animae*.[1] This is the Office of the Dying. Framed by the Litany of the Saints, with which the Order opens, and by a number of litany-like supplications, which form the transition to the Lessons and Psalms, there is a group of three famous orisons. Of these, the first and second are old; they can be traced back to the Sacramentaries of the eighth century. The third is of a more recent date. As Saint Peter Damian is said to have inspired its setting, the prayer cannot antedate the eleventh century.[2] Although composed at different periods, the first prayer and the third are nevertheless in a close inner relationship. Both refer to the journey of the soul, the one to the departure, *Profectio*, from this world, the other to the arrival, *Adventus*, in heaven. The wishes for the arrival are clothed in the following words:

> May your soul, which is departing from the body, be met by the brilliant host of Angels, may it be received by the court of Apostles, welcomed by the triumphant army of resplendent Martyrs, surrounded by the lilied array of rubiate Confessors, greeted by the jubilant choir of Virgins, and embraced by the blessed peace in the bosom of the Patriarchs. . . .

Reprinted, with permission, from *The Art Bulletin*, XXVI (1944), 207–231.

[1] The sources of the various prayers of this Order, which is also found in the Breviary, are studied and carefully analyzed by L. Gougaud, "Étude sur les *Ordines commendationis animae*," *Ephemerides Liturgicae*, XLIX (1935), 3–27. For some of the pre-Christian as well as Early Christian background see Arthur D. Nock's "Postscript" to the study of C. B. Welles, "The Epitaph of Julius Terentius," *Harvard Theological Review*, XXXIV (1941), 103–109.

[2] The interrelation between a letter of Peter Damian (*Ep.*, VIII, 15; Migne, *PL*, CXLIV, col. 497) and the prayer *Commendo te* is evident though the proportion of dependency may be disputed. V. Thalhofer and L. Eisenhofer, *Handbuch der katholischen Liturgik* (2nd ed., Freiburg, 1912), II, 460, assume that Peter Damian was familiar with the prayer. Gougaud, *op. cit.*, 12ff, maintains that the prayer "est formée du texte d'une lettre de saint Pierre Damien," and he proves that the prayer was introduced into the Order very late, probably not earlier than the 16th century. Nock, *op. cit.*, 106, emphasizes that the ideas found in the prayer are indeed very old. There is reason to believe that Peter Damian depended upon a "vocabulary" current in the West at the latest since Carolingian times when the categories of the Litany of the Saints, introduced on the Continent in the early 8th century, began to pervade equally poetry, liturgy, and even the conceptions of the secular state. For an example, see *infra*, note 7.

All the ranks of the celestials, who together form the mystical body of Christ, are expected to come to meet, in a solemn and formal manner, the soul which is guided to the city of heaven by Saint Michael, the Christian Psychopompos. Once more, at the Exequies, this dignified meeting is remembered when the clergy sings "In paradisum deducant te Angeli: in tuo adventu suscipiant te Martyres et perducant te in civitatem sanctam Ierusalem."[3] The soul's arrival after its long journey is visualized as a transcendental *entrée joyeuse* into celestial Jerusalem.

The idea underlying these prayers is very old.[4] The punctilio of the reception in the citadel of heaven corresponds to the receptions accorded kings or high dignitaries on their arrival at the gates of a city on earth. This parallelism is not accidental. The modern mind, probably under the influence of conceptions of the Renaissance, may think of the honors due to the "Majesty of Death," and so find the royal honors offered to the soul justifiable and appropriate.[5] From an ecclesiastical point of view it may be more important to remember that the soul ascending to heaven belongs to one anointed, anointed on the death-bed. A solemn liturgical reception is prescribed by the Church for those consecrated with the holy balm, and according to a decree of Pope Honorius III of 1221, the liturgical reception was even considered a prerogative reserved exclusively for God's Anointed, for kings and bishops.[6] Consequently, a kingly reception of the soul at the gates of the celestial city appears as "correct" and in agreement with ecclesiastical etiquette.

In fact, the difference between the *adventus regis* and the *adventus animae* appears sometimes as slight. A poem *Ad regem suscipiendum* of the ninth century, written by Notker for one of the numerous meetings of royalty at the gates of the Abbey of St. Gall, impresses us by its similarity with the prayer associated, rightly or wrongly, with the name of St. Peter Damian.[7] The poet greets the king and wishes that at his entry he may be met by the celestial militia descending from heaven, by the chaste choir of virgins under the

---

[3] See, in the same Order, the prayer *Delicta iuventutis:* "Suscipiat eum sanctus Michael Archangelus Dei, qui militiae caelestis meruit principatum. Veniant illi obviam sancti Angeli Dei et perducant eum in civitatem caelestem Ierusalem." For the earliest version of the prayer, see Migne, *PL*, CLI, cols. 925f, and Nock, 103ff. The prayer of the Exequies as quoted above was introduced in the 10th century; cf. Gougaud, in *Jahrbuch für Liturgiewissenschaft*, VII (1927), 301, no. 320.

[4] Likewise old is the opposite idea, namely, that the phalanxes of demons come to meet the soul. See M. W. Bloomfield, "The Origin of the Concept of the Seven Cardinal Sins," *Harvard Theological Review*, XXXIV (1941), 121ff, especially p. 126, the *Vita S. Joannis Eleemosynarii*, chap. xl: "...obviant ei (animae) cum ascenderit a terra in coelum chori daemonum, singuli in proprio ordine. Obviat ei chorus daemoniorum superbiae, investigat eam, si habeat opera eorum. Obviat chorus spiritum detractionis. ... Obviat iterum superius daemones fornicationis..." Migne, *PL*, LXXIII, col. 375.

[5] The concept of the "Majesty of the Dead" is very old (cf. *infra*, note 88, the study of D. E. L. Haynes), but certain modern connotations seem to stem from the Renaissance when, e.g., the custom was revived to

transport the dead body in a triumphal car. The subject seems to be as yet unexplored; cf. Leopold Ettlinger, "The Duke of Wellington's Funeral Car," *Journal of the Warburg and Courtauld Institutes*, III (1939–40), 254ff.

[6] Potthast, *Regesta pontificum Romanorum* (Berlin 1874–75), no. 6584; Ludwig Biehl, *Das liturgische Gebet für Kaiser und Reich* (Paderborn, 1937), 146. Whether the papal ordinance ever was observed seems doubtful; we find in the Pontifical of Durandus († 1296 A.D.) an *Ordo ad recipiendum... principem processionaliter*, and princes were not anointed in the 13th century. Cf. Pierre Batiffol, *Études de liturgie et d'archéologie chrétienne* (Paris, 1919), 22; see also the modern *Pontificale Romanum* which contains, after the Orders for the Reception of Emperors and Kings, an *Ordo ad recipiendum processionaliter principem magnae potentiae*.

[7] *MGH, Poetae*, IV, 324, no. x:

1. Ave beati germinis
   invicte rex et inclyte,
   omnis tibi militia
   occurrat ovans celitum.

2. Intacta Christi genetrix,
   mater honora, virginum
   chorum pudicum socians,
   tibi procedat obviam.

3. Agonithete apostoli,
   victoriosi martyres
   omnesque sancti ordines
   semper vocent te laudibus...

leadership of St. Mary, by the apostles umpiring in the *agon* of life, by the martyrs who are the victors in this competition, and by the other holy ranks who raise their voices in acclamation of the royal comer. These images, it is true, are suggestive also of the athletic metaphors in the homilies of St. John Chrysostom, which in Latin translation were eagerly read at St. Gall.[8] But they are indicative, above all, of the analogies of the two receptions: both the soul at its entry into the celestial city and the king at his entry into a city on earth are to be met, it is hoped, by all the ranks of the celestials.

The ceremonial of the king's liturgical reception has been laid down in the various *Ordines ad regem suscipiendum*.[9] In these Orders, there are minutely prescribed the details of the celebration: the costumes of the clergy as well as those of the children, who always have a prominent place at liturgical receptions; the ritual, which includes the aspersion of the comer, his descent from the horse to kiss the Gospels, and his censing; the chants of the clergy; finally the arrangements for the procession of cross-bearers, bearers of holy water, thuribels, candles and sacred books, not to mention all the others who conduct their secular lord and likeness of the Lord in Heaven under a canopy into the city (pl. 20, fig. 46).[10] The oldest setting of these Orders, to our knowledge, is the one found in the Cluniac *Consuetudines* of the Abbey of Farfa, which may fall still in the tenth century although the manuscript was written about 1039.[11] Another early Order of this kind comes from the Abbey of Saint-Yrieix near Limoges.[12] There is reason to believe that the

[8] J. A. Sawhill, *The Use of Athletic Metaphors in the Biblical Homilies of St. John Chrysostom* (Princeton, 1928), 113, the "Index of Athletic Terms," *s.v.* ἀγωνοθέτης. Homilies of John Chrysostom are found in the library catalogue of St. Gall of the middle of the 9th century as well as in that of 841–872 A.D., also in the catalogues of Reichenau of 822–838 A.D. and of the second half of the 9th century; cf. Paul Lehmann, *Mittelalterliche Bibliotheks-kataloge Deutschlands und der Schweiz*, I (Munich, 1918), 80, 84, 253, 265.

[9] These Orders as well as those for the reception of bishops and prelates, princes and queens, are as yet neither sifted nor classified, but Mr. William A. Chaney, in Berkeley, has undertaken to deal with this subject. The fundamental study on the *Adventus* and the reception of royalty in the Hellenistic and Early Christian periods is Erik Peterson, "Die Einholung des Kyrios," *Zeitschrift für systematische Theologie*, VII (1930), 682–702 (here quoted as Peterson); see *DACL*, V: 1 (1922), cols. 197ff, *s.v.* "Epiphanie"; Maskell, *Monumenta ritualia ecclesiae Anglicanae* (2nd ed., Oxford, 1882), II, cliv ff; Biehl, *op. cit.*, 141ff, 166ff; C. Erdmann, "Kaiserliche und päpstliche Fahnen im hohen Mittelalter," *Quellen und Forschungen aus italienischen Archiven und Bibliotheken*, XXV (1933–34), 11ff. For the Roman and Byzantine usage see, in addition to Pfister, "Epiphanie," *RE*, Supplement IV (1924), cols. 310ff, §§ 36ff, and A. Deissmann, *Licht vom Osten* (4th ed., 1923), 314ff, the admirable discussions of both A. Alföldi, "Die Ausgestaltung des monarchischen Zeremoniells am römischen Kaiserhofe," *Römische Mitteilungen*, XLIX (1934), 88ff (here quoted as Alföldi), and André Grabar, *L'Empereur dans l'art byzantin* (Paris, 1936), 234ff, and *passim* (hereafter quoted as Grabar). For the Roman coinage see Paul L. Strack, *Untersuchungen zur römischen*

Reichsprägung des zweiten Jahrhunderts (Stuttgart, 1931–33), I, 110, 130, and II, 152ff, 160ff, and Jocelyn M. C. Toynbee, *The Hadrianic School* (Cambridge, 1934); see also *infra*, note 38.

[10] Paris, Bibl. Nat. Ms. Fr. 2813, fol. 457ᵛ, late 14th century; cf. Delachenal's edition of *Les Grandes Chroniques de France: Jean II et Charles V* (Paris, 1910ff), IV, pl. xxxiii, and II, 197f, for the description of the *Entrée* of Emperor Charles IV and his son at Cambrai, in 1377 A.D.

[11] *Consuetudines Farfenses*, chap. xxxii, ed. Bruno Albers, *Consuetudines monasticae*, I (Stuttgart, 1900), 170; also in *MGH, Scriptores*, XI, 547; Biehl, p. 168. The Order has its place among chapters dealing with processions: chap. xxix, "De processionibus"; chaps. xxx–xxxi, "De sanctorum reliquis qualiter deferatur … processionaliter"; chap. xxxii, "Ad regem deducendum"; chap. xxxiii, "Ad episcopum deducendum"; chap. xxxiv, "Item ad abbatem." The sequence of Orders has been changed in later times, but substantially the Orders are still found in the present *Pontificale Romanum*, into which they have been incorporated apparently through the medium of William Durandus; cf. Batiffol, *op. cit.*, 22; V. Leroquais, *Les pontificaux manuscrits des bibliothèques publiques de France* (Paris, 1937), I, xiiif.

[12] Paris, Bibl. Nat. Ms. Lat. 903, fol. 68, contains the following antiphon, which is inserted between Holy Thursday and Good Friday: "*Ad regem ducendum.* Benedictus deus patrum tuorum faciens misericordiam cum domo patris tui sit dominus deus tuus tecum detque omnes inimicos tuos sub pedibus tuis et stabiliat regnum tuum in pace, ut per te nomen magnum glorificetur in saecula. …*" A facsimile is found in *Paléographie musicale*, XIII (1925), fol. 135f, to which Professor Manfred F. Bukofzer kindly called my attention.

codification of the reception ceremonial first took place in monastic circles,[13] and the great number of poems *In adventu regis*, which have been handed down from the Abbey of St. Gall, may remind us that no town or city was visited by mediaeval monarchs so frequently as were the favored royal monasteries. However this may be, the liturgical reception as such was very much older than the codification of its ritual. From the Carolingian period there have been transmitted large numbers of *Versus ad regem suscipiendum*, and among the poets of these chants we find all the renowned names of that epoch, Theodulf of Orléans and Walafrid Strabo, Sedulius Scotus and Hartmann, as well as Notker of St. Gall, while other authors have remained anonymous.[14]

The general idea reflected in these verses may be gathered conveniently from a poem *In adventu regis*, which is found in a manuscript of Metz of the early tenth century.[15] The eulogizing poem refers apparently to Charles the Bald who, in the first line, is hailed "Ave sacer et alme Imperator Carole." There follow the *vota*, the good wishes for the emperor and his house as well as for his powerful and successful government of the world:

> The necks of all peoples shall bend to thee,
> The kingdoms of earth shall submit to thee,
> That ever thou mayst rule in eternity.
> Heaven rejoice and Earth jubilate:
> A new Constantine has irradiated this world,
> A famous Charles, offspring of saints,
> Whom God has elected to rule the nations. ...

We easily recognize the timeless features of this monarch. They are those of the Prince of Promise, of the Messianic world ruler, and have been traditional with the image of Christian emperors and kings ever since Constantine the Great. The ruler is shown in

[13] According to B. Capelle, "Le *Kyrie* de la messe et le Pape Gélase," *Revue bénédictine*, XLVI (1934), 135, the Roman Bibl. Angelica Ms. B.3.18, fol. 181, of the eleventh century, contains an *Ordo ad regem suscipiendum*. The provenance of the manuscript could not be ascertained at present. Lessons "In adventum episcopi" (with Luke 10, 1–7, as the pericope) are found in the Franco-Roman Evangelary of *ca.* 750 A.D. The earliest manuscript of this type (Douai, Bibl. Mun., Ms. 12) comes from the abbey of Marchiennes; cf. Theodor Klauser, *Das römische Capitulare Evangeliorum* (Liturgiegeschichtliche Quellen und Forschungen, no. 28; Münster, 1935), I, 131, 136ff and 170, n. 343. The same Lectionary contains a Lesson "In adventum iudicum" (p. 171, no. 350). The visit of royal judges or officials would naturally be more important to the regular clergy than to the secular clergy so that this instance, too, suggests the monastic origin of the mediaeval Reception Orders, which seem to stem from the Gallican orbit.

[14] Most of these verses are found in the St. Gall Ms. 381; cf. *MGH, Poetae*, IV, 323ff, nos. viii–xii, xiv–xviii. Theodulf wrote a poem *De adventu Hludowici Augusti Aurelianos* (814 A.D.) in Sapphic stanzas (*ibid.* I, 528, no. xxxvii); see the eighth stanza, which is indicative of the performance:

> Hoc chorus cleri populique turba
> Safficum carmen recinens precetur,
> Det Hludovico ut deus imperandi
>   Tempora longa.

His famous hymn *Gloria, laus et honor tibi sit, rex Christe redemptor* (*ibid.*, I, 558, no. lxix) is likewise an *Adventus* chant to be sung by children on Palm Sunday, i.e., on the "Entry of Christ." For Walafrid Strabo's *Adventus* chants to Lothair and Charles the Bald, cf. *ibid.*, II, 405ff, nos. lxiii–lxiv, and for those of Sedulius Scotus *ibid.*, III, 183, 217, nos. xv, lx (see also pp. 185, 220, nos. xviii, lxvi, *De adventu Franconis episcopi*). New chants were composed for every royal reception, since the monks of St. Gall boast of having received King Conrad I "novis laudibus dictatis"; cf. *Casus Sangallenses*, in *MGH, Scriptores*, II, 84.

[15] It is published by A. Prost, "Caractère et signification de quatre pièces liturgiques composées à Metz en latin et en grec au IXᵉ siècle," *Mémoires de la société nationale des antiquaires de France*, XXXVII (1876), 209ff; see also 212ff, *Item in adventu presulis*. The content of the manuscript and some considerations not here to be discussed suggest that the emperor addressed is Charles the Bald and not Charlemagne.

harmony with the universe which rejoices whenever he makes his "appearance," and the city, too, that he visits is in unison with the whole cosmos. Thus, the little city of Metz, exulting at the *felix adventus* of the Prince of Peace, the *Rex pacificus*, appears, in that moment, as the center and navel of the world, a timeless Zion:

> City, be happy, Heaven, rejoice!
> Jubilate, Metz, at the King's Advent.
> The King of Peace arrives at your gate
> To bring for ever blissful joy. . . .

And those who have gone to meet the Expected One are to join in the salutation, *Benedice, benedice, benedice!*[16]

This, with minor variations, is the type of chant sung at the royal or imperial receptions. Sometimes the prince would be compared to Solomon.[17] Sometimes his *Adventus* would be hailed as the dawn of a new Golden Age: peace and happiness are to rule, fertility is to be his companion, Spring is to return anon that the arid pastures may cover themselves with new verdure and the meadows with flowers.[18] Or else, the Messianic note may be anticipated and struck by the ruler himself when he announces his coming: the chancery of Frederick II produced the most daring manifestoes of that kind.[19] Until the late

---

[16] Colla gentium   Tibi sternantur,
      Regna mundi   Tibi subdantur,
      Ut in perpetuum   Regnes per evum.
      Exulta polus   Letare tellus,
      Constantinus novus   Effulsit in mundum,
      Carolus preclarus   Progenie sancta,
      Quem deus elegit   Regere gentes. . . .

The subjection of the *gentes* is a recurrent image in connection with Messianic rulership; see, e.g., *supra*, note 12, and also the intention for the emperor in the *Orationes solemnes* on Good Friday; see also F. E. Brightman *Liturgies Eastern and Western* (Oxford, 1896), I, 407. For the title and acclamation *Novus Constantinus* see Henri Grégoire, *Recueil des inscriptions grecques chrétiennes d'Asie Mineure* (Paris, 1922), I, 22; A. D. Nock, "Studies in the Graeco-Roman Beliefs of the Empire," *Journal of Hellenic Studies*, XLV (1925), 93, n. 8; O. Treitinger, *Die ost-römische Kaiser- und Reichsidee nach ihrer Gestaltung im höfischen Zeremoniell* (Jena, 1938), 131, n. 4. With the words "progenie sancta" (paralleling, as it were, Horaces's "Divis orte bonis") the poet alludes to St. Arnulph as patron of the Arnulfingians (Carolingians). See also Hincmar's address to Charles the Bald at the latter's coronation in Metz, in 869 A.D. (*PL*, CXXXVIII, col. 740) and the refrain

      Salve regum sancta proles
      Care Christo Carole

in Walafrid Strabo's *Adventus* chant for Charles the Bald, *MGH, Poetae*, II, 406. See also A. M. Friend, "Two Manuscripts of the School of St. Denis," *Speculum*, I (1926), 67f. The text of the verses concluding the poem is:

      Gaude civitas,   Letare polus,
      Exulta Mettis   De adventu regis.
      Rex pacificus   Advenit tibi,
      Letitiam ferens   Gaudiumque per evum. . . .

[17] See, e.g., Sedulius (*MGH, Poetae*, III, 217):
      Rex tuus mitis, sapiens, honorus,
      Pacifer ductor Salemonis instar
      Nunc venit Caesar, tuus, alma, princeps,
           Filia Sion. . . .

[18] See, e.g., Notker of St. Gall, in the last stanza of the poem quoted *supra*, note 7:
      Hec ipsa gaudent tempora
      Floreque verno germinant,
      Adventus omni gaudio
      Quando venit optatior.
Or, Walafrid Strabo to Lothair (*MGH, Poetae*, II, 405, no. lxii):
      Innovatur nostra laetos
      Terra flores proferens:
      Ver novum praesentat aestas,
      Cum datur te cernere. . . .
Or, the lines of Sedulius (*ibid.*, III, 183, no. xv):
      Hos comitetur—amen—victoria, pompa, trophea,
           Pax, ardens virtus, intemerata salus;
      Linguosi populi dextra laevaque locati
           Hos primo timeant, hinc venerentur, ament;
      Aurea saecla novis contexant ordine sceptris,
           Disponant Francis prospera regna suis. . . .

[19] *MGH, Constitutiones*, II, 304ff, nos. 219, 221; cf. E. Kantorowicz, *Kaiser Friedrich der Zweite*, I (Berlin, 1927), 467ff, and II (Berlin, 1931), 202, 289ff. See also the poem of Marquard of Ried (*Contin. Scotorum*, in *MGH, SS.*, IX, 625) in the praise of Frederick II on his entry into Jerusalem:
      Adveniente Dei famulo magno Friderico
      Sol nitet, aura tepet, aqua bullit, terra virescit. . . .
      Jerusalem gaude. . . .
      Rex quia magnificus Jesus olim, nunc Fridericus,
      Promptus uterque pati, sunt in te magnificati.

Middle Ages this tone was to linger on. It predominated at the magnificent entrances of French kings and Burgundian dukes, and the *tableaux vivants*, then called "mysteries," explained by the means of seemingly indispensable scrolls the various aspects of the Messianic symbolism of the *felix adventus*.[20] Time and again it has been announced on these occasions that the comer is the Expected One and that accordingly the city, whose gates have been flung open to him, is another Zion.[21] For whenever a king arrived at the gates of a city, celestial Jerusalem seemed to descend from heaven to earth.[22] It is as though, through the magic balm of the Anointed, both king and city are transformed as they approach one another; every terrestrial city becomes another Jerusalem at the Advent of the Anointed, and the ruler at his entry becomes more and more a likeness of Christ. In other words, the liturgical celebration of an *Adventus* reflects, or even stages, the Christian prototype of Messianic entries, that is, the Lord's triumphant Entry as king into Jerusalem on Palm Sunday.

There is ample evidence to prove this assertion. It is countenanced, for example, by the protocol of the entry into Rome of the Exarch of Ravenna which became the model of the receptions of Frankish kings and German emperors.[23] At various distances from the city the prince was met by various delegations. At thirty miles he was received by the judges and officials of Rome with their banners. At one mile there were lined up the

---

[20] In 1458, at the Entry of Philip the Good in Ghent, there were staged tableaux of the Prophets holding in their hands scrolls with inscriptions such as

> Ecce nomen domini venit de longinquo (Is. 30, 27);
> Ecce venit desideratus cunctis gentibus (Hag. 2, 8);
> Benedictus Dominus Deus Israel, qui misit hodie te in occursum meum (1 Kings 25, 32).

The symbolism of world-redeemer was indicated by the display of a copy of Van Eyck's Altar so as to allude to the "Ecce agnus Dei" and the redemption of man; cf. Jean Chartier, *Chronique de Charles VII*, chap. 283, ed. Vallet de Viriville (Paris, 1858), III, 80ff; Otto Cartellieri, *Am Hofe der Herzöge von Burgund* (Basel, 1926), 57, 223. Attention may be called to the fact that Bible verses beginning with *Ecce* or *Benedictus* are adduced preferably. The same seems to be true with reference to the antiphons in the time of Advent, an observation intimated to me by Professor M. F. Bukofzer. For the Royal Entries of the French Kings see Théodore Godefroy, *Le cérémonial de France* (Paris, 1619); for those of the English Kings, see Robert Withington, *English Pageantry* (Cambridge, Mass., 1918), I, 124ff, 222ff; also E. K. Chambers, *The Mediaeval Stage* (Oxford, 1903), II, pp. 166ff, and George R. Kernodle, "Renaissance Artists in the Service of the People," *Art Bulletin*, XXV (1943), 59ff. The papal entries deserve to be studied. Pope Julius II, for example, held his triumphal entry into Rome, after the conquest of the Romagna, on a Palm Sunday; cf. Marino Sanuto, *Diarii*, VII (Venice, 1882), 43.

[21] Cf. *supra*, note 17. See also the Annalist of London (quoted by Withington, *op. cit.*, I, 125) on the Entry of Edward II, in 1308, where it is said that London appeared "quasi nova Jerusalem"; *Annales Londinenses*, ed. Stubbs (London, 1882), 152.

[22] The Descent of Jerusalem (Apoc. 21, 2) is of course a very popular topic in texts, liturgy, and art, especially in the earlier Middle Ages. For significant later changes, see

A. L. Mayer, in *Jahrbuch für Liturgiewissenschaft*, XIV (1938), 166ff.

[23] "Sicut mos est exarchum aut patricium suscipiendum"; cf. *Liber pontificalis*, ed. L. Duchesne (Paris, 1886–92), I, 496f. The reception of Charlemagne, in 774, was *not* that of an emperor. At the imperial receptions the pope himself proceeded to the sixth milestone to meet the emperor; cf. Paulus Diaconus, *Hist. Lang.*, V, chap. 11, *MGH, Scriptores Langobardorum*, p. 149, and *Liber pontificalis*, I, 343, with reference to the Emperor Constans II, "cui sexto ab urbe miliario Vitalianus papa cum sacerdotibus et Romano populo occurrit" (A.D. 663). The reception of Charlemagne thus was modelled after that of the exarch; it remained authoritative for all imperial receptions in Rome during the Middle Ages. Cf. *Liber pont.*, II, 88 (Louis II, in 844) and *ibid.*, II, 300 (Henry V, in 1111). See, in general, E. Eichmann, "Studien zur Geschichte der abendländischen Kaiserkrönung," *Historisches Jahrbuch*, XLV (1925), 24ff. The Roman ceremonial as described in the *Liber pontificalis* has clearly influenced the Milanese Order of the Royal Reception; cf. Magistretti, *Monumenta veteris liturgiae Ambrosianae* (Milan, 1897), I, 121ff, and for the date of this Order, Eichmann, "Zur Geschichte des lombardischen Krönungsritus," *Historisches Jahrbuch*, XLVI (1926), 528f. The reception at 30 miles is reminiscent of the 30 stadia mentioned by Josephus, *Bell. Jud.*, VII, 101, at the *Adventus* of Titus in Antioch; see Peterson, p. 694. For a strange interrelation between mileage and apostles, see the Felician Epitome of the *Liber pontificalis*, ed. Mommsen, *MGH, Gesta pontificum*, I, 134, in the *Vita* of Pope John I (523–526): "Qui, dum introissent omnes ... cum Johanne*m* papa Constantinopolim, occurrerunt eis a miliario XII in honore apostolorum [sc. omnis civitas cum cere*os* et cru*ces*]," a passage which had escaped me and to which Mr. W. A. Chaney, in Berkeley, kindly called my attention.

Roman militias with the patrons of the seven regions and with the school children, who all waved palm leaves and olive branches and sang their chants. Here the lower clergy, too, received the prince, carrying the "venerable crosses" and forming the solemn procession. Finally, at the steps of St. Peter's the prince was met by the pope and the high clergy. Prince and pontiff would embrace each other, then join hands and walk together, the prince at the right of the pope, into the cathedral, while the clergy and all the faithful would acclaim the comer and shout "*Benedictus qui venit in nomine Domini.*"

This acclaim, if anything, makes it quite evident that the Entry of Christ into Jerusalem on Palm Sunday was the prototype after which the receptions of mediaeval princes were modelled. This evangelical prototype, to be sure, made each individual representative of the temporal kingship transcendent at his entry. However, the recourse to the biblical model established also the unbroken tradition from antiquity in so far as the Christian ceremonial of royal receptions appears, with few *mutatis* and even fewer *mutandis*, as the continuation of the ceremonial observed at the epiphanies of Hellenistic Kings and Roman Emperors. This is not surprising. After all, Jesus, at the gates of Jerusalem, was received as the Hellenistic King of the Jews. Very correctly, therefore, St. John, when describing the Lord's Entry, employs the expression *Hypantesis*, while St. Paul, when describing the Lord's reception at his Second Coming, uses the word *Apantesis;* and the meeting of Jesus as a child with Simeon the High Priest is celebrated in the Eastern Church as the feast of *Hypapante* (*occursus domini;* the feast of Purification in the Western Church).[24] All these terms are synonymous. They signify the official meeting of kings or high dignitaries when they arrive at a city and make their "Appearance," their *Epiphany* or *Parousia*, so that both St. John and St. Paul as well as the Eastern Church apply to the receptions of Christ the technical terms for the constitutional welcome of royalty.[25]

Owing to several excellent modern studies on this solemnity and its constitutional background, the main features of the Hellenistic-Roman as well as early Christian receptions stand out very clearly and can be easily summarized.[26] The *Apantesis*, or solemn reception, was usually ordered by decree, after the magistracies of the city concerned had passed an official resolution. The arrival of the ruler, it is true, was supposed to evoke public joy. But it is to be remembered that the joy may have been dampened by the taxes which invariably resulted from the king's presence, no matter whether these duties were collected under the name of *parousiai* in Roman Egypt or were called, more prosaically, "fodder," *fodrum propter adventum regis*, in the districts surrounding mediaeval Rome.[27] As regards the ceremonial, it was similar to the one customary in Byzantine and

[24] John 12, 13: ἐξῆλθον εἰς ὑπάντησιν αὐτῷ; 1 Thess. 4, 17: εἰς ἀπάντησιν τοῦ κυρίου εἰς ἀέρα. For *Hypapante* cf. *infra*, notes 73, 123.

[25] Peterson, p. 693; cf. Moulton and Milligan, *The Vocabulary of the Greek Testament* (London, 1930), 53: "...a kind of technical term for the official welcome of a newly arrived dignitary." Also the term *Dies adventus* designating Palm Sunday would be incomprehensible unless we realize its "constitutional" connotations; see, e.g., F. C. Conybeare and A. J. Maclean, *Rituale Armenorum* (Oxford, 1905), 182.

[26] Cf. *supra*, note 9, especially Peterson, who offers a valuable collection of places and discusses the subject with all the circumspection to be expected of this scholar. Alföldi's study is fundamental for imperial Rome.

[27] For the παρουσίαι cf. U. Wilcken, *Griechische Ostraka* (Leipzig, 1899), I, 274ff; A. Deissmann, *op. cit.* (*supra*, note 9), 280ff; Rostovtzeff, *The Social and Economic History of the Hellenistic World*, III (Oxford, 1941), 1561, and A. C. Johnson, *Roman Egypt* (Baltimore, 1936), 620ff. The costs did not always run as high as those of the reception of Tiridates in Rome (66 A.D.), as then they

Frankish Rome. The population lined up at the city-gates or at some distance from the city, arranged in accordance with the political organization of a Hellenistic community: the civil authorities, the soldiers, the priests and priestesses, the gymnasiarch with the ephebes and youngsters, the *paidonomos* with the school children, the citizens proper, the women and virgins, and finally the other inhabitants of the town. White garments were prescribed to all participants and so was the wearing of wreaths. To carry torches, to burn incense, to pour out aromatic oils, or to strew flowers were traditional marks of respect. Often we learn that the images of gods or cultual objects were carried to meet the rulers, that the temples were open, that sacrifices were offered, and that the newly arrived prince immediately entered the main sanctuary of the city. We find also the official chants of welcome and the acclamations by which the ruler was hailed as "bene-factor and saviour" (εὐεργέτης καὶ σωτήρ) so that even the Messianic note, or rather the symbolism of world-saviourship, goes back to pre-Christian times or non-Christian customs.[28]

No item that we are familiar with at the royal receptions in the Christian age seems to be missing in the Hellenistic orbit, although some features must be translated. The order of society, for example, and its arrangement changed, as the antique political organi-zation was supplanted by that of the Church.[29] The insignia of the gods were replaced by the victorious symbol of the last antique Deity, by "the venerable crosses with which it is the custom to receive emperors and kings."[30] And the pagan *xoana* made way for the

amounted to 800,000 *sestertii* daily, but were charged to the public treasury; cf. Cassius Dio, LXII, 4. The medi-eval *fodrum* comprised all kinds of taxations, among these, however, also the tax *in adventu regis;* cf. H. Brunner, *Deutsche Rechtsgeschichte,* II (Leipzig, 1892), 229; J. Ficker, *Forschungen zur Reichs- und Rechtsgeschichte Italiens,* II (Inns-bruck, 1869), p. 7, § 215, and p. 309, § 337; Ernst Mayer, *Italienische Verfassungsgeschichte,* I (Leipzig, 1909), 315ff, with note 64 ("fodrum propter adventum regis et pape"). The Dissertation of Post, *Über das Fodrum* (Strassburg, 1880), was not accessible to me. In later times the *mansionaticum* or *gistum* was linked up with the *Adventus;* cf. Dom Ursmer Berlière, "Le droit de gîte épiscopale lors d'une joyeuse entrée," *Mélanges Paul Fournier* (Paris, 1929), 17f.

[28] To the material collected by Peterson, whose dis-cussion here has been closely followed, there may be ad-duced a few additions. The imperial images, when sent out to the provinces, were received with the same ceremonial as the emperors *in persona;* cf. Helmut Kruse, *Studien zur offiziellen Geltung des Kaiserbildes im römischen Reich* (Paderborn, 1934), 34ff, who quotes (pp. 41ff) an interesting *Adventus* chant from a Cairo Papyrus of 566 A.D., sung at the reception of an imperial image. The ceremonial was faithfully transferred to the reception of relics of saints (*supra,* note 11) when their worship began in the fourth century and when imperial honors were cumulated also on these objects of veneration; see St. Jerome's polemical treatise *Adversus Vigilantium,* Migne, *PL,* XXIII, col. 344 (*ca.* 404 A.D.); F. J. Dölger, *Antike und Christentum,* III (Münster, 1932), 248ff. See also the re-liquary procession, preceded by the emperor and high

dignitaries with candles carried in their hands, in the famous ivory of Trier (Delbrück, *Die Consulardiptychen* [Berlin, 1929], N. 67, pp. 261–270). Constantius, when re-ceiving the bodies of Saints Andrew, Luke, and Timothy, was the first emperor to partake in an *Adventus* of relics, and he created a sensation by so doing; cf. Jerome, *op. cit.,* Migne, *PL,* XXIII, col. 343. See also the homily of St. John Chrysostom (Migne, *PG,* LXIII, cols. 468ff.) refer-ring to the translation of the relics of St. Phocas under the Emperor Arcadius. For the reception with torches and incense, see Alföldi, p. 89; Kruse, p. 39, note 4; L'Orange and von Gerkan, *Der spätantike Bildschmuck des Konstantins-bogens* (Berlin, 1939), 97; see also our pl. 14, fig. 21, where, at the reception of Galerius, the torchbearing citizens as well as the deity expecting the emperor in front of an open temple can be distinguished clearly. For the Messianic character of the *Adventus* in pre-Christian times, see Alföldi, pp. 88f. The *Soter* acclamation survived not only in Byzantium (see Nikephoros Bryennios, II, chap. 5; Migne, *PG,* CXXVII, col. 103; Treitinger, *op. cit.,* 231ff), but also the pope was gradually steeped with soteriological elements; cf. *Liber pont.,* I, 451, the reception of Pope Stephen II (752–757): "Venit pastor noster et post Deo salus noster." Cf. *ibid.,* I, 430, for Pope Zacharias.

[29] Peterson, p. 695.

[30] *Liber pont.,* II, 88. Already Guido Panciroli, *In notitiam dignitatum,* chap. xxiv, in J. G. Graevius, *The-saurus antiquitatum Romanarum* (Utrecht, 1698), VII, 1399D, has indicated that the papal and archiepiscopal privilege of displaying a processional cross is derived from an imperial prerogative; cf. Kruse (*supra,* note 28), 76ff.

wooden or painted images of the saints. Even so the similarities remain startling. In imperial Rome, *Fortuna Redux* was responsible for the emperor's happy return and arrival. In Constantinople, at least on one occasion, it was the *Hodegetria*, the most holy image of "St. Mary the Conductress," which was carried to meet the emperor. She conducted him through the Golden Gate, whose inscription commemorated the *aurea saecla* of bygone days, and through the city to the temple of St. Sophia where the emperor attended the sacrifice.[31]

These processions and honors originally were due the gods. In the Hellenistic Age they were conferred on the kings. The king's appearance at the gates of a city compared with, or was, the epiphany of a god. This explains the soteriological or "Messianic" character of the ceremony, a trait which was to outlast fifteen or more Christian centuries.[32]

In continuation of the Hellenistic ruler-worship there developed the celebration of the *Adventus Augusti* in imperial Rome.[33] Augustus, in the great account of his exploits, devotes two paragraphs to the enumeration of all the honors showered on him at his return from Syria in 19 B.C. He emphasizes that by decree of the Senate part of the praetors and of the tribunes of the people, together with one of the consuls, were sent as far as Campania to meet him. Other decrees were passed that yearly "the day on which Augustus entered the city [October 12] should be honored with sacrifices by the whole population and be held sacred for evermore." Italian cities made the day when first he appeared at their gates the beginning of their year, thus starting a new era with the Emperor's Epiphany.[34] Briefly, Octavian's *Adventus* and Entry with its complex symbolism of imperial world-saviourship parallels the Lord's Epiphany and Entry into Jerusalem—a pre-Christian Palm Sunday, as it were.

We may pass over all the other occasions when an emperor's arrival prompted a city to make this day the beginning of a new era or when Rome indulged in celebrations because the GENIUS POPULI ROMANI INTRAVIT URBEM.[35] As late as the fourth century, in the Calendar of 354, we find on record the public feast-days of the *Adventus Divi*, one of which (October 29) refers to Constantine's entry into Rome after his victory of the

---

[31] Nikephoros Gregoras, IV, 2, ed. Schopen (Bonn, 1829), I, 87; Georgios Pachymeres, II, 31, ed. Niebuhr (Bonn, 1835), I, 160ff; Gibbon, ed. Bury (London, 1898), VI, 465. See also, for the Golden Gate, Robert of Clari, *The Conquest of Constantinople*, transl. by E. H. McNeal (New York, 1936), 108f; Strzygowski, "Das goldene Thor in Konstantinopel," *Jahrbuch des Deutschen Archäologischen Instituts*, VIII (1894), 5.

[32] See in general Pfister, "Epiphanie," *RE*, Suppl. IV, cols. 310ff; Alföldi, 88ff, and, for *Juppiter Imperator* as a model, Max Radin, "Imperium," *Studi in onore di Salvatore Riccobono*, II (Palermo, 1936), 23-45. Ammianus Marcellinus (XXII, 9) says bluntly "urbique propinquans in speciem alicuius numinis"; and substantially the same idea was applied to the pope, as the *Liber pontificalis*, II, 446, reports: "Exierant obviam sibi [Pope Alexander III] extra urbem ... vultum eius intuentes tamquam vultum Jesu Christi cuius vices in terris regit."

[33] Alföldi, p. 88ff, discusses admirably the development and growth of the *Adventus* in imperial Rome as well as its "Messianic" character.

[34] *Res gestae Divi Augusti*, chaps. 11-12; Cassius Dio, LI, 20, 3; Suetonius, *Augustus*, chap. 59. Cf. Pfister, in *RE*, Suppl. IV, col. 311, who compares the beginning of a new era on the occasion of the epiphany of an emperor with the new era beginning with the Epiphany of Christ. The custom of starting the era with the date of a ruler's Entry lingered on until the fifth century. Gaiseric, King of the Vandals, began his era not with his accession, but with the *annus ab ingressu Carthaginis* (Oct. 19, 439); cf. Mommsen, "Das römisch-germanische Herrscherjahr," *Neues Archiv*, XVI (1891) 62ff.

[35] Alföldi, p. 91, fig. 3; see also E. Babelon, "Un nouveau médaillon en or de Constantin le Grand," *Mélanges Boissier* (Paris, 1903), 49ff. See our pl. 13, figs. 6, 7.

Milvian Bridge, an event commemorated also on the Arch of Constantine and invested by posterity with a definitely religious glamour.[36]

Gradually the *Adventus* began to be reflected in the imperial coinage. Coins commemorating an "arrival" first were struck in Greece to celebrate the visit of Nero. From Trajan onward, Rome, too, issued coins and medallions referring to an *Adventus Augusti*.[37] The designs of these coins vary. Of Hadrian,[38] who visited almost every province of the Empire, we know a whole set of *Adventus* coins showing him as he is met by the *Natio*, the personification of the country which he visits: Mauretania (pl. 13, fig. 1), Cilicia (pl. 13, fig. 2), Judaea (pl. 13, fig. 3) and others. The *Natio* receiving the emperor carries a palm leaf (pl. 13, fig. 1), a *vexillum* (pl. 13, fig. 2), or else some other symbol in her left hand, while with her right she usually offers the libation over an altar, the sacrifice *ob adventum felicem Augusti*. She usually appears alone. Only Judaea forms an exception, as she is frequently represented with children surrounding her (pl. 13, fig. 3) or greeting the guest with palm branches (pl. 13, fig. 4). The children, to be sure, symbolize the Roman colony, the *Iudaea renascens*, which gradually was recovering after the Jewish Rebellion. Here, in the place of Old Jerusalem destroyed by Titus, Hadrian had founded a New Jerusalem calling it Aelia Capitolina, and it was the Greek, not the Jewish, youth to which the design of the coins seems to allude. Yet the question very reasonably may be raised whether in fact it is by coincidence only that on Hadrian's coins of Judaea children should go out with palm branches to meet the imperial "Benefactor and Saviour of the World" before the city where, according to the narration of the Gospel, children with palm leaves had in a like way greeted the Messianic King of Israel at his Entry.[39]

Another peculiarity is sometimes displayed by the *Adventus* coins of Alexandria (pl. 13, fig. 5). Here the *Natio* is replaced by the national deities of Egypt, Serapis and Isis. We see an altar, but no sacrifice. Instead the god is shown as he shakes hands with Hadrian while Isis lifts her *sistrum* to welcome the Empress Sabina. It has been suggested that the gods greet the majesties as their temple-sharing (σύνναοι) and throne-sharing (σύνθρονοι) equals. The suggestion has been rejected, as "the type of the emperor meeting the god is familiar and does not imply temple-sharing."[40] However, throne-sharing in connection with an *Adventus* must have been likewise a familiar concept and a trait well known in the Hellenistic world. Christ, after his Ascension and at his *Adventus* in

[36] *CIL*, I, 352, 397; cf. p. 346, for the two *Adventus Divi* on July 18 and 21, as well as p. 350, for a *Profectio Divi* on September 27. See also Babelon, *op. cit.*, 51.

[37] Strack, *Untersuchungen*, I, 131. See our pl. 13, fig. 18.

[38] The Hadrianic *Adventus* coins have been studied most efficiently by Miss Jocelyn M. C. Toynbee in her delightful book on *The Hadrianic School* (Cambridge, 1934). Fundamental, in addition to Strack's second volume, is of course H. Mattingly, *Coins of the Roman Empire in the British Museum*, III (London, 1936).

[39] For our pl. 13, figs. 1–4, see Strack, II, pl. xiii, nos. 757, 748, 752, and pl. xiv, no. 719; cf. pp. 152ff. For *Iudaea renascens* see Strack, II, 162, pl. xiii, nos. 752, 753, 755, and pl. xiv, no. 719. Mattingly, *op. cit.*, III, clxxii, follows Strack's interpretation, and so does

Miss Toynbee, pp. 119ff, whose discussion of "Judaea's children" here has been followed very closely. A coin similar to our pl. 13, fig. 3 is found in Toynbee, pl. v, no. 4; cf. p. 121, note 1.

[40] Strack, II, 164, pl. vi, no. 314, pl. xiii, no. 743; Toynbee, pp. 42ff, pl. ii, nos. 20–21. Wilhelm Weber, *Untersuchungen zur Geschichte des Kaisers Hadrianus* (Leipzig, 1907), 316f, and Strack, *loc. cit.*, as well as other scholars hold that the coin indicates a "temple-sharing." A. D. Nock, "Σύνναος θεός," *Harvard Studies in Classical Philology*, XLI (1930), 19f, however, is probably correct in not recognizing these coins (see also Toynbee, pl. xi, no. 1) as evidence for temple-sharing. Toynbee, p. 43, note 2, and Mattingly, III, clxxi f, carefully avoid making any decision in this respect.

heaven, becomes the *Synthronos* of God. He shares the throne sitting on the right of the Father, and this idea is repeated later on over and over again in benedictions for the mediaeval ruler who, it is hoped, may share in afterlife the throne of Christ and rule in *condominium* with the *christus* "cuius typum gerit in nomine."[41]

The Alexandrian *Adventus* type with Serapis and Isis was used as a model by Commodus, though with a few changes. The emperor stands alone, but behind him we find a Victory crowning him with her right hand while a palm branch is held in her left (pl. 13, fig. 5a).[42]

Although gradually superseded by other designs, the Hadrianic type of *Adventus* coins survived until the end of the third century when Carausius, Emperor of Britain (287–293 A.D.), once more presents himself joining hands with a *Natio*, Britannia. The design is conventional, but the legend of the coin is startling. *Expectate veni*—"Come, O Expected One"—is the motto, which betrays unmistakably the strength of that Messianic current and world-redeemer mysticism that manifests itself increasingly at the imperial Advent (pl. 13, fig. 9).[43] Constantine the Great, probably for his *Adventus* in Milan in 313, had a gold medallion struck displaying his profile together with that of *Sol invictus*, who has the emperor's features, while the emperor, in turn, shows on his shield the chariot of the Sun-God and is styled *Invictus Constantinus* (pl. 13, figs. 6, 7).[43a] Moreover, Constantine's father Constantius was hailed at the reconquest of Britain in 296 as the "Restorer of Eternal Light," an acclamation found as a legend on his magnificent gold medallion, which was struck at his *Adventus* in England, showing the conqueror on horseback while conquered *Londinium* kneels before him at the gate of the city (pl. 13, fig. 8).[44]

Not only the defeated *Natio* in her humiliation rouses our attention but also the city-gate motif on an *Adventus* coin. A very famous and telling example of an *Adventus* with city-gate is offered by a bronze medallion of Marcus Aurelius (pl. 13, fig. 10). The emperor, who in the Hadrianic *Adventus* series is usually *togatus*, here wears a uniform, the lance in his right hand. Two standard-bearers *aquilifer* and *vexillifer*, march before him; behind, a Victory holds a wreath over the head of the Caesar. The city is Rome. To

---

[41] The Christian version of the idea of "throne-sharing" and the survival of this idea by transference has as yet not been studied. It clearly survived in Byzantium; cf. Constantine, *De caerim.*, II, 1, ed. Reiske (Bonn, 1829), I, 521, II, 600; E. Kantorowicz, "Ivories and Litanies," *Journal of the Warburg and Courtauld Institutes*, V (1942), 73, note 3. For the royal *condominium* with Christ see P. E. Schramm, "Das Herrscherbild in der Kunst des frühen Mittelalters," *Studien der Bibliothek Warburg*, 1922/3 (1924), 222ff., and "Die Krönung in Deutschland bis zum Beginn des Salischen Hauses," *Zeitschrift der Savigny-Stiftung für Rechtsgeschichte*, kan. Abt., XXIV (1935), 317ff., §§ 14 and 17, with reference to the Coronation Order of Mainz of the 10th century.

[42] Mattingly, *Coins of the Roman Empire in the British Museum*, IV (London, 1940), pl. xcix, no. 15; Toynbee, pp. 45ff., and pl. xi, nos. 2, 3. It is not an *Adventus* coin proper, but the design is based upon the "arrival" pattern.

[43] After H. A. Grueber, in *Numismatic Chronicle*, ser. 3, XX (1900), pl. iii, no. 8. Cf. Percy H. Webb, "The Reign

and Coinage of Carausius," *ibid.*, ser. 4, VII (1907), 70, and pl. 1, no. 9; Toynbee, pp. 64ff, and pl. xii, no. 6.

[43a] Cf. E. Babelon, *op. cit.*, 49.

[44] J. Babelon and A. Duquénoy, "Médaillons d'or du trésor d'Arras," *Aréthuse*, I (1924), 46ff, and pl. vii, no. 2; Toynbee, p. 65, and pl. xii, no. 10; Grabar, p. 234, no. 3. The "arrival" here is symbolized by a ship just as in the very first *Adventus* coins which were struck by Corinth and Patras for Nero; cf. B. V. Head, *Catalogue of Greek Coins in the British Museum: Corinth* (London, 1889), 70ff, and pl. xviii, nos. 4, 6; B. Pick, in *Zeitschrift für Numismatik*, XVII (1890), 182ff., 190. It is, however, not here the intention to deal with the "arrival" by boat, which is represented, e.g., in the spiral reliefs of the Column of Trajan (cf. Lehmann-Hartleben, *Die Trajanssäule* [Berlin and Leipzig, 1926], 84ff, pl. xix) and mentioned in *Dig.*, 1, 4, 5, 16, a place to which Professor Max Radin kindly called my attention. For the redeemer mysticism see also the obverse of the *Adventus* medallion of Constantine the Great (pl. 13, fig. 6), *supra*, note 35.

the left, in the background, there rises the temple of *Fortuna Redux*, whose worship came increasingly into prominence under the emperors. To the right, we see the Arch of Domitian through which the emperor is about to enter the city.[45]

It is likely that Rome on this occasion—probably in A.D. 174—granted an arch to Marcus Aurelius in celebration, not of a triumph, but of his *Adventus* after years of strenuous warfare.[46] Arches commemorating an "arrival," and not a triumph proper, are rare altogether; and *Triumphus* and *Adventus*, though closely related with each other, are not the same thing.[47] However, an arch had been erected in Brindisi for Octavian on his arrival in 30 B.C., and if a similar building were put up in Rome for the Emperor Marcus, this would indeed indicate that by the second century the *Adventus* had become an integral and independent element within the imperial theology of triumph and victory.[48] From Trajan onward at the latest, the reliefs of the triumphal arches display quite often the *Adventus Augusti*. The panels of the *Adventus* Arch of Marcus, for instance, representing the emperor's "arrival" and "reception," were used for the decoration of the Arch of Constantine in which again the scene of this emperor's *Ingressus* was given a prominent place.[49] One of the most complete representations of an imperial *Adventus* is actually found on a triumphal arch, that of Constantine's co-emperor Galerius, at Salonica (pl. 14, fig. 21).[50] The cavalcade, with the emperor seated in a cart (like Constantine on his Roman triumphal arch), has departed from a city to the left and approaches one to the right, apparently Salonica. At the city-gate the people come to meet the emperor: first citizens with torches and flowers, then soldiers with their standards. On the rocks in the background, we see an open temple with the deity standing in the entrance and awaiting Galerius, head of the "Jovian" Dynasty or even the very Genius of Jupiter.[51] The scene is flanked by two Victories, indicating the close relationship between *Adventus* and *Victoria*.

The Galerius relief is interesting because it displays at the same time the emperor's

[45] See Max Bernhart, *Handbuch zur Münzkunde der römischen Kaiserzeit* (Halle, 1926), pl. LXXX, no. 6. The coin has been discussed frequently; cf. H. Stuart Jones, "Notes on Roman Historical Sculptures," *Papers of the British School at Rome*, III (1905), 259ff, and pl. XXIX, no. 6; J. Liegle, "Architekturbilder auf antiken Münzen," *Die Antike*, XII (1936), 220, fig. 21. For the emperor's solemn entry through the Arch of Domitian see also L'Orange-Gerkan, *Konstantinsbogen*, 79, no. 1.

[46] Cf. Kähler, *s.v.* "Triumphbogen," *RE*, VIIA: 1 (1939), 390f, § 32, who holds that the arch was built in 174 A.D., when Marcus returned for a short time to Rome; Jones, *op. cit.*, 261ff, seems to share this opinion. But the emperor's return to Rome in that year is disputed; cf. Wilhelm Weber, *Rom, Herrschertum und Reich* (Stuttgart, 1937), 319, who denies it, and Mattingly, IV, cxlvii, who leaves it an open question whether the return was only desired or really took place.

[47] Jean Gagé, "La théologie de la victoire impériale," *Revue historique*, CLXXI (1933), 26ff, stresses that in the second, and especially in the third, century "l'avènement du prince, non moins que ses succès militaires, doit être considéré comme une révélation victorieuse." The coins show the same design for *Adventus, Profectio, Victoria, Gloria Romanorum,* and similar subjects (see pl. 13, figs.

13–20). Alföldi, p. 90, calls attention to the fact that by the second century the former "moderation" of the emperors relative to the celebration of the *Adventus* had disappeared. Also, the *Fortuna Redux* became increasingly important in imperial Rome; cf. Otto, *s.v.* "Fortuna," *RE*, VII (1912), 37ff. Despite these similarities it is necessary to distinguish carefully between *Adventus* and *Triumphus;* cf. Peterson, p. 693, note 3.

[48] Kähler, *op. cit.*, 407, § 6, for the Arch of Brindisi. The complement to an *Adventus* arch is that erected for the *Profectio;* cf. Kähler, 415, § 8, for the Arch of Claudius at Boulogne.

[49] In addition to Trajan's *Adventus* on the Beneventan Arch there may have been yet another representation of an "arrival" of this emperor; see the interesting discussion by Miss Toynbee, pp. 43ff, and pl. XXIII, no. 4, on the slab in the Louvre. On the Arch of Marcus Aurelius there were represented either two *Adventus* or a *Profectio* and an *Adventus;* cf. Jones, *op. cit.*, 261ff, and pl. XXIV, nos. 3–4; L'Orange-Gerkan, *Konstantinsbogen*, 185, pl. XLVII, a–b, and, for the *Ingressus* of Constantine, *ibid.*, 74ff, 87ff.

[50] Kinch, *L'arc de triomphe de Salonique* (Paris, 1890), 20ff, pl. VI; Grabar, *L'empereur*, 228, n. 4.

[51] See Mattingly, in *Cambridge Ancient History*, XII, (London, 1939), 329ff, on the coinage of the tetrarchy.

"arrival" and the "meeting," *Adventus* and *Occursus*. This is not the case in the medallion of Marcus Aurelius (pl. 13, fig. 10) on which only the "arrival" is represented. The solemn "meeting" is likewise omitted on a type of *Adventus* coin which seems to be started, under Marcus Aurelius, by a coin of his son Commodus. The emperor alone is pictured. He is on horseback and salutes with his right hand (pl. 13, fig. 11).[52] This type is long-lived. It is found as late as the fifth century on a gold coin of Valentinian III (425–455) riding a horse with rich trappings. Even more impressive is the last coin of this series, an *aureus* celebrating the *Adventus* of Marcian (450–457). This emperor, who may be styled the first true representative of *Dei gratia* rulership, is figured, like his Western predecessor Honorius (pl. 13, fig. 12), with a halo, as had been the custom since the late third century. The act of address on these later coins, though seemingly traditional, is reminiscent of what has been called the "magic gesture," a felicitous expression for a salute midway between rhetorical gesture and blessing.[53]

Closely related with this group of coins showing the emperor alone on horseback is an *Adventus* of Septimius Severus (pl. 13, fig. 13).[54] He appears on a prancing or galloping horse, with a standard-bearer hastening before him as *cursor*.

We may wonder whether this galloping horseman may have exercised an influence on the great scene of an *Adventus* which is depicted on the wall of the subterranean chamber of Aurelius Felicissimus in Rome and is claimed as a work of the middle of the third century (pl. 15, fig. 26).[55] In the center, standing out against a rectangular yellow background (perhaps the façade of a temple), a horseman is seen on a galloping mount. His right hand is raised, not because he performs the gesture of address or salute, but because he holds a scroll in his hand with which he seems to wave to the dignified congregation of men pouring out of the gate of a city εἰς ἀπάντησιν αὐτῷ—to meet him. Whoever the horseman may be, and whatever the city in the stables of which we see a lonely ass, this probably gnostic representation of an *Adventus* is in many respects preparatory to the scenes of the Entry of Christ into Jerusalem which begin to appear on Christian sarcophagi in the fourth century, that is, at a time when in general the symbolism of imperial art migrated, as it were, from the palace to the church.[56]

Attention may be called to two specimens. The famous sarcophagus in the Lateran Museum (pl. 14, fig. 23)[57] shows the Entry in the right part of the front side. Christ is

[52] Bernhart, *Handbuch*, pl. LXXX, no. 4; Mattingly, *Coins*, IV, pl. LXVI, no. 6, and pl. XC, no. 10.

[53] For Valentinian, see Grabar, pl. XXIX, no. 9; for Marcian, see F. Gnecchi, *I medaglioni Romani* (Milan, 1912), I, 40, and Hugh Goodacre, *A Handbook of the Coinage of the Byzantine Empire* (London, 1928), I, 37. The coin here reproduced (pl. 13, fig. 12; cf. Gnecchi, I, pl. XIX, no. 10) is an *aureus* of Honorius which matches the coin of Marcian. For the "magic gesture" of *Sol invictus* as adopted by the emperor, cf. L'Orange, "*Sol invictus imperator.* Ein Beitrag zur Apotheose,"*Symbolae Osloenses*, XIV (1935), 86–114, and L'Orange-Gerkan, pp. 176, 180, and *passim*.

[54] After Gnecchi, III, pl. XCII, no. 8.

[55] Joseph Wilpert, "Le pitture dell' ipogeo di Aurelio Felicissimo presso il Viale Manzoni in Roma," *Atti della pontificia accademia Romana di archeologia, Memorie*, I:2 (1924), pp. 37–39, pl. XX. Wilpert stresses the gnostic origin of the painting; however, his interpretation of the horseman (Epiphanius?) is not quite convincing. The *Adventus* coin of Septimius Severus has been adduced in this connection also by G. Bendinelli, "Il monumento sepolcrale degli Aureli al Viale Manzoni in Roma," *Monumenti antichi*, XXVIII (1923), 347, fig. 25, cf. pl. X; see also Grabar, p. 234, note 1.

[56] Wilpert, *I sarcofagi cristiani antichi*, II (Rome, 1932), pp. 312f. Pre-Constantinian specimens of the Entry at least are not known.

[57] Marion Lawrence, "City-Gate Sarcophagi," *Art Bulletin*, X (1927), fig. 34, facing p. 27; C. R. Morey, *Early Christian Art* (Princeton, 1942), 133, and fig. 136.

mounted astride the "colt of an ass," which despite its tiny stature piaffes just as proudly as the chargers of the emperors at their *Adventus*. A familiar gesture is the raising of the right hand of the rider who here gives the benediction rather than the salute. Familiar are also the city-gate, the figure bending its knee before the triumphant comer (pl. 13, figs. 4, 8), and the *pedisequus*—the figure following the mount (perhaps St. Peter)—who performs with his right hand a gesture reminiscent of the Victory holding the wreath over the head of the emperor (pl. 13, figs. 5a, 10). And similar features can be detected easily in a relief from St. John Studion in Constantinople (p. 14, fig. 22).[58]

The sarcophagi exhibit a type of Christ's Entry which on the whole became traditional and here may be called the "historical" concept, since a faithful and realistic account of the biblical narration is intended. For all that, however, the influence of the imperial *Adventus* imagery cannot be mistaken, a dependency of which scholars have not been heedless.[59] In this connection there have been adduced, among other evidence, the ivory covers of the Gospels of Etschmiadzin of the sixth century.[60] The two covers, though referring to the lives of Mary and Jesus respectively, are yet interrelated through the images in the lower section of the tablets. They both show Christ as the θεὸς ἐπιφανής, as they display the two *adventus in carne* and at the same time the two scenes in which, according to the Gospels, the Lord's kingship has been unambiguously recognized. In the tablet of Mary we find the *Adoration of the Magi* who come to worship the cosmos-child as King of the Universe. The other tablet contains the *Entry into Jerusalem* when Jesus was worshiped as King of Israel (pl. 14, fig. 25).[61] The rhythm of this *Entry* is closely related to a type of *Adventus* coin to be discussed in the next section. There is, however, one figure which brings the *Natio* coinage of Hadrian back to our mind. In the right corner of the carving we recognize—in the place of the customary city-gate—the *Natio*, the personification of Jerusalem, with a mural crown on her head and the *cornucopiae* in her left hand, who comes to meet the King of the Jews. And in a similar way it is the *Hierosolyma* that spreads the rug before the Lord in another ivory carving, in the *cathedra* of Bishop Maximianus of Ravenna (pl. 14, fig. 24).[62] The borrowing from imperal images here is quite manifest.

There is yet another feature of the Etschmiadzin *Entry into Jerusalem* which should not be passed over, namely the two *cursores* preceding, or accompanying, the rider on the left side of his horse. They appear as two standard-bearers in the *Adventus* medallion of Marcus Aurelius (pl. 13, fig. 10), and in later representations this couple is found quite frequently. They appear, for example, in the fresco of St. Demetrius in Salonica where the haloed Emperor Justinian II is depicted at his triumphal entrance into Salonica in

---

[58] Lawrence, *op. cit.*, fig. 46, and pp. 40ff.

[59] See Grabar, pp. 234ff, and *passim*, on whose rich material I am drawing here.

[60] Strzygowski, "Das Etschmiadzin-Evangeliar," *Byzantinische Denkmäler*, I (Vienna, 1891), pl. I; Grabar, pp. 235ff.

[61] For the parallelism of *Adoration* and *Entry*, see also

Jean Gagé, "Σταυρὸς νικοποιός. La victoire impériale dans l'empire chrétien," *Revue d'histoire et de philosophie religieuses*, XIII (1933), 398, note I.

[62] Morey, *Early Christian Art*, 262 and fig. 90. See also *infra*, note 87a and pl. 17, fig. 33a for the personification of Egypt in the representations of the "Flight."

688 A.D. (pl. 15, fig. 28).[63] Also, this couple of *cursores* is found in a miniature of the Bible of San Paolo of the ninth century, where King Solomon is seen, conducted to Gihon, place of his coronation, by Zadok the priest and Nathan the prophet (pl. 15, fig. 27).[64]

These last two images are also remarkable because they betray the reverse current of influence. The imagery of Christ's Entry into Jerusalem, in itself moulded after the imperial model, now begins to shape the *Adventus* of the Christian monarchs. This development has been briefly outlined above in connection with the liturgy and with the antiphon *Benedictus qui venit*, which was sung at the ruler's reception. Now we may realize that imagery and liturgy speak, as it were, the same language.[64a]

It would be relatively easy to outline the further development: to show how the ceremonial of the *Adventus* was taken over by bishops and patriarchs, and how, at the receptions of these princes of the Church, above all at that of the Roman Pontiff, the *imitatio imperatoris* quite logically was blended with the *imitatio Christi*.[65] Suffice it here to adduce a miniature of the late fifteenth century displaying the *Adventus* of a cardinal legate, who rides neither a horse (as does the emperor) nor an ass (as does the Lord) but is seated on a mule as are King Solomon and Saint Charlemagne in mediaeval legends (pl. 16, fig. 29).[66]

[63] Grabar, pl. VII, no. 2. I see no argument opposing the conjecture that this *Entry* should represent the triumphal *Adventus* of Justinian II in 688 A.D. On this event and its importance to the church of St. Demetrius in Salonica new light has been shed by A. Vasiliev, "An Edict of the Emperor Justinian II, September, 688," *Speculum*, XVIII (1943), 1–13.

[64] A. Boinet, *La miniature carolingienne* (Paris, 1913), pl. cxxv. Entries of Solomon are rare on the whole; see, however, Wilhelm Neuss, *Die katalanischen Bibelillustrationen um die Wende des ersten Jahrtausends und die altspanische Buchmalerei* (Bonn and Leipzig, 1922), pl. x, fig. 26, and pp. 24, 78; G. Swarzenski, *Die Salzburger Malerei* (Leipzig, 1908), pl. xxxvii, fig. 121. The coronation place Gihon may have something to do with the annual throne procession of Jehovah. However, we know too little about this ceremony to seek for possible influences on other triumphal processions in Jerusalem. See Hans Schmidt, *Die Thronfahrt Jahwes am Fest der Jahreswende im alten Israel* (Tübingen, 1927).

[64a] L. A. Celati, in *Bollettino della società Piemontese di archeologia e belle arti*, VIII (1924), 99, publishes a coin of Philip of Savoy, Prince of Achaia and Morea (1301–1324), bearing the legend *Benedictus qui venit in nomine domini*. It may be that in the later Middle Ages *Adventus* coins have been struck again, but it is beyond the power of the present author to survey the problem. A Renaissance medallion shows clearly the *Adventus* design, the Emperor Maximilian with Mars as *cursor* and with *Justitia* and *Fides* as attendants; cf. G. F. Hill, "L'école des médailleurs de Mantoue," *Aréthuse*, I (1924), 62, and pl. xi, no. 3. The *Adventus* type with an angel preceding is found in a coin glorifying St. Peter's escape from prison, which was struck under Pope Clement VII, in 1529; cf. Camillo Serafini, *Le monete e le bolle plumbee pontificie del medagliere Vaticano* (Milan, 1910), I, pl. xxxii, nos. 9–11, p. 207.

[65] The problem deserves a special study. See, however, Peterson, p. 690, on the entry of Athanasius into Alexandria. As far as the Holy See is concerned, the most important passages are found in the *Liber pontificalis*, I, 275, 390, 427, 447, and *passim;* see also II, 446, for the emperor-like reception of Pope Alexander III "quod nulli Romanorum pontificum recolitur factum" (a queer and hardly correct statement considering the implications of the *Constitutum Constantini;* cf. *infra*, p. 73f). Pope Julius II, after his conquest of the Romagna, delayed his triumphal entry into Rome until Palm Sunday, 1507; cf. Marino Sanuto, *Diarii*, VII (Venice, 1882), 43.

[66] Pontifical of Antoine de Châlons, Bishop of Autun (1485–1500), in Autun, Bibl. Mun. Ms. 129, fol. 100; Leroquais, *Les pontificaux manuscrits*, pl. cxiii. For the mount of Solomon, see 3 Kings 1, 38; for Charlemagne's riding a white mule to Jerusalem, see G. Rauschen, *Die Legende Karls des Grossen im 11. und 12. Jahrhundert* (Leipzig, 1890), 119. Occasionally, however, also the Lord is depicted on a mule, e.g., in the Gospels of Belgrade of the thirteenth century mentioned by A. Grabar, *Recherches sur les influences orientales dans l'art balkanique* (Paris, 1928), 81. The mount of the pope was a horse (*Constitutum Constantini*, § 16, *infra*, p. 73; see also *Ordo Romanus I*, chap. 2, and *IX*, chap. 6, Migne, *PL*, LXXVIII, cols. 937, 1007, as well as the later *Ordines*, e.g., *Ordo XI*, chap. 21; *XII*, chap. 6; *XIII*, chap. 8, etc., *ibid.*, cols. 1033, 1067, 1110), and that it was a white horse is suggested not only by images (e.g. our pl. 20, fig. 45) and by the tax imposed on Reichenau and Bamberg to furnish annually two white horses for the Holy See (cf. Klewitz, "Die Krönung des Papstes," *Zeitschrift der Savigny-Stiftung für Rechtsgeschichte*, kan. Abt. XXX [1941], 117) but also by other sources which quite often mention the "albus (candidus) equus" or the "blanke perd," e.g., Suger, Romuald of Salerno, the *Sachsenspiegel* and others; cf. Robert Holtzmann, *Der Kaiser als Marschall des Papstes* (Berlin and Leipzig, 1928), p. 8, n. 4; p. 11, n. 2; p. 13, n. 4; p. 17, n. 1. See also Gertrud Bing, "The Apocalypse Block-Books and Their Manuscript Models," *Journal of the*

2. Ecce mitto angelum meum...

The *Benedictus qui venit*... stands as a motto for practically all the representations of an *Adventus* which have hitherto been discussed. By this acclamation Christ was received at his Entry on Palm Sunday; it was sung as an antiphon to greet the Vicars of Christ, kings and emperors; and equivalents of this salutation—"Benefactor and Saviour of the World"—may be read from the lips of those represented on marbles or coins as they welcome a Roman Emperor: the torchbearing citizens and standard-bearing soldiers, the Countries, Cities, or Gods. We have labelled this the "historical" concept of the *Adventus*.

However, the "historical" type is not the only one to indicate an *Adventus*. In its stead we find frequently another concept which neither anticipates nor recalls the events on Palm Sunday, nor even alludes to them. This other type may be called the "eschatological" *Adventus*. It responds with the verse "*Ecce mitto angelum meum...*," which is still prescribed in the present *Pontificale Romanum* as au antiphon for the reception of emperors. It figures, as early as the tenth century, in the Order of Farfa for the reception of kings (*supra*, p. 39). And, ever since the tenth century, it serves as an *Introitus* in Orders of Royal and Imperial Coronations, when the prince is conducted into the cathedral and up to the altar.[67]

What does this verse imply? It has been suggested that the reference is Exodus 23, 20, when God on Mount Sinai promises Moses:

> Behold I will send my angel who shall go before thee, and keep thee in thy journey, and bring thee into the place that I have prepared.

But this suggestion is not quite correct.[68] The text in the *Pontificale Romanum* shows that the antiphon refers to the Gospels, whose writers in fact quote the prophecy of Malachi 3, 1, when applying to St. John the Baptist the words, "Behold I send my angel before thy face, who shall prepare thy way before thee."[69] The harbinger thus is considered in

---

Warburg and Courtauld Institutes, V (1942), p. 154, note 1: "Equus albus mater ecclesia est" — with reference to the first Rider. It is significant of the intellectual changes which took place in the 13th century that a break in this tradition should occur under Pope Celestine V, the Spiritualist among the popes, who in 1294 at his entry into Aquila rides an ass which two kings lead by the bridle. Here the *imitatio Christi* is quite obvious. In 1305, Pope Clement V rides a white mule at his coronation in Lyon; cf. Holtzmann, *op. cit.*, p. 16, note 3.

[67] Within the rite of the coronation the verse first appears in the Order of Mainz, *ca.* 961 A.D.; cf. Schramm, "Die Krönung in Deutschland," 233ff, 311. Via Mainz, the verse was received in Rome (perhaps in Ottonian times), where it is found, later on, in the Order of Cencius Savelli (*Liber censuum*, ed. P. Fabre and L. Duchesne [Paris, 1905–1910], I, p. 1*), and from Rome it may have wandered to Milan; cf. Magistretti, *Monumenta veteris liturgiae Ambrosianae*, I (Milan, 1897), p. 124. In Milan we find also a clear distinction between the "historical" and the "eschatological" entry. When the king to be crowned is received at the gates of the city, the procession sings *Benedictus qui venit*, and when he enters the cathedral in procession, the antiphon *Ecce mitto angelum*

meum is chanted; cf. Magistretti, pp. 121ff, and *supra*, note 23, and for the *Introitus* also *infra*, note 73. The *Ecce mitto* is found also in the Order of the Milanese coronation of Henry VII (1311 A.D.) where it figures as the tenth and last antiphon to be sung before the king arrives at the altar; cf. *MGH, Leges*, II, 504. Schramm, *op. cit.*, p. 235, note 2, seems to assume that the *Ordo Farfensis* (cf. *supra*, note 11) was influenced by the Order of Mainz. I am inclined to believe that the Cluniac Order of Farfa simply reflects the earlier, Gallican, custom which is likewise reflected by the Order of Mainz. The antiphon *Ecce mitto* as a reception chant was, almost certainly, "Gallican" by origin and not "Roman"; cf. *infra*, note 73.

[68] Schramm, *op. cit.*, 311; Eichmann, "Studien zur Geschichte der abendländischen Kaiserkrönung," *Historisches Jahrbuch*, XLV (1925), 33, and LII (1932), p. 309, n. 147. They both seem to refer to the Order of Milan (*MGH, Leges*, II, 504) where in fact Exod. 23, 20, was sung. See, however, *infra*, notes 69, 73.

[69] The text of the *Pontificale Romanum* is "Ecce mitto angelum meum, qui praeparabit viam tuam ante faciem meam" which varies slightly from any one of the biblical texts to which the antiphon refers, namely Mal. 3, 1; Matt. 11, 10; Mark 1, 2; Luke 7, 27.

the Gospels as the ἄγγελος, or messenger, of God who shall prepare the way of Jesus, the Messiah. Accordingly, John the Baptist sometimes is represented in late Byzantine art with wings, that is as an angel.[70]

This verse, when chanted to an emperor or king at his reception, may be interpreted in two ways. Either the emperor himself, who is addressed, is considered the "angel" sent by God—and this interpretation would fall in with the well-known character *angelicus* of the mediaeval ruler,[71] or the underlying idea is that God's angel may walk before the emperor, conduct him and prepare his way. In this case the emperor, the *christus Dei*, logically would compare with Christ "cuius typum gerit in nomine."[72] The antiphon, in this case, would stress the Messianic rather than the angelic character of the monarch; as St. John the Baptist, who compares with an angel, is the precursor of the Lord, so is the angel of God visualized as the forerunner—or quite precisely as the *cursor*—of the Messianic king and Prince of Promises.

The second interpretation is doubtless the one which is correct. The emperor is not himself the angel; he is the Anointed of God, and before him there shall walk God's angel as a celestial attendant or *cursor*. The correctness of this interpretation is countenanced by the immediate source of the *Adventus* antiphon. Whence derives the inspiraton of chanting this verse at the *Adventus* of an emperor? The answer is very simple: from the *Adventus Domini*. For "Ecce mitto angelum meum..." were the first words of the first Lesson read on the first Sunday of Advent as the prophecy of the Coming of the Lord. In this place the Malachi prophecy is found at least in the Missal of Bobbio of the seventh century and it is used similarly in other early Hispano-Gallican Lectionaries as well. What might have been assumed anyhow here is confirmed: this particular antiphon for the reception of kings originated in the Hispano-Gallican Church and not in the Roman. Rome welcomed the ruler "historically" by chanting "Benedictus qui venit." The Hispano-Gallican Church received the Anointed "eschatologically" with the Old Testament verse "Ecce mitto angelum meum."[73]

For our purpose it is of some importance that the second interpretation is supported

---

[70] Walter Haring, "The Winged St. John," *Art Bulletin*, V (1922), 35–40; N. L. Okunev, "Arilje, un monument de l'art serbe du xiiie siècle," *Seminarium Kondakovianum*, VIII (1936), pl. ix, no. 2, and p. 256; Kantorowicz, "Ivories and Litanies," 71f. The only other saint who occasionally is represented with wings, though for different reasons, seems to be St. Francis; cf. Beda Kleinschmidt, "San Francesco und das Purgatorium," *Gesammelte Aufsätze zur Kulturgeschichte Spaniens*, II (1930), 400ff, and pl. opp. p. 400.

[71] Its basis is probably 2 Kings 14, 17–20.

[72] Schramm, *op. cit.*, 317. In this sense the verse is quoted in the *Adventus* oration of Eustathius of Salonica when he addresses Emperor Manuel Comnenus; cf. W. Regel, *Fontes rerum Byzantinarum* (St. Petersburg, 1917), p. 60, lines 15ff.

[73] See Migne, *PL*, LXXII, cols. 457f, for Bobbio, and *ibid.*, col. 172, for Luxueil. In the *Liber comicus* the passage is read on the fourth Sunday of Advent, cf. G. Morin, *Anecdota Maredsolana*, I (Maredsous, 1893), 7f. In the

Missale mixtum the words figure on the second Sunday of Advent (Matt. 11, 10). On the fifth Sunday of Advent they are found in the Lectionary of Milan; cf. G. Godu, "Épîtres," *DACL*, V, col. 290, whose lists (cols. 261ff.) offer a convenient survey of the early pericopes. It is noteworthy that some Gallican sacramentaries begin the liturgical year, not with Advent, but with Christmas. The Advent period thus concludes, not opens, the liturgical year so that *adventus* has the meaning of *parousia* and refers to the Second Coming of Christ at the end of time; cf. Hans von Schubert, *Geschichte der christlichen Kirche im Frühmittelalter* (Tübingen, 1921), 668f. Rome has changed this custom, and the eschatological Lesson from Malachi was replaced by Matt. 11, 2–10, where the *Ecce mitto* refers to the First Coming of Christ; cf. Klauser, *Das römische Capitulare Evangeliorum*, I, 42, 89, 127, 167f, 182f. The pericope from Malachi figures in Rome on *Hypapante* or *Occursus Domini* (Feb. 2), and it is alluded to in the *Introitus* on Epiphany and on the Octave of Epiphany; but it is not connected with the Second Coming.

also by imagery. Once more we have to hark back to the imperial coins of Rome. An almost infinite number of *Adventus* coins is available which show, with insignificant variations, the following design: the emperor, riding a quick step and raising his right hand in the act of address, is followed by a standard-bearing *pedisequus* and is preceded by a winged *cursor*, a Victory of course, who carries a *tropaeum* in her left hand and a crown in her right (pl. 13, figs. 7, 15).[74] Substantially the same type of coin was used to symbolize the *Victoria Augusti* (pl. 13, fig. 16),[75] a custom making it obvious that the *Adventus Augusti* has been incorporated into the general imperial theology of Triumph, Glory, and Victory. Accordingly, the same design was stamped also on the late series of *Gloria Romanorum* coins of which by far the most impressive specimen is the large gold medallion of Justinian I (pl. 17, fig. 35) with the legend *Salus et Gloria Romanorum:* a winged Victory carrying the *tropaeum* on her left shoulder and, with her right hand, leading by the bridle the richly harnessed horse of the haloed emperor. A star beaming over the lance of the rider has magical meaning (cf. pl. 16, figs. 31, 32; pl. 17, figs. 33a, 34).[76]

If we allow for the change from pagan Victory to Christian angel—a traditional feature of iconographical development—it appears that the antiphon "Ecce mitto angelum meum" is indeed a most suitable translation into words of an image which was displayed by imperial art as late as the sixth century. Moreover, Justinian's *Victoria* with crown and palm branch became the model of the gold coins of Germanic kings. We find her on the coins of the Ostrogoths in Italy. She appears, if in a barbarized design, on those of the Visigoths in Spain from the sixth century to Roderic, the last king (710–711). And the *Victoria-Angelus*, the ἄγγελος νικοποιός, of the Byzantine emperors standing frontally with cross and globe in its hands, is displayed also on the coins of the Merovingian kings of Gaul.[77]

The "translation" of imagery into words is perhaps not quite as rare as might be assumed. The *Adventus* design with a winged Victory serving as *cursor* was applied also to coins celebrating the *Profectio Augusti*.[78] It seems natural that the emperor's "victorious

---

[74] Gnecchi, pl. cxviii, no. 2. The earliest Roman *Adventus* coin, a bronze medallion of Trajan (our pl. 13, fig. 18; *ibid.*, pl. xxxviii, no. 1) displays likewise the procession; but *Felicitas*, and not *Victoria*, precedes the emperor; cf. Strack, I, 130.

[75] Gnecchi, pl. cvi, nos. 5–6. See, in general, Gagé, *Rev. Hist.*, CLXXI (1933), 26ff. Other triumphal representations are closely related to this pattern; see, for instance, H. v. Fritze, "Die Münzen von Pergamon," *Abhandlungen der Berliner Akademie*, 1910, Abh. 1, pl. vii, and many other similar coins which, however, shall not be discussed here.

[76] Grabar, pl. xxviii, no. 4; cf. pl. xvii, no. 2, the Silver Disc from Kerch. Mrs. Arthur Strong, *Apotheosis and After Life* (New York, 1915), 109, styles the medallion directly an *Adventus*; so does Dalton (*infra*, note 87) along with others.

[77] In general, see M. J. de Morgan, "Évolutions et révolutions numismatiques," *Mélanges Gustave Schlumberger* (Paris, 1924), 288f, pl. ix. For France, see A. Blanchet and A. Dieudonné, *Manuel de numismatique française*, (Paris, 1912), I, 200, 207, figs. 174, 175, 180;

the word *Victoria* is found on Merovingian coins as late as the seventh century, *ibid.*, 202. Locally the *Gloria Romanorum* type remained the model (*ibid.*, 241, 339) until the Carolingians replaced it by the *Christiana Religio* coinage. Cf. *infra*, note 82.

[78] This series begins with Trajan (pl. 13, fig. 19; Bernhart, pl. lxxx, 9), cf. Strack, I, 218, who indicates (p. 130, n. 520) that the *Decursio* coinage was the basis of both the *Profectio* and the *Adventus* (pl. 13, fig. 18; Gnecchi, pl. xxxviii, no. 1) of Trajan. For the *Profectio* on Greek pottery see Walter Wrede, "Kriegers Ausfahrt in der archaisch-griechischen Kunst," *Athenische Mitteilungen*, XLI (1916), 222–374, an article to which Professor H. R. W. Smith kindly called my attention. For Jewish representations of the *Profectio*, referring to Job 2, 11, see G. Wodtke, "Malereien der Synagoge in Dura und ihre Parallelen in der christlichen Kunst," *Zeitschrift für Neutestamentliche Wissenschaft*, XXXIV (1935), 61, and pl. 2, and *The Excavations at Dura-Europos* (New Haven, 1936), VI, pl. xlvii. For a Jewish *Triumphus*, referring to Esther 6, 11, Dura offers likewise an example, cf. Wodtke, *loc. cit.*; see also A. W. Byvanck and G. J. Hoogewerff, *La*

departure" and his "victorious arrival" should belong together and supplement each other as antitypes. Triumphal arches were built for both the *Profectio* and the *Adventus;* in the reliefs of the arches representations are found referring to both events; in the Roman calendars annual celebrations are listed for both the *Profectio Divi* and the *Adventus Divi;* finally the coins show very often the same design for an *Adventus* and for a *Profectio* (pl. 13, figs. 14, 17, 19, 20).[79]

It is noteworthy that the military-technical term of *Profectio* has been passed on to the liturgy. This reminds us that on a great number of occasions on which Rome would offer a sacrifice to the gods of the state, or strike a coin commemorating the event connected with a sacrifice, the Church has established an oration or even a mass. This liturgical "continuity" made itself felt, above all, in the Hispano-Gallican rite where it lasted until the ninth century, when much of it began to fade away. We still find, for example, in the *Breviarium Gothicum* hymns for the various *Natales* of the king, the anniversaries of his birthday and of his day of accession. These days were traditionally celebrated in imperial Rome as well as in Byzantium, but this custom fell into desuetude in the West by the ninth century. In the *Breviarium Gothicum* there follows after the hymns for the royal anniversaries an *Ymnus in profectione exercitus* which was to be sung on the days of fasting until the army returned.[80] Moreover, in the Sacramentary of Gellone, whose texts may fall in the reign of King Pepin, there is still found an archaic *Missa in profectione hostium* which disappears thereafter, although some prayers have survived as an *Oratio pro exercitu.* In the first prayer of this mass God is entreated not only to lend light to his army marching in the dark but also to order his angel that it may walk before the Frankish chosen people now marching into battle; and the biblical precedent referred to is the angel conducting Israel by day and by night on its march from Egypt to the Land of Promise.[81]

It may be purely by coincidence that the image of the *Profectio* mass matches the symbolism of the *Profectio* coins. However, there is one item which allows us to link up, indirectly at least, the image of the prayer with the images of the coins. In a chapter of the *City of God*, St. Augustine discusses the question "Whether, if the highest power

miniature hollandaise (The Hague, 1926), Texte, pl. vi, no. 23, and I, 109, and Edgar Wind, "The Subject of Botticelli's *Derelitta*," *Journal of the Warburg and Courtauld Institutes*, IV (1940/41), 114ff. Cf. Eichmann, "Das *Officium Stratoris et Strepae*," *Historische Zeitschrift*, CXLII (1930), 18.

[79] *Supra*, notes 36, 47–49. The parallelism is obvious already in the coins of Trajan (pl. 13, figs. 18, 19); compare also the *Adventus* of Septimius Severus (pl. 13, fig. 13; Gnecchi, pl. xcii, no. 8) with the *Profectio* of Marcus Aurelius (pl. 13, fig. 14; Gnecchi, pl. lxi, no. 5), or the *Adventus* of Tacitus (pl. 13, fig. 15) with the *Profectio* of Severus Alexander (pl. 13, figs. 17, 20; Gnecchi, pl. xcix, no. 9, and pl. ci, no. 8). See also Haynes, pl. 1 (in the article quoted *infra*, note 88), or Babelon, *Mél. Boissier*, 52. For the inner connection of *Profectio* and *Triumphus* (*Adventus*) see the instructive passages of Livy (XLII, 49; XLV, 39, 11) adduced by Richard Laqueur, "Das Wesen des römischen Triumphs,"

Hermes, XLIV (1909), 225. See also Radin, *Studi . . . Ricco bono*, II, 25f.

[80] The problems here breached will be treated separately in a study on "Charles the Bald and the *Natales Caesarum.*" For the hymns mentioned see Migne, *PL*, LXXXVI, col. 917; *Analecta hymnica*, XXVII (1897), 269ff. The most elaborate Orders for the king's *Profectio* (as well as for his *Adventus*) are found in the Visigothic Liturgy; cf. M. Férotin, *Le Liber Ordinum* (*Monumenta ecclesiae liturgica*, V [Paris, 1904]), cols. 149–156, nos. xlviii–l. See also A. Heisenberg, "Kriegsgottesdienst in Byzanz," *Aufsätze zur Kultur- und Sprachgeschichte vornehmlich des Orients, E. Kuhn zum 70. Geburtstag* (Munich, 1916), 252, and *Euchologium Sinaiticum*, ed. Jean Frček (Paris, 1933), 28f, *Patrologia Orientalis*, XXIV, 691ff.

[81] Gerd Tellenbach, "Römischer und christlicher Reichsgedanke in der Liturgie des frühen Mittelalters," *Sitzungsberichte der Heidelberger Akademie*, 1934/5, Abh. 1, pp. 67ff.

belongs to Jove, Victory also ought to be worshipped."[82] Augustine of course denies the power of Jupiter and fights against the possibility that *Victoria* should depend upon the father of the Capitoline Gods.

> Do they say, perhaps, that Jupiter sends the goddess *Victoria*, and that she, as it were, acting in obedience to the king of gods, comes to those to whom he may have despatched her, and takes up her quarters on their side?
>
> This indeed is truly said, not of Jove, whom they, according to their own imagination, feign to be the king of the gods, but of Him, who is the true Eternal King, because he indeed sends, not *Victoria* who is without substance, but His angel, and causes [through it] whom he pleases to conquer.

Here the replacement of the winged Victory by a victory-granting angel, an ἄγγελος νικοποιός, is plainly demonstrated. Augustine's passage, of course, does not imply that the Franks now systematically "translated" *Victoria* into an angel. But the angel walking before the army became the power securing victories just as the *Victoria* walking before the emperors had promised victory. And in this case it is not even necessary to stress the influence of the *City of God* on the Frankish Empire in general terms, since there is at our disposal specific evidence to make it certain that Augustine's words about Victory were deeply engrained in the Frankish consciousness. In his *Mirror of Kings*, Hincmar of Reims devotes a whole chapter to this very passage of the *City of God*.[83] Moreover, in the likewise Carolingian collection of *Sentences Useful for the Affairs of the State* we find the same passage under the headline:[84]

> Victoriam ab omnipotente per angelum suum, cui voluerit et ubi iusserit, dari.

Thus, the Roman *Profectio* coins and the Frankish *Profectio* mass are indirectly linked together through the medium of St. Augustine who here, as usual, acts as the main voucher of the unbroken, though "translated," tradition.

However this may be, the general influence of the *Profectio-Adventus* type of coin on Christian imagery is an undeniable fact. It has been mentioned before (p. 50) that the Entry of Christ as carved into the ivory cover of the Gospels of Etschmiadzin displayed the *Hierosolyma* in the form of the *Natio* of Hadrianic *Adventus* coins (pl. 14, fig. 25). It may be added here that we find in the ivory the same hasty quick-march of the procession which occurs time and again in the numismatic documents of the *Adventus-Profectio* type. Furthermore, there is a Coptic relief now in Berlin of the fifth or sixth century, in which the scheme of *cursor*-horseman-*pedisequus* is applied as clearly as possible to describe the Lord's Entry. The Lord is seated on an ass; one angel serving as *cursor* leads the mount by

---

[82] *De civit.*, IV, chap. 17, cf. chap. 15. I am glad to have chanced upon an obvious allusion to this passage by Harold Mattingly, "The Roman 'Virtues'," *Harvard Theological Review*, XXX (1937), 117: "Victory no longer flew over the battlefield. ... But God still sent his angel to bear triumph to the side to which he pleased to accord it, and the angel, with palm and cross, still appeared on the coinage. ... There must be other such survivals by

transference that would repay investigation." See also *supra*, note 77.

[83] Hincmar, *De regis persona et regio ministerio*, chap. XII, Migne, *PL*, CXXV, cols. 842ff.

[84] *Capitula diversarum sententiarum pro negociis rei publice consulendis*, chap. V; cf. G. Laehr and C. Erdmann, "Ein karolingischer Konzilsbrief und der Fürstenspiegel Hincmars von Rheims," *Neues Archiv*, L (1933), 120.

the bridle while a second angel follows as *pedisequus* (pl. 16, fig. 30).[85] A similar design has been mentioned with reference to a Serbian Gospel Book where Christ, as he approaches Jerusalem, is followed by an angelic attendant (for a similar scheme see pl. 18, fig. 39).[86] Also, the composition of the relief of St. John Studion (pl. 14, fig. 22) is reminiscent of this scheme, which no longer can be called a faithful "historical" representation of the Entry. This concept is not justified by the narration of the Bible. The biblical report has been blended with, or even superseded by, an *Adventus* motif borrowed from the imperial imagery. The Entry on Palm Sunday and the imperial *Adventus* procession appear as interchangeable concepts, and the historical Palm Sunday reception with the acclaim "Benedictus qui venit" has been replaced by the "eschatological" Advent of an imperial saviour whose way is prepared by a winged genius—"Ecce mitto angelum meum."

This is not the place to dicuss similar representations of gods in Near Eastern art, at Dura-Europos and in Syria (pl. 17, fig. 36), or to account for the great number of works of applied art displaying a similar subject (pl. 16, figs. 31, 32).[87] Nor shall there be ventured a guess to explain why this *Adventus*, i.e., the "Horseman-Angel" motif, appears so frequently as an apotropaic symbol on amulets (pls. 16–17, figs. 33, 34), a feature most startling in the case of an *encolpium*, now lost but known from a drawing, in which the *Flight to Egypt* is represented as a genuine *Adventus* with the *Natio*, Egypt, receiving the Holy Family, with Joseph acting as *cursor*, and with the star projecting from above just as in the medal of Justinian (pl. 17, fig. 33a).[87a] However, in order to clarify the eschatological essence of these representations at least it should be mentioned that the scheme of

[85] G. Duthuit, *La sculpture copte* (Paris, 1931), pl. xva; Grabar, p. 235, n. 3. With this relief there should be compared the famous Byzantine embroidery at Bamberg, cf. Grabar, pl. vii, no. 1.

[86] Grabar, p. 236, n. 1, and the same author's *Recherches sur les influences orientales dans l'art balkanique* (Paris, 1928), 81.

[87] Relief from Khirbet-el-Hamam, Syria, late second or early third century; cf. C. Hopkins, in *The Excavations at Dura-Europos*, VI, pl. xxx, and pp. 233f; see also P. S. Ronzevalle, "Notes et études d'archéologie orientale," *Mélanges de l'Université Saint-Joseph*, XXI (Beyrouth, 1937), pls. xvi, 3, vi, vii, xvii, and p. 56. For the development of the motif in Far Eastern art, see Carl Schuster, "Motives in Western Chinese Folk Embroideries," *Monumenta serica*, II (1936/37), 40ff, an article to which Dr. Diether von den Steinen, in Berkeley, called my attention. The motif of "Horseman with Angel" is found, e.g., in a rock crystal gem from Alexandria; cf. O. M. Dalton, *Catalogue of Early Christian Antiquities and Objects from the Christian East ... of the British Museum* (London, 1901), p. 13, no. 84; see *ibid.*, p. 109, no. 543, for the *tabula ansata* from Tyre which Dalton rightly compares with the medallion of Justinian.

[87a] For the amulet from Koula, near Izmir, see *Bulletin de correspondance hellénique*, XVII (1893), 638, and for the one from Cyzicos, see Paul Perdrizet, in *Revue des études grecques*, XVI (1903), p. 47, fig. 1. These amulets should be compared with the *Gloria Romanorum* medallion of Valens; cf. Grabar, pl. xxviii, no. 3. See also the article

"Amulettes," *DACL*, I, col. 1847 (cf. col. 3033), and above all the broad discussion by Erik Peterson, Εἷς θεός (Göttingen, 1926), 82–130 (especially pp. 86f, 106f, 119f). The soteriological components of the imperial *Adventus-Victoria* imagery have been fused with apotropaic elements characteristic of amulets. Emperor and Victory have been turned into the haloed horseman Solomon-Sisinnius and the angel Araaph or Arlaph (Raphael?). They have also the appearance of the star in common with the Justinian medallion; with the Valens medallion that of the Evil Devicted. The details of this "transference" from *Adventus* design into an apotropaic symbol are as yet rather obscure; but the fact itself is countenanced by another amulet, the famous *encolpium* preserved in a Dal Pozzo drawing; cf. E. B. Smith, "A Lost Encolpium and Some Notes on Early Christian Iconography," *Byzantinische Zeitschrift*, XXIII (1914–20), 217ff. For in this case the personification of the *Aegyptus* makes the *Adventus* idea evident, an iconographic pattern to the longevity of which Professor C. R. Morey kindly called my attention. It is found in the Menologium of Basil II; cf. *Il menologio di Basilio II* (Codices e Vaticanis selecti, VIII; Turin, 1907), fol. 274, and p. 75, including note 2; it became traditional in the rural churches of Asia Minor; cf. G. de Jerphanion, *Les églises rupestres de Cappadoce* (Paris, 1925), Texte, I, 79, 117, 160, 188, 216, 274, 332, 534 (with indications as to the plates). The *Aegyptus* is found also in an enamel of Notre Dame at Huy of the thirteenth century; cf. Charles Cahier, *Nouveaux mélanges d'archéologie, d'histoire et de littérature sur le moyen âge* (Paris, 1874–77), II, 152ff.

these Entries is identical not only with the triumphant *Adventus* as found in imperial coins but also with Etruscan eschatological scenes, which, there is every reason to believe, served as a model of the coins. These scenes represent the last journey, the solemn *Profectio*, of the dead to the underworld whither the soul is conducted by attendants who sometimes are pictured as winged *Lases* (pls. 17–18, figs. 37, 38). That the Etruscan funeral procession, leading the dead *ante faciem*, before the terrifying face of the Lord of the Lower Regions (pl. 17, fig. 37), has been turned in imperial Rome into a procession-in-state of the soul (pl. 18, fig. 39), which now is equipped with the symbols of victory, may be due to the impact of the mystery religions and their belief in an apotheosis after death.[88] Death, as it conferred divinity, initiated a triumph—an attitude toward life and death which closely approaches that of Christianity. And there is no verse in the Bible which could "translate" the eschatological essence of these scenes into words more accurately than the prophecy "Ecce mitto angelum meum qui praeparabit viam ante faciem meam."

* * *

We are now in a position to distinguish clearly between two different concepts of the *Adventus*.[89] The first refers to the "historical" Entry. Iconographically it is a true arrival. Liturgically it is echoed by the likewise "historical" antiphon "Benedictus qui venit in nomine Domini." The second concept refers to the "eschatological" Advent. Iconographically it is dominated by the *praecursor* motif, which compares to the biblical office of St. John the harbinger and, sometimes winged, precursor. Liturgically it is echoed by the antiphon "Ecce mitto angelum meum," which in turn is credited to refer to the Advent of Christ.

To realize that there are two basic ways of representing an *Adventus* is important because this enables us to recognize, in images as well as in texts, the *Adventus* scene even though this idea may not present itself in the familiar "historical" forms of the Entry on Palm Sunday. The "eschatological" *praecursor* motif may just as well dominate the ruler's "arrival." Moreover, this distinction will prove helpful to solve some problems which hitherto appeared as obscure or even as insolvable.

3. Two Panels in the Doors of Santa Sabina

It is needless to emphasize the singular importance which the doors of Santa Sabina on the Aventine Hill in Rome have for students of Early Christian art. The wood carvings in the various compartments of the doors have been convincingly ascribed to an Italo-

---

[88] See the brilliant discussion of D. E. L. Haynes, "Mors in Victoria," *Papers of the British School at Rome*, XV (1939), 27–32, to which the author feels greatly indebted; cf. *ibid.*, pl. 1, fig. A, for the Funeral Relief of the 3rd century A.D. in the Terme Museum in Rome (our pl. 18, fig. 39); cf. pl. II. See further Giulio Quirino Giglioli, *L'arte etrusca* (Milan, 1935), pl. CCXLII, fig. 2, and pp. xii and 44, for the Sarcophagus of Vulci (4th century B.C.) in the Ny Carlsberg Museum at Copenhagen (our pl. 18, fig. 38), and Andreas Rumpf, *Katalog der etruskischen Skulp-*

turen (Berlin, 1928), p. 33, and pl. 42, no. E 58, for the cinerary cist from Malacena (4th century B.C.) in Berlin (our pl. 17, fig. 37).

[89] Cf. Grabar, p. 234, who distinguishes between a "realistic" and a "symbolical" representation of the *Adventus*. The terms "historical" and "eschatological," which here are used, have very much the same meaning though from a different point of view. With Cyril of Jerusalem (*infra*, note 136) we might distinguish also between Christ the King and Christ the Judge.

Gallic school which flourished in Northern Italy during the fourth and fifth centuries.[90] The date of the doors, which represent after those of San Ambrogio in Milan the earliest monument of its kind, is *ca.* 430 A.D. The carvings are unique in many respects, or even without parallel.

All the more deplorable is the fact that several panels of these doors have hitherto defied any attempt to explain satisfactorily the scenes represented in them. This holds good, above all, for the two panels which will be discussed here. They have been referred to as the "enigmatic," the "mysterious," panels of Santa Sabina, and they have not ceased to puzzle scholars. Wiegand, whose book on Santa Sabina still is recognized as the authoritative study,[91] has styled one of these panels the "Christian Roman Empire" (pl. 19, fig. 40). This explanation has been generally accepted, and it has been advanced, though somewhat reluctantly, even by so critical a scholar as Professor C. R. Morey, the last to have dealt with these carvings.[92] It is, at any rate, a far better suggestion than the one offered occasionally by others who hold that the panel represents "Zacharias announcing to the children of Judah the name of the new-born Baptist," or King Solomon in a rôle not identified.[93] Iconographically the scene was believed to be, as it were, a ἅπαξ λεγόμενον, which, however, it is not. Yet, by the customary means of comparison and of detecting parallels, the riddle probably could not be solved.

What does the image represent? In the upper part a man is seen whose majestic appearance, whose chlamys and general attire suggest a ruler—emperor or king—although he is bareheaded and wears neither diadem nor crown. He stands at the curtained entrance of a building, a palace, temple, or church, which has a cross on its roof. The two towers may, but need not, belong to the building proper; they might as well indicate the "city" in back of the building.[94] The position of the majestic man in the chlamys is such that his vertex is crowned by the triangular pediment of the building, an arrangement usually indicating a special, even divine, honor intended for the person thus represented.[95] The man in the chlamys, therefore, is of a rank higher than the angel who stands at his left in front of the masonry wall which forms the long side of the building, and who makes with his hands almost the same gesture as the man in the chlamys. Both

[90] See for this school A. C. Soper, "The Italo-Gallic School of Early Christian Art," *Art Bulletin,* XX (1938), 145–192, especially pp. 169f. It amounts to what E. Weigand has called the Celto-Roman School; cf. *Byzantinische Zeitschrift,* XXX (1930), 587ff, XXXII (1932), 63ff, and XXXV (1935), 212, 430, 433f, also in *Kritische Berichte zur kunstgeschichtlichen Literatur,* III (1930/31), 55ff.; see also F. Gerke, "Malerei und Plastik in der theodosianisch-honorianischen Zeit," *Rivista di archeologia cristiana,* XII (1935), 146ff.

[91] J. Wiegand, *Das altchristliche Hauptportal an der Kirche der hl. Sabina* (Trier, 1900), 52ff. His interpretation has been almost generally accepted, see, e.g., E. Weigand, in *Byzantinische Zeitschrift,* XXX (1930), 594f; W. Koehler, in *Mediaeval Studies in Memory of A. Kingsley Porter* (Cambridge, Mass., 1939), I, 134, and others; see however *infra,* note 93. A critical discussion of the extensive literature on the doors of Santa Sabina here is not intended. It can be dismissed all the more easily as the

interpretation advanced in these following pages takes a course different from that of previous studies.

[92] Charles Rufus Morey, *Early Christian Art* (Princeton, 1942), 140.

[93] For "Zacharias in the Temple" see Kondakov, in *Revue archéologique,* New Ser., XXXIII (1877), 370; Corrado Ricci, in A. Colasanti, *L'Arte bisantina in Italia* (Milan, n.d.), 9. For "Solomon" see A. Venturi, *Storia dell'arte italiana,* I (1901) 481f; L. Bréhier (cf. *infra,* note 129) holds that the building represents the Basilica of the Holy Sepulchre and that the bearded man in the chlamys is Constantine the Great (!); in general, see J. Wiegand, *loc. cit.*

[94] Morey, *op. cit.,* p. 140, and p. 219 n. 291. Cf. *infra,* note 100 and our pl. 19, fig. 44.

[95] For the pediment and its symbolism see Alföldi, "Insignien und Trachten der römischen Kaiser," *Römische Mitteilungen,* L (1935), 127–134.

the chlamydate, who in every respect occupies the honorary place, and the angel are acclaimed with the customary gesture by two groups of men arranged in two superimposed registers. Those in the upper plane, perhaps "senators," wear the toga, while citizens in dalmatics and *paenulae* occupy the lower register.[95a] In each section, the figure to the left seems to hail the angel, whereas the two others are turned to the man in the chlamys. In this respect, too, the chlamydate is the one specially favored, as he has twice the number of *acclamantes*.

These acclaiming groups are the only well-known subject within the whole representation, as they appear recurrently in Roman and Christian art. A sestertius of Hadrian, for instance, shows the emperor, standing in front of the temple of Divus Julius and under the pediment of the building, in an attitude which is vaguely reminiscent of that of the *chlamydatus* in the panel of Santa Sabina. He addresses soldiers who acclaim him (pl. 19, fig. 43).[96] On the other hand, the two registers of *acclamantes* are found on the monument of Porphyry, a charioteer of the Blues in Constantinople, who stands on his quadriga like a triumphant hero while receiving at his entry into the Circus the applause of the people (pl. 18, fig. 42).[97] The acclaiming group is found also in the miniature of the Bible of San Paolo, where the people hail King Solomon at his *Adventus* in Gihon (pl. 15, fig. 27).[98] Had there not been the angel in the Sabina panel, the scene might well have passed for an "Epiphany" of a ruler who receives at the city-gate the acclaims due on that occasion. The angel, however, if innocently, seems to have obscured the scene and to have foiled the interpreters. It has been suggested that "the relief is an allegory of the Empire as constituted of emperor (under the divine guidance represented by the angel), the senate, and the people."[99] But "allegory" means usually an *ultima ratio*, when no other explanation offers itself. It fits badly with the other representations of the door, none of which is "allegorical." They all refer to the Bible.

The presence of the angel should have been a hint rather than a handicap. A ruler with angel and acclaiming people suggests, almost a priori, an *Adventus*, provided that we can emancipate ourselves from the idea that this scene always must be depicted in the classical manner of the Lord's Entry into Jerusalem on Palm Sunday. But once we know that an *Adventus* may as well be "eschatological" and thus reflect the verse "Ecce mitto angelum meum" the solution becomes in fact very simple. A checking of the Bible for the few places where the verse is quoted is sufficient to make the meaning of the panel quite obvious. The carving refers to Malachi 3, 1–2:

> Behold I send my angel and he shall prepare the way before my face. And the
> Lord [κύριος], whom you demand, and the Angel of the Covenant, whom you

95a Delbrück, *Die Consulardiptychen* (Berlin, 1929), 33ff.

96 Bernhart, *Münzkunde*, pl. LXXVIII, no. 2.

97 A. Mordtmann, "Das Denkmal des Porphyrius," *Athenische Mitteilungen*, V (1880), pl. XVI, and pp. 295ff.303; A. M. Woodward, "Some Notes on the Monument of Porphyrios at Constantinople," *Annual of the British School at Athens*, XVII (1910/11), 88–92. Cf. Morey, p. 140, for the Probianus Diptych.

98 They are seen on the left side of the canopy, likewise in a lower plane.

99 Morey, *loc. cit.* The present writer adduced the panel in a similar way (*Journal of the Warburg and Courtauld Institutes*, V, [1942], 73) to illustrate the *character angelicus* of the ruler; but this interpretation turns out to be wrong.

desire, shall suddenly come to his Temple. Behold he shall come, saith the Lord of Hosts [Κύριος Παντοκράτωρ]. And who may abide the day of his coming [εἴσοδος, *adventus*], and who shall stand when he appeareth?

The last of the Jewish Prophets, the so-called "Malachias," who wrote between 500 and 450 b.c. and whose short prophecy forms the last book of the Old Testament and therewith the transition from the Old to the New, announces the sudden (ἐξαίφνης) coming of the Messianic ruler to dwell again in his temple and among his chosen people. The Lord is to return together with the Angel of the Covenant, his *praecursor*, who shall prepare the way before him. The scene which is shown in the panel refers, almost verbatim, to this promise. It is the sudden, flash-like *Adventus*, the Epiphany of the *Kyrios* before his temple, the cross on the roof of which foreshadows the New Covenant and, maybe, the second advent to come. Both he and his angelic forerunner are acclaimed ("diagonally") by those "who have demanded" him and "that have desired" the angel; they have "abided the day of his advent and stand, when he appeareth," to form the ἀπάντησις at his coming.

This, I believe, is the only possible and consistent explanation of the image, all the more so as it is confirmed by another document. A miniature, which in this connection has escaped notice, offers the iconographic evidence. In the Bible of Santa Maria of Ripoll in Catalonia, the so-called Bible of Farfa of the early eleventh century, we find, at the beginning of the Book of Malachi, the illustration of the verse "Ecce mitto angelum meum" (pl. 19, fig. 44).[100] The *Kyrios Pantokrator* stands in front of the city-towers rather than of the temple. The angel at his side is placed outside the complex of buildings; he seems to give account of his preparation of the way. The cheering people are replaced by baffled people who come out of a city-gate to the right in order to stare at, or to receive, the Lord.[101] This illustration removes the last doubt about the intentions of the artist of the Sabina doors: he has wished to represent the sudden *Adventus* of the Messianic world-ruler and of his angelic forerunner at the gate of the temple.

* * *

The arrangement of the oblong panels of the doors of Santa Sabina was originally such that events of the Old Testament corresponded to those of the New. Although this *dittochaeic* order was deranged in early times so that the original composition today is

[100] Wilhelm Neuss, *Die katalanischen Bibelillustrationen um die Wende des ersten Jahrtausends und die altspanische Buchmalerei* (Bonn and Leipzig, 1922), pl. LXII, fig. 190. The towers here are clearly those of the city and not of the temple (*supra*, note 94). It is remarkable that in this illumination the *Kyrios Pantokrator* should appear likewise bearded, chlamydate, and bareheaded (he is even lacking the halo surrounding the head of the angel). The parallel thus forms rather important evidence for the close relations between Early Spanish and Early Christian art. I am greatly indebted to Professor Morey for several suggestions and corrections and to Dr. W. L. M. Burke for valuable information about the imagery of

Malachi 3, 1, in the collections of the Princeton Index of Christian Art.

[101] Another representation of Malachi (Neuss, *op. cit.*, pl. XXXVI, fig. 111) alludes to the prophet's relationship with John the Baptist (through the medium of the verse "Ecce mitto angelum meum"), whereas a third—in the Gumpert Bible—refers to his foreshadowing of Christ; cf. G. Swarzenski, *Die Salzburger Malerei* (Leipzig, 1908), pl. XLI, fig. 129. A man with an angel in, or in front of, a temple is found once more in the Bible of Ripoll (Neuss, pl. XXXI, fig. 97; see also J. D. Bordona, *Spanish Illumination* [Florence and Paris, 1930], I, pl. XLI); but here, as in other cases, the picture refers to Ezekiel 40, that is to the "Vision of the Temple Restored."

disputed, it has never met with serious objections that the Malachi *Adventus* should be paired with a second enigmatic representation which has been called the *Ecclesia*: the Church juxtaposed with what has been considered the representation of the "Christian Roman Empire." About this panel (pl. 19, fig. 41) Professor Morey writes as follows:[102]

> The last of the four panels in this register contains the enigmatic relief which cannot be an *Ascension*, in view of the occurrence of this scene already in the preceding panel,[103] and which has never found a satisfactory explanation. The youthful Christ stands in a glory surrounded by the four beasts' heads symbolic of the Evangelists, holding a scroll on which is incised a garbled rendering of the letters of the famous ΙΧΘΥC acrostic.[104] The letters A and Ω are carved in relief beside the figure. An arc of heaven identified by sun and moon which project from it, separates this celestial apparition from the earthly group below, in which two figures, apparently Peter and Paul, hold a wreath above a female standing between them and gazing upward toward the Saviour. A reasonable interpretation considers this the personification of the Church, *Ecclesia*.

There is little to be added to this clear description except, perhaps, that in addition to sun and moon there are found five stars in the celestial vault. But this is probably unimportant. Objectionable, however, is the way in which the strange object, allegedly "held" by the two male figures, is introduced without reservation as to other possibilities as a "wreath." A rapid glance at the panel informs us that this object, to say the least, is a curious kind of a wreath, with a "handle" pointing upward and thus prolonging the vertical arm of the two arms which form a cross within a circle. Moreover, the manner in which the two male figures "hold" this object is not such as to dissipate serious doubts concerning the success of their efforts. The left figure, probably St. Paul, pushes his left hand right through the circle while the other, whom we may call St. Peter, seems to touch it at a tangent. Besides, this object has been discussed time and again. It has even been dubbed, quite seriously, a hanging global lamp braced by metal bands of which we see, as it were, the "equator" and the "meridian of Greenwich" while the circle itself forms the 90° meridian. The prolongation of "Greenwich," so to speak, northward, was considered a chain by which the lamp was suspended in heaven. However, those advocating the lamp theory have found it difficult to explain what service a lamp might render when sun, moon, and stars are shining and the cask of Diogenes is missing.[105]

The interpretation of the panel has to proceed from this strange object which dominates the center, if not of the whole panel, at least of the lower part. That the object represents

[102] Morey, *op. cit.*, 139.

[103] It is difficult to understand why A. C. Soper, *op. cit.*, 167, 169, fig. 40, and also F. van der Meer, *Maiestas Domini: Théophanies de l'apocalypse dans l'art chrétien* (Città del Vaticano, 1938), 255f, have decided to style this panel an *Ascension*. The *Ascension of Christ*, paralleled by that of Elijah, is represented in another panel in a manner which reminds F. J. Dölger, *Sol Salutis*, 2nd ed. (*Liturgie-* *geschichtliche Forschungen*, Heft 4/5; Münster, 1925), p. 212, of the apocryphal *Gospel of Peter*; cf. *infra*, note 129.

[104] Morey, p. 219, n. 289; F. J. Dölger, ΙΧΘΥC: *Das Fischsymbol in frühchristlicher Zeit* (Rome, 1910), I, 209ff, explains the unusual arrangement of the acrostic.

[105] These theories have been discussed by Wiegand, *Das altchristliche Hauptportal*, 82ff.

a cross with a "ring" or "wreath" has been realized already by Grisar and Wiegand; but they failed to base their solution of the problem on this fact and thought of an act of crowning of the *Ecclesia*.[106]

The thing that has puzzled most has been the "handle," the seemingly strange prolongation of the vertical arm in the upper (i.e., in the wrong) direction. But this is not puzzling at all. In fact, the explanation is so simple that the present writer hardly dares to proffer it. We need only turn the image around to recognize without difficulty a cross with a crown of light, the σταυρὸς φωτοειδής, diving headlong from above. That is to say, the "luminous cross" is diving, or rather descending, from heaven to earth, and as it approaches, it is received and gently supported by the two apostles. They stretch out their hands, of course not after the ring of light which is immaterial, but after the wood itself in order to receive or maybe to greet it. They do not lift it. Their hands meet it in mid-air. They almost seem to move toward it together with the woman in rapture, whom perhaps we may call St. Mary[106a] and whose eyes are fixed ecstatically on the descending cross just as are the eyes of the men. The little group comes to meet the descending cross while it still is in the air. They are assembled, as it were, εἰς ἀπάντησιν τοῦ κυρίου εἰς ἀέρα, for the "meeting of the Lord (or his cross) in the air," as this had been prophesied by an authentic utterance of the Lord, by a λόγος κυρίου as transmitted by St. Paul. But St. Paul in 1 Thessalonians 4, 15, where he describes the Lord's Second Coming, does not mention the cross. St. Matthew (24, 30), to be sure, expounds the appearance of "the sign of the Son of Man," which usually has been interpreted as the cross. But according to Matthew the sign was to appear in heaven, and neither this evangelist nor any other writer of the canonical books of the Bible suggests a descending to earth, an independent activity of the cross, which, in the panel, is shown as the Lord's *praecursor* and harbinger while its master is still standing above the celestial vault.

Is there any evidence that the cross, at the Lord's Second Coming, should act as a *prodromos?* In a sermon ascribed to St. Augustine, the Lord's Second Coming is compared to the *Adventus* of a king in a city.[107] Soldiers carrying the royal standards on their shoulders precede the king and announce his coming by the clash of their arms. Similarly, the divine entry of the celestial king, when he descends from heaven, shall be announced to the trembling earth by the triumphant standard, whose splendor will be so bright that it shall outshine sun and moon and make the stars fall from above. It will be carried on

---

[106] With few exceptions (cf. *supra*, note 103) this interpretation seems to have been generally accepted; see, e.g., *DACL*, I, cols. 3027f. See, however, L. Bréhier, *infra*, note 129.

[106a] The set of three persons is remindful of the trio in the *Ipogeo* of Aurelius Felicissimus—cf. Wilpert, *Atti ... di Archeologia, Memorie*, I: 2 (1924), pl. III, and p. 19, and, more specifically, of some *Ascensions* (Rabula). The female figure between Peter and Paul need not be Mary. She might be the "Bride" (Apoc. 22, 17) that says "Come." If, however, the panel be considered an illustration of 1 Thess. 4, 15–16, there is no reason why St. Mary should

not be among those "that are alive, that are left," or among "the dead that shall rise first and meet the Lord," just as the two apostles. See, for the rising of Peter and Paul, Pseudo-Chrysostomos, *De laudibus S. Pauli*, Migne, *PG*, LXIII, cols. 798f.

[107] *Sermo* CLV, Migne, *PL*, XXXIX, cols. 2051f: "Quemadmodum enim ingredientem regem in civitatem exercitus antecedit, praeferens humeris signa atque vexilla regalia ...: ita Domino descendente de coelis praecedet exercitus Angelorum, qui signum illud, id est triumphale vexillum, sublimibus humeris praeferentes divinum regis coelestis ingressum terris trementibus nuntiabunt."

the shoulders of a host of angels to precede the Lord. The unknown author of this homily follows, on the whole, the description offered by St. Matthew (24, 27ff), except for one detail: the standard of the cross is not only expected to appear in heaven; it is to be carried before the descending King of Glory on the shoulders of angels just as the Victory carries the *tropaeum* or as the legionaries carry their standards before the Caesar at his *Adventus*. This concept is certainly reminiscent of the *cursor*-motif, but it does not fit exactly with the panel of Santa Sabina where the cross is not carried by angels but, while descending, acts, as it were, independently and by itself.

The comparison of the Lord's Second Coming with the *Adventus* of the Basileus may put us on the right track. This comparison was a popular topic of Eastern homiletic. Not to mention other authors,[108] it is found occasionally in the homilies, genuine or spurious, of St. John Chrysostom on which the author of the sermon ascribed to St. Augustine draws heavily. Chrysostom uses the comparison with the imperial *Adventus* in connection with both the Entry into Jerusalem and the Second Coming of Christ.[109] As far as the latter is concerned, he draws a curious parallel. He refers to 1 Thessalonians 4, 16, and asks,

> Why, if Christ is about to descend, are we going to be taken up in the clouds? For honor's sake. For when the Basileus enters a city, those that are in the state of honor go out to meet him; the criminals, however, remain in the city and there expect their judge.

In a similar way, continues Chrysostom, when the Lord arrives on his Advent, those that have professed Him shall go to meet Him in mid-air while the iniquitous have to stay where they are and expect their Judge.[110]

This metaphor is drawn out by the unknown author of a spurious sermon ascribed to St. John Chrysostom.[111] This author, too, distinguishes between two groups, those having professed the Lord and those having contemned Him. In this connection he recalls certain "imperial images" (βασιλικαὶ εἰκόνες) displaying several registers. In one of the registers there is seen the glorious galaxy of imperial satellites, in the other there are the barbarians conquered by the emperor.[112] Both the satellites and the barbarians worship the Basileus; but the former venerate him voluntarily because they adore the emperor, whereas the barbarians lie in the dust before him because they are forced to do so. Similar scenes, says the author, shall be seen at the Second Coming of the Lord, or rather at the appearance of that "terrible and glorious insignia" (φοβερὸν ἐκεῖνο καὶ ἔνδοξον σημεῖον), the cross.

---

[108] To the places adduced by Peterson, pp. 699ff, add Proclus of Constantinople (434–447), Migne, *PG*, LXV, col. 773/4A. See also Kruse (*supra*, note 28), p. 35, n. 2; p. 72, n. 4; p. 74ff.

[109] See, e.g., the Palm Sunday sermon (spurious) in Migne, *PG*, LXI, col. 715; and the Ascension sermon, *ibid.*, L, col. 450f.

[110] *In Epist. I ad Thessal.*, Sermo VIII, Migne, *PG*, LXII, col. 440. This comparison as well as its interpretation is found frequently in Eastern writings; cf. Peterson, p. 701, n. 1.

[111] Migne, *PG*, LIX, cols. 649ff. Cf. Grabar, p. 80.

[112] On these images see Peterson, p. 701; Delbrück, *Die Consulardiptychen*, p. 12, n. 30; Grabar, pp. 253ff, who makes it obvious that the writer must have had in mind reliefs similar to those in the base of the Obelisk of Arcadius.

Fig. 1. Hadrian, sestertius (Rev.): Adventus Mauretaniae. Fig. 2. Hadrian, sestertius (Rev.): Adventus Ciliciae. Fig. 3. Hadrian, sestertius (Rev.): Adventus Judaeae. Fig. 4. Hadrian, sestertius (Rev.): Restitutor Judaeae. Fig. 5. Hadrian, sestertius (Rev.): Adventus Alexandriae. Fig. 5a. Commodus, aureus of Alexandria (Rev., enlarged). Fig. 6. Constantine, gold medallion (Obv.): Constantine and Sol Invictus. Fig. 7. *Idem* (Rev.): Adventus. Fig. 8. Constantius Chlorus, gold medallion (Rev.): Redditor Lucis Aeternae, Londinium. Fig. 9. Carausius, denarius (Rev.): Expectate Veni. Fig. 10. Marcus Aurelius, aureus (Rev.): Adventus. Fig. 11. Commodus, sestertius (Rev.): Adventus. Fig. 12. Honorius, aureus (Rev.): Adventus. Fig. 13. Septimius Severus, bronze medallion (Rev.): Adventus. Fig. 14. Marcus Aurelius, sestertius (Rev.): Profectio. Fig. 15. Tacitus, bronze medallion (Rev.): Adventus. Fig. 16. Gordianus, bronze medallion (Rev.): Victoria. Fig. 17. Severus Alexander, bronze medallion (Rev.): Profectio. Fig. 18. Trajan, seven denarius piece (Rev.): Adventus. Fig. 19. Trajan, sestertius (Rev.): Profectio. Fig. 20. Severus Alexander, bronze medallion (Rev.): Profectio.

Pl. 14　　　　　　　　　　　　　　　THE KING'S ADVENT

Fig. 21. Salonica, Arch of Galerius: Adventus.

Fig. 22. Istanbul, Museum of Classical Antiquities,
relief from St. John Studion: Entry of Christ.

Fig. 25. Erivan, State Repository of MSS, Etschmiadzin Gospels, ivory cover (detail):
Entry of Christ.

Fig. 24. Ravenna, Archiepiscopal Palace,
Cathedra of Maximianus: Entry of Christ.

Fig. 23. Rome, Lateran Museum, sarcophagus (detail): Entry of Christ.

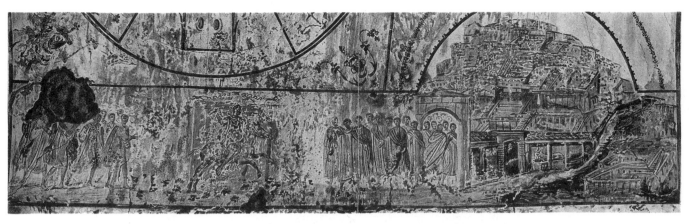

Fig. 26. Rome, Hypoge of Aurelius Felicissimus, wall painting: Gnostic Adventus.

Fig. 27. Rome, San Paolo f.l.m. Bible, fol. 185^v: Entry of King Solomon (reduced).

Fig. 28. Salonica, St. Demetrius, wall painting: Entry of Justinian II.

Pl. 16   THE KING'S ADVENT

Fig. 31. London, British Museum, *tabula ansata* from
Tyre: Adventus (?) (reduced).

Fig. 29. Autun, Bibl. Mun., Pontifical, MS 129, fol. 100:
Entry of a Cardinal Legate (reduced).

Fig. 32. London, British
Museum, rock crystal
gem from Alexandria:
Horseman with Angel.

Fig. 33. Amulet from Cyzicus:
Solomon-Sisinnius with Angel.

Fig. 30. Berlin, Staatl. Museen, Coptic relief from Sohag: Entry of Christ.

Fig. 33a. Windsor Castle, No. 9070, Dal Pozzo
drawing of amulet: Flight into Egypt.

Fig. 35. Paris, Bibl. Nat., gold medallion of Justinian I, Rev.:
SALUS ET GLORIA ROMANORUM.

Fig. 34. Amulet from Koula (near Izmir):
Solomon-Sisinnius with Angel.

Fig. 36. Damascus, Museum, relief from Khirbet-el-Hamam
(near Homs): Horseman God.

Fig. 37. Berlin, Staatl. Museen, Etruscan Cinerarium from Malacena: Eschatological Scene.

Pl. 18   THE KING'S ADVENT

Fig. 38. Copenhagen, Ny Carlsberg Glyptotek, Etruscan sarcophagus
from Vulci: Eschatological Scene.

Fig. 42. Istanbul, Museum of Classical Antiquities, Monument
of Porphyry the Charioteer: Entry into the Circus.

Fig. 39. Rome, Terme Museum: Roman funeral relief.

Advent of the Kyrios.   Second Coming of Christ.

Figs. 40-41. Rome, S. Sabina, panels of the wooden doors.

Fig. 43. Hadrian, sestertius
(Rev.): Acclamation.

Fig. 44. Vatican, Bible of Ripoll (MS Lat. 5729), fol. 252: Advent of the Kyrios.

Pl. 20   THE KING'S ADVENT

Fig. 45. Rome, SS. Quattro Coronati, wall painting:
Constantine and Pope Sylvester, Officium Stratoris.

Fig. 46. Paris, Bibl. Nat. MS fr. 2813, fol. 467ᵛ: Entry of Emperor Charles IV (enlarged).

Before the Advent of the Saviour [there appears] the royal standard, vulgarly called *signum* [which] foreruns the Advent of Christ glorified by angels. There shall appear the cross *on earth*, overshadowing the sun, obscuring the moon..., the standard outshining the ray of the light.

To the cross, that is to the messenger and *praecursor* of the Lord, there falls the task of separating the just from the iniquitous, those being allowed to come to meet the Lord from those being condemned to wait for the Judge.[113] Here indeed we find the cross preceding the Lord, descending to earth, and at the same time acting as the Lord's vicar, like a living being.

Whence derives this weird image of the cross acting single-handedly, forerunning, or even striding before the Lord at his Advent? This conception was apparently quite popular in early Christianity. Origen, St. Jerome and others have read the *Apocalypse of Elijah* in which it is said:[114]

When the Anointed comes, he shall come in the form of a dove, surrounded by a wreath of doves, and he shall walk on the clouds of heaven and the sign of the cross shall march before him.

And a similar wording is found in the *Apocalypse of Sophonias*.[115]

Christ coming with the wreath of doves may occasionally have influenced works of art;[116] but more relevant for our present purposes is the reference which is made to the walking cross. It is found also in the *Epistola Apostolorum*, likewise an apocryphal work, which was written, perhaps in Asia Minor, about 160–170 A.D. and which contains the conversations of the Lord with His disciples after the Resurrection. Here the Lord says:[117]

Verily, I say unto you, I shall come like the Sun when he rises..., and while my standard of the cross will stride before me, I shall come to earth to judge the quick and the dead.

---

[113] Migne, *PG*, LIX, cols. 649f: Πρὸ δὲ τῆς παρουσίας τοῦ Σωτῆρος, ὥσπερ βασιλικὸν σημεῖον, τὸ λεγόμενον σίγνον κατὰ τὴν κοινὴν συνήθειαν, προτρέχει τῆς Χριστοῦ παρουσίας, ὑπὸ τῶν ἀγγέλων δοξαζόμενον. Φανήσεται ὁ σταυρὸς ἐπὶ τῆς γῆς, σκέπων ἥλιον, ἀμβλύνων σελήνην ... (col. 650) τότε φανεὶς ὁ σταυρὸς ἐλέγξει τὴν τόλμαν, καὶ βεβαιώσει τὴν Ἐκκλησίαν· τότε ἀποκριθήσονται οἱ ἀντιλέγοντες, καὶ δοξασθήσονται οἱ ὑπακούσαντες· τότε πᾶσα ἡ κτίσις προσκυνήσει τῷ Υἱῷ τοῦ Θεοῦ.

[114] See, in general, W. Bousset, *Der Antichrist in der Überlieferung des Judentums, des neuen Testaments und der alten Kirche* (Göttingen, 1895), pp. 56ff, 154ff; Dölger, *Sol Salutis*, pp. 215ff. For the *Apocalypse of Elijah*, a work translated into Coptic as early as the third century, see G. Steindorff, *Die Apokalypse des Elias* (Texte und Untersuchungen zur Geschichte der altchristlichen Literatur, New Ser., II, 3a; Leipzig, 1899), p. 87. See also Theodor Zahn, *Geschichte des neutestamentlichen Kanons*, II (Erlangen, 1890), 801ff; O. Bardenhewer, *Geschichte der altchristlichen Literatur* (2nd ed., Freiburg, 1913–32), II, 707ff.

[115] L. Stern, "Die koptische Apocalypse des Sophonias," *Zeitschrift für ägyptische Sprache und Altertumskunde*, XXIV (1886), 124; Steindorff, *op. cit.*, 22ff; Bardenhewer, *op. cit.*, II, 708.

[116] See the description of the images in the apse of St. Felix in Nola in Paulinus of Nola, *Epistola*, XXXII, chaps. 10 and 14, ed. Hartel (Vienna, 1894), pp. 286, 289; Bousset, *op. cit.*, 56. See also the mosaic in the apse of St. Clement in Rome where twelve doves are seen in the cross; Wilpert, *Die römischen Mosaiken und Malereien der kirchlichen Bauten vom IV. bis XIII. Jahrhundert* (2nd ed., Freiburg, 1917), pl. 117; cf. *ibid.*, pl. 88, and *DACL*, XII, 174, fig. 8489, for the mosaic of Albenga.

[117] C. Schmidt, *Gespräche Jesu mit seinen Jüngern nach der Auferstehung* (Texte und Untersuchungen etc., Ser. III, XIII; Leipzig, 1919), 56ff; cf. p. 341 for the relations to the *Apocalypse of Elijah*, and p. 402 for the date; Bardenhewer, *op. cit.*, I, 596ff.

This work, which is extant in Ethiopic and Coptic translations only, draws on the *Apocalypse of St. Peter*.[118] "St. Peter" in his revelation, like St. Paul in the Epistle to the Thessalonians, refers, when reporting the events due at Christ's Second Coming, to an authentic utterance of the Lord, to a λόγος κυρίου. This is what, according to "Peter," the Lord said:

> Verily, the Advent of the Son of Man is not known; but as a lightening shineth forth from the east unto the west, so shall I come on the clouds of heaven with a great host in all my glory; in my glory shall I come with my cross striding before my face.

A question arises here. If, at the Lord's Second Coming, the cross is to descend first, it must, on some earlier occasion, have ascended to heaven. When and how did that happen? The answer is given by "Peter," who at any rate is consistent in his images. For in the so-called *Gospel According to St. Peter* we find the exact inversion of the report on the Advent. "Peter" narrates the events at the Lord's Resurrection, which originally was considered to be one with His Ascension, and tells us how the soldiers who were on guard at the tomb saw two angels entering the sepulchre:[119]

> Thereupon they see how there come back from the tomb three men [instead of two]; and the two support the one, and a cross follows after them. And of the two, the heads reach unto heaven, but the head of the one, whom they support, towers beyond the heavens. And a voice was heard from above, saying: "Hast thou preached to the departed?" And the answer was heard from the cross, saying: "Yea."

Thus, at the Resurrection, which here is identical with the Ascension, the cross walked behind the Lord, so to speak, as his *pedisequus;* and logically it would walk before the Lord as *cursor* at his eschatological return.

Here indeed we find the concept of the "walking cross." Pseudo-Peter seems to have been the main source of this uncanny image which was widespread in the Christian Antique, especially among the Orientals. Two Eastern authors here shall be adduced because their writings fall within some sixty years of the doors of Santa Sabina. One is Cyril of Jerusalem (died 386), who in his discussion of the Second Coming quite plainly declares, "The genuine and proper sign of Christ is the cross. The sign of the luminous cross

[118] M. R. James, "A New Text of the Apocalypse of Peter," *Journal of Theological Studies*, XII (1911), 38; H. Duensing, "Ein Stücke der urchristlichen Petrusapokalypse enthaltender Traktat der äthiopischen pseudoklementinischen Literatur," *Zeitschrift für die neutestamentliche Wissenschaft*, XIV (1913), 66; cf. Zahn, *op. cit.*, 810ff; Bardenhewer, I, 610–615.

[119] *The Gospel according to Peter*, chaps. 39–41, ed. Walter R. Cassels (London, 1894), 137; Bardenhewer, I,

524–529; James, *op. cit.*, 577ff, and *Journal of Theological Studies*, XXXII (1931), 275ff, on the relations between Peter's Gospel and his Apocalypse. For the analogy concerning the cross of Ascension and Second Coming see Hugo Koch, in *Theologische Literaturzeitung*, XLVI (1921), 203, and Dölger, *Sol Salutis*, 218. For the speaking cross, see also M. R. James, *Apocrypha anecdota* (Cambridge, 1893), 159f, 162.

precedes the King."[120] The other is St. Ephrem the Syrian (died 373), who in a less specific way says:[121]

> Then, while all behold it, there appears in the heights the terrible and holy sceptre of the great King. Everyone recognizes it and recalls the word of the Lord by which he announced it. There will appear the sign of the Son of Man in heaven and all shall be in certainty that behind it there shall appear the King.

Through Cyril and Ephrem, and probably through other channels as well, the image of the cross preceding the Lord eventually reached the Middle Ages and exercised its influence on apocalyptic thought in general as well as on artistic representations.[122]

A tradition flowing in a broad stream with many ramifications must be accounted for. There is no plausible reason to assume that an Italian artist of the early fifth century could not, or should not, have been acquainted with these ideas. It is true that the *Apocalypse of St. Peter* is not canonical. But neither is the Proto-Evangelium of James, and yet the great majority of the representations of Mary depends on this apocryphal work. Moreover, among the mosaics of the triumphal arch in Santa Maria Maggiore (432–440), which in general is devoted to Epiphany scenes in the life of the Lord, we find one scene depicting the youthful Jesus at his *Adventus* in Sotine, as he is received by Aphrodisius, the governor of that city; another scene represents, in an excitingly syncretistic fashion, the *occursus Domini* (*Hypapante*, Presentation in the Temple), or rather the meeting of the *redemptio saeculi*, of the Child initiating the *saeculum novum*. Both scenes depend on pseudo-Matthew.[123] To draw on apocryphal writings was anything but unusual in Early Christian art.[124] Why then should pseudo-Petrus form an exception, who still was read regularly once a year as a Lesson in Palestinian churches as late as A.D. 440?[125] That his popularity was

[120] Cyril of Jerusalem, *Katechesis XV: De secundo Christi adventu*, chap. XXII; Migne, *PG*, XXXIII, cols. 899f: Σημεῖον δὲ ἀληθὲς ἰδικὸν τοῦ Χριστοῦ ἐστιν ὁ σταυρός. Φωτοειδοῦς σταυροῦ σημεῖον προάγει τὸν βασιλέα. Cf. Bousset, *op. cit.*, 155, and the passages quoted by him.

[121] The various redactions of Ephrem's sermon here are not regarded; see the text offered by Bousset, p. 155ff.

[122] Bousset, pp. 155ff. See also the Latin version (8th century) of a sermon ascribed to Ephrem and published by C. P. Caspari, *Briefe, Abhandlungen und Predigten aus den zwei letzten Jahrhunderten des kirchlichen Altertums und dem Anfang des Mittelalters* (Christiania, 1890), 220: "...adveniet filii hominis signum, et prodiens apparebit Dominus cum virtute magna et maiestate multa, signo praeeunte eum salutaris ligni, necnon et omnibus virtutibus caelorum cum universo choro sanctorum signum sanctae crucis gestantibus humeris, praecedente ante illum tuba angelica...." Narrations such as this may have influenced the imagery of the Last Judgment where sometimes the cross is found preceding the Lord, e.g., in Fra Angelico's Triptych in Rome and probably in a great number of other works of art which here it is not intended to examine. See, however, the interesting *Last Judgment* in Rome (about 1040–1080), published by Deoclecio Redig de Campos, "Eine unbekannte Dar-

stellung des jüngsten Gerichts aus dem elften Jahrhundert," *Zeitschrift für Kunstgeschichte*, V (1936), 126, fig. 2. In the *Judgment* of Torcello the cross preceding the Lord is part of the imagery of the *Etimasia*. This, according to a suggestion of Professor Morey, might raise the question whether the texts adduced here might apply on the explanation also of this type of images.

[123] For the *Adventus* at Sotine see Wilpert, *Römische Mosaiken*, I, 489ff, pls. 66–68; Grabar, p. 228; De Waal, "Die apokryphen Evangelien in der altchristlichen Kunst," *Römische Quartalschrift*, I (1887), 190. The "Presentation" refers to pseudo-Matthew, chap. 14, as has been pointed out brilliantly by Grabar, pp. 216–225; for the connection with the *Saeculum Novum* coinage, see Gagé, "Saeculum Novum," *Transactions of the International Numismatic Congress in London, June 30–July 3, 1936* (London, 1938), 182ff, pl. XIV, 4–5, and his study "Le Templum Urbis et les origines de l'idée de *Renovatio*," *Mélanges Franz Cumont* (Brussels, 1936), 170ff. The concept of the Presentation is clearly that of the *occursus domini*; cf. *supra*, note 73, for the liturgy of the feast. [Edd. note: the mosaic here referred to is the main subject of "*Puer Exoriens*," above, pp. 25–36 and pl. 11, fig. 1.]

[124] De Waal, *op. cit.*, 173ff, 272ff, 391ff.

[125] Sozomenos, *Hist. eccl.*, VII, chap. 19; Migne, *PG*, LXVII, col. 1478.

greater apparently in the East than in the West means very little in that period of continuous exchanges, nor is this fact prejudicial as to the origin, Eastern or Western, of the artist. It is well known that the West was familiar with the *Apocalypse of Peter*. The *Muratorian Fragment*, for which Roman origin seems to be ascertained, mentions (about 200 A.D.) among the sacred books of the Church "apocalepse etiam iohanis et petri" though the author may add "quam quidam ex nostris legi in ecclesia nolunt."[126] Other lists such as the *Catalogus Claramontanus*,[127] here may be left aside. But at least it should be mentioned that Harnack conjectured influences of pseudo-Peter on the Acts of several Gallican martyrs, and additional evidence has since been made available.[128]

It now is fairly easy to integrate those concepts into the scene of the Sabina panel. The relief undoubtedly refers to the Second Advent of Christ, a topic rare in later but popular in Early Christian art.[129] The Lord Himself appears in the glory, still above the heavens; but His forerunner, the "luminous cross," which at the Second Advent takes the place of St. John announcing the *agnus Dei* of the First Advent, has already reached the space between heaven and earth. The globe of light surrounding the σταυρὸς φωτοειδής is a well known feature; it matches the description offered by Paulinus of Nola:[130]

> Crucem corona lucido cingit globo...
> Crux cingitur orbe coronae...

That the cross dives headlong from heaven to earth is likewise nothing that should baffle us. We need recall only the numerous representations of angels diving headlong from above to below. The cross here takes their place. Perhaps we should also take into account the cross of St. Peter which stands upside down, a feature which may, or may not, be considered an additional allusion to Peter or to Rome, though without influencing the general content of the tablet.

---

[126] The most convenient edition with facsimile is found in *DACL*, XII (1935), cols. 543ff, *s.v.* "Muratorianum."

[127] Zahn, *op. cit.*, II, 159.

[128] Harnack, *Die Petrusapokalypse in der alten abendländischen Kirche* (Texte und Untersuchungen *etc.*, XIII:1; Leipzig, 1895), pp. 71–73, refers to the Acts of Felix of Valence, Fortunatus, and Achilles, of Ferreolus and Ferrutio, of Dorothea and Theophilus. This conjecture compares favorably with the surmise that the artist of the Sabina doors depended on the Italo-Gallic School. Harnack's suggestion since has been supported by a manuscript in Épinal in which pseudo-Peter is quoted ("... ut apud Danielem et apud Petrum in Apocalypsi eius scriptum est"); cf. M. R. James, in *Journal of Theological Studies*, XII (1911), 383, who (pp. 380ff) discusses also possible influences of Peter on the *Shepherd of Hermas*.

[129] Grabar, pp. 249ff. Christ with the Apostles and two angels blowing the trumpets (in the St. Gall cod. 51) may likewise refer to the Second Coming; cf. E. Kantorowicz, "Ivories and Litanies," pl. 20b. In the West, in later centuries, it is preferably the *Adventus in nubibus* which we find depicted, e.g., in the various *Beatus* manuscripts; cf. W. Neuss, *Die Apokalypse des heiligen Johannes in der altspanischen und altchristlichen Bibelillustration* (Münster, 1931),

II, pls. 28–42, figs. 45–62; see also Georgiana Goddard King, in *Art Studies*, VIII (1930), 22, and fig. 7. An *Ascension*, or *Resurrection*, in accordance with the *Gospel of Peter*, i.e., with the cross following behind the Lord, does not seem to exist. Hubert Schrade, *Ikonographie der christlichen Kunst*, I: *Die Auferstehung Christi* (Berlin and Leipzig, 1932), 7f, mentions, it is true, the *Gospel of Peter* but no pictorial evidence; see also Schrade's "Zur Ikonographie der Himmelfahrt," *Vorträge der Bibliothek Warburg 1928–29* (Leipzig and Berlin, 1930), 74ff, 182. Dölger, *Sol Salutis*, 212, believes that the *Ascension* in the door of Santa Sabina betrays the influence of Peter, but his assertion is not convincing.

Subsequently, and after having sent the manuscript of this study to the press, I have noticed that Louis Bréhier, *La sculpture et les arts mineurs byzantins* (Paris, 1936), 79, n. 8, has styled the panel *La Seconde Venue*. He does not substantiate this interpretation and maintains that Peter and Paul lift (above the head of Mary) "un disque timbré de la croix." The connection with the other panel has not been recognized by Bréhier; cf. *supra*, note 93.

[130] *Ep.* XXXII, chap. 10, ed. Hartel, I, 286. See, e.g., the cross in the apse of S. Apollinare in Classe (Morey, fig. 183).

As yet undiscussed is the group in the lower part of the panel. We may call the three figures Peter, Paul, and Mary. They represent, as it were, those "that are alive, that are left," and who come to meet in mid-air the cross and therewith the Lord who is to follow behind His banner. It is as though they say "Ἔρχου," "Come," as "the Spirit and the bride and he that heareth say, Come" (Apoc. 22, 17). Or, the scene may interpret St. Paul's message (1 Thess. 4, 15–16; see above, note 106a), to which a sentence referring to the cross in accordance with "Peter" should be added:

> For the Lord himself shall come down from heaven [preceded by the standard of the cross] . . . and the dead who are in Christ shall rise first. Then we who are alive, who are left, shall be taken up together with them in the clouds to the meeting with the Lord in the air (εἰς ἀπάντησιν τοῦ Κυρίου εἰς ἀέρα).

Iconographically, the representation on the door of Santa Sabina can be brought into line, without difficulty, with other representations of the Second Coming. These have been competently discussed by Grabar,[131] who emphasizes at the same time their close relationship with the Last Judgment. It is true that the cross preceding the Lord is a subject which is found in representations of the Last Judgment rather than in those of the Second Coming. But there is no doubt that the artist of Santa Sabina intended to represent the scene preceding the Judgment, that is, the Advent proper, a scene which in contradistinction to the terrifying grandeur of the public and general judgment is a more intimate, more mysterious and more exclusive scene, as it would be a small group of elected only that are worthy to come and meet the Lord or His forerunner, the cross.

The interpretation of the panel as the Second Coming, furthermore, is strongly supported by the fact that this panel forms the antitype for the Malachi prophecy. The *Kyrios* of the Old Testament is paralleled by the King of Glory of the New, and the *Adventus* of the Lord of the Temple corresponds with that of the Lord of the Judgment. In either case the Messianic ruler is to come "suddenly," "like the lightning" (ἐξαίφνης, ὥσπερ ἡ ἀστραπή), while both are supposed to act, after their epiphany, as judges. In the first case, the *praecursor* of the Kyrios is the Angel of the Covenant, in the second it is the cross. Also, the cross is striving upward in the first panel and downward in the second. Finally the acclaiming groups in the first panel find a parallel in the expectant group of the second. And the *dittochaeic* composition suggests anyhow that an *Adventus* of the Old Testament should correspond with one of the New and that the prophecy of the First Covenant should find its last fulfilment in the events of the Second.

As the contrast, or parallelism, of the two scenes seems to be unique in works of art, the question must be raised whether it was the artist himself who contrived the antithesis of Malachi's prophecy and the Lord's promise of a second return. It is most unlikely that this composition should have been the artist's personal invention; and, in fact, it is not difficult to discover his sources. It seems to the present writer that in the discussion of the *dittochaeic* compositions one important source has been neglected, the Lectionaries, or

---

[131] Grabar, pp. 228, 249ff.

rather the Lessons. It is to be remembered that the Lessons, in early times, were tripartite, that is, they were taken not only from the Epistles and Gospels but also from the Old Testament, especially from the Prophets. If we now check the oldest Lectionary of the Western Church that has been preserved completely, namely the *Liber comicus* of Silos (*ca.* 657–667 A.D.), we there find for the fourth Sunday of Advent the following Lessons:[132]

LECTIO LIBRI MALAZIE PROPHETE [Mal. 3, 1–4]:
Haec dicit dominus. Ecce ego mittam angelum meum etc.

EPISTOLA PAULI APOSTOLI AD TESALONICENSES PRIMA [1 Thess. 5, 14–23]:
Fratres rogo vos—in adventum domini nostri ihesu xpi serbetur.

LECTIO SANCTI EUANGELI[I] SECUNDUM MARCUM [Mark 1, 1–8]:
Initium euangelii ihesu xpi filii dei, sicut scriptum est in esaya propheta, Ecce mitto angelum meum ante faciem tuam—ille vero baptizabit vos in spiritu sancto.

We may add the last Lesson of the third Sunday of Advent, that is, the one preceding in the *Liber comicus* those quoted above, namely:

LECTIO SANCTI EUANGELII SECUNDUM MATHEUM [Matt. 21, 1–9]:
(The description of the Entry in Jerusalem on Palm Sunday, ending with the verse: "Benedictus qui venit in nomine domini".)

Allowing for the fact that Lesson 1 Thess. 5, 14–23, is prescribed in the *Liber comicus*, and not 4, 15–16, which the artist seems to have had in mind, we find here the whole complex of *Adventus* quotations which we have been dealing with in these pages: the Entry, the Malachi prophecy, the eschatological Second Coming, and the reference to John the Baptist and Forerunner. Nearest to the Mozarabic Lectionary is the Missal of Bobbio, as might have been expected.[133] Here we find for the first Sunday of Advent the Lessons Malachi 3, 1–6, James 5, 7–12, 19–20 (referring to the Second Coming), and Matthew 11, 2–15 (referring to the Forerunner), that is, a selection similar to that of the *Liber comicus*. And as an Advent Lesson we find at least the Malachi verses also in the Lectionary of Luxueil.[134] Briefly, the Lectionaries, just as the panels of Santa Sabina, contrast Malachi's prophecy with the promise of the Lord's Second Coming, or rather they present a synopsis of the various Advents.

The Lectionaries thus make it obvious whence the artist may have borrowed his inspiration. The origin of the various systems of pericopes admittedly is obscure; it is not our intention to intrude into this jungle. However, there is no reason to object to the relevance of the Lessons in connection with the Sabina doors on the grounds that our Lectionaries do not go as far back as the early fifth century. Advent was celebrated in

---

[132] G. Morin, *Anecdota Maredsolana*, I (Maredsou, 1893), 7ff.

[133] Migne. *PL*, LXXII, cols. 457ff; cf. Edmund Bishop, *Liturgica historica* (Oxford, 1918), 178ff, on the Missal.

[134] Migne, *PL*, LXXII, cols. 171ff ("In Vigiliis Natalis Domini"). Cf. *supra*, note 73.

Rome by that time,[135] and the Lessons existed even though there may not have been Lectionaries. It here may suffice to adduce Cyril's *Katechesis* on the Second Coming of Christ.[136] Cyril begins his discussion by pointing out that every event in the life of the Lord seems to have happened twice and to have a parallel. When referring to the *Adventus*, Cyril compares the Entry into Jerusalem, when Jesus appeared as the Lord of the Temple, to the Second Coming, when he shall appear as the Lord of the Judgment. That is, he makes the "historical" *Adventus* become transparent against the background of the "eschatological" *Adventus*, and *vice versa*, just as in the *Didache* (chap. 10) the hope for the Second Coming is combined with the Palm Sunday acclaim: "Let Grace come and let this world pass away. Hosanna to the son of David!" Cyril brings these two Advents into relationship with Malachi, in whose prophecy they both are foreshadowed. The *Kyrios Pantokrator* first is to come as the Lord of the Temple (Mal. 3, 1–4) and he then is to perform the function of Lord of the Judgment as indicated in verse 3, 5: "And I will come to you in judgment. . . ." In Cyril's *Katechesis* we thus find identically the same contrast by parallelism which is produced by the later Lectionaries, and this antithesis, which was doubtless popular, as St. Augustine likewise refers to it in the *City of God*,[137] had been put into words at least some sixty years before the artist in Rome set to work and carved the two scenes in the doors of Santa Sabina.

Everything now falls into its place. Cyril of Jerusalem and the Lectionaries support, in an unambiguous way, the interpretation of the Sabina panels which here has been advanced. There can be no doubt that the two "enigmatic" reliefs represent the two Advents, that of the *Kyrios* at the door of his temple and that of the Lord before the Day of Judgment.

4. EPILOGUE

Palm Sunday and Second Coming, "historical" and "eschatological" *Adventus*, those are two themes which should be clearly distinguished from one another. Yet, it is in the nature of things, and of mediaeval thinking in particular, that occasionally the one

---

[135] The Roman celebration of Advent seems to go back to *ca.* 430 A.D., cf. *DACL*, I, cols. 2249f, 3224. The oldest Roman Lectionary, now dated *ca.* 645, contains the following Lessons for the 4th, 3rd, and 2nd Sundays of Advent: Matt. 21, 1–9 (Entry into Jerusalem); Luke 21, 25–33 (Second Coming); Matt. 11, 2–10 (*Ecce mitto*). In essence, these pericopes deal with the same ideas as those found in the *Liber comicus* (cf. *supra*, note 132); see Klauser, *Das römische Capitulare Evangeliorum*, I, 42; cf. pp. 89, 127, 167f, 182f. The *Adventus* idea in the liturgy deserves a special study. Some material, especially with reference to the Breviary, has been offered, however, by Ildefons Herwegen, "Das Königtum Christi in der Liturgie," *Ehrengabe deutscher Wissenschaft dargeboten von katholischen Gelehrten: Festschrift Prinz Johann Georg Herzog zu Sachsen* (Freiburg, 1920), 147–168.

[136] Migne, *PG*, XXXIII, cols. 899f.

[137] *De civ.*, XVIII, chap. 35; he first quotes the verses Malachi 3, 1–2, and then goes on to say: "Hoc loco et primum et secundum Christi praenuntiavit adventum; primum scilicet, de quo ait *Et subito veniet in templum suum*; id est in carnem suam. . ., secundum vero ubi ait *Ecce venit, dicit Dominus exercituum*. . ., significavit utique etiam Judaeos secundum scripturas, quas legant, Christum quaerere et velle." See also *De civ.*, XX, chap. 25. The two Advents are mentioned also by St. Jerome, *Ep.*, CCXXI, chap. 11, Migne, *PL*, XXII, col. 1036, who refers to 1 Thess. 4, 14ff, and says: "Duos autem esse adventus Domini Salvatoris. . ., primum in humilitate venerit, et postea sit venturus in gloria." See Irenaeus, *Adversus haereses*, IV, chap. 33, 1, ed. A. Stieren, (Leipzig, 1853), p. 666. The "dittochaeic" concept of the two Advents is found also in a Romanos hymn; cf. T. M. Wehofer, "Untersuchungen zum Lied des Romanos auf die Wiederkunft des Herrn," *Sitzungsberichte der Wiener Akademie*, CLIV (1906), Abh. 5, pp. 47f, 110.

concept would supersede or even take the place of the other.[138] More rarely it seems that the two forms of the *Adventus* were blended. However, there is a very well known, if strange, evidence for the linking of the two Advents which requires discussion here.

A peculiar, in fact unique, Palm Sunday performance took place in Russia during the sixteenth and seventeenth centuries.[139] Although originally common to several of the greater Russian cities such as Novgorod, Kazan, Astrakhan, and others, the great pageantry eventually was restricted to the imperial residence, Moscow. In Moscow, there moved on Palm Sunday a solemn and magnificent procession from the Uspenskij Cathedral to the Jerusalem Church. The ceremony began with the recital of St. Matthew's narration of the Lord's Entry into Jerusalem. The patriarch himself, who on this occasion took the place of Christ, recited the words of the Lord, saying, "Go into the place over against you, and straightway ye shall find an ass tied, and a colt with her: loose them, and bring them unto me." Thereupon two clerics would go and bring an ass, which was mounted by the patriarch to carry him to the "Jerusalem" Church. This clearly is the staging of the "historical" Entry of Christ. But the "eschatological" idea was likewise represented. For after the patriarch had been seated on the ass, the Tsar, trimmed with all the insignia and symbols of his imperial power, took the ass by the bridle with his "sceptre-glorious" hands and walked as the *cursor* of "Christ" before the mount of the patriarch until they reached "Jerusalem." It is true, the Tsar led the ass in a very indirect and symbolic way. The rein was very long, and the Tsar's "sceptre-glorious" hand supported by two high courtiers, merely touched its end, while the middle of the long rein was held by the Tsarevitch or else by the most dignified boyar of the empire. Moreover, the ass's bridle proper was held by one of the men of the patriarch. Hence, the Tsar's service as *cursor* was, emphatically, a symbolic act. Nevertheless the Tsar led the ass of the patriarch—as the Angel leads the mount of Christ (cf. pl. 16, fig. 30).

Whence did this Moscovite ritual stem? We should expect from Byzantium, but this is not so. The Byzantine emperor was very careful to stay at home on Palm Sunday. It was an impossible idea for a Byzantine emperor to walk, to say nothing about leading the mount by the bridle, while his patriarch was riding. The Byzantine emperor, therefore, for all his liking to celebrate publicly the great festivals of the Church, stayed at home on Palm Sunday. He celebrated the day with a great procession, *Peripatos*, within the palace where he himself would stage the Lord's Entry into Jerusalem after his own imperial fashion.

Whence then did Moscow borrow the ritual? As far as the rôle of the patriarch is concerned the rite of Jerusalem was authoritative. "Sic deducetur episcopus in eo typo quo tunc Dominus deductus est" writes the Aquitanian Pilgrim in the fourth century as she describes how the bishop walked in procession on Palm Sunday; and the bishop's

---

[138] Cf. *supra*, p. 221.

[139] For the following see Georg Ostrogorsky, "Zum Stratordienst des Herrschers in der Byzantinisch-Slavi-schen Welt," *Seminarium Kondakovianum*, VII (1935), 193ff, an excellent study to which the present writer owes the material here adduced.

riding on the back of an ass was likewise a custom of that patriarchate, though a later one, reflecting the well-known Syrio-Palestinian stagelike realism.[140]

However, the imperial duty of leading the mount of the patriarch on Palm Sunday is a feature exclusively Russian and its source has been made perfectly evident by Georg Ostrogorsky, whose excellent study is merely paraphrased in the present pages. The source may truly be called "troubled." It is the forgery of an interpolation inserted in a forged document. The forged document is the *Donation of Constantine.* The interpolation is the famous sentence referring to the *officium stratoris* of the emperor which probably was later inserted into the passage referring to the *frygium*, the later tiara. This is the text:[141]

> With our own hands we have placed on his most holy head the *frygium*, which by its white splendour indicates the splendid resurrection of the Lord; and for the deference of the blessed Peter we held the bridle of his horse, rendering to him the service of equerry, and ordered that all his successor pontiffs, and they alone, shall wear the very same *frygium* in processions. In imitation of our empire. . . .

By misinterpreting the sentence in which the *frygium* and its being worn at processions are discussed, and by linking it with the clause in which the *officium stratoris* is treated, the Metropolitan Makarij of Moscow produced, in 1550, the following version:

> Also we order that this rite and custom [of leading the horse by the bridle] shall be rendered at processions, in imitation of our emperorship, to all the pontiffs after him [i.e., Pope Sylvester].

Whether this was a deliberate misinterpretation or a mistake must be left undecided. However, what was good for Constantine and the Roman patriarch was good also for the Russian emperor, successor of Constantine, and the patriarch of the Third Rome. Thus, the source of the Russian ceremony is, as it were, a forgery "raised to the third power." Yet, the misinterpretation led, eventually, to that queer blending of the "historical" with the "eschatological" *Adventus* which we found in the Russian rite.[142]

But what are the implications of the imperial *officium stratoris* as recorded in the "original" *Constitutum Constantini?* It is obvious that by the middle of the eighth century, when the forged document was drafted, the *Adventus* and its symbolism had entered into a new phase. The ritual of the solemn receptions originated as an honor rendered to the

---

[140] For the Aquitanian Pilgrim see L. Duchesne, *Christian Worship* (5th edition, London, 1931), pp. 505ff, and for the later usages at Jerusalem, Ostrogorsky, *op. cit.*, 198. For the spreading of the Palm Sunday procession in the West, see Adolf Franz, *Die kirchlichen Benediktionen im Mittelalter* (Freiburg, 1909), I, 470ff. The Western rite of the *Palmesel* procession is of a later date (first evidence is 973 A.D.) and has little to do with the Russian performance. The "Feast of the Ass" on New Year's Day is certainly connected with "Advent" or "Epiphany" (cf. Zach. 9, 9). But it is beyond the scope of this study to deal with these subjects. Cf. Karl Young, *The Drama of the Medieval Church* (Oxford, 1933), I, 94ff.

[141] The study of Robert Holtzmann, *Der Kaiser als Marschall des Papstes* (Schriften der Straßburger Wissenschaftlichen Gesellschaft in Heidelberg, New Ser., VIII, 1928), is fundamental for the *officium stratoris*. The theory according to which the sentence referring to the *officium stratoris* is an interpolation (Holtzmann, pp. 24f), seems to be the one generally accepted. The manuscript transmission does not suggest an interpolation, and the present writer accepts this theory somewhat reluctantly.

[142] Ostrogorsky, pp. 200ff.

gods at their epiphany. Then, when the Hellenistic rulers were placed among the deities of the state, these kings at their "Epiphanies" were received with the same divine honors. The Roman emperors in turn, when celebrating their "Messianic" *Adventus* as redeemers of the world, followed the model of the Hellenistic kings; and so did the writer of the Fourth Gospel when using, in connection with the Lord's Entry into Jerusalem, the legal or constitutional term *Hypantesis*. The model of Christ's Entry finally moulded the ceremonial of the reception of Christian emperors and mediaeval kings whose Messianic-eschatological nature and mission were visibly and audibly stressed on that occasion. On the other hand, the imperial Roman solemnity, as it was owed also to the high officials of the state at their *Adventus*, influenced the receptions of bishops and patriarchs. By the middle of the eighth century the pope, too, fell in. Emperor-like receptions had been granted to him long before.[143] Now, however, he claimed an extraordinary, an extravagant, honor such as never before had been demanded by, or had been offered to, a human being: the world-ruling emperor, himself a Messianic-eschatological figure, was to act as the pontiff's *cursor* and to lead the horse by the bridle when the pope rode in triumph or made his epiphany at an *Adventus* (pl. 20 fig. 45).[144]

Often it has been emphasized that the *Donation of Constantine* was the vehicle by means of which the papacy eventually secured a position not to be matched by any spiritual or any temporal dignitary on earth. Surely, the sight of the emperor serving as equerry to the pope could not possibly be surpassed or outdone by any prerogative or privilege of any terrestrial power. In this respect, the document indeed reflects the notorious papal ambition of gaining absolute power within the Church and over the secular state. But there is a way other than the traditional ecclesiastico-political of approaching the problem, and to this other aspect our attention is called by the "eschatological" character of the papal Triumph and Advent.

Almost never with regard to the early Middle Ages, and rarely otherwise, has the question been raised, What is the position of the pope within Christian eschatological thinking? Has he at all an individual eschatological standing or a Messianic function comparable with that of the emperor, the classical exponent of these speculations? The answer to these questions, it seems, has to be in the negative in view of the early Middle Ages and in the affirmative as far as the later periods are concerned. It is far beyond the scope of this study even to intimate an outline of the growth of papal Messiahship because such an endeavor would call for an account of all the papal efforts to secure for the Roman pontiff the Messianic-eschatological functions reserved by tradition to the Roman emperor. It would require a survey of the struggle between Papacy and Empire

[143] Cf. *supra*, note 65.

[144] Holtzmann, *op. cit.*, does not clearly distinguish between *Triumphus* and *Adventus*, that is, the two occasions on which the pope is offered the equerry service of emperors, kings and princes. However, pp. 40ff, he briefly indicates the connection with pre-Christian usages and images, though without recognizing the Epiphany or *Adventus* character of the ceremony, of which Luther still seems to have been aware; see his *Passional Christi und* *Antichristi*, 1521, in the Weimar Luther edition, IX, 709, and pls. 17, 18, where he sets the Entry of Christ into Jerusalem against the Pope on horseback: "Der Bapst magk gleych wie der Keysser reytten, und der keysser ist seyn thrabant," Our pl. 20, fig. 45 (cf. Wilpert, *Römische Mosaiken*, pl. 269) is one of the rare representations of the *officium stratoris* (13th century; Rome, SS. Quattro Coronati).

under these aspects, of the papal revolution, of the crusades, and of the various claims of the pope to represent the *verus imperator* of this world and to appear, also in imagery, in the *Majestas* reserved to the emperor and Christ.[145]

One step, and perhaps the one most important, in this direction certainly is marked by the *Constitutum Constantini* and, in it, by the passage referring to the *officium stratoris* of Caesar. The "eschatological" *conductus* at the hands of a Victory or an Angel had been a symbolic prerogative of both the emperor on earth and the emperor in heaven. Now the pope insists upon being conducted by the "Messianic" emperor himself. The space beyond time opens its gate to the pope. He enters through it by the end of the thirteenth century. In Gothic and Renaissance imagery, at long last, the papal tiara, replacing the imperial crown of the Romanesque age, would adorn the King of Glory; it is seen even on the inclined head of a *Volto santo*. From the whirlpools of the Spiritualist Movement there arose the vision of a Messianic *Papa Angelicus*, a papal antitype of the Messiah-emperor to come before the end; and simultaneously there emerged—an inevitable correlate—the vision of the *Papa Antichristus*.[146] The papacy therewith was projected plainly into the Messianic-apocalyptic space, and one may meditate on whether "the white horse which is the Church"[147] had been marshalled thither by the angel invisibly holding the bridle or by the emperor of this world visibly performing the *officium stratoris*.

[145] The earliest representations of the pope enthroned originated in the twelfth, or perhaps late eleventh, century; cf. Gerd Ladner, "I mosaici e gli affreschi ccclc-siastico-politici nell' antico Palazzo Lateranense," *Rivista di archeologia cristiana*, XII (1935), 265–292. For Urban II in the *Majestas*, see also Bordona, *Spanish Illuminations*, I, fig. 76.

[146] The problem has been recognized and discussed with regard to the later Middle Ages by Friedrich Baethgen, "Der Engelpapst," *Schriften der Königsberger Gelehrten Gesellschaft*, X (1933), 75–119. See also Ernst Benz, *Ecclesia spiritualis* (Stuttgart, 1934), 366ff.

[147] Cf. *supra*, note 66.

THE PROBLEM OF MEDIEVAL WORLD UNITY

T HE SLOGAN of Medieval World Unity, whatever may have been its origin, has been popularized by the School of Romanticism.

> Those were beautiful, brilliant times when Europe was *one* Christian country, when *one* Christendom dwelled in this humanly shaped continent, when *one* great unity of action joined together the remotest provinces of this broad and wide spiritual empire.

With these words the German Novalis begins his treatise on *Christendom or Europe*, written in 1799; and in 1800, Fichte would echo: "The people of the new Christian Europe can be looked upon as *one* nation."

The enthusiasm for the Middle Ages, a period then rediscovered, did not always carry Romantic minds to these lofty abstractions, and the strong antipathy toward the "Dark Ages," fostered by classicism and enlightenment, put on a wholesome brake. Nevertheless, it gradually became a commonplace to maintain that the Middle Ages, for all their wars and profound discords, represented a pattern of world unity and uniformity which had since been lost. Scholars and popular writers liked to emphasize that Europe, owing to the one faith professed by all, represented one great family of nations guided by either emperor and pope together or by the Holy See alone; that there was a commonwealth with customs and institutions alike in all countries and a language—Latin—common to all, with letters and learning on common ground and with a common foreign war, the crusades, which made the diverging ambitions converge in one great common task.

This, approximately, was the image of Medieval World Unity which the Romantic School passed on to the following generations. Even Ranke, though himself not a Romanticist, succumbed to this spell; infatuated with his conception of the commonwealth of Romanic and Germanic peoples, he, too, went as far as to use the expression of a "Romano-Germanic Nation."

Today, the historian finds it difficult to defend the case of Medieval World Unity on similar lines and in a similarly sanguine way. With some reservations he might be willing to admit that Western Europe appears, from a very distant point of view, as an entity, despite its serious and dangerous cracks. Cracks cause a pot to leak and prevent it from performing its task of holding liquids, but are no objection to the fact that even a cracked pot is still a pot. Yet the historian will vehemently refuse to acknowledge the much-hailed unity of language, letters and learning, of customs, education and crusading spirit,

Reprinted, with permission, from the *Annual Report of the American Historical Association for 1942*, III (1944), 31–37.

or even of ecclesiastical matters, as soon as he takes into account the Greco-Slav common-wealth of nations centered in Byzantium. That is to say: the fascinating conception of Medieval World Unity collapses and a mirage dissolves when the dome of Santa Sophia rises on the horizon.

The historian, today, cannot dismiss Byzantium as an intellectual parenthesis. He will not exclude Europe beyond the Adriatic Sea from his account, nor draw a frontier or establish an intellectual customs port at Venice, nor ignore the existence of South-Eastern Europe in order to preserve belief in "Medieval World Unity." We cannot simply forget that Constantine's creation of an Empire-Church, his fusion of Roman Empire and Christian Church served—with due alterations and due forgeries—as a basis for political thinking and acting during the Middle Ages until roughly 1300 A.D., until in the West the "Byzantine style" was abolished in every respect. In essence, the medieval western world produced no one new political solution to surpass, to improve or to replace that of Constantine; the Carolingian or Ottonian Empire-Churches as well as the Grego-rian Church-Empire are only paraphrases of the Constantinian tune.

Byzantium belongs to "our world," although the disparity of Romano-Germanic West and Greco-Slav East may defy every effort to construct a world unity. There is no unity of Eastern and Western customs or standards; there is no unity of language and letters or of the fundamentals of education. Where, if at all, has St. Augustine his shrine in Byzantine education? To the Western mind the idea of the "City of God" is basic and cannot be thought away. But did it exercise any appreciable influence on the East, and are we allowed to transfer the *Civitas Dei* ideology to Byzantine conditions? Not to mention a unity of political matters, even the unity of the Church is a most problematic and delicate matter. Shaky ever since the Iconoclast Struggle, at the breaking point in the ninth century, and definitely broken in the eleventh when the Reform Papacy launched anew the ship of St. Peter, the ecclasiastical union remained a dream and only the schism between East and West survived.

Thus, we seem to have run a car with a fragile cargo of World Unity at full speed in a blind alley. For this is the impasse: we have to admit that the Greco-Slav commonwealth belongs to Europe, but in so doing we realize that World Unity has gone to pieces. It is no longer a pot, leaking perhaps and full of cracks but still a pot, that we hold in our hands; the potsherds have definitely fallen asunder while we face the intricate question: "Is a handful of potsherds still a pot?" The housewife, rightly, says "No" and throws the pieces into the garbage. The archaeologist, rightly, says "Yes," gathers the pieces from the garbage, puts them into a glass case and visualizes the pot as an entity although in reality it is not.

The Middle Ages stood by the archaeologist. His ability to look at mere fragments in a glass case and yet see the whole vessel as it should appear and to forget completely its fragmentary state, this ability was native to the medieval mind. It is the main feature which the Romano-Germanic nations have in common with one another and also with Byzantium. Therefore, if it be our desire to defend the myth of Medieval World Unity, we should remember that indeed this unity was myth, nay, that it was this very "Myth of Unity" which East and West alike professed. In other words, the "Myth" is the seemingly nebulous though yet quite solid substance of Medieval World Unity.

This is not really surprising. The medieval mind set the Whole before the parts and found it easier than we do to acknowledge a totality, even an imaginary one. The absence of unity was considered a momentary defection which could be overlooked because sooner or later the unity would have to be restored. A united world was indispensable for achieving that state of perfection which, it was generally recognized, would be established just before time ends and doomsday dawns. Thus, the medieval Myth of World Unity has a predominantly messianic or eschatological character. Against this background the myth stands out and becomes almost reality.

Medieval World Unity was a part of the Christian eschatology, and therefore does not refer to this earth and its surface alone; it embraces the whole depth of Space and is in fact a Unity of the Universe. This consideration should prevent us from confounding medieval ideas of World Unity with modern ideas of International Unity. "International," the word in itself, proceeds from a negation, from the desire to rule out and bridge the differences prevailing between the peoples living on the surface of this globe. Medieval thought started out from the affirmative. The Whole was not achieved by adding the parts but it was set before the parts. Men visualized the universe as one articulated totality which embraces Earth and Heaven alike. Individual and community both appear as organic members of the cosmos. They had their places assigned within the totality of Space and had their functions assigned within the totality of Time. The unity of the universe, which today we find difficult to envisage, was definitely an *a priori* of medieval imagination. From the outset, therefore, we miss the essential point if we do not consider Medieval World Unity to encompass Earth as well as Heaven, with the one referring to the other, reflecting the other, and flowing over into the other.

This idea of World Unity is neither purely transcendental nor purely material. It dwells in the stratum of thinner air in which medieval Realism and medieval Sacramentalism have their abode; or else it may be called reasonably a part of that "Christian Myth" whose relationship with "Christian History" has recently been discussed by Lynn White in a brilliant and suggestive way.

The Unity of the Universe: a great myth it is, a myth which East and West have in common. It manifests itself daily in the Eastern and Western Churches alike, despite the profound differences between the rituals. Daily, at the solemn entrance of the clergy bearing the Gospel, would the Eastern Church pray:

> Cause that with our entrance, there may be an entrance of Holy Angels, ministering together with us, and with us glorifying thy goodness.

And the Western Church beseeches God that he may send his angels to carry to the celestial altar the gifts laid out on the altars on earth. When the hymn of the "Thrice Holy" is chanted, the visible Church is chiming in with the "never silent glorification" of the celestial beings, and the "Holy" is echoed by animate and inanimate nature, by beast, birds, and insects, by mountains and stars, rivers and valleys, so that the universe—

not the surface of this earth—becomes a harmonious and articulated One that choruses with the chant of the Church and is tuned with the chant of the celestials. Accordingly, in the eucharistic preface, which precedes this hymn, man is styled a "Citizen of the Universe" (κοσμοπολίτης ἄνθρωπος) and the "Adornment of the Cosmos" (κόσμου κόσμος).

In addition to this active flowing-over of the one sphere into the other, the visible Church, in a more static way, is also a reflection of the Celestial Jerusalem. And as the City of Heaven is but one and undivided, therefore its likeness on earth should display undivided unity, too. For unity is of God, and division or conflict is the work of Lucifer. Hence, the early Church would ask God to bring together his *Ecclesia* "just as the bread has become one from many grains grown on many hills."

> Bring them together from every people and every country and every town and every hamlet and every house so as to form one living universal Church.

Soon, however, Eastern and Western Churches would pray less timidly and more triumphantly:

> Be mindful, O Lord, of thy Holy Catholic and Apostolic Church which *is* from end to end of the Universe.

Here the universal unity of the Church, which the faithful hope will be established at the end of Time, is anticipated as a spiritual reality within Time. And yet the Church is not heedless of the great variety of Churches—Roman and Gallican, Byzantine, Syrian, Egyptian, Armenian, and others—and consequently would pray also

> for the peace of the whole world, and for the welfare of the Holy *Churches* of God and the Oneness (ἕνωσις) of them all.

The diversity of the churches and the oneness of The Church—both are realities though realities of a different kind which do not exclude each other. Accordingly, Charlemagne—in the *Libri Carolini* in which he fights the Byzantine decisions concerning the veneration of images—would stress the various Churches in all parts of the world and yet, almost in the same breath, reproach the Greeks for having cut the *vinculum ecclesiasticae unitatis.*

What is true for the Church is true for the people. In the early Western Church we find the prayer:

> God, who hast made the diversity of all peoples to be *one* in the confession of thy name, give us the will and the power to do what thou hast prescribed, that in thy People called to eternity there be *one* faith of mind and *one* piety of action.

Here the factual diversity of peoples is set against the eschatological unity of the *One* People, the unity for which the Western Church prays also in the *Orationes solemnes,* the ancient litany still sung on Good Friday and containing intentions

> for the Heretics and Schismatics that they may find their way back into the Church;

for the unfaithful Jews that finally they may recognize the Lord;

and for the Pagans that they may forget their idols and be converted to the faith of the living God.

On these intentions, almost to the letter, there draw the hundreds of politico-messianic prophecies, prognostications, and Sibylline oracles which pervade medieval literature and which promise the oneness of this world to be effectuated before the break of the Last Day.

The materialization of these hopes and expectations was the task not only of the Church but also of the secular power. For a third time, we encounter the twofold reality of oneness and diversity. Eastern and Western rituals have the following prayer in common:

We pray for our most Christian Emperor, that God may subdue to him all the barbarous nations for the sake of our perpetual peace.

This reminds us of the very complex problem of the Roman Empire, providentially established *ad praedicationem Evangelii*, and of its mission to safeguard universal peace, to renew the World Unity and thus to prefigure on earth the world dominion of the transcendental cosmocrator. Needless to say that the Church, at least the Western, would have been terrified at the attempt of any monarch to subjugate in fact the "whole world." Even Charlemagne was almost too heavy a burden for the Church. And yet, the *idea* of such world unification was fondled incessantly by the Church and exercised a permanent spell upon the minds of people. Most suggestive, in this connection, is a ninth-century prayer, probably from St. Gall, where we find the words:

Holy Trinity, extend the Roman Empire to the remotest boundaries of the earth; let its shores be washed by the Ocean that girds its borders... But our princes may so rule in this world that the world shall not rule over them.

The plural "princes" does not seem to refer, at least not here, to the plurarity of the Byzantine Emperors, but to the various kings and princes ruling within the imaginary Roman Empire. Hence, in addition to the multitude of Churches and the *one* Church, to the multitude of nations and the *one* People, we find here the multitude of princes and the *one* and universal Roman Emperor, all of them joined together without effort.

It is obvious that the conception of World Unity has nothing whatever to do with what today would be called reality. In East and West alike, the Roman Empire was not considered a political unit but a supra-political idea, an almost sacramental entity. Therefore it makes no difference whether this Empire be called Roman or Christian. In fact, from the ninth century onward it became the custom, at least outside of the city of Rome itself, to pray for the "Christian Empire" and not for the *Imperium Romanum* and to entreat the Godhead for the victory of the "Christian army," the *exercitus Christianus*, although politically a Christian Empire existed as little as a Christian army. Mythically, however, or eschatologically, these were nevertheless realities. Thus, for all the variety which the physical eye perceives and which reason does not deny, the spiritual eye would always be able to view the Oneness as the truer reality.

The vision of the unity to come proved stronger than the perception of the disparity that was, and general convention made it easy to establish spiritually that which did not exist materially. Examples offer themselves by the hundreds. We need think only of All Souls' Day, that most popular feast introduced by Odilo of Cluny, and its universal unity of souls, hapless and unredeemed, that dwell in a plane between the planes of Heaven and World. Or, we might think of the idea of spiritual kinship, of the *cognatio spiritualis*, which universally comprised the clergy and also the kings. All monks are *fratres*, all bishops are brothers to one another as well as to the pope who, in turn, is recognized as their spiritual father. The Byzantine Emperor would address the Frankish monarch his "spiritual brother" (πνευματικὸς ἀδελφός) and would style minor rulers, such as those of Bulgaria or Armenia, his "spiritual children" (πνευματικὰ τέκνα), a usage replaced or augmented in later times by a likewise hypothetical blood relationship and the mutual application of *consanguineus*, "Cousin." Or, we may think of the universality of spiritual punishment found in the formulae of penalty in thousands of papal, imperial or royal charters, that *sententia terribilis* according to which he that infringes the rights granted in a charter incurs "the wrath of Almighty God and all the saints... that he be condemned to suffer with the devil and his most bloody splendors and with Judas, the traitor, the eternal sea of flames." This indeed is a language comprehensible to both East and West, and it is significant of the general changes of mind that this spiritual condemnation should be abandoned in the thirteenth century and be replaced by the more local but more effective *indignatio imperatoris* (*vel regis*), the emperor's or king's indignation.

There are countless other ways to illustrate the nature of Medieval World Unity. The Byzantine claim to represent the Roman world empire and the proud title of Byzantium's soldiers as "champions of the whole world" (οἰκουμένης πρόμαχοι); similar claims in the West developing by slow degrees in the Ottonian period, when Rome became the ideal capital of the new empire; the effectiveness of the imperial "Rome-idea" as a basis of the Hohenstaufen universalism and of Barbarossa's catchword "One God, one pope, one emperor"; the apostolic Rome-idea, on which the papal *Una sancta* theory throve, and Innocent's motto "One flock and one shepherd"—the implications until the times of Dante are always the same: Medieval World Unity, as conceived in East and West, is primarily eschatologic and its reality is identical with the Lord's real presence in the sacraments.

THE CAROLINGIAN KING
IN THE BIBLE OF SAN PAOLO FUORI LE MURA

NOTHING is problematic about the approximate date of the magnificent Carolingian Bible which for a long time had been deposited in the Roman monastery of San Callisto before it was entrusted to the care of the Benedictine monks of the Abbey of San Paolo fuori le mura. Artistic considerations make it impossible to suggest for that precious manuscript, whose ceremonial throne image is closely related to that of the St. Emmeram *Codex aureus* in Munich, a date other than the latter half of the ninth century. This was a period when the Carolingian school of painting, which Professor Albert M. Friend ingeniously tried to locate in St. Denis, was at its best.[1] Since the Bible is dedicated to a king named "Charles," leaving us the choice between either Charles the Bald or Charles the Fat, the work must have been executed in the sixties, seventies, or eighties of the ninth century.[2] The reduction of that still rather wide chronological margin depends entirely upon the person of the king to whom the Bible was dedicated; that is, whether the king, ceremoniously represented on fol. 1^r (pl. 21, fig. 1), should be identified as Charles II or Charles III. Needless to say, both the Bald and the Fat Charles found their intercessors and champions among modern scholars until finally the law of gravity seems to have prevailed: the scale of Charles the Fat, as might be expected, appeared as the heavier one.[3]

One clue for solving the question has been given by the artist himself. He has covered the disc-like globe in the left hand of the prince with one of those highly artificial and complicated monograms (Fig. A, below, p. 90) which had become the fashion in Greek and Roman

Reprinted, with permission, from *Late Classical and Mediaeval Studies in Honor of Albert Mathias Friend, Jr.*, ed. Kurt Weitzmann *et al.* (Princeton, 1955), 287–300.

[1] Albert M. Friend, "Carolingian Art in the Abbey of St. Denis," *Art Studies*, I (1923), 67–75; "Two Manuscripts of the School of St. Denis," *Speculum*, I (1926), 59–70.

[2] *MGH, Poetae*, III, 257 (No. VI, 1): "Hunc Karolum regem"; also 258, 55: "... rex Karolus ore serenus."

[3] Apart from Mabillon and Montfaucon, who took it for granted that the manuscript should be ascribed to Charles the Bald (cf. Dümmler, in: *Neues Archiv*, IV [1879], 536, § IV; also Pertz, in: *Archiv*, V [1824], 456), this ascription has been favored, for example, by Comte P. Durrieu, "Ingobert, un grand calligraphe du IXe siècle," *Mélanges offerts à Émile Chatelain* (Paris, 1910),

1ff; Friend, *op. cit.*, p. 71, n. 5; A. Boeckler, *Abendländische Miniaturen* (Berlin and Leipzig, 1930), 37ff, though tending towards Charles the Bald, leaves the question undecided. For Charles III, see H. Janitschek, *Die Trierer Ada-Handschrift* (Leipzig, 1889), p. 99, n. 3, who believed that the manuscript was written ca. 881, that is, even before Charles III became King of France (also Traube; below, note 6); F. F. Leitschuh, *Geschichte der Karolingischen Malerei* (Berlin, 1894), p. 87, at least adds a question mark: "auf Befehl des Königs Karl (des Dicken?)." Later, however, Georg Leidinger, *Der Codex Aureus der Bayerischen Staatsbibliothek in München* (Munich, 1921–1925), VI, 123, talks about "das dem Münchener Codex aureus am nächsten stehende Prachtwerk der karolingischen Buchkunst..., die Bibel Karls des Kahlen in San Paolo fuori le mura." See below, notes 5ff.

antiquity and survived throughout the Middle Ages.[4] Unfortunately that monogram is ambiguous too; it may be deciphered as containing a reference to either Charles the Bald or Charles the Fat and to either one of their queens, Richildis or Richardis, and therefore it is of little help. Indirectly, perhaps, it may offer an additional clue, though only after the problem has been attacked and solved or clarified in a different fashion.

The chief argument in favor of Charles III as against his literature-inspiring and art-patronizing uncle has been extracted from a line of the verse inscription filling the purple panel under the throne image and, as usual, interpreting the meaning of the scene. Two verse lines refer to the veiled queen who, followed by another woman, probably a lady-in-waiting, approaches the throne from the king's left (pl. 21, fig. 1). They read:

Nobilis ad laevam coniunx de more venustat,
Qua insignis proles in regnum rite paretur.

Beautifying as usual is the noble consort on the left,
By whom distinguished issue may be rightfully given to the realm.

It is not really the whole couplet that is supposed to decide date and fate of the manuscript. It is a single word, the subjunctive *paretur*, which prompted a group of scholars to assume that the royal couple addressed by the poet was as yet without children. Against Mabillon and Montfaucon this theory was produced, in 1824, by G. H. Pertz.[5] It gradually became the vulgate opinion within the *Monumenta Germaniae Historica*. Reluctantly, and almost withdrawing in a footnote the decision made in the text, even Ludwig Traube[6] accepted the suggestion of Pertz, which through C. Schnaase and H. Janitschek had already started to pervade also the works of art historians.[7] *Monumenta* tradition and art history happily came to cooperate in the works of Percy Ernst Schramm. After a careful investigation of the whole matter and after weighing almost all the pros and almost all the cons, Schramm nevertheless followed the lead of Traube and Pertz chiefly because he felt he had to make a decision *à tout prix*.[8] His authority, safe under the

---

[4] On monograms, see V. Gardthausen, *Das alte Monogramm* (Leipzig, 1924); also s.v. "Monogramm," *RE*, XXXI (1933), 133–143; and for early Christian times, H. Leclercq, s.v. "Monogramme," *DACL*, XI:2 (1934), 2369–2392.

[5] Pertz, *Archiv*, V, 456f.

[6] Traube, in his edition of *MGH, Poetae*, III, 242, § VI: "Cum Pertzio tamen crediderim Karolum III esse quo auctore codex scriptus est, i.e. intra 880 et 88; nam ... de Karolo Calvo propter coniunctivum I, 14 [reference to the poem, *op. cit.*, 257] cogitari nequit." In the footnote (n. 2), however, he shows that he feels rather uncomfortable: "Haud scio an haec, dum Pertz et Schnaase [see next note] ... mihi imponunt, confidentius pronuntiaverim. Nam quod Schnaase ... adfirmat, potest errare; quod autem rex orbus dicitur, contra suadet, ut de Karolo Calvo cogitemus." He then refers to E. Dümmler, *Geschichte des Ostfränkischen Reiches* (Berlin, 1865), I, 589ff, 758, that is, the very places which actually would prove that the codex, after all, refers to Charles the Bald.

[7] Janitschek, *op. cit.*, 99; he overstresses the meaning of *rite paretur* in the sense of legitimacy, for the line merely parallels the *rite gubernat* which refers to the king (line 6); C. Schnaase, *Geschichte der bildenden Künste im Mittelalter*, 2nd ed. (Düsseldorf, 1865–1879), III, 640, n. 2, actually preceded Janitschek, and exercised some influence on Traube.

[8] Schramm, "Umstrittene Kaiserbilder aus dem 9. bis 12. Jahrhundert," *Neues Archiv*, XLVII (1928), 478, makes it perfectly clear that Charles II was as good a candidate as Charles III; but then he decides abruptly for the latter without offering any other reason than the authority of Traube and Pertz. In his admirable work *Die Deutschen Kaiser und Könige in Bildern ihrer Zeit: 751–1152* (Leipzig and Berlin, 1928), 64f, that attribution appears as an established fact, and also the caption of pl. 41 does not betray by a question mark Schramm's former wavering. For a good plate, see A. Boinet, *La miniature Carolingienne* (Paris, 1913), pl. cxxi.

carapace of Traube's authority, practically decided the matter by drawing a conclusion which seemed straightforward and simple enough. Charles the Bald (so the argument runs) had descendants; Charles the Fat had none. The poet had expressed the hope that the queen may give noble princes to the realm. Was it too bold then to conclude that the subjunctive (*paretur*), which in Latin carries also the burden of a Greek optative, referred to Charles the Fat without children and therefore desirous of issue, whereas the same subjunctive precluded the identification with Charles the Bald who had issue and therefore could not reasonably be desirous of more?

Psychology is perhaps not so good a guide in Carolingian family relations, nor are straightforward solutions always the best. Three persons celebrating their birthday on the same day discover that together their ages amount to 99 years: does that necessarily imply that each participant is 33 years old? Straightforwardness with regard to royal offspring has often enough wrought havoc with datings of manuscripts or attributions of poems and other documents. Emperor Henry II was made a saint, not to mention other miracles, for his Joseph-like marriage. Do we have to blush for him, or for the Church which mistakenly canonized him, when we find that a form of Laudes casts a shadow on his chastity by indiscreetly acclaiming his *nobilissima proles*? I do not think so; for the acclamatory formula, which has puzzled scholars of rank, had the meaning of a *potentialis*: had there been offspring, the princes would have been acclaimed as *nobilissima proles*. That is all. The formula does not indicate, nor is it meant to indicate, a historical fact.[9] Things are no better when the historian jubilates because younger kings, *precellentissimi filii reges*, are acclaimed, *was gerade auf Ludwig den Frommen passt*.[10] Unfortunately it is the live essence of liturgical formulae that, in one way or the other, they always "fit the occasion," since that is what they are there for: if offspring there be, the formula will be sung; and if there be none, it will not be sung; and if it were sung nevertheless, no great harm would be done because its presaging solemnity might "fit" an occasion to come. The scholarly criticism concerning the offspring, however, may have grossly misleading effects, which brings us back to unlucky Charles without children. The St. Gall MS 381 contains a number of poems "For the Reception of Kings," that is, poems sung for a king's *adventus* at the gates of the monastery. One of those chants is formed almost verbatim, with some lines transposed, after the "Blessings" of Deut. 28, 3 ff:

> Blessed shalt thou be when thou comest in,
> and blessed shalt thou be when thou goest out.

[9] See, for those Laudes, F. Leitschuh, *Katalog der Handschriften der kgl. Bibliothek zu Bamberg* (Bamberg, 1898), I:1, 147; also *PL*, CXL, 54f, and *Acta Sanctorum*, July, III, 699. To solve the nonexistent mysteries of a *proles regalis* in the Laudes of Conrad II has been tried in vain by W. Wattenbach, in *Neues Archiv*, II (1877), 439. Similar efforts of F. E. Warren, *The Liturgy and Ritual of the Celtic Church* (Oxford, 1881), to solve the problems of some Irish *nobilissima proles* in an *Exultet* have been indicated by Edmund Bishop, *Liturgica Historica* (Oxford, 1918), p. 297, who warns of the "very common pitfalls" of those formulae and adds that it is "very unsafe to attempt strict historical deductions from liturgical formulae, new or old." See also his remarks on p. 13, where he sounds another warning.

[10] See E. Eichmann, "Die Ordines der Kaiserkrönung," *Zeitschrift der Savigny-Stiftung für Rechtsgeschichte*, kan. Abt., II (1912), 10, who overlooked that this was simply the standard formula of the Franco-Roman Laudes (see my *Laudes regiae* [Berkeley and Los Angeles, 1946], pp. 105ff, 109, n. 146); but others were no more fortunate in other respects (see *Laudes*, p. 55, n. 142, or p. 107, n. 140).

> Blessed shalt thou be in the city,
> 　　and blessed shalt thou be in the field.
> Blessed shall be the fruit of thy body, and the fruit of thy ground.
> Blessed shall be thy basket and thy store...

The modern literary critic who maintains that the words *Benedictus fructus ventris tui* "speak against attribution to Charles III whose marriage was without issue, so that to all likelihood the lines referred to Louis the German," borders on blasphemy and leaves us uncertain as to whether to laugh or cry. Those Blessings of unsurpassed simplicity, dignity, and beauty "fit" every occasion, every Charles and Louis and Henry, simply because they are "Blessings," and therefore they are found already in the *Liber responsalis* as a fitting form for the reception of any and every king, be he even a king without a fruit of his body or a basket or a store.[11] The literary critic did not fare better with another *susceptaculum* composed of four lines from Hosea 12, 5f and a burden *Salve proles regum invictissimorum* intercalated after every line and serving also as an opening. We are told that the *proles* must refer to children of a ruling king, which allegedly would "fit" only the sons of Louis the German, among them Charles III, and only before August 28, 876, when Louis the German died. Why sons should stop being "offspring of most unconquered kings" after the death of their father is a mystery of literary criticism which none will be desirous of penetrating; but the greeting *salve proles regum* fitted every ruling Carolingian king of the ninth century, since there were none who had not kings as fathers and grandfathers.[12] It is a futile occupation to try to extract allusions where there are none, just as futile as the effort to determine the month or season of the year of a king's reception when a poem says: "When thou comest, the flowers bloom and the pastures turn green again."[13] Nor should we be startled when we find that a number of

---

[11] W. Bulst, "Susceptacula regum," *Corona Quernea: Festgabe Karl Strecker* (Schriften des Reichsinstituts für ältere deutsche Geschichtskunde, VI; Leipzig, 1941), 105f. It is the merit of Dr. Bulst to have excavated the technical term *susceptacula* and to have collected the St. Gall chants sung at the reception of kings; but his ascriptions, practically throughout, are doubtful and often untenable. See, for the *Benedictus tu in civitate etc.*, the responsories *In susceptione regum* of the *Liber responsalis; PL*, LXXVIII, 828C.

[12] Bulst, *op. cit.*, 103ff. Dr. Bulst assumes that, because in the Laudes the acclamation of the *proles regalis* refers to the younger princes, *proles* is always used, so to speak, in view of future generations and not of past. This, however, is wrong. A mature emperor or king could still be *proles regalis*. Instead of long arguments, it suffices to quote Walahfrid Strabo for a reception of Charles the Bald:

> Salve *regum sancta proles*
> Care Christo Carole.

See *MGH, Poetae*, II, 406, No. 64. In another poem of that kind, Charles the Bald is greeted on his entry into Metz:

> Carolus praeclarus *Progenie sancta*
> Quem Deus elegit   Regere gentes.

Cf. A. Prost, "Caractère et signification de quatre pièces liturgiques composées à Metz," *Mémoires de la société*

nationale des antiquaires de France, XXXVII (1876), 209f. There was no panegyric poetry which did not stress the γένος of the praised, and the pattern as established by Simonides and Pindar, poured into rules by Aphthonius and Menander, and transmitted, for example, by Themistius and Himerius to the East, and by Claudian and others to the West (see, for the latter, L. B. Struthers, "The Rhetorical Structure of the Encomia of Claudius Claudianus," *Harvard Studies in Classical Philology*, XXX [1919], 49–88), was of course received by the Carolingian poets and preachers. See, for example, Hincmar's allocution to Charles the Bald at the latter's coronation in Metz (869) which, though for special reasons, is a long praise of Charles' ancestry; see *MGH, Capitularia*, II, 340, 28ff, No. 276; also Friend, "Two manuscripts," p. 67, and below, n. 47. See also E. R. Curtius, *Europäische Literatur und lateinisches Mittelalter* (Bern, 1948), 164, for the panegyric technique (*formula laudis*) in the Middle Ages.

[13] In Egypt, to be sure, the Nile rises on that occasion; see my remarks on that *congaudere* of nature in "Kaiser Friedrich II. und das Königsbild des Hellenismus," p. 192, nos. 69–70. For the imperial "Spring" metaphor, it is sufficient to quote Horace, *Carmina*, IV, 5, 6ff:

> Instar veris enim voltus ubi tuus
> Adfulsit populo, gratior it dies
> Et soles melius nitent.

charters of Charles III contain prayer-like formulae for the ruler's *proles*: it has been recognized long ago that as historical evidence for or against descendants those formulae are completely worthless.[14]

The question arises whether the lines under the ceremonial throne image of "King Charles" in the Bible of S. Paolo likewise are without value. After all, to express the hope that a queen may give "distinguished descendants" to her kingdom was a very natural expectation because, once more, that was what a queen was there for, whether her name be Hermintrude or Richildis or Richardis. But let alone the possibility that a generality was expressed, does that wish, even when couched in the subjunctive *paretur*, necessarily imply that the queen has never before borne children at all? For one thing, the queen, after having given birth to several children, may have been expectant again when the inscription was composed. The subjunctive, all by itself, would not exclude that possibility. Or else, her children may have died or been crippled or otherwise incapacitated. Why, then, should it not be desirable that the queen give birth to other and perhaps more fortunate children? But even if we wink at the experts and assume that the queen of "King Charles" was meant to be as yet without offspring, it would demand a good portion of hard-boiled credulity to accept any proposition which ruled out the possibility that the verse might yet refer to a queen, or to two queens, married to Charles the Bald.[15]

Charles II was married twice. His first consort Hermintrude died October 6, 869. She had given birth to many children, to at least four sons, so that (to use the words of a bishop) "the loyal subjects were to be congratulated for having the best hopes" for a secured succession to the throne.[16] However, during the last three or four years of Hermintrude's life the succession came to rest on one son alone, on Louis, a stammerer, whom (according to the same bishop) God had destined "to undergo suffering as all the faithful know to their sorrow," and for whom Charles the Bald showed little sympathy.[17] It is true, a brother of Louis, Karloman, was alive; but that prince had been given up to religious life; he was abbot of St. Médard and did not count as a possible successor to the throne, although on a later occasion he made two unfortunate and abortive efforts to seize power, whereupon he was blinded by his father. Two other sons of Queen Hermintrude died within a year. Lothair, abbot of St. Germain, who had always been in ill health, died in 865. And Charles, King of Aquitaine, had an accident while hunting, and died on September 29, 866.[18] This prince was already a dying man when Charles the Bald, after having been married to Hermintrude for 24 years, asked the Frankish bishops assembled in Soissons to grant his consort a solemn coronation and unction.[19]

[14] See Paul Kehr, in his Introduction of *MGH, Diplomata Karoli Tertii*, p. xl: "Als historische Zeugnisse sind diese formelhaften Bestimmungen ... ohne Bedeutung."

[15] It must be admitted that, for example, Leidinger or Schramm (above, notes 3, 8) did not rule out entirely another solution as did Pertz and others.

[16] See the *Adlocutio duorum episcoporum* at the consecration of Queen Hermintrude, in 866; *MGH, Capitularia*, II, 453, 37, No. 301: "... in quorum nobilitate ... fideles illius [regis] spem maximam se habere sunt gratulati."

[17] *Ibid.*, p. 454, 1: "... aliquibus [filiis scil. Hludowico et Karolo Aquitaniae] ... suo iudicio talem passionem permisit incurrere, sicut fideles illius agnoscunter dolore." See also Dümmler, *Ostfr. Reich*, I:2, 483, 589f.

[18] Dümmler, *Ostfr. Reich*, I:2, 590, n. 80, for Lothair; 588ff and 759ff, for Karloman; 543f, for the accident of Charles of Aquitaine.

[19] *Annales Bertiniani, ad a.* 866, ed. Waitz (*Script. rer. German.*, 1883), 82f.

Separate coronations of princesses were not a very old custom in the Carolingian house; but by 866 they were not unusual either. Charles the Bald himself had ordered his daughter Judith crowned, in 856, before she was married to King Eathelwulf of East Anglia. Thereafter, in 862 and 865 respectively, Lothair II had his two queens crowned.[20] Hence, Charles the Bald seems to have followed simply the new custom of which he himself had been the initiator by the coronation of Judith, when after a long marriage he finally demanded a solemn consecration for his consort Hermintrude. But the newly established custom was not the chief reason for the solemnity which took place on August 25, 866, in Soissons. In an allocution which preceded the coronation proper, two bishops put forth that the Frankish kingdom rested on the succession of princes of the blood and that the house of Charles II had been met by various afflictions during the last year, and finally they said quite bluntly: "Therefore the king demands that there be extended the episcopal blessing to his wife that the Lord may deign to give him through her that issue from which the holy Church may have solace and the realm the necessary defense... if God so wills and cooperates." The bishops concluded their address to the people by referring to Abraham and Sarah who in far more advanced years than the king and queen were nevertheless blessed with a son, Isaac, and they asserted that the prayers of priests and their supplications might make the mercy of God inclined to cooperate and to connive at the king's demands.[21]

In other words, Charles the Bald hoped that the consecration and unction of his queen might have the effects of a *Fruchtbarkeitszauber*. To attribute extra-sacramental powers to a sacramental act was, of course, nothing unusual. Baptism not only freed man from the consequences of the original sin, but was believed also to have supranatural healing powers as experienced, according to the legends, by Constantine the Great. To the consecration of the Byzantine emperor the Patriarch of Antioch, Theodore Balsamon, ascribed the same effects as to baptism, that is, to do away with all the crimes and sins of the emperor's former life.[22] That idea was still favored in fourteenth-century France when Jean Golein, a clerk in the surroundings of Charles V, declared that the king by his anointment was "telement nettoié de ses pechiez come celui qui entre nouvellement en religion esprouvée: que aussi comme ou baptesme les pechiez sont pardonnez...."[23] And even in Elizabethan England the Crown jurists held that the descent of the Crown "wipes away imperfections."[24] The same was true with regard to holy orders;[25] and also concerning the sacrament of marriage a decretal of Pope Alexander III expounded:

[20] For the coronation of Judith, see Schramm, "Ordines-Studien II," *Archiv für Urkundenforschung*, XV (1938), 8ff, and, for the coronations of other queens, 11, n. 5; see also his *Der König von Frankreich* (Weimar, 1939), I, 21ff.

[21] *MGH, Capitularia*, II, 453f, esp. 454, 3ff: "Propterea petit benedictionem episcopalem super uxorem suam venire, ut talem sobolem ei Dominus de illa dignetur donare, unde sancta ecclesia solacium et regnum necessariam defensionem ... annuente et cooperante Domino possit habere." That Hermintrude's unction was supposed to have the effects of a fertility charm has, of course, been noticed before; see Schramm, *König von Frankreich*, I, 24f.

[22] *PG*, CXXXVII, 1156; Marc Bloch, *Les rois thaumaturges* (Strasbourg, 1924), 198, 476.

[23] Bloch, *op. cit.*, 483.

[24] Edmund Plowden, *Commentaries or Reports* (London, 1816), 238; the same idea was repeated by Sir Edward Coke, Sir Francis Bacon, Sir William Blackstone, and other English Jurists.

[25] Bloch, *op. cit.*, 483, n. 2, quotes Bernard of Clairvaux saying that entering into a monastic order *secundum baptisma nuncupetur* (*PL*, CLXXXII, 889).

"Such is the power of matrimony that those born out of wedlock become legitimate after matrimony has been entered on."[26] It is therefore not surprising to find that Charles the Bald ascribed to the touching with chrism the power to restore fertility to his aging queen.

The decisive thing here, however, is that Queen Hermintrude's coronation was staged, *expressis verbis*, for the purpose of calling down on her the blessings of heaven for further descendants. It is, therefore, difficult to understand why the supplication of the dedicatory poem in the Bible of S. Paolo—"by whom there be given progeny"—should have "fitted" only Charles III *because* he had no children, and not Charles the Bald *although* he had children.[27]

These considerations would allow the poem to be written, and the Bible to be executed, around 866 when everyone knew that the king was hoping for more sons. Since, however, Queen Hermintrude died on October 6, 869, it would seem safe to set the date of the Bible after 866 and before 869. "Before 869" is actually the date suggested by Professor Friend, though for different reasons.[28] However, there yet remains another, and preferable, possibility of linking the manuscript to Charles the Bald.

The celestial blessings which Charles II had hoped for failed to materialize. When Queen Hermintrude died, the king waited only a few months to get remarried. Already on January 22, 870, Charles' marriage with his former mistress, Richildis, sister of the Count of Provence, was solemnized.[29] Apart from other reasons, the haste of his second marriage may be explained also by the king's desire to secure the succession to the throne. However, Charles' second marriage remained without issue. In 875, Queen Richildis had a miscarriage. In 876, she was pregnant again; but the son to whom she gave birth on the road when fleeing from Heristal, after the defeat of Charles near Andernach at the hands of his German nephew, died after a few months.[30] That is to say, Charles the Bald actually did remain without descendants from his second queen. At long last, the subjunctive *paretur* suggesting a marriage without issue seems justified and may nevertheless refer to Charles the Bald, and not to the childless Charles III. Everything "fits," and with regard to Queen Richildis it may be said: *Nihil obstat.*

There is more to all that than a joke and a hypothesis. A charter of Charles the Bald has been preserved which is quite relevant, but which hitherto has been overlooked by those trying to date and locate the Bible of S. Paolo. This oversight is pardonable. The editor of the document dated it 846—wrongly, to be sure, because Queen Richildis is mentioned. The charter therefore must fall after 870. Further, Charles is called king, and not emperor, and therefore it must fall between 870 and 875. Actually, the charter is now competently dated May 12, 871.[31] At that time, Charles made a grant to Notre

---

[26] "Tanta est vis matrimonii, ut qui antea sunt geniti, post contractum matrimonium legitimi habeantur." Cf. c. 6 X, 4, 17; E. Friedberg, *Corpus iuris canonici* (Leipzig, 1881), II, 712.

[27] Traube (above, note 6), however, when quoting Dümmler, apparently recognized that the "although" deserved to be considered.

[28] Friend, "Carolingian Art," p. 71, followed Durrieu too closely when assuming that the monogram contained the cipher of Hermintrude; see below, note 36.

[29] *Annales Bertiniani, ad a.* 870, ed. Waitz, p. 108; Dümmler, *Ostfr. Reich*, I.2, 758f.

[30] *Ann. Bert., ad a.* 875 ("aborsu filium peperit"), and *ad a.* 876 ("et fugiens, subsequenti nocte galli cantu in via peperit filium"); Waitz, pp. 126, 132f.

[31] The charter, edited by Jules Tardif, *Monuments historiques* (Paris, 1866), 98f, No. 152, was dated by him May 12, 846. The second volume of the great edition of charters of Charles the Bald by M. Georges Tessier, *Recueil des actes de Charles II le Chauve, roi de France*, I:840–860

Fig. 1. Rome, San Paolo f.l.m. Bible, fol. 1ʳ: Charles the Bald (reduced).

Fig. 2. Rome, San Paolo f.l.m. Bible, fol. 185ᵛ: King Solomon (reduced).

Fig. 3. Paris, Bibl. Nat. MS lat. 1141, fol. 2ᵛ: Coronation of a Frankish Prince (reduced).

Pl. 24   THE ARCHER IN THE RUTHWELL CROSS

Fig. 1. Ruthwell Cross, uppermost section: Archer.

Fig. 2. London, Brit. Mus. Cotton MS Claudius B. IV, fol. 36ᵛ: Ishmael with Hagar and his Egyptian Wife.

Dame of Paris in which he placed the abbey of St.-Éloi under the jurisdiction of the bishop of Paris. When making that grant, the king expressed the hope that a donation to the cathedral of *Maria Genetrix* might bring profit to king and queen from the Virgin. And, says the text, to gratify the bishop's petition pleases the king all the more because the *Virgo Genetrix*, for the sake of the whole Christian people, might in return grant him and the queen descendants. Actually, the thought of royal descendants pervades the entire document, which contains also a clause stipulating that the canons of Notre Dame as well as the monks of St.-Éloi were held to celebrate annually not only the ordinary anniversaries of Louis the Pious and Empress Judith, the king's parents, but also the king's birthday and day of consecration, the birthday of Queen Richildis, and the wedding anniversary of the royal couple. Those were stipulations which had become customary in Charles the Bald's later years.[32] In addition, however, there follows once more a reference to the expected royal progeny, as the charter adds: "Moreover, the present and future bishops shall celebrate with the continuous assiduity of prayers and masses, together with all the clergy under their authority, the birth of our offspring if it should come to pass that such be granted by the prolific Virgin; and a refection shall be held with the greatest care in both congregations on the day of the birth of our offspring if, as we said, such shall have been granted by the Mother of God."[33]

It is evident that the thought of additional descendants occupied the mind of Charles the Bald not only after 866 when he lost an able-bodied son by accident and had Queen Hermintrude crowned for the clearly defined purpose of securing more children, but also after his second marriage when he was possessed by the same idea. The charter for Notre Dame shows that the king's hopes and wishes had been transferred to his new queen. And while in 866 Charles the Bald had placed his hopes in a sacramental action and in the supplications of the priests, he now turned to the *fecunda Virgo Genetrix* herself who, in so many respects, had taken over the functions of the Roman goddess *Fecunditas*.

If we take all those dispositions of Charles the Bald into consideration, it becomes almost incomprehensible that, on account of the disputed verse line, the attribution of the S. Paolo Bible to Charles the Bald could ever have been ruled out highhandedly and straightforwardly because that king had children and Charles III had none. The attribution to Charles the Bald, however, eliminates also other acknowledged difficulties:

(Paris, 1943), was not yet available to me so that I still have to rely on the edition of Tardif. The charter, however, which belongs to the small group of documents carrying the Byzantine *legimus* in red ink, has been dealt with in another connection by M. Tessier, "Diplôme de Charles le Chauve pour Saint-Philibert de Tournus," *Bibliothèque de l'École des Chartes*, XCIII (1932), 201, where the correct date is given. See also Jusselin, in *Le Moyen Âge*, XXXIX (1929), 231.

[32] The charter is badly mutilated, but its contents are clear. The bishop of Paris, petitioning the king, "deprecatus est ut ob nostrae mercedis coniugisque reginae ... [Vir]ginis intemeratae genitricis Mariae emolumentum" the abbey be placed under the bishop of Paris. "Cuius petitionibus eo cessimus libentius quo nostrae utilitati profuturum perspeximus amplius, et ob domini nostri Jhesu Christi suaeque virginis [matris hon]orem ... et utilis ... [propter?] nobis in salutem populi Christiani a genitrice virgine prolis attributionem...." The stipulations concerning the anniversaries will be discussed in my forthcoming study, long overdue, on "Charles the Bald and the *Natales Caesarum*."

[33] The king orders the bishop to celebrate "nativitatem praeterea amabilimae coniugis nostrae, Richildis reginae, kalendis Augustis, et copulam secundum Dei voluntatem nostrae coniunctionis, insuper et ortum prolis nostrae, si a fecunda virgine impetrando data fuerit, sub continua orationum missarumque assiduitate cum omni clero sibi commisso, praesens futurusque antistes celebret, et refectio in utraque congregatione, in die ortus prolis nostrae, si, ut diximus, a genitrice Dei data fuerit, studiosissime peragatur."

first, how to explain the improbable fact that a French scriptorium which evidently was closely attached to the West-Frankish dynasty should have donated one of its most precious manuscripts to an Eastern Carolingian ruler who certainly was not held in high esteem;[34] and second, how to ignore the book's dedication to a "king," whereas Charles III's relations to France fell in the period when he was emperor.[35] Even though inaccuracies with regard to the title might be taken into account if everything else pointed in the other direction, there is nevertheless no reason for simply brushing aside a piece of perfectly sound evidence.

One point is as yet in need of clarification: was the queen approaching the throne Charles II's first consort Hermintrude, or was she Richildis, the second queen, whom he married in 870? Here the monogram on the orb may be of some help (Fig. A). Schramm thought of deciphering the monogram as *Christe, conserva Karolum et Richardim* or something to that effect; he admitted, however, that the weird agglomeration of characters could be read just as well *et Richildim*, whereas it seemed more difficult to extricate the letters for *et Hermintrudim* from the intricate design.[36] That, if nothing else, may settle this question of Hermintrude versus Richildis. It will probably be safe to identify the veiled princess in the miniature with Queen Richildis.[37]

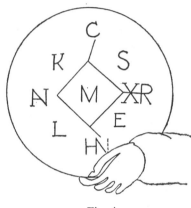

Fig. A

There are, however, some good additional reasons for that ascription. Professor Schramm, keen observer that he is, has stressed most emphatically the uniqueness of a queen's representation in a Carolingian painting.[38] Pictures of consorts are indeed very rare in Carolingian art. Their names are occasionally mentioned on coins; there is a medaillion picture of the Empress Judith on the front page of Hrabanus Maurus' commentary on the Book of Judith; and there exists—if genuine—a gem displaying a female head with the inscription RICHILDE.[39] But in a highly ceremonious picture, showing the king in full regalia seated on his throne, the simultaneous representation of a royal consort, even in the reduced size in which she appears in the S. Paolo Bible, was unique in that period. Even in later times, in the works of Ottonian art when queens were re-

[34] Schramm, "Umstrittene Kaiserbilder," 478, as well as in *Die deutschen Kaiser und Könige etc.*, 64f, takes it as an effluence of Charles III's imperial dignity and his reunion of the empire of Charlemagne "that the so-called School of Corbie executed for him, the scion of the Eastern Frankish line, a Bible which represents the apex of book illumination of that generation." The happiness of that reunion of the empire may have been less great in France than in the East Frankish parts of the empire.

[35] This fact has been hushed up to make the attribution to Charles III possible. Janitschek and Traube, however, were ready to date the Bible "between 880 and 888," that is, even before Charles III began to rule over France; see above, notes 3 and 6.

[36] Schramm, "Umstrittene Kaiserbilder," 479f, is

probably correct against Pertz, *Archiv*, V, 454ff, and other suggestions. Without being an expert in the deciphering of monograms, I too find it difficult to reconstruct the name *Hermintrudis*. The flatness of the globe which appears more like a disc, is, however, not necessarily a sign of degeneration; it agrees with Byzantine and Near Eastern art where angels are not rarely seen holding a disc-globe with the monogram of Christ or the cross or other symbols.

[37] It seems devious to me to try to identify the second lady, behind Richildis, as Charles II's first queen Hermintrude.

[38] Schramm, *Deutsche Könige und Kaiser*, 65.

[39] Schramm, *op. cit.*, 51, for Angilberga; pl. 16, for Empress Judith; fig. 37a, for the gem of Richildis.

presented more often, a devotional pattern prevailed depicting the queen crouching with the king at the feet of Christ or being crowned by Christ;[40] but also the Ottonian throne images do not seem to take cognizance of queens at all. Considering, therefore, the quite extraordinary display of a queen in the Bible of S. Paolo and her explicit mention in the explanatory verse, we are bound to think of some special occasion for which the manuscript may have been executed; and it will not appear farfetched if we now conclude that the Bible of S. Paolo was executed on the occasion of Charles the Bald's marriage to Richildis.

This hypothesis would justify the presence of the queen in the ceremonious throne image. It may even explain the fact that the queen makes her appearance veiled, and not crowned. Also the verse inscription expressing the hope that the newly wedded queen may give birth legitimately to noble descendants would find a very natural explanation. It is true, a difficulty remains: Queen Hermintrude died on October 6, 869, and Charles' marriage to Richildis took place on January 22, 870. How could the voluminous Bible of S. Paolo have been written and illustrated within less than four months? To begin with, it would be reasonable to argue that the Bible was not dedicated on the very day when the wedding was celebrated, but on some other suitable occasion in the course of the wedding year. Even the possibility should not be ruled out completely that the Bible may have been made for the wedding anniversary, since Charles the Bald, contrary to all Western custom, had ordered the liturgical celebration of his wedding anniversaries in various monasteries and cathedrals. At St. Denis this custom can be traced as far back as 862; the observance of the anniversary of his marriage to Queen Richildis was ordered by the king for St. Stephen's of Lyon in 870, and in the following year for Notre Dame of Paris and the abbey of St.-Éloi.[41] However, the Bible manuscript itself furnishes us with some clues. It has been observed that all the full-page miniatures as well as a great number of pages containing large initials or incipits have been subsequently pasted into the Bible; that the images betray the hands of several artists; and that the illustrations were executed hastily (some of the ornamental borders remained unfinished, and the purple panels inserted for inscription in gold lettering remained sometimes vacant).[42] In other words, to a Bible text which was ready in writing, the images were added with some speed and for some special purpose. It can hardly be doubted that this special purpose should be sought somehow in connection with the king's second marriage in 870.

Every bit of evidence, in addition to reason and probability, therefore compels us to abandon Pertz' quite arbitrary attribution of the manuscript to Charles the Fat, an attribution hinging upon a subjunctive wrongly related, on a disregard of the title

[40] *Ibid.*, pls. 65, 66, 71b, 81, etc.

[41] See Tardif, *Monuments* (above, note 31), p. 118, No. 186, for St. Denis; Bouquet, *Recueil des historiens des Gaules et de la France*, VIII, 622, No. 223, for Lyons; and above, note 33, for Paris and St.-Éloi.

[42] During a recent visit to Rome, I had occasion to inspect the S. Paolo Bible. I am greatly indebted to Dom Ambrosius Wirth for admitting me to the Library, and to Dom Ildefonso Tassi, the learned librarian of S. Paolo, for discussing with me the many problems of the Codex and for calling my attention to the observations summarized in the text. All detailed evidence must be left to the future editor of the manuscript.

"king," and on some mysterious devotion of a French monastery to its unpleasant and gauche East-Frankish lord. As a wedding gift for Charles III the manuscript cannot be taken into account. Charles the Fat was married in 862, when no French scriptorium would have dreamed of honoring that unknown prince. And whether Charles III was really so desirous of having an offspring, as has been rashly assumed, may reasonably be doubted. Archbishop Hincmar of Reims may have known more than we know today about Charles III's wishes when he reported that, in 873, the young king, in a fit, exclaimed that he did not touch his wife (*quia uxorem suam carnali commercio non contingeret*);[43] and at a later time, in 887, so we are told, Charles declared publicly that never during his long married life had he had intercourse with Queen Richardis (*publice protestatur numquam se carnali coitu cum ea miscuisse*).[44] True or not, it was, as numerous legends concerning Richardis show,[45] public gossip that something was wrong with this king's married life. Therefore, it would have been exceedingly tactless to remark on his expected descendants, as it would have been an incomprehensible *faux pas* to display, contrary to all tradition, the unfortunate Empress Richardis in a throne image of Charles III. That, it would seem, finishes off Pertz' unhappy suggestion and severs, once and for all, any connection of Charles the Fat with the Bible of S. Paolo.

Being restored to Charles the Bald, the Bible of S. Paolo returns again to its proper surroundings and to the place to which it belongs and from which it should never have been removed: to the great number of precious manuscripts which were produced in the surroundings of Charles the Bald, and probably commissioned by him, in the sixties and seventies of the ninth century. But do we know anything about the scriptorium in which that extravagant Bible could possibly have originated? Beyond guesswork nothing certain can be said. There is, however, some little observation which, for what it is worth, should not be passed unmentioned.

In addition to the throne image of Charles the Bald, the Bible of S. Paolo contains yet a second throne image, that of King Solomon (pl. 22, fig. 2). The King of Wisdom, throned like his Frankish successors under a magnificent canopy, is about to decide the case of the two harlots and to pronounce his famous judgment. He is represented as a mature man, the face framed by a full dark beard. In the upper register King Solomon is seen once more, this time on the way to Gihon, his coronation place. Riding a white mule, he is preceded by Nathan the Prophet and Zadoc the priest. Again, as in the central picture, Solomon is bearded; and he is dressed in a long gown which reaches down to his ankles even while sitting on his mount. Finally, in the upper right corner we recognize Solomon's anointing at the hands of Zadoc while Nathan assists on his right side. This

[43] *Annales Bertiniani, ad a.* 873, ed. Waitz, p. 122.

[44] Regino of Prüm, *Chronicon, ad a.* 887, ed. Kurze (*Script. rer. german.*; 1890), p. 127. According to that chronicle, Richardis herself is supposed to have made a statement to the effect that she "ab omni virili commixtione se inmunem esse profitetur." She went, in 887, to a monastery to become a nun (see next note).

[45] Already the account of Hincmar (i.e., the *Ann. Bertin.*), and even more so that of Regino of Prüm, have

novelistic features and come close to the pattern of hagiographic legends. For the later legends concerning the virginal *sancta Richardis imperatrix*, see Dümmler, *Ostfränkisches Reich*, II, 285f, esp. nos. 70–73. Whatever the truth may be, there is no doubt but that ever since 873 some grave disturbances of Charles III's married life were generally known and common talk. The only really startling thing is that scholars of highest rank should have been taken in by Pertz' superficial and rash conclusion.

type of coronation scene—the king between two haloed priests or saints—was anything but conventional in Carolingian art. We have to descend probably to the Bamberg Apocalypse, where Otto III is crowned by Saints Peter and Paul, before we encounter once more this variation of an otherwise well-known pattern.[46] Nevertheless, Carolingian art did produce, perhaps only a year or two earlier than the anointment of Solomon, a scene of that kind. The frontispiece of the unfinished sacramentary, cod. lat. 1141 of the Bibliothèque Nationale (pl. 23, fig. 3), shows the coronation "by the Hand of God" of a haloed prince in Frankish garment, flanked by two likewise haloed bishops. Professor Friend has identified the figures as King Clovis attended by St. Remi and St. Arnulf of Metz; but more recently, the two bishops have been disclosed to represent Popes Gelasius and Gregory the Great, whose Sacramentaries were authoritative in the Frankish Empire, whereas the extremely youthful king has been called Charlemagne.[47] What attracts our attention, however, is not so much the whole coronation scene and its meaning as the young *coronandus* of MS 1141. For apparently under his influence, King Solomon, the *coronandus* of the S. Paolo Bible (pl. 22, fig. 2), has completely changed his appearance. Instead of being bearded, as he was before, he is beardless, and instead of wearing a long gown reaching down to the ankles he wears a short tunic which leaves his feet in high boots and his knees visible. In short, Solomon at his coronation has been replaced by another personage: instead of a Jewish king there appears, all of a sudden, a youthful beardless "Clovis" in Frankish attire who resembles the haloed prince of the unfinished Metz sacramentary as a brother (pls. 22–23, figs. 2, 3).[48] How that picture slipped into the Solomon scenes will probably never be known. It is an "iconographic interpolation" caused perhaps by the fact that the artist, for depicting the coronation scene, turned to MS 1141 for a model, but then failed to assimilate the central figure of his model to the Solomon type of the Biblical image.

The inferences of this observation might be rather far-reaching. MS 1141 could not easily have left the scriptorium in which it originated, since it was as yet unfinished; nor could it, for that very reason, have been widely known in 870 or 871 when the S. Paolo Bible was worked on. Would that imply that the painter of the "interpolated prince" worked in the same scriptorium in which the as yet unfinished MS 1141 was deposited

[46] Schramm, *Die deutschen Könige und Kaiser*, pl. 78, cf. pl. 83.

[47] Friend, "Two Manuscripts," 66ff (cf. Schramm, *op. cit.*, 58), identified the three figures on the basis of Hincmar's address at the Lotharingian coronation of Charles the Bald, in 869; see *MGH, Capitularia*, II, 340, 22ff (see above, note 12). New findings, however, bring new solutions. Professor André Grabar called my attention to the study of J. Croquison, "Le 'Sacramentaire Charlemagne'," *Cahiers archéologiques*, VI (1952), 55–70 (with pls. XVI–XVIII), who has shown—convincingly, as I believe—that the two bishops were meant to be Pope Gelasius (carrying the closed book) and Pope Gregory the Great (carrying the open book), the two representatives of the liturgy valid in the Frankish Empire. The identification of the youth with Charlemagne, so treacherously obvious from the point of view of liturgical history,

seems to me less satisfactory: a ruler who died at the age of 72 would not easily be represented, half a century or more after his death, in the extremely youthful age displayed by the central figure, which is lacking all the familiar features of Charlemagne known from other representations. The possibilities to identify the young prince more convincingly are not yet exhausted. See, e.g., below, note 49.

[48] I have also inspected MS 1141, hoping to find that the color scheme of its representation of Solomon, compared with the same in the Bible of S. Paolo, might provide some additional clues. The agreements, however, are too general to allow any conclusions—mantle: red with gold dots; boots: blue; trousers: red; tunic: yellow with light violet (MS 1141) or light violet and lacking the yellow (S. Paolo MS).

or waiting to be finished?[49] And was the scriptorium of MS 1141, as Professor Friend suggests, the abbey of St. Denis? And if that were correct, would then the slip of the painter of the S. Paolo Bible, owing to the interrelations with MS 1141, draw all the other manuscripts of the so-called "School of Corbie" to the scriptorium in which MS 1141 was executed, presumably St. Denis?

The present author can only pose, not answer, those questions. For to solve those problems would be the task not of the historian but of the art historian, which the author of this contribution in honor of Bert Friend is not.

[49] Friend, "Two Mss," naturally dated MS 1141 ca. 869–870, since he connected it with Charles' coronation at Metz, which would bring the Sacramentary and the Bible of S. Paolo chronologically very close together. M. Croquison (above, note 47) makes no indication as to the date, though he too thinks of Charles the Bald "who may have ordered it for the liturgical service in his palace chapel." Professor E. A. Lowe (to him as well as to Professor Kurt Weitzmann I am greatly indebted for stimulating advice and criticism) kindly informed me that, while accepting 870–871 as the date of the Bible of S. Paolo, he would be inclined to attribute to MS 1141 a date of 10 to 20 years earlier. It would seem good to recall that not only Charlemagne was interested in liturgical matters, but that this was true also of Charles the Bald. We know, e.g., that Charles the Bald occasionally ordered to celebrate before him the old Gallican mass, just as he had the liturgies of Jerusalem and Constantinople celebrated in his presence, but that he decided for the Roman mass: "sed nos sequendam ducimus Romanam Ecclesiam in missarum celebratione." Cf. Mabillon, *De liturgia gallicana libri tres*, praef., c. 3, in *PL*, LXXII, 103–104. Would that allow us perhaps to identify the young prince between the two representatives of the ancient and the modern liturgies with Charles the Bald?

THE ARCHER IN THE RUTHWELL CROSS

Two HIGHLY suggestive studies were devoted some time ago to the Ruthwell Cross, a monument of probably the seventh or eighth century, near the English-Scottish border, which combines classical elements with others of Anglian or Celtic origin. One study was written by the late Professor Saxl,[1] and the others one by Professor Meyer Schapiro.[2] They were published almost simultaneously, in Spring 1945, although owing to the contingencies of wartime communications it so happened that the authors were barely informed of each other's doings.[3] Whereas Professor Saxl stressed the Mediterranean origin of the iconographic items and of some stylistic elements of the representations sculptured in the Cross and its shaft, Professor Schapiro broadly discussed the religious meaning of the reliefs. The latter's interpretation of the Cross, which he came to regard as a landmark of Insular asceticism reflecting ideals of the Egyptian desert fathers, appears particularly persuasive. In fact, most of the subjects represented in the Cross fall in with the idea of the solitary life of the hermits in the deserts of Egypt or Syria: the Lord's Temptation and his adoration by the beasts of the desert; St. John the Baptist; the hermits Paul and Anthony; St. Mary Magdalen, who was believed to be a recluse; the Flight into Egypt—those are the outstanding themes alluding to the life in the desert.

There is, however, one figure to which neither Saxl nor Schapiro paid much attention; that is, the kneeling archer (pl. 24, fig. 1) in the upper part of the Cross. In the caption of figure 1 (no. 9) of his article, Schapiro introduced him as "Archer Aiming at Bird," referring thereby to the bird, apparently an eagle, carved in the uppermost stone of the Cross.[4] Whether the archer really "aims" at the bird, may be open to doubts; but as a working hypothesis we may accept the suggestion. The symbolism of the eagle in Christian art and lore opens the field widely to speculation.[5] Saxl held that "the eagle at the summit must undoubtedly be interpreted as a symbol of the Ascension,"[6] but he did not combine the archer with the bird. Instead, the archer reminded him of Psalm 90, 6, "the arrow that flieth by day," and of two archers in the representation of Psalm 90 in the Utrecht Psalter who point their weapons at Christ shown as he treads lion and adder

Reprinted, with permission, from *The Art Bulletin*, XLII (1960), 57–59.

[1] F. Saxl, "The Ruthwell Cross," *Journal of the Warburg and Courtauld Institutes*, VI (1943), 1–19.

[2] Meyer Schapiro, "The Religious Meaning of the Ruthwell Cross," *Art Bulletin*, XXVI (1944), 232–245.

[3] M. Schapiro, 233, n. 4, suggests, however, that at least he was informed about Saxl's forthcoming article.

[4] Schapiro (plate facing p. 232) calls attention to the fact that the upper part of the Cross has been reversed. Both archer and bird are better recognizable in Saxl's study, pl. 4, b and d. For the drawing of that section of the Cross (pl. 24, fig. 1) I am greatly obliged to Miss Anna C. Esmeijer, in Princeton.

[5] See T. Schneider, art. "Adler," *Reallexikon für Antike und Christentum*, I, cols. 91ff.

[6] F. Saxl, *op. cit.*, 6.

under his feet.[7] Saxl's reference to that Psalm is easily explained by the fact that Christ is represented in the central section of the Cross standing on adder and lion, which, however, do not represent the conquered fiend but the desert animals adoring the Lord. Schapiro referred to the figure of the archer in a footnote only. He believed that the archer and the bird did not have a "definite religious sense," and explained the scene as "one of the oldest mediaeval examples of secular imagery at a terminal point of a religious monument."[8] He thus seemed to think of a hunting scene of a more or less ornamental character, disconnected from the great theme of desert life which otherwise he found so strongly emphasized in the carvings of the Cross.

It is surprising that apparently neither Saxl nor Schapiro have recalled—not even in order to refute it—one Biblical model that seems to fit so well into the composition of the Ruthwell Cross and almost thrusts itself upon the reader, especially the reader of Schapiro's illuminating discussion. Genesis 21, 12–21, narrates the cruel story of Abraham's treatment of Hagar, the bondwoman from Egypt, and her son Ishmael. At the imperious bidding of Sarah, who had watched Ishmael playing with her son Isaac (according to legendary tradition, Ishmael had jokingly aimed his bow at Isaac),[9] Abraham was forced to remove Hagar from his house. He gave her a loaf of bread and a skin filled with water and sent her away together with Ishmael, the son whom she had born unto him. Hagar wandered into the wilderness of Beersheba, in the Negeb, where the water was soon consumed. She cast the starving child under a shrub, and sat herself down "a good way off, as it were a bowshot," to avoid being bound to witness the death of her child. God, however, seeing her distress, opened her eyes, whereupon she noticed a well of water. She filled the empty skin and gave the lad to drink. "And God was with the lad; and he grew and dwelt in the wilderness, and became an archer (*moratus est in solitudine factusque est iuvenis sagittarius*); and he dwelt in the wilderness of Paran [in the Sinai Peninsula], and his mother took him a wife of the land of Egypt."

If really, as Schapiro pointed out so convincingly, the carvings in the Ruthwell Cross were centered on themes of the Egyptian desert and of the ascetic life in the wilderness in general, it would not appear too farfetched to identify the archer with Ishmael. The rabbinic tradition has it that Ishmael became the teacher and master of all archers, and in another tradition it is said that "he aimed at birds."[10] It is true, of course, that he was not an anchorite, although according to one tradition he became a penitent during the lifetime of Abraham.[11] Moreover, the fact that "God was with him" and protected him in the desert has to be taken into account, and John Chrysostom makes this feature the focal point of his exegesis of Genesis 21, explaining that there was even greater security for a man dwelling in the desert, provided that God was his friend, than for one living in the cities; Chrysostom returned to this subject once more, thus interpreting Ishmael

[7] Utrecht Psalter, fol. 53ᵛ, ed. E. DeWald (Princeton, 1932), pl. LXXXIV.

[8] M. Schapiro, *op. cit.*, 238, n. 57.

[9] B. Beer, *Leben Abraham's nach Auffassung der jüdischen Sage* (Leipzig, 1859), 49; see also Louis Ginzberg, *The Legends of the Jews* (Philadelphia, 1947), I, 263f (a work

to which Professor Kurt Weitzmann kindly called my attention).

[10] B. Beer, *op. cit.*, 169, n. 515.

[11] Max Seligsohn, art. "Ishmael," *The Jewish Encyclopedia*, VI, cols. 647f.

chiefly as a pious man living in the desert.[12] For all that, however, Ishmael as an archer represented another type of desert dweller than the hermits, one who through the descendants born to him by his Egyptian wife became the eponymic forebear of the Ishmaelites or *Agareni*, the Arab tribes[13] that according to the legend turned against Israel[14] and eventually, by accepting the faith of Mahomet, also turned against the Christian religion. This, then, was the fulfillment of the divine promise (Genesis 16, 13) that went to Ishmael even before he was born, saying: "He shall be a wild man. His hand will be against all men, and all men's hands against him." And this is also the reason why, according to the legend, the angels protested against showing the well to Hagar: "Why should Ishmael have water, since his descendants will destroy the Israelites by thirst?"[15]

It would be difficult to tell whether or not the shooting at the eagle of the Ascension (if we accept Saxl's interpretation of the bird) should be considered significant of the hostility of the Ishmaelites against Israel and against the new chosen people of Christ. We should not forget that the eagle may symbolize, on the basis of Psalm 102, 5, and of Isaiah 40, 31, the community of the chosen with God.[16] Also, it must remain undecided whether the archer in the Ruthwell Cross is really aiming at the bird (as suggested by Schapiro) or shooting in vain (comparable to the archers in the Utrecht Psalter), or not shooting at the bird at all. The iconographic pattern, however, of Ishmael the archer shooting at a bird is not without a parallel, though it is rare. It is actually found in Insular art. British Museum, Cotton MS Claudius B.IV, an Aelfric Heptateuch from St. Augustine's in Canterbury, of the second quarter of the eleventh century, displays in a drawing (fol. 36[v]) a handsome, rather princely-looking youth, Ishmael, who points his arrow at a bird perched on top of an extravagantly stylized tree and big enough to be identified with an eagle (pl. 24, fig. 2).[17] His mother Hagar, seated to the left side of the tree, makes a gesture that suggests that she wishes to stop the youthful archer from shooting the bird, whereas the young Egyptian woman, Ishmael's wife, seems to soothe the anxiety of her mother-in-law. The representation of Ishmael the archer, though suggested by the Bible, does not belong to a fixed cycle of pictures; but it is found occasionally, for example in a Rembrandt etching, where the lad is shown as an archer even in his father's house, at the time when Abraham was host to his three angelic visitors.[18] Again, the legendary tradition mentions that Ishmael was present on that occasion.[19]

[12] John Chrysostom, *In cap. xxi Genes.*, *Homilia XLVI*, c. 2, *PG*, LIV, col. 425; cf. c. 4, cols. 427f.

[13] Genesis 25, 12–18.

[14] B. Beer, *op. cit.*, 171; Seligsohn, in *Jewish Encyclop.*, VI, col. 647.

[15] B. Beer, *op. cit.*, 51; Seligsohn, *loc. cit.*

[16] T. Schneider, "Adler," *RAC*, I, col. 92.

[17] Francis Wormald, *English Drawings of the Tenth and Eleventh Centuries* (London, 1952), pl. 19a and p. 67 (n. 28); cf. pp. 39f, for the hypothesis that "the original lying behind the Aelfric Heptateuch must have been an important early Christian MS," though the artist would probably have followed "a good tenth century copy." I am obliged to Dr. Rosalie B. Green for calling my at-

tention to this drawing. The eagle, it is true, is found quite often in the reliefs of ancient Christian sarcophagi, holding in its beak the wreath surrounding the Christogram above the triumphal Cross; this is best visible in a sarcophagus at Arles and Avignon (J. Wilpert, *I sarcofagi cristiani antichi* [Rome, 1929–1936], II, pl. 146, fig. 2; see, for other examples and for the literature on the subject, Schneider, "Adler," *RAC*, I, col. 92). But even should that wreath-holding eagle be more than a decorative element, it is iconographically too different from the eagle in the Ruthwell Cross to have any relevance here.

[18] Bartsch 29, Etching of 1656, to which Professor Erwin Panofsky obligingly called my attention.

[19] Cf. B. Beer, *op. cit.*, 39, n. 414.

The story of Ishmael is referred to once more in the Bible: by St. Paul, in his Epistle to the Galatians 4, 22–31. The story is garbled, because the Apostle, introducing Ishmael as the son *secundum carnem* as distinguished from Isaac, Abraham's son *secundum promissionem* or *secundum spiritum* tries to demonstrate that it is always the son according to the flesh who will persecute the son according to the spirit and to promise, and "even so it is now."[20] Therefore he claims that Ishmael *persecuted* Isaac, a statement refuted by St. Jerome,[21] whose words later were taken over verbatim by the *Glossa ordinaria* on the Bible.[22] The Apostle may have followed a Haggadah or Targum tradition when he maintained that Ishmael persecuted Isaac,[23] just as Jerome followed legendary tradition when he broadly discussed the issue of inheritance which allegedly separated Ishmael from Isaac.[24] Thereafter, however, Jerome fell in with St. Paul's arguments and held that those living carnally will always persecute with Ishmael the Isaacs, that is, those baptized and rising again with Christ and setting their affection on things above, not on things on earth (Col. 3, 2),[25] or, as Augustine said, always persecute the *sursum Jerusalem*.[26]

Whether it could be argued that the archer in the Ruthwell Cross carvings is aiming at, and therewith persecuting, a *sursum Jerusalem* or one of its equivalents, will remain a matter of interpretative speculation. Less speculative is perhaps another bit of evidence, that of the Lectionaries, which seems to connect the Ishmael story with the season of Lent. The First Sunday of Lent has, according to oldest Roman usage, the Gospel of Matthew (4, 1–11) describing the Temptation of Christ in the wilderness.[27] Since in that passage (verse 6) Satan refers to Psalm 90, 11, we find that the Gradual, and the *Tractus* thereafter, are covered by Psalm 90: "Thou shalt tread upon the lion and the adder."[28] The Genesis passage about Ishmael (21, 12–21) is, of course, absent from the Roman system of pericopes, because the Old Testament, if we except Psalter und Prophets, is read only on few occasions. In the Mozarabic *Liber Commicus*, however, the Genesis passage is read on the Thursday of the First Week of Lent, whereas the prophecy about Ishmael (Genesis 16, 12) belongs to the Lesson of the preceding day, Wednesday after the First Sunday of Lent.[29] Rome has the Ishmael story nevertheless in the Epistle on the Fourth Sunday of Lent, the passage (Galatians 4, 22–31) that in the *Liber Commicus* is read on the Nativity of St. John the Baptist, a day likewise connected with the idea of the wilderness.[30] While all that may be inconclusive, the pericopes show none the less

[20] For a hodiernal application of the Pauline version, see Erik Peterson, "Die Kirche aus Juden und Heiden," in his *Theologische Traktate* (Munich, 1951), 241ff.

[21] Hieronymus, *In Epist. ad Galat.*, c. IV, 29–31, Migne, *PL*, XXVI, col. 419AB: "Non puto invenire nos [*non* in text is wrong] posse ubi Ismael persecutus fuerit Isaac."

[22] *PL*, CXIV, col. 582B.

[23] B. Beer, *op. cit.*, 49. See, however, also Genesis 16, 12: "manus eius contra omnes."

[24] Hieronymus, *loc. cit.* For the expulsion of Ishmael as an act of disinheritance, see B. Beer, *op. cit.*, 49, also 61.

[25] Hieronymus, *op. cit.*, col. 420A: "Hodie quoque hi qui ... vivunt carnaliter persequuntur eos qui ex aqua et spiritu nati sunt et cum Christo resurgentes ea quaerunt quae sursum sunt, non deorsum. Faciant quod volunt: cum Ismaele persequantur Isaac. ..."

[26] Augustinus, *Epistolae ad Galatas expositio*, § 40, *PL*, XXXV, cols. 2133f.

[27] T. Klauser, *Das römische Capitulare Evangeliorum* (Liturgiegeschichtliche Quellen und Forschungen, 28; Münster, 1935), I, pp. 19 [no. 56], 65 [no. 64], 107 [no. 60], 146 [no. 73], 175 [no. 64].

[28] For the *Tractus*, which is characteristic of the mass in Lent, see J. A. Jungmann, *Missarum Sollemnia*, 2nd ed. (Vienna, 1949), I, 531f. The inner connection of the Temptation with Psalm 90 has been pointed out by F. Saxl, *op. cit.*, 2, and by M. Schapiro, *op. cit.*, 233.

[29] *Liber Commicus*, ed. Fray Justo Perez de Urbel and Atilano Gonzales y Ruiz-Zorilla (Monumenta Hispaniae Sacra, Ser. Liturgica, II; Madrid, 1950), I, 102f and 96f.

[30] *Liber Commicus*, II, 447f.

that Ishmael has some right to be present in a climate in which the ideas of asceticism and desert life prevail.[31]

I believe, therefore, that we may safely work with a hypothesis holding forth that the archer in the Ruthwell Cross refers to Ishmael in the wilderness. This, at any rate, seems a more satisfactory solution than the assumption according to which a purely decorative configuration, having no religious meaning at all, was displayed by archer and eagle in the summit of the Ruthwell Cross.

[31] See above, nn. 11 and 12, for the concept of Ishmael as a penitent.

THE QUINITY OF WINCHESTER

W<small>RITTEN</small> between 1012 and 1020 A.D., the manuscript of the *Officia* of the New Minster has long been appreciated as a remarkable specimen of the Winchester School of painting. Among other illustrations, the manuscript contains a most puzzling drawing which, though generally known for thirty years or more, has not yet received the attention that this strange image deserves.[1] Only one student of art, hitherto, has made a serious effort to explain the meaning of this representation.[2] His suggestions, however, go far astray and have failed to hit the mark, mainly because the subject has been treated as an isolated phenomenon, regardless of the parallels in contemporaneous imagery.

The drawing (pl. 25, fig. 1) belongs to the *Officium Trinitatis*.[3] But instead of showing an image of the Holy Trinity, as might well be expected, the artist has produced an astounding medley of divine figures. Prominence has been given, undoubtedly, to two almost identical male figures, which occupy the right half and the center of the little image. The head of each is surrounded by a cruciform-halo. Each holds a book in his left hand while the right hand indicates that a sprightly conversation is being carried on. They are evidently God the Father and God the Son. The Son is seated at the right hand of the Father, a posture which accords with the texts of many a prayer and many a passage of the New Testament, and which, of course, is authorized by the first verse of Psalm 109 (110). The Son occupies the center of the image. The Virgin Mary is seen at his right hand, an appropriate place when we think of the numerous legends of Mary's Assumption and her Coronation in Heaven. Here, however, such scenes are not yet alluded to. Their illustration belongs to an altogether later period.[4] The Winchester drawing shows Mary holding in her right arm the Infant Jesus, who is distinguished by a little cruciform-halo and a book in his left hand. The rhetorical gesture of his right hand manifests his partici-

Reprinted, with permission, from *The Art Bulletin*, XXIX (1947), 73–85. The original has this prefatory note:

For the kind permission to reproduce Figures 7, 10, 11, 35, I wish to express my thanks to the British Museum, to the Very Reverend The Dean of Winchester, and to Dr. Erwin Rosenthal, at Berkeley. My thanks are due also to Professors Walter J. Fischel and George H. Williams, at Berkeley; to Mr. T. D. Kendrick of the British Museum; to the Frick Art Reference Library in New York; to the Index of Christian Art at Princeton; and to the Warburg Institute in London, for information, suggestions, and courtesies. Finally I am greatly indebted to Mr. Francis Wormald, of the British Museum, for valuable information and suggestions, for several manuscript photographs, and for calling my attention to the Trinity in the Harley Manuscript.

[1] British Museum, Cotton MS Titus D. XXVII, fol. 75ᵛ. See British Museum, *Schools of Illumination* (London, 1914), I, 10, and pl. 12b; Eric G. Millar, *English Illuminated Manuscripts from the Xth to the XIIIth Century* (Paris and Brussels, 1926), I, 19, and pl. 24b. See also next note and below, n. 36, as well as J. B. MacHarg, *Visual Representations of the Trinity* (Columbia University Diss., Cooperstown, N. Y., 1917), 103.

[2] Alfred Hackel, *Die Trinität in der Kunst* (Berlin, 1931), 69ff.

[3] See *Schools of Illumination*, I, 10.

[4] *Infra*, n. 8.

pation in the dialogue which is being carried on between the Father and the Son. Mary is without a halo. She wears a crown which almost serves as a nest for the dove seated on her head. The dove, the Holy Ghost, also has the cruciform-halo, a symbol which thus, very oddly, appears four times in the drawing.

The group of five persons is framed by a studded circular aureole. Within that circle we find God the Father, the Son, and the Virgin seated on a similarly studded semi-circular vault which indicates the celestial globe. Here the vault serves, as indeed it often does, as a celestial throne, a bench-throne which unites the main figures. The feet of Christ rest on a shackled and wriggling figure, Lucifer, whose body cuts through the lower part of the circular aureole of heaven. In the depth below, the fanged jaws of Hell are wide open and ready to devour him. The infernal jaws, of course, are below the circle of the celestial sphere; and so are the two personages who are squeezed, right and left, into the spandrels of the underworld. They are Judas and Arius, according to the inscriptions. Both are naked, and their feet shackled. Judas has a crook in his left hand, perhaps a reminder of his forfeited office of apostle.[5]

Were it not for the left group—Mary, the Infant Jesus, and the dove—we would readily call the image an illustration of the first verse of Psalm 109 (110): "The Lord said unto my Lord: Sit thou at my right hand, until I make thine enemies thy footstool." However, what the artist shows is not the Two Persons of Psalm 109—i. e., the "Binity," which is often depicted (pls. 25–27, figs. 4–7, 9, 10)[6]—nor even the Trinity, which later on, though without proper reason, frequently illustrates Psalm 109 (pl. 27, fig. 10; pl. 32, fig. 34).[7]

---

[5] Satan sometimes carries a crook; see, e.g., Kurt Weitzmann, *Die byzantinische Buchmalerei des 9. und 10. Jahrhunderts* (Berlin, 1935), pl. LXXXIII, fig. 526. The crook as carried by Judas has barbs, which is a curious feature.

[6] In addition to the Utrecht and Canterbury Psalters (pl. 25, figs. 2, 3) see pl. 25, fig. 4, the *Officia* of Westminster (Maidstone Museum MS, fol. 32v), published by E. G. Millar, "Les principaux MSS à peinture du Lambeth Palace à Londres," *Bulletin de la société française de reproduction de MSS à peintures*, 8e Année (1924), pl. XI, fig. f; also our pl. 27, fig. 9, the Ormesby Psalter (Oxford, Bodl. Libr. MS Douce 366, fol. 147v), in Millar, *English Illuminated Manuscripts*, II, pl. 4; cf. our pl. 26, figs. 5 and 6; also our pl. 26, fig. 7, the matrix of the seal of Godwin the Minister (eleventh century), in the British Museum; see O. M. Dalton, *Catalogue of the Ivory Carvings of the Christian Era ... in the ... British Museum* (London, 1909), 32f, No. 31; A. Goldschmidt, *Die Elfenbeinskulpturen* (Berlin, 1926), IV, 19ff; and M. H. Longhurst, *English Ivories* (London, 1926), 10, 74ff., who with Dalton stresses the relationship with the Winchester Offices and the Utrecht Psalter, but styles that representation of Psalm 109 a "Holy Trinity trampling on Sin." The assumption is that a small piece of ivory, which is broken away above the heads, displayed the dove. However, Mr. T. D. Kendrick, of the British Museum, has been kind enough to inspect the seal once more and to inform me that he does not think it is possible to identify with certainty the object above the two heads. The mutilation is regrettable, since the Godwin seal might have represented our earliest

Western evidence of a Trinity with dove formed on the basis of Psalm 109 (110). For the seal itself, see also F. Wormald, "The Seal of Nectan," *Journal of the Warburg Institute*, II (1938–1939), 70, and pl. 13e.

[7] The Belgrade Psalter (pl. 32, fig. 34; Belgrade, Nat. Libr. MS, fol. 189) is of course very late, but it may have preserved an earlier iconographical type; cf. J. Strzygowski, "Die Miniaturen des serbischen Psalters in München," *Abhandlungen der kaiserlichen Akademie in Wien*, LII (1906), 57, fig. 26; cf. pl. XXXVII, fig. 85, for the Serbian Psalter in Munich, where Christ, sitting on the *left* side of the Father, is seen with the dove in his lap. Cf. A. Baumstark, "Frühchristlich-syrische Psalterillustrationen in einer byzantinischen Abkürzung," *Oriens Christianus*, V (1905), 313, for the introduction of the dove into illustrations of Psalm 109 (110). The Princeton Index of Christian Art files as the earliest evidence of this type the Gospel Book of Pembroke College, Cambridge, of the early twelfth century (MS 120, fol. 6); M. R. James, *A Descriptive Catalogue of the Manuscripts in the Library of Pembroke College, Cambridge* (Cambridge, 1905), 124. See, however, below, p. 106. In the Winchester Bible (pl. 27, fig. 10), the Trinity illustrates the so-called Gallican version of the psalm and alludes to the "Messianic" interpretation; the Hebrew version (right), showing two kings, may render the "historical" interpretation (cf. pl. 26, fig. 5). Messianic and historical interpretations were interlaced and exchangeable anyhow. When the king entered into a city or visited a monastery, the verse *Dixit Dominus* (Ps. 109:1) was sung at Vespers, indicating that the historic

Il is a Quaternity of God the Father, the Son, St. Mary, and the Holy Ghost; or, if we add the Infant on the lap of the Virgin, we face the seemingly unique representation of what logically must be called a "Quinity."

It is strange enough to find the Virgin seated on one throne with the Trinity, and it is a most unusual composition at that early date when the cult of Mary was not yet at its climax and when even the familiar Coronation of the Virgin, or her throne-sharing with Christ, was as yet iconographically undeveloped.[8] In fact, we have to go on to the fifteenth century to meet another Μαρία σύνθρονος, a Virgin sharing the throne with the Trinity. One of the few specimens of a genuine "Quaternity" is found, for example, in the Book of Hours of Jean sans Peur, Duke of Burgundy; and the very competent editor of the manuscript has rightly stressed the extraordinary composition of that miniature (pl. 28, fig. 12).[9] The crowned Virgin appears there as the central figure on the celestial throne. She is seated between God the Father at her right side and the Son at her left, a place reminiscent almost of the "theology" of the Emperor Julian, who styled the Great Mother the *synthronos* of Zeus, and Helios, the *synthronos* of the Mother.[10] In the Franco-Burgundian miniature the Holy Spirit seems to be missing. However, around the three sharers of the celestial throne there floats, or rather flows, a belt-like circle which is doubtless supposed to represent the Spirit. In that case, the Third Person of the Trinity envelops the three sharers of the throne equally, whereas in the Winchester drawing the Holy Spirit seems to be attached exclusively to the Virgin. He becomes, as it were, one with her.

This unity of the Virgin with the Spirit has prompted a far-fetched interpretation of the figure.[11] It has been assumed that the drawing betrays the influence of Early Christian doctrines, according to which the Holy Ghost was considered as female, nay, as the Mother of Christ. It is true that in several gnostic writings the Spirit appears as a woman; and an echo of this doctrine is found still in the *Didascalia Apostolorum*, in which the bishop is said to take vicariously the place of God the Father, and the deacon that of the Son, whereas the Holy Ghost is said to be represented by the deaconess.[12] Most of those

event was conceived in the light of the prophecy, or that the messianic promise had become "history" at the king's advent. See the *Antiphonae de susceptione regum* (to which Mr. W. A. Chaney has kindly called my attention) in the gallicized *Liber responsalis*, in Migne, *PL*, LXXVIII, col. 828C, and *Art Bulletin*, XXVI (1944), 208–210. Mr. W. Oakeshott, *The Artists of the Winchester Bible* (London, 1945), 16 (cf. pl. xxxviii) dates the design "*ca.* 1210."

[8] See Marion Lawrence, "Maria Regina," *Art Bulletin*, VII (1925), 156. The type of Mary as "Thronesharer" with Christ after the pattern of S. Maria in Trastevere—see J. Wilpert, *Die römischen Mosaiken und Malereien* (Freiburg, 1917), 1167, fig. 532—is not found before the twelfth century.

[9] V. Leroquais, *Un livre d'heures de Jean sans Peur, duc de Bourgogne (1404–1419)* (Paris, 1939), pl. xiv. Related representations are found not rarely in connection with the Virgin's Coronation. See also the hermetic "Quaternity" (early fifteenth century) in the *Buch der heyligen Dreyualdekeit* (Berlin, Kupferstichkabinet MS 78 A.11); cf. G F. Hartlaub, "Signa Hermetis," *Zeitschrift des deutschen Vereins für Kunstwissenschaft*, IV (1937), 109,

fig. 6, where the dove is likewise on the head of the Virgin Mary.

[10] Julianus Imp., *Oratio*, V, 167B: ὁ μεγὰς Ἥλιος, ὁ σύνθρονος τῇ Μητρί; and 179D: ὦ θεῶν καὶ ἀνθρώπων μῆτερ, ὦ τοῦ μεγάλου σύνθωκε καὶ σύνθρονε Διός.

[11] Hackel, *loc. cit.* Equally far-fetched is the general setting into which the drawing has been placed by Hermann Kantorowicz, *Studies in the Glossators of the Roman Law* (Cambridge, 1938), 186.

[12] See H. Usener's "Dreiheit," *Rheinisches Museum*, LVIII (1903), 41ff, and *Das Weihnachtsfest* (Bonn, 1911), 118ff, as well as E. Norden, *Agnostos Theos* (Berlin, 1913), 229ff. *Didascalia Apostolorum*, II, 26 (= c. IX), ed. by R. H. Connolly (Oxford, 1929), p. 89, and the notes on p. 88; see also the *Odes of Solomon*, XXXVI, 3, ed. by R. Harris and A. Mingana (Manchester, 1920), II, 384f, and J. H. Bernard, "The Odes of Solomon," *Journal of Theological Studies*, XII (1911), 28 (where, however, the Order of Severus should be ruled out). Further, J. A. Jungmann, *Die Stellung Christi im liturgischen Gebet* (Liturgiegeschichtliche Forschungen, Heft 7–8; Münster i. W., 1925), 148, n. 91.

doctrines—unknown or unnoticed during the Middle Ages—appear irrelevant to the Winchester drawing. However, one well-known patristic work, St. Jerome's *Expositions on the Prophets*, should probably be accounted for. For here, in fact, the Saint quotes the Aramaic Gospel of the Ebionites and adduces from this source, which has been looked upon as the original version of the Gospel of St. Matthew, the curious sentence "modo tulit me *mater mea spiritus sanctus* in uno capillorum meorum." But the scholarly Jerome explains also that there is no reason for feeling scandalized at the phrase "Just now my Mother the Holy Spirit has carried me by one hair (to Mount Tabor)," since in Hebrew and Aramaic the word for "spirit" (*ruach, rucha*) is feminine, just as it is neuter in Greek (*pneuma*) and masculine in Latin. But, says Jerome, this makes no difference, and he adds rather daringly: *In divinitate nullus est sexus.*[13]

No doubt Jerome's *Expositions* were known in England as well as on the Continent. But there is no reason to believe that the Winchester master has borrowed his inspiration for representing the oneness of the Spirit with Mary from Jerome or, through him, from a gnostic source. The Winchester drawing actually does not require any gnostic interpretation. It can be explained most satisfactorily from its own environment and direct sources, among which, it is true, St. Jerome will turn out to be of major importance.

It is obvious that the group of the Virgin Mary, the Infant, and the dove has been tacked on to the other two figures without an original inner connection. Admittedly, the artist has succeeded marvellously in bracing and enlivening the scene. The Infant argues, Mary listens attentively, and only the dove appears incommunicative. Yet, there is no question that the "Binity," Father and Son, forms the original nucleus of the image. From these two figures, therefore, the interpretation must start.

The model of the Binity is found in the Utrecht Psalter (pl. 25, fig. 2), or in one of its derivations, among which the MS Harley 603 is perhaps of a date earlier than the Winchester drawing.[14] The divergences of the drawing from its model are relatively insignificant. In the Utrecht Psalter the two figures illustrating Psalm 109 are youthful and beardless; in the Winchester drawing both are bearded, whereas in the Canterbury Psalter, a twelfth-century copy of the Utrecht Psalter, the Son alone has a beard (pl. 25, fig. 3).[15] Moreover, in the Psalters, both Utrecht and Canterbury, the left figure, the Son, alone has a cruciform-halo, and only the right figure with plain halo is seated on the celestial globe, whereas the left is seated on a bench (pl. 25, fig. 2) or on a rounded throne with low back and armrests (pl. 25, fig. 3). Also the feet of the cross-nimbed figure rest on

[13] Hieronymus, *In Iesaiam*, c.XL,9, and *In Michaeam*, c.VII,7, in Migne, *PL*, XXIV, col. 405A, and XXV, col. 1221D; cf. Usener, *op. cit.*, p. 118, n. 18. The variant "Videbitis Regem regum *procedentem a matre* (instead of *a Patre*)" in the *Magnificat* antiphon *In nativitate Domini*, which is found in some manuscripts of the Breviary, does not refer to the Holy Spirit at all, but to the Virgin; see Anselm Manser, "Christkönigszüge im römischen und benediktinischen Adventsgottesdienst," *Heilige Über-lieferung* (Festschrift für Abt Ildefons Herwegen, ed. O. Casel; Münster i. W., 1938), 133.

[14] E. T. De Wald, *The Illustrations of the Utrecht Psalter* (Princeton, 1932), pl. CI (fol. 64v). The Harley MS 603, fol. 56v, is a faithful copy of the Utrecht Psalter.

[15] M. R. James, *The Canterbury Psalter* (London, 1935), fol. 199v, and p. 37. The description offered by the editor ("the Father on a throne and the Son with book on a rainbow; under the Father's [!] feet are two prostrate *enemies*") is hardly correct, since it disagrees with the text of the Psalm. The enemies form the footstool of the *Son*, who sits practically always at the right side of the Father. For an exception (Serbian Psalter; above, n. 7), see the suggestions of Baumstark, *op. cit.* p. 317.

two enemies, whereas the figure in the Winchester drawing makes only *one* enemy, Lucifer, his footstool.

We have to concentrate, for a moment, on the haloes as represented in the Psalters. The distinction between cross-haloed and plain-haloed divinities is anything but unusual, or clear, in the Utrecht Psalter. Whatever may have been the reason for thus distinguishing between the divine persons in the other drawings of that Psalter (and it might be worth while investigating the matter), in the model of the Winchester drawing the cause is a curious, though very common, interpretation of the first words of Psalm 109: "The *Lord* said unto my *Lord*." Usually the Lord that speaks would be considered as God the Father, and the Lord spoken to, either as King David: the "historical" interpretation (pl. 26, fig. 5; pl. 27, fig. 10); or as Christ: the "messianic" interpretation (pls. 25–27, figs. 4, 6, 7, 9, 10).[16] The difference was not too great, since David himself was "messianic" and was both the ancestor and prefiguration of Christ. The commentators on the Psalm, therefore, hold that David and Christ are almost exchangeable here. "Qui filius Dei est, ipse et filius David est," writes Jerome. And St. Augustine explains, "Filius David secundum carnem, dominus David secundum divinitatem; sic Mariae filius secundum carnem et Mariae dominus secundum maiestatem."[17] The Utrecht Psalter, however, does not make the distinction between God the Father and Christ (David), but distinguishes between the Son of God and the Son of man, or else between the "Lord of David" and the "Son of David." In other words, the plain-haloed figure is not God the Father but the youthful *Filius Dei*, co-equal with the Father,[18] who receives as his throne-sharer in heaven the cross-haloed and likewise youthful *Filius David*, the incarnate Christ. The difference is accentuated also by the seat. The *Filius Dei* is seated on the celestial globe as King of the Universe; the incarnate *Filius David* sits on a throne.[19]

---

[16] For the "historical" conception, see, in addition to (pl. 27, fig. 10) the Winchester Bible (above, n. 7), also (pl. 26, fig. 5) the *Luttrell Psalter* (fol. 203), ed. by E. G. Millar (London, 1932), pl. 158. See also pl. 32, fig. 33, the Jerusalem Psalter (*infra*, n. 19). In the Chludoff Psalter—Moscow MS 129, fol. 111ᵛ—a photostat of which I owe to the kindness of the Frick Art Reference Library in New York, David stands before the throne of Christ, and the Divine Hand, emanating rays, stretches downwards from heaven. The underlying idea, quite foreign to the West, is very similar to that represented in the Jerusalem Psalter.

[17] Hieronymus, *Tractatus in Librum Psalmorum*, cix, ed. G. Morin, *Anecdota Maredsolana*, III, 2 (Maredsou, 1897) 198, and *Breviarium in Psalmos*, cix, in Migne, *PL*, XXVI, cols. 1163f.; Augustinus, *In Joannis Evangelium*, viii, 9, *ibid.*, XXXV, col. 1456, and *Enarratio in Psalmos*, cix, *ibid.*, XXXVII, cols. 1449f; see also Cassiodorus, *Expositio in Psalterium*, cix, *ibid.*, LXX, col. 793, and Beda, *Retractatio in Actus Apostolorum*, ii, 34, ed. M. L. W. Laistner, *Bedae Venerabilis Expositio Actuum Apostolorum et Retractatio* (Cambridge, Mass., 1939), 104.

[18] For reasons of convenience, and in accordance with the Princeton Index of Christian Art, De Wald, in his edition of the Utrecht Psalter (p. 5, n. 3), styles the Christ before the Incarnation the "Christ-Logos." Except

in a symbolical form (Hand of God, etc.), God the Father is not represented in the Utrecht Psalter. He is replaced by the co-equal Christ-Logos, who thus becomes the Creator God, in full agreement with the general christocentric concepts prevalent during the earlier Middle Ages; see, for an Anglo-Saxon example in a very prominent place, the Laws of King Alfred, *Introductio*, § 3, ed. Felix Liebermann, *Die Gesetze der Angelsachsen* (Halle, 1903–1916), I, 26f: "on VI dagum Crist geworhte heofonas 7 eorðan." By the twelfth century, the Trinity occasionally replaces the Creator Christ-Logos. See, for the general problem, Adelheid Heimann, "Trinitas Creator Mundi," *Journal of the Warburg Institute*, II (1938–1939), 42ff, 45, n. 4, whose article "L'Iconographie de la Trinité," *L'art chrétien*, I (1934), has not been accessible to me.

[19] The sharing of one bench-throne is found more frequently than the enthronement on two different seats. The two seats are equal (pl. 26, fig. 6) in the *Stuttgart Psalter* (fol. 127ᵛ), ed. by E. T. De Wald (Princeton, 1930). The difference of the seats is strongly accentuated in a Greek Psalter (pl. 32, fig. 33) at Jerusalem of *ca.* 1053–1054—Hagios Taphos MS 53, fol. 162ᵛ—published by Baumstark, in *Oriens Christianus*, V, pl. vii, 1, and pp. 316ff. The Father is represented by the *etoimasia*, the "empty" throne with back and armrests, whereas Christ,

Christ *secundum quod Deus*, addressing Christ *secundum quod homo* and bidding the latter to sit down at his right side, may appear as a strange fashion of interpreting the phrase "Dixit *Dominus Domino* meo." However, according to the patristic and other authorities, this duplication of the Second Person is correct. It is soundly based upon the various glosses explaining the psalm. The gloss, added to Psalm 109 in the Canterbury Psalter and phrased apparently after the text of the *Glossa ordinaria*, even begins with the summary *Materia est Christus secundum utramque naturam*. Moreover, in the explanation following thereafter, the human nature of the one seated at the right side of the one whose nature is divine is stressed time and time again.[20] In essence, the gloss goes back here to the authority of St. Jerome. He was probably the first author within the Latin tradition to emphasize that the throne-sharing Jesus was not Christ *secundum divinitatem* —who, of course, held the throne of heaven from eternity—but Christ *secundum humanitatem*, who rose from the dead and ascended in the flesh.[21]

This uncanny duplication of the Second Person of the Trinity—rare in Western and very common in later Eastern art[22]—has been adopted not only by the master of the Utrecht Psalter but also by that of the Winchester *Officia*. It is evident, however, that the concept of the double nature of Christ had to be modified by the Winchester artist, since the subject he wished to illustrate was not Psalm 109, but the Office of the Trinity. In a Trinity, God the Father could not well be absent nor could he be represented vicariously by the co-equal Son. The artist, therefore, when adjusting himself to the new task, quite obviously had to face certain difficulties.

*   *   *

We have to bear in mind that in the early eleventh century the representation of a Trinity was a relatively new and uncommon topic. Popular enough, it is true, were the symbolic Trinities showing, say, in connection with the Baptism, the divine hand in the clouds, the descending dove, and Jesus in the Jordan. But an "anthropomorphic" Trinity

---

the *Dominus* of the kneeling David, sists on a throne without back. In the Albani Psalter, the Father is seated on a globe and points with his hand at an empty throne at his right side; see Adolph Goldschmidt, *Der Albanipsalter in Hildesheim* (Berlin, 1895), 120.

[20] James, *Canterbury Psalter*, p. 3, claims that a great body of the glosses in that psalter is taken from "the 9th century (and earlier) *Glossa ordinaria*." See, however, on the *Glossa ordinaria*, Beril Smalley, *The Study of Bible in the Middle Ages* (Oxford, 1941), 31ff, 39ff, and her fully justified doubts as to the date of the *Glossa* and Walahfrid Strabo's "authorship." It is interesting to note, with regard to the general christological changes developing during the twelfth and thirteenth centuries, that the Two-Natures interpretation of Psalm 109, so basic with the early commentators, is almost without interest to the expositors of the psalm from the twelfth century onwards. See, for the earlier interpreters, in addition to Jerome, Augustine (*Enarratio in Psalmos*, cix), and Cassiodorus (*supra*, n. 17), also Pseudo-Bede, *In Psalmorum Librum Exegesis*, in Migne, *PL*, XCIII, col. 1033 (on the authorship of this work, see M. L. W. Laistner, *A Hand-List*

of Bede Manuscripts [Ithaca, N. Y., 1943], 159); and for the later commentaries, e.g., Petrus Lombardus, in Migne, *PL*, CXCI, col. 997, or Honorius Augustod., *ibid.*, CXCIV, col. 693 (among the works of Gerhoh of Reichersperg).

[21] Hieronymus, ed. Morin, *op. cit.*, p. 198, and *Breviarium in Psalmo*, in Migne, *PL*, XXVI, col. 1163f. It was accepted also in the East; see Ioannes Chrysostomos, *In Ascensionem*, c.3, Migne, *PG*, L, col. 446. See also Theodore of Mopsuestia, whose interpretation of Psalm 109 is known through the medium of Cosmas Indicopleustes, *Topographia*, V (Migne, *PG*, LXXXVIII, cols. 254f.), and who in some respects agrees with the conventional exegesis, although in this Psalm (as in Psalms 2, 8, and 44) he sees his opportunity for stressing most emphatically a succession in time of the divine after the human nature; cf. H. Kihn, *Theodor von Mopsuestia und Junilius Africanus* (Freiburg, 1880), §§ 459ff, 454ff; F. Baethgen, "Der Psalmenkommentar des Theodor von Mopsuestia," *Zeitschrift für die alttestamentliche Wissenschaft*, V (1885), 75ff; and below, notes 45 and 62.

[22] See below, p. 117.

was, iconographically, as yet a type almost unknown in the West. To be sure, anthropomorphic Trinities were not lacking entirely, and it is quite surprising to find that most
of the early efforts in that direction were carried out by Anglo-Saxon artists.[23] Nevertheless, of the later conventional types toward which the Winchester master was groping
—the three male figures, identical or not, or the two male figures with the dove hovering
between them (pls. 26–27, figs. 8, 10)—there were no antecedents in Western art.[24] This,
however, may not hold good for the East. The three male figures, seated on one throne,
represent a type that can be traced back to the Coptic circle of art, to the sixth century or,
perhaps, the seventh.[25] The type of the two *synthronoi* with the dove between them is
found in the somewhat archaic Belgrade Psalter (pl. 32, fig. 34, and above, n. 7) which,
though itself late mediaeval, is credited with representing a tradition of long standing.

This is certainly correct in view of the non-Christian tradition. Not to mention specimens antedating the Christian era, there is a famous and frequently discussed Egyptian
amulet in the British Museum, belonging to the first or second century after Christ,
which forms an early representation of that pattern of triune deity (pl. 29, fig. 20).[26]
Moreover, certain "prototypes" as developed by the imperial art of the later Roman
Empire have to be accounted for. The *synthronismoi* of two or three emperors, frontally
aligned, are commonly known (pl. 29, figs. 18, 19), and their relationship to later images
of the Trinity, though hitherto uninvestigated, is almost self-evident (cf. pl. 26, fig. 8).[27]
But it has hardly been emphasized in this connection that large numbers of gold coins,
of a date as late as the Theodosian era, are available showing the imperial throne-
partners in the unity of a winged demon. For we see the two emperors, not with a dove,
but with another "bird," a *Victoria*, floating between their haloed (pl. 29, fig. 22), or
simply diademed (pl. 29, fig. 21), heads and, on some coin issues, even ready to crown

[23] If we disregard the Trinity of the Lateran Sarcophagus (see, e.g., Heimann, "Trinitas creator mundi,"
p. 43) and a perhaps dubious one in a Lorsch MS, to
which the explanation of "Trinity" has been added by
another, if contemporary, hand (Bibl. Vat., MS Pal. Lat.
834, fol. 28; cf. A. Goldschmidt, *German Illumination*
[Florence and Paris, 1928], I, pl. 61), the oldest Western
anthropomorphic Trinities turn out to have originated in
England: the one in the Sherborne Pontifical (Paris,
Bibl. Nat. lat. MS 943, fols. 5ᵛ, 6, 6ᵛ; see Leroquais, *Les
pontificaux manuscrits des bibliothèques publiques de France*
[Paris, 1937], plates. viii–x); another in the British
Museum, Harley MS 603, fol. 1 (see below, n. 70); and
a third, of *ca*. 1050 A.D., in the Psalter of Bury St. Ed-
mund's (Vat. Regin. MS lat. 12, fol. 88), for the knowledge of which I am indebted to the friendliness of Mr. F.
Wormald.

[24] For pl. 26, fig. 8, see *infra*, n. 69; and for pl. 27,
fig. 10, *supra*, n. 7.

[25] The claim of Miss Heimann, "Trinitas creator
mundi," p. 46, as to the "Byzantine," that is, Eastern
origin of this Trinity, is doubtless correct. However, the
Trinity in the Homilies of the Monk James (see, e.g.,
H. Omont, in *Bulletin de la société française de reproduction de
MSS*, XI année [1927], pl. xix), usually considered as the
earliest evidence for the three throned figures, has antecedents which I intend to discuss in another connection.

[26] See W. Spiegelberg, "Der Gott Bait in dem
Trinitäts-Amulett des Britischen Museums," *Archiv für
Religionswissenschaft*, XXI (1922), 225ff; Hugo Gressmann, *Die orientalischen Religionen im hellenistisch-römischen
Zeitalter* (Berlin and Leipzig, 1930), 51f, and for the
earlier literature on the amulet, O. Weinrich, *Neue
Urkunden zur Sarapisreligion* (Tübingen, 1919), 28. For the
interesting inscription on the back of the triangular green
stone ("One is Bait, one is Hathor, one is Akōri; their
power is one. Be greeted, father of the universe; be
greeted, trimorphous god"), see Spiegelberg, *loc. cit.*, and
for the acclamation, Erik Peterson, Εἷς Θεός (Göttingen,
1926).

[27] For the three emperors—Constantine II, Con-
stantius, and Constans (pl. 29, fig. 19)—see O. Seeck, "Zu
den Festmünzen Constantins und seiner Familie," *Zeit-
schrift für Numismatik*, XXI (1898), pl. iii, 6; cf. Jocelyn
M. C. Toynbee, *Roman Medallions* (Numismatic Studies,
V; New York, 1944), 199. For the two emperors (pl. 29,
fig. 18), Valens and Valentinian, see Friedrich Kenner,
"Römische Medaillons," *Jahrbuch der kunsthistorischen
Sammlungen des Allerhöchsten Kaiserhauses*, XI (1890), pl. iv,
No. 536, facing p. 76, and for other similar coinages,
Toynbee, *op. cit.*, p. 175, and pls. iii, 7; xxxi, 1.
See also *supra*, n. 25, and for the Christian interpretation
of the triad, Garrucci (*infra*, n. 30), pl. 189, fig. 7.

them (pl. 30, fig. 23). Nor has an early specimen of this type, a medallion issued by the Dyarchy, attracted attention, although it actually displays a god with his human-imperial incarnation, his co-ruler and *synthronos*, at his right side and with a Victory hovering above and between them: Hercules with Diocletian's colleague Maximian, the first *Augustus* of the Herculian dynasty (pl. 30, fig. 24).[28]

How easily those types were translated into the language of Christian imagery is strikingly disclosed by a gold medallion of the emperor Constans with his brother Constantius II, which recently has been published for the first time (pl. 30, fig. 25). The two emperors, both in "liturgical" attire and haloed, are enthroned as usual, though turned towards each other as if in conversation. Only the divinity has been changed; for between their heads there now hovers not the *Victoria* as unifier, but the Christogram, the ✗ of Constantine's labarum. The intrinsic value of the image is still the same as before, a manifestation of the imperial glory and triumph. But the emperors, formerly bound together *in unitate Victoriae*, now appear as one *in unitate victoriae Christi*, since the victorious Christ has taken the place of Victory to secure, now as ever, the emperors' triumph over the *barbarae gentes*.[29]

It may appear relevant to mention here that the scheme of the two emperors with the winged *Victoria* has survived in the coinage of the Germanic tribes and that it is found on a Frankish gold one-third *solidus* as well as on an Anglo-Saxon thrymsa of the seventh century.[30] Decisive, however, for the transition from imperial to Christian concepts are documents of a different kind: the gold-glasses of the Early Christian period. Here the "survival by transference" of the coin images can be grasped almost at a glance, even though the throned figures themselves have been exchanged, and not only the unifying deity. Roman martyrs, preferably Peter and Paul, the Roman apostles, are the favorite figures displayed by the gold-glasses. Sometimes their busts are shown facing each other, sometimes the figures in full sit on chairs. As the "unifier" hovering above the apostles'

[28] For the emperors without halo (pl. 29, fig. 21), see H. A. Grueber, "The First Corbridge Find," *Numismatic Chronicle*, ser. iv, vol. XIII (1913), 35, and pl. v, 6; for the haloed emperors (pl. 29, fig. 22), see Pearce, *ibid.*, ser. v, vol. XVIII (1938), pl. xiv, 8; and *ibid.*, pl. xiii, 5, for Victory crowning the emperors (pl. 30, fig. 23). The type goes back at least to the era of Diocletian; see Kenner, "Nachtrag zu dem Münzfunde aus Brigetio," *Numismatische Zeitschrift*, XXIII (1891), 91, and pl. viii, 3. For the bronze medallion of Hercules and Maximian, both crowned by Victory (HERCULIO MAXIMIANO AUG.; obverse: JOVIO DIOCLETIANO AUG., with the portrait of Diocletian), see F. Gnecchi, *I medaglioni romani* (Milan, 1912), III, 124, and pl. cxxiv, 1. Iconographically, this type falls in, I guess, with the well-known "winged creatures as spandrel fillers," which have been so ably discussed by Karl Lehmann, "The Dome of Heaven," *Art Bulletin*, XXVII (1945), 1–27, especially 18f; see also B. Rowland, Jr., "Gandhāra and Early Christian Art," *ibid.*, XXVIII (1946), 44ff.

[29] This medallion, highly suggestive and so very telling in view of the "transition," was first published by Miss Toynbee, *op. cit.*, pl. xxxi, 1, and p. 179, n. 181; see also pl. xxxiii, 6, 7, and *passim*, for the emperor as

triumphator gentium barbararum by virtue of the Labarum, a type which in connection with certain litanies will be discussed elsewhere. Hercules sharing the throne with the emperor Maximian (pl. 30, fig. 24) also has a Christian parallel: St. Demetrius of Thessalonica as throne-sharer of Manuel Angelos, Emperor of Thessalonica; cf. Longuet, "Deux monnaies de Manuel l'Ange Comnène Ducas, empereur de Thessalonique (1230–1262)," *Revue numismatique*, ve sér. vol. VII (1943), 138. The function of Victory has been taken over here by St. Michael, who in full military attire is displayed on the obverse.

[30] See, for France, P. le Gentilhomme, "Trouvaille de monnaies d'or des Mérovingiens et des Wisigoths," *Revue de la numismatique*, ive sér., vol. XXXIX (1936), pl. iii, 40, and pp. 100f, 123, n. 138; for England, Charles Oman, *The Coinage of England* (Oxford, 1931), pl. i, 5, and p. 6, and G. C. Brooke, *English Coins* (London, 1932), pl. i, 9, who (p. 4), when describing the thrymsa, rightly calls the winged creature "Victory or Angel." A very good reproduction of the English coin is offered by N. T. Belaiew, "On the Geographical Distribution of the Sceattas," *Seminarium Kondakovianum*, VIII (1936), pl. vii, 10; cf. p. 217.

heads there may be seen, similar to the imperial medallion, the Christogram (pl. 30, fig. 26a), or a large crown (pl. 30, fig. 26b); or the two symbols might be combined so that the sacred characters are surrounded by the knotted wreath of immortality (pl. 30, fig. 26c). On other glasses, the unifier is Christ himself, "coming on the clouds of heaven" and ready to crown his martyrs with, says Prudentius, the *corona civica aeternae curiae*, the crown of the kingdom beyond and of the martyrs and saints (pl. 30, fig. 26d).[31] Gone are the Caesars. Their successors are the Roman apostles and martyrs, crowned rulers and Caesars of the second Rome—a highly suggestive illustration and most faithful mirroring of Prudentius' verses, of the sermons of Pope Leo the Great, and of the spirit which, half a millennium later, dictated *O Roma nobilis* and the cycle of related poems.

One gold-glass, however, rouses our attention in particular. Its general design (pl. 30, fig. 26d) is traditional: two seated figures with the plain-haloed *Christus coronator* hovering above and between them. According to the inscriptions, the figure to the right is the Protomartyr St. Stephen, and the one to the left is Christ. No doubt, the latter, indeed, is meant to be Christ; the teacher's scroll in his left hand and the quartered globe at his feet duly justify the inscription. It is startling, however, that Christ should appear twice in the same image. He is, at the same time, the one who crowns and who is crowned, who imposes the crown on the martyrs and who receives it as the *martys synthronos* of the Protomartyr. For Christ himself is the "faithful and true martyr" according to the Johannine writings (Apoc. 1, 2, 5; 3, 14, 15; John 18, 37), and his alignment with Stephen, therefore, makes perfect sense. Yet, the image has perplexed modern scholars, who usually assumed an error on the part of the artist and rejected the possibility "che egli (il Salvatore) incoroni sè stesso." However, to Early Christian minds a concept such as "He that crowneth and is crowned, that imposeth the crown and receiveth it" would have come most naturally; and a similar idea is expressed very strongly in the Byzantine liturgies (below, p. 116). Even in the light of the Utrecht Psalter and the Winchester drawing the possibility of a "reduplication" of Christ in imagery should not be ruled out; rather should it be accepted that the Christ Son-of-Man is crowned here by the haloed Christ Son-of-God or Christ-Logos.[32]

In the design of the gold-glass, at last, the figure of Christ has been included in that ancient scheme of the two throned figures with a third hovering in the heights above and between them. The next step, however, was long delayed. For a corresponding ar-

---

[31] See for pl. 30, figs. 26 a–d, R. Garrucci, *Storia della arte cristiana* (Prato, 1873), pls. 181, 2; 179, 2 (for a photograph, see P. Ducati, *L'arte in Roma dalle origini al sec. VIII* [Bologna, 1938], pl. ccxliii, 1); 183, 8; 189, 3. There is any number of similar designs with small variations to be found in those plates; see, e.g., pl. 181, 1, and 3–6; pl. 182, 1; 184, 3, etc. Prudentius, *Peristephanon*, II, 555f, addressing St. Stephen: "Aeternae in arce curiae / gestas coronam civicam"; cf. Garrucci, *op. cit.*, text vol. II, p. 145. For the wreath surrounding a symbol as well as for the symbolism of the knot, see E. R. Goodenough, "The Crown of Victory in Judaism," *Art Bulletin*, XXVIII (1946), 139–159, especially 150ff.

[32] Garrucci *op. cit.*, II, 165ff, claims that the inscription has been displaced and that the figure to the left was meant to be St. Laurence; Hermann Vopel, *Die altchristlichen Goldgläser* (Archäologische Studien zum christlichen Altertum und Mittelalter, V; Freiburg, 1899), 54, believes that the artist simply stuck to the traditional pattern of representing *Christus coronator* even though this cliché did not fit the actual design. Much more correct is the opinion (quoted by Vogel, p. 54, n. 4) of W. Smith and S. Cheetham, *Dictionary of Christian Antiquities* (London, 1880), II, 1399, who consider one figure as Christ the teacher on earth, whereas "the other shows Him as seen by St. Stephen in vision from heaven."

rangement of the Holy Trinity, reflecting, as it were, the doxology *Qui tecum vivit et regnat* with the ensuing *in unitate Spiritus sancti*, does not seem to occur in Western art before the beginning of the twelfth century.[33]

*   *   *

At any rate, to the master of the Winchester drawing this scheme must have been unknown. In his effort to produce a Trinity, therefore, he could not yet rely upon an established pattern of his subject. He had to develop his scheme more or less by himself on the basis of the imagery then known, and known to him. He chose a very suitable model, the Psalter illustrations of Psalm 109. There was but one pitfall. Through the agency of this model in the Utrecht conception, the idea of the "double nature" crept into his design. It thrust itself upon the artist, although the difficult problem *utriusque naturae*, all by itself, had nothing to do with a Trinity. However, the artist deviated from his model. In the Winchester drawing the "double nature" is not reflected in the group to the right, in the Two Persons, where this feature is found in the Utrecht Psalter. For in the drawing the two male figures are not distinguished from one another. They both have cruciform-haloes; they are seated together on one bench; and the divine Son, now bearded like the Father, has become the peer of the Father instead of assimilating himself to the youthful type of his own incarnation. Since the group to the right represented, quite obviously, the Father and the divine Son, the Winchester master, to solve his problem, moved the representation of the "double nature," as it were, to the left, that is, he added to the "Binity" of the Psalter model the left group: Mary with the Infant Jesus and the dove.

It may be mentioned immediately that this left group was as little a result of the artist's own inventive imagination as was that of the "Binity." That additional subject, too, was borrowed from the Utrecht Psalter. To identify the model, we have to turn to those liturgical formulae which allude to Psalm 109 and to the Son's throne-partnership with the Father: to the *Gloria* ("Qui sedes ad dexteram Patris") and the Apostles' Creed ("Ascendit ad coelos, sedet ad dexteram Dei Patris"). The illustrations of *Gloria* and *Credo* display, in the Utrecht Psalter (pl. 28, figs. 13, 14) as well as in its derivations (pl. 28, figs. 15, 16), the Virgin Mary approaching God on the throne of heaven, with the dove on her head (both without halo) and with the Infant (cross-haloed) in her arms. The editor of the Utrecht Psalter correctly has labelled each of those drawings as "Trinity," if a symbolical Trinity. Yet, on closer inspection, one discovers that those "Trinities" illustrating *Gloria* and *Credo* are just as strange as the one in the Winchester *Officia* and that they, too, in fact, display "Quinities." The drawing illustrating the *Gloria* shows, in addition to the Father, and to Mary with the Infant Jesus and the dove, yet another symbol, the Lamb of the Apocalypse—with, or without, its victorious cross-staff— representing, as it were, Christ *secundum quod Deus*. And in the *Credo* illustration we find the *Etoimasia*, the "empty throne," prepared on a globe, which is also a symbol of the divine Christ (pl. 28, figs. 14, 16; cf. pl. 32, fig. 33). In other words, through the symbols

[33] For the doxology in this connection, see Fulgentius, *Epistola* XIV, c.35, in Migne, *PL*, LXV, col. 424, the Fourth Question proposed to him by the African Deacon Ferrandus.

of Lamb and Throne, both apocalyptic, the *divinitas Christi* appears to be indicated, whereas the *humanitas Christi* is represented, in both prayers, by the Infant Jesus, the Incarnate, in the arms of his mother.

When now we turn back to the Winchester drawing, it is easy for us to account for the artist's intentions, as well as for his models. The two Persons in the right section of the image represent the Father with the Son—the Son *secundum divinitatem* and in his appearance the likeness of the Father. To produce a Trinity it would have been sufficient to add a dove. But this the artist, apparently, considered as insufficient, because by the simple addition of the Holy Spirit to the "Binity" he would have ignored Christ *secundum humanitatem.* He therefore contrived the expedient of setting forth the human nature of Christ by representing the Incarnation itself: the Virgin Mother and, closely attached to her, the Holy Spirit. Hence, the throned *Christus Deus* and the Infant *Jesus homo* in the arms of Mary belong together; together they form, as it were, one Person, the divine and the incarnate Christ, that is, the "complete" Saviour *secundum divinitatem* and *secundum humanitatem.* The enigmatic character of the drawing thus derives from the artist's strange endeavor to show the Second Person in its two natures simultaneously. In fact, the whole group—the enthroned Christ, the Infant, and the Virgin—together form the Second Person of the Trinity, to which there has been added the Third Person, the dove.

A few words may be said about the dove, which appears, to say the least, thoroughly uninterested in the *sacra conversazione* of its co-equals. It turns its back toward that group. But it would be unjustified to charge the bird with impoliteness or even indifference. The dove, here a symbol also of the vehicle of the Incarnation, should be compared with similar representations, for instance, with the Annunciation in the Chludoff Psalter (pl. 29, fig. 17), where the dove nests on St. Mary's head and halo in a manner similar to that of the Winchester drawing, that is, alighting from the right side.[34] We may recall that in Early Christian art, in scenes of divine ascensions and descensions, the right side often indicates both "East" and "Heaven."[35] This symbolism, however, has seemed indecisive to the master of the Utrecht Psalter (pl. 28, figs. 13, 14; cf. figs. 15, 16). In the Psalter, the dove's head is consistently turned toward the Infant Jesus, so that the direction of its bill simply depends upon whether the Child is carried in the right arm of the Virgin or in the left. In the Winchester drawing the Infant is in Mary's right arm— hence the dove turns its back to the group of Father and Son and seems to be occupied with Mary alone. This "oneness" of Mary and the dove refers to the Incarnation. There is no need to assume "gnostic" influences upon the artist in order to elucidate his drawing, a suggestion all the more irrelevant as the design of the left group, centering on Mary, was not an independent creation of the artist.

---

[34] J. J. Tikkanen, "Die Psalterillustrationen im Mittelalter," *Acta Societatis Scientiarum Fennicae,* XXX: 5 (1903), 49, fig. 63. The iconographic type, of course, is much older, as is illustrated by the gold-foils found in Mycenae and showing the goddess with the dove on her head; see H. Schliemann, *Mycenae* (New York, 1878), 180, fig. 267; Wolfgang Reichel, *Über vorhellenische Götterculte* (Vienna, 1897), 77, figs. 31–32. In more recent literature see also G. H. Karo, *Die Schachtgräber von Mykenai* (Munich, 1930–1933), 305, and M. P. Nilsson, *The Minoan-Mycenaean Religion and Its Survival in Greek Religion* (London-Paris, 1927), 340ff.

[35] See F. J. Dölger, *Die Sonne der Gerechtigkeit und der Schwarze* (Münster i. W., 1918), 37ff ("Rechts und Links, Osten und Westen in religiöser Bewertung").

The originality of the Winchester master, on the whole, appears limited. It is restricted —if we except one item— to the combination of the Psalter illustrations of Psalm 109 with those of the *Gloria* and the Creed, which refer to that psalm. This, in itself, is a matter of major interest, since the fact that Psalm 109 is fundamental to the development of the iconography of the Trinity (pl. 27, fig. 10; pl. 32, fig. 34) has not yet been studied sufficiently.[36]

The connection of the Winchester drawing with Psalm 109, however, is also revealing with regard to another detail. Only through the medium of that Psalm can we understand the presence of the third group of figures in the image, the "enemies" serving the Son as a footstool. In the Utrecht Psalter (pl. 25, fig. 2, also 3, 4; cf. pl. 27, fig. 9) the feet of the *Dominus* rest on two anonymous enemies, in full agreement with the text of the psalm. In the Winchester drawing there is but one enemy, Lucifer,[37] whereas the *inimici* suffering in Hell form the "footstool" in a rather indirect and detached fashion. Moreover, these enemies no longer are anonymous; they are named; they are Judas and Arius. It is true that Judas and Arius are sometimes put into parallel in theological writings.[38] Yet, it is also true that the presence of Arius in the *Officia* of Winchester would remain obscure unless we realize that this figure is inspired quite plainly by the gloss, or glosses, to the 109th Psalm.

We have to remember that Psalm 109 had been in the very center of the struggles between the orthodox Christians and the heterodox Arians. The orthodox champions had tried to prove the equality of the Son with the Father by calling upon the evidence of that Psalm, asserting that its words manifested the co-equality of the two *synthronoi*. The Arians, claiming the inferiority of the Son to the Father, ridiculed those alleged proofs. Mockingly they said that the metaphor of the Son sitting at the right side of the Father proved next to nothing; from this evidence one might as well deduce the superiority of the Son over the Father because *qui est in dexteram, ipse est maior*.[39] To this St. Ambrose found it easy to reply: *Divinitas gradus nescit*.[40] Still, the Arians continued to heckle and to minimize the significance of the throne-partnership as described in the Psalm. They

---

[36] According to Tikkanen, *op. cit.*, p. 213, n. 2, the contamination of the two subjects (psalm and *Gloria* or Creed) has been noticed already by J. O. Westwood, in *Reports Addressed to the Trustees of British Museum on the Age of MSS* (London, 1874), 10 (not accessible to me). Hackel, *Die Trinität*, p. 64, hardly more than mentions the *logos synthronos*. The meaning of the Winchester drawing has been recognized already by J. A. Herbert, *Illuminated Manuscripts* (London, 1911), 117, who has suggested that it symbolizes "the human as distinct from the divine character."

[37] The crown-like tufts of hair and the snout-like nose are characteristic of the representations of the devil in the Winchester School; see the *Register* of New Minster, in *Schools of Illumination*, I, pl. 13, b, or the *Liber Vitae* of New Minster, in Millar, *English Illuminated Manuscripts*, I, pl. 25, b, as well as the Harrowing of Hell (Cotton MS Tiberius C.VI) in W. Worringer, "Über den Einfluss der angelsächsischen Buchmalerei auf die frühmittelalterliche Monumentalplastik des Kontinents," *Schriften der*

Königsberger Gelehrten Gesellschaft, VIII:1 (1931), pl. x, fig. 12. The artist may have alluded to Ps. 109,3 ("ante luciferum te genui"), when replacing the customary *inimici* by Enemy, for *lucifer*, the morning-star, is occasionally interpreted as *Lucifer*, the devil; see, e.g., Pseudo-Beda, in Migne, *PL*, XCIII, col. 1034B; Honorius Augustodunensis, *ibid.*, CXCIV, col. 695D. See also our pl. 26, fig. 7.

[38] See, e.g., Beda, *Expositio Actuum Apostolorum*, I, 18 and 20, ed. Laistner, p. 12, lines 17 and 24.

[39] A. Spagnolo and C. M. Turner, "An Arian Sermon from a MS in the Chapter Library of Verona," *Journal of Theological Studies*, XIII (1912), 20ff. The Arian arguments against the relevance of Psalm 109 have been refuted in patristic literature time and time again; see, e.g., Hieronymus, *In Ps. cxlviii*, ed. Morin, 308ff, and *passim*.

[40] Ambrosius, *De fide*, II, c.12, especially § 105, in Migne, *PL*, XVI, col. 606.

claimed that according to the selfsame verse the Son shared the divine throne not as an equal but only because he had been "ordered" to do so—*quia iussus sedet ad dexteram*. And they concluded that the Father who ordered was greater than the Son who obeyed.[41]

In short, the Arians, though quite ready to acknowledge the mediatorship of the Son, refused to recognize a status of the Glorified co-equal with that of the Father. "Gloria Patri *per* Filium" was the wording of the Arian doxology which, though having an old tradition and orthodox background, made the Orthodox gradually, as it were, "*Per-conscious*" and prompted them to emphasize all the more vigorously that the King of Glory shared the throne with God as a co-equal.[42] The orthodox defense eventually resulted in an actual overstress of the God-equal kingship of the triumphant Christ at the expense, perhaps, of his priesthood, a feature which was to impress itself deeply upon the whole development of Western civilization in both the Middle Ages and the age of the Reformation.[43]

Psalm 109, at any rate, was in the center of the christological discussions of the early Church, and it thus happened that St. Jerome, too, took a stand in those disputes of his times. In his *Commentary* on Psalm 109,[44] Jerome distinguishes between the two natures of Christ and asserts that the words of the psalm were spoken to Christ the man, and not to Christ the God.

> The God does not sit; it is the assumption of the flesh who is seated. To him, who is man, who has been received into heaven, order is given to sit. This we are saying as against the *Arians* and those who maintain: "Greater is the Father, who orders him to sit, than the one, to whom that order is being given!"

Hence, through the *Commentary* of Jerome the name of Arius came to be connected with Psalm 109 so closely that the reference to Arianism remained a permanent requisite in many of the later expositions on that psalm. It is, therefore, on the strength of Jerome's gloss, or of one of its derivatives, that the Winchester artist placed Arius as "enemy" under the foot of the Lord.[45] Only through the gloss do we understand both features: (1) the presence of Arius in a Trinity and (2) the artist's urge to represent the two natures of Christ.

---

[41] See, e.g., Hieronymus, ed. Morin, p. 309, who argues: "Una natura iubet et facit: Deus iubet, Deus facit. Iubet pictor ut pingat pictor, et pictor pingit quod pingi praeceperat." See also Pseudo-Beda, *PL*, XCIII, col. 1034C.

[42] See the interesting discussion of Fulgentius, *Epistola*, XIV, 35–37, in Migne, *PL*, LXV, col. 425C, and for the problem, J. A. Jungmann, *Die Stellung Christi im liturgischen Gebet* (Münster, 1925), 180ff, 184ff.

[43] Jungmann, *op. cit.*, 103f, 188ff, especially 195ff; see also O. Casel's review of Jungmann in *Jahrbuch für Liturgiewissenschaft*, VII (1927), 181, No. 51.

[44] Hieronymus, ed. Morin, p. 198.

[45] See, e.g., Cassiodorus, in Migne, *PL*, LXX, col. 794A, who forms one of the main sources of mediaeval psalter exegesis; or Beda, *Expositio Actuum Apostolorum*, II, 34, ed. Laistner, p. 20, lines 24ff, who interprets Psalm 109, 1, on the basis of Hieronymus, *Commentarioli in Psalmos*, ed. Morin, *op. cit.*, III: 1, p. 80. This, I believe, clearly evidences that the "Nestorianism" of the Winchester artist results from a secondhand "anti-Arianism" rather than from a direct touch of Nestorian doctrines. However, we should be aware of the fact that a sub-current of Nestorian ideas, supplied by Theodore of Mopsuestia (above, n. 21) and, to a lesser degree, by Junilius Africanus was certainly permeating Celtic and Anglo-Saxon Psalter exegesis; see G. I. Ascoli, *Il codice Irlandese dell' Ambrosiana* (Archivio glottologico Italiano, V; Rome, 1878), and James W. Bright and Robert L. Ramsay, "Notes on the 'Introductions' of the West-Saxon Psalms," *Journal of Theological Studies*, XIII (1912), 520–558 (esp. p. 524f); see also M. L. W. Laistner, "Antiochene Exegesis in Western Europe during the Middle Ages," *Harvard Theological Review*, XL (1947), 21, 26f.

Fig. 1. London, Brit. Mus., Offices of New
Minster, Winchester (Cotton MS Titus D.
XXVII, fol. 75ᵛ): Officium Trinitatis.

Fig. 3. Cambridge, Trinity College, Canterbury
Psalter (MS R. 17-1), fol. 199ᵛ: Psalm 109
(enlarged).

Fig. 2. Utrecht Psalter, fol. 64ᵛ: Psalm 109
(enlarged).

Fig. 4. London, Maidstone Mus., Offices of Westminster, MS, fol. 32ᵛ: Psalm 109.

Fig. 7. London, Brit. Mus., seal of Godwin
(Ivory, 11th Cent.): Psalm 109 (enlarged).

Fig. 5. London, Brit. Mus., Luttrell Psalter (Add. MS 42130), fol. 203:
Psalm 109.

Fig. 6. Stuttgart Psalter, fol. 127ᵛ: Psalm 109.

Fig. 8. Paris, Bibl. Nat., Book of Hours (MS lat. 757),
fol. 222ᵛ: Trinity (reduced).

Fig. 10. Winchester Cathedral Library, Winchester Bible: Psalm 109 (reduced).

Fig. 11. Washington, National Gallery, Rosenwald Collection: Christ in Abraham's Bosom (reduced).

Fig. 9. Oxford, Bodleian, Ormesby Psalter (MS Douce 366), fol. 147ᵛ: Psalm 109.

Pl. 28   THE QUINITY OF WINCHESTER

Fig. 12. Paris, Bibl. Nat., Book of Hours of Jean sans Peur (MS lat. n.a. 3055), fol. 159ᵛ: Trinity with Mary.

Gloria in Excelsis.   Credo.

Figs. 13-14. Utrecht Psalter, fols. 89ᵛ-90 (enlarged).

Gloria in Excelsis.   Credo.

Figs. 15-16. Cambridge, Trinity College, Canterbury Psalter (MS R. 17-1), fols. 278ᵛ-279.

Fig. 17. Moscow, Historical Museum, MS 129 ("Chludoff Psalter"), fol. 45: Annunciation (Ps. 44, 11).

Fig. 18. Vienna, Kunsthistorisches Museum, gold medallion: Valens and Valentinian.

Fig. 19. Gold medallion, 338 A.D.: Constantine II (center) with Constans and Constantius II (enlarged).

Fig. 20. London, Brit. Mus., Egyptian amulet of green stone, 1st-2nd Cent. A.D.: Triune Deity.

Fig. 21. Gold solidus: Valens and Valentinian I with Victory (enlarged).

Fig. 22. Gold solidus: Theodosius I and Gratian, haloed, with Victory (enlarged).

Pl. 30   THE QUINITY OF WINCHESTER

Fig. 25. Gold medallion:
Constans and Constantius II
with Christogram.

Fig. 23. Gold solidus: Theodosius I
and Gratian Crowned by Victory
(enlarged).

Fig. 24. Bronze medallion:
Hercules and Maximian
Crowned by Victory.

Fig. 26a. Bibl. Vaticana,
gold-glass: Peter and Paul
Crowned by Christ.

Fig. 26b. Vatican, Museo
Cristiano, gold-glass: Peter
and Paul.

Fig. 26c. Gold-glass
(cf. n. 31): Peter
and Paul.

Fig. 26d. Bibl. Vaticana,
gold-glass: Christ and St.
Stephen crowned by Christ.

Fig. 27a. Aureus: Postumus
and Hercules (enlarged).

Fig. 27b. Bronze medallion:
Postumus and Hercules.

Fig. 28. Gold medallion: Probus
and *Sol Invictus* (enlarged).

Fig. 29a. Gold medallion:
Constantine I and *Sol Invictus.*

Fig. 29b. Solidus: Constantine I
and *Sol Invictus* (enlarged).

Fig. 30. Mt. Athos, Lavra, St. Nicholas, wall painting:
King of Kings and High Priest.

Fig. 31. Mt. Athos, Lavra, St. Nicholas, wall painting: Divine Liturgy ("Thou that offerest and art offered").

Fig. 32. Mt. Athos, Lavra, St. Nicholas, wall painting: Divine Liturgy ("That acceptest and art distributed").

Pl. 32   THE QUINITY OF WINCHESTER

Fig. 33. Jerusalem, Greek Patriarchate, Hagios Taphos MS 53, fol. 162ᵛ: Psalm 109.

Fig. 34. Belgrade Psalter (extinct), fol. 189: Psalm 109.

Fig. 35. London, Brit. Mus. MS Harley 603, fol. 1: Trinity (reduced).

The composition of the Winchester drawing, by now, has become perfectly conclusive. From Jerome's time-bound anti-Arian arguments in his *Commentary* on Psalm 109 there derived the figure of Arius. In this respect the artist worked independently: Arius does not appear in the Utrecht Psalter. From the same gloss there further derived what may have appeared to the artist as a dogmatic necessity: the distinction between the *humanitas* and the *divinitas* of Christ. This distinction had been carried through already by the master of the Utrecht Psalter. However, in the Psalter the subject of the "two natures" had been indicated very discretely either by a halo-variant or by the introduction of the Lamb or the Throne, at any rate in a purely symbolical fashion. The Winchester master has by far outstripped his model. The topic of the two natures, which may have appeared to him as indispensable even in the picture of a Trinity, has been emphasized so forcefully that, in fact, the image might be taken to display an antithesis rather than a synthesis of the God-Christ and His human manifestation.

It might be held that the artist, involuntarily and certainly *optima fide*, has depicted an almost "Nestorian" christology by splitting the two natures of Christ; his work, to be sure, is not in agreement with the "unsevered and unseparated" of Chalcedon or with the corresponding phrases of the Athanasian Creed. Also it might be held that his efforts to meet the requirements of St. Jerome's gloss have led him to introduce a Virgin Mary that appears as a *christotokos*, mother of Christ, rather than a *theotokos*, Mother of God. The artist certainly did not wish to indicate a polarity of the two natures; but his attempt to illustrate the *Officium Trinitatis* on the basis of Psalm 109 has resulted in a garbled rendering of the triune Deity. He has produced a weird "Quinity," which—it may be mentioned by the way—is in no respect a forerunner of the mariolatrous Quaternities of the later Middle Ages. The "Quinity of Winchester," after all, is meant to be a Trinity, in fact so orthodox and anti-Arian a Trinity that it is on the verge of overbalancing the dogma and turning it to the contrary.

* * *

The Winchester Trinity, though probably unique and without a true parallel, reflects nevertheless a rather broad and general artistic or human problem. The difficulty of representing at once the two natures and yet avoiding their, so to speak, "frontal" meeting in the same image has not really been mastered by the artist; it has led him to his quasi-"Nestorianism." This difficulty, however, is restricted to mediaeval and, for that matter, to Christian art in general as little as is the underlying problem itself. It all reappears with any representation of the two natures of any deified human being; and it all turns up unfailingly as soon as the divine, instead of being recognized as an immanent component of the human, begins to lead a life of its own—and vice versa. In this respect there has been much more of "Nestorianism" in history than might be assumed.

Problems of that kind were known to some extent even in Greece where, for example, a divine Heracles was worshipped as distinct from Heracles the man and hero.[46] "Those

---

[46] For the problem, see A. D. Nock, "The Cult of Heroes," *Harvard Theological Review*, XXXVII (1944), 142ff, and Wilfred L. Knox, *Some Hellenistic Elements in Primitive Christianity* (London, 1944), 39f.

Greeks," writes Herodotus,[47] "I think, are most in the right who have established and practise two cults of Heracles, sacrificing to one Heracles as to an immortal and calling him the Olympian, but bringing offerings to the other as to a dead hero." This was a simple solution. A greater difficulty arose whenever and wherever the deity that received the honors was identical with the one who paid those honors as high priest or worshipper. The reliefs in the temple of Abu Simbel, in Nubia, show Ramses II, the king and therewith the head of all cults in Egypt, as he inaugurates his own sanctuary and worships his own image.[48] This may appear as strange, or even ridiculous, to the modern mind; but we should be careful when applying such qualifications, even though they may be found in antique literature itself. Athenaeus, for instance, disapproves of Alexander the Great who, vested in the gods' attire and adorned with their insignia, received almost divine worship and, at the same time, offered to them the sacrifices.[49] Similar situations could turn up very easily in the Roman Empire: the emperor as *Pontifex Maximus* would offer sacrifices and also, at least in the provinces, receive them. In fact, Cassius Dio ridicules Caligula because he consecrated himself to his own service as Jupiter Latiaris, αὐτὸς ἑαυτῷ ἱερᾶτο.[50] Later, in the third century, after the Tetrarchy had established the "Jovian" and "Herculian" dynasties, the situation became even more complex and involved, when "the Genius of each emperor, itself divine and an object of worship, was declared to be the very Genius of Jupiter and Hercules themselves."[51]

It is one thing, however, to believe in the simultaneity of the two natures, and to write about it, or even to act accordingly; and it is another thing to represent the two natures in an image—sculpture, coin, or painting. "It was easy for the poet to find in Nero *in uno et Martis vultus et Apollinis*, but how was the sculptor or painter to render this subject?"[52] The Roman engravers, who had to sink the dies for coins displaying the image of the imperial *deus et dominus*, sometimes may have struggled heavily to solve that difficult problem. It was easy enough to represent the emperor as god by furnishing him with the

[47] Herodotus, II, 44; Nock, *op. cit.*, p. 142.

[48] J. Baillet, *Le régime pharaonique* (Blois, 1912), I, 395; the difference does not appear as too great in this connection if really the king should worship only his *Ka*, as is suggested by Nock, "Σύνναος Θεός," *Harvard Studies in Classical Philology*, XLI (1930), 14, n. 1, since the representation of the *Ka* itself leads continuously to the "duplication" of a figure in imagery; see, e.g., Adolf Erman, *Die Religion der Ägypter* (Berlin and Leipzig, 1934), 54, 210.

[49] See Athenaeus, XII, 537F, quoting Ephippos; E. Neuffer, *Das Kostüm Alexanders des Grossen* (Diss. Giessen, 1929), 11f, 39ff; cf. Eitrem, "Zur Apotheose," *Symbolae Osloenses*, XV–XVI (1936), 137, who adduces several examples of "self-worship." Another kind of "duplication" seems to have started with Philip II of Macedonia, who, when celebrating the marriage of his daughter (at Aigai, 336 B.C.), had his enthroned image allocated to those of the twelve gods to watch the play in the theatre; that is to say, the king *in natura* was to preside over the performance (had he not been murdered on that occasion) whereas the king *in effigy* was to attend as the "thirteenth god" in the midst of the twelve gods; cf. Diodorus, XVI,

92, 5. See, also, for Alexander, Elias Bickermann, "Die römische Kaiserapotheose," *Archiv für Religionswissenschaft*, XXVII (1929), 25, note 2. The whole article is relevant to the problem here under discussion.

[50] Dio, LIX, 28, 5; Eitrem, *op. cit.*, p. 127. For the very broad problem implicit in αὐτὸς ἑαυτῷ, and its connection with the godhead which is αὐτοπάτωρ, Father and Son at the same time (τίκτων αὐτὸς ἑαυτόν, ἐποίησεν αὐτὸς ἑαυτόν), see the material collected by Julius Amann, *Die Zeusrede des Ailios Aristeides* (Tübinger Beiträge zur Altertumswissenschaft, XII; Stuttgart, 1931), 31ff and 50ff.

[51] Harold Mattingly, in *The Cambridge Ancient History* (Cambridge, 1939), XII, 330, whose definition is well illustrated by the medallions; cf. Toynbee, *Roman Medallions*, pl. III, 15–16. See also Mattingly, in his review of Miss Toynbee's book, in *Numismatic Chronicle*, ser. VI, vol. IV (1944), 126, concerning the legend IOVI DIOCLETIANO AUG.

[52] Alföldi, "Zur Kenntnis der römischen Soldatenkaiser: II," *Zeitschrift für Numismatik*, XXXVIII (1928), 192, a study to which I owe very much.

attributes of the deity, but it was hard to represent him as at once god and man. Various efforts by the Roman or provincial die-sinkers led in that direction, and at least one of the resulting solutions, repeatedly applied during the third century, deserves our attention.[53] Postumus, the Gallic emperor, seems to have started issuing a type of coin which, by means of jugate busts, combines the profile images of the emperor and of Hercules, a Hercules, to wit, whose features were so strongly assimilated to those of his human-imperial double that they suggested almost identity (pl. 30, figs. 27a, b).[54] The same holds good for the jugate busts of Probus and *Sol invictus*, the emperor's *comes* (pl. 30, fig. 28).[55] Coins of Carus show the emperor with the same god and in the same configuration, and in this case the inscription DEO ET DOMINO CARO AUG(*usto*) seems to indicate the intention of a human-divine duplication even more clearly.[56] Finally, if we pass over some other combinations,[57] a gold medallion of the early fourth century (pl. 30, fig. 29a) displays the profile of *Invictus Constantinus*, who on his shield exhibits the chariot of the Sun-deity, and at the same time the jugate profile bust of a *Sol invictus* whose features strike us as representing—especially in a *solidus* of the same type (pl. 30, fig. 29b)—almost a twin likeness of Constantine the Great himself.[58]

"Co-equality" with the god, as suggested by the coin inscriptions of Carus and others before him, probably was not always intended. The god might be honored as the *comes* or *consors* of the emperor, and the emperor, in his turn, might appear as the god's duplication in the flesh.[59] However, the iconographical solution of representing the emperor as both "god" and "lord" at the same time is interesting because it is reminiscent, at least in one respect, of Christian solutions. The master of the Utrecht Psalter, for example, when representing the incarnate Christ at the side of the divine Christ (or "Christ-Logos"), distinguishes the otherwise identical figures merely by a slight variance of the

[53] Alföldi, *loc. cit.*, discusses various solutions, including the one to be discussed here.

[54] For pl. 30, fig. 27a, see Harold Mattingly and Edward A. Sydenham, *The Roman Imperial Coinage* (London, 1923–1933), V: 2, pl. XIII, 11; see also pl. XIII, 9–10. The similarity is less striking in pieces such as pl. 30, fig. 27b, after Gnecchi, *Medaglioni*, pl. CXVI, 7, where the beards differ and the god's nose and forehead are formed more nobly than the emperor's; see also Alföldi, *op. cit.*, pl. VII, 10, and Toynbee, *Medallions*, pl. XLVI, 8. See, for the general religious background of the jugate heads, H. Usener, "Zwillingsbildung," *Kleine Schriften*, IV (1913), 334ff, especially 355f. Another interesting form of "reduplication" is mentioned by Suetonius, *Caligula*, 22, 3: "Templum etiam numini suo proprium et sacerdotes et excogitissimas hostias instituit. In templo simulacrum stabat aureum iconicum *amiciebaturque cotidie veste, quali ipse uteretur*." See also the study of Bickermann, above, note 49.

[55] Pl. 30, fig. 28; Toynbee, pl. II, 7; see also Gnecchi, pls. CXIX, 7, and CXXI, 1–3.

[56] The legend is found before, e.g., under Aurelian; cf. W. Kubitschek, "*Dominus et Deus* auf Münzen Aurelians," *Zeitschrift für Numismatik*, N.F. VIII (1915), 167ff, and in general for the title *Dominus et Deus*, Franz Sauter, *Der römische Kaiserkult bei Martial und Statius* (Tübinger

Beiträge, XXI; Stuttgart, 1934), 36ff.; also Alföldi, "Insignien und Tracht der römischen Kaiser," *Mitteilungen des deutschen archäologischen Instituts, Römische Abteilung*, L (1935), 92ff, who in his article quoted above (n. 52) stresses the fact "dass ein Doppelwesen gemeint ist"; see also Mattingly concerning Diocletian, above, n. 51.

[57] See Mattingly-Sydenham, *s.v.* "Hercules, Juppiter, Sol," for Probus, Victorinus, Carausius, Diocletian with Sol, for Probus with Hercules, and for Postumus and Diocletian with Juppiter; see, for a jugate bust with Saturn, also Alföldi, "Der neue Weltherrscher der vierten Ekloge Vergils," *Hermes*, LXV (1930), 382, n. 2; W. H. Roscher, *Ausführliches Lexicon der griechischen und römischen Mythologie* (Leipzig, 1884–1937), II, col. 1461.

[58] The beautiful medallion (cf. *Art Bulletin*, XXVI [1944], fig. 6) is now splendidly reproduced by Miss Toynbee, *op. cit.*, pl. XVII, 11; see also J. Maurice, *Numismatique Constantinienne* (Paris, 1908–1912), II, 238ff, and E. Babelon, in *Mélanges Boissier* (Paris, 1903), 49f. For pl. 30, fig. 29b, see Maurice, *op. cit.*, p. 236, pl. VII, 14; also Alföldi, "The Helmet of Constantine with the Christian Monogram," *Journal of Roman Studies*, XXII (1932), pl. II, 15–16.

[59] See, for the gods as the emperors' *comes*, the forthcoming study of A. D. Nock, in *Journal of Roman Studies*, XXXVIII (1947).

halo: a plain one for the *Deus*, and a cruciform-halo for the *Dominus*. This distinction by means of the "headgear" is most conspicuous in the medallions of Probus or Constantine: the god, whose features are identical with those of the emperors, wears the radiate crown whereas Probus is helmeted and Constantine laureate. This parallel does not suggest a "borrowing" from imperial coins on the part of the mediaeval artist; it merely implies a similar solution of a task which by its very nature was difficult to solve.

When now we turn back again to the general period of the Winchester drawing, we find that difficulties of a pertinent kind were felt by the Church itself. This is evinced, above all, by the Council of Constantinople in 1156.[60] The question had arisen whether the sacrifice of the mass should not be offered solely to the Father and the Holy Spirit, since Christ as the High Priest could not offer himself to Himself; or else, the idea of Christ the High Priest had to be discarded. In other words, the problem had turned up whether the straight and square confrontation of the two natures of Christ—as Offerer and as Recipient of the sacrifice—was still compatible with the Chalcedonian Creed or whether this duplication produced a "Nestorian" split in the unity of the Double Nature. A high member of the Eastern hierarchy, Soterichus, patriarch-elect of Antioch, and a small group of bishops following him, therefore had objected to a prayer to be said at the "Great Entrance" while the Cherubic Hymn was being sung, which contained the formula: "Thou art He that offerest, and art offered; and that acceptest and art distributed."[61] This prayer, which in the Byzantine liturgies can be traced back to the ninth century at the latest, appeared to the Patriarch as "Nestorian" because he felt that it placed the sacrificial Christ—*secundum humanitatem*—almost antithetically against Christ *secundum divinitatem*, who received the sacrifice, and that therefore it suggested "two Christs." The synod rejected the scruples of the patriarch-elect; it even declared him incapable of being invested with his high office. The matter, however, relevant to the problem here at issue is that among the authorities which the assembly adduced in order to prove the orthodoxy of the formula, we find Psalm 109.[62] This reference is significant, since indeed the first verse of the psalm seemed to suggest a similar duplication—*Dominus Domino*.[63] The synod meant to demonstrate by this quotation that the abrupt confrontation of the two natures was in full agreement with the dogma, since they believed the psalm to emphasize not the severance, but the oneness, of the two natures.

It has seemingly never been investigated—and to do so is far beyond the scope of this study—to what extent the decision of 1156, confirming so energetically (as it does) the concept of Christ the High Priest, may have been responsible for the development of an

---

[60] The Acts of the Council are published by Angelo Mai, *Spicilegium Romanum*, X (1844), 1–93; cf. K. J. Hefele, *Konziliengeschichte* (Freiburg, i. Br., 1886), 567ff; Jungmann, *op. cit.*, p. 210. For the allegation on the part of the iconoclasts saying that the iconophiles were "Nestorians," see G. B. Ladner, "Origin and Significance of the Byzantine Iconoclastic Controversy," *Mediaeval Studies*, II (1940), 148f.

[61] F. E. Brightman, *Liturgies Eastern and Western* (Oxford, 1896), I, 318, 34 (Basil), 378, 5 (Chrysostomos), 431, 6 (Armenian).

[62] See Mai, *op. cit.*, p. 48f, where the Council refers to Cosmas Indicopleustes' *Prooemium in Psalterium*. See above, note 21.

[63] In the Hebrew original, of course, there is no duplication, since the *Tetragrammaton* (Jehovah) addresses the *ādhōn*, as has been pointed out already by Hieronymus, *Commentarioli in Psalmos*, ed. Morin, *op. cit.*, III, 1, p. 80. The duplication results from the translation which renders the sign standing for Jehovah likewise with *Dominus* (κύριος).

iconographical subject which began to make its appearance in the wall-paintings of Eastern churches in the twelfth century, or shortly thereafter.[64] We have to think, in the first place, of the type of the Χριστὸς ἀρχιερεύς, the Christ in episcopal—and that is, sacrificial—attire, a representation which became very common in the decorations of Orthodox churches (pl. 30, fig. 30), whereas it remained almost unknown in the West.[65] In the second place, however, we have to recall the great cycles of the "Divine Liturgy" illustrating almost programmatically that very verse which had caused the trouble in 1156: "Thou art He that offerest, and art offered [p. 31, fig. 31]; and that acceptest and art distributed [pl. 31, fig. 32]." Did not, dogmatically, the Council of 1156 free the way to, and even encourage, those images in which the divine Christ in episcopal apparel is shown as he dismisses and blesses the cortège of angels carrying the sacrificed human Christ, and, at the same time, as he receives paten and chalice from the procession of angels vested in the raiment of priests and deacons?[66] In those paintings, indeed, the duplication of "Offerer" and "Recipient" is shown most clearly, in a straightforward fashion the "naturalism" of which by far surpassed the concept of the Winchester drawing. Eastern art felt unshocked at the portrayal of Christ confronting Himself in even more than one aspect. It felt unembarrassed at displaying the divine-human duplication in that naturalistic and forthright fashion which despite (or through?) its undeniable hieratic grandeur, its stern dignity, and its almost inexhaustible symbolism evokes somewhat bewildering, not to say uncanny, feelings in the unprepared occidental spectator.

Even at the complete loss of this element of breath-taking emotion and sacred awe, the West has preferred to represent the two natures separately, either the one or the other. The God and the Man, when shown in the same panel, would be distributed to two different registers: in a lower compartment, the Madonna with the Infant, or the Crucified; in an upper, the exalted "King of Glory." It is like distributing the two natures to the two sides of a coin, a solution actually suggested by a seal of Charles the Bald: on the obverse side, an acclamation to the King of Glory; on the reverse, a supplication to the Son of Man.[67] In all that there is tension, too, but not the awesome and perplexing tension that results from the duplication of a figure, from man's meeting squarely with his own otherness, his divine or deified self.[68] Nor is anything like it to be found in the later

[64] For the date of the illustrations (twelfth to fifteenth centuries), see J. D. Ştefănescu, "L'Illustration des liturgies dans l'art de Byzance et de l'Orient," *Annuaire de l'institut de philologie et d'histoire orientales*, I (1932), 22ff, and for the illustrations of the "Great Entrance," p. 72ff.

[65] D. V. Aïnalov, "Nouveau type iconographique du Christ," *Seminarium Kondakovianum*, II (1928), 24, traces the concept of Christ the Priest to the apocryphal tradition of the sixth century which has influenced the illustration of Luke 4, 14f. This, however, does not match exactly the type of Christ officiating in the Divine Liturgy, for which L. Bréhier, "Une nouvelle théorie de l'histoire de l'art byzantin," *Journal des savants*, N.S. XII (1914), p. 36, suggests Cappadocian origin. See, for pl. 30, fig. 30, G. Millet, *Monuments de l'Athos* (Paris, 1927), pl. 262, fig. 1 (St. Nicholas, in Lavra). The very rare

Western representations of *Christus Pontifex Maximus* will be discussed elsewhere.

[66] See, for pl. 31, figs. 31–32, Millet, *op. cit.*, pls. 256, 2 and 257, 2; see also pl. 262, 1–2, and in general the discussion of Ştefănescu, *supra*, n. 64.

[67] Obverse: *Gloria sit Christo Regi victoria Carlo.* Reverse: *Jesu Nate Dei Carlum defende potenter.* See B. de Montfaucon, *Les monuments de la monarchie française* (Paris, 1728–1733), I, 274, pl. xxi, 9.

[68] For the general problem of the "celestial second self" (*himmlischer Doppelgänger*), see Richard Reitzenstein, *Die hellenistischen Mysterienreligionen* (3rd ed., Berlin and Leipzig, 1927), 178ff:

Ich gehe meinem Abbild entgegen,
    Und mein Abbild geht mir entgegen. . . .

Western images of the Trinity. True, the Trinities sometimes show three identical divine figures (pl. 26, fig. 8), perplexing through the triplication of the same; but in these images the human nature of the Second Person suffers restriction—the manifest deficiency which the Winchester artist tried to overcome. Another type, very popular in later times, shows the "Throne of Grace," that is, the Father holding the crucified Christ before him, with the dove hovering in the center or the upper part of the image; but in this case, the unity and co-equality of the Three Persons remain in the sphere of the dogma without convincing the eye alone. These Trinities lack the inner tension, human or hieratic, which is absent also from the monstrous three-faced, three-headed, or three-busted Trinities which eventually were severely censured by the Church.[69]

We realize that to abandon the face-to-face confrontation of the two natures in one pictorial composition meant also to abandon a very strong and effective element of stir and commotion. And yet, it has been demonstrated by one, admittedly singular, specimen that it was not altogether beyond artistic reach or possibility to depict, if on a very different level, a meeting of god or man with his other self, a "meeting" which contained a maximum of tension and inner emotion, and which yet avoided, through its simple humanity, the perplexities of duplication or triplication.

The unfinished, not too well-known Trinity, which has been sketched on the first folio of the MS Harley 603, is seemingly a *hapax gegrammenon*, a unique piece, and at the same time a masterpiece. There is no reason to reject the assumption that the sketch is contemporary with the main part of the codex—itself a copy of the Utrecht Psalter—and that therefore an Anglo-Saxon master working in the first decades of the eleventh century should be held responsible for that image (pl. 32, fig. 35).[70]

In a rather large mandorla a simple throne-bench is decked with the customary roll-shaped cushion. On this God the Father is seated. A cruciform halo surrounding his head frames the soft waves of his parted hair. His feet rest on a footstool. His ankles, or rather the heels of his feet, are about to touch while the knees fall far apart and thus form a lap. In the lap, and balanced by the right knee, the Son is held, whose little feet are dangling in the air. The Son carries in the left hand a globe which appears very large, somewhat out of proportion with his stature. The Son is of an unusual age, neither babe nor adult. He may be seven, or ten, or twelve; one cannot tell. He is without halo, but

[69] For pl. 26, fig. 8, see V. Leroquais, *Les livres d'heures manuscrits des bibliothèques publiques de France* (Paris, 1927), pl. IX. The earliest Western specimen of this type seems to be the Trinity in Herrad of Landsberg's *Hortus deliciarum*; cf. Heimann, "Trinitas Creator Mundi," p. 46, pl. IV, c, who discusses also some of the "monster" Trinities (*monstrum in rerum natura*, according to Archbishop Antonine of Florence). Pope Urban VIII had those images publicly burned in 1628; cf. Usener, "Dreiheit," p. 182. For the "Throne of Grace," see MacHarg, *op. cit.*, p. 71ff. (*supra*, n. 1). A related concept within Eastern art has been reproduced by Helen Rubissow, *The Art of Russia* (New York, 1946), pl. 2, to which Professor G. H. Williams, in Berkeley, has kindly called my attention. The fourteenth-century icon shows the Infant Jesus, with the dove in his chest, on the knees of the Father. The type can be traced back, in the East, to the twelfth century (see H. Gerstinger, *Die griechische Buchmalerei* [Vienna, 1926], pl. XVIII, and p. 34f) and may be even older. It is most interesting to note that the representation of the anthropomorphic Holy Spirit was forbidden by Pope Benedict XIV (1740–58).

[70] The manuscript is well known; see, e.g., Herbert, *Illuminated Manuscripts*, p. 115f. Reproductions of the Trinity, however, are not known to me, nor does the Princeton Index seem to have this Trinity in its files. Mr. Francis Wormald, of the British Museum, has most kindly called my attention to this Trinity and has also provided me with a print of the image. To determine date, school, hand, or stemma of the sketch is beyond my present possibilities, and a more searching study than the one offered here must be left to the experts.

he shares, as it were, the Father's crown of light and pain. A scroll—does it indicate the *Verbum?*—winds across the Child's chest and over his right shoulder. It is held by the Father in the left hand and is gently supported by his right, which, at the same time, supports the cheek of the Child. On the scroll, where it passes over the Father's left arm, and almost vertically above the globe, the dove has placed its feet. The Spirit that "bloweth as it listeth" seems surprised at realizing what Oneness it has produced. And the surprise is even greater with the four strange-looking angels which surround, and supposably carry, the mandorla. They are the angels "desirous to look,"[71] the angels who, curious and furtive, yearn to watch the mystery that comes to pass behind the curtain of light formed by the mandorla.

An enthroned figure with the Child on its lap, all by itself, is anything but a rare and unfamiliar topic. Abraham, a bit stiff and hieratic, may be seen occasionally holding not only Lazarus but also the Infant Jesus on his knees (pl. 27, fig. 11).[72] This, however, is subject matter belonging to a slightly later period. Here we may forget about it all the more readily as the one and only relevant model of the composition reveals itself at the first glance: the Madonna, the enthroned Virgin Mary with the Babe on her lap or her knees. Two remarkable changes of the model appear as the ingenious device of the artist. First, the Babe no longer is a babe, an "Infant Jesus." He is far too advanced in age to depend on the Mother or to sit on her lap. His nourishment is of a kind different from the milk of his Mother's breast. He has ceased to be, as it were, *Mariae filius*. Still, he is not yet the Teacher, the adult Christ, not yet *Mariae dominus*, though his boyhood does not permit us to forget entirely that the Child was born in the flesh by a mortal Mother. This impression, however, is counterbalanced, or even eclipsed, by the second change which the artist has contrived. The place of the Mother has been taken by the Father. The birth *in carne* has been supplemented and supplanted, most visibly, by the *generatio in spiritu*, as befits the age of the boy. If ever a "Generation in the Spirit" has been convincingly demonstrated, and in a manner both delightful and stirring, it is in this Anglo-Saxon sketch. The delicacy of the feelings which it discloses seems to make the most delicate Madonna appear somewhat coarse and with some residuum of the *christotokos*. The scene showing the Son in the arms of his Father has the touch of an unsurpassed purity and chastity, the touch of a loving tenderness which differs from that of a mother and yet includes it. Moreover, it has the touch of simplicity without rusticity, of that simple beauty and unbroken passion which are so familiar to us from the figures on Greek vases and from the verses of early Greek lyrics.

The Son is doubtless the Father's equal. It is not only the physical features—the double-curve of the lips, the strangely drawn brows vaulting over the half-closed lids of

---

[71] Compare 1 Peter 1, 12 concerning the mysteries of salvation "which things angels desire to look into." In the sense of angelic curiosity, which tries to glimpse behind the curtains of the Holy of Holies, this verse was quoted by Moses Bār Kēphā (813–903) in his *Exposition of the Liturgy*; see R. H. Connolly and H. W. Codrington, *Two Commentaries on the Jacobite Liturgy* (London, 1913), 67. The verse fairly describes the curious eyes of the angels surrounding the mandorla.

[72] See the delightful study of Erwin Rosenthal, "Abraham and Lazarus. Iconographical Considerations of a Medieval Book Painting," *The Pacific Art Review*, IV (1945–1946), 7ff. Cf. Gerstinger, *loc. cit.*, (above, note 69).

slightly slanted eyes, the long straight nose—which betray the co-equality. It is, above all, the Child's spirit which has been awakened to equal that of the Father. Anselm's pressing question, posed more than two generations later, *Cur Deus homo? Cur homo Deus?*, has found a clear and forthright answer in this embracement without words, and with thought silenced. The mute oneness of Father and Son beyond word or thought solves, as it were, the mysteries of incarnation and deification. The Son that lifts and lends his face to the Father and still clings to the globe of the universe, the Father that bends his head down to the Son, they both seem to be melting away in that timeless moment of surrender, one spirit, one flesh, each meeting his own self in the other, each God and man at the same time. What difference does it make who holds the globe! It is as though the Father, while with half-closed eyes he presses the cheek of the lad to his cheek, were speaking not through the medium of word or thought but through the co-equal rhythm of the pulses: "What difference which of us should hold the globe! What difference who has created this universe! We ourselves do not know. What I have created, is your creation; for what I have done, has been done for you, and therefore by you. If your nature be human, I am man too. And if I be the creating God, you are the creating God too." Here there is no split. It is the true Oneness of the Two Natures. And it is all human or, which is the same, all divine. And it is both at once.

Goethe, in his notes on the paintings of Philostratus, discusses the relationship between Heracles and his son Telephos as depicted by the Greek master. He calls the conception "infinitely tender" (*unendlich zart*), and he meditates: "Unfortunately, the more modern art[73] has been hindered by religious accidents from forming the most delightful proportions, the relations of father to son, of fosterer to infant, of educator to pupil, whereas surely ancient art has handed to us the most delicious documents of that kind."[74] Goethe, as always, has struck the vital chord; his verdict has proved, on the whole, to be justified. To the rule, however, the Harley Trinity forms the exception. Like so many works of Anglo-Saxon art, this sketch discloses an un-Roman lyrical undercurrent. It is as though from far away "a glance has flashed" to meet the artist. There does not seem to occur, in the Middle Ages, an epistrophe of his concept.

[73] "Modern," here, is used by Goethe in the humanistic sense, for example, of Petrarch, *De rebus familiaribus*, VI, 2 (edited by J. Fracassetti [Florence, 1859], I, 314): "dicantur antiquae quaecumque ante celebratum.... Christi nomen, novae autem ex illo usque ad hanc aetatem."

[74] *Goethes Werke*, ed. H. Grimm (Weimar, 1898),

XLIX: 1, p. 129: "Leider war die neuere Kunst durch religiöse Zufälligkeiten verhindert, die köstlichsten Verhältnisse nachzubilden: den Bezug vom Vater zum Sohn, vom Ernährer zum Säugling, vom Erzieher zum Zögling, da uns doch die alte Kunst die herrlichsten Documente dieser Art hinterliess." Cf. p. 72: "Hercules als Vater: unendlich zart und zierlich."

[*Ed. Note.* We know of two changes in the above essay which were planned by the author, based upon communications he had received from friends. P. Leo Eizenhöfer pointed out that the Virgin is standing, not seated, in the Winchester miniature (pl. 25, fig. 1; cf. pp. 101–102). Prof. Erwin Panofsky found that the dove representing the Holy Spirit is indeed pictured in the Burgundian miniature (pl. 28, fig. 12; cf. p. 102); it can be seen faintly in our reproduction, standing on the belt-like circle where it passes in front of the figure of Christ.]

DEUS PER NATURAM, DEUS PER GRATIAM

A NOTE ON MEDIAEVAL POLITICAL THEOLOGY

D<small>R. GEORGE H. WILLIAMS</small>' recent study on the Norman Anonymous of 1100 A.D., published as an extra number of this review,[1] may be taken as an excuse for delving once more into the highly suggestive pamphlets of this anti-Gregorian royalist. In a paragraph headed *Christus per naturam, Christus per gratiam* Dr. Williams, able and stimulating, discusses the Christology—perhaps we should say: political Christology— of that courageous mediaeval publicist,[2] thereby commendably calling attention to a hitherto somewhat neglected topic: the bearing of Christology on the relationship between Church and State.[3] It is, however, not the christological aspect of the *natura-gratia* problem which will be dealt with in the following pages, but the historical and doxographic sides of it. Dr. Williams, it is true, has indicated the immediate, or possibly immediate, sources of his author's political theories, but it would have exceeded by far the proper tasks of his analysis to trace every theorem back to its origins.[4] Although the building up of an unbroken *catena philologica* is not intended here either, it may yet prove not quite useless to spread out in the present paper some material, casually collected and perforce incomplete, which might elucidate the adaptation to Christian thought of an axiom of Hellenistic political theory.

* * *

The crucial sentence to which Dr. Williams' chapter-heading alludes is found in the tractate *De Romano Pontifice*, but its essence is rendered more concisely in the tractate *De Consecratione Pontificum et Regum* in which the Norman Anonymous puts forth with

Reprinted, with permission, from *The Harvard Theological Review*, XLV (1952), 253–277.

[1] George H. Williams, *The Norman Anonymous of 1100 A.D.* (Harvard Theological Studies, XVIII; Cambridge, 1951.) In the present "Note" the discussion of many a problem that might have been interesting and even essential has been omitted or sidestepped. I have consciously avoided embarking on interrelated problems, all of them subtle and complicated, and have preferred to concentrate on the one question which the title indicates. Besides the obligations acknowledged in the footnotes I wish to thank Professor Harold F. Cherniss for many fruitful conversations, suggestions, and improvements; for similar courtesies my thanks go to Professor Arthur

D. Nock and Dr. George H. Williams, both at Harvard, to Professor Ludwig Edelstein, at Johns Hopkins, and Professor Theodor E. Mommsen, at Princeton University.

[2] Williams, 128ff.

[3] See Williams' Foreword, p. vii, for the original title of his doctoral dissertation. Meanwhile Dr. Williams has elaborated this problem in his study "Christology and Church-State Relation in the Fourth Century," *Church History*, XX (1951), No. 3, pp. 3–33, No. 4, pp. 3–26, in which he touches also upon the problems discussed in the present "Note."

[4] Williams, 57f, nos. 168ff, has collected the parallels within the writings of his author and has indicated several relevant antecedents.

greatest vigor his ideas about the proportions prevailing between the divine power and the royal power.[5]

> The king's power is the power of God, but it is God's by nature, the king's by grace.[6]

Although a line of distinction has been drawn between divine power and royal power, that clear distinction itself will turn out to be extremely useful for blurring the borderline between divine and royal powers; it will be peculiarly useful to the Anonymous for exalting the king and proving, in the first place, his vicariate of Christ. For the author logically continues:

> Also, the king is *Deus et Christus*, but by grace; and whatsoever he does, he does not simply as a man but as one who has been made *Deus et Christus* by grace; and even he who is *Deus et Christus* by nature, does what he does through his vicar through whom vicariously he acts.[7]

In a preceding section of the same tractate the author examines the position of kings and priests according to the Old Testament. He quotes (quite traditionally, as will be seen presently) the versicles Exodus 22, 28 ("*Diis* non detrahes et principi populi tui non maledices"), and Psalms 81, 6 ("Ego dixi: *dii estis*"), in order to conclude that both the anointed king and the anointed priest were through their anointment *dii* or, as he puts it, were *Deus et Christus*. He stresses explicitly that those anointed on earth are *Deus et Christus* not only according to name (*nomen*) but also according to essence (*res*):

> Nam nisi rem haberent, falso designarentur hoc nomine [sc. dii et christi].[8]

The anointed participate in the divine name and essence, though not without some restriction; they participate

> not by nature but by grace, since only Christ, Son of God and Son of man, owned both [name and essence] by grace as well as by nature. For he is God by nature and deified by none, is holy by nature and sanctified by none. But I said also "by grace" because according to his human nature he is deified and is sanctified by the Father.[9]

---

[5] *MGH, Libelli de lite*, III, 662ff. I shall quote this tractate simply by quoting page and line.

[6] 667,36f: "Potestas enim regis potestas Dei est, Dei quidem est per naturam, regis per gratiam."

[7] 667,37–40; "Unde et rex Deus et Christus est, sed per gratiam, et quicquid facit non homo simpliciter, sed Deus factus et Christus per gratiam facit. Immo ipse, qui natura Deus est et Christus, per vicarium suum hoc facit, per quem vices suas exequitur." For *Deus factus*, see, e.g., Augustine, *De fide et symbolo*, c. 9, *PL*, XL, 189: "Non enim sunt naturaliter dii, quicumque sunt facti atque conditi ex patre per Filium dono Spiritus sancti." See also Augustine, *De civ.*, X, 1, ed. Hoffmann (*CSEL*, 40), I, 447: "[Deus] facit suos cultores deos"; also IX, 23, Hoffmann, I, 440f, and below, nos. 19, 65. For *vicarius*

Christi, see now, in addition to the standard studies of Harnack and Rivière, also Michele Maccarrone, "'Vicarius Christi' e 'vicarius Petri' nel periodo patristico," *Rivista di Storia della Chiesa in Italia*, II (1948) 1–32, and "Il Papa 'vicarius Christi,' Testi e dottrina del sec. XII al principio del XIV," *Miscellanea Paschini* (Rome, 1949), II, 1–37.

[8] 665,17–23.

[9] 665,24ff: "... non tamen per naturam, sed per gratiam, quia solus Christus, filius Dei et filius hominis, hoc habet et per gratiam et per naturam." This argument (Christ *deus per gratiam*) has been often discussed in earlier times and has been canvassed also by Peter the Lombard, e.g., *Sententiae*, III, dist. X, passim, *PL*, CXCII, 777f.

Thus Christology enters into the picture only to be carried over, in an unusual fashion, to the royalist theory. For now the Christ-like anointed on earth is, so to speak, bound to receive his two natures, too. At the anointment, says the author, the spirit of the Lord and his deifying power "leaped" into the anointed (*insiliebat in eos*) changing them into different men. In that moment, and from that moment on, they become truly "figure and image" of the God-man (*Christi figura fierent et imago*), inasmuch as the anointed on earth now becomes a *gemina persona*, that is,

> one person by nature, the other by grace.... In view of one person he is, by nature, an individual man; in view of the other he is, by grace, a Christus, that is, a God-man.[10]

To be sure, the author himself has made a leap in his thinking, for the point of reference for nature and grace has changed. In the one case, "nature" is what makes the king equal to all other human beings, whereas "grace," which leaps into him at his anointment, exalts him over all other men and makes him quasi God and Christ. Contrariwise, in the case of the God-man, "nature" indicates the higher order, that of divinity, whereas "grace" refers only to the humbled Christ in human flesh, co-equal with all other men.

That the anointed on earth share also, to some extent, in the divine "nature" is a different matter; for through the New Covenant those anointed become "more certainly and more truly participants of the divine grace and nature." They become "one with God and Christ by the spirit of adoption," they are *dii et christi per adoptionis spiritum*. Again the author has made a leap in his argumentation, and a significant one it is. "Adoption," which has here taken the place of "grace," is normally understood to be accomplished by the baptismal unction. Hence, what in fact was meant to distinguish every Christian and to make every Christian a "king and priest," now has been appropriated as a special privilege of those anointed at the rites of consecration and ordination.[11] In other words, a ritual act which refers to Christians in general has been reduced to appear as a purely royal and priestly prerogative, a method of twisting which can look back to a long line of ancestors.

The Norman Anonymous, however, prefers to employ his formula of nature and grace. In the tractate *De Romano Pontifice* he discusses once more the investiture problem and defends the custom according to which the king invests the bishop with the *temporalia*.

---

[10] 664,20ff: "Itaque in unoquoque gemina intelligitur fuisse persona, una ex natura, altera ex gratia... Una, qua per conditionem naturae ceteris hominibus congrueret, altera qua per eminentiam deificationis et vim sacramenti cunctis aliis precelleret. In una quippe erat naturaliter individuus homo, in altera per gratiam Christus, id est Deus-homo." This is the mediaeval version of the later Tudor theory of the King's two Bodies (natural and politic); see F. W. Maitland, "The Crown as Corporation," *Selected Essays* (Cambridge, 1936), 104–127, and my forthcoming study on that subject.

[11] 667,2ff. For the *consortes divinae naturae*, see 2 Peter 1, 4. For the baptismal meaning of adoption (cf. Rom.

8,15–23; 9, 4; Gal. 4,5), see L. Wenger, Art. "Adoption," *Reallexikon für Antike und Christentum*, I, 107f (e.g., Hesych: υἱοθεσία = ἅγιον βάπτισμα), also col. 108, for the Pauline antithesis of Son of God φύσει and sons of God θέσει (Gal. 4, 8): "qui natura non sunt dii"). See, above all, the introductory prayer of the *Benedictio Fontis*: "ad recreandos novos populos, quos tibi fons baptismatis parturit, spiritum adoptionis emitte"; H. A. Wilson, *The Gelasian Sacramentary* (Oxford, 1894), 84. It should be added that on other occasions the Anonymous uses the idea of adoption in the normal way, that is, referring to all Christians; see Williams, 143ff, and passim.

> For when the king grants the investiture he is not a layman that grants it, but the *christus Domini*. That is, a *christus Domini* ruling by grace together with him (*per gratiam ei conregnans*) who is *Christus Dominus* by nature. ... Verily, that *christus per gratiam*, the king, serves the *Christus per naturam*.[12]

Here the king's character of *christus per gratiam* leads not only, as often it does, to a vicariate of Christ[13] but to a "throne-sharing" with the *Christus per naturam*—the king by grace a *synthronos* of the God.

* * *

The arguments of the Norman writer may be startling but they are startling only in their application to the Church-State struggle of post-Gregorian Europe and their integration into a complex system and a well-proportioned edifice of mediaeval royalism. Apart from that, his arguments have their set place within a very long tradition.

The special variety of the antithesis of nature and grace as exhibited by the Anonymous is the essential factor of his system. His antithesis is not the customary one which restores man to his original nature and therewith to immortality. This version, of course, forms the theme of Ephesians 2, 3–5: "By nature we were children of wrath. ... But God ... has quickened us together with Christ: by grace ye are saved." It is the theme also of St. Augustine's treatise *De natura et gratia* and his other anti-Pelagian writings.[14] But it does not describe the antithesis favored by the Norman author. According to *his* version "nature" is not used in the lower sense of something in need of being remedied and redeemed by "grace." Nature appears as the higher quality (God by nature) and grace as the lower (god by grace).

The views of the Anonymous have antecedents. In an address to the bishops assembled at Ravenna, in 877, Pope John VIII referred to the events of Christmas 875 when he elevated Charles the Bald to the imperial dignity. The pope, for reasons closely connected with the political situation at that time, chose to bestow rather highflown titles upon his protégé. He referred to him as the *christus* whom God anointed with the oil of gladness above his fellows (Psalms 44, 8; Hebrews 1, 9), a prince "constituted by God as saviour of the world" (*a Deo constitutus salvator mundi*),[15] and then explained to what effect God had established Charles as the prince of his people:

> ad imitationem ... veri Regis Christi filii sui ..., ita ut quod ipse [Christus] possidet per naturam, iste [imperator] consequeretur per gratiam.[16]

---

[12] 685,42ff; 686,4.

[13] See also 668,39: "Nec puto quod aliquis iustius debeat ea prerogare quam Christus ex natura per Christum ex gratia, sanctus ex natura per sanctum ex gratia." See below, n. 65, for the "throne-sharing" of all men with Christ.

[14] *PL*, XLIV, 247ff.

[15] For the political situation, see Williams, 58, n. 169; P. E. Schramm, *Der König von Frankreich* (Weimar, 1939), I, 36ff; and, for the general papal predicaments in that period, F. Engreen, "Pope John the Eighth and the Arabs," *Speculum*, XX (1945), 318–330. For the *salvator mundi* title, see Heinrich Linssen, "ΘΕΟΣ ΣΩΤΗΡ: Entwicklung und Verbreitung einer liturgischen Formelgruppe," *Jahrbuch für Liturgiewissenschaft*, VIII (1928), 32ff, 70f, who however, does not consider the mediaeval ruler epithets. But on *soter* cf. also Nock in *The Joy of Study*, ed. Sherman E. Johnson (N. Y., 1951), 127ff.

[16] Bouquet, *Recueil des Historiens des Gaules*, VII, 694ff; Mansi, *Concilia*, XVII, Appendix, p. 172.

Pope John's oration was not to fall into oblivion. It found its place in at least two canonical collections: in that of Anselm of Lucca the earlier redaction of which may fall in the year 1083, and in that of Cardinal Deusdedit, written between 1085 and 1087.[17] Other canonical collections may contain that document, too. At any rate, there is evidence that the address of Pope John VIII was known to two prominent contemporaries of the Norman Anonymous, and it may have attracted the attention also of others.

The similarity between the address of Pope John and the arguments of the Norman publicist is striking. The papal formula, however, is of even greater interest, since two notions, new to us, here make their appearance: (1) the *imitatio* of Christ, the genuine supreme King; and (2) the antithesis of owning (*possidet*) and achieving (*consequeretur*). All that was implicitly expressed by the Norman writer as well; but it is said more powerfully by the pope and it adds some new flavor to the formula contrasting divinity by nature and divinity by grace.[18]

That formula was applied by Pope John VIII to kingship: in imitation of Christ, King eternal and universal, the Carolingian emperor ascended by grace to a dignity which Christ owned by nature. Such reference to kingship was unwarranted by the *natura-gratia* formula taken all by itself. In the Commentary on the Psalms, ascribed probably wrongly to Bede, the same topic appears in connection with the 81st Psalm, as indeed it often does. To the divine title *Deus deorum* (Psalms 81,1 and 49,1) the author remarks:

> [that refers to him] through whom all those who are not gods by nature, but become gods by grace (*per gratiam dii fiunt*), are deified (*deificantur*).

> One is God by nature, many [are gods] by grace; one is born (a God) from the Father's substance, many have become [gods] by his grace.

The distinction between "being God" and "becoming gods," which is equivalent to the papal *possidere-consequi*, is certainly put forth very vigorously. Then the author comments upon *dii estis* (Psalm 81,6),

> that is, ye may be gods if ye will have done what I shall order ye to do. And ye all, without exception, may be "sons of the most High—sons, that is, by adoption, and gods by grace."[19]

The commentator is more cautious than the Norman Anonymous in keeping apart adoption and grace. And he certainly does not think of kings.[20] He talks about the

---

[17] Anselm of Lucca, *Collectio canonum*, I, 79, ed. M. Thaner (Innsbruck, 1906–1915), 52f; *PL*, CXLIX, 489 (here numbered I, 78); Deusdedit, IV, 92, ed. Victor Wolf von Glanvell, *Die Kanonessammlung des Kardinals Deusdedit* (Paderborn, 1905), I, 439.

[18] Above, n. 7; also 664,19f: "... ut in regendo populo Christi Domini figuram vicemque tenerent et in sacramento preferrent imaginem."

[19] *In Psaltorum Librum Exegesis*, LXXXI, *PL*, XCIII, 924D, 926A; see also, for Psalm 49,1, p. 740BC: "Unus namque Deus est per naturam, multi per gratiam; unus

natus est ex substantia Patris, multi facti ex eius gratia. ." The author here draws heavily from Augustine, *Enarratio in Psalmos*, XLIX, 2, *PL*, XXXVI, 565 (see below, n. 21). For the authorship of the Psalter Exegesis, see M. L. W. Laistner, *A Hand-List of Bede Manuscripts* (Ithaca, N. Y., 1943), 159.

[20] Nor do others; see, e.g., Augustine, *De fide et symbolo*, c. 9 (above, n. 7), and *Enarratio*, XLIX (above, n. 19). Cassiodorus, one of the sources of Pseudo-Bede, says in the *Expositio in Psalterium*, XLIX, 1: "Dii dicuntur homines, qui bonis conversationibus gratiam supernae

baptized as sons of adoption who potentially may become also "gods by grace," provided that they obey the divine commandments. In other words, he talks about Christians in general, about the *justi et deificati*, whereby the "deification" again refers to Man in general.[21]

Nevertheless, the interpretation of *dii* in the restricted sense of kings and princes must have existed and even have been fairly common, as may be gathered from Jerome's Tractates on the Psalms. In his exposition of Psalm 81, Jerome says epigrammatically: *Quod dii sumus, non sumus natura, sed gratia*.[22] And he adds:

> God did not say: "I have said: ye are gods" with regard to kings and princes, but to all: to all those to whom I have equally given body, soul, and spirit[23] have I also equally given divinity and adoption. Equally we all are born, emperors and paupers.

Jerome would hardly have bothered to emphasize so strongly the potential deification of all men and to refute a singling out of rulers had there not existed some tendency to interpret (suggested perhaps by Exodus 22, 28) the "gods" of the Old Testament as kings and princes. In fact, Eusebius, when discussing the 81st Psalm, thinks of the θεοί as mentioned therein in terms of ἡγούμενοι καὶ ἄρχοντες, and so did others.[24] Even Chrysostom would answer the question "Whom does he call gods in that place?" with "The rulers."[25] Jerome, of course, did not polemize against Eusebius, but against a common opinion, whereas the one man against whom he really struggles throughout, Origen, is far from giving so much as a thought to kings or princes. Origen, who actually seems to have fathered the conventional interpretation of Psalm 81 (contrasting, in that

Majestatis accipiunt... Ita ergo filii dicuntur sicut et dii, quia utrumque gratia praestat utique, non natura"; and similarly LXXXI, 6: "(filii) per gratiam utique, non per naturam," since only Christ "proprie dicitur Dei Filius" whereas the others are sons only κατ' ἀναλογίαν; *PL*, LXX, 348D, 594CD. Also Justin Martyr, *Dialogus*, c. 124, ed. E. J. Goodspeed, *Die ältesten Apologeten* (Göttingen, 1914), 245, stresses the fact that *all* men may become sons of God; to Irenaeus, *Adv. haer.*, III, vi, 1, ed. Harvey, II, 22, those having received the grace of the adoption appear as the "gods." It would be easy to collect similar places in great numbers.

[21] Pseudo-Bede, *In Psalt.*, XLIX, *PL*, XCIII, 740B: "Deus deorum, id est Deus iustorum, Deus deificatorum. Si enim est iustificans, est et deificans, quia de iustis dictum est: 'Ego dixi: Dii estis'." The Justification betrays Augustinian ideas; see *Enarratio*, XLIX, 2, *PL*, XXXVI, 565: "Manifestum est ergo, quia homines dixit deos, ex gratia sua deificatos, non de substantia sua natos... Qui autem iustificat, ipse deificat, quia iustificando filios Dei facit."

[22] *Tractatus in Librum Psalmorum*, LXXXI, 1, ed. G. Morin, *Anecdota Maredsolana* (Maredsous, 1897), III: 2, 77; see also Williams, p. 72, n. 214, who adds a few more places (Augustine, the Glossa ordinaria, etc.) for *dii* as applied to all Christians, an interpretation which was, of course, well known to the Norman Anonymous as well; see Williams, 144f, 146f, passim.

[23] The Pauline trichotomy (1 Thess. 5, 23) should be noted; cf. Erich Dinkler, *Die Anthropologie Augustins* (Stuttgart, 1934), 255ff; also F. E. Brightman, "Soul, Body, Spirit," *Journal of Theological Studies*, II (1901), 273ff, for the Eastern liturgies; the trichotomy, however, is found also in the West despite later "emendations"; see, e.g., H. A. Wilson, *The Gelasian Sacramentary* (Oxford, 1894), 70, in the Benediction of Oil for Anointing the Sick: "tutamentum corporis, animae et spiritus."

[24] Eusebius, *In Psalmos Commentaria*, LXXXI, *PG*, XXIII, 988B; see also XLIX, 2 (col. 433D): The Seventy θεοὺς ἐκάλεσαν τούς τε ἄρχοντας καὶ κριτάς, ὅπερ ἴδιον μόνου Θεοῦ. For later times see, e.g., Euthymius Zigabenus, *PG*, CXXVIII, 853f, with reference to Exod. 22, 28. Antonius Melissa, *Loci communes*, II, 3 (al. CLXXIII), *PG*, CXXXVI, 1020B, apparently reproducing John Chrysostom, interprets Exod. 22, 28, in the sense that the "gods" are the "priests" as opposed to the "princes" mentioned in the second half of the versicle; see, however, next note; and, for the great variety of interpretations, the summary by J. J. Reeve, art. "Gods," *International Standard Bible Encyclopaedia* (Chicago, 1915), II, 1270–1272.

[25] John Chrys., *Expositio in Psalmos*, XLIX, *PG*, LV, 240f, who gives as the first meaning of θεοί that of princes: τίνας ἐνταῦθα λέγει θεούς; Τοὺς ἄρχοντας. He, too, refers to Exod. 22, 28, while discussing Ps. 49, 1: Θεὸς θεῶν.

place, the God by nature with the gods by grace), may be likewise responsible for the exegesis of the word "gods" in the sense of "nothing but a name."

> To those created by God the *name* [gods] has been conferred, though not by nature but by grace.

> Although they [the gods] are powerful and seem to have been given that *name* by grace, yet none of them is found similar to God in either power or nature.[26]

To expound the term "gods" as a mere name or speech, a λόγος ψιλός, was an expedient adopted also by other interpreters. Theodore of Mopsuestia, for example, says very pointedly that those styling themselves "gods" do not prevail in the nature of God, but that they have received, merely by grace, the name of god which is a pure matter of speech.[27] And Theodoret of Cyrus explains even more straightforwardly that

> God the creator of all has a divine nature, not the mere name [of God], whereas man has only the name "Image [of God]," but is lacking the thing itself.[28]

The setting over of ὄνομα against πρᾶγμα in that connection explains why the Norman Anonymous exclaimed almost angrily: "Nisi rem haberent, falso designarentur hoc nomine."[29]

We may neglect here the numerous authors who, in the midst of the christological struggles, used the antithesis of God-by-nature, god-by-grace chiefly to prove that the Second Person of the Trinity was co-equal and consubstantial with the First. The Son, like the Father, was God φύσει whereas all others, "be they sons and gods on earth or in heaven,"[30] were "gods" only χάριτι, or were "sons of God" only θέσει, by adoption. This is what Athanasius expounds, time and again, in his Orations against the Arians;[31] and some arguments of John Chrysostom[32] and Cyril of Alexandria[33] have a similar intention. Their purpose is to show that Christ, like the Father, is "God by nature" and that he is the only "Son of God," and that in comparison with the Son's natural divinity

---

[26] Origen, *In exodum Homilia VI*, c. 5, ed. Baehrens, I, 196,22f; also *Homilia VIII*, c. 2, Baehrens, I, 200,25. The *nomen* interpretation is applied by others as well (see, e.g., John Chrys., *PG*, XLVII, 758f) and may go back, in the last analysis, to the λεγόμενοι θεοί of 1 Cor. 8, 5.

[27] *In evang. Joannis*, X, 35, *PG*, LXVI, 760D. See also the *Scholia vetera in Joannem*, X, 34, *PG*, CVI, 1260CD, which come very close to Theodore's text. Since in John 10,34, the versicle Ps. 81,6, is quoted most authoritatively by Christ himself, the exegesis of John frequently is concerned with the interpretation of θεοί.

[28] Theodoret, *Quaestiones in Genesim*, I, 20, *PG*, LXXX, 108A.

[29] Above, n. 8.

[30] Athanasius, *Oratio I*, c. 39, a quotation from 1 Cor. 8, 5. (See next note.)

[31] Athanasius applies that antithesis very often; see, e.g., *Contra Arianos Oratio I*, cc. 8, 39; *Oratio II*, cc. 51, 61; *Oratio III*, c. 6, and passim, *PG*, XXVI, 29A, 93A, 272C, 273C, 277A, 334A. Some of his definitions are interesting: *Or. I*, 8, the gods by *charis* are set over against Christ,

"the true image of the Father's *ousia*"; *Or. I*, 39, the "true and one Son of the true God," who is God, not as a reward for virtue (μισθὸς ἀρετῆς), but φύσει κατ' οὐσίαν, is distinguished from πάντες ὅσοι υἱοί [τοῦ Θεοῦ] τε καὶ θεοὶ ἐκλήθησαν, εἴτε ἐπὶ γῆς, εἴτε ἐν οὐρανοῖς (see below, n. 76); *Or. II*, 59, the "Becoming" sons of God by adoption is stressed: τὸ μὲν γὰρ 'γενέσθαι', διὰ τὸ μὴ φύσει, ἀλλὰ θέσει αὐτοὺς λέγεσθαι υἱούς φησι; and in the same chapter he contrasts κατὰ χάριν with κατὰ φύσιν; *Or. II*, 61, he discusses the nature-grace problem with regard to Christ alone who is the Bringer of grace rather than the Son by grace (above, n. 9).

[32] John Chrys., *In Joannem Homilia III (al. II)*, c. 2, *PG*, LIX, 39.

[33] Cyril plays throughout with the *nomen* interpretation (above, nos. 26, 28, 29): men are only "called" gods; see, e.g., *In Psalmum LXXXI*, *PG*, LXIX, 1205; *In Joannis Evangelium*, I, c. 10 (to John, 1, 18), *PG*, LXXIII, 179AB; VII (to John 10, 34) *PG*, LXXIV, 25C, 32A; see also, for the problem of adoption, I, c. 9 (to John 1, 13), *PG*, LXXIII, 153f.

and divine sonship the so-called deification of man by grace or man's adoption to sonship of God cannot detract from the uniqueness of the God-man.

We may turn instead to another aspect of the problem, one which has been conjured up in the address of Pope John VIII when he declared: the emperor achieved by grace a dignity *ad imitationem Regis Christi* who was the true King by nature. Without raising as yet the question how *imitatio* entered into that picture, it should be taken, for the present moment, simply as a fact that the very complex cluster of notions connected with *imitatio Dei* or *homo imago Dei* has been linked with the problem of nature and grace; or that, biblically speaking, Psalm 81, 6 (*dii estis*), is inextricably conjoined with Genesis 1, 26: *Faciamus hominem ad imaginem et similitudinem nostram*. That combination is fairly illustrated by Cyril of Alexandria, who, in his exegesis of the Fourth Gospel, declares that all men were adopted (by grace) to the likeness of Christ, God by nature, because images are always to the likeness of the archetype.[34]

Cyril, of course, does not speak of kings, he speaks of men in general. On the basis of Genesis 1, 26, however, man and king become easily interchangeable. Theodoret of Cyrus, for example, discusses in one of his *Quaestiones* the Genesis verse and asks what it means.[35] Some people, writes Theodoret, seek man's likeness to God in an anthropomorphic conception of the deity; others hold that man's God-likeness should be sought in the sphere of the invisible, of the soul. Philo, who seems to have started within the Greek-speaking world that kind of discussion on Genesis 1, 26, had decided in favor of the invisible, the soul.[36] Theodoret, however, declared both opinions wrong. Man is the likeness of God above all with respect to dominion (κατὰ τὸ ἀρχικόν), that is, to his lordship over nature:

> Just as God himself has the lordship over all and everything, so he gave man the lordship over the living creatures lacking reason.

In other words, man is the image of God chiefly because he is ruler like God. Theodoret admits other possibilities as well, since the similitude of man with God may result also from imitations of the archetype (ὡς ἀρχετύπου μιμήματα). Man, after a limited fashion, is a creator; he too makes images; he rules and judges in imitation of God (βασιλεύει ἄνθρωπος καὶ κρίνει κατὰ μίμησιν τοῦ θεοῦ); but man is imperfect in all that because God creates without labor and without time (δίχα πόνου καὶ χρόνου), gives life to his images, and is omniscient—all of which is beyond man's abilities. These considerations lead Theodoret to his statement, quoted above, that man has only the "name" of God's image but lacks the essence.

This conclusion apparently did not satisfy Anastasius Sinaita, a most popular seventh-century author, whose influence on late Byzantine and early Russian thought and art has as yet to be studied. In his *Quaestiones* he quotes Theodoret and reproduces the latter's text almost verbatim. However, he deviates where Theodoret declares that man has

---

[34] Cyril, *In Joannis Ev.*, V, c. 5 (to John 8, 42), *PG*, LXXIII, 884D, and *passim*.
[35] Theodoret, *Quaest. in Gen.*, I, 20, *PG*, LXXX, 104ff.

[36] Philo, *De opificio*, 69, Cohn-Wendland, I, 23, 2ff, in addition to other places; cf. Harry A. Wolfson, *Philo* (Cambridge 1948), I, 116, 347, *passim*.

only the "name" of God's image, and instead connects the idea of man's rulership after the divine model with Psalm 81, 6, and says that the kingly men, as marked out by Theodoret, are sometimes called "gods" in Holy Scripture although there is a great difference between those gods and God: "God is God by nature, man by grace."[37] And Anastasius concludes that man is of the likeness of God in view of his intellect, his free will, and his kingly rule. Concerning the emphasis on rulership Anastasius may have followed Diodorus of Tarsus whose interpretation of Genesis 1, 26, has been added (probably by a later editor) to Theodoret's exegesis; for Diodorus states quite bluntly:

In what respect is man the image of God? According to his rulership and power.[38]

This theme is echoed, even more strongly, in the West. The so-called Ambrosiaster, writing in Rome during the pontificate of Pope Damasus (366–384), likewise explains in his *Quaestiones*: "In dominatione imago Dei factus est homo,"[39] only to go even a step further in a later Question. Man, writes he, is the image of God for the purpose that One be made quasi Lord on whom all others depend, for

[man] has the imperium of God, as it were, as his vicar, because every king has the image of God (*habens imperium dei quasi vicarius eius, quia omnis rex dei habet imaginem*).[40]

The oscillation between the notions of man, of man a king, and of royal office could hardly be more irritating than in the case of Ambrosiaster.

At any rate, by building up a doctrine of man's original kingship and of man's essentially royal character those authors come to create a theory fluctuating between *homo imago Dei* and *rex imago Dei*. They are—perhaps with the exception of Ambrosiaster—far from singling out the professional king as the only image of God, but their concept of "man" in general is, like that of Philo,[41] avowedly royal. The idea of man's inner kingship is found everywhere in early Christian literature, and it has been expounded in a truly grand fashion, for example, by Gregory of Nyssa in his vision of man's natural imperial sovereignty, in his lapidary statement "Where the power of ruling prevails, there prevails the image of God," and in his stirring apostrophe: "Thou art a kingly being, Man"— ἀρχικὸν εἶ ζῷον, ἄνθρωπε.[42]

---

[37] Anastasius Sinaita, *Quaestiones*, XXIV, Migne, *PG*, LXXXXIX, 541ff, esp. 544D, 545B. I am much obliged to Professor André Grabar, of Dumbarton Oaks, for calling my attention to this author and his influence on later Byzantine thought.

[38] *PG*, LXXX, 108CD: Πῶς οὖν Θεοῦ εἰκὼν ὁ ἄνθρωπος; Κατὰ τὸ ἀρχικὸν, κατὰ τὸ ἐξουσιαστικόν. I am grateful to Professor G. B. Ladner for mentioning this place to me. See also, for Chrysostom, above, n. 25; further, Ps. Athanasius, *Quaestiones in Vet. Test.*, LV (to Gen. 1, 26) *PG*, XXVIII, 733B: Just as God βασιλεύει, ἄρχει, ἐξουσιάζει in the universe, οὕτω καὶ ὁ ἄνθρωπος ἄρχων καὶ βασιλεὺς καθέστηκε πάντων τῶν ἐπιγείων πραγμάτων.

[39] (Ambrosiaster), *Quaestiones Veteris et Novi Testamenti*, XLV, 3, ed. Souter (*CSEL*, 50), 82, 20. See also Williams, 175ff, for the problem *Rex imago Dei, sacerdos Christi*.

[40] *Op. cit.*, CVI, 17, Souter, 243, 12ff. It would be probably worth while to study Ambrosiaster within the framework of the Eastern *Quaestiones* literature, since the similarities are rather remarkable.

[41] See, e.g., Philo, *De opificio*, 148, ed. Cohn-Wendland, I, 51f. The kingliness and godliness of the Sage, who in many respects is comparable to the vision of the kingly man as created originally by God, will not be considered here; see, for some aspects of the problem within the Philonic context, Goodenough, *The Politics of Philo Judaeus* (New Haven, 1938), esp. 90ff, 98ff, *passim*, and below, n. 81.

[42] Gregory Nyss., *De hominis opificio*, 4–5, and *In verba 'faciamus hominem' Oratio I*, in *PG*, XLIV, 136f, 264f. For the connections with Philo and Plato, see Harold F. Cherniss, *The Platonism of Gregory of Nyssa* (University of California Publications in Classical Philology, XI; Berkeley, 1934), 29f. (nos. 43f, p. 75); cf. 82, n. 45.

What matters here is only the combination of the antithesis "God-by-nature, god-by-grace" with the broad idea of *homo-rex imago Dei* and of the God-vicariate of the "image." In this respect not only is Ambrosiaster illuminating but so also is a brief remark of Aponius, an author of the fifth century too little explored, who in his commentary on the *Canticum canticorum* observes:

> What Christ is by *nature*, is achieved by those whom ... he has placed as his vicars, through the *image*.[43]

Aponius thinks in the first place of the apostles, in the second of the apostles' episcopal successors, that is, of Church officers; however, the *religiosissimi reges* appear to him also as "vicars of God."[44] More remarkable is the fact that in Aponius' work we find "grace" replaced by "image," and we may wonder whether his version of the problem, centered as it is in "image" and "imitation," does not come closer to the original strata than the Christian notion of grace.

It will be appropriate, though at first glance seemingly not fitting, to adduce here that famous christological argument of St. Basil which later, during the controversy on images, was repeated over and over again.[45] Basil, like all the other anti-Arian christological champions, endeavored to demonstrate the oneness of God the Father with God the Son and defeat the opinion that "two Gods" were involved in the orthodox dogma. For that purpose he avails himself, among other arguments, of a comparison with imperial images also, and declares: the emperor and the emperor's image are not two emperors even though the same respects are paid to the image as to the emperor himself;[46] nor, for that matter, are there two Gods, since the identity of the Son—who is the perfect "Image" of the Father—with the divine archetype is absolute and therefore greater than that of the emperor's image with the imperial archetype. For in the emperor's case identity of image and archetype, so far as it goes, is achieved by imitation (μιμητικῶς), whereas the identity of the Son with the Father—not "achieved" at all—is one by nature (φυσικῶς).[47]

---

[43] Aponius, *In Canticum Canticorum*, ed. H. Bottino and J. Martini (Rome, 1843), p. 235 (Lib. XII, *ad Cant.* VIII, 10). In addition to Harnack, "*Vicarii Dei vel Christi* bei Aponius: Ein Beitrag zur Ideengeschichte des Katholizismus," *Delbrück-Festschrift* (Berlin, 1908), 37–46, see Michele Maccarrone, "*Vicarius Christi e Vicarius Petri* nel periodo patristico," 20ff (see above, n. 7). Cf. Williams, 176, n. 586.

[44] Aponius, p. 202 (Lib. X, *ad Cant.* VII, 5).

[45] Basil, *De Spiritu sancto*, c. 45, *PG*, XXXII, 149C, and *Homilia XXIX contra Sabellianos*, c. 4, *PG*, XXXI, 608A. For the later repetitions of that passage by John of Damascus, see Kenneth M. Setton, *Christian Attitude towards the Emperor in the Fourth Century* (New York, 1941), 199, n. 9. Basil's comparison has its antecedents in the writings of Athanasius; see next note.

[46] All that is expressed, in essence, already by Athanasius, *Contra Arianos*, III, 5, *PG*, XXVI, 332A.B. who (333A) stresses that the oneness of the Son with the Father is οὐ κατὰ χάριν but according to the *ousia* of God which here takes the place of *physis*. See, for the survival of the Athanasian argument in Pseudo-Athanasius and John of Damascus, Setton, *op. cit.*, 199, n. 8. The seemingly strange comparison of Christ with the imperial images derives from the concept that Christ was the perfect *image* of the Father, even his *mimetes* (Ignatius, *Ad Philad.*, 7, 2: μιμητὴς τοῦ πατρὸς αὐτοῦ). The comparison with imperial images is found time and again; see, e.g., Sirarpie der Nersessian, "Une apologie des Images au septième siècle," *Byzantion*, XVII (1944–45), 60f, for Chrysostom (*In inscriptionem altaris homilia* I, c. 3, *PG*, LI, 71f) and for the Armenian tractate on images by Vrt'anes K'ert'ogh (shortly after 600 A.D.); also Gregory Nyss., *De hominis opificio*, 4–5 (above, n. 43), and *De professione Christiana*, in *PG*, XLVI, 245A, a place to which Professor Werner Jaeger kindly called my attention. The otherwise very useful study of Helmut Kruse, *Studien zur offiziellen Geltung des Kaiserbildes im römischen Reich* (Paderborn, 1934) is less satisfactory with regard to the Christian problems.

[47] *PG*, XXXII, 149C: ὃ οὖν ἐστιν ἐνταῦθα μιμητικῶς ἡ εἰκών, τοῦτο ἐκεῖ φυσικῶς ὁ Υἱός.

We face a new antithesis, that of *physis* and *mimesis*, which presumably was looming at the back of all the theorems discussed in these pages; and it leads directly to the Hellenistic origins of the nature-grace formula.

*   *   *

The "Pythagorean" tractates *On Kingship*, the fragments of which have been transmitted by Stobaeus, discussed by Goodenough, and re-edited, translated, and commented on by Delatte, were composed probably not earlier than the first or second centuries A.D., which does not preclude reflection of ideas of the Hellenistic period.[48] One of the fragments goes under the name of Sthenidas of Lokri.[49] The author elaborates the *topos* of the wise king:

> The King must be a wise man, for so he will be an imitator and emulator of the first God.

> He [the God] is the first king and ruler by Nature [and by Being], the king only by Becoming and by Imitation. The one rules in the entire universe, the other on earth; the one governs and vivifies all things forever, in himself possessing wisdom, the other has only understanding within Time.[50]

The similarity, especially of the central section, with the Christian doctrines is striking. The resemblance of thought would reach identity of thought if we disregard for the present moment the fact that there has been set over against the God and universal King "by nature" a royal demi-god, not "by grace," but by "imitation." We should not forget, however, to what extent the idea of *imitatio* had penetrated the Christian—and Jewish—theories of kingship.[51] Moreover, there is in Sthenidas' parallelogram of divinity and kingship also the remarkable antithesis of Being (*ousia*) and Becoming (*genesis*) which matches the *esse* or *possidere* as opposed to *fieri* and *consequi* in the Christian versions of that thought. The antithesis of ἀεί and ἐν χρόνῳ, intensifying that of nature

---

[48] Stobaeus, IV, vi, 22; vii, 61–64, ed. Hense, IV, pp. 244f, 263–279; Erwin R. Goodenough, "The Political Philosophy of Hellenistic Kingship," *Yale Classical Studies*, I (1928), 55–102; Louis Delatte, *Les Traités de la Royauté d'Ecphante, Diotogène et Sthénidas* (Liège and Paris, 1942), according to whose edition the texts are quoted here, whereas the English translation follows that of Goodenough. For the date of the texts, see Delatte, 284f, and *passim* (especially the arguments on pp. 87 and 108f); the date seems to be accepted by the reviewers; see, e.g., M. P. Charlesworth, in *Classical Review*, LXIII (1949), 22f; J. S. Morrison, in *Journal of Hellenic Studies*, LXIX (1949) 91f; A. D. Nock mentioned some doubts because there is no evidence "that any Gentile read Philo" (see also Charlesworth, p. 23, n. 1).

[49] For the name Sthenidas, see Delatte, 283.

[50] Stobaeus, IV, vii, 63; Delatte, 45f, cf. 56 and 274ff; for "vivifies" (ζωοῖ), see 103f, 107.

[51] Above, n. 16. For the Byzantine emperor as *mimetes* of God and Christ, see Baynes (below, n. 78), who indicates Eusebius as the mediator of those ideas which, however, are found throughout (Agapetos). For the Jewish strand, see the Letter of Aristeas, 188, 210, 281; Goodenough, *Politics of Philo*, 90ff; see also Nock (below, n. 81), 215: "Jews and Christians alike accepted the philosophical view that the king was the counterpart of God and that it was his duty to imitate the moral excellences of divinity." In general, see Michaelis, art. "μιμέομαι, μιμητής," in: *Theologisches Wörterbuch zum Neuen Testament*, ed. G. Kittel (Tübingen, 1939), IV, 661–678, who, however, does not consider the ritual *mimesis* of myths (see Sallustius, c. iv, ed. Nock [Cambridge, 1926], p. 8) or the spiritualization of the painter's *mimesis*: the mass-celebrating priest a "painter" imitating the true mass in heaven; see, e.g., R. H. Connolly, *The Liturgical Homilies of Narsai* (Cambridge, 1909), 46, *passim*; R. H. Connolly and H. W. Codrington, *Two Commentaries on the Jacobite Liturgy* (Oxford, 1913), 35, cf. 17; also the *Nestorian Order of Baptism*, in H. Denzinger, *Ritus Orientalium* (Würzburg, 1863), I, 336f; Chrysostom, *In Actus Homilia XXX*, 4, *PG*, LX, 226–228, where the Holy Spirit is the painter of the truly "imperial" (divine) images.

and imitation, likewise is reflected in the Christian texts.[52] Moreover, the concept of the royal *dii et christi* and of kings as mediators between God and men is marked out very clearly in all the Pythagorean political tractates. Diotogenes, for example, another Pythagorean, holds that the God-imitating king, who himself is the Animate Law, "has been metamorphosed into a deity among men"—of course not by grace, but by *mimesis*.[53] And Diotogenes resumes also the theme of *physis* and *mimesis* when he contrasts the God, who "by nature" is the best of all things most honored, with the king, who "by imitation" is best on earth and among men.[54]

Other parallels are frequent and suggestive. We are reminded of the Norman Anonymous and his distinction between the king as an ordinary individual man and the king as *Deus et Christus* by grace when we read how Ecphantus, a third Pythagorean, explains the geminate nature of his king:[55]

> On the earth and among us, man has the best nature of all; but more divine is the king who claims the lion's share of the better elements in the common nature.

> He is like other men in his tabernacle,[56] inasmuch as he is formed of the same material; but he is fashioned by the supreme Artificer, who in making the king used himself as archetype.

Ecphantus thus establishes also a king of two bodies or two natures, one human and the other god-like—again, not god-like by grace, but by *mimesis*.

In addition to that, Ecphantus availed himself of the stratagem to claim for the king exclusively what normally would refer to man in general, a method not dissimilar to that applied by the Norman Anonymous when he represented the ordinary baptismal unction and "adoption" as though it implied a special privilege of his royal and priestly anointed.[57] Ecphantus borrowed the second sentence of the afore-mentioned passage verbatim from another Pythagorean, Eurysus, who was quoted by Clement of Alexandria.[58] But Eurysus, in his Περὶ τύχας, does not talk about kings at all, he talks about man:

[52] For ὡσία in that place, see Delatte, 45, 270; cf. *supra*, nos. 31, 46; and for the antithesis of Time and Eternity, above, n. 35.

[53] Delatte, 39,11, and 255; Goodenough, 68. For the kings as Animate Law, see the recent study by Artur Steinwenter, "ΝΟΜΟΣ ΕΜΨΥΧΟΣ: Zur Geschichte einer politischen Theorie," *Anzeiger der Wiener Akademie*, LXXXIII (1946), 250ff, and Delatte, 245ff.

[54] See, for this passage (Stobaeus, IV, vii, 61, Hense, 265, 5), the commentary of Delatte, p. 254.

[55] See above, n. 10. Goodenough, 76; Delatte, 25f, 28 (the passage has been transmitted twice by Stobaeus), and the important commentary, pp. 179ff. Delatte has not made use of the Philonic parallel adduced by Goodenough *Politics* (above, n. 41), 99, a Philo fragment transmitted by Antonius Melissa, *Loci communes*, II, c. 2 (al. CIV), *PG*, CXXXVI, 1012B: Τῇ μὲν οὐσίᾳ τοῦ σώματος ἴσος παντὸς ἀνθρώπου ὁ βασιλεύς, τῇ ἐξουσίᾳ δὲ τοῦ ἀξιώματος ὅμοιός ἐστι τῷ ἐπὶ πάντων Θεῷ. This passage is verbatim repeated by the composer of the Russian Laurentian Chronicle, ed. P. Bychkov (3rd ed., Archeographic Commission; St. Petersburg, 1898), p. 351 (ad a. 1175), who actually quotes Philo, though he purports to quote Chrysostom, when he writes: "By his earthly nature the Tsar is like all men; by the power of his rank, however, he is like God." I am grateful to Dr. Michael Cherniavsky, at Princeton, for having called my attention to this passage. See also below, n. 72.

[56] For σκᾶνος and its equivalents, rendered by the Vulgate (2 Ptr. 1, 13–14) as *tabernaculum* and meaning the dwelling place of the soul, which is the body, see Delatte, 181. The word is used also with regard to the incarnate Christ, e.g., Augustine, *Enarrationes in Psalmos*, XC, 5, *PL*, XXXVII, 1163: "In ipso tabernaculo Imperator militavit pro nobis." According to the Acts of the Persian Martyrs, it is used also by King Shapur to designate his own body ("so long as I remain in my tabernacle"); cf. Oskar Braun, *Ausgewählte Akten Persischer Märtyrer* (Bibl. d. Kirchenväter; Kempten and Munich, 1915), 3, where the translator's question-mark may be safely omitted.

[57] Above, n. 11.

[58] Clement, *Stromata*, V, 5, 29; Goodenough, 76, n. 75, gives that parallel, but Delatte, 177ff, discloses its true implications.

> Man is like the others [*i.e.*, created beings] in his tabernacle, inasmuch as he is formed of the same material [*sc.* as the animals]; but he is fashioned by the supreme Artificer, who in making him [man] used himself as archetype.

In other words, Eurysus said that the Demiurge created *man* in his own image and likeness, a concept for which he may have drawn inspiration from various sources, most likely however from Genesis 1, 26.[59] Ecphantus, while taking over that statement verbatim, twisted it by changing "animals" into "men," and "man" into "king," and thus adapted Eurysus' statement to the king exclusively, claiming for him alone what had been said of man in general. Stratagems of that kind were rare in classical times when texts were not synonymous with absolute authority; and even the Jewish interlocutor supporting Celsus against the Christian exegesis complains that scores of prophecies had been claimed for Jesus, or by Jesus, which might just as well have been claimed to refer to countless others.[60] This tendency to establish and then to monopolize claims was daily bread in mediaeval thought, when words of the Bible were applied and adapted and turned around as circumstances demanded—on the greatest scale by Joachim of Fiore. More relevant to the present problem is a phrase of Petrus de Vinea, the imperial logothete and court orator, who in his great eulogy on Frederick II praised his emperor as the one *quem supremi manus opificis formavit in hominem*. What he did was merely to twist by a new application Genesis 2, 7: *Formavit Deus hominem;* but since Vinea certainly did not want to proffer a truism, he evidently wished to imply that his emperor exclusively and by special privilege had been formed by the hand of the supreme Artificer himself.[61] Or, the most famous example of those twists, 1 Cor. 2, 15: *Spiritualis iudicat omnia, et ipse a nemine iudicatur.* By a process as tortuous as it is revealing, that verse in which St. Paul demonstrates the inner sovereignty of man endowed with the Spirit supposedly came to mean (and in practice it did mean and still does) that the pope exclusively was that *pneumatikos* to whom the Apostle referred, and that he alone owned, in a forensic sense, the privilege of judging all and being judged by none.[62] This twisting method of "monopolizing by exclusion" was indeed a very mediaeval method: the office claimed what was valid for man at large. It is a method of putting office above man, indicating at the same time the shift from man to office. The wheel turned full circle only when, with Dante, "Man" himself, or "being Man," became an office.

A related method of twisting, and of changing application, may be observed in view of the *dii* of the Old Testament, and thereby some light will be shed on the *natura-gratia* formula so closely connected with the "gods." Clement of Alexandria, when referring

[59] Delatte, 179, gives parallels from Timaeus, but believes that Eurysus was inspired by Genesis 1, 26.

[60] Origen, *In Celsum*, I, 50, ed. Koetschau, 101, 17.

[61] Huillard-Bréholles, *Vie et correspondance de Pierre de la Vigne* (Paris, 1865), 426, No. 107; see, for a fuller discussion, Kantorowicz, "Kaiser Friedrich II. und das Königsbild des Hellenismus," *Varia Variorum: Festgabe für Karl Reinhardt* (Munster and Cologne, 1952).

[62] The material has been neatly summed up by Albert Michael Koeniger, "Prima sedes a nemine iudicatur,"

Beiträge zur Geschichte des christlichen Altertums und der byzantinischen Literatur: Festgabe Albert Ehrhard (Bonn and Leipzig, 1922), 273–300. As usual, the papal maxim finally became a cornerstone of royal absolutism; see, e.g., Salmasius, *Defensio regia pro Carolo I.* (Paris, 1650—first published in 1649), ch. VI, 169: "Rex a nemine iudicari potest nisi a Deo"; and p. 170: "... illum proprium (regem esse), qui iudicat de omnibus et a nemine iudicatur."

to Psalm 81, 6, interprets "gods" as those endowed with *pneuma* or *gnosis*,[63] those who are made perfect and therefore immortal,[64] and he styles those human "gods" the *synthronoi* of the Saviour, ranking them with or after the angels.[65] Occasionally he illustrates the words of the 81st Psalm by quoting Empedocles on the sages that become gods,[66] just as on another occasion he explains man's becoming like unto God by quoting Heraclitus: ἄνθρωποι θεοί, θεοὶ ἄνθρωποι.[67] For Clement the "gods" were exalted (that is, redeemed or saintly) men and angels, which was true for Jerome too and for others as well.[68] Eusebius and others recognized them as rulers and princes. Jerome expressly rejected that idea, and thought rather of all men or at least of all Christians. Theodoret and his predecessors or followers—they depended directly or indirectly on Philo—think of the royal man as Image of God. Rufinus tells a spurious story about Constantine the Great who allegedly addressed the bishops assembled at Nicaea as "gods."[69] Pseudo-Isidorus, in the forged letters of Popes Anacletus, Marcellus, Melchiades, and others, repeats Rufinus' statement, styling the bishops now quasi *ex cathedra* "gods."[70] Finally, Pope Nicholas I allows *dii* to refer to the pope: ". . . pontificem quem constat a pio principe Constantino Deum appellatum, nec posse Deum ab hominibus iudicari manifestum est." Nothing could be more telling than the new twist from the plural *pontifices* to the one Roman Pontiff, and from the "gods" to the one God "who obviously cannot be judged by man." Surely this was "monopolizing by exclusion."[71]

---

[63] *Stromata*, II, xx, 125, 5, and IV, xxiii, 149, 8, Stählin, II, 181, 314; see also *Protrepticos*, XX, 123, Stählin, I, 86, 18.

[64] *Paedagogus*, I, vi, 26, 1, Stählin, I, 105, 22. Immortality is, *per se*, divinity: εἰ οὖν ἀθάνατος γέγονεν ὁ ἄνθρωπος, ἔσται καὶ θεός (Hippolytus, *Sermo in sanctam theophaniam*, c. 8, *PG*, X, 860A). See G. W. Butterworth, "The Deification of Man in Clement of Alexandria," *Journal of Theological Studies*, XVII (1916), 159ff, and in the same volume (257ff) some further notes on the subject by Cuthbert Lattey, who points out that "deification" does not imply polytheism, but sanctifying grace. For the Christian deification in general, see J. Gross, *La divinisation du chrétien d'après les pères grecs* (Paris, 1938); also M. Lot-Borodine, "La doctrine de la déification dans l'église grecque," *Revue de l'histoire des religions*, CV–CVII (1932–1933), and the remarks as well as bibliographic notes of A. D. Nock, in *The Journal of Religion*, XXXI (1951), 214f.

[65] *Stromata*, VII, x, 56, 6, Stählin, III, 41, 24. Lattey (above, n. 64), p. 261, stresses that the usage of the word *synthronos* indicates a connection of Christian deification with Ptolemaic king-worship; the connecting link, however, should be sought in Psalm 109 (110), 1, a problem which I shall discuss elsewhere on a broader basis. For the equation with angels, see also Friedrich Andres, "Die Engel- und Dämonenlehre des Klemens von Alexandria," *Römische Quartalschrift*, XXXIV (1926), 131ff; Williams, 162, n. 548. The idea, widely spread in the East and especially in the early Church, was that Christ himself represented the "God of gods" with regard to deified men ("gods") who shared the throne with him; see, e.g., Irenaeus, *Adv. haer.*, III, vi, 1, ed. Harvey, II, 22; Athanasius, *Contra Arianos*, I, c. 39, *PG*, XXVI, 92f. The

idea is found also in the West: Augustine, *Enarrat. in Ps.*, XLIX, 1, *PL*, XXXVI, 565 (with regard to the *dii facti*); Cassiodorus, *Expos. in Ps.*, XLIX, *PL*, LXX, 348D ("Deus autem deorum est Dominus Christus"). This became finally the generally accepted interpretation, see Peter the Lombard, *Comment. in Ps.*, XLIX, 1, *PL*, CXCI, 475B.

[66] *Stromata*, IV, xxiii, 149, 8, Stählin, II, 314, 26; Diels, fr. 146.

[67] *Paedagogus*, III, i, 2, 1, Stählin, I, 236, 25; Diels, fr. 67.

[68] Jerome, *Commentarioli in Ps.*, LXXXI, 1, ed. G. Morin, *Anecdota Maredsolana*, III:1 (Maredsous, 1895), p. 63: "[dii] angeli sive sancti." See above, n. 20 (Cassiodorus), n. 21 (Pseudo-Bede), n. 65 (Athanasius, Augustine). Augustine prefers to think of men rather than of angels: ". . . non frustra in scripturis sanctis expressius homines nuncupatos deos quam illos immortales et beatos, quibus nos aequales futuros in resurrectione promittitur." *De civ.*, IX, 23, Hoffmann, I, 440ff; cf. X, 1, and XV, 23, Hoffmann, I, 447, and II, 112.

[69] Rufinus, *Hist. eccl.*, I, 2, *PL*, XXI, 468. See also *Didascalia Apostolorum*, II, 34, ed. R. H. Connolly (Oxford, 1929), 96, 17ff, for the bishop as king and god.

[70] See the letters of Pseudo-Anaclet, c. xix; Pseudo-Marcellus, c. x; Pseudo-Melchiades, c. xi, ed Hinschius, *Decretales Pseudo-Isidorianae* (Leipzig, 1863), 76, 228, 248, and *passim*; the places have been collected by Dr. Schafer Williams, *Visio aetatis aureae ecclesiae Pseudo-Isidorianae* (unpubl. Ph. D. Diss., Berkeley, 1951.)

[71] Nicolaus I, *Ep.*, 86, *PL*, CXIX, 961, *MGH, Epistolae*, VI, 486, 17ff; cf. Jean Rivière "Sur l'expression *Papa-Deus* au moyen âge," *Miscellanea F. Ehrle* (Rome, 1924), II, 279, who correctly refers to Exod. 22, 28, and Ps. 81, 6, but concludes that Nicholas wished to appear

We now see that with the interpretation of *dii* in the sense of "anointed on earth"—kings and priests—the Norman Anonymous was in good company, including that of his seventeenth-century opposite number, Bossuet.[72] At any rate, his arguments were based on a very definite and very sound tradition. This is true also with respect to the "God-by-nature, god-by-grace" formula which customarily was connected with the *dii* of the 81st Psalm. The usefulness of that formula for political theory hinged, of course, on the interpretation of *dii* in the sense of kings. That was originally not the case. It is true that the contrast of *physis* and *mimesis*, which in the last analysis is Platonic,[73] was adapted by the Pythagoreans to political theory as a means of harmonizing the state with the cosmos, of attuning men to the king and the king to God, and thereby also of exalting the king and making him for cosmic reasons as similar as possible to the godhead.[74] The Christian version of the *physis-mimesis* contrast had originally nothing whatever to do with political ideas. The attuning of earth to heaven was achieved by other means, chiefly through the liturgy, whereas the new *physis-charis* formula served different purposes. Origen, who may have introduced that formula to explain those puzzling *dii* of the Old Testament, used the contrast of nature and grace for apologetic ends; and it retained its apologetic character also when applied to christological thought as a defense and weapon against Arians and other heterodox. The formula then served, above all, to demonstrate that Christ was truly "God by nature" and not identical with that plurality of "gods" who, if they were gods at all and not by name only, were Christian "sons by adoption" or "gods by grace." Only through the adaptation of *dii* to a restricted group of men, to kings or bishops, did the *natura-gratia* formula become available also for political theory and political theology.

To summarize, the mediaeval formula of "God-by-nature, gods-by-grace," which has been thrown into focus by the twelfth-century Norman royalist, goes back to the Pythagorean or Hellenistic antithesis of "God by *physis*, god by *mimesis*," which the post-classical or late antique philosophers have combined with their theories on kingship. To what extent certain other and older distinctions—φύσει θεοί and θέσει θεοί, men immortal and gods mortal, man a terrestrial mortal god and god a celestial immortal man[75]

merely as *primus inter pares*. For the principle of mono-polizing by exclusion, see Friedrich Heiler, *Altkirchliche Autonomie und päpstlicher Zentralismus* (Munich, 1941), 270ff, esp. 274f. Gregory the Great (*Reg.*, V, 36, *MGH*, *Epistolae*, I, 318, 15ff) uses the Rufinus story with reference to priests in general, and Gregory VII, in his letter to Bishop Hermann of Metz (*Reg.*, VIII, 21, ed. Caspar, 553), gives the story an unmistakably hierarchic tendency.

[72] "Vous êtes des Dieux, mais des Dieux de chair et de sang, de boue et de poussière"; quoted by Fritz Hartung, "L'état c'est moi," *Historische Zeitschrift*, CLXIX (1949) 20. As Dr. M. Cherniavsky kindly points out to me, the same arguments were used in Russia, around 1500, by the Abbot of the Volokolamsk Monastery, Joseph Sanin, *Illuminator*, c. 16, in: *Pravoslavnyi Sobesednik* (Kazan, 1857), Parts 3–4, pp. 602f: "You are gods and the sons of the most High... God has placed you in his place on his throne, because the Tsar in his nature is like all men, but in his power he is like the supreme God." See above, n. 55.

[73] See Michaelis (above, n. 51), 663ff, also for the increase of the word μιμέομαι and its derivatives in the works of Philo; Cherniss (above, n. 42), 62, for the Platonic usage of that figure of speech; and Henry G. Meecham, *The Epistle to Diognetus* (Manchester, 1940), 143f, for the commonplace character.

[74] See especially the tractate of Diotogenes; Delatte, 37ff (cf. 270ff); Goodenough, 71ff.

[75] The relevant places have been collected by Bywater, in his edition of Heraclitus (Oxford, 1877), 26f, and by R. Walzer, *Eraclito* (Florence, 1939), 101f; see also Carl Langer, "Euhemeros und die Theorie der φύσει und θέσει θεοί," *Angelos*, II (1926), 53ff. As late as the 11th century, the Byzantine emperor is addressed θεὸς ἐπίγειος, though χάριτι (V. Valdenberg, "Nikoulitza et les historiens contemporains," *Byzantion*, III [1927], 97; cf. R. Guilland, "Le droit divin à Byzance," *Eos*, XLII [1947], 142, 149), and to Hobbes (*Leviathan*, c. XVII) the sovereign is a *Deus mortalis*.

—would demand consideration cannot be decided here. The way, however, in which Clement of Alexandria quoted the Heraclitean ἄνθρωποι θεοί, θεοὶ ἄνθρωποι, and Athanasius, following St. Paul (1 Cor. 8, 5), introduced the sons of God and gods εἴτε ἐπὶ γῆς, εἴτε ἐν οὐρανοῖς allows us to wonder whether those older distinctions, even though expounded in a new non-dialectical and more appropriate fashion, may not have been contributive, too.[76] At any rate, in the antithesis of "God-by-nature, gods-by-grace" we have to recognize the Christian equivalent of at least one aspect of pre-Christian deification, deification by *mimesis*.[77] It is certainly not the only political theorem which survived during the Middle Ages by transference.[78]

The "transference" itself, however, demands a few words of comment. How did the Hellenistic *mimesis* change into the Christian *charis*, or how did *imitatio* enter into the *natura-gratia* scheme? One has to start from the dogmatic truism that man achieved his God-likeness and regained his original immortality as "Image of God" through the medium of divine grace, manifested and activated through the Incarnation. Not by his proper nature, but by divine grace does man become like God. Apart from the deification from above, however, it is in man's proper power to become and be like God by imitation of the Godhead, whereby the notion of *mimesis* implies not merely active imitation, but also "ontologically" the Being like unto God, as the Living Image of Him. Hence the two notions of *gratia* and *imitatio*, appearing so often almost interchangeable, are in fact interrelated through the medium of *imago Dei*. Man the Image of God is the fundamental idea which *charis* and *mimesis* have in common and to which they can be reduced. There is hardly a difference between *eikon* and *mimesis*, just as in *charis* the idea of εἰκὼν τοῦ θεοῦ is included. Gregory of Nyssa's χριστιανισμός ἐστι τῆς θείας φύσεως μίμησις[79] is probably the formulation bringing us as close as we can hope to come to determining the transition from imitation to grace.

The difference between *mimesis* of pagan thought and *gratia* of Christian thought remains nevertheless considerable. According to the Hellenistic philosophers it was an act of man's own virtue to become God-like and be the God's perfect imitator; it was an act of purely human effort and human industry: *deorum virtus natura excellit, hominum autem industria*, as Cicero puts it.[80] According to Christian teaching, however, man could not by his proper human power alone, despite his free will, hope to be restored to his divine Being and divine immortality: this was possible by the intervention of grace only, since every natural virtue became of merely relative value without *veri Dei verus cultus*. Even if the possibility of a completely sinless virtuous man were admitted, writes Augustine, this man would yet be without sin not by his own natural efforts and merits but by divine grace.[81] In other words, the supranatural was interposed between man

---

[76] Above, nos. 31, 67; cf. n. 11, and below, n. 81.

[77] Hans Joachim Schoeps, *Aus frühchristlicher Zeit* (Tübingen, 1950), 298f.

[78] Delatte, 152ff; N. H. Baynes, "Eusebius and the Christian Empire," *Mélanges Bidez* (Annuaire de l'Institut de Philologie et d'Histoire Orientales et Slaves, II; Brussels, 1934), 13ff; Steinwenter (above, n. 53); also the study mentioned above, n. 61.

[79] Greg. Nyss., *De professione*, PG, XLVI, 244C; also 244D; and *In verba* 'faciamus hominem,' Or. I, PG, XLIV, 273D. Cf. Cherniss, 62.

[80] Cicero, *Topica*, 76; cf. Delatte, 277, also for additional places.

[81] Augustine, *De natura et gratia*, c. 42 (49), PL, XLIV, 271; also *De civ.*, XIV, 13: "Dii enim creati non sua veritate, sed Dei participatione sunt dii. Plus autem ap-

and his deification. And the supranatural—that is, grace—had to be interposed if redemption were to make sense. It was this antinomy of Classical and Christian attitudes which was overcome when Dante, despite his full recognition of the celestial paradise of grace, unlocked a *paradiso terrestre* to man's proper *virtù*.

petendo minus est... Illud itaque malum, quo, cum sibi homo placet tamquam sit et ipse lumen, avertitur ab eo lumine, quod ei, si placeat, et ipse fit lumen." The idea of grace in connection with imitation and deification is found already in the *Epistle to Diognetus*, X, 4, ed. Meecham, 86, who in his commentary (p. 134) stresses that "it is the divine grace and initiative that enables men to imitate God." On the other hand, A. D. Nock pointed out that there were many aspects of Christian "imitation of God" and that the purely human efforts towards imitation were considered effective too (*Journal of Religion*, XXXI [1951], 214, in his review of Meecham which unfortunately came to my knowledge only after having finished the present study). However, also the pagan antecedents of Christian deification had many aspects. It was the current view of pagan philosophy in the post-classical era that the philosopher or the sage shared, one way or another, the life of the gods either by his nature or by his training (see also above, n. 41). It should be stressed, however, that for Plato the ὁμοίωσις θεῷ existed only κατὰ τὸ δυνατόν (*Theaet.* 176B) whereas Plotinus, when quoting that passage (*Enn.* II, 1), omitted the modification and allowed man to become god-like or even god without such restriction (cf. II, 6). In that generalization, the Neo-Platonists certainly ap-

proximated Christian deification, a fact very strongly felt by Augustine. He fought the *Platonici* on the ground of their failure to make it clear that their immortals were, like good Christians, gods *a summo Deo facti*; for if the Platonists would only admit that their gods were not *per se ipsos beati*, there would be little difference between their teaching and that of Christians who, in agreement with many passages of Holy Scripture, likewise called their exalted men *dii* (*De civ.*, IX, 23). Hence pagan and Christian deification, despite all obvious contrasts, did not appear totally incomparable, and the convergent trends might be exposed in a far more subtle and satisfactory fashion than by the essay of O. Faller, "Griechische Vergottung und christliche Vergöttlichung," *Gregorianum*, VI (1925), 426ff. For that purpose the most recent studies on Epicurus should be considered too, since they suggest a fellowship of the sage with the gods by some kind of homogeneity rather than as a result of supreme efforts. Further investigations in that direction might succeed in establishing a new link between pagan god-likeness and Christian deification by grace. See A. H. Armstrong, "The Gods in Plato, Plotinus, Epicurus," *Classical Quarterly*, XXXII (1938), 190–196; Norman W. De Witt, "The New Piety of Epicurus," *Transactions of the Royal Society of Canada*, 3rd Ser., XXXVIII (1944), 79–88.

INALIENABILITY

A NOTE ON CANONICAL PRACTICE AND THE ENGLISH CORONATION OATH IN THE THIRTEENTH CENTURY

IN TWO LETTERS, one of 1233 and the other of 1235, Pope Gregory IX referred to the Coronation Oath of King Henry III of England.[1] In the letter of 1233, Pope Gregory reminded the king that, at the time of Henry's coronation in 1216, he, the young king, had sworn a corporeal oath "de regni Angliae iuribus et honoribus conservandis ac revocandis alienatis illicite vel distractis."[2] In the second letter, that of 1235, the pope stressed once more that "in coronatione tua iuraveris, ut moris est, iura, libertates et dignitates conservare regales."[3] It is well known that a "non-alienation clause" by which the king swore not to alienate the rights of the Crown and to revoke what had been alienated, did not form part of the customary tripartite oath which, with slight changes, had survived from Anglo-Saxon times.[4] That standard oath has been quoted by Bracton, and there is every reason to believe that Bracton reproduced, with substantial accuracy, the oath which the English king in the thirteenth century actually professed.[5] The papal letters, however (which, as Mr. Richardson proposes in a highly suggestive study, may

Reprinted, with permission, from *Speculum*, XXIX (1954), 488–502.

[1] Nothing could be farther remote from the present writer's ambition than to rehearse at full length once more the vexed question of the English Coronation Oath and Edward II's "fourth clause." All that is intended here is to communicate a few observations which may or may not prove relevant to the problem of inalienability, and which have little to do with the aims of the subtle studies of B. Wilkinson ("The Coronation Oath of Edward II," *Essays in Honour of James Tait* [Manchester, 1933] 405ff, and "The Coronation Oath of Edward II and the Statute of York," *Speculum*, XIX [1944], 445ff) or with the investigations of Percy Ernst Schramm (*History of the English Coronation* [Oxford, 1937], 204ff, and "Ordines-Studien III: Die Krönung in England," *Archiv für Urkundenforschung*, XV [1938], 349ff, 357ff), although they have something to do with the numerous studies of H. G. Richardson, summed up in his penetrating article on "The English Coronation Oath," in *Speculum*, XXIV (1949), 44–75. Where Mr Richardson stopped the present brief note wishes to continue, if only with a very limited goal.

[2] W. Shirley, *Royal and Other Historical Letters of the Reign of Henry III* (London, 1862), I, 551.

[3] Rymer, *Foedera*, I:1, 229, and, for the correct date (1 July), Potthast, 9952; cf. Richardson, p. 51, nos. 43, 44.

[4] The problem has been clearly recognized by Professor C. H. McIlwain, *The Growth of Political Thought in the West* (New York, 1932), 379: "It is a curious fact calling for further investigation, that in no surviving contemporary form of the English medieval coronation oath is there to be found any provision touching the inalienability of regalian rights; and yet the statements just cited, and a number of others, seem to leave no doubt that in the thirteenth and fourteenth centuries at least, the English king at his coronation did take some kind of solemn engagement under oath not to dismember his realm nor to 'blemish' the rights of his Crown..." The history of the tripartite Anglo-Saxon oath has been efficiently and conveniently summed up by Schramm, *Coronation*, 179ff.

[5] Bracton, *De Legibus*, fol. 107, ed. Woodbine, II, 305. For the recension which Bracton used, and for the slight changes resulting from the *oratio obliqua*, see Richardson, pp. 44f, nos. 3–4; also Fritz Schulz, "Bracton on Kingship," *English Historical Review*, LX (1945), 137, 145ff.

even have repeated phrases used by the royal scribes),[6] indicate that Henry III must have sworn at some time something about maintaining the rights of the Crown and refraining from alienations. In other words, there must have existed, in addition to the standard tripartite oath, some further promise or clause concerning non-alienation which curiously did not go on record and of which we have only indirect knowledge through the papal letters.

This assumption becomes almost a certainty in the case of Edward I. No additional clause appended to the standard oath taken by King Edward has been recorded, and yet the king himself, only a few months after his coronation, referred in a letter to Pope Gregory X to an oath sworn at his coronation by which, as Edward asserted, the king was "astricted" to conserve the rights of the Crown.[7] On seven other occasions—the reader may be sent back again to Mr. Richardson's exhaustive study[8]—King Edward repeated that assertion. Finally, Pope Clement V alluded likewise to that clause of the coronation oath. We are, therefore, compelled to believe that in fact both Henry III and Edward I took at the time of their coronations some additional oath which, for one reason or another, has escaped codification. When finally at the coronation of Edward II a fourth clause was added, it differed in content widely from what his two predecessors must have sworn.[9]

Nevertheless, the non-alienation issue had not disappeared from the oath of Edward II entirely. Mr. Richardson, who has sifted and inspected the relevant material with great care and ingenuity, has remarked very correctly that in liturgical books not all that is said is always codified (as occasionally, for example, the *Laudes*);[10] and we may add that not all that is codified, is always said (as, for example, the commemoration of the emperor in the *Orationes solemnes* on Good Friday).[11] In the *Liber regalis*, a service book from the beginning of Edward II's reign, which may have been used at the coronation itself, Mr. Richardson has discovered an anonymous additional note saying "that the king at his coronation has to swear to maintain undiluted the rights of his kingdom."[12] In that note, perhaps a reminder to the celebrant, the anonymous cleric made a perfectly

---

[6] Richardson, p. 52, has tried to reconstruct from Gregory's answer to Henry III, in 1233, the work of the royal clerks who, as he suggests, may have borrowed from Innocent III's bull of 1215 (condemnation of Magna Charta). However, the papal chancery itself could independently have drawn from the Innocentian bull by checking, so to speak, the file "England" in the papal archives.

[7] *Parliamentary Writs*, I, 381f.:"... et iureiurando in coronacione nostra prestito sumus astricti quod iura regni nostri servabimus illibata." See below, n. 60.

[8] Richardson, p. 49f.

[9] For the oath of Edward II itself, see the studies by Wilkinson and Schramm (above, n. 1), but also Richardson's earlier studies. Richardson, p. 60ff, has demonstrated that the non-alienation promise was actually embedded in the first clause of Edward II's oath, that is, in the reference to the Laws of Edward the Confessor, including the interpolation from the *Leges Anglorum*. The problem of inalienability in the *Leges Anglorum* will not be dealt with here. It should be mentioned, though, that the findings of Richardson, as put forth in the *Bulletin of the Institute of Historical Research*, XVI (1938), 7 and 10,

and in *Transactions of the Royal Historical Society*, 4th Series, XXIII (1941), 149f, defeat the thesis of Schramm, *Coronation*, p. 206, and in *Archiv f. Urk. Forsch.*, XV (1938), 350, according to which the *rex Edwardus* of the oath of 1308 supposedly referred, not to the Confessor, but to Edward I. See below, n. 64.

[10] Richardson, p. 46.

[11] See, e.g., Edmund Bishop, *Liturgica Historica* (Oxford, 1918), 297: "... the present Roman Missal, in which we may read, but do not say, a commemoration of the 'Emperor'." In the more recent editions of the *Missale Romanum* (e.g., the New York edition of 1937), the commemoration of the emperor has dropped out completely. Similar examples may be found time and time again. What about the acclamation, for example, to the *nobilissima proles* in the *Laudes* of Emperor Henry II, whose saintliness was founded also in his Joseph-like marriage and who certainly had no *proles* worth the acclamation? See my *Laudes regiae* (Berkeley and Los Angeles, 1946), 99, n. 119.

[12] Richardson, in *Bull. of the Inst. of Hist. Res.*, XVI (1938), 11.

scholarly allegation to the *Liber Extra*, the Decretals of Gregory IX. That is, he quoted in a juristic manner a decretal of Pope Honorius III, originally directed (in 1220) to the Archbishop of Kalocsa in Southern Hungary, in which the pope complained of certain alienations made by King Andrew II of Hungary although that king "in sua coronatione iuraverit iura regni sui et honorem coronae illibata servare."[13]

This decretal, first identified apparently by Professor Schramm,[14] has been quoted by Mr. Richardson according to Friedberg's authoritative edition of the *Corpus iuris canonici*.[15] Unfortunately, the philologically best edition is not always the one most useful to the historian. The Krüger-Mommsen-Schoell edition of the *Corpus iuris civilis*, for example, is next to useless for the mediaevalist, because it lacks the index of *initia* of the individual laws and, in the edition of the *Novellae*, even that of the rubrics.[16] The old sixteenth-century editions of both Roman and canon laws, despite their dubious readings, not only are far more convenient and even indispensable for verifying mediaeval allegations but also yield materially more to the mediaevalist than the modern editions because—and that above all—they contain the otherwise almost inaccessible ordinary glosses.[17] But, alas, *glossae non leguntur*—and therewith we historians deprive ourselves of the accumulated scholarship of many generations while endeavoring at the same time individually to reassemble materials which schools of glossators have collected already 700 years ago. Had Mr. Richardson checked, not indeed the best edition, but one of the old glossed editions of the Gregorian Decretals, the present paper would have been superfluous, because the gloss would have sent him in the same direction as it sent me, when, in the course of a little investigation on the notion of "Crown" in canon law, I naturally chanced upon the decretal of Honorius III. He would have found most or all of the allegations which are used in the following pages and, as I believe, clarify that fourth or additional clause of the coronation oath of Henry III, sworn to apparently also by Edward I and perhaps even by Edward II.

* * *

It has been observed recently by Professor Marcel David that after the age of the church reform in the eleventh century the old *professio fidei* made by a bishop at his consecration changed into a *iuramentum fidelitatis*, and that this change affected, in the course of the twelfth century, also the secular sphere when the king's coronation *promissio* was gradually transformed into a coronation *iuramentum*.[18] This change was paralleled by

---

[13] The allegation *Extra de iureiurando, intellecto*, etc., refers to *Liber Extra*, title *De iureiurando*, chapter *Intellecto*, that is, to c. 33 X, 2, 24.

[14] See Schramm, in *Arch. f. Urk. Forsch.*, XVI (1939), 284. Wilkinson, in *Speculum*, XIX (1944), 450, n. 1, apparently overlooked Schramm's remark, because he has thoroughly misunderstood the canonistic reference.

[15] Richardson, p. 48, n. 26, quoting E. Friedberg, *Corpus iuris canonici* (Leipzig, 1881), II, 373.

[16] See Hermann Kantorowicz, "Die Allegationen im späteren Mittelalter," *Arch. f. Urk. Forsch.*, XIII (1935), 15–29, esp. 25f.

[17] Throughout I am quoting canon law according to a glossed standard edition in three volumes (Turin, 1588), and Roman law according to a glossed standard edition in five volumes (Venice, 1584), without reference to volume or page.

[18] Marcel David, "Le serment du sacre du IXᵉ au XVᵉ siècle," *Revue du Moyen Age Latin*, VI (1950), esp. 168ff. (published also separately, Strasbourg, 1951); see also the review by Schramm, in *Zeitschrift der Savigny-Stiftung für Rechtsgeschichte*, germ. Abt. LXIX (1952), 542–547.

the development of the episcopal oath itself and of its wording. Under the influence of feudal law, which began to spread in the States of the Church during the eleventh century,[19] as well as more generally under the impact of the imperializing tendencies which transformed the Church administration into a centralized papal monarchy,[20] the ancient oath of office taken by bishops and prescribed by the *Liber diurnus* was replaced by a new form.[21] Whereas the ancient formularies of the *Liber diurnus* demanded from the bishop assurances mainly in matters of faith and of devotion to the papal head of the Church, the new oath was rather a politico-administrative oath of office and fealty in which the word "faith" no longer had a place.[22]

The oldest form of the new oath goes back, so far as we know, to 1073. It is the oath which Archbishop Wibert of Ravenna, at his ordination, swore to Pope Alexander II; for, the three North Italian metropolitans (Ravenna, Milan, Aquileia) were consecrated by the pope himself.[23] The oath contained seven clauses,[24] of which the last three referred exclusively to certain episcopal duties: (V) to the reception of papal legates, (VI) to the appearance at synods when summoned by the pope, and (VII) to the annual visits *ad limina Apostolorum*.[25] The first four clauses, however, were of a different nature. The bishop (I) swore fealty and obedience to St. Peter, the Church, and the pope, including the pope's legitimate successors; (II) forswore acts of treason in counsel and action; (III) promised secrecy with regard to everything the pope might intimate to the bishop either directly or through envoys or in writing; and (IV) swore to defend the *papatus Romanus* and the *regalia sancti Petri*.[26]

---

[19] Karl Jordan, "Das Eindringen des Lehenswesens in das Rechtsleben der römischen Kurie," *Arch. f. Urk. Forsch.*, XII (1931), 13–110, esp. 44ff.

[20] See, for the imperialization of the papacy, P. E. Schramm, "Sacerdotium und Regnum im Austausch ihrer Vorrechte," *Studi Gregoriani*, II (1947), 403–457, esp. 436ff; also my *Laudes regiae*, 135ff, and the article "Dante's 'Two Suns'," *Semitic and Oriental Studies Presented to William Popper* (Berkeley and Los Angeles, 1951), 229, for the "Sun-Papacy"; and for some additional features (the papal "omni-insular theory"), Luis Weckmann, *Las Bulas Alejandrinas de 1493 y la Teoría Política del Papado Medieval* (Mexico, 1949), esp. 37ff.

[21] For the history of the episcopal oath, see the very thorough study of Th. Gottlob, *Der kirchliche Amtseid der Bischöfe* (Kanonistische Studien und Texte, IX; Bonn, 1936), a book which should be consulted throughout even when not mentioned in the footnotes. For the early oaths, see *Liber diurnus*, Nos. 73 (*Promissio fidei episcopi*), 74 (*Cautio episcopi*), 75 (*Indiculum episcopi*), and 76 (*Indiculum episcopi de Langobardia*), ed. Th. von Sickel (Vienna, 1889), pp. 69ff, 74ff, 79f, 80f; the edition in Migne, *PL*, CV, 67ff, is confusing. The forms have been reprinted by Gottlob, pp. 170ff, and analyzed, pp. 11ff.

[22] This item, of course, has been noticed by Gottlob, p. 45, who indicates (p. 122) that the essence of the ancient *Promissio fidei* is contained in the first clause of the new oath: "Ego ... ab hac hora in antea fidelis ero Sancto Petro etc." This, in fact, is the opinion of Innocent IV, quoted by Johannes Andreae, *Novella in Decretales* (Venice, 1612), fol. 184, on c. 4 X, 2, 24 (*Ego.N.*),

gl. *Sancto Petro*: "id est fidem quam beatus Petrus servavit et docuit, fideliter observabo." However, *fidelis ero* refers to fealty rather than to faith; accordingly Johannes Andreae (*loc. cit.*), when glossing on *fidelis*, sends the reader to Hostiensis who glossed on that word under the title *De feudis* of the Decretals; see his *Summa aurea* (Venice, 1586), col. 972, on X, 3, 20, n. 10. See, for the controversy, below, n. 29.

[23] See Gottlob, pp. 20ff, 44f. The claims of the papacy to the two formerly Lombard ecclesiastical provinces and to that of the Exarchate of Ravenna are of course very old.

[24] For the form of Wibert's oath, see Deusdedit, *Collectio canonum*, V, c. 423, ed. Wolf von Glanvell (Paderborn, 1905), I, 599; *Liber censuum*, No. 148, ed. Fabre und Duchesne (Paris, 1910), I, 417; Gottlob, pp. 176f; also Gregory VII, *Registrum*, I, 3, ed. Caspar (Berlin, 1920), 6, n. 3.

[25] Those clauses agree with the standard oath (below, n. 35), which Johannes Andreae, *loc. cit.*, calls the *Forma iuramenti septem capitula continens*. For the bishops' annual visits to Rome, see Januarius Pater, *Die bischöfliche visitatio liminum ss. Apostolorum* (Veröffentlichungen der Görresgesellschaft: Sektion für Rechts- und Sozialwissenschaft, XIX; Paderborn, 1914). That *limina Apostolorum* finally came to mean not Rome, but the pope, has been clearly expressed by Johannes Andreae, who renders only the common opinion when he glosses *Limina*: "limina enim apostolorum esse intelliguntur, ubi est papa... qui liminibus illis praeest et qui fungitur vice et auctoritate eorum (sc. apostolorum)."

[26] "Papatum Romanum et regalia sancti Petri adiutor ero ad retinendum et defendendum, salvo meo ordine,

Clauses I–IV agree, minor changes notwithstanding, with the first four clauses of the oath of fealty taken by Robert Guiscard in 1059.[27] It is not impossible that, a few months earlier than the Norman prince, Archbishop Wido of Milan delivered a similar oath;[28] but the form of Wido's oath is not preserved, and therefore Guiscard's oath of 1059 represents to us the earliest pattern of the first four clauses which were to be included into the new episcopal oath. Although that new episcopal oath implied neither vassalage nor feudal tenure in the proper sense of those words—with regard to the *spiritualia* this actually would have been simony[29] — the general influence of feudal thought is nevertheless evident. This influence can be traced back to Fulbert of Chartres (975–1029?). Fulbert, when asked what an oath of fealty should contain, gave his expert opinion in a letter (1020 A.D.) addressed to Duke William of Aquitaine, and the points enumerated by Fulbert match, by and large, clauses I–IV of both the Guiscard oath and the new episcopal oath.[30] The authority of Fulbert's letter in later times is easily explained, for in the course of the twelfth century it was included by Gratian in his *Decretum*,[31] and it was

contra omnes homines." The notion of *regalia sancti Petri*, abundantly used or perhaps even introduced by the Reform Papacy, indicates yet another feature of the "imperialization" of the papal Church (above, n. 20). The term appears not only in the oaths of the Norman princes and in the oaths and *promissiones* of many German kings and emperors—see, e.g., *MGH, Const.*, I, 564, 14, No. 394 (oath of Conrad, son of Henry IV, to Urban II, in 1095), or *ibid.*, 168, 17, No. 115 (*Promissio* of Lothair, in 1133), or 201, 26, No. 144; also 353, 29, No. 250 (Barbarossa), and, in a slightly different form (negotiations with Henry V), 159, 31, No, 107, also 163, 29, No. 110—but also in the writings of the political pamphleteers of that period. See, e.g., the *Dialogus de Pontificatu*, in *MGH, Libelli de Lite*, III, 538, 30; also Gerhoh, *De investigatione Antichristi*, I, c. 69 (*ibid.*, 389, 10), who claims that it was the duty to defend *et regalia atque pontificalia beati Petri*. The antithesis of *regalia* and *pontificalia* reflects the *rex et sacerdos* idea which dominates the Reform Papacy and which Gerhoh (388, 45) expresses quite bluntly when he says that the bishops, since they possess not only the *sacerdotalia* of tithes and oblations but also the *regalia* on the part of their king, may claim to be *quodammodo et reges et sacerdotes domini*; they are therefore entitled to demand obedience on the part of the people and even an oath of fealty *ad defensionem videlicet regalium simul et pontificalium beati Petri*. See, in that connection, also *Descriptio Lateranensis Ecclesiae*, c. 9, ed. R. Valentini and G. Zucchetti, *Codice topografico della Città di Roma* (Fonti per la Storia d'Italia, XC; Rome, 1946), III, 345, 5 (including the variant reading in the footnote), where the pope is styled *sacerdos regalis et imperialis episcopus*. Those concepts were supported by Justinian's *Novella* IX in its mediaeval interpretation (Rome as *patria legum, fons sacerdotii*). — Also the notion *papatus* (absent from the *Liber diurnus*) became current at the same time; for whereas the considerably older notions of *pontificatus* and *patriarchatus* designated umambiguously the spiritual aspects of the office, *papatus* could be easily adjusted to encompassing also the temporal sphere and thus to fall in with the *rex et sacerdos* theories. Hence, Innocent IV interpreted the word *papatus* of the oath as

meaning *principatus tam in spiritualibus quam in temporalibus;* see Johannes Andreae, *loc. cit.* (above, n. 22). All those terms are very much in need of being carefully investigated. It is noteworthy that both the word *fidelis* (clause I) and the words *regalia sancti Petri* (clause IV) have been eliminated from the episcopal oath as prescribed for the bishops of the United States of America; see Gottlob, p. 99, n. 103.

[27] For Guiscard's oath, see Deusdedit, *Coll. canonum*, III, c. 285, ed. Glanvell, 393f; *Liber censuum*, No. 163, ed. Fabre and Duchesne, I, 422; and, for the repetition of the oath in 1080, Gregory VII, *Registrum*, VIII, 1a, ed. Caspar, p. 514.

[28] Gottlob, p. 43.

[29] See c. 11 X, 5, 41, a decretal of Lucius III: "Indignum est et a Romanae ecclesiae consuetudine alienum, ut pro spiritualibus facere quis homagium compellatur." See also gl. *homagium* on that decretal: "id est sacramentum fidelitatis, quod pro aliquo spirituali facere quis non debet, cum sit illud simoniacum..." Since, however, all the decisive words—such as *fidelitas, beneficium, etc.* —were ambiguous (see above, n. 22), they were open to feudal interpretation as well. See, for the controversy on that point, Gottlob, pp. 115ff, who (esp. pp. 120, 125) proves convincingly that the episcopal oath was not really a feudal oath. However, Pope Innocent II, at the Lateran Council of 1139, himself remarked that "Romani pontificis licentia ecclesiastici honoris celsitudo quasi foeudalis iuris consuetudine suscipitur et sine eius permissione legaliter non tenetur." Mansi, *Concilia*, XXI 534, quoted by E. Eichmann, *Die Kaiserkrönung im Abendland* (Würzburg, 1942), II, 172; see also p. 178, for the parallelism of episcopal and feudal oaths, and, for a very striking later example, F. Baethgen, "Die Promissio Albrechts I. für Bonifaz VIII.," *Aus Politik und Geschichte: Gedächtnisschrift für Georg von Below* (Berlin, 1928), 75–90.

[30] Fulbert of Chartres, *Epistolae*, 58; Migne, *PL*, CLXI, 229CD.

[31] *Decretum*, c. 18, C. XXII, q. 5, ed. Friedberg, I, 887, with n. 157.

included in the *Libri feudorum* as well.[32] Hence, through Fulbert's letter the feudal background of the new episcopal oath finds a plausible explanation. Only in one respect did the oaths imposed by the Holy See show a remarkable deviation from feudal norms: the defense of the personal lord, the pope, has been supplemented by a defense of the impersonal *papatus Romanus* and the likewise impersonal *regalia sancti Petri*, two notions which hardly antedate the eleventh century and which are probably coinages of the Reform Papacy.[33]

The oath which Wibert of Ravenna took in 1073 became, with minor changes,[34] the "standard form" which, appropriately modified, was to serve many other purposes as well.[35] It was included in the *Liber Extra* of Pope Gregory IX, in 1234, and therewith became the official norm within the Roman Church.[36] It still contained no more than the seven clauses followed by the customary corroboration: *Sic me Deus adiuvet et haec sancti Dei evangelia.* What a surprise, then, to find around 1200 A.D. scattered references to some additional oath! In a decretal of Pope Celestine III (1191–98), originally a letter addressed to Archbishop William of Ravenna, the metropolitan was reminded of his "oath of fealty" by which "he was held to alienate nothing from the Holy See."[37] Similarly, Pope Innocent III, Celestine's successor, reminded the archbishop of Milan in a letter, which likewise became a decretal, that the archbishop was "held astricted by his oath not to reinfeudate anew without previous consultation with the pope."[38]

The parallel of canon law evidence with available evidence concerning England is striking: in England, an official oath of only three clauses, and yet a frequently mentioned non-alienation clause; in Rome, an official oath of seven clauses, and yet repeated allusions to some additional non-alienation clause. With regard to Rome, however, we are more fortunate than with regard to England, because forms containing the "eighth clause" of the episcopal oath are indeed known.

Forms containing clause VIII begin to make their appearance by the time of Pope Gregory IX. The earliest one so far known refers by chance to Archbishop Edmund Abingdon of Canterbury, consecrated in 1234. It has been transmitted in the *Liber censuum* with the forms of Archbishops Marianus of Tuam (1235), Jarlerius of Upsala

---

[32] *Libri feudorum*, II, 6 (in Vol. IV of the *Corpus iuris civilis*; above, n. 17). Karl Lehmann, *Die Entstehung der Libri feudorum* (Rostock, 1891; also in *Festschrift der Rostocker Juristenfakultät zum 50 jährigen Doktorjubiläum Sr. Excellenz des Staatsrathes Dr. von Buchka*), pp. 34f, claims that the *epistola Philiberti* (i.e., Fulberti) came very early into the collection of the *Libri feudorum* and is found already in the twelfth-century Cod. Par. 4615 (see p. 17).

[33] This has been noticed also by Eichmann, "Die römischen Eide der deutschen Könige," *Zeitschrift der Savigny-Stiftung für Rechtsgeschichte*, kan. Abt. VI (1916), 172. See also above, n. 26.

[34] One of the changes refers to the phrase "pape . . . suisque successoribus, qui *per meliores cardinales* intraverint." The standard oath has replaced the italicized words by *canonice* (*catholice*, in the oath of King John [see below, n. 35], is an error and must be corrected), because in the meantime the papal decree of election of Alexander III (c. 6 X, 1, 6; Friedberg, II, 51) had established the

principle of the two-thirds majority; cf. Gottlob, 58, n. 81.

[35] The standard form agreed basically with the oath taken by all sorts of papal dependents: by the papal vice-chancellor and the papal notaries (M. Tangl, *Die päpstlichen Kanzleiordnungen von 1200–1500* [Innsbruck, 1894], 33ff, Nos. 1 and 3), by the Roman Senator, the community of Tibur, and by the papal feudatories (*Liber censum*, Nos. 59, 144, 67, edd. Fabre and Duchesne, pp. 313, 415, 341); cf. Baethgen, "Promissio," 81ff (above, n. 29). The form was used also for the feudal oath of King John; see Stubbs, *Select Charters*, 280f, and below, nos. 50, 51.

[36] See c. 4 X, 2, 24, ed. Friedberg, II, 360.

[37] See c. 8 X, 3, 13, ed. Friedberg, II, 514 (Jaffé-Loewenfeld, 17049): "cum ex sacramento fidelitatis tenearis Apostolicae Sedi nihil alienare."

[38] See c. 2 X, 3, 20, ed. Friedberg, II, 525 (Potthast, 3525): "iuramento tenearis astrictus non infeudare de novo, Romano pontifice inconsulto."

(1236), Peter of Rouen (1237), and Martin of Léon (probably Martin Arias: 1239).[39] We know, however, also the forms of Raoul of Lyon (1234)[40] and of Raymond of Peñafort, who became archbishop of Tarragon after 1234.[41] That is to say, forms containing that "eighth clause" make their appearance suddenly and simultaneously in the thirties of the thirteenth century. In that clause VIII, which was simply tacked on to clause VII (annual visits *ad limina Apostolorum*), the archbishop swore that he would not sell, give away, pawn, reinfeudate, or otherwise alienate, *inconsulto Romano pontifice*, the property pertaining *ad mensam archiepiscopalem*, that is, pertaining to the "table possessions" of the archbishopric, which served for the support of the archbishop and a few other purposes.[42]

To what extent the non-alienation clause was felt to be something additional becomes strikingly clear when we turn to another thirteenth-century formulary, referring to Amanieu II of Armagnac, archbishop of Auch, who was consecrated in Rome in 1263. This is, seemingly, a rather late date. In fact, however, the formulary is archaic—as archaic as the manuscript itself in which it has been transmitted and which served Professor M. Andrieu for the reconstruction of the Roman pontifical of the twelfth century.[43] In the formulary of Auch we find the customary seven clauses of the standard oath as prescribed by canon law in the *Liber Extra*; there follows the corroboration, and thereafter, in no organic connection whatsoever with the oath proper, comes the non-alienation clause. It will simplify the matter if the oath, beginning with the seventh clause, be quoted here in full.

(VII) Apostolorum limina singulis annis aut per me aut per meum nuntium visitabo, nisi eorum absolvar licentia.

Sic me Deus adiuvet et hec sancta Dei evangelia.

---

[39] *Liber censuum*, Nos. 198–198d, edd. Fabre and Duchesne, pp. 449f; cf. No. 147, p. 416.

[40] *Lib. cens.*, No. 54b, p. 287.

[41] Tangl, *Kanzleiordnungen*, p. 50, No. XVIII; cf. Gottlob, p. 56f.

[42] "Possessiones vero ad mensam mei archiepiscopatus pertinentes non vendam neque donabo neque inpingnorabo neque de novo infeudabo vel aliquo modo alienabo inconsulto Romano pontifice. Sic me Deus adiuvet et hec sancta evangelia." The phrase *inconsulto Romano pontifice* was used, in that connection, already by Innocent III (above, n. 38). The English writ *De non procedendo rege inconsulto*, famous through Sir Francis Bacon (*Works*, ed. James Spedding [London, 1870], VII, 687ff), has nothing to do with the canonistic formulae. For the *mensa episcopalis*, see A. Pöschl, *Bischofsgut und mensa episcopalis* (Bonn, 1908–1911); also his "Bischöfliche Tafelgüter oder Urbare," *Zeitschrift des historischen Vereins für Steiermark*, XXVI (1931), 141–153.

[43] The form, as yet unknown to Gottlob, was published by Michel Andrieu, *Le Pontifical romain au moyen-âge* (Studi e Testi, 86; Vatican City, 1940), I, 290f; cf. p. 51, for the manuscript, date, and other details. The manuscript Vat. lat. 7114 is late thirteenth century, but reflects conditions of the preceding century. For example, the form of *laudes*, in the Coronation Order *Ad ordinandum imperatorem secundum Occidentales*, is out of date and belongs to the twelfth century and to the era of Benedict of St. Peter, though in one respect an effort has been made to modernize them (cf. my *Laudes regiae*, pp. 237f). Moreover, the Coronation Order *secundum Occidentales* which, such as it stands, has never been used, belongs to a much earlier period and to an ideology different from the late thirteenth century; see C. Erdmann, *Forschungen zur politischen Ideenwelt des Frühmittelalters* (Berlin, 1951), 72ff. That two manuscripts of this Coronation Order originated in the diocese of Auch—that is, Vat. lat. 7114, and the so-called *Codex Gemundensis* (from the Cistercian monastery of Gimont, diocese of Auch; see Erdmann, p. 76, n. 1, an addition by Dr. R. Elze)—is most remarkable. It will not be hazardous to conclude that also clause VIII of the episcopal oath reflects an earlier stage; it certainly gives the impression of being older than the standardized clause VIII as quoted above (n. 42), and like the *Laudes* and the Coronation Order it was superannuated by the time the manuscript was written. Therefore, also, it was not the superannuated Auch form of the episcopal oath, but the one referred to above (nos. 39–42), which finally was taken over by the Pontifical of Durandus and therewith became the common usage of the Roman Church. See, for the Durandus form, Andrieu, *op. cit.*, III, 392, including footnote 33, which refers to bishops consecrated in Rome.

(VIII) Predia, possessiones, ornamenta ecclesiastica, que iuris sunt N. ecclesie, nunquam alienabo, nec vendam, nec in pignora ponam, neque alicui sine communi consensu capituli vel potioris partis et sanioris consilii in beneficio vel feudo dabo. Que distracta sunt, vel in pignore posita, ut ad ius et proprietatem eiusdem N. revocentur ecclesie, fideliter laborabo.

The non-alienation promise, which in this case referred not only to the mensal property of the see, but to all properties, possessions, and church valuables *que iuris sunt N. ecclesie*, is clearly an *ad hoc* addition quite loosely connected with the standard oath of the Decretals.

What are the implications of this practice? It appears that canon law provided for a standard episcopal oath of seven clauses, but that in some instances an eighth clause was appended forswearing alienation and promising revocation of properties belonging either to the *mensa episcopalis* or to the church as such; that is to say, of possessions allowing the bishop personally "to live on his own" or of possessions serving the general and public utility of the see. But on what occasions was that promise added? At that point the glosses shed some light on the procedure. Bernard of Parma, who composed the *Glossa ordinaria* on the Decretals of Gregory IX around 1245, remarked on the decretal of Celestine III: "Every bishop who is *immediately under the pope*, swears to him that he will not alienate property of the Church, nor give it away in tenure."[44] A century later, Baldus glossed the standard oath of seven clauses of the *Liber Extra*. At the very end of his interpretation he alleged the decretal of Innocent III and added the brief remark: "The *Liber Extra* notes that the *exempti* have to swear also (*etiam*) that they will not alienate Church property without having consulted the pope."[45] Other glosses, not readily accessible to me,[46] would probably make similar statements; but the two glosses adduced here are sufficient to clarify the matter. The glossators indicate that certain bishops were obliged to take an additional oath concerning non-alienation, although such an oath was neither prescribed by the standard oath nor on record in the body of canon law. The group of bishops bound to add that eighth clause to their oaths were designated as *exempti* or *immediate sub papa*. Now, those who were *nullo medio* directly under the pope were, in the first place, the papal suffragans of the pope's own ecclesiastical province and

---

[44] See gl. *sacramento*, on c. 8 X, 3, 13: "Nam quilibet episcopus *qui immediate domino pape subest*, iurat ei fidelitatem quod non alienabit bona ecclesie, nec in feudum dabit de novo, et idem iuramentum prestent alii episcopi suis metropolitanis." Gottlob, p. 65, n. 108, holds that the glossator was inaccurate when talking about *bona ecclesiae* in general, and not specifically about the *possessiones ad mensam pertinentes*. The observation of Gottlob is of peculiar interest: apparently Bernard of Parma, the composer of the *Glossa ordinaria*, still referred to the older form as transmitted by the pontifical of Auch ("possessiones...que iuris sunt N. ecclesie"; see above, n. 43), a form necessarily unknown to Gottlob. For the oaths of the suffragans to their metropolitans, which may be disregarded here, see Gottlob, pp. 138–169; also p. 183, for the late forms of that oath.

[45] Baldus, *In Decretalium volumen commentaria* (Venice edition of 1580, fol. 249r), on c. 4 X, 2, 24, n. 14: "Extra no. quod *exempti debent etiam iurare* quod non alienabunt proprietates ecclesiae Romano Pontifice inconsulto, de feu. c. 2. de reb. ecc. non ali. (= c. 2 X, 3, 20)."

[46] Johannes Andreae, *loc. cit* (above, n. 22), introduces the oath form as pertinent to the *episcopi qui sunt exempti*, and adds in gl. *nullo medio*: "idem servatur in aliis, si confirmationem, consecrationem vel pallium a papa recipiunt." But he is silent, just as is Hostiensis, about the non-alienation clause. The early glossators, including those of the *Compilatio prima* which contained already the standard oath, might have been of great interest to this study, but unfortunately they were inaccessible to me.

jurisdiction—by and large, the bishops within the States of the Church—; second, the archbishops of Ravenna, Milan, and Aquileia, heading the three North Italian ecclesiastical provinces within, as it were, the *pomerium* of the papal power or under the pope as the "Primate of Italy" (although this title—but not the claim—was of a later date); third, certain exempt bishoprics such as Bamberg, Puy, the Corsican sees, and indeed very many others as well, which, for one reason or the other, depended *nullo medio* on the Holy See. To these there were added, at the latest during the thirteenth century, most of the metropolitans and other recipients of the *pallium* who were likewise *nullo medio* under the pope, although not all of them had to swear to the eighth clause.[47]

At what time exactly the additional oath was introduced it would be difficult to tell. At the Roman synod of 1078, Pope Gregory VII decreed that no bishop consecrated by the pope himself—that is, one who was *nullo medio* under the pope—was allowed to hand out possessions of his church as fiefs without the consent of the pope.[48] This, however, was simply a decree, and it had, all by itself, nothing to do with the episcopal oath of office; whereas the decretals of Celestine III and Innocent III make it clear that by the end of the twelfth century the eighth clause had already been added to the oaths of at least the North Italian archbishops, perhaps in agreement with the pattern preserved in the Auch formulary. On the other hand, the sudden accumulation of evidence in the 1230's of metropolitans swearing to the eighth clause would suggest that—earlier individual cases notwithstanding—it became a more general practice only under Gregory IX to make the metropolitans at large take the oath of the *exempti* in Italy.

However that may be, the practice observed in Rome around 1200 is as obvious as the tendency of expanding the number of the bishops who depended on the Holy See *nullo medio* and therefore had to take the non-alienation oath. It all amounted to the development of the new custom according to which those who were, so to say, "tenants-in-chief" of the pope, had to add to the standard oath of seven clauses an eighth clause in which they promised not to alienate the properties of their episcopal sees.

The canonical procedure may shed some new light on the practice observed in England and alluded to so frequently in the correspondence between English kings and the Holy See. To the English standard oath there was added, apparently, a non-alienation clause which was not legally codified. Its absence, however, no longer needs to startle us,

---

[47] The oath at the reception of the pallium (cf. above, n. 46) was substantially the same as the standard oath; see *Liber censuum*, No. 148, ed. Fabre and Duchesne, p. 417. Not all metropolitans and primates, however, were bound to include clause VIII; see, e.g., the form of the primate of Bulgaria in which the additional clause is lacking (Innocent III, *Registrum*, VII, 11; Migne, *PL*, CCXV, 295A; Gottlob, p. 54f); and whether it was included in the form valid for the Latin patriarchs in the East (Gottlob, p. 55f), is doubtful.

[48] Gregory VII, *Reg.*, VI, 5b, c. 30, ed. Caspar, 402, 16: "Ut nulli episcopi predia ecclesiae in beneficium tribuant sine consensu pape, si de sua sunt consecratione." Cf. Gottlob, p. 57. Since this was a decree, but not yet part of the oath, the non-alienation clause is still lacking in the oath of Aquileia of the eleventh century; Gregory

VII, *Reg.*, VI, 17a, 4, ed. Caspar, pp. 428f. The exempt bishoprics are listed in the *Liber censuum*, edd. Fabre and Duchesne, I, 243; see the notes 247ff, and also Gottlob, pp. 64ff. For a Bamberg form, see Raynald, *Annales ecclesiastici, ad a.* 1206, §13. Gottlob, p. 57, assumes probably correctly that the non-alienation clause was introduced for the metropolitans at large by the time of Gregory IX, but that it had been added previously for such sees as were, for one reason or another, in particularly close relationship with the Holy See. For the distinction between inalienable Church property and a bishop's alienable private property, the jurists often referred to the *Decretum*, c. 13, D. XXVIII ("De Syracusanae"), a problem neatly put forth by the author of the *Summa Parisiensis*, ed. Terence P. McLaughlin (Toronto, 1952), p. 28.

for the corresponding clause was absent also from the standard oath of the Decretals. Furthermore, the addition of the non-alienation clause to the English coronation procedure finds a plausible explanation: Cardinal Guala Bicchieri, who in 1216 acted as the papal legate to England and who administered the oath to Henry III,[49] simply followed the practice known to him because observed, by that time, in Rome; that is, that the *exempti* who were *nullo medio* under the pope, swore not only the standard oath, but promised also, and additionally, not to alienate possessions of their *episcopatus*. The impersonal *episcopatus*, of course, was sensibly replaced by the likewise impersonal *corona*; but otherwise the English king and "tenant-in-chief" of the Holy See was treated —at least with regard to the additional non-alienation oath—like the episcopal "tenants-in-chief," the *exempti*.

While the connection of coronation and non-alienation oath thus gains a high degree of probability, it still remains perfectly legitimate to ask whether the additional clause was appended to the three clauses of the English coronation oath proper or rather to the oath of fealty sworn to the pope—a question which raises immediately the problem whether or not King John, in 1213, took that non-alienation oath. Unfortunately, it does not seem possible to answer those questions satisfactorily. The feudal oath of King John[50] has, like other oaths of papal feudatories and papal officials,[51] the first four clauses in common with the standard episcopal oath, notwithstanding the insertion of a special clause, taken from the old *Liber diurnus* oath, of which Pope Innocent III availed himself on other occasions as well.[52] The similarity of King John's feudal oath with the then current episcopal oath might suggest that indeed already under this king the non-alienation clause of the *exempti* was added to the oath of fealty by which the king recognized the papal overlordship. This hypothesis—and beyond the sphere of the hypothetical we cannot move—would further suggest that the non-alienation clause was tacked on to the oath of fealty rather than to the three clauses of the English coronation oath when, in 1216, an oath of fealty to the pope first entered into the English coronation ceremonial.

There remains, however, yet another factor to be considered. In 1220, four years after the coronation of Henry III, Pope Honorius III wrote the letter (above, p. 140) to the archbishop of Kalocsa in which he demanded that King Andrew II of Hungary revoke certain alienations because "at his coronation, he [the king] had sworn to maintain undiluted the rights of his realm and the honor of his Crown."[53] This letter, we recall,

---

[49] See Richardson, pp. 55, 74.

[50] Stubbs, *Select Charters*, 9th ed. (Oxford, 1921), 280f.

[51] See above, n. 35, also n. 34.

[52] The insertion reads: "Eorum [i.e., pope and successors] damnum, si scivero, impediam et removere faciam si potero: alioquin quam citius potero, intimabo vel tali personae dicam quam eis credam pro certo dicturam." The sentence is taken from the ancient *Indiculum episcopi* of the *Liber diurnus*, No. 75 (above, n. 21). Innocent III added that phrase also to the oath of the Bulgarian primate; see above, n. 47. Also, the words *papatus* and *regalia sancti Petri* have been replaced by "*Patrimonium beati Petri* et specialiter *regnum Angliae* et

regnum Hiberniae adiutor ero ad tenendum et defendendum contra omnes homines pro posse meo."

[53] See c. 33 X, 2, 24, and above, n. 13. It would be worth while to investigate the influence of that Honorian decretal of 1220. Gregory IX repeated it substantially in a letter to King Andrew II of Hungary (31 January, 1233; see Potthast, 9080), and sections of it were reiterated also in the letter to Henry III of 1235 (above, n. 2). It should not be underestimated to what extent the papal chancery used the same phrasings on the recurrence of similar situations. The Golden Bull of King Andrew II of Hungary, for example, brought about a similar reaction on the part of the Holy See as King John's issuance of Magna Charta; see Josef Deér, "Der Weg zur

passed by 1234 into the *Liber Extra*, so that the basic ideas of that letter became binding law within ecclesiastical practice. We have no means to determine whether the King of Hungary had really taken a non-alienation oath at his coronation. But whether he did so or not appears of minor importance compared to the fact that apparently the Holy See by that time was already proceeding on the assumption that an oath of that kind was customarily taken by any king at his coronation, just as it was taken by an ever-expanding group of high-ranking princes of the Church at their consecration.[54] In other words, in Rome the existence of certain royal obligations towards the impersonal crown was taken for granted at a time when that idea had as yet barely penetrated secular political thought.[55] *Ut moris est* ("as is the custom"), wrote Pope Gregory IX to Henry III in 1235[56]—the "custom," we may add, according to the assumption unilaterally represented by the Holy See, and probably with regard not only to England, but to the European kingdoms at large. Even though it can be proved easily that this assumption was substantially wrong—for example with regard to France[57]—there is nevertheless no reason to doubt that in England the papal legate Guala would have seen to it that the facts, in one way or the other, corresponded to the papal assumption and that in agreement with canon law[58] some non-alienation promise was made by the king.

There is no ambiguity concerning the influence of Canon Law with regard to Edward I. By this time, the decretal of Honorius III mentioning in so many words the inalienable rights of the Crown, began to be effective at the royal court too. When Edward, ten months after his coronation, referred for the first time to the obligations deriving from his coronation oath, his clerk or legal adviser—perhaps Francis Accursius or Stephen of S. Giorgio[59]—quoted the Honorian decretal saying that the king was obliged "to maintain undiluted the rights of the realm" and added, by an interesting twist of the

---

Goldenen Bulle Andreas' II. von 1222," *Schweizer Beiträge zur allgemeinen Geschichte*, X (1922), 133ff, 136.

[54] Certain coincidences should be noted; Gregory's *Liber Extra* was commissioned in 1230 and finished in 1234; the oaths of metropolitans begin to show the non-alienation clause regularly and generally after 1234; and Pope Gregory's letters to Henry III fall in the same period, 1233 and 1235. Should it have been in these years only that the pope "assumed" that a king at his coronation took customarily an oath concerning the inalienability of Crown property? The Honorian decretal to Hungary was certainly earlier than 1234, and so were the decretals of Celestine III and Innocent III concerning the North Italian archbishops. However, it may have been Gregory IX who started to generalize what had been incidental.

[55] Georges de Lagarde, *La Naissance de l'esprit laïque au declin du moyen âge*, I: *Bilan du XIIIᵉ siècle* (Vienna, 1934), 158, n. 23, remarks that the idea of inalienability of rights of the state "a été une des plus lentes à pénétrer." For a few remarks on the continental development, see Schramm, *Coronation*, 198f, and "Das kastilische Königtum in der Zeit Alfonsos des Weisen (1252–84)," *Festschrift Edmund E. Stengel* (Münster and Cologne, 1952), 406; and, for Spain, also Gifford Davis, "The Incipient Sentiment of Nationality in Mediaeval Castile: the *Patrimonio real*," *Speculum*, XII (1937), 351–358.

[56] Above, n. 3, also n. 54. Most surprisingly, the same phrase had been used by Prince Louis of France in his declaration of 1215, in which he asserted that King John "in coronatione sua solempniter, *prout moris est*, iurasset se iura et consuetudines ecclesie et regni Anglie conservaturum." Cf. Richardson, pp. 51, 54. The French prince, of course, knew full well that such an oath was not the *mos* of France, at least not by that time (see next note).

[57] See Schramm, *Der König von Frankreich* (Weimar, 1939), I, 237, nos. 1 and 7, for the introduction of the non-alienation clause in the French coronation ceremonial in 1365. Actually, a few lines had to be erased in King Charles V's private de luxe edition of the ritual in order to squeeze the new clause into the old version of the oath.

[58] We may think of the decretals of Celestine III and Innocent III; above, nos. 37, 38.

[59] See, for Accursius as well as Stephen of S. Giorgio, G. L. Haskins and E. H. Kantorowicz, "A Diplomatic Mission of Francis Accursius," *English Historical Review*, LVIII (1943), 424ff; also 424, n. 4; for Stephen, see also Robert Weiss, "Cinque lettere inedite del Cardinale Bendetto Gaetani (Bonifacio VIII)," *Rivista di Storia della Chiesa in Italia*, III (1949), 157–164, esp. 162ff; there is, however, still much unedited material on that South Italian clerk at the court of Edward I.

romano-canonical maxim *Quod omnes tangit*, that by his oath the king was bound also "to do nothing that touches the Diadem of this realm without having resorted to the counsel of prelates and magnates."[60] *Obiter*, because far beyond the scope of this paper, it may be remarked that the decretal of Honorius III concerning the Hungarian crown furthered also the development of the notion of "Crown" in connection with the idea of the inalienability of royal rights and possessions. The notion of Crown, it is true, was quite common in England ever since the twelfth century especially with regard to fiscal and iudicial matters; but it was only in the course of the thirteenth that the impersonal crown achieved constitutional importance.[61]

It is hard to believe that Edward I, only ten months after his coronation and at a time when everyone concerned would have known what the king had promised on that occasion, should have tried to fabricate a story about a coronation promise which in fact he had not made.[62] The contrary seems to be true: that is, the papal assumption concerning a generally practiced non-alienation promise made by a king at his coronation must have met with the facts also in the case of Edward I. That Edward utilized that promise in pursuit of his own interests by turning it against the Holy See does not mitigate the probability that he made the additional promise. It seems less likely, though, that the same can be said of Edward II whose non-alienation promise has to be extracted (as Mr. Richardson has shown)[63] from the reference to the Laws of the Confessor contained in the first clause of the new coronation oath.[64] However, Edward II himself seems to have referred to an "oath which he had sworn to maintain the laws of the land and the estate of the Crown" when, in 1321, he refused to grant the barons letters of pardon;[65] and the note in the *Liber regalis*, citing once more the Honorian decretal concerning the king of Hungary, shows that the idea of the king's non-alienation promise was engrained as deeply in the minds of the clergy as certainly it was in the minds of fourteenth-century jurists. "Take notice," wrote Baldus, "that all kings in the world have to swear at their coronation to conserve the rights of their realm on the honor of

---

[60] *Parliamentary Writs*, I, 381f: "... et iureiurando in coronacione nostra prestito sumus astricti quod iura regni nostri servabimus illibata nec aliquid quod diadema tangat regni eiusdem absque ipsorum [prelatorum et procerum] requisito consilio faciemus." Richardson, 49f, has clearly recognized the influence of the Honorian decretal on the wording of that letter. The strict observation of the *cursus*, however, should be noticed too; also the fact that the oath, normally called *iuramentum* or *sacramentum*, here is called solemnly *iusiurandum*, apparently in allusion to the legal title *De iureiurando* under which the Decretal of Honorius III to Hungary had found its place in the *Liber Extra* (above, n. 13); finally, *diadema* for *corona* is unusual in the products of the English chancery and might indicate the Italian scribe. See further Gaines Post, "A Romano-Canonical Maxim, *Quod omnes tangit*, in Bracton," *Traditio*, IV (1946), 197–252; Antonio Marongiu, *L'Istituto parlamentare in Italia dalle origini al 1500* (Rome, 1949), 65–78, has devoted a chapter to that maxim, but his suggestion that Edward I may have borrowed it from the summons

of Rudolph of Habsburg for the Diet of Nürnberg in 1274, is defeated by the far earlier evidence from England as assembled by Post.

[61] See the extremely useful study by Fritz Hartung, *Die Krone als Symbol der monarchischen Herrschaft im ausgehenden Mittelalter* (Abhandlungen der Preussischen Akademie der Wissenschaften, 1940, Phil.-hist. Kl., Nr. 13; Berlin, 1941), esp. 6–19, for the notion of the Crown in England.

[62] I differ here from Wilkinson, "Coronation Oath," *Speculum*, XIX (1944), 448ff.

[63] See above, n. 9.

[64] See, for this point, also the forthcoming study by Robert S. Hoyt, "The Coronation Oath of 1308," *Traditio*, X (1954), which, through the kindness of its author, I was able to read in manuscript long after the present paper had gone to the press.

[65] Johannes de Trokelow, *Annales*, ed. H. T. Riley, Rolls Series (London, 1866), p. 109, quoted by Hoyt, *op. cit.*, note 85: "... iuramentum quod de legibus terrae et statu coronae manutenendis fecerat..."

the Crown,"[66] which undoubtedly was true in the latter half of the fourteenth century when Baldus wrote. But the jurists noticed the parallelism of royal and episcopal oaths at an earlier date. Already the *Glossa ordinaria* on the Honorian decretal indicates that the bishops too, and not only the kings, have to promise not to alienate.[67] Lucas de Penna, writing in the fifties of the fourteenth century, holds that bishops and kings are "equiparate" with regard to their oaths concerning alienation.[68] And his contemporary Petrus de Ancharano says quite straightforwardly: "The king, at the time of his coronation, swears not to alienate the things of his kingdom; similarly, the bishops swear [not to alienate] the rights of their bishopric."[69] Related ideas may have prompted the English cleric who, in 1308, added the note to the *Liber regalis.*

To summarize, the non-alienation promises of Henry III and Edward I, so often referred to by both the Holy See and the king, must probably be taken as a historical fact. Their very existence, at any rate, cannot be ruled out on the ground that they did not go on record; for the non-alienation oath of the clergy also formed an additional clause which was not part of the standard oath as prescribed by canon law. Most interesting, however, and revealing is yet another point related to what perhaps may be termed "constitutional semantics." A feudal oath had been adopted by the Church. It had been transformed into an episcopal oath at a time when the papal monarchy was in its formative stage. Owing to that appropriation by the Church, however, the feudal vassalitic oath became an oath of office binding the bishop, not as a vassal, but as an "officer," and binding him not only to the pope personally but also to the abstract institution, the *papatus,* and to the bishop's own office, the *episcopatus.* Later on, the ecclesiastified and now pseudo-feudal oath returned in a new guise to the secular state as an obligation on the part of the king to protect an impersonal institution, the Crown. To be sure, a development in that direction was well on its way in England even before King John's surrender to the Holy See. Nevertheless, as a result of that event, of the early application of canonistic practice and maxims to England as a papal feudatory state, and of an objectively false or incorrect assumption on the part of the Holy See, the canonistic doctrine of "Inalienability" was articulated and became the norm in England much earlier than in other European countries.

[66] Baldus, on c. 33 X, 2, 24, n. 3, *In Decretales* (Venice, 1580), fol. 261ᵛ: "Nota quod omnes reges mundi in sua coronatione debent iurare iura regni sua conservare et honorem coronae."

[67] See c. 33 X, 2, 24, gloss *Regni sui:* "Sic et episcopi iurant in sua consecratione, quod iura sui episcopatus non alienabunt..."

[68] Lucas de Penna, *In tres libros* (Lyon, 1582), 564, on

C., XI, 58, 7, n. 8: "Nam aequiparantur quantum ad hoc etiam iuramentum super his praestitum de alienatione facta non revocando (?) episcopus et rex. Ita et principi alienatio rerum fiscalium ... noscitur interdicta."

[69] Petrus de Ancharanus (1330–1416), on c. 33 X, 2, 24, n. 1, *Super Decretales* (Bologna, 1581), fol. 291: "Rex iurat tempore suae coronationis non alienare res regni sui. Similiter episcopi iurant sui episcopatus iura."

KINGSHIP UNDER THE IMPACT OF SCIENTIFIC JURISPRUDENCE

Participants of a Symposium which was arranged to demonstrate from various points of view the characteristic features of "Twelfth-Century Europe," will be inclined, despite the additional heading "and the Foundations of Modern Society," to fall under the spell of Charles Homer Haskins' great vision and ingenious thesis of "The Renaissance of the Twelfth Century." Although the subject I have proposed to discuss here would seem to confirm rather than refute Haskins' thesis, it is not at all my intention to deal with "Renaissance" features or analyze twelfth-century kingship *sub specie iurisprudentiae renatae*.[1] It is my intention to stick more closely to "the Foundations of Modern Society" and point out certain effects which a disciplined scientific jurisprudence—reborn or not —seems to have had upon the idea of medieval kingship.

What unquestionably distinguished, in the public sphere, the twelfth century from the preceding centuries was the sheer existence of a learned jurisprudence.[2] Law, of course, there always existed, even in the darkest of the so-called Dark Ages. It will be quite sufficient here to recall the impressive sets of Dooms of the Anglo-Saxon kings, the Lombard edicts, the Visigothic law collections, or the *Capitularia* of the Carolingians in order to understand that the earlier Middle Ages were anything but lawless. These *leges barbarorum*, however, were characterized by the fact that according to their claims and their applicability they all were provincial and not universal; second, that they were the work not of professional jurists but of jurisprudential laymen, even though many a feather may have been borrowed from scientific—that is, Roman—law; finally, that those laws, which represented the customs of a tribe or a region, were administered by jurisprudential laymen (kings, counts, clerics, noblemen, or *missi* of any kind) and not by learned and scientifically trained judges. A similar situation prevailed within the

Reprinted, with permission, from *Twelfth-Century Europe and the Foundations of Modern Society*, edd. M. Clagett, G. Post, R. Reynolds (Madison, Wisc., 1961), 89–111. The original has this prefatory note:

Surgery prevented the present author from being a full-time participant of the Symposium on "Twelfth-Century Europe and the Foundations of Modern Society." He was, however, able to prepare this paper which his friend, Professor Gaines Post, was kind enough to deliver for him and even to defend in the discussion—an act of making a colleague's cause his own for which the author remains a grateful debtor.

[1] Charles Homer Haskins himself has surveyed brilliantly "The Revival of Jurisprudence" in Chapter VII of his *Renaissance of the Twelfth Century* (Cambridge, 1939), 192–223.

[2] The truly important achievement of the so-called "rebirth of Roman law" was the evolution of a scientific jurisprudence and a jurisprudential method; this point has been stressed repeatedly, most emphatically, e.g., by Woldemar Engelmann, *Die Wiedergeburt der Rechtskultur in Italien durch die wissenschaftliche Lehre* (Leipzig, 1938).

realm of ecclesiastical law. True enough, the canons of the councils, decrees of popes, and certain laws of the Christian emperors—apart from Scripture and patristic tradition— formed *a priori* a body of ecclesiastical law which, however, was as yet unsifted and unorganized. A period of regional-provincial collections of canonical material (African, Hispanic, Gallican, Italian) was followed by a period of private collections of a more universal character, of which a respectable number was produced between the Caro- lingian age and that of Gregory VII. Thereafter, however, the forces released by the Church Reform and the Struggle over Investitures broadened the universalistic outlooks. After the efforts of Burchard of Worms and Ivo of Chartres, a compendious and organized body of canon law was privately composed, round 1140, by the Bolognese monk Gratian, the *Decretum Gratiani*.[3] Nor can we doubt that it was by the power of the same forces that the body of Roman law was reactivated which, in its turn, was not without influence on the work of Gratian.[4] Hence, a universal ecclesiastical law and a universal secular law made their appearance, within a generation or two, in the early twelfth century.

The intricate problem of the survival of Roman law during the Middle Ages and the process of its so-called revival shall concern us here as little as the question of who first made Bologna the home of legal studies, Pepo or Irnerius.[5] It is quite sufficient for our present purpose to know that in the pamphlet literature of the Struggle over Investitures Roman law was not infrequently, if only sporadically and unsystematically, applied to bolster the imperial position as well as to undermine it;[6] further, that around 1100, or a little later, Irnerius taught Roman law at Bologna; finally, that around 1140 Gratian composed in Bologna his *Decretum*. At any rate, two independent, though eventually interdependent, sets of law, both universal according to claims and applicability, came into existence in the twelfth century. The scientific interpretation of these sets of law became a "must" owing to the numerous contradictions and other difficulties, and it gave birth to a methodical study of sources and parallels, and therewith to a legal science which, in the course of time, mothered our modern historico-philological method. That is to say, once the two bodies of law, Roman and canon, were placed before the scholar, there resulted also the challenge to understand, interpret, and apply the law scientifically —comparable to the effects issuing from Holy Scripture and leading to numerous ex- positions on the books of the Bible or, as happened later, to the effects of the *corpus Aristotelicum* and its commentation in the age of scholasticism. Canonistic studies (hitherto a branch of theology) and secular jurisprudence (hitherto a branch of rhetoric) became

---

[3] A succinct and admirably organized survey of sources and history of canon law to roughly 1300 has been offered by Alphons M. Stickler, *Historia Iuris Canonici Latini*, I: *Historia Fontium* (Turin, 1950); a brief general survey, including canon law in England, was given by the Lord Bishop of Exeter, R. C. Mortimer, *Western Canon Law* (Berkeley and Los Angeles, 1953).

[4] For some aspects of the interrelations between the Struggle over Investitures and the reactivation of Roman law, see Karl Jordan, "Der Kaisergedanke in Ravenna zur Zeit Heinrichs IV.," *Deutsches Archiv*, II (1938), 85–125. For Gratian and Roman law, see the report of

Stephan Kuttner, "New Studies on the Roman Law in Gratian's Decretum," *The Seminar*, XI (1953), 12–50.

[5] For the few documents referring to Pepo, see Hermann Kantorowicz and Beryl Smalley, "An English Theologian's View of Roman Law: Pepo, Irnerius, Ralph Niger," *Mediaeval and Renaissance Studies*, I (1941–43), 237–52.

[6] For example, Petrus Crassus (cf. Jordan, "Kaiser- gedanke") bolstered, and Manegold (see below, note 28) undermined the imperial position by means of Roman law.

each a science in its own right. Legal science acquired the rank of "moral philosophy"; it became autonomous and soon rose to be a challenge to theology.[7]

Moreover, through the concentration of the new legal studies in the city of Bologna and their combination with the study of the notariate and with the *ars dictandi*, a broad layer of legally trained men and minds began to spread, especially in Italy where the jurists became the foremost representatives of the Italian intelligentsia, a legal profession the like of which did not exist in the earlier Middle Ages. This change did not escape contemporary observers who in prose and in jingling verses began to complain that the study of the two lucrative arts—jurisprudence and medicine—tended to eclipse the study of literature, and of letters in general, as well as of theology. These complaints were repeated over and over again, from the time of Stephen Langton, who was not the first to do so, to Dante who was not the last.[8]

Another consequence of the new study of law was perhaps more decisive. In former days, law was a matter dealt with by kings, grandees, and wise old men—by *witan* of every pattern—and it was administered by noblemen, clerics, and others enjoying the king's confidence. Beginning with the twelfth century, however, law became a matter to be treated with scientific accuracy, and justice was administered (the later, the more exclusively) by judges trained in the laws and in legal thinking. This evolution resulted in a remarkable change of the earlier medieval social stratification. As the number of Doctors of Laws increased (wrote, around 1180, Ralph Niger), the jurists in their pride demanded to be called not doctors or masters, but *domini*, lords;[9] that is, they assumed a title normally reserved to noblemen and prelates who represented the two ruling classes during the earlier Middle Ages. From the twelfth century onward, the two knighthoods of former days (the *militia armata* of chivalry and the *militia inermis* or *celestis* of the clergy) were complemented or supplemented by a third knighthood of jurists, the *militia legum* or knighthood of law, and soon of letters at large (*militia litterata* or *doctoralis*).[10] Roman law stipulated that a *filius familias* could dispose freely of his *peculium castrense*, that is, of

---

[7] Hermann Kantorowicz, *Studies in the Glossators of the Roman Law* (Cambridge, 1938), 37f, n. 4. Haskins, *Renaissance*, 199, ascribes the separation of civil law from rhetoric to Irnerius, and (p. 215) of canon law from theology to Gratian. To Hostiensis, *Summa aurea*, prooem., nos. 9–10 (Venice, 1586, col. 6), canon jurisprudence was a third *scientia* apart from theology and civil law, a *tertium genus, ex ingenio quasi permixtum,* a *scientia permixta,* because it embraces both the spiritual and the temporal. For the method, see Erich Genzmer, "Die justinianische Kodifikation und die Glossatoren," *Atti del Congresso Internazionale di Diritto Romano: Bologna,* I (Pavia, 1934), 380ff.

[8] The jingle: "Dat Gallienus opes et sanctio Iustiniana./ Ex aliis paleas, ex istis collige grana," quoted by Stephen Langton as well as by the *Glossa ordinaria,* on *Const. omnem,* v. 'ditissimi,' is sure to be much older; cf. H. Kantorowicz, "An English Theologian's View" (above, note 5), 246, n. 2; see also Haskins, *Studies in Mediaeval Culture* (Oxford, 1929), 47, for the rivalry between law and theology, and p. 25, for the "lucrative branches of knowledge." See Dante, *Paradiso,* IX, 133ff, and Michele

Maccarone, "Teologia e diritto canonico nella *Monarchia,* III, 3," *Rivista di Storia della Chiesa in Italia,* V (1951), 23f.

[9] Ralph Niger, *Moralia regum,* c. XIX, ed. H. Kantorowicz, "An English Theologian's View," 250, lines 31ff: "Procedente vero tempore, aucto numero legis peritorum inpinguatus est dilectus, et recalcitravit in tantum ut legis doctores appellarentur domini, indigne ferentes appellari doctores vel magistri." Cf. p. 247, n. 2. Later the title *dominus* was an established fact. See, e.g., Lucas de Penna, *Lectura . . . super tribus libris Codicis,* on *Cod.* 12, 15 (Lyon, 1544, fol. 231voa): "[doctores legum] qui etiam sunt ab omnibus honorandi nec debent ab aliis quantumcumque maximis in eorum litteris appellari fratres, sed domini. contrarium facientes puniendi sunt." Lucas de Penna actually refers to Innocent IV, *Apparatus,* on X, 2, 15, n. 5 (Lyon, 1578, fol. 200), who mentioned the *sententia dominorum.*

[10] H. Fitting, *Das Castrense peculium in seiner geschichtlichen Entwicklung und heutigen gemeinrechtlichen Geltung* (Halle, 1871), 531ff, has summed up the essential material. For *militia doctoralis,* see Baldus, on *Cod.* 7, 38, 1, n. 1 (Venice, 1586, fol. 28).

everything he had earned as a soldier (*miles*) or as a public official, as a lawyer, or otherwise in the service of the Prince. The medieval jurists interpreted the word *miles*, "soldier," in the medieval sense of "knight"; and since Roman law "equiparated" the lawyer and the *miles* or knight, the glossators began to claim knighthood for the jurist.[11] This claim was put up, at the latest, by the great Placentinus who died in 1192; it was repeated by Azo and the *Glossa ordinaria* on Roman law composed by Accursius around 1230, and by many others as well. And thus it happened that by the second half of the thirteenth century the doctor's cap was generally recognized as an equivalent of the *cingulum militare* of knighthood.[12] By applying the terminology of Roman law to the conditions of the high Middle Ages (in fact, by misinterpreting Justinian's laws) the jurists further arrived at the theory that every Doctor of Laws who had taught at a university for twenty years had the rank of a count.[13] However that may be, the tombs of the great jurists in Bologna display, without an exception, the title *Dominus*, Lord, before the name of the deceased.

The social rise of legal intelligentsia certainly reflected the general importance of the learned jurists and their authority to which eventually all princes, secular and spiritual, paid their respects. Justinian had styled Ulpian his friend (*amicus*) and father (*parens*) just as he styled the jurists Theophilus and Dorotheus his predecessors (*antecessores*) and gave them the title of *viri illustres*.[14] It was natural for the medieval jurists to make the most of Justinian's words. Azo, for example, said quite bluntly that legal science "effects that the professors of law rule solemnly over the *orbis terrarum* and sit in the imperial court judging in a lordly fashion tribes and nations, plaintiffs and defendants."[15] Bracton repeated, and enlarged on, Azo's words, changing, however, "emperor" and "imperial" into "king" and "royal."[16] And Cynus of Pistoia exclaimed: "Thou seest, o student,

---

[11] The relevant places are *Cod.* 2, 7, 4 and 14; see also 2, 6, 7 (*nobilissimos*). These laws refer to *advocati* only, but the medieval jurists expanded the reference to *jurisperiti* in general. See also *Instit.*, prooem. (below, note 42), and *Cod.*, prooem. *Summa rei publicae*, prol.

[12] Fitting, *Castrense peculium*, 543, n. 1, for Placentinus (*milites literatoria militantes*); Azo, *Summa Institutionum*, on prooem., n. 2 (Lyon, 1530, fol. 268), distinguished three *militiae*: "Est ergo militia alia armata, alia inermis, alia literata." Already Guido Faba, *Summa dictaminis*, I, n. 28, ed. A. Gaudenzi, in *Propugnatore*, III (1890), 309, addresses a *magister* as *litteratorie militiae cingulo redimito*. This may be a figurative expression; however, the later formularies contain a form for the promotion to the doctorate, saying: "...celebri militia et militari cingulo [te] decoramus teque consortio, ordini et numero milicie legum doctorum et professorum aggregamus"; cf. H. Kaiser, *Collectarius perpetuarum formarum Johannis de Geylnhusen* (Innsbruck, 1900), form 49; see, in general, Fitting, *Castrense peculium*, 547ff.

[13] *Cod.* 12, 15.

[14] *Cod.* 8, 37 (38), 4: "Secundum responsum Domitii Ulpiani...iuris consulti amici mei." *Cod.* 4, 65, 4: "... ad Domitium Ulpianum praefectum praetorio et parentem meum ..." *Inst.*, prooem., § 3: "...Theophilo et Dorotheo viris illustribus antecessoribus [nostris]." That the word *nostris* was usually omitted has been

stressed by François Hotman (Hotomanus, *In quatuor libros Institutionum* [2nd ed.; Venice, 1569, 5]; on *Inst.*, prooem., 3, v. "Antecessoribus nostris"), who like all the glossators and commentators pointed out that "father" and "predecessor" referred to the jurisprudents to whom Justinian allocated himself.

[15] Azo, *Summa Institutionum*, prologue *Quasimodo geniti* (Lyon, 1530, fol. 267ᵛᵒ), ed. F. W. Maitland, *Select Passages from the Works of Bracton and Azo* (Selden Society, VIII; London, 1895), 3: "[scientia iuris] velut almifica dominatrix nobilitat addiscentes ... et ut vera per omnia fatear, iuris professores per orbem terrarum fecit solemniter principari et sedere in imperiali aula tribus et nationes, actores et reos ordine dominabili iudicantes." That the Bolognese Master Boncompagno served as a ghost writer of Azo's prologue is of little or no importance in this connection; cf. Hermann Kantorowicz, *Glossators of the Roman Law*, 227, n. 3a.

[16] Bracton, *De legibus*, fol. 1b, ed. Woodbine, II, 20; ed. Maitland, 7 (with his notes on p. 15): "... quia nobilitat addiscentes... et facit eos principari in regno [Azo: *per orbem terrarum*] et sedere in aula regia [Azo: *imperiali*] et in sede ipsius regis quasi throno Dei, tribus et nationes, actores et reos ordine dominabili iudicantes ...." For Bracton's additions, see Ernst H. Kantorowicz, *The King's Two Bodies* (Princeton, 1957), 160; his changes (*orbis terrarum: regnum; imperiali: regia*) are sug-

how much the [legal] science effects which makes the jurisprudent a father and friend of the Prince."[17] Indeed, the twelfth, thirteenth, and fourteenth centuries were the golden age of the jurisprudents. As the jurists became the chief advisers and councillors of princes, the princes became more and more dependent on them. As early as 1115 we find Irnerius in the entourage of Emperor Henry V, where he also served as a judge.[18] Further, no medievalist will have missed the stories about Barbarossa conversing with, and seeking the counsel of, the learned Four Doctors of Bologna. Moreover, the professional jurist became the professional administrator of justice, the professional judge. Gone were the times when the customs and laws of a country were remembered by the wise old men only and when some sort of natural reason, combined with certain social standing, made a person fit to sit in court as a judge. What counted in the age of the new jurisprudence was that the judge arrived at his sentence in a scientific, rational fashion, which among other things excluded ordeals by fire or water, and that he judged according to his lawbooks or was able—as in England—to expound the common law scientifically as a professional. By gradually monopolizing the administration of justice, the legal profession, however, began to encroach upon the position of the king himself in his capacity of judge. The medieval king could, and would, sit in court if he so pleased and could himself adjudicate the cases before him. This custom died slowly. Frederick II still sat in court; so did Henry III of England as well as Edward I and Edward II.[19] Later something changed. It is true, the king was the fountain of justice; he was supposed to interpret the law in case of obscurity; the courts were still the "king's courts" and the king was still considered the judge ordinary of his realm whereas the judges, who derived their power from him, acted only as delegate judges. For all that, the custom arose that the king should not pass judgment himself: *Rex aut Imperator non cognoscunt in causis eorum*, "king and emperor do not pronounce judicially in their causes," says Andreas of Isernia quite explicitly.[20] Cynus uses approximately the same words (*Imperator causas suas non*

---

gestive with regard to the broader subject of *rex est imperator in regno suo* (see below). That the judge, "as judge," is "sitting in the seat of the King (concerning his justice)," was an axiom defended ardently by Sir Edward Coke, in the case of Floyd and Barker, *Twelfth Part of the Reports*, 25.

[17] Cynus of Pistoia, *In Codicem*, on *C.* 4, 65, 4, n. 2 (Frankfurt, 1578, fol. 276ᵛ): "Notandum quod Imperator vocat Ulpianum parentem suum, sic respectu scientiae aetatis [cf. *Glossa ordinara* on *C.* 4, 65, 4], vocat eum amicum, infra de contra. sti. l. secundum [= *C.* 8, 37 (38), 4]. Nam sic legitur in Chronicis, Alexander Imperator praecipuum habuit amicum Ulpianum et Paulum etiam, et vides, studiose, quantum potest scientia: quia facit legum peritum patrem praecipuum [principium?], facit etiam amicum, secundum Augustinum est animi custos et secundum Ieronymum est alter ego." The passage from Cynus was occasionally quoted in later times; see e.g., Johannes Oinotomus, *In quattuor Institutionum . . . libros*, on *Inst.*, prooem., 3, n. 1 (§ *cumque hoc*), (Venice, 1643, 4).

[18] Haskins, *Renaissance*, 199; Jordan, "Kaisergedanke," 126.

[19] For Frederick II as judge, see Fedor Schneider, "Toscanische Studien," *Quellen und Forschungen aus italienischen Archiven und Bibliotheken*, XII (1909), 52ff; cf. 65: "serenissimo imperatore ibidem presentialiter existente." Cf. Julius Ficker, *Forschungen zur Reichs- und Rechtsgeschichte Italiens* (Innsbruck, 1868), I, 296f, § 162; also III, 362f, §§ 612f. The imperial presence seems to have been restricted to cases of high treason (that is, cases in which the ruler could act as *iudex in causa propria* even in early modern times), and although the emperor occasionally might pronounce the judgement *ore proprio* (Ficker, 297, n. 2), he would normally remain silent and leave the procedure to the judges or speak through his *logothetes*.

For England, see W. Holdsworth, *A History of English Law* (7th ed.; London, 1956), I, 34f, 205ff (*Coram rege* court). See, for a few later cases, S. B. Chrimes, in his edition of Sir John Fortescue's *De Laudibus Legum Angliae* (Cambridge, 1942), 150, on Ch. VIII, line 32: "proprio ore nullus regum Angliae iudicium proferre visus est."

[20] Andreas of Isernia, *In usus feudorum commentaria*, on *Feud.*, II, 55 ("De prohibita alienatione feudi"), n. 84 (Naples, 1571, fol. 281ʳᵒ⁻ᵛᵒ).

ipse cognoscit: sed iudices alios facit), but adds: "*Licet quando velit, et ipse possit in re sua iudex esse.*"[21] Indeed, it was common opinion that in cases pertaining to the fisc the prince could be *iudex in causa propria*, and, as Bracton shows, also in cases of high treason[22] —opinions well prepared by Pope Innocent IV discussing the limitations of a bishop's competency to pass judgment on himself.[23] Normally, however, the king was supposed to judge exclusively through his judges who were juristic professionals and who, in lieu of the king, were expected to have all the pertinent laws present to their mind, *in scrinio pectoris*.[24]

From the end of the thirteenth century onwards, jurists also gave a reason for that custom. The South-Italian Andreas of Isernia, writing around 1300, was hardly the first to make the blunt statement that the king has to rely upon his jurisprudents because *raro princeps iurista invenitur*, "rarely will a prince be found who is a jurist."[25] In similar terms, Sir John Fortescue explained that it was unfit for a king "to investigate precise points of the law . . . but these should be left to your judges and advocates . . . and others skilled in the law. In fact, you will render judgment better through others than by yourself, for none of the kings of England is seen to give judgment by his own lips, yet all the judgments of the realm are his. . . ." And Fortescue added that the legal experience necessary for judges is scarcely attainable in twenty years of study.[26] It was this doctrine which finally brought about one of the fiercest clashes between Sir Edward Coke and King James I. At a Star Chamber session, the king, taking his seat on the normally empty throne, declared he would ever protect the common law. "No," interjected Sir Edward Coke, "the common law protects the king." The angry king, shaking his fist at Coke, later argued that "he thought the law was founded upon reason, and that he and others had reason as well as the judges." To that Coke replied calmly that indeed the king had excellent gifts by nature, "but his Majesty was not learned in the laws of his realm of England, and causes which concern the life, or inheritance, or goods, or fortunes of his subjects, are not to be decided by natural reason, but by the artificial reason and judgment of law, which. . . requires long study and experience before that a man can attain to the cognizance of it."[27]

---

[21] Cynus, on *Cod.* 7, 37, 3, n. 1 (fol. 445ᵛ).

[22] Cf. Lucas de Penna, *Super tribus libris Codicis*, on *Cod.* 11, 58, 7, n. 16 (Lyons, 1544, fol. 185): "Est enim princeps iudex in causa sua" whenever *causae fiscales* are concerned, or when he revokes things alienated *in praeiudicium dignitatis et coronae*." Bracton, fol. 119b, ed. Woodbine, II, 337, concerning treason or lese majesty, judged by "court and peers" with the king, too, acting as judge, but "debent pares associari, ne ipse rex per seipsum vel iustitiarios suos sine paribus actor sit et iudex."

[23] Innocent IV, *In quinque libros Decretalium apparatus*, on X, 5, 40, 23, n. 3 (Lyon, 1578, fol. 369ᵛ).

[24] Cynus, on *Cod.* 6, 23, 19, n. 1 (fol. 367): "Nota hoc ad quod haec lex quotidie allegatur, quod princeps habet omnia iura in scrinio sui pectoris. quod non intellegas ad literam, quia multi imperatores ignoraverunt iura, *et maxime hodie ignorant*, sed intelligi debet in scrinio sui dectoris, id est, in curia sua, quae debet egregiis abundare Doctoribus, per quorum ora loquatur iuris religiosissimus princeps [cf. *Inst., prooem.*]."

[25] Andreas of Isernia, on *Feud.* I, 3, n. 16, 'Qui success. ten.' (fol. 21ᵛ): "Potest dici, quod quia princeps multos habet in suo consilio peritos . . . [allegation of *Cod.* 6, 23, 19; above, n. 24] et ideo dicitur Philosophiae plenus . . . raro enim invenitur princeps Iurista." Cf. *ibid., praeludia*, n. 25, fol. 3ᵛᵒ: ". . . et maxime Iurisperiti, et qui cum eis [imperatoribus] erant, per quos dicuntur [imperatores] habere omnia Iura in pectore . . . [alleg. *Cod.* 6, 23, 19] et Philosophiae legalis plenitudinem . . . cum Principes rari sciant iura . . . Item Imperator non facit leges, sed Iurisperiti approbati per eum, ut Tribonianus et alii." Matthaeus de Afflictis (d. 1523,) *In Utriusque Siciliae . . . Constitutiones*, on *Liber augustalis*, I, 37, n. 12, and II, 30, n. 1 (Venice, 1562: I, fol. 157, and II, fol. 65ᵛ), repeats Andreas of Isernia almost verbatim.

[26] Fortescue, *De Laudibus*, ed. Chrimes (above, note 19), c. VIII, 22f.

[27] Coke, *Twelfth Part of the Reports*, 63–65; for the other sources see Catherine Drinker Bowen, *The Lion and the Throne* (Boston and Toronto, 1956), 304f, 622; Roland

Raro princeps iurista invenitur: the modern idea of a king who no longer is supposed to take causes out of his courts and give judgment upon them himself, originated from the stratum of scientific jurisprudence which emerged in the twelfth century. The new jurisprudence, which so often has been claimed (and rightly so) as supporting royal absolutism, in this case put some restrictions on royal arbitrariness by depriving the king from functioning actively on the bench as supreme judge. Roman law, however, had the effect of bridling the king in other respects as well.

During the great strife between Pope Gregory VII and Emperor Henry IV both curialists and imperialists began to make use of the *lex regia* or *lex de imperio* for the purpose of arguing whether or not an emperor could be deposed. The law, transmitted by the *Digest*, the *Code*, and the *Institutes* of Justinian, advanced the doctrine that the *imperium*, originally vested in the *populus Romanus* and its *maiestas*, had been conferred by the Roman people upon the Roman emperor. This act, in itself, was double-edged, as it touched upon two principles diametrically opposed to each other. It could imply (and this was the opinion of the imperial party) that the Romans had renounced the supreme power once and for all, and had irrevocably bestowed it upon the Prince, or rather upon the Prince's office. On the other hand, the same law allowed the curialists to defend the opposite thesis: that each Prince had been appointed individually by the Roman people as the administrator of the empire, and that this appointment was not at all irrevocable. Manegold of Lautenbach (*ca.* 1085) even went so far as to say that a prince who failed as a governor could be chased away just as a farmer could chase away an unfaithful swineherd.[28] The prince thus became an employee of the sovereign people, since the supreme power was supposed to rest always and imprescriptibly with the sovereign people of Rome.

We notice that herewith the principle of popular sovereignty was foreshadowed during the Struggle over Investitures, and may add that it permeated the ideologies of the twelfth century. For one thing, the City-Romans in the days of Arnold of Brescia defended this idea when Barbarossa prepared to come for his coronation to Rome, and the Roman leaders claimed that the citizens of the Eternal City alone were entitled to dispose of the imperial diadem—an argument to which Barbarossa answered that he held his *imperium* from God alone and from God directly.[29] The history of Rome in the thirteenth and fourteenth centuries actually centered upon the theory of Roman popular sovereignty until finally, in 1328, an emperor, Louis of Bavaria, actually received the diadem at the hands of the senators and people of Rome, not in St. Peter's, but on the

G. Usher, "James I and Sir Edward Coke," *English Historical Review*, XVIII (1903), 664ff, esp. 667ff.

[28] Eugenio Dupré Theseider, *L'Idea imperiale di Roma nella tradizione del medioevo* (Milan, 1942), 255ff, offers a useful collection of extracts from legal texts concerning the *lex regia;* see, for a discussion of the *lex regia,* Fritz Kern, *Gottesgnadentum und Widerstandsrecht im früheren Mittelalter* (Leipzig, 1914), 251ff. (256, n. 471, the passage from Manegold of Lautenbach, *MGH, Libelli de lite,* I, 365, 18ff); E. Schoenian, *Die Idee der Volks-*

souveränität im mittelalterlichen Rom (Leipzig, 1919), esp. 58ff; for the older literature, see Kantorowicz, *Kaiser Friedrich der Zweite, Ergänzungsband* (Berlin, 1931), 85ff, to which there should be added Karl Jordan, "Der Kaisergedanke in Ravenna," *Deutsches Archiv,* II (1938), 110ff; Fritz Schulz, "Bracton on Kingship," *EHR,* LX (1945), 153ff.; Walter Ullmann, *The Medieval Idea of Law as Represented by Lucas de Penna* (London, 1946), 48ff.

[29] Dupré Theseider, *L'Idea imperiale,* 153–60.

Capitoline Hill.[30] It is true, of course, that the civilians during the twelfth and thirteenth centuries and beyond were inclined to uphold the origin of the imperial power directly from God; but they also left no doubt that indeed the ancient Roman *populus* acted within its right when it claimed to be the ultimate source of the imperial power, whereas opinion was divided with regard to the claims of the medieval City-Romans or, for that matter, with regard to any medieval *populus*. It was finally as a result of the intransigence of the hierocratic theory, according to which the emperor depended not on God directly but on the pope, that the Roman lawyers, and some moderate canonists as well, recognized the popular origin of the imperial power, and used the idea of popular sovereignty as a means to freeze out the papal claims. Hence the jurists, while always ready to support the notion of the direct, divine origin of imperial power, tried to combine it with the argument of the popular origin of imperial power. The *Glossa ordinaria* of Accursius therefore neatly combined "God" and the "people" as the two sources of imperial authority and thereby came close to the, so to say, final formulation of John of Paris around 1300: *populo faciente et Deo inspirante*.[31]

To the debate on the *lex regia* the twelfth-century jurists contributed after their fashion by glossing on that law: Irnerius and Roger, Pillius, Placentinus, and Azo as well as canonists such as Rufinus, Bazianus, and the authors of anonymous works.[32] The arguments of the *lex regia* in favor of the popular origin of imperial power were used against papal claims by Frederick II, and against papal as well as imperial claims by the Senator Brancaleone and by Cola di Rienzo, and culminated of course in the doctrine of Marsilio of Padua.[33]

On the other hand, the context in which the *lex regia* was quoted in the *Digest* and the *Institutes* seemed to support the budding royal absolutism, for it was quoted in order to substantiate the sentence which for centuries remained the pith of absolutist desires: *Quod principi placuit, legis habet vigorem*. "What has pleased the Prince, has the force of law," for the Prince legally owned the power to legislate after the people had conferred the *imperium* upon him. Roman law, however, also provided the means to check unscrupulousness on the part of the prince. As opposed to the absolutists, the constitutionalists referred to a law in the *Code*, the *Digna vox*, in which the legislator frankly declared himself bound to the law: "It is a word worthy of the majesty of the ruler that the prince professes himself bound to the law: so much does our authority depend upon the authority of the law."[34] Therewith the gates were flung open to the problem of whether the prince be "above the law" or "under the law." It shall not be denied that the problem itself existed before, but it became articulate with the reactivation and the exegesis of Roman law, and gained additional importance by the question whether and to what extent the

---

[30] In general, see Paul Schmitthenner, *Die Ansprüche des Adels und Volks der Stadt Rom auf Vergebung der Kaiserkrone während des Interregnums* (Historische Studien, 155; Berlin, 1923); see Depré Theseider, *L'Idea imperiale*, 237ff, for the coronation of Louis of Bavaria.

[31] See my remarks in *The King's Two Bodies* (Princeton, 1957), 296ff.

[32] See Dupré Theseider, *L'Idea imperiale*, 257ff, and, for the canonists, Friedrich Kempf, *Papsttum und Kaisertum bei Innocenz III.* (Miscellanea Historiae Pontificiae, XIX; Rome, 1954), 214, n. 52.

[33] See, for Frederick II, Brancaleone, and Rienzo, Dupré Theseider, *L'Idea imperiale*, 173ff, 197ff, 307ff.

[34] *Cod.* 1, 14, 4.

ruler was bound to local customs.[35] The jurists, of course, were fully aware of the glaring contradiction presented by Roman law itself, of the antinomy between the maxims *princeps legibus solutus* and *princeps legibus alligatus*, and they tried to discuss away the discrepancy by stressing that the prince, though not fettered by the law, should voluntarily bind himself to the law, especially to the laws he himself may have issued. On the basis of this antinomy John of Salisbury felt prompted to interpret the prince as being at once an *imago aequitatis* and a *servus aequitatis*, just as Frederick II claimed to be at once "Father and son, lord and servant of Justice."[36] It was perhaps Thomas Aquinas who, in his orderly fashion, overcame the apparent legal impasse when he explained that indeed the prince was *legibus solutus* with regard to the *vis coactiva*, the coercive power of man-made positive law which received its power from the prince anyhow; on the other hand, Aquinas held that the Prince was bound to the *vis directiva*, the directive power of natural law to which he should submit voluntarily—and for that purpose Aquinas, too, quoted the *Digna vox*.[37] This cleverly phrased opinion by Aquinas, combining most of the earlier arguments, offered a way out of the dilemma which was acceptable to both adversaries and defenders of the more absolutist concepts of kingship. It was still quoted by Bossuet, while Louis XIV himself acknowledged its essence.[38]

We recognize that Roman law had its say in eminently political and ethical matters, sponsoring, as it did, both popular sovereignty and royal absolutism, both a kingship above the law and one bound to the law, and that thereby, to say the least, it kept the discussion moving. To some extent we probably should connect (as A. J. Carlyle did) the conflict among the jurists about the *lex regia* with the conflict between the new lawbooks and the customs, or the customary law, of the land.[39] There is, however, an ethical substratum in this dispute as well as in the *Digna vox* itself: "It is worthy of the majesty of the ruler that the prince professes himself bound to the law."

Political ethics, to be sure, were influenced by Roman law in very many respects. For one thing, there developed, beginning in the twelfth century, a growing awareness of the transpersonal, or "public," character of the commonwealth, the *res publica*. On the basis of Roman law John of Salisbury styled the prince a *persona publica*, a *potestas publica;*[40] and it did not take long before one began to learn that also the fisc (whose characteristics were broadly discussed in the Tenth Book of Justinian's *Code*) was a public institution which "never died" and therefore survived the individual prince. This was true also of the "Crown" in the abstract and in a suprapersonal sense of the word which began to be used in France and in England as early as the twelfth century; Suger of St. Denis and

[35] For the place accorded to customs by Roman law, see *Dig.* 1, 3, 32–40.

[36] *Policraticus*, IV, 2, ed. Webb, I, 238, lines 15f; *Liber augustalis*, I, 31, ed. Huillard-Bréholles, *Historia diplomatica Friderici Secundi* (Paris, 1852ff.), IV, 33; also Dupré Theseider, *L'Idea imperiale*, 179.

[37] Aquinas, *Summa theologica*, I–IIae, qu. XCVI, a. 5, ad 3; cf. R. W. and A. J. Carlyle, *A History of Mediaeval Political Theory in the West* (London, 1928), V, 475f; Jean-Marie Aubert, *Le droit romain dans l'œuvre de Saint*

Thomas (Bibliothèque thomiste, XXX; Paris, 1955), 83f.

[38] Kantorowicz, *The King's Two Bodies*, 136, n. 154.

[39] A. J. Carlyle, "The Theory of the Source of Political Authority in the Mediaeval Civilians to the Time of Accursius," *Mélanges Fitting* (Montpellier, 1907), I, 181–94.

[40] *Policraticus*, IV, 2; Gaines Post, "The Theory of Public Law and the State in the Thirteenth Century," *Seminar*, VI (1948), 42–59.

Henry I of England (under whom the office of "coroner," charged with maintaining judicial and fiscal rights of the crown, came into being) may stand here as the landmarks. Slightly more emotional was the notion of *patria* applied to the kingdom in twelfth-century literature, in France (*Song of Roland*) as well as in England (Geoffrey of Monmouth). Moreover, a few years ago Gaines Post showed how much the two laws, Roman and canon, contributed to giving currency to the idea of *patria* which likewise implied a transpersonal concept of public perpetuity: to fight for the *patria*, to die for the *patria*, even to kill without qualms one's father or brother for the sake of the *patria*, to procreate children for the *patria*, or to pay special taxes *pro necessitate* or *pro defensione patriae*. All those were ideals (no matter whether we like them or not) which were disseminated by the two laws and the new jurisprudence.[41]

Those political or public ethics inevitably influenced also the image of the ruler. The *prooemium* of Justinian's *Institutes* opens with a philosophical remark of general importance: "The imperial majesty must needs be not only decorated with arms, but also armed with laws that it be able to govern rightly in either time, in war and in peace." This opening of the authoritative juristic textbook not only suggested a farewell to the purely military ideal of a kingship relying upon the sword, but also contained a challenge for a king to act as a legislator. The dialectics, however, of the formula *armis decorata—legibus armata* conjured an image of majesty rooted in far deeper layers, and the humanistically well-versed jurists of the Renaissance recognized that Justinian's formula was a transformation of Greek ideals and that it reflected the *optimum* of rulership expounded in Plato's *Republic:* kings who philosophize and philosophers who rule as kings. Emblematic drawings rendering the gist of Justinian's formula were not rare in the Renaissance. They showed a king brandishing a sword in one hand and a book in the other, until finally an *impresa* of the sixteenth century, bearing the moto *Ex utroque Caesar* (an allusion to Justinian's *utrumque tempus*), changed the meaning of the book in the prince's left hand, which now no longer was supposed to represent "Laws" specifically, but "Letters," because "by these two, that is, Arms and Letters, Julius Caesar... was made the lord of the whole world." Or else, the book stood for "Arts" in general, as explained by the accompanying verse: "*A Prince's* most ennobling parts/Are skill in *Armes*, and love of *Arts*."[42]

That kind of dialectical tension was, so to speak, daily bread in the twelfth century, in which not only the ideals of "knight" and "cleric" merged, as, for example, in the orders of knighthood as well as in courtly poetry,[43] but in which also the *rex literatus* appeared as another ideal. In a way, John of Salisbury anticipated the Renaissance motto when he declared (and he was not the first to do so) that an illiterate king was nothing but an *asinus coronatus*.[44] John of Salisbury does not refer to the Prologue of the *Institutes*,

---

[41] See Kantorowicz, *The King's Two Bodies*, 173ff, for the fisc, and 232ff for *patria*; Gaines Post, "Two Notes on Nationalism in the Middle Ages: I. *Pugna pro patria*," *Traditio*, IX (1953), 281ff.

[42] The decisive places are *Institutes*, prooem., and *Cod.*, Constitution *Summa rei publicae*. For the problem, see Ernst H. Kantorowicz, "On Transformations of Apolline

Ethics," *Charites: Studien zur Altertumswissenschaft*, ed. Konrad Schauenburg (Bonn, 1957), 265–74.

[43] This is more or less the theme of the valuable study of Reto R. Bezzola, *Les origines et la formation de la littérature courtoise en Occident (500–1200)* (Bibliothèque de l'École des Hautes Études, fasc. 286; Paris, 1944).

[44] *Policraticus*, IV, 6, ed. Webb, I, 254, line 25.

though he quotes it in another connection. But Glanville, the great English jurisprudent under King Henry II, opened the prologue to his *De legibus* with the very words of the *Institutes*, changing only Justinian's *imperialem maiestatem* into the more modest and appropriate *regiam potestatem*. His paraphrase then wandered to the Scottish lawbook commonly called the *Regiam Maiestatem;* it served the writer of *Fleta* to formulate his prologue, and it is found also in a spurious proem to Bracton's *De legibus*, whereas the genuine Bracton drew directly from the *Institutes* or from Azo's *Summa Institutionum*.[45] If we add the late medieval tractates on the subject of "Knighthood and Jurisprudence," *De militia et iurisprudentia*, we not only recognize the influence of the prologue to the *Institutes*, but also begin to see more clearly the bearings of the "legal knighthood," the *militia legum*, to which, as early as the twelfth century, the jurists aspired.[46]

Scientific jurisprudence gradually began to change the vocabulary of statecraft, and the new vocabulary began to influence statecraft itself. If those concerned continuously read and heard and had discussions about whether the people or the prince should be recognized as the true founder of law; or about the fact that the prince is not only decorated with arms, but also armed with laws; that the prince is *legibus alligatus*, though in some respects he be *legibus solutus*, and that what pleases him has the strength of law, then indeed it should not be surprising to find that the prince accepted and grew into the new role of legislator. Indeed, the law-making king began to eclipse the law-preserving king of earlier centuries, and the *rex legislator* superseded the more religiously tinted *rex iustus*. The image of Justinian and Tribonian began to obscure that of Melchizedek, whose name was translated *rex iustitiae*.[47] That is to say, under the impact of jurisprudence and juristic rationalism the ideal of liturgical kingship began to disintegrate. Its roots had been undercut anyhow by the papacy of the Church Reform. Now it fell to Justinian's lawbooks and their vocabulary to replace and, in a secular sense, restore some of the religious values of kingship, which had determined, as an effluence of the ruler's liturgical consecration (then still considered a sacrament), the image of kingship in the centuries preceding the Struggle over Investitures.

At the height of that struggle, around 1100, the so-called Norman (or York) Anonymous defended more vigorously than any other author the idea of Christ-centered, liturgical kingship, and therewith that of the priestly character of the king who was "not quite a layman," nay, was (as a result of his anointment) a *rex et sacerdos*. Forty years later, in King Roger II's prologue to his Assizes (1140), the shift from liturgy to law becomes manifest in a peculiar way. The position of "king and priest" was claimed, after a fashion, also by Roger II; but he regained his quasi-priestly character not through the Church (this was impossible after the Gregorian Age), but through the high pretensions of Roman legal philosophy, extracted from the prologue to the *Digest*, where the juris-

---

[45] See, on these prologues, Kantorowicz, "The Prologue to *Fleta* and the School of Petrus de Vinea," *Speculum*, XXXII (1957), 231–49, and, for the earlier times, P. E. Schramm, *Kaiser, Rom und Renovatio* (Leipzig and Berlin, 1929), I, 282f.

[46] See, e.g., Flavio Biondo, *Borsus, sive de militia et iurisprudentia*, ed. B. Nogara, *Scritti inediti e rari di Biondo Flavio* (Rome, 1927), 130ff. See also above, note 10.

[47] See Andreas of Isernia, *In usus feudorum*, praeludia, n. 25, fol. 3vob, on the legislating prince: "Item, imperator non facit leges, sed iurisperiti approbati per eum, ut Tribunianus et alii..." For, the prince *est raro iurista*.

prudents were compared to priests. The ancient liturgical language still reverberated in King Roger's prologue, but its spirit was that of Justinian. Like Justinian, the Sicilian king called his lawbook an oblation to God, an offering of mercy and justice, and then continued: "By this oblation the royal office assumes for itself a certain privilege of priesthood; wherefore some wise man and jurisprudent [in the *Digest*] called the law-interpreters Priests of Justice."[48] That is to say, the point of reference of this new ideal of priest-kingship was no longer the Anointed of God of the *Books of Kings* and the *Psalter*, but the legislator and jurisprudent as depicted in the lawbooks of Justinian.

The metaphorical quasi priesthood of the jurisprudents, and thereby of the king who was the *iudex iudicum* of his kingdom, was frequently discussed and interpreted by the glossators. In a twelfth-century collection of legal word definitions, the author, drawing from the *Institutes*, expounded under the heading *De sacris et sacratis* the new (or, in fact, very old) dualism: "There is one thing holy which is human, such as the laws; and there is another thing holy which is divine, such as things pertaining to the Church. And among the priests, some are divine priests, such as presbyters; others are human priests, such as magistrates, who are called priest because they dispense things holy, that is laws."[49] That doctrine of bipartition was carried on in the law schools. The *Glossa ordinaria* refers to it, and Baldus, in the fourteenth century, still defended the thesis that *legum professores dicuntur sacerdotes*, for (says he) there is a *sacerdotium spirituale* as well as a *sacerdotium temporale*—just as Bracton distinguished between *res sacrae* pertaining to God and *res quasi sacrae* pertaining to the fisc.[50] This general mood of the glossators was curiously epitomized by Guilelmus Durandus, the great jurist and liturgical expert at the end of the thirteenth century, who referred to the glossators when he declared, not at all disapprovingly, "that the emperor ranked as a presbyter according to the passage [in the *Digest*] where it is said: 'Deservedly we [the jurisprudents] are called priests'." It is remarkable that here a positive effort was made to derive the prince's nonlaical character not from his anointment with the holy balm and his consecration, but from Ulpian's solemn comparison of judges with priests.[51]

In this connection we may recall also that it was in the days of Barbarossa only, and not before, that the medieval empire began to be styled "the holy empire," *sacrum imperium*—and every medieval historian should feel uneasy when in his textbook he constantly reads that Charlemagne, in 800, was crowned emperor of the "Holy Roman Empire," a statement teeming with mistakes and misconceptions and as anachronistic as talking about the guns of Alexander or the paratroopers of Caesar. *Sacer*, in the language of Roman law, meant no more than "imperial," though in medieval Latin it may have had more Christian-ecclesiastical connotations. It was, at any rate, from Roman law that Barbarossa borrowed the epithet *sacrum* for his *imperium*, and it would spoil the

---

[48] F. Brandileone, *Il diritto Romano nelle leggi Normanne e Sveve del regno di Sicilia* (Turin, 1884), 94. See, for this problem, Kantorowicz, *The King's Two Bodies*, 117–23.

[49] *Petri Exceptionum appendices*, I, 95, ed. H. Fitting, *Juristische Schriften des früheren Mittelalters* (Halle, 1876), 164.

[50] Bracton, fol. 14, ed. Woodbine, II, 57f.

[51] Durandus, *Rationale divinorum officiorum*, II, 8, 6 (Lyons, 1565, fol. 55vo): "Quidam etiam dicunt ut not. ff. de rerum divis. l. sancta [*Dig.* 1, 8, 9: the prince dedicates *sacra loca*] quod fit presbyter, iuxta illud: 'Cuius merito quis nos sacerdotes appellat' [*Dig.* 1, 1, 1]."

specific flavor of both the time of Charlemagne and the age of Barbarossa with its new jurisprudence to use uncritically the epithet "sacred" for the events of 800. And one more little warning should be sounded. We are far too often inclined to talk about "secularization" of ecclesiastical thought and institutions in connection with the modern state. Secularization certainly there was—when, for example, the marriage of Christ to the universal Church, or the marriage of the bishop to his local church, was by analogy transferred to the political sphere, the jurists pointed out that the king was wedded to his realm as a "mystical groom."[52] But we find little of that "secularization" in the twelfth century. What happened then was not a secularization of the spiritual, but rather a spiritualization and sanctification of the secular. *Sacrum imperium* was not a borrowing from the vocabulary of the Church; it was a para-ecclesiastical designation in its own right, though when reintroduced it replaced the old antithesis of *sacerdotium* and *regnum* by the more coördinating and complementary designations of *sancta ecclesia* and *sacrum imperium*, holy Church and sacred empire. In other words, the sacred character of the empire, and of the emperor himself, no longer drew its strength from the idea of the *christus domini*, from the altar, or from the Church, but it was a secular sacredness *sui iuris* and *sui generis* apart from the Church, a concept which eventually found its most eloquent interpreter in Dante and his vision of two Paradises, one imperial-terrestrial and the other ecclesiastical-celestial.

It would be wrong to assume that the dualism of sacredness and holiness was produced by Roman law alone. From Justinian there derived the vocabulary, the technical term *sacrum imperium;* Roman law, however, represented but one current within a very complex evolution, as may be grasped from many examples. The Christ-centered kingship of the earlier Middle Ages found one expression in the ruler's title of honor, *vicarius Christi*. In the thirteenth century, however, this title became rarer, and without disappearing completely it was replaced by that of *vicarius Dei*, "Vicar of God." What this change implied was again a loosening of the ties with which the medieval prince was linked to the altar, to the sacrificial God-man who was not only the eternal King but also the eternal Priest. What had happened is again a rather complex evolution of which no more than two strands shall be mentioned here. On the one hand, the dogmatic-theological development of the twelfth century towards defining the real presence of Christ in the Sacrament produced a new accentuation of the very ancient idea of the presence of Christ in the person of the vicariously mass-celebrating priest. The *Decretum Gratiani* quoted a number of places in which bishops and priests were styled *vicarii Christi;* but by the end of the twelfth century *vicarius Christi* became almost exclusively the title of honor of the supreme hierarch, the Roman pontiff.[53] On the other hand, the hierocratic terminology found an unexpected ally in Roman law. For, the civilians, relying upon the vocabulary of Justinian's lawbooks and on Roman authors such as Seneca and Vegetius, began to style the emperor *deus in terris*, *deus terrenus*, or *deus praesens*, taking it for granted

---

[52] See, on the marriage of the prince to his realm, Kantorowicz, *The King's Two Bodies*, 212–23, and, for *Reipublicae mysticus coniunx*, René Choppin, *De domanio* *Franciae*, III, tit. 5, n. 6 (Paris, 1605, p. 449).

[53] See, for those changes, Kantorowicz, *The King's Two Bodies*, 89–93.

on the basis of their sources that the prince was above all "vicar of God" and not "vicar of Christ." In fact, the designation *vicarius Christi* for the emperor would not have been within the range of legal language at all. Thus it happened that the Christocentric ideal of rulership dissolved also under the influence of Roman law, and gave way to a more theocentric concept. Henceforth, a papal *Christus in terris* (to use an expression of Arnald of Villanova) found a counterpart in an imperial *deus in terris*.[54]

Another bifocality may be discerned with regard to the universalism of the Roman Empire and the territorial monarchies, and herein again Roman law plays an important role. It was in the twelfth century only that Roman law, by which (as was commonly imagined) in ancient times the whole *orbis terrarum* had been governed, became the new *Kaiserrecht*, the valid law of the medieval lords of the *sacrum imperium*. The universalistic character of Roman law was taken for granted even before its reactivation in the twelfth century: around 1050, the hope was voiced by Anselm the Peripatetic that the ancient universalism was to be restored not *armis*, but *legibus*: "Legibus antiquis totus reparabitur orbis" ("By the ancient laws the whole world shall be repaired").[55] It was a hope still shared by Dante, among many others.

Moreover, independently of Roman law, the universality of the Roman Empire appeared throughout the Middle Ages as an established fact, because St. Jerome's identification of the prophet Daniel's Fourth World Monarchy with the empire of the Romans held sway. In the twelfth century the universalistic tendencies inherent in both Roman law and Roman Empire were linked to the Hohenstaufen emperors, and these medieval princes were backed not only by dreams and myths, but also by the reality of law itself. That union was consummated by the time of Barbarossa, at the latest. The landmarks are the Diet of Roncaglia of 1158, the assertion of the Four Doctors that the medieval emperor was the *dominus mundi*, and the decision of Barbarossa to incorporate one of his own laws, the *Authentica Habita* or *Privilegium scholasticum* granting to students universal safety, into Justinian's *Code*, an act emphasizing that Barbarossa considered himself the direct successor of the ancient Roman emperors[56] The universality of the empire, however, was not only one of space but also one of time. Daniel's Fourth Empire (that is, in Jerome's interpretation, the Roman Empire) was to last until the end of the world. This was a myth. But the myth now was backed by jurisprudence since the lawbooks of Justinian stated over and over again that "the empire is forever," *Imperium semper est*. And whereas Jerome's mythical sempiternity referred to the Roman Empire alone, the statement of the lawbooks *Imperium semper est* had implications in the sense that every *universitas*, large or small, was juristically "forever." In other words, the juristic (though not the mythical) sempiternity of the empire was transferable to, and easily adopted by,

[54] *Ibid.*, 92, nos. 16f.

[55] See F. Dümmler, "Gedichte aus dem XI. Jahrhundert," *Neues Archiv*, I (1876), 177, line 25. For the problem, see P. E. Schramm, *Kaiser, Rom und Renovatio*, I, 279ff, and the recent study by Hermann Krause, *Kaiserrecht und Rezeption* (Abh. d. Heidelberger Akad., 1952, N. 1; Heidelberg, 1952).

[56] The Fourth (Roman) Empire was eventually fused with a Fifth Empire, that of Christ; cf. Aquinas [Tolomeo of Lucca], *De regimine principum*, III, 12f, ed. Joseph Mathis (2nd ed.; Turin and Rome, 1948), 53ff; also C. N. S. Woolf, *Bartolus of Sassoferrato* (Cambridge, 1913), 318ff. For the *Authentica Habita*, see *Cod.* 4, 13, 5 post; *MGH, Constitutiones*, I, 249, no. 176.

the territorial monarchies, in fact by any *universitas* or *communitas regni*, even though they were lacking the eschatological-mythical background of the eternal Roman Empire. Subsequently, the claims to universalism on the part of the Hohenstaufen emperors and their successors were challenged by the lords of the territorial monarchies; and the best challenge was to claim the same, or at least similar, prerogatives for the territorial states. This, then, was the climate in which, from the twelfth century onward, some fundamental political dogmas began to develop in the individual monarchies, culminating finally in the famous sentence *Rex superiorem non recognoscens est imperator in regno suo*, "A king not recognizing a superior is emperor within his realm." As a result of this maxim, some special imperial prerogatives, as, for example, the right of appointing notaries public or of legitimizing illegitimate children, were passed on to the kings deeming themselves emperorlike within their realms.[57]

In addition to these fairly well-defined imperial prerogative rights, however, there was passed on to the kings also the whole compound of legal philosophy contained in the imperial Roman law. For example, the *lex Julia maiestatis* concerning the crime of lese majesty was now appropriated by the kings although in the *Digest* and the *Code* it referred only to the emperor and to the *maiestas* of the Roman people.[58] Further, the statement of St. Jerome, embedded in canon law and saying: *Exercitus facit imperatorem*, "The army creates the emperor," was transferred to the king: *exercitus facit regem*.[59] Also, the famous maxim, derived from the *Code* and declaring that "the emperor has all the laws in the shrine of his breast," was transferred not only to the pope, the *verus imperator*, but also to the king of France; for, a French jurist (probably Thomas of Pouilly, *ca.* 1296–97), says in so many words that "of the King of France it may be said, as it is said of the emperor, that all the laws, especially those pertaining to this kingdom, are shut in his breast."[60] That, furthermore, the Roman emperor was *terra marique dominus*, "lord over land and sea" and over the elements as well, was a notion going back to antiquity. It was applied not at all rarely to Frederick II. Then, in a lawsuit concerning the association (*pariage*) of Philip IV of France and a French bishop, one of the royal legists, Guillaume de Plaisian, pointed out that the French king, since he was "emperor in his realm," had command over land and sea, whereupon the bishop mockingly answered: "Whether the king be emperor in his realm, and whether he command over land and sea and the elements, and whether the elements would obey if the king gave orders to them, is

---

[57] For the *Rex imperator* theory, see Post, in *Traditio*, IX (1953), 296ff, with a critical discussion of some recent studies on the subject (Calasso, Ercole, Mochi Onory); for the imperial prerogatives, see W. Ullmann, "The Development of the Medieval Idea of Sovereignty," *EHR*, LXIV (1949), 1ff.

[58] *Dig.* 48, 4; *Cod.* 9, 8. For example, Andreas of Isernia, *In usus feudorum*, on *Feud.* I, 5, n. 13 (fol. 32ᵛᵒ–33ʳᵒ), applies the *lex Julia maiestatis* perpetually to the king of Sicily, and so do the other Neapolitan jurists.

[59] *Decretum*, c. 24, D. XCIII: *exercitus imperatorem faciat*. John of Paris, *De potestate regia et papali*, c. XV, ed. Dom Jean Leclercq, *Jean de Paris* (Paris, 1942), 222, line 8, still makes a distinction: *nam populus facit regem et exercitus imperatorem.* Jean de Terre Rouge, *Tractatus de iure futuri successoris legitimi*, I, art. 1, conclusio 24, in François Hotman, *Consilia* (Geneva, 1586), Appendix, 34: *exercitus populi facit regem sive imperatorem*. Cf. E. E. Stengel, *Den Kaiser macht das Heer* (Weimar, 1910), also in *Historische Aufsätze Karl Zeumer gewidmet* (1910), 262–75.

[60] Fritz Kern, *Acta Imperii Angliae et Franciae ab a. 1267 ad a. 1313* (Tübingen, 1911), No. 271, p. 200, lines 12ff: "et de eo (rege Franciae) potest dici, sicut de imperatore dicitur, videlicet quod omnia iura, precipue competentia regno suo, in eius pectore sunt inclusa." The whole legal opinion discusses imperial rights appropriated by the French king.

irrelevant to the points at stake."[61] How deeply engrained the belief in the king's power of commanding the elements actually was, even as late as the seventeenth century, may be gathered from the *Diary* of Samuel Pepys who, seeing in the summer of 1662 King Charles II riding in his barge in a downpour of rain, made the telling entry: "But methought it lessened my esteem of a king, that he should not be able to command the rain."[62] Finally, there should at least be mentioned a philosophical concept transmitted from Greek philosophy through the agency of Roman law, which was reapplied to the Hohenstaufen emperor and transferred to the pope in the twelfth century, until in the thirteenth it was passed on to the territorial kings: the idea of the prince as the *lex animata*, the "living" or "animate law." The usefulness of this concept for the theory of absolutism is almost self-evident, especially when, under the influence of Aristotle, the *lex animata* was turned into a *iustitia animata*. For not only was the king said to be present in all his law courts, in which finally he was present also vicariously through his image, his state portrait, or his coat of arms, but there was also a good reason for asserting that the king's will, theoretically, had the force of law: being himself the animate law, the king could do no wrong, since "whatever he did would be *ipso facto* just."[63]

To be sure, it is a long and very involved and complicated way that leads from the twelfth century to the absolutist theories of sovereignty. Nor can this rapid survey claim to have done more than barely touch upon a few problems. For all their brevity and skimpiness, however, the present remarks may suffice to demonstrate that in a discussion of "Twelfth-Century Europe and the Foundations of Modern Society" the impact of jurisprudence on government cannot easily be neglected.

---

[61] For the rule over land and sea as a rhetorical commonplace applied to Hellenistic kings, see A. Momigliano, "Terra Marique," *Journal of Roman Studies*, XXXII (1942), 53–64, and, for its application to the *dea Roma*, C. M. Bowra, "Melinno's Hymn to Rome," *ibid.*, XLVII (1957), 25. For Frederick II, see Kantorowicz, *Kaiser Friedrich der Zweite, Ergänzungsband*, 204f. For Philip IV, or rather his crown jurist Guillaume de Plaisian, and the Bishop of Gévaudan, see *Mémoire relatif au Paréage de 1307*, ed. A. Maisonobe, in *Bulletin de la société d'agriculture, industrie, sciences et arts du Département de la Lozère* (Mendo, 1896), 521, 532; Plaisian asserted "quod dominus Rex sit imperator in regno suo et imperare

possit terre et mari," to which the bishop replied: "Porro utrum dominus Rex sit imperator in regno suo et utrum possit imperare terre et mari et elementis et, si obtemperarent ipsa elementa, si eisdem imperaret, ... nichil ad propositum nec contra Episcopum facit."

[62] See Samuel Pepys' entry on July 19, 1662.

[63] For the *lex animata* theory, see Kantorowicz, *The King's Two Bodies*, 127ff; Krause, *Kaiserrecht* (above, note 55), 37ff; and, for the age of absolutism, William Farr Church, *Constitutional Thought in Sixteenth-Century France* (Cambridge, 1941), 251, also 47 (n. 10), 58, 70, 97, and *passim*.

THE PROLOGUE TO *FLETA* AND THE SCHOOL
OF PETRUS DE VINEA

Not the least among the many obvious advantages of a new edition of an old text is that the unaccustomed setting, print, and size may render even a familiar text unfamiliar and cause the reader's eye to rest on passages which formerly he may have failed to notice. In John Selden's seventeenth-century editions of that summary of English or (better) Bractonian law which passes under the puzzling name of *Fleta* the Prologue is somewhat lost. Printed in italics on a single sheet following the title page, it is seperated from the text proper by many pages of *Tituli capitulorum*, and from some copies in our public libraries the lonely Prologue sheet may have even vanished entirely.[1] In the handsome new edition of *Fleta* prepared for the Selden Society by the distinguished Dioscuri of English mediaeval studies, Mr. Richardson and Professor Sayles, the author's Prologue cannot easily be missed.[2] In the margin of the English translation which runs parallel with the Latin text, the editors have indicated the sources from which Fleta drew, and, if we disregard an isolated Biblical reference to Ezekiel, it turns out that all the marginal quotations refer to the Prologue of Glanville's *De legibus Angliae*.[3] The opening words of Glanville and therefore of Fleta, it is true, are ultimately a paraphrase of the Prologue to Justinian's *Institutes* adapted to the royal dignity (replacing *Imperatoriam maiestatem* by the more modest *Regiam potestatem*); but since Fleta copied verbatim the text of Glanville, and not that of the Roman textbook, the editors of Fleta were probably correct in leaving the indirect borrowing from the *Institutes* unmentioned.

Glanville addressed his Prologue to Henry II and praised this king in high-flown words. Fleta, writing in or shortly after 1290, used his model's dithyrambs to exalt King Edward I. And the same precious words were used a third time, when the author of the *Regiam Maiestatem*, the Scottish version of Glanville, addressed his sovereign lord, the

Reprinted, with permission, from *Speculum*, XXXII (1957), 231–249.

[1] *Fleta, seu Commentarius Iuris Anglicani* (London, 1647; 2nd ed., 1685); cf. Ioannis Seldeni, *Ad Fletam Dissertatio*, ed. David Ogg, Cambridge Studies in English Legal History (Cambridge, 1925).

[2] *Fleta*, edited with a translation by H. G. Richardson and G. O. Sayles, Selden Society, LXXII (London, 1955), vol. II. Vol. 1, containing the introduction, has not yet been published. To assess the date of Fleta is difficult. Mr Richardson kindly informed me that the book must have been in the making before the expulsion of the Jews (July–October 1290); that, however, the submission of Scotland, referred to in II, c. 13, suggests a date not earlier than 1292 or even 1296; consequently, *Fleta* in its present form would get a date 1296–1300, but an origin many years previously. There is, of course, no way to tell at what stage of the work the Prologue was written.

[3] Glanvill, *De Legibus et Consuetudinibus Regni Angliae*, ed. George E. Woodbine (Yale Historical Publications: Manuscripts and Edited Texts, XIII; New Haven, 1932).

king of Scots.[4] There seems to have been in thirteenth-century England a serious shortage of panegyric vocables. John Selden, no doubt, felt fully justified in drawing the treacherously obvious conclusion: "therefore little can be deduced from such eulogies."[5] The present paper intends to demonstrate, on the contrary, that very much can be deduced from such eulogies.

* * *

For no obvious reason, the editors of the new *Fleta* indicate only where the borrowings from Glanville begin, but not where they end. In fact, the writer of *Fleta* has inserted into the Prologue of Glanville a long passage, followed by a minor one. His style undergoes a sudden change: the sentences roll forth in perfect rhythms, and at the end of a clause the *cursus velox* is hardly ever omitted. Moreover, Glanville's eulogies of Henry II are not only augmented by new sets of images, but soar to a most surprising and, if one may say so, most un-English pitch.[6] Edward I, quite unexpectedly, appears like another paradisian Adam, a cosmic ruler, "whom the great Artificer's hand formed into man."[7] He appears as the messianic prince, announced by Isaiah, in whose days "spears are turned into reaping-hooks and swords beaten into ploughshares," who binds the contrasting elements, "so that crooked is turned into straight, and rough are turned into smooth paths, levelling the depths with the heights and the heights with the depths by a marvellous art."[8] *Ad memoriam futurorum* the famous deeds of Edward should not only be written down "with the pen in codes," but be "graven on the rocks with the chisel."[9] Rarely has a mediaeval English king been glorified in similar terms. If the feelings towards his king ran so extravagantly high on the part of a man whom Edward I, as we are led to assume, put into jail, the expression of those feelings might serve as a *document humain* characterizing the generous and noble mind of both Fleta and the "English Justinian." Unfortunately, however, those intercalated passages are no more Fleta's own invention than is the main body of his Prologue, which was fathered by Glanville. They, too, are borrowed, and the story of those borrowings is so interesting that it seems worth the while to make the details of the case more generally known.

[4] See Thomas Thomson, *Regiam Majestatem and Glanvill*, in: *The Acts of the Parliaments of Scotland* (London, 1844) I, 185ff, cf. H. G. Richardson, "Roman Law in the *Regiam Majestatem*," *The Juridical Review*, LXVII (1955), 155–187, who suggests a date "in the 1240's."

[5] Selden, *Ad Fletam*, X, 1, ed. Ogg, p. 183. Selden's phrasing is not quite as epigrammatic as that of Ogg's English translation; cf. p. 182: "Adeoque laudes illae . . . non ita in argumentum heic trahendae." What Selden means to say is that those eulogies are of little value for an individual characterization of Edward I, since originally they were supposed to characterize Henry II. Even that is only half-correct, since a great portion of the Prologue to *Fleta* was actually written in praise of Edward I—though not by the author of *Fleta*. See below, p. 174.

[6] The insertions (ed. Richardson-Sayles, p. 1, line 13, to p. 2, line 11, and p. 2, lines 26–31) have attracted peculiarly little attention. For example, N. Denholm-Young, "Who wrote 'Fleta'?," in his *Collected Papers on Mediaeval Subjects* (Oxford, 1946), 69, says that the Prologue "except for three sentences is Glanville's prologue," meaning thereby only the final paragraphs (p. 3, lines 10–21). Apparently Denholm-Young took interest only in this final section, for a scholar so familiar with the *cursus* as Denholm-Young is (see *op. cit.*, 26ff, on "The Cursus in England") could not have missed the *clausulae* prevailing in the inserted sections. About Woodbine's opinion, expressed in his editions of Bracton's *De Legibus et Consuetudinibus Angliae* (New Haven, 1915), I, 17, and of Glanville, p. 184, v. *Prologus*, see below, Appendix.

[7] Richardson-Sayles, p. 2, line 4f.

[8] *Ibid.*, p. 2, line 8f, where the text should read: "ut prava in directa, et aspera in vias [conversa] sint planas." See below, no. 37, line 6f, and Isai. 40, 4.

[9] *Ibid.*, p. 1, line 15ff. Cf. Job 19, 24.

One text which served Fleta for the embellishment of his Prologue was the great *Eulogy* for the Emperor Frederick II which, in the manuscripts, is usually ascribed to the imperial prothonotary and logothetes, Petrus de Vinea (*Epistolae*, III, 44), and recently has been ascribed, with some good reasons and some bad, to Nicolaus de Rocca, Vinea's most gifted pupil.[10] What Fleta took from the *Eulogy* becomes evident by reproducing Fleta's insertions in parallel with the relevant passages of Vinea, III, 44, and underscoring the concordances, whereas passages italicized or set in boldface type may be disregarded for the present moment.[11]

FLETA, Prol.

[Quam eleganter aut quam strenue, quam callide hostiumque obviando maliciis excellentissimus rex noster Edwardus hostilitatis tempore armatam excercuerit miliciam nemini venit in
5 dubium, cum iam *in omnem terram exierit laus eius* et in omnes fines magnalia eius] *et intonuerunt longe lateque mirifice* verba sua *in terminos orbis terre. Quis ergo posset amplo famine prepotens eius ample preconia laudis exprimere cuius ab*
10 tempore *nature cunabilis gesta conspicua memorialibus sunt commendenda perpetuis et cuius etate crescente cum tempore facta magnifica calamo sunt exaranda codicibus, sed celte pocius sculpenda scilicibus ad memoriam futurorum? Quis unquam*

5. in-eius] cf. Ps. 18, 5; cf. Eugen Müller, *Peter von Prezza* (Heidelberg, 1913), 140, No. 19. 7. verba sua] nomen suum St. 8. posset] possit St, P. 10. tempore] ipsis St. 12. calamo-codicibus, ad-futurorum] cf. StC. atque Job 19, 24. 14. unquam posset] inquam possit St.

VINEA, III, 44

Grandis namque progressus materie ... et ex tele diffuse contextu, que de preconio (9) summi Cesaris hostes cedentis orditur, ne quid ex contingentibus obmittatur, manus scribentis tremescit (21) et stupet. *Quis* enim *posset amplo famine prepotens* (8) tanti principis insignia promere in cuius pectus confluunt quicquid virtutes habent...? Non Plato, non Tullius (22) ....

8. posset] possit St, P; prepotens] St, P. prepotentis Vin

[10] The *Eulogy*, as this piece may be called here for reasons of convenience, has been edited several times; see Petrus de Vineis, *Epistorarium*, III, 44, ed. Simon Schard (Basel, 1566), 467ff, and, for a slightly better edition, A. Huillard-Bréholles, *Vie et correspondance de Pierre de la Vigne* (Paris, 1865), 425f, No. 107. Neither of these editions is satisfactory. More recently Karl Pivec, "Der Diktator Nicolaus von Rocca: Zur Geschichte der Sprachschule von Capua," *Innsbrucker Beiträge zur Kulturwissenschaft*, I (1953), 135–152, has made a new edition of the *Eulogy*, based upon Dietrich of Nieheim's *Viridarium imperatorum et regum Romanorum* (written in 1411), an author who in his turn reproduced it from a so-called Vinea collection; see also the new edition of the *Viridarium* by A. Lhotsky and K. Pivec, in *MGH, Staatsschriften des späteren Mittelalters*, V:1 (Stuttgart, 1956), 70f. Although Pivec (on the basis of the *Viridarium*, but without considering the full text transmission [below, n. 16]) was able to correct a few errors of Schard and Huilard-Bréholles, his own rather high-handed emendations have brought new mistakes into the text; and while his attribution of that piece to Nicolaus de Rocca is appealing and probably correct, his comparisons of style are not at all convincing. See, for the involved problem, the review by Rudolf M. Kloos, in *Deutsches Archiv*, XI (1955), 567f. I am greatly indebted to Dr. Kloos for a number of suggestions he made in connection with the present paper.

[11] The text of *Fleta* is that provided by Richardson-Sayles with one or two obvious emendations (e.g., above, n. 8). The text of the *Eulogy* follows, on the whole, that of Huillard-Bréholles, but considers also that of Pivec where readings are improved; the task of a new edition of that piece of rhetoric remains with the *Monumenta Germaniae Historica*. Fleta's quotations from the *Eulogy* are scattered all over the inserted part of his Prologue; therefore the line numberings of Fleta's insertion are added to the *Eulogy* in parentheses. In order to avoid repetition, I have integrated the parallels from two letters of Stephen of San Giorgio. Hence, simple underscoring means (in all four pieces) parallels with the *Eulogy* of Vinea (or Rocca); *italics* means parallels with Stephen of San Giorgio's *Laudes* for Edward I (see below, p. 174f); finally, **boldface** implies parallels with Stephen's letter to the king of Castile (see below, n. 37). In the apparatus of all the texts the following sigla are used:

[ ] = Glanville (i. e., bold brackets).
RS = Richardson-Sayles (edition of Fleta).
St = Stephen of San Giorgio: *Laudes* for Edward I.
StC = Stephen of San Giorgio: Letter to Castile.
Vin = *Eulogy* edited by Huillard-Bréholles.
P = *Eulogy* edited by Pivec.

15 *posset explicare sermonibus graciarum uberes dotes*
eius qui statura decorus placet aspectibus, speciosus
forma pre filiis hominum desideratur a gentibus,
qui trahit effluencia largitatis ut adamas, qui sic
apparet in oculis omnium graciosus ut favorem
20 *quasi possideat omnis carnis? Porro lingue de-*
ficiunt, ora subcumbunt, labia tremefiunt, et
facundia subticet Tulliana. Hic est enim de quo
scriptum est '<u>*Aquila grandis magnarum alarum,*</u>
<u>*longo membrorum ductu, plena plumis et varietate,*</u>'
25 *et hic est cuius emissa de pharetra nunquam rediit*
sagitta retrorsum, cuius gladius eductus ut pro-
deret non est reversus inanis, dum sic incessanter
dimicaret in hostes ut magnificus semper in bellicis
actibus triumphator. Surgite igitur, O animosi et
30 *iuvenes bellicosi, explicate vexilla, clangite tubis,*
et festum agite tanto regi, qui viriliter sumens ab
adolescentia sua scutum et ad viriles annos usque
perveniens indefecte pugnavit et strenue pro iure
suo. Si quis ergo Martis aditare *prelia concupiscit,*
35 *festinus regem hunc adeat, qui docet manus inperi-*
tas ad prelium et humeros pulcre parat ad sarcinas
ponderum bellicorum. Hic revera etiam est <u>quem</u>
summi <u>manus</u> Artificis <u>formavit in hominem,</u>
qui, sub libra mansuetudinis et levamento
40 clemencie cuncta deliberans, <u>utpote pacis ami-</u>
<u>cus, caritatis patronus, iuris conditor, potencie</u>
<u>filius,</u> populum sibi subditum <u>perpetua racione</u>
<u>gubernat,</u> pacis ligans federibus universa, ut
prava, indirecta et aspera in vias sint **planas,**
45 yma summis summaque ymis arte quadam
mirabili coequando. **Et cum magnum ita iudicet**
sicut parvum, non est apud eum accepcio
muneris vel persone.
    [Quam iuste — racione promptissimus]. Sub
50 eius namque temporibus, que sibi Dominus in
tempore feliciter longiora prolonget, <u>fomenta</u>
<u>malicie destruuntur,</u> virtutum germina hinc inde
pulalant, in spicis grana fructificant, et pacis
orrea lucupletantur, ita quod lancee vertuntur
55 in falces, gladii conflantur in vomeres et quicquid
quisquam effrenis audet et inmoderate presumit
ambicio sue potentis auctoritatis censura casti-
gat.
    [Leges autem Anglicanas....]

Hunc siquidem terra, pontus adorant et ethera
satis applaudunt, <u>utpote</u> qui mundo verus imperator a divino provisus culmine <u>pacis amicus,</u>
charitatis patronus, iuris conditor, <u>iusticie con-</u>
servator, <u>potentie filius,</u> mundum <u>perpetua ra-</u>
cione gubernat (40).

Hic est de quo Ezechielis verba proclamant
'<u>*Aquila grandis magnarum alarum, longo ductu*</u>
<u>*membrorum, plena plumis et varietate* multiplici.'</u>
Hic est (25) de quo loquitur Ieremias. . . .

Talem namque totus orbis vocabat in dominum,
talem requirebat iusticie defensorem, qui in
potentia strenuus, *in strenuitate preclarus,* **in**
claritate benignus, . . . in providentia foret hu-
manus. In eo denique insita forma boni, tanquam
livore carens, climata <u>ligat</u> (43) et elementa
coniungit, ut conveniant flammis frigora, iungan-
tur arida liquidis, planis associentur aspera, et
directis invia maritentur (44). Sub eius namque
<u>temporibus</u> (50) destruuntur <u>fomenta malicie,</u>
<u>virtus</u> (52) securitatis inseritur: itaque <u>gladii</u>
<u>conflantur in vomeres</u> (55), pacis federe (43)
suffocante timorem . . . O miranda divina clementia . . ., perituro mundo de tam mundo
principe . . . providisti, qui *ex omni parte beatus,*
strenuus in toto . . ., <u>quem supremi manus</u>
<u>opificis formavit in hominem</u> (38), ut tot rerum
habenas flecteret et cuncta sub iuris ordine
limitaret. O utinam divina provisio . . . annos
augusti regnantis augeres! . . . .

18. qui] et St. 23. Aquila-varietate] cf. Ezech.
17, 3. 24. varietate] decora add. St, multiplici
add. ¡Vin. 26. proderet] per deret St. 27. in-
cessanter] strenue add. St. 29. actibus] extiterit
add. St. 29. o animosi] o quirites et milites St.
31. et festum] et diem festum St. 33. indefecte]
indefesse St. 33. iure suo] populo christiano St.
34. aditare] adiscere St. 44. prava-planas] prava
in directa et vias aspera convertuntur in planas
StC.; cf. Is. 40, 4. 44. et cum-persone] StC, cf.
2 Chron. 19, 7. 50. que-prolonget] cf. Vin. 53.
51. fomenta] fermenta emend. RS. 55. gladii-
vomeres] cf. Is. 2, 4.

15. terra-ethera] cf. infra, n. 36; Ovidii *Metam.*
I, 15, laudat P. 16. mundo] mundus emend. P.
19. iusticie conservator] om. RS, St, P. 20.
mundum-gubernat] cf. Boethius, *Consol.,* III,
metr. 9; racione] relatione Vin. 27. multiplici]
decora St, om. P. 36. vocabat] vocavit emend.
P; cf. Kloos *Deutsches Archiv,* XI, 567. 39. insita-
liquidis] cf. Boethius *l.c.,* Kloos, *l.c.,* 186f. 46.
federe] guerrarum add. P. 51. hominem]
homine isto P; rerum-flecteret] Ovidii *Metam.,*
II, 169, laudat P, sed pauca habet ad rem; cf.
Boethius, *Consol.,* III, metr. 2. 53. annos] animos
emend. P; annos-augeres] tales acclamationes
saepissime inveniuntur; cf. Fleta, 50 (que-
prolonget); StC, 27 (Augeat-vite vestre).

The parallels are so striking that no comment is needed. It is true, Fleta's predilection for picking isolated half-sentences from the *Eulogy* and strewing them like orange-blossoms on the reader's path is slightly baffling. This oddity, however, may find an explanation later.

More perplexing is the fact that Fleta knew the *Eulogy* at all. Admittedly, letters of Petrus de Vinea or his school were known in England long before and were used, for example, by the clerks of Henry III at the time when that king embarked on his hapless Sicilian adventure.[12] In that case, however, the originals were official writings issued by the imperial chancery; and although we are not at all sure how some of them happened to be known in England, those official letters could have been collected as models of style by the recipients.[13] The *Eulogy*, however, was a piece of a very different character. It was a panegyric oration with which Frederick II actually may have been greeted on some occasion, just as it was customary on festal days to honor the Byzantine emperors by a panegyric address.[14] More likely, however, the *Eulogy* was not recited, but was merely a written encomium. The recently discovered encomia of Abbot Nicholas of Bari, which in style and content are closely related to the *Eulogy*, make it clear that this literary genre was cultivated in the surroundings of Frederick II.[15] Panegyrics of that kind, however, whether actually recited or only written, could not normally be popularized by the recipient, who was the prince. They were, as in Antiquity, collected and released by the author himself, and therefore consigned to rhetorical or epistolary collections, to "letter books" in the broadest sense of the word. Hence, all the private productions (private as opposed to pieces issued officially by the chancery) of Vinea and Rocca and others have reached us in such collections, no matter whether these letter books were destined to sail under the name of Vinea or another famous *dictator*, or were nameless and represented indiscriminately letters by many authors.[16] The possibility that the

---

[12] See E. Kantorowicz, "Petrus de Vinea in England," *Mitteilungen des Österreichischen Instituts für Geschichtsforschung*, LI (1937), 43–88.

[13] "Transmission through the recipient" explains, for example, the fact that some twenty imperial writings (including a letter of Walter of Ocra to Henry III) found their way into the chronicles of Roger of Wendover and Matthew Paris; cf. Otto Vehse, *Die amtliche Propaganda in der Staatskunst Friedrichs II.* (Munich, 1929), 216–236; see p. 218, n. 111, the list of letters used by Matthew Paris; cf. Kantorowicz, "Petrus de Vinea in England," 75f.

[14] Solemn addresses were due to the Byzantine emperors especially on the day of Epiphany (6 January), but also on other occasions—a performance, descending from Antiquity, which survived until the end of the Byzantine empire. Unfortunately, only a few of the mediaeval speeches are accessible in modern editions; see, however, W. Regel, *Fontes rerum Byzantinarum* (St. Petersburg, 1917), or Max Bachmann, *Die Rede des Johannes Syropulos an den Kaiser Isaak II. Angelos* (Diss. Munich, 1935). A *Corpus Panegyricorum Byzantinorum* is a long-felt and urgent desideratum of every student engaged in Byzantine studies, since those encomia are among our most valuable sources for the history of political ideas and intellectual history in general. It would not be

too difficult to show that the Byzantine phraseology affected also the panegyrics of orators in the surroundings of Frederick II, as, for example, the eulogies of Abbot Nicholas of Bari (see next note).

[15] R. M. Kloos, "Nikolaus von Bari, eine neue Quelle zur Entwicklung der Kaiseridee unter Friedrich II.," *Deutsches Archiv*, XI (1954–55), 166–190. There are three panegyrics: one on the Constitutions of Melfi (*Liber augustalis*), and one each for Frederick II and Petrus de Vinea. For Petrus de Vinea, of course, there exists yet another encomium, written by Nicolaus de Rocca; see Vinea, *Ep.*, III, 45, ed. Schard, 470; ed. Huillard-Bréholles, *Pierre de la Vigne*, p. 289, No. 2.

[16] See the highly suggestive paper by Hans Martin Schaller, "Zur Entstehung der sogenannten Briefsammlung des Petrus de Vinea," *Deutsches Archiv*, XII (1956), 114–159. According to Schaller, the *Eulogy* (Vinea, III, 44) is found in both the large and small six-book collections (pp. 121, 129), in the large five-book collection (p. 132), though not in the shorter one (p. 134), and in some of the collections not organized in books (p. 141). Whether the author of the *Eulogy* was Petrus de Vinea or Nicolaus de Rocca makes no difference here nor, probably, with regard to the transmission of the text.

Eulogy for Frederick II could have been transmitted separately, and not within the framework of some *Epistolarium*, therefore should probably be ruled out.[17]

To cut a long argument short, we have to assume that the author of *Fleta* had at his disposal some Vinea collection from which he culled his rhetorical flowers. This would not be impossible at all. The Vinea collections, as we know them, were composed in the late thirteenth century—perhaps in Paris, perhaps at the Curia, perhaps independently at both places—and Fleta wrote around 1290 or at any rate before 1300.[18] All that sounds reasonable enough. Why should Fleta not have owned a copy of the famous *Epistolarium*? It would be one more warning to the historian not to neglect the Sicilian material when working on English problems of legal and intellectual history in the thirteenth century.[19] In fact, however, Fleta was in a far more curious position. He may have derived his knowledge of epistolary models both from the recipient and from the author himself.

In the Necrology of Montecassino an entry is found on 23 October: "Obbiit Magister Stephanus de sancto Georgio scriptor domini pape et consiliarius et secretarius regum anglie et sicilie."[20] The entry is correct. Master Stephen of San Giorgio, a fairly well-known man, served many lords, and with many at the same time.[21] Between 1281 and 1285, we meet him as chamberlain and chaplain in the entourage of Cardinal Hugo of San Lorenzo in Lucina, an Englishman who, when still Master Hugo Atratus of Evesham, had served as a royal clerk under Edward I.[22] Edward I in 1283 appointed Stephen his proctor at the papal court in Rome. At the Roman Curia Stephen had the office of a papal *scriptor*. Finally, in those perilous years when the conflict between Naples and Aragon, as a result of the Aragonese conquest of Sicily, became the major problem of European politics and diplomacy, Stephen took up service also with King Charles II of Naples, his native lord.[23]

[17] This is true also with regard to the copy transmitted through Dietrich of Nieheim (above, n. 10), since Dietrich avowedly reproduced his text from a Vinea collection.

[18] See Schaller, *op. cit.*, 126ff, 132ff.

[19] In addition to the study mentioned above (n. 12), see also a remark about Bracton and the Sicilian law books in my "Mysteries of State," 70, n. 16.

[20] Mauro Inguanez, *I Necrologi Cassinesi* (Rome, 1941), I, 23 October ("Il necrologio del codice Cassinese 47"), quoted by R. Weiss (see next note), p. 164, n. 43.

[21] See T. F. Tout, *Chapters in the Administrative History of Mediaeval England* (Manchester, 1920), II, 24, n. 1, who has summed up a few dates from the Patent Rolls; the fullest biographical account has been given by Robert Weiss, "Cinque lettere inedite del Card. Benedetto Gaetani (Bonifacio VIII)," *Rivista di Storia della Chiesa in Italia*, III (1949), 162ff; see also G. L. Haskins and E. H. Kantorowicz, "A Diplomatic Mission of Francis Accursius and his Oration before Pope Nicholas III," *English Historical Review*, LVIII (1943), 424, n. 4, and the study by Taylor qoted below (n. 31). Service with more than one lord at the same time was nothing extraordinary; Galfridus Anglicus, e.g., was simultaneously clerk to the kings of Castile and England (cf. Denholm-

Young, "The Cursus in England," in *Collected Papers*, 33f), and there are many other examples available.

[22] The *Collegium cappellanorum domini Hugonis Cardinalis* addresses Stephen repeatedly as *concappellanus;* see Paris, B. N. MS. lat. 8567, f. 18, where (f. 20ᵛ) the chaplains write to another chaplain "per Stephanum de Sancto Georgio, Camerarium ipsius Cardinalis." For Hugo Atratus of Evesham, cf. *Calendar of Close Rolls, 1272–79*, 158. He became a cardinal in 1281 and died in 1285. Stephen was absent from England in the early 1280's (see below). May we assume that he accompanied the new cardinal to the Curia as a chaplain and chamberlain of the cardinal's household?

[23] For Stephen's appointment as Edward's proctor, see *Patent Rolls, 1281–1292*, 86. He became *scriptor domini pape* (according to Weiss, "Cinque lettere," p. 163, n. 37) between 1285 and 1287 at the latest; in 1288 (20 August), he is certainly mentioned in this capacity in papal letters; cf. Ernest Langlois, *Les Registres de Nicolas IV* (Paris, 1905), I, 34, Nos. 211, 212. He could not have taken up service with Charles II prior to the latter's liberation from Aragonese captivity by the treaty of Campfranch, in October 1288 (see below, n. 52ff); in 1289, he drafted Charles II's proclamations announcing the king's coronation at the hands of the pope (Rieti, 26 May; below,

That Stephen of San Giorgio was a South Italian cannot be doubted. His brother Peter of San Giorgio, who received from Edward I the title of a "king's chaplain," was a monk in Montecassino. Thomas of San Giorgio, *magister racionalis* of King Charles II of Naples, may have belonged to the same family, although the name "de Sancto Georgio" was not too rare in Italy.[24] Decisive however, is the fact that the correspondence of Stephen has been handed down to us in a Paris manuscript (Bibl. Nat. MS. lat. 8567) which contains almost exclusively material connected with South Italians. In addition to Stephen's letters we find in it the correspondences of Nicolaus de Rocca and Leonardus de Benevento as well as the letter book of Berard of Naples.[25] Berard of Naples, incidentally, had an English prebend and was granted the title of "king's clerk" by Edward I, although this busy papal notary was permanently occupied at the papal court.[26] That, to be sure, was nothing abnormal in the thirteenth century, when the English Church became a hunting ground of Italian ecclesiastics and other beneficiaries who never so much as saw their prebends.

The same, however, was not true with Stephen of San Giorgio, who likewise was a royal clerk under Edward I. In the Patent Rolls his name first appears in 1274, when he was granted a benefice at the church of Bureford, in the diocese of Hereford,[27] to which were added subsequently other benefices in the dioceses of Lincoln and London.[28] That Stephen was not only a titular *clericus regis*, but was active in the king's service, is evidenced by a number of letters of Edward I which, according to the entries, were written "per magistrum Stephanum de sancto Georgio."[29] About the length of time he spent without interruption in England nothing certain can be said until Stephens's cor-

n. 55). Benedetto Gaetani, in letters to Edward I in June 1290, repeatedly styled Stephen "vestro et excellentis Principis domini C[aroli] Sicilie Regis illustris clerico" (Weiss, *op. cit.*, 159f, Nos. II and III).

[24] For Peter of San Giorgio, see *Patent Rolls, 1272–1281*, p. 143 (27 May, 1276); on that occasion Stephen is referred to as "King's clerk." Cf. H. Finke, *Acta Aragonensia* (Berlin and Leipzig, 1908–22), II, 642, for Thomas of San Giorgio. See also E. G. Léonard, *Histoire de Jeanne Ire* (Monaco and Paris, 1932), II, 398, for one Matteo di San Giorgio "du diocèse du Mont-Cassin, notaire apostolique et notaire de la Chambre" (for both references my thanks go to Professor Theodor E. Mommsen). It would be difficult to tell from which place Stephen originated; the relations to Montecassino would perhaps suggest San Giorgio a Liri (southeast of Pontecorvo), near the frontier of the Kingdom of Naples and the States of the Church; another San Giorgio was near Benevento, and a third one in Calabria; see E. Sthamer, *Die Bauten der Hohenstaufen in Unteritalien*, Ergänzungsband I: *Die Verwaltung der Kastelle* (Leipzig, 1914), Index, *s.v.* Giorgio. At any rate, the South Italian family of that name has nothing to do with the English St. George family, a relationship which Tout, *Chapters*, II, 24, n. 1, took into consideration.

[25] A detailed analysis of B.N. lat. 8567 is not intended here. See, for the MS, the brief description by Huillard-Bréholles, *Pierre de la Vigne*, 256f; also a few remarks by L. Delisle, in *Notices et Extraits*, XXVII: 2 (1879), 100;

and especially F. Kaltenbrunner, "Römische Studien III," *Mitteilungen des Instituts für Österreichische Geschichtsforschung*, VII (1886), 114ff. I have referred to the MS repeatedly; see, e.g., *Laudes Regiae* (Berkeley and Los Angeles, 1946), p. 30, n. 55, and indirectly also in *EHR*, LVIII (1943), 424, n. 4; I still intend to edit the numerous letters of this important MS so far as they refer to England.

[26] See *Patent Rolls, 1272–81*, 143, 336. His name appears quite often in *Ancient Correspondence* (e.g., Vol., XIII, No. 182a; vol. XIX, No. 19); also, in B.N. lat. 8567, fol. 13, there is a letter "T. Thesaurarius Anglie Magistro B[erardo] de Neapoli per Stephanum [de Sancto Georgio]." The name of the treasurer of the Wardrobe was Thomas Beke (Tout, *Chapters*, II, 160, also p. 14), who held that office from 1274 to 1280. This is not, however, the place to sum up Berard's relations with England.

[27] *Patent Rolls, 1272–81*, 76.

[28] *Ibid.*, 209, 242.

[29] See, e.g., B.N. lat. 8567, fols. 19–19^v, and three more letters on fol. 22; these letters are addressed to curials or to the pope; there is good reason to believe that Edward's letter of 1275, to Pope Gregory X, in *Parliamentary Writs*, I, 381f, was written also by Stephen; cf. E. H. Kantorowicz, "Inalienability," *Speculum*, XXIX (1954), 500, n. 59, See also above, n. 26, for the treasurer's letter written by Stephen.

respondence has been thoroughly studied, sifted, and dated. His name, however, is twice mentioned in the "Household Ordinance of 1279" where he figures as a clerk of the Wardrobe.[30] The correctness of this information is confirmed not only by the fact that Stephen wrote letters for the treasurer of the Wardrobe, Thomas Beke, but also by a letter in the Paris manuscript which he provided with the telling salutation: "Sociis suis clericis Guardarobe Regie, Stephanus salutem."[31] Entrusted with various missions, Stephen was obliged to travel, off and on, between Rome and the English court. In 1282 he was certainly at the papal Curia. For in that eventful year, when Peter of Aragon conquered Sicily and Edward I went to war to quell the rebellion in Wales, he wrote from Italy to the English chancellor, Robert Burnell, to inquire about the king and queen and "tocius regni status," and also about the royal expedition against the Welsh "rebels and traitors."[32] On 11 December of that year, Prince Llywelyn met his death. On 22 January 1283, only six weeks after that event, Stephen wrote, probably from Orvieto, an exuberant letter to his associates of the Wardrobe to felicitate them and their king on that magnificent victory.[33] In the following year (1284) we find Stephen himself in Wales, staying with Edward I at Aberconewey.[34]

Stephen of San Giorgio must have felt great admiration for Edward I. For he composed, either in connection with the Welsh war or on some other occasion, a panegyric about Edward, *Laudes de domino Odduardo Rege Anglie*, in which he exalted especially the military prowess of that king, praising him as a teacher of warfare to the chivalrous youth and a master in the trade of Mars. Since this eulogy, as yet unpublished, will lead us straightway back to Fleta's Prologue, it may be printed here in full length.[35]

Laudes facte de domino Odduardo Rege Anglie, per Stephanum de Sancto Georgio
(Paris, B. N. MS. lat. 8567, fols. 14ᵛ–15ʳ).
(*circa* 1283–1284)

Inter magnificos et praeclaros alumpnos, quos pregnantis nature peperit uterus et mamma lactavit, in unum profecto scilicet excellentissimum principem dominum Odduardum Anglie Regem Illustrem graciarum suarum dona et divinarum suarum dotes natura mater specialiori quadam opulentia dinoscitur adunasse, ut sicut suorum splendorum natalium
5   altique sanguinis generositate prepollet, sic ex omni parte beatus et hinc inde dotatus in felicitate muneribus sceptro ac dyademate non indignus, plenus fastigiis potentiaque suf-

[30] Tout, *Chapters*, II, 160 and 163 ("sire Esteuene de sein Jorge").

[31] See, for this letter (B. N. lat. 8567, fol. 3ᵛ), Kantorowicz, "A Norman Finale of the Exultet and the Rite of Sarum," *Harvard Theological Review*, XXXIV (1941), 134; also *Laudes Regiae*, p. 30. The letter, most gratifyingly, has been edited and translated by A. J. Taylor, "The Death of Llywelyn ap Gruffydd," *The Bulletin of the Board of Celtic Studies*, XV (1953), 20ff. There is another letter of Stephen in B.N. lat. 8567, fol. 1ᵛ, which is addressed "Sociis et amicis clericis Illustris Regis anglie." See above, n. 26, for Thomas Beke's letter "per Stephanum."

[32] Taylor, *op. cit.*, p. 207, n. 3; Stephen inquired about the "processus regalis expedicionis contra rebelles et proditores Wallenses." On 27 September 1282 Stephen sent a report about Peter of Aragon's conquest of Sicily; see *Lists and Indexes*, XLIX: Diplomatic Documents,

No. 1587 (the document is unfortunately in very bad shape).

[33] Above, n. 31.

[34] Taylor, *op. cit.*, 207, n. 3, quoting *Exchequer Accounts*, 351/12, m.5, mentions ℓ 54 paid to Stephen for his expenses when bringing, in October 1284, letters from the Curia to King Edward at Aberconewey. See also Rymer, *Foedera*, I:2, 648, Edward's letters to various cardinals and curials (4 and 5 October 1284, from Montalto in Wales) in which he refers to the news and rumors "quos idem clericus noster [Stephanus de sancto Georgio] ex parte vestra nobis viva voce retulit."

[35] B.N. lat. 8567, fol. 14ᵛ (*italics* refer to Fleta's Prologue, underscoring to Vinea, III, 44). The date, of course, is quite uncertain; but since Edward's military virtues are so strongly emphasized, we may want to think of the Welsh campaign. His other campaigns would be too late, since Stephen died in 1290.

fultus, strenuitate preclarus, claritate sublimis, sublimitate flexibilis vivat et regnet Rex
ipse cum Regibus gloriosus. Cuius nempe fama concelebris tantam iam redolet suavitatem
odoris, ut *in omnem terram exiverit* sonus *eius et intonue*rit *longe lateque mirifice* nomen
10   suum *in terminos orbis terre. Quis ergo possit amplo famine prepotens eius ample preconia*
laudis exprimere cuius ab ipsis *nature cunabulis gesta conspicua memorialibus sunt* (f. 15ʳ)
comendanda perpetuis et cuius etate crescente cum tempore facta magnifica calamo sunt ex-
aranda codicibus, sed celte potius sculpenda scilicibus ad memoriam futurorum? Quis,
inquam, possit explicare sermonibus graciarum uberes dotis eius, qui statura decorus placet
15   *aspectibus speciosus forma pre filiis hominum desideratur a gentibus, qui trahit effluentia*
largitatis ut adamas, et *sic apparet in oculis omnium graciosus ut favorem quasi posideat*
omnis carnis? Porro lingue deficiunt, ora succumbunt, labia tremefiunt et facundia subticet
Tulliana. Hic est enim de quo scriptum est: 'Aquila grandis magnarum alarum, longo
membrorum ductu, plena plumis et varietate decora.' *Et hic est cuius emissa de pharetra nun-*
20   *quam rediit sagitta retrorsum, cuiusque gladius eductus ut* perderet *non est reversus inanis,*
dum sic incessanter strenue dimicaret in hostes ut magnificus semper in bellicis actibus
extiterit triumphator. Surgite igitur, o quirites et milites *et iuvenes bellicosi, explicate vexilla,*
clangite tubis et diem *festum agite tanto Regi, qui viriliter sumens ab adolescentia sua scutum*
et ad viriles annos usque perveniens, indefesse pugnavit et strenue pro populo christiano. *Si*
25   *quis ergo Martis adiscere prelia concupiscit, festinus hunc Regem adeat, qui docet manus*
imperitas ad prelium et humeros pulchre parat ad sarcinas ponderum bellicorum.

In marg.] optima est. 1. preclaros-uterus] cf. Vinea, *Ep.*, III, 45, ed. Schard, 470: 'satis
preclaros alumnos longe lateque per orbem nature pregnantis peperit uterus.' 5. ex-beatus]
cf. Vin, 49. 6. potentia-claritate] cf. Vin, 37. 9. exiverit] cf. Ps. 18, 5; StC, 9. 12. calamo-
futurorum] StC, 12. 14. decorus-aspectibus] cf. Gen., 49, 22; Nicolaus de Bari, ed. Kloos
(supra, n. 15), 174, nos. 81–82. 15. speciosus-ghominum] cf. Ps. 44, 3; Nicolaus de Bari, 175,
n. 87a. 18. Aquila etc.] cf. Esek., 17, 3; Vinea, *Ep.*, III, 45, ed. Schard, 472. 21. dimicaret]
dimicarit MS. 22. et milites] superscr. MS. 25. docet-prelium] cf. Ps. 143, 1; Nicolaus de
Bari, 174, n. 77.

Even without the help of italics to mark the agreements it would have been obvious that
Fleta, in the intercalated section of his Prologue, reproduced verbatim the *Laudes de
domino Odduardo* of Stephen of San Giorgio. Fleta actually proceeded quite skilfully. He
copied Glanville's Prologue until he arrived at the quotation of Psalm 18, 5: "in
omnem terram exierit laus eius" (line 5). This versicle, however, is quoted also in
Stephen's *Laudes* (St. 9), a pleasant coincidence which saved Fleta even the small trouble
of inventing a suitable transition: the Psalter enabled him to change horses in midstream
without danger or effort and thence to ride at a lively gait with Stephen until, on line 37,
he abandoned that charger or the charger him. The textual changes Fleta saw fit to
make were insignificant. Line 7 (St. 9), he changed "nomen suum" into "verba sua";
line 29 (St. 22), he eliminated the Roman Quirites and added to the more native yeomen
a second epithet, "animosi"; and line 33 (St. 24), he replaced "pro populo christiano" by
"pro jure suo." All other changes seem to be casual omissions or careless mistakes.

We have to return once more to the *Eulogy* for Frederick II. Being a South Italian
trained to express himself in the style of the *tuba Capuana* (Petrus de Vinea) Stephen of
San Giorgio must have known almost by heart the *Eulogy*, which served as a paragon of
panegyrical plenty. It was at the tip of his pen whenever he wished to praise a king or
even the *Rex regum*, Christ.[36] Hence, a few quotations from the *Eulogy* for Frederick

[36] See below, n. 37, the encomium to the king of
Castile. In a Christmas sermon (B.N. lat 8567, fol. 17ᵛ),
Stephen praises the Saviour "quem terra, pontus, ethera
colunt, adorant, predicant," which should be compared
with *Eulogy*, lines 15f. Whatever the ultimate source of
those words may be, Stephen borrowed them from the
Eulogy. Also the answers of the *collegium cappellanorum* to
this sermon (fol. 18) is full of echoes of the *Eulogy*, which in
itself is a resonance of Boethius, *Consolatio*, III, metr. 2 and
9; cf. Kloos, in *Deutsches Archiv*, XI (1954–55), 186f., 568.

slipped into his *Laudes* for Edward (lines 5, 6f, 10f, 18f). In other words, some of the sprinkled quotations from the *Eulogy* which Fleta invested in his Prologue, were not taken directly from the original, but came to him through the agency of Stephen's *Laudes*. Fleta, nevertheless, had more than a slight knowledge of the original; for where Stephen's *oeuvre* steps out, the Frederician *Eulogy* steps in. After a longer quotation borrowed again from Glanville, Fleta unmistakably surrendered to the Sicilian original (lines 37ff, 49ff). That is to say, Fleta had at his disposal two encomia: the *Eulogy* and the *Laudes*.

These two sources, however, fail to fill another gap. On line 46ff, Fleta has a quotation only partly covered by 2 Chronicles 19, 7: "non est enim apud Dominium Deum ... personarum acceptio nec cupido munerum." Fleta says: "Et cum magnum ita iudicet sicut parvum, non est apud eum accepcio muneris vel persone." This "filler," however, was borrowed by Fleta from another encomium of Stephen of San Giorgio, from the praise for the king of Castile, probably Sancho IV. This letter, hitherto unpublished, is as follows.[37]

(Lodi, Whit-Thursday [*ca* 1288])

Illustri Regi Castelle, Stephanus devotum terre osculum ante pedes.

Inter alios Reges et principes orbis terre, quos unitas fidei orthodosse connectit, quosque reddit celebris fame relatio gloriosos. Fama vestra, Rex Inclite, dulci personans in auribus hominum melodia magnificentiam vestram pullulat prerogantius excellere, ut de aliis quibus latera vestra sunt predita

5 taceatur, virtutis quadruplicis maiestate. Volat siquidem ipsam nec subticet quod Prudentia, qua presencia pulchre quis ordinat, futura previdet et preterita recordatur; Fortitudo, qua **prava in directa et vias aspera** convertuntur in **planas**; Iustitia, qua redditur unicuique ius suum; ac Largitas, qua munifica dextera beneficia conferuntur, in vestri cordis armario vel archivo sua tabernacula posuerunt. Satis est enim mundo notorium, immo iam *in omnem terram sonus exivit*, quod cuncta, que vos, prin-

10 ceps egregie, qui prudentia nostis per distinctionem temporum concordare scripturas, magnifice peregistis hucusque, decreta nunc agitis et agenda decernitis, sale prudentie sunt condita et condita sapientia, ac pre sue dignitatis titulo *calamo sunt scribenda codicibus ad memoriam futurorum.* Id autem universalis tenet opinio quod velut athleta fortissimus contra perfidiam agarenice feritatis pro fide catholica dimicantes et per fortitudinis robur excitantes potencie vestre vires sarracenorum duritiam

15 domuistis, et gladius vester qui vinci nusquam potuit, regna regnis adiciens potenter subditas sibi faciat barbaras nationes. Nec latet, inquam, angulos mundi huius, magnifice domine, immo est iam in auribus hominum divulgatum, quod equa lance iustitie subditorum vestrorum merita trutinans regia manus vestra et reddens unicuique iura sua, regit in iustitia populos, gubernat in pace subiectos. **Et dum** auctoritas vestra sacra **ita magnum iudicat sicut parvum, non est apud eum accepcio**

20 **muneris vel persone.** Illud etiam non ignoratur, munifice domine, per cardines orbis terre quod largiflua manus vestra sic se petentibus aperit affluenter, ut quicquid a vobis iuste petitur vel honeste vel etiam flagitatur, ex dono sine quolibet improperio largiatur claudi nescia et inscia non donare. (15ᵛ) Quid plura. Nullus unquam a latere vestro vacuus, nullus inops, nullus gratia vestra non preditus dicitur recessisse. Feliciter igitur ego reputans ex premissis eos qui vestris gratis merentur

25 astare conspectibus et ex hiis maiestatis vestre personam amabilem, brachiis fidei, devotionis et amoris amplexans, in ea parvitate qua dego, totum me serviciis vestris offero, totum me vestre potentie pedibus recommendo. Augeat vobis dominus dies letos et protrahat feliciter terminum vite vestre. Amen.

Datum Laudi die quinto a patre filioque procedens suos replevit apostolos charismatibus spiritus

30 almus.

2. in marg.] optima.   8. in archivo] superscr. MS.   9. exivit] vide St, 9.   12. in marg.] nota.   16. subditas-nationes] cf. Missale Romanum, *Orationes solemnes in Passione Domini.*   18. in marg.] nota. 22. flagitatur] flagitator MS.   27. Augeat-vestre] vide Vin, 54.

[37] Paris, Bibl. Nat. MS lat. 8567, fol. 15ʳ. Without a full investigation of Stephen's itinerary, it is not at present possible to date this laudatory letter beyond "Lodi, Whit-Thursday." In 1288, however, Stephen of San Giorgio was active in arranging the settlement between Aragon and Charles II of Naples; Castile was lined up with France against Aragon. It may have been at that time, or a year later, that he addressed the king of Castile who, in that case, would have been Sancho IV. Had this laudatory letter been addressed to Alfonso X, it would perhaps have been possible to say more than the generalities in which Stephen indulged.

This letter interestingly illustrates Stephen's method of transferring laudatory words from one king to another. The underscored words (line 6; cf. Is. 40, 4) reveal, at the same time, that Fleta's lines 43f were not borrowed from the *Eulogy* directly (line 43) but from Stephen's paraphrase. To be sure, Fleta may have used other letters of the South Italian *dictator* as well. It seems, however, that he had before his eyes the letter to Castile—which is all the more note-worthy as this letter follows, in the Paris MS. 8567, immediately after the *Laudes* to Edward. Did there exist, as early as 1290, a "letter book" of Stephen of San Giorgio, arranged by the author himself? And could Fleta have owned such a book, or seen and used it? There are no answers to those questions. Be that as it may, we know now that Fleta's Prologue is a queer cento made up of Glanville's Prologue in praise of Henry II, of the Vinea-Rocca *Eulogy* for Frederick II, of Stephen's *Laudes* for Edward I, and of the same author's encomium for the king of Castile. Fleta seems to have been a collector of panegyrics.

Naturally the question poses itself how it happened that Fleta had access to the *dictamina* of Stephen of San Giorgio. We recall that the South Italian master was a clerk of the Wardrobe and that one of his effusions—the congratulations on the defeat and death of Llywelyn—was addressed to his associates in the Wardrobe. This letter, no doubt, was deposited in the archive of the Wardrobe, the records of which, unfortunately, have not survived.[38] In the same archive the *Laudes de domino Odduardo* would have been kept. These *Laudes* were not addressed to the king himself, but were an encomium *about* the king. Certainly Stephen would have submitted a copy of that piece of rhetorical art to King Edward as well. But if this laudation was shown or given to any group of courtiers, as its purpose demanded, the author's colleagues in the Wardrobe would have been the first to receive it.

The problem can now be reduced to the simple question whether Fleta himself perhaps belonged to the Wardrobe. For if that were true, he would have had access to Stephen's pronunciamentos through the Wardrobe archive and could have known that encomium, so to speak, as a recipient or on the recipients' end of the line. On the other hand, however, should Fleta have belonged to the Wardrobe, there would have existed also a possibility that he knew the author and drew his knowledge from the author directly.

Who was, or who wrote, Fleta? It has always been suspected that the mysterious anonymous who claimed to have composed his tractate *in Fleta*, in the prison in Fleet Street, was a man closely attached to the king's household. It would have been a convenient hypothesis to assume that Fleta was identical with John of Fleet, a Wardrobe clerk under Edward I, and that he wrote his book in some manor called Fleet; but for various reasons this hypothesis does not work.[39] Not so long ago, however, N. Denholm-Young tried to crack the riddle of Fleta's identity, and it seems that in connection with

---

[38] Tout, *Chapters*, I, 34; see also Kantorowicz, "Petrus de Vinea in England" (above, n. 12), p. 67, n. 89.

[39] Cf. Francis M. Nichols, in his edition of Britton (Oxford, 1865), Introd., pp. xxvff; Tout, *Chapters*, II, 34ff; Denholm-Young, "Who wrote 'Fleta'?" in: *Collected Papers*, 78; cf. 69f, where he mentions Fleet "as the name of manors elsewhere in England." For John of Fleet, see Tout, *Chapters*, VI, Index, *s.v.* "Fleet." There are several men of that name, but none seems to have held office earlier than the 1290's.

the South Italian Master Stephen the arguments of Denholm-Young can be broadened and strengthened.

Very cautiously, though with very good, indeed excellent, reasons, Denholm-Young identified Fleta with one Matthew de Scaccario or Matthew Cheker.[40] Of Fleta's lack of originality the Prologue is a glaring example. A similar lack of originality eventually could become the device for singling out Matthew Cheker as the hypothetical composer of the anonymously transmitted tractate. Anonymity, of course, was considered good style among the jurists around 1300. Roffred of Benevento, whose works were known in England,[41] suppressed his name ("I have not mentioned the name of the composer"); but then he referred to Karolus (de Tocco) of Benevento as his teacher and added that he, the pupil, was a native of the same town; and thereby he surrendered his secret. Andreas of Isernia declared quite in general that "like honest men who do not care for pomposity" some authors did not head their works epigrammatically by the mention of their name.[42] Why the author of *Fleta* played that game of anonymity we do not know; but he revealed his name when he copied Bracton just as, in his Prologue, he copied Glanville or Stephen of San Giorgio. Bracton explained that a writ was invalidated if the name of the recipient was misspelt and illustrated this item by misspelling his own name: Henry of *Brocheton* or even *Brachton*, instead of Bracton, would make a writ invalid. Fleta, unoriginal as he was, transferred that explanation to his own name and pointed out that a writ was not valid if it said "Matthew, the son of William," instead of "Matthew, the son of Peter." The name of Matthew, being not too frequent in England, eventually led Denholm-Young to identify "Fleta" with Matthew de Scaccario, otherwise Matthew Cheker.[43]

Matthew's biographical notes have been collected by Denholm-Young, and they may be summed up quickly so far as they are relevant to the present problem. From 1277 to 1283 Matthew Cheker belonged to the king's household, first as a yeoman (*valettus regis*), later as a squire. He was employed in the Wardrobe and his name appears several times in connection with the Wardrobe treasurer and payments made to the soldiers. In the years of the Welsh rebellion and thereafter we find him repeatedly in Wales or occupied

---

[40] Denholm-Young, *op. cit.*, 68–79, as well as his paper "Matthew Cheker," *ibid.*, pp. 80–85 (both papers were first published in *Eng. Hist. Rev.*, 1943 and 1944). H. G. Richardson, in his review of Denholm-Young's book in *Law Quarterly Review*, LXIII (1947), 376ff (to which Mr Richardson himself kindly called my attention), expressed his willingness to admit that some Matthew closely connected with the king's household may have been the author of *Fleta*, but he objects to the identification, current since Selden, of *in Fleta* with "in Fleet Prison." He suggests instead that the book was given its name on the basis of a *jeu de mots*, "because in it the reader will 'fleetly' find his law. Fleta then signifies a handy compendium. . . ." Richardson, however, does not offer any evidence to support this interpretation, which, though interesting, does not appear self-evident to me. Sir Maurice Powicke, *The Thirteenth Century, 1216–1307* (Oxford, 1953), 356, n. 2, mentions the "attractive identification" of Denholm-Young.

[41] R. J. Whitwell, "The Libraries of a Civilian and Canonist and of a Common Lawyer, An. 1294," *Law Quarterly Review*, XXI (1905), 394, shows that Master Peter de Peckham had in his library a copy of *Ranfredus Beneventanus*, that is, Roffred Epiphanii of Benevento, who was appointed a law professor at the University of Naples by Frederick II and died in 1243.

[42] Cf. Giovanni Ferretti, "Roffredo Epifanio da Benevento," *Studi Medievali*, III (1908), 239, n. 8: "Ut audivi a domino meo Ka. Beneventano, cuius ego discipulus sum, qui hoc opus condidi et nomen non apposui conditoris et eiusdem sum patrie habitator." Feretti (p. 238, n. 2) quotes also Andreas of Isernia, *In Usus Feudorum Commentaria*, praeludia, n. 17 (Naples, 1571, fol. 2ᵛ): ". . . compilator et compositor huius operis, qui in palam conscripta deduxit: sed forte noluit nomen suum epigrammate superscribi, sicut faciunt viri honesti, non curantes de pompis. . . ." Andreas, however, had mentioned his name in the preceding *prooemium*.

[43] Denholm-Young, *op. cit.*, 72ff.

with Welsh affairs. In 1287 he served his king in some legal matters. Later, in connection with the judicial inquiry of 1289 and the fall of Adam of Stratton, whose attorney he became, Matthew was accused, rightly or wrongly, of having tampered with documents, one of the chief crimes of Adam of Stratton himself. The result was that Matthew, in 1290, was sent for two years and two days to the Fleet prison.[44]

If we think of mediaeval prisons as places of utter brutality and of conditions which only our enlightened humanitarianism has gradually overcome and changed for the better, we shall have to revise our opinion considerably with regard to the Fleet. Gentleman prisoners who were willing to pay and live on their own, had their chambers furnished with their tapestries and books, and were allowed to live in reasonable comfort. Matthew Cheker, it seems, passed his term of arrest in particular ease. He could come and go more or less as he pleased, go to Christmas parties and the like, attend service in the church of the Carmelites or a court session in Westminster, until this gay atmosphere of a *Fledermaus* prison came to an abrupt end. In January 1292 he had to stand another trial on account of his extravaganzas, and was convicted; the time he had spent in Fleet did not count, and he was sent for two years and two days to the Tower, where his comforts were considerably reduced.[45]

Matthew's guilt or innocence are of no interest here. What matters is that in Fleet prison Matthew indeed could have written his tractate, if he so desired. In this respect, our most important piece of evidence is a list, apparently drafted when he left Fleet prison, of his belongings and chattels ("Bona et catalla Mathei de Escheker").[46] In this inventory we find among many other items an interesting catalogue of books which he had in Fleet. In addition to belletristic books of *Poytrie* and *Romauns*, a *Summa* on alchemy, and a primer, we find therein a *Decretum Gratiani*, a *Digestum novum*, the *Summae* of Hengham, the *peciae* of Britton's legal tractate in twenty-six quires, and other law books, statute books, and records.[47]

Perhaps we would have expected to find Glanville among Matthew's books, and we may be disappointed that the inventory does not mention in so many words *Epistolarium Petri de Vinea* or a letter book of Matthew's friend, Stephen of San Giorgio. For it will not be too hazardous to assume that "Fleta," Matthew Cheker, was personally acquainted with the South Italian Master Stephen. From 1277 to 1279/1280 both men were members of the king's household and held appointments in the Wardrobe. They may

---

[44] *Ibid.*, 80f, for the early period and Matthew's connection with the Wardrobe.

[45] The whole story is told by two legal documents: *Select Cases in the Court of King's Bench under Edward I*, ed. G. O. Sayles, Vol. II (Selden Society, LVII; London, 1938), Introd., p. cliv; and *Select Cases in the Exchequer of Pleas*, edd. Hilary Jenkinson and Beryl E. R. Formoy (Selden Society, XLVIII; London, 1932), 141ff; see Denholm-Young, *op. cit.*, 74f.

[46] Cf. Whitwell (above, n. 41), pp. 399f, and his interpretation of the document, pp. 394ff. Here we find also the "pictured tapestry" (*Taminan depictum*) mentioned.

[47] *Ibid.*, p. 400: "Item. xxvj. pecie de Summa Britton." Denholm-Young, p. 75, inadvertently mentions Bracton instead of Britton. *Pecie* (*petie*) are the numbered quires of an official copy of a standard manuscript made by professional scribes under the supervision of a university (Paris, Bologna, Oxford, and very few others); cf. Denholm-Young's review (*op. cit.*, pp. 177ff.) of the authoritative work on this subject by Jean Destrez, *La Pecia dans les mss. universitaires du XIIIe et du XIVe siècle* (Paris, 1935); see also K. Christ, "Petia: Ein Kapitel mittelalterlicher Buchgeschichte," *Zentralblatt für Bibliothekswesen*, LV (1938), 1–44; and, for the importance of the *petiae* of the University of Paris for the redaction of the Petrus de Vinea letter books, see H. M. Schaller (above, n. 16), pp. 123ff.

have met also in Wales, in the years after the defeat of Llywelyn, when Stephen again was in the entourage of Edward I. Matthew may have asked Stephen for a copy of the *Laudes de Odduardo Rege*, may have asked him for other laudations praising other princes, and may have received from Stephen the *Eulogy* for Frederick II and the letter to the king of Castile. We cannot possibly tell how and when and where those two men met, or what they were talking about; but the Prologue to *Fleta* indicates that Matthew Cheker made use of the writings of his Wardrobe associate, Stephen of San Giorgio, and there is no reason to assume that he did not get those panegyrics from the "horse's mouth."

One more little item should be considered which may be meaningful or may just belong to the "Department of Curious Coincidence." Among the chattels of Matthew Cheker we find: "Item unum Kalendarium. Forma concordie et pacis inter Regem Karlium et Alfusum Regem Dragonie, et alia diversa Minuta eiusdem Mathei."[48] *Kalendarium* may be anything in the form of a list: a list of records, for example, or of entries of any kind; Bracton's list of chapter headings, his "table of contents," was called *Kalendarium*.[49] More important, however, is the fact that the person who drafted the list of Matthew's books "singled out for special notice"[50] the form of a peace treaty between King Charles II of Naples and King Alfonso III of Aragon. How did this instrument get into Matthew's scholarly luggage?

We know, of course, how actively King Edward participated in the numerous efforts to settle the differences between Aragon and Naples arising from the Sicilian Vespers (1282), from the capture of Naples' heir to the throne (Prince Charles of Salerno) by a Siculo-Aragonese admiral (1284), and from the death of Charles of Anjou (1285). Under the sponsorship and arbitratorship of Edward I a number of treaties were concluded between the rival powers, only to be broken, to result in a new impasse, or to be foiled, like the treaty of Tarascon (1291), by the sudden death of the Aragonese signer.[51] One treaty, however, that drafted and signed at Campfranch (Campofranco) in October 1288, had at least one positive result: the liberation of the Prince of Salerno. It was a complicated treaty, and its numerous clauses and provisos called for a great number of instruments. One of those instruments, the one concerning the terms of liberation of the Prince of Salerno, bears the signature of a witness we are interested in, "Master Stephen of San Giorgio, Clerk of the Lord King of England."[52] In the same capacity Stephen put his signature also under the oath of King Alfonso III of Aragon.[53] In other words, Stephen belonged to the strong English delegation which Edward I had despatched to

---

[48] Whitwell, *op. cit.*, 400.

[49] It is, of course, impossible to tell, or even to guess, what kind of a *kalendarium* Matthew had among his belongings; it was, however, some isolated list, since it is not mentioned among his books but among all sorts of odds and ends. Perhaps it was the "Calendar" of the numerous instruments of the Anjou-Aragon treaty itself.

[50] Denholm-Young, *op. cit.*, 75.

[51] See, on those protracted negotiations, Ludwig Klüpfel, *Die äussere Politik Alfonsos III. von Aragonien (1285–1291)*, (Abhandlungen zur Mittleren und Neueren Geschichte, XXXV; Berlin and Leipzig, 1911–1912). *Fleta*, III, c. 6

(cf. Selden, *Ad Fletam*, X, 4, ed. Ogg, p. 188), mentions a "decree [concerning the inalienability of the *res Coronae*] made by all Christian kings at Montpellier in the fourth year of King Edward, son of King Henry." This puzzling "decree" (though certainly wrongly dated and probably misunderstood) should perhaps be viewed against the background of those negotiations between Anjou and Aragon, at which several kings were present while others were represented by their envoys. It is futile, however, to make guesses without a detailed investigation of the issue.

[52] Rymer, *Foedera*, I:2, 691.

[53] *Ibid.*, 693.

Campfranch, headed by the chancellor, Bishop Robert of Bath and Wells, and including such indispensables as John de Lacy and Peter of Chavent, then still steward of the king's household, and others.[54]

During the following years Stephen of San Giorgio was occupied almost perpetually with Angevin-Aragonese affairs. In May 1289, at Rieti, the liberated Prince of Salerno was finally crowned King Charles II of Naples by the Orsini Pope Nicholas IV; and it was Stephen who drafted the solemn proclamations by which the king announced his coronation to his subjects and to foreign courts.[55] When, in 1290, the theater of negotiations shifted to Provence, Stephen moved too. He was working together with the two cardinals charged with achieving a peace, one of them being Benedetto Gaetani, cardinal-deacon of San Nicola in Carcere Tulliano, later Pope Boniface VIII. In June of that year the cardinals decided to send Master Stephen of San Giorgio to King Edward to report about the miseries of the *reformatio pacis*.[56] In Paris, on his way to England, he met Charles II, who likewise wrote to Edward to tell him that Master Stephen would convey to him all the information obtainable about the treaties.[57] Thus Stephen traveled once more to England—in his pouch the acts of the affair "Naples versus Aragon." It was his last voyage to the British Isles; on 23 October 1290, Stephen of San Giorgio died.

Was Matthew Cheker involved in those diplomatic negotiations between Naples and Aragon? Certainly not. How, then, did he happen to have that "forma concordie et pacis" in his scholarly apparatus, and how did he get it? Through Stephen of San Giorgio? We do not know. Nor do we know what may have been bundled together with that treaty. The inventory of Matthew's chattels only says laconically: "forma concordie et pacis . . . et alia diversa Minuta."

APPENDIX

About the Prologue to *Fleta*, Professor Woodbine (above, n. 6) has made certain statements which might be relevant to the present investigation, but need qualification, since they are liable to be misunderstood. In his edition of Bracton's *De legibus* (I, p. 17, n 1), Woodbine remarked that there is "a simple explanation of the fact that the prologue to Glanvill precedes the text of Fleta," because the Glanville prologue is found "in some of the Bracton MSS." This opinion was repeated once more when Woodbine (in his edition of Glanville [1932], p. 184) commented on Glanville's prologue: "Fleta has an extended form of the same prologue, a fact which is rather good evidence that the writer of Fleta was using a manuscript of Bracton's treatise which also contained *it* [italics mine]. Two MSS of Bracton which have *it* are still extant—Middle Temple MS 6 Seat A.E.15 and Trinity College, Cambridge, MS 0.3.52. The most cursory reading of the opening lines of

---

[54] *Ibid.*, 694. Peter de Chavent swears for his king, Edward I, concerning the hostages to be handed over to the king of Aragon; see, for Chavent's stewardship, Tout, *Chapters*, VI, 41, also II, 26, and, for his connections with "Fleta," II, 34f. Denholm-Young, p. 78, thinks it "possible that Matthew, at some time before 1287, was a member of Peter de Chavent's household."

[55] See B.N. lat. 8567, fols. 20ᵛ–21: "Rex fidelibus suis super coronatione sua, per Stephanum."

[56] Cf. Robert Weiss, "Cinque lettere" (above, n. 20), 159f, Nos. II and III. See also T. S. R. Boase, *Boniface VIII* (London, 1933) 18ff.

[57] Rymer, *Foedera*, I:2, 738 (28 July 1290).

Bracton will reveal that he had read, and was more or less using, the prologue of Glanvill."

These remarks contain two assertions and one hypothesis. To begin with the last assertion, it is not at all clear what Woodbine means when he refers to "the opening lines of Bracton." Does he refer to the genuine Bracton (I mean the one he edited 1915–1942) or to the Bracton of the two MSS which he quoted in the preceding sentence? He could not have meant the genuine Bracton of his edition because the most cursory reading of the opening lines of Bracton's "Introduction" reveals instantly that they have no similarity whatever with Glanville's prologue, if we except the paraphrase of Justinian's proem to the *Institutes*—and there Bracton was guided by Azo and the text of the *Institutes*, and not by Glanville. If, however, Woodbine referred only to the two MSS, this would imply that their prologues represented the genuine Bracton; in that case, however, he certainly should have printed the texts of those prologues in his edition or at least in his apparatus. But the Bracton text Woodbine edited and the peculiar prologues of the two MSS are mutually exclusive, and an inspection of the two MSS will show that it would be more than hazardous to draw from those prefaces any conclusion about what the authentic Bracton "had read, and was more or less using."

Moreover, Professor Woodbine seems to maintain (in the first sentence quoted above) that Fleta's "extended form of the same [Glanville] prologue" was borrowed from one of the Bracton MSS "which also contained *it*." This, however, cannot possibly be the meaning of his assertion, because the extended form of the prologue is not found in the two Bracton MSS quoted by him; it is found exclusively in the prologue to *Fleta*, as the borrowings from South Italian stylists would have suggested anyhow.

Finally, there remains the hypothesis. Professor Woodbine assumes that the writer of *Fleta* "was using a manuscript of Bracton's treatise which also contained it [the Glanville prologue]" and that "two MSS. of Bracton which have it are still extant." Unfortunately, the two MSS (I am greatly obliged to the kindness of A. Haleran, Esq., Librarian of Trinity College, Cambridge, and H. A. C. Sturgess, Esq., Librarian and Keeper of the Records of the Honourable Society of the Middle Temple, for providing me with photostats of the prologues) bear out neither the assertions nor the hypothesis of Prof. Woodbine.

Trinity College, Cambridge, MS. 0.3.52, fol. 1vo, contains a prologue which is nothing but an abstract of *Institutes* 1, 1–2, and of Bracton's *De legibus*, I, 1–3 (fols. 1–2a). It begins with the words of the proem of the *Institutes* adjusted to regal rank, but has nothing at all to do with Glanville, as a comparison of the Incipits may show:

Trinity Cambridge MS	*Glanville*
Regalem potestatem non solum armis, set legibus oportet esse armatam, *ut utrumque tempus bello*rum et *pacis* recte gubernetur non solum hostilibus preliis, sed per prudentiam Iuris et legum calumpni autem [sic] iniquitatem expellat.	*Regiam potestatem non solum armis* contra rebelles [et gentes] sibi regnoque insurgentes *oportet esse* decoratam, *sed* et *legibus* ad subditos et populos pacificos regendos decet esse ornatam, *ut utraque temp*ora, *pacis* scilicet et *bell*i, gloriosus rex noster ita feliciter transeat . . . .

In other words, any similarity between the Trinity Cambridge MS and Glanville evaporates after the fifth word (*armis*), and the few other parallels are easily explained by the common source, the proem of the *Institutes*. Hence, a more thorough reading of the Trinity Cambridge MS of Bracton reveals that the writer of the Pseudo-Bractonian prologue did *not* use Glanville for a model and that consequently this preface could *not* have been used by the writer of *Fleta*.

The situation is different with regard to the Middle Temple MS 6 Seat A.E.15, for which Woodbine uses the siglum *LT*. This prologue, it is true, repeats verbatim (apart from a small number of readings) the prologue of Glanville and, more specifically, the *beta* tradition of the Glanville text (cf. Woodbine's edition, p. 17). It does not, however, contain the South Italian additions of the prologue to *Fleta*. We may wonder whether really "the presence of this [Glanville] prologue in some of the Bracton MSS.—it is found in others besides *LT*—offers a simple explanation of the fact that the prologue to Glanvill precedes the text of Fleta," as Woodbine suggests (*De legibus*, I, p. 17, n. 1). To begin with, there are no other Bracton MSS besides *LT* which have the Glanville prologue; there are not even two, since the Trinity Cambridge MS has to be eliminated completely. Hence, *LT* is unique; it is (to our knowledge) a *hapax gegrammenon*, written in the late thirteenth or early fourteenth century. Nothing, of course, is impossible. The author of *Fleta* may have chanced upon the Middle Temple MS, provided that it was written before he wrote. If he saw it, he did not use it. For Fleta follows throughout the *alpha* tradition of Glanville, whereas *LT* represents the *beta* tradition. Moreover, on one occasion the writer of *LT* skipped three words ("tempore pacis ipse [pacis auctor et] amator"), whereas both Glanville (p. 23, the line before the last) and Fleta (p. 2, line 13) have the three words bracketed in the parenthesis. That is to say, Fleta did not copy *LT*, and of another Bracton MS prefaced by the Glanville prologue we have no knowledge. We therefore have to abandon the hypothesis that Fleta borrowed his prologue from a Bracton MS.

What the Middle Temple MS actually proves is a certain popularity of the panegyrical Glanville prologue even at a time when Glanville's work was out of date. The prologue of Glanville was used in the 1240's to preface the Scottish *Regiam Majestatem*; it was used in the 1290's to preface *Fleta*, and probably around 1300 to preface, in *one* case, also Bracton's *De legibus*. It would be legitimate to ask whether perhaps the Glanville prologue survived independently as a piece of panegyric rhetoric. Of this we have no evidence; but Fleta's cento might suggest an answer in the affirmative.

PLATO IN THE MIDDLE AGES

T HERE is the charming story about Goethe's friends in Rome who, on a moonlit night shuttled back and forth for many hours in a ferry-boat on the Tiber because one of the party had proposed to remain upon the water until their customary dispute was settled: Raphael or Michelangelo? There are other pairs of names—Mozart or Beethoven, Alexander or Caesar, Caesar or Brutus, or

> Hoc unum semper quaeris, superetne Maronem
> Tullius, an maior sit Cicerone Maro

—which likewise typify the two possible though different ways of mastering a cosmos by means of respectively equal faculties, and between which individual mind and mankind have shuttled through more than one night. But all these disputes are of recent date compared with the almost 2300 years which have passed away since—according to a legend—Plato, when entering his classroom and missing, that day, Aristotle among his pupils, exclaimed: "The classroom is empty; the Intellect is missing!" Though the contest between Platonic and Aristotelian concepts of the world has never come to a rest, the acme of their great struggle must be sought, undoubtedly, in the Middle Ages, because in this period of spiritualized and abstract thinking every problem of the Universals reflected directly upon life itself. The mediaeval contest between the two Greek masters was concluded officially, it has often been said, by Raphael, by his representation of the two Dioscuri in the School of Athens where Plato, armed with the *Timaeus*, points towards heaven and, at his side, Aristotle, holding the *Ethics* in his left hand, performs with his right a gesture almost of blessing this earth. The dispute was settled by the artist's sage and simple way of realizing that only by putting the two doctrines in gear with one another were heaven and earth kept in motion; it was settled by the simple exchange of the "or" between the two names for an "and."

Efforts to reconcile the two doctrines are as old as is the strife itself. Had Boethius not been executed, the Middle Ages might have started with this very "and" in which they eventually ended. For it had been Boethius' intention to render into Latin the complete works of both Plato and Aristotle in order to prove their "essential concord," and modern

Reprinted, with permission, from *The Philosophical Review*, LI (1942), 312–323. This is a review article of the following two books:

Raymund Klibansky, *The Continuity of the Platonic Tradition during the Middle Ages. Outline of a Corpus Platonicum Medii Aevi* (London, The Warburg Institute, 1939) 58 and 5 plates.

PLATO LATINUS, edidit Raymundus Klibansky, Volumen I: *Meno interprete Henrico Aristippo* edidit Victor Kordeuter, recognovit et prefatione instruxit Carlotta Labowsky (Londinii: In aedibus Instituti Warburgiani, MCMXL), xxi and 92.

scholars have sometimes raised the question whether there would have been a "Middle Ages" proper had not Boethius been prevented from accomplishing his gigantic task. However, he bestowed upon mankind neither the *Plato latinus* nor the *Aristoteles latinus*. The Middle Ages became acquainted with the works of the two masters in an indirect and tortuous way; and, in tracing back this queer path of human intellect, it remained ultimately with our generation to make up, in a very different sense, for what had been withheld from students by Boethius' death: the Latin Plato and Aristotle.

Some ten years ago, the Union Académique Internationale, relying upon the singular experience of the late Father Lacombe, undertook an edition of the *Aristoteles latinus*, that is, of all the Latin translations, ancient and mediaeval, of Aristotelian works and their commentaries. And fortunately the old spirit of rivalry between Peripatos and Academy broke out, once more, and resulted in a plan to produce the indispensable supplement of the Latin Aristotle, a *Plato Latinus* as a part of a *Corpus Platonicum Medii Aevi*. Under the auspices of the British Academy and the Union Académique Internationale, supported also by the Mediaeval Academy of America, the Warburg Institute in London has embarked upon an edition of the Corpus of mediaeval Platonic writings, for which Dr. Raymond Klibansky, Lecturer in Mediaeval Philosophy and Fellow of Oriel College, Oxford, is responsible as general editor. Anybody having a faint knowledge of the work done by the Warburg Institute and of its aims—it proceeded from the private foundation of the late Dr. Aby Warburg, is now affiliated with the University of London, and has been devoted, from its very origin, to investigations of the tradition of the classical heritage during the Middle Ages and its transmission to Modern Times—will admit that no task could agree more perfectly with the abilities of this learned corporation than that of editing a "Mediaeval Plato." On the other hand, the erudition and editorial experience of Dr. Klibansky, an expert Platonist through his studies in Proclus, Master Eckhart, and Nicholas of Cusa, are a pledge for the scholarly standard of this enterprise and, as may be hoped in spite of all the unforeseen obstacles,[1] for its successful and uninterrupted completion.

The main burden of the undertaking is, of course, with the editor and organizer. It is hardly an exaggeration to maintain that almost half the work is done when once a way is seen through the labyrinth of Platonic tradition, the works to be published are selected, and the program is drafted. The difficulty that the organizer has to face is not really the embarrassing amount of material, as in the case of the *Aristoteles latinus*, it is the concealment, or even the occult nature, of mediaeval Platonism. Plato's influence, says Klibansky, "is less apparent in the official teaching of schools and faculties, than in the esoteric doctrine of small circles and single outstanding thinkers. For this reason very shadowy notions are still prevalent concerning the nature and meaning of mediaeval Platonism." Plato's rule over the mediaeval mind was sound; but it was noiseless. Plato

---

[1] Klibansky, in the Preface of his book, lets us visualize the technical difficulties. His book had been printed in Germany; the military preparations during the summer 1939 delayed the issue; the outbreak of the war made it necessary to print the book anew in England. The edition of the *Meno* was printed in Bruges shortly before Belgium was occupied.

was not greeted by any spectacular *entrée joyeuse* with a flourish of trumpets such as greeted Aristotle when he conquered and mesmerized the occidental mind in the thirteenth century; and when Plato finally made his official appearance in the Renaissance he was received, as it were, with the respectful and solemn silence which was essential to the hypostasis of the Logos. Moreover, Plato in the Middle Ages rarely exercised his power in a direct way through his own works. He was effective, in a refracted way, through the works of others, while he himself remained in the background or appeared in disguise. Thus, when in the thirteenth century the foes of Aristotle shouted "Saint Augustine!" and when, in the fourteenth, Petrarch and the early humanists used against Aristotle the battle-cry "Tullius!" it was in fact Plato who was at the bottom of these fights. But the shrewdest disguise of the Divus was his use of his pupil's garb. The *Liber de pomo* which pretended to be Aristotle's last conversation with his friends—King Manfred of Sicily had it translated into Latin from a Hebrew version—was in fact an Arabic paraphrase or imitation of Plato's *Phaedo;* the so-called *Theology of Aristotle*, a Syrian pamphlet turned into Arabic, was an extract from the last three books of Plotinus' *Enneads;* and the *Liber de causis*, that famous transformation of Proclus' *Elements*, whose influence during and after the thirteenth century was almost immeasurable, was likewise received as an Aristotelian work until St. Thomas Aquinas discovered its Neoplatonic origin (Klibansky, 14, 16).

We can see where the great difficulties of drafting the program of the Corpus Platonicum must be sought. It is not enough to keep apart the three main currents of Platonic tradition, the Arabic, the Byzantine, and the Latin, with their tributaries. There are likewise subterranean Platonic streams, *e.g.* in Aristotle's genuine works, which come into view and disappear again and whose very existence, not to mention influence, is not easily ascertained. In this dimness, however, Klibansky's clear, concise, and very complete survey of *The Continuity of the Platonic Tradition*, which precedes and explains the program, is an excellent and very useful guide. It is to be hoped that this unpretentious short sketch providing firsthand information may be read and reread as thoroughly as possible, because its study would prevent teachers and students of Philosophy and of "History from Adam to Adolf" from further retailing, or memorizing, atrocious errors concerning Plato in the Middle Ages.

Klibansky's sketch has some particular aims, too. It fights the two customary modern conceptions of mediaeval Platonic tradition "as either Platonism, as was formerly, or Neoplatonism, as is now, the rule." Klibansky champions instead an unbiassed and more correct conception of mediaeval Platonism "which is neither the doctrine of Plato (*i.e.* Plato's own thought) nor that of Plotinus or Proclus, but, based on Hellenistic thought, nourished by the religious experience, Christian, Jewish, or Islamic, of later centuries, and intimately fused with teachings from Stoic and other philosophies, is, in fine, something new and individual, difficult to bring under a simple heading." Indeed, to seek out the particular mediaeval character of mediaeval Platonism and to set aside any catchword derived from points of view other than mediaeval is the only possible approach to the problem. What Klibansky means might be described, very vaguely, as a

Platonism which may, or may not, be amalgamated with either Neoplatonic or the original Platonic thoughts, but which is always a "religious Platonism" and whose functions, varying with the times and the schools, may be recognized as sometimes supporting the official religions, sometimes reviving them, or sometimes even engulfing theology, as theology had engulfed Platonism in another period. But, as far as the Western world is concerned, its function never would cease to be "Christian" and this, perforce, separates mediaeval and Renaissance Platonism from Plato himself as well as from Plotinus. It is this religious Platonism which survives the Middle Ages and appears, without a break of tradition, as the Platonism of the Renaissance. Klibansky is eager to offer proofs against those advocating that the Renaissance Platonism had nothing to do with the Platonic studies of the Middle Ages, and his case is indeed very strong. The manner in which the mediaeval manuscripts were transmitted, the extensive use made by Renaissance scholars of practically all of the mediaeval Platonic writings, finally the testimony of Marsiglio Ficino himself (published by Klibansky in Appendix II, pp. 42–47), all these arguments make it difficult to insist upon a break between Mediaeval and Renaissance Platonism. After all, Dr. Klibansky's thesis matches perfectly with the more modern method of interpreting historical phenomena strictly from their own conditions without carrying other slogans into history; and it matches likewise with the more modern view taken of the "Problem of the Renaissance" according to which even the so-called "antique" character of this period ever continues to display thoroughly mediaeval and transcendental features in addition to, or in spite of, the new estimation of this present world.

These most important reflections, interesting and fundamental though they are in themselves, are but side issues of a sketch whose main purpose is to comment on the program of the Corpus Platonicum by discussing the continuity of Platonic tradition. It is admirable how safely Klibansky can pilot the raft with his reader on this Alpheus which really originates in "Arabia" and emerges in Sicily. That a *Plato Arabus* is to form an important division of the Corpus is of course foreseen by the editor. Yet he does not aspire to an absolutely complete edition of all the Arabic texts referring to Plato, least of all to publishing those Arabic versions of Platonic dialogues of which a considerable number were translated, early in the ninth century at Baghdad, by Nestorian and Monophysite Christians, Syrian as well as Arab. His intention is to include in Section I of the *Plato Arabus* (1) a description of the Arabic manuscripts devoted to Platonic philosophy and (2) a collection of the scattered quotations from Plato to be found in the works of the Arabic philosophers, scientists, and historians.

The edition of texts begins with the commentaries, paraphrases, and discussions of Plato's works in Arabic. Note must, of course, be made of the difference between the originally Greek commentaries, pre- and post-Neoplatonic, which were translated into Arabic and are often preserved in translation only, and the genuine Arabic discussions and expositions of Plato's works. Of the latter (Section II: "Arabic writings on and paraphrases of Plato's works") it is planned to publish a paraphrase of Plato's *Republic* by Averroes, extant only in Samuel ben Jehuda's Hebrew translation of the lost Arabic text. Averroes, however, represents the very end of the "heroic age" of Arabic philosophy. In the earlier period, in the tenth century, Al-Fārābī was the outstanding scholar and Platonist. Those of his works not available in modern editions are to be published now in the Corpus, *e.g.*, his paraphrase of Plato's *Laws* (as yet unedited) and his book *On the Trend of Plato's and Aristotle's Philosophy* (known from a Hebrew work of the thirteenth century) the original Arabic text of which has been discovered quite recently in Istanbul.

This work of Al-Fārābī (*cf.* Append. I, pp. 39f) promises to be the more interesting as it may produce new knowledge of a certain Greek *Introduction to Platonic Philosophy* which was Al-Fārābī's source. This Hellenistic work itself is lost, but it must have been of a relatively early date as it is mentioned by Cicero (*Acad. post.*, I, 4, 17); and it may be interesting, too, for its tendency to harmonize Platonic and Aristotelian doctrines, a tendency which occasionally became palpable with Neoplatonists, *e.g.*, with Porphyry and the Neoplatonist Simplicius' exposition of Aristotle's *De Caelo* as well as with Boethius and with Al-Fārābī himself. It is a trend which eventually makes the ascriptions of Platonic and Neoplatonic writings to Aristotle somewhat comprehensible.

This Hellenistic *Introduction* calls our attention to the fact that by no means all the Greek commentaries used by Arabic scholars were "Neoplatonic," as is usually assumed. Klibansky rightly stresses this point when discussing the summary of eight Platonic dialogues by Galen, a work which—like Plutarch's lost commentary on the *Timaeus* —belonged to the earlier, pre-Neoplatonic stage of Plato exegesis. Of this summary by Galen it is planned to publish the *Paraphrase of the Timaeus* from an Aya Sofya manuscrpt in Constantinople, along with some fragments of other parts. They are to form a section (III: "Translations of Greek writings on Plato") from which students of classics may profit directly because some Greek texts will be made available, at least in their Arabic versions. Among these there will be found Theon of Smyrna's *About the order in which one ought to read the works of Plato, and about their titles*, one of the writings which endeavored to systematize the works of Plato by arranging them in tetralogies.

While, according to Dr. Klibansky, the commentaries antedating the Neoplatonic period were appreciated above all by Arabic scientists, the clearly Neoplatonic commentators, Porphyry and Proclus, were preferred by the Arabic philosophers. In order to realize the Neoplatonic influence exercised by Arabic scholars on the Western mind, one need only be reminded of Avicenna[2] and his doctrine of the eternal emanation of the world from God and, further, of the *Liber de causis* whose reception in the West coincided with that rising tide of Platonism in the twelfth century which resulted, on the one hand, from Michael Psellus' revival of Platonic philosophy in Byzantium with its ensuing European ramifications, and on the other hand from the new estimation of Pseudo-Dionysius, John the Scot, and Boethius' theological tractates. The *Liber de causis*, by which this movement was furthered, as well as the so-called *Theologia Aristotelis*, of which a new manuscript has been discovered in Leningrad, will represent Section VI of the

---

[2] R. de Vaux, O. P., *Notes et textes sur l'Avicennisme latin aux confins des XIIe–XIIIe siècles* (Paris: J. Vrin, 1934), argues for the existence of a Latin Avicennism corresponding to that of a Latin Averroism.

Arabic Plato ("Arabic Recastings of Neoplatonic Works"). Section IV is reserved to the *Vitae* and the *Dicta Platonis*. The Arabic biographies of Plato draw mostly from the sources of Diogenes Laertius; the sayings of Plato, genuine or attributed to him, are found in Arabic collections such as the *Dogmata philosophorum*, a work very popular in the West after a Spanish translation had been made at the court of Alfonso X in the thirteenth century. Section V will deal with *Plato Pseudoepigraphus*, a legendary but nevertheless most important branch of Platonic tradition, which refers to Plato the Physiognomist as well as to *Plato Alchimista* and *Plato Magus*.

The Oriental Plato would be incomplete if its Whences and its Whithers were neglected. The Whence of Arabic studies in Plato refers to the Syrian literature, the indispensable link between Arabic writers and the Hellenistic, ultimately the Greek, philosophy. The Whither is frequently represented by Hebrew scholars whose translations helped to connect Arabic philosophy with that of the West. Moreover, Jewish philosophy, in itself, was occasionally impregnated by Neoplatonic thought. Ibn Gabirol's *Fons vitae*, translated by John of Spain and Gundissalinus into Latin in the twelfth century, is the outstanding work of this group; but the Neoplatonic undercurrent is conceivable, as Klibansky indicates, even in some of the problems discussed by Maimonides. These subsidiary currents, the Syrian and the Hebrew, cannot be disregarded; and it is therefore part of the project to add an Appendix including a *Plato Hebraeus, i.e.*, a survey of the Hebrew translations of Platonic literature, and a *Plato Syrus* in which the remains of literature about Plato in Syriac, along with the Latin translation, are to be collected.

It is to be regretted that the second main center of Platonic studies, Byzantium, will be put aside for the time being, although the editor consoles us with the assurance that "the documents for the continuous history of Byzantine Platonism, now widely scattered, will be collected some time, it is to be hoped, in the *Plato Byzantinus*." He of course is fully aware of the importance of Byzantine Platonic studies. Theologically the works of Pseudo-Dionysius exercised an almost boundless influence.[3] Philosophically Plato's reviver in Byzantium was Michael Psellus, whose school continued without interruption until Plethon and Bessarion transferred the Byzantine Platonism to Florence; here it was absorbed by the Academy of Marsiglio Ficino and fused with other mediaeval Platonic currents. Most interesting are Byzantium's Eastern radiations. We have some knowledge about her indirect influence in Persia, where shortly before 500 Nestorian refugees from the University of Edessa established a "Hippocratean Academy" and where, after the closure of the Platonic Academy in 529, the Athenian Academicians found an asylum at the court of Chosroes I, for whom a scholar named Ouranios is said to have made a translation of the Platonic dialogues into Persian. The traces of this activity are certainly much too dim to permit a special section in the form of a *Plato Persicus*, although it might be worth while to gather the few items known. These considerations do not hold good as far as Armenia is concerned. Klibansky himself, by pointing out that the impulses

---

[3] Klibansky, 25, proffers a striking textual agreement of Pseudo-Dionysius with a passage in Plato's *Parmenides*.

created by Psellus led to the Armenian translation of Plato's dialogues by Gregorius Magister, indicates this Byzantine sphere of influence. But the Armenian activity, together with the Neoplatonic movement in Georgia, is all the more interesting if we take into account the Armenian studies of the sixth century focussing on Philo but dealing also with Plato.[4] Thus an appendix similar to that of the Hebrew and Syriac Plato and treating the *Plato Armeniacus* would be most desirable; together with the notes on the Persian Plato it would broaden our views of those remote Platonic centers through which Greek learning eventually passed into Inner Asia.[5]

What interests us most is, however, the influence on the West, and this leads us to the *Plato Latinus* which is to represent the *pièce de résistance* of the project. The Platonic tradition in the West was undoubtedly under the sway of an unlucky star. Latin versions of Plato were rare at all times. Cicero's translation of the *Protagoras* and Apuleius' of the *Phaedo* did not survive; and Boethius never carried out his plan. Thus the Middle Ages received of Platonic texts nothing but parts of a Latin *Timaeus* by Cicero, Chalcidius' version of this dialogue, and fragments of the great myth at the end of the *Republic* through Macrobius' comments on the *Somnium Scipionis*. Taken altogether, the Middle Ages knew of Plato's works as much as we know of the pre-Socratic philosophers, but were lacking their "Diels." To publish, as it were, the Diels of mediaeval Platonism, that is to comb through the ancient Latin authors known to the Middle Ages for Platonica, and likewise through the writings of the Latin Fathers, is the first task of the *Plato Latinus* (Section I: "The ancient and mediaeval Latin translations of Plato's writings"). It is needless to stress all the problems which would be greatly clarified if we had an exact survey of all the Platonic materials which mediaeval scholars could have possibly borrowed from Cicero (*e.g.*, passages from the *Phaedo*, the *Phaedrus*, the *Laws*), from Priscian (fragments of Apuleius' version of the *Phaedo*), from Claudianus Mamertus' *De statu animae*, from Boethius, from the Grammarians, furthermore from St. Augustine, from the Greek Fathers in Latin translation, and even from Aristotle's works in Latin. There will be much of laborious "gold-panning," often with an output of a few cents only, but it is one of the most essential divisions, especially for the earlier Middle Ages. Later on, in the twelfth century, it is true, the first mediaeval versions of Plato were made in Sicily, where a court official of the Norman William I, Henricus Aristippus, translated the *Meno* and the *Phaedo* from Greek into Latin. The Greek, or Byzantine, intellectual life of Southern Italy in the eleventh and twelfth centuries will need several careful investigations before we can judge why a man such as Henricus Aristippus became interested in Platonic

---

[4] In addition to the studies of F. C. Conybeare, many of them in the *American Journal of Philology*, XII–XVI (1891–95), see Hans Lewy, *The Pseudo-Philonic 'De Jona', the Armenian Text with a critical Introduction* (London, 1936), who mentions, 13f, an Armenian sixth-century translation of the *Book of Ideas;* as Klibansky, 41, refers to "an unknown Arabic treatise *On the Platonic Ideas*, found in Constantinople, MS Aya Sofya 2457, and in Cairo," it would certainly be important to examine along with the Arabic also the Armenian version, although the similarity of the title does not necessarily involve a tallying of the

texts. On Gregorius Magister see the recent study of M. Leroy, "Grégoire Magistros et les traductions arméniennes d'auteurs grecs," *Annuaire de l'institut de philologie et d'histoire orientales*, III (1935), 263–294.

[5] There is very little known about Plato in Central Asia; on W. L. Lorimer's article "Plato in Afghanistan and India," *American Journal of Philology*, LIII (1932), 160ff, see Klibansky, 41; A. Weber in *Sitzungsberichte der Preussischen Akademie der Wissenschaften* (Berlin, 1890), 901ff, is quite superficial; see also *Journal of the Asiatic Society of Bengal*, XXX (1861), 151ff.

studies and eventually, through the Norman channels, passed on his knowledge to England, to Oxford. In the thirteenth century conditions were much more favorable; but then the philosophical studies focussed on Aristotle's works rather than on Plato's. Nevertheless, William of Moerbeke translated Proclus' commentary on the *Timaeus* and, above all, that on the *Parmenides*, in which, as Klibansky found out many years ago,[6] a great part of the original dialogue was embedded. In the humanist age, the activity of Plato-translators, such as Chrysoloras and Leonardo Bruni, made other dialogues available, and a complete survey of the Latin versions preceding Ficino's final standard translation of Plato will be added to the first part of the *Plato Latinus*.

For our knowledge of mediaeval thought the commentaries on Plato are as important as the texts. Greek commentaries in Latin translation, unless they reached the West fragmentarily through Arabic writers, were available not earlier than the thirteenth century, the time of William of Moerbeke. His translations of the Proclus commentaries, furthermore a fifteenth-century version of the *Theologia Platonis* along with Simplicius' exposition of the *De caelo* (a Neoplatonic commentary on Aristotle translated in the thirteenth century) and Nicholas of Cusa's Marginalia to his manuscripts of Plato and Proclus: all this material is to form Section III ("The mediaeval Latin translations of the Greek commentaries on Plato").

Section II, "The ancient and mediaeval Latin commentaries of Plato's writings," promises to reveal real *terra incognita*. Not one item in this group has been hitherto published, with the exception, of course, of Chalcidius' commentary on the *Timaeus*, known and widely read throughout the Middle Ages. This dialogue, therefore, found the greatest number of mediaeval commentators, most famous of all William of Conches. The complete text of his commentary has been recently discovered and will now be published with its different redactions, along with the anonymous commentary found in an Oxford Corpus Christi manuscript and with *Timaeus*-glosses preserved in manuscripts at Florence, Leyden, London, Paris, and other places. Moreover, the glosses on Chalcidius in several manuscripts (Durham, Munich, Orléans, Vienna) together with those of Petrarch are to be edited. There follow the commentaries on Macrobius and on the latter's commentary on the *Somnium Scipionis*, such as the Glosses of Avranches and those in Cologne and Munich, furthermore a newly discovered commentary on Macrobius by William of Conches. Finally there is the *Phaedo*, which became known very late and became popular very slowly; nevertheless we shall find an *Examinatorium in Phaedonem Platonis* by John Dogget, chaplain to Richard III, later Provost of King's College, Cambridge. At any rate, we may expect to find many surprises in this section.

As in the Arabic Plato, two sections of the *Plato Latinus* (Sections IV and V) are devoted to the *Vita et dicta Platonis* and to *Plato pseudoepigraphus*. Also there is projected a collection of quotations from and references to Plotinus in Latin authors (Section VI). And finally there is yet another chapter (Section VII) which may rouse the curiosity either of the

---

[6] R. Klibansky, "Ein Proklusfund und seine Bedeutung," *Sitzungsberichte der Heidelberger Akademie*, 1928/29, Abh. 5, discovered that this commentary preserved the end of Plato's *Parmenides*, which is lost in the Greek manuscripts.

philosopher or the historian or the classical scholar: that is, the *Iconographia Platonis*. The collection of Plato's images is as important as that of texts, and the editor himself has made a start by adding to his sketch five plates representing Plato the prophet of Christ, the physician, the philosopher. But of course, Plato's influence on the arts cannot be exhausted by an iconography. Not where Aristotle but where Plato rules does art begin to develop all its abilities. It is significant that the brilliant discussion of artistic theories in the Middle Ages by E. Panofsky, likewise a publication of the Warburg Institute, bears the title "*Idea*." It is significant, too, that the most important justification of ecclesiastical imagery in the iconoclast struggles was set forth by the Neoplatonist Theodore of Studios.[7] The aesthetic influence of Plato is immense, perhaps as a result of his likewise aesthetic conception of God as beautiful. From Boethius' verse ". . . pulchrum pulcherrimus ipse / Mundum mente gerens similique in imagine formans. . ." and from Pseudo-Dionysius' praise of the divine beauty there is one straight line leading to Ficino's words in his commentary on the *Phaedrus:* "Deum tandem amamus ut pulchrum quem iam pridem dileximus ut bonum." Plato as an instigator of artistic theories and an inspirer of artists is certainly not one of the least important of his radiations.

So much about the program. What the volumes of the *Corpus Platonicum* will be like may be gathered from the edition of Plato's *Meno* in the translation of Henricus Aristippus, published as the first volume of the *Plato Latinus*. The editorial work is shared by Mr. Victor Kordeuter and Miss Charlotte Labowsky, while five authorities—W. D. Ross, R. A. Nicholson, F. M. Powicke, C. W. Previté-Orton, and F. Saxl—have acted as a board of advisers. The get-up of the book—it was printed in Bruges—is simple and appropriate. Preface and commentaries are written in Latin. Very careful indices, Greek-Latin as well as Latin-Greek, make the text valuable for research. The Stephanus pagination is noted in the margin. Of the life and the works of Henricus Aristippus, a Greek courtier of William I of Sicily and ambassador at Byzantium for a short time, Haskins has carefully collected all the information available; the editors of the *Meno* were right to follow, in their preface, his thorough studies and to disregard what "plurimis verbis, levissimis rationibus" has been suggested by others. The edition is based on five manuscripts, each of which has its interesting history. As far as can be judged from the variants, the editors were right to use as the basic text the Oxford Corpus Christi MS 243, written at Utrecht, which John Whethamstede, Abbot of St. Albans, gave to Duke Humphrey of Gloucester. None of the texts are really good, though they are not as bad as the often queer language of the translations suggests. Aristippus' Latin, as far as his own style is concerned—it is known from the prologues to his translations—, proves to be that of a scholar who acquired his *dictamen* according to the rules of early twelfth-century teachers in Italy: an inclination towards rimed prose, no *cursus*, but as yet without the "punnings," the alliterations and the exaggerations of the French style at the end of that

---

[7] *Cf.* Erwin Panofsky, '*Idea*', *ein Beitrag zur Begriffsgeschichte der älteren Kunsttheorie* (Studien der Bibliothek Warburg, V; Leipzig, 1924); G. B. Ladner, "Origin and Significance of the Byzantine Iconoclast Controversy," *Mediaeval Studies*, II (1940), 142ff, and his fuller account of the doctrine of the Neoplatonic iconophiles in *Zeitschrift für Kirchengeschichte*, L (1931), 1ff.

century. Of this training very little is apparent in the translation. For Aristippus translates literally, including every Greek particle, and preserves the Greek word-order. The result is often only a sequence of Latin words which make almost no sense or are comprehensible only when read with the Greek text. "Deinceps nequaquam visus est tibi nosse?" has the simple meaning of οὐκ ἐδόκει σοι εἰδέναι; ("Then you did not consider that he knew?"). As for the particles, it is sometimes almost like translating the French "tiens, tiens" into English "hold, hold," not to mention real blunders (the imperative πειρῶ = try, is constantly translated "experior"). Fortunately the Greek apparatus with which the editors have equipped the text helps the reader along. The Latin text, by the way, does not agree exactly with any Greek codex known today, although most of the readings can be traced to one Greek manuscript or another. The translation is certainly obscure; it is but a dim reflexion of the Platonic charm. Nevertheless its influence was not insignificant, as Aristippus' versions were known to Roger Bacon, were used at the Sorbonne, in Oxford and Padua, and were studied carefully by Petrarch and Salutati as well as by Nicholas of Cusa.

To the modern scholar this twelfth-century version is mainly of historical interest as an important item of mediaeval Platonism. But it is obvious that the true value of the single volume can be judged only within the framework of the projected general edition of mediaeval Platonic writings. It is to be hoped that peaceful times may permit the swift completion of the comprehensive program which the editor of the *Corpus Platonicum Medii Aevi* has outlined.

AN "AUTOBIOGRAPHY" OF GUIDO FABA

Among prominent Bolognese masters of rhetoric and *dictamen* in the thirteenth century, Guido Faba enjoys a special reputation. His glory, though modest, is twofold. He is considered the most influential master of the *stilus supremus* which exercised its peculiar spell on the writings of almost every European chancery of that age; and he has a little national shrine in Italy because, owing to his works in the vernacular, he figures as the initiator of an Italian rhetoric, one who, "primus ad Italos," transferred the rules of Latin *dictamen* to Italian prose.[1] Guido Faba was not a man of genius. However, he may be regarded as the truest exponent of Bolognese school-tradition as it had gradually developed during the course of the preceding century, a master who, in his turn, conveniently transmitted this tradition through his treatises and his way of teaching.[2] The stupendous number of manuscripts in which his works have survived permits us to guess at his influence and relative importance. But a survey of the Faba manuscripts which are scattered through every European library is unfortunately still lacking. They have never

Reprinted, with permission, from *Mediaeval and Renaissance Studies*, I (1943), 253–280.

[1] This has been stressed frequently, ever since Guido Faba's *Parlamenti ed Epistole* were published by A. Gaudenzi, *I suoni, le forme e le parole dell'odierno dialetto della città di Bologna* (Turin, 1889), 127ff; concerning the problem of Guido's authorship cf. *infra*, note 17. Of the second work of Guido containing vernacular models, the *Gemma purpurea*, fragments have been published by Rockinger, "Briefsteller und Formelbuecher des elften bis vierzehnten Jahrhunderts," *Quellen und Eroerterungen zur bayerischen und deutschen Geschichte*, IX (1863), 185ff., under the title of *Doctrina ad inveniendas ... materias;* more elaborate is the edition and the discussion by E. Monaci, "Su la Gemma purpurea e altri scritti minori volgari di Guido Faba o Fava," *Rendiconti della R. Accad. dei Lincei*, IV (1888), 399ff; the same author's *La Gemma purpurea del maestro Guido Fava ricostituita nel testo volgare* (Rome: Nozze Spezi-Salvadore, 1901), has not been available to me. Faba's influence on Dante's prose is mentioned frequently though vaguely; see, e.g., Giulio Bertoni, "La prosa della Vita nuova di Dante," in his *Poeti e poesie del medio evo e del rinascimento* (Modena, 1922), 159ff; but the subject has been treated carefully by A. Schiaffini, "La tecnica della Prosa rimata nel medio-evo latino, in Guido Faba, Guittone e Dante," *Studi romanzi*, XXI (1931), 7–115. On the Latin text of the *Gemma purpurea* see also Gaudenzi, "Sulla cronologia delle opere dei dettatori bolognesi da Buoncompagno a Bene di Lucca," *Bullettino dell' Istituto Storico Italiano*, XIV (1895), 127ff (quoted here as Gaudenzi, *Cronologia*).

[2] This at least was Master Guido's own opinion; in his *Summa dictaminis* he says: "Magister Guido ubique diligitur, quia sua dictamina comprobantur." Cf. Schiaffini, 37. But it is impossible to tell, at the present stage of investigations, what in Guido Faba's writings is his own invention and what must be considered Bolognese school tradition. Emmy Heller, "Die Ars dictandi des Thomas von Capua," *SB. Heid. Ak.*, 1928/29, Abh. 4 (Heidelberg, 1929), 52f, notes 21, 22 (see also the footnotes to her edition of the "Ars dictandi"), considers the great number of parallels between Guido Faba and Thomas of Capua as a result of a similar training, i.e. of the school tradition. Agreements with Buoncompagno (*infra*, note 20), with Master Bene (*infra*, note 26), and with other *dictatores* can be easily collected. Conformities with Petrus de Vinea are likewise abundant; they may go back to note-books taken down in courses of lectures at Bologna. On the other hand, there is evidence for Guido Faba's direct influence on the Capuan school of epistolary style; see, e.g., Gerhart Ladner, "Formularbehelfe in der Kanzlei Kaiser Friedrichs II. und die 'Briefe des Petrus de Vinea'," *Mitteilungen des Oesterr. Instituts für Geschichtsforschung*, Erg. Bd. XII (1932), 168ff; the conformity of a Faba *exordium* with Frederick's letter to Bologna (*Regesta Imperii*, V, 3777), mentioned by Ladner, p. 175, n. 3, perhaps indicates Faba's influence on Peter of Prezza, a pupil of the Capuan school. However, we are groping in the dark without adequate editions of Faba's works and of the letter collections of the 13th century.

been examined systematically, and are uncollected and unsifted, so that we are still in need of the most primitive foundations for an appraisal of this once famous teacher of style. It would therefore, at present, be difficult to substantiate the conventional opinion about the effectiveness of his teaching, or to measure his influence on the style of letter-writing of the generations that followed him; and even the many parallels and reminiscences, to be found in later writings, of phrases and idiomatic sayings transmitted by Guido Faba are puzzling to the student rather than enlightening.

Our knowledge of his life is likewise fragmentary and by no means detailed. This might be due simply to the nature of things. The careers of the masters of *dictamen* are wrapped in obscurity unless these rhetors achieved a distinguished position in the political world. Thomas of Capua, for instance, is fairly well known because, as papal notary under Innocent III, thereafter Cardinal Deacon, finally Cardinal Priest of Santa Sabina and an eminent diplomat of the Holy See, he stands out clearly against the background of the Papal Court whose most gifted *dictator* he was.[3] There is also the life of Petrus de Vinea, which receives light from the *magna curia* of Frederick II, from the writer's own tragic fate, and from the sombre glow of Dante's hell.[4] And other stylists, too, such as Berard of Naples or Marinus of Eboli, are quite well known because they left their traces as *S.R.E. vice-cancellarii*.[5] This floodlight of the courts, papal or imperial, is rarely turned upon the schoolmasters of Bologna. Master Buoncompagno is perhaps the only one whose life is relatively easily traceable. It is not merely that he himself, in his works, makes the full light play continuously on the facets of his scurrilous and eccentric personality, but also that he has been studied more intensively than most of the other *dictatores*.[6] And if our knowledge of Guido Faba's life and career is as yet scanty, the main reason for this deficiency must be sought not in the lack of source-material but in the badly neglected study of his works, many of which are still unpublished. Half a century ago, Gaudenzi, the editor of several important works of this author,[7] laboriously, and

---

[3] See the studies minutely worked out of Emmy Heller, *supra*, note 2, and "Der kuriale Geschäftsgang in den Briefen des Thomas von Capua," *Archiv für Urkundenforschung*, XIII (1935), 198–318, where 126 of about 690 letters of Thomas' *Summa dictaminis* are published. The antiquated edition of this work by S. F. Hahn, *Collectio monumentorum* (1724), I, 279ff, will some day, it may be hoped, be replaced by Mrs. E. Heller's edition, in spite of all obstacles.

[4] See the most recent study on this subject by Leonardo Olschki, "Dante and Peter de Vinea," *The Romanic Review*, XXXI (1940), 105ff; cf. *infra*, note 34, on the problem of "envy" in the writings of the Bolognese students.

[5] Kaltenbrunner, "Roemische Studien III: Berard von Neapel," *Mitteil. d. Oesterr. Instituts für Geschichtsforschung*, VII (1886), 21ff; see also L. Delisle in *Notices et Extraits des manuscrits de la Bibl. Nationale*, XXVII: ii (1879), 87–168. For Marinus see Fritz Schillmann, *Die Formularsammlung des Marinus von Eboli*, I (Bibl. d. Preussischen Histor. Instituts in Rome, vol. XVI; Rome, 1929), and C. Erdmann, "Zur Entstehung der Formelsammlung des Marinus von Eboli," *QFiAB*, XXI (1929/30), 176ff.

[6] In addition to the well-known book of Carl Sutter, *Aus Leben und Werken des Magisters Buoncompagno* (1894), where editions and literature are listed on p. 24, see Gaudenzi, *Cronologia*, 88ff, and his edition of the *Rhetorica novissima* (*Bibliotheca Juridica Medii Aevi*, vol. II [1901]), as well as F. Baethgen, "Rota Veneris," *Deutsche Vierteljahrsschrift für Literaturwissenschaft und Geistesgeschichte*, V (1927), 37–64, and his edition of the *Rota Veneris* (*Texte zur Kulturgeschichte des Mittelalters*, ed. Fedor Schneider, Heft 2 [Rome, 1927]).

[7] The *Summa dictaminis*, the *Dictamina rhetorica*, and the *Epistolae* were published by Gaudenzi in *Il Propugnatore*, n. s.. III: i–ii (1890); V: i–ii (1892); VI: i–ii (1893); the *Exordia* have been published for the greater part by Oswald Redlich, *Eine Wiener Briefsammlung zur Geschichte des deutschen Reiches und der österreichischen Länder in der zweiten Hälfte des XIII. Jahrhunderts* (Vienna, 1894), 317ff, though not all of the *exordia* are to be ascribed to Guido Faba; nor does the order match exactly Faba's *Exordia inter amicos et socios;* e.g., the first model ("Ordo rationis expostulat") is found as no. 59 in Redlich's collection. Cf. also Rockinger, *op. cit.*, 185ff.

13*

often controversially, collected some of Guido Faba's biographical dates;[8] to the information offered by him have clung the few students who have occupied themselves, usually by incidence or only in passing, with Guido Faba's personality, though Gaudenzi himself indeed furnished his discussion with more than one question mark.[9]

The dates so far gathered can be summed up briefly. Guido Faba must have been born before 1190 because a document which he signs as witness in 1210 introduces him as *magister* in Bologna. By that time, he must have concluded his studies and, although gifted students then graduated at a comparatively early age, we may assume that he was at least of age in 1210. Thus his studies were completed during the first decade of the thirteenth century, at the time when Thomas of Capua was applying himself to his studies at Vicenza, a daughter university of Bologna, and when Buoncompagno, apparently Faba's rival in later years, was already teaching rhetoric, grammar, and *dictamen* at Bologna. It has been questioned whether or not Guido Faba was Bolognese by birth. One of his works carries a dedication "in the honour, glory, and praise . . . of *dominus* Aliprand Faba, podestà of Bologna, whose . . . fame, adorned by martial glories, illuminates the whole clan (*totam illuminat parentelam*)."[10] This dedication, it is true, seems to suggest a blood relationship between Guido Faba and the Bolognese podestà Aliprand Faba, the latter a native of Brescia. Hence Guido Faba would have been likewise a Lombard, not a native of *Bologna la grassa*, and the designation "Bononiensis," added sometimes to his name, would indicate not his true home but merely his home by choice, where he is known to have lived in 1210 and subsequently.[11] Some ten years later, in 1219/20, a notary Guido Faba is mentioned several times in Bolognese documents.[12] Yet scholars have refrained from identifying him with the master of *dictamen*, partly because Guido, in his later years, appears to have been a chaplain and partly because in Bologna, according to the statute of 1250, clerics were not permitted to take charge of a

[8] Gaudenzi, *Cronologia*, 118ff.

[9] Gaudenzi's editions are notoriously careless and his collections of biographical notes may be contestable in many points, but his discussion is not as bad as his colleagues tried to make out; their knowledge of Guido Faba was no more sound; least of all that of F. Torraca, "Per la storia letteraria del secolo XIII," *Rassegna critica della letteratura italiana*, X (1905), 102ff, whose "corrections," almost from first to last, prove to be even more incorrect than the suppositions of the reprimanded Gaudenzi.

[10] Gaudenzi, *Cronologia*, 119f. The dedication is published in part by Rockinger, *op. cit.*, 179f; the reading "fidelissimus clericus et devotus" is found in many manuscripts so that Torraca's emendation "fidelissimus amicus," though suggestive, is unconvincing and certainly wrong; his conclusions concerning Guido's chaplaincy are likewise wrong, cf. *infra*, note 46. Aliprand Faba was podestà at Bologna in 1229; his greatest glory was a victory over the people of Modena, Parma, Rimini, and Pavia near San Cesario (1229, Sept. 4); cf. Muratori, *Scriptores*, XVIII, 110, 256. Giuseppe Manacorda, *Storia della scuola in Italia* (Milano, 1914), I: i, 264, styles Guido Faba a Brescian; but not all Fabas were from Brescia, as may be concluded from the fact that an

Everardus Faba was podestà of Brescia in 1215 (cf. *Regesta Imperii*, V, 12618).

[11] It is true, in the legal instrument quoted by Gaudenzi, *Cronologia*, 119, Guido is styled merely "magister Faba"; following this Torraca, *op. cit.*, 102, rejects the identity of this "magister Faba" with Guido Faba because "Faba," according to Torraca, can also be a Christian name. Torraca's arguments are flimsy in this spiteful controversy. His evidence is contestable, and besides "Faba" was not Guido's family name but a nickname which he acquired in his early youth; cf. *infra*, note 33. Guido's mastership in 1210 fits into his curriculum very smoothly.

[12] *Chartularium Studii Bononiensis*, I (Bologna, 1909), 27, no. xxx; 29, no. xxxi; 47, no. li; *Statuti delle società del popolo di Bologna*, ed. A. Gaudenzi in *Fonti per la storia d'Italia* (Rome, 1896), II, 441, where a "Guido Faba filius Nicolai" is mentioned in the roll of Bolognese notaries in 1219. Gaudenzi, *Cronologia*, 120, takes the possibility of two Guido Fabas, a master and a notary, into consideration; Torraca, 103, takes it for granted that there were at least two namesakes and in addition to these still a master Faba and another Guido; cf. however, G. Zaccagnini "Per la storia letteraria del Duecento," *Il libro e la stampa*, VI (1920), 120.

professional notariate of the city.[13] It has likewise been doubted whether a certain "Guido scriba domini episcopi," mentioned in a Bolognese legal instrument of 1221, is to be considered the same as Master Guido Faba, the stylist.[14] Furthermore, Guido's training as a lawyer has been doubted by Gaudenzi, who nevertheless admits that the master of *dictamen* may have acquired a modest knowledge of canon law because there are some formularies extant showing Guido in the position of a papal *judex delegatus*.[15] This commission does not necessarily involve any close relationship between Guido and Rome, although he mentions incidentally that he had been at the *Curia Romana* and that he had there learned to use correctly the *salutationes* of the different ranks of cardinals.[16] His teaching at Bologna is said to have comprised the fifteen years between 1225 and 1240. Then some chance—we know not what—seems to have carried him to Siena. It is true that the Ghibelline party, about 1240, made efforts to call into life a Tuscan *studium* at Siena; but it seems unlikely that Guido had anything to do with this new foundation. Guido Faba died about 1245, perhaps in Siena. But it must be emphasized that our knowledge of his Sienese period is based merely on conjectures and that, when all is said, the later years of Guido Faba remain as obscure as his earlier years.[17]

A picture of Guido's years of apprenticeship, in many respects more accurate and more reliable than the one outlined, can be gathered from a work of his, the *Rota nova*. Saving the title and a short analysis of the manuscript offered by N. Denholm-Young,[18] this treatise has been hitherto unknown. It is preserved, apparently, in but one thirteenth-century manuscript, Oxford, New College MS. 255, which may have come to England before 1330. The *Rota nova* opens, in this manuscript, a series of Guido Faba's writings of which, in fact, only the *Dictamina rethorica* (fol. 23–40)[19] has been published from other manuscripts. Of the remaining treatises many contain well-known models of letters,

[13] Gaudenzi, *Cronologia*, 120 with n. 3.

[14] *Ibid.*, 151, n. 2.

[15] They are published by Rockinger, *op. cit.*, 182ff, and may be only exercises or models which refer to the time of Gregory IX; see also *infra*, n. 62.

[16] *Summa dictaminis*, no. LIV, ed. Gaudenzi in *Il Propugnatore*, n. s. III: i (1890), 322: "Una tamen ecclesia est Rome, que habet titulum 'Ecclesiam baptismalem', ut in curia intellexi." Cf. E. Heller, *Die Ars dictandi des Thomas von Capua*, p. 49, n. 10, and p. 27.

[17] Gaudenzi, *Cronologia*, 150, admits that his suggestions might appear like "fantasticherie." His interpretation is based upon the fact that in the *Parlamenti ed Epistole* (cf. *supra*, note 1) a great number of allusions to Siena are found. Torraca, *op. cit.*, 104f, therefore declines to believe in Guido Faba's authorship of this work and suggests that a Master Guido of Siena, of whom we know nothing but the name, was the author. In his *Manuale della letteratura italiana* (Florence, 1926), I: i, 73f, he seems to have corrected his opinion and attributes the work to Guido Faba. The latter's authorship should not be doubted; the little work is found in a Vatican manuscript along with Guido Faba's authentic writings. Moreover, there are many agreements between this work and Guido's *Littere stili secularis*, found in the Oxford, New College MS. 255, fol. 6ᵛ, 8ʳ–15ᵛ, which are followed by

the *Littere prosaici dictaminis stili ecclesiastici* on fol. 16ʳ. Also, the exchange of letters between *Carnisprivium* and *Quadragesima*, which is found on fol. 49ʳ⁻ᵛ, reappears in the *Gemma purpurea* (cf. Monaci in *Rendiconti dei Lincei*, IV [1888], 404) as well as in the *Parlamenti*, ed. Gaudenzi (cf. *supra*, note 1), 157f. Torraca overestimates the significance of Guido's various denominations and is inclined to split "magister Guido," "magister Guido Bononiensis," "Guido Faba sancti Michaelis cappellanus," and "Guido Faba notarius" into four different persons. This method is unjustifiable; the differing forms of the name are often found in one and the same work and the discussion following here will make it clear that the various titles all refer to the same person. For the *Studium* at Siena cf. H. Rashdall, *The Universities of Europe* (2nd ed., Oxford, 1936), II, 31f: "a kind of School occurs in 1240." The *Studium* opened in 1246; thus it is not quite impossible that Guido had, after all, something to do with this new school.

[18] The MS. is described by H. O. Coxe, *Catalogus Codicum Manuscriptorum in Collegiis Aulisque Oxoniensibus* (Oxford, 1852), I, 91; the writings of Guido Faba have been analysed by N. Denholm-Young, "The Cursus in England" in *Oxford Essays in Mediaeval History presented to H. E. Salter* (Oxford, 1934), 94f.

[19] Gaudenzi, in *Il Propugnatore*, n. s. V: i, 86ff; V: ii, 58ff.

though in a framework which differs considerably from the redactions found in other manuscripts. There is no doubt that the treatises in the New College manuscript represent Guido Faba's lectures at Bologna in which he offers to his pupils his customary material but changes the arrangement and general presentation as any lecturer, then or now, would do when repeating a course. This practice holds good also for the *Rota nova*. The doctrinal part of this treatise is found on fol. 1r–6v; the prologue has been placed by mistake on fol. 7r–v, so that this leaf interrupts a second work, the *Littere stili secularis*,[20] which begins on fol. 6v and is continued on fol. 8r. The doctrinal part and the models of the *Rota nova*, but not the prologue, agree almost to the letter with Guido's *Summa dictaminis*.[21] In conformity with the latter, the *Rota nova* contains two sections, one dealing with mistakes and their avoidance ("De vitiis evitandis"), the other with the rules of *dictamen* ("De regulis"). The main difference between the *Summa* and the *Rota* lies in their presentation. The *Summa* is an ordinary schoolbook with a proem whose phrasing is clearly influenced by Azo and Buoncompagno,[22] whereas the *Rota* is garbed in a more mystic mantle, for, in the latter, the two sections on mistakes and on rules are styled *Ala prima* and *Ala secunda*, in reference to the two wings of the Archangel Michael. This somewhat cryptic relationship is elucidated by a miniature (fol. 1r, at the beginning of the *Ala prima*), and it is explained in the prologue to which the present article is to be devoted.

Not only is this prologue stuffed with rebus-like allusions; the breath of an allegorical mysticism is felt in every sentence of this piece of elaborate prose which reveals itself as a manifesto dictated by the celestial powers and which, in its first sentence, strikes the chord of the *Rhetorica mystica* with full force:

[20] The short prologue (fol. 6v) being as yet unprinted may be published here:

> Incipiunt littere stili secularis facte comparativum, positivum et superlativum, id est quod de qualibet materia sunt tres epistole diverse.
>
> Viris providis et discretis multa laude et honore dignis, strenuis sociis et amicis specialibus, universis scolaribus et honorabilibus viris notariis Bononie commorantibus floribus eloquentie purpuratis presbyter Guido ecclesie sancti Michaelis fori medii cappellanus, solo nomine dictus magister, salutem et aurire aquas de fontibus scientie salutaris. Quamvis multa supersint negotia et fatigationes tante precesserint, que me reddere possint a vestris petitionibus excusatum, sociali tamen dilectione convictus, cui posse totum non presumerem denegare, illud diligenter attendens quod omne bonum in commune deductum clarius elucescit, stilum rethorice dulcedinis in utraque curia presentialiter assuetum communicare nuntio liberaliter universis.

The phrase "solo nomine magister" is, of course, nothing but a formula of devotion or humility; it is used by Albert of Samaria, cf. Krabbo in *Neues Archiv*, XXXII (1906), 73 ("B. Tusculanus solo nomine dictus episcopus"), 78 ("B. solo nomine Reginus antistes"), as well as by Henricus Francigena, cf. Odebrecht in *Archiv für Urkundenforschung*, XIV (1936), 247 ("solo nomine magister R."), and by Buoncompagno in the prologue of his *Liber decem tabularum*, cf. L. Delisle in *Annuaire-Bulletin de la société de l'histoire de France*, VII (1869), 152. Thus the suggestion of Pio Rajna "Per il Cursus medievale e per Dante," *Studi di filologia italiana*, III (1932), 31, n. 2, that this phrase was a satirical and later addition or that it indicated the author's being no longer alive, cannot be accepted.

[21] Cf. Denholm-Young, *op. cit.*, 94; the *Summa dictaminis* is published by Gaudenzi, cf. *supra*, n. 7.

[22] The *Incipit* is "Quasi modo geniti infantes lac concupiscentie rationabile sine dolo cum exultatione suscipite." This reference to 1 Peter 2, 2, which is the *Introitus* of the mass on the Sunday after Easter, is likewise the *Incipit* of Azo's *Summa Institutionum* (Lyons, 1540, f. 168v): "Quasimodo geniti pueri vel adulti lac iuris concupiscite." Owing to an indiscretion of Buoncompagno it is known that he himself was the 'dictator' of the prologue at least of Azo's *Summa Codicis* ("Cum post inventionem"); see *Rhetorica novissima*, X, 1, ed. Gaudenzi, p. 292: "Pro certo ego ipse in prologo summe Azonis dixi..."; cf. Hermann Kantorowicz, *Studies in the Glossators of the Roman Law* (Cambridge, 1938), 227. However, the *dictamen* of Azo's *Summa Institutionum* shows also some remarkable agreements with Buoncompagno's *Rhetorica novissima*, IX, 5, ed. Gaudenzi (cf. *supra*, n. 6), p. 289, so that Guido Faba's borrowing from Azo might as well imply his borrowing from Buoncompagno. Moreover, the flowery style of Guido's *Summa dictaminis* with its luxuriance of lilies, roses, violets, "cynnamomum et balsamum" is much more reminiscent of Buoncompagno's style than the other writings of Guido.

Let the heavens rejoice and let the earth be glad; let the sea roar, and the fulness thereof; glory be to all creatures that are created in the state of reason because the divine magnificence discloses itself by ordering the Christian people to celebrate and commemorate in homage this very day on which this holy letter has been written.

This *arsis* is, rhetorically, not without moment. The garb discloses the effort to raise the subject to almost giddy heights and to link it with the universe so that each sentence inevitably receives a mounting emphasis from the general tenor. The author styles his *pronunciamento* a *littera sacra* which is received and hailed by the cosmos, by Heaven, Earth, and Sea, and the Christian People are supposed to hold their breath while listening to the good news addressed to every rational creature. A miniature displaying sun, moon, and stars in the blue circle of a firmament surrounded by two white rings puts the cosmic character of the "holy letter" very clearly before the reader. That letters and manifestoes of Emperors, and occasionally of Popes, should be styled *litterae sacrae*, had become customary during the twelfth century as a result of the revival of Roman Law and Roman legal language. Guido Faba's letter, however, claims to be sacred, not *ex officio*, but as a product of rhetorical art and because a "man of genius" raises his voice. Guido Faba, admittedly, does not want to be taken too seriously in his claims. He uses all the illustrious phrases and metaphors with a certain amount of the self-irony which is palpable in all his writings.[23] For he is well aware of the discrepancy between the enormous pretensions of his images and the humbleness of his subject—a discussion of the blunders and rules of *dictamen*. Nevertheless, his rhetorical ability to produce an awe-inspiring tone, fit to address a world-wide audience, should not be underestimated. On the one hand, his manifesto is merely another token of the general tendency, noticeable among the rhetors as well as the jurists of that age, to raise their arts to a sphere of quasi-holiness in order to compete with theology. On the other hand, there sounds, throughout Guido Faba's rhetorical burlesque, very distinctly the tone of the great imperial as well

---

[23] See, e.g., New College MS. 255, fol. 42, the *Invectiva magistri contra scolares malitiosos et tenaces*, which ends:

> Illuminet itaque dominus de celorum habitaculo dura corda (*Eccl.*, 2, 10) et iniquitates non respiciat sed ignoscat faciatque dono sue gratie salutaris, quod indignatio magistri Guidonis aliquo remedio mitigetur, ut, dum manum suam ad benediccionem extenderit, quasi spiritus sancti gratia descendat scientia dictaminis super omnes.

Very similar to the tone of the *Rota nova* is the prologue of the *Gemma purpurea* ("Gemma claritatis refulsit in habitaculo domus mee," printed by Gaudenzi, *Cronologia*, 127f) or that of the *Summa de virtutibus* as yet unpublished:

> Apperiat dominus corda nostra, qui aperuit occulos ceci nati, et reseret labia obmutescentis, qui os Zacherie aperuit prophetantis, et virtus spiritus paraclyti, que venit in discipulos domini, descendere de celorum habitaculo nunc dignetur, que rore superne gratie nos illustret, ut recto zelo et pura conscientia decorati ei laudes reddamus omni tempore, quas tenemur, et repleti suavitate virtutum iugiter possimus in suis mirabilibus delectari. Cum itaque lingua carnis consonare debeat lingue mentis et

mens, nisi vite spiraculo polleat, in lege dei nequeat cogitare, tali premisso initio, quod principium est bonorum et finis, ad nostrum secure propositum accedamus. In precedenti quidem parte divina oppitulante clementia de vitiis breviter est notatum. Quare de virtutibus supponamus, quibus mediantibus incentivum delinquendi compescitur et creatura creatori debite famulatur. Attende igitur, o lector, lege continue, disce serio et lecta memorie recommenda, que tibi de mensa domini apponuntur, quoniam in hiis utilitas evidens apparebit non momentanea sed eterna, non vilium divitiarum sed celestium epularum, non tantum ad corporis incrementum verum sed ad anime salutiferum nutrimentum. Nota igitur studiose et teneas diligenter, quod in scripturis quattuor virtutum genera designantur...

The text published is mainly based on Clm. 23497, fol. 37, which has been collated with Clm. 21565 (fol. 67), Clm. 16124 (fol. 66ᵛ), and Clm. 23505 (fol. 76ᵛ); Gaudenzi, *Cronologia*, 125, published the part from "Quare" to "nutrimentum," but left out the "prologo enfatico."

as papal manifestoes of the thirteenth century, a tone which cannot be mistaken and which has its inner truth as soon as the alloy of self-irony is dropped and the subject is in harmony with the stirring solemnity of the language. As far as the sheer elements of rhetoric are concerned—the ability to connect every matter directly with the universe, the economical and therefore most effective use of scriptural phrases in order to preserve or restore the sonority of the language, and the rolling rhythms of the *clausulae*—there is no difference between Guido Faba's semi-farcical proems and the thundering bulls of Gregory IX, the apocalyptic pamphlets of Rainer of Viterbo,[24] or the solemn proclamations of Petrus de Vinea. All these writings were published as truly *litterae sacrae* and in fact directed to the "Christian People." Nor should it be disregarded that the *dictatores* of these bulls, pamphlets, and proclamations had received that very same rhetorical training the teaching of which was Guido Faba's profession, or that Dante, in his letters as well as when he styled his great vernacular song

> . . .il poema sacro
> al quale ha posto mano e cielo e terra. . . (Par. XXV, 1)

was, after all, still a pupil of this school of rhetoric. It cannot be maintained that Guido Faba was the inventor of this cosmic tenour, but, to our knowledge, he was the first to have taught it systematically and to have trained in it several generations of scribes.[25]

After having struck the note in the first sentence of the proem, Guido Faba faces the more difficult task of preserving it and of establishing a direct connection between the celestial powers, the teaching of rhetoric, the city of Bologna, and his own person in particular.

It cannot be denied that the author solves his task with considerable skill. Celestial Piety, Guido Faba explains, took in her care Latin Eloquence, which had been abandoned by the "purple science of *dictamen*," and deigned to listen in her royal chamber to the implorations of her serfs.

> And as the divine love had made Saint Peter the keeper of the keys and conferred upon him the power of binding and loosing, so did it want to see Bologna exalted also in the profession of Rhetoric, Bononia who deserves to be called "Good in

---

[24] Cf. Elisabeth v. Westenholz, *Kardinal Rainer von Viterbo* (Heidelberg, 1912).

[25] It is beyond the scope of this article to present an analysis of the style of letters in the 13th century, but I may deal with this subject on another occasion. One feature significant of this style may, nevertheless, be indicated here: that is, the ideal of a synthesis of Solomon and Cicero, of preacher and rhetor. Jacob of Dinant, master of rhetoric at Bologna, or Reggio, later in the 13th century, explains in the prologue to his *Ars arengandi*, published by André Wilmart, *Analecta Reginensia* (Studi e Testi, LIX; Vatican, 1933), 121: "Salomon huic (sc. arti) primus auctor nec Tullius ymus Dicitur. . . ." That Cicero is claimed the model of the *dictatores* is old tradition; it is true also with Guido Faba who styles himself "Tullii et Ciceronis heredem"; cf. Gaudenzi, *Cronologia*, 127, and *infra*, Appendix, § 6. Of Solomon, Guido wishes "quod in magisterio stili prosaici preesset filiis hominum et prodesset"; see *infra*, Appendix § 6 and also *Summa dictaminis*, ed. Gaudenzi, in *Il Propugnatore*, n. s. III: 1 (1890), 287: "Sapientia Salomonis per quam viri scolastici decorantur et clarescit machina mundi." Guido Faba himself published two treatises, *De sapientia Salomonis* and *De proverbiis Salomonis*, which are found in many manuscripts, e.g., in Clm. 23497, fol. 8ᵛ, Clm. 16124, fol. 16, and in others. This prominence given to Solomon and the style resulting from it was not invented by Guido Faba. Buoncompagno's prose abounds in images borrowed from the Psalms and from Solomon, but he remains in the playful grounds of a pseudo-poetic sphere; whereas Guido Faba, by his application of biblical language to secular subjects, conquers, as it were, a new dimension because through his solemn language he contrives to connect almost every subject directly with the universe.

every concern"[26] and has been entrusted already with the foundation of other branches of knowledge.

That Bologna should be the mother and mistress of every knowledge, such was the will of divine providence which had bestowed on the city the privilege of being the source of every intellectual enlightenment until the end of time. Guido conceives this grant as a legal act, or as a notarial privilege, corroborated by the signatures of all the angels and by the consent of the knighthood of the celestial hosts (§ 4). He therefore warns masters and students never to abandon Bologna and thus to contravene or despise this celestial grant.

> Let masters and students, if they can, transplant their studies to another place. They should know that they cannot teach or learn elsewhere, but will only err like sheep that do not return to the fold and venture to kick against the pricks of the Lord which are hard for those daring to encroach upon the Holy Ghost. (§ 5)[27]

This last passage alludes obviously to an actual event which permits us to date the *Rota nova* quite accurately. In 1224, Frederick II had founded the university of Naples which, for obvious reasons, could not compete with the old reputation of Bologna. In the years immediately following (1225/26), the political conditions in Lombardy forced the Emperor to outlaw Bologna along with other North Italian cities. This ban included the schools of the cities; thus also the university of Bologna was declared closed. But the last thing that Frederick II wished was to have the students and masters suffer for the recalcitrance of Bologna's rebellious citizens. He tried to find a way out and, at the same time, to fish in the waters which he had troubled. At the imperial court, they even thought of transplanting the whole *studium* of Bologna to Naples. Frederick's letter in which he forbade his subjects to continue or attend lectures at Bologna was, at the same time, an invitation to masters and students to come to easy-going Naples and to continue the studies there in beautiful surroundings. But a resolution of the Council of Bologna shows that the city decided to defy the imperial demands.[28]

Thus the *Rota nova* can be dated 1225/26, as these are obviously the events which Guido Faba has in mind.[29] Masters and students, he says, would be unable to continue their studies at another place because only Bologna was privileged by the angels to be

---

[26] The pun "Bononia—bona omnia" was very popular; see, for instance, the prologue of Magister Bene's *Candelabrum*, published by Gaudenzi, *Cronologia*, 151: "alitum bonitatis a Bononia contrahentes" and "sicut nomen nomini, sic nostra devotio ... ipsius respondeat bonitati"; see also K. Hampe, "Zur Gründungsgeschichte der Universität Neapel," *SB. Heid. Ak.*, Jahrg. 1923, Abh. 10 (1924), 14, cf. 11f. The power of binding and loosing (cf. Matth. 16, 19) refers, in the *Gemma purpurea*, to Guido himself, not to Bologna: "cui secreta huius scientie pandebantur et ligandi atque solvendi speciosa vel deformata dictamina potestatem distributor contulerat gratiarum." Cf. Gaudenzi, *op. cit.*, 127f.

[27] For the special relationship of the Spiritus sanctus to *dictamen* see the texts *supra*, n. 23. and *infra*, n. 39.

[28] Cf. Gaudenzi, in *Archivio storico italiano*, ser. V, vol. XLII (1908), 356, 360.

[29] Guido Faba's warning, it is true, could refer to any other of the Bolognese migrations of which many took place between 1220 and 1230. For entirely different reasons, however, the *Rota nova* appears to have been written in 1225/26 (cf. *infra*, p. 210). That Guido Faba recognized Naples as a competitor of Bologna can be gathered from two student letters exchanged between Bologna and Naples; cf. Haskins, *Studies in Mediaeval Culture* (1929), 30, n. 2; they are found also in the New College MS. 255, fol. 41v, where they belong to a treatise called *Littera magistri missa scolaribus Bononie et lecta per omnes scolas civitatis omnium artium*. It therefore seems likely that Guido Faba would allude, also in the *Rota nova*, to the imperial invitation in 1225/6.

the mother of every branch of knowledge and, above all, of rhetoric and *dictamen*. This consideration brings Guido's own person to the fore. In order to provide some evidence for his assertion that Bologna was the mother of rhetoric, he had only to point to himself as the God-sent master of eloquence. He raises his voice, once more, and bids the universe keep silence, for to speak is the prerogative of "Tullian experience and of Cicero's plenty" as well as of the wisdom of Solomon whom God wished to make excel in the mastery of prose style before the sons of men.[30]

> Therefore, Bologna, thou almost too perfect and happy creation, thou mayest rejoice, and with thee thy citizens all chant to the Most High, for out of thee has come the Man who is able to enlighten the ignorance of yore as well as the modern confusion, and to cleanse both by means of his letters. (§ 7).[31]

Is it necessary to add that this "Man," introduced almost with the words of St. Matthew (2, 6) when he announces the coming of Christ, is Guido Faba who now begins to narrate the story of his life? And thus begins the part of the prologue (§§ 8–15) which deserves our full attention. It offers a real autobiography of the writer and has but one disadvantage: the author's pleasure in representing the story of his life and his sufferings in so periphrastic a way and in so mystical a disguise—though in agreement with the whole style of his proem—makes it not at all easy to extract from this tissue the simple facts.

The first facts that can be gathered from Guido's report are that he was born in Bologna,[32] and furthermore, that his name "Faba" was a nickname which was the result of the antics and buffooneries for which he had been famous as a boy.[33] Thus the hypothesis of his kinship with the Bolognese podestà from Brescia, Aliprand Faba, collapses. The dedication of his *Summa dictaminis*, in which it is said that the podestà's fame illuminates the whole clan, must be considered as a joke meaning that everyone who, for one reason or another, calls himself "Faba," participates in the podestà's glory; and, inasmuch as Guido bears this nickname, he too becomes famous thanks to the glory of his namesake. More than that can hardly be gathered from the dedication.

After having introduced himself, the author begins to tell us about his studies (§ 8). Like all the teachers of *dictamen* as well as their successors, the humanists in the fourteenth

---

[30] Cf. *supra*, n. 25.

[31] It is remarkable that a similar allusion to Matth. 2, 6 should be found in Frederick II's (or Petrus de Vinea's) famous letter to Jesi, the Emperor's Bethlehem; cf. *MGH, Constitutiones*, II, 304, no. 219. Master Bene praises Bologna in a similar way because he, Bene, had dwelled there: "Letetur itaque nobilissima Bononia et exultet..., gaudeat in perpetuum, quia de tenebris errantium iam meruit liberari. Sit enim nomen meum memorabile, quia licet clara Florentia nos genuit, fructum tamen scientie... a Bononia contrahentes ipsam precipue matrem nobilium studiorum debemus et volumus semper magnifice honorare." Gaudenzi, *Cronologia*, 151. Bene was a contemporary of Guido Faba and probably the latter's successor as scribe to the Bishop of Bologna; see R. Davidsohn, *Ge-*

schichte von Florenz, IV, 156. Guido Faba's praise of Brescia—"o Brixia terra nobilis, nunc gaude beata, que tantum lilium protulisti etc."—refers to the author's namesake, the podestà of Bologna, cf. Rockinger, *op. cit.*, 180. What the Bolognese "school tradition" was like can be judged from these eulogies of the birthplaces and similar examples.

[32] "Ex te natus est homo ille," cf. *infra*, Appendix, § 7.

[33] I do not know how the phrase "qui ab effectu rei hoc prenomen faba annis puerilibus acquisivit" could be explained otherwise; "fabas dicere" means to indulge in jokes and buffooneries. As Guido himself considers "Faba" a *prenomen*, which may have been applied to him particularly during his youth, the expression "magister Faba" in the document of 1210 is less startling; cf. *supra*, n. 11.

and fifteenth centuries, Guido Faba complains of the persecutions of Envy.[34] He was too good a student of rhetoric to pass through his studies without becoming the object of this vice, and therefore he had to give up the *studium litterarum*, that is the general humanistic studies, to which he had been devoted and in which he had made considerable progress.[35] Presumably, he abandoned these studies after having acquired the master's degree which he first used, as has been mentioned before, in 1210.

There follows a strange passage in Guido's autobiography (§§ 8–11). He mentions that after having given up the *litterae* he stooped to learning the blacksmith's trade in addition to his former studies. At the end of two years, however, when he was an advanced student of this craft, God called him away from the smithy by means of three signs and wonders.

> A piece of unforged iron, which came red-hot from the workshop, slipped away and hopped about by order of the Thunderer and, bouncing up, it suddenly fell upon the floor; with this leap, however, it injured and burnt his [Guido's] bare foot so that he had to limp for the rest of his life (§ 9).

There followed a second "miracle." When Guido heated the iron once more and began to beat it on the anvil with a heavy hammer, a tiny scale, red-hot, penetrated the pupil of his eye so that the sight of the craftsman, who had been working too strenuously, was impaired (§ 10). But this was not all. There came what Guido called the third miracle: from the same piece of red-hot iron his tongue was injured.

> Thus by this threefold suffering he understood the revelation of the mystery and, after having recovered his senses, he began to cry and to assert most humbly before all people that, by means of these three signs, the Holy Trinity called him away from this craft (§ 11).

At last, contrite and chastened, he made haste to return to the studies of literature which he had foolishly given up, whereupon masters and students of Bologna displayed their pleasure at the return of the Prodigal Son and rejoiced: "The sheep that was lost is found and he who was dead is alive again."

This is Guido's report of how, by divine summons, he was induced to leave hammer and anvil and to devote himself to literature. It is, as it were, the hagiographic part of his

---

[34] The complaint about envy is a constantly recurrent topic in the writings of the masters of *ars dictandi*; cf. Albert of Samaria's prologue to the *Dictaminum precepta* ("licet emulorum mordeatur invidia") in Oxford, Bodl. MS. Laud. misc. 569, fol. 146 (it is mistakenly attributed to Henricus Francigena), Hugh of Bologna in Rockinger, *op. cit.*, 53f; likewise Henricus Francigena in the prologue to his *Aurea gemma* in a passage not printed by Haskins, *Studies in Mediaeval Culture* (1929), 178; the prologues to every work of Buoncompagno contain laments on envy; so does the *Liber de floribus* of Boto da Vigevano (cf. Bertoni, *Il Duecento* [Milan, s. a.], 278f), and the same holds good for practically all the pre-humanist masters as well as for their successors, the humanists. There is certainly much truth in these complaints because the social position of successful *dictatores* such as Petrus de Vinea (cf. *supra*, n. 4, the discussion of Olschki) and others necessarily aroused feelings of envy; see also *infra*, n. 57. There is a clear relationship between envy and the saying: "Aptus rethoricus equitat cum principe primus"; cf. H. Walther, "Beiträge zur Kenntnis der mittellateinischen Literatur," *Zentralblatt für Bibliothekswesen*, XLIX (1932), 273. Sociologically the problem of *invidia* in the earlier centuries would be the more interesting if the assertion of J. Huizinga, in the first chapter of his admirable book *The Waning of the Middle Ages* (London, 1924), proves true, according to which *superbia* and *avaritia* come to the fore with the rise of bourgeoisie in the later Middle Ages.

[35] "...in quo profecerat competenter."

narration. But what is the meaning of his working in the smithy and that of his painful experiences? It is clear that the blacksmith's trade proper cannot have been his new occupation. At least, this may be concluded from the phrase that he stooped to learn the new craft "in addition" to his former studies.[36] This term can be explained satisfactorily only if his apprenticeship in the smithy was connected, in some way or other, with his studies in the field of literature. At first glance, it could be assumed that some punning and twisting of "Faber" and "Faba" was at the bottom of it. By chance, however, we learn what Guido had in his mind. Stephen of Tournai, the famous canonist, wrote a letter, about 1180, to Heraclius, Bishop of Cæsarea, who was then staying in the Holy Land. Stephen reminds his friend of the times they had spent together as students in Bologna.

> Often I pray, in copious prayers, that our former facetious prattle may be atoned for. We called the pleadings of the toga-bearing barristers "trade-marketings," the lawsuits of the litigating parties "battles of the blind," the lecture-rooms of the Bolognese "blacksmiths' workshops." In the meantime, we have followed different ways of studies; I took up the joinery of Bulgarus which once I had laughed at, you the Calvary of the cross.[37]

The expression "smithy" was Bolognese slang and signified the Bolognese Law Schools. Therefore, if Guido Faba demeaned himself in the blacksmith's trade for two years, after his graduation in literature, this meant in plain words that he had devoted himself, in accordance with a then popular curriculum,[38] to the study of Law after having accomplished that of Letters.

The work in the Law School, however, did not agree with him; or, according to Guido's metaphors, he became lame, half-blind, and acquired a heavy tongue. He risked losing the former versatility which he had acquired when studying rhetoric. Law made him unlearn what Rhetoric had taught. And in the gifts of grace, bestowed upon him by Rhetoric, must be sought the *tertium comparationis* of his miraculous afflictions emanating from the Trinity. Jesus, on the sea of Galilee, had made the dumb speak, the lame walk, and the blind see (Matth. 15, 31); that is, he performed the miracle which Rhetoric was likewise able to perform.[39] Law, however, was about to undo this miracle of Rheto-

---

[36] "...ad artem fabrilem descenderet addiscendam."

[37] Cf. Migne, *PL*, CCXI, 355, ep. lxiii: "Jocosas olim confabulationes nostras fructuosis oro sepius orationibus expiari. Togatorum advocationes *mercimonia*, litigantium conflictus *cecorum pugnas*, Bononiensium auditoria *fabriles* diximus *officinas*. Inter hec diversa secuti studia sumus, ego, quod irriseram, *carpentariam* Bulgari, vos calvariam Crucifixi." Bulgarus, of course, is the famous Doctor of Law.

[38] That Guido Faba had really the Law School in mind, may be gathered from one of the letters in his *Dictamina rhetorica*, in which a student writes to his uncle: "Cum in hoc anno in grammatica profecerim competenter, leges audire desidero in futuro"; cf. Gaudenzi in *Il Propugnatore*, V: 1 (1892), 109, no. lxi, and compare this phrasing with that found in § 8 of the *Rota nova*: "... ut

litterarum omisso studio, in quo profecerat competenter, ad artem fabrilem descenderet addiscendam."

[39] This parallelism between Christ, or the *Spiritus sanctus*, and the *ars dictaminis* is startling rather than rare. It is found in Guido's prologue to his *Summa de virtutibus* (cf. *supra*, n. 23). It is found very explicitly in Jacob of Dinant's *Summa dictaminis* (ed. Wilmart, *Analecta Reginensia*, 146): "Solum hoc in laudem presentis operis ad presens sufficiat in prologo premittere, quod ars dictandi non immerito Dei filio, quod est verbum patris quo pater dixit et facta sunt (Psalm 148, 5) et ars ipsius et mens, per quandam apropriacionem potest licet subtiliter acceptari, quanvis et spiritu sancto possit similiter atribui, qui est ille spiritus, qui scienciam habet vocis, qui super discipulos die pentecostes in linguis apparuit, quia quos repleverit eloquentes facere consuevit." And the paral-

ric, and the Holy Trinity thought it fit to "reveal this mystery" to Guido by a threefold visitation. Hence, after two years, Guido gave up law and returned to letters.

Even so he was not happy. He studied day and night, but earned no money, or too little, so that finally he became wasted in body. Skin and bone, all that was left of him, decided that for the sake of regaining flesh—and in that they were supported by the "anxiety of the spirit and a macerated mind"—he should give up letters once more; they decided that

> he should be delivered to the pastime of the tanners, he, Guido, who avoided the acknowledged evil by means of dog droppings and of puncturing with an awl with which people prepare the skins which they stretch, thereafter, with their teeth (§ 13).

This passage, again, is anything but clear. Was it that his wasted body was considered good enough for the flayer only? And, if so, what had that to do with "dog droppings" and with stretching skins with the teeth? Once more, it is merely by chance that a parallel solves this rhetorical charade. About 1300, Jacopo da Cessole wrote a book *De moribus hominum et officiis nobilium sive super ludo scacchorum*.[40] This became one of the most popular mediaeval books on chess because, using as symbols a set of chess-men, the author discussed in a philosophical and edifying way the classes of human society. He begins by discussing the duties of the King and Queen. Thereafter follows a discussion of the chess-men now called Bishops, which then were styled *alphiles*[41] but were viewed by Jacopo da Cessole as Judges. The Queen's Bishop, on the black square, was Judge for criminal jurisdiction, and the King's Bishop, on the white square, Judge for cases of civil law. The Pawns in front of the officers represented, according to the author, different groups of the working class. The Queen's Bishop's Pawn, seated in front of the criminal Judge, represented the wool-weavers, tailors, barbers, skinners, curriers, tanners and notaries, that is all the professions "qui circa pellem operantur."[42] Hence, because the notaries concerned themselves with parchment, they were placed among the tanners and all the others whose occupation was the preparing of skins.[43] This queer division of society was

---

lelism is found, once more, in a letter of John Whetham-stede, Prior of Gloucester College in Oxford and Abbot of St. Alban's, whose writing in general is influenced by the Italian doctrines of rhetoric. On his way to Siena, Whethamstede met an Italian master of Rhetoric, "resurgentem etsi non Christum alterum, tamen habuimus alloquentem nobis oratorem Tullium. ... Venientes tamen in Galilaeam [Siena!], audientesque a discipulis eius qualiter vir ille erat alter Cicero, qui, quo modo Christus in Judaea divina fecerat virtute et audire surdos et mutos loqui, ita ipse in Italia arte Rhetoricae muto-rum linguas fecit disertas, vigore eloquentiae surdorum aures reddebat attentas, et pauperes vi linguae docuit evangelizare...." Cf. Johannes Amundesham, *Annales Monasterii S. Albani*, ed. H. T. Riley (Rolls Series 28, 5), I, 136f, A.D. 1423. That a scale flew into Guido's eye and destroyed it, is an inversion of Acts 9, 18, where it is said that the scales fell from the eyes of St. Paul. That is to say, Law blinded Guido who had gained his sight previously by means of Rhetoric. The idea of a quasi-salvation attained through Rhetoric (and in a similar way through every branch of knowledge), significant for the *dictatores* and other scholars of that age, needs a special discussion.

[40] On Jacopo's biographical dates, cf. F. Novati, in *Il libro e la stampa*, III (1909), 45ff. The *Super ludo scacchorum* has been edited, along with the German poetical paraphrase of 1337, by Ferdinand Vetter, *Das Schachzabelbuch Kunrats von Ammenhausen* (Bibliothek älterer Schriftwerke der deutschen Schweiz, Ergänzungs-band; Frauenfeld, 1887–92).

[41] For the etymology of this word (derived from the Arabic 'al fil', the elephant) see Vetter, *op. cit.*, xxxvi and 166ff, about these chess-men as judges.

[42] *Ludus scacchorum*, III, c. 3, ed. Vetter, 450, has the rubric "De officio lanificum et carnificum et scriptorum et omnium qui circa pellem operantur."

[43] *Ibid.*, 451: "Hii omnes lanifices appellantur, quia aut notarii aut pelliparii aut coriarii circa pellem ipsam operantur." See also *ibid.*, 467f on the notaries in particular; and, 806, on the arrangement of the chess-men according to Jacopo da Cessole.

obviously not simply invented by Jacopo da Cessole; for Guido Faba's prologue to the *Rota nova* discloses that at least in Bologna University slang the notaries, long before, were considered *cerdones*.[44]

The solution of Guido Faba's cryptic narration now encounters no difficulties. That dog dirt was used for the currying of any sort of white leather, hence also of vellum, is familiar to every reader of *Des deutschen Spiessers Wunderhorn*.[45] That the notaries braced and stretched the parchment into shape by holding it with their teeth and stretching it with the hands may have been a trick of penman's craft to make the skins appropriately supple. And the "puncturing with an awl" seems to allude to the "bodkin" by means of which the "red tape," or rather the silk or wool string for attaching the seal, was drawn through the parchment. Consequently, the whole passage has the following meaning: in order to avoid the 'notorious evil' of starvation and emaciation, Guido Faba's skin, bones, spirit, and mind held a council on how to recover flesh and they finally persuaded their master to become a "tanner," a notary, and to make money. Guido Faba obeyed. He had recourse to the *tabellionatus ars* and could boast that he deserved to be styled "master of masters in both courts,"[46] in civil as well as in canon law.

But Guido felt dissatisfied before long with his new profession. The notariate was rendered distasteful by much discomfort and fatigue as well as by the enemies he acquired "because he refused to deviate either to the right or to the left." He therefore "communed with himself, took shelter with God, and stayed for two years with the Bishop of Bologna" (§ 14). Actually, Guido Faba is known to have been the scribe of Bishop Henry of Bologna in 1221. But he seems to have had some quarrel with the Bishop, as can be gathered from a model letter[47] as well as from the last section of Guido's prologue (§ 15).

The last paragraph is likewise far from easy to understand. Guido explains that, at the courts of the mighty, little care is taken for the salvation of the soul, but great care for temporal comfort.

> And as he did not want to dwell in the blackguardism, the treachery, and the deceits of the flesh, he recalled his former freedom, took in hand the care of the Chapel of Saint Michael, was there promoted to the sacerdotal office, began to rebuild the chapel along with the dilapidated houses, endured patiently all the persecutions and offences of the neighbours whose party was supported surreptitiously by the clerics of the city, and had a new temple erected in honour of the Archangel Michael.

If this narration is to be taken literally, it would mean that Guido Faba had become a priest at San Michele di Mercato di Mezzo in Bologna, that he rebuilt this chapel as well

---

[44] The satirical poem *De uxore cerdonis*, ed. by Nie-wöhner in *Zeitschrift für deutsches Altertum*, LXV (1928), 65ff, refers to a real tanner.

[45] See in Gustav Meyrink's *Des deutschen Spiessers Wunderhorn* (Munich, 1925), the short story, "Wozu dient weisser Hundedreck?"

[46] Cf. *supra*, n. 20, the last sentence of the prologue to the *Littere stili secularis*, where Guido stresses his experience "in utraque curia".

[47] Cf. Rockinger, *Briefsteller und Formelbuecher*, 181: "Conqueritur sanctitati vestre magister G., capellanus ecclesie sancti Michahelis Bononie, de domino Heinrico Bononie episcopo, qui quandam summem pecunie, quam in servicium eius expendit de sua voluntate pariter et mandato, iniuste detinet et reddere contradicit." This, together with the unfriendly description of the episcopal court, makes it unlikely that Guido was on particularly good terms with Bishop Henry.

as the surrounding houses, and that he finally built a new chapel dedicated to the Archangel. But the preceding parts of the prologue have made it clear that a literal interpretation would certainly be out of place.

That Guido became a priest cannot easily be denied. He states too positively that he was promoted to the sacerdotal office; and too often, in his writings, does Guido style himself "cappelanus" or "sacerdos" of St. Michael's, although just as frequently he calls himself "magister Guido Faba sancti Michaelis Bononiensis."[48] Yet the question must be raised whether this chaplaincy may not have been a "clerical" office in a figurative sense. Guido writes that he left the episcopal court in order to regain his former freedom. Apparently, he has in mind the academic freedom of a scholar, of a teacher of the arts, grammar and rhetoric, but hardly the esoteric freedom, the "libertas animi," of priesthood, unless this latter freedom was combined with a good prebend which would permit him to lead a carefree life. But this is certainly not the whole story, and there are some facts which at least make us wonder whether Guido, in his "sacred letter," really wants to stress his belonging to the clergy of the Church of Bologna or whether he was not simply a *clericus* of St. Michael's in a secular, scholarly sense.

His guardianship of the chapel of St. Michael and his title as "magister sancti Michaelis Bononiensis" may put us on the right track. It seems as though the name of this chapel stands for the "cathedra," the professorship, of grammar and *dictamen* which Guido mentions in the last sentence of his proem. We must not forget that the ideal academic classroom such as that visualized by Master Buoncompagno did not yet exist.[49] Classes were held, in Bologna and elsewhere, in convents, churches, or chapels.[50] Moreover, students as well as teachers belonged "to a chapel." Just as Oxford students today would be introduced as "so-and-so of St. John's," or "of Corpus," or "of Magdalen," so it was the usage, in Bologna, to append to a master's or student's name the name of his convent or chapel, which could, but need not, be the same as that of the parish. Thus there may be found, especially in official charters, designations such as "Johannes de Arquata, de capella sancti Archangeli," or "Corbellanus capelle sancti Martini de Aposa,"[51] designations which indicated not only the chapel proper but the whole "block" to which the chapel belonged. Consequently, the additional "de capella sancti Archangeli" or "qui moratur in capella sancti Prosperi" referred also to the *hospicia* in the adjacent houses.[52]

[48] New College MS. 255, fol. 6ᵛ: "presbyter Guido ecclesie sancti Michaelis fori medii cappellanus" (cf. fol. 15ʳ, 40ᵛ.) See also Gaudenzi, *Cronologia*, 123. The ancient Mercato di Mezzo is to-day the Via Rizzoli; see the map in Francesco Cavazza, *Le scuole dell' antico studio bolognese* (Milan, 1896). The chapel of St. Michael is between the Palazzo del Podestà and Mercato di Mezzo, cf. Guido Zaccagnini, *La vita dei maestri e degli scolari nello Studio di Bologna nei secoli XIII e XIV* (Geneva, 1926), who offers a 17th-century map (following p. 4) on which the chapel can be located. The title of chaplain in connection with Guido's name occurs frequently; cf. *supra*, n. 47; Pertz, *Archiv*, VII (1842), 68. Often, however, he is styled simply "sancti Michaelis Bononiensis," cf. Rockinger, 179; Clm. 7205, fol. 98; New College MS. 255, fol. 15ʳ, 40ᵛ. All this makes it hard to doubt that he really was a chaplain.

[49] Cf. Sutter, *Aus Leben und Schriften des Magisters Boncompagno* (Freiburg i. B. and Leipzig, 1894), 40, n. 3.

[50] Cf. Cavazza, Zaccagnini, *opp. cit.*

[51] See, for instance, the documents published by Cavazza, *op. cit.*, Appendix, or Luigi Colini-Baldeschi, "Lo studio di Bologna e la Marca d'Ancona," *Studi e memorie per la storia dell'Università di Bologna*, V (1920), 111ff, where any number of items can be found, especially in the Bolognese acts of indictment.

[52] This becomes quite clear from the document (1327, May 11) published by Cavazza, *op. cit.*, Appendix, no. xliv.

From late thirteenth- and early fourteenth-century documents it can be gathered that at least two, perhaps three chapels of St. Michael were connected with the study of grammar and rhetoric in Bologna. In 1304 and 1320, there is mentioned a "Raynerius magister gramatice professor capelle Sancti Michaelis de Lambertaciis sive Sancti Remedii."[53] In 1325, we find a "magister Albertinus de Mascheriis de Placentia, ordinarius lector in Bononia gramatice facultatis capelle Sancti Michaelis de Leproseto."[54] There are also innumerable documents in which students of the Faculty of Arts are mentioned "de capella sancti Archangeli."[55] And does not Guido style himself, in exactly the same way, "magister Guido Faba sancti Michaelis"?

If all this is taken into account, the narration of Guido Faba is at last cleared up. Notwithstanding the possibility of his enjoying St. Michael's as a prebend, his entering upon the guardianship of this chapel means above all that he was entrusted with the instruction of grammar and *dictamen* at this chapel. Thus, if Guido explains that he rebuilt it and the dilapidated houses surrounding it, he means to say that he reorganized the neglected study of *dictamen* at St. Michael's, including the adjacent houses and *hospicia* where the students lived. And if he complains of persecutions inflicted on him by envious neighbours supported by malevolent *clerici*, he seems to hint that his colleagues, the scholars (called also *clerici*), instigated his neighbours, namely other masters or perhaps the students "de capella sancti Michaelis," to frustrate his efforts. Finally, if he announces that he built a new temple or shrine in honour of St. Michael, this means that he was writing a new book, the *Rota nova*. This last item is commented upon by Guido himself. His book, says he, was composed by order of the Archangel; and it was appropriately called the "New Wheel" for its similarity with the Wheel of Fortune.

> As the status of any person undergoes multifarious changes through something new, so did he, Guido, ascend from a lower rank to a higher. And, while sitting professorially on the throne of the Wheel, he holds in his hand the two wings which the angel presented to him, the one destined to cut down all the blunders of *dictamen*, the other to make known the rules by which the knowledge of *dictamen* and of the ornate style is acquired, lest without these wings—even birds cannot fly without wings—students should set out to fly;[56] for irreparably they fall to the ground who hasten forward to forbidden things.

In the manuscript, these sentences are illustrated by a miniature which precedes, on fol. 1ʳ, the "First Wing," the first section of the doctrine proper. An angel, who has but

---

[53] Cf. G. Zaccagnini, "Giovanni di Bonandrea, detta-tore e rimatore, e altri grammatici e dottori in arti dello Studio Bolognese," *Studi e memoire p. l. stor. dell'Univ. di Bologna*, V (1920), 172, n. 4.

[54] Cf. L. Frati, "Grammatici Bolognesi del Trecento," *Studi e memorie p. la stor. dell'Univ. di Bologna*, IV (1920), 32f. This chapel was also called Santa Tecla, cf. Cavazza, *op. cit.*, Appendix, no. xliii, p. xxxi.

[55] Colini-Baldeschi, *op. cit.*, 116, 124, et passim; Cavazza, nos. xliv, xlx, pp. xxxiif.

[56] Their motto may have agreed with Guido's statement "Cum summa sapientia divitiarum quasi mater sublimet ignobiles, pauperes et mendicos, ad ipsius habendam notitiam studere debet quilibet deli-genter" (New College MS. 255, fol. 40ᵛ; cf. *Il Propugnatore*, n. ser. VI: 1 [1893], 91), or with the words of Peter of Prezza, a pupil of Peter de Vinea, "in scientia captes famam, in fama alios prevenias ad honorem, in honore divicias consequaris"; cf. Eugen Müller, *Peter von Prezza, ein Publizist der Zeit des Interregnums* (Heidelberg, 1913), 135ff, No. 15; cf. *supra* n. 34.

one wing on his shoulder, hands the other pinion to a *magister* who is enthroned near a rotating wheel and is garbed not in the black robe of a priest but in the dark-blue tabard of the philosophers.[57] These items seem to support the suggestion that the chaplaincy of Guido, who may or may not have been a cleric of the Church, signifies in the first place what we would call the "St. Michael Professorship of Rhetoric" in Bologna.

There remains nothing but to sum up the results of our investigation. With the reliable dates which can be ascertained from Guido Faba's autobiography and which are supported by documents, a basis is gained for establishing the chronology of his life between 1210 and 1225. A few dates are countenanced by other sources, for instance that he was a *magister* in 1210, that he became a notary earlier than 1218 (he was appointed under Otto IV), that he still was a notary in 1220 and was scribe to the Bishop of Bologna in 1221 and 1222. Thus Guido Faba, the son of Nicholas[58] and a Bolognese by birth, had concluded his studies of literature by 1210 and thereafter took to the Law School for two years, presumably from 1211–1213. Around 1213, he may have returned to studying, or rather teaching, the humanistic sciences—literature, grammar, and rhetoric. We do not know exactly how long it took his body to become so wasted that its owner, once more, had to change his profession; but if we assume that Guido dedicated himself to the *humaniora* for another three years, from 1213–1216, this conjecture may be fairly exact. It would agree with the fact that Guido was appointed a notary under Otto IV; and, on the other hand, it would leave a margin of four or five years for the period in which he worked in this new profession. The *matricula* of notaries in Bologna begins, unfortunately, not earlier than 1219.[59] By that time, however, Guido must have gathered considerable experience as a notary; for the city elected him to accompany the proctors of Bologna to Viterbo when a pending lawsuit between Pistoia and Bologna was arbitrated before the law-court of Cardinal Hugh of Ostia, the papal legate in Lombardy and Northern Italy.[60] Guido's position as a member of this committee of arbitration can be

---

[57] From the dark-blue gown of philosophers came the Christian hood and the priestly garb; cf. Philipp Oppenheim, *Das Moenchskleid im christlichen Altertum* (Freiburg, 1931), 218ff. On the academic dress see Zaccagnini, *La vita dei maestri e degli scolari nello studio di Bologna nei secoli XIII e XIV* (Geneva, 1926), 69, and the plates offered by him as well as by Cavazza, *op. cit.* In general see H. Rashdall, *The Universities of Europe in the Middle Ages* (Oxford, 1936), III, 385ff; L. H. Dudley Buxton and Strickland Gibson, *Oxford University Ceremonies* (Oxford, 1935), 19–32; H. P. Stokes, *Ceremonies of the University of Cambridge* (Cambridge, 1927), 43–48. See also the interesting plates in the article of T. Sandonnini, "Di un codice del XIV secolo e dell' antico studio modenese," *Atti e memorie della R. Deputazione di Storia Patria per le provincie Modenesi*, ser. V, vol IV (Modena, 1906), 94, 101, 104.

[58] Cf. next note.

[59] It is published by Gaudenzi, *Statuti delle società del popolo di Bologna*, II (Fonti per la storia d'Italia; Rome, 1896); on p. 441, line 87, there is an entry: "Guido Faba,

filius Nicolai, O." As we know from other sources (*infra*, n. 61) that Guido acted as a notary of the city of Bologna in 1219 and also that he was a notary before entering the service of the Bishop of Bologna, there cannot be the slightest doubt that the entry refers to the master of *dictamen*, in spite of Torraca, *op. cit.*, 103. The "O" that follows the entry refers to the Emperor Otto IV, the Welf. Although Otto was deposed in 1215, the Guelf towns, including Bologna, continued to recognize him as Emperor even after his death (May, 1218); cf. Julius Ficker, *Forschungen zur Reichs- und Rechtsgeschichte Italiens*, II (Innsbruck, 1869), § 372, p. 417f; hence Guido Faba was nominated notary under Otto IV, although he was appointed by the city; see Ficker, *op. cit.*, II, § 247, p. 71ff, on the manner of appointing notaries in the Italian towns and in Bologna.

[60] On the legateship of Hugh of Ostia cf. Guido Levy, *Registro del Cardinale Ugolino d'Ostia* (Fonti per la storia d'Italia; Rome, 1890) and *Archivio della società romana di storia patria*, XII (1889), 241ff.

traced as late as October 1220,[61] shortly before he took up service with the Bishop of Bologna to whom he may have been recommended by his activity at the Cardinal's court of arbitration.[62] Bishop Henry of Bologna left for Rome, in November 1220, to attend the coronation of Frederick II. On this occasion the Bishop may have completed his suite by taking Guido Faba into his service as a scribe. This would explain also Guido's sojourn in Rome. He attended the coronation as a member of Bishop Henry's staff and gathered his information about the *salutationes* at the Papal Court. This position was kept by Guido for two years, 1221 and 1222.[63] By 1223 he must have given up his service with the Bishop and started teaching at St. Michael's in Bologna. According to the last section of his autobiography, Guido began to reorganize the studies at St. Michael's; and, a few years after having taken charge of this chapel, he began to build a new shrine for the Archangel, that is to write his *Rota nova*. This would indicate, approximately, the year 1225 or 1226, a date likewise probable because of his warning to the masters and students not to leave Bologna and go to Naples.[64]

About Guido's later years we learn nothing. Nevertheless, we have been able to gather, from the queer narration in the *Rota nova*, quite a number of positive dates for Guido Faba's years of training.

APPENDIX

Guido Faba, Prologue to the *Rota nova* (ca. 1226).

Oxford, New College MS. 255, fol. 7[r-v].

1. Letentur[a] celi et exultet terra, commoveatur mare cum plenitudine sua[65] et glorientur universe rationabiles creature, quia dei virtus recolitur et divina magnificentia declaratur, que sub veneranda memoria diem presentem, in qua hec littera sacra describitur, collendam indicit populo christiano. 2. Respiciens quidem celestis pietas latinum eloquium, purpurata dictaminis scientia desolatum, [de][b66] excelso sancto habitaculo regni sui preces servorum supplicantium misericorditer voluit exaudire, et sicut beatum Petrum clavicularium suum fecit, ei ligandi simulque solvendi potestate concessa,[67] ita civitatem Bononie, que bona vere per omnia dici potest,[68] prout in aliis facultatibus susceperat fundamentum, in hac rethorica profexione voluit sublimare. 3. Et sic altitudine divini conscilii scientiarum matrem in terris eam esse voluit et magistram,[c] a qua sicut a capite

---

[61] In connection with the lawsuit Bologna versus Pistoia he is found in 1219, in the *Liber censuum communis Pistorii*, ed. Q. Santoli (Pistoria, 1915), I, 70, on July the first; in the *Registro Grosso* in *Chartularium studii bononiensis*, ed. Nordi and Orioli (1909), I, 27, no. xxx, on July 15; in the *Registro Novo* in *Chartularium*, I, 47, no. li, on Sept. 26; in the *Registro Grosso* in *op. cit.*, I, 29, no. xxxi, on October 16, at Viterbo; and for the last time in his capacity as notary in the *Liber censuum comm. Pistorii*, I, 82; cf. Zaccagnini, "Per la storia letteraria del Duecento," *Il libro e la Stampa*, VI (1912), 120, n. 5.

[62] His activity as a *judex delegatus* (cf. *supra*, note 15) if it ever took place, cannot antedate 1227 because the documents refer to Pope Gregory IX. That Guido really held such an office should not be denied completely; in the New College MS., 255, fol. 15[r], Guido takes leave from his pupils "dum nuper in Lombardiam accedere festinarem pro quibusdam magnis negotiis exequendis."

[63] Gaudenzi, *Cronologia*, 151, n. 2.

[64] Cf. *supra*, n. 28 sq.

[65] Ps. 95, 11.

[66] Cf. MS. fol. 42: "de celorum habitaculo"; and *supra*, n. 22.

[67] Matth. 16, 19; cf. *Gemma purpurea*, *supra*, n. 26.

[68] "Bononia = bona omnia"; cf. *supra*, n. 26.

---

a) Letentur *corr. ex* Letent *c*.

b) *del. c*.

c) magistriam *c*.

vel a fonte singuli viventes lumen accipiunt et doctrinam, nec tanta dignitate sibi celitus attributa deo propitio usque ad finem seculorum spoliari poterit per aliquam potestatem. 4. Fuit namque hoc privilegium angelorum subscriptionibus roboratum, et omnis militia superioris exercitus hiis consensit. 5. Transferant itaque se magistri vel scolares alibi, si possunt, gratia studiorum scientes quod nec docere poterunt nec doceri, sed errant sicut oves, nisi redeant ad ovile, conantes domini[d] calcitrare contra stimulum,[69] quod est durum, cum dona spiritus sancti presumunt minuere. 6. Taceat igitur totus mundus, et Tulliana peritia necnon et facundia Ciceronis[70] loquatur, et a finibus terre austri regina veniat audire sapientiam Salomonis,[71] qui, licet ymaginem gerat hominis speciosam,[72] repletus tamen virtute multiplici pronuntiat verba tam melliflua et decora, ut gemmarum pulcritudinem superent et splendorem, auro purissimo et amenis floribus adornata, de quo recte dicitur et cantatur "In utero quippe matris sue rore suavitatis venustavit eum dominus et implevit,"[73] volens quod in magisterio[e][74] stili prosaici preesset filiis hominum et prodesset. 7. Gaudeas siquidem, Bononia, vere felix prenimium et formosa facta, excelsa meritis et virtute, et tecum cives omnes laudes resonent ad superna, quia ex te natus est homo ille,[75] qui veterum ignorantiam et confusionem modernam clarificet suis epistolis atque mundet. 8. Hic nempe Guido ab ipsis cunabilis[f] nominatus, qui ab effectu rei hoc prenomen Faba annis puerilibus acquisivit, cuius future prudentie ac utilitati humane cepit antiqui hostis malitia taliter invidere, ut litterarum omisso studio, in quo profecerat competenter, ad artem fabrilem descenderat addiscendam, in qua provectus biennio iam elapso tribus fuit miraculis a domino revocatus. 9. Nam ferrum vivum,[76] ut fervens exiverat de fabrica magistrali, altitonantis[77] iussu prosiluit et volavit et rediens velociter cecidit[g] super terram et per spaltum decoxit nudum pedem ipsius taliter et combuxit, quod incepit continuo claudicare. 10. Iterum vero, dum secundario idem ferrum calefieret ab eodem et super incudem forti maleo tunderetur, ardens squama eius pupillam oculi subintravit,[78] que lumen turbavit nimio laborantis. 11. Et cur verbis immoramur! Tertia vice recepit eiusdem ferventis ferri vulnera lingua sua; et sic triplici dolore afflictus revelationem misterii recognovit, et in se reversus plorans humiliter cepit

---

[69] Act. 9, 5; 26, 14.

[70] The affected separation of Tullius from Cicero occurs also in other writings of Guido Faba, cf. *supra*, n. 25.

[71] Matth. 12, 42.

[72] Is. 44, 13.

[73] Luc. 1, 15.

[74] "...eius stili... magisterium" is a phrase used by Thomas of Capua, *Ars dictandi*, ed. E. Heller (*supra*, n. 2), 11.

[75] Micha, 5, 2; Matth. 2, 6; cf. *MGH, Const.* II, 304, No. 219, and *supra*, n. 31.

[76] "Ferrum vivum," here, has a double meaning; it is not only "natural, unforged" iron but also "alive" because it hops and leaps about as though it were alive.

[77] "Altitonans" was obviously Bolognese school tradition; cf. Buoncompagno, *Rhetorica novissima*, V, 3, 4, ed. Gaudenzi (*supra*, n. 6), 262; Boto da Vigevano, *Liber de floribus* (a pupil of Buoncompagno), ed. Bertoni, *Il Duecento* (Milan, s. a.), 278: "Si michi altitonans Jhesus Christus centum linguas ferreas tribuisset...." In the

Renaissance these Jovian attributes of Christ, not rare in early Christianity (see, e.g., F. J. Dölger, *Antike und Christentum*, III [1932], 227f), became almost daily bread among the Humanists; see, for instance, the very charming and classicistic Sapphic ode of Lyppus Florentinus, recited before the Pope:

> Alma quae coelo resides sereno
> Virgo, quae trini es genetrix tonantis,
> Audias nostras modulante voces
> Carmine plectro...

Cf. V. Cian, "Per Bernardo Bembo," *Giornale storico della letteratura italiana*, XXXI (1898), 78f, n. 3.

[78] Act. 9, 18: "ceciderunt ab oculis eius tamquam squamae."

---

d) conant *lacuna* ni *c*.

e) magistro *c*.

f) cunabilis *corr. ex* gunabilis *c*.

g) cecicidit *c*.

coram omnibus protestari, quod eum hoc trino signo sancta trinitas a tali officio revocabat. 12. Demum sic contritus et flagellatus ad male dimissum studium rediit festinanter, de quo magistri Bononie pariter et scolares gaudium habuerunt dicentes: "Ovis que perierat est inventa et qui mortuus fuerat nunc revixit."[79] 13. Ad hec, cum in studio die noctuque sollicite laboraret, attenuatum est corpus eius; et ossa cum pelle consilium inierunt, quibus spiritus anxietas et animi maceratio sociata pro carnis receptione communiter decreverunt, quod dimissis litteris cerdonum sollatio iungeretur, qui per putredinem caninam, quibus pelles aptantur que postea dentibus extenduntur, et per puncturam subule[h] malum cognitum evitavit. 14. Tandem ad tabellionatus artem recurrens in utraque curia magister nominari promeruit magistrorum;[80] sed cum talis actus angustia non modica premeretur tam pro fatigationibus quam pro inimicitiis acquisitis, quia declinare nolebat ad dexteram vel sinistram, ad dominum refugium est conversus annis duobus pro scriba domini bononiensis episcopi commorando. 15. Verum quia in curiis non saluti animarum sed temporalibus commodis providetur, nolens in carnis truffis baruffis vel mendaciis commorari de libertate pristina recordatur, sicut placuit omnium conditori, curam capelle sancti Michaelis suscepit, in qua feliciter ad sacerdotalis ordinis officium est promotus, et rehedificans ecclesiam ipsam cum domibus ruinosis post vicinorum multas persecutiones et scandala, que substinuit patienter, quorum partem clerici fovebant civitatis latenter, novum templum fabricari fecit archangelo Michaeli, cuius preceptionibus et mandatis ystoriam hanc descripsit, que Nova rota meruit appellari, quia, sicut novitate status cuiuslibet diversimode variatur, ita per mutationem prefatam de minori ascendit ordine ad maiorem sedensque in rote solio cathedratus alas duas, quas ab angelo habuit, retinet manu dextra, in una quarum omnium epistolarum vitia resecantur et in alia continentur regule, que faciunt ad scientiam dictaminis et ornatum, [ne][i] sine quibus alis, sicut nec absque pennis aves volare possunt,[81] aliqui properent ad volatum, quia sine remedio ruerent, qui ad hec prohibita festinarent. Explicit rota.

[79] Luc. 15, 24.

[80] On his mastery of *dictamen* and law *in utraque curia* cf. *supra*, n. 20 and n. 46.

[81] Cf. Thomas of Capua, *Ars dictandi*, ed. Heller, 10: "volare volentes antequam pennas idoneas produxerint ad volandum." See also *ibid.*, 11, note *a*, for a similar phrasing ("quin ymmo et volare conantes prius quam pennas produxerint ad volandum") in the *Formularium* of Arnold of Protzan, in *Codex diplomaticus Silesiae*, V (Breslau, 1862), 2.

h) subole *c*.
i) *add. ed.*

PETRUS DE VINEA IN ENGLAND

Die geschichte der englischen Kanzlei ist noch nicht geschrieben. Von der Chancery als Verwaltungsbehörde wird man sich zwar dank zahlreicher neuerer Arbeiten,[1] wenn auch nicht ohne einige Mühe, ein Bild machen können. Über die Kanzlei als *scriptorium*[2] aber wissen wir noch herzlich wenig und womöglich noch weniger über die Entwicklung des lateinischen Sprachstils, dessen sich die englischen Kanzlisten während der dem Eroberungszeitalter folgenden Jahrhunderte in ihren Schriftstücken bedienten. Das gilt weithin zwar auch für die Entwicklung des Sprachstils anderer Länder. Aber wenigstens die Urkundensprache der päpstlichen, der kaiserlichen, der französischen Kanzlei wie der Kanzleien italienischer Städte und deutscher Territorialherren sind mehrfach zum Gegenstand von Untersuchungen gemacht worden, und zumindest glaubt man, die großen Linien der Stilentwicklung schon erkennen zu können. Für England fehlen jedoch selbst entsprechende Vorarbeiten; auch vermittelt uns keine englische Diplomatik eine Kenntnis etwa von Ursprung und Artung des anglo-normannischen und angiovinischen Kanzleistils — schon deshalb nicht, weil es bis heute eine englische Diplomatik nicht gibt.[3] Hier klafft eine empfindliche Lücke.

Umso dankbarer wird man es daher begrüßen, daß jetzt für einen wichtigen Teilbezirk kanzleisprachlicher und damit sprachgeschichtlicher Forschung wenigstens eine erste Bresche gelegt ist durch die gut fundierte Untersuchung von N. Denholm-Young

Reprinted, with permission, from *Mitteilungen des Österreichischen Instituts für Geschichtsforschung*, LI (1937), 43–88.

[1] T. F. Tout, *Chapters in the Administrative History of Mediaeval England* (Manchester, 1920–33) bietet I, 127ff einen knappen Überblick, neben zahllosen wertvollen Einblicken an den verschiedensten Stellen seines großen Werkes. Wichtige Informationen bei Henry C. Maxwell Lyte, *Historical Notes on the Use of the Great Seal of England* (London, 1926). Für die frühe normannische Periode vgl. H. W. C. Davis, *Regesta Regum Anglo-Normannorum* (Oxford, 1913), I, Einl., XIff und C. H. Haskins, *Norman Institutions* (Cambridge, Mass., 1918), 52ff und *passim*; ferner für Heinrich I.: J. H. Round, "Bernard, the King's Scribe," *Engl. Hist. Rev.*, XIV (1899), 417–430; für Heinrich II.: L. Delisle, *Recueil des Actes de Henri II concernant la France* (Paris, 1909), Einl.-Bd. 88ff; für Heinrich III.: F. M. Powicke, "The Chancery during the Minority of Henry III," *Engl. Hist. Rev.*, XXIII (1908), 220–235; L. B. Dibben, "Chancellor and Keeper of the Seal in Henry III's Reign," *Engl. Hist. Rev.*, XXVII (1912), 39–51; für Eduard II.: T. F. Tout, *The Place of the Reign of Edward II in English History* (Manchester 1914), S. 319ff; eine umfassendere Arbeit liegt vor für Eduard III. von B. Wilkinson, *The Chancery under Edward III* (Manchester, 1929); für die vornormannische Zeit vgl. jetzt die umfangreiche Untersuchung von Richard Drögereit, "Gab es eine angelsächsische Königskanzlei?" *Arch. f. Urk.-Forsch.*, XIII (1935), 335–436.

[2] Das *scriptorium* als königliches Sekretariat stand ursprünglich mit dem Amte des Kanzlers in einem sehr viel lockereren Zusammenhang, als dies auf dem Kontinent üblich war. Der Kanzler, bis Thomas Becket ein niederer Kleriker, war vor allem Siegelbewahrer. Die Schreibstube hingegen unterstand dem *magister scriptorii*, der als *clericus qui praeest scriptorio* zeitweilig auch den Titel eines Protonotars führte und als solcher dem Kanzler untergeordnet wurde. Der Name *scriptorium* blieb der Kanzlei bis zur Zeit König Johanns eigentümlich; vgl. Tout, *Chapters*, I, 131, 134; Hubert Hall, *Studies in English Official Historical Documents* (Cambridge, 1908), 374ff; Wilkinson, a. a. O., 189ff.

[3] M. Déprez, *Études de diplomatique anglaise. Le sceau privé, le sceau secret, le signet* (Paris, 1908), bietet keinen Ersatz und verfolgt andere Ziele.

über den "Cursus in England."[4] Allerdings handelt es sich bei dem Gebrauch des Kursus in der englischen Kanzlei — das zeigt die Untersuchung schlagend — eher um ein der englischen Kanzlei gerade nicht eigentümliches Element, um ein Pfropfreis, das in England weit weniger als in anderen Ländern mit dem Stamm wirklich verwuchs. Die ganze hochentwickelte Kunst des lateinischen Sprachstils, welche Italien, Frankreich, Deutschland und andere Länder des Kontinents seit dem 12. Jahrhundert pflegten, fand in England nur spärlich, in die englische Kanzlei nur spät Eingang. Vor allem ist festzustellen, daß die Kunst des Sagens und das Sagen als Kunst in die Schreibstuben Englands niemals mit solcher Macht einbrach, daß — wie zumal in Italien — die Kanzlisten gleichsam nicht mehr anders konnten, als ihre Sätze mit sorgfältig kadenzierten Schlüssen ausklingen zu lassen und ihre Briefe nach ganz bestimmten ästhetischen Regeln aufzubauen. Auch der schöne Ehrgeiz nach sprachlicher Überlegenheit der eigenen über andere Kanzleien, der im Süden förmliche Kanzlei- oder Dictatorenwettkämpfe hervorrief,[5] blieb England fremd. Man wußte dort von solchem Ehrgeiz nichts, und die Regeln der *ars dictandi* zu beobachten, das Schriftstück durch eine prunkvolle oder auch gedankenschwere Arenga einzuleiten, es nach festen Gesetzen zu gliedern und aus ihm der Form nach jeweils ein kleines Kunstwerk zu gestalten: das alles machte in den Schreiben der englischen Kanzlei niemals den Kern aus, blieb in England fast immer ein entbehrliches Beiwerk.[6]

Dementsprechend ist eine eigene englische Literatur der *ars dictandi* nur in bescheidenstem Umfang hervorgebracht worden, und bedeutendere sowie einigermaßen wirksame Werke dieser Art entstanden nur in unverhältnismäßig später Zeit. Bis zum Ende des 14. Jahrhunderts begnügte man sich, derartige Werke vom Kontinent zu beziehen, aus Frankreich und aus Italien.[7] Und ebenso auffallend ist es, daß ein Unterricht im *dictamen* an Englands ältester Universität, in Oxford, erst spät nachzuweisen ist. Das mag an der Überlieferung liegen, da die frühesten erhaltenen Statuten von Oxford erst aus der Zeit um 1350 stammen, und sicherlich konnte man auch früher schon in England das *dictamen* erlernen.[8] Aber es bleibt doch bezeichnend, mit welcher Beiläufigkeit diese ganze

---

[4] "The Cursus in England," in *Oxford Essays in Mediaeval History presented to H. E. Salter* (Oxford, 1934), 68-103. Meine im folgenden vorgetragenen einleitenden Bemerkungen basieren vielfach, auch wo dies nicht eigens gesagt wird, auf der Arbeit von Denholm-Young, dem ich persönlich für zahlreiche Hinweise zu Dank verpflichtet bin.

[5] Dieser Ehrgeiz ist gleich bei der Einführung des Kursus an der päpstlichen Kanzlei anzutreffen, vgl. etwa die berühmte Stelle im *Liber Pontificalis* in der Vita Gelasius' II. (ed. Jos. M. March [Barcelona, 1925], 163), wo die Berufung des Johannes von Gaëta an die päpstliche Kanzlei damit begründet wird, *ut per eloquentiam sibi a Domino traditam antiqui leporis et elegantie stilum, in sede apostolica iam pene deperditum... reformaret ac leoninum cursum lucida velocitate reduceret.* Vgl. ferner die Bemerkung Gregors IX. über die *dictoris facunditas* in dem Schreiben Friedrichs II.: Huillard-Bréholles, *Historia diplomatica Friderici Secundi* (Paris, 1852–61), IV, 444, und C. H. Haskins, *Mediaeval Culture* (Oxford, 1929), 127; dazu die Bemerkungen Friedrichs II. über den Kanzleikrieg:

Winkelmann, *Acta Imp.*, I, 261, n. 286, sowie die allgemeinen Bemerkungen bei Niese, *HZ*, CVIII (1913), 531; F. Gräfe, *Die Publizistik in der letzten Epoche Friedrichs II.* (Heidelberg, 1909), 3ff; O. Vehse, *Die amtliche Propaganda in der Staatskunst K. Friedrichs II.* (München, 1929), 168ff.

[6] Daß die *scriptores* der englischen Kanzlei gelegentlich auch *dictatores* genannt werden, z. B. *Cal. Pat. R. 1247–58*, S. 424, 549, besagt noch nichts über eine Kenntnis des kunstgerechten *dictamen*, wie Tout, *Chapters*, I, 133 Anm. 1 anzunehmen scheint; überdies sind die a. a. O. genannten gascognischen *dictatores* lediglich Bevollmächtigte für die Friedensverhandlungen gewesen.

[7] Vgl. die Listen der in England vorhandenen Hss. von *artes dictandi* bei Denholm-Young, 92ff; s. auch 73ff.

[8] Daß man innerhalb der Oxforder Artistenfakultät um 1254 den römischen Kurialstil und den Kursus soweit beherrschte, um eine päpstliche Bulle sachgemäß fälschen zu können, zeigt die Bulle *Dolentes* Papst Innocenz' IV.; vgl. Matth. Paris, ed. Luard, VI, 293, n. 146; Digard, *Bibl. Écol. Chart.*, LI (1890), 389, 408ff. In den Schriftstücken der Universitätskanzlei von Oxford begegnet der Kursus

Disziplin in Oxford behandelt wurde und daß dort die *ars dictandi* einen Teil des Unter-
richts nur der Grammatik, nicht wie in Italien der Rhetorik und Rechtskunde ausmachte.[9] Um der sprachlichen Korrektheit willen, so scheint es, nicht um die Wirksamkeit der Sprache zu steigern, wurde in Oxford das *dictamen* gelehrt.

Vergebens wird man daher in Englands königlichen Erlassen und Schreiben, vergebens auch in der Mehrzahl der privaten Korrespondenzen[10] bis tief ins 13. Jahrhundert
hinein jenen durchgängigen Gebrauch der Satzrhythmik, jenes wohldurchdachte Aus-
wiegen der Satz- und Briefteile, das ganze pomphafte rauschende Schreiten der feierlichen lateinischen Prosa suchen, durch die einem die Schreiben ganz besonders der
italienischen Stilisten Bewunderung abnötigen. Vergebens wird man aber auch die
etwas weniger anspruchsvolle und weniger pathetische, gleichsam klassizistischere und
grazilere Handhabung der Sprache suchen, wie sie in Orléans und in Tours, den Stätten
des *stilus gallicus* im Gegensatz zum *cursus curie romane*, gepflegt wurde.[11] Das offizielle
England blieb von dieser Bewegung zunächst unberührt, das sonstige England wenig berührt, und als man sich dann die Lehren der *ars dictandi* und des Kursus allmählich doch
anzueignen, als der in ihnen geforderte Sprachstil die Kanzleien der Eduarde doch end-
lich zu beeinflussen begann, da war diese Spätblüte mittelalterlicher Latinität in dem
dafür maßgebenden Land, in Italien, bereits am Verblättern. Seit den 80er Jahren des
13. Jahrhunderts wurde die Allherrschaft des Kursus an der päpstlichen Kurie durch-
brochen,[12] und die endgültige Preisgabe des *stilus grandiloquus* oder *stilus supremus*, wie ihn
noch Dante in seinen Briefen schrieb, setzte im Grunde bereits mit Petrarca ein, der —
obwohl der mittelalterlichen Briefkunst noch tributär — dennoch schon einem ganz
anderen Stilideal zustrebte. Die Briefe werden intimer, dienen der privaten, nicht
der öffentlichen Mitteilung. Die Stimme senkt sich, oft bis zum Flüstern. Die veränderte
Rhythmik des Lebens veränderte eben auch die Rhythmik der Sprache, was sprach-
technisch darin zum Ausdruck kam, daß — auch in der lateinischen Dichtung — die
Akzentbewertung mittelalterlichen Stils von den Humanisten verworfen wurde zugunsten der, freilich niemals erstorbenen, quantitativen Silbenbewertung der Antike.
Eine Generation nach Petrarca waren die Satzschlüsse bei den Modernen bereits ver-
pönt, und wie im Bereiche der Poesie die Rhythmik der Metrik wich, so vergaß man im
profanen Bereich überhaupt die Möglichkeit einer rhythmischen Prosa.[13]

---

nicht vor 1288, vgl. H. Anstey, *Munimenta academica* (London, 1868), I, 43ff; besser noch in dem Schreiben des
Kanzlers Simon (1293), ebda. I, 62f.

[9] Denholm-Young, 73. Es ist keine Frage, daß nach
dem Statut von Oxford (Strickland Gibson, *Statuta
antiqua Universitatis Oxoniensis* [Oxford, 1931], 20) niemand
Grammatik lehren durfte, *nisi prius fuerit examinatus de
modo versificandi et dictandi et de auctoribus et partibus..*, eine
Bestimmung, die noch öfters wiederholt wird; vgl. etwa
das Statut von ca. 1380 (ebda. S. 169). Dennoch bin ich
im Zweifel, ob hier wirklich jene durch die Summen der
ars dictandi vermittelte hohe Stilkunst gemeint ist; denn
de modo versificandi et dictandi wurde zu allen Zeiten des
Mittelalters, bekanntlich auch zur Zeit Karls d. Gr. ge-
prüft und unterrichtet, es fragt sich nur wie.

[10] Die Briefe eines Grosseteste nennt Denholm-

Young, S. 84 mit Recht "shockingly unrythmical"; erst
John Peckham, der freilich einen Bolognesen in seiner
Kanzlei beschäftigte, schreibt einen Kurialstil.

[11] Vgl. die Literatur bei Haskins, *Mediaeval Culture*,
190, Anm. 1.

[12] N. Valois, *Bibl. Écol. Chart.*, XLII (1931), 266f;
Bresslau, *Urkundenlehre* II, 1, (2. A.), 368f.

[13] Interessant ist in diesem Zusammenhang die Bemerkung Salutatis, welche A. C. Clark, *The Cursus in
Mediaeval and Vulgar Latin* (Oxford, 1914), S. 21 anführt:
*Cum omnia michi placeant, super omnia michi gratum est quod
more fratrum ille sermo rythmica lubricatione non ludit. Non est
ibi syllabarum equalitas que sine dinumeratione fieri non solet,
non sunt ibi clausule que similiter desinant et cadant...*, doch
dürfte hier mehr an Isokolie und Reimprosa gedacht sein
als an den Kursus.

Die eigentliche Aufnahme der Stilkunst in England, wie fragmentarisch auch immer, erfolgte also erst zu einer Zeit, als der Höhepunkt bereits erreicht, wenn nicht schon überschritten war, als außerdem die Vulgärsprachen — in England bekanntlich das Französische, nicht das Englische[14] — in den Kanzleien bereits Verwendung fanden. Das alles mag dann zusammengewirkt haben, um zu verhindern, daß der hohe Stil in England noch in ähnlicher Weise Allgemeingut werden konnte wie etwa in Italien.

Damit ist allerdings noch nicht die andere Frage beantwortet, weshalb wohl das humanistischen Regungen doch stets offene England sich überhaupt nur so langsam und zögernd dieser literarischen Mode erschloß, die im 12. und 13. Jahrhundert einen so wesentlichen Bestandteil der abendländischen Geisteskultur ausmachte, und weshalb dort wohl die frühhumanistische Kunst des hohen Briefstils fast nur widerwillig nachgeahmt wurde. Es ist nicht ganz leicht, hierfür Gründe anzugeben. Ganz gewiß darf man nicht Unkenntnis verantwortlich machen. Jedes päpstliche Schreiben seit der Mitte, jedes kaiserliche seit dem Ende des 12. Jahrhunderts wies ja zumindest den Gebrauch des Kursus auf,[15] und die theoretische Lehre des *dictamen* drang selbstverständlich auch nach England, obwohl nicht in ihrer frühen Form.

Die erste Periode der *ars dictandi* mit ihrem Zentrum in Bologna und einem Nebenzentrum in Pavia sah als ihre Vertreter Grammatiker und Legisten, welche die ihnen offenbar aus der Praxis bekannten Regeln des Briefaufbaues und gewisse Briefformeln zusammenstellten, dabei jedoch den außerhalb der Kurie erst wenig gebräuchlichen Kursus, den sie selbst wohl kaum anwandten, auch in ihren Schriften nicht lehrten. Das gilt auch von Alberich von Monte Cassino, dem ältesten uns bekannten Verfasser eines Lehrbuches der *ars dictandi*, dem man auf dem Weg über seinen Schüler Johann von Gaeta die Einführung des Kursus in der päpstlichen Kanzlei zuschreibt.[16] In dieser ersten Epoche der Stilkunst, während welcher von Italien aus die Lehre wie die Lehrbücher sich über Frankreich und, wiewohl langsamer, auch über Deutschland verbreiteten, wurde England, das zumindest in den Tagen Lanfrancs und Anselms in Canterbury selbst eine hohe Stufe des Briefstils erreicht hatte, anscheinend noch nicht getroffen. Das läßt auch der an sich zwar wenig beweisende Mangel an englischen Handschriften von Autoren dieser Epoche vermuten.[17]

Die Bekanntschaft mit der *ars dictandi* wurde England vielmehr erst durch Frankreich vermittelt, das in der zweiten Epoche seit der Mitte des XII. Jahrhunderts die in Italien

[14] Immerhin gibt es auch eine Urkunde Heinrichs III. von 1258 in englischer Sprache, vgl. Rymer, I, 378, und Maitland, "Outlines of English Legal History," in *Collected Papers*, II, 436.

[15] In anderer Beziehung wußte die englische Kanzlei sehr wohl von der päpstlichen zu lernen, vgl. Denholm-Young, 68, n. 2, für den kurialen Einfluß auf die englische Schrift.

[16] Haskins, a. a. O., 172, u. Albericus Casinensis in *Casinensia* (Monte Cassino, 1929), 115ff; die hier vorgetragene Periodeneinteilung folgt weitgehend den durch Haskins vermittelten Erkenntnissen.

[17] Hss. dieser ersten Epoche fehlen in England nicht vollständig. So ist eine fälschlich dem Henricus Franci-

gena zugeschriebene *Aurea gemma* in einer Hs. des 12. Jhdts. im Oxford, Bodl. Laud. Misc. 569, gemeinsam mit Auszügen des Bernhard von Bologna, zusammengestellt für den Gebrauch von Cisterziensern, erhalten (vgl. Haskins, 178f. 182), und eine andere *Aurea gemma*, die wirklich Francigenas Werk ist, findet sich — nach freundlicher Mitteilung von Dr. C. Erdmann, dem ich für mehrfache Hinweise Dank schulde — in einer Pariser Hs., Bibl. Nat. lat. 2904, die englischen Ursprungs ist und noch dem 12. Jhdt. angehört. Das Vorkommen der zu diesem Traktat gehörenden Musterbriefe in einer Hs. des Richard von Bury aus dem 14. Jhdt. (s. u. Anm. 110) ist hier nicht von Interesse.

empfangenen Anregungen in eignen Schulen, in Orléans und Tours, weiter entwickelte, zeitweilig sogar die Führung an sich nahm und auf Deutschland wie rückwirkend auch auf Italien und auf das geistig von Frankreich stark abhängige normannische Sizilien entscheidenden Einfluß gewann.[18] Von den Italienern unterschieden sich die französischen Schulen dadurch, daß das juristische Element ganz zurücktrat, daß die Lehre außerhalb von Kanzlei und Grammatikschule auch von den philosophierenden Literaten rezipiert wurde[19] — Alanus von Lille ist ein klassischer Vertreter dieser Richtung, aber auch einzelne Schüler von Chartres — und daß hier der Kursus nicht nur Anwendung fand, sondern geradezu als Lehre in die *artes dictandi* eingefügt wurde. In Frankreich erlernten jetzt einzelne Engländer wie Johann von Salisbury die Kunst des *dictamen*, und mit Peter von Blois hätte die Stilkunst wohl auch in den Kanzleien Englands Wurzel schlagen können. Denn obwohl er nicht Engländer von Geburt war, so lag doch sein Hauptwirkungsfeld als Kanzler des Erzbischofs von Canterbury in England, und gerade weil er in Palermo, Rom, Bologna und Tours in gleicher Weise heimisch war, wäre Peter von Blois wie kein anderer geeignet gewesen, hier den Mittler zu spielen. Das geschah jedoch nicht. Wie weit auch seine Briefe, deren Auswirkung leider noch nicht hinreichend untersucht ist, damals verbreitet waren: seine kleine Lehrschrift der *ars dictandi* fand in England keinen Anklang. Nur in einer einzigen Cambridger Handschrift ist sie uns erhalten.[20] Gewiß war einer der berühmtesten Sprachmeister der Zeit um 1200 der Herkunft nach Engländer: Gottfried von Vinsauf. Aber sein Wirkungsfeld wie das so vieler seiner literarischen Landsleute — Johann von Garlandia gehört etwa zu ihnen — lag in Frankreich, und wenn auch seine Werke in der Heimat früh bekannt und durch seinen englischen Zeitgenossen Gervasius von Melkley (um 1208) weiter verbreitet wurden, so galt doch das Interesse nicht seiner *Ars dictaminis*, sondern seinen Lehren der *Ars versificatoria*.[21]

So blieb auch die zweite Epoche ohne eigentliche Wirkung auf den englischen Prosastil. Die Schulen Frankreichs vermittelten wohl einige Kenntnis des *dictamen;* auf den englischen Kanzleistil aber übten sie keinen erkennbaren Einfluß aus. Überhaupt sollten für England, soweit es sich dem hohen Stil erschloß, nur die Werke der dritten Epoche fruchtbar werden, also die der Bologneser und der süditalienischen Schule des 13. Jahrhunderts. Man läßt diese dritte Epoche gewöhnlich mit Albert von Morra und Transmundus beginnen. Es ist die Frage, wieweit das richtig ist. Denn Transmundus dürfte Franzose gewesen sein und sein Verhältnis zu den italienischen Diktatoren bedarf noch der Klärung.[22] Albert von Morra aber gibt nur die Regeln für den an der Kurie gebrauchten Kursus, und über seinen eigenen Briefstil oder gar über dessen Verwandtschaft mit dem der Bologneser und Capuaner Schule wissen wir schlechterdings nichts. Richtig ist nur das eine, daß diese beiden dazu beigetragen haben, die Kursuslehre — die

---

[18] Haskins, 190ff.

[19] Niese, *HZ*, CVIII (1913), 484.

[20] Auszüge bei Langlois, *Not. et Extr.*, XXXIV: 2 (1895), 23ff; E. S. Cohn, "The Manuscript Evidence for the Letters of Peter of Blois," *Engl. Hist. Rev.*, XLI (1926), 43ff.

[21] Denholm-Young, 72ff; S. 93 ein Hinweis auf die Verbindung des Gervasius von Melkley mit Alanus von Lille.

[22] Vgl. W. Holtzmann, *Neues Archiv*, XLVIII (1930), 412, Anm. 1; E. Heller, *S.-B. Akad. Heidelberg*, 1929, H. 4, Exkurs.

kuriale der eine, die französische der andere — nunmehr zum Allgemeingut auch der italienischen Diktatoren zu machen, die sich ihrerseits wieder vorwiegend dem Notarsberuf zuwandten. Die in Frankreich vervollkommnete Stilkunst und die kurialen Gepflogenheiten trafen hier also zusammen mit dem Notariat, das heißt: mit der Juristerei.

Damit ist der Schlüssel zu der außerordentlich großen Wirkung der italienischen Schulen des 13. Jahrhunderts gegeben. Während die *ars dictandi* in Frankreich im Literarischen wurzelte und vom Literarischen her neben Dichtung, Philosophie und Briefstil auch die Urkundensprache durchdrang, fand sie in Italien ihren Schwerpunkt in der Jurisprudenz, ging dadurch ein in die Sphäre des Staates, eroberte sich hier die Kanzleien auch der kleineren, ja kleinsten Gestirne und entfaltete von der juristisch durchgebildeten Kanzlei aus ihre ungeheuere Wirkkraft — man kann sagen: in allen Ländern Europas. Dem konnte sich auch England nicht ganz entziehen. Seit der zweiten Hälfte des 13. Jahrhunderts fanden Thomas von Capua, Buoncompagno, Guido Faba, Petrus de Vinea, Laurentius von Aquileja in England Eingang, und auf diese Meister geht mittelbar oder unmittelbar alles zurück, was man dort im *stilus supremus* hervorgebracht hat.

Allein, gerade die eigentümliche Verbindung von Juristerei und *ars dictandi* — kennzeichnend schon für die erste, mehr aber noch für die dritte Epoche der Stilkunst — setzte ihrem Eindringen in die englische Königskanzlei von vornherein gewisse Grenzen. Denholm-Young macht darauf aufmerksam,[23] daß die englische Kanzlei wie auch die anderen englischen Behörden im 12. Jahrhundert bereits einen so ausgeprägt eignen bürokratischen Stil, so eigentümliche Formen und feste Formeln entwickelt hatten, daß man von ihnen innerhalb des eignen Landes nicht mehr abweichen oder durch Einfügung des Kursus eine Änderung herbeiführen mochte. Das ist ganz gewiß richtig. Und weiter: der englische Verwaltungsapparat, der seit der gleichen frühen Zeit die beweiskräftige Registrierung aller Schriftstücke vorsah, würde für England auch jenes bekannte Argument des Peter von Blois hinfällig werden lassen, der als Zweck der Einführung des Kursus an der päpstlichen Kanzlei die Verhütung von Fälschungen angegeben hatte.[24]

Aber es ist, wie mir scheint, nicht allein die Eigentümlichkeit der englischen Verwaltung, sondern mindestens ebenso die eigenartige Gestaltung des englischen Rechtswesens dafür verantwortlich zu machen, daß in England von Anfang an der Gebrauch des *stilus supremus* ein auf wenige Gelegenheiten beschränkter Luxus blieb. Johann von Bologna, Notar des Erzbischofs von Canterbury Johann Peckham, stellt in seiner um 1285 abgefaßten und seinem Herrn gewidmeten Schrift eine in diesem Zusammenhang recht interessante Betrachtung an. Er spricht sich über die weite Verbreitung von Rechtsinstrumenten in Italien aus und begründet sie damit, daß die Italiener als vorsichtige Leute gleichsam von allem, was sie untereinander abmachten, auch ein öffentliches Instrument zu besitzen wünschten. Englischen Gewohnheiten aber laufe das zuwider, da die Engländer nur im Falle wirklicher Erfordernis und darum nur sehr selten ein

---

[23] A. a. O. 85: "by the time the Cursus was becoming fashionable in England, chancery phraseology had become stereotyped."

[24] Bresslau, *Urkundenlehre*, II, 1 (2. A.), 365 Anm. 5.

Rechtsinstrument verlangten.[25] Das ist nun eine der rein völkerpsychologischen Begründungen, wie sie damals Mode wurden,[26] und als solche zweifellos ebenso zutreffend und auch heute noch gültig wie interessant. An dem eigentlichen Problem aber geht diese Begründung dennoch vorbei. Nicht die englische Vertrauensseligkeit machte Notariats- und Rechtsinstrumente unnötig, sondern die *consuetudines* des englischen Rechts kannten nicht die gleichen Notwendigkeiten wie die römischen Rechtsgepflogenheiten, ja sperrten sich gegen die den Italienern geläufigen Rechtsformen. Damit aber wird ein sehr wesentliches Moment in unsere Betrachtungen einbezogen. Denn bei aller selbstzwecklichen Freude an der schönen Sprachform[27] hatten doch gerade die italienischen Stilisten von jeher betont, daß ihre Kunst nicht nur ästhetischem, sondern auch praktischem Zwecke diente, und zumal seit dem beginnenden 13. Jahrhundert hatten die stilistischen Handbücher ausgesprochenermaßen den Zweck, Notare in der Abfassung juristischer Dokumente zu unterweisen[28] — jene bekannte Wandlung der *ars dictandi* zur *ars notaria*,[29] die ja schon längst abgeschlossen war, als 1285 Johann von Bologna seine Schrift dem Erzbischof von Canterbury überreichte. Auch diese Schrift hatte zum Ziel, Notare in die Geheimnisse juristischer Geschäftsgänge einzuweihen.[30]

Es ist leider niemals hinreichend untersucht worden, welchen Einfluß Sprache und Stil nicht allein der Bibel, der Kirchenväter, der Liturgie und der lateinischen *auctores* sondern auch des römischen Rechts auf die Diktate der italienischen Stilisten gehabt haben, obwohl bisweilen — zumal bei der Capuaner Schule — dieser Einfluß förmlich mit Händen zu greifen ist.[31] Aber auch ohne eine solche Untersuchung kann, wie gesagt, über die Zusammenhänge von Rechtsstudium und *ars dictandi*, zumindest in Italien,

[25] Seine *Summa* bei Rockinger, "Briefsteller und Formelbücher des XI. bis XIV. Jhdts.," *Quellen u. Erörterungen*, IX (1906), 595ff, besonders 604: *Licet tractatus instrumentorum in Ytalie partibus necessarie sit diffusus, pro eo quod Ytalici tamquam cauti quasi de omni eo quod ad invicem contrahunt, habere volunt publicum instrumentum, quod quasi contrarium est in Anglicis, videlicet quod nisi necessarium esset non nisi rarissime petitur instrumentum.* Vgl. Denholm-Young, 85.

[26] Die im XIII. Jhdt. einsetzende und dann in der Renaissance einen breiteren Raum einnehmende Völkerpsychologie ist nicht zu verwechseln mit jenen stereotypen Urteilen des einen Volkes über das andere, wie sie z. B. Kern, *HZ*, CVIII (1913), 237ff für den Deutschen, Langlois, *Rev. Hist.*, LII (1893), 313ff für den Engländer in französischer Auffassung zeigen. Gemeint sind hier die sehr viel tiefer gehenden Betrachtungen, die etwa Friedrich II. über die Verschiedenheiten von Italienern und Deutschen anstellt und über die Petrarca, *Epp. Sen.*, II, 1 (jetzt bei Burdach, *Petrarcas Briefwechsel mit deutschen Zeitgenossen*, 253, n. XIV) berichtet; ein anderes Beispiel: Kantorowicz, *K. Friedrich II.*, 379; auch das Urteil des Guido v. d. Sabina (Clemens IV.) über die Römer mag hierhin gehören: *Reg. Imp.*, V, n. 9482.

[27] Vgl. etwa Buoncompagnos Äußerung: *cursus vocatur, quia cum artificialiter dictiones locantur, currere sonitu delectabili per aures videntur cum beneplacito auditorum;* Ch. Thurot, *Notices et Extraits*, XX: 2 (1868), S. 480; ein paar weitere Beispiele bei E. Norden, *Antike Kunstprosa*, II, 959f.

[28] Ein paar Bemerkungen bei Rockinger, *Über Formelbücher vom 13.–16. Jhdt.* (München, 1855), 38f, 103ff. Allgemein vgl. Fitting, *Die Anfänge der Rechtsschule zu Bologna* (Berlin und Leipzig, 1888), 15ff, 79ff; L. J. Paetow, *The Arts Course at Mediaeval Universities* (Urbana, 1910), 71f. Die Schrift des Albert von Morra war betitelt: *Forma dictandi, quam Rome notarios docuit mag. Albertus qui et Gregorius VIII. papa.* Vgl. auch neben zahlreichen anderen Beispielen das *Prooemium* der *Ars dictandi* des Thomas von Capua: E. Heller, *S.-B. Heidelberg*, 1929, 51.

[29] Bresslau, a. a. O., 256; Paetow, 82ff.

[30] S. u. Anm. 33.

[31] Als Beispiel diene etwa Vineas Brief an die Römer: BF (*Reg. Imp.*, V.), 2160 oder der Stiftungsbrief für die Universität Neapel: BF, 1737, der sich gedanklich eng an Azo im *Prooemium* zu seinem Institutionenkommentar anschließt, vgl. Niese, *HZ*, CVIII (1913), 521, Anm. 2, auch 517. Azo selbst zeigt die Verbindung von Stilkunst und Rechtssprache gerade in diesem *Prooemium* ganz vorbildlich; er wirkte damit wiederum nach England hinüber, wo um die Mitte des 13. Jhdts. Bracton ihn verwendet; vgl. den Paralleldruck von Bracton und Azo bei F. W. Maitland, *Select Passages from the Works of Bracton and Azo* (Selden Society, VIII; London, 1895). Ein paar gute Bemerkungen bei Rockinger, *S.-B. München*, phil. hist. Kl., 1861, 119ff; Rashdall, *Universities of Europe in the Middle Ages*, I² (Oxford, 1936), 109f, 124f; vgl. auch O. Vehse, *Die amtliche Propaganda . . . Friedrichs II*, 159f; G. Ladner, *MÖIG.*, Erg.-Bd., XII (1932) 166, Anm. 1.

kein Zweifel bestehen.[31a] In England hingegen haben innerhalb der Sphärc des weltlichen Rechts derartige Zusammenhänge nicht bestanden, im Gegenteil: wie sich die englischen *consuetudines* gegen die römischen — civilen, aber auch kanonistischen — Rechtsformen und Rechtsbräuche sperrten, so sperrten sie sich auch in hohem Maße gegen die römische Rechtssprache und die römischen Rechtsbegriffe, die man in England großenteils unanwendbar fand oder entbehrlich glaubte. Studium des Rechts und Studium der *ars dictandi* haben sich in England nicht gegenseitig ergänzt, sondern gehörten verschiedenen Bereichen an. Dies der wesentliche Unterschied zu allen italienischen, ja vielleicht kontinentalen Verhältnissen! England ist ja auch niemals ein Land des gewerbsmäßigen Notariats geworden, wenigstens nicht in dem Ausmaß wie kontinentale Länder, insbesondere Italien. Für die englischen Kanzlisten, die erst in der Spätzeit Eduards I., nachdem der Bolognese Franciscus Accursius nach England berufen war, eine juristische Schulung zeigten,[32] waren daher auch die Handbücher des *dictamen* anscheinend entbehrlich, soweit diese auf England fremde Rechtsanschauungen Bezug nahmen. Und das traf immerhin für eine große Zahl der italienischen Werke zu. So konnte noch Johann von Bologna am Ende des 13. Jahrhunderts darüber spotten, daß gleichsam das ganze englische Königreich nur über einige wenige Clerks verfügte, die sich in einem seiner Auffassung nach geordneten Rechtsgang überhaupt auskannten.[33] Aber wie immer auch: Rezeption der *ars dictandi* — zumal in der späteren Form der *ars notaria* — und Rezeption des römischen Rechts und seiner Denk- wie Sprachwelt stehen in einer, im einzelnen vielleicht noch recht problematischen Wechselbeziehung.

Vergegenwärtigt man sich nun, daß vor der Zeit Bractons, also vor der Mitte des 13. Jahrhunderts, das römische Recht in England eine recht geringe praktische Wirksamkeit entfaltete,[34] so wird es einen nach dem Gesagten nicht wundern, daß auch die *ars dictandi* vor dieser Zeit in England und insbesondere an der englischen Kanzlei ohne Einfluß geblieben ist. Erst zusammen mit dem römischen Recht nahm man offenbar auch die Stilkunst auf, und tatsächlich haben Aufnahme der *ars dictandi* und Aufnahme

---

[31a] Bresslau, 256; Fitting, 79ff, für die Verbindung beider Disziplinen bei Irnerius. Die grammatisch-rhetorisch-dialektische Bildung beherrschte auch Paucapalea, den Albert von Samaria in einem Brief einer ungedruckten Fassung seiner *Ars dictandi* anredet: *aristotelici(s) disciplinis admodum eruditus;* Clm. 22267, f. 89 (datiert: 1115); freundlicher Hinweis von Dr. C. Erdmann. Über Albert von Samaria vgl. Haskins, 173ff; Krabbo, *Neues Archiv,* XXXII (1906), 71ff.

[32] Tout, *The Place of Edward II in English History,* 61f.

[33] Rockinger, *Briefsteller und Formelbücher,* S. 601. In der Widmung an Johann Peckham heißt es: *Cum igitur sollempnis vestra curia et regnum Anglie quasi totum careat, qui secundum formam romane curie vel ydoneam aliam qualemcumque noticiam habeant eorum, que ad artem pertinent notarie, set per nonnullos clericos acta causarum, processus iudicum, diffiniciones litium et alia... inter homines emergencia conscribantur etc.* Man mag die ganze Verachtung des Bolognesen für das englische Gewohnheitsrecht in Abzug bringen und mit Übertreibung rechnen: dennoch stimmt, was er sagt, mit allen sonstigen Beobachtungen überein, daß nämlich eine allgemeinere Kenntnis römischer (civiler

wie kanonistischer) Rechtsgänge in England nicht vorhanden war, sondern das zu seiner Zeit in der Tat nur *nonnulli clerici* diese Verfahren beherrschten. Das ist sogar im 14. Jhdt. kaum anders gewesen, als man sich für diese Zwecke päpstlicher- oder kaiserlicherseits approbierter Notare bediente; vgl. Denholm-Young, 86.

[34] Über das römische Recht in England allgemein: Paul Vinogradoff, *Roman Law in Mediaeval Europe* (2. A., Oxford, 1929), 97ff; W. S. Holdsworth, *History of English Law,* II (2. A. London 1923), *passim;* D. Ogg in der Einleitung zu seiner Ausgabe von I. Selden, *Ad Fletam dissertatio* ... [1647], (Cambridge, 1925). Für das römische Recht vor Bracton vgl. F. de Zuluetta, *The* Liber pauperum *of Vaccarius,* (Selden Society, XLIV; London, 1927) und: William of Drogheda, *Mélanges de Droit Romain dédiés a G. Cornil* (Gent, 1926), II, 641–57; F. Joüon des Longrais, "La conception de la Saisine du XIIe au XIVe siècle," *Études de Droit Anglais,* I (Paris, 1925). Zweifellos zu geringe Einwirkung schreibt dem römischen Recht zu F. W. Maitland, *Select Passages from the Works of Bracton and Azo,* Einleitung; Pollock-Maitland, *History of English Law,* I (2. A., 1898), 120ff.

des römischen Rechts in England auch zeitlich miteinander Schritt gehalten. Die vielfachen Auflehnungen der englischen Stände während des 13. Jahrhunderts gegen die Einführung römisch-italischer Rechtsformen und Rechtsanschauungen überhaupt[35] bedeutete also zugleich eine Ablehnung Bolognas als Ganzen. Bologna als ein Sammelbegriff, als Schule der beiden römischen Rechte und als Schule des hohen Stils hat einfach für England nicht die gleiche Bedeutung gehabt wie für den Kontinent, obwohl natürlich englische Studenten auch in Bologna, zumal seit der ersten Hälfte des 13. Jahrhunderts, vielfach anzutreffen waren;[36] aber in die englische Kanzlei sind sie allem Anschein nach nur selten gelangt. So haben gerade die ersten Wellen der Wirkung Bolognas das offizielle England erst spät erreicht und sich auch dann noch an den vorhandenen festen Formen gebrochen. Erst als England sich der Rechtsschule Bologna unter vielen Vorbehalten ein wenig erschloß — sinnbildlich hierfür die Berufung des Franciscus Accursius durch Eduard I., den man den englischen Justinian nannte — erschloß es sich mit der gleichen Verhaltenheit auch der Stilschule dieser Stadt.[37]

Dies sind, wie mir scheint, die wichtigsten Gründe für die späte und zögernde Aufnahme der italienischen Stilkunst auch der dritten Epoche in England und an der englischen Kanzlei. Daß freilich die französischen Einflüsse der vorausgehenden Epoche ebenfalls so geringe Wirkung ausübten, ist auf die gleiche Weise nicht zu erklären. Über die literarische Bildung der englischen Kanzlisten wird man sich nicht leicht ein Urteil bilden können. Aber Literatur einerseits, Politik wie Verwaltung andererseits gehörten offenbar ganz getrennten Sphären an und haben sich in England mit seiner hochentwickelten Bürokratie nicht mehr in der gleichen Weise durchdrungen wie in Frankreich und in Italien, wo sich die Bürokratie erst mit den literarisch geschulten Juristen und den juristisch geschulten Literaten entwickelte. Und schließlich lag für eine literari-

---

[35] In der Ablehnung des römischen Rechts trafen sich in England zeitweilig Könige und Barone, vgl. Roger Bacon, *Compendium studii* c. 4, ed. Brewer, *Rogeri Bacon opera... inedita* (London, 1859), 420; *MGH, SS*, XXVIII, 579 betr. eines allerdings wohl legendären Verbotes des römischen Rechts unter König Stephan. Für Heinrich III. und sein Verbot des Studiums römischen Rechtes — in Übereinstimmung vielleicht mit den bekannten päpstlichen Verboten — vgl. *Cal. Close R.*, *1234–37*, 26 (1234 Dez. 11.). Die Barone lehnten auf dem Tage von Merton 1235/36 jede Änderung der Gesetze auf Grund ultramontaner Einflüsse ab: *nolumus leges Anglie mutare;* vgl. Bracton, *Note Book* (ed. Maitland), I, 104–8; für ihre Ablehnung der *leges imperiales* auf dem Tage von Berwick-upon-Tweed (1292) vgl. Rishanger, *Ann. Regni Scotie* (ed. Riley, Rolls Series), 255. Zu den heftigsten Gegnern des römischen Rechts und der Juristen gehörte, wenn auch aus anderen Gründen, Roger Bacon; vgl. sein *Compendium studii* a. a. O.; ferner die gehässigen Bemerkungen des Matth. Paris., III, 531, 491, 495; IV, 14; V, 427f, 638f, sowie das gefälschte Papstschreiben ebda. VI, 293, n. 146; dazu Digard, *Bibl. Écol. Chart.*, LI (1898), 381–419.

[36] Haskins, *Studies in Mediaeval Science* (Cambridge, Mass., 1924), S. 185, Anm. 131, kündigt eine Arbeit seines Schülers Paul B. Schaeffer über diese Fragen an. Tamassia, "Odofredus," *Atti e Memorie della Romagna*, Ser. III, t. XII (1894), 72, bringt einige Angaben des Odofredus († 1265) über englische Studenten in Bologna; vgl. auch Hessel, *Bologna*, 417. Daß die Engländer als Nation in Bologna schon um 1115 vertreten waren, zeigt ein Brief in der *Ars dictandi* des Albert von Samaria (Clm. 22267, f. 89; vgl. oben Anm. 31a); denn in einem fingierten Studentenbettelbrief eines offenbar italienischen Studenten aus Bologna werden die *Normanni, Galli, Britanni, Allobroges, Guascones* genannt als die *gentes et fere nationes, inter quas habito*. Allerdings werden hier, da nur Stämme Galliens genannt sind, unter den *Britanni* wohl die Bretonen zu verstehen sein. Die Allobroger sind die Flamen, wie auch Mittarelli, *Annal. Camald.*, IV, 560, n. 351 (a. 1240) zeigt, wo als neu hinzugekommene Nation lediglich noch die Spanier angeführt werden, sonst aber die gleichen Völker wie bei Albert von Samaria, die nun freilich nicht mehr als *fere nationes* gelten. Vgl. auch Rashdall, *Universities*, I, 184, Anm. 4, für die Zeit um 1265.

[37] Ein Brief des Franciscus Accursius im Publ. Record Office, Ancient Corresp. XVII, n. 182 (1279 Jan. 4), gedruckt bei Langlois, *Rev. Hist.*, LXXXVII (1905), 66, an den König gerichtet, zeigt selbstverständlich den hohen Stil des Bolognesen; interessant ist es zu sehen, daß hingegen der Brief seines englischen Gesandtenkollegen, der gleichzeitig mit ihm an der Kurie weilte, den unschönen Stil der englischen Kanzlisten aufweist; Langlois, a. a. O., 65f.

sche Bildung innerhalb der englischen Kanzlei wohl auch nicht die gleiche Notwendigkeit vor wie in anderen Ländern, wie ganz besonders in Italien und Deutschland. Denn
man wird noch an etwas anderes erinnern müssen. Der hohe Stil hatte, sofern man überhaupt von einem Zweck reden will, genau wie die Rhetorik den einen Sinn, die Wirksamkeit der Sprache zu steigern, das zu Sagende in seiner akustisch wirksamsten und
überzeugendsten Form vorzubringen. Der *stilus supremus* ist daher, wie man heute sagen
würde, auch ein Mittel der politischen Propaganda gewesen — unentbehrlich in den
kanzleimäßig ausgetragenen Feldzügen und dem hohen Sprachgefühl der Damaligen
vermutlich ganz gemäß.[38] Derartige in Manifesten, Flugschriften und Briefen ausge-
kämpfte Fehden, wie sie Kaiser- und Papstkanzlei durch Jahrhunderte zu bestehen, wie
sie die Staufer mit den italienischen Städten auszufechten hatten, wie sie in kleinerem
Umfang im politischen Italien und auf philosophisch-literarischem Gebiet in Frankreich
an der Tagesordnung waren, das Entwickeln von ganzen sogenannten Weltanschau-
ungen in Manifesten — das alles hat England trotz innerer und äußerer Kriege nicht gekannt. Nie hat das tönende Manifest — im tiefsten Grunde auch unenglisch — den
Kampf der Waffen begleitet. Den Weg in die Öffentlichkeit zu suchen, das Bearbeiten
der öffentlichen Meinung und das Werben um sie mit den Mitteln der Rhetorik war
damals nicht Englands Sache. Und somit entfiel die Notwendigkeit, die Macht des
Worts in der Politik zu erproben.

Wenn dennoch auch die offizielle Kanzlei seit dem späteren 13. und vor allem im
14. Jahrhundert sich in besonderen Fällen der gehobenen rhythmischen Prosa bediente,
so geschah dies, soviel wir wissen, nur im Verkehr mit auswärtigen Höfen, die selbst im
Hochstil zu schreiben pflegten. Denholm-Young weist darauf hin, daß in der Epoche von
1306–1358 die an fremde Höfe, insbesondere an die Kurie gerichteten Briefe gesondert
in den Roman Rolls aufbewahrt wurden. Das geschah freilich aus verwaltungstechni-
schen Gründen.[39] Durchblättert man aber diese bei Rymer gedruckten Briefe, so bemerkt man in der Tat, daß sie größtenteils nach allen Regeln der Stilkunst abgefaßt
und entgegen sonstigem englischem Kanzleibrauch z. B. auch mit Arengen versehen
sind.[40] Sie stellen gewissermaßen ein Kompendium der rhytmisierten Schriftstücke
der englischen Kanzlei dar, wie man sie außerhalb der Roman Rolls nur ausnahms-
weise antrifft.

In dieser Epoche, also von Eduard I. bis Eduard III., ist auch die Mehrzahl der
italienischen Lehrbücher des *dictamen* nach England gekommen, deren Handschriften
heute in englischen Bibliotheken ruhen. Besonders zahlreich sind die Handschriften des

---

[38] Über diese Fragen vgl. Erdmann, "Die Anfänge der
staatlichen Propaganda im Investiturstreit," *HZ*, CLIV
(1936), 491ff; ferner Vehse, *Amtliche Propaganda*, 137f; H.
Wieruszowski, *Vom Imperium zum nationalen Königtum*
(München u. Berlin, 1933), 59. Für die Qualität der
Sprache hatte man ein sehr deutliches Gefühl, vgl. etwa
Andreas v. Isernia's Bemerkung zu *Liber Augustalis*, I,
tit. 31: *pulchre dictata est hec lex* (*Constitutiones Regni Siciliae*
[Neapel, 1773], 81) oder die Bemerkungen von Salimbene
(*MGH, SS*, XXXII, 383f) über das Diktat des Thomas
von Capua.

[39] Denholm-Young, 88. Die Roman Rolls sind ursprünglich ein Teil der die gesamte Auslandskorrespon-
denz umfassenden Treaty Rolls gewesen, die dann in
einzelne Abteilungen wie French Rolls, Almain Rolls
etc. aufgespalten wurden. In den ersten 18 Regierungs-
jahren Eduards II. (1307–25) waren die Roman Rolls
und die French Rolls vereinigt, was im Druck bei Rymer
vermerkt wird; vgl. M. S. Giuseppi, *A Guide to the Mss.
Preserved in the Public Record Office*, I (1923), 38–40.

[40] Für das Fehlen der Arengen vgl. Denholm-Young,
88.

Guido Faba, dessen Einfluß sich in England wie anderwärts geltend machte.[41] Auf ihn, auf Thomas von Capua, auf Richard von Pofi, aber auch auf Petrus de Vinea weisen die damals oder wenig später in England selbst entstehenden Summen der *ars dictandi* als Stilmuster ausdrücklich hin.[42] Es ist daher nicht weiter überraschend, daß man in den Roman Rolls auf zahlreiche Exordien stößt, welche deutlich genug die italienische Schule und gelegentlich auch ganz unverkennbar den Einfluß von Briefen des Petrus de Vinea verraten.[43] Und die Bedeutung dieses großen sizilischen Sprachbildners für das spätmittelalterliche England geht schließlich auch hervor aus der großen Zahl von Handschriften seines Briefbuches, die sich in England vorfinden und die fast ausnahmslos dem 14. Jahrhundert angehören.[44]

II.

Indessen ist es kaum beachtet, daß schon vor dem Zeitalter der drei Eduarde, daß schon in der Kanzlei Heinrichs III. etwa seit den 40er Jahren des 13. Jahrhunderts der

[41] Denholm-Young, 92ff. verzeichnet von Guido Faba's *Summa de modo dictaminis* 10 Hss., von den *Exordia* 5, von den *Arenge* 5, je drei von den *Dictamina rhetorica* und *De arte conscribendi epistolas* und je eine der *Citationes* und der *Rota nova;* dazu kommt noch eine Anzahl verloren gegangener Hss., die wir aus mittelalterlichen Bibliothekskatalogen kennen. Thomas von Capua ist mit 10, Richard von Pofi mit 9, Buoncompagno mit 1 Hs. vertreten. Für Petrus de Vinea s. u. Anm. 44.

[42] Um 1386 entstand die *Summa* des Johann de Briggis, vermutlich Fellow von Merton College in Oxford, der Peter von Blois, Petrus de Vinea, Thomas von Capua, Mattheus de Libris, Guido von Bologna (Faba) als Vorbilder eines hohen Stils empfiehlt; vgl. Denholm-Young, 100f, der noch auf einige anonyme und nicht hinreichend untersuchte Summen des 14. Jhdts. hinweist. Eine derselben (Oxford, Balliol Coll. Ms. 263, f. 4', ca. 1400) empfiehlt gleichfalls die Lektüre des Petrus de Vinea, Richard von Pofi, Guido Colonna u. a.

[43] Eine genauere Analyse der Briefe zumal Eduards II. auf Beeinflussung durch Petrus de Vinea ist hier nicht beabsichtigt. Einige Beispiele aus den Roman Rolls mögen genügen. Rymer, II, 1, S. 20, ein Brief Eduards II. an den Papst (1307 Dez. 10) zeigt mit PdV., VI, 30 völlige Übereinstimmung in der Arenga:

PdV, VI, 30.

Ad hoc summi dispensatione consilii pre aliis principibus optinuimus monarchiam dignitatis et imperii Romani suscepimus diadema, ut etsi alia...

Rymer, II, 1, S. 20.

Ad hec summi dispensatione consilii optinuimus monarchiam regie dignitatis, ut in regno nostro Anglie aliisque terris sub ditione nostra constitutis...

Rymer, II, 1, S. 49, ein Brief an den König von Frankreich und fast gleichlautend an die Kurie (1308 Juni 16), klingt in der Arenga (*Naturalis rationis instinctus necnon firma spes nobis suggerit...*) an sizilische Kanzleiwendungen an, ohne daß ich die entsprechende Stelle anzugeben wüßte; doch nimmt der Brief späterhin in Absatz 3 den Typ sizilischer Herrschaftsarengen auf, wie er in Sizilien

seit dem 12. Jhdt. üblich war: *Sane post regni... gubernacula per nos Deo volente suscepta...;* dazu wäre zu vergleichen Pirro, *Sicilia sacra,* I, 393: *Regni gubernaculum... nos ad hoc divino munere dignoscimur suscepisse...,* wozu noch weitere Beispiele bei Ladner, "Formularbehelfe in der Kanzlei Kaiser Friedrichs II. und die Briefe des Petrus de Vinea," *MÖIG,* Erg.-Bd., XII (1932), 131f zu vergleichen wären. Auch die Dispositio dieser gleichen Briefe: *requirimus, monemus et hortamur attente* entspricht, worauf mich Dr. Ladner freundlichst aufmerksam machte, gleichfalls sizilischem — aber auch päpstlichem — Kanzleibrauch. Bei dem engen Zusammenhang zwischen sizilischer und päpstlicher Kanzlei mag überhaupt die eine oder andere Wendung auch auf Thomas von Capua oder einen anderen päpstlichen Diktator zurückgehen. So ist beispielsweise Rymer, II, 1, S. 5 (1307 Sept. 6 an den Papst): *Inter ceteras studii nostri sollicitudines...* zu vergleichen mit Potthast, 20027. Auch ein Incipit wie Rymer, II, 1, S. 20: *Exultat ecclesia Anglicana...* ist nicht unbedingt mit PdV., II, 1, oder II, 45, oder Winkelmann, *Acta Imp.,* I, n. 702, in Verbindung zu bringen, da in beiden Fällen die Karsamstagsliturgie der Kerzenweihe (*Exultet iam angelica turba*) das Vorbild ist. Immerhin würde eine systematische Untersuchung der englischen Königsbriefe des 14. Jhdts. eine ganze Anzahl von Übereinstimmungen mit PdV.-Briefen zutage fördern.

[44] Die Mehrzahl der in England befindlichen Vinea-Hss. ist bei Pertz, *Archiv,* VII (1839), 890ff und Huillard-Bréholles, *Pierre de la Vigne,* 266ff aufgeführt; einige Ergänzungen bietet die Liste bei Denholm-Young, 98, der noch eine Hs. s. XIV. aus Edinburgh (Univers. Libr., Laing Ms. 351 = 182 des Gesamtkatalogs von C. R. Borland) nennt; doch enthält diese Hs., f. 1–22, nur *Flores.* Beachtenswert auch der Hinweis auf einige verschollene Hss., die M. R. James, *Ancient Libraries of Canterbury and Dover* (Oxford, 1904), S. 299, no. 956ff, anführt, von denen jedoch no. 958 — gleichfalls nur *Flores* enthaltend — jetzt im Britischen Museum (Royal Ms. 11 A XII) zu finden ist. Über eine Hs. aus dem letzten Drittel s. XIII. s. u. Anm. 112.

Gebrauch des Kursus in der auswärtigen Korrespondenz hier und da anzutreffen ist.[45] Selbst völlig durchrhythmisierte Briefe fehlen nicht ganz,[46] die, obgleich weit entfernt von stilistischer Vollkommenheit, doch seltsam abstechen von den primitiv kakophonen und antirhythmischen Satzschlangen, welche die englische Kanzlei jener Zeit sonst hervorbrachte.[47] In den beiden folgenden Jahrzehnten, also zwischen 1250 und 1270, nimmt die Zahl der rhythmisierten[48] wie der einigermaßen stilgerecht gebauten Briefe[49] naturgemäß noch zu, obwohl sie im Ganzen immer noch selten sind. Und in dieser Epoche ist merkwürdiger Weise schon Petrus de Vinea als Stilmuster in der englischen Kanzlei nachzuweisen.

Petrus de Vinea war in England kein Fremder. Im Gegenteil: ihn als den einzigen der großen italienischen Klassiker der *ars dictandi* verbanden auch persönliche Beziehungen mit dem englischen Hof.[50] Sie rühren her aus der Zeit der Eheschließung Kaiser Friedrichs II. mit Isabella von England (1235). Damals ging Petrus de Vinea als Brautwerber seines Herrn nach London, um mit dem König über die Bedingungen der Heirat, über Höhe und Zahlweise der Mitgift zu verhandeln und um schließlich, damaliger Sitte gemäß, des Kaisers Ring der Braut an den Finger zu stecken und sie dadurch seinem Herrn zu vermählen. Wir sind über diese Vorgänge und über Vineas Tätigkeit in London

---

[45] Denholm-Young, 88, spricht nur von ein bis zwei Beispielen, doch ist die Zahl erheblich größer.

[46] Als Beispiel zwei Briefe von 1245 (Juni 8): *Cal. Close R. 1242–47*, 356, anläßlich des Konzils von Lyon an Kaiser und Papst gerichtet. Der Papstbrief, ohne Arenga zwar, setzt rhythmisch richtig ein: *Cum sollempnes nuncii nostri...* und schließt mit Velox: *...vestro conspectui presentare*. Der Brief an den Kaiser zeigt fortlaufenden Rhythmus, wobei einem achtmaligen *Velox* ein zweimaliger *Planus* gegenübersteht.

[47] Als Ausnahme anzusehen ist auch ein Brief des Richard v. Cornwall vom Jahre 1241 bei Matth. Paris., IV, 138ff, der völlig rhythmisch gebaut ist. Aber der Brief ist in Sizilien geschrieben und der Diktator war vermutlich ein Südländer. Daß Richards späteres deutsches Königtum einen Einfluß auf die englische Kanzleisprache gehabt hätte, ist nach den Untersuchungen von P. Zinsmaier, "Ein verschollenes Formularbuch der Reichskanzlei im Interregnum," *MÖIG*, XLVIII (1934), 54f. kaum anzunehmen; Vinea zumindest kommt garnicht in Betracht.

[48] Briefe, die, an sich schlecht stilisiert, dennoch mit *Velox* ausklingen, sind in der auswärtigen Korrespondenz mehrfach anzutreffen, z. B.:

Rymer, I, 392 (1259 Dez. 19 an den Papst):...*habere dignemini excusatam*.
Rymer, I, 394 (1260 Febr. 5 an Frankreich):...*curabimus adimplere*.
Rymer, I, 395 (1260 März 10 an Frankreich):...*habere dignemini commendatum*.

Immerhin ist zu bemerken, daß diese Briefe in Frankreich geschrieben sind, so daß mit anderen Kanzleibeamten zu rechnen ist.

[49] Geradezu verdächtig gut ist ein Brief an die Kurie (1254 Febr. 12: *MGH, Epp. Pont.*, III, n. 446, 407; BFW, 13926), der allerdings auch nicht in England, sondern in der Gascogne ausgefertigt ist. Ebenso überraschend ist

das Glückwunschschreiben an Alfons X. von Kastilien anläßlich seiner römischen Königswahl: Rymer, I, 367. Hier könnte man nach den Ausführungen von Denholm-Young, 77ff., auf die Vermutung kommen, daß Galfridus Anglicus, Verfasser einer um 1280 geschriebenen *Scientia epistolaris* und vermutlich mit Gotfried von Eversley identisch, der Diktator gewesen sein könnte. Denn dieser Engländer, der am kastilischen Hof als Notar beamtet war, stand gleichzeitig in englischem Dienst: *vester notarius et noster clericus* nennt ihn Eduard I. Er starb 1283 und ist erst in den 70er Jahren nachzuweisen; aber seine Familienverhältnisse zeigen, daß er jedenfalls nicht in ganz jugendlichem Alter gestorben sein kann, so daß auch eine frühere Verwendung möglich ist. — Auffallend ist die beträchtliche Zahl ausländischer Notare an der kastilischen Kanzlei, welche allerdings die Arbeit von Miss E. S. Procter, "The Castilian Chancery during the Reign of Alfonso X," in *Oxford Essays in Mediaeval History Presented to H. E. Salter* (Oxford, 1934), 104–122, nicht erwähnt. Ich notierte drei italienische Notare, von denen zwei auch schon vor dem römischen Königtum Alfonsos X. in der kastilischen Kanzlei begegnen. Petrus v. Reggio wird 1271 als Protonotar genannt (BF, 5518, 5519), ist jedoch schon 1256 in diesem Amt nachweisbar, als er ein ins Spanische übertragenes Werk ins Lateinische übersetzte und zwar zusammen mit Aegidius de Tebaldis aus Parma, Notar des kastilischen Königs; vgl. M. Steinschneider, *Die europäischen Übersetzungen aus dem Arabischen* (Wien, 1904), 3, n. 9; F. M. Powicke, *The Mediaeval Books of Merton College* (Oxford, 1931), 142, Anm. Und drittens ist 1266 Bonaventura de Senis als Notar in Kastilien nachzuweisen, vgl. Daumet, *Mémoire sur les relations de la France et de la Castille de 1255 à 1320* (Paris, 1913), 149, n. III; ebda. wird ein *Henricus dictus Tuscanus* als *miles et major portarius aule* genannt, ein Zeichen nur für die offenbar nicht geringe Durchsetzung des kastilischen Hofes mit Italienern.

[50] Vgl. Huillard-Bréholles, *Pierre de la Vigne*, 20ff.

durch Urkunden wie durch Chronisten recht gut unterrichtet,[51] und einige Briefe König Heinrichs III.[52] bestätigen noch, welche hohe Bedeutung man in Westminster der Mission des Petrus de Vinea beimaß. Weniger bekant ist es, daß der König damals dem sizilischen Großhofrichter in feierlicher Beurkundung eine nicht unbeträchtliche Schenkung zukommen ließ.[53] Bis ein entsprechendes Lehensgut frei würde, so hieß es in der Schenkung, sollten Vinea und seine Nachkommen vom englischen König und dessen Nachkommen alljährlich 40 Mark erhalten, die jeweils zu Ostern beim Exchequer zahlbar seien. Diese Lehens- oder Pensionsangelegenheit hielt durch mehr als ein Jahrzehnt, bis zu Vineas Sturz, die persönlichen Beziehungen des Logotheten mit dem englischen Hof in Fluß. Die Rolls geben darüber Auskunft, daß Vinea tatsächlich seine Pension einigermaßen regelmäßig erhalten hat und daß im Laufe von 12 Jahren zumindest neunmal die ihm zustehenden Gelder angewiesen worden sind. Die Zahlung erfolgte jeweils bei passender Gelegenheit. Einmal, im Jahre 1237, ist ein päpstlicher Notar Walter der Geldüberbringer.[54] Das nächste Mal sollte Sergius Vulcanus, ein Campanier, der 1239 als Bote des Kaisers in England weilte, das Geld mitnehmen;[55] doch es stellte sich damals heraus, daß der Elekt von Valence, Wilhelm v. Savoyen, bei seinem Aufenthalt am kaiserlichen Hoflager den Betrag schon an Vinea ausgezahlt hatte.[56] Im Jahre 1240

---

[51] W. Kienast, *Die deutschen Fürsten im Dienste der Westmächte*, II, 1, 76, Anm. 1 hat die in Frage kommenden Stellen zusammengetragen.

[52] BFW, 11154–59.

[53] Einzig Kienast, a. a. O., 76, Anm. 2, erwähnt die Schenkung; vgl. auch den Hinweis von Hampe, *HZ*, CXLVI (1932), 461, Anm. Da diese wie die folgenden Registereintragungen nur als Regest bekannt sind, benutze ich die Gelegenheit, anmerkungsweise hier die Texte abzudrucken. Die Rolls wie vieles andere Material einzusehen hat mir das Record Office in freundlichster Weise gestattet. 1235 Mai 1. Westminster. — *Rex Archiepiscopis etc. salutem. Sciatis nos concessisse et hac carta nostra confirmasse pro nobis et heredibus nostris dilecto nobis magistro Petro de Vinea, magne curie imperialis iudici, quod ipse et heredes sui singulis annis percipiant ad scaccarium nostrum Pasche quadraginta marcas de dono nostro, donec nos vel heredes nostri eidem magistro Petro vel heredibus suis providemus in aliquo tenemento ad valentiam quadraginta marcarum annuatim. Quare volumus et firmiter precipimus pro nobis et heredibus nostris, quod predictus magister Petrus et heredes sui singulis annis percipiant ad scaccarium nostrum Pasche quadraginta marcas de dono nostro, donec nos vel heredes nostri eidem magistro Petro vel heredibus suis providimus in aliquo tenemento ad valentiam .xl. marcarum annuatim sicut predictum est. Huius testibus venerabilibus patribus E(dmundo) Cantuariensi archiepiscopo, tocius Anglie primate R(ichardo) Dunelmiensi J(oscelino) Bathoniensi W(altero) Carleoliensi et W(ilelmo) Exoniensi episcopis R(ichardo) comite Pictavie et Cornubie H(uberto) de Burg, comite Kantiensi J(ohanne) de Lascy, comite Lyncolniensi et comestabulo Cestriensi W(ilelmo) de Fear, comite Derbicensi Rado filio Nicholai Johanne filio Philippi Amauritio de Sancto Amando*

Bartholomeo Pecche et aliis. Datum per manum venerabilis patris R(adulfi) Cycestriensis episcopi cancellarii nostri apud Westmonasterium prima die Maii. Charter Roll, 19 Henry III, membr. 11; Regest: *Cal. Chart. R. 1226–57*, S. 200.

[54] 1237 Mai 19. Westminster. — *Rex thesaurario et camerario suis salutem. Liberate de thesauro nostro magistro Waltero notario domini pape quadraginta marcas ad opus Petri de Vinea de anno regni nostri xxi⁰ de annuo feodo suo .xl. marcarum, quas percipit singulis annis ad scaccarium nostrum, non obstante precepto nostro, ne denarios alicui liberaretis. Teste rege apud Westmonasterium, xix. die Maii.* Liberate Roll, 21 Henry III, membr. 9; Regest: *Lib. R.*, I, 270.

[55] 1239 Juli 4. Westminster. — *Rex thesaurario etc. Liberate de thesauro nostro Sergio Vulcano nuncio magistri Petri de Vinea ad opus ipsius magistri Petri .xl. marcas de anno regni nostri xxiii⁰ de annuo feodo suo .xl. marcarum. Teste rege etc.* Am Rande: *Pro magistro Petro de Vinea. Memorandum quod electus Valentiensis solvit ei in Italia .xl. marcas de feodo suo, ut idem Sergius protestatus est.* Lib. R. 23 Henry III membr. 9; Regest: *Lib. R.*, I, 400. Sergius Vulcanus entstammte einer bekannten Beamtenfamilie aus der Gegend von Neapel und Sorrent, vgl. Kantorowicz, *Kaiser Friedrich II.*, Erg.-Bd., 273.

[56] Vgl. die in der vorigen Anmerkung zitierte Randnotiz. Über die Anwesenheit des Elekten von Valence, Onkels der Königin, am kaiserlichen Hoflager in Italien 1238/39 unterrichtet auch *Lib. R.*, I, 365, 1239 Febr. 9. Danach wurden an einen florentinischen Kaufmann, Clarius Hugelini, 1000 Mark zurückgezahlt, welche dieser für des Königs Angelegenheiten dem beim Heere des Kaisers weilenden Elekten gegeben hatte. Der Elekt, der einst vom Kaiser das *cingulum militare* erhalten hatte (BF, 2179), weilte beim kaiserlichen Heere als Beauftragter des englischen Königs, mit dessen Truppenkontingent er über die Placentiner einen Sieg erfocht; vgl. BFW, 13265a, BF, 2375b, 2383a. Er starb am 1. Nov. 1239 in Viterbo; vgl. Kienast, a. a. O., 85.

dient ein florentinischer Kaufmann Fulginus,[57] das Jahr darauf Vineas Diener[58] als Überbringer des Geldes. Die Raten für 1244 und 1245 nimmt Walter v. Ocra, damals Gesandter des Kaisers in London, nach Italien mit,[59] während uns für 1242[60] und 1248[61] nur die einfachen Zahlungsanweisungen vorliegen und in einem anderen Falle lediglich der Name des süditalienischen Boten, jedoch nicht das Jahr, für das die Zahlung gelten sollte, überliefert ist.[62]

Für die nahen Beziehungen Vineas zum englischen Hof aber spricht weiterhin die Tatsache, daß auch seinem Neffen Johannes de Vinea, Dekan von Capua, in späterer Zeit Jahrgelder in Höhe von 20 Mark unter den gleichen Bedingungen gewährt worden sind. Die Schenkung als solche datiert erst vom 8. Januar 1244,[63] und Zahlungen sind für 1244,[64] 1245[65] und 1248[66] aus den Rolls nachzuweisen. Jedoch schon ein halbes Jahr vor der Gewährung jener Jahrgelder, schon am 8. August 1243 findet sich in den Patent Rolls eine Eintragung, daß dem Johannes de Vinea, Scholaren zu Paris, 20 Mark Sterling oder deren Gegenwert in Mark von Paris oder Tours zu zahlen seien — eine

[57] 1240 Juli 4. Westminster. — *Rex eisdem salutem. Liberate de thesauro nostro Fulgino, mercatori de Florentia, ad opus magistri Petri de Vinea .xl. marcas de hoc anno regni nostri xxiiii⁰ de annuo feodo suo .xl. marcarum, quas percipit ad scaccarium nostrum de dono nostro. Teste rege apud Westm. iiii. die Julii.* Lib. R. 24 Henry III membr. 10; Regest: *Lib. R.,* I, 477.

[58] 1241 Oktober 11. Westminster. — *Rex etc. Liberate etc. Anredo de la More servienti magistri Petri de Vinea ad opus ipsius Petri .xl. marcas de hoc anno regni nostri xxv⁰ de annuo feodo etc. Teste rege etc.* Lib. R. 25 Henry III membr. 3; Regest: *Lib. R.,* II, 78.

[59] 1245 November 17. Westminster. — *Rex etc. Liberate etc. magistro Waltero de Ocra ad opus magistri Petri de Vinea .xl. marcas de termino sancti Michaelis anno etc. xxviii⁰ et eidem Waltero .xl. marcas de termino Pasche anno xxix⁰. Et eidem Waltero .xx. marcas ad opus magistri Johannis Decani Capuani de annuo feodo suo, quod ipsi percipiunt ad scaccarium nostrum. Liberate etiam eidem magistro .xl. marcas ad expensas suas et cuiusdam militis socii sui, nunciorum domini imperatoris, versus partes suas de dono nostro. Teste rege etc.* Lib. R. 29 Henry III membr. 15; Regest: *Lib. R.,* II, 277.

[60] 1242 Juni 19. Sainte. — *Rex magistro Petro de Vinea imperialis aule iudici salutem. Respicientes ad laudabile obsequium vestrum, quod multociens nobis prestitistis, et ad meritorum vestrorum exigenciam nos promittimus, quod quam cito se facultas optulerit, providebimus vobis in quadraginta libratis terre de aliqua excaeta nostra. Interim autem vobis concedimus .xl. libras annuas sterlingorum percipiendas ad scaccarium nostrum Londonie. Teste rege etc.* Pat. Roll 26/27 Henry III membr. 13; Regest: *Cal. Pat. R. 1232–47,* 309; vgl. unten Anm. 76 über den Zeitpunkt dieser Pensionserneuerung.

[61] 1248 August 22. Woodstock. — *Rex Claro Hugelino salutem. Rogamus vos attente quatinus faciatis habere magistro Petro de Vinea .xl. marcas, magistro Johanni de Capua nepoti eius .xx. marcas et magistro Waltero de Ocra .xl. marcas, in quibus eis tenemur pro feodo suo de termino Pasche proximo preteriti. Et nos illas vobis in Anglia cum inde litteras vestras recepimus, reddi faciemus. In cuius etc. Teste rege apud Wodestock, xxii. die Augusti.* Pat. Roll 32 Henry III membr. 3; Regest: *Cal. Pat. R. 1247–58,* 26; in Abschrift von R. Pauli in Berlin, Staatsbibl. *Ms. Lat.* 385, f. 28; vgl. Kantorowicz, *Friedrich II.,* Erg.-Bd., 130.

[62] 1245 November 17. Westminster. — *Rex etc. Liberate de thesauro nostro Emerico Mauclerk .lx. marcas ad opus magistri Petri de Vinea de annuo feodo suo .lx. marcarum, quas ei concessimus percipiendas ad scaccarium nostrum. Texte etc.* Lib. R. 29 Henry III membr. 15; Regest: *Lib. R.,* II, 277; *lx* statt *xl* ist selbstverständlich ein Versehen, das jedoch auf die Eintragung *Cal. Close R. 1242–47,* 217, vom 1. August 1244 zurückgehen dürfte; der Überbringer wird hier *Mauclerk de Avers* genannt; vgl. auch unten Anm. 65.

[63] 1244 Januar 8. Westminster. — *Rex concessit Johanni de Vinea, decano Capuano, nepoti magistri Petri de Vinea .xx. marcas singulis annis percipiendis ad scaccarium Pasche, quamdiu regi placuerit. In cuius etc. Teste rege etc. — Consimiles litteras habet magister Walterus de Ocra de .xl. marcis singulis annis percipiendis ad idem scaccarium.* Pat. R. 28 Henry III membr. 10; Regest: *Cal. Pat. R. 1232–47,* 415.

[64] 1244 Januar 10. Westminster. — *Rex thesaurario etc. Liberate etc. magistro Waltero de Ocra, clerico et nuncio domini imperatoris .xl. marcas de termino Pasche anno etc. xxviii⁰ de annuis .xl. marcarum, quas ei concessimus percipiendas ad scaccarium nostrum. Liberate etiam eidem Waltero .xl. marcas pro expensis suis, quas fecit in adventu suo a domino imperatore ad nos in Angliam de dono nostro. Liberate etiam eidem Waltero .xx. marcas ad opus magistri Johannis, decani Capuani, de termino Pasche anni eiusdem de annuis .xx. marcarum. quas concessimus eidem Johanni percipiendas ad scaccarium nostrum. Teste rege apud Westmonasterium, x. die Januarii.* Liber. R. 28 Henry III membr. 16; Regest: *Lib. R.,* II, 209.

[65] Vgl. Anm. 59; doch liegt für das gleiche 29. Jahr Heinrichs III. noch eine andere Anweisung vor: 1245 Mai 5. Reading. — *Rex etc. Liberate etc. Almerico de Aversa* (vgl. oben Anm. 62) *.xx. marcas ad opus Johannis de Vinea de anno etc. xxix⁰ de annuo feodo suo .xx. marcarum. Teste rege etc.* Lib. R. 29 Henry III membr. 8; Regest: *Lib. R.,* II, 302. Die Zahlung von 1245 November 17 (oben Anm. 59) kann auch nicht für das 28. Jahr (1244) gelten, da für dieses Jahr die Zahlung bereits angewiesen wurde; vgl. Anm. 64. Es muß sich wohl um ein Versehen handeln, wie auch *Cal. Close R. 1242–47,* 217, zeigt.

[66] Vgl. oben Anm. 61.

Anordnung, die nur insofern widerrufen wurde, als inzwischen John Mansel die Summe an Vineas Neffen bereits gezahlt hatte.[67] Diese Eintragung, welche die bekannte Für-sorge Vineas für die Glieder seiner Familie nur bestätigt, verdient einiges Interesse. Denn wir wissen über Johannes de Vinea sehr wenig[68] und jede Nachricht über ihn ist uns daher willkommen. Am 6. Februar 1240 wird er einmal als Bürger von Capua erwähnt.[69] Am 17. April 1243 geht er im Auftrage des Kaisers nach Verona und erhält den üblichen Geleitsbrief,[70] der ihm vielleicht nur als Paß zur Reise nach Oberitalien und Frankreich diente. Denn im August des gleichen Jahres war er jedenfalls, wie die englischen Rolls zeigen, in Paris anzutreffen. Aus den päpstlichen Registern erfahren wir dann in den Jahren 1248[71] und 1249,[72] daß sich Johann de Vinea das Amt eines Dompropstes an der Kapitelkirche von Atina angemaßt hatte, woraus hervorgeht, daß dieser Neffe des sizilischen Logotheten tatsächlich Kleriker war. Jetzt erhalten wir über die dazwischen-liegenden Jahre von 1244 bis 1248 auf dem Umweg über England die Nachricht, daß er in dieser Zeit Dekan von Capua gewesen ist, wodurch eine andere entlegene Notiz zum Jahre 1247 erwünschte Bestätigung findet.[73] Auch der Bildungsgang dieses Höflingsnepoten ist jetzt zu übersehen. Wir besitzen von ihm einen Brief, in welchem er zwei Freunden zum Tode eines dritten gemeinsamen Freundes kondoliert.[74] Er weist sich in diesem Schreiben nicht nur dem Stil nach als ein Schüler Vineas aus, sondern bekennt sich aus-drücklich als solchen. Wie andere Angehörige des Vineakreises mag er an der kaiser-lichen Kanzlei seine Ausbildung als Stilist empfangen haben, wurde dann jedoch für die kirchliche Laufbahn bestimmt und nach Paris geschickt, um Theologie zu studieren. Dort mag er sich den Magistertitel erworben haben, den ihm die englischen Writs seit dem Januar 1244 zugleich mit dem Titel eines Dekans von Capua beilegen. Ja, sein kurzer Aufenthalt in Paris, der kaum länger als ein halbes Jahr gedauert haben kann, mag eigens dem Zwecke gedient haben, dort den Titel zu erhalten, der damals in Neapel für Theologen vielleicht nicht verliehen wurde. Überdies wird Petrus de Vinea seinem Neffen die beste Ausbildung haben geben wollen, und die war für Theologen nur in Paris zu holen — im Notfall eben auf Kosten des Königs von England.[75]

---

[67] 1243 August 8. Bordeaux. — *Rex etc. rogat magistrum Egidium thesaurarium domus templi Parisiis, quod Johanni de Vinea scolari Parisiis facit habere .xx. marcas sterlingorum vel ad valentiam. .xx. marcas parisiensis monete vel turoniensis et ut pre-dictas .xx. marcas vel eorum valenciam ei reddi facit ad Puri-ficationem beate Marie anno etc. xxviii°. In cuius etc. Teste rege etc.* Diese Zahlungsanweisung ist durchstrichen und am Rande eine Notiz: *Quia reddita fuit littera at J. Mansel liberavit ei .xx. marcas.* Pat. R. 27 Henry III membr. 5; Regest: *Cal. Pat. R. 1232–47*, S. 390.

[68] Ein paar Notizen bei Huillard-Bréholles, *Pierre de la Vigne*, 101ff. Die Angaben über die Familie des Petrus de Vinea etwa bei De Blasiis, *Pietro della Vigna* (Neapel, 1860), 208, oder bei Capasso-Jannelli, *Pietro della Vigna* (Caserta, 1882), 58f, sind durchaus widerspruchsvoll. Die persönlichen und Familienverhältnisse des Petrus de Vinea bedürften dringend einer neuen Untersuchung.

[69] BF, 2778; H-B, V, 729.

[70] BF, 3357; H-B, VI, 82.

[71] Berger, n. 4433; *MGH, Epp. pont.*, II, 424, n. 598.

[72] Berger, n. 4644; *MGH, Epp. pont.*, II, 486, n. 680.

[73] De Blasius, a. a. O., 285 bringt einen Urkundenaus-zug, in dem Johann de Vinea im August 1247 als Dekan der Kirche von Capua genannt wird; vgl. ebda., S. 208, und Capasso-Jannelli, a. a. O., 58.

[74] Huillard-Bréholles, *Pierre de la Vigne*, 334, n. 34; vgl. 103f.

[75] Das war damals offenbar ein ganz üblicher Weg. In der Ancient Correspondence, III, n. 14, findet sich ein Brief des ja auch dem Kaiserhof sehr nahestehenden Kardinals Johann Colonna an den englischen König, in dem er bittet, seinen Neffen, *Oddonem nomine, qui scientie illectus amore ad effugandas ignorantie tenebras Parisiis scolasti-cis disciplinis insistit, nec habeat, unde possit ibidem honeste sicut convenit sustentari,* durch Gewährung einer Pfründe oder einer Pension zu unterstützen. Über diesen Nepoten, Otto Colonna, habe ich nichts weiteres feststellen können; jedenfalls ist er nicht zu verwechseln mit dem bekannteren Nepoten dieses Kardinals, der 1226 in Paris studierte und später Erzbischof von Messina wurde; denn der hieß Jo-hann Colonna; vgl. Gerardus de Fracheto, *Vitae fratrum Or-dinis Praedicatorum*, ed. B.M. Reichert (Louvain, 1896), 177.

Andererseits sind die fast selbstverständlichen Zusammenhänge mit der großen Politik bezeichnend. Seit 1242 war Heinrich III. von England ganz besonders bemüht um die Gunst des Kaisers, den er im Juni 1242 zu einem Bündnis gegen Frankreich zu gewinnen suchte. Da ist es zunächst einmal auffallend, daß der englische König unter dem gleichen Datum seines Bündnisvorschlages die Schenkung an Petrus de Vinea nochmals bestätigt.[76] Sechs Monate später, nach einem ungünstigen Ausgang seines französischen Krieges, bedurfte Heinrich III. der kaiserlichen Hilfe gegen den Grafen von Toulouse.[77] Er schreibt von Bordeaux aus am 8. Januar 1243 in dieser Angelegenheit an den Kaiser. Seinen Brief aber sandte er mit einem schmeichelhaften Begleitschreiben zunächst an Petrus de Vinea, den er auffordert, des Königs Bitten beim Kaiser wirksam zu unterstützen.[78] Damals mag Vinea auch um das Stipendium für seinen Neffen gebeten haben, das wenige Monate später gewährt wurde. Diese kleinen Gefälligkeiten des englischen Königs sowie Vineas Fürsorge für seinen Neffen wird man nicht gleich als Bestechung ansehen und als solche dem leider immer noch wenig bekannten Sündenregister des Logotheten[79] zuaddieren dürfen. Schließlich hatten auch andere kaiserliche Höflinge[80] englische Lehen inne, die an sich je nur modernen Ordensverleihungen entsprechen, so vor allem Walter v. Ocra,[81] einer der engsten Vertrauten des Kaisers, der von Heinrich III. Jahrgelder in gleicher Höhe wie Petrus de Vinea selbst erhielt. Neben dem Wunsch, den Kaiser in seinen Beamten, Gesandten und Freunden zu ehren, wird freilich für den englischen König auch bestimmend gewesen sein, sich für alle Fälle in der kaiserlichen Umgebung ein paar einflußreiche Fürsprecher zu sichern.

Dennoch bleibt in der ganzen Beziehung Vineas zum englischen Hof noch eine Frage offen. Anscheinend in seinen späteren Jahren schreibt Petrus de Vinea einen merkwürdigen Privatbrief an den König von England. Er versichert darin dem König, daß

---

[76] 1242 Juni 17–19. BFW, 11391–93; vgl. oben, Anm. 60; Kienast, a. O., 105, Anm. 1.

[77] BFW, 11402; H-B, VI, 906, Kienast, a. a. O., 107, Anm. 2.

[78] BFW, 11403; H-B, VI, 907; vgl. Huillard-Bréholles, *Pierre de la Vigne*, 23. Mit mündlichem Bescheid ging gleichzeitig Avelard v. Semingham als Bote an den Hof des Kaisers: *Cal. Pat. R. 1232–47*, 357.

[79] Vgl. etwa F. Schneider, *QF*, XXII (1930–31), 57f, 80f.

[80] Philipp de Sesso, Kleriker der Kirche von Reggio, erhielt auf Bitten des Kaisers ein englisches Kirchenlehen oder wenigstens die Provision auf ein solches im Werte von 40 Mark; *Cal. Pat. R. 1232–47*, 219, vom 8. Mai 1238. Für entsprechende Kammerlehen, die der Kaiser an einflußreiche Persönlichkeiten in Frankreich verlieh, vgl. Kienast, 112ff.

[81] Die Schenkung an Walter v. Ocra datiert erst von 1244 Januar 8, vgl. oben, Anm. 63. Zahlungen sind für 1244 (oben, Anm. 64) und für 1248 (oben, Anm. 61) bereits nachgewiesen; eine weitere Ordre findet sich Lib. R. 29 Henry III membr. 15; Regest: *Lib. R.*, II, 277; 1245 November 17. Westminster. — *Rex etc. Liberate de thesauro nostro magistro Waltero de Ocra .xl. marcas de termino Pasche anno etc. xxix⁰ de annuo feodo suo .xl. marcarum. Teste rege etc.* — Walter v. Ocra war gleichsam der ständige Geschäftsträger des Kaisers in England, erst-

mals i. J. 1236 (*Cal. Pat. R. 1232–47*, 146; BFW, 11179 11182), um dann, sehr zur Beunruhigung des englischen Königs, nach Irland zu gehen: *Cal. Close R. 1234–37*, 368; BFW, 15066; Liebermann, *Neues Archiv*, XIII (1888), 217. Im folgenden Jahre 1237 war er zumindest für 33 Tage in London (*Lib. R.*, I, 288 vom 18. August 1237), aber sicherlich länger in England, da er bereits am 5. Juli dort gewesen sein muß, als ihm ein silberner Becher im Gewicht von 4 Mark zum Geschenk gemacht wird (*Cal. Close R. 1234–37*, 466). Auch 1239 scheint er in London gewesen zu sein, da er bei einem Unglück im Tower einigen Sachschaden erlitt, der ihm ersetzt wird (*Lib. R.*, I, 396 vom 26. Juni 1239). Über seinen Aufenthalt von 1241 unterrichtet *Lib. R.*, II, 80f. 1243 ging er zuerst als Gesandter nach Frankreich (BF, 3366, 3367); aber Ende des Jarhres war er wieder in England (*Cal. Close R. 1242–47*, 146, vom 18. Dezember 1243), wo er für längere Zeit blieb; denn 1244 weilt er mindestens durch 10 Monate dort, wohl aus Anlaß des Parlaments von London (BF, 3205), da er im Januar 1244 (*Lib. R.*, II, 209) und im November (*Lib. R.*, II, 277) dort anzutreffen ist. Die zahlreichen und oft ausgedehnten Aufenthalte in England, die fast einer ständigen diplomatischen Vertretung gleichkommen, trugen ihm in England auch die Bezeichnung als *nuntius consuetus* des Kaisers ein, vgl. Matth. Paris, *MGH, SS*, XXVIII, 419.

alle seine eigene Person betreffenden bösartigen Gerüchte zerstreut seien und daß seine Treue beim Kaiser wiederum in Vollkommenheit erstrahle. Gleichzeitig aber bittet Vinea, der durch des Königs Gnade schon unter dessen Getreue aufgenommen sei — eben als Inhaber eines englischen Lehens — ihn nun auch in Englands Bürgerschaft aufzunehmen, auf daß er nicht nur ein ergebener Lehensmann des Königs sei, sondern auch gelte als Sohn und Bürger des englischen Königreiches.[82] Vinea will also, wie wir heute sagen würden, die englische Staatsangehörigkeit erwerben. Ein absonderlicher Wunsch für ein Zeitalter, das nach unseren Vorstellungen den Begriff der Staatsangehörigkeit gar nicht kannte! Doch das trifft zumindest auf die englisch-französischen Verhältnisse jener Jahre doch nicht mehr ganz zu.[83] Gerade nach jenem Krieg von 1242/43, der für England erfolglos verlief, hat nämlich Ludwig IX. von Frankreich eine Bestimmung erlassen (1244), die früheren englischen Bestrebungen übrigens nahekam, wonach Doppelvasallen, da sie nicht zwei Herren dienen könnten, entweder für Frankreich oder für England zu optieren hätten, auf daß dann ein jeder Lehensträger entweder dem französischen oder dem englischen König *inseparabiliter adhereat*.[84] Es ist eine erste Durchbrechung des lebensrechtlichen durch den nationalstaatlichen Gedanken, und dieses Novum mag immerhin einiges Aufsehen erregt haben. Es wäre denkbar, daß Petrus de Vinea — selbst ein Doppelvasall durch seine sizilischen und englischen Lehen — in irgendeiner Form auf diese Bestimmung Bezug hatte nehmen und nun auf diese Weise den Engländer seiner Treue hatte versichern wollen. Merkwürdig bleibt der Fall trotzdem.

Die Beziehungen des Logotheten zu England lassen sich bis zum Jahre 1248 verfolgen. Im August dieses Jahres werden ihm wie auch seinem Neffen und Walter v. Ocra zum letzten Mal die Jahrgelder angewiesen.[85] Wenige Monate später erfolgt Vineas Sturz und damit hören seltsamer Weise auch die Zahlungen an die beiden anderen Süditaliener auf. Ihre Namen erscheinen in den Rolls nicht wieder — auch dies für uns nicht erklärlich. Nur einmal noch, im Jahre 1256, taucht der Name des Petrus de Vinea unvermutet auf, als nämlich König Heinrich III. für seinen Sohn Edmund, den Thronprätendenten von Sizilien, über die süditalischen Liegenschaften seines einstigen Günstlings nunmehr zugunsten eines päpstlichen Nepoten verfügte.[86]

III.

In dieser gleichen Zeit, als Heinrichs III. sizilisches Abenteuer zwar alte Träume der normannischen Könige wieder aufleben ließ, jedoch den englischen Adel aufs tiefste zu beunruhigen begann, machte sich nun erstmals die Wirkung Vineas als Stilisten in England bemerkbar. Im Jahre 1253 war an der Kurie unter Innocenz IV. nach mancherlei

---

[82] Huillard-Bréholles, *Pierre de la Vigne*, S. 303, n. 8: *Apulus vester a vobis in fidelem regis per regie munificentie gratiam adoptatus adoptari in municipem Anglie supplicat per eandem, ut non solum devotus fidelis regis et domini, sed regni filius habeatur et civis.*

[83] Zum folgenden H. Mitteis, *Lehnrecht und Staatsgewalt* (Weimar, 1933), 551.

[84] Mitteis, a. a. O.; Matth. Paris (ed. Luard), IV, 288.

[85] Oben Anm. 61.

[86] *Cal. Close R. 1254–56*, 407f; BFW, 13998; vgl. auch *MGH, Epp. pont.*, III, 315, n. 346.

Fehlschlägen und anderweitigen Versuchen der Plan aufgetaucht, den jungen Edmund v. Lancaster, des englischen Königs erst achtjährigen Sohn, mit dem Königreich Sizilien zu belehnen. Der Tod Innocenz' IV. hatte die Ausführung des Planes verzögert. Erst sein Nachfolger Alexander IV. hat nach weiterem Verhandeln die Belehnung Edmunds am 9. April 1255 vollzogen.[87] Seit 1256 führte der Prinz sein eigenes Siegel als *SICILIE REX*,[88] doch hat selbstverständlich eine eigne sizilische Kanzlei in England niemals bestanden. Vielmehr besorgte die englische Kanzlei auch die sizilische Korrespondenz, obwohl diese mit der Zeit einen beträchtlichen Umfang annahm. In der Hauptsache wurden von Seiten Englands Briefe nur mit der Kurie und mit italienischen Bankhäusern, den beiden eigentlichen Eroberern Siziliens, in dieser Angelegenheit gewechselt. Aber man trat doch auch mit einzelnen sizilischen Persönlichkeiten, mit einzelnen Adelsgruppen und mit süditalischen Städten in unmittelbare Verbindung. Lag es da nicht nahe, sich mit den Siziliern selbst in dem ihnen seit Jahrzehnten vertrauten Tone der *tuba capuana*, in der Sprache des Petrus de Vinea zu verständigen?

Leider ist die sizilische Korrespondenz nur ganz trümmerhaft auf uns gekommen. Das mag damit zusammenhängen, daß, wie einem Memorandum vom 30. November 1255 zu entnehmen ist, die sizilischen Briefe in der Wardrobe aufbewahrt worden sind, und deren Archiv ist verloren.[89] Spuren dieser Korrespondenz sind zwar noch mehrfach nachzuweisen. So verzeichnet das Register des Walter Stapeldon, Bischofs von Exeter, aus dem Anfang des 14. Jahrhunderts noch ganz genau, in welcher Truhe zu seiner Zeit einige zwanzig Bullen König Edmunds für seine sizilischen Untertanen aufbewahrt wurden;[90] aber mit ganz wenigen Ausnahmen sind diese Urkunden verschollen.[91] Weiter findet sich in den Patent Rolls eine Notiz über Briefe des Podestà von Aquila und eines *comitis Tucye una cum aliis literis de negotio Appulie et Cicilie*.[92] Aber auch diese Briefe sind verloren

---

[87] BFW, 8974. Für die Frage der Thronkandidatur Walter E. Rhodes, *EHR*, X (1895), 19ff; Rodenberg, *P. Innocenz IV. u. das Königreich Sizilien* (Halle, 1892), 154ff; Karst, *Geschichte Manfreds... bis zu seiner Krönung* (Berlin, 1897), 99ff; Tenckhoff, *P. Alexander IV.* (Paderborn, 1907), 35ff.

[88] Die Anfertigung eines Siegels hatte i. J. 1254 schon Papst Innocenz IV. gefordert: Potthast, 15388. Ein metallenes Faksimile der Bulle Edmunds im Brit. Mus. (XLIII, 73). Die Vs. zeigt das Bild eines kindlichen Königs mit Krone, Lilienszepter und Apfel auf einer Thronbank sitzend, die Füße auf einem Schemel. Die Umschrift lautet: *Eadmundus: Dei: Gracia: Sicilie: Rex*. Die Rs. zeigt das englische Wappen in dreieckigem Schild; Umschrift: *Eadmundus: Natus: Regis: Anglie: Illustris*. Vgl. W. De Gray Birch, *Catalogue of Seals... in the Brit. Mus.*, VI (London, 1900), 146, n. 21647. Der Gebrauch einer Goldbulle Edmunds ist verschiedentlich nachzuweisen, vgl. Rymer, I, 360, 405 u. ö. Gelegentlich werden die sizilischen Schriftstücke auch mit dem englischen Königssiegel versehen und zwar mit der Begründung, daß Edmunds Siegel nicht zur Hand sei, vgl. *Cal. Pat. R. 1247–58*, 508. Englische Sachen Edmunds wurden jedenfalls nicht mit dem sizilischen Königssiegel gesiegelt, vgl. etwa Rymer, I, 387. Das sizilische Siegel hat 1255 offenbar noch nicht existiert, da König Heinrich III. in einem Memorandum von 1255 Nov. 30 anordnet, daß

alle Urkunden in Sachen Siziliens unter seinem eigenen Siegel gesiegelt werden sollten, vgl. Rymer, I, 332; *Cal. Pat. R. 1247–58*, 451.

[89] Memorandum von 1255 Nov. 30 bei Rymer, I, 332 betreffs Siziliens: *transscripta omnium privilegiorum sigillata sunt sigillo... venerabilis patris... Bononiensis episcopi et commissa in gardroba nostra salvo custodienda*. Über den Verlust des Wardrobe-Archivs vgl. Tout, *Chapters*, I, 34f.

[90] *Kalendare de bullis papalibus*, um 1323 verfaßt, ed. Palgrave, *Ancient Calendars and Inventories of the Exchequer*, I (London, 1836), erwähnt S. 28 eine Anzahl päpstlicher Bullen betreffs Siziliens, S. 142 Briefe Heinrichs III. an italienische Kaufleute und ca. 20 Bullen König Edmunds für Sizilien. Bei den S. 100 genannten *Provisiones de libertatibus et statutis de Regno Siciliae* dürfte es sich um die der Kurie gegenüber eingegangenen Verpflichtungen für Freiheit der Kirche u. ä. handeln. Über das zur "Treasury of the Receipt" gehörende Register des Bischofs Stapeldon vgl. Giuseppi, I, 210.

[91] Hierher gehören vielleicht Edmunds Schreiben bei Rymer, I, 335 (1256 Januar 13), 359 (1257 Juni 26), 405 (1261 März 20 und 21); dazu die Beglaubigungen Rymer, I, 310.

[92] *Cal. Pat. R. 1247–58*, 661 (1258 Januar 23); doch ist *Tucye* statt *Cucye* zu lesen, obwohl auch mit dieser Lesart wenig anzufangen ist, da *Tuscia*, woran man denken könnte, hier nicht in Betracht kommt.

gegangen.[93] Ebenso wissen wir, daß ein süditalischer Adliger, Johann v. Eboli, dem König geschrieben hat; doch kennen wir nur des Königs Antwortschreiben.[94] Immerhin sind Briefe von Süditalienern an den König von England noch in einiger Zahl vorhanden,[95] während englische Briefe an süditalische Empfänger — und sie gerade interessieren hier — nur spärlich vertreten sind. Dazu kommt, daß es sich meistens nur um Beurkundungen handelt, die so kurz und formelhaft gehalten sind, daß aus ihnen für das Diktat nichts zu entnehmen ist.

Eine Ausnahme macht ein Päckchen von vier Briefen, das sich abseits von Archiv und Registratur erhalten hat. Die Abtei Burton-upon-Trent in der Grafschaft Stafford hat im 13. Jahrhundert ein Annalenwerk begonnen, das mit der Klostergründung (1004) einsetzt, etwa vom Jahre 1214 ab die gleichzeitigen Ereignisse selbständig verarbeitet und besonders wertvoll geworden ist durch die große Zahl der eingestreuten Dokumente, die dem jeweiligen Annalisten — wie so häufig gerade in England — offenbar von amtlicher Seite zur Verfügung gestellt worden sind.[96] Anläßlich des Berichtes über die sizilische Kandidatur des jungen Edmund bringt nun der Annalist zum Jahre 1257 jene vier Briefe aus der sizilischen Korrespondez des Königs.[97] Brief I ist an den König gerichtet: eine Anzahl sizilischer Adliger, die in Rom weilen, sind die Absender; sie bitten den König um sein Kommen und beglaubigen den Johann v. Montefusculo als ihren Boten.[98] Brief II ist ein Schreiben des Königs von England an die Leute von Teano, in welchem er diesen mitteilt, daß er im kommenden Sommer nach Sizilien aufbrechen wolle, um dort

---

[93] Einen an Heinrich III. gerichteten Brief aus Aquila findet man Rec. Off. Ancient Correspond., XLVII, n. 29; aber der Absender ist nicht der Podestà, sondern der Prior Angelo v. Aquila. Ein Bote dieser Stadt, Aligno v. Aquila, ist jedoch 1257 Juni 24 tatsächlich in England nachweisbar, vgl. *Cal. Close R. 1256–1259*, 68. Für die damalige Verbindung dieser Stadt mit der Kurie vgl. BFW, 9084, 9090 (Oktober 1256), woraus man allerdings auf entsprechende Beziehungen auch zu England schließen kann; 1257 war Aquila im Aufstand gegen Manfred (BF, 4701 b).

[94] *Ann. Burton.*, S. 400: *devotio vestra, quam... carissimo nato nostro per nobilem virum Johannem de Montefusculo verbis et litteris polliciti estis servare...*

[95] 1) Podestà, Rat und Gemeinde von Brindisi an König Edmund mit der Bitte, *regnicolas Scicilie infelices a iugo servitutis* zu befreien. — Undatiert, ca. 1256–58. Rec. Off., Diplomatic Documents, n. 9, vgl. *Lists and Indexes*, XLIX (London, 1923). Für die Beziehungen Brindisis zum Hl. Stuhl und damit zu England vgl. BFW, 9017 (1255) und den folgenden Brief.

2) Robert v. Bari an Heinrich Wengham, Kanzler des Königs von England, mit der Bitte sich beim König und der Königin für Roberts Verwandte in Brindisi zu verwenden, *qui pro devocione Romane Ecclesie nec minus ad exaltationem Edmundi illustrissimi regis Sicilie dampna non modica passi sunt.* — Undatiert, ca. 1256–58; Rec. Off., Ancient Correspond., XLVII, n. 39.

3) Angelo, Prior v. Aquila, berichtet Heinrich III. über die Fortschritte Manfreds und teilt mit, daß zumindest 100 Ritter für 4 Monate angeworben werden müßten, um Aquila, *que cum alis suis regni Sicilie januas claudit et aperit,* halten zu können, wofür er das nötige

Geld an die Kurie anzuweisen bittet. Undatiert, ca. 1256–58; vgl. oben Anm. 93; gedruckt bei Langlois, *Rev. Hist.*, LXXXVII (1905), 64; Arndt, *Studien zur inneren Regierungsgeschichte Manfreds* (Heidelberg, 1911), 198.

4) Sizilische Adlige zu Rom bitten Heinrich III. um sein baldiges Kommen und beglaubigen bei ihm den Johann v. Montefusculo als ihren Boten. — Rom, 1256 März 18; *Annal. Burton.*, 397; s. u. Anm. 101, 102.

5) Sizilische Adlige zu Pisa beglückwünschen Heinrich III. zur Erhebung seines Sohnes Edmund zum König von Sizilien; sie teilen ihm mit, daß Pisaner und Genuesen Sizilien auf gemeinsame Kosten erobern wollten und darüber mit dem Papst verhandelten; sie beglaubigen den Johannes de Alfario, *militem civem Neapolitanum,* als ihren Boten beim König. Pisa, 1258 August 14; Rec. Off., Ancient Correspond., XLVII, n. 37. Die Absender sind: *Leonardus de Aldigerio, Johannes de Scalecta, Nicholaus Bisala milites cives Messane et alii de eadem terra et Sicilie insule, Cormaginus de Griffo et fratres, Richardus Carachulis et Stephanus Bonifacii milites cives Neapolitani, judex Maceus Mougelli de Salerno et Jacobus Crispus miles de eadem terra... ab eodem regno eiecti... Leonardus de Aldigerio* war 1255, als Messina die päpstliche Hoheit anerkannte, zum Podestà dieser Stadt gemacht worden, vgl. Potthast, 16001; Jamsilla bei Muratori, *Rer. It. SS.*, VIII, 552f; Barth. Neocastr. c. 4 bei Muratori, ebda., XIII, 1019. — Auf diesen Brief und einen der anderen machte mich vor Jahren Prof. W. Holtzmann freundlicher Weise aufmerksam.

[96] Vgl. Luard in der Einleitung der *Annal. Monastici*, I, xi, xxixf.

[97] *Annal. Burton.* (*Annal. Monastici*, I), 397ff.

[98] S. o. Anm. 95, n. 4.

die Sarazenen und andere Feinde der Kirche zu vernichten. Brief III ist an den Edlen
Johann v. Eboli gerichtet mit der Bitte, für die Sache der Kirche und Englands nach
Kräften zu wirken. Der Empfänger von Brief IV war Graf Thomas (II.) v. Aquino,
Schwiegersohn Kaiser Friedrichs II. und zeitweiliger Parteigänger der Kirche, dem der
König gleichfalls seine baldige Ankunft meldet und den er ermahnt, sich nicht von seiner
Treue gegen die Kirche abbringen zu lassen. Mit Ausnahme von I, der das Datum: 1256
März 18 trägt, ist keiner der Briefe datiert. Aber sie mögen alle noch ins Jahr 1256 oder
in den Anfang 1257 zu setzen sein, da der König mehrfach davon spricht, daß er im
kommenden Sommer sich zur Heerfahrt nach dem Süden aufmachen werde. Damit aber
kann nur der Sommer 1257 gemeint sein. Denn nach den abschließenden Vereinbarungen
mit der Kurie war ihm zur Eroberung des Königreiches als Termin, bis zu welchem der
Feldzug anzutreten sei, der Juni 1257 gesetzt worden und eine ihm nachträglich ge-
währte Fristverlängerung von drei Monaten — also bis zum September 1257 — änderte
nichts an der Tatsache, daß im Sommer 1257 der Eroberungszug vor sich gehen sollte.[99]
Dazu kommt, daß im Frühjahr 1257 tatsächlich in London mit päpstlichen Bevollmächtigten über die Entsendung eines Kriegskapitäns — Heinrich v. Kastilien war
dafür ausersehen — verhandelt wurde.[100] In diese Zeit werden daher auch die Briefe an
die Süditaliener gehören. An ihrer Echtheit zu zweifeln liegt keine Veranlassung vor.
Die Reihe der Absender von I kann keine Erfindung sein,[101] und der in dem gleichen
Brief und in III genannte Bote Johann v. Montefusculo, ein sehr genau bekannter Süditaliener, läßt sich aus den Patent Rolls tatsächlich als damals in England weilend nachweisen.[102] Die Verbindung Englands mit Teano ist genau so wahrscheinlich wie die mit
anderen Städten, mit Aquila, Brindisi, Messina; denn auch Teano war damals päpst-
lich.[103] Und wenn in IV gerade Graf Thomas v. Aquino zur Treue ermahnt wird, so ist
daran zu denken, daß der Graf damals wirklich noch Anhänger der Papstpartei war: ihn
traf, im Gegensatz zu andern ehemaligen Parteigängern der Staufer, im Jahre 1255
nicht der päpstliche Bann, und erst im September 1257 ist der Graf im Gefolge Manfreds
nachweisbar, mit dem er schon vorher sympathisierte.[104] Seine Haltung mußte Anfang

---

[99] Rymer, I, 350; für die Fristverlängerung vgl. BFW, 9087.

[100] Rymer, I, 359 vom 28. Juni 1257.

[101] Die Absendernamen sind im Druck, jedoch auch in der Hs. Brit. Mus., Vespas. E. III f. 65ᵇ, von der mir Mr. Sven E. Berg von Worcester College in Oxford freund- licher Weise Photographien besorgte, mehrfach ver- stümmelt. *Petrus Rufus de Caliba, comes Cantanzarus* ist natürlich der frühere Marstallmeister des Kaisers, sein Neffe *Jordanus Ruphus* ist gleichfalls bekannt (vgl. Kan- torowicz, *Fried. II.,* Erg.-Bd., 157f.), wenn auch nicht als *canonicus Treponensis*; doch mag hier eine Sigle ausgefallen sein, so daß *can. Trepon.* nicht als Apposition zu Jordanus Rufus gemeint sein muß. Die Siglen der Bischöfe von Squillace (*T.* = Thomas) und von Ariano (*J.* = Jacobus) sind richtig, die des Bischofs von Nicastro (*B.* statt *S.* = Samuel) vielleicht bloß verschrieben; völlig irrig *G. de Messana, Clunensis (episcopus),* da das sinnlose *Clunensis* auch nicht durch *Clusinensis* zu emendieren ist, indem 1257 dort ein Bischof Petrus saß. Hinter *Cataldus de Taranto* fehlt im Druck *Johannes de Cassano.* Der *magister*

Johannes de Pascha, procurator Sancti Nicholai de Baro ist in dieser Eigenschaft nachweisbar, vgl. *Cod. Barese,* VI, 107, n. 71. *Gauterus de Sisaulo* dürfte der schon BF, 2710, und hernach mehrfach im Register Friedrichs II. (vgl. H-B, V, 675, 676, 721, 815) genannte Messinese *Walter v. Fisaulo* sein; und *Angelus de Riso* kann man wohl mit dem BFW, 9052 genannten *Angelus de Riso Baroli* identifizieren.

[102] Er war Neffe des Großhofjustitiars Richard v. Montefusculo, der 1246 in die große Verschwörung der sizilischen Barone verwickelt war. Johann v. M. floh damals nach Rom, erhielt seine sizilischen Güter vom Papst bestätigt (Berger, n. 2890ff.) und blieb gleich seinen Brüdern Giffred und Richard (vgl. Berger, n. 2902) ein besonderer Günstling des Papstes; vgl. *MGH, Epp. Pont.,* III, 122, n. 140. Über seine Anwesenheit in England s. auch *Cal. Pat. R. 1247–58,* 629, 639 (1258 Mai 7, Juni 28).

[103] BFW, 8824ᵇ, 8839. Für Aquila und Brindisi s. o. Anm. 93, u. 95, n. 3; für Messina oben Anm. 95, n. 5, BFW, 9011 und Karst, *Geschichte Manfreds,* 135f.

[104] BF, 4665; H. Arndt, *Innere Regierungsgeschichte Man- freds,* 161f.

1257 als unsicher gelten, und Heinrichs III. Ermahnungen, er möge der Kirche die Treue bewahren, dürften daher durchaus begründet gewesen und keineswegs ohne bestimmten Anlaß vorgebracht worden sein.

Was den Stil dieser Briefe anbelangt, so ist bei allen dreien (II, III, IV) nur zu sagen, daß Petrus de Vinea Pate gestanden hat. Am interessantesten ist in dieser Beziehung II, der Brief an Teano. Denn er ist zu seinem größten Teil wörtlich einem Schreiben des Petrus de Vinea nachgebildet, dem bekannten Diplom zur Ernennung der kaiserlichen Statthalter in Italien, das uns in verschiedenen Fassungen erhalten ist.[105] Nur die Schlußsätze weichen entsprechend dem ganz anderen Zweck des Schreibens von der Vorlage ab. Doch selbst in den Schlußsätzen sind noch einzelne Wendungen ganz unverkennbar Vinea-Briefen entnommen. Ich stelle zunächst die beiden Briefe einander gegenüber:[106]

<table>
<tr><td style="text-align:center">Petrus de Vinea</td><td></td><td style="text-align:center">Annales Burtonienses</td></tr>
<tr><td>

Ad extollenda iustorum preconia et reprimendas insolentias transgressorum prospiciens e celo iustitia in populis *regnantium constitu*it[a]) *solia et diversorum* principum potestates. Caruisset namque libenter humana conditio iugo dominii nec libertatem a se, quam eis natura donaverat, homines abdicassent, nisi quod impunita licentia scelerum in evidentem perniciem humani generis redundabat, et ex necessitate quadam oportuit naturam subesse iustitie et servire iudicio libertatem. Sed *nec exquiri extrinsecus*[b]) *decuit speciem aliam creature,*

</td><td style="text-align:center">

5

10

15</td><td>

Ad necessarium *regimen populorum*[1]) *et* gentium *diversorum*[2]) *constitu*ta sunt in orbe terrarum dispensatione celesti[3]) *regnantium solia et* pontificum dignitates.

Nec enim *exquiri extrinsecus decuit aliam speciem creature, cui*[a']) *se representata*

</td></tr>
</table>

<table>
<tr><td>

[a]) *erexit* BCDEFGM; vgl. Anm. 3.
[b]) *decuit extrinsecus* EFG; *extrinsecus exquiri* D.

</td><td>

[a']) *cum* Hs.

</td></tr>
</table>

[1]) *Ad regimen populorum:* Vinea, z. 21f.
[2]) *et diversorum:* Vinea, z. 5.

[3]) *dispensatione celesti* außer in EFG auch in dem sonst gänzlich abweichenden Formular für Pandulf v. Fasanella, *MGH, Const.,* II, 306, n. 223: *In imperiali solio constituti, quod ex celesti dispensatione feliciter optinemus.*

---

[105] Tatsächlich weicht das Schreiben der *Annal. Burton.* in Kleinigkeiten von jedem der uns bekannten Formulare ab, über die Ficker, *Forschungen,* II, 519f, § 413 und Ladner, *MÖIG.,* Erg.-Bd., XII (1932), 104ff zu vergleichen ist. Am nächsten kommt es in Arenga und Text dem Diplom für Enzio (*A = MGH, Const.,* II, 300, n. 216) in der *Conclusio* einem anderen Diplom für Enzio (*B = MGH, Const.,* II, 301, n. 217), und dem Diplom für Ezzelino (*D =* PdV, V, 1), erhalten in den Hss. von Wolfenbüttel und Montpellier (vgl. Ladner, a. a. O., 105). Ein weiteres Formular kennen wir in der Ausfertigung für Friedrich v. Antiochien (*C = MGH, Const.,* II, 373, n. 266) und schließlich drei Ausfertigungen in einer verkürzten Form, nämlich für Meinhard v. Görz (*F = MGH, Const.,* II, 378, n. 270), für Thomas v. Savoyen als Generalvikar von Pavia aufwärts (*E =* ebda., 379, n.

272) und als Generallegaten der westlichen Lombardei (*G =* ebda., 381, n. 273). Die Arenga ist außerdem noch erhalten in der Sammlung des Marinus v. Eboli (*M*), die nach einer Photographie des Cod. Vat. Lat. 3976 einsehen zu können ich der Freundlichkeit Herrn Dr. F. Schillmanns danke. Für eine weitere Verwendung der Arenga in einem Briefbuch des 13. Jhdts. vgl. Anhang. Dem Text ist die Fassung von *A* zugrunde gelegt, jedoch mit der *Conclusio* von *D*, da es hier auf die Übereinstimmung mit Petrus de Vinea ankommt. Es sind nicht alle Varianten verzeichnet, sondern nur einige, welche die Verwandschaft mit *A* zu erhellen geeignet sind.

[106] *Kursiv* bedeutet wörtliche Übernahme der Vorlage, S p e r r u n g bezeichnet Anklänge an andere Vinea-Briefe.

cui[c]) se representatu per hominem celestis imago subiceret,[c]) sed homo prelatus est homini, ut gratiorem prelaturam efficeret identitas speciei. Potissime tamen ad regimen populorum divina sententia prefecit Imperium, dum ostensa sibi figura numismatis in redditione census pre ceteris regibus Cesaree fortune fastigium presignivit. Cui diversimodas subdidit nationes, non ob hoc solum, ut eis imperando preesset, sed ut ipsis pacis et iustitie copiam ministrando prodesset. Inter illas[d]) multarum igitur occupationum curas, quibus fluctuantis pelagi more pro salubri reipublice statu noster spiritus continue fatigatur, meditatione sollicita revolventes, quod Romaniole provincia utique nobilis et pars Romani Imperii preciosa diu provisione iustitie caruisset, propter quod tam filios et indigenas comitatus predicti quam advenas in provinciam venientes in personis injurias et in rebus damna non modica novimus fuisse perpessos et ibidem iura Imperii multipliciter diminuta, ne talentum nobis in eis[e]) creditum negligenter absondere videamur, utpote qui rationem villicationis nostre sumus in examine stricti iudicii reddituri: ad hoc[f]) dirigimus[g]) aciem mentis nostre, ut ad statum pacificum regionis ipsius imperialis provisionis instantia salubriter intendamus. Quia[h]) tamen circa alias partes imperii ad presens necessario detinemur, ne terra predicta tantisper fructu nostre providientie careat, cui potencie nostre presenciam proximam pollicemur: ecce de tua prudentia et fidelitate confisi te de latere nostro generalem legatum tocius comitatus predicti ad eum velut conscientie nostre conscium pro conservatione pacis et iustitie specialiter destinamus, ut vices nostras universaliter geras ibidem.[h])

---

per hominem celestis ymago subiceret; sed homo prelatus est homini, ut gratiorem prelaturam efficeret identitas speciei. Potissime nempe

divina clementia pretendit hec solia, dum ostensa sibi figura numismatis in reddicione census utrorumque fastigia designavit, quibus diversimodis[b']) subdidit nationes, non ob hoc solum, ut eis imperando preessent, sed ut ipsis pacis et iusticie copiam ministrando prodessent. Inter multas igitur occupationum curas, quibus

noster spiritus fatigatur, ad inducta summi pontificis meditatione sollicita animo revolventes, quod regnum Cicilie, provinciarum Italie decus, hortus[c']) ecclesie per intestinas clades et bella Saracenorum ac quorundam suorum complicum seu fautorum, enormiter immo crudeliter laceretur,

et ne talentum nobis in ipso per summum pontificem creditum negligentia abscondere videamur,

ad hoc direximus aciem mentis nostre, ut ad reformationem et statum pacificum regionis ipsius regalis provisionis instantia intendamus. Quia tamen ad presens pro munitione quam tale tantumque[4]) requirit negocium[4]) decentius ordinanda ad partes istas detinemur, ne terra tantis predita[d']) defectu careat providentie, cui potentie nostre nolumus deesse presenciam: ecce quod ad ordinandum, qualiter barbare nationes suisque complicibus necessarium obstaculum opponatur, necnon ad elidendum eorum aditus et conatus, nobiles et industrios viros conscientie nostre conscios, tales ad sacram Apostolicam sedem de latere nostro speciales dirigimus nuntios et legatos, quid ad conservationem vestram et aliarum civitatum et castrorum, que hucusque fidem et devotionem Ecclesie servare procedent, celeriter prout viderint expedire, donec nos in manu potenti et[e'])

---

[c])–[c]) cui — subiceret fehlt M.
[d]) Inter alias D.
[e]) in eis fehlt D.
[f]) folgt: procurandum D.
[g]) direximus BC.
[h]) AD; ganz abweichend nach Quia tamen C; [h])–[h]) Quia — ibidem fehlt B.

[b']) so Hs.
[c']) ortus Hs.
[d']) so Hs.
[e']) ex Hs.

[4]) Vinea, z. 83.

Quapropter *fidelitat*i tue firmiter
et districte precipiendo mandamus,
quatenus ad statum pacificum regio- 75
nis ipsius et reparationem nostrorum
et imperii iurium in eandem fidem
tuam et sollicitudinem, sicut gratiam nostram caram diligis, sic
efficaciter et diligenter impendas, 80
ut in te diligentie tue testimonio
electionis nostre iudicium com-
mendetur, dum *talem tanto negoti*o
duximus preponendum, ex cuius fide
et industria serenitatis nostre salu- 85
bre propositum de observatione
virium regionis eiusdem singulis
exprimatur.

⁵) Vgl. etwa PdV, II, 9: *in manu
forti et bracchio extenso personaliter nos
conferre..*; PdV, II, 26: *nostre potentie
bracchium..*; PdV, II, 27: *in bracchio
potentie nostre*. Vgl. Ps. 135, 12; Ezech.
20, 33.

extento brachio⁵) veniamus ad con-
terendum, manu coadiutrice divina,
barbaras nationes. Ideoque *fidelitat*em
vestram attentius confortamus, *quatenus
ad* cepte fidelitatis perseverantiam industria vestra se potenter et prudenter
exerceat de nostris viribus et succursu
estate futura infallibiliter spera-
turi⁶). Nos enim paratis rebus et copia
gentium aggregata felices gressus et
potentiam nostram in Appuliam
dirigimus⁷), hostes Barbaricos, Exercituum Domino favente, de Christianorum finibus ad ultimum eorum
exterminium exclusari. Vobis autem
adesse curabimus ad reformationem
optati regiminis et honoris.

⁶) Auch diese Wendung häufig, vgl.
Winkelmann *Acta Imp.*, I, n. 935, 710, z.
34; PdV, V, 129 u. ö.
⁷) Vgl. PdV, V, 129: *felices... gressus
dirigere;* Winkelmann, *Acta Imp.*, I, n.
428, 366, z. 7, u. ö.

Die Vorlage ist, wie die Gegenüberstellung zeigt, fast wörtlich ausgeschrieben. Wenn
auch derartig weitgehende Übereinstimmungen in den beiden anderen Briefen nicht
nachzuweisen sind, so fehlt es dennoch nicht an Anklängen, die ohne das Muster von
Vinea-Briefen undenkbar wären. Zumal III, der Brief an Johann v. Eboli, ist durchsetzt
mit Wendungen, die einem aus der sizilischen Kanzlei vertraut sind. Ein paar Gegen-
überstellungen mögen das verdeutlichen:

Annal. Burton.

Noscat igitur vestra nobilitas per presentes, quod... *ad*
destructionem et *ultimum* Saracenorum Lucherie de
Christianorum finibus *exterminium* eorumque *complicum
et* fautorum, qui universalis Ecclesie fidem nefanda cre-
dulitate deducti errores conantur fedare contagio, necnon
ad reformationem regni Cicilie paratis rebus et *copia*
virium aggregata, *felices gressus* et potentiam nostram
estate futura tempore, quod Reges et principes *ad* prelia
processuri aptum sudoribus bellicis eligerunt, infallibiliter
in Apuliam dirigemus.

Petrus de Vinea

Winkelmann, *Acta Imp.*, I, n. 428, S. 366, z. 6ff.: cum
nos in *estate futura ad ultimum exterminium* nostrorum
rebellium (vgl. H-B, II, 421: in *exterminium... complicum
et* sequacium) persone nostre laboribus parcere non
volentes *gressus nostros* ad partes vestras cum multitudine
gentis et *copia* thesaurorum instanter et *feliciter* prepara-
mus.
PdV, V, 126: Cum pro congregando felici exercitu ad
extremam depopulationem nostrorum rebellium *tempore
congruenti*, eo videlicet, *quo reges* solent *ad* bella *procedere...*

Der Wendung: *tempore congruenti* (PdV, V, 126) entspricht: *temporis congruentia* in III;
PdV, V, 1, und *Annal. Burton.*, II: *conscientie nostre conscium* wird in III zu: *mentis nostre
conscia littera.* Auch die in II durch Sperrdruck hervorgehobene Wendung: in *manu potenti
et extento brachio* kehrt in III — und zwar diesmal richtig zitiert — wieder,¹⁰⁷ und so
wären noch andere Übereinstimmungen anzuführen.

In Brief IV an den Grafen von Aquino ist es vor allem das Exordium,¹⁰⁸ das an Vinea-
Briefe anklingt, ohne daß ich die absolute Übereinstimmung hätte feststellen können;

¹⁰⁷ S. o. Anm. 5 des Brieftextes.
¹⁰⁸ *Inter meditaciones et curas multimodas, quibus nostra
solicitatur intencio, illud* (hier hat der Abschreiber eine
Reihe von Worten ausgelassen; nach PdV, I, 23 wäre

etwa zu ergänzen: *occurrit nostre considerationis precipuum, ut)
votis vestris sub nostri tutela regiminis tranquillitatis et pacis
vigeat plenitudo.* Für die Feststellung mehrerer Parallelen
bin ich Dr. G. Ladner in Rom zu Dank verpflichtet.

ähnlich lautet immerhin PdV, 1, 23; ferner eine Stelle in PdV, V, 1, sowie in Winkelmann, *Acta Imp.* I, n. 916, S. 689. Und auch an sonstigen Anklängen fehlt es nicht, obwohl sie nicht so stark vorherrschen wie in den beiden anderen Briefen. Dennoch: über die Benutzung von Briefen des Petrus de Vinea in der englischen Kanzlei um das Jahr 1256/57 kann kein Zweifel bestehen.

IV.

Es erhebt sich nun die Frage: wie kam die englische Kanzlei zu jenen Briefen, die ihr als Vorlage dienten? Da wird man zunächst daran denken, daß schließlich England im Laufe von rund zwei Jahrzehnten eine recht beträchtliche Anzahl von Briefen, Rundschreiben, Manifesten der sizilischen Kanzlei erhalten hat. Der Gedanke läge nahe, daß man an der englischen Kanzlei diese Briefe gesammelt hätte, daß also mit einer Sammlung ähnlich vielleicht der des Jean de Caux an der französischen Kanzlei[109] zu rechnen wäre. Wir sind über die englischen d. h. die in England selbst entstandenen Briefsammlungen vorerst noch gar nicht unterrichtet. Gefehlt haben sie ganz gewiß nicht, wie z. B. der *Liber epistolaris* des Richard de Bury aus der ersten Hälfte des 14. Jahrhunderts zeigt.[110] Auch das Rotbuch des Exchequers wäre hier zu nennen,[111] obwohl sich kaum sagen läßt, nach welchen Gesichtspunkten — sachlichen oder stilistischen — die darin überlieferten Briefe ausgewählt worden sind. Aber es ist nicht sehr wahrscheinlich, daß die englische Kanzlei um die Mitte des 13. Jahrhunderts bereits aus stilistischen Gründen ein Briefbuch aus Kanzlei-Eingängen angelegt hätte. Dem stünde auch anderes entgegen. Denn so sorgfältig die von der Kanzlei ausgehenden Briefschaften registriert wurden, so sorglos verfuhr man anscheinend mit den Eingängen: erst seit dem 13. Jahrhundert dachte man überhaupt daran, sie aufzubewahren, und erst aus der Zeit Eduards I. sind diese Bestände in etwas größerem Umfang, wenn auch längst nicht etwa vollständig erhalten.[112] So ist es auch zu erklären, daß uns von den vielen an England gerichteten Staatsbriefen Friedrichs II. auf kanzleimäßigem Wege — von dem halboffiziellen Rotbuch des Exchequers abgesehen — nichts erhalten ist, und man wird vergebens die in Betracht kommenden Fonds nach Kaiserbriefen der ersten Hälfte des 13. Jahrhunderts durchsuchen.

Was wir an England-Briefen der sizilischen und der Reichskanzlei des 13. Jahrhunderts kennen, ist durch das Briefbuch des Petrus de Vinea selbst, vor allem aber durch

---

[109] Langlois, *Not. Extr.*, XXXV : 2 (1897), 795ff; vgl. über diese Sammlung auch H. Wieruszowski, *Vom Imperium zum nationalen Königtum* (Munich-Berlin, 1933), 77ff., deren S. 80 geäußerte Vermutung, daß die Vinea-Briefsammlungen wenn nicht in Frankreich selbst, so doch auf dem Wege über fremdländische Kanzleien entstanden seien, ich mir jedoch nicht zu eigen machen möchte.

[110] *Historical Mss. Commission, 4th Report*, Appendix I (London, 1874), 379ff. Auch die Hs. Brit. Mus., Addit. Ms. 24062 gehört vielleicht hierher. Eine Untersuchung über die englischen Briefsammlungen bereitet W. A. Pantin von Oriel College in Oxford vor; vgl. dessen Edition einer späteren *Ars dictandi* in: *Bull. of the John Rylands Library*, XIII (1929), 3–59.

[111] *The Red Book of the Exchequer*, ed. Hubert Hall (London, 1896).

[112] Vgl. etwa die Bemerkungen von W. Holtzmann, *Archiv. Zs.*, XXXIX (1932), 11; F. Bock, *MÖIG.*, Erg.-Bd., XII (1932), 200ff. Die Eingänge zu registrieren, war überhaupt wenig üblich, vgl. etwa für die Kurie die Bemerkungen von Schwalm, *Neues Archiv*, XXV (1899), 570. Doch macht mich Prof. F. Bock freundlicher Weise darauf aufmerksam, daß in Venedig Einlaufregister aus dieser Zeit vorhanden sind, die "Libri Commemoriali" im Archivio di Stato zu Venedig.

Mattheus Parisiensis auf uns gekommen,[113] der freilich mit dem Rotbuch des Exchequers und einer gleichfalls Briefe Friedrichs II. überliefernden Handschrift des Britischen Museums in einem noch ungeklärten Zusammenhang steht.[114] Nicht weniger als zwanzig Briefe der kaiserlichen Kanzlei sind in seine Chronik eingestreut. Mit drei Ausnahmen[115] sind sie alle an England gerichtet, davon vier an Richard v. Cornwall,[116] einer an den englischen Adel,[117] die übrigen an König Heinrich III.[118] Diese Briefe sind dem Chronisten allem Anschein nach im Original zugestellt worden; der Chronist selbst rühmt sich seiner Verbindung mit den Clerks des Exchequers.[119] Aber Mattheus bringt diese Briefe doch nur ihres historischen Inhalts wegen, nicht aus literarisch-stilistischen Gründen, also nicht wegen ihrer schönen Diktion; auf dem Weg über ihn konnten daher diese Briefe nicht Stilmuster werden — außer für den Chronisten selbst.[120]

Dennoch wurden die Briefe der kaiserlichen Kanzlei auch als literarische Produkte bereits im England des 13. Jahrhunderts gewürdigt, wie sich aus einigen wenigen anderen Indizien schließen läßt. An Hss. des Petrus de Vinea sind in England gemeinhin nur solche des 14. Jahrhunderts bekannt. Indessen befindet sich in der Bibliothek von Queen's College in Oxford das Fragment eines Vinea-Briefbuches,[121] das zweifellos noch

[113] Ein Schreiben, das Jerusalemmanifest vom 27. März 1229 (BF, 1738) ist durch Roger Wendover überliefert.

[114] Das Rotbuch des Exchequers enthält neben Papstbriefen und Briefen des Königs von Frankreich folgende Briefe der kaiserlichen Kanzlei (ed. H. Hall, Einl., S. c–ciii, n. 129, 132, 135, 136, 137, 138):
1) BF, 2087 (1235 April 25) an franz. König betr. der englischen Heirat des Kaisers, dazu der Brief Gregors IX. in dieser Angelegenheit (BFW, 7076).
2) BF, 2910 (1240 März 16) Rundschreiben.
3) BF, 3129 (1240 Juli 28) desgl.
4) BF, 3139 (1240 Sept. 13) desgl.
5) BF, 3205 (1241 Mai 18) desgl.
6) BF, 3551 (1246 April 15) desgl.
7) BF, 3579 (1246 August) W. v. Ocra an Heinrich III.
8) BF, 3495 (1245 Juli 31) Rundschreiben (an engl. Adel).
9) BF, 3541 (1246 Februar) Rundschreiben.
Von n. 1 abgesehen handelt es sich also nur um Manifeste der kaiserlichen Kanzlei, die in der gleichen oder in nur wenig abgewandelter Form an alle europäischen Höfe geschickt wurden. — Sieben dieser Manifeste bringt auch Matth. Paris. in seiner Chronik: n. 2 (ed. Luard, III, 631), n. 4 (IV, 65), n. 5 (IV, 125), n. 6 (IV, 570), n. 7 (IV, 575), n. 8 (IV, 538), n. 9 (IV, 475). — Aber auch Brit. Mus., Hargrave Ms. 313, f. 103 (vgl. Liebermann, NA, X (1885), 594; H. Hall, Red Book, I, Einl., S. Lf) enthält fünf dieser Schreiben: n. 3, 4, 6, 8, 9. — In dem Briefbuch des Petrus de Vinea finden sich fünf Briefe des Rotbuches: n. 3 (PdV, I, 36), n. 4 (PdV, I, 34), n. 5 (PdV, I, 19) n. 6 (PdV, II, 10), n. 9 (PdV, I, 2). — Wie im Einzelnen das Rotbuch, Matth. Paris., Hargrave Ms. 313 und das Briefbuch des PdV zusammenhängen, wäre noch zu untersuchen, vgl. Liebermann, MGH, SS, XXVIII, 81, Anm. 21. Unabhängig vom Rotbuch enthält Matth. Paris. noch folgende Schreiben des PdV-Briefbuches: PdV, I, 6 (BF, 2427) an die Kardinäle; PdV, I, 7 (BF, 2430) an die Römer;

[115] BF, 2427, PdV, I, 6 (1239 März 10) an die Kardinäle; BF, 2430, PdV, I, 7 (1239 April 20) an den römischen Senator; BF, 3217 (1241 Juli 3) Tatarenmanifest in der Fassung an den König von Frankreich.

PdV, I, 21 (BF, 2431) an die abendl. Könige; PdV II, 50 (BF, 2291) an Richard v. Cornwall.

[116] BF, 2291, PdV, II, 50 (1237 Dez. 4); BF, 2312 (1238 Febr. 11); BF, 2316 (1238 März 3); BF, 3460 (1245 Febr. 27).

[117] BF, 3495 (1245 Juli 31).

[118] BF, 2431, PdV, I, 21 (1239 April 20); BF, 2531 (Herbst 1239); BF, 2910 (1240 März 16); BF, 3019 (1240 April 25); BF, 3139, PdV, I, 34 (1240 Sept. 13); BF, 3205, PdV, I, 9 (1241 Mai 18); BF, 3216 (1241 Juli 3) = Tatarenmanifest in der Fassung für England; BF, 3264 (1242 Jan. 30); BF, 3422 (1244 März 28); BF, 3541, PdV, I, 2 (Frühjahr 1246); BF, 3551, PdV, II, 10 (1246 Apr. 15). Weiter ist ein Brief des W. v. Ocra an den König hier überliefert: BF, 3579 (Sommer 1246).

[119] Matth. Paris., V, 627; vgl. H. Hall, Red Book, I, Einl., xixf, xxxiif. Nach Liebermann, MGH, SS, XXVIII, 82 hätte der Chronist sein Material auch von Richard v. Cornwall erhalten. Die Annahme von Luard in seiner Ausgabe des Matth. Paris., IV, S. x, daß das Briefmaterial an das St. Albans-Kloster gesandt sei, um dort aufbewahrt zu werden, ist nicht überzeugend.

[120] S. u. Anm. 153.

[121] Queen's College Ms. 389 B. Die Hs. vereinigt Fragmente verschiedenartigster Herkunft aus dem Besitze des Colleges, größtenteils von alten Bucheinbänden stammend, die in unbekannter Zeit zu einem Codex zusammengebunden und in der Bodleiana aufbewahrt wurden. Mr. Denholm-Young, der mich freundlicherweise auf die Hs. aufmerksam machte, hat im Jahre 1932 die Bruchstücke geordnet, soweit möglich identifiziert — die Identifizierung der Vinea-Fragmente ist W. Holtzmann zu danken — und Stück für Stück säuberlich auf starke weiße Papierblätter aufgezogen, so daß jetzt ein Band nach Art der Ancient Correspondence des Record

dem 13. Jahrhundert angehört und das, wie aus den Fragmenten zu ersehen ist, eine der sog. "eingeteilten" Sammlungen darstellt, deren älteste ja noch ins 13. Jahrhundert gehören. Allerdings ist die Hs. nicht englischen Ursprungs, und so bleibt die Frage offen, wann sie nach England gekommen ist. Interessanter ist vielleicht eine Hs. des 12. Jahrhunderts der Bodleiana[122] — Martial und andere lateinische Autoren enthaltend und von Huillard-Bréholles schon beschrieben —, die auf dem letzten Blatt neben anderen Schreibübungen auch eine Abschrift von Friedrichs II. Brief an die Kardinäle vom 10. März 1239 enthält. Nicht daß dieser weitverbreitete Brief in England bekannt war, fällt dabei ins Gewicht, sondern daß es ganz offensichtlich eine englische Kanzleihand der 60er bis 70er Jahre des 13. Jahrhunderts gewesen ist, die das freie Blatt des älteren Codex mit diesem Vinea-Brief ausgefüllt hat. Als Stilmuster aber hat ein kaiserliches Manifest jedenfalls einem anderen Schreiben gedient, das der Zeit Heinrichs III. entstammt, heute leider nur als ein in der Mitte von oben nach unten durchrissener Fetzen in die Bände der Ancient Correspondence eingeklebt ist[123] und dessen Exordium folgendermaßen beginnt:

> *Illis felicitatem ascribit antiquitas, qui ex alieno...*
> *stantiam statum solidant futurorum. Sane dum in pert...*

womit zu vergleichen ist PdV, I, 2:

> *Illos felices describit antiquitas, quibus ex alieno prestatur cautela periculo.*
> *Status namque sequens formatur ex principio precedentis...*

Auch hier ist nicht die Kenntnis des über alle Länder verbreiteten Manifestes auffallend,[124] sondern die Tatsache, daß dieses Manifest als Stilmuster von einem Engländer verwendet wurde.

Gewiß wird man diese wenigen Zeugnisse in ihrer Tragweite nicht überschätzen dürfen. Aber sie zeigen immerhin, daß Petrus de Vinea in England auch im 13. Jahr-

---

Office entstanden ist. Die Spuren des früheren Mißbrauchs der Pergamente als Bucheinbände sind sehr merkbar; viele Fragmente sind in schlechtem Zustand und verstümmelt. Fol. 12–15ᵛ enthält Stücke aus dem III. Buch der PdV-Sammlung in einer nicht-englischen Schrift des XIII. Jhdts. Die vier jetzt vorhandenen Teile auf f. 12, 13, 14, 15 bildeten ursprünglich zwei Doppelblätter. An den früheren Umbruchstellen sind die Pergamente jedoch durchgetrennt, so daß aus den einstigen Doppelblättern vier einzelne Blätter entstanden, die jetzt in falscher Reihenfolge liegen. Es enthält:

f. 12:	PdV, III, 14	beginnend: *(dividen)das utque cuiuslibet*
f. 12ᵛ:	PdV, III, 15–18	bis: *lactabat filios, nutriebat...*
f. 14:	PdV, III, 18	beginnend: *(nutriebat) providos...*
f. 14ᵛ:	PdV, III, 21–22	bis: *de vobis audire veri(dica)*
f. 15:	PdV, III, 37	beginnend: *(qualem) me dimiseritis...*
f. 15ᵛ:	PdV, III, 40	bis: *ut per arida...*
f. 13:	PdV, III, 40	beginnend: *(arida) climata gelidum...*
f. 13ᵛ:	PdV, III, 41	bis: *me iacente desideratum...*

Die dazwischenliegenden Briefe, III, 22–III, 37, die im gedruckten PdV etwa den gleichen Raum einnehmen wie die vorliegenden Briefe, werden gleichfalls zwei Doppelblätter ausgemacht haben. — Zwei weitere Fragmente des Briefbuches finden sich f. 8 und f. 9, die PdV, I, 20–21 enthalten.

[122] Oxford, Bodl. Ms. Auct. J. 1. 8 (2482); vgl. Huillard-Bréholles, *Pierre de la Vigne*, 271. Die Hs. saec. XII. enthält 140 Blätter; f. 138 beginnen Epigramme des Martial, deren letzte 27 Verse die obere linke Ecke von f. 140ᵛ noch einnehmen. Der Rest des Blattes ist mit Schreibübungen ausgefüllt. In der rechten oberen Ecke von einer englischen Kanzleihand der Brief PdV, I, 6 (BF, 2427), der uns noch durch Matth. Paris, III, 548 und *Annal. Stad.*, *MGH, SS*, XVI, 364 überliefert ist. Weiter enthält das Blatt die bekannten Streitverse: *Fata monent etc.* in der von Holder-Egger, *Neues Archiv*, XXX (1904), 337, als "englische Fassung" bezeichneten Form; vgl. ebda. 339.

[123] Record Office, Anc. Corresp., II, n. 131.

[124] Es findet sich auch im *Red Book* und im Hargrave Ms. 313, s.o. Anm. 114.

hundert nicht ganz ohne Wirkung geblieben war, und es ist durchaus denkbar, daß die Zahl solcher Zeugnisse in Laufe der Zeit sich noch wird vermehren lassen. Was man aber vergebens suchen wird, ist die Vorlage für den Brief an Teano, ist das Schreiben PdV, V, 1. Und das ist ganz erklärlich. Denn PdV, V, 1 ist ein Diplom zur Ernennung der höchsten kaiserlichen Beamten, der Generallegaten und Generalvikare. Es war nur für den internen Gebrauch der kaiserlichen Verwaltung in Italien bestimmt, hatte für außenpolitische Propaganda gar keinen Wert und fand Verwendung ausschließlich in dem italischen Staat Kaiser Friedrichs II., nicht in Sizilien. Auf dem Wege über die Propaganda hatte dieses Diplom, das ja vor allem die Befugnisse der Statthalter umschrieb, niemals an die englische Kanzlei gelangen können. Auch dem Mattheus Parisiensis ist es daher unbekannt geblieben, wie es selbstverständlich auch in der französischen Sammlung des Jean de Caux fehlt. Wie hätte dieses Diplom auch ins Ausland gelangen können? Welches Interesse konnte man für dieses Verwaltungsformular haben? Sollte es durch einen Zufall, vielleicht gar durch einen der Empfänger nach England verschlagen sein, um dann bei passender Gelegenheit von der englischen Kanzlei ausgewertet zu werden?

Das Diplom ist uns — von kleineren Abweichungen abzusehen — in zwei verschiedenen Fassungen und in sieben Ausfertigungen für fünf verschiedene Empfänger überliefert. Die ursprüngliche längere Fassung kennen wir in den Ausfertigungen für Enzio als Generalvikar der Romaniola und als Generallegaten der Lombardei; weiter für Friedrich v. Antiochien und für Ezzelino.[125] Überliefert ist uns diese Fassung lediglich durch Hss. des PdV-Briefbuches. Von der jüngeren Fassung mit einer erheblich verkürzten Arenga, die mindestens seit 1248 ausschließlich gebraucht wurde, ist uns ein Diplom im Original erhalten: die Ernennung des Thomas v. Savoyen zum Generallegaten der Lombardei.[125a] Seine Ernennung zum Generalvikar von Pavia aufwärts kennen wir aus einem Transsumpt des Jahres 1310.[125b] Schließlich ist uns durch die Marseiller Registerauszüge noch die Ausfertigung für Meinhard v. Görz als Generalkapitän der Steiermark erhalten.[125c] Der Empfängerkreis ist natürlich erheblich größer gewesen — aber wie sollten diese sizilischen Beamten und italienischen Fürsten dazu gekommen sein, ihr Statthalterdiplom nach England zu schicken? Ein Umstand freilich könnte an die Übermittlung durch den Empfänger denken lassen. Denn einer der hohen Beamten, Thomas v. Savoyen, stand in sehr naher Beziehung zum englischen Hof. Er war durch die Königin Eleanor ein Onkel Heinrichs III. und weilte wie fast alle Savoyarden zum großen Ärger der Engländer sehr häufig am englischen Hof — zuletzt noch in den

---

[125] Der Vermutung von Ladner, *MÖIG.*, Erg.-Bd., XII, (1932), 105, Anm. 1, daß in der Tat Ezzelino zum Generalvikar der östlichen Lombardei *(a Pavia inferius)* ernannt worden ist, möchte ich mich anschließen; es geht schließlich nicht an, ganz präzise Angaben wie das zweimal wiederholte *in Lombardia a Pavia inferius* willkürlich in *Romaniola* abzuändern und dementsprechend dann *vicarius generalis* durch *legatus*, *Ezzelinus* durch *Entius* zu ersetzen. In Betracht käme das Jahr 1238, in dem wir über die Einrichtung des Generalvikariats *a Papia superius* unterrichtet werden (Kantorowicz, Erg.-Bd., 195), dem an sich die gleichzeitige Einrichtung des Sprengels *a Papia inferius* entsprechen würde. Über diesen Sprengel beginnen unsere sonstigen Nachrichten aber erst 1239. Um 1238 könnte Ezzelino, was mit seiner damaligen Stellung auch am besten zusammenpassen würde, das Generalvikariat, freilich nur für kürzere Zeit, innegehabt haben.

[125a] *MGH, Const.*, II, n. 273.

[125b] *MGH, Const.*, II, n. 272.

[125c] *MGH, Const.*, II, n. 270.

Jahren 1254 und 1257/58,[126] als die englische Thronkandidatur für Sizilien bereits die abendländische Politik beschäftigte. Und Thomas von Savoyen wußte daraus ja auch Nutzen zu ziehen, indem er sich von England mit dem Fürstentum Capua beschenken ließ.[127] Aber abgesehen von der Unwahrscheinlichkeit, daß der Savoyarde mit den Originalurkunden oder deren Abschriften nach England gereist wäre, will es der Zufall, daß wir über den Verbleib gerade der Diplome des Thomas v. Savoyen unterrichtet sind[127a] und daß weiter gerade seine Diplome die spätere Fassung mit verkürzter Arenga aufweisen, während der Teano-Brief die ursprüngliche längere Fassung als Vorlage benutzt und ausgeschrieben hat. Damit entfällt diese Hypothese.

Eine weitere Möglichkeit bestände darin, daß die Kurie dieses Schriftstück — vielleicht zusammen mit anderem sizilisch-staufischem Material — dem König von England als künftigem Herrn Siziliens zur Verfügung gestellt hat. Derartiges Material war zweifellos im Besitz der Kurie, und selbst das fragliche Dokument konnte dort schon damals bekannt gewesen sein: ihres philosophischen Gehaltes wegen hatte Marinus v. Eboli die Arenga des Statthalterdiploms in seine Sammlung eingereiht.[128] Gewiß ist diese Sammlung nicht vor 1268 entstanden, und so käme dem in unserem Fall genau so wenig Bedeutung bei wie der noch späteren Verwendung des Diploms durch Gregor X. oder Berard v. Neapel.[129] Aber es bleibt natürlich die Möglichkeit offen, daß schon vor der Sammlung des Marinus v. Eboli staufische Materialien an der päpstlichen Kanzlei gesammelt waren, und das wäre wichtig insofern, als der Vorgänger des Marinus als *S. R. E. vicecancellarius*, Jacob Buoncambio, später Bischof von Bologna, im Jahre 1255 in den Angelegenheiten Siziliens vom Papst nach England geschickt wurde.[130] Und wir wissen, daß damals Jacob als Bischof von Bologna jenem geheimen Rat Heinrichs III. angehörte, in dessen Schoß allein über die sizilischen Fragen Beschlüsse gefaßt werden sollten, unter Umgehung von Adel und Klerus. Die Zusammenarbeit dieses absolutistischen Kabinets mit der Kurie aber war außerordentlich eng. So erfahren wir durch einen Zufall, daß die Transskripte aller Sizilien betreffenden Privilegien mit dem Siegel des Jacob Buoncambio, des päpstlichen Bevollmächtigten und Bischofs von Bologna, versehen und in der Wardrobe aufbewahrt werden sollten.[131] Nun weilte der Bischof in der Zeit, als Heinrich III. den Brief an Teano sandte, zwar schon seit langem nicht mehr in England; aber es ist vielleicht doch nicht ganz von der Hand zu weisen, daß durch ihn, den ehemaligen Vizekanzler der Kurie, jenes als Vorlage dienende Diplom nach England gelangt ist, freilich wohl in einer Briefsammlung.

Denn man wird von vornherein die Annahme ausschließen müssen, daß, etwa gleich den Manifesten und anderen Schreiben, das Diplom isoliert der englischen Kanzlei in die Hände geriet. Man wird im Gegenteil noch weiter gehen müssen: da ja auch andere

[126] Mugnier, *Les Savoyards en Angleterre au XIII*ᵉ *siècle* (Chambéry, 1890), 113; L. Wurstemberger, *Peter II. von Savoyen*, I, 344; W. Kienast a. a. O., II, 1, S. 144.

[127] 1254 Oktober 3; Rymer, I, 308; BFW, 13943.

[127a] Vgl. Anm. 125a und 125b.

[128] Die Arenga ist bei Marinus überschrieben: *Cause propter quas imperium est inventum*; vgl. Schillmann, *Die Formularsammlung des Marinus v. Eboli*, I (Rom, 1929), 137, n. 508; s. o. Anm. 105.

[129] Vgl. Anhang.

[130] BFW, 8981, 8990, 8994.

[131] S. o. Anm. 89 und *Cal. Pat. R. 1247–58*, 451; über den geheimen Rat des Königs vgl. die Bemerkungen von Ch. Bémont, *Simon de Montfort* (engl. Übers. v. E. F. Jacob, Oxford, 1930), 130f.

Vinea-Briefe in den englischen Schreiben anklingen, so wird man an eine Sammlung von Erzeugnissen der staufischen Kanzlei — eben an eine Sammlung sog. Vinea-Briefe — zu denken haben, die damals nach England gebracht worden ist. Und da erscheint es als das Nächstliegende, daß diese Sammlung auf dem direkten Weg nach England gelangte, nämlich aus Sizilien.

Es darf nicht vergessen werden, daß für die süditalischen Guelfen der englische König oder dessen Sohn Edmund als der vom Papst belehnte und darum rechtmäßige König Siziliens zu gelten hatte. Die Beziehungen zwischen den beiden Königreichen — schon einmal im 12. Jahrhundert sehr intensiv[131a] — waren in jenen Jahren wieder außerordentlich lebhaft geworden, so daß England bisweilen von Siziliern geradezu überschwemmt schien. Die Durchsetzung des englischen Klerus mit Italienern — auf andere Ursachen zurückgehend — bleibe hier unerörtert. Doch ist immerhin selbst als Dekan von St. Paul in London ein Süditaliener, Walter von Salerno, in jenen Jahren nachzuweisen.[132] Wichtiger ist es, daß es damals auch an namhaften süditalienischen Juristen in England nicht fehlte. Im engeren Dienste des Königs und als seinen ständigen Vertreter an der Kurie in Sachen Siziliens, der oft genug auch in England weilte, trifft man immer wieder auf Robert von Bari, uns sehr genau bekannt als späterer Protonotar Karls von Anjou, der in dem Verfahren gegen Konradin 1268 den Vorsitz führte.[133] Weiter begegnen wir in England während jener Jahre vielfach dem Judex und Magister Innocenz v. Trani, der gleichfalls durch lange Zeit im unmittelbaren Dienst des Königs stand.[134] Aus den Rolls erfährt man, daß der Kaufmann Sampson v. Salerno, der in England lebte, ein besonderer Schützling des Königs war,[135] während des Königs Schwägerin Sancha, Gräfin von Cornwall, sich für eine Johanna v. Apulien verwandte.[136] Sizilien war zweifellos damals in England Mode, und der junge Edmund, der künftige König des süditalischen Reiches, legte gelegentlich sogar apulische Tracht an.[137] Selbst im Palast und Marstall trifft man Apulier. Fortunat, der unselige Hofnarr, der sich des Königs handgreiflichen Scherzen ausgesetzt sah, war freilich ein Lucchese,[138] aber Leopardi, der italienische Arzt der Königin,[139] mag aus Salerno hervorgegangen sein, und in dem Marstall des Königs war die Wartung des Elefanten, den ihm 1255 der König von Frankreich zum Geschenk gemacht hatte, einem Kalabresen anvertraut, Henricus de Fiore, der — wie auf einer der Zeichnungen des Mattheus Parisiensis zu sehen ist — in der für die Falkner und Jäger Friedrichs II. üblichen Tracht seinen Dienst verrichtete.[140] Apulien war also im damaligen England recht stark vertreten — viel stärker etwa als im

---

[131a] Vgl. Haskins, *EHR*, XXVI (1911), 433ff.

[132] Matth. Paris., V, 432, 678; VI, 307f; nicht in Betracht kommt hier die große Zahl der mit Pfründen versehenen Süditaliener, die niemals nach England gekommen sind.

[133] *Cal. Close R. 1256–59*, 253 (1258 Aug. 4); BFW, 13978, 14252 u. ö.; vgl. Hampe, *Konradin*, 318, Anm. 5.

[134] *Cal. Close R. 1256–59*, 53 (1257 Mai 12); *Cal. Pat. R. 1256–58*, 570 (1257 Juli 20); er ist schon in der Zeit Innocenz' IV. mehrfach in England nachzuweisen, vgl. Bliss, *Calendar of Papal Registers*, I, 258, 298 und 395 für einen späteren Aufenthalt unter Urban IV.

[135] *Cal. Close R. 1254–56*, 26, 81 (1255 Jan. 19, Mai 9); *Cal. Close R. 1256–59*, S. 185 (1258 Jan. 10).

[136] *Cal. Close R. 1254–56*, 265 (1256 Januar 22).

[137] Matth. Paris., V, 623f.

[138] *Cal. Close R. 1259–61*, 59 u. ö.; vgl. A. E. Stamp, "The Court and Chancery of Henry III," in *Historical Essays in Honour of James Tait* (Manchester, 1933), 310.

[139] W. H. Blaauw, *The Baron's War* (2. Aufl., London, 1871), 27.

[140] M. R. James, "The Drawings of Matthew of Paris," in *The Walpole Society 1925–1926* [XIV] (Oxford, 1926), 7, Taf. VI.

Deutschland Friedrichs II. — und die vielen Gesandtschaften aus dem Süden, die seit Edmunds Thronkandidatur in England aus- und eingingen, brachten einen neuen Einstrom des süditalischen Elements, das sich schon vorher erfreulicher Weise auch in Gestalt von Goldaugustalen im königlichen Schatz niedergeschlagen hatte.[141] Wir wissen nicht, in wessen Auftrag im Juni 1257 die *nuncii Apulie* Peter v. Rieti, Simon v. Spoleto, Taddeus v. Batza (Bancia?) und Aligno v. Aquila in London weilten.[142] Aber außer ihnen war zwischen 1256 und 1258 im Auftrag sizilischer Prälaten und Adliger zu Rom Johann v. Montefusculo,[143] war als Beauftragter sizilischer Adliger zu Pisa Johannes de Alfario,[144] waren Gesandte des Podestà von Aquila,[145] des *comes Tucye*[146] — wer immer dieser Graf gewesen sein mag — in England anzutreffen; und weiter lernte man Robert v. Apulien als Prokurator des Franciscus von Neapel,[147] einen Kleriker Gentilis als Boten des Grafen Roger v. Celano[148] in England kennen neben dem sizilischen Marschall der Papstpartei Roger Fimette von Lentini,[149] der wie Johann Colonna, der Erzbischof von Messina,[150] sich im Auftrage der Kurie zeitweilig in England aufhielt.

Angesichts dieser sizilischen Invasion ist nichts wahrscheinlicher, als daß damals eine Sammlung von Briefen der sizilischen Kanzlei oder eben: ein Vinea-Briefbuch nach England miteingeführt worden ist und daß einer der sizilischen Gesandten, sei es auf Veranlassung des englischen Königs oder der Kurie oder noch wahrscheinlicher: aus eigener Initiative und zu eignem Gebrauch, ein derartiges Briefbuch nach England mitgebracht hatte, dessen Spuren wir in den fraglichen Briefen begegneten. Und auf ein Briefbuch, nicht etwa auf ein Paket zufälliger sizilischer Kanzleiakten, weist noch anderes hin. Denn das in England als Vorlage benutzte Schreiben war für die Süditaliener kanzleimäßig schon veraltet und nur noch von literarischem Wert, da man spätestens seit 1248 das als Vorlage benutzte Formular gar nicht mehr gebrauchte, es vielmehr durch ein kürzeres ersetzt hatte. Gerade die ursprüngliche längere Fassung aber ist — und zwar vermutlich schon sehr früh — zu einem Bestandteil der Briefsammlung des Petrus de Vinea geworden; denn sowohl Marinus v. Eboli wie die, anscheinend aus Berard v. Neapel schöpfende, Madrider Briefsammlung wie das Schriftstück der englischen Kanzlei folgen der älteren längeren Fassung. Es ist offenbar die Fassung, die von Vinea selbst herrührte und als Modell in die frühesten, vielleicht an der kaiserlichen Kanzlei selbst noch zusammengestellten Briefbücher einging.[151]

[141] *Cal. Pat. R. 1247–58*, 314.

[142] *Cal. Close R. 1256–59*, 68 (1257 Juni 24).

[143] S. o. Anm. 102; er ist noch einmal 1261 in England nachzuweisen, vgl. Rymer, I, 405.

[144] Anc. Corresp., XLVII, n. 37 (1258 Aug. 14).

[145] *Cal. Pat. R. 1247–58*, 661 (1258 Jan. 23).

[146] Ebda.

[147] *Cal. Pat. R. 1247–58*, 643 (1258 Aug. 1).

[148] *Cal. Close R. 1256–59*, 22 (1258 Aug. 4).

[149] *Cal. Pat. R. 1247–58*, 629 (1258 Mai 7); 639 (1258 Juni 28) u. ö.; er war, von Friedrich II. verbannt, unter Konrad IV. wieder ins Königreich zurückgekehrt, vgl. Karst, *Geschichte Manfreds*, 136ff, 152 und ist nicht zu verwechseln mit einem Predigermönch gleichen Namens,

der gleichzeitig in Sizilien für den Papst und für England tätig war, vgl. Rodenberg, *Innocenz IV. u. d. Königr. Sizilien*, 98, Anm. 4; *MGH, Epp. Pont.*, III, 67, n. 85ff.

[150] 1256 Nov. 9 erfolgt seine Entsendung nach England (BFW, 9086, 9087); für seinen Aufenthalt in England vgl. *Cal. Pat. R. 1247–58*, 551 (1257 April 21) und ebda. 567 (1257 Juni 26); für seine Rückkehr nach Rom ebda. 592 (1257 Mai 10); s. o. Anm. 75.

[151] Daran ändert die Tatsache nichts, daß auch die kürzere Fassung des Diploms in Vinea-Briefbüchern vorkommt z. B. in *Vat. Palat. Lat.* 955, vgl. Ladner, *MÖIG.*, Erg.-Bd., XII, (1932), 106 zu D. 5. Übrigens ist hier die Arenga noch etwas länger als in den übrigen Diplomen dieses Typs, vgl. *MGH, Const.*, II, 380, z. 36ff.

Wenn man sich nun in England dieses ursprünglichen Modells, das um 1238/9 an der kaiserlichen Kanzlei gebraucht wurde, nicht aber des seit 1248 gültigen "modernen" Formulars bediente, so scheint eine andere Erklärung als die des Vorhandenseins eines Vinea-Briefbuches kaum mehr möglich. Für die Tatsache selbst aber: daß man sich in jenen Jahren an der englischen Kanzlei überhaupt der Vinea-Briefe als Vorlage bediente, liegt die Erklärung nahe genug. Man wollte die schön stilisierten Schreiben der neuen sizilischen Untertanen ganz einfach in einem adäquaten Stil beantworten und suchte genau die Sprache und den Ton zu treffen, den die Süditaliener seit Jahrzehnten zu hören gewohnt waren, legte also auch in den Briefen gleichsam apulische Tracht an — das dem mittelalterlichen Denken einzig gemäße, allbekannte und naheliegende Mittel jeder neuen Dynastie, in die äußeren Formen der vorangegangenen möglichst unmerklich hineinzuwachsen.

Es bliebe noch die Frage offen, ob nicht einer der in England weilenden Apulier jene Briefe, die uns durch die Annalen von Burton überliefert sind, diktiert haben könnte. Das ist selbstverständlich möglich. Wie wir wissen, haben zumindest die päpstlichen Bevollmächtigten, aber doch wohl auch einzelne Sizilier an den Beratungen über die Zukunft des süditalischen Königreiches teilgenommen. Wir wissen auch, in welchen nahen Beziehungen der Bischof von Bologna, Jacob Buoncambio, zu dem Rate des Königs gestanden hat und erfahren gelegentlich, daß auch Johann Colonna, der Erzbischof von Messina, über die geplanten Maßnahmen zur Entsendung eines Kapitäns nach Sizilien an den Papst berichtet hat.[152] So wäre es immerhin möglich, daß die fraglichen Briefe etwa im Auftrage des mit den lokalen Verhältnissen wohlvertrauten Johann Colonna von einem Apulier-Sizilier diktiert worden sind. Indessen, die Überlieferung der Briefe in einer englischen Chronik, die in großer Anzahl Erzeugnisse der englischen Kanzlei ausgeschrieben hat und offenbar zur Kanzlei in nahen Beziehungen stand, nötigt uns dennoch, die Briefe — wer immer ihr Diktator war — als Erzeugnisse der englischen Kanzlei anzusprechen, die ja nicht ohne weiteres Fremden die eignen Befugnisse abgetreten haben wird. Schließlich ist ja die englische Kanzlei durchaus nicht ganz ohne jede Kenntnis des gehobenen Stils gewesen, wie die angeführten Beispiele zeigten, und überdies: wo die unmittelbare Vorlage des Vinea-Briefes fehlt, fallen auch die englischen Schreiben stilmäßig sofort erheblich ab. Wie leicht man aber bei Kenntnis von Vinea-Briefen wenigstens Ton und Sprechweise der kaiserlichen Kanzlei nachzuahmen vermochte, auch wenn man in der *ars dictandi* weniger bewandert war, das zeigt etwa das Beispiel des Mattheus Paris, der es mit Leichtigkeit fertigbrachte, auf Grund echter Briefe recht geschickt kaiserliche Schreiben zu ergänzen, wenn nicht zu erfinden, oder gar ganze kaiserliche Reden und Ansprachen zu erdichten, die durchaus vineamäßig klingen.[153]

Aber gleichgültig, ob ein Engländer oder ob ein Apulier — wie etwa Heinrich v. Isernia am böhmischen, Peter v. Prezza und Nicolaus v. Trani am meissenschen Hof — für den hohen Briefstil der englischen Kanzlei verantwortlich zu machen ist. Das Wesentliche liegt doch in der Tatsache selbst, daß sich schon um 1256/57 der Gebrauch

---

[152] *Cal. Pat. R. 1247–58*, 567 (1257 Juni 26).   [153] O. Vehse, *Die amtliche Propaganda... Friedrichs II.*, 219ff., 224f.

16*

einer wie immer gearteten Sammlung von Briefen des Petrus de Vinea an einer fremden Kanzlei nachweisen läßt. Und weiter: es ist, soviel ich sehe, überhaupt die früheste Übernahme des Diktats, die erste Verwendung von Vinea-Briefen als Stilmustern an einer fremdländischen Kanzlei, von der wir wissen. Dabei sehe ich von den rein sachlichen Entlehnungen und inhaltlichen Übernahmen einzelner Programmpunkte kaiserlicher Reformmanifeste durch den französischen Adel ab, die längst bekannt sind.[154] Für die gewiß noch nicht hinreichend durchforschte Auswirkung Vineas aber ist diese Übernahme seines Diktats durch die englische Kanzlei nicht ohne Belang. Wir wissen Einiges über seine Wirkung in Meissen und Böhmen, in Österreich und an den Reichskanzleien der Habsburger, Luxemburger und Ludwigs des Bayern; wir wissen, daß die Briefe nachgewirkt haben in Sizilien und Aragon, in Neapel und Frankreich, an Kanzleien italienischer Städte, vielleicht auch an einzelnen Kardinalskanzleien und an der päpstlichen Kurie; wir kennen seinen Einfluß auf Dante, Petrarca, Rienzo, auf Briefstil und Gesetzgebung Karls IV.[155] Von einer praktischen Auswirkung der Vinea-Briefe auch in England — und dies schon wenige Jahre nach Vineas Tod — wußten wir bisher nichts. Aber es handelt sich nicht darum allein. Petrus de Vinea war wie der staufische Monarch, in dessen Namen er sprach, eine schlechthin europäische Geistesmacht, die so verschiedenartiges geistiges Gut mit sich führte und auch locker machte, daß die unwahrscheinlichsten Auswirkungen nicht überraschen können. So rückt vielleicht auch jene bekannte Diktat-Übereinstimmung sizilischer Verordnungen mit dem berühmten Reskript Simons v. Montfort vom Jahre 1264,[156] das man als die Geburtsurkunde des englischen Unterhauses anzusehen pflegt, nunmehr in ein anderes Licht, und der Zusammenhang wird weniger problematisch, als es bisher der Fall hatte sein müssen.

ANHANG

Die Hs. des Escorial, d. III. 3., eine Papier-Hs. des 14. Jhdts. spanischer Provenienz, von der ich durch die Liebenswürdigkeit meines einstigen Schülers, Herrn Angel Ferrari in Madrid, eine Anzahl von Photographien erhalten konnte, stellt eine Sammlung der verschiedensten Briefe aus den verschiedensten Ländern dar. Ihr Inhalt ist durch die sehr genauen Angaben von A. Antolín, *Catálogo de los Códices latinos de la Real Biblioteca del Escorial*, I (Madrid, 1910), 464ff recht gut zu übersehen. Fol. 100–102v — im Katalog als Gruppe XI bezeichnet — enthält ein Testament Kaiser Friedrichs II., auf das mich Dr. C. Erdmann aufmerksam machte, eine Stilübung zweifellos italienischer Herkunft, die jedoch nicht ganz ohne Interesse ist und auf die ich an anderer Stelle zurückkomme. Gruppe XII, beginnend mit f. 103, enthält im wesentlichen Papstbriefe, die aus der

[154] Gräfe, *Die Publizistik... Friedrichs II.*, 229ff., bes. 233.

[155] Für die Nachwirkung der Vinea-Briefe in den Kanzleien vgl. Kantorowicz, Erg.-Bd., 113f; Ladner, a. a. O., 95, Anm. 1; Wieruszowski, *Vom Imperium zum nationalen Königtum*, 58–83; Burdach, *Rienzo u. d. geistige Wandlung seiner Zeit*, 14ff., 348, u. *passim*.

[156] Winkelmann, *Jahrbücher Kaiser Friedrichs II.*, II, 412, bringt als erster die Stellen bei Ryccard. Sangerm. (ed. Gaudenzi) 144 und Rymer, I, 2, 92f., das Reskript vom 14. Dezember 1264, miteinander in Verbindung; vgl. Kantorowicz, Erg.-Bd., 114; Wieruszowski, a. a. O., 130f.

Sammlung des Berard v. Neapel stammen. Legt man die Numerierung der Berard-Briefe (B) von Kaltenbrunner, *MÖIG*, VII, (1907), 557ff zugrunde, so entspricht

n. 1 = B. 35 = P. 18635	n. 10 = B. 343 = P. 20989	n. 19 = B. 286 = P. 20838
n. 2 = B. 36 = P. 18619	n. 11 = B. 344 = P. 20990	n. 20 = B. 369 = P. 21072
n. 3 = B. 37 = P. 18633	n. 12 = B. 207 = P. 20613	n. 21 = B. 209 = P. 20612
n. 5 = B. 284 = P. 20857	n. 13 = B. 208 = P. 20614	n. 22 = B. 384
n. 9 = B. 311 = P. 20969	n. 18 = B. 287 = P. 20845	n. 23 = BF, 4608

Da mehrfach die Reihenfolge der Berard-Briefe gewahrt ist, so kann kein Zweifel darüber bestehen, daß der Sammlung des Escorial mittelbar oder unmittelbar u. a. auch Berard zugrunde gelegen hat. Über Berard und die von ihm abhängigen italienischen Brief-sammlungen ist freilich noch längst nicht soweit Klarheit geschaffen, um sagen zu können, ob auf ihn auch die Briefe XII, 14 (f. 115^{r-v}) und XII, 15 (f. 115^v–116^v) zurückgehen. Beide vermag ich bei Berard nicht nachzuweisen, was freilich wenig besagen will. In beiden Fällen handelt es sich um Stilübungen in Nachahmung päpstlicher Briefe, denen jedoch Diktate Vineas als Vorbild dienten. Beide Briefe gehören auch inhaltlich zu-sammen, da beide an Prälaten und Bevölkerung eines Landes — n. 14: Dänemarks, n. 15: Spaniens — gerichtet sind mit dem Befehl, sich der Sache eines unmündigen Königs und einer die Regentschaft führenden Königin-Witwe anzunehmen. Während der Brief an Dänemark jedoch nur einzelne Anklänge an das uns hier interessierende Schreiben PdV, V, 1, das auch dem englischen Brief als Muster vorlag, aufzuweisen hat, ist das Exordium des Briefes an Spanien dem des Statthalterdiploms Friedrichs II. wörtlich gefolgt. Inhalt-lich weist es in die Zeit der kastilischen Thron- und Bürgerkämpfe, die seit dem Tode des Infanten Fernando de la Cerda (1275) durch Jahrzehnte das unglückliche Land nicht zur Ruhe kommen ließen. Unter der Königin wird wohl Maria de Molina, Witwe Sanchos IV., zu verstehen sein, die seit 1295 für ihren Sohn Fernando IV. die Regent-schaft führte und in der Tat von allen Seiten aufs schwerste bedrängt wurde. Daß es sich um eine Stilübung handelt, geht wohl schon aus dem in einem Papstbrief undenkbaren Titel eines *rex* bzw. einer *regina Yspanie* hervor, und der Brief hat für uns nur Interesse, weil er die Benutzung des Statthalterdiploms in einer Berard v. Neapel nahestehenden Sammlung zeigt und für die Verbreitung Vineas auch in Kastilien einen Beitrag liefert. — Ich drucke ihn hier ab, wobei *Kursiv*schrift Entlehnungen aus dem Statthalterdiplom kenntlich macht.

Prelatis et universitati Hyspanie (fol. 115^v–116^v).

Ad extollenda iustorum preconia et reprimendas insolentias transgressorum[a] *prospiciens e celo iustitia erexit*[1] *in populis regnantium solia et diversorum principum potestates. Caruisset namque libenter humana conditio jugo dominii nec libertatem a se, quam eis natura donaverat, homines abdicassent, nisi quod impunita licentia scelerum in evidentem perniciem humani generis redundabat. Et sic*[2] *ex*[b] *necessitate quadam oportuit naturam subesse iusticie et servire iudicio libertatem. Nec*

---

[a] Am Rande: *(m)ultum plena.*	[1] So auch BCDEFGM; s. o. S. 233, Anm. 105.
[b] *ex* getilgt.	[2] So auch EFG.

exquiri extrinsecus decuit ad populorum regimen speciem alteram[3] *creature, sed homo prelatus est homini ut graciorem prelaturam efficeret ydempnitas speciei.* Poro *non ob hoc solum* dominos subditis *sententia divina prefecit, ut eis dominando preessent, sed ut ipsis pacis et iusticie copiam ministrando prodessent,* ut appensis in statera iudicii meritis singulorum condignis dignos prosequantur favoribus et in facinorosos exerceant debite gladium ultionis et ut subditi colla humilient mandatis et beneplacitis dominorum eisque debitam reverentiam, ad quam ipsi tenentur, impendant et circa iura ipsorum eis liberaliter exhibenda nostri mandato pareant redemptoris, qui *hostensa sibi figura numismatis* que sunt dei deo et que sunt cesaris cesari reddenda constituit et precepit. Cum enim ex deo regnent reges et principes principentur[c], hii, qui resistere terrenis potestatibus moliuntur, manifeste videntur divinis dispositionibus obviare, ac propter hoc celestem contra se iram provocant, dampnificantur frequenter in temporalibus et nonnunquam animarum pericula, quod est dampnosius, incurrere dinoscuntur. Cupientes itaque ut vos iura debite devotionis et fidei karissimo in Christo filio nostro... pupillo illustri regi Yspanie, hoc maxime[d] tempore, quo ipsum adversariorum suorum tenet carcer inclusum, prompta liberacione ac liberali promptitudine impendatis, presertim cum nos ipsum eiusdemque regnum sub nostra et apostolice sedis protectione duxerimus admittendum, universitatem vestram monemus etc. quatenus eidem regi et karissime in Christo filie nostre... vidue illustri regine Yspanie matri et tutrici eiusdem obedientes ac intendentes fideliter et devote, circa defensionem dicti regni et liberationem ipsius omnem, quam postestis, exhibeatis opem et operam efficacem, nec permitatis eandem reginam et dictum regnum, prout in vobis est, ab eorum adversariis aliquatenus molestari, ita quod crescatis exinde meritis apud deum, penes nos gratia et apud homines clara fama dictusque rex vestre constantis fidelitatis et constancie fidelis obsequia suo loco et tempore congruis retributionibus prosequatur.

[c] Darüber: *dominentur.*   [d] *maximo.*   [3] Sonst stets *aliam.*

ANONYMI "AUREA GEMMA"

I<small>N A FUNDAMENTAL</small> study on the *artes dictandi* in Italy during the twelfth century, C. H. Haskins contrived a means of cutting a highway through a jungle.[1] The difficulty of dealing with these manuals of written eloquence, of ascertaining their date, place of origin, and authorship, and of disentangling the web of mutual borrowing is well known. Of a vast material, only a fragment has been published; and, with a few exceptions, the editions are anything but critical. Of the three sections into which the *artes dictandi* were gradually divided—the prologue, the *ars* proper (i.e. the doctrine), and the model letters—it is mainly the prologues and letters which offer a clue to dating and locating the writings, since the doctrinal section usually abounds in traditional and formalized rhetorical rules. But even the prologues and letters are often liable to fool the student of *artes dictandi*. Sometimes the author omitted his name intentionally;[2] sometimes he wrote two or more prologues to practically the same manual;[3] and on other occasions the author would borrow so extensively from his predecessors or contemporaries that it is hard to tell which treatise is whose.[4] Also, there are the copyists who complicate the investigations. For their teaching and for the use of their classes, the schoolmasters liked to fuse the works of several authors or to change name and initials mentioned in prologues and letters in order to adjust the imported texts to new surroundings.[5] Finally, there is

---

Reprinted, with permission, from *Medievalia et Humanistica*, I (1943), 41–57. The original has this prefatory note:

It is the author's intention to substantiate in this present article a statement made in his study on "Petrus de Vinea in England," *Mitteilungen des Österreichischen Instituts für Geschichtsforschung*, LI (1938), 48, n. 17, where he maintained that ascription to Henricus Francigena of an *Aurea gemma* found in an Oxford manuscript (*infra*, n. 10) was not correct. He is greatly indebted to Dr. Carl Erdmann from whose profound knowledge he like many another scholar has greatly profited, and who placed at the author's disposal, years ago, photostats of practically all the manuscripts here under discussion.

[1] C. H. Haskins, *Studies in Mediaeval Culture* (Oxford, 1929), 170–192.

[2] See, e.g., the preface to John of Garland's *Epithalamium*, published by L. J. Paetow, "Morale Scolarium of John of Garland," *Memoirs of the University of California*, vol. IV, no. 2 (Berkeley, 1927), 101, n. 87: "Auctor nomen suum tacuit, dicens: 'Nomen celo meum quia non a nomine labor, Si sponsa placeat virginis iste labor.' Auctor est hystoriographus..."Anonymity was considered good style especially among the lawyers; see, in general,

Hermann Kantorowicz, *Studies in the Glossators of the Roman Law* (Cambridge, 1938), 213f., and also Giovanni Ferretti, "Roffredo Epifanio da Benevento," *Studi medievali*, III (1908), 238f., who quotes (*ibid.*, n. 2) the interesting statement of Andreas of Isernia: "Compilator et compositor huius operis... noluit nomen suum epigrammate superscribi, sicut faciunt viri honesti non curantes de pompis."

[3] See, e.g., *infra*, App. I–III, and the author's study on Guido Faba forthcoming in *Mediaeval and Renaissance Studies* (London: The Warburg Institute).

[4] See, e.g., *infra*, App. V, for Henricus Francigena's dependency on Hugh of Bologna, and also *infra*, n.12.

[5] A good example is the so-called Manual of Bishop Benno of Meissen in the Wolfenbüttel MS 56.20, fol. 1–4^v, which has been recognized as a recasting of Hugh of Bologna's *Rationes dictandi*. Not only is the name of the author replaced by that of the Saxon bishop, but also "Bononiensis" is sometimes exchanged for "Boemiensis" so as to equip the manual with the proper local coloring; cf. A. Bütow, *Die Entwicklung der mittelalterlichen Briefsteller bis zur Mitte des 12. Jahrhunderts, mit besonderer Berücksichtigung der Theorien der 'Ars dictandi'* (Greifswald Dissertation, 1908), 44f.

yet another intricacy which has to be taken into account; for sometimes the prologues, which were composed usually with special care, show a tendency to independence and to lead a life of their own. Severed from the work to which they originally belonged they make their unexpected appearance along with doctrines and model letters of another writer and thus present themselves as parts of works to which in fact they do not belong. This, however, is a peculiarity not only of the *artes dictandi*. Recently, and with reference to the proems of legal writings in the twelfth century, it has been emphasized in a most picturesque way that "many mediaeval writings resemble those luckless earthworms the heads and tails of which, having been separated by the ploughshare, wriggle away in different directions never to meet again in this world."[6]

This statement, if pathetic and mournful, is all too true. In the case with which this article is concerned, the separation of head and tail has resulted in a little monster apparently presenting itself with two heads which have grown onto the tail of an *ars dictandi* of the twelfth century. The manual under discussion is not unknown to students. Its prologues, however, deserve further inspection not only for the sake of disentangling a confused problem of authorship but also for determining a certain development of the *artes dictandi* in so far as they pretended to be "literature."

The two prologues are found in a manuscript in Leipzig (L)[7] at the end of an *ars dictandi* and of a collection of model letters. The first prologue is headed by a rubric "Prologus precedentis operis quod dicitur aurea gemma."[8] Since in this prologue it is the title of the treatise, *Aurea gemma*, which is explained elaborately, it may here be called L^t. There follows a second rubric "Alius prologus de eodem"[9] which provisionally may be cited as L^x. These two prologues are found also in an Oxford manuscript (O)[10] in which they precede—so far correctly—the doctrinal part and the letters. From this manuscript, Haskins has published the first prologue, namely the discussion of the *titulus* (O^t), and the first sentence of the second prologue (O^x) without indicating a new rubric.[11] He was correct because O does not distinguish between the two *prooemia; O* offers merely one very long prologue the context of which tallies completely with the two prologues found at the end of L.

The question arises whether we have to account for two prologues or only one, that is to say whether L or O is correct. The problem now becomes complicated. Haskins has published the prologue in O as that of an *ars dictandi* written by Henricus Francigena, a master of *dictamen* not too well known who, however, taught in Pavia after 1120, whose name suggests French, perhaps Provençal, origin and who depends on Bologna, especially on Hugh of Bologna, as far as his art is concerned.[12] Haskins seemed to be fully entitled

---

[6] Hermann Kantorowicz, *op. cit.*, 226.

[7] Leipzig, Univ. Bibl. MS 350, fol. 146ᵛ–132; on the manuscript see R. Helssig, *Katalog der lateinischen und deutschen Handschriften der Universitäts-Bibliothek zu Leipzig*, I (Leipzig, 1926–35), 520; Botho Odebrecht, "Die Briefmuster des Henricus Francigena," *Archiv für Urkundenforschung*, XIV (1926), 233.

[8] The prologue begins "Liber librorum sicut cantica canticorum"; cf. *infra*, Appendix IV.

[9] It begins "Sociorum assidua pulsatione coactus"; cf. *infra*, Appendix III.

[10] Oxford, Bodl. MS Laud. misc. 569, fol. 178ᵛ–190ᵛ; cf. Haskins, *op. cit.*, 178; Odebrecht, *op. cit.*, 233.

[11] Haskins, 179.

[12] For Henricus Francigena, see, in addition to Bütow, *op. cit.*, 30ff, and Haskins, 178ff, the more recent study of Odebrecht, *op. cit.*, 231f, who indicates in his edition of Francigena's letters the borrowings and makers it clear (p. 236) that Francigena drew on Hugh of Bologna's work, not vice versa.

to ascribe this work to Henricus Francigena; other scholars had done so before him.[13] In fact, *O* contains among its model letters 14 of the 32 letters which we may be sure formed Francigena's original collection as it is transmitted in other manuscripts.[14] Moreover, from the prologue of Francigena's genuine *ars dictandi*, likewise published by Haskins,[15] it is known that this teacher had called his manual, rather pretentiously, *Aurea gemma*.

However, the observation has been made before that L^x, and accordingly O^x, show some similarity with a proem whose author is indubitably Albert of Samaria.[16] This master, as far as we know, is a predecessor of Henricus Francigena *in arte dictandi*. He is credited with having been the first teacher of the new *dictamen* at Bologna. Also, he seems to have been the first to have added to the theoretical part of his manual some practical examples, i.e. the model letters.[17] The similarity of $L^x O^x$ with the proem of Albert's *Dictaminum precepta* suggested a borrowing on the part of Henricus Francigena; but a closer inspection of the prologues indicates more than a simple "taking over," since Albert proves to be the author of $L^x O^x$. One prologue of Albert's treatise has been published from a manuscript of Reinhardsbrunn (*R*),[18] another is found in a manuscript in Munich (*M*).[19] The prologue in *M* addresses itself to the students of philosophy in Bologna, the one in *R* to a pupil of Albert, a monk.[20] Owing to the different addressees, the introduc-

[13] For instance, H. O. Coxe, *Catalogus codicum manuscriptorum Bibliothecae Bodleianae*, II (1885), 407; Bütow, 32, did not know the Oxford manuscript, but he considered the *ars dictandi* in *L* a work of Francigena; see also N. Denholm-Young, "The Cursus in England," in *Oxford Essays in Mediaeval History presented to H. E. Salter* (Oxford, 1934), 96.

[14] *O* contains the numbers 1–6, 12, 13, 16, 20–23, 27 in Odebrecht's edition.

[15] Haskins, 178f., based his edition on Paris, Bibl. Nat. MS lat. nouv. acq. 610, fol. 27; see Appendix V.

[16] Bütow, 43; Odebrecht, 233, who notes that one of the prologues in *L* agreed with *O*; but it escaped his attention that *O* also contains the second prologue of *L*.

[17] For Albert of Samaria, see Haskins, 173ff, and his study "An Early Bolognese Formulary," in *Mélanges H. Pirenne* (Brussels, 1926), 201–210, in which he deals mainly with the manuscript in Berlin, Staatsbibl. Cod. lat. 181 (Philipps, 1732); see, however, W. Holtzmann in *Neues Archiv*, XLVI (1925), 34ff.

The name "de Samaria" has puzzled scholars to some extent. Haskins, 174, n. 4, and *Mélanges H. Pirenne*, 202, n. 3, is inclined to follow Tiraboschi, *Storia della letteratura italiana* (Milan, 1823), IV, 637f., who suggested that Henry of Settimello's surname "Samaritanus" (cf. Muratori, *Antiquitates Italicae*, III, 916, who quotes "Carmina Henrici Samariensis"; the manuscripts are classified by Niewöhner in *Zeitschrift für deutsches Altertum*, LXV [1928], 65) derived "dalla misera a cui era stato ridotto" and had the meaning of "poor, unfortunate." This explanation is not satisfactory. In addition to Albert of Samaria himself, who at least taught at Bologna, and Henry of Settimello (Samaritanus), who at least was educated at Bologna, we know the Bolognese poet and member of the so-called "Sicilian School," Ranieri Samaritani. In fact, the family dei Samaritani was quite prominent in Bologna. About 1200, there was one Matheus de Samaritanis, whose son Lambertinus died before 1272 and was the

father of Raynerius de Samaritanis (probably the poet) and two other sons, Bornius and Bonifatius; cf. L. Frati, "Notizie biografiche di rimatori italiani dei secoli XIII e XIV," *Giornale storico della letteratura italiana*, XI (1888), 125ff, and "Grammatici Bolognesi del Trecento," *Studi e memorie per la storia dell' università di Bologna*, IV (1920), 38; see also the documents published by Lino Sighinolfi, "Salatiele e la sua *Ars notariae*," *Studi e memorie ... di Bologna*, IV (1920), 148f., where the branch of Guido de Samaritanis with his children Johanna, Bertholomeus, and Bertholucius is mentioned in 1289; also one Guillielmus de Samaritanis is mentioned in 1290; cf. Luigi Colini-Baldeschi, "Lo studio di Bologna e la Marca d'Ancona," *Studi e memorie etc.*, V (1920), 102. Thus, Albert of Samaria is sure to belong to this family of the Bolognese nobility, all the more so as he is styled a nobleman ("ut Samaritanus nobili genere natus," "te namque nobili prosapia ortum"); cf. Haskins, 174, n.5, and 175, § 1. Pio Rajna, "Per il *cursus* medievale e per Dante," *Studi di filologia italiana*, III (Florence, 1932), 29, even suggests that Albert may have been the "capostipite" of this family. Whence the name derives is a different problem. We may, however, assume that it had a local meaning referring perhaps to an infirmary or a chapel, unless the name is to be connected with the Holy Land.

[18] Now Pommersfelden, MS 2750, fol. 49r; cf. H. Krabbo, "Der Reinhardsbrunner Briefsteller aus dem zwölften Jahrhundert," *Neues Archiv*, XXXII (1906), 54ff., Bütow, 23ff., Haskins, 173f.

[19] Munich, Cod. lat. 22267, fol. 82r, a most interesting manuscript to which Dr. Erdmann called my attention; see my article on "Petrus de Vinea in England" (quoted in the first note), 52, n. 31a, and Erdmann in *Deutsches Archiv für Geschichte des Mittelalters*, IV (1940), 320.

[20] The addressee, not Albert, was a monk; Krabbo, 71, committed an error in his emendation; cf. Haskins, in *Mélanges Pirenne*, 202, and *infra*, Append. II.

tory sentences of the prologues in R and M differ from one another. This disagreement, however, is restricted to the dedicatory *exordium* (R^e and M^e), whereas the context which follows is identical in both manuscripts. Of this common context, one paragraph refers to the title of the work ($R^t M^t$) whereas the main part represents the *materia* ($R^m M^m$), that is the subject-matter treated on a background of philosophical views and other more general considerations.[21] In short, the prologues of Albert of Samaria contain three main sections: the dedicatory *exordium* in which the recipient is addressed (R^e and M^e, differing from one another), the discussion of the title (R^t and M^t) and the *materia* (R^m and M^m).

If we now compare Albert's prologues in R and M with the second prologue in LO, hitherto cited as $L^x O^x$, we find that all four manuscripts offer the same *materia* so that we are in a position to establish the equation $R^m = M^m = L^m = O^m$. This agreement of the four manuscripts is all the more welcome as the text transmitted as badly in LO as in RM can be improved considerably by means of the variant readings. That the *exordium* in LO (now cited as $L^e O^e$) deviates from both R^e and M^e is not surprising, as it is directed to yet another group of recipients, to Albert's *socii*. However, Albert's authorship of this paragraph can not easily be contested because the style, tenor, and metaphors of $L^e O^e$ are very similar to R^e and especially to M^e.[22] Thus, as a first result of our investigations, we may register the fact that we have gained three versions of Albert's prologue to his *Dictaminum precepta*. Since the complete texts of Albert's various prologues are either not edited or offer room for improvement, I publish in Appendix I the complete prologue with the dedicatory introduction of M, and in Appendices II and III the variant dedications of R and LO.

However, a reservation should be made regarding the general agreement of the prologues in R and M with those in LO. LO, it is true, contain a dedicatory *exordium* and the discussion of the *materia*, but they do not contain Albert's discussion referring to the title *Dictaminum precepta* ($R^t M^t$). Yet the section on the title is not lacking because LO offers instead that first prologue ($L^t O^t$) in which the title *Aurea gemma* is explained circumstantially (Appendix IV). It is this title, though not the title alone, which seemed to justify the assumption of Henricus Francigena's authorship of the whole work, whereas the agreements with Albert's treatise suggested merely a heavy drawing on, the *Dictaminum precepta*. But this view is no longer tenable. Except for the title *Aurea gemma*, the prologue in LO has nothing in common with Francigena's authentic prologue whose first part has been published by Haskins from a Paris manuscript[23] and which I publish completely on the basis of three manuscripts in Appendix V.

---

[21] On the *materia*, see Hermann Kantorowicz, *op.cit.*, 37f.

[22] The first sentence of $L^e O^e$ is simply a recasting of the last sentence of M^e:

M^e: *Naturalis* igitur *ratione* iure perfusus vestrique amoris hortatu compulsus precipuum quoddam atque *perutile aggressus sum opus*, non ingenii confidentia, sed vestre supplicationis sedula instantia.

L^e O^e: Sociorum assidua pulsatione coactus, *naturalis* etiam *rationis* incitamento astrictus, *aggressus sum* rem arduam, sed professionis officio iniunctam et ... satis idoneam, *opus* difficile, sed tamen *perutile*.

The statements in M^e ("mentes desidia torpentes" or "fugienda lasciviarum illecebra") are phrased as admonitions in $L^e O^e$ ("desidiam ponite, lasciviam fugite"). Furthermore, in $L^e O^e$ we find the phrase "spernuntur aspera et spinosa dictamina," which is found in R ("spernat aspera et spinosa dictamina"), cf. Krabbo, *op. cit.*, 78, and M, fol. 85^v ("spernat aspera et spinosa dictamina Alberici monachi insolubilia").

[23] Haskins, *op. cit.*, 178f.

The dedicatory passage in *LO* as well as the *materia* have proven to be written by Albert of Samaria. A closer inspection of L^tO^t shows that at least its main idea is taken also from Albert of Samaria, from a letter in which he advises the budding *dictator* to emulate Cicero as well as Saints Gregory, Augustine, Jerome, and Ambrose.[24] This idea, it is true, has been couched somewhat more pompously in D^tO^t and the diction has undergone a certain embellishment, but it would be not at all far-fetched to ascribe even L^tO^t to Albert of Samaria and to draw the conclusion that he, too, wrote a work called *Aurea gemma*.[25] This hypothesis seems to be supported by yet another argument which deserves being mentioned. Odebrecht, in a careful study of Francigena's letters, emphasizes that the theoretical or doctrinal part (i.e. the *ars dictandi* proper) in *O* was not composed by this master, whereas indeed a short part of his doctrine is found in *L*. To be exact: *O*, fols. 178^r–186^v, and *L*, fols. 142^r–144^v, contain the very same doctrine; but the two manuscripts differ from one another in that only *L*, fols. 144^v–145^v, offers a few additional paragraphs taken from Francigena's genuine *Aurea gemma*. However, Odebrecht does not mention that the complete doctrine which *L* and *O* have in common and which is not Francigena's work presents itself as a comprehensive collection of those rules and theoretical advices which Albert of Samaria has inserted between the letters which illustrate his rules.[26]

Thus, it may be a matter of discussion whether the manual, at least the version in *O*, should be called plainly a work of Albert of Samaria; but the attribution to Henricus Francigena is almost without basis. Except for the title *Aurea gemma* and several model letters, there is nothing in *O* to indicate Francigena's authorship; and even the small theoretical section in *L* is added quite pointlessly, because more than one subject dealt with in this *additamentum* has been treated already in the preceding section which is Albert's work and which *L* and *O* have in common.[27] It would be more correct, at any rate, to style the manual in *LO* an *ars dictandi* based upon Albert of Samaria, but containing a few interlarded quotations taken from Henricus Francigena's work, than to ascribe the whole treatise to the latter. However, neither Francigena nor Albert can be claimed as the composer proper of the little work. Even if we assume the most extensive borrowings of Francigena from Albert, it would hardly be plausible that Francigena, being himself the author of an independent and complete theory of the *dictamen*, should have borrowed the complete doctrine of Albert while adding but a few paragraphs of his own theory. On the other hand, Albert cannot be claimed as the author because model letters of Francigena (and in *L* parts of his doctrine) are indeed found in the treatise; and

---

[24] Krabbo, 78; the letter is found also in *M*, fol. 85^v.

[25] Another work of Albert is mentioned by Delisle, *Cabinet des manuscrits de la Bibliothèque Nationale*, II (Paris, 1870), 548, n. 264, from a catalogue of the library of St. Pons de Temières whose date is 1276 and in which an entry is found "introductiones perscicarum(!) edite ab Alberto Samaritano." Manitius, *Geschichte der lateinischen Literatur des Mittelalters*, III (Munich, 1931), 306, emends "Prisciani" for "perscicarum"; it is more likely, however, and paleographically quite comprehensible that we should read "Introductiones prosaicarum (sc. dictaminum)," all the more so as this title then was quite popular; see, e.g., Bernard of Bologna's *Introductiones prosaici dictaminis*, which are discussed by Haskins, *op. cit.*, 182.

[26] The agreements are mentioned, though not analysed carefully enough, by Bütow, *op. cit.*, 39; see also p. 35 with regard to the Wolfenbüttel MS 56.20. The works of the two authors have been fused at an early date, but to disentangle them requires a critical edition of Albert's work.

[27] E.g., the sections on the "salutationes" and "similitudines."

since Albert wrote at a somewhat earlier date than Francigena, the convenient expedient of Albert's borrowing must be ruled out.

There remains but one explanation: the manual is a later compilation which drew on the works of both Albert and Francigena.[28] Exactly this is exposed in plain words by the anonymous author of L^tO^t. He declares to have called his work *Aurea gemma* "eo quod *ex fontibus doctorum* quasi ex auro et gemma sit compositus et informatus." The writer of this first prologue in *LO* does not even pretend to have composed a book of his own invention. From the works of the *doctores*, namely of Albert of Samaria and Henricus Francigena, he gathers all that he considers as gold and gems and combines these pieces to form a new work. He even puffs up the manual and advertises it for the very reason that it represents a compilation of two acknowledged authorities. To this new work Albert contributed the main part of the theory and of the prologue, while Francigena, in addition to a number of letters and a few theoretical rules (in *L*), provided above all the name of the new treatise: *Aurea gemma*.

How the compiler procceded is now obvious. He took a prologue of Albert of Samaria, omitted the paragraph referring to the humble title *Dictaminum precepta*, borrowed the more suggestive title *Aurea gemma* from Francigena, and prefaced the new prologue by a short interpretation of the title, the "book-jacket" of the new compilation, so to speak. He would probably have borrowed also the introductory paragraph from Francigena's genuine work, had this *dictator* offered an adequate discussion of the title. Francigena, however, did not trouble to expatiate on the meaning of *Aurea gemma;* he simply mentions the title: "hunc libellum qui Aurea gemma intitulatur."[29] Hence the anonymous compiler had to pen a few sentences of his own invention. In harking back to Cassiodorus' *Exposition of the Song of Songs* he explains that the treatise, for its outstanding qualities, deserves to be styled the "Book of Books," but that its choiceness suggested another title:

> As gold is more precious than any other metal and a gem by nature is clearer and brighter than any other stone, so is this book more excellent than all breviaries of all authors. Therefore, it might have been called "Gold" or "Gem"; but we can connect also the gold with the gem and by this combination produce something even more beautiful and seemly, namely a "Golden Gem." For this reason, and because its composition and information derive from the sources of the doctors, as it were from gold and gems, let its name be "The Golden Gem."

It is a question of little importance whether we, today, appreciate this far-fetched and

---

[28] The later date is countenanced also by the fact that *L*, fol. 145^v, shows a change of the papal initial, I(nnocent II) for C(alixtus II), so that the copy falls in the period 1130–1143; cf. Bütow, 33.

The relations between the four manuscripts may become clearer by a diagram:

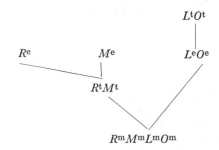

[29] Cf. *infra*, Append. V.

manneristic way of interpreting a book title. What matters is to know whether it met with the taste of the contemporaries. And in raising this question we eventually may realize that this mannerism betrays the tendency toward a new ideal of style which urges us to link this short paragraph to a later rather than to the earlier type of prologues to *artes dictandi*.

We must take into account the endeavors of the masters of *dictamen* to increase the reputation of their modest art by passing their works off as products of literature proper, in a way similar to the works of the ancient authors on rhetoric. To reconquer for the new written eloquence the sovereign rank of ancient rhetoric, to make the "idea" of *dictamen* a collective noun for philosophy, dialectic, grammar, political science, and other branches of education[30] and thus compete with the all-embracing idea of rhetoric of by-gone days, as well as to establish the new art as an autonomous discipline, as a mental and moral training in its own right and independent of theology[31]—all this was aimed at by the masters of *dictamen*. In short, the art of *dictamen* was considered a, or rather the, subject of general education. Hence originates the pretension of these teachers to offer in their writings something more dignified than simple manuals and textbooks. They claimed to produce works of truly literary value—an endeavor furthered by the insertion of letters which were generally acknowledged as "literature"—and accordingly had to provide their manuals with the accoutrement of literary works.

On the background of these pretensions it is worth our while to inspect rapidly the development of the titles of the *artes dictandi* and their interpretation in the prologues. The history of book titles, most likely, will never be written, interesting though this chapter of cultural history might be. Names of books, like many other things, reflect the intellectual disposition of an age; and it is obvious that titles such as "The Castle of Otranto" or "The Cloister and the Hearth" disclose a temperament and rhythm of life quite other than "The Moon and Sixpence" or "Look Homeward, Angel." The ancient grammarians had established certain rules concerning prologues and titles as well; and from one of their works may have been derived that queer explanation of the etymology and the meaning of *titulus* which occasionally is found in mediaeval writings and can be

[30] Not to mention scores of places where the dictamen would be styled "artium liberalium imperatrix" (Boncompagno, *Bonconpagnus*, c. II, in Rockinger, *op. cit.*, 128f), or "Dei gratia universalis rei publice mediatrix, consulum, oratorum, iudicum generalis magistra" (Wattenbach, in *Archiv für Kunde österreichischer Geschichtsquellen*, XIV [1855], 92), or in other similar terms, it may suffice to refer to Albert of Samaria, *infra*, Append. I: "... dictatorem oportet cognoscere grammaticam, rethoricam, dialeticam, eloquentie studia huic operi necessaria ... Que omnia, qualiter dicatori sint necessaria, in sequentibus monstrabo per singula. Absque harum igitur aliquantula saltim scientia nulla erit dictandi notitia." With rhetoric as a center, Richard McKeon, "Rhetoric in the Middle Ages," *Speculum*, XVII (1942), 1–32, touches upon a similar problem.

[31] I intend to deal with this problem in another connection. See, however, the verses of Udalrich of Bamberg,

written about 1125, in which theology ("divini expositores"), along with *artes* and *auctores*, becomes almost an "ancilla artis dictandi":

> ... nam calles munere Christi
> Artem dictandi, quam credimus esse legendi
> Artes, auctores, divinos expositores
> Precipuum fructum, per quam secernere doctum
> Scimus ab indocto.

Cf. C. Erdmann, "Die Bamberger Schule im Investiturstreit," *Zeitschrift für bayrische Landesgeschichte*, IX (1936), 3; Dümmler, in *Neues Archiv*, XIX (1894), 226, verses 27ff. Albert of Samaria, too, and correspondingly the Anonymous (*infra* Append. IV; Krabbo, *op. cit.*, 78), make the authors and fathers serve with the *ars dictandi* which, in itself, eventually becomes the "gradaria ad virtutes"; Eugen Müller, *Peter von Prezza* (Heidelberg, 1913), 135f.

traced back at least to the later Carolingian period. *Titulus,* it is said, derived from Titan, the Sun, "because as Titan's presence illuminates the world so does the title elucidate what is to follow in the book." Without a title a book was considered dumb.[32] It seems as though Alberic of Monte Cassino, who is usually claimed as the founder of the new *dictamen,* alludes to this *titulus a Titane* explanation when discussing the title of his own manual, the *Radii dictaminum.* This title, says he, is nothing but a *color,* yet he expects his book to be a ray, at least metaphorically, illuminating the dark. However, the name of his manual (it was called also *Flores rethorici*) makes it quite clear what the reader could hope to find in the book, and the same holds good for the titles of other manuals. Alberic called his second treatise simply *Breviarium de dictamine;* Albert of Samaria, as we know, chose the title *Dictaminum precepta;* Hugh of Bologna wrote *Rationes dictandi prosaice,* Bernard of Bologna *Introductiones prosaici dictaminis,* and other masters wrote treatises bearing similar titles.[33]

As long as the content of a book was thus clearly indicated by its title, it was sufficient simply to mention in the prologue, without a commentary, the *inscriptio operis.* Taste and fashion, however, changed in the twelfth century, and a lengthy and somewhat allegorical interpretation of the title became indispensable when the masters of the new eloquence began to put their literary pretensions into practice, fell in with the general intellectual and literary currents of their time, and published their manuals under such poetical or mystical names that the reader could not possibly guess what kind of book the extravagant title might cover. In fact, the masters of the *dictamen* did nothing but accommodate themselves to the then popular predilection for establishing cosmic or occult relationships of everything with anything; and hence it became their desire not to clarify, but to mystify the all too trivial subject-matter of their textbooks. Inevitably, the choice of the allegorical title retroacted upon the content of the prologues. The reader was led, so to speak, through the peristyle of a solemn and beautifully couched preface, in which the secret of the allegorical title was disclosed, before he was to approach the shrine of Eloquence on whose altar, of course, he would find nothing but the arid and bony rules of the *dictamen prosaicum,* a useful but by no means mysterious matter.

[32] Cf. *Commentum in Donati artem minorem* in Einsiedeln, MS 172, fol. ult., quoted by H. Keil, *Grammatici Latini,* Suppl. (Leipzig, 1870), p. xlii, note:

> Hoc quod in capite librorum scribitur, diversis nominibus a doctoribus appellatur. Dicitur enim capitulus, dicitur titulus, dicitur elencus, dicitur prologus, dicitur prefacia, dicitur argumentum, dicitur prooemium, dicitur clavis. Capitulus dicitur eo quod in capite ponitur. Titulus a Titane, id est a sole, quia sicut sol oriens sua presentia mundum inluminat, ita et titulus sequentia librorum manifestat; nam si titulum abstuleris, quodam modo mutus est liber. Inde quidam in epistola sua ad familiarem dixit: "Titulum frontis erade hunc, muta fit pagina."

The explanation "titulus a Titane" is found as a scholion of Remigius of Auxerre, pupil of Heiric, to the word "titulo" in the preface to Phocas' *Ars de nomine et verbo* (Keil, *op. cit.,* V, 410, line 18); cf. Manitius, "Zur karolingischen Literatur," *Neues Archiv,* XXXVI (1910), 48. Remigius quotes it also in his *Expositio super Donatum minorem,* cf. Henricus Keil, *De grammaticis quibusdam latinis infimae aetatis commentatio* (Erlangen Program, 1868), 24, who publishes the passage from a 12th century manuscript (Paris, Bibl. Nat. lat. suppl. 292). The phrase is found also in John of Garland's *Distigium;* cf. L. J. Paetow, *op. cit.* (cf. *supra,* n. 2), 135, and A. Wilmart, *Analecta Reginensia* (*Studi e Testi,* vol. 59; Vatican, 1933), 254.

[33] Cf. Haskins, *op. cit.,* 171ff; for Alberic cf. H. M. Willard, "The Use of the Classics in the *Flores rhetorici* of Alberic of Monte Cassino," *Haskins Anniversary Essays in Mediaeval History* (Boston and New York, 1929), 351–363, especially 355, n. 15, for the explanation of the word "radium."

By far the best known representative of this new style is the Master Buoncompagno. His works display the strangest titles and carry such odd names that indeed the author was compelled to comment elaborately upon them so as to link the name to the book. In his prologue to a work called *Palma*, Buoncompagno explains that this palm-tree stands for his victory over enviers. Or, a discussion of Noah's dove carrying the famous bough to the ark opens the prologue to the *Oliva* whose name, says the author, was to indicate that from this book "procedes not the oil of adulation but the liquor of sincerety." A third book was called *Cedrus* for a reason certainly not easy to guess. Buoncompagno holds that the two preceding books had exalted his name over that of his adversaries like a Cedar of Lebanon, not to mention the fact that the cedar "for its golden color and its spicy taste excels in beauty all other fruits." And after a similar pattern he interprets a fourth work, the *Myrrha*, which he considers remindful of the resurrection because people used myrrh to embalm corpses.[34] Buoncompagno's contemporary was the Bolognese master Guido Faba, who commented on the title *Gemma purpurea* in a corresponding way and who wrote a most cryptic introduction to his *Rota nova* in which the Wheel of Fortune is turned into a Wheel of Eloquence on the summit of which the pupils receive from the hands of their teacher angelic wings enabling them to fly.[35] It can hardly be maintained that these and similar explanations greatly clarified the matter. However, these masters formed a school. Bonus of Lucca calls one of his works *Cedrus Libani*, another one *Mirra correctionis* "because it pours forth a fragrance like that of myrrh which by its occult power kills the worms and protects the flesh from putridness."[36] Master Bene of Bologna explains that he called his book *Candelabrum* because it was divided in eight parts and therefore displayed a similarity to a chandelier of eight brackets.[37] Other *dictatores* invented names of a different kind. Thomas of Armannino wrote a treatise called *Microcosmus* which at least left room for a Macrocosmos to come.[38] John Bondi of Aquileia wrote a *Lucerna*—in allusion to Psalm 117, 105: "Thy word is a lamp to my feet and a light to my path"— which he wanted not to be hidden under a bushel but to be exalted over the *Candelabrum* of Master Bene.[39]

Later in the thirteenth century, as *dictamen* and jurisprudence together gave birth to the new *ars notaria*, the fashion also affected the writings of lawyers. *Aurora* became a most popular title of their works. There was the *Aurora* of Rolandinus Passagerii, the *Aurora novissima* by Peter de Unzola, and an *Aurora novella* by Pietro de' Boattieri.[40] *Rosaria* and *Margeritae*, as a rule, fall into a different category, since they simply indicate *florilegia*.[41]

[34] Carl Sutter, *Aus Leben und Schriften des Magisters Boncompagno* (Freiburg i. B. and Leipzig, 1894), 105f, 67, 69, 71f.

[35] On the *Gemma purpurea*, see A. Gaudenzi, "Sulla cronologia delle opere dei dettatori bolognesi da Boncompagno a Bene di Lucca," *Bullettino dell' istituto storico italiano*, XIV (1895), 127f; for the *Rota nova*, see E. H. Kantorowicz, "An Autobiography of Guido Faba," *supra*, n. 3.

[36] Concetto Marchesi, "Due grammatici latini del medio evo," *Bullettino della società filologica romana*, XII (1910), 23–37.

[37] Gaudenzi, *op. cit.*, 151f.

[38] Bertoni, "Il *Microcosmo* di Tommasino d'Arman-

nino," *Archivum Romanicum*, V (1921), 19–29; cf. Zaccagnini, in *Il libro e la stampa*, VI (1912), 126f.

[39] Munich, Cod. lat. 9683, fol. 48–61ᵛ, begins: "Lucernam pedibus meis et lumen semitis meis"; cf. Rockinger, *op. cit.*, 954.

[40] Cf. Savigny, *Geschichte des Römischen Rechts im Mittelalter* (2nd ed.; Heidelberg, 1850), V, 543, 549; Guido Zaccagnini, "Le epistole in latino e in volgare di Pietro de' Boattieri," *Studi e memorie per la storia dell' università di Bologna*, VIII (1924), 213–248; Fedor Schneider, in *QFiAB*, XVIII (1926), 191ff.

[41] For these titles, see Hermann Kantorowicz, *Studies in the Glossators of the Roman Law*, 17.

However, there is a *Rosa novella* by Pietro de' Boattieri, a title which the author considers most suitable because he found a parallel between the rules of his art and the rose "which, while growing between the foliage, spreads its fragrance through its blossoms and is willing to produce fruits welcome to those who see and smell."[42] How much, or how little, these and other usages of the masters of style influenced the early Bolognese poetry and the *dolce stil nuovo* cannot be discussed here. However, it should not be forgotten that technically, not of course artistically, the prologues to the works of Dante fall in this line of development, for he explains the titles of his writings in very much the same manner as his contemporaries and fellow-countrymen, the masters of the *dictamen*.[42a]

These mystico-poetical names of books and their corollary, the allegorical prologues, make their first appearance, at least as far as the *artes dictandi* are concerned, in Francigena's and Pseudo-Francigena's *Aurea gemma*. That is to say: Henricus Francigena seems to have been the first master to choose a poetico-allegorical name for his manual, and the "Anonymous" the first to interpret the title of an *ars dictandi* in the manner indicated. Why this title should have become as popular as it actually did is difficult to tell. However, there is a third *Aurea gemma* extant in a manuscript of Weissenau in Suabia and a fourth in a manuscript of Admont in Steiermark.[43] A fifth *Aurea gemma* is attributed, rightly or wrongly, to John of Garland;[44] and yet another is said to have been one of the sources of Herrad of Landsberg, whose trends of thought were so greatly influenced by the scholar known as Honorius Augustodunensis, probably an Austrian.[45] Whether Herrad's *gemma* was really *aurea*, or whether it was rather a *Gemma animae*, is difficult to discover since the *Hortus deliciarum* was destroyed by fire at the bombardment of Strasbourg in 1870. However, Honorius, that standard-bearer of the new symbolism, mysticism, and mystagogical theology, explains the title of his great liturgical work, called *Gemma animae*, in quite a familiar way; for in the prologue he says that he chose that title "quia videlicet velut aurum gemma ornatur, sic anima divino officio decoratur."[46] To be sure, there is no indication whatever that allows us to assume that Honorius exercised an influence on the Italian masters of epistolary style, although he was actually a contemporary of Henricus Francigena as well as of our "Anonymous." Nevertheless, the coincidence is at least illustrative in so far as it shows that the general mystico-allegorical climate of the twelfth century, which drew its strength from many a source, began to affect also the works of the Italian rhetors. And the first testimony of this movement within the *ars dictandi* circles is apparently the anonymous *Aurea gemma* with which we have been here concerned.

---

[42] Fedor Schneider, *op. cit.*, 270.

[42a] See the prologue to the *Convivio* and especially the letter to Can Grande (*Ep. X*, §§ 6ff.).

[43] Haskins, 180f, 181, n. 1.

[44] Paetow, 144.

[45] Cf. Manitius, *Geschichte der lateinischen Literatur des Mittelalters*, III (1931), 1011.

[46] *PL*, CLXXII, 543.

APPENDICES

I

ALBERTUS DE SAMARIA (1).

Manuscripts: *Munich, Cod. lat.* 22267, *fol.* 82ʳ (= *M*)
Pommersfelden, MS 2750, *fol.* 49ʳ (= *R*)
Leipzig, Univ. Libr. MS 350, *fol.* 146ᵛ (= *L*)
Oxford, Bodl. Laud MS misc. 569, *fol.* 178ᵛ (= *O*)
M contains §§ 1–3, *R* §§ 2–3, *LO* contain § 3.

H. Krabbo, "Der Reinhardsbrunner Briefsteller aus dem zwölften Jahrhundert," *Neues Archiv*, XXXII (1906), 72f, has published §§ 2–3 from *R*. The first sentence of § 1 (*M*ᵉ, until 'titubarent') has been published recently by Ludwig Ott, *Untersuchungen zur theologischen Briefliteratur der Frühscholastik* (Beiträge zur Geschichte der Philosophie und Theologie des Mittelalters, vol. XXXIV; Münster i. W., 1937), p. 4, n. 6.

§ 1 (*M*ᵉ). Albertus Samaritanus bononiensibus scolaribus philosophicis studiis inherentibus.

Si doctrine studiis, ut vanis fabulis rebusque caducis et nihilo profuturis, at non nunquam pericula prestantibusᵃ mortalium pectora insudarent, nequaquam res humane tot casibus vacilarent nec hominum animi tot et tantis ignorantiarum calamitatibus titubarent, sed ex inscitie cecitate depulsa eo claritudinis pervenirent, ubi aᵇ mortalitate ad immortalitatem procul dubio pertransirent.[1] Ceterum mentes desidia torpentes nil altum sapere, nil utile concupiscere, nil honestum queunt istumve capescere. Sectantur voluptatum pestifera gaudia et cupiunt nancisci vere virtutis premia. Quod, quantum a calle longius errant quantumque a vertitate abhorreant, cogeret illos videre necessitas, nisi eos deprimeret caliginose cecitatis densitas. Non enim id, quod conantur, valent inertia adipisci nec, quod nituntur, assequi. Hinc erigenda est mentis acies, deponenda carnalis moles, fugienda lasciviarumᶜ illecebra [et]ᵈ mollicies; totisque nisibus [oportet] corporis, ut ait Crispusᵉ, uti servitioᶠ, animi frui imperioᵍ, [quorum aliud nobis est]ʰ commune cum summis. aliud commune cum infimis. Ad hoc utilitas nos invitatⁱ et natura consequenterᵏ incitatˡ. Naturalis igitur rationisᵐ iure perfusus vestrique amoris

---

[1] This ethical viewpoint is remindful of the distich
   Instrue preceptis animum, ne discere cessa;
   Nam sine doctrina vita est quasi mortis imago.
Cf. *Catonis Disticha*, III, 1, ed. Baehrens, *Poetae latini minores* (1881), III, 226. See also the famous *monitum* of Seneca
   Vive vacans studio quasi nunquam sis moriturus,
which was used like a proverb; see, e.g., *Florilegium Gottingense*, published by Ernst Voigt in *Romanische Forschungen*, III (1887), 293, n. 113. See also the words of Seneca (*Epistolae*, LXXXII, 3) "Otium sine litteris mors est et vivi hominis sepultura," quoted, e.g. ,by John of Salisbury, *Policraticus*, ed. Webb (1909), I, 17, line 29. Cf. *infra*, Appendix II.

ᵃ prestantis *M*.
ᵇ ab *M*.
ᶜ lascivarum *M*.
ᵈ aut 'et' aut verbum om. *M*.
ᵉ cripus *M*.
ᶠ 'utis' lacuna 'vitio' *M*.
ᵍ impo *M*.
ʰ excidit fol. 82ʳ altera pars ultimae lineae; emendatio sequitur Sallust., *Catil.*, I, 1, 2.
ⁱ non vitat *M*.
ᵏ consequeriter *M*.
ˡ irritat *M*.
ᵐ omnis *M*, sed cf. *infra*, Append. III: 'naturalis ... rationis incitamento'.

hortatu compulsus precipuum quoddam atque perutile[n] aggressus sum opus, non ingenii confidentia, sed vestre supplicationis sedula instantia.

§ 2 ($M^t R^t$). Petitis[o][2] nempe et indesinenter[p] flagitatis, ut DICTAMINUM[q] PRECEPTA tradam et, introductionis imitans modum, modos[r] epistolarum ostendam, rem quidem utilem, multo[s] tamen[s] difficilem, preclarum opus, sed grande onus. Vestri[t] tamen amore[u] commotus[v] leve mihi videtur tam pergrave onus. Ad legenda itaque hec vos summopere invitans oro et moneo: ponite desidiam, adhibete diligentiam, estote[w] tenaces[x] memoria, legendi assiduitas adhibeatur[y] eximia[z].

§ 3[m]($M^m R^m L^m O^m$). Inter[a] breve[b] enim[c] temporis spacium[d], si meis ammonitionibus obsecundare[e] volueritis[e], huius artis scientiam[f] adipisci[g] valebitis ac[h] per nostrarum regularum conpendiosam[i] traditionem prosaicarum[j] epistolarum poteritis comprehendere rationem[k], quam[k] specialiter vestre utilitati[l] enucleandam[m] suscepi[n], generaliter tamen omnibus profuturam nullius sperna[o] invidia. Primum[p] itaque dictatorem oportet[q] cognoscere grammaticam, rethoricam, dialeticam[r], eloquentie studia huic operi[s] necessaria[t]. Grammatica enim[u], cum sit recte loquendi scientia, verba cum nominibus[v] docet[w] coniungere[x] ceterasque[y] dictiones congrua[z] ratione[a] disponere. Hec[b] autem sunt fundamenta et[c] huius artis initia[d] et primordialia indicia[d]. Rethorica vero[e] distincte[f], ornate[fg], expolite[h] componere[i] unicuique sexui[j] et[k] persone[l] et etati[m] necnon[n] ordini[o] et[p] dignitati[q] congrua accidentia[r] distribuere[s], ordinem et modum discernere. Diale-

---

[2] R being dedicated to a single person (cf. *infra*, Appendix II) always has the second person of the singular; it seemed unneccessary to indicate this continually in the apparatus.

[n] proutile M.
[o] Petis R.
[p] non desinenter M.
[q] tibi add. R.
[r] epistolarum modum R.
[s] om. M.
[t] Tui R; cf. n. 2.
[u] amoris supplicatione R.
[v] committo M.
[w] sit R.
[x] tenax maxime R.
[y] habent M.
[z] om. R.
[a] et R.
[b] om. R.
[c] etenim LO, omne R.
[d] spacium temporis OR.
[e] obtemperaveritis LO.
[f] noticiam L, peritiam O.
[g] capere L, attingere O, adhipisci R.
[h] 'ac – invidia' om. LO, et ins. 'Atque ne (Atnequam O) diu lectorem suspensum teneam, huius (huius teneam O) opusculi ianuam intrare cupientibus (volentibus O) pandam'.
[ijk] om. M.
[l] humilitati R.
[m] enudendam M.

[n] fasce. i. M.
[o] om M.
[p] Primo LO.
[q] oportet dictatorem LO.
[r] rethoricam sequ. LO.
[s] om. O.
[t] necessarium M.
[u] etenim R.
[v] pulcre add. O.
[w] om. M.
[x] om. M., construere R.
[y] certas L, certas personas O.
[z] certa propositionis LO.
[a] lege LO.
[b] 'Hec – indicia' om. LO, ins. 'Dialectica – concludere'; vide infra.
[c] id est M.
[d] indicia – initia R.
[e] autem LO.
[f] et add. LO.
[g] ornate, distincte R.
[h] expulite M.
[i] dissere LO, et add. R.
[jk] om. M.
[l] personi M, 'persone et' om. LO.
[m] et etati om. M.
[n] et LO.
[o] om. L.
[p] om. LO.
[q] om. O.
[r] ac necessaria L.
[s] reddere LO, 'ordinem – discernere' om LO.

tica^t autem^u proponere^v et^w assumere monstrat^x et concludere. Que^y omnia, qualiter^z dictatori^a sint^b necessaria, in sequentibus^c monstrabo^d per singula. Absque^e harum^f igitur^g aliquantula saltim scientia^h nulla erit dictandi^i noticia^k. Sunt tamen nonnulli^l adeo facilia^m habentes ingenia, qui^n ignoratis harum artium^o preceptis^o perpulchra^p componant dictamina. Quod tamen illis^q non^r arte accedit^q, sed$^{r'}$ natura; omnis enim ars a natura sumit^s initium. Que, dum^t secundum^u Platonem^v inest anime per naturam, ignoratur tamen^w a plerisque^x, nisi a^y magistro^z discant^a per^b carnis hebetis^c coniecturam^d. Excitatur ergo a doctoribus^e torpens^f animus, et quasi e^g somno vigilans^h naturaliter meminit que docentur^i.

^{t} dyaleticam O, vide supra b.
^{u} vero LO.
^{vw} propositionem LO.
^{x} demonstrat L, decet O.
^{y} Quia O.
^{z} equaliter M.
^{a} dictanti L, dictaturis O.
^{b} sunt M, sint dictatori R.
^{c} sequenti O.
^{d} demonstrabo L.
^{e} Ergo absque LO.
^{f} illarum LO.
^{g} 'igitur – saltim' om. LO.
^{h} noticia L, communione O, scientia saltim R.
^{i} scientia et add. R.
^{k} peritia LO.
^{l} adeo nonnulla M, qui add. O.
^{m} fallatia O.
^{n} ut L, ubi O.
^{o} preceptis artium L; partium (preceptis om.) O.
^{p} pulchra O, perpulchra R.

^{q} accidit eis O, accidit illis L.
^{r} om. R, arte non L.
$^{r'}$ non R.
^{s} simit R.
^{t} om. LO.
^{u} iuxta L, om. MR.
^{v} om. MR.
^{w} tamen ignoratur LO.
^{x} populis que L.
^{y} per L.
^{z} doctorem L, doctoribus O.
^{a} discatur LOR.
^{b} pro M.
^{c} ebetis L, habetis MO.
^{d} coniuncturam O, coniunctionem debilitatur L.
^{e} magistris R.
^{f} torpes R.
^{g} a LO.
^{h} evigilans L.
^{i} docetur LMR.

APPENDIX II

ALBERT OF SAMARIA (2).

Manuscript: *Pommersfelden, MS* 2750, *fol.* 49^r (= *R*).

H. Krabbo, *op. cit.*, 71, has published this section. It seemed unnecessary to repeat his apparatus.

(R^e) Adalbertus Samaritanus superno munere monacho^{a1} Ti., suo discipulo amantissimo, ad meliora semper proficere.

Inter cetera egregii bona ingenii precipue hoc approbo, quod video phylosophie deditum ad eius studium inhianter [mentem] erigere. Singulare etenim privilegium sapientie post quoque mortem^b facit vivere, sic econtrario desidia, mater inscientie,

---

[1] According to Krabbo's interpretation, Albert of Samaria would have been a monk; but the solution of "monti" is more likely to be "to the monk of T." (or: "to the monk Ti. . . ."); cf. Haskins, in *Mélanges H. Pirenne*, p. 203, No. 2: "Albertus superno munere siquid est G. Cremonensi scolastico carissimo socio"; see also *ibid.*, p. 204, No. 5, 205, No. 9; Krabbo, 76. "G. superno munere si quid est W. honeste indoli adolescenti."

---

^{a} monti R; monachus Ti. emend. Krabbo.
^{b} mortalem R.

noverca sapientic torpescendo [facit]^c perimere.^{2} In adolescentuli itaque lasciva etate constitutus et circa hec tempora amori atque labori deditus doctrine merito es laudabilis, cum et tue etatis et paribus studiorum prebes exemplum, iuvenibus rudimentum, senibus experimentum. Huius igitur tam preclari studii effectione^d ulnis te cordis amplectens tuis peticionibus, licet arduis, libens acquiesco, non mei ingenii confidentia, sed tue supplicationis sedula instantia.^{3}

^{2} This ethical conception is likewise reminiscent of the places quoted *supra*, Append. I, n. 1.
^{3} There follow §§ 2 and 3 printed in Appendix I.

^{c} praecedente 'perimere' add. Krabbo.
^{d} effectionum. *R*.

APPENDIX III

ALBERT OF SAMARIA (3).

Manuscripts: *Oxford, Bodl. MS Laud misc.* 569 (= *O*)
Leipzig, Univ. Libr. MS 350 (= *L*).

C. H. Haskins, *Studies in Mediaeval Culture* (1929), 179, published the first sentence from *O*.

(*O*^{e}*L*^{e}) Sociorum^a assidua pulsatione coactus, naturalis etiam^b rationis incitamento astrictus, aggressus sum rem arduam^c, sed professionis officio iniunctam^d et prosaicas orationes^e fingere cupientibus satis idoneam, opus difficile, sed tamen perutile^f. Non enim, ut ait Marcus^g Cato, Platonis sententiam imitans, solis nobis nati sumus, sed toti mundo natura nos^h peperit, educavit et^i docuit^k.^{1} Verum, quia ab hominibus^l nostrorum temporum spernuntur aspera et spinosa dictamina^2 et non amplectuntur diffusa sed^m brevia, quedam^n pro capacitate ingenii sub^o brevitate perstrinximus^p, et compendiosa traditione sociis nostris tradere dignum duximus, quod, licet emulorum mordeatur invidia, sapientium tamen iudicabitur^q dignum^r censura, quod caritas amicis^s petentibus communibus^t etiam^u utilitatibus preparabat^v, brevitas et utilitas commendabat. Oro itaque et moneo vos, socii, desidiam ponite, lasciviam fugite, vanas et ineptas fabulas devitate, studium adhibite, sollerti meditatione^w hanc veram^x traditiunculam legite, sollicita indagatione discutite, sagaci intellectu capite, tenaci memorie commendate.^{3}

^{1} Cf. Cicero, *De off.*, I, 7, 22. The quotation is found frequently; see, e.g., *Opusculum de accentibus*, ed. Ch. Thurot, in *Notices et extraits des manuscrits de la Bibliothèque Nationale*, XXII: 2 (1868), 25.
^{2} Cf. *supra*, p. 44, n. 22.
^{3} There follows Appendix I, § 3.

^{a} praecedit lemma in *L*: 'Alius prologus de eodem.'
^{b} et *O*, sum *L*.
^{c} arduam rem *L*.
^{d} non iunctam *L*, non invictam *O*
^{e} prosaicam orationem *L*.
^{f} pro utilitate *O*.
^{g} Mag. *O*.
^{h} om. *O*.

^{i} om. *O*.
^{k} edocuit *O*.
^{l} omnibus *O*.
^{m} om. *O*.
^{n} quadam *O*.
^{o} sed *O*.
^{p} perstringimus *O*.
^{q} iudicabit *LO*.
^{r} om. *O*.
^{s} omissis *L*.
^{t} cum omnibus *O*.
^{u} om. *O*.
^{v} imperabat *O*.
^{w} moderatione *L*.
^{x} om. *L*.

APPENDIX IV

ANONYMUS SAEC. XII (*ca.* 1130–1143).

Manuscripts: *Leipzig, Univ. Bibl. MS* 350, *fol.* 146 (= *L*)
Oxford, Bodl. MS Laud misc. 569, *fol.* 178^v (= *O*).

C. H. Haskins, *op. cit.*, 179, has published the prologue from *O*.

Incipit ecce liber qui^a dicitur Aurea gemma.[1]

(*L^{t}O^t*) Liber^b librorum sicut cantica canticorum per excellentiam liber iste dicitur,[2] eo quod maxima utilitas et maior quam in ceteris in eo contineatur^c. Intendit enim dictandi doctrinam^d perficere et construere et quodlibet imperfectum formare^e, Tullium in rethorica arte probatissimum^f imitando, Gregorii, Augustini, Jeronimi atque Ambrosii vestigia in dictaminis varietatibus sequendo: Tullium in faceta locutione et verborum compositione, Gregorium in dulcedine et suavitate, Augustinum in callida et subtilissima argumentatione, Jeronimum in sententiarum pondere, Ambrosium in rethorica^g disputatione.[3] Quanto igitur aurum cunctis metallis preciosius et gemma naturalis ceteris lapidibus clarior et lucidior^h, tanto liber^i iste omnium^k auctorum^l breviariis^m cunctis^n invenitur eminentior.^{o} Aurum itaque vel^p gemma potest dici; sed^q aurum gemme adiungas et utriusque^r coniunctione^s quiddam^t pulcrius et decentius, id est^u auream gemmam, facias. Vocetur^v itaque Aurea gemma, eo quod ex fontibus doctorum quasi ex auro et gemma^w sit compositus et informatus.[4]

---

[1] The headline is a hexameter; it is destroyed in *L*.

[2] Cf. Cassiodorus, *Expositio in Cantica Canticorum*, in Migne, *PL*, LXX, 1056: "Sicut enim dicitur 'Rex regum et Dominus dominantium' ..., sic dicitur Canticum canticorum ob excellentiam et dignitatem."

[3] Cf. Krabbo, *op. cit.*, 78; see also the letter in *M*, *fol.* 85^v, quoted *supra*, n. 24.

[4] There follow Appendix III and Appendix I, § 3.

---

a 'Incipit – qui' om. *L*, et ins. 'Prologus precedentis operis quod'.
b om. *O*.
c contineatur in eo *O*.
d doctrinam dictandi *L*.
e informare *L*.
f om. *O*.

g theorica *O*.
h splendidior *O*.
i libet *O*.
k omni *O*.
l ac add. *L*.
m abreviator *O*.
n libris *O*.
o om. *O*.
p et *O*.
q si add. *L*.
r utramque *O*.
s adiunctione *L*.
t quidam dulcius et *O*.
u idem *O*.
v vocatur *L*.
w gemmis *L*.

APPENDIX V

HENRICUS FRANCIGENA.

Manuscripts: *Paris, B. N. MS lat. n. acq.* 610, *fol.* 27 (= *P*)
Paris, B. N. MS lat. 2904, *fol.* 111 (= *Pa*)
Wolfenbüttel, MS 56.20 *Aug.* 8°, *fol.* 66 (= *W*).

C. H. Haskins, *op. cit.*, 178f, published the first part (until 'Papie composuit') from *P*.

Petro, divino munere Severiane domus canonico[a], sacerdoti glorioso[b], Henricus[c] Francigena, amicorum eius amicissimus, salutem et peticionem cum humanitatis[d] familiaritate.

Crebris[1] *vestre dilectionis*[e], dilectissime Petre, *fatigatus precibus, honestissime*[f] vestre *peticioni*[g] opere precium duxi[h] nullatenus *denegare*, quod meam parvitatem *dudum*, scilicet[i] *opuscula dictandi* componere, *promisisse recolo*. Scribam *itaque non invitus*, tum rogatu[k] vestro[l], quem sinceritatis brachiis[m] Deo teste[n] et consciencia mea[o] complector[p], tum[q] *communi utilitate* dictancium *raciones dictandi prosaice*, non tantum ex armariolo nostri[r] ingenii, verum etiam diversorum sentencias *in unum colligendo. Quibus* doctrinam *rudibus*, solamen provectis, discretis[s] remigium breviter[t] et commode tradere concupisco *tali*[u] sub condicione, ut, quibus[v] nostre Muse liber[w] placuerit[x], deinceps ad aliorum nugas et musitationes[y], que pocius eos[z] impediunt quam expediunt[a], *recurrere* nullatenus adtemptent[b]. *Si*[c] *vero livor* [sit] *edax*[d] illorum, qui *nichil fructus in se* videntes[e] *facibus*[f] *invidie et*[g] *acerbitatis*[h] *odio*[i] *accensi* temerario ausu[k] meum[l] librum[m] *mordere, rodere, lacerare* presumpserint: vos queso[n] eis[o] rebelles estote[n] ut decet[p]. Incipiamus igitur[q] celesti[r] favente gratia et vestra cogente dilectione[s].

Quocienscunque aliquis[t] prosaice sine vicio egregias[t] componere litteras[u] desiderat, opere precium est, ut primum dictandi originem[v], deinde ordinem et[w] materiarum distinctionem[x] perfecte[y] noscat, ut recte tramite[z] incedere per altos dictaminis montes[a] leviter valeat. Legat igitur studiosus[b] dictator[c] hunc[d] libellum, qui Aurea[e] gemma intitulatur, quem Henricus[f] Francigena[g] ad utilitatem desiderancium dictare Papie com-

---

[1] *Italics* indicate literal borrowing from Hugh of Bologna's *Rationes dictandi*, ed. L. Rockinger in *Quellen und Erörterungen zur bayerischen und deutschen Geschichte*, IX: 1 (Munich, 1863), 53ff.

[a] *M. PPa*
[b] gloriosam *W.*
[c] om. *W*; E. *Pa.*
[d] humilitatis *Pa*, unanimitatis *W.*
[e] dilectionis vestre *Pa.*
[f] 'Petre – honestissime' om. *W.*
[g] peticionibus *W.*
[h] om. *Pa.*
[i] om. *Pa.*
[k] conrogatu (tum om.) *Pa.*
[l] om. *Pa.*
[m] om. *Pa.*
[n] om. *PaW.*
[o] 'teste' hic ins. *Pa.*
[p] complectri *P.*
[q] et in *P.*
[r] om. *Pa.*
[s] desertis *Pa.*
[t] breve *W.*
[u] om. *Pa.*
[v] quibuslibet *PPa.*
[w] om. *PPa.*
[x] placuerint *PPa.*
[y] musiciones *Pa*, inusitationes *W.*
[z] vos *Pa.*
[a] expediant *P.*

[b] attendam *Pa.*
[c] Sed (om. 'vero') *Pa.*
[d] edacium *W.*
[e] in se videntes fructus *Pa.*
[f] fascibus *W.*
[g] om. *W.*
[h] accerbitatis *W.*
[i] hodio *W.*
[k] ausi *PaW.*
[l] om. *P.*
[m] librum meum *Pa.*
[n] 'quesco' sequ. 'estote' *Pa.*
[o] ei *P.*
[p] condecet *W.*
[q] om. *PPa.*
[r] sceleste *Pa.*
[s] 'Prefatio' add. *P.*
[t] 'egregias' sequ. 'aliquis' *W.*
[u] litteras componere *Pa.*
[v] originem dictandi *W.*
[w] om. *W.*
[x] distictione *W.*
[y] perficere *Pa*, om. *W.*
[z] 'vel ordine' add. *P.*
[a] montes dictaminis *W.*
[b] studiose *Pa.*
[c] dictatur *P.*
[d] huc *W.*
[e] om. *W.*
[f] E. *Pa.*
[g] Francigena Henricus *P.*

posuit. Perlecto vero[h] libro[h], que in eo sunt, retineat et[i], quociens[k] dictare voluerit, retenta carmini[l] suo, secundum[m] quod[n] precipit[o] liber[p], caute interserat[q], ne[r] despiciat[s] nostre paupertatis Musam. Leviter enim[t] et compendiose hoc in volumine[u] dictaminis eciam[v] minus intelligentes aliquem[w] fructum[x] percipere[y] possunt[z]. Quibus nos[a] provectiores[b] condescendentes[c] non quasi[d] natando[e] per profundum, sed simplici via dictaminis egregium iter calcavimus[f]. Unde a[g] legentibus veniam supplicando[h] petimus, ut, si quid absonum et[i] indiscrete[k] positum hoc in paupertino[l] tractatu nostre[m] negligencie temeritate inveniatur[n], si[o] non[p] displiceat[q], nostre debilitatis[r] viribus indulgeant, et si[s] corrigere poterint[t], corrigant. Nos vero adhuc multa addere voluimus[u] et[v] forsan[w] quedam que ibi sunt[x] extirpate. *Ceterum ne[y] in[z] prologis scribendis[a] nichil* vel parum *profuturis[b] videamur[c]* tempus con*terere*, faciamus[d] *finem prefacioni.*

[h] om. *Pa.*
[i] quam add. *W.*
[k] quocumque *Pa.*
[l] carminis *W,* retenti carmine *Pa.*
[m] om. *W.*
[n] que *W.*
[o] precepit *Pa.*
[p] liber precipit *W.*
[q] interiesserat *P,* interserast *Pa.*
[r] Nec *Pa.*
[s] decipiat *W.*
[t] om. *Pa.*
[u] volumines *Pa.*
[v] ut *Pa,* om. *W.*
[w] aliquam *Pa.*
[x] frustra vim *Pa.*
[y] capere *Pa.*
[z] possit *Pa.*
[a] om. *Pa.*
[b] provectiones *W,* om. *Pa.*
[c] condicemur *Pa.*
[d] que *Pa.*
[e] notando *PaW.*
[f] calcabimus *W.*

[g] om. *Pa.*
[h] suplicando *W.*
[i] non *W.*
[k] indiscretum *Pa,* discrete *W.*
[l] paupererimo *P.*
[m] om. *PaW.*
[n] negligenciam (temeritate om.) inveniunt *Pa.*
[o] sed *PaW.*
[p] om. *W.*
[q] despiciant *Pa.*
[r] debilitati *Pa.*
[s] om. *Pa.*
[t] poterant *P.*
[u] volumus *W.*
[v] ad *W.*
[w] fortasse *Pa,* forsant *W.*
[x] inest *Pa.*
[y] Ceteri me *W.*
[z] om. *Pa.*
[a] cribendis *W.*
[b] profuturi *P.*
[c] videamus *PaW.*
[d] faciam *P,* 'igitur' add. *W.*

KAISER FRIEDRICH II. UND DAS KÖNIGSBILD DES HELLENISMUS

(MARGINALIA MISCELLANEA)

I N EINEM ANREGENDEN Werk über die Apotheose im Spiegel des hellenistisch-spätantiken Herrscherporträts hat Hans Peter L'Orange an Hand gewisser Einzelzüge wie Haartracht und Himmelsblick einen Bildtypus herausgestellt, den er mit Alexander dem Großen beginnen läßt und dessen Fortleben er bis zu dem Staufenkaiser Friedrich II. verfolgt.[1] Ob diese Linienführung sachlich in allen Einzelheiten richtig ist, stehe nicht zur Erörterung.[2] Auch mag es hier gleichgültig sein, daß der diadem-gekrönte bärtige Kopf im Besitze des Kaiser-Friedrich-Museums ganz gewiß nicht Friedrich II. darstellt.[3] Nach Ausweis der Münzen und des Kopfes vom Capuaner Brückentor, dessen Abguß wiederzufinden Ernst Langlotz kurz vor dem Zweiten Weltkrieg geglückt ist, war die offizielle Bildauffassung des Kaisers (und nur um ein offizielles Porträt könnte es sich doch handeln) eine gänzlich andere. Wenn ferner die kaiserlichen Parteigänger oberitalienischer Städte sich damals die *barbarasi* nannten, so ermutigt der Parteiname gewiß nicht, ein bärtiges Haupt als Bildnis des letzten Staufenkaisers zu identifizieren.[4]

Der Kopf entstammt jedoch allem Anschein nach der süditalienischen Bildhauerschule des 13. Jahrhunderts, und da der Künstler, einem spätantiken Modell nacharbeitend, den Kopf mit der ἀναστολὴ τῆς κόμης, den flammenden Locken des Sonnengottes, versehen hat, so läßt sich L'Oranges weiter Bogenspannung, durch die er Hellenistisches und Staufisches zu verbinden weiß, eine innere Berechtigung nicht absprechen. Im Gegenteil, das archäologische Problem, das der ausgezeichnete Osloer Gelehrte damit angedeutet hat, läßt die Frage aufkommen, in welchem Maße hellenistisches Gut überhaupt in der Umgebung Friedrichs II. wirksam gewesen ist, und bis zu welchem Grade es statthaft

Reprinted, with permission, from *Varia Variorum: Festgabe für Karl Reinhardt* (Münster-Köln, 1952), 169–193.

[1] H. P. L'Orange, *Apotheosis in Ancient Portraiture* (Instituttet for Sammenlignende Kulturforskning, Ser. B, Skrifter, XLIV; Oslo, 1947).

[2] Einwände bezüglich einiger Einzelheiten (Interpretation von Nero) machte Miss Jocelyn M. C. Toynbee, in *Numismatic Chronicle*, 6th ser., vol. VII (1947), 126–149, doch berühren diese das Hauptproblem nicht. L'Oranges Arbeit ist nicht auf ein interessantes, wenn auch späteres und außerhalb seines Arbeitsfeldes liegendes Problem eingegangen: wieweit die ἀναστολὴ τῆς κόμης, die

"Sonnenfrisur," etwa auf die Haartracht Ludwigs XIV. eingewirkt hat. Aber der Kult des *Roi soleil* ist noch niemals systematisch auf seine Quellen hin untersucht worden.

[3] L'Orange, *Apotheosis*, 129, Fig. 97, versieht übrigens die Zuweisung des mittelalterlichen Portraitkopfes selbst mit einem Fragezeichen. Anscheinend stammt die Deutung als "Friedrich II." von A. Venturi, *Storia dell' Arte Italiana* (Mailand, 1904), III, 540, und Fig. 519.

[4] Es wäre zu hoffen, daß Langlotz seinen Fund veröffentlicht, selbst wenn der Abguß etwas enttäuschend ist. Zur Bartlosigkeit, vgl. Kantorowicz, *Kaiser Friedrich der Zweite: Ergänzungsband* (Berlin, 1931), 258f.

ist, auch die Züge des hellenistischen Herrschertyps in das historische Bild dieses Kaisers einzuzeichnen.

Das Thema "Friedrich II. und der Hellenismus" ist begreiflicherweise schlechthin unausschöpflich. Was — so wird man fragen dürfen — ist denn nicht, mit Einschluß des Christentums, letzten Endes hellenistischen Ursprungs gewesen? Ganz gewiß würde dies gelten für die Rezeption des Aristoteles. Sieht man aber von all dem hier ab, so trägt doch der ganze sonstige gelehrte Betrieb am Kaiserhofe den Stempel des Hellenismus. Die Physiognomiker, Astrologen, Menschen- und Tier-Mediziner, die Botaniker, Zoologen, die Optiker und Alchimisten, sie alle arbeiten mit Material, das letztlich hellenistischer Herkunft ist. Selbst wenn man das Thema auf das hellenistische Königsbild einzuschränken sucht, so bleibt des Vagen immer noch genug. Die Arbeiten von Andreas Alföldi und anderen haben es klargestellt, daß Tracht und Zeremoniell der weltlichen wie geistlichen Herrscher des Mittelalters weitgehend und ganz direkt vom Hellenismus bestimmt waren.[5] Ein Gelehrtenleben hindurch hat ferner Franz Kampers in immer erneuten, wenn auch nicht immer ganz glücklichen Anläufen versucht, von Friedrich II. her zum Hellenismus die Brücke zu schlagen. Dabei bewegten sich seine Fragen meist in dem schwer faßbaren Wolkenraum von Kaisersage und Kaisermystik, und seine Arbeiten werden dinglicher nur da, wo sie sich mit einem ganz konkreten Begriff wie dem der *Fortuna Augusti* beschäftigen.[6]

Nun haben jedoch in jüngster Zeit die Arbeiten von Erwin R. Goodenough[7] und Louis Delatte[8] über die hellenistischen Königsspiegel, deren Fragmente bei Stobaeus überliefert sind, das Problem der hellenistischen Staatsphilosophie sehr viel schärfer beleuchtet; und auf der Grundlage der Papyri und Inschriften hat Wilhelm Schubart weiterhin das Gesamtbild noch um wesentliche Einzelzüge bereichern und ergänzen können.[9] Diese und andere Arbeiten[10] haben mit verblüffender Deutlichkeit gezeigt, in welchem bisher ungeahnten und durchaus nicht-erkannten Ausmaß Königsideal und Staatstheorie des Hellenismus im Mittelalter weitergewirkt haben. Die hellenistische Königsphilosophie hat in sehr wichtigen Einzelheiten zunächst das spätantike, dann das

---

[5] A. Alföldi, "Die Ausgestaltung des monarchischen Zeremoniells am römischen Kaiserhofe," *Mitteil. d. Deutschen Archäol. Inst., Röm. Abt.*, XLIX (1934), 118ff, und "Insignien und Tracht der römischen Kaiser," *ebda.*, L (1935), 171ff; auch Richard Delbrück, "Der spätantike Kaiserornat," *Antike*, VIII (1932), 21ff, und die Arbeiten von Percy Ernst Schramm. Für die Kirche, vgl. Theodor Klauser, "Abendländische Liturgiegeschichte: Forschungsbericht und Besinnung," *Eleutheria* (Bonner theologische Blätter für kriegsgefangene Studenten, I., 1944), 10f, und vor allem jetzt *Der Ursprung der bischöflichen Insignien und Ehrenrechte* (Bonner akademische Reden, I; Krefeld, 1949), eine Arbeit, der man nur baldige Fortsetzung wünschen kann.

[6] F. Kampers, "Die *Fortuna Caesarea* Kaiser Friedrichs II.," *Hist. Jahrb.*, XLVIII (1928), 208ff. Kampers hat sich leider manche einfache Linie verbaut durch Annahme eines "rätselvollen Überlebens" oder "dunklen Erinnerns" in bezug auf antike Elemente. Der "Sonnenkult" Friedrichs II., z. B., hat seine klare Brücke zum

byzantinischen Hofstil etwa in dem Gedicht des Eugenios von Palermo auf König Wilhelm von Sizilien; vgl. Leo Sternbach, "Eugenios von Palermo," *BZ*, XI (1902), 449.

[7] Erwin R. Goodenough, "The Political Philosophy of Hellenistic Kingship," *Yale Classical Studies*, I (1928), 55ff, sowie *The Politics of Philo Judaeus* (New Haven, 1938), 86ff.

[8] Louis Delatte, *Les Traités de la Royauté d'Ecphante, Diotogène et Sthénidas* (Bibl. de la Fac. de Philos. et Lettres de l'Univ. de Liège, Fasc. XCVII; Lüttich-Paris, 1942).

[9] W. Schubart, "Das hellenistische Königsideal nach Inschriften und Papyri," *Archiv für Papyrusforschung*, XII (1936), 1ff, "Das Königsbild des Hellenismus," *Antike*, XIII (1937), 272ff, und "Das Gesetz und der Kaiser," *Klio*, XXX (1937), 54ff.

[10] Unzulänglich sind mir zur Zeit H. E. Stier, *Nomos basileus* (Diss. Berlin, 1927), und P. Zancan, *Il monarcato ellenistico nei suoi elementi federativi* (Padua, 1934).

byzantinische Kaiserbild beeinflußt, von dem wiederum manche Züge eingewoben sind in die Herrscherauffassung, der man am Hofe Friedrichs II. gehuldigt hat.

Auf welche Weise etwa die hellenistischen Königstheorien in das byzantinische Denken einmündeten, hat Norman H. Baynes an einem Beispiel verdeutlicht, indem er auf die Vermittlerrolle des Eusebius hinwies.[11] Es handelte sich dabei ganz besonders um die Vorstellung des hellenistischen Königs als eines "Nachahmers" der Gottheit, eines θεομιμητής,[12] der sinngemäß in Byzanz immer stärker zu einem χριστομιμητής abgewandelt wurde, zu demjenigen also, der gleichsam von Amts wegen den Gottmenschen fast bühnenmäßig vergegenwärtigte und auf Erden die Christusrolle spielte — ein Gedanke, der wiederum das östliche Hofzeremoniell aufs stärkste mitbestimmt hat.[13]

Daß die *mimesis* nicht das einzige Theorem hellenistischer Herrscherphilosophie gewesen sein konnte, das vom Altertum ins Mittelalter hinübergewirkt hat, wäre von vornherein zu erwarten gewesen. Leider hat jedoch die mittelalterliche Historik, falls nicht neuere Arbeiten hier übersehen sind, diese neuerschlossenen hellenistischen Königsspiegel bisher fast völlig unbeachtet gelassen, sehr zu ihrem eigenen Schaden.[14] Eine Ausnahme bildet dabei Artur Steinwenter,[15] der, als Rechtshistoriker dem Begriff des νόμος ἔμψυχος und seiner Geschichte nachgehend, auf jene Stobaeus-Fragmente und die Arbeit von Goodenough zurückgegriffen und naturgemäß auch die, in letzter Zeit vielfach behandelten, Reden des Themistius berücksichtigt hat, deren Topoi in die byzantinische Rhetorik geradeso eingingen wie die des Eusebius in die theologisch gefärbten Staatslehren der Byzantiner.[16] Daß im Westen für die Lehre vom Mittlertum des

---

[11] N. H. Baynes, "Eusebius and the Christian Empire," *Mélanges Bidez* (Annuaire de l'Inst. de Philol. et d'Hist. Orient. et Slaves, II; Brüssel, 1934), 13ff. Siehe auch, für das Weiterwirken in Byzanz, Delatte, *Traités*, 152ff, und eine hingeworfene, wenn auch äußerst fundierte Bemerkung von Louis Robert, *Hellenica*, IV (1948), 100, bezüglich der "continuité des habitudes littéraires et des clichés moraux et politiques, de la fin du IIIᵉ siècle à l'époque justinienne." Siehe ferner, für die in den hellenistischen Königstraktaten so außerordentlich wichtige φιλανθρωπία, neben den Arbeiten von Schubart (Anm. 9), den Aufsatz von H. I. Bell, "Philanthropia in the Papyri of the Roman Period," *Hommages à Joseph Bidez et à Franz Cumont* (Collection Latomus, II; Brüssel, 1948), 31ff, für Byzanz besonders 35f, wo jedoch das unendlich weite Feld der östlichen Liturgie für diese Begriff nicht ausgewertet worden ist.

[12] Für den Begriff und seine Geschichte, vgl. etwa Michaelis, s. v. μιμέομαι , in G. Kittel, *Theologisches Wörterbuch zum N.T.*, IV (Stuttgart, 1942), 661ff.

[13] Otto Treitinger, *Die oströmische Kaiser- und Reichsidee nach ihrer Gestaltung im höfischen Zeremoniell* (Jena, 1938), bes. 125ff.

[14] Kenneth M. Setton, *Christian Attitude Towards the Emperor in the Fourth Century* (Studies in History, Economics and Public Law... of Columbia University, vol. 482; New York, 1941), bringt den Übergang schon zum Ausdruck, und Goodenough schließt seinen Aufsatz ("Political Philosophy") mit einem Ausblick auf das Mittelalter (100f). Aber selbst der ungewöhnlichen Belesenheit von Wilhelm Berges, *Die Fürstenspiegel des hohen und*

späten Mittelalters (Leipzig, 1938), scheinen die hellenistischen Spiegel entgangen zu sein.

[15] Artur Steinwenter, "ΝΟΜΟΣ ΕΜΨΥΧΟΣ: Zur Geschichte einer politischen Theorie," *Anzeiger der Wiener Akademie*, LXXXIII (1946), 250ff. Auf Grund von Delatte, *Traités*, 245ff, wären noch einige Ergänzungen zu machen, die jedoch die von Steinwenter gezeichneten Entwicklungslinien, insbesondere der späteren Zeit, nicht wesentlich beeinflussen. Nur als Kuriosum sei vermerkt, daß der Sultan Melik Nassir Mohammed von Ägypten sich in einem Schreiben an Kaiser Andronicus III. (1328–1341) ἡ ζωὴ τῆς δικαιοσύνης εἰς τὸν κόσμον bezeichnet, was doch wohl als eine Umschreibung von νόμος ἔμψυχος aufzufassen ist; vgl. W. Regel, *Analecta Byzantino-Russica* (St. Petersburg, 1891), 57, 7.

[16] Zuletzt etwa Pietro de Francisci, *Arcana Imperii* (Mailand, 1948), III:2, 114ff, und vorher Johannes Straub, *Vom Herrscherideal in der Spätantike* (Stuttgart, 1939), 160ff. Vgl. auch Kampers, "Fortuna," 223. Für die Nachwirkung des Themistius in Byzanz, vgl. die Arbeiten von Vladimir Valdenberg, in *Byzantion*, I und II, vor allem "Le idee politiche di Procopio di Gaza e di Menandro Protettore," *Studi Bizantini e Neoellenici*, IV (1935), 67ff, bes. 73f. Die ideengeschichtlich so wichtige Themistius-Forschung wird erst dann den vollen Gehalt der Reden ausschöpfen können, wenn die veraltete und überdies schwer erhältliche Ausgabe von Dindorf (Leipzig, 1832) ersetzt sein wird durch die Neuausgabe und englische Übersetzung, die Professor Glanville Downey, in Dumbarton Oaks, vorbereitet.

Kaisers als *lex animata* Friedrich II. eine besonders wichtige Stellung einnahm, ist verständlich durch die hier einmal völlig unproblematische Überlieferung des Begriffs: Justinian hat die Prägung des Themistius fast wörtlich in seine Novelle 105 übernommen.[17] Durch das erneuerte Studium des römischen Rechtes ist dann die Lehre von der *lex animata* schon im 12., vor allem aber im 13. Jahrhundert wieder fruchtbar geworden, und dadurch indirekt auch die hellenistische Lehre vom Mittlertum des Herrschers.[18] Glossatoren wie Rhetoren des "juristischen Jahrhunderts" konnten nicht umhin, sich mit der Anschauung auseinanderzusetzen, daß "Gott den Herrscher als das beseelte Gesetz zu den Menschen herabgesandt hat."

*   *   *

Im Zusammenhang mit der Lehre von der *lex animata* verdient jedoch ein weiterer Topos Beachtung. In seiner großen Prunkrede auf Friedrich II., die ihrer Gattung nach, wenn auch weniger den Bildern nach, der östlichen Enkomien-Literatur angehört, hat Petrus de Vinea, der kaiserliche Logothet, seinen Herrn gepriesen als den *pacator iustissimus ... quem supremi manus opificis formavit in hominem, ut tot rerum habenas flecteret et cuncta sub iuris ordine limitaret.*[19] Ich hatte diese Zeilen vor vielen Jahren mit der Adams-Spekulation des 13. Jahrhunderts in Verbindung gebracht: der Kaiser ist wie Adam — und damit wie der "neue Adam", Christus — von Gott selbst erschaffen — oder gezeugt.[20] Ob und wieweit diese Idee mitgeschwungen hat, bleibe vorerst dahingestellt. Sie war jedoch nicht allein maßgebend; denn das Bild von dem Herrscher, "den des höchsten Werkmeisters Hand selbst zum Menschen geformt hat," ist nicht erst im 13. Jahrhundert geprägt worden. Die einzige Parallele, die ich seinerzeit heranziehen konnte, war eine Stelle bei Benzo von Alba, einem Panegyriker der Zeit Heinrichs IV., der seinen Kaiser ansprach als *de coelo missus, non homo carnis.*[21] Aber diese Parallele paßt nicht recht. Woran Benzo, dem zumindest einzelne Stichworte des römischen Rechtes bekannt waren,[22] gedacht haben mag, war eher die *lex-animata*-Lehre: der Kaiser ist der von Gott zu den Menschen Herabgesandte (Benzos: *de coelo missus*), und zwar als das lebendige oder beseelte Gesetz selbst (Benzos: *non homo carnis*). Gehört auch das Bild, das Benzo benutzte, dem gleichen, oder wenigstens einem verwandten Ideenkreis an, so ist es doch nicht identisch mit Vineas Kaiser, "den des höchsten Werkmeisters Hand selbst zum Menschen geschaffen hat." Die schlagende Parallele findet sich jedoch in einer der hellenistischen Staatstheorien.

[17] Vgl. *Nov. Just.*, 105, 2, 4, mit Themistius, *Or.* XIX, 228a (Rede über die Philanthropia des Kaisers Theodosius); hierzu Steinwenter, 251 und 260. Übrigens sagt schon Menander (*Basilikos logos*, 11, ed. Bursian, *Abh. Akad. München*, 1882, 97, 25f), daß der König τῇ δ' ἀληθείᾳ τὴν καταβολὴν οὐρανόθεν ἔχει.

[18] Nachweise bei Steinwenter, 252ff; vgl. Berges, *Fürstenspiegel*, 49; auch meinen *Ergänzungsband*, 86, 99.

[19] Huillard-Bréholles, *Vie et Correspondance de Pierre de la Vigne* (Paris, 1865), Anh. No. 107, S. 426.

[20] Vgl. *K. Friedrich II.* (Berlin 1927), 476; ferner die Analyse von Ernst Benz, *Ecclesia Spiritualis* (Stuttgart, 1934), 227ff, bes. 231. Ob das Stück wirklich gesprochene

Rhetorik oder Stilübungsrhetorik ist, ist schwer zu sagen. Angesichts der sehr lebendigen Panegyrik in Byzanz und auch im Laskaridischen Reich von Nicaea, zu dem der Hof engste Beziehungen hatte (vgl. etwa meinen *Ergänzungsband*, 133), sind derartige Ansprachen an den Kaiser sehr wohl möglich gewesen. Für den hier verfolgten Zweck wäre das übrigens gleichgültig, da es nur auf das Vorhandensein des Topos ankommt.

[21] Benzo, *Ad Heinricum*, VI, c. 7, *MGH, SS*, XI, 669, 1; vgl. meinen *Ergänzungsband*, 108.

[22] Vgl. P. E. Schramm, *Kaiser, Rom und Renovatio* (Leipzig-Berlin, 1929), I, 281f, 284.

In der Schrift Περὶ βασιλείας stellt der "Pythagoräer" Ekphantos eine Betrachtung über die Kosmosregionen an, wie sie in besserer Überlieferung in der hermetischen Κόρη κόσμου erhalten ist.[23] Jede der Regionen wird regiert von einem Herrscher, der innerhalb seines Bereiches der Gottheit jeweils nächstverwandt ist. In der Himmelsregion herrschen die Götter selbst; im Äther herrscht Helios über die Sterne; in der Luftregion herrscht Selene über die Seelendämonen.

> Bei uns auf der Erde ist zwar der Mensch das Bestgeborene, das Göttlichere aber ist der König, der innerhalb der allen gemeinsamen Menschennatur am Besseren den Löwenanteil hat.
>
> Den übrigen Menschen gleicht er durch sein Gehäuse insofern, als er aus dem gleichen Stoffe gefertigt ist; aber er ist von dem höchsten Werkmeister geformt, der ihn fertigend sich selbst zum Vorbild nahm (τὸ μὲν σκᾶνος τοῖς λοιποῖς ὅμοιος, οἷα γεγονὼς ἐκ τᾶς αὐτᾶς ὕλας, ὑπὸ τεχνίτα δ'εἰργασμένος λῴστω, ὃς ἐτεχνίτευσεν αὐτὸν ἀρχετύπῳ χρώμενος ἑαυτῷ).
>
> Der König ist also das eine und einzige Geschöpf, das des oberen Königs inne wird (κατασκεύασμα δὴ ὦν ὁ βασιλεὺς ἓν καὶ μόνον ἐννοητικὸν τῶ ἀνωτέρω βασιλέως); und während er seinem Fertiger von jeher bekannt war, ist er den von ihm Beherrschten ein solcher, den man in seinem Königtum wie in einem Lichte erblickt.[24]

Auf die königliche Mittlerlehre, die hier wie anderwärts in den "pythagoräischen" Königstraktaten sehr deutlich formuliert ist und die im Umkreis Friedrichs II. gleichfalls wiederkehrt, sei nicht weiter eingegangen.[25] Der entscheidende Satz jedoch über den göttlichen Techniten, der selbst den König geformt hat, stimmt inhaltlich mit Vineas Lobrede völlig überein.

Wie ist Vinea nun dazu gekommen, einen Gedanken des Ekphantos in solch erstaunlicher Ähnlichkeit zu wiederholen? Grundsätzlich wird mit zwei Möglichkeiten zu rechnen sein: Vinea könnte den gleichen Gedanken gehabt und ihm in seiner bibelnahen Sprache Ausdruck gegeben haben, oder aber es wäre mit einer indirekten Überlieferung zu rechnen, da er ja die Stobaeus-Fragmente selbst nicht gekannt haben kann.

Hinsichtlich der ersten Möglichkeit, der der Gedankengleichheit, lohnt es schon, einige Erwägungen anzustellen. Vineas Ausdrucksweise — *quem supremi manus opificis formavit in hominem* — lehnt sich ganz offenkundig an Genesis 1, 27 f. an: *Formavit ergo Dominus Deus hominem...* Gott als *supremus opifex* oder *artifex* (λῷστος τεχνίτης) ist natürlich ein ganz herkömmliches Bild, so alt wie die Interpretation des Sechstagewerkes selbst. Geht man nun von der Genesis-Stelle aus, so hätte Vinea im Grunde nichts anderes getan, als das vom Menschen und seiner Erschaffung generell Gesagte nunmehr in be-

---

[23] Stobaeus, I, 49, 45, ed. Wachsmuth, I, 407; ed. Walter Scott, *Hermetica* (Oxford, 1924), I, 494ff; Delatte, *Traités*, 154 und 174ff.

[24] Die hier zitierte Stelle ist bei Stobaeus zweimal überliefert, IV, vi, 22, ed. Hense, 245, und IV, vii, 64, Hense, 272; neue Edition bei Delatte, *Traités*, 25f und

27f, cf. 47f; Goodenough "Political Philosophy," 76, und *Politics of Philo*, 98f, übersetzt die Stellen.

[25] Vgl. Delatte, Index s. v. "Roi médiateur"; auch Goodenough, *Politics of Philo*, 98, mit anderen interessanten Stellen; für Friedrich II. im Zusammenhang mit der *lex animata*, vgl. Steinwenter, 263; auch meinen *Ergänzungsband*, 83ff; s. unten, Anm. 31.

sonderer oder gar ausschließlicher Weise auf den Kaiser und seine Erschaffung zu beziehen. Friedrich wäre demnach DER Mensch, der neue Urvater gewesen, der wiederum eins war mit der ganzen Menschheit, als deren Inbegriff Vinea seinen Herrn denn auch darstellt.[26]

Es ist nun außerordentlich bezeichnend, daß in diesem Falle Vineas Methode genau die gleiche gewesen wäre wie die des Ekphantos. Jener Satz des Ekphantos findet sich wörtlich auch bei Clemens von Alexandrien, der ihn jedoch anführt als Zitat aus einer Schrift Περὶ τύχας eines' anderen "Pythagoräers," des Eurysos.[27] Eurysos ist ganz gewiß nicht von Ekphantos abhängig gewesen.[28] Denn das Eurysos-Zitat bei Clemens bringt, trotz wörtlicher Übereinstimmung, einen fundamental anderen Gedanken zum Ausdruck, der bestimmt der ursprüngliche ist. Eurysos spricht nämlich gar nicht vom König, sondern vom Menschen im allgemeinen.

> Sein Gehäuse hat er (der Mensch) mit den übrigen Geschöpfen (den Tieren) gemeinsam insofern, als er aus dem gleichen Stoffe gefertigt ist. Aber er (der Mensch) ist von dem höchsten Werkmeister geformt, der ihn fertigend sich selbst zum Vorbild nahm.

Mit anderen Worten, Clemens von Alexandrien führte das Zitat aus Eurysos an als Bestätigung der Lehre vom Menschen als *imago Dei*, eine Lehre, die — von Genesis, 1, 27 ganz zu schweigen — in einen völlig anderen Zusammenhang gehört, schon damals ihre lange Geschichte hinter sich hatte und eine noch längere Geschichte in künftigen Jahrhunderten entfalten sollte.[29]

Es wäre also Ekphantos gewesen, der anscheinend als erster den Satz von der Menschenerschaffung im allgemeinen auf die der Königserschaffung im besonderen, ja in einem ausschließlichen Sinne, übertragen hätte.[30] Die Ähnlichkeit zwischen Vinea und Ekphan-

---

[26] Benz, *Ecclesia Spiritualis*, 231.

[27] Clemens, *Stromata*, V, 5, 29, ed. Stählin, II, 344, 20; Goodenough, "Political Philosophy," 76, n. 75, bezieht die Stelle auf den König; korrekter bei Delatte, *Traités*, 177.

[28] Delatte, *Traités*, 178 und 285.

[29] Vgl. Delatte, 178ff, mit Material zur *homo imago Dei*-Lehre, von der es übrigens auch eine trinitarische Version gibt: *homo qui ad imaginem sanctae Trinitatis conditus est* heißt es z. B. in einer der vielen Antworten auf Karls d. Gr. Rundfrage über die Taufe (Migne, *PL*, XCVIII, 939 C). Für die Durchführung dieser Lehre, vgl. etwa Anastasius Sinaita, *Quaestio II* (Migne, *PG*, LXXXIX, 344C), wo der Mensch als ναὸς ἔμψυχος τοῦ θεοῦ aufgefaßt wird, der den Vater, den Sohn als Hohepriester und das Pneuma als Feuer der Wahrheit in sich trägt. Die Auslegung ist wesentlich durch das pluralische "Wir" in Gen., 1, 26–27, bestimmt worden, das schon Philo Schwierigkeiten bereitete, der jedoch den Plural auf die bei der Schöpfung des Menschen mittätigen δεύτεροι bezog; vgl. für die Stellen Harry A. Wolfson, *Philo* (Cambridge, Mass., 1948), I, 387, Anm. 18. Von christlicher Seite wurde dann der Plural auf die Trinität bezogen; vgl. etwa Athanasius, *Contra Arianos Oratio I*, c. 18, bei Migne, *PG*, XXVI, 49A, oder Gregor von

Nyssa, *De hominis opificio*, c. 6, bei Migne, *PG*, XLIV, 140BC; für weiteres Material s. H. Pinard, "Création," *Dictionnaire de théologie catholique*, III, 2111ff, bes. 2118f, und für das ikonographische Problem Adelheid Heimann, "Trinitas creator mundi," *Journal of the Warburg Institute*, II (1938–1939), 42ff.

[30] Es wäre interessant, dem Oszillieren zwischen "Menschenerschaffung" und "Königserschaffung" im einzelnen nachzugehen. Die Ähnlichkeit des Menschen mit Gott (Gen., 1, 27) ist zu Zeiten fast gewohnheitsmäßig dahin interpretiert worden, daß Gott und Mensch einander durch die βασιλεία angeglichen seien, ein Gedanke, der (von Philo und Origenes zu schweigen) in großartiger Weise zum Ausdruck gebracht worden ist von Gregor von Nyssa, *De hominis opificio*, c. 4f, bei Migne, *PG*, XLIV, 136f, worauf mich freundlicherweise Professor Werner Jäger aufmerksam machte. Hier ist geradezu eine Theorie der menschlichen Souveränität, oder der Souveränität des königlichen Menschen, formuliert worden; schwächer dann bei Theodoret, *Quaestiones in Genesim*, c. XX, bei Migne, *PG*, LXXX, 104ff, und bei Anastasius Sinaita, *Quaestio XXIV*, bei Migne, *PG*, LXXXIX, 541ff. Vgl. zum Thema auch Johannes Hehn, "Zum Terminus 'Bild Gottes'," *Festschrift Eduard Sachau* (ed. Gotthold Weil, Berlin, 1915), 36–52. Der

tos liefe demnach einzig darauf hinaus, daß beide die *homo imago Dei*-Lehre einseitig zu einer aufs äußerste gesteigerten *rex imago Dei*-Lehre umgebogen hätten. Durch dieses einfache Mittel wäre der König nunmehr als der einzige von Gott selbst nach seinem Ebenbild Erschaffene hingestellt worden; und da dem König ganz selbstverständlich die Aufgabe zufiel, seine Untertanen sich selbst und dadurch Gott anzugleichen, so war er kraft der μίμησις zu einer Art Mittlerwesens erhoben, um somit als "letzter der Götter, aber erster der Menschen" zu wirken — Gedanken, die weder Ekphantos noch Vinea noch auch der päpstlichen Staatslehre fremd waren und die auch, wiewohl in anderer Brechung, in der *lex animata*-Lehre vorherrschen.[31] All das würde demnach in der Hauptsache besagen, daß der König in fast ausschließlichem Maße die *imago Dei* gewesen sei. Es ist nur eine äußerste Überspitzung der sonst schon fast banal zu nennenden und allgemeingültigen Anschauung des Mittelalters, der gemäß der König zwar im besonderen, aber keineswegs exklusiven Sinne als *imago Dei* verehrt wurde.

Andererseits ist jedoch auch die Möglichkeit einer Kontinuität der Überlieferung nicht von der Hand zu weisen. Es ließen sich wahrscheinlich sehr viele Stellen aus der byzantinischen Panegyrik anführen, die in irgendeiner Form die Gedanken des Ekphantos aufnehmen und weiterspinnen. Delatte hat eine Anzahl solcher Fälle zusammenstellen können, in denen des Ekphantos Lehre wenigstens anklingt.[32] Hier sei, weil der zeitliche Abstand von Vinea relativ gering ist, nur auf eine unbeachtete Parallele aus der byzantinischen Hofrhetorik verwiesen. In einer anonym überlieferten Leichenrede auf den im Jahre 1180 verstorbenen Kaiser Manuel Komnenos sagt ein Rhetor:[33]

> Weh mir, o Kaiser, Gebilde Du der Hände des besten Werkmeisters, Gottes (πλάσμα χειρῶν ἀριστοτέχνου θεοῦ); Du beseeltes Goldbildnis der Königsherrschaft (βασιλείας χρυσοῦν ἀφίδρυμα ἔμψυχον), das — Glut des Herzensfeuer zwar, doch auch eine Hämmerung von Drangsal und Mühen — auf dem gedrungenen Amboß der Standhaftigkeit von dem Demiurgen weise und kunstrecht zu einer Stele der Tapferkeit gefertigt (εἰς ἀνδρείας στήλην πρὸς τοῦ δημιουργοῦ σοφῶς φιλοτεχνηθέν) und, wie auf einer Schaubühne der königlichen Warte, den Menschen als Ur-Idee aufgerichtet worden ist (πρὸς ἀρχετυπίαν ἀνθρώποις... ὀρθωθέν).

Trotz aller Künstelei und durch allen Schwulst rhetorischer Überladenheit hindurch ist doch noch, obwohl gleichsam flachgedrückt durch das Gehämmere des göttlichen Bildhauer-Schmiedes, der ursprüngliche Gedanke zu erkennen: der von des göttlichen Aristotechniten Hand zum Bild, und damit den übrigen Menschen zum Vorbild, geformte Kaiser, ein lebendes Goldbildnis der Ur-Idee aller Königsherrschaft oder, wie es ein Dichter des späten 13. Jahrhunderts ausdrückt, ein ἔμψυχον ἴνδαλμα ψυχῆς τῆς

Übergang von Adam zu König, und von König zu Adam, fehlt denn auch nicht in Byzanz: εἵνεκα δὲ βασιλέως κόσμος, δῆλον ὡς σύ, βασιλεῦ, τῷ κόσμῳ ψυχή. Ἀδὰμ μὲν οὖν ὁ πρῶτος γεγονὼς τῷ κόσμῳ ψυχὴ καὶ βασιλεὺς κτλ. Vgl. Theodoros Hyrtakenos, bei Boissonade (s. u. Anm. 34), I, 251. Hier wird also der Kaiser, wie Adam, zur Weltseele.

[31] Vgl. *Kore kosmou*, ed. Scott, I, 496, 12, eine häufig angeführte Stelle, z. B. bei F. Boll, *Aus der Offenbarung*

Johannis (Leipzig-Berlin, 1914), Anh. II ("Könige als Offenbarungsträger"), 137. Für die papale Theorie genügt es hier, auf Innocenz III. hinzuweisen: *inter Deum et hominem constituti*, Ep. VI, 86, Migne, *PL*, CCXV, 88C, und die berühmte Stelle im *Sermo de diversis*, II, ebda., CCXVII, 658.

[32] Delatte, *Traités*, 152ff.

[33] W. Regel, *Fontes rerum byzantinarum* (St. Petersburg, 1917), Fasc. 2, p. 195, 7–12.

βασιλικωτάτης.[34] Der Leichenredner hat freilich die Metapher des Ekphantos ihres metaphysischen Gehaltes nahezu entledigt, indem er die *imago Dei* allzu dinglich als ein von Gott — hier gewissermaßen einem berußten Hephaistos gleichend — mit Hammerschlägen gefertigtes Goldbild versteht. Aber dieser dingliche Bildcharakter des Königs hat sehr viele Parallelen,[35] hervorgerufen vielleicht durch die tatsächliche Bedeutung, die im Osten dem Kaiserbild selbst noch in christlicher Zeit zukam.[36]

Angesichts der Byzanznähe des staufischen Großhofes wäre es durchaus statthaft, wenigstens die Möglichkeit offen zu lassen, daß traditionelles Gedankengut der hellenistischen Königsspiegel in byzantinischer Brechung auf Vinea und die Capuaner Rhetorenschule hinübergewirkt hat, selbst wenn sich eine bestimmte Quelle nicht mehr so eindeutig feststellen läßt wie etwa im Falle der Lehre von der *lex animata*.[37] Und die Frage der Überlieferung läßt sich auch nur allgemein, aber kaum eindeutig lösen in bezug auf einen anderen juristischen Begriff.

*   *   *

Die Paragraphen I, 16–19 des *Liber augustalis*, der großen Konstitutionen-Sammlung, die Friedrich II. 1231 in Melfi für sein süditalisches Königreich veröffentlicht hat, und

---

[34] So in dem *Prokypsis*-Gedicht (Nr. 19) des Manuel Holobolos, bei J. F. Boissonade, *Anecdota Graeca* (Paris, 1833), V, 181, 4; zur Datierung (1295) vgl. A. Heisenberg, "Aus der Geschichte und Literatur der Palaiologenzeit," *Sitz.-Ber. München*, 1920, Abh. 10, 124f. Andererseits war natürlich der Patriarch eine εἰκὼν ζῶσα Χριστοῦ καὶ ἔμψυχος; cf. Peter Charanis, "Coronation," *Byzantion*, XV (1941), 53, Anm. 23.

[35] Ein paar Beispiele bei Delatte, *Traités*, 154, 157, 180, die sich aus späterer Literatur leicht vermehren ließen. Nikephoros Blemmides, z. B., nennt seinen Kaiserspiegel geradezu βασιλικὸς ἀνδριάς und verlangt, daß der gute Kaiser ein κανών sei, strahlender als der vielbesungene Kanon des Polyklet (c. 6); Migne, *PG*, CLXII, 667C, vgl. 633B. Oder Theodoros Hyrtakenos, der mit Bezug auf den Kaiser sagt: εὗρεν Ἀνδρία τὸν ἔμψυχον ἑαυτῆς ἀνδριάντα (Boissonade, *Anecd. Gr.*, I, 262). Andererseits findet sich in den liturgischen Büchern der Ostkirche überraschend häufig der Ausdruck "Statue" oder "Stele," wo der Westen bestimmt nur "Bild" gebrauchen würde: στήλη ἔμψυχος καὶ ἔμπνους εἰκών heißt es beispielsweise in einem Stichos für St. Ignatius (*Menaia*, editio Romana, 1888ff, III, 416, zum 29. Januar). Für den Gebrauch von ἔμψυχος (s. auch oben, Anm. 29) bieten die östlichen liturgischen Bücher gleichfalls eine völlig unausgeschöpfte Quelle, die auch zur Lehre von der *lex animata* sowie zu deren Verständnis noch manches beitragen könnte. Übrigens sei auch daran erinnert, daß in der theurgischen Praxis die Belebung von Götterstatuetten etwas ganz übliches war: man machte das ἄγαλμα des Gottes ἔμψυχον; vgl. E. R. Dodds, "The Theurgy," *Journal of Roman Studies*, XXXVII (1947), 62ff. Der gleichsam magische Charakter der Empsychie, im Osten soviel stärker entwickelt als im Westen, würde eine Untersuchung lohnen.

[36] Helmut Kruse, *Studien zur offiziellen Geltung des Kaiserbildes im römischen Reich* (Paderborn, 1934); Treitinger, 204; siehe auch Sirarpie Der Nersessian, "Une apologie des images au septième siècle," *Byzantion*, XVII (1944–45), 60ff, und wohl aus dem gleichen Jahrhundert, oder weniger früher, eine koptische Predigt, in der sehr anschaulich die Aufstellung und das Asylrecht des Kaiserbildes beschrieben wird, freilich nur, um die Superiorität eines Muttergottesbildes darzutun; cf. William H. Worrell, *The Coptic Manuscripts in the Freer Collection* (University of Michigan Studies, Humanistic Series, X; New York, 1923), 375. Max Bachmann, *Die Rede des Johannes Syropulos an den Kaiser Isaak II. Angelos (1185–1195)* (Diss. München, 1935), 32 (zu p. 16, 32), denkt bei den Worten ἀγγελικαὶ εἰκονομορφαί an die Ikonen des Angelos, durch die, da überall aufgestellt, das Reich quasi mit "Engeln" angefüllt und in einen Himmel auf Erden verwandelt sei.

[37] Ähnliches gilt auch von der Lehre der Erschaffung der Königsseelen, die bei Friedrich II. und dem dynastisierten 13. Jahrhundert eine gewisse Rolle spielt; vgl. etwa den Brief (wohl Stilübung) an Conrad IV. bei Huillard-Bréholles, *Hist. diplom. Friderici Secundi* (Paris, 1852ff), V, 275, für die *infusio subtilis et nobilis animae* bei Königen. Man denke auch an Pierre Dubois. Einfacher zu erklären ist das Fortleben eines anderen Axioms des dynastischen Gedankens. *CIL*, III, 710 (Diocletian und Maximian): *diis geniti et deorum creatores;* ähnlich schon vorher bei Seneca, *Consolatio ad Marcum*, XV, 1: *Caesares qui dis geniti deosque genituri dicuntur* (vgl. F. Cumont, *Textes et monuments relatifs aux mystères de Mithra* [Brüssel, 1899], I, 291, n. 5), wozu die christliche Version unter Philipp IV. von Frankreich ganz folgerichtig lautet: *sancti reges Francorum ... cum generent sanctos reges;* vgl. Dom Jean Leclercq, "Un sermon prononcé pendant la guerre de Flandre sous Philippe le Bel," *Revue du moyen âge latin*, I (1945), 170; auch meinen Aufsatz "Pro patria mori in Mediaeval Thought," *AHR*, LVI (1951), 483. Die Quelle dürfte in diesem Falle Vergil sein; *Aeneis*, IX, 642: *dis genite et geniture deos.*

zwar gleichzeitig in lateinischer wie in griechischer Sprache, haben schon den Zeitgenossen ein gewisses Erstaunen abgenötigt. Der Kaiser spricht hier von einer seltsamen Einrichtung zum Schutze des individuellen Besitzes wie dem des Individuums und seiner Angehörigen gegen Gewalt durch das Rechtsmittel der privaten *defensa*.[38] Die *defensa* ist ein Friedegebot, das nicht ein Beamter sondern jegliche Privatperson einem Angreifer von Besitz oder Personen auferlegen kann, indem er den Kaiser anruft — *per invocationem nostri (sc. imperatoris) nominis*.[39] Der unrechtmäßig Angegriffene suchte sich also zu schützen durch Anrufung des Kaisernamens, wobei die Formel lautete: *ex parte imperatoris defendo*, oder auch: *prohibeo te ex parte regis (imperatoris) quod me offendere non praesumas*. Daraufhin galt der Angriff, wenn er dennoch erfolgte, gleichsam als ein Angriff auf die Person des Kaisers selbst, und der Fall wurde demgemäß, unter Ausschluß aller Lokalgerichtsbarkeit, direkt vor das Hofgericht gezogen. Die *defensa* diente unter anderem auch dazu, die königliche Gerichtsbarkeit gegenüber den lokalen Gewalten auszudehnen.[40]

Über die Herkunft dieser Einrichtung ist bisher keine Einigkeit erzielt worden. Daß die Paragraphen unter Friedrich II. formuliert worden sind und erst 1231 ihre endgültige Fassung erhielten, steht wohl fest. Ebensowenig kann aber bezweifelt werden, daß die *defensa* schon unter den Normannen bestanden hat. Ein Dokument vom Jahre 1227 zeigt, daß noch vier Jahre vor der Gesetzgebung von Melfi nicht nur der Herrscher, sondern auch der zuständige Erzbischof oder ein Lokalbeamter angerufen werden konnten.[41] Aus normannischer Zeit ist ein Fall aus dem Jahre 1163 bekannt geworden, der in der Chronik der Abtei Casauria überliefert ist.[42] Weiter haben einzelne Gelehrte versucht, durch ein Zurückdatieren des Stadtrechts von Trani ins elfte Jahrhundert die *defensa* noch früher anzusetzen.[43] Andere haben daran gedacht, die Institution aus dem normannischen Recht herzuleiten und sie mit dem *Haro*-Ruf in Verbindung zu bringen. *Haro* ist jedoch, wie das englische *hue and cry* oder das hochdeutsche *zeter* lediglich ein "Gerüft", das juristisch als ein Beweismittel der handhaften Tat diente, und dieser *Haro*-Ruf, der freilich zunächst ein Alarmgeschrei war, hatte im 13 Jahrhundert nichts zu tun mit einem privaten Selbstschutz *per invocationem nominis regis*.[44]

[38] Huillard-Bréholles, *Hist. dipl.*, IV, 17ff; der Glosse wegen benutze ich die Cervoni-Ausgabe: *Constitutionum regni Siciliarum libri III... sumptibus Antonii Cervonii* (Neapel, 1773), 35ff und für den griechischen Text die Ausgabe von C. Carcani (Neapel, 1786).

[39] *Liber aug.*, I, 16. Die Literatur ist angeführt bei Hans Niese, *Die Gesetzgebung der normannischen Dynastie im Regnum Siciliae* (Halle, 1910), 32, n. 4. Neuere Arbeiten sind mir nicht bekannt geworden, doch schließt das deren Existenz nicht aus.

[40] Für die erste Formel, vgl. Niese, 34, n. 3, auf Grund des *Chron. Casauriense* (unten, Anm. 42), wo allerdings *veto*, nicht *defendo* steht; für die zweite Formel vgl. Andreas v. Isernia, Cervoni-Ausgabe des *Lib. aug.*, p. 35. Federico Ciccaglione, *Manuale di storia del diritto italiano* (Mailand, ohne Jahr), II, 163f, § 589, der im übrigen byzantinische Herkunft vermutet, betont die Ausdehnung der kaiserlichen Gerichtsbarkeit gegenüber den lokalen Gewalten.

[41] C. A. Garufi, "La *defensa ex parte domini imperatoris* in un documento privato del 1227–28," *Rivista italiana per le scienze giuridiche*, XXVII (1899), 190ff. Leider ist mir die Zeitschrift, die einen großen Teil der italienischen Arbeiten über die *defensa* enthält (vgl. Niese, p. 33), gegenwärtig nicht zugänglich. Ich kenne die Arbeit Garufis nur aus der Besprechung im *Archivio storico siciliano*, ser. II, vol. XXIV (1899), 344.

[42] *Chronicon Casauriense*, bei Muratori, *Rer. It. SS.*, II, 1009, eine Urkunde, auf die erstmals Niese, S. 34, für die *defensa* aufmerksam gemacht hat.

[43] Cipolla, "Un dubbio sulla data degli *Ordinamenti* tranesi," *Rendiconti dei Lincei*, ser. v, vol. V (1896), 267ff, der die *Ordinamenti* von Trani nicht 1063, sondern 1363 datiert; vgl. hierzu auch L. S. Villanueva, in *Arch. stor. sicil.*, ser. II, vol. XXI (1896), 403. Die *defensa* wird in Trani, wie übrigens auch anderwärts in späterer Zeit, auferlegt *da la parte de la mia signoria*.

[44] Über den *Haro*-Ruf, vgl. Niese, S. 33, n. 4, und seine Kritik an E. Glasson, "Étude historique sur la clameur de Haro," *Nouvelle revue historique de droit français et étranger*, VI (1882), 397ff, 517ff. Für die germanische Institution des Gerüftes, vgl. jetzt L. L. Hammerich, *Clamor* (Kgl. Danske Videnskabernes Selskab, XXIX:1; Kopenhagen, 1941).

Was Friedrich II. bezweckte, als er 1231 für das ganze Königreich einheitlich die Anrufung des Herrschernamens bei Auferlegung der *defensa* anordnete, sagt das Gesetzbuch selbst ganz deutlich; es war, neben vielem anderen, eine Manifestation der zumindest potentiellen Allgegenwart des Kaisers: *et sic nos etiam qui prohibente individuitate personae ubique praesentialiter esse non possumus, ubique potentialiter adesse credamur.*[45] Der Glossator Andreas von Isernia, der unter den ersten Anjous schrieb, bemerkte hierzu sehr richtig: *Juxta illud: "An nescis longas regibus esse manus?"*[46] Ungehorsam gegenüber einer auferlegten *defensa* war daher auch gleichbedeutend mit einer Verachtung des kaiserlichen Namens, so daß das Gesetzbuch die Erwartung aussprechen konnte, daß selbst bei fälschlich gebotener *defensa* der zu unrecht Betroffene zunächst gehorche und sogar sein gutes Recht für den Augenblick preisgebe *ob reverentiam culminis nostri.*[47]

Das sind Anschauungen, die von einem einfachen Gerüft weit entfernt sind. Hingegen ist die Idee der potentiellen Allgegenwart des Kaisers um so näher verwandt der antiken, zumal spätantiken Vorstellung von der Allgegenwart der Kaiser-*numina.*[48] So ist denn auch die bisher einzige einwandfreie Parallele zu der sizilischen Kaiserinvokation bei einem römischen Schriftsteller der Zeit Mark Aurels gefunden worden.[49] In den Metamorphosen des Apuleius (III, 29) wird erzählt, wie der unselige, in einen Esel verwandelte Lucius sich gegen seine Peiniger und ihre Schläge zu schützen suchte. Er beschloß *ad auxilium civile decurrere et interposito venerabili principis nomine tot aerumnis me liberare.* Er entschloß sich also dafür, zwischen sich und seine Peiniger den Namen des Kaisers zu "interponieren." In einem thessalischen Marktort angelangt, will er in dem Menschengewimmel der Griechen *genuino sermone,* also doch wohl in seiner eignen angeborenen Sprache, den Namen des Kaisers anrufen *(nomen augustum Caesaris invocare temptavi).* Aber Lucius konnte natürlich nur in ein Eselsgebrüll ausbrechen, *reliquum autem Caesaris nomen enuntiare non potui.* Daß sein unmelodisches Brüllen die Peiniger nur dazu herausforderte, mit ihren Lederriemen um so kräftiger auf den Esel einzuschlagen, hat mit der Sache selbst nichts mehr zu tun, da ja die Eselstreiber nicht wissen konnten, daß sie sich damit beinahe einer Verachtung des Kaisernamens schuldig gemacht hätten.

---

[45] *Liber aug.,* I, 17 (gegen Ende); Huillard-Bréholles, *Hist. diplom.,* IV, 20.

[46] Cervoni-Ausgabe, p. 41, Glosse zu *ubique potentialiter.*

[47] *Liber aug.,* I, 19.

[48] Cl. Mamertinus, *Paneg. genethl. Maximiano,* c. 14, p. 286, 13–17, ed. W. Baehrens: *ubicumque sitis, in unum licet palatium concesseritis, divinitatem vestram ubique versari, omnes terras omniaque maria plena esse vestri. Quid enim mirum si, cum possit hic mundus Iovis esse plenus, possit et Herculis* [d. h. *Maximiani*]? Cf. Leo Berlinger, *Beiträge zur inoffiziellen Titulatur der römischen Kaiser* (Diss. Breslau, 1935), 65 (auch 62, Anm. 220). Für die "virtuelle Omnipräsenz" des byzantinischen Kaisers, vgl. Franz Dölger, "Die Kaiserurkunde der Byzantiner als Ausdruck ihrer politischen Anschauungen," *HZ,* CLIX (1939), 235, Anm. 2. Der Absolutismus legalisiert später die Omnipräsenz des Königs. Vgl. z. B. Sir William Blackstone, *Commentaries on the Laws of England,* p. *270 (alle Ausgaben haben die gleiche Paginierung): "A consequence of (t)his prerogative is the legal *ubiquity* of the king. His majesty in the eye of the law is always present in [all his courts ... It is the regal office, and not the royal person, that is always present in] court, always ready to undertake prosecutions, or pronounce judgment for the benefit and protection of the subject." Das ist genau die gleiche Anschauung, die der *Liber augustalis* durch die Antithese *praesentialiter — potentialiter* zum Ausdruck bringt.

[49] Francesco Schupfer, "La *defensa* e l'asino di Apuleio," *Riv. ital. per le scienze giurid.,* XXI (1896), 422ff; *ibid.,* XXX (1905), 185; Villanueva, in *Arch. stor. sicil.,* ser. II, vol. XXI (1896), 402ff; auch Nino Tamassia, "Nuovi studi sulla *defensa,*" und "Ancora sulla *defensa,*" *Atti del R. Istituto Veneto,* LX (1900–1901), 343ff und 685ff, wo jedoch die *preces* für den Kaiser oder an ihn verwechselt werden mit der rechtlichen *invocatio* des Kaisernamens. Es sei übrigens bemerkt, daß in Apuleius' Vorbild, Lukian, *Asinus,* c. 16 (584), es einfach heißt ἐπεὶ δὲ πολλάκις "ὦ Καῖσαρ" ἀναβοῆσαι ἐπεθύμουν was eher nach einem Seufzer klingt, als nach einem rechtlichen "Interponieren" (s. unten) des Kaisernamens.

Die Stelle zeigt ganz deutlich, daß im 2. Jahrhundert, als Apuleius, der Isisgläubige aus dem numidischen Madaura, seine Metamorphosen schrieb, eine der sizilischen *defensa* durchaus wesensverwandte Einrichtung bestand und dem Dichter — sei es aus Thessalien oder aus Numidien oder vielleicht nur aus Gebräuchen der Kulte — bekannt war, nämlich sich durch die Anrufung des Kaiser-Namens, und damit des Kaiser-Numens, gegen Angriffe zu schützen. Auffallend ist es nur, daß sonst im römischen Bereich so wenig von dieser Einrichtung bekannt ist. Denn daß Gräber und andere Stätten und Stiftungen unter den Schutz des Kaisers gestellt werden, hat mit dem durch Kaiserinvokation zu erreichenden momentanen Rechtsschutz nichts gemeinsam.

Woran jene Invokation viel eher erinnert, ist vielleicht das Asylrecht der Kaiserstatuen und der Schutz, der dem zukommt, der ein Kaiserbild berührt. In diesem Falle wird zwar nicht der Name des Kaisers, wohl aber das Bildnis der Kaisers "interponiert," und es ist bekannt, daß dieses Bildnis-Asylrecht zu dem unstatthaften Mißbrauch geführt hat, nun einfach stets eine Münze bei sich zu tragen, um somit jeden Augenblick das Münzbild des Kaisers "interponieren" zu können oder es wie ein Amulett dem Verfolger vorzuhalten.[50] Der Unterschied zwischen der *defensa* und dem *ad statuas confugere* ist natürlich der, daß im ersten Fall der unschuldig Angegriffene den Namen des Kaisers interponiert, während im Falle des Statuen-Asyls der schuldig Verfolgte sich durch Flucht zur Kaiserstatue den Häschern entzieht. Gemeinsam ist jedoch die Stellvertretung des Kaisers durch Namen oder Bild. Nun ist das Asylwesen in Rom, wenn auch verklärt durch das legendäre Asylrecht des Romulus, erst im Jahre 42 v. Chr. eingeführt worden, während es in Ägypten schon zur Ptolemäerzeit bestand.[51] Sollte dies vielleicht zum Verständnis beitragen dafür, daß auch der Namensruf, wie ihn Apuleius beschreibt, sich auf den Brauch im ptolemäischen Ägypten zurückführen läßt?

Die einschlägigen Stellen hat Wilhelm Schubart aus den Papyri zusammengetragen und besprochen, und es kann hier nur das von ihm Gesagte wiederholt werden.[52] Ein Tebtunis Papyrus des 2. Jahrhunderts v. Chr. meldet, daß in einem Dorf ein Mann im Bade überfallen worden sei. In seiner Beschwerde über den Vorfall bekundet der Betroffene, daß, "als der um mich beschäftigte Diener den König um Hilfe rief, mehrere Leute herbeikamen."[53] Daß der König selbst gerade in der Nähe des dörflichen Badehauses geweilt habe, ist mehr denn unwahrscheinlich. Gemeint ist, daß der Junge den Königsnamen ausstieß, woraufhin die Leute zu Hilfe eilten. Ähnlich heißt es bei einer anderen Gelegenheit: "Als ich zum König rief mir beizustehen, hörten mich einige von den anderen und eilten herbei."[54] Wenn ferner die Tempelsklaven der Bubastis an den mächtigen Finanzbeamten Zenon schreiben, es hätte sich eine Anrufung des Königs er-

---

[50] L. Wenger, "Asylrecht," in *Reallexikon für Antike und Christentum*, I: 6 (1943), 836ff; Mommsen, *Strafrecht*, 458ff; cf. *Dig.*, 47, 10, 38: *ne quis imaginem imperatoris in invidiam alterius portaret.*

[51] Friedrich von Woess, *Das Asylwesen Ägyptens in der Ptolemäerzeit und die spätere Entwicklung* (Münchener Beiträge zur Papyrusforschung, V; München, 1923), bes. 108, 210; s. oben, Anm. 36.

[52] W. Schubart, "Das hellenistische Königsideal," *Arch. f. Papyrusforschung*, XII (1936), 16.

[53] Tebt. III, 798, ed. Hunt und Smyly, *The Tebtunis Papyri*, III (1933), 251f: τοῦ παιδαρίου βοήσαντος τὸν βασιλέα, was die Herausgeber übersetzen: "Having shouted for help in the king's name."

[54] *Berliner Griechische Urkunden*, III, 1007.

übrigt, da ja er, Zenon, gegenwärtig sei,[55] so entspräche das etwa der Anrufung der Lokalgewaltigen des vor-friderizianischen Rechts in Sizilien.

Es ist natürlich richtig, daß in diesen Fällen der Königsnamen auch als Alarmgeschrei diente, um Hilfe herbeizurufen. Aber es ist doch außerordentlich bezeichnend, daß man, um Lärm zu schlagen, eben nicht "zeterte", sondern den Namen des Königs anrief, also etwa schrie βασιλεῦ βοήθει, so wie man später gerufen hätte Χριστὲ βοήθει. Es bleibt ferner bestehen, daß man den Königsnamen anrief, wenn ein Angriff, eine Mißhandlung oder ein sonstiger Rechtsbruch drohte oder stattfand, und in dieser Beziehung stimmt dann der Brauch in Ägypten durchaus überein mit dem bei Apuleius beschriebenen Verfahren: der Name des Ptolemäerkönigs wurde wie der des Kaisers "interponiert", geradeso wie später der Name Christi oder Gottes gleichsam interponiert wurde. Die Rechtsbedeutung dessen hat Schubart sicher richtig umschrieben, wenn er sagt, daß durch die Anrufung des Königs die Tat "öffentlich" wurde und damit zur Hilfeleistung verpflichtete. Daneben hat jedoch die Invokation des Herrschernamens auch etwas Soteriologisches. Der Herrscher ist ἀλεξίκακος. Durch seine Allgegenwart ist er nahe, auch wenn er leiblich fern ist. Sein Zorn erreicht den Missetäter, und "am Zorne des Königs stirbt man."[56]

Es ist wohl kaum zu bezweifeln, daß die Papyri und Apuleius die gleiche Rechtsanschauung wiedergeben. Dies scheint weniger wahrscheinlich hinsichtlich der ἐκβόησις oder καταβόησις, die, gleichfalls in ptolemäischen Papyri nachweisbar, dann im byzantinischen Recht eine gewisse Rolle spielte und schließlich in dem weitverbreiteten Νόμος γεωργικός (vermutlich 7. Jahrhundert) einen Niederschlag fand.[57] Das Verfahren ist nach den wenigen Andeutungen des Agrargesetzes nicht deutlich zu rekonstruieren, doch handelt es sich darum, daß man, vorwiegend bei Besitzstörung, das "Geschrei" erhob, das heißt: bei den lokalen Beamten (im Jahre 441 war es der Proconsul der Provinz Asia) "Einspruch" oder Klage erhob.[58] Daß dieser Einspruch mit Berufung auf

---

[55] Cairo P. Zenon, 59 451, ed. C. C. Edgar, *Zenon Papyri*, III (Cairo, 1928), 175.

[56] Die Stellen bei Cumont, *L'Egypte des astrologues* (Brüssel, 1937), 212, Anm. 1.

[57] Cf. Louis Bréhier, "L'Εκβόησις dans le droit populaire à Byzance," *Miscellanea Guillaume de Jerphanion* (Orientalia Christiana Periodica, XIII; Rom, 1947), 33ff; Henri Grégoire, "Miettes d'histoire byzantine," *Anatolian Studies for Sir William Mitchell Ramsay* (Manchester, 1923), 157f; für die Datierung des Agrargesetzes, vgl. Georg Ostrogorsky, *Geschichte des byzantinischen Staates* (München, 1940), 54, Anm. 1.

Hierher gehören, wie mir scheint, auch einige der von Schubart, 16, angeführten Papyri. *Berliner Griechische Urkunden*, VIII, 1762, 3f. (= W. Schubart und D. Schäfer, *Spätptolemäische Papyri* [Berlin, 1933], 40), z. B., spricht davon, daß "am folgenden Tage noch viel mehr Menschen zum Tore des ... kamen und die Hilfe der Königinnen und Truppen anriefen (καὶ ἐπεβοῶντο τὰς βασιλίσσας καὶ δυνάμεις)." Die Leute verlangten die Entfernung eines Missetäters und seiner Genossen aus dem Gau. Darauf kam der Stratege aus Alexandrien, vertröstete die Leute und versprach, der Regierung zu berichten. Hier handelt es sich jedoch nicht, wie bei dem

Überfall im Bade, um die Abwehr einer imminenten Gefahr, sondern darum, den Willen der Bewohner durchzusetzen durch einen "Appell" an die — selbstverständlich nicht anwesende — Königinnen (des Jahres 58 v. Chr.) und die Truppen, d. h., wie die Herausgeber erklären, an die "Königsmacht als Ganzes." Der Fall ist viel ähnlicher der von Grégoire mitgeteilten ephesischen Inschrift v. J. 441 n. Chr. als etwa der Apuleius-Stelle. Das gleiche scheint mir der Fall zu sein bci *PSI*, VI, 551, (=*Pubblicazioni della Società Italiana per la ricerca dei Papiri greci e latini*, ed. G. Vitelli, M. Norsa etc. [Florenz, 1920], VI, 2), vom Jahre 272/1 v. Chr., wo, wie auch Schubart annimmt, der König wohl anwesend war, als man an ihn appellierte; vielleicht auch im *P. Cairo Zenon*, 59520, S. 233, bei dem der Sachverhalt Schubart als zweifelhaft erschien. Ich würde denken, daß es sich um die von Bréhier beschriebene καταβόησις handelt, eine Anklage also oder ein Einspruch. Doch muß ich die Entscheidung Berufeneren überlassen, da ich mich in den schwierigen Rechtsproblemen Ägyptens nicht auskenne.

[58] Grégoire, a. a. O. Walter Ashburner, "The Farmers' Law," *Journal of Hellenic Studies*, XXXII (1912), 90 und 94f, übersetzt die einschlägigen Stellen (§§ 32 und 81) demgemäß auch mit *complain*.

den Herrscher erfolgte, ist wohl für Ägypten, doch nicht für Byzanz bezeugt, und nur die Tatsache, daß anscheinend das Delikt der Besitzstörung dabei im Vordergrund stand, ließe vielleicht an einen Zusammenhang mit der *defensa* des sizilischen Gesetzbuches denken.[59]

Der Glossator der sizilischen Konstitutionen, Andreas von Isernia, erklärt mehrmals, daß das *ius defensae* ein *ius novum* darstelle.[60] Das ist so nicht richtig, da die *defensa* unter Anrufung des Königs oder einer Lokalgewalt schon vor 1231 bestand. Vielleicht beschränkte sich die Neuerung Friedrichs II. einfach darauf, daß er die *defensa* aus dem Lokalbereich endgültig herausgelöst hat, um für das ganze Königreich die Auferlegung der *defensa* durch Anruf des Kaisernamens vorzuschreiben. Das Delikt wurde damit unweigerlich — gleichsam als ein *placitum coronae* — vor das Hofgericht gezogen. Es ist dabei gar nicht unmöglich, daß Friedrichs "Neuerung" direkt auf Apuleius zurückging, wenigstens in der Formulierung: *nomen augustum Caesaris invocare* bei Apuleius klingt an die zweimalig wiederholte *invocatio nostri nominis* im Gesetzbuch doch so stark an, daß eine Abhängigkeit glaubhaft erscheint. Mit Apuleius war man damals durchaus vertraut. Johann von Salisbury hat ihn vielfach benutzt.[61] Eine Handschrift der Metamorphosen in beneventanischer Schrift läßt sich im 12. Jahrhundert in Monte Cassino, also im sizilischen Königreich, nachweisen.[62] Es liegt kein Grund vor zu vermuten, daß den "Apuliern" Apuleius unbekannt gewesen und ihnen die Bedeutung des Kaiseranrufs entgangen sein sollte.

Trifft diese Annahme zu, so hätte Friedrich II. durch die Vermittlung des Apuleius *de facto* gar nicht römischen, sondern hellenistischen oder ptolemäischen Brauch wiederhergestellt. Dies würde allerdings nur für die Invokation des Kaisernamens gelten, denn dem Rechtsmittel der *defensa* selbst mögen andere Rechtanschauungen zugrunde liegen.

* * *

Eine dritte kleine Beobachtung sei hier abschließend angefügt, deren Auswertung, wenn sie überhaupt Wert hat, anderen überlassen bleiben mag. Es handelt sich um ein Gedicht, das den Einzug Friedrichs II. in Jerusalem, am 17. März 1229, verherrlicht.

Aus den *Casus Sancti Galli* hat jüngst Walter Bulst die Bezeichnung *susceptacula regum* zutage gefördert und damit höchst dankenswerter Weise den *terminus technicus* wieder eingeführt für eine Gattung von Liedern, die zum feierlichen Empfang eines Herrschers, eben *ad regem suscipiendum*, gedichtet und vorgetragen wurden.[63] Solche Gedichte für den *Adventus* oder die *Epiphanie* eines Herrschers, oder auch Bischofs, sind überaus zahlreich aus spät- und nachkarolingischer Zeit überliefert. Später treten sie zurück und werden seltener, vielleicht weil dann die strengeren Formen des liturgischen Empfangs für die freieren literarischen Erzeugnisse wenig Spielraum mehr ließen. Erst im Spätmittelalter

---

[59] Oben, Anm. 57, bezüglich Ägyptens.

[60] *Liber aug.*, Cervoni-Ausgabe, 35 und 38; siehe auch meinen *Ergänzungsband*, 95.

[61] Vgl. die Ausgabe des *Policraticus* von Clemens C. I. Webb (Oxford, 1919), I, xxxiv, wo allerdings nicht die Metamorphosen benutzt sind.

[62] Cf. E. A. Lowe, *The Beneventan Script* (Oxford, 1914), 12; die beiden berühmten Apuleius-Hss. der Laurentiana in beneventanischer Schrift sind doch wohl von Monte Cassino.

[63] Walther Bulst, "Susceptacula regum," *Corona Quernea: Festgabe Karl Strecker* (Leipzig, 1941), 97ff.

tritt die Adventus-Dichtung wieder sehr stark hervor, und zwar gab dann, ähnlich wie in der Musik,[64] die Liturgie selbst durch Lockerung oder gar Zerfall ihrer Strenge den Stoff her für die so beliebten *tableaux*, die — bereichert noch um renaissancehaft klassizistische Motive — den nunmehr auch staatsrechtlich wichtig gewordenen Einzug, die *entrée joyeuse* eines Fürsten verherrlichten.[65]

In Byzanz ist der Verlauf ein etwas anderer gewesen. Aus einer sehr reichen Tradition schöpfend hat die Epiphanie-Dichtung und -Rhetorik stets und zu allen Zeiten ihren festen Platz im Kaiserzeremoniell behalten. Dabei galt diese zeremonielle Dichtung und Redekunst nicht nur dem Empfang und Einzug selbst, wenn der Kaiser siegreich oder nach längerer Abwesenheit wieder in seine Hauptstadt zurückkehrte, sondern sie war unerläßliches Beiwerk bei jeder "Epiphanie" des Kaisers, jedem offiziellen Erscheinen in feierlicher Form. Überhaupt ist ja im Osten ganz ähnlich wie in der Antike die Idee der Epiphanie, die immer zugleich eine Manifestation des Göttlichen einschloß, im Kult wie im Leben von unendlich größerer Bedeutung gewesen als im Westen. Das trifft zu für die liturgischen Handlungen der Kirche—man denke etwa an die Krönung von Täufling oder Brautpaar — aber auch für die Liturgie des Hofes. Hierhin gehörte dann auch jene Zurschaustellung des Kaisers an bestimmten Kirchenfesten (Weihnachten und Epiphanien) und an bestimmten Hoffesten (Krönung und Hochzeit), wenn sich der Basileus auf einer mit Stoffen und Teppichen reich verkleideten Estrade, genannt *prokypsis*, dem Volke zeigte. Das Zeremoniell verlangte dabei, daß die Vorhänge, die zunächst den Kaiser verhüllten, im gegebenen Augenblick und nach vorbereitendem Ruflied — richtigen κλητικά — plötzlich zurückgezogen wurden, um den Blick auf den Kaiser freigebend gleichsam seine, und zugleich die göttliche, Epiphanie zu symbolisieren. Bei dieser Schaustellung traten dann Poeten und Rhetoren in ihre Rechte, die in mehr oder minder festgeprägten Formen dieses höchst artifizielle "Erscheinen" des Kaisers feierten.[66]

Von den karolingischen *susceptacula* wie von den byzantinischen Epiphaniegedichten unterscheidet sich das Gedicht auf Friedrich II. insofern, als es nicht eigentlich zur Empfangs- oder Erscheinungsfeier selbst gedichtet worden ist, sondern nur des Kaisers Adventus, seinen Einzug in Jerusalem, beschreibt. Dies geschieht allerdings in einer Weise, die dem sonst für Empfänge und Einzüge üblichen Ideengehalt völlig gleichkommt. Daß der Dichter, ein Passauer Kanoniker namens Marquard von Ried, selbst im Heiligen Land anwesend und somit Augenzeuge war, als Friedrich II. in Jerusalem einzog, wäre an sich möglich gewesen. Bezeugt ist das nicht, und die Inserierung des Gedichtes in die im Wiener Schottenkloster entstandene Fortsetzung der Klosterneuburger Annalen weist nur auf die gleichen Bezirke im Südosten des Reiches hin, in denen Mar-

[64] Vgl. Manfred F. Bukofzer, *Studies in Medieval and Renaissance Music* (New York, 1950), besonders 217ff über den Ursprung der spätmittelalterlichen Meß-Cyklen aus dem Bröckeln der Liturgie.

[65] Vgl. Kantorowicz, "The King's Advent and the Enigmatic Panels in the Doors of Santa Sabina," *Art Bulletin*, XXVI (1944), 210, Anm. 20. P. E. Schramm, *Der König von Frankreich* (Weimar, 1939), I, 204, mit Anm. 5. Das Material über die spätmittelalterlichen *entrées* ist zwar unendlich, dennoch würde es sich lohnen, das neue staatsrechtliche Element herauszuarbeiten, durch das das liturgische Element des frühen Mittelalters völlig verdeckt wird — ein Beitrag zu dem sehr viel weiteren Thema "Vom liturgischen Königtum zum Rechtskönigtum von Gottes Gnaden."

[66] Ich gehe auf Einzelheiten hier nicht ein, die ich in anderem Zusammenhang besprechen werde; vgl. die klassische Darstellung der *prokypsis* von August Heisenberg, "Aus der Geschichte und Literatur der Palaiologenzeit," *Sitz.-Ber. München*, 1920, Abh. 10, bes. 85ff.

quard, um 1240 Propst von Matsee im Salzburgischen, auch sonst zu suchen ist.[67] Aus dem relativ umfangreichen Gedicht seien hier zwei Versgruppen angeführt, die für den *Adventus augusti* bezeichnend sind:[68]

Subdita sunt elementa Deo: quos foverit ille,
Illa fovent, e converso quos urserit urgent.
Adveniente Dei famulo magno Friderico
Sol nitet, aura tepet, aqua bullit, terra virescit.
Fons inquam Syloe qui multis aruit annis,
Nunc quasi congaudens producit aquas salientes...

Jerusalem gaude nomen domini venerare
Magnifica laude: vis ut dicam tibi quare?
Rex quia magnificus Jesus olim, nunc Fridericus,
Promptus uterque pati, sunt in te magnificati.
Obtulit ille prior semet pro posteriore
Et pro posterior sua seque prioris honore,
Hic Deus, ille Dei pius ac prudens imitator.

Die erste Gruppe der hier angeführten Verse diene lediglich dazu, den "messianischen" Charakter klarzustellen, der fast stets, oder doch sehr häufig, in die Adventus-Dichtung eingewoben ist. Die vier Elemente sind Gott untertan; doch sie gehorchen dem Diener Gottes und darum begünstigen sie den Kaiser bei seinem Einzug (*adveniente Dei famulo*). Die Sonne, hier das Element des Feuers vertretend, brennt nicht, sondern sie strahlt; die Luft ist lau; das Wasser sprudelt; die Erde schmückt sich mit neuem Grün; und der seit vielen Jahren trockene Siloam-Quell bringt springende Wasser hervor, um seine Mitfreude am Erscheinen des Kaisers zu bezeugen. Das alles ist gewiß kein versteckter Hinweis darauf, daß es Frühling ist, obwohl ja Friedrich II. im März in Jerusalem einzog. Gemeint ist natürlich jener messianisch zeitlose Frühling, der kalenderwidrig auch im Sommer, Herbst oder Winter herrschen würde, sobald der Gesalbte erscheint.[69] In Ägypten, zum Beispiel, hätte die Epiphanie des Herrschers oder seiner Beauftragten ein Steigen des Nils zur Folge.[70]

Worauf es hier jedoch ankommt, ist nicht die messianische Stimmung des Advents, sondern der in der zweiten Versgruppe enthaltene antithetische Vergleich des in Jerusalem einreitenden Kaisers mit Christus am Palmsonntag, die durch ein *hic-ille* eingeführte *christomimesis* des Kaisers: *Hic Deus, ille Dei pius ac prudens imitator.* Vergleiche des Herrschers mit Gott oder Christus sind überaus häufig im Mittelalter: der König ist

---

[67] Über Marquard von Ried, E. Winkelmann, *Jahrbücher der deutschen Geschichte: Kaiser Friedrich II.* (Leipzig, 1897), II, 78, Anm. 3f.

[68] *Continuatio Scotorum, MGH, SS,* IX, 625.

[69] Das sagt völlig eindeutig, z. B., Walafried Strabo (*MGH, Poetae,* III, 183, No. XV): *Innovatur nostra laetos | Terra flores proferens: | Ver novum praesentat aestas, (!) | Cum datur te cernere...* Bulst (oben Anm. 2) hat viel zu viele

historische "Data" aus den *susceptacula* herauszulesen versucht; richtig Wolfram von den Steinen, *Notker der Dichter* (Bern, 1948), I, 495 ("Wenn du kommst, ist Frühlingswetter").

[70] *P. Berlin,* 10580, 42f; *Berliner Klassikertexte,* V (1907), 119, zur Begrüßung des *praefectus praetorio Orientis:*
ἐκ σέθεν εἰς κτητῆρας ἀθέσφατον ἔπλετο ὕδωρ.
Νεῖλος ἀρουραβάτης ἐπεθύσατο δ' αὔλακι γαίης...

quasi oder *sicut Deus in terris.* Antithesen wiederum würden das Unterscheidende zwischen der göttlichen Allmacht und der königlichen Teilmacht hervorheben. Das ist hier jedoch nicht der Fall. Die Antithetik dient vielmehr dem Vergleich; sie dient dazu, den Unterschied zu verwischen oder ihn vergessen zu machen und den Bild-Parallelismus zwischen dem einziehenden Kaiser und dem einziehenden Gott hervorzuheben. Das Erregende an jener Apostrophe der Einzugsstadt Jerusalem besteht gerade in dem Element der Gleich- oder Ein-ebnigkeit von Gott und Kaiser, die hier durch das Bild des Einzugs erzeugt wird, und in dem der wechselseitigen Bedingtheit, indem der Gott für den Kaiser das Bild und Vorbild aufgestellt, der Kaiser aber das Bild des Gottes erneuert und ins Gedächtnis zurückgerufen hat. "Dieser ein Gott, jener des Gottes frommer und kluger Mime." Diese Art, die *christomimesis* nicht durch Aufzählung von Tugenden wie *justitia, aequitas, clementia,* sondern gleichsam als aktives Bild bühnenmäßig zu vergegenwärtigen, ist im Westen sonst eher den Schilderungen von Heiligen vorbehalten: sie sind es vor allen anderen, die wie Franziskus sichtbar in den Fußtapfen ihres Herrn wandeln und als die wahren Nachahmer Christi auch ihrem Herrn Ähnliches verrichten. Mit Bezug auf Kaiser und Könige ist jedoch solche Bildgleichheit begreiflicherweise selten, wenn man von dem Sitzen auf dem Königsthron oder Richterstuhl absieht. Erst die spätmittelalterliche, und zumal französische, Königsmystik hat die Bildgleichheit von Herrscher und Gottheit auch in andere Bereiche, wie in das des Wunderwirkens, hineinprojiziert.

All dies ist anders im Osten, wo gerade jene Art des antithetischen Bildvergleiches hundertfach zu belegen ist, zumal in der Epiphaniedichtung.[71] Es genüge hier, nur eines der Epiphanie-Gedichte anzuführen, die bei der Prokypsis am Epiphanienfest, im Osten bekanntlich die Feier der Taufe Christi, vorgetragen wurden. Der Verfasser ist Theodoros Prodromos, ein gefeierter Dichter der Komnenenzeit, der Johannes Komnenos (1118–1143) mit folgenden Versen begrüßte:[72]

Ἰδοὺ διπλῆ πανήγυρις, διπλῆ χαρὰ Ῥωμαίοις,
λουτρὰ Χριστοῦ, καὶ τρόπαια λαμπρὰ τοῦ βασιλέως·
Χριστὸς ἐλούθη δι' ἡμᾶς λουτρῷ τῷ τῶν ὑδάτων,
ἄναξ ἐπλύνθη δι' ἡμᾶς λουτρῷ τῷ τῶν ἱδρώτων·
ὁ μὲν συντρίβει κεφαλὰς ἐν ὕδατι δρακόντων,
ὁ δὲ συγκλίνει κεφαλὰς ἐπὶ τῆς γῆς βαρβάρων·
ὁ μὲν τοὺς ἐμφωλεύοντας ὄφεις ἀποκτιννύει,
ὁ δὲ συγκλείει φωλεοῖς τοὺς πρὶν ἀνέτους Πέρσας·
τὸν μὲν τὸ πνεῦμα μαρτυρεῖ περιστερᾶς ἐν εἴδει,
τὸν δ' ἡ λευκὴ περιστερὰ τῆς νίκης καταγγέλλει·
τὸν μὲν φωνὴ παρὰ πατρὸς υἱὸν ἀνακηρύττει,
τὸν δὲ Περσῶν ὀλοθρευτὴν τὰ πράγματα βοῶσι·

---

[71] Es genügt hier, auf die Akklamationen hinzuweisen, die unaufhörlich, unter Verwendung der Texte der jeweiligen Festtagsliturgie, Kaiser und Gottheit antithetisch vergleichen; Treitinger, *passim*; einige gute Beobachtungen vom Musikalischen her bei Jacques Handschin, *Das Zeremonienwerk Kaiser Konstantins und die sangbare Dichtung* (Baseler Rektoratsprogramm, 1940–41; Basel, 1942).

[72] Theodoros Prodromos, *Poemata*, XVI, 1–17, ed. Angelo Mai, *Novae patrum bibliothecae* (Rom, 1853), VI, 412.

δοκῶ φωνῆς ἐξ οὐρανοῦ δευτέρας ἐπακούειν
βοώσης πάλιν ⟨τοῖς⟩ λαοῖς, οὗτος ὁ βασιλεύς μου·
οὗτος εἰς ὃν εὐδόκησα, τούτῳ καὶ πειθαρχεῖτε·
ἀμφότεροι καθαίρουσι τὴν βασιλίδα πόλιν
λουτροῖς ἀναγεννήσεως καὶ παλιγγενεσίας...

Das würde in einfacher Übersetzung etwa lauten:

Sieh da, zweifache Feier, zweifache Freude den Römern:
Christi Bad und des Kaisers glänzende Siegesmale.
Christus ward für uns gewaschen im Bad des Wassers,
Der Herrscher ward für uns gespült im Bad des Schweißes.
Jener zermalmt im Wasser Drachenköpfe,
Dieser beugt auf Erden Barbarenköpfe.
Jener tötet die Schlangen im Höhlenschlupf,
Dieser verschließt die einst dreisten Perser in ihrem Schlupf.
Jenen bezeugt der Geist in Taubengestalt,
Diesen vermeldet das Weiß der Siegesstaube.
Jenen kündet des Vaters Stimme als Sohn,
Diesen rufen die Taten aus als Perser-Verderben.
Mir scheint, ich hört zum zweitenmal vom Himmel eine Stimme,
Die wieder Völkern zuruft: "Dies ist mein König,
An ihm hab ich Gefallen, und ihm gehorcht."
Sie beide reinigen die Königsstadt
Durch Bäder von Wieder- und von Neugeburt.

Das Gedanken- oder Bilderschema dieser Verse bedarf kaum des Kommentars. Wie in den Versen auf den Einzug Friedrichs II. in Jerusalem bildet hier der antithetische Vergleich das wesentliche Stilmittel. Daß uns die Vergleiche eines *tertium* zu entbehren scheinen, liegt an uns, nicht an dem Dichter, der sich nur der herkömmlichen Metaphern bedient. Für den Westen ist der 6. Januar das Fest der heiligen Drei Könige. Für den Byzantiner ist es das Fest der Taufe Christi, das wiederum als Siegesfest gesehen wird. Hundertfach wiederholen die Stichoi der östlichen Liturgien, aber auch die Malereien, das Bild des im Jordan auf die Drachen tretenden Christus. Umgekehrt aber ist der Sieg über den Drachen dem über Barbaren oder andere Kaiserfeinde schon auf Münzen und Medaillen der konstantischen und nachkonstantischen Zeit gleichgesetzt worden: das Labarum mit den Kaiserbildern auf den Drachen aufgepflanzt oder der Kaiser, den Kreuzstab in der Hand, mit dem Fuße auf eine Schlange mit Menschenkopf tretend.[73] Ebenso ist die Geisttaube über dem Jordan auch die Siegestaube, die oft genug in ihrem

[73] Für das Labarum über der Schlange (*Spes publica*), vgl. Jules Maurice, *Numismatique Constantinienne* (Paris, 1908), I, Tafel IX, 2, und dazu die bekannte Beschreibung des Palastgemäldes, in dem Konstantins Sieg über Licinius als Drachensieg gefeiert wird, bei Eusebius, *Vita* *Constantini*, III, 3. Für den auf die Schlange mit Menschenkopf tretenden Kaiser, vgl. Babelon, "Attila dans la numismatique," *Revue numismatique*, sér. IV, vol. XVIII (1914), 301ff, Abb. 3–8.

Schnabel den Siegeskranz trägt, um Christus zu krönen.[74] Und die Katharsis des Reiches durch den Schweiß des Kaisers ist gleichfalls ein seit frühester Zeit unendlich oft wiederholtes Bild.[75] Der Osten, der weit mehr als der Westen jedes Fest Christi bildhaft als Siegesfest auszulegen vermag, ist darum auch unendlich viel reicher an Möglichkeiten, den Kaiser mit Christus zu vergleichen, als der Westen. Der kaiserliche *christomimetes* in Byzanz wandelt *ex officio* unaufhörlich in den Fußtapfen seines göttlichen "Mitkönigs" wie im Westen nur ein heiliger Franziskus.[76] Das ergibt dann auch jene Verflochtenheit von Kaiser und Gottmensch, die es gestattet, die Himmelsstimme den Kaiser gleichsam als Sohn verkünden zu lassen oder von Kaiser und Christus als den "zwei Sonnen" Neu-Roms zu singen.[77]

Zwei weitere Beispiele seien hier angefügt, weil sie noch näher an die Zeit oder Umgebung Friedrichs II. heranführen. Nikephoros Blemmides, ein Rhetor und Gelehrter der Laskaridenzeit, der unter anderem auch eine Leichenrede auf Friedrich II., den Freund und Schwiegervater des Kaisers Johann Vatatzes, verfaßte, schrieb auf die Geburt eines kaiserlichen Prinzen ein überschwängliches Gedicht. Der Neugeborene ist Sohn des Helios, Kind der Selene (Ἡλίου τέκνον παμφαοῦς, λαμπρᾶς σελήνης γόνε). Vom Vater hat er die Intellektualität (νοερότης), von der Mutter die Besonnenheit oder Enthaltsamkeit (σωφροσύνη). Dann folgen die Vergleiche:

> Der Jungfrau Kind ist Christus; du das der Keuschesten.
> Der Vater Christi ist höchste Vernunft, Allherrscher, Allregierer;
> Dein Vater ist der höchste Intellekt bei uns auf Erden.
> Der Vater Christi [Dein Vater?] ist durchs Los Selbstherrscher, Selbstregierer;
> Denn von Christus stammt der *christos*, und du bist Gesalbter durch diesen.

Es folgt dann noch ein Vergleich mit den drei Magiern, die einst Christus aufsuchten, während jetzt die Untertanen den Neugebornen suchen, um ihm Gold zu bringen.[78] Das

---

[74] Zugrunde liegt Psalm 73, 13: συνέτριψας τὰς κεφαλὰς τῶν δρακόντων ἐπὶ τοῦ ὕδατος. Damit wird dann Christi Taufe zum Kampf gegen und Sieg über den Drachen; vgl. Carl-Martin Edsman, *Le baptême de feu* (Acta Seminarii Neotestamentici Upsaliensis, IX; Leipzig-Uppsala, 1940), 46ff. Für einige bildliche Darstellungen, vgl. J. Strzygowski, *Iconographie der Taufe Christi* (München, 1885); vgl. auch *Dictionnaire d'archéologie chrétienne et de liturgie*, II, 346ff. Eines der schönsten Dokumente für die Tauf-Siegeskrönung ist ein Goldmedaillon der Dumbarton Oaks Collection, in Washington, die Herabkunft der Geisttaube mit dem Siegeskranz darstellend, und eines der interessantesten eine Stele aus T'alin (Armenien) des 6. Jahrhunderts, deren Kenntnis ich Professor Sirarpie Der Nersessian verdanke; doch wird dieses Thema in anderem Zusammenhang zu behandeln sein.

[75] Vgl. etwa, von anderen Prodromos-Gedichten abgesehen, Manuel Holobolos (oben, Anm. 34), XVI, 3ff, bei Boissonade, V, 177; dazu Heisenberg, a. a. O., 119. Daß der Kaiser *sudorum rivos* vergieße auch bei Cl. Mamertinus, *Gratiarum actio*, c. 6, p. 136, ed. W. T. Baehrens; ed. H. Gutzwiller, *Die Neujahrsrede des Konsuls Claudius*

Mamertinus vor dem Kaiser Julian (Basel, 1942), 36.

[76] Die Gottheit als συμβασιλεύς des Kaisers sehr häufig in den Akklamationen angerufen; cf. Constant. Porph., *De caerimoniis*, I, 5, (ed. Reiske, p. 47,6) auch II, 19 (p. 612, 4), II, 43 (p. 650, 4 und 22), und *passim*. Siehe auch die Gegnerschaft gegen diesen Anspruch bei den Franken: *Libri Carolini*, I, 1, ed. Bastgen (*MGH, Concilia*, II Suppl.), 8ff., auch 130, 180f (mit Anm. 2).

[77] Prodromos, XVIII, ed. Mai, a. a. O., 413; s. auch Kantorowicz, "Dante's 'Two Suns'," *Semitic and Oriental Studies presented to William Popper* (Berkeley, 1951), 217–231.

[78] A. Heisenbergs Ausgabe des *Nicephorus Blemmydes* (Leipzig, Teubner, 1896), 110f; Raffaele Cantarella, *Poeti Bizantini* (Mailand, 1948), No. XCII, vol. I, 210; II, 240, die italienische Übersetzung. Die einschlägigen Zeilen lauten:

παρθένου τόκος ὁ Χριστός, σὺ τῆς σωφρονεστάτης·
Χριστοῦ πατὴρ ὁ πρῶτος νοῦς, παντάναξ, παντοκράτωρ,
καὶ σοῦ πατὴρ ἐν νοεροῖς τοῖς καθ' ἡμᾶς ὁ πρῶτος,
Χριστοῦ [*fortasse leg.* καὶ σοῦ?] πατήρ κληρουχικῶς αὐτάναξ, αὐτοκράτωρ·
ἐκ γὰρ Χριστοῦ χριστός ἐστι, καὶ σὺ χριστὸς ἐκ τούτου...

gleiche Schema findet sich bei einem süditalischen Griechen, Nikolaus von Otranto, wohl der Sohn von Friedrich II. Großhofnotar Johann von Otranto, der zur Feier des Malers Paulus von Otranto den Apostel Paulus als literarische Staffage benutzt.

> Ein einziger Paulus nur war unter den Aposteln;
> Und nur ein Paulus ward geboren unter Malern.
> Es spricht in Worten jener bis zum heutigen Tag;
> So spricht in Bildnissen die Malerei.
> Jener die Leuchte des gesamten Erdenrunds,
> Dieser die Zier in allem Kirchenbau.[79]

Es ist fraglos, daß diese antithetischen Vergleiche, die auf der Basis des ὁ μὲν — ὁ δέ Gottheit und Herrscher gleichsam in-eins-setzen und auf eine Ebene bringen, ein äußerst beliebtes und immer wiederkehrendes Stilmittel bilden.[80] Es findet sich natürlich auch bei Rednern und Predigern. So sagt Eustathius von Thessalonich, der Homerscholiast, in einer Epiphanienrede vor Kaiser Manuel Komnenus: "Der Allkönig (παμβασιλεύς) Jesus hat gegen den mit Blutschuld befleckten ewigen Tod das gewaltige Siegeszeichen aufgerichtet; du aber, o Retter-Kaiser (ὦ σῶτερ βασιλεῦ), hast — so wage ich es zu sagen — gegen den menschenverderbenden Krieg gefochten und hast dieses totbringende Übel in die Tiefe hinabgeschleudert."[81]

Die Geschichte solcher Vergleiche von Gottheit und Fürst mittels der Antithese im einzelnen zu verfolgen, geht hier nicht an. Sie finden sich überall in Byzanz, im lateinischen Bereich etwa bei Corippus.[82] Die römischen Kaiser-Panegyriker des 3. Jahrhunderts sind voll solcher Bilder genau wie die römischen Kaiserdichter — man denke etwa an Martials Vergleiche von Domitian mit Hercules und anderen Göttern.[83] Das früheste solcher Epiphanie-Gedichte, das wir kennen und das Gottheit und König gleichsam auf einen Nenner bringt, um schließlich sogar den gegenwärtigen König über die abwesenden und "ohrenlosen" Götter zu stellen, sind jene Ithyphalloi, die dem Demetrius Poliorketes bei seinem Einzug als Befreier Athens im Jahre 290 v. Chr. vorgetragen wurden und die dann den Athenern wie ein moderner "Schlager" in den Ohren lagen.[84]

---

[79] J. N. Sola, "De Codice Laurentiano X plutei V," *Byzantinische Zeitschrift*, XX (1911), 381:

Παῦλος μὲν εἷς ἦν τοῖς ἀποστόλοις μόνος,
καὶ Παῦλος εἷς πέφυκεν ἐν τοῖς ζωγράφοις·
λαλεῖ δ' ἐκεῖνος μέχρι τοῦ νῦν ἐν λόγοις,
λαλεῖ πίναξιν οὕτως ἡ ζωγραφία·
λάμπης ἐκεῖνος ἁπάσης οἰκουμένης,
οὗτος δὲ κόσμος ἁπάσαις ἐκκλησίαις...

[80] Siehe, z. B., Manuel Holobolos, XVIII, 1ff, ed. Boissonade, V, 179; auch das oben (Anm. 77) angeführte Gedicht des Prodromos sowie dessen XII. Gedicht (Mai, a. a. O., 411) zur Weihnachts-Prokypsis.

[81] Regel, *Fontes rerum byzantinarum*, 27, 22ff. Für den griechisch-sizilischen Umkreis vgl. etwa die Palmsonntagspredigt des Philagathos vor König Roger II., bei Migne, *PG*, CXXXII, 541B, gedruckt als Homilie XXVI des Theophanes Kerameus, wo der Glanz der Auferstehung mit dem des Königshofes kontrastiert wird. Vgl. Ernst

Kitzinger, "The Mosaics of the Capella Palatina in Palermo," *Art Bulletin*, XXXI (1949), 281, mit Anm. 68 für die Verfasserschaft der Homilie.

[82] Corippus, *In laudem Justini*, II, 428, ed. Partsch, 137 (*MGH, AA. ant.*, III: 2), sagt, ganz ähnlich wie nach ihm Marquard von Ried; *ille est omnipotens* (sc. *Christus*), *hic omnipotentis imago*. Überhaupt sind gewisse Übereinstimmungen doch merkwürdig; vgl., z. B., Corippus, I, 361, ed. Partsch, 126: *Omnia Justino praebent elementa favorem, Omnia congaudent;* siehe auch II, 94ff, ed. Partsch, 129.

[83] Cf. Franz Sauter, *Der römische Kaiserkult bei Martial und Statius* (Stuttgart, 1934), 81f, und *passim*.

[84] Der Text bei Athenaeus, VII, 253 D, auch in den *Collectanea Alexandrina*, ed. J. U. Powell (Oxford, 1925), 173f; dazu Victor Ehrenberg, "Athenischer Hymnus auf Demetrius Poliorketes," *Antike*, VII (1931), 279ff, und vor allem O. Weinreich, "Antikes Gottmenschentum," *Neue Jahrbücher*, II (1926), 646ff.

Das Gedicht, dessen Anfang nicht erhalten ist, wird mit einem Vergleich von Demeter und Demetrius begonnen haben. Beide mögen als Athen besonders nahestehend und zugehörig gefeiert worden sein; denn der Dichter fährt dann fort:

> So wie die größten und die liebsten Götter sind
>> Sie der Stadt erschienen;
> Denn hierher hat Demetrios und Demeter
>> Hergeführt der Kairos.
> SIE kam, um die hochheiligen Mysterien
>> Koros zu begehen;
> ER aber ist gleich einem Gotte schön und heiter
>> lächelnd gegenwärtig...

Es ist erstaunlich, wie wenig an diesem Schema die christliche Dichtung im Grunde verändert hat. Von dem Spielen mit dem theophoren Namen ganz zu schweigen,[85] ist es vor allem die erstrebte Gleichebnigkeit von Gottheit und Herrscher bei ihrer Epiphanie, die als das Konstante erscheint, aber auch der durch ein ὁ μέν – ὁ δέ eingeleitete antithetische Vergleich, der dann von den Byzantinern — natürlich im Sinne von Christus und Basileus — bis zur Ermüdung wiederholt wird. Erst in Byzanz ist allerdings das schematische "Ableiern" solcher Vergleiche, vielleicht nach dem Vorbild östlicher Liturgien,[86] zur wirklichen Mode geworden.

Wie der Passauer Dichter dazu kam, in etwas überrschender Weise jenes Schema auf Friedrich II. anzuwenden, läßt sich kaum beantworten. Interessanter als die Quellenfrage wäre es, die andere Frage zu stellen, wie es denn kam, daß der Westen überhaupt die antithetischen Bildvergleiche von Herrscher und Christus so selten benutzt hat und daß μίμησις offenbar im Osten und Westen Verschiedenes bedeutete.

Dies wäre freilich ein sehr großes Thema, das nicht einfach im Vorbeigehen behandelt werden kann. Hier waren nur einige Lesefrüchte zu bergen; und nicht mehr war beabsichtigt, als durch wenige, allzu flüchtig gezogene Linien, ohne allen Anspruch au schlüssige Lösungen, ein Problem zu umreißen, das durch seine Geschichte der Lockenfrisur des Sonnengottes der klassische Archäologe angeregt hat. Die hellenistisch-staufische Bogenweite der hier nur angedeuteten Fragen aber mag Karl Reinhardt, dem Freund der Frankfurter Jahre, erneut bestätigen, wie sehr über Meilen und Zeiten hinweg und trotz Schranken und Schweigens der mittelalterliche Historiker des Graecisten bedarf.

---

[85] Für das Spielen mit dem Namen Manuel (Emmanuel-Christus) siehe, z. B., Eustathius von Thessalonich, bei Regel, *Fontes*, 57, 1, oder Theodoros Prodromos' *Epithalamium*, 71, bei Carl Neumann, *Griechische Geschichtsschreiber und Geschichtsquellen des zwölften Jahrhunderts* (Leipzig, 1888), 67: σὺ γὰρ ὡς χριστομίμητος χριστώνυμος ὑπάρχεις.

[86] Es wäre dabei vor allem an die Paradigmengebete und an die Σήμερον-Stichoi (bei der Epiphanien-Wasserweihe) zu denken; vgl. A. Baumstark, "Paradigmengebete ostsyrischer Kirchendichtung," *Oriens Christianus*, Ser. II, vol. X–XI (1923), und ders., "Die *Hodie*-Antiphonen des römischen Breviers und der Kreis ihrer griechischen Parallelen," *Die Kirchenmusik*, X (1909), 153ff.

ZU DEN RECHTSGRUNDLAGEN DER KAISERSAGE

1. Ein Angebliches Testament Kaiser Friedrichs II.

VOR MEHR ALS einem halben Jahrhundert hat Scheffer-Boichorst auf ein Testament Friedrichs II. aufmerksam gemacht, von dem er vermutete daß es eine "Stilübung" sei. Das Stück war ihm nur fragmentarisch bekannt; hätte er das Ganze gesehen, so hätte er wohl keinen Augenblick gezögert, sich noch sehr viel bestimmter auszusprechen.[1] Vor längerer Zeit hat sodann der Verfasser dieser Zeilen, von dem immer wieder verblüffenden Spürsinn des unvergeßlichen Carl Erdmann auf eine Handschrift des Escorial (d. III. 3) verwiesen, sich mit diesem Testament beschäftigt, das er als eine "Stilübung zweifellos italienischer Herkunft" bezeichnete, die jedoch "nicht ganz ohne Interesse" sei und auf die er an anderer Stelle zurückzukommen versprach.[2] Dieses Versprechen ist, wie so viele Arbeitsversprechen, bisher nicht eingelöst worden, und wenn dies heute dennoch geschieht, so gab den Anlaß dazu die Heidelberger Dissertation von Dr. Gunther Wolf, die jüngst in der Form eines längeren Zeitschriftenaufsatzes erschienen ist.[3]

In der Stadtbibliothek zu Besançon stieß Dr. Wolf im Verlaufe anderer Arbeiten auf die Abschrift des bislang nur unvollständig veröffentlichten Testaments, dessen Text in dem genannten Escorialensis, einer Papierhandschrift der ersten Hälfte des 14. Jahrhunderts, überliefert ist (E). Abgesehen von der Arenga und mancherlei Zusätzen stimmt das Stück — zumal in den eigentlichen Testamentsbestimmungen — weitgehend mit dem von Weiland veröffentlichten Testament überein (W), dessen Authentizität nicht zu bezweifeln ist.[4] Dr. Wolf bringt darum auch den Text von E dankenswerter Weise in Parallelkolumne mit den einschlägigen Stellen von W zum Abdruck.[5] Es schließt sich

Reprinted, with permission, from *Deutsches Archiv*, XIII (1957), 115–150.

[1] P. Scheffer-Boichorst, *Zur Geschichte des XII. und XIII. Jhdts.* (Berlin, 1897), 268ff.

[2] E. Kantorowicz, "Petrus de Vinea in England," *MÖIG*, LI (1937), 86ff.

[3] Gunther Wolf, "Ein unveröffentlichtes Testament Kaiser Friedrichs II.," *Zs. f. d. Gesch. d. Oberrh.*, CIV (1956), 1–51. Enthusiasmus und Arbeitseifer gepaart mit Finderfreude sind dieser Arbeit gewiß nicht abzusprechen, und man hätte nur gewünscht, daß diese Qualitäten sich an einem tauglicheren Objekt entfaltet hätten sowie unter sachverständiger Leitung, die wiederum der Entwicklung kritischer Fähigkeiten zugute gekommen wäre.

[4] *MGH, Const.*, II, Nr. 274, S. 282–289. Zu den von Weiland angeführten Gründen für die Echtheit des Testaments, die aus der Überlieferung hervorgeht, sei noch hinzugefügt, daß Manfred nicht nur sich mehrfach auf das Testament bezieht und dessen Bestimmungen korrekt zitiert (BF, 4633, 4635, 4637 u. ö.), sondern daß auch das Diktat seiner Erlasse und Briefe sich oft eng an den Wortlaut des Testaments anschließt; vgl. z. B. den Brief an die Palermitaner (BF, 4633; B. Capasso, *Hist. Diplom. Regni Siciliae* [Neapel, 1874], S. 5f), beginnend *Etsi primi parentis ... incauta transgressio*, mit den ersten Worten des Testaments; oder, in dem gleichen Brief (Z. 11), *divus Cesar genitor noster rebus humanis assumptus* mit Weiland, S. 385, Z. 13: *ut rebus humanis absumpti vivere videamur*. Dergleichen ließe sich noch mehrfach nachweisen. Es ist immerhin bezeichnend, daß sich ähnliche Niederschläge des Testaments E anscheinend nicht finden.

[5] Vgl. Wolf, S. 4ff, der es leider verabsäumt hat, das keineswegs kurze Stück nach Paragraphen unterzuteilen oder die Zeilen zu numerieren. Soweit möglich, zitiere

284

eine "Echtheitskritik" an, in der die Möglichkeit einer Fälschung oder einer Stilübung in durchaus nicht überzeugender Weise abgelehnt wird. Datiert wird das Stück, weil es angeblich eine Verschlechterung des kaiserlichen Gesundheitszustandes erkennen lasse, auf etwa eine Woche nach W (also etwa 7.–13. Dezember 1250). Die Absonderlichkeit eines Doppeltestaments wird damit erklärt, daß W "Staatstestament," E jedoch "Privat-testament" sei. Einem kurzen Abschnitt über "Theologie und Staatsauffassung" folgt eine Besprechung der Legate und Titel sowie ein Vergleich mit anderen Herrscher-testamenten der Zeit. Da fast alle Schlüsse mit der Echtheitsfrage stehen und fallen, genügt es hier, sich allein mit dieser zu befassen.[6]

Testament E findet sich in der Handschrift (f. 100–102^v) zusammen mit Stücken des Berard von Neapel, denen wiederum solche aus dem Briefbuch des Thomas von Capua eingesprengt sind — genauer aus der Zehn-Buch-Redaktion der Thomas-Briefe, die wohl um 1268 von dem päpstlichen Notar Jordan von Terracina zusammengestellt wurde. Zu diesen Einsprengseln gehört z. B. ein Papstbrief *Prelatis et universitati Hyspanie* [sic] (115$^{r\text{-}v}$) und ein solcher an Dänemark (115^v–116^v).[7] Es handelt sich also, zumindest in den hier in Betracht kommenden Teilen der Handschrift, um eine vorwiegend aus kurialen Briefbüchern schöpfende Zusammenstellung von Stücken verschiedenartiger Herkunft, in die dann auch E hineingeraten ist, das ich hier behelfsmäßig als "literarisch zugestutzte Überarbeitung" von W bezeichnen möchte. Mit E haben nun die beiden Papstbriefe gemein, daß alle drei Dokumente sich in den Arengen ein wenig an das bekannte Statthalterdiplom Friedrichs II. (Vinea, *Epistolae*, V, 1) anlehnen, das ja zusammen mit dem Prooemium des *Liber augustalis* Stilübungen nicht selten zum Vorbild

---

ich E hier nach den Paragraphennummern der Parallel-kolumne von W. Die wenigen Textverbesserungen sind nicht wesentlich: S. 5, Z. 11 v. u.: *et velut* statt *velut;* ebda. Z. 10 v. u. ist das Fragezeichen nach *poeticum* sinn-entstellend und zu streichen; Z. 2 v. u.: *karissimi* für *carissimi;* S. 6, § 2: *subbreviloquio* statt des sinnstörenden *sub breviloquio* [*breoiloquio* ist doch wohl Druckfehler]; S. 6, § 6: *salvationis nostre* statt *Salvatoris nostri;* S. 8, Z. 1: *adquires* statt *adimis.* Die Zeichensetzung ist willkürlich und besser in der Hs. als im Druck.

[6] Damit werden natürlich auch die Betrachtungen über "Staatstestament" und "Privattestament" (Wolf, S. 21ff) hinfällig, die an sich recht fragwürdig sind (s. unten, Anm. 28). Als Kriterien für die Echtheit werden sowohl Abweichungen von als auch Übereinstimmungen mit echten Dokumenten beigebracht. S. 15 wird z. B. gesagt, es "schwäche wieder den Verdacht einer Fäl-schung ab," daß der Notarstitel eine völlig ungewöhn-liche, ja einmalige Fassung habe (s. unten im Text zu Anm. 26). Umgekehrt heißt es S. 12, eine Fälschung sei unwahrscheinlich, weil sich in E "alle von Vehse be-merkten Stilmittel" fänden, ferner der "bei Friedrich II. beliebte Adamstopos" und schließlich "wörtliches Zitat aus dem Corpus Iuris Civilis." Die Verwendung des all-bekannten Kanzleistils und der rhetorischen Mittel be-sagt natürlich genauso wenig wie Zitate aus dem Corpus Iuris Civilis, das ja kein dem kaiserlichen Gebrauch vor-behaltenes Geheimwerk war; und was schließlich den Adamstopos anbetrifft, so darf man daran erinnern, daß

es ja das Wesen einer Fälschung ist, sich einem Original nach Möglichkeit anzupassen (s. unten Anm. 35 zur Ver-wendung des Statthalterdiploms). Was weiterhin zur Entkräftung der Ansicht, es handle sich um eine Stilübung angeführt wird, bleibt nahezu unverständlich, so etwa die Bemerkung (S. 17, Anm. 40): "Wie hätte das aragonesische Königshaus Interesse an der Abschrift (um 1340!!) gehabt [Ausrufezeichen sind Zitat], wäre E eine Stilübung gewesen?" Oder ebda. die Bemerkung: "Berthold v. Hohenburg, Richard v. Caserta und Walter v. Ocra etwa, die alle Friedrich überlebten, hätten einer Interpolation ihrer Namen in die Zeugenliste eines un-echten Testaments sicher nicht tatenlos zugesehen!" Was hatte das aragonesische Königshaus mit einer Brief-sammlung zu tun? Und was hätten die großen Herren des Kaiserhofes wohl gegen einen Stilschüler oder Stil-meister unternehmen sollen?

[7] Den Spanienbrief habe ich *MÖIG*, LI (1937), 87f abgedruckt. Erst nachträglich machte mich freundlicher-weise Frau Dr. Emmy Heller darauf aufmerksam, daß dieser Brief auf die Sammlung des Thomas von Capua zurückgehe, ebenso der an Dänemark, und auch (nach gütiger Mitteilung von Herrn Dr. R. M. Kloos) noch zwei weitere, die bei S. F. Hahn, *Collectio monumentorum*, I (1724), 350 und 384 gedruckt sind. Für den Charakter derartiger Briefsammlungen höchst lehrreich ist die Ab-handlung von H. M. Schaller, "Zur Entstehung der sog. Briefsammlung des Petrus de Vinea," *Deutsches Archiv*, XII (1956), 114ff, bes. 142ff.

gedient hat.[8] In der langatmigen, von einer Unzahl rhetorischer Fragen geschwellten Arenga von E ist denn auch ein Kernsatz des Diploms *(ex necessitate quadam oportuit naturam subesse iusticie et servire iudicio libertatem)* sofort zu erkennen, freilich schulmäßig "verschönt" und zugleich verballhornt: *et sic oportet miserrime, oportuit et oportebit in posterum legem nature subesse peccato et iugo servitutis servire libertatis iudicium.*[9] Von der Häufung der Tempora *(oportet, oportuit, oportebit in posterum)* ganz abgesehen hat der Verfasser — vorgeblich der mit dem Tode ringende, dennoch sein allerletztes Testament diktierende Kaiser[10] — durch Wortmacherei nur Unklarheiten geschaffen: statt daß als Konsequenz von Adams Fall hinfort "die (menschliche) Natur der Gerechtigkeit unterstellt und die Freiheit dem Richterspruch hörig werden mußte," heißt es nun, daß "die *lex nature* der Sünde unterstellt und der Richterspruch der Freiheit dem Joch der Knechtschaft hörig werden muß, mußte und müssen wird". Während in W König Konrad zum Erben bestimmt wird *in imperio et in omnibus aliis empticiis et quoquomodo acquisitis,* also "im Reich und allen käuflich oder sonstwie erworbenen" Pertinenzen, wird daraus in E eine längere Aufzählung, unterbrochen durch die typische Entschuldigung für Weitschweifigkeit *ut subbreviloquio utamur,* die dann ihrerseits zu neuer Weitschweifigkeit führt: *in omnibus et singulis bonis nostris, que nostro subiacent dominio, vel subesse debent, sub celo, super terram, ab oriente usque in occidens, ab aquilone usque in meridiem*[11] — rhetorische Amplifikationen also, die für jeden, der mit derartigen Produkten vertraut ist, die rhetorisch-literarische "Stilübung" kenntlich machen. Das gleiche gilt für das danach Folgende; denn wo W kurz und bündig im üblichen Stil sagt *in subsidium Terre Sancte,* heißt es in E *in recuperatione terre sancte ultra mare sive sanctissimi sepulcri salvationis nostre.*[12] Wenn in W bestimmt wird, daß nach kinderlosem Tode der legitimen Söhne der legitimierte Manfred folgen solle, fügt E die nichtssagende Klausel hinzu: *Deinde succedat, cui lex permiserit.*[13]

Von solchen rhetorischen Schulpfropfungen wimmelt das Stück, doch sind andere Änderungen aufschlußreicher. In Frage kommen da zunächst ein paar geographische Einzelheiten im Zusammenhang mit den Schenkungen. Es ist verständlich, daß der weniger bekannte *ducatus Stirie* durch den viel geläufigeren *ducatus Suavie* ersetzt wird.[14] Auch daß der Stilist für süditalische Flecken kein sonderliches Interesse zeigt, wird man

---

[8] Z. B. Vinea, *Epp.,* III, 68 und 69. Das gleiche gilt natürlich auch von echten Stücken; vgl. etwa Manfreds Statthalterdiplom (*MGH, Const.,* II, Nr. 422, S. 553) oder den Brief Heinrichs III. von England an Teano (*MÖIG,* LI [1937], 71ff). Die necessitas erscheint dabei fast als ein Schlagwort ghibellinischer Anschauungen und in Manfreds Aufruf an die Römer wird sie gar personifiziert: *Respondet mundi deposcens Necessitas: Nemo nisi maximi filius cesaris (MGH, Const.,* II, Nr. 424, S. 565, Z. 12). Es ist bezeichnend, daß dieses Kennwort in E weggelassen worden ist; s. unten, Anm. 27 für die Tendenz des Stückes.

[9] Wolf, S. 5, Mitte.

[10] Ebda. S. 20, auch 17f und 21, Anm. 1, wobei überall die Worte *sine scriptis* eine verhängnisvolle Rolle spielen; s. unten, Anm. 33.

[11] Ebda., S. 6, § 2.

[12] Ebda., § 6.

[13] Ebda., S. 8, § 2. Diese *lex* versteht Wolf, S. 11f, 29, 39

u. ö. seltsamer Weise als die *lex regia.* Das ist ein Mißverstehen der Funktion der *lex de imperio,* durch die dem Princeps die Vollgewalt der Legislation (wenn man will: die Souveränität) übertragen wurde, die aber nicht die Sukzession regelt (so S. 29: "Nach der die Nachfolge im Kaisertum erfolgt"), wie besagtem Manfred (oder dessen Notar Petrus de Prece) auch durchaus bekannt war; vgl. den Römeraufruf, *MGH, Const.,* II, Nr. 424, S. 564, Z. 11f: *cum illa [sc. lex regia] in iure condendo, non enim circa electionem et formam imperii alloquatur.* Was der Stilkünstler sich bei der *lex* gedacht hat, ist nicht klar; er könnte natürlich an den Enkelsohn Friedrich gedacht haben oder andere im Testament genannte Nachkommen, oder an das Wahlrecht der Kurfürsten, oder an die verschiedenartigen Rechte des Papstes — falls er sich überhapt etwas gedacht hat und nicht einfach Worte gemacht hat.

[14] Wolf, S. 6, § 4; vgl. S. 32f, wo mit Recht *Suavie* zugunsten von *Stirie* zurückgewiesen wird.

ihm nicht verargen dürfen. Bekanntlich erhielt Manfred neben dem Monte Santangelo als Hauptapanage das Fürstentum Tarent. Dieser Principat, obwohl in Normannenzeiten des öfteren ähnlichen Zwecken dienend,[15] war doch mehr oder weniger in Vergessenheit geraten und daher von neuem und ad hoc zusammenzustellen. Demgemäß werden in W die Grafschaften aufgezählt (Monte Scaglioso, Tricarico und Gravina); ferner wird der Manfred zustehende Küstenstrich definiert *(a maritima terre Bari usque Polianum);* Polignano, südlich von Bari, mit allen Pertinenzen wird hinzugefügt und die allgemeine Ausdehnung bestimmt "von Porta Roseto bis zum Quell des Bradano *(fluminis Brandani"*).[16] Das Gesamt dieser Ländereien formte also das Fürstentum Tarent. Der Verfasser von E machte sich die Sache leichter und weniger umständlich. Er setzte Manfred zum Erben ein *in principatu Tarentino* und *in comitatu de Bari*[17] —letzteres ein zumindest unüblicher Ausdruck, da die Kanzlei stets von der *terra Bari* spricht, und auch sachlich nicht ohne weiteres zutreffend. Andererseits aber zeigte sich der Testator in E großzüger als sein Vorgänger in W; denn zu der Reihe apulischer Schenkungen fügte er unerwartet, und gleichsam ex machina, noch den *comitatus Ildebrandischus* hinzu, also die toskanische Grafschaft der Aldobrandesca. Zunächst wäre man dem Verfasser zuzutrauen bereit, es sei der wenig bekannte *Brandanus*-Fluß bei ihm zu *Ildebrandischus* geworden. Aber so einfach liegen die Dinge doch nicht. In der Ausstattung Manfreds mit der Aldobrandesca könnte sich nämlich, wenn man so will, ein Körnchen Wahrheit finden lassen; ja bei einigem Geschick hätte sich sogar auf Grund dieser Verleihung ein gar nicht übles Echtheitsplaidoyer zugunsten von E aufbauen lassen, wenn die Absonderlichkeit einer toskanischen Dotation für Manfred, und zugleich die krasseste aller Abweichungen von W, dem Herausgeber von E bloß aufgefallen wäre.[18]

Zur Klärung der Interpolation wird es sich nicht vermeiden lassen, auf einige Einzelheiten hinzuweisen, die der Zeit gleich nach dem Tode des Kaisers angehören. Seit dem Umschwung in Florenz im Oktober 1250 zuungunsten der Kaiserpartei war die Reichsherrschaft in der Toskana am Zerfall. Um zu retten was noch zu retten war, suchte die kaiserliche Verwaltung mit Hilfe des ghibellinischen Siena wenigstens die Maremma und Aldobrandesca zu sichern. Über diese Versuche gibt nun eine seit ihrer Veröffentlichung durch Ficker durchaus nicht unbeachtete Urkunde Auskunft. Im Rate von Siena wurde am 4. Januar 1251 ein Schreiben verlesen, das vom 31. Dezember 1250 datiert war (also mehr als zwei Wochen nach dem Tode des Kaisers) und in dem der Generalvikar des Sprengels "Von Amelia bis Corneto und in der Aldobrandesca und Maremma" befiehlt, der Kommune Siena die Grafschaft der Aldobrandesca zum Schutz gegen Reichs-

---

[15] Roger II. gab das Fürstentum Tarent seinem zweiten Sohne Tankred (vgl. Erich Caspar, *Roger II.* [Innsbruck, 1904], 428); als letzter hielt es wohl Wilhelm III. von Sizilien.

[16] *MGH, Const.,* II, S. 385f, § 3.

[17] Wolf, S. 7, § 3; vgl. S. 34.

[18] Wolf, S. 34, bemerkt lediglich: "Weiter [d. h. zu den apulischen Ländereien] erhält Manfred den comitatus Ildebrandis [sic], der die Orte ... umfaßt." Zehn Flecken sind aufgezählt auf Grund von BF, 441, einer Beleihungsurkunde Ottos IV. von 1210. Wolf hat es sich anscheinend gar nicht klargemacht, daß in E Manfred zu den süditalischen Liegenschaften noch eine toskanische Grafschaft zugesprochen wird, wie er freilich auch dem Leser nicht klarzumachen versucht, wo eigentlich diese zusätzliche Grafschaft liegt, die doch gar nicht zu den kalabrischen Besitzungen paßt. Infolgedessen ist er mit allzu großer Sorglosigkeit über die Tatsache hinweggegangen, daß ihm hier zur Geschichte Toskanas eine einzigartige "Quelle" zur Verfügung stand, mit der er sich zumindest hätte auseinandersetzen dürfen.

feinde und Rebellen zu übergeben *pro parte serenissimi domini nostri et illustris viri domini Manfredi, filii sui.*[19] War also Manfred vielleicht doch zum Grafen der Aldobrandesca gemacht worden, wie es E vorsah? Denn warum sonst die Nennung seines Namens im Zusammenhang mit der Grafschaft? Der Sachverhalt ist natürlich längst erkannt worden.[20] Aus höchst plausiblen Gründen — im wesentlichen wohl um Zeit zu gewinnen — hat die kaiserliche Verwaltung im römischen Tuszien zunächst den Versuch gemacht, die Ereignisse zu Fiorentino in der Capitanata nicht sofort bekanntzugeben und damit das Ableben des Kaisers noch zu verschleiern (wenn man will: "geheimzuhalten").[21] Bis gegen Ende Januar 1251 gab also die Verwaltung in scheinbarer Unbefangenheit vor, noch im Namen des Kaisers zu handeln, jedoch unter Hinzufügung des Namens Manfreds, der ja bis zur Ankunft Konrads IV. als *balius* der Kaiserherrschaft in Italien eingesetzt war — ein Umstand, der dem Generalvikar natürlich nicht unbekannt sein konnte.[22] Daß diese Nennung Manfreds als die Folge von Bestimmungen anzusehen ist, wie sie spätestens im Testament W festgelegt wurden, geht aus einem Dokument vom 27. Januar 1251 hervor, in dem sich die Gemeinde Grosseto denen von Siena unterwirft "zu Ehren" des Kaisers und Manfreds und gleichzeitig verspricht, Siena gegen alle zu unterstützen außer *contra imperatorem et dominum Manfredum predictum et filios et heredes ipsius imperatoris.*[23] Die Nennung der Söhne und "Erben" deutet in diesem Falle doch wohl eindeutig auf das Testament hin, selbst wenn die Fiktion immer noch aufrechterhalten wurde, daß der Kaiser am Leben sei. Dementsprechend erfolgte also die Nennung Manfreds — nicht, weil er Graf der Aldobrandesca, sondern weil er für Konrad IV. Reichsverweser in Italien war.

Es wäre nun durchaus möglich, daß der Verfasser von E die Kompetenzen Manfreds nicht erfaßt und darum nicht unterschieden hat und daß er ihm aus diesem Grunde die Aldobrandesca als Erbe zusprach. Der wahre Sachverhalt wird aber vermutlich sehr viel einfacher und viel weniger "staatsrechtlich" sein. In der Aldobrandesca und Maremma waren seit Jahren die Verwandten Manfreds, die Lancias, als kaiserliche Beamte tätig. Spätestens seit 1249 unterstand der Verwaltungsbezirk Manfreds Onkel Galvano Lancia, der dort als Generalvikar fungierte. Nachdem dann (wohl im Januar 1251) Galvano Lancia Toskana verlassen hatte, um sich nach Sizilien zu begeben, blieb als Reichsvikar der Maremma und Aldobrandesca sein Sohn zurück, der für uns erstmals am 8. Januar

---

[19] Ficker, *Forschungen*, IV, Nr. 416, S. 427f, dazu II, S. 518f, § 411; BFW, 13779. Zum Problem selbst hat August Karst, *Geschichte Manfreds vom Tode Friedrichs II. bis zu seiner Krönung* (Berlin, 1897), 3f, Anm. 4, alles relevante Material zusammengestellt. Vgl. auch nächste Anm.
[20] Vgl. Fedor Schneider, "Toscanische Studien V," *QFiAB*, XIII (1910), 1ff, bes. S. 2, Anm. 5.
[21] Zur Frage der "Geheimhaltung" von Friedrichs Tod in der Toskana vgl. die Kontroverse zwischen Davidsohn und Schneider in *QFiAB*, XIII (1910), 245–254 und 255–272, bei der man im wesentlichen Schneider, der Fickers Argumente verteidigt, wird folgen müssen.
[22] Im Gegensatz zu Schneider, a. a. O., 261, Anm. 1, sehe ich keinen Grund, warum dem Generalvikar die Einsetzung Manfreds zum *balius in Italia* nicht auf Grund des Testaments bekannt sein konnte. Manfred selbst zitiert es ja wörtlich am 15. Dezember in seinem Brief an

Palermo (s. o., Anm. 4). Im übrigen mag natürlich für den Eventualfall des Todes des Kaisers die Verweserschaft Manfreds auch längst zuvor und außer-testamentarisch geregelt worden sein. Daß die "Geheimhaltung" des Todes im römischen Tuszien von Galvano Lancia, und nicht von Manfred, ausgegangen sei, ist eine ansprechende Hypothese von Karst, a. a. O.
[23] Ficker, *Forschungen*, IV, Nr. 417, S. 428f; BFW, 13786. Daß die Exceptionsklausel die "Söhne und Erben" auch sonst einschließen kann, ist selbstverständlich wahr. Der Zeitpunkt und die Umstände, unter denen Grosseto die Verpflichtung auf sich nahm, deuten aber doch darauf hin, daß es sich hier nicht um potentielle, sondern um aktuelle Nachkommen und "Erben" handelt. Schneider, a. a. O., S. 10f hat ganz gewiß recht, wenn er sagt, daß schon am 27. Januar keiner mehr daran glaubte, daß der Kaiser noch lebe.

1251 nachweisbar ist und späterhin mehrfach in Erscheinung tritt. Sein Name war Manfred Lancia.[24] Daß ein des Dictamens Beflissener den Reichsvikar in der Aldobrandesca mit dem Kaisersohn vertauschte, ist nicht nur verzeihlich, sondern auch äußerst naheliegend. Auf diese Weise ist wohl die toskanische Grafschaft in das Testament E hineingeraten, wobei es freilich weniger verzeihlich gewesen wäre, hätte wirklich der sterbende Kaiser seinen Sohn Manfred mit dessen Vetter Manfred III. Lancia verwechselt.

Im übrigen ist der Irrtum des Verfassers von E recht willkommen, weil es immerhin einen ungefähren Anhalt für die Datierung des Stückes gibt — vermutlich 1251. Es ist wohl auch anzunehmen, daß der Verfasser irgendwo im mittleren Italien beheimatet war, was möglicherweise eine andere Frage klären könnte: daß nämlich der in W genannte Notar Nikolaus von Brindisi in E ersetzt wird durch den, zumindest in der Anconitaner Mark bekannten, kaiserlichen Richter Nikolaus von Calvi,[25] obwohl hier der Sachverhalt weniger offenkundig ist als im Falle Manfreds und der Aldobrandesca.

Daß der Verfasser von E etwa im Interesse Manfreds gearbeitet hätte, scheint nicht wahrscheinlich. Im Gegenteil, Mehreres weist wohl eher darauf hin, daß er irgendwie mit kurialen Kreisen liiert war, was der Charakter der Escorial-Sammlung ohnehin nahelegen würde. So erhält z. B. der Notar Nikolaus den eigentümlichen und sonst nicht belegbaren Titel *sacri imperii et nunc dicti imperatoris Frederici notarius*, d. h. der "Reichsnotar" wird hier zum "Privatnotar" des *quondam imperator*, dem ja vom Papst das Reich abgesprochen ist.[26] Wenn in W (§ 6) der Kaiser 100 000 Goldunzen fürs Heilige Land aussetzt *pro salute anime nostre*, so wird in E diese Wendung unterdrückt. Andererseits, wenn in W der Kaiser bestimmt, daß der Kirche *restituantur omnia iura sua, salvis in omnibus . . . iure et honore imperii*, so wird in E wiederum die Salvierungsklausel unterdrückt, dafür aber gesagt, Friedrich habe bestimmt *reddere et restituere omnia iura omnesque rationes . . . que et quas possidemus iniuste*, eine Verschärfung, die schon Scheffer-Boichorst dazu führte, das Stück als "Stilübung" zu bezeichnen.[27] Und wenn schließlich, um von kleineren Änderungen zu schweigen, in W der Kaiser den Söhnen auferlegt, die testamentarischen Dispositionen zu beachten (§ 19), so befiehlt in E der Kaiser *ex autoritate nobis a iure concessa* (ein zumindest überflüssiger Zusatz, da ja jeder Testator aus der Autorität des Rechtes heraus seine Dispositionen trifft), daß das Testament *sit lex a nostra magestate autenticata;* und wenn in W *universis fidelibus* bei ihrem Treueid *(sub sacramento fidelitatis)* befohlen wird, daß sie *predicta omnia illibata teneant et observent*, so wird in E konsequenterweise der Satz über Untertanen und Treueid wiederum ausgelassen, dafür aber das auch gegen die Söhne gerichtete grobe Geschütz einer dem "Tyrannen" gemäßen Pönformel aufgefahren: *ut contradictores huius rei ultimo supplicio tanquam nobis rebelles et proditores omnimodo iudicentur.*[28] Die Tendenz der Überarbeitung bedarf keiner weiteren Worte.

[24] Über Manfred III. Lancia vgl. Schneider, a. a. O., S. 5ff, 15ff; BFW, 13781.

[25] Wolf, 15, Anm. 35a.

[26] Ebda., S. 15 und 49.

[27] Ebda., S. 6, § 17; Scheffer-Boichorst, S. 270. Zur Tendenz vgl. auch oben Anm. 8 (Fortlassen der *necessitas* und Ersetzen der *iustitia* durch *peccatum*).

[28] Ebda., S. 8, § 19, schon von Pertz als unecht angesehen und von Scheffer-Boichorst, a. a. O., S. 270 angezweifelt. Für die Tendenz siehe auch oben, Anm. 8, letzte Zeile. Wolf, S. 21f., schließt gerade aus der Fortlassung der *fideles* etc., daß E ein Privattestament sei. Es sei hier obiter bemerkt, daß die Unterscheidung zwischen Staats- und Privattestament höchst unglücklich

Von der Arenga zum Rechtsinhalt leitet E über, indem es den Kaiser die tiefsinnige Betrachtung anstellen läßt, "der Tod sei nichts anderes als das Ende des Lebens, das man im Zeitlichen zu führen glaube".[29] Nach einer kleinen Vorlesung oder Belehrung darüber, daß "nach der Norm des [römischen] Civilrechts Ihr, geliebteste Söhne, in dieser Welt unsere eigene Person darstellt,"[30] entschließt sich der kaiserliche Patient, um nicht "intestat" zu verscheiden, nunmehr noch ein "nunkupatives Testament" zu verfassen. Hätte der Kaiser dieses Nunkupativ-Testament nicht gemacht, so wäre er freilich immer noch nicht intestat verstorben, da er ja angeblich acht Tage zuvor W ausgefertigt hatte.[31] Das Unglück wäre auch sonst nicht zu groß gewesen, da das Vorhandensein von Söhnen irgendwelche Intestatserben ohnedies ausschloß;[32] und der bei Privatleuten gefährlichste Intestatserbe, der Fiskus, kam in diesem Fall ja nicht in Betracht. Aus dieser Besorgnis heraus also brauchte der Kaiser sich kaum veranlaßt gesehen zu haben, nun noch ein *nuncupativum testamentum quod sine scriptis dicitur* zu hinterlassen, wie es das römische Recht z. B. im Falle angeborener oder erworbener Blindheit wie auch im Falle von Analphabetentum des Testators und sonstigem Unvermögen vorsieht, wobei der Testator, falls sieben Zeugen mit dem Notar als achtem anwesend sind, weder eigenhändig die Namen der Erben einträgt, wie das sonst seine Pflicht war, noch auch den eignen Namen eigenhändig unterschreibt.[33] Dies erklärt dann wohl auch in E die Siebenzahl (in W sind es 9 bzw. 10 und der Notar) der *testes rogati* — letzteres ein technischer Begriff (der Gegensatz sind die im Strafprozeß befohlenen oder gezwungenen Zeugen), der in einer Fassung von W auch vorkommt, in E aber wieder pleonastisch erweitert wird *(ad hoc vocatis et rogatis)*, und aus dem keine weiteren Schlüsse gezogen werden können.[34] Das alles ist lediglich

ist. Ein Staatstestament gibt es im Grunde gar nicht (*respublica non habet haeredem, quia semper vivit in semetipsa*, sagt Baldus, *Consilia*, III, 159, n. 5 [Venedig, 1575, fol. 45ᵛ], wie gewiß schon viele vor ihm), weil ja jedes Testament privatrechtlich ist; und wenn ein Herrscher (wie etwa Karl d. Gr.) sein Reich unter die Söhne aufteilt, so überrascht uns eben die Tatsache, daß hier das Reich "privatrechtlich" behandelt wurde. Daß im übrigen dem Privatrecht entnommene Maximen (wie etwa das bekannte *Quod omnes tangit, ab omnibus comprobetur* [Cod. 5, 59, 5, 2]; hierzu Gaines Post, *Traditio*, IV [1946], 179ff) formbildend und schließlich maßgebend auch für das öffentliche Recht werden konnten, ist eine im Spätmittelalter allenthalben zu beobachtende Erscheinung. Einen rechtlichen Unterschied zwischen W und E vermag ich nicht zu entdecken.

[29] Wolf, S. 5 und dazu S. 23, wo das Wort *[finis vite...] credite* trotz besserer Einsicht (S. 5, Anm. 3b) als Imperativ aufgefaßt wird.

[30] S. unten, S. 133.

[31] Wolf, S. 13, Anm. 27, und S. 19f.

[32] Cod. 6, 14, 2: *existente filio... nemo potest intestato heres existere;* und dazu Glossa ordinaria, v. "*existere*": ... *per suum heredem quivis alius excluditur*.

[33] Da Cod. Theod. 4, 4, 2–5–7 nicht (oder nur fragmentarisch durch Justinians Codex) bekannt waren, so kommt für das Nunkupativ-Testament im wesentlichen in Betracht Cod. 6, 22, 8 (*ut carentes oculis seu morbo vel ita nati per nuncupationem suae condant moderamina voluntatis, praesentibus septem testibus... tabulario etiam: ... ut sine scriptis*

testentur), und Cod. 6, 23, 21, 1 und 4 (*Quod si litteras testator ignoret vel subscribere nequeat, octavo subscriptore pro eo adhibito eadem servari decernimus... Per nuncupationem quoque, hoc est sine scriptura, testamenta non alias valere sancimus, ut supra dictum est...*). Wolf ist (vgl. S. 23, Anm. 11) diesen rechtlichen Fragen aus dem Wege gegangen, "zumal über den Einfluß des römischen Rechts auf das Mittelalter in Einzelnen auch unter den Fachleuten noch mancherlei Unklarheit herrscht." Das ist möglich; was uns jedoch angeht, ist allein, was sich die Juristen des 13. Jhdts. für Gedanken gemacht haben und wie sie z. B. das nunkupative Testament interpretierten. In dieser Beziehung ist denn auch die Glossa ordinaria zu Cod. 6, 22, 8, v. "*per nuncupationem*" ganz klar: *per testamentum nuncupativum sine solennitate, non tamen sine scriptura, ut inst. e. §. cecus* [= Inst. 2, 12, 4]. *Sed quare dicitur hoc nuncupativum, cum tamen habeat tantam similitudinem cum scripto? Resp. quia testator non signat, nec subscribit, nec nomen heredis scribit, quod in eo* [sc. *test. scripto*] *esset necesse*. Über die Bedeutung und Entwicklungsgeschichte der *nuncupatio* in der klassischen und nachklassischen Jurisprudenz, auf die hier nicht näher eingegangen werden soll, vgl. B. Kübler v. "Testament (juristisch)," in Pauly-Wissowa, *RE*, V A: 1 (1934), Sp. 990, 993, 996. — Aus der Wendung *sine scriptis dicitur* lassen sich Schlüsse auf sizilische Konzepte, Beurkundungsvorgänge u. ä. nicht ziehen (s. oben, Anm. 10).

[34] Vgl. etwa Dig. 22, 5, 11; Wolf, S. 9 und 13. Zu den Zeugennamen, soweit sie in E nicht mit denen von W übereinstimmen, sei bemerkt, daß *Rozardus de la Cerr...*

ein gewisses Sich-Brüsten mit juristischen Kenntnissen auf Seiten des Stilisten, bar aller historisch-realen Grundlagen.

Nach dem hier Ausgeführten ist es wohl offenkundig, daß E lediglich ein — vermutlich von kurialer Seite — literarisch zugestutztes Muster eines Kaisertestaments darstellt, das der Auswahl von Berard- und Thomas-Briefen vorangestellt worden ist. Dabei bleibt es in diesem Zusammenhang gleichgültig, ob man ein solches Stück eine Stilübung oder eine Verunechtung zu nennen vorzieht. Schlüsse über tatsächliche Vorgänge in den letzten Tagen des Kaisers lassen sich daraus nicht ziehen; sie beruhen notwendig auf einer falschen Voraussetzung, nämlich auf der der Echtheit des Testaments. Trotzdem lohnte es, dieses angebliche Testament zu veröffentlichen; denn als Verunechtung hat es für gewisse Anschauungen in den Jahren nach dem Tode des Kaisers natürlich einen Quellenwert, und zwar einen gar nicht uninteressanten.[35] Ein Passus des Testaments hilft uns zumindest, gewisse Grundlagen der Kaisersage schärfer als bisher zu erfassen, vor allem den für die Entstehung der Kaisersage entscheidenden Sibyllenspruch *Vivit et non vivit.*

2. VIVIT ET NON VIVIT

Ein der Erythräischen Sibylle zugeschriebenes Vaticinium, das bald nach dem Tode Friedrichs II. entstanden sein mag, fand verhältnismäßig rasch beträchtliche Verbreitung.[36] Soweit bekannt findet sich in dieser Weissagung die früheste Spur der Sage vom fortlebenden Kaiser, die um das Motiv von des Kaisers Wiederkehr wie um weitere

---

natürlich zu Acerra zu ergänzen ist, vielleicht Graf Roger von Acerra, der in einer Papsturkunde von 1255 als verstorben erwähnt wird (BFW, 8978). Interessant ist der Zeuge *archiepiscopus Neapolitanus* insofern, als der Stuhl 1250 nur einen Elekten hatte, Berard Caraccioli, der erst 1252 konsekriert wurde. Auch diese Tatsache hat Wolf nicht stutzig gemacht, obwohl er sie (S. 48; vgl. S. 13) selbst vermerkt. Dies ist eines der vielen Anzeichen dafür, daß der Stilist mit den Verhältnissen im Süden nicht vertraut war, also wohl in Mittelitalien zu suchen ist.

[35] Der einzige Anhaltspunkt zur Datierung von E scheint mir, wie schon bemerkt, in der Erwähnung der Aldobrandesca als Dotation Manfreds zu liegen, was bedeuten würde, daß die Überarbeitung wohl ganz bald nach dem Tode des Kaisers, also im Jahre 1251, entstanden ist. Zur Entstehung selbst läßt sich nichts Genaueres sagen. Testament W ist wohl schon in den ersten Monaten des Jahres 1251 in Mittel- und Oberitalien bekannt geworden, wie vielleicht auch die Überlieferung erkennen läßt (*MGH, Const.,* II, S. 382f). Der allem Anschein nach kurialen Kreisen nahestehende Verfasser von E hat dies Testament gekannt und sich offenbar beeilt, es literarisch "interessant" zu machen, indem er es zurechtstutzte. Daß er W kannte, ergibt sich unbezweifelbar aus dem ersten Halbsatz der Arenga, den er fast wörtlich übernahm, wobei er jedoch den stilgerechten, die Anfangsworte verflechtenden, rhythmisch schweren Einsa z von W: *Primi paréntis incáuta transgréssio,* in einen Hexameter verwandelte: *Adam primus parens sic posteris legem indixit.* Statt der kurzen uninteressanten Einleitung von W hat der Verfasser dann eine "interessante" Arenga

fabriziert: in rhetorische Fragen eingekleidete Banalitäten über den Tod; eine zum Teil baren Unsinn enthaltende Verballhornung des Statthalterdiploms, dessen Einflechtung jedoch den Eindruck erwecken sollte, "echt friderizianisch" zu klingen, wie es ja auch nicht anders sein konnte, da es angeblich der sterbende Kaiser selbst war, der "nunkupativ" die Worte wählte. Zur weiteren Dramatisierung, und auch um die eignen juristischen Kenntnisse ins Licht zu setzen, fügte der Verfasser dann das Nunkupativ-Testament ein. Reportagemäßig uninteressant war die Mehrzahl der echten Bestimmungen (§§ 7–16 in W), während die Apanagierung der Söhne seit vielen Jahren ein Gegenstand allgemeinen Interesses war (s. unten, Anm. 60). Die die Söhne betreffenden Abschnitte hat er denn auch im allgemeinen richtig reproduziert, wenn auch teils "verschönt," teils verkürzt (wie die langweilige Aufzählung von apulischen Gütern), teils mißverstanden, teils aber auch erweitert, indem er die im Testament Nichtgenannten so bedachte, wie sich das aus der Situation um 1251 zu ergeben schien. Obwohl nicht ohne kuriale Tendenz, hat der Überarbeiter wohl doch keinen anderen Zweck verfolgt als den der literarischen Reportage. Politische Absichten lagen ihm gewiß ganz fern.

[36] Vgl. für das Vaticinium O. Holder-Egger, "Italienische Prophetien des 13. Jhdts.," *NA,* XV (1890), 155ff, und für die Datierung in die ersten Jahre nach dem Tode des Kaisers, S. 149f; ferner F. Kampers, *Die deutsche Kaiseridee in Prophetie und Sage* (München, 1896), 84ff und *passim,* und Hampe (s. u., Anm. 42), S. 7.

Sagenstoffe vermehrt und seit 1519 in steigendem Maße auf Barbarossa übertragen, schließlich im Zeitalter der Nachromantik eine Art politischer Verwirklichung fand, von der das Kyffhäuserdenkmal ein spätes, wenn auch vielleicht nicht glückliches, Zeugnis ablegt. In der sozusagen "ursprünglichen" Fassung des Sibyllinums werden nun die "Adlerhennen" aufgezählt, die dem "Adler" — d. h. Friedrich II. — "Adlerjunge" beschert haben: die maurische Konstanze von Aragon, die orientalische Isabella von Jerusalem, die britannische Isabella Plantagenet, die deutsche Konkubine Adelheid (Mutter Enzios) und die gallische (d. i. lombardische) Bianca Lancia. Dann heißt es vom Kaiser selbst: "Verborgenen Todes wird er die Augen schließen und fortleben; tönen wird es unter den Völkern 'Er lebt und lebt nicht,' denn eines von den Jungen und von den Jungen der Jungen wird überleben."[37]

Eine spätere verkürzte Form der Erythräa bezieht sich, wie mir scheint, in diesem Teil eher auf das Königreich Trinacria, d. h. die Insel Sizilien. Vorangeschickt wird hier, daß ein "Junges der Jungen" von der "gallischen Henne," also von Bianca Lancia, überlebe. Dann kommt das Kernstück: "Sein Tod wird verborgen und unbekannt bleiben, und tönen wird es im Volke: 'Er lebt und lebt nicht'."[38] Ein *pullus pullorum* wird zwar einleitend noch genannt, aber der Spruch selbst, *Vivit et non vivit*, ist kausal nicht mehr so deutlich mit dem Vorhandensein von Söhnen und Enkeln verknüpft wie in der früheren Fassung. Die Weissagung wurde später von Fra Salimbene in seiner Chronik mehrfach zitiert, und in keinem Falle fehlt der entscheidende Satz *Vivit et non vivit*, auf den auch andere Autoren deutlich anspielten.[39] Es fällt dennoch auf, daß Salimbene nur ein einziges Mal den vollen Spruch erwähnt mit Nennung der *pulli*, und auch da ist das Fortleben des Kaisers bereits abgelöst von den Deszendenten, die an den anderen Stellen schon garnicht mehr erwähnt werden.[40]

Seltsamerweise hat man es bisher verabsäumt, die schlagende Parallele zu diesem Spruch heranzuziehen, die doch manches verdeutlicht. In dem Kapitel zum Lob gutgeratener und gutgezogener Kinder heißt es bei Jesus Sirach (30, 4): *Mortuus est pater ... et qua si non est mortuus, similem enim reliquit post se.* Das Sibyllium *Vivit et non vivit* wendet also nur ins Affirmative, was Jesus Sirach gleichsam negativ ausgedrückt hat: *mortuus est et quasi non est mortuus.* Genauer gesagt: der Vater stirbt zwar, ist jedoch nicht tot, weil er ja "seinesgleichen hinter sich gelassen hat." Das Fortleben des Vaters ist verbürgt im Sohne. Das ist nun offenbar genau das Gleiche, was der Sibyllenspruch — zumindest in

---

[37] Holder-Egger, a. a. O., S. 166 für die *gallinae* und S. 168 für den Spruch: *Oculos eius morte claudet abscondita supervivetque; sonabit et in populis: "Vivit, non vivit," uno ex pullis pullisque pullorum superstite.*

[38] Holder-Egger, *NA*, XXX (1905), 333f: *Et dabitur ei quinta [Gallicana] gallina, que claudet oculos suos, uno tantum ex pullis [pullisque* ist m. A. nach überflüssiger und eher fehlleitender Zusatz Holder-Eggers] *pullorum superstite; cuius mors erit abscondita et incognita, sonabitque in populo: "Vivit" et "Non vivit."* Ich bin mit Rudolf M. Kloos, "Ein Brief des Petrus de Prece zum Tode Friedrichs II.," *Deutsches Archiv*, XIII (1957), S. 156, Anm. 20, gleichfalls der Ansicht, daß die kürzere Fassung viel später als 1254 zu datieren ist und womöglich in die Zeit um 1270 und

eher noch später gehört. Zu beachten ist, z. B., daß das *in populis* der längeren Fassung verwandelt ist zu *in populo*, was anscheinend auf Trinacria zu beziehen wäre. Doch liegt es mir fern, das Sibyllinum neu auszudeuten zu wollen.

[39] Salimbene de Adam, ed. Holder-Egger, *MGH, SS*, 174, 243, 347, 537 stets in der Form *in populis*, nicht *in populo*. Vgl. für einen Anklang das Schreiben des Petrus de Prece bei Kloos, a. a. O., S. 152, Anm. 5, der mit Recht auf die Sächsische Weltchronik verweist (*MGH, Dt. Chron.*, II, 258, c. 399).

[40] Nur S. 537 hat Salimbene die volle Fassung mit dem Nachsatz über die *pulli*, die aber keine entscheidende Rolle spielen. S. 174, 243, 347 hat der Spruch eine ganz andere Bedeutung, da von den Nachkommen nicht mehr die Rede ist.

der ursprünglichen längeren Fassung — zum Ausdruck bringen wollte: *Vivit, non vivit, uno ex pullis pullisque pullorum superstite.* Schon in der zweiten, kürzeren Fassung der Erythräischen Sibylle ist der Kausalsatz, oder kausale Ablativus absolutus, fortgelassen, der wie bei Jesus Sirach das Fortleben des Vaters begründet durch das Überleben von — und darum in — Kindern. Statt dessen wird vielleicht schon in der späteren Sibylle und ganz gewiß bei Salimbene das Fortleben gleichsam mystifiziert: "Sein Tod wird verborgen und unbekannt bleiben," und darum wird es heißen "Er lebt und lebt nicht." Nicht so sehr wegen des Fortlebens in den Kindern, sondern wegen der Verborgenheit des Todes lebt der Vater, der Kaiser, geheimnisvoll weiter. Das ist natürlich ein vollkommen anderer und neuer Gedanke, der vielleicht durch die höchst zweifelhafte, in jedem Fall nur regionale und ganz kurzfristige, sogenannte "Geheimhaltung" des Todes Friedrichs II. durch Manfred irgendwelchen Nahrungsstoff erhalten hat.[41] Diese mystifizierte Version soll uns hier nicht weiter angehen, wohingegen die Weissagung "Er lebt und lebt nicht" im Zusammenhang mit der Frage dynastischer Sukzession doch von erheblichem Interesse ist.

Um zunächst bei den Sibyllen zu bleiben, so hat Karl Hampe einen Brief oder eine Flugschrift der Leute von Tivoli veröffentlicht, in dem diese den Tod des Kaisers beklagten (ca. Januar 1251).[42] Was die Sibylle — doch wohl die Tiburtina — verheißen habe, nämlich, daß "zu seiner Zeit die Schollen fruchtbar sein würden," das habe der Kaiser erfüllt, dessen messianisches Kaisertum nunmehr der Sohn, Konrad IV., fortsctzcn würde. Dabei bedienten sich die Tiburtiner in ihrer Flugschrift des Vergleichs mit der Sonne: "Gleich der Sonne, wenn sie von der Himmelsachse in das westliche Meer sinkt, so hinterläßt Friedrich im Westen eine Sonne als Sohn, deren Morgenröte im Osten schon zu leuchten beginnt, während noch die Sterne am Himmelsgewölbe funkeln."[43] Auf das Mythologumenon braucht hier nicht näher eingegangen zu werden, da es bekannt genug ist: der lugubre Tod des Helios an jedem Abend, jedem Wintersolsticium, und sein Wiedererscheinen an jedem Morgen, jedem Jahresbeginn als ein νήπιος ἀνατέλλων.[44] Worauf es hier ankommt, ist die Identität zwischen Vater und Sohn oder,

---

[41] Zu der Geheimhaltung des Todes vgl. oben, Anm. 21, die Kontroverse zwischen Davidson und Fedor Schneider in *QFiAB*, XIII (1910), 245–272, bei der kaum viel mehr herauskommt als ein quasi sibyllinisches "Verheimlicht und doch nicht verheimlicht."

[42] K. Hampe, *Eine frühe Verknüpfung der Weissagung vom Endkaiser mit Friedrich II. und Konrad IV.* (S.-B. Heidelberg, 1917, Nr. 6).

[43] Ebda., S. 18, auch S. 11. Hampe übersetzte *solem genitum* mit "Sonnensohn," was der Bedeutung nicht ganz gerecht wird, genau wie *sol puer* nicht "Sonnenknabe" ist, sondern die noch "knabenhafte Sonne." Da Sonne im Deutschen weiblich ist, könnte man geneigt sein, *sol genitus* mit "Tochter-Sonne" zu übersetzen, was zwar den Sinn träfe, wegen der Beziehung auf Konrad IV. jedoch nicht angängig ist. Ich habe deswegen die Wendung mit "Sonne als Sohn" übersetzt.

[44] Für diesen Ausdruck der Zauberpapyri vgl. Franz Boll, *Griechische Kalender* I (S.-B. Heidelberg, 1910, Nr. 16), S. 42, 35. Der Mythos von Helios, der täglich als Knabe seinen Lauf beginnt, war natürlich ganz genau bekannt.

Der mit Unrecht oder Recht dem Alexander Neckam (gest. 1217) zugeschriebene sog. Mythographus III, c. 8, 4, ed. G. H. Bode, *Scriptores rerum mythicarum Latini tres* (Celle, 1834), 201, Z. 30ff, sagt: *[Solem = Apollinem] imberbem pingunt, quod singulis diebus renascendo quasi iunior videatur,* und interpretiert weiterhin den Beinamen Phoebus als *novus,* und zwar *quod revera sol in ortu suo quotidie novus appareat.* Ähnlich schon der Mythographus II (c. 19, ed. Bode, S. 81, Z. 8). Auf dem Mythographus III fußte dann Petrus Berchorius (Pierre Bersuire), der Freund Petrarcas, der um 1340 schrieb und später unter dem Namen Thomas Walleys gedruckt worden ist (*Metamorphosis Ovidiana* [Paris, 1515–16], fol. VI). Dessen Exegese wurde dann, wie jüngst Sabine Krüger, *DA*, XII (1956), 210f gezeigt hat, von Dietrich von Nieheim für seine Scholien zur Alexandersage benutzt. Zur Überlieferung vgl. H. Liebeschütz, *Fulgentius Metaphoralis* (Leipzig-Berlin, 1926), bes. 15ff, 41ff; E. Panofsky, *Hercules am Scheidewege* (Leipzig, 1930), 11ff und *passim.* Zum sterbenden Helios vgl. besonders F. J. Dölger, *Sol Salutis*[2] (Münster, 1925), 343ff und *passim.*

um im Bilde zu bleiben, zwischen der scheidenden und der aufgehenden Sonne, die zwar wechselt, aber dennoch stets die gleiche Sonne bleibt. Die Identität gewährleistet dabei auch die Kontinuität: wie der Vater so wird der Sohn ein Friedefürst sein, "dem Manfred mit den übrigen Brüdern, vom Vater weise und bestimmt bevollmächtigt, die Pfade der kaiserlichen Majestät bereitet." Kurz, das Bild des Jesus Sirach, wonach der Vater zwar gestorben, jedoch nicht tot sei, weil er *similem reliquit post se*, ist hier auf die Sonne übertragen, die zwar allabendlich dem Tode verfällt, aber doch nie wirklich tot ist, weil sie sich allmorgendlich erneuert — *aliusque et idem nasceris*, wie Horaz im Säkulargedicht (10f.) den Sonnengott anredet.

Wenig später schrieb der Notar und spätere Vicekanzler der jüngeren Staufer, Petrus de Prece, einem Ungenannten einen Brief, in dem er die Behauptung zurückwies, es sei mit dem Tode Friedrichs II. das Kaisertum der Staufer erloschen: wenn wirklich, wie gesagt würde, der "Adler der Frühe" verstorben sei, so lebe er doch weiter in vielen überlebenden Adlerjungen, die aus ihm hervorgegangen seien.[45] Die Anlehnung an die Erythräische Sibylle ist deutlich genug und vom Herausgeber des Briefes auch voll gewürdigt worden.[46] Zu unterstreichen wäre noch, daß hier — anders als bei Salimbene — nicht das leiseste Schwanken vorhanden ist, wie denn die Sibylle zu interpretieren und das Fortleben des Kaisers zu begründen sei: *vivit in pullis superstitibus*. Es lohnt, sich dieser Tatsache zu erinnern. An anderer Stelle spricht Petrus de Prece davon, daß das "himmlische Haus der Augusti ununterbrochen *(perpetuo)* in seinen Gestirnen leuchte,"[47] und daß überhaupt dem *illustrissimum germen ab augustorum sanguine longo legittime derivatum*[48] eine besondere Mission innewohne, wie dies natürlich längst beobachtet worden ist.[49] Dabei ist aber in diesen Stücken fast durchgängig das dynastische Element dem persönlichen Element, dem individuellen Throninhaber, übergeordnet, am stärksten vielleicht in Manfreds Römermanifest, das gleichfalls Petrus de Prece zum Verfasser hat.[50] Hampe hat sehr richtig bemerkt, daß in dem Brief der Tiburtiner persönliche Eigenschaften des "Endkaisers" von Friedrich II. auf Konrad IV übertragen worden sind, obwohl doch der Begriff selbst sich gegen jede Pluralisierung sperren müßte.[51] In dieser Hinsicht geht Petrus de Prece wohl noch einen Schritt weiter, wenn er Konradin als Erneuerer einer *felix etas* und der *aurea saecula* verheißt,[52] wie freilich schon vor ihm Manfred die Wiederkehr der *aurea tempora* unter Konrad IV. erwartet hatte.[53] Es ist fast wie in spätrömischer Zeit, als von jedem neuen Kaiser bei seinem Regierungsantritt gleichsam automatisch der Beginn eines goldenen Zeitalters proklamiert wurde.[54] Was dort jedoch am Kaiseramt

[45] Vgl. die Edition des Briefes von R. M. Kloos, *DA*, XIII (1957), 169–170: ...*de orientali videlicet aquila quam dicitis occidisse, que si pro certo decessit ut fertur, vivit tamen in pullis multis superstitibus ex eodem.*

[46] Kloos, a. a. O., S. 170, Anm. 7.

[47] Vgl. Eugen Müller, *Peter von Prezza, ein Publizist des Interregnums* (Abh. Heidelb., 1913), S. 75, und den Text *(ut tanquam coelestis Augustorum stellata syderibus perpetuo radiaret)* bei Del Re, *Cronisti e scrittori* (Napoli, 1868), II, 679, § 23.

[48] Vgl. Kloos, "Petrus de Prece und Konradin," *QFiAB*, XXXIV (1954), 97, § 9.

[49] Vgl. Kantorowicz, *Erg.-Bd.*, S. 222ff.

[50] *MGH, Const.*, II, Nr. 424, S. 559ff. Es sollte betont werden, daß Petrus de Prece als der Hauptherold des staufischen Dynastiekultes betrachtet werden muß, vielleicht neben Heinrich von Isernia.

[51] Hampe, a. a. O., S. 14.

[52] Kloos, *QFiAB*, XXXIV (1954), 98, § 10.

[53] BF, 4633, Capasso, *Hist. diplom.*, S. 6 (an die Palermitaner): *ut ... aurea iam rediisse tempora gratulentur.*

[54] A. Alföldi, "Der neue Weltherrscher der IV. Ekloge Vergils," *Hermes*, LXV (1930), 369–384, bes. 375; auch *Röm. Mitt.*, L (1935), 89 und *passim*. Der Topos durchzieht noch die karolingische Hofdichtung (Sedulius u. a.).

hing, wird nach 1250 weitgehend mit der Dynastie verknüpft, die ja — wie das personifizierte Amt selbst — ihre eigene Kontinuität, ja Sempiternität hatte.

Dieser Kontinuität hat schon zu Lebzeiten des Kaisers der Abt Nikolaus von Bari Ausdruck gegeben.[55] In seinem Enkomium auf Friedrich II. verhieß er dem Reiche der Kaisererben Dauer bis zum jüngsten Gericht: die *progenies* werde herrschen bis zum Ende der Welt, weil mit dem Geschlecht "am Tag seiner Bewährung das Fürstentum ruhe" (Ps. 109,3) und in all seinen Vikaren Christus gegenwärtig sei.[56] Daß für Nikolaus von Bari das *imperiale semen* gleichsam vom Himmel kommt *(de celo venit)* und darum allen anderen Fürstenhäusern überlegen ist, gehört in einen anderen Zusammenhang — ein Gedanke, der in Manfreds Römermanifest dann breit ausgesponnen ist.[57] Die Idee der Fortdauer hingegen ist nicht weniger eindeutig dargelegt in Manfreds Brief an Konrad IV., in dem sich auch das Sonnenbild der Tiburtiner wiederfindet: " Es sank die Sonne der Welt, die unter den Völkern leuchtete; es sank die Sonne der Gerechtigkeit; es sank der Urheber des Friedens;" den Völkern aber erwachse Hoffnung, ja völlige Gewißheit und sicheres Vertrauen, denn "mag auch jene Sonne sich zum Untergang bereitet haben, so ist doch d u r c h   d e n   O r d o einer gewissen K o n t i n u i t ä t ihr erneutes Leuchten in Euch [sc. Konrad IV.] gegeben, und so glaubt man nicht, daß der Vater abwesend sei, da man hofft er lebe im Sohne."[58] Der Manfredbrief bringt im Grunde nur das, was schon das echte Kaisertestament (W) ausgesprochen hatte: der Kaiser sagte darin, er disponiere für seine Söhne, "damit wir, wiewohl menschlichen Dingen entrafft, dennoch zu leben scheinen."[59]

Es ist also nicht ganz von ungefähr, daß in der Erythräischen Sibylle der Gedanke des kaiserlichen Fortlebens — *Vivit et non vivit* — erscheint und zunächst auch ganz richtig mit den Nachkommen, den *pulli*, verknüpft worden ist; das heißt, es handelte sich auch in dem Sibyllinum zunächst um nichts anderes als um das Fortleben der kaiserlichen

---

[55] Kloos, "Nikolaus von Bari, eine neue Quelle zur Entwicklung der Kaiseridee unter Friedrich II.," *DA*, XI (1954), 166–190, veröffentlichte erstmals die ganz ungewöhnlich interessanten Stücke, die, obwohl in vielem nur Bekanntes bestätigend, dennoch ein völlig neues Licht auf den "Kaiserkult" unter Friedrich II. werfen.

[56] Vgl. das Enkomium auf Friedrich II., § 11 (Kloos, S. 172f). Ausgehend von Genesis 49, 10 [Jakob seine Söhne um sich versammelnd] bezieht Nikolaus die Segnung des Juda auf Friedrich II: "Es wird das Szepter nicht entwendet werden von der Hand des Herrn Friedrich noch der Stab des Herrschers von seinen Lenden ... 'donec veniat qui mittendus est,' id est Christus ad iudicium, hoc est usque ad finem mundi, que progenies imperabit, quia 'secum est principium in die virtutis suae'* [Ps. 109, 3], id est Christus in omnibus suis vicariis."* Das dynastische Moment ist in den Lobsprüchen des Nikolaus überaus stark vertreten, und obwohl in ihnen die biblischen Bezüge dominieren, so gibt es doch zahlreiche Verbindungslinien zu der Feier der *Cesarea stirps*, die wir von Petrus de Prece (etwa in Manfreds Römermanifest) her kennen. Zur Kontinuität auch oben, Anm. 47.

[57] Vgl. Kloos, S. 170, § 4 für die Preisung der *nobilitas generis*, die sich von Kaisern und Königen herleitet: *qui de celo venit* [Joh. 3, 31], *super omnes est, id est, qui de imperiali*

semine descendit, cunctis nobilior est. Derartiges kennen wir sonst eigentlich nur zum Preis der französischen Dynastie (und auch da im Grunde erst seit dem Ende des 13. Jhdts.), wobei natürlich die staufisch-römischen *divi imperatores* durch die *sancti reges* Frankreichs ersetzt werden; vgl. etwa (um von Dubois und allbekanntem Material zu schweigen) Dom Jean Leclercq, "Un sermon prononcé pendant la guerre de Flandre sous Philippe le Bel," *Rev. du moyen âge latin*, I (1945), 165–172, besonders S. 169, Z. 21: [die *sancti reges Francie*] *sanctitatem generant, cum generent sanctos reges.* Zu vergleichen ist Vergil, *Aeneis* IX, 642: *dis genite et geniture deos;* auch Seneca, *Consol. ad Marcum*, XV, 1: *Caesares qui dis geniti deosque genituri dicuntur*, und eine (natürlich damals nicht bekannte) Inschrift: *diis geniti et deorum creatores* (*CIL*, III, 710: Diocletian und Maximian). In der Kriegspredigt ist das Ersetzen der *dii* durch *sancti* ganz offenkundig.

[58] BF, 4634; Huillard-Bréholles, *Hist. dipl.*, VI, 811: ... *ut licet occasum sol ille petierit, p e r c u i u s d a m t a m e n c o nt i n u a t o n i s   o r d i n e m relucescat in vobis ... et sic pater abesse non creditur, dum vivere speratur in filio.*

[59] *MGH, Const.*, II, S. 385, Z. 12f: *sic de imperio ...[et filiis nostris]* duximus disponendum, ut rebus humanis absumpti vivere videamur.

Dynastie, um das Fortleben des Kaisers in Sohn und Enkel, und nicht etwa um das rätselhafte Fortleben der individuellen Person selbst, Friedrichs II. Die vielfache Beschäftigung mit den Söhnen in Kundgebungen und Relationen jeglicher Art mag dem Sibyllenautor Derartiges nahegelegt haben;[60] und in diesen allgemeinen Rahmen gehört auch das in der Escorial-Handschrift überlieferte Testament E.

Dieses Testament ist für das tiefere Verständnis der ganzen Theorie des dynastischen Fortlebens um so wichtiger, als wir in ihm eine deutliche Wendung ins Juristische wahrnehmen. Die Arenga, die sich zunächst rein rhetorisch in biblisch-philosophischen und poetischen Betrachtungen über den Tod ergeht, gleitet dann hinüber in juristisches Gedankengut, um schließlich zu den konkreten Erbschaftsbestimmungen zu gelangen. Der sterbende Kaiser habe sich dabei direkt an seine Söhne gewandt:

> *Videntibus itaque nobis in mundo personaliter plus non posse consistere . . . per substitutum fulgere procuramus et vivere, cum iuxta legum civilium normam, o filii karissimi, nostram personam propriam presentetis in mundo. Scriptum est enim: "Qui videt me, videt et patrem meum"* (Joh. 14, 9).[61]

Es lohnt, diesen Paragraphen genau durchzuinterpretieren. Der leitende Gedanke des ersten Halbsatzes entspricht etwa dem Statthalterdiplom, zumal in der Fassung von 1240 für Pandulf von Fasanella: der Kaiser, so heißt es da, setzte einen Generalvikar ein *quia presentialiter ubique adesse non possumus, ubi longe lateque potentialiter preminemus.*[62] Der gleiche Gedanke war schon vorher in einem der *Defensa*-Gesetze des *Liber augustalis* erörtert worden[63] und findet sich auch in einer Stilübung der Briefsammlung des Petrus de Vinea wieder sowie in den Statthalterdiplomen Konrads IV.[64] Diese Statthalter sind (z. B. im Falle Enzios) *persone nostre speculum,*[65] sie sind *tamquam nostre ymaginarium visionis*[66] oder auch *quasi partes . . . corporis [nostri].*[67] Diese Idee der kaiserlichen Stellvertretung ist in dem Testament gleichsam von den Statthaltern auf die Erben übertragen: da der Kaiser *personaliter* nicht mehr in der Welt sein kann, so wolle er durch einen Ersatzmann leuchten und leben — *per substitutum fulgere et vivere.* Die Übertragung dieser Idee schließt jedoch

---

[60] Vgl. für Friedrich II. und seine Söhne im Jahre 1247, Kantorowicz, *Erg.-Bd.*, S. 302ff, die Nachrichten der Piacentiner Annalen und des Mainardin von Imola; vgl. ebda., S. 307, Anm. 26.

[61] Wolf, a. a. O., S. 5f.

[62] *MGH, Const.*, II, Nr. 223, S. 306, Z. 37f.

[63] *Lib. aug.*, I, 17; vgl. dazu Kantorowicz, "Invocatio nominis imperatoris," *Bollettino del Centro di Studi Filologici e Linguistici Siciliani*, 3 (1955), 35–50. Hinzuzufügen wäre noch PdV, II, 8, ein Manifest an die Römer, wo es heißt: *licet nostra non sit ubique corporalis praesentia, nostrae tamen ad longinquos orbis terminos laxantur habenae.*

[64] PdV, III, 69. Für Konrad IV., vgl. *MGH, Const.*, II, Nr. 344, S. 452, Z. 2ff: *Verum cum per individuitatem persone simul et semel ubique personaliter nostra serenitas adesse non possit, ut noscant subditi longas regibus esse manus* [Ovid, *Ep.* XVI, 166] . . . Das mehrfache Zitieren der Ovidstelle im Umkreis der sizilischen Staufer ist auffallend; cf. Kloos, *DA*, XI (1911), 175, § 16, für Nikolaus von Bari; ferner Marinus de Caramanico, v. "*Ubique potentialiter*" zu Liber

Augustalis, I, 17 (Cervoni-Ausgabe [Neapel, 1773], S. 41); s. auch Kantorowicz, "Invocatio," S. 40, Anm. 21. An die staufischen Vorlagen (ohne die Ovidstelle) lehnte sich dann auch die Kanzlei Karls von Anjou an; vgl. etwa R. Trifone, *La legislazione angioina* (Neapel, 1921), 77, Z. 18.

[65] *MGH, Const.*, II, Nr. 217, S. 302, Z. 5.

[66] Ebda., Nr. 422, S. 554, Z. 5. Zugrunde liegt hier, wie in zahlreichen ähnlichen Fällen, etwa Cod. 7, 62, 16 (Cod. Theod. 11, 30, 11): Vikare und Richter "*qui imaginem principalis disceptationis accipiunt.*" Vgl. etwa Lucas de Penna, zu Cod. 11, 40, 4, n. 1 (*In Tres Libros* [Lyon, 1582], S. 446), zum Worte *imagines: Alias ponitur [imago] pro simulatione vel fictione . . . eo quod id quod agitur veritatis figuram repraesentat. Sic delegatus dicitur imago delegantis. supra de appel. etiam* (= Cod. 7, 62, 16).

[67] Petrus de Vinea, III, 69, ed. Huillard-Bréholles, *Hist. dipl.*, IV, S. 246. Zugrunde liegt hier Cod. 9, 8, 5 rubr.: *nam et ipsi [sc. senatores] pars corporis nostri sunt.*

eine nicht unwesentliche Veränderung ein: die Statthalterdiplome und verwandte Zeugnisse implizieren eine kaiserliche Ubiquität, eine Allgegenwart des Kaisers im Raume; Testament E jedoch, wie übrigens auch das echte Testament W, impliziert sozusagen eine kaiserliche Sempiternität, eine immerwährende Gegenwart des Kaisers in der Zeit.[68]

Hierbei ist nun der Wortlaut von E nicht ohne Bedeutung; denn *per substitutum* oder *per subrogatum vivere* ist juristischer terminus technicus. Dig. 5, 1, 76 behandelt die Frage, ob ein Gerichtshof, bei dem im Laufe des Verfahrens ein oder mehrere Richter ausgeschieden und durch andere ersetzt seien (*et alii fuerunt eis substituti* heißt es in der Glossa ordinaria des Accursius zu diesem Gesetz), noch den gleichen Gerichtshof darstelle. Die Frage wird bejaht, denn: eine Legion, von deren Mannschaft viele gefallen und durch andere ersetzt seien, bleibe stets die gleiche Legion; ein Volk sei heute das gleiche, das es vor hundert Jahren war, obwohl keiner der damals Lebenden noch am Leben sei; ein Schiff, dessen Planken nach und nach allesamt ersetzt seien, bleibe dennoch das gleiche Schiff; und eine Schafherde, so fügt die Glosse hinzu, bleibe durch Substitution stets die gleiche Herde. In diesem Sinne bleibt daher der Gerichtshof immer der gleiche, auch *tribus vel duobus iudicibus mortuis et aliis subrogatis*.[69] Diese Anschauung galt ganz allgemein für alle Arten von Verbänden: *in collegiis ... semper idem corpus manet, quamvis successive omnes moriantur et alii loco ipsorum substituantur*, sagt etwa Bracton.[70] In all diesen Fällen handelt es sich um das Fortleben der *forma* oder *species*, wie es denn auch in Dig. 5, 1, 76 ausdrücklich erwähnt wird.[71] Daß nun die Substitution oder Subrogation das Mittel zur Sempiternisierung ist, haben die späteren Juristen unzweideutig ausgesprochen. Dig. 8, 2, 33, z. B., erörtert eine perpetuelle Servitut zur Erhaltung einer "ewigen Wand" (*paries aeternus*) an einem Gebäude. Dazu sagt korrigierend die Glosse zum Worte '*aeternus*': *id est sempiternus. nam aeternum dicitur quod semper fuit et est: ut Deus sempiternus dicitur, quod incepit et non desinet; ut anima et angelus et haec servitus*, was späterhin Bartolus und Baldus lapidar zusammenfaßten: *perpetuatio fit per successionem sive subrogationem*.[72]

Soviel vorerst zum Ausdruck *per substitutum vivere*. Die Substitutionsidee ist jedoch von allem Anfang aufs engste verquickt mit dem Erbrecht — und daher schließlich auch mit dem dynastischen Thronfolgerecht. Inst. 3, 1, 3 heißt es: *Et statim morte parentis quasi*

---

[68] Für die kaiserliche Ubiquität vgl. meinen oben (Anm. 63) zitierten Aufsatz.

[69] Glos. ord. zu Dig. 5, 1, 76, v. "*proponebatur.*" Ich zitiere die Accursius-Glosse nach der 5-bändigen Ausgabe des *Corpus iuris civilis*, Venedig, 1584.

[70] Bracton, *De legibus et consuetudinibus Angliae*, fol. 374b, ed. Woodbine (New Haven, 1915–1942), S. 175, ed. Travers Twiss (Rolls Series), V, S. 448.

[71] Vgl. den Schluß-Satz: *quapropter cuius rei species eadem consisteret, rem quoque eandem esse existimari*, wobei die Glosse v. "*rei species*" erklärend sagt: *id est forma*, und der kaum spätere Odofredus bemerkt (zu Dig. 5, 1, 76 [Ausgabe Lyon, 1550, fol. 209ᵛ]): *unde ex quo remanet idem genus vel eadem species, licet non sit eadem qualitas, tamen eandem rem iudicamus.*

[72] Bartolus zu Dig. 8, 2, 33 (Ausgabe Lyon, 1555, fol. 222); Baldus zur gleichen Stelle (Ausgabe Venedig,

1586, fol. 311). Vgl. übrigens auch Bartolus zu Cod. 11, 9, 2, n. 1 (zit. Ausg., fol. 37ᵛ), v. "*aeternus*": *inproprie [princeps] dicitur aeternus: tamen imperator respectu officii, quod non debet habere finem, potest dici sempiternus.* Interessant ist, wegen seiner Stellungnahme zur aristotelischen Lehre von der Anfangs- und daher auch Endlosigkeit der Welt, Angelus de Ubaldis zu Dig. 8, 2, 33, n. 2 und 4 (Ausgabe Venedig, 1580, fols. 185ᵛ–186). Auch er wendet sich zunächst gegen den Mißbrauch des Wortes *aeternus* und sagt: *Nota sub sole nihil possibile est aeternum, fit tantum aeternitas per successionem seu subrogationem*; mit der Glosse unterscheidet er dann zwischen *aeternus* und *sempiternus*, gibt zu, daß die Seele und die Engel kein Ende haben, lehnt aber den Begriff für eine Servitut ab, *quia impossibile est aliquid esse sub sole sine fine, et ideo mundus habebit finem secundum fidem, licet princeps philosophorum fuerit in opinione contraria motus rationibus naturalibus.*

continuatur dominium. Zu den Worten "*quasi continuatur*" bemerkt dabei die Glosse: ...
pater et filius unum fictione iuris sunt.[73] Diese juristische Fiktion einer Identität von Vater
und Sohn, Erblasser und Erben, ist natürlich ein ganz allgemein verbreiteter Gedanke,
zumal Cod. 6, 26, 11 (worauf sich auch die Glosse beruft) dafür die gesicherte Grundlage
bildet: *Natura pater et filius unum fictione iuris sunt.* Andererseits wird die *continuatio dominii*
durch Dig. 28, 2, 11 festgestellt, indem das Gesetz sagt, die erbenden Söhne, selbst wenn
nicht ausdrücklich als Erben eingesetzt, "gälten schon zu Lebzeiten des Vaters in gewissem Sinne als die Herren" des väterlichen Besitzes *(etiam vivo patre quodammodo domini
existimantur).* Schließlich wurde von den Juristen gern die Glosse "*Quam filii*" zu Dig. 50,
16, 220 herangezogen, wo es heißt, daß der Vater die eigene Natur im Sohne zu erhalten
trachte: *quaelibet res conservationem sui desiderat, ut videat pater suam naturam in filio conservari.*
Die gleiche Lehre einer quasi-Identität von Vater und Sohn vertrat auch die Kanonistik.
Decretum C. I q. 4 c 8 sagt mit Bezug auf Erzeuger und Sohn: *unus erat cum illo.*[74] Aus
dem Ausdruck *rex iuvenis* in C. XXIV q. 1 c. 42 leitete man die Lehre her (entsprechend
Dig. 28, 2, 11), daß der Sohn schon zu Lebzeiten des Vaters König sei,[75] während die
Glosse "*primatus*" zu C. VII q. 1 c. 8 herhalten mußte, um auf Grund von Deut. 21, 17
über die Primogenitur abzuhandeln.[76] Daß dabei die Kanonisten weitgehend wiederum
auf das römische Recht Bezug nahmen, ist selbstverständlich. Zenzelinus de Cassanis,
z. B., allegiert in der Glosse "*sublimitatem eorum*" zur Bulle *Execrabilis* ausdrücklich die
Glosse "*quasi continuatur*" zu Inst. 3, 1, 3, wenn er sagt: *pater et filius   eadem persona
fingatur esse.*[77] All diese Stellen wurden immer wieder herangezogen, und es versteht sich,
daß davon auch die kaiserliche Kanzlei nicht unberührt blieb. In einem Briefe Friedrichs II. von 1233 z. B. findet sich ein Niederschlag dieser Lehre, wenn darin gesagt
wird, daß Vater und Sohn durch die Liebe, *sicut innate beneficio gratie, una persona censetur.*[78]

Wir verstehen jetzt besser, was der Stilist des Testamentes E im Sinne hatte, wenn er
den sterbenden Kaiser die Söhne belehren läßt, daß sie "gemäß der Norm des römischen
Rechts" des Kaisers Person darstellten: er bezog sich offenbar auf Cod. 6, 26, 11 oder auf
die Institutionenglosse "*quasi*" oder ähnliche Stellen. Ebenso ist in diesem Sinne Manfreds Brief an Konrad IV. zu verstehen, wenn er sagt daß "durch den Ordo einer gewissen Kontinuität" die väterliche Sonne nunmehr in ihm, Konrad, von neuem leuchte,
so daß man glaube, der Vater sei nicht abwesend, vielmehr hoffe man, er lebe im Sohne
weiter; und im gleichen Atem kommt Manfred dann auf das Erbrecht zu sprechen.[79]
Ferner, wenn Konrad IV. in einem Brief an den Justitiar von Abruzzo (verfaßt von Petrus
de Prece) von sich selbst sagt, daß nach dem Willen Gottes *iam genitor noster revixit in filio,*

---

[73] Die Glosse zitiert dabei Cod. 6, 26, 11.

[74] Friedberg, I, Sp. 419f; die Stelle ist einem Briefe
Augustins entnommen. Für die Glossa ordinaria be-
nutze ich die 3-bändige Ausgabe des *Corpus Iuris Canonici*
(Turin, 1588).

[75] Friedberg, I, Sp. 983f. Auf Dig. 28, 2, 11 beruft sich
dann z. B. Petrus de Ancharano, *Consilia*, LXXXII, n. 2
(Ausgabe Venedig, 1574, fol. 40): *[heredes] etiam vivo
patre quodammodo domini existimantur.* Vgl. unten Anm. 86.

[76] Cf. Friedberg, I, Sp. 569 zum Erstgeburtsrecht
Esaus.

[77] Extrav. Joann., XXII, tit. III (Ausgabe Friedberg,
II, Sp. 1207.)

[78] Böhmer, *Acta imperii selecta*, Nr. 301, S. 265.

[79] S. oben, Anm. 58, und anschließend: *nec creditur
tam pretiosa hereditas amisisse patronum, dum eius confidit
invenire dominium tam suave, tam placidum in herede.* Die
quasi-Personifizierung der Erbschaft war üblich auf
Grund der vielzitierten *lex mortuo* (Dig. 46, 1, 22: *quia
hereditas personae vice fungitur*). Vgl. darüber Gierke,
Genossenschaftsrecht, III, S. 362, zur *hereditas iacens*, auch
S. 203.

so gehört auch das vielleicht noch zu dem Topos von der Einheit von Vater und Sohn.[80] Man wird sich nämlich in diesem Zusammenhang auch an die, im wesentlichen aristotelischen, Zeugungs- und Vererbungslehren der Antike erinnern müssen, die in der Scholastik wieder zu Ehren kamen; denn auch diese Lehren führten zur Annahme einer psychisch-physischen "Identität" von Vater und Sohn, und sie blieben daher seitens der Juristen keineswegs unbeachtet.[81]

Es bereitet nunmehr auch keine Schwierigkeiten, das Bibelzitat Johannes 14, 9, das der Verfasser des Testaments E unmittelbar folgen läßt, richtig einzureihen und zu bewerten. Nach römischem Recht, so habe der Kaiser angeblich gesagt, stellten die Söhne des Kaisers Person in der Welt dar: "Es steht nämlich geschrieben: 'Wer mich sieht, sieht auch meinen Vater'." Hier ist es nun zur Abwechslung die theologisch-dogmatische Wesensgleichheit von Gottvater und Gott dem Sohn, durch welche die Identität von Vater und Sohn *fictione iuris* erhärtet wird. Es wäre jedoch ein totales Verkennen der Methode juristischen Argumentierens im Spätmittelalter, wollte man annehmen, der Autor von E stünde mit dieser theologischen Überhöhung einer juristischen Fiktion allein. An Beispielen für diese Methode besteht wahrlich kein Mangel,[82] und die genaue Parallele für den vorliegenden Fall bietet sich in der Tat bei einem französischen Juristen, Jean de Terre Rouge, der bald nach 1400 einen Traktat über das Thronfolgerecht in Frankreich schrieb.[83]

Den Anlaß zu dem Traktat gab der seit 1381 offenkundige Wahnsinn Karls VI. von Frankreich und die danach unter dem Druck burgundischer Ansprüche resultierende Frage, ob der Dauphin *rege vivente* zur Thronfolge und Regierungsübernahme berechtigt sei. Jean de Terre Rouge untersucht eingehend die Gründe, die für die Nachfolge des Sohnes, und zumal des Erstgeborenen sprechen, und kommt dabei zu einer ganzen Anzahl von "Schlüssen," deren einige hier erwähnt seien. Vater und Sohn, obwohl man sie unterscheide, gelten dennoch in Bezug auf Art und Natur als ein und derselbe, und zwar nicht nur im Hinblick auf die allgemeine Gattungsnatur des Menschen, sondern auf die partikulare Natur des Vaters: im Samen des Menschen sei, wie Aristoteles und Thomas von Aquino dargelegt hätten, *quaedam vis impressiva, activa, derivata ab anima generantis et a suis remotis parentibus* wirksam, *et sic est identitas particularis naturae patris et filii*.[84] Terre

---

[80] BF, 4619; Winkelmann, *Acta imperii inedita*, I, Nr. 488, S. 408, Z. 29, herangezogen von Kloos, *DA*, XIII (1957), S. 164, Anm. 60, nach dem der Brief Diktat des Petrus de Prece ist.

[81] Vgl. darüber die umfassende Arbeit von Erna Lesky, *Die Zeugungs- und Vererbungslehren der Antike und ihr Nachwirken* (Abh. d. Akad. d. Wiss. in Mainz, Geistes- und Sozialwiss. Kl., 1950, Nr. 19 [1951]); und für die Scholastik A. Mitterer, *Die Zeugung der Organismen, insbesondere des Menschen, nach dem Weltbild des hl. Thomas von Aquin und dem der Gegenwart* (Wien, 1947); s. auch in *Zs. f. kath. Theol.*, LVII (1933), 491–556. Vgl. unten, Anm. 84.

[82] Vgl. Kantorowicz, "Mysteries of State: An Absolutist Concept and its Late Mediaeval Origins," *Harvard Theological Review*, XLVIII (1955), 65–91, insbes. S. 76ff.

[83] Iohannes de Terra Rubea, *De iure futuri successoris legitimi in regiis hereditatibus*, gedruckt als Anhang zu Francisci Hotomani (Hotman), *Consilia* (Geneva, 1586), 27–62. Eine gute Analyse des Traktats gibt André Lemaire, *Les lois fondamentales de la monarchie française d'après les théoriciens de l'ancien régime* (Paris, 1907), 54ff; vgl. auch John Milton Potter, "The Development and Significance of the Salic Law of the French," *EHR*, 52 (1937), 235–253; William Farr Church, *Constitutional Thought in Sixteenth-Century France* (Cambridge, Mass., 1941), 28f. In Betracht kommen hier im wesentlichen die Konklusionen von Tract. I, art. 2, S. 35ff.

[84] Tract. I, art. 2, Concl. 1: *quod pater et filius, licet distinguantur, supposito tamen unum idem sunt specie et natura nedum communi (quia uterque homo), sed etiam in natura particulari patris. Probatur conclusio: nam secundum Philosophum in semine hominis est quaedam vis impressiva etc., ut haec habentur et notantur per sanctum Thomam in 1. parte, quaest. ult. art. 1 [cf. Summa Theol., I, q. 119, art. 1, resp. 2;*

Rouge berührt dann die kanonistische Lehre, nach der in Bezug auf das Amt Amts-vorgänger und Amtsnachfolger als eine Person zu gelten haben,[85] und erhärtet dies da-durch, daß nach den Anschauungen des Erbrechts der Sohn schon zu Lebzeiten des Vaters *dominus cum patre rerum patris* sei, so daß das von Vater und Sohn gleichsam gemein-schaftlich überlagerte *dominium* auf den Erben ohne Unterbrechung übergehe.[86] Da nun Vater und Sohn ihrer Natur nach gleich seien, so lassen sich auf dieses Verhältnis auch die Worte der Schrift anwenden, etwa das Wort des Paulus (Römer 8, 17): *Si filius ergo heres*; oder das Wort des Johannes-Evangeliums (16, 15): *Omnia quaecunque habet Pater, mea sunt;* oder das Wort des Vaters im Gleichnis vom Verlorenen Sohn (Lukas 15, 31): *Fili, tu semper mecum es, et omnia mea tua sunt,* wozu der Autor hinzufügt: *scilicet per identitatem paternae naturae.*[87] Es sei hier nicht weiter auf diese ins Dynastische getragenen christo-logischen und biblischen Beweise eingegangen; denn das Gesagte genügt vollständig, um zu erkennen, in welchen gedanklichen Rahmen der Passus des Testaments E gehört: die Söhne stellen des Kaisers eigene Person in der Welt dar, denn es steht geschrieben *Qui videt me, videt et Patrem meum.* Der Sachverhalt ist durch den französischen Juristen der späteren Zeit wohl völlig geklärt, und das einzig Überraschende ist die Tatsache, daß diese Anschauungen schon um 1250 voll entwickelt waren.

Ein später Autor mag uns noch in anderer Beziehung zu Hilfe kommen, Johannes Gerson, der in seinem reichhaltigen Traktat *Vivat Rex* auf die Identität von Vater und Sohn zu sprechen kommt und dabei gleichzeitig andeutet, daß auch noch in anderer Be-ziehung der Vater im Sohne fortlebe. Gerson nennt den Dauphin den "ersten und wahren Erben des Königs" und schließt dann folgende Betrachtung an:

> Est enim [*Delphinus*] tanquam una cum rege persona, secundum Sapientis dictum Ecclesiastici XXX; "*Mortuus est pater et quasi non est mortuus, reliquit enim similem filium post se.*" Pater post naturalem, aut civilem, mortem in filii sui adhuc vivit persona.[88]

Hier wird das dem Sibyllenspruch "Er lebt und lebt nicht" so nahe verwandte Wort des Jesus Sirach "Er ist tot und ist gleichsam nicht tot" ausdrücklich auf die Identität von Vater und Sohn, König und Thronfolger angewandt. Gerson fügt jedoch hinzu, daß der Vater nach seinem "natürlichen oder zivilen Tod" in der Person seines Sohnes noch fort-lebt. Mit anderen Worten, er unterscheidet de facto zwei verschiedene Tode des Vaters: den natürlichen Tod des Fleisches und den juristischen Tod als König, der ja auch durch Abdankung oder, wie im Falle Karls VI., durch Regierungsunfähigkeit eintreten konnte. Gerson projiziert also die ganze Lehre des *per substitutum vivere* gleichzeitig auf den

---

auch I, q. 118, art. 1, ad 3]. Die einschlägigen Aristoteles-steilen, obwohl besonders zahlreich in *De generatione animalium*, sind doch weit verstreut; vgl. Harold Cherniss, *Aristotle's Criticism of Plato and the Academy* (Baltimore, 1944), 470f.

[85] Concl. 2: *quod sub ratione illius identitatis consuetudo transfert regnum et regni successionem in primogenitum... sicut quando scribitur abbati vel alicui praelato vel officiario seculari vel ecclesiastico, intelligitur scriptum esse sub ratione praelaturae et officii, ut c. quoniam abbas. de offic. delegat.* [c. 14 X 1, 29; Friedberg, II, 162; s. unten, Anm. 90]. *Filiatio enim nihil aliud est, quam illa identitas particularis naturae praesens*

penetrans in filium, ut l. liberorum, de verb. signif. cum gloss. [Dig. 50, 16, 220, v. "*Quam filii*"; vgl. oben, S. 298].

[86] Concl. 4: *quod quia filius est idem cum patre vivente..., ipse est (secundum philosophum) aliquid patris...* Concl. 5: *quod filius vivente patre est quodammodo dominus rerum patris cum eo: ita quod post mortem patris novam hereditatem acquirere non censetur, sed magis dominium (quod habebat) continuare et plenam administrationem consequi...*

[87] Concl. 3 enthält alle diese Bibelstellen.

[88] Gerson, *Vivat Rex*, I, consid. iv, in: *Opera omnia*, ed. Ellies du Pin (Antwerpen, 1706), IV, S. 591. Die Rede wurde 1405 gehalten.

physischen König und auf die Königswürde, die *Dignitas*, die ja *per substitutum* ihre eigene Kontinuität und Sempiternität hat gleichsam "bis ans Ende der Tage." Auf diesen zivilen Tod des Königs, oder vielmehr auf sein ziviles Leben und Fortleben kommt Gerson nochmals zurück. Er führt nämlich aus:

> *De secunda Regis vita verba faciemus, civili videlicet et politica, que status regalis dicitur aut dignitas. Estque eo melior sola vita corporali, quo ipsa est diuturnior per legitimam successionem....*[89]

Das zivile oder politische Leben ist also gleichbedeutend mit dem *status regalis*, der personifizierten *Dignitas* oder dem Amt; und dieses zivile oder politische "Leben" der *Dignitas* steht um so höher als es durch legitime Sukzession längerwährend ist als das bloß leibliche Leben.

In den wenigen hier angeführten Sätzen des Johannes Gerson ist im wesentlichen der gleiche Problemkreis umrissen, der den bisherigen Ausführungen zugrunde lag und der auch in dem angeblichen Testament des Kaisers (E) angedeutet ist. Denn wenn der Kaiser durch das Testament Anstalten trifft, "durch einen *substitutus* zu leuchten und zu leben," und sich zu diesem Zweck an die Söhne wendet, die juristisch seine eigene Person darstellen, so ist damit doch Ähnliches ausgesagt wie von Gerson. Es sind die gleichen Voraussetzungen, von denen beide ausgehen, was natürlich auch für Terre Rouge noch zutrifft. Während uns nun Gersons Zitat aus Jesus Sirach wieder zu dem Sibyllenspruch zurückführen könnte, drängt seine Theorie von einer *secunda Regis vita*, die sich in der *Dignitas* manifestiere, in eine andere Richtung, der hier noch nachzugehen ist.

Die Lehre von der Identität von Vater und Sohn, oder König und Thronfolger, ebenso wie die Idee des Fortlebens in einem *substitutus*, wurzelt nämlich zu allem anderen auch in einem Bereich, in dem Jurisprudenz und Mythologie zusammenstoßen, wodurch wiederum die juristischen Argumente in gewissem Sinne dem Sibyllinum näherrücken. Dies geschieht anscheinend erstmals in der Glosse zum Worte "*substitutum*," die sich in der von Bernhard von Parma um 1241 (oder 1245) verfaßten Glossa ordinaria zu den Dekretalen Gregors IX. findet. Bernhard glossierte die Dekretale *Quoniam abbas* (c. 14 X 1, 29) Papst Alexanders III., in der der Papst das Verfahren des Abtes von Leicester billigte, nach dem Tode des Abtes von Winchester zusammen mit dessen neugewähltem Amtsnachfolger *(abbatem Vincestriae de novo substitutum)* als *iudex delegatus* zu fungieren. Zur Begründung führte der Papst an, daß die ursprüngliche Bestallung nur unter Nennung des Ortsnamens (Abt von Winchester) und nicht mit Nennung des Personennamens[90] er-

[89] *Ibid.*, II prol.; *Opp.*, IV, S. 592. Der Gedanke, daß der König "zwei Leben" — oder noch mehr — habe, ist gleich in der einleitenden Akklamation ausgesprochen: *Vivat [rex] corporaliter, vivat politice et civiliter, vivat spiritualiter et indesinenter...*

[90] c. 14 X 1, 29; Friedberg, II, Sp. 162: *quia sub expressis nominibus locorum et non personarum commissio literarum a nobis emanavit...* Auf die Tatsache, daß die Bestallung ihrerseits entweder von der individuellen päpstlichen Person oder vom Papste kraft seines Amtes vorgenommen werden konnte, sei hier nicht eingegangen, zumal der gewählte Papstname (z. B. Alexander III. im Gegensatz zu Rolandus Bandinelli) seinerseits als unpersönliche Dienstbezeichnung aufgefaßt werden

konnte. Vgl. etwa zum Liber Sextus, Prooem., die Glossa ordinaria, v. "*Bonifacius*," über die päpstliche Namensänderung: *Respondetur hoc fieri, ut ostendatur ad permutationem nominis, factam mutationem hominis: cum enim prius esset purus homo, nunc vicem veri Dei gerit in terris.* Vgl. auch Baldus zum Liber Extra, Prooem., rubr., n. 5f (*In Decretalium volumen commentaria* [Venedig, 1580], fol. 3): *Non ergo istud nomen, Gregorius, est nomen primae impositionis, sed secundae. Propter dignitatem apostolatus fit nova creatura, et nomen proprium tacetur tanquam minus excellens, et nomen secundae inventionis, id est pontificale, debet exprimi. Et ideo si scribetur Papae sub nomine proprio batismali, posset ratione dicere:* "*Istae literae non diriguntur mihi*," *vel quia videtur in contemptum.* Baldus kommt dann darauf zu sprechen, daß, im Gegensatz

folgt sei und sich daher ohne weiteres auch auf jeden Nachfolger im Amt beziehe. Dieses Verfahren mag älterer Praxis entsprochen haben; aber erst Papst Alexander III. hat die bestehende Praxis rationalisiert und damit ein juristisches Prinzip formuliert, dessen Bedeutung die Rechtslehrer der nachfolgenden Zeit unschwer begriffen. Technisch unterschied man fortan klar zwischen Person und Amt, zwischen einer *delegatio facta personae* und einer *delegatio facta dignitati*, die erstere zeitlich beschränkt durch (bestenfalls) die Lebensdauer des Bestallten, die letztere zeitlich unbegrenzt, weil am Amt haftend.[91] Um 1215 hat dann Damasus in einer Glosse zu *Quoniam abbas* das entscheidende Wort geprägt: *Dignitas nunquam perit, individua vero quotidie pereunt.*[92] Als hernach die Dekretale in die offizielle Sammlung Papst Gregors IX. einging (1232), erhielt sie die den Inhalt wiedergebende Aufschrift: "Eine Delegation, die einer Würde [d. h. einem Würdenträger] ohne Nennung des Eigennamens gemacht ist, geht auf den Nachfolger über."[93] Etwa zehn Jahre später gibt dann auch die Glossa ordinaria des Bernhard von Parma den Grund für die nun längst übliche Praxis an: Vorgänger und Nachfolger in einer Würde seien als eine Person zu verstehen *(pro una persona intelliguntur)*, denn "die Würde stirbt nicht," *Dignitas non moritur.*[94] Die Fiktion der Identität von Amtsvorgänger und Amtsnachfolger war in den gleichen Jahren auch von Papst Innocenz IV. in seinem Dekretalenapparat fortmuliert worden,[95] und als Schlagwort *Dignitas non moritur* umschrieb die hinfort herrschende Lehre.

Uns gehen hier nicht die zahlreichen Varianten und Anwendungen des Themas an: daß die Kirche immerwährend ist, *quia Christus non moritur;*[96] daß die *regia dignitas nunquam moritur*, auch wenn der individuelle König stirbt;[97] daß der Princeps nur Gott verpflichtet sei *et dignitati suae quae perpetua est;*[98] oder daß die *regia maiestas nunquam moritur*[99] — Variationen des gleichen Themas, die schließlich in England um die Mitte, in Frankreich gegen Ende dse 16. Jahrhunderts einmünden in die berühmte Formel, die den west-

zum Papst, der Kaiser seinen Namen nicht ändere; das gelte auch für Justinian, der trotz seiner *dignitas alta* dennoch *nomen proprium idem perseverat, licet coruscatione dignitatis polleat.* An anderer Stelle zögert Baldus (zu Dig., Prooem., rubr., n. 30 [Venedig, 1586, fol. 2ᵛ]), die päpstliche Namensänderung als *effectus rei vel alicuius officii designativum* aufzufassen. Die englischen Kronjuristen folgerten schon aus dem Gebrauch des *Pluralis maiestatis*, daß eine Handlung des Königs amtlich und nicht privat sei; vgl. etwa Plowden, *Reports* (s. u. Anm. 100), S. 175 b, wo der Vorsitzende Richter Brook zu diesem Zweck *Magna Carta* von 1215 c. 17 anführt: *sequantur curiam nostram.*

[91] *De ordine iudiciario*, c. 42, ed. Agathon Wunderlich, *Anecdota quae processum civilem spectant* (Göttingen, 1841), 84; cf. Gierke, *Genossenschaftsrecht*, III, S. 271, Anm. 73. Der Traktat war früher dem Damasus zugeschrieben, doch anscheinend zu Unrecht; cf. S. Kuttner, *Repertorium der Kanonistik* (Studi e Testi, 71; 1937), 428, Anm. 3.

[92] Gierke, III, S. 271, Anm. 73, der auch zeigt, daß schon Gotfried von Trani (schrieb ca. 1232, starb 1245) das Prinzip auf das Kaisertum übertrug. Die Definition des Damasus ging dann wörtlich ein in die Glos. ord. zu c. 14 X 1, 29, v. "*substitutum.*"

[93] Friedberg, II, Sp. 162.

[94] Glos. ord. zu c. 14 X 1, 29, v. "*substitutum.*"

[95] Gierke, III, S. 272, Anm. 77, für die Personenidentität von Amtsvorgänger und -nachfolger, die konsequenterweise ineinsgesetzt wird mit der von Erblassr und Erbe; vgl. etwa Johannes Andreae in seiner Glos. ord. zum *Liber Sextus (De regulis iuris*, c. 46; Friedberg, II, S. 1123), v. "*Is qui in ius*": . . . *quia haeres censetur eadem persona cum defuncto, successor cum praedecessore.*

[96] Johannes Andreae, *Novella in Decretales Gregorii IX* (Venedig, 1612), zu c. 4 X 2, 12, n. 5; vgl. Pierre Gillet, *La personnalité juridique en droit ecclésiastique* (Mecheln, 1927), 178. Als *Dignitas* ist natürlich auch der Heilige Stuhl unsterblich, ebenso das Imperium etc. Von zahllosen früheren Stellen abgesehen, vgl. etwa, wegen der scharf betonten Dauer durch Sukzession, Albericus de Rosate, zu Dig. 5, 1, 76, n. 1 (Venedig, 1584, fol. 304ᵛ): *Sedes apostolica non moritur, sed semper durat in persona successoris . . . et dignitas imperialis semper durat . . . et idem in qualibet dignitate, quia perpetuatur in persona successorum . . .*

[97] So z. B. Mattheus de Afflictis, in seiner Glosse zu *Liber aug.*, II, 35, n. 23 (*In utriusque Siciliae Neapolisque sanctiones et constitutiones* [Venedig, 1562], II, fol. 77).

[98] Baldus, zu c. 33 X 2, 24, n. 5 (*In Decretalium volumen commentaria* [Venedig, 1580], fol. 261ᵛ): *Unde imperator . . . non obligatur homini, sed Deo et dignitati suae, quae perpetua est.*

[99] Baldus, zu c. 7 X 1, 2, n. 78 (*In Decret . . .*, fol. 18).

lichen Monarchien zum Eckstein dynastischer Dogmatik wird: *Le roi ne meurt jamais.*[100] Es ist freilich längst nicht genügend bekannt, daß diese Formel sich in direkter Filiation vom 12. Jahrhundert, genauer: von Papst Alexanders Dekretale *Quoniam abbas*, herleitet. Was hier jedoch allein unser Interesse beansprucht, ist die Glosse "*substitutum*" Bernhards von Parma zu dieser Dekretale. Dem Einwand, daß die Bezeichnung "Abt dieses oder jenes Ortes" in Wirklichkeit nur "an Stelle des Eigennamens" stehe, begegnete der Glossator damit, daß er sagte, "Abt von Winchester" sei nicht *proprium nomen, sed singulare . . . et appellativum similiter*, sei also „einzigartig," oder eine Person aussondernd, und zugleich appellativ. Das Seltsame aber ist, daß Bernhard hinter *singulare* einen Vergleich einschiebt, *ut Phoenix*; das heißt: "Abt von Winchester" sei ein Einzelnes, ein Einzelwesen "wie der Vogel Phönix."[101]

Vielleicht mag dieser Vergleich der unsterblichen *Dignitas* und ihrer vielfachen Inkarnationen mit dem Vogel Phönix uns Heutigen abstrus erscheinen, auch wenn wir uns daran erinnern, daß dieser Märchenvogel ein in jeder Beziehung außergewöhnliches Geschöpf war. Denn in jedem gegebenen Augenblick gab es in der Welt ja nur einen einzigen Phönix, der nach einer Lebensdauer von 500 oder mehr Jahren von der Sonne sein Nest in Flammen setzen ließ, selbst die Glut mit den Schwingen anfachte, und schließlich im Feuer den Tod fand, während von den glühenden Aschen — aus einer Raupe oder Puppe auskriechend — sich der neue Phönix erhob.[102] Die volkskundlichen Züge des Phönix-Mythos, widerspruchsvoll in zahllosen Einzelheiten, sind hier von geringerer Bedeutung. In heidnischer wie in christlicher Kunst und Literatur war der Phönix ein Sinnbild der Unsterblichkeit, der Zeitenerneuerung und des Aion. Er diente daher — von der Jungfräulichkeit seiner Zeugung noch ganz abgesehen — auch als ein Sinnbild der Auferstehung Christi und der Christen überhaupt, aber auch als Sinnbild der ewigen Erneuerung und Dauer römischer Kaisermacht.[103] Diese Art der Symbolik interessierte jedoch die mittelalterlichen Juristen nur peripher, obwohl Johannes Andreae

---

[100] Für England vgl. etwa Edmund Plowden, *Commentaries or Reports* (London, 1816), S. 177f für einen Fall (Hill v. Grange) vom Jahre 1554–55, wo die Richter über Akte argumentieren, bei denen der Königstitel zum Namen des Königs hinzugefügt war: "*And King is the name of continuance, which shall always endure as the head and the governor of the people, as the Law presumes . . . and in this the King never dies.*" Im Verlaufe des Arguments erklärte dann einer der Richter, indem er die Essenz von *Quoniam abbas* wiedergibt, "*that the Dignity always continues . . . And then when . . . the relation is to him as King, he as King never dies, although his natural Body dies; but the King in which name it has relation to him, does ever continue . . . From whence we may see that where a thing is referred to a particular king by the name of King, in that case it may extend to his heirs and successors . . .*" Für Frankreich vgl. Jean Bodin, *Les six livres de la république*, I, c. 8 (Paris, 1583 [Erstausgabe 1576], S. 160): "*Car il est certain que le Roy ne meurt jamais, comme l'on dit . . .*" was wohl doch zeigt, daß dieses Wort schon vorher verbreitet war, also wohl in England und Frankreich annähernd gleichzeitg aufkam.

[101] Die Glosse zu c. 14 X 1, 29 ist zu lang, um hier ganz zitiert zu werden; der einschlägige Absatz lautet: *Sed*

videtur quod idem sit, etsi non exprimatur proprium nomen; quia hoc nomen abbas talis loci, loco proprii nominis est . . . Sed non est proprium nomen, sed singulare, ut phoenix, et appellativum similiter . . .

[102] Über den Phönix vgl. Jean Hubaux und Maxime Leroy, *Le mythe du Phénix* (Bibl. de la fac. de philos. et lettres de l'université de Liège, 82; Liège und Paris, 1939); ferner E. Rapisarda, *L'Ave Fenice di L. Cecilio Firmiano Lattanzio* (Raccolta di studi di letteratura cristiana antica 4; Catania, 1946); A.-J. Festugière, in *Monuments Piot*, XXXVIII (1941), 147ff; auch Carl-Martin Edsman, *Ignis divinus* (Lund, 1949), 178–203. K. Burdach, *Rienzo und die geistige Wandlung seiner Zeit. Vom Mittelalter zur Reformation*, II, 1 (Berlin, 1913–1928), S. 83ff. und *passim* bringt weniger zur "Phönixerwartung" des 13. Jhdts. als man erwarten würde.

[103] Vgl. das Phönixgedicht des Laktanz (unten, Anm. 109), Vers 163ff; dazu Hubaux und Leroy, S. 6f, 115, und insbesondere Festugière, a. a. O., S. 149f. Für den Phönix im Kaiserkult und auf Münzen, vgl. etwa J. Lassus, in *Monuments Piot*, XXXVI (1936), 81–122, und Henri Stern, *Le Calendrier de 354* (Paris, 1953), 145ff.

in seiner Glosse zu *Quoniam abbas* auch die folkloristischen Züge des Phönixmythos be-
handelte.[104] Worauf die Juristen mit dem Phönix-Gleichnis hinauswollten, zeigt am
besten eine Glosse des Baldus zu der Dekretale Alexanders III. Baldus zog nämlich aus
Bernhard von Parmas Vergleich der *Dignitas* mit dem Vogel Phönix einen philosophisch
einwandfrei richtigen Schluß: "Der Phönix ist ein höchst einziger und einzigartiger
Vogel, in welchem die ganze Spezies im Individuum erhalten wird."[105] Für Baldus also
war der Phönix einer der seltenen Fälle, in welchen das Einzelwesen gleichzeitig die
ganze Gattung darstellte, so daß hier nun wirklich einmal Gattung und Individuum
zusammenfielen und die Gesamt-Potentialitäten der Phönixgattung im Phönixindividu-
um volle Aktualität wurden. Die Gattung war natürlich unsterblich oder sempitern, das
Individuum hingegen sterblich. Der sagenhafte Vogel verfügte demnach über eine seltsame Zwienatur: er war sowohl Phönix wie die gesamte "Phönixheit," war Individuum
und Gattung, war zugleich singulär und kollektiv, da die ganze Spezies "Phönix" sich
in nie mehr als einem einzigen Exemplar reproduzierte — Eigenschaften also, die der
Vogel Phönix einerseits mit den Engeln gemein hatte, andererseits aber mit der *Dignitas*
geistlicher oder weltlicher Fürsten, der ja wiederum ein *character angelicus* eigentümlich
war.[106]

Mit dem Vogel Phönix war nun juristisch die *Dignitas* insofern vergleichbar, als auch
bei der Abts-, Bischofs-, Königs- oder sonstigen Würde in jedem Augenblick nur ein
Einziger der Repräsentant der korporativ erfaßten "Gattung" — d. h. der langen Reihe
von Amtsvorgängern und Amtsnachfolgern — war. Die Idee des *Per substitutum vivere* war
bei dem Phönix ebenso vollkommen ausgeprägt wie die der "Identität im Wechsel der
Glieder";[107] und wenn es je eine gleichsam notorische Identität oder Einheit von "Vater
und Sohn" gab, so gewiß im Falle des legendären Phönix. Gerade diese Einheit war es
nämlich, die als ein besonderer Charakterzug des Wundervogels von allen antiken
Autoren ganz scharf hervorgehoben wurde. "Am geburtstäglichen Todestag ver-
scheidend und nachfolgend; wiederum ein Phönix, wo schon keiner mehr war; wiederum
er selbst, der soeben nicht war; ein anderer und doch derselbe," so beschreibt Tertullian
das Fortleben des Phönix.[108] Lactanz, nicht weniger gedrängt in seinen Bildern, sagt:
"Sich selbst ist er selbst der Sproß, ist sein eigener Vater und sein eigener Erbe ... Er
ist der Gleiche und doch nicht der Gleiche, der er selbst ist und doch nicht er selbst"
*(Ipsa sibi proles, suus est pater et suus heres ... Est eadem sed non eadem, quae est ipsa nec ipsa
est ...).*[109] Und ähnlich Claudian: "Er ist der Vater, und er ist sein Sproß, und keiner ist

---

[104] Johannes Andreae, zu c. 14 X 1, 29, n. 30f *(Novella* [oben, Anm. 96], fols. 206ᵛ–207).

[105] Baldus, zu c. 14 X 1, 29, n. 3 *(In Decretalium,* fol. 107): *Est autem avis unica singularissima, in qua totum genus servatur in individuo.* Den generischen Charakter der *Dignitas* unterstreicht noch Sir Edward Coke, Calvin's Case, in: *Reports,* VII, fol. 10 b: *"It is true that the King in genere dieth not, but, no question, in individuo he dieth."*

[106] Auf angelologische Fragen wie die der Individua-tion der Engel sei hier nicht weiter eingegangen; vgl. zur Orientierung Überweg-Baumgartner, *Grundriß der Gesch. d. Philos. d. patrist. und scholast. Zeit¹⁰* (Berlin, 1915), 498

und 580, und, für die von Thomas von Aquino abweichen-de Auffassung des Duns Scotus, Etienne Gilson, *Jean Duns Scot* (Paris, 1952), S. 399ff. Engel, Phönixe und Würden (oder Körperschaften) haben jedenfalls zahlreiche Züge gemein; vgl. oben, Anm. 72.

[107] Hierfür Gierke, *Genossenschaftsrecht,* III, 270ff, 277.

[108] Tertullian, *De resurrectione mortuorum,* XIII, 2: *...natali fine decedens atque succedens, iterum phoenix ubi nemo iam, iterum ipse qui non iam, alius idem.*

[109] Laktanz, *Carmen de ave Phoenice,* Vers 167ff, ed. Hubraux und Leroy, a. a. O., S. XV, mit leichter Ab-weichung von der Ausg. Brandt's in *CSEL,* XXVII, 146.

der Erschaffer ... Der der Zeuger gewesen, schießt nun hervor als die gleiche Geburt und er folgt als ein neuer ... O Glücklicher du, und Erbe deiner selbst."[110]

Es lohnt vielleicht darauf aufmerksam zu machen, daß der Phönix nicht nur Vater und Kind seiner selbst, sondern immer wieder auch "Erbe seiner selbst" genannt wird, z. B. auch von Ambrosius.[111] Dies mag dazu beigetragen haben, daß bei Behandlung der Frage der Sukzession den Juristen das Phönixgleichnis überhaupt einfiel, da ja die Identität von Vater und Sohn, Vorgänger und Nachfolger gewohnheitsmäßig im Zusammenhang mit dem Erbrecht erörtert wurde. Es ist im übrigen durchaus möglich, daß der Vergleich der *Dignitas* mit dem Vogel Phönix nicht erst von Bernhard von Parma eingeführt wurde, sondern auf frühere Glossatoren zurückging. Hier genügt es jedoch festzustellen, daß jedenfalls zu Anfang der 40er Jahre das Phönixbild zur Verdeutlichung der vielzitierten Dekretale *Quoniam abbas* schon im Umlauf war. Auch darauf sei noch verwiesen, daß in dem von Petrus de Vinea verfaßten Kampfmanifest *Levate in circuitu* (1239, April 20) deutlich auf die Dekretale Alexanders III. angespielt wurde,[112] und ebenso, daß man Friedrich II. selbst schon zu Lebzeiten gelegentlich als "Phönix" bezeichnete.[113] Das alles soll nicht überwertet werden; auch läßt es sich nirgends erweisen, daß die Sibyllentexte sich an die Phönixerzählungen angelehnt hätten, selbst wenn in den echten Sibyllen der Phönix einmal erwähnt wird.[114] Dennoch stehen sich Phönixerwartungen und Sibyllenprophetie nahe genug, und ebensowenig darf es übersehen werden, daß Aussagen über den Phönix wie z. B. *est eadem sed non eadem* oder *est ipsa nec ipsa est* inhaltlich wie formal nächstverwandt sind dem Spruch der Erythräa *Vivit et non vivit*. Zusammen mit Jesus Sirachs *Mortuus est et quasi non mortuus est* waren sie auf den gleichen Ideenkomplex bezogen.

Es ist nicht schwierig, das Gesagte nunmehr zusammenzufassen und die einfachen Schlüsse zu ziehen. Von den verschiedensten Gesichtspunkten herkommend und unter Zuhilfenahme der verschiedensten Bilder und Gleichnisse wurde in der ersten Hälfte des 13. Jahrhunderts die Idee der Dynastie gleichsam ausgearbeitet oder rationalisiert und auch für das Kaisertum, für die staufische *Caesarea stirps*, in Anspruch genommen. Dabei spielte die Lehre von der Identität von Vater und Sohn, Erblasser und Erben, Monarchen und Thronfolger, Amtsvorgänger und Amtsnachfolger die wohl wichtigste Rolle. Diese Lehre wurde vom Kaiser selbst wie von den Kaisersöhnen in mehr oder

---

[110] Claudian, *Phoenix*, Vers 24, 69f., 101, ed. Hubaux und Leroy, S. XXIff:

> *Sed pater est prolesque sui nulloque creante* ...
> *Qui fuerat genitor, natus nunc prosilit idem*
> *Succeditque novus* ...
>   ... *O felix heresque tui.*

[111] Ambrosius, *Expositio in Ps. CXVIII*, c. 13, ed. Petschenig, in *CSEL*, LXII, 428, Z. 19: ...*et sui heres corporis et cineris sui factus*. Bei Hubaux und Leroy, a. a. O., S. 199ff wird das *heres*-Problem ganz ungenügend behandelt.

[112] Auf die nicht unerheblichen kanonistischen Einschläge bei Petrus de Vinea hat kürzlich Brian Tierney, *Foundations of the Conciliar Theory* (Cambridge, 1955), S. 77ff. aufmerksam gemacht. Auf *Quoniam abbas* nimmt Bezug *MGH, Const.*, II, S. 297, Z. 23ff: *non in contemptu papalis officii vel apostolice dignitatis... set persone prevaricationem arguimus*.

[113] Nikolaus von Bari (ed. Kloos, *DA*, XI [1954] S. 170, § 5) vergleicht Friedrich wegen seiner Einzigkeit mit dem Phönix, wie dies später zum allgemeinen Hofstil der Renaissance-Monarchen gehörte: *Magnus est dignitate honoris... Ipse est sol in firmamento mundi... Unus est et secundum non habet, fenix pulcherrima pennis aureis decorata*. Daß Friedrich selbst *(De arte venandi cum avibus,* II, c. 2) den Phönix erwähnt, freilich nur um Plinius' Theorie von der Zwiegeschlechtigkeit des Vogels abzulehnen, ist hier natürlich ohne Belang.

[114] Vgl. *Sibyllinische Weissagungen*, VIII, 139, ed. A. Kurfess (München, 1951), S. 166.

weniger allgemeinen Worten herangezogen. Sie lag dem Sonnenglcichnis zugrunde, dem Scheiden der alten und dem Aufgehen der neuen Sonne, die doch immer die gleiche bleibt — *aliusque et idem*. Das "Fortleben im Sohne" war in dem angeblichen Testament juristisch interpretiert als ein *per substitutum vivere*. Die Juristen selbst anerkannten das Prinzip der "Dauer im Wechsel," des Fortlebens eines Gerichtshofes, einer Legion, eines Volkes, einer Herde, eines Schiffes trotz Substitution aller Komponenten, ja machten die Substitution geradezu zum Lebensprinzip einer ewigen Dauer: *perpetuatio fit per successionem et subrogationem*. Das römische Erbrecht kanonisierte die Identität von Erblasser und Erben als eine *fictio iuris*, und die Kanonisten vertraten die gleiche Anschauung auf Grund einiger Sätze des Decretums. Hinzu kamen die Zeugungs- und Vererbungslehren der Antike, die — von der Scholastik rezipiert — gleichfalls das Einssein von Vater und Sohn aus quasi naturwissenschaftlichen Gründen vertraten und die vielleicht mitverantwortlich waren für die am Kaiserhofe jedenfalls vertretene Lehre von der besonderen Subtilität der Königsseelen.[115] Herangezogen wurden auch die evangelischen Zeugnisse für die Wesensgleichheit von Vater und Sohn. Von der Kanonistik zuerst erfaßt, von den Zivilisten jedoch alsbald übernommen, verbreitete sich die eine Identität von Amtsvorgänger und Amtsnachfolger voraussetzende Lehre der *Dignitas quae non moritur*, die schließlich hinführte zu dem Motto: *Le roi ne meurt jamais*. Und diese Lehre wurde wiederum verquickt mit dem Mythos vom Vogel Phönix, in dem Unsterblichkeitsglauben, Fortleben durch Substitution und Identität von Erzeuger und Erzeugtem zusammenflossen.

In diesen allgemeinen Zusammenhang reiht sich nun das unter dem Namen der Erythräischen Sibylle nach 1250 in Umlauf gesetzte Vaticinium ohne weiteres ein. Der alte Adler "lebt und lebt nicht, da eines der Adlerjungen und ein Junges der Jungen überlebt." Es bleibt dabei unbenommen, den nach dem Physiologus sich stets selbstverjüngenden Adler mit dem Phönix in Verbindung zu bringen, dessen Stelle der Adler auch sonst oft genug eingenommen hat.[116] Diese Spekulationen scheinen mir jedoch ganz überflüssig und nebensächlich zu sein, da das angeblich rätselhafte *Vivit et non vivit* sich völlig zwanglos aus den Anschauungen, auch den Rechtsanschauungen, der Zeit erklären läßt.

Viel seltsamer ist dann freilich die Abwandlung der rationalen juristischen Argumente ins Sagenhafte, ist der Prozeß der Mystifikation. Der Kernspruch *Vivit et non vivit*, so lange er mit dem Überleben der Nachkommen, und das heißt mit den dynastischen Hoffnungen, verbunden blieb, war nicht "mystischer" als das Stichwort *Dignitas non*

---

[115] Vgl. den Brief an König Konrad (vermutlich eine Stilübung) bei Huillard-Bréholles, *Hist. dipl.*, V, S. 274f: *Immo tanto se maiori nota notabiles faciunt principes inscii quam privati, quanto nobilitas sanguinis per infusionem subtilis et nobilis anime facit ipsos esse pre ceteris susceptibiles discipline.* Die zugrunde liegende Lehre läßt sich nicht eindeutig feststellen, doch kommt sie wohl am nächsten der Lehre von der Erschaffung der Königsseelen in der Kore kosmou, fragm. XXIV, ed. A. D. Nock und A.-J. Festugière, *Corpus Hermeticum*, IV (Paris, 1954), 52ff. Von dem Corpus Hermeticum war damals jedoch wohl nur der *Asclepius* bekannt. Man kann natürlich auch an die Lehre von den *rationes seminales* denken; vgl. Lesky, a. a. O. (oben, Anm. 81), S. 164ff, auch 172f; Hans Meyer, *Geschichte der Lehre von den Keimkräften von der Stoa bis zum Ausgang der Patristik* (Bonn, 1914), bes. 184ff. für Augustin und Macrobius als Vermittler der Lehre.

[116] Hubaux und Leroy, *Le mythe du Phénix* (s. Index s. v. "Aigle") haben diese Parallele vielleicht zu weit getrieben. Immerhin ist die Ähnlichkeit von Adler und Phönix auf Grund des Physiologus gegeben, wo die beiden Vögel nacheinander behandelt werden (cc. 8 und 9).

moritur, regia maiestas non moritur, oder *Le roi ne meurt jamais.* Der Spruch war, sozusagen, auf diese Lehren hin angelegt und hätte wie in den westlichen Monarchien in sie einmünden können. Dies geschah jedoch nicht. Statt dessen wurde der Satz schon von Salimbene verbunden mit dem persönlichen, physischen Tode des Kaisers unter angeblich seltsamen Umständen, das heißt mit der durchaus legendären und unhistorischen *mors abscondita* des Kaisers. *Vivit et non vivit* erschien damit als das Resultat des "verborgenen Todes" und wurde nunmehr auf ein rein persönliches mystisch-physisches Fortleben des kaiserlichen Individuums bezogen, und nicht mehr auf das unpersönliche und überpersönliche Fortleben der Dynastie oder der *Dignitas.* Die ursprünglichen Zusammenhänge waren somit verwischt, und die Mystifikation lag den Joachiten und hernach den Transalpinen offenbar mehr und näher am Herzen, als die logischen Schlüsse der Civilisten und Kanonisten — Schlüsse, die mangels einer Dynastie im nachstaufischen Reiche auch keinen rechten Nährboden fanden.

So geht die Kaisersage im Grunde zurück auf das Mißverstehen der rationalen, juristischen Argumente für eine Kontinuität der Dynastie und eine Sempiternität der *Dignitas,* was natürlich keineswegs ausschließt, daß Mißverständnisse — ähnlich wie Fälschungen — historische Fakten erster Ordnung sein können, die selbst wiederum Geschichte machen. Es ist jedoch kaum übertrieben zu sagen, daß die Sage vom Fortleben des in den Berg entrückten und im Berge schlummernden Kaisers *qui non moritur* das irrational-verschwommene oder legendäre Gegenstück bildet zu dem juristisch-rationalen Dogma der westlichen Monarchien: *Le roi ne meurt jamais.*

PRO PATRIA MORI
IN MEDIEVAL POLITICAL THOUGHT

CHRISTMAS, 1914. Belgium then was occupied by the German armies. Cardinal Mercier, the ultrapatriotic primate of Belgium and archbishop of Malines, was in many respects the champion of the intellectual resistance of his country against the occupying power. To comfort his flock and to encourage his fellow citizens the cardinal distributed on Christmas Day, 1914, his famous pastoral letter *Patriotism and Endurance*. In it he developed some challenging ideas about the relations between patriotism and religion, and about the otherworldly effects of death on the battlefield. "Who does not feel that patriotism is 'consecrated,' and that an attack on the national dignity is a sort of sacrilegious profanation?" The cardinal had been asked whether the soldier who fell in the service of a just cause ("and that ours clearly is") was a martyr. The Prince of the Church had to answer that, in a strict and theological sense, the soldier was not a martyr, because he died arms in hand, whereas the martyr gives himself up to his executioners without resistance.

> But if you ask me what I think of the eternal salvation of a brave man, who consciously gives his life to defend the honor of his country and to avenge violated Justice, I do not hesitate to reply that there is no doubt whatever that Christ crowns military valor, and that death christianly accepted assures to the soldier the salvation of his soul. ... The soldier who dies to save his brothers, to protect the hearths and the altars of his country, fulfills the highest form of love. ... We are justified in hoping for them the immortal crown which encircles the foreheads of the elect. For such is the virtue of an act of perfect love that, of itself alone, it wipes out a whole life of sin. Of a sinner instantly it makes a saint.[1]

To this pastoral letter some objections were raised immediately, and not only on the part of the German governor-general, the cultured and educated Baron von

Reprinted, with permission, from *American Historical Review*, LVI (1951), 472–492. The original has this prefatory note:

This paper, read at the joint luncheon of the American Historical Association, Pacific Coast Branch, and the American Philosophical Association, Pacific Division, on December 29, 1949, at Mills College, in Oakland, California, is published here with few minor changes and some additions. The intention of this address, which had to meet the fields of interest of both historians and philosophers, is clearly not to exhaust the subject but to outline with a few strokes the, in fact, much more complicated problem. I am greatly indebted to Professors Ludwig Edelstein and Leonardo Olschki for various valuable suggestions.

[1] The pastoral letter has been published often; see, e.g., *A Shepherd among Wolves: War-Time Letters of Cardinal Mercier*, selected by Arthur Boutwood (London, n.d.), 46f, whose translation I use here.

Bissing.[2] On March 25, 1915, Cardinal Billot, a patriotic Frenchman, severely censured the words used by his confrère in the Sacred College. "To say," he wrote, "that the mere fact of dying consciously for the just cause of the Fatherland 'suffices to assure salvation' means to substitute the Fatherland for God . . ., to forget what is God, what is sin, what is divine forgiveness."[3]

If two eminent Princes of the Church disagree so profoundly on a fundamental matter of life and death, and of life after death, we may be sure that the reasons for such a basic disagreement are to be sought in a distant past and that the whole problem has a long history. In fact, to the ears of the professional medievalist almost every word of Cardinal Mercier's pastoral letter has the familiar ring of a long-established tradition. And since the involved problem has both a historical and a philosophical background, it may be fitting to trace, if in a necessarily sketchy fashion, the early development of the idea *Pro patria mori* within the political concepts of the medieval Christian world.[4]

*   *   *

Every schoolboy reading his first Latin sentences would soon learn in what high esteem Greek and Roman antiquity held those who died in battle for their community, *polis* or *res publica*. The reasons were many and complex. There was, in earlier times, the religious fear of a return of the dead, later the religious desire to apotheosize the dead.[5] The quasi-deification of war heroes was fully developed by the fifth century B.C. at the latest. We need only to think of Sparta. But we may think also of that broad alley on the Athenian Kerameikos, the Dromos, where on either side official tombs honored those who had died in battle for their city, and where Pericles delivered the funeral speech in which he placed the first victims of the Peloponnesian War among the immortals.[6] Or we may recall the lines of Vergil where Aeneas sees in the Elysian plains, dwelling together with priests and poets and prophets, those who had suffered for the fatherland (*ob patriam pugnando volnera passi*), and who, as the true predecessors of the crowned martyrs and confessors of the Church, had "their brows bound with snowy fillets," the insignia of agonal victory like the crown with which the fillet so often was combined.[7] And we need only to mention the name of Cicero or that of Horace, whose second "Roman Ode" (III, 2) is alluded to

[2] For the German reaction, see D. J. Cardinal Mercier, *Cardinal Mercier's Own Story* (New York, 1920), 45ff. The correspondence between Cardinal Mercier and Baron von Bissing, or Baron von der Lancken, makes peculiarly interesting reading for the historian, for there is a striking contrast between the debasement and brutalization of style, language, and human standards which has taken place between the two world wars and the courteous form, the generally humane tone, and the occupying power's great patience which those letters disclose.

[3] Cardinal Billot's response is known to me only from the excerpts quoted by Franz Cumont, *Lux perpetua* (Paris, 1949), 445, who has called attention to the conflicting opinions of the two cardinals.

[4] I do not find that the problem, though deserving a monographic study, has been discussed before. Carl

Erdmann, *Die Entstehung des Kreuzzugsgedankens* (Stuttgart, 1935), touches upon related ideas and adduces relevant material.

[5] See, e.g., Cumont, pp. 332ff.

[6] George Karo, *An Attic Cemetery: Excavations in the Kerameikos at Athens* (Philadelphia, 1943), 24f.

[7] Vergil, *Aeneid*, VI, 660ff; for the fillets, see Eduard Norden, *P. Vergilius Maro Aeneis Buch VI* (Leipzig, 1903), 293; for the connection of fillet and crown (surviving in the bows adorning our funerary wreaths), see Erwin R. Goodenough, "The Crown of Victory in Judaism," *Art Bulletin*, XXVIII (1946), 139ff, especially p. 150, and for the connection with the diadem, Andreas Alföldi, "Insignien und Tracht der römischen Kaiser," *Römische Mitteilungen*, I (1935), 146; cf. Richard Delbrück, "Der spätantike Kaiserornat," *Antike*, VIII (1932), 7f.

in the title of the present paper, in order to conjure up that huge compound of ethical values which in Rome were inseparable from the death *pro patria* and which later were revived by Petrarch and the early humanists, with their new standards of civic virtues and merits.

In Greek as well as in Roman antiquity, the term πατρίς or *patria* referred chiefly, if not exclusively, to the city. Only barbarians were named, like modern nationals, after their country, and only barbarians were *patriōtai*, whereas the Greeks were proud of being *politai*, citizens. The city, of course, would include the surroundings, which might even be expanded, as sometimes in Roman poetry, to the whole of the Italian peninsula. To the Stoics, it is true, and to the other philosophical schools as well, the notion of *patria* may have meant the universe, the *kosmos* of which they were citizens. But then this was a philosophical or religious, and not a political, conception. For the Roman Empire or the *orbis Romanus* would not have been referred to as *patria*, and if a soldier, when killed in the defense of Gaul or Spain or Syria, died nevertheless a hero's death *pro patria*, it was a death for the *res publica Romana*, for Rome and all Rome stood for—her gods, perhaps the *Dea Roma*, the imperial *pater patriae*, or Roman education and life in general—but not for the territory he happened to defend.[8] *Patria*, most certainly, did not mean the same thing at all times, but usually meant the city.

Although Greek and Roman antiquity had made heroes of and almost deified the victims of war, and although the ancient model otherwise determined medieval thought in more than one respect, the Western mind in the feudal age was reluctant or failed to accept those views. Civic death *pro patria*, whatever "*patria*" then may have designated, had lost its religious flavor and semireligious connotations. Christianity was certainly one factor causing that change. With regard to the Christians, "every place abroad is their fatherland, and in their fatherland they are aliens," says the writer of the "Letter to Diognet."[9] The ties fettering man to his *patria* on earth, already slackening in the Late Empire, had lost their value. "Why should that man be praised?" asks Saint Augustine. "Because he was a lover of his city? This he could be carnally. . . . But he was not a lover of the City above."[10] And in the *City of God* (especially V, 18) Augustine assembles scores of examples to show that, if the Romans did their great deeds for human glory and an earthly city, it should be far easier for Christians to do similar things for the love of the *patria aeterna*. How much easier for a Christian to offer himself up for the eternal fatherland if a Curtius, leaping into the chasm, made the supreme sacrifice to obey the false gods! The Christian, according to the teaching of the Fathers had become the citizen of

[8] The *orbis Romanus* (see, in general, Joseph Vogt, *Orbis Romanus* [Tübingen, 1929]) was both linked to and set over against the *urbs;* see, e.g., the legend *vota orbis et urbis* on coins of Constantine and Licinius, which has survived in the papal blessing *urbi et orbi*. But the *orbis Romanus*, except in a philosophical sense and when coinciding with *oikoumene*, would not have been *patria* despite the lines (Rutilius Namatianus, *De reditu suo*, I, 63 and 66):

Fecisti patriam diversis gentibus unam . . .
Urbem fecisti quod prius orbis erat.

[9] Quoted by Karl Ludwig Schmidt, *Die Polis in Kirche und Welt* (Rektoratsprogramm der Universität Basel, 1939), 47, a book offering several clues to the present problem; see Migne, *PL*, II, 1173C.

[10] Augustine, *Contra Gaudentium*, I, 37, in Migne, *PL*, XLIII, 729. The chief evidence is Book V of the *Civitas Dei*, especially V, 18, where the great deeds of individual Romans for their purely terrestrial *patria* are adduced to encourage even greater Christian deeds *pro aeterna patria*.

a city in another world. Ethically, death for the carnal fatherland meant little if compared with that for the spiritual *patria*, Jerusalem in Heaven, or with the true models of civic self-sacrifice, the martyrs, confessors, and holy virgins. The saints had given their lives for the invisible community in heaven and the celestial city, the true *patria* of their desires; and a final return to that fatherland in Heaven should be the normal desire of every Christian soul while wandering in exile on earth.

> *Nostrum est interim*
> *mentem erigere*
> *Et totis patriam*
> *votis appetere*
> *Et ad Jerusalem*
> *a Babylonia*
> *Post longa regredi*
> *tandem exsilia*

sings Abelard,[11] who may stand here for thousands of others who have uttered the same idea. After all, in the exequies—not to mention many other places in the liturgies—the priest would entreat God that the holy angels be ordered to receive the soul of the defunct and to conduct it *ad patriam Paradisi*. Heaven had become the common fatherland of the Christians, comparable to the κοινή πατρίς which in ancient times had designated the netherworld.[12]

If religiously and ethically the Christian idea of *patria* was well defined, the same cannot be said of the political meaning of *patria* during the centuries of Western feudalism. To be sure, the word itself existed and it was used time and again. But its meaning—much more closely related to antiquity than to modern times—was practically always "native town or village," the home (*Heimat*) of a man. A knight going to war might make provisions for returning home safely (*sanus in patriam fuero regressus*), or a person might return to a town or county *ad visendam patriam parentesque*.[13] This, though most generally the meaning of *patria*, did not necessarily exclude a lingering on of the broader and more exalted ancient notion of "fatherland" into Christian times. The monks of early Frankish monasteries, for example, might be held to pray *pro statu ecclesiae et salute regis vel patriae*

---

[11] Abelard, Hymn 29, "Sabbato ad Vesperas," in Guido Maria Dreves, *Analecta Hymnica*, XLVIII (1905), 163, No. 139. The stanza (4) is preceded by three stanzas describing the celestial city and the court of the King of Heaven.

[12] See Plutarch, *Moralia*, 113C, ed. by William R. Paton and Hans Wegehaupt (Leipzig, 1925), I, 234, 2.

[13] The examples, chosen at random, could easily be multiplied *ad infinitum*. For those quoted, see *Formulae Sangallenses* in *MGH, Leges*, V, 401, 23, and 402, 17; *MGH, Briefe der deutschen Kaiserzeit*, V: *Briefsammlungen der Zeit Heinrichs IV.*, ed. by Erdmann and Fickermann, 369, 3, and *passim*. Even in much later times, and not only in Italy, would *patria* refer to the city. When Philip IV of France made a treaty with the bishop of Verdun, a bishopric then belonging to the empire, and demanded that the bishop "*per se et gentes suas tenetur patriam iuvare pro posse suo et defendere bona fide una cum gentibus nostris*," the stipulation referred not to France as *patria* but to the city of Verdun; Fritz Kern, *Acta Imperii, Angliae et Franciae* (Tübingen, 1911), No. 155, pp. 103, 10. The plural *patriae*, e.g., in a document of Rudolf Habsburg mentioning *patriae et provinciae ad imperium spectantes* (see *MGH, Leges* IV, vol. III, No. 653, p. 654, 2), means cities; cf. Ausonius, *Ordo nobilium urbium*, XVII, 166 (Bordeaux): "*Haec patria est, patrias sed Roma supervenit omnes.*" Also in the letters of Rather of Verona (*MGH, Briefe der deutschen Kaiserzeit*, I, ed. by Fritz Weigle, 49, 4, and *passim*) the word has a local meaning.

or "for the eternal salvation and the happiness of king or fatherland";[14] and even the title *pater patriae* might be occasionally applied to a medieval prince,[15] cases in which *patria* certainly meant more than just the native village. Those, however, were formalized phrases of ancient tradition, and they reflected medieval "patriotism" as little as the bookish reproductions from Vergil, Horace, and other classical authors in the works of medieval poets and writers.[16]

For all that, however, a warrior's heroic self-sacrifice did exist in the Middle Ages; only, the man would offer himself up for his lord and master (rather than for a territory or an idea of "state"), comparable to the martyr's death for *his* Lord and Master. The political sacrifice of a knight would have been personal and individual rather than "public," and it was that personal sacrifice resulting from the relations between lord and vassal, or from the idea of personal fealty, which medieval literature has so abundantly praised and often glorified. A vassal would follow the duke of Champagne or defend the count of Burgundy against aggression. But it would be the "duke" or the "count," and not some "eternal Burgundy" or an "idea of Champagne" for which it would have been worth while to shed one's blood, even though the ancient personifications of provinces survived in medieval imagery.[17] In any event, *patria* had lost the emotional content which had characterized it in antiquity, while on the other hand *patria* was as yet far from coinciding with a national territory or a territorial state as in modern times.

Like other great changes in history leading to modern civilization a change in the concept of *patria* can be traced to the twelfth and thirteenth centuries. The transformation implied that indeed the classic emotional values of *patria* were recovered as they descended, so to speak, from heaven back to earth; but it implied also that henceforth the notion of "fatherland" might well transcend the ancient city limitations and refer to a national kingdom, or to the "crown" as the visible symbol of a national territorial community.[18]

Within certain limited fields that development can be grasped almost statistically. Taxation, for instance, may be used as an example for illustrating the re-emergence of the notion of *patria*. The feudal aids which were due on three occasions—ransom for the

[14] The formula occurs so often in early Frankish documents, while disappearing later, that it must be of ancient origin and must go back to some *supplicatio*; see, e.g., *Formulae Marculfi*, in *MGH, Leges*, V, 40, 19, and 43, 2, or the Council of Compiègne, in 757, *MGH, Concilia*, II, 62, 13. On the other hand there should not be excluded a possible relation with the Visigothic formula *princeps vel gens aut patria* (see *Lex Visigothorum*, in *MGH, Legum Sectio I*, vol. I, index, *s.v.* "patria"), which comes closer to antique concepts of public law than the Frankish form, which is attenuated. In the Carolingian *Leges Saxonum*, for example, the meaning of *patria* is purely local (see *MGH, Fontes iuris Germanici antiqui in usum scholarum*, 24, 27, 46ff). For Visigothic Spain, see the recent study of Floyd Seyward Lear, "The Public Law of the Visigothic Code," *Speculum*, XXVI (1951), 1–23, who stresses (p. 20, n. 42) the difficulty of reaching positive conclusions in view of terminology.

[15] Percy Ernst Schramm, *Kaiser, Rom und Renovatio* (Leipzig and Berlin, 1929), I, 80f, II, 93.

[16] The model of Horace, *Odes*, III, 2, is quite obvious, e.g., in Richer, *Historiae*, I, 8, ed. by Georg Waitz (Hanover, 1877), 77: "*decus pro patria mori egregiumque pro christianorum defensione morti dare*"; cf. Erdmann, *Kreuzzugsgedanke*, 22, n. 62, also for the parallelism of *patria* and *christianorum defensio*.

[17] It is quite sufficient to recall the famous throne-images of Otto III (Munich Gospels, Bamberg Josephus), or the Byzantine haloed city-goddesses; see, for the latter, Kurt Weitzmann, *The Joshua Roll* (Princeton, 1948), figs. 65, 67, 69, 71, 73, and, for the Aegyptus in Palermo, Ernst Kitzinger, "The Mosaics of the Cappella Palatina in Palermo," *Art Bulletin*, XXXI (1949), 280, and fig. 8.

[18] In Italy, of course, *patria* was practically always the city or city-state, though with Dante and Petrarch the country of Italy, too, began to become *patria*. In a somewhat broader sense the terms *Latium* or *Ausonia* were used in antiquity; see also below, n. 27.

feudal lord, knighting of his eldest son, dowry for his eldest daughter—were personal lordly taxes which had nothing whatsoever to do with the country, nation, or *patria* in either an ancient or a modern sense. By the twelfth century, however, the fourth case of the later *aide aux quatre cas* (the German *Vierfallsbede*) made its appearance: a taxation *pro defensione regni*.[19] Professor Strayer, in a most stimulating little study, has pointed out that Louis VI of France, when facing an attack from across the Rhine (1124), went to St. Denis, took the Oriflamme from the altar, offered prayers *pro defensione regni*, and made grants to the abbey dedicated to St. Denis, the patron saint of France and the dynasty. That is to say, "for the defense of the realm" divine help was needed, and it was secured by *giving* to the church.[20] At the end of the thirteenth century, however, the proportions were definitely reversed. *Pro defensione regni* the king no longer gave; he took. He imposed a tax to meet the emergency of the realm, and *pro necessitate regni* he imposed the tax also on the church.[21]

It is well known to what extent the pattern of those taxes *pro defensione* or *pro necessitate regni* followed the pattern of the crusading taxes—tenths, fifteenths, twentieths—which were levied from the whole church, or parts of it, by the Holy See *pro defensione (necessitate) Terrae Sanctae*. For, the goal of the crusades has usually, and in early times always, been formulated in terms of a defensive war, a defense of the Christian brothers and churches in the Holy Land, and not as a war of aggression against the infidels.[22] Already the Norman kings of Sicily had begun to transfer the idea of a defensive war to their own realm and accordingly took taxes *pro defensione (necessitate) regni*.[23] In order to simplify here a rather complicated issue, and for the sake of brevity, we might say: What was good for the *regnum Christi regis*, Jerusalem and the Holy Land, was good for the *regnum regis Siciliae* or *Franciae*. If a special and extraordinary taxation was justifiable in the case of an emergency in the kingdom of Jerusalem and for its defense, it seemed also justifiable (especially in the age of the purely secularized crusades, such as those against the Hohenstaufen and Aragonese) to meet the emergencies of the Sicilian kingdom or those of France in the same fashion. After all, "Emergency begins at home."

Once established, that tax did not disappear again; only the terminology used in levying it changed occasionally. The old argument *pro defensione (necessitate) regni*—

[19] For the twelfth century, see the letter of Martin IV to Charles of Anjou (Nov. 26, 1283) after the Sicilian Vespers. The pope states that even before Frederick II, who is said to have introduced, after his return from the Holy Land, *subventiones et collectae ordinariae*, the Sicilian (Norman) kings had imposed, as an extraordinary tax, *collecte ... pro defensione ipsius regni*; cf. *Les Registres du Pape Martin IV* (Paris, 1913), No. 488, p. 225; also *Les Registres du Pape Honorius IV* (Paris, 1886), No. 96, p. 75. Pope Martin seems to have investigated the matter rather thoroughly for he writes: "*de modo subventionum etc. nichil aliud potuit inveniri nisi quod antiquorum habet relatio.*" For Frederick II's *collectae*, see Ernst Kantorowicz, *Kaiser Friedrich der Zweite*, Erg. Bd. (Berlin, 1931), 99.

[20] Joseph R. Strayer, "Defense of the Realm and Royal Power in France," *Studi in Onore di Gino Luzzatto* (Milan, 1949), 289ff.

[21] This, of course, was the whole issue of *Clericis laicos*. See also Strayer, *op. cit.*, 290, and *passim*.

[22] Erdmann, *Kreuzzugsgedanke*, 321; somewhat different was the Charter of Alfonso VII for the Confraternity of Belchite (1136) which was founded "*ad Christianorum defensionem et Sarracenorum oppressionem*"; see Percy Ernst Schramm, "Das Kastilische Königtum und Kaisertum während der Reconquista," *Festschrift für Gerhard Ritter* (Tübingen, 1950), 111. In Spain the whole development was different in so far as crusading idea and national idea or patriotism coincided. Also crusaders' songs would show the idea of annihilation of the Moslems: "*Illuc debemus pergere Saracenos destruere*"; Dreves, *Anal. Hymn.* XLVb (Leipzig, 1904), 78, No. 96, stanza 7.

[23] Above, n. 19.

sometimes amplified by the expression "for the defense of the king," the supreme feudal lord—remained valid throughout and has not disappeared even now in the twentieth century.[24] In addition, however, in the second half of the thirteenth century, and especially in France, we find a tax imposed *ad tuitionem patriae* or *ad defensionem patriae*.[25] And in 1302, after the French defeat at Courtrai, Philip IV or his officers asked subventions from the clergy "for the defense of the native fatherland which the venerable antiquity of our ancestors ordered [us] to fight for, because they preferred care for the fatherland even to love for their descendents."[26] Here, then, that crucial word *patria* appears in a fairly modern sense, referring to a territorial national state and harking back to the model of ancient times. In other words, by the end of the thirteenth century the national monarchy of France was strong enough and sufficiently advanced to proclaim itself as *patria* and to impose taxes, including church taxes, *ad defensionem natalis patriae*.

But was it worth dying for that fatherland as the martyrs died for the *patria* in heaven? Perhaps we should draw a parallel between the "holy soil" of the *Terra Sancta* overseas and the "holy soil" of *la doulce France*, the French fatherland. The emotional ring of names such as *Latium* or *Ausonia* in the verses of Ovid or Vergil—"*ecce tibi Ausoniae tellus; hanc arripe velis*" ("Lo, yours is Ausonia's soil; sail and seize it!")—or the strong emotion dwelling, for instance, in Pliny's praise of Italy—*Haec est Italia dis sacra*, a land *numine deum electa*—all that had been recovered for France by the *Chanson de Roland* and the other *chansons de geste*.[27] The kingdom of France, *Francia*, whose very name suggested the fatherland of the free (*franci*), was the land of the new chosen people;[28] she too was, so to say, a *Francia Deo sacra*[29] for whose sacred soil it was worth while, and even sweet, to make

[24] These questions have been studied in recent years most successfully by Gaines Post; see, above all, "Plena potestas and Consent in Medieval Assemblies," *Traditio*, I (1943), 371ff, and "The Theory of Public Law and the State in the Thirteenth Century," *Seminar*, VI (1948), 42ff, esp. 55ff. See Strayer, *op. cit.*, 292; "*tam pro capite nostro, tam pro corona regni defendenda*"; and in general his paper "The Laicization of French and English Society in the Thirteenth Century," *Speculum*, XV (1940), 76ff, esp. 82ff.

[25] Strayer, "Defense of the Realm," 292, n. 7, 294, n. 6.

[26] On August 29, 1302, Philip IV writes to the clergy of the bailiwick of Bourges: "*ad defensionem natalis patrie pro qua reverenda patrum antiquitas pugnare precepit, eius curam liberorum preferens caritati ...*" Quoted by Georges de Lagarde, "La Philosophie sociale d'Henri de Gand et de Godefroid de Fontaines," *Recueil de travaux d'histoire et de philologie*, 3me sér., fasc. 18 (1943), 88, n. 1. It is apparently that kind of phraseology which Strayer, "Laicization," 85, n. 2, alludes to; see also Jean Leclercq, *Jean de Paris et l'ecclésiologie du XIIIᵉ siècle* (Paris, 1942), 18, n. 5, and in *Revue du moyen âge latin*, I (1945), 166, n. 6; Frantz Funck-Brentano, *Mémoire sur la bataille de Courtrai* (Paris, 1891), 87, *passim*, and *Philip le Bel en Flandre* (Paris, 1897), 424.

[27] *Aeneid*, III, 477; Pliny, *Nat. Hist.*, III, 39ff, 138. It seems strange that *Ausonia* and *Ausones* preserved its emotional power in Byzantium. In the poems, e.g., of Theodoros Prodromos (12th century), ed. by Angelo Mai,

Patrum nova Bibliotheca (Rome, 1853), VI, 399ff, Constantinople is called Αὐσόνων πόλις (X, 21), the emperor is ὁ τῶν Αὐσόνων ἥλιος (IV, 10) or Αὐσόνων αὐτοκράτωρ (X, 171); see also poems I, 65; II, 17; VI, 13; XIX, 53; XX, 13, as well as the poems of Manuel Holobolos (13th century), ed. by Jean François Boissonade, *Anecdota Graeca* (Paris, 1833), V, 159ff, e.g., II, 6 (p. 161); IV, 1 (p. 163); V, 16 (p. 165), etc. The Byzantine court tradition can be easily traced back to—it may even have been started by—Optatianus Porfirius, *Carmina*, XV (III), 10: "*maxime Caesar / Ausoniae decus o, lux pia Romulidum*"; cf. X (XXI), 13; XVI (X), 38: "*O lux Ausonidum*"; VII (XXIII), 2: "*magne / Ausonidum ductor.*"

[28] Percy Ernst Schramm, *Der König von Frankreich* (Weimar, 1939), I, 137, 228, and *passim*, has collected some material; see also Helmuth Kämpf, *Pierre Dubois* (Leipzig and Berlin, 1935). For *Franci* = *liberi*, see, e.g., Alexander of Roes, *Memoriale*, c. 17, ed. by Herbert Grundmann and Hermann Heimpel, *Die Schriften des Alexander von Roes* (Deutsches Mittelalter: Kritische Studientexte der Monumenta Germaniae Historica, IV; Weimar, 1949), 38, 13, and *passim*; also Wilhelm Berges, *Die Fürstenspiegel des hohen und späten Mittelalters* (Leipzig, 1938), 76f; Leclercq, *Jean de Paris*, 170f, lines 103ff.

[29] One example for many: Richier, *La vie de Saint-Remi*, ed. by W. N. Bolderston (London, 1912), line 61: "*Molt fait dieus aperte monstrance / D'especial amour a France*"; or line 114: "*A bien Dieus [en] France eslargie / La grace dou Saint Esperite.*" For France as the "*doux royaume de Jésus Christ*," see Kämpf, p. 111. See also below, n. 41.

the supreme sacrifice, while to defend and protect her would imply a quasi-religious value comparable to charity.

Actually the *defensio Terrae Sanctae* becomes directly relevant to that complex problem once we ask what was the reward for those fighting and perishing for the Holy Land.

* * *

The decrees of the Council of Clermont, in 1095, established the indulgences for the crusaders in a canonically perfectly correct and unimpeachable fashion. The second Canon of Clermont states quite unambiguously: "This expedition shall be considered an equivalent of all penitence" (*iter illud pro omni poenitentia reputetur*).[30] That is, all punishment which church discipline might have decreed against a penitent—fasts, alms, prayers, pilgrimages—should be forgotten and atoned for by the crusade. The crusading campaign itself was the atonement. It was a remission of those temporal punishments which the church had the power to impose—but not a remission of sins. This distinction, the neglect of which was so characteristic of Luther's contemporaries, was meaningless also to the contemporaries of the crusades. All our sources mention, strangely enough, not the remission of ecclesiastical punishment but the remission of sins, the *remissio peccatorum*, as the reward of the crusaders. Even Pope Urban II, although at Clermont the matter had been phrased correctly, was careless when claiming in his letters that the crusade effected a *remissio omnium peccatorum*. And this idea was generally current among clergy and laity alike.[31]

On the strength of this premise the death of a crusader in battle would easily appear as a new martyrdom. The crusader, certain of the remission of all his sins, was assured of his entry straight into Paradise and might expect, for his self-sacrifice in the service of Christ the King, the martyr's crown in the life hereafter. A crusader's song reflects this assumption quite clearly:

> He that embarks to the Holy Land,
> He that dies in this campaign,
> Shall enter into heaven's bliss
> And with the saints there shall he dwell.[32]

This idea was still shared by Dante. His ancestor, Cacciaguida, was slain as a crusader in the Second Crusade. The poet, therefore, will meet his venerable forbear in the heaven of Mars where the champions of God and the martyrs have their place in the peace of Paradise. Cacciaguida himself explains: "*E venni dal martiro a questa pace.*"[33] This was not only the language of poets and of public opinion. Ivo of Chartres, the greatest canon lawyer around 1100, collected in his *Decretum* and in the *Panormia* a number of relevant passages, and reproduced, along with others, also a passage from a letter of Pope

---

[30] Erdmann, *Kreuzzugsgedanke*, 316.
[31] *Ibid.*, 294, 317.
[32] Dreves, *Anal. Hymn.*, XLVb, 78, No. 96; Erdmann, *Kreuzzugsgedanke*, 317:

Illuc quicumque tenderit,
Mortuus ibi fuerit,
Caeli bona receperit,
Et cum sanctis permanserit.

[33] *Paradiso*, XV, 148.

Nicholas I (858–867) in which the pope declared that any soldier killed in the defense of faith against pagans or infidels would be received as a citizen in the kingdom of heaven. "For if one of you should be killed, the Almighty knows that he died for the truth of faith, the salvation of the *patria*, and the defense of Christians; and therefore the soldier will attain the aforementioned reward."[34] The importance of this passage should be sought not only in the fact that Nicholas I could promise in good faith the celestial *patria* to those who died in the defense of faith or of the *patria* in this world,[35] but that Ivo of Chartres in his collections called back to memory a number of utterances about *patria* which eventually were to form a good basis for later discussions.[36] In some respects the later theories are foreshadowed also in a letter of Urban II, who wrote: "None who shall be killed in this campaign for the love of God *and his brothers* shall doubt that he will find remission of his sins and the eternal beatitude according to the mercy of God."[37] Here the parallelism of "love of God and love of his brothers" is of some importance because it was the Christian virtue of *caritas* which finally was to work as a lever to justify ethically, or even to sanctify, war and death for the fatherland.

Two generations after Ivo and Urban, around 1170, the poet of the *Chanson de Roland* muses about the Frankish-French warriors of Charlemagne: "*Se vos murez, esterez seinz martirs*"—"And if you die, you shall be holy martyrs."[38] It is true, of course, that the warriors of Charlemagne supposedly were fighting the Saracens in Spain and therefore equaled crusaders. However, to the French people of the twelfth and thirteenth centuries those Frankish soldiers had become French soldiers while Charles himself figured as "emperor of France." Death *against* the Saracens therefore was at the same time death *for* the French emperor and French brothers and compatriots, a fact which gave the "martyrdom" of the slain also a national flavor. Priority, to be sure, was held by death for the supreme lord, divine or feudal. At a council at Limoges, in 1031, where the truce of God was discussed, a vassal of the duke of Gascogne was told: "For your lord you have to accept death... and for this loyalty you will become a martyr of God."[39] Here the crown of martyrdom descended upon those suffering death for their feudal lord. By the middle of the thirteenth century, however, the crusader idea of a holy war was all but completely secularized, and its place was taken by a quasi-holy war for the defense of the realm or of the nation symbolized by the "crown" of France. A poet of that age, Richier, glorifying Rheims and its first bishop, St. Remy, styled the crown of France the most precious of all relics and declared that those who were killed in protection of the

---

[34] Ivo, *Decretum*, X, 87, in Migne *PL*, CLXI, 720; Erdmann, *Kreuzzugsgedanke*, 248.

[35] "*quisquis ... in hoc belli certamine fideliter mortuus fuerit, regna illi coelestia minime negabuntur. Novit enim omnipotens, si quislibet vestrorum morietur, quod pro veritate fidei et salutatione patriae ac defensione Christianorum mortuus est, ideo ab eo praetitulatum praemium consequetur.*"

[36] Ivo, *Decretum*, X, 93, 97, with places from another letter of Pope Nicholas I (*MGH, Epistolae*, VI, 585, 11f) and from Ambrose.

[37] Paul Kehr, *Papsturkunden in Spanien*, I: *Katalanien* (Abhandlungen Göttingen, N. F. XVIII: 2; Berlin, 1926),

287f, No. 23: "*In qua videlicet expeditione si quis pro Dei et fratrum suorum dilectione occuberit, peccatorum profecto suorum indulgentiam et eterne vite consortium in venturum se ex clementissima Dei nostri miseratione non dubitet.*"

[38] *Chanson de Roland*, line 1134; cf. Cumont, *Lux perpetua*, 445. Leonardo Olschki, *Der ideale Mittelpunkt Frankreichs* (Heidelberg, 1913), 14ff.

[39] Migne, *PL*, CXLII, 1400B: "*Debueras pro seniore tuo mortem suscipere, ... et martyr Dei pro tali fide fieres.*" Cf. Marc Bloch, *Les rois thaumaturges* (Strasbourg, 1924), 244, n. 3.

crown should be saved in the life after death. Thus they were rendered equal to saints or martyrs. God himself, argues the poet, sanctifying "the king, the crown, and the realm" in which the grace of the Holy Spirit had been multiplied, has sent from high heaven the holy balm of anointment *por la corone deffendre*.[40]

The voice of the poet was echoed by that of the priest. When Philip IV of France started his disastrous campaign against the craftsmen and peasants of Flanders—a war marking in so many respects the watershed between two ages—an unknown cleric delivered a sermon on the king's departure to war. He preached on 1 Maccabees 3, 19–22, a passage which in any century would readily lend itself as a *locus classicus* for self-righteously interpreted warfare: "*They* march against us in the plenty of pride and lawlessness. . . . *We*, however, will fight for our souls and laws; and the Lord himself will crush them before our faces." To prove the just cause of the French, the preacher first exalted the saintly character at large of the *nobiles et sancti reges Francorum*. They are saints (1) for their love of purity to the effect that, whereas other princely races were stained, the blood royal of France has remained perfectly pure; (2) for their protection of holiness in view of the church; (3) for their spreading of holiness because they procreate holy kings (*cum generent sanctos reges*); (4) for their working of miracles by healing scrofula, the "king's evil"—arguments apparently representing the common opinion in the surroundings of Philip IV and very well known from the political tractates of Pierre Dubois. There follows of course that the cause of those royal saints is perforce the cause of Justice herself, whereas the Flemings are fighting for an unjust cause ("*cum autem nos bellemus pro justitia, illi pro injustitia*"). The wicked Flemings are almost congratulated because through the king's war against them they have a chance to be, as it were, "liberated" from their injustice and conquered by the holy king of France rather than by evil. On the other hand, death on the battlefield for a just cause receives its reward. "Since the most noble kind of death is the agony for justice, there is no doubt but that those who die for the justice of the king and realm [of France] shall be crowned by God as martyrs." The "agony for justice," exemplified by Christ, is the price paid for the crown of martyrdom, and this "justice" is that of the king of France and his realm. The preacher, however, demands the sacrifice for the holy king for yet another reason. He demands it not on the grounds of the old feudal ties of lord and vassal but on the grounds of the new organological concept of the state. The king, said he, is the head, the subjects are the members of the body politic. Natural reason commands that all members be not only directed by the head and serving the head but also willing to expose themselves for the head. Moreover, the king's peace is the peace not only of the realm but also of the church, of learning, virtue, and justice, and it permits the concentration of forces for the acquisition of the Holy Land. "Therefore he who carries war against the king [of France], works against the whole church, against the Catholic doctrine, against holiness and justice, and against the Holy Land." Here the equation of "war for France" and "war for the Holy Land"

[40] Richier, lines 46ff, p. 40; Bloch, *loc. cit.* For the notion of "crown," see Fritz Hartung, "Die Krone als Symbol der monarchischen Herrschaft im ausgehenden Mittelalter," *Abhandlungen der Preussischen Akademie* (1940), No. 13 (Berlin, 1941), esp. for France 19ff. Further, see Richier, lines 61f, 73ff, 114ff, pp. 41ff; and above, n. 29.

has been carried through. We seem already to hear Joan of Arc saying: "Those who wage war against the holy realm of France, wage war against King Jesus."[41]

The preacher, by adducing the organological concept of state, has struck a new tone which demands consideration of yet another topic: the realm as *corpus mysticum*.

* * *

Whereas the concept of the church as the *corpus Christi* goes back to St. Paul (1 Cor. 12, 12), the term *corpus mysticum* has no biblical tradition. In fact, it is far less ancient than might be expected. *Corpus mysticum* first appeared in Carolingian times, and it then referred not at all to the church, or to the oneness and unity of Christian society, but to the Eucharist. It designated the consecrated host, the mystical body of Christ.[42] This, with few exceptions, remained the official meaning of *corpus mysticum* until the middle of the twelfth century, that is, until well after the great dispute about transubstantiation which is connected with the name of Berengar of Tours. In response to Berengar's doctrine and that of heretical sectarians, who tended to spiritualize and mystify the Sacrament of the Altar, the church was compelled to stress most emphatically not a spiritual or mystical but the *real* presence of the human Christ in the Eucharist. The Sacrament now was termed significantly the *corpus verum* or *corpus naturale*, or simply the *corpus Christi*, the name under which also the feast of *Corpus Christi* was instituted in the Western Church, in 1264. That is to say, the Pauline term originally designating the Christian church now began to designate the host, whereas the notion *corpus mysticum*, hitherto used to describe the host, was gradually transferred, after 1150, to the church as an organized body. It was finally through Pope Boniface VIII and the bull *Unam sanctam* that the doctrine of the church as "one mystical body the head of which is Christ" (*unum corpus mysticum cuius caput Christus*) was defined and dogmatized.

Now the term *corpus mysticum* as a designation of the church in its sociological and ecclesiological aspects was adopted in a critical moment of church history. After the investiture struggle there arose, for many reasons, the "danger of too much stress being laid on the institutional, corporational side of the Church" as a body politic.[43] It was the beginning of the so-called secularization of the medieval church, a process which was balanced by an all the more designedly mystical interpretation of the administrative

---

[41] The interesting document has been published by Dom Jean Leclercq, "Un sermon prononcé pendant la guerre de Flandre sous Philippe le Bel," *Revue du moyen âge latin*, I (1945), 165–72. For the general background, see Kämpf, *Pierre Dubois*, who publishes a similar sermon by Guillaume de Sauqueville (pp. 109–11). The maxim of the anonymous preacher (Leclercq, p. 172, lines 163ff), "*si ipsi volunt ab iniustitia vinci, orabimus ut a potestate et exercitu regio devincantur. Melius est enim eis a rege vinci quam a malo et in iniustitia perdurare*," indicates the theory according to which war is made *ex caritate*. This in fact was the current scholastic doctrine; see Harry Gmür, *Thomas von Aquino und der Krieg* (Leipzig and Berlin, 1933), 7f; see also p. 46 for the theory that the king waging a just war acts "*ex zelo iustitiae, quasi ex auctoritate Dei*." In a similar fashion all the other theories of that remarkable

sermon could be analyzed as reflections of contemporary thought. For the two quotations, see pp. 170, 87ff ("*cum enim nobilissimum moriendi genus sit agonizare pro iustitia, non dubium quin isti qui pro iustitia regis et regni moriuntur, a Deo ut martyres coronentur*") and pp. 170, 65ff. ("*Igitur qui contra regem invehitur, laborat contra totam ecclesiam, contra doctrinam catholicam, contra sanctitatem [sc. regis] et iustitiam et Terram Sanctum*").

[42] The history of the term *corpus mysticum* has been settled, in a brilliant study, by Henri de Lubac, *Corpus mysticum* (Paris, 1944), also in *Recherches de science religieuse*, XXIX (1939), 257ff, 429ff, and XXX (1940), 40ff, 191ff.

[43] I follow here the stimulating article by Gerhart B. Ladner, "Aspects of Mediaeval Thought on Church and State," *Review of Politics*, IX (1947), 403ff, esp. 414f.

body. The new term *corpus mysticum* linked the building of the visible church organism, it is true, with the former liturgical sphere; but, at the same time, it placed the church as a body politic or a political organism on one level with the secular bodies politic which by that time began to assert themselves as self-sufficient communities. Moreover, the terminological change coincided with that moment in the history of Western thought in which corporational and organological doctrines began to pervade political theories anew and to form decisively the political thinking of the high and late Middle Ages— when, for example, John of Salisbury wrote those famous chapters of his *Policraticus* in which he compared the commonweal of the state with the organism of the human body.[44]

In addition to the organological concept of the spiritual and secular communities there was yet another set of corporational doctrines, deriving from, or closely related to, the new study of Roman law, which began to exercise its powerful influence on the concepts of church and state alike. They reached their first full growth when, by the middle of the thirteenth century, the great lawyer-pope Innocent IV introduced or elaborated the notion of the *persona ficta*, the fictitious or (as we would call it) juristic person, that abstraction of any aggregate of man—corporation, community, or dignity—without which modern society could not easily exist.[45] Under the impact of those ideas, soon augmented and ethicized by Aristotelian social doctrines, the former liturgical term *corpus mysticum* lost much of its transcendental meaning. To what extent the purely sociological and juristic features began to dominate may be gathered from Aquinas, who quite juristically defined the church also as *persona mystica* instead of *corpus mysticum*.[46] That is, the mysterious materiality which the term *corpus mysticum* had still preserved was here abandoned and exchanged for the juristic abstraction of the "mystical person," which was synonymous with the lawyers' "fictitious person."

While the lofty idea of the church as *corpus mysticum cuius caput Christus* filled itself with secular corporational and legal contents, the secular state, striving after its own exaltation and quasi-religious glorification, itself adopted the term "body mystical" and used it for its own justification and its own ends. Already Vincent of Beauvais in the mid-thirteenth century mentions the *corpus reipublicae mysticum*.[47] The lawyers began to distinguish five or more *corpora mystica*—village, city and province, realm and universe.[48] Baldus defined the *populus* not simply as the individuals of a community, but as "men assembled into

---

[44] *Policraticus*, V, c. 2, ed. by Clemens C. J. Webb, I, 282ff. Most instructive for the origins of the organological concepts is Wilhelm Nestle, "Die Fabel des Menenius Agrippa," *Klio*, XXI (1926–27), 350ff, who shows to what extent St. Paul has reproduced current stoic ideas (358f). The line leading from Stoicism ("*socii eius [dei] sumus et membra*"; Seneca, *Ep.* 92, 30) to the Christian *Christi sumus membra* (Rom. 12, 4) and further to Roman law (see *Cod. Theod.* 9, 14, 3 [In Eutropium, Sept. 4, 397]: "*virorum illustrium qui consiliis et consistorio nostro intersunt, senatorum etiam, nam et ipsi pars corporis nostri sunt*," a passage to which Professor Otto Maenchen kindly called my attention) should be investigated even beyond Otto von Gierke, *Das deutsche Genossenschaftsrecht* (Berlin, 1881), III, 134ff. For John of Salisbury's alleged source, Pseudo-

Plutarch's *Institutio Trajani*, see Hans Liebeschütz, "John of Salisbury and Pseudo-Plutarch," *Journal of the Warburg and Courtauld Institutes*, VI (1943), 33ff, who shows convincingly, it seems to me, that Pseudo-Plutarch is Salisbury himself.

[45] Gierke, III, 246ff.

[46] See, e.g., Thomas Aquinas, *Summa theol.*, III, q. 48, a. 2, ad 1: "*Dicendum quod caput et membra sunt quasi una persona mystica.*" See Lubac, in *Recherches de science religieuse*, XXIX (1939), 461, n. 4.

[47] *Speculum doctrinale*, VII, c. 15 (erroneously cited as c. 8 by Gierke, III, 548, n. 75.)

[48] Gierke, III, 545, n. 64, quoting Antonio de Rosellis; see also Fritz Kern, *Humana civilitas* (Leipzig, 1913), for the five corporations of medieval political thought.

one mystical body" (*hominum collectio in unum corpus mysticum*).[49] And in England as well as in France the terms *corpus politicum* and *corpus mysticum* were used, without clear distinction, to designate the people and the state.[50]

In any event, before the end of the thirteenth century secular communities, large and small, were to be defined as "mystical bodies," meaning simply any polity, any *corpus morale et politicum*[51] in the Aristotelian sense. There was, of course, no difficulty whatsoever in combining Aristotelian concepts with ecclesiastical terminology. Godfrey of Fontaines, a Belgian philosopher of the late thirteenth century, integrated very neatly the *corpus mysticum* into the Aristotelian scheme. "Everyone is by nature part of a social community, and thereby also a member of some mystical body." That is to say, man is by nature a "social animal." As an *animal sociale*, however, man is "by nature" also part of some "mystical body," some social body collective or aggregate, which Dante easily defined as "Mankind" and which others may define, as need be, in the sense of *populus* or *patria*, no matter whether referring to the kingdom of France or the city-state of Florence or any other social community and corporation.[52] From the works of Aristotle a new halo had descended upon the organisms of human society.

*   *   *

It will not be difficult now to draw some conclusions. Once the *corpus mysticum* has been identified with the *corpus morale et politicum* of the people and has become synonymous with nation and "fatherland," death *pro patria*, that is for a mystical body corporate, regains its former nobility. Death for the fatherland now is viewed in a truly religious perspective; it appears as a sacrifice for the *corpus mysticum* of the state which is no less a reality than the *corpus mysticum* of the church. It all implies a recovery of certain ethical values and moral emotions which, with regard to the secular state, had been practically absent during the earlier Middle Ages, and yet so dominant in Greek and Roman antiquity. This, however, does not mean simply a paganization of the idea *pro patria mori*. Humanism had its effects, but the quasi-religious aspects of death for the fatherland clearly derived

---

[49] Gierke, III, 432.

[50] In England the term is found very often in Lancastrian times; see, e.g., *Rotuli Parliamentorum*, IV, 367, in a parliamentary sermon of the *legum doctor* William Lynwode (1430–31); John Fortescue, *De Laudibus Legum Angliae*, c. 13, ed. by Stanley B. Chrimes (Cambridge, 1942), 30, 17 and 28; see also the sermons of Bishop John Russel, of Lincoln (1483), quoted by Stanley B. Chrimes, *English Constitutional Ideas of the Fifteenth Century* (Cambridge, 1936), 180, 185. For France, see Hartung, "Die Krone," 29, quoting Jean de Terre Rouge (*ca.* 1420).

[51] Gierke, III, 548, n. 75.

[52] Godfrey of Fontaines, *Quaestiones ordinariae*, I, 2, 5, ed. by Odon Lottin (Louvain, 1937), p. 89; cf. De Lagarde, *op. cit.*, 64. It may be mentioned here that in the thirteenth century also the royal title begins to change from *rex Francorum* to *rex Franciae*, indicating the territorialization of the state; see Schramm, *Der König von Frankreich*, I, 111, n. 1; see also Strayer, "Laicization," 81f, cf. 85, n. 3. On the other hand, the new definiteness of national boundaries is reflected also by the national limitation of ecclesiastical provinces, unknown in the earlier Middle Ages; see, for a few good remarks, Gerd Tellenbach,"Vom Zusammenleben der abendländischen Völker im Mittelalter," *Festschrift für Gerhard Ritter* (Tübingen, 1950), 19f. In England the title *Rex Angliae* became the general custom under Henry II. Interesting, in this connection, are the remarks of Sir Francis Bacon on the importance of a country's name as a unifier of the country. When, at the *entrée joyeuse* of James I, in 1603, Bacon suggested the name of Great Britain for the united crowns of England and Scotland, he remarked: "For name, though it seem but a superficial and outward matter, yet it carrieth much impression and enchantment." And he reminds the king of the power dwelling in the name of Graecia for the Greek resistance against Persia, in that of Helvetia to knit together the Swiss confederation, and in that of Spain as "a special means of the better union and conglutination of the several kingdoms." Cf. Stanley Thomas Bindoff, "The Stuarts and Their Style," *EHR*, LX (1945), 207. See, for Spain, also Schramm, "Das kastilische König- und Kaisertum," 109f.

from the Christian faith, the forces of which now were activated in the service of the secular *corpus mysticum* of the state.

Pope Urban II had qualified the crusader's death on the battlefield as "charity" when he glorified death *pro Dei et fratrum dilectione*. In the thirteenth century, the *amor patriae* was commonly interpreted as *caritas*.

> *Amor patriae in radice charitatis fundatur*—Love for the fatherland is founded in the root of a charity which puts not one's own things before those common, but the common things before one's own. ... Deservedly the virtue of charity precedes all other virtues because the merit of any virtue depends upon that of charity. Therefore the *amor patriae* deserves a rank of honor above all other virtues.

This is the opinion of Tolomeo of Lucca in his continuation of Aquinas' *De regimine principum*.[53] And in the same chapter, in which by and large he follows Saint Augustine, Tolomeo adduces Cicero saying that to all of us the parents and children, relatives and household members are dear, but that "the fatherland embraces *caritate* all those relations. What good citizen would hesitate to welcome death if it were profitable for the fatherland?" The examples drawn from Roman antiquity which Tolomeo had borrowed from Augustine were repeated by Dante with even greater emphasis.[54] He talks about the Roman *Decii* as the "most sacred victims" (*sacratissimae victimae*) and recalls "that ineffable sacrifice" (*illud inenarrabile sacrificium*) of Cato, of Romans, that is, who for the salvation of their *patria* or its liberty did not shun the darkness of death. "Whoever designs the good of the state designs the goal of law." This was the *thema probandum* of Dante's chapter which opens up a new legal-philosophic aspect of death for the fatherland.

To what extent actually a hero's death *pro patria* was religiously defended and defined may be gathered from the philosophers of the late thirteenth century, an age steeped in Aristotelian and often Averroistic modes of thought. Remigio de' Girolami, a Florentine who had studied in Paris and who seems to have been Dante's teacher, was a corporationalist in the extreme.[55] Although he did not, like Dante, confess the Averroistic corporationalism of the collective soul, he nevertheless almost sacrifices the individual soul to the collective state. To Remigio the *patria*, the city community, takes precedence over both family and individual. Man is bound to love his *patria* more than himself; he should love it immediately after God "for the similitude which the city has with God." The universe, he argues, is more perfect an image of God than the city, but the city—a small universe—is more perfect an image of God than the individual. That is, for the sake of the *corpus mysticum* of the city Remigio strangely devaluates the physical individual

[53] Thomas Aquinas, *De regimine principum*, III, c. 4, ed. by Joseph Mathis (Rome and Turin, 1948), 41. For Aquinas himself, see *Summa Theologiae*, I, 60, 5, Resp.: "*Est enim virtuosi civis ut se exponat mortis periculo pro totius reipublicae conservatione*"; also II–II, 101, 3, 3 ("*pietas se extendit ad patriam*..."), with the good commentary on *patria* according to Aquinas, in *Die Deutsche Thomas-Ausgabe* (Heidelberg, 1943), XX, 343ff. In general, see Hélène Pétré, *Caritas* (Louvain, 1948), 35ff.

[54] *Monarchia*, II, 5. See the very important study of Theodore Silverstein, "On the Genesis of *De Monarchia*, II, V," *Speculum*, XIII (1938), 326ff.

[55] For Remigio's *De bono communi*, see Richard Egenter, "Gemeinnutz vor Eigennutz," *Scholastik*, IX (1934), 79–92; see also Martin Grabmann, *Mittelalterliches Geistesleben* (Munich, 1926), I, 361ff, and "Studien über den Einfluss der aristotelischen Philosophie," *Sitzungsberichte der bayerischen Akademie*, 1934, No. 2, 18ff. The social aspects of *De bono communi* have been elucidated by De Lagarde, *op. cit.*, 65, and "Individualisme et corporatisme au moyen âge," *Recueil de travaux d'histoire et de philologie*, 2me sér., XLIV (1937), 39.

who alone, according to Genesis, was created in the likeness of God. The Florentine, however, with some reservations went so far as to maintain that the personally guiltless citizen, if he could prevent his country from being eternally condemned to hell, should readily take upon himself his own eternal condemnation, even prefer it to being saved himself while his city was condemned. That means advocating not a simple *pro patria mori* in the sense of suffering a natural death. It is an attempt to defend even the eternal death of the soul, the jeopardy of individual salvation and of the beatitude of the life eternal for the sake of the temporal fatherland.[56]

Cicero could ask with Posidonius (*De officiis*, I, 45, 159) whether really the community was always and under any circumstances to be placed above the virtues of moderation and modesty. And his answer was a clear No.

> For there are things, partly so dirty, partly so disgraceful and vile that the wise man will not do them even for the sake of the fatherland and its conservation. ...Such things, therefore, he would not take upon himself for the sake of the *res publica*, nor will the *res publica* wish to accept them for herself.

Hence, the self-denial of the Christian patriot of Florence goes far beyond the wise moderation which the classical author demands, at least with regard to the sage.

Also in the Aristotelian and Averroistic circles at Paris similar problems must have been widely discussed. Henry of Ghent, though far from siding with the absurdity of his contemporary, Remigio de' Girolami, yet takes a stand against the scholarly selfishness of true or fictitious Averroists who held that the philosopher should not sacrifice his speculative life, and therewith his beatitude of this world, if it conflicted with his civic duties.[57] Henry is one who strongly defends the sacrifice of temporal death for the fatherland but who no less strongly objects to spiritual death: for the temporal state man is not entitled to sacrifice the salvation of the soul. Moreover, he warns of a false death *pro republica:* for example, if a man chooses death on the battlefield not for his fatherland but for his own rashness; or if, instead of defending the justice and innocence of his country, he strives to acquire only honor and glory for his country in defiance of all justice—something called "imperialism" in modern language. For all that, Henry of Ghent vehemently rebukes the cowards who run away instead of fighting. Rather than to fly, the soldier should choose to die on the battlefield *pro patria et republica* in accordance with Cicero's device *Patria mihi vita mea carior est*—"The fatherland is dearer to me than my life." And in this connection Henry of Ghent gives, as it were, the final blessing to death *pro patria:* he compares the death of a citizen for his brothers and his community to the supreme sacrifice of Christ for mankind.[58]

It is against the background of the secularized idea of the *corpus mysticum*—implying that the state as an abstract notion or the state as a juristic person finally achieved its

---

[56] For the problem, which has been clearly recognized by Egenter, *op. cit.*, 89ff, see also Post, "The Theory of Public Law" (above, n. 24), 48, who remarks that according to the scholastic philosophers "the salvation of one's soul is the only private right that is superior to the public utility, except in the case of a bishop, who cannot, says Pope Innocent III, resign his office to save his own soul if he is needed to help others to salvation."

[57] De Lagarde, "Henri de Gand," 80ff, upon whose excerpts I have to rely, since the *Quodlibets* of Henry of Ghent are not accessible to me.

[58] *Ibid.*, 87.

semi-religious or natural-religious exaltation—that we can fully understand a tractate of Enea Silvio Piccolomini, later Pope Pius II, which in 1446 he dedicated to the Habsburg emperor Frederick III.[59] With other teachers, this learned humanist maintains that the prince (the emperor) is entitled to take away the private property even of meritorious citizens in the case of an emergency of the state.[60] The ruler may demand even more than property: he may demand *ad usum publicum* also the lives of the citizens.

> It should not [writes Enea Silvio] appear too hard when we say that for the benefit of the whole body a foot or hand, which in the state are the citizens, must be amputated, since the prince himself, who is the head of the mystical body of the state, is held to sacrifice his life whenever the commonweal would demand it.

Not rarely do we find in the writings of curialists that the Roman pontiff is styled the head of the *corpus mysticum* of the church.[61] In Enea Silvio's writing, however, we find a new version of the old theme. The "mystical body of the church the head of which is Christ" has been replaced here by the "mystical body of the state the head of which is the prince." And so as to make the parallel quite unambiguous Enea Silvio reminds his princely reader that Christ sacrificed himself voluntarily although he, too, was *princeps et rector* as the head of the church.[62]

Here the parallelism of spiritual *corpus mysticum* and secular *corpus mysticum*, of the mystical body's divine head and its princely head, of self-sacrifice for the heavenly transcendental community and self-sacrifice for the terrestrial metaphysical community has reached a certain point of culmination. And from this high-point onward the historian will find it easy to coast down that road which ultimately leads to early modern, modern, and ultra-modern statisms.

---

[59] Enea Silvio, *De ortu et auctoritate imperii Romani*, ed. by Gerhard Kallen, *Aeneas Silvius Piccolomini als Publizist* (Stuttgart, 1939), 80ff.

[60] For *necessitas non habet legem*, see Post, "The Theory of Public Law," 56.

[61] Enea Silvio, *De ortu*, 82, 418ff. For the pope as head of the *corpus mysticum*, see, e.g., Hermann of Schilditz, *Contra haereticos*, II, c. 3, ed. by Richard Scholz, *Unbekannte kirchenpolitische Streitschriften aus der Zeit Ludwigs des Bayern* (Rome, 1914), II, 143f ("*ita se habent omnes fideles ad capud ecclesie, quod est Romanus pontifex, in corpore mistico ecclesie*"); see also Alvarus Pelagius, *Collirium*, ed. by Scholz, *op. cit.*, II, 506 ("*ecclesia que est corpus Christi misticum . . . ibi est, ubi est caput, scilicet papa*").

[62] If *pro patria mori* became an act of *caritas* and equivalent to *pro Deo (Christo) mori*, it might be expected, as Professor Philip Merlan kindly pointed out to me, that accordingly *patriam trahere*, treason against the fatherland, would be paralled by *Deum (Christum) trahere*. In fact, Dante, *Inferno*, XXXIV, describes Brutus and Cassius sharing the punishment of Judas. This idea, however, has a long history, since every treasonable act would be interpreted by means of biblical exemplarism as a repetition of the treason of Judas. See, e.g., *Poenitentiale Valicellanum*, cc. 50 and 51, where it is said that not only a person delivering another man up to his enemies shall be judged like Judas, but also "*si quis castellum vel civitatem*

aut alicuius munitionem in manus inimicorum spiritu Judae tradiderit"; Hermann Joseph Schmitz, *Die Bussbücher und Bussdisziplin der Kirche* (Mainz, 1883), I, 376f, quoted by Ferd. Koenen in *Deutsches Dante-Jahrbuch*, VII (1923), 93, n. 11. Moreover, the *crimen laesae maiestatis* was customarily made parallel with the crime of the lese majesty of God; see Ernst Kantorowicz, *Kaiser Friedrich*, Erg. Bd., 110. Relevant to the problem is the study of Maxime Lemosse, "La lèse-majesté dans la monarchie franque," *Revue du moyen âge latin*, II (1946), 5–24, who very neatly points out how the notion *laesa maiestas* was replaced in the West by the feudal concept of *infidelitas* (personal treason as opposed to public treason); how the substance of *laesa maiestas* as a public crime was retained as a result of the religious or ecclesiological status of the king (Alcuin, *Epist.*, III, 12, in *MGH, Epist.*, IV, 24: "*In necem regis nemo communicare audeat, quia christus Domini est . . . et omnis quisquis tali sacrilegio assenserit . . . Judae traditori sociatus sempiternis cremabitur incendiis*"); and how finally after the Bolognese revival of Roman law the ancient *laesa maiestas* reappears without abolishing the Christian concept of the king's religious nature. Both trends concur in the interpretation of suicide as treason or felony because through this crime "the king, being the head, has lost one of his mystical members." Edmund Plowden, *The Commentaries or Reports* (London, 1816), 261.

It would be wrong to underrate the role which humanism and revived antiquity have played in the emotional revaluation of the ancient *pro patria mori* in modern times. The mainspring, however, is that at a certain moment in history the "state" in the abstract or the state as a corporation appeared as a *corpus mysticum* and that death for this new mystical body appeared equal in value to the death of a crusader for the cause of God. And it may be left to the reader to figure out all the distortions which the central idea of the *corpus mysticum* has suffered by its transference to national, party, and racial doctrines in more distant and in most recent times. The so-called "Tombs of Martyrs" of the National-Socialist movement in Munich, or the gigantic streamer *Chi muore per Italia non muore* covering, on Christmas, 1937, the façade of the Milan cathedral for the commemoration service for the dead soldiers of the Fascist Italian divisions in Franco's Spain, illustrate some of the recent nationalistic ravings which so terribly distort an originally venerable and lofty idea.

On the other hand, the disenchantment of the world has progressed rapidly, and the ancient ethical values, miserably abused and exploited in every quarter, are about to dissolve like smoke. Cold efficiency during and after the Second World War, together with the individual's fear of being trapped by so-called "illusions" instead of professing "realistic views," has done away with the traditional "superstructures," religious as well as ideologic, to the effect that human lives no longer are sacrificed but "liquidated." We are about to demand a soldier's death without any reconciling emotional equivalent for the lost life. If the soldier's death in action—not to mention the citizen's death in bomb-struck cities—is deprived of any idea encompassing *humanitas*, be it God or king or *patria*, it will be deprived also of the ennobling idea of self-sacrifice. It becomes a cold-blooded slaughter or, what is worse, assumes the value and significance of a political traffic accident on a bank holiday.

*   *   *

Needless to say, the two cardinals quoted in the introduction are far remote from those debasing tendencies which belong anyhow to a later period: both regarded the soldier's death on the battlefield as a true sacrifice which—with or without otherworldly reward—bestowed a final shimmer of human nobility on the human victim. When now we turn back to re-read Cardinal Mercier's pastoral letter of Christmas, 1914, we realize that the words he used, which then appeared so challenging, are in fact fully justified by a very long tradition of ecclesiastical doctrine and Western political thought in general. Those words did not express his private opinion or willful interpretation. Much can be said also, however, in support of Cardinal Billot's view. From a theological-dogmatic basis, he rejected the sentence expounding that "death christianly accepted assures to the soldier the salvation of the soul," because, he claimed, this was substituting the fatherland for God. And indeed, this substituting tendency has become more and more obvious since 1914. History, we might venture to say, supported Cardinal Mercier; theology, Cardinal Billot. But who was right and who wrong, in the crucial matter of the soldier's eternal salvation, cannot be decided by either the historian or, after the split between faith and reason, the philosopher.

DANTE'S "TWO SUNS"

Two ends have been set by Providence, that ineffable, before man to be contemplated by him: the blessedness, to wit, of this life which consists in the exercise of man's proper power and is figured by the terrestrial paradise; and the blessedness of eternal life which consists in the fruition of the divine aspect, to which his power may not ascend unless assisted by the divine light. And this blessedness is given to be understood by the celestial paradise.

Man, according to the two ends set before him, is in need of a twofold directive power: the Roman Pontiff to lead mankind in accordance with things revealed to eternal life; and the Roman Emperor to direct the human race to temporal felicity in accordance with the teachings of philosophy.

This is, in the words of a famous passage of the *Monarchia*, Dante's view of a world order such as it should be but was not, owing to the incessant strife between papacy and empire for the supreme position in this world.[1] The discord between the two supreme authorities has been, time and again, deplored by the poet as the mainspring of Italy's, and indeed the world's, political and moral disaster around 1300. The contest between the two universal powers concerning some alleged supremacy of one over the other appeared to Dante as a struggle devoid of substance and foundation. The two offices, so he ponders, defy comparison altogether, since their tasks are fundamentally different. If, however, a comparison of Pontiff and Emperor be desired, the first thing to do would be to reduce both to a common denominator allowing comparison.

Of such common denominators Dante adduces two in his *Monarchia*.[2] Both Pontiff and Emperor are, above all, men. Therefore they must be measured by the standard of man, by the *humanitas* which personally they represent. "As men they have to be referred to the *optimus homo* who is the measure of all others and, as it were, their Idea—whosoever this 'best man' may be. That is, they have to be referred to him who is mostly one in his own kind." In other words, the very "Idea of Man," the man—"whosoever he may be"—that encompasses most perfectly the human race and "is mostly one in his kind," is the standard of both Pontiff and Emperor so far as they are men. This is not only a truly "humanistic" argument by which Dante transfers the theoretical strife of many centuries to a completely new plane; it falls in also with the political doctrines of that age which had learned to distinguish more clearly than before between man and his

Reprinted, with permission, from *Semitic and Oriental Studies Presented to William Popper* (University of California Publications in Semitic Philology, XI; Berkeley and Los Angeles, 1951), 217–231.

[1] *Monarchia*, III, xvi, 7.
[2] *Ibid.*, III, xii, 7ff.

office, between king and crown.[3] So far as the *offices* of Pontiff and Emperor are concerned, so Dante continues, it is obvious that both offices derive from the same source, which is God. The common denominator of the offices, therefore, is "either God himself in whom all disposition is universally united, or some substance inferior to God," some of the celestial intelligences, in which the deity appears in a more particularized form.[4]

As *humanitas* in Dante's scheme is always peculiarly concentric with *deitas*, it becomes almost natural that the human and the divine should appear also as the two planes which Pontiff and Emperor have in common. Only when reduced to these two denominators, it seems to Dante, could the two powers become comparable at all. However, when reduced to the human and divine planes the two powers would cease to be in a state of competition concerning the supremacy of either one or the other; for in the mirror of human perfection and of the divine being, or the celestial beings, Pontiff and Emperor are equal anyhow.

These, by and large, are the arguments which Dante expounds in the *Monarchia*. In the *Divina Commedia*, however, he reduces the two universal powers to yet another denominator to prove their equality when, in addition to *humanitas* and *divinitas* of Pontiff and Emperor, the poet refers to the Roman character they have in common, to their *Romanitas*. In fact, nothing could be more Dantesque than this triad of Man, God, and Rome.

The sixteenth Canto of the *Purgatorio* has as its essence the meeting of Dante with the Lombard Marco. Dante had inquired of Marco about the causes of vice and sin, since some people placed those causes in the heavens whereas others sought them below on earth.

> Brother,
> The world is blind, and truly thou comest from it,

begins Marco's reply. He explains that Necessity deriving from stellar influence must be refuted although indeed the heavens set man's impulses in motion. Yet, Reason and Freewill are given to man to secure the victory of his better nature. Therefore, it is solely man's fault, not that of the stars, if vice and sin predominate on earth. Man's soul was created simple; and as it "sprung from a joyous maker," it knows no other desire than to return to Him. The soul, however, for its return to God, needs guidance; it needs the laws to curb it, and needs a ruler, the Emperor, who discerns *della vera cittade almen la torre*, "of the true city at least the tower." With this remark the Lombard turns from the sphere of theology and natural philosophy to that of political philosophy. Laws, says he, certainly there are, yet none puts them to work because the shepherd—the Pontiff—who leads the flock,

> though chewing the cud hath not the hoofs divided.

---

[3] Fritz Hartung, "Die Krone als Symbol der monarchischen Herrschaft im Mittelalter," *Abhandlungen der Berliner Akademie*, 1940, No. 13 (1941); also E. Kantorowicz, "Christus-Fiscus," *Synopsis: Festgabe für Alfred Weber* (Heidelberg, 1948), 225ff, and Gaines Post, "The Theory of Public Law and the State in the Thirteenth Century," *Seminar*, VI (1948), 42ff.

[4] *Monarchia*, III, xii, 11: "vel ipse Deus..., vel aliqua substantia Deo inferior."

He is not *kashér*. True enough, he "ruminates"; he ruminates the theological knowledge of generations, but does not fulfill the other requirement of the Law: to discern Good from Evil as indicated by the cloven hoofs. The flock, the ignorant crowd, becomes like its leader sinful and corrupt and desires "whereof he is greedy." Hence, neither stars nor nature is responsible for the corruptness of the world, but the fault is with evil leadership. The Pontiff has engulfed the Emperor, has joined to his pontifical staff the imperial sword. And the result: both Empire and Church go ill because united in one hand they cease to fear each other.

What should the right order of the world be? What had it been like so long as the world was good? Here Marco hints at Rome.

> Soleva Roma, che il buon mondo feo,
>   due soli aver, che l'una e l'altra strada
>   facean vedere, e del mondo e di Deo.

> (She that had made the good world, Rome, was wont
>   To have TWO SUNS which made plain to sight
>   Both one road and the other, world and God.)

For centuries, ever since the age of Gregory VII, a dangerous image had gained influence on the political theory of the papacy: Sun and Moon as symbols of Church and Empire.[5] Although the sheer coexistence of two celestial luminaries of unequal size proved, all by itself, less than nothing in view of the relations of *regnum* and *sacerdotium*, the metaphor had yet been taken as evidence for the inferiority of the Moon-Empire to which only some reflected light was granted from the Sun-Papacy. Dante, in the *Monarchia*, had denied and ridiculed the validity of the Sun-Moon symbol as evidence in political matters.[6] Now, in the *Comedy*, he abolishes it, and no more than two words are needed to do away with that specter: *due soli*. Pope and Emperor, to Dante two coördinate and equal powers with different tasks, no longer reflect a major and a minor light: they are "Two Suns" which jointly illuminate the world to lead the human race to the two goals which "Providence, that ineffable, has set before man": the terrestrial paradise and the celestial. And from this greater concept Dante cannot exlude Rome. From Rome there shall shine forth the Two Suns to bring light to man and shed light on his path—from Rome, the capital of the World and the Empire as well as of Italy. Pontiff and Emperor, coequals when measured by the standards of Man and God, are coequals also with regard to Rome and to their solar characters. Rome, according to the poet, "was wont to have two suns." And by the power of two luminaries of equal grandeur Rome had created the "good world," a world such as it had been, so we might say, as long

---

[5] For the Sun-Moon symbolism of papacy and empire, see Konrad Burdach, *Rienzo und die geistige Wandlung seiner Zeit* (=*Vom Mittelalter zur Reformation*, Vol. II, 1; Berlin, 1913–1928), 273ff, 332ff, and *passim*; also Percy Ernst Schramm, *Kaiser, Rom und Renovatio* (Leipzig and Berlin, 1929), I, 124f, n. 5, and II, 64, line 31.

[6] *Monarchia*, III, iv. See also the objections to this chapter by Dante's contemporary adversary, the Dominican Guido Vernani; Thomas Käppeli, "Der Dantegegner Guido Vernani O.P. von Rimini," *Quellen und Forschungen aus italienischen Archiven und Bibliotheken*, XXVIII (1937–1938), 144ff.

as an Emperor *a Deo coronatus* and a Pontiff *a Deo electus* still balanced, supported, and checked one another.[7]

It is by means of that rather bold new metaphor that Dante tries to overcome the effects of the theocratic Sun-Moon symbolism. There is nothing obscure about his intentions. He wishes to emphasize, once more, that the secular sphere exists in its own right, that the celestial paradise is sided by a terrestrial paradise of equal dignity, and that Philosophy and Theology, Empire and Papacy are of equal rank. Yet, that new metaphor itself—Two Suns shining forth from Rome—strikes us as strange and hardly less fantastic than the old Sun-Moon symbolism serving as the evidence for papal supremacy. If taken in a literal sense, the idea of two suns over Rome appears even monstrous, frightening rather than comforting. The appearance of a second sun, an anhelion, was a bad omen for the Romans in ancient times, as may be gathered from Livy;[8] and Claudian, too, uses the image of *gemini soles* purely in the negative to indicate the monstrosity of an epoch.[9] For all that, however, Dante's image of the Two Suns was, in a politico-theological sense, not at all foreign to Roman thought, nor, for that matter, to medieval thought.

In fact, we need only to turn to Byzantium in order to find the image of the Two Suns not too rarely in the language of poetry and rhetoric. The plurality of emperors, customary in Constantinople, would have challenged unfailingly the court poets and rhetors to compare their emperors with two, or even more, suns just as they were used to comparing the imperial couple, basileus and basilissa, with sun and moon.[10]

We may, however, forget about those obvious comparisons, and turn to what may be called the original version of Dante's image of the Two Suns of Rome.

Theodoros Prodromos, a well-known and indeed prolific poet of the Comnenian age,[11] has written among many other works a great number of poems for John II Comnenus (1118–1143)—epinikia, epithalamia, epitaphia, and, following Byzantine court etiquette and court demands, also several poems for the *prokypsis*.[12] The *prokypsis* was a wooden

---

[7] See E. Kantorowicz, *Laudes regiae* (Berkeley and Los Angeles, 1946), 105, 145.

[8] Livy, XXIX, 14; cf. Pliny, *Nat. Hist.* II, 31f.

[9] Claudian, *In Eutropium*, I, 7.

[10] Examples of this solar duality are very numerous; see, e.g., Theodoros Prodromos (cf. next note), *Poemata*, I, 6, ed. Mai, *Patrum nova bibliotheca* (Rome, 1853), VI, 399:

ἥλιε καὶ παρήλιε δύο λαμπροὶ φωστῆρες
πατὴρ καὶ τέκνον βασιλεῖς...

XIV, 23, ed. Mai, p. 412:

'Ρωμαίων ἥλιε λαμπρέ...

μετὰ τῶν παρηλίων σου τῶν σεβαστοκρατόρων.

Manuel Holobolos (see below), II, 14, ed. J. F. Boissonade, *Anecdota Graeca* (Paris, 1833), V, 161:

Στηρίζοι τούσδε τοὺς λαμπροὺς ἡλίους τῶν Αὐσόνων,
πατέρα τε καὶ τὸν υἱὸν...

Theodoros Hyrtakenos, ed. Boissonade, *op. cit.*, I, 258 (last lines):

Ὢ δυοῖν ἡλίων ἐν δίσκῳ φωσφορούντων ἑνί...

Cf. Otto Treitinger, *Die oströmische Kaiser- und Reichsidee nach ihrer Gestaltung im höfischen Zeremoniell* (Jena, 1938), 117ff; *ibid.*, 115, for the comparison of the emperor with

Helios, and of the empress with Selene, which is very frequent indeed.

[11] For the literature on Prodromos, see, in addition to K. Krumbacher, *Geschichte der byzantinischen Literatur* (2d ed.; Munich, 1897), 359 and *passim* (see Index), the very complete bibliography by Konrad Heilig, "Ostrom und das Deutsche Reich um die Mitte des 12. Jahrhunderts," in T. Mayer, K. Heilig, C. Erdmann, *Kaisertum und Herzogsgewalt im Zeitalter Friedrichs I.* (Schriften des Reichsinstituts für ältere deutsche Geschichtskunde, IX; Leipzig, 1944), 237, n. 3. The poems of Prodromos referred to here are found in Mai (see n. 10), VI, 399ff, and in the essay on Prodromos by Carl Neumann, *Griechische Geschichtsschreiber und Geschichtsquellen im zwölften Jahrhundert* (Leipzig, 1888), 37ff.

[12] For the *prokypsis*, see August Heisenberg, "Aus der Geschichte und Literatur der Palaiologenzeit," *Sitzungsberichte der Bayerischen Akademie*, 1920, Abh. 10, 85ff; Treitinger, *op. cit.*, 112ff. The Hellenistic and Late Antique models of the ceremony deserve further investigation; for some suggestions see M. A. Andreeva, in *Seminarium Kondakovianum*, I (1927), 157ff. (Russian).

platform or tribune which, appropriately draped with tapestries and golden curtains, was erected in the open to serve the imperial ceremonial on the two main ecclesiastical feasts, Christmas and Epiphany (January 6), as well as on a few other occasions, at weddings in the royal house or, in later times, coronations also. To this *prokypsis* their majesties had to ascend, while the front of the platform was still veiled, by a back step. When they had arranged themselves on the tribune, the curtains were flung open: the emperors, now visible to court and army, who were assembled in front of the platform, made their "epiphany" and received the acclamations which were due on that occasion. It was probably after those acclamations that a court poet or orator had to address the emperor. The speaker was expected, as it were, to interpret the meaning of this highly dramatic pageantry by putting it into some relation with the festal event. It was almost traditional that those poems alluded to the emperor as the *Helios basileus*, the Sun-Emperor, who like the rising sun had risen on the *prokypsis*. In a more or less skillful fashion the poet would try also to parallel the imperial epiphany with that of Christ: on Christmas, with the epiphany in the flesh in the cave-stable of Bethlehem; and on Epiphany, with that in the baptismal waters of the Jordan.

One of those *prokypsis* poems of Theodoros Prodromos for the "Feast of Lights," as Byzantium called the Epiphany, is devoted, almost in its entirety, to the theme of the Two Suns.[13]

> Light up, Rhomaean City! And once more: Light up.
> Bask in the double beams of your Two Suns.
> You have the Sun of Justice, here, the Father's
> Reflected splendour, naked in the Jordan.
> And, there, you have the Sun of Monarchy,
> The Father's vicar, shining in the palace.
> Oh, what lights flood on thee today, City of Rome!
> What beams shoot down on this earth's face!...

In this manner Prodromos carries through his comparison between the Two Suns, one divine and the other imperial. The city, of course, is not that Rome on the Tiber which the Byzantines have learnt to despise and hate, but the New Rome, the Second Rome on the Bosphorus. This other Rome owns Two Suns, but not emperor and pope, of course, nor even emperor and patriarch of Constantinople. It is Christ himself, the Sun of Justice (Ἥλιος τῆς δικαιοσύνης), who is the city's great luminary together with the emperor. To raise the question of "supremacy" would be ridiculous, since one is man, the other God. Still, the emperor-sun rises "together" with the Sun of Justice because he, the emperor,

---

[13] Poem XVIII, ed. Mai, p. 413:

Φωτίζου πόλις ρωμαΐς, πάλιν ἐρῶ φωτίζου·
διπλαῖς αὐγάζου ταῖς αὐγαῖς ἐκ δύο τῶν ἡλίων·
ἔχεις ἐκεῖθεν ἥλιον τὸν τῆς δικαιοσύνης,
τὸ τοῦ πατρὸς ἀπαύγασμα γυμνὸν ἐν Ἰορδάνῃ·
ἔχεις ἐντεῦθεν ἥλιον τὸν τῆς μονοκρατίας,
τὸν τοῦ πατρὸς διάδοχον λαμπρὸν ἐν ἀνακτόροις·
ὢ πόσα φῶτα σήμερον τὴν Ῥώμην φρυκτωροῦσιν·
ὢ πόσαι τὸ περίγειον ἀκτῖνες δᾳδουχοῦσιν·

ἀλλ' ὁ Χριστὸς μὲν ἥλιος καὶ ποιητὴς ἡλίου·
σὲ δ' ἥλιον τὰ πράγματα, σκηπτοῦχε, μαρτυροῦσιν...

The Light and Sun symbolism is dominant in the liturgies of practically all churches on the feast of Epiphany, particularly in the Eastern churches; see, e.g., P. Hendrix, "La Fête de l'Épiphanie," *Congrès d'Histoire du Christianisme: Jubilé Alfred Loisy* (Paris and Amsterdam, 1928), II, 213ff, 226ff; Treitinger, *op. cit.*, 117, n. 350.

is the recognized *christomimetes*—the imitator, even impersonator, of Christ—whom the Byzantines, in view of his share in the world government, would go far to style their "second God" (δεύτερος θεός).[14]

The emperor a "Sun" as the *mimetes* of Christ: this is the leading idea which yet another Byzantine poet has developed. Manuel Holobolos,[15] a thirteenth-century court poet serving under the first Palaeologan emperors, Michael VIII and Andronikos II, likewise compares his *Helios basileus* with Helios-Christ. He wonders, when comparing the Two Suns with each other, how the divine Sun of Justice found space in the "narrow disk" of the cave of Bethlehem, and how the huge imperial Sun could be encompassed by the small wooden scaffold of the *prokypsis*. But he is quick to explain this "miracle" by emphasizing that the emperor, after all, was the perfect *mimetes* of Christ.[16]

This, however, is only one aspect of the emperor's Sun-likeness. For the Byzantine basileus is "Sun" not only because he imitates, impersonates, and stages Christ. This, to be sure, was the Christian version by which the imperial Sun-rulership was made more palatable to an age which rarely—except in the paganizing circles of rhetoric schools— was conscious of the pagan origin and substratum surviving in this solar ruler-worship. For in fact the emperor was also "Sun" in his own right ever since the times of Constantine, in whom a far older Roman tradition came to end.[17] Theodoros Prodromos, in a poem to Emperor Manuel I, actually strikes the right chord when he, too, hints at the emperor's *christomimesis* and at his theophoric name (Manuel = Immanuel), but adds:

Thee, the Christos, I dare style Phoibos too.[18]

We realize that the emperor is "Sun" as the Christ-imitating prince, and that he is another Phoibos as well, a Sun-God independent of the Christian God. The verse reflects, even in that late period, the essence of the earlier and original triangle of Emperor, Christ, and *Sol invictus*. It conjures up, once more, the competition of "Suns" so fateful in the critical century of transition. That Christ and Emperor could appear to the Byzantines as "Two Suns" becomes plausible once we recall that both could claim,

---

[14] For the concept of μίμησις (θεομίμησις, χριστομίμησις), see the material collected by Michaelis, s.v. μιμέομαι, in Gerhard Kittel, *Theologisches Wörterbuch zum Neuen Testament*, IV (Stuttgart, 1942), 661–678, esp. 666, n. 8, in connection with the ruler cult. For the Hellenistic period, see Erwin R. Goodenough, "The Political Philosophy of Hellenistic Kingship," *Yale Classical Studies*, I (1929), 55ff, and for the Constantinian age, N. H. Baynes, "Eusebius and the Christian Empire," *Mélanges Bidez* (Annuaire de l'Institut de Philologie et d'Histoire Orientales, II; Brussels, 1934), 13–18. For the emperor as δεύτερος θεός, see Max Bachmann, *Die Rede des Johannes Syropulos an den Kaiser Isaak II. Angelos* (Munich Diss., 1935), 11, line 15, who adduces more material; for the problem in general, H. Volkmann, "Der Zweite nach dem König," *Philologus*, XCII (1937), 285ff; F. J. Dölger, *Antike und Christentum*, III (1933), 121; and for the early connection with the Sun-God, Reitzenstein, *Poimandres* (Leipzig, 1904), 278ff.

[15] M. Treu, "Manuel Holobolos," *Byzantinische Zeitschrift*, V (1896), 538ff; Heisenberg, *op. cit.*, 112ff, who

discusses all the *prokypsis* poems of Holobolos as edited by Boissonade, *op. cit.*, V, 159ff.

[16] Compare Holobolos, II, 16–18, with IV, 1–3; Boissonade, 161, 163. The distinction between the "Sun-Gods" and their disks is interesting; see below, n. 32. The "contraction of the sun" to a size fitting in a narrow space was a very popular *topos*. See, e.g., Ephrem, *Hymnus in Epiphaniam*, II, 9, ed. Lamy, I, 16: "...celebret Solem nostrum [i.e., Christum] quod eousque suam contraxit amplitudinem vehementiamque temperavit, ut posset internus animae purae oculus eum aspicere." See also Usener, *Weihnachtsfest* (below, n. 44), 365f.

[17] Treitinger, *op. cit.*, 119f, has outlined very clearly the pagan as well as the Christian strata of the imperial Sun-rulership.

[18] τοίγαρ τολμῶ σε τὸν Χριστὸν καὶ Φοῖβον ὀνομάσαι·
σὺ γὰρ ὡς χριστομίμητος χριστώνυμος ὑπάρχεις.
Neumann (above, n. 11), 67, lines 70f; Heilig, *op. cit.*, 247, emends τοίγαρ (for οὐ γάρ). What matters here is only the comparison of the emperor with both Christ and Apollo in one verse.

independently and yet interdependently, a solar character, and that each was the central figure of a solar theology.

The Roman imperial-solar theology, such as it began to develop in the first century B.C., has too many facets to allow an unambiguous definition. The borderline between comparison and identity of a ruler with the Sun-God—or with any other deity—was never clearly drawn. In fact, full identity of the ruler with the god would almost rule out the possibility of "duplication." The main idea which could lead to a gemination of the celestial body was that the emperor represented a "new Sun," a νέος Ἥλιος, a *Sol novus*.[19] The Asiatics honoring Caligula must have had some gemination of the Sun in mind when they declared in an inscription:

> The new Sun, Gaius Caesar Augustus Germanicus, ... shall
> with his own rays radiate together (with Helios).[20]

The verb "to radiate together" (συναναλάμπειν) indeed would suggest the idea of a second sun; and the fact that Caligula shines "with his own rays" (ἰδίαις αὐγαῖς) makes it rather obvious that the imperial "new Sun" is at the same time credited to be a second sun beside, or even competing with, the heavenly disk. A similar idea is expressed by the distichs in which the island of Rhodes declares:

> I, Rhodes, once the island of Helios, am now Caesar's,
> And I boast of equal light from each.
> I was near extinguished when a new ray gave light to me,
> Helios, and aside thy brilliance shone Nero.[21]

The imperial *neos Helios* has doubled the sun: Helios and Nero shine together on the human race, just as Caligula emanating his own beams doubled the brilliance of the natural sun.[22]

That the conception of the ruler as a "new Sun" was not of Roman origin may be taken for granted. The whole compound of solar ideas originated in the Near East. One might be inclined to consider Pharaonic tradition, since the rulers of Egypt were consistently identified with Rē' and praised without end as the Sun of Egypt:

---

[19] For the designation of a ruler as a "new" god (Dionysos, Helios, etc.), whereby comparison and identification remain fluctuating notions, see A. D. Nock, "Notes on Ruler-Cult," *Journal of Hellenic Studies*, XLVIII (1928), 33ff. For Christ as "sol novus" see Ambrosius, *Sermo* VI, Migne, *PL*, XVII, cols. 635ff.

[20] Dittenberger, *Sylloge Inscr. Graec.*, 3d ed., 1917, No. 798: ὁ νέος Ἥλιος Γάϊος Καῖσαρ Σεβαστὸς Γερμανικὸς συναναλάμψαι ταῖς ἰδίαις αὐγαῖς ... ἠθέλησεν. Cf. F. Sauter, *Der römische Kaiserkult bei Martial und Statius* (Tübinger Beiträge zur Altertumswissenschaft, Heft 21; Stuttgart, 1934), 141; see, for related expressions, *Papyri Osloenses*, Fasc. III, ed. Eitrem and Amundsen (Oslo, 1936), No. 126, 4, and p. 188; also No. 52, 18, Fasc. II (1931), p. 128. The sun metaphors were applied also to high officers. The praetor Brutus was styled *Sol Asiae* (Horace, *Sat.* I, 7, 24). Later, an epigram from Gortyn celebrates Leontios, pretorian prefect of Illyria in 412–413, γῆς Ἰλλυρίδος δεύτερον ἠέλιον; Louis Robert, *Hellenica* (Paris, 1948), IV, 15.

[21] *Anthologia Palatina*, IX, 178 (Antiphilus of Byzantium):

> Ὡς πάρος Ἀελίου, νῦν Καίσαρος ἁ Ῥόδος εἰμὶ
> νᾶσος, ἴσον δ' αὐχῶ φέγγος ἀπ' ἀμφοτέρων.
> ἤδη σβεννυμέναν με νέα κατεφώτισεν ἀκτίς,
> Ἅλιε, καὶ παρὰ σὸν φέγγος ἔλαμψε Νέρων.

Cf. Sauter, *loc. cit.*; H. P. L'Orange, "Domus aurea—Der Sonnenpalast," *Serta Eitremiana* (Oslo, 1942), 69f, whose thesis of Nero's Sun-emperorship, however, seems to be carried too far; cf. J. M. C. Toynbee, "Ruler-Apotheosis in Ancient Rome," *Numismatic Chronicle*, 6th ser., VII (1947), 126ff.

[22] See below, n. 40, for the survival of those ideas, and above, n. 19, for the *neos Helios*.

(Turn) thy face unto me, thou rising Sun,
That illumineth the Two Lands with its beauty!
Thou Sun of mankind, that banisheth the dark from Egypt,
Thou art like thy father Rē', who ariseth in the firmament.[23]

However, the very identity of the Egyptian king with the Sun makes a doubling as expressed in the cult of the Roman emperors less likely, although there is much fluctuation, also in Egypt, in the relationship of ruler and godhead.[24]

Perhaps it will be more profitable to think, in the first place, of Persia, whose model has so decisively influenced the Hellenistic as well as the imperial solar theology in its formative period. If we may believe Pseudo-Callisthenes, the Achaemenid kings already displayed that official title which later the Sassanids adopted: ὁ Ἡλίῳ συνανατέλλων, "The one rising together with Helios."[25] Again it is the "together," the simultaneous rising of Helios and King, which evokes the impression of a duplication of the sun. And incidentally we find that very phrase in a Roman poem. When greeting Domitian on the day of his new consulate, at the beginning of the new year, Statius exclaims:

Atque oritur cum sole novo, cum grandibus astris . . .
(And he rises together with the new sun, with the great stars . . .)

Statius' phrase *oritur cum sole* matches verbatim the Ἡλίῳ συνανατέλλων of the Persian title. And in Statius we find also that element of competition between imperial sun and physical sun which later became so momentous: *Clarius ipse nitens*—he, the emperor, shines clearer and brighter than the sun and the heavenly bodies.[26]

The idea of a duplication of the sun has been expressed in the Roman Empire in various forms, though usually more by implication than explicitly. Imperial-divine geminations were anything but rare in the Empire, since the emperor could become the impersonator of any deity, and vice versa.[27] Just as Juppiter or Mars was hailed as "Augustus" of the Romans,[28] so did the Sun-God become "Lord of the Roman Empire": SOL DOMINUS IMPERII ROMANI appears on coins of Aurelian,[29] who for himself chose

[23] Cf. Ivan Engnell, *Studies in Divine Kingship in the Ancient Near East* (Uppsala, 1943), 6; and in general, Jules Baillet, *Le Régime pharaonique* (Paris, 1912), I, 13ff, and *passim*.

[24] Baillet, *op. cit.*, I, p. 15, 4, seems to think of "Two Suns." A certain "duplication" (King and Ammon) is certainly intended by the statues of Thutmose III, at Medinet Habu and Karnak, where king and god appear as *synthronoi*; cf. Uvo Hölscher, *The Excavations of the Eighteenth Dynasty: The Excavations of Medinet Habu*, II (Chicago, 1939), Pl. III, facing p. 12, and figs. 43, 44, on page 51.

[25] *Historia Alexandri Magni*, ed. W. Kroll (Berlin, 1926), I, 36, 2 (p. 40), also I, 38, 2–3, and 40, 2 (pp. 42, 45). The title seems to be authentic, since Antiochus of Commagene uses similar titles (*synthronos* of Mithras). For the Sassanids (Chosroes II), see Theophylact Simokattes, *Hist.*, IV, 8, 5; Carl Clemen, *Griechische und lateinische Nachrichten über die persische Religion* (Religionsgeschicht-

liche Versuche und Vorarbeiten, XVII: 1; Giessen, 1920), 193; also Arthur Christensen, *L'Empire des Sassanides* (Copenhagen, 1907), 88.

[26] Statius, *Silvae*, IV, 1, 3–4; Sauter, *op. cit.*, 139.

[27] Usener, "Zwillingsbildung," *Kleine Schriften*, IV (1913), 334ff; A. D. Nock, "The Emperor's Divine *Comes*," *Journal of Roman Studies*, XXXVII (1947), 102ff, especially 108, with n. 56; E. Kantorowicz, "The Quinity of Winchester," *Art Bulletin*, XXIX (1947), 81ff.

[28] For the gods as emperors see Nock, "Studies in the Graeco-Roman Beliefs of the Empire," *Journal of Hellenic Studies*, XLV (1925), 84ff, esp. 93. The archaeological material—gods in the uniform of emperors, even including Christ—would probably yield further interesting aspects of the problem.

[29] For Aurelian see Mattingly and Sydenham, *The Roman Imperial Coinage*, V: 1 (1927), 258f, cf. 301, and Pl. VII, 110, 112; see also Kantorowicz, "The Quinity of Winchester," 82, n. 56.

the style DEUS ET DOMINUS (NATUS). This would imply that indeed there were two *domini* of the Empire, *Sol* and Aurelian.

Further, we may think of the very broad idea of the Sun-God as the emperor's companion.[30] SOL INVICTUS COMES AUGUSTI seems very close to "duplication," especially when we consider coins displaying the jugate busts of Emperor and *Sol*, where the similarity of the features of emperor and god suggests that "twinship" was aspired to.[31] It is as though a *biga* of suns was to protect the empire.[32] This concept did not exclude an element of competition. Statius' verses had exalted the imperial sun over the physical; and the coins inscribed ORIENS AUGUSTI or CLARITAS AUGUSTI apparently reflect ideas which would hallow the "Rise" and the "Brightness" of the sun as exclusively imperial monopolies.[33]

It is remarkable that those ideologies and solar theologumena do not break off with the introduction of Christianity. To Eusebius the Christian emperor Constantine still is the one "rising together with the Sun" (ὁ Ἡλίῳ συνανατέλλων);[34] and the image of the two suns—imperial and physical—will continue to be used by the Byzantine court poets and orators. Corippus, in his panegyric on the accession of Justin II (565), produces in some detail his arguments for twin suns with which the Roman capital was blessed. When describing the emperor's elevation on the buckler he avails himself of the familiar sun metaphors. Four selected young men, writes Corippus,[35] lift the "tremendous disk of the shield," and, standing on it, the Emperor Justin becomes manifest:

> . . . Now he is present, the greatest benefactor of the common world, to whom kings bend their necks in subjection, before whose name they tremble, and whose divinity they worship. There he stands on that disk, the most powerful prince, having the looks of the Sun. Yet another light shines forth from the city. This day is truly a marvel, for it allows Two Suns to rise together at the same time. Or did my song carry me beyond its proper bounds? Perhaps it puzzles you that I say Two Suns are rising together and at once. But those are not empty words. The mind of the Just [sc. Justin] resplends more than the sun. It

---

[30] See, for that whole idea, Nock, "The Emperor's Divine *Comes*," 102–116. Alföldi, *The Conversion of Constantine and Pagan Rome* (Oxford, 1948), 59, understands the *comes Augusti* merely as "the lackey of the Emperor." See Nock, 103, against this interpretation in the sense of subordination of the *comes*.

[31] See Kantorowicz,"Quinity," figs. 27–29; *Panegyrici Latini*, VII, 21, ed. Baehrens, p. 177, 15 (to Constantine): "vidisti teque in illius (sc. Solis comitantis) specie recognovisti."

[32] Nock, "*Comes*," 114, n. 108, directs attention to the fact that occasionally a distinction is made between the disk of the visible sun and Helios, or Apollo. Perhaps one should add Tertullian, *Apolog.* XVI, 10: "habentes ipsum (i.e. solem = Christum) ubique in suo clypeo." Also Ovid, *Met.* XV, 192, seems to take the disk as the shield of Phoebus ("Ipse (sc. Phoebi] dei clipeus terra cum tollitur una Mane rubet"). See, further, Corippus, below, n. 37; Holobolos (above, n. 16), II, 17, and IV, 2, ed. Boissonade, V, 161, 163. Both Christ and emperor, as *Helioi*, seem to be distinguished from the disk belonging to them (which is not identical with the physical sun).

[33] I shall discuss these coins in another connection.

[34] Eusebius, *Vita Const.* I, 43, ed. Heikel, p. 28, 11.

[35] Corippus, *In laudem Iustini*, II, 145ff, ed. Partsch, in *MGH, Auct. ant.* III, p. 130:

> . . . nunc maximus orbis
> communis benefactor adest, cui subdita reges
> colla parant, nomenque tremunt et numen adorant.
> adstitit in clipeo princeps fortissimus illo
> solis habens speciem. Lux altera fulsit ab urbe.
> Mirata est pariter geminos consurgere soles
> una favens eademque dies. Mea carmina numne
> mensuram transgressa suam? mirabere forsan
> quod dixi geminos pariter consurgere soles.
> Nec vacuis verbis nec inanibus ista figuris
> ore feres prolata meo, si dicta rependis.
> Mens iusti plus sole nitet. Non mergitur undis,
> Non cedit tenebris, non fusca obtexitur umbra.

Cf. J. A. Straub, *Vom Herrscherideal der Spätantike* (Forschungen zur Kirchen- und Geistesgeschichte, XVIII; Stuttgart, 1939), 134; see also L'Orange, "Domus aurea," 70.

does not merge into the ocean; it does not yield to darkness; nor is it obscured by a black shadow.

This is not the place to give any detailed analysis of Corippus' lines. The elevation on the buckler appears to the poet as the epiphany of the *Euergetes*.[36] On his huge disk the emperor rises like another sun; he appears, like the *mystes* in the cults, *ad instar Solis*.[37] The spiritualization of the sun as the "mind of the Just" has its long tradition,[38] and the metaphors adduced to evidence the superiority of that new "Sun of Virtue" over the physical sun are derived, almost verbatim, from the language of Christian writers.[39] What matters here is only the image of the Two Suns, the physical sun and the imperial. This image lingers on in the Byzantine court language until it loses all its substance. An *epinikion* of Theodoros Prodromos for John II Comnenus may illustrate this style:

> Sun-Basileus divine, bringer of light and radiance,
> Thou hidest the sun, thou shinest upon the morning earth.
> Thou art to rise henceforth and beam the rays from heaven.
> Thou puttest the east to flame, lustrest the eve.
> Thy mock-sun is the other sun rising as thy companion.[40]

There is still the old duality of suns. But the emperor has outshone Helios, and the physical sun serves only as the parhelion of the true luminary, the emperor.

The twinship of emperor and physical sun, or of emperor and Phoibos, though surviving in the rhetorical flowers of the paganizing Byzantine court poetry, had lost its meaning as well as its last touch of "reality." Yet, the old symbol of the Two Suns regained, and retained, some of its former values whenever the outworn pagan image was replaced by the new symbol-values of Christian thought. Already Corippus strikes that note. It was probably nothing but a play on the name of Justin which prompted Corippus to interpret his imperial luminary as the "mind of the Just." However, since his main arguments for the superior power of the "inner" Sun, the "Sun of the Just," are borrowed directly from ecclesiastical or even liturgical language, it may well be that the imperial *Sol Justi* was expected to evoke associations with the divine *Sol Justitiae*, Christ.

The designations of *Sol Justitiae* (Malachi 4, 2) and of *Oriens* (Luke 1, 78; cf. Zach. 3, 8; 6, 12) form the basis of the solar veneration and solar theology which were rampant in

---

[36] The formula *nunc–adest* is typical for the epiphany in an almost liturgical sense. For the *benefactor*-εὐεργέτης title in the ruler cult, see, for the earlier times, Eiliv Skard, *Zwei religiös-politische Begriffe* EUERGETES-CONCORDIA (Avhandlinger Norske Videnskaps-Akademi, Oslo, 1931: 2; 1932), 6–66; for the Roman period, Leo Berlinger, *Beiträge zur inoffiziellen Titulatur der römischen Kaiser* (Breslau Diss., 1935), 49, 67, 77.

[37] The *ingens clipei orbis* (line 137), the size of which may be gathered from Byzantine miniatures, is quasi the disk of the sun (*clipeus solis*) on which the emperor *solis habens speciem* rises. Cf. Apuleius, *Met.* XI, 24, where Lucius is presented to the people as another sun.

[38] See, e.g., for the sunlike rise of virtue in man's soul, Philo, *Legum alleg.* I, 45, ed. Cohn, I, 72, quoted by

F. J. Dölger, *Sol Salutis* (2d ed.; Münster, 1925), 150, n. 2; see also Nock, "*Comes*," 114, n. 8.

[39] See below, n. 47 (Maximus of Turin), also n. 45 ("Sun without setting").

[40] Prodromos, X, 121ff, ed. Mai, p. 409:

> Ἥλιε θεῖε βασιλεῦ φωσφόρε σελασφόρε,
> ἀπέκρυψας τὸν ἥλιον, λάμψας εἰς γῆν ἑῴαν·
> σὺ γοῦν λοιπὸν ἀνάτελλε, σὺ γοῦν ἀκτινοβόλει,
> τὴν ἕω καταπύρσευε δᾳδοῦχε τὴν ἑσπέραν,
> κἀκεῖνος ὡς παρήλιος σοὶ παρανατελλέτω.

A similar idea in Holobolos, I, 1–4, ed. Boissonade, p. 159, where the physical sun, blinded by the glamour of the rising imperial sun, flees to the West. Scores of similar *colores* could be collected; see Treitinger, *Die oströmische Kaiser- und Reichsidee*, 115ff.

the cult of Christ.[41] They appear from the earliest times of the Christian era, and they were perpetuated above all in the Eastern liturgies, but are almost as frequently found in the Western service.

> O Oriens,
>
> splendor lucis aeternae,
>
> et *sol iustitiae*,

is the beginning of one of the *O*-Antiphones in the Advent office of the present Roman breviary, and similar examples could be adduced in great numbers. That the new spiritual Sun was without competition and that from the very beginning this divine light eclipsed the natural sun was, of course, the common and current interpretation on the part of the Church. "He, the *only* Sun, has risen from on high," writes (with Luke 1, 78) Melito of Sardes in the times of Marcus Aurelius.[42] "He will rise above the sun," writes Justin Martyr.[43] He, the "new Sun,"[44] differing from the natural sun, is the "Light without evening" and "Sun without setting."[45] His is the *plenitudo claritatis*, who is "our Sun, the true Sun," writes Zeno of Verona.[46] And in Maximus of Turin we find the model of Corippus' arguments; for, writes Maximus, whereas the "old Sun" of the material world suffers eclipses, is excluded from the houses by walls, is obscured by clouds, and lends its light also to crimes and sins of men, the true Sun of Justice knows none of those deficiencies. A concept of Two Suns, divine and natural, is of course impossible in a system in which the new Sun has quasi-monopolized the "Light of the World" and owns the *plenitudo claritatis*, the plenty, or even the totality, of brightness.[47]

Yet, there was a time when the Sun of Justice was in competition, not with the physical sun, but with the "unconquered Sun," the *Sol invictus* of the pagan religion; that is, with the very deity which, in its turn, so long had been the *alter ego* of the Roman emperors. It is true, occasionally a Christian poet might identify the new Sun of Justice with the pagan solar deity: *Salve, o Apollo vere*, is the invocation by which Paulinus of Nola addresses Christ;[48] and this salute is paralleled by Sophronius' *Phaeton Christos*.[49]

---

[41] For the following, see Dölger, *Sol Salutis*, as well as his *Die Sonne der Gerechtigkeit und der Schwarze* (Münster, 1918).

[42] Dölger, *Sol Salutis*, 156, n. 3.

[43] *Ibid.*, 153.

[44] Christ, the *sol novus*, as opposed to the physical sun, the *sol vetus*: Maximus of Turin (attributed to Ambrose), in a Christmas sermon, Migne, *PL*, XVII, cols. 635f; cf. H. Usener, *Das Weihnachtsfest* (2d ed.; Bonn, 1911), 366f. See also Ephrem, *Hymnus in Epiphaniam*, II, 9, ed. Lamy, I, 16: "sol iste, qui aestu suo terram urit, nobiscum celebret Solem nostrum."

[45] For φῶς ἀνέσπερον, see, e.g., Methodius († 312), *Symposium*, XI, 31, in W. Christ and M. Paranikas, *Anthologia Graeca Carminum Christianorum* (Leipzig, 1871), 34 (Ζωῆς χοραγός, Χριστέ, χαῖρε, φῶς ἀνέσπερον); see, ibid., 174, Cosmas Melodus, *Hypapante Canon*, lines 86f (a burden which is four times repeated); also p. 198, line 59; or p. 256, for Metrophanes' *Trinity Canon*, line 63 ([Φῶς] τριλαμπὲς ἀνέσπερον). See also the *Hirmos*'Ησαΐας φῶς ἰδὼν ἀνέσπερον, which was sung, e.g., on December

24, January 5, February 2, as well as on many other days; *Mēnaia*, editio Romana, 1892, II, 621; III, 80, 483, etc. Even more popular was the image of Christ as ἄδυτος Ἥλιος, which, e.g., through Sophronius, *Oratio*, in Migne, *PG*, LXXXVII: 3, col. 4004, was passed on to the liturgy, although the image is much older; see, e.g., Methodius of Olympos, *Sympos.* IV, 5; VI, 5; VIII, 3; ed. Bonwetsch (1917), 51, 21; 69, 22; 84, 24; see also Christ and Paranikas, *Anthologia*, 173, 251, 256, and *passim;* also F. C. Conybeare, *Rituale Armenorum* (Oxford, 1905), 417 (δ), 432, etc. See also F. J. Dölger, "Christus als Licht ohne Abend," *Antike und Christentum*, V (1936), 8ff.

[46] Zeno, *Tract. IX, De nativitate Domini et majestate,* Migne, *PL*, XI, col. 417B, a sermon recently analyzed by Dölger, *Antike und Christentum*, VI (1940), 1–56 (not yet accessible to me).

[47] *PL*, XVII, cols. 635ff, esp. §§ 3–4; here also (col. 636D) the expression *sol justus et sapiens* (above, nn. 35, 39).

[48] Paulinus of Nola, *Carmen* II, 51, ed. Hartel, p. 349.

[49] *PG*, LXXXVII: 3, col. 3760B.

Those identifications with the pagan god are relatively rare, since the true momentum of the solar theology and solar nomenclature of Christ was that it served as a weapon against the solar henotheism of the *Invictus*, the emperor's celestial double. The history of the final arrangement between the Two Suns, the Christian *Sol Justitiae* and the imperialized *Sol invictus*, has often been traced.[50] The emperor, as it were, changed his celestial patron and antitype by exchanging the "Unconquered Sun" for the "Sun of Justice." But through this exchange the ancient Hellenistic-Roman solar theology had a chance to survive in a Christian garb. Thus we find in the Byzantine Empire, beside the deflated solar imagery of the paganizing poets and rhetors, a well-rounded tradition of "Sun-Rulership," since the imperial "heliomimetes" became a *christomimetes*, and therewith again the living twin image of a Sun, of the "Sun of Justice" in heaven.[51] Nothing can be more telling than the fact that many solar metaphors which henceforth would be applied to the emperor were actually Christian coinages for Christ, the New Sun. We have noticed Corippus' borrowing, directly or indirectly, from Maximus of Turin. And when we read the Byzantine acclamations hailing the "rise without evening of the imperial power" or praising the "inexhaustible font" of the imperial Sun, we know that these acclaims have transferred to the emperor *colores* which were borrowed from the liturgy of the Church.[52]

This, then, appears to be the origin of the Byzantine concept of the Two Suns. They are represented by Christ and the Emperor, the Two Suns of Rome on the Bosphorus. And we now may ask whether this vast compound of ideas is relevant, in any respect, to Dante's image of Pope and Emperor as the Two Suns of ancient Rome on the Tiber. It would be foolish to assert that Dante's line

> Soleva Roma, che il buon mondo feo,
> due soli aver ...

depended directly on the Byzantine model, and even more so to insist that Dante consciously followed Byzantine "ideas." Nevertheless, we should not underestimate the effectiveness of the original imperial Sun-Rulership.

It was the Reform Papacy of the eleventh century which created that image of the two great luminaries as symbols of the two universal powers on earth: the sun equaling the pope; the moon, the emperor. This new symbolism is interesting all by itself. The creation of a "Sun-Papacy" falls in with the trend of Church reform to imperialize the papal office, that is, to materialize the Donation of Constantine to the letter, and to claim imperial prerogatives for the Holy See to an extent which, though known in

---

[50] From Usener ("Sol invictus," in: *Das Weihnachtsfest*, 348ff) to Alföldi, *Conversion of Constantine* (above, n. 30), there is an enormous literature on the subject.

[51] This development has been outlined very neatly by Treitinger, *op. cit.*, 117ff; see also A. Grabar, *L'Empereur dans l'art byzantin* (Paris, 1936), for the general problem.

[52] Constantine Porph., *De caerimoniis*, I, 78, ed. Reiske, p. 375, 6, and ed. Vogt, II, 176, 17ff: ...ἑορτάζει τὴν σὴν ἀνέσπερον ἀνάληψιν τῆς αὐτοκρατορικῆς ἐξουσίας,

ὁ δεῖνα, τὸ ἀκένωτον φρέαρ τῆς οἰκουμένης. For *akenotos* as an epithet of Christ, see *De caerim*. I, 2, ed. Reiske, p. 40, ed. Vogt, I, 33, 19. See also Eustathius of Thessalonike, *Manuelis Comneni laudatio funebris*, c. 71, PG, CXXXV, col. 1025B, who praises the dynasty as a "sun without setting" (φωσφορήσοι...εἰς ἄδυτον). All those adjectives have been transferred from the ecclesiastical cultual language to the language of the imperial cult.

outlines, had not yet become visible in all details. The extravagant claims of the *Dictatus Papae*; the crown adorning the papal tiara; the imperial purple (*cappa rubea*) as worn by the pope; the imperialized acclamations (*laudes*) as sung to the pope; the papal coronations and crown-wearings; the omni-insular theory (that is, the papal claim to overlordship over all islands); the organization of a papal court after the model of secular princes; the papal feudal lordship over princes, and the papal claim to the vicariate of the empire should an interregnum occur; the adoption of the imperial title *vicarius Christi* or *Dei*, as well as inummerable other items, are indicative of the same general development: the pope has become, according to canonistic interpretation, the *verus imperator*.[53] To this concept of a Caesarean Papacy we may now add a new feature: the Pope as Sun. Indeed, the Roman Pontiff, who as Vicar of Christ became *ipso facto* also the antitype of the *Sol Justitiae*, has entered as Helios-Pope on the full legacy of the Roman emperors.

For all that, the original solar qualities of the emperor were not quite forgotten, even though the part which in general the idea of Sun-Rulership played in the West was negligible as compared with that which it played in the East.[54] We have at our disposal some evidence which is rather important in view of the problem of the Two Suns. Cardinal Humbert of Silva Candida, the champion of Church reform in the eleventh century, rejected, on one occasion, the efforts of some people who tried to compare the emperor to the sun. He declares that such comparisons were futile, since they would lead the people to set a second sun, the imperial, over against the papal sun so that those people in fact *soli alterum solem apponant*, "place another sun at the side of the sun."[55] This duplication of the sun could not find the approval of the cardinal, who just mentions it as a curiosity. He does not tell us who the people were that considered the emperor the "Sun." However, Cardinal Humbert, this staunch fighter against the Byzantines, cannot have been ignorant of the fact that the Byzantine emperor was traditionally called the *Helios basileus*; and, on the other hand, there must have been some recollection of the emperor's solar character even in the West—as indeed some miniatures would suggest[56] —if the cardinal considered it worthwhile to pillory those styling the emperor the "Sun."

It must have been from those two sources, Byzantine influx and Western recollection, that the thirteenth century experienced that rather baffling revival of imperial-solar concepts under Frederick II. In the both apocalyptic and messianic climate of that age the idea of the Sun-Emperor could not easily be separated from that of the Savior-

---

[53] The main features of the imperialized papacy have been collected recently by Percy Ernst Schramm, "Sacerdotium und Regnum im Austausch ihrer Vorrechte," *Studi Gregoriani*, ed. G. B. Borino (Rome, 1947), II, 403–457; see, for the omni-insular theory, Luis Weckmann, *Las bulas alexandrinas de 1493 y la teoría política del papado medieval* (México, 1949), esp. 209ff; and in general E. Kantorowicz, *Laudes regiae* (Berkeley and Los Angeles, 1946), 136ff, and *passim*.

[54] See, in general, Franz Kampers, *Vom Werdegang der abendländischen Kaisermystik* (Leipzig and Berlin, 1924), who has tried to trace, in this as well as in his other writings, the solar ideas in the Middle Ages, though not too successfully. See below, n. 56.

[55] Humbert, *Adversus simoniacos*, III, c. 21, *MGH, Libelli de lite*, I, 225, 24: "ut modo ei (sc. sacerdotali dignitati) velut lunae solem saeculares potestates praeponant, modo velut soli alterum solem apponant, modo—quod tamen rarissime fit—in solo filiationis nomine velut filium patri supponant." The solution which Dante provides in the last chapter of the *Monarchia* comes very close to the third alternative: "Illa igitur reverentia Caesar utatur ad Petrum, qua primogenitus filius debet uti ad patrem."

[56] See, e.g., Otto Brendel, "Der Schild des Achilles," *Die Antike*, XII (1936), pl. 15, facing p. 280.

Emperor. In fact, Frederick II appeared as *Sol* in a prophecy from Tibur.[57] Also, a North Italian poet writes

Sol novus est ortus, pax, gloria, semita, portus...,

a line reflecting the messianic atmosphere hovering around that emperor and, in its first part, reminiscent of Statius.[58] *Sol mundi* is Frederick in the eyes of a South Italian poet,[59] whereas Manfred, Frederick's son, styles his father *Sol mundi, auctor pacis,* and even *Sol Justitiae.*[60] About the influence of the Byzantine court style in Frederick's surroundings there can be little doubt. We know the Greek panegyrics written by South Italian officials, and their idioms correspond with the language of the Latin orators of the Sicilian court.[61]

This, however, was also the air which Dante breathed. He may not have known the Byzantine poetry of his time. But he knew Statius. He knew Petrus de Vinea and his Letter Book. He knew most certainly the North and South Italian poets of his age. His own letters were couched in the style of the imperial chancery of Frederick II and of the Bolognese. Little wonder that his Savior-Emperor, the Luxembourg Henry VII, appears not only as the "Lamb of God, which taketh away the sin of the world," but also as *Sol noster,* as the *Titan exoriens,* or the *Titan pacificus.*[62] It is true, in the *Monarchia* the emperor's solar character is not stressed, and in one of his letters of that period, in which he avails himself of the then current symbols, Dante condescends to give the emperor the designation of "Moon"; for the poet rebukes the Florentines, who had assumed quasi-imperial rights, for having duplicated *Delia* (Diana), whereas they did not dare duplicate also *Delius* (Apollo), that is, the Sun-Pope.[63] The idea of a gemination of the great luminaries thus had been in Dante's mind, if in a negative sense, long before he wrote that Canto of the Purgatory in which he glorifies former Rome's "Two Suns." In those lines he does what Cardinal Humbert had objected to: he sets another Sun at the side of the papal Sun. He actually reinstates the emperor in his proper place as the *Sol mundi,* in full agreement with the trends of thought of his time, and he does so without denying to the papal *Vicarius Christi* the representation of the Sun of the World.

In short, the lines of the Lombard Marco are not simply a whim, or a flash of poetic inventiveness (though they are that as well); they are an act of reinstatement of the emperor in his old rights. It is the language of his own time, it is the then customary solar apostrophes of the imperial power, which have led Dante to his duplication of the Sun and to his seemingly strange and irrational metaphor of Rome's *due soli.*

---

[57] K. Hampe, "Eine frühe Verknüpfung der Weissagung vom Endkaiser mit Friedrich II. und Konrad IV.," *Sitzungsberichte der Heidelberger Akademie,* 1917, Abh. 6, p. 18, and p. 11, some additional notes on solar veneration.

[58] Orfinus of Lodi, ed. Ceruti, in *Miscellanea di storia Italiana,* VII (1869), 45, cf. 38; see above, n. 26.

[59] E. Winkelmann, *Acta imperii inedita* (1880), I, n. 725, p. 571, 5, a letter of Magister Terrisius of Atina.

[60] Huillard-Bréholles, *Historia diplomatica Friderici Secundi* (Paris, 1861), VI, 811. For a few other places see Kantorowicz, *Kaiser Friedrich der Zweite,* Ergänzungsband, 251.

[61] See Kantorowicz, *Kaiser Friedrich ...,* 133, 205. For the Norman-Byzantine Sun-Kingship in panegyrics, see, e.g., Eugenios of Palermo, ed. L. Sternbach, in *Byzantinische Zeitschrift,* XI (1902), 449, 8: ἀμβλύνεται φῶς ἡλίου σαῖς ἀκτῖσι (to King William of Sicily); cf. line 11: ἀνέσπερον βλέπων σε λαμπρὸν φωσφόρον.

[62] Dante, *Epist.* VII, 1–2; V, 1.

[63] *Epist.* VI, 2.

DIE WIEDERKEHR GELEHRTER ANACHORESE
IM MITTELALTER

Des weisen los ist Einsamkeit — doch gewiß nicht immer äußere Abkehr von der Welt. Wer abseits lebt, ist nach Aristoteles weniger als Mensch: ein Tier, oder mehr als ein Mensch: ein Gott. So wäre es Hybris gewesen, sich von den Menschen zu sondern, und gerade den Strahlendsten, Göttlichsten der hellenistischen Weisen diente das Wissen, um unter den Menschen weilend Menschen zu finden, nicht die Einsamkeit zu suchen. "Wer das Tiefste gedacht, liebt das Lebendigste."

Dem Lebendigsten in Palästra und Agora zu begegnen war dem christlichen Denker des Mittelalters mit wenigen Ausnahmen versagt: das wahre Leben war in andere Welten entrückt, und ein Weiser, der beim Symposion philosophierend und scherzend die Nacht durchzechte, wäre nicht mehr als Weiser geglaubt worden. Als Weiser galt der fromme Asket, der dieser Welt entsagte, in der Einöde hauste und, fast als ein Heiliger verehrt, nun wirklich "mehr war als Mensch." Zu ihm, dem Klausner, ging, wie Geschichte, Legende und Dichtung hundertfach melden, wer immer in christlichen Läuften Worte der frommen Weisheit zu finden hoffte.

Allein, Weltflüchtigkeit kannte auch die Antike. Es waren die Nicht-mehr-Weisen oder die Schüler der zum gelehrten Wissen gewordenen Weisheit, die in der müder werdenden sinkenden Zeit das Ideal philosophisch-gelehrter Anachorese priesen und lebten — ein Ideal, das sich dann im Schauer der Mysterien- und Jenseitslehren verwandelte, sich je später je mehr religiös verfärbte und das schließlich mit dem aus ganz anderen und dennoch verwandten Schichten aufsteigenden christlichen Willen zur Anachorese verwuchs. Sich vielfach vermischend flossen in spätantik-frühchristlicher Zeit gelehrte und religiöse Motive der Weltflucht so sehr ineinander, daß zwischen Weisheitssuche und Gott-suche bisweilen kaum zu unterscheiden war. Auch äußerlich nicht. Denn der schwere dunkle Philosophenmantel war buchstäblich zum Eremiten- und Mönchskleid geworden: *graeculi* hatte man im späten Rom die christlichen Asketen genannt, weil sie den Mantel der Philosophen trugen.[1] Und wie zahlreich sind die Schilderungen früher Asketen, die in der Einsamkeit Gott dienten und ein philosophisches Leben führten! Noch der Heilige Hieronymus, einen Fasttag mit der Lektüre Ciceros beschließend, sah sich im Traum vor ein Tribunal gestellt, das zu seinem Entsetzen entschied, er sei gar kein Christ, sondern Ciceronianer. Und fast konnte man das Wort des Minucius Felix

---

[1] Tertullian, *De pallio*, ed. Öhler, I, 913ff. Philipp Oppenheim, *Das Mönchskleid im christlichen Altertum* (Freiburg, 1931), 218–224.

verallgemeinern: entweder seien die Christen tatsächlich Philosophen oder die Philosophen seien schon Christen gewesen.[2]

Mit dem steigenden Mittelalter löste sich dieser Zustand des Gleichgewichts: die Schale, welche die Philosophie trug, wurde leichter und leichter. In dem gleichen Jahre, in welchem die platonische Akademie ihre Tore schloß (529), gründete der Heilige Benedikt das Kloster auf dem Monte Cassino. Nicht gelehrte Suche nach der Weisheit dieses Lebens trieb in die Einsamkeit, sondern das Verlangen, unangefochten vom Fleisch, entsündigt und geheiligt schon hier ein engelgleiches gottgeweihtes Jenseitsleben zu führen. Die Klosterheiligkeit bestimmte die neue Klostergelehrtheit: ein Weltentsagen aus anderen als fromm-religiösen Gründen war der Zeit fremd geworden und eine Weltflucht, die nicht auch mit allem gelehrten Streben Gott allein geweiht und der ewigen Seligkeit zu dienen bestimmt war, dem Mittelalter kaum noch denkbar.

Wie ein Kampfruf konnte es daher klingen, als Peter Abaelard sich im Preis einer fast säkularen gelehrten Anachorese erging, diese dem Mönchtum seiner Tage entgegenstellte und in der "Geschichte seines Unglücks" (1132) erklärte: "Was also jetzt bei uns die Mönche, soweit sie diesen Namen in Wahrheit verdienen, aus Liebe zu Gott ertragen, das ertrugen aus Liebe zur Weisheit die Philosophen, die bei den Heiden als die Adligen galten."[3] Aber als ein Kampfruf — es sei denn gegen die Behauptung einiger Zeloten, daß mit dem Beruf des Mönchs sich eine Beschäftigung mit weltlichen philosophischen Schriften niemals vertrage[4] — war diese und manche ähnliche Bemerkung kaum gedacht. Denn der Lehrer des "Ja und Nein" zwang zu keiner Entscheidung, sondern stellte nur gegenüber und stellte nur fest ... stellte fest, daß neben dem geistlichen ein philosophisches weltliches Klausner- und Mönchtum auch möglich sei, daß dessen Ethos einst von nicht minderem Rang war als das der Mönche und daß bei den Heiden die Philosophen als die wahren Adligen galten. Diese Feststellung aber hieß, ungewollt dem mittelalterlichen Möchtum sein Absolutes zu nehmen und es durch ein anderes Bild zu relativieren. All die vielen Stellen, die Abaelard aus Philosophen und Kirchenvätern zusammentrug und die auf Ähnliches hinwiesen, stellten auch nur fest und relativierten weiter, daß die *vita solitaria* nicht allein den Gottgeweihten, sondern auch den Philosophen die rechte Lebensform darbiete und daß wie für den Mönch, so für den Gelehrten Ehelosigkeit Erfordernis bleibe.[5] "Welches Durcheinander von Scholaren und Kammerzofen, von Schreibpulten und Wiegen, von Büchern oder Schreibtafeln und Spinnrocken, von Griffel oder Schreibrohr und Spindeln! Wer, der sich theologischen oder philosophischen Betrachtungen hingeben will, könnte das Plärren der Kinder, den besänftigenden Singsang der Ammen, den Lärm des Gesindes aushalten? wer jene beständigen scheußlichen Schmutzereien der Kleinen ertragen?" Er führt Theophrasts Wort an, der Weise möge nicht heiraten, und dazu des Hieronymus Ausruf: "Wen von

---

[2] Vita philosophica der Asketen z. B. Eusebius, *Hist. eccl.*, VI, 9, 10; VII, 32, u. ö. Vgl. O. Zöckler, *Askese und Mönchtum* (Frankfurt, 1897), I, 176ff. Heimbucher, *Orden und Kongregationen der kathol. Kirche*[3] (Paderborn, 1933–34), I, 61ff. — Hieronym., *Ep.*, 22, 30, Migne, *PL*, XXII, 416. Minuc. Fel., *Octav.*, 20, 1, ed. Bönig, S. 30,

dazu als Beispiel die Bekehrung etwa des Victorin bei Augustin, *Conf.*, VIII, 3–5; vgl. Ernst Benz, *Marius Victorinus* (Stuttgart, 1932), 3ff.

[3] *Opera*, ed. V. Cousin (Paris 1849), I, 14.

[4] Ebda., I, 18.

[5] I, 13.

den Christen muß nicht ein Theophrastus mit solchem Worte beschämen!"[6] Nicht um
der künftigen Seligkeit willen und nicht wegen des heiligen, sondern wegen des be-
schaulich-philosophischen Gelehrtenlebens dieser Welt pries Abaelard Weltabkehr und
Ehelosigkeit, und bezeichnenderweise erteilte er Dispens nur den sehr Reichen, die —
sofern göttlichen oder philosophischen Studien überhaupt zugeneigt — in ihren weiten
Palästen dem Ehe-Ungemach leichter entgehen könnten als der für gewöhnlich arme
Gelehrte.[7] Damit war ohne eigentlichen Angriff der tiefere Sinn von Möchtum und
frommer Askese aufgehoben oder doch ins rein Praktische, Zweckmäßige, Vernünftige
umgewandt. Gerade die Ausnahme, die Abaelard den Reichen zugestand, zeigt deutlich,
wie für ihn der jenseitsgerichtete Gehalt von Asketen- und Klausnertum völlig zurück-
treten konnte — keineswegs immer zurücktrat! — und wie leicht er die von der Trans-
zendenz her bestimmte mönchische Lebensform mit einem ganz anderen, säkularen Inhalt zu füllen wenigstens imstande war.

Abaelards eigner schicksalsvoller Lebensweg spricht vernehmlicher als alle Argumente:
er selbst sollte ja zeitweilig ein gelehrtes Leben in der Einsamkeit führen und darin Vielen
ein Vorbild werden. Nach seiner Verstümmlung, nach seinem Zwist im Kloster St. Denis,
in das er als Mönch eintrat — "aus Verwirrung und Scham mehr, ich gestehe es offen,
als aus demütiger Bekehrung"[8] —, nach der Verbrennung seiner Schrift über die Dreieinigkeit auf dem Konzil von Soissons, nach mancherlei sonstiger Unbill hatte sich
Abaelard in einer einsamen Gegend im Gebiete von Troyes niedergelassen und hier aus
Stroh und Binsen seine Klause errichtet. Hier fanden ihn später seine Schüler und andere
junge Adepten der Weisheit. Sie folgten ihm in die Einöde, sie führten um der Wissenschaft willen ein Einsiedlerleben gleich ihm, sie teilten sein Los, bauten ihre elenden
Hütten nahe der seinen und nahmen um den Preis der philosophischen Unterweisung
dieses harte Leben in Kauf — "Eremiten mehr als Scholaren," wie Abaelard meinte.
Ihm selbst stiegen heidnische Philosophen als Vorbilder auf: Pythagoras mit seinen
Schülern, Platon, der für seine Akademie einen Ort fern der Stadt in ungesunder Lage
gewählt habe, der jüdische Prophet Elisa mit seinen Jüngern, von denen Hieronymus
als "Mönchen jener Zeit" gesprochen hatte.[9] Immer wieder kommen ihm diese Vergleiche in den Sinn, und wenn er die Lebensweise seiner Schüler überdachte, wie sie sich
von Kräutern und trocknem Brot nährten, auf Binsenlagern schliefen, von Rasen-
bänken statt von Tischen speisten, nur um seinen Unterricht zu genießen, so urteilt er
selbst: "Man hätte glauben können, sie wollten wahrhaftig den früheren Philosophen
nachleben."[10]

Freilich, die weltliche Philosophie hat Abaelard, wie er sagte, seinen Schülern nur als
Lockspeise zugeworfen, um sie in Wirklichkeit der Theologie zu gewinnen.[11] Doch nicht
um ein gottgeweihtes heiliges Leben zu führen, sondern um geistig zu leben, um des
Geistes willen entstand jene eigenartige Siedlung weltlicher gelehrter Klausner, die als
Schutzpatron dem "Geist der Wahrheit" unterstehen sollte. Denn die Kapelle, die

---

[6] I, 13.
[7] Ebda.
[8] I, 16.

[9] I, 26.
[10] *Eos priores philosophos imitari crederes:* I, 25.
[11] I, 17f.

Abaelard bei seiner Klause errichtet und zunächst der Dreieinigkeit unterstellt hatte, wurde nach der Ankunft seiner Schüler ausgebaut und dem "Parakleten" geweiht, dem Heiligen Geist als Tröster oder — wie es nach dem von Abaelard angeführten Wort des Johannes weiterhin heißt[12] — "dem Geiste der Wahrheit, welchen die Welt nicht kann empfangen, weil sie ihn nicht sieht und nicht weiß: ihr aber werdet ihn erkennen." Die Wahl dieses durchaus ungewöhnlichen Kirchenpatrons trug Abaelard Angriffe ein: es ginge nicht an und widerspreche dem Herkommen, so sagten seine kirchlichen Feinde, eine Kirche dem Geist ganz allein, von der Trinität abgetrennt, zu weihen und man witterte einen geheimen Zusammenhang mit Abaelards verurteilter Trinitätslehre, der man vorrückte, daß sie die Einheit aufspalte und einen Tritheismus, eine Dreigötter-lehre vertrete. Mochte die Anklage auch schief, den wahren Kern nicht treffend, theolo-gisch überdies widerlegbar gewesen sein, so hatten die Ankläger doch Richtigeres ge-meint: daß nämlich Abaelard die Ergebnisse philosophischer Wahrheitssuche mit selbst-herrlichem Anspruch neben die Glaubenswahrheiten stellte — wenn auch ohne diese selbst anzutasten — und daß er den erkennden Geist, an dem er die Richtigkeit offen-barter Glaubensinhalte maß, als ein Selbständiges herauszulösen drohte aus jener mystischen Einheit der "Geistseele," in der das Dogma der Kirche den Geist um-klammert hielt. Nicht eigentlich die Trinität, wohl aber die Geistseele, die dogmatisch spätestens mit dem Athanasianum festgelegte Einheit von νοῦς und ψυχή, hatte er auf-gespalten.

Aber das Zeitalter, das den Geist als Selbständiges aus seinen bisherigen Bindungen löste und zwischen Geist und Seele wieder schärfer zu unterscheiden lernte,[13] brach mit Abaelard — obwohl nicht durch ihn allein — unweigerlich an. Und in diesem Zu-sammenhang muß man auch die sich anbahnende Herauslösung und Verselbständigung des gleichsam nur gelehrten Sektors des Möchtums verstehen. Ohne etwa das Mönchtum seiner Tage zu verneinen, hat Abaelard doch aus diesem die rein gelehrte Lebensbetätigung herausgebrochen und damit ein selbstständiges philosophisches Mönchtum möglich ge-macht, das primär dem forschenden — freilich noch Gott erforschenden — Geiste geweiht war ... eine neue *vita contemplativa* unter dem Primat des Geistes allein, nicht im Zeichen der sich Gott als Ganzes darzubringenden Geistseele. Damit aber war nicht nur eine Aufspaltung, eine Säkularisation des bisherigen Mönchgedankens eingeleitet, sondern auch der Weg geöffnet zu dem Kult des philosophischen Lebens und der Vernunft überhaupt, der geistig die Folgezeit bestimmen sollte. Bald ging das Sprichwort um:[14]

---

[12] I, 27; vgl. Joh. 14, 16. 14, 26.

[13] Die Problematik der Geist-Seele-Frage bricht im 12. Jhdt. wieder auf, oftmals im Anschluß an Augustin, der noch vielfach trichotomistisch (d. h. zwischen Geist Seele Leib unterscheidend) dachte (vgl. etwa: *De fide et symbolo* c. 23 u. ö.), obwohl er dichotomistisch (zwischen Leib und Geistseele unterscheidend) lehrte; vgl. Erich Dinkler, *Die Anthropologie Augustins* (Stuttgart, 1934), Anh. I, S. 255–266: "Dichotomie oder Trichotomie?" Für das 12. Jhdt. vgl. etwa den Alcher von Clairvaux (gest. 1171) zugeschriebenen pseudo-augustinischen Traktat: *De spiritu et anima*, Migne, *PL*, XL, 779–831; ferner Germain Morin, "Un traité inédit d'Achard de Saint-Victor," in: *Festschrift für M. Grabmann* (Münster, 1935), 251–262: *De discretione animae spiritus et mentis*. Ins 12. Jhdt. gehört wohl auch die Übersetzung von Costa-Ben-Lucas Traktat: *De differentia spiritus et animae* (ed. C. S. Barach, Innsbruck, 1878), die vielleicht auf Adelard v. Bath zurückgeht; vgl. Haskins, *Studies in the History of Mediaeval Science* (Cambridge, Mass., 1924), S. 33, n. 66. J. B. Heard, *The Tripartite Nature of Man* (Edinburgh, 1872), kommt für den Historiker kaum in Betracht.

[14] P. Lehmann, "Mittellateinische Verse...vom An-fang des 13. Jhdts.," in: *S.-B. Akad. München*, 1922, 2. Abh., S. 22.

Auro quid melius? Jaspis.
Quid iaspide? Sensus.
Quid sensu? Ratio.
Quid ratione? Nihil.

Das Bestreben, Philosophen- und Mönchtum in eine Parallele zu setzen, sie zu koordinieren, ja dem Gelehrten Anteil zu geben an der Weihe des Mönchs, blieb bestehen. Der Philosophenmantel ging als Talar wieder an den Gelehrten zurück — seit damals, zum Beispiel in Oxford und Cambridge, auch von den Scholaren getragen, deren Colleges die Idee von Gelehrtenklöstern ganz ursprünglich vermitteln. Um die Mitte des dreizehnten Jahrhunderts ist die Beiordnung von Gelehrten- und Priestertum oder von Gelehrten- und Mönchtum schon fast Gemeingut. Selbst ein so populäres Werk wie die "Image du Monde," eine gereimte Enzyklopädie des Weltwissens, um 1247 von einem Lothringer in französischer Sprache verfaßt, rühmt ähnlich wie Abaelard die antiken Philosophen, die als Eremiten gelebt und in Armut ihre Tage verbracht hätten. Um der Wissenschaft willen seien viele von ihnen umgekommen, weil sie vor ihren Fürsten das Wahre und Richtige verkündeten. Sie werden dem Reimer zu "Märtyrern" wie ihre Reisen dementsprechend zu "Pilgerfahrten" werden aus Liebe zur Wissenschaft, vergleichbar höchstens den Bettelmönchen seiner Zeit, die der Welt entsagten, arm blieben und das Studium pflegten.[15] Religiöse Aufhöhung des Philosophen und Säkularisation des Denkens beginnen ineinanderzugreifen und sich gegenseitig zu ergänzen.

Aber die neuen und stärksten Antriebe zu einem wirklichen Kult weltlicher philosophischer Gelehrsamkeit, der sich im dreizehnten Jahrhundert fast selbst überschlug, kamen doch von einer ganz anderen Seite. Aristoteles, dessen geschlossenes Werk nebst den Schriften seines Kommentators Averroes bald nach der Jahrhundertmitte nahezu vollständig vorlag, nahm das Denken seiner Anhänger wie Gegner völlig gefangen. Zum erstenmal lag der Welt wieder ein einheitliches System vor, welches nicht jenseitsbestimmt, sondern philosophisch war. Kein Wunder, daß es in dieser Zeit des sich ohnehin lockernden Glaubens über Einzelne fast wie ein Rausch kam: ein Rausch des Intellekts, der sich selbst genügenden Vernunft. Die extremen Aristoteliker, die sogenannten "lateinischen Averroisten" der Pariser Artistenfakultät: ein Siger von Brabant, ein Boethius von Dacien, die den Gegensatz ihrer aristotelisch-averroistischen Lehren zum katholischen Dogma nicht scheuten oder ihn bestenfalls in der Feststellung einer doppelten — einer theologischen und einer philosophischen — Wahrheit auflösten, traten damals hervor und erklärten, daß das philosophische Denken und philosophische Leben letztes Ziel und letzte Glückseligkeit des Menschen in sich selbst berge. Sie verfochten Lehrsätze, wie den, daß ein "Leben ohne Wissenschaft den Tod bedeute und das Grab eines niederen Menschen," daß es "kein höheres Lebensziel und keine höhere Lebensform gebe als sich der Philosophie zu weihen," daß "keine anderen Weisen in dieser Welt seien als allein die Philosophen," daß "der Intellekt die letzte Vollendung des

---

[15] Ch. V. Langlois, *La connaissance de la nature et du monde au moyen âge* (Paris, 1911), 70ff, 107f; über Verfasser und Abfassungszeit ebda. 49ff.

Menschen bleibe," daß "alles dem Menschen erreichbare Gute in den intellektuellen Kräften des Menschen beschlossen liege."[16] Eine Autarkie des Menschen, sofern er Philosoph ist, wird von ihnen verkündet, und das αὐταρκες ὄν, das einst der platonische Demiurg durch den νοῦς dem Kosmos verliehen, wird von dem Philosophen-Individuum jetzt wieder für sich beansprucht, somit den geistigen Menschen, der Teil hat an der Weltvernunft, als einen sich selbst genügenden Kosmos verstehend.

Hier begegnet zum erstenmal im Mittelalter die das Jenseits ausschließende oder überflüssig machende Selbstvollendung und Selbsterlösung des Menschen durch den Intellekt: das irdische Paradies des Philosophen, dem sich kein himmlisches Paradies des Gläubigen und Mystikers neben- und überordnet. Diese Ethik der averroistischen Lehre entwickelt in knappster Form Form Boethius von Dacien. *De summo bono sive de vita philosophi* nennt er seine Schrift,[17] in der er das philosophische Leben schlechthin als das höchste Gut, als die letzte Glückseligkeit des Menschen preist. Nur der Philosoph, der die Leidenschaften beherrschend glücklich und selbstzufrieden ist, lebt nach der kosmischen Ordnung der Natur *(secundum ordinem naturalem)*, während die anderen, die den Sinnen und Begierden erliegen, im Grunde gegen ihr eigenes Glück, gegen die höchste dem Menschen beschiedene Lust lebten. Trotz eines unleugbar asketischen Zuges ist aber eine Annäherung an das christliche Asketentum nicht mehr zu erwarten: die Idee des Klausner- oder des Mönchtums wird nirgends gestreift. Dem hätte schon des Aristoteles Lehre vom Menschen als ζῷον πολιτικόν entgegengestanden, und gerade dem Glücklichen empfiehlt die Nikomachische Ethik, nicht als Einsiedler zu leben.[18] Die für den Weisen geforderte Abtötung aller nicht-geistigen Leidenschaften, welche die Ruhe und Sammlung des Philosophen stören und beeinträchtigen könnten, hätte allerdings — wenigstens für die *vita contemplativa* — eine gelehrte Zurückgezogenheit nahelegen können. Aber ausgesprochen ist das wohl nirgends, und es ist auch nicht zu vergessen, in welchem Maße der Averroismus eine Philosophie geistiger Lebenslust war, die in ihrem Trachten nach rein diesseitiger Glückseligkeit und Frohheit einen stark genüßlich-hedonistischen Zug nicht entbehrt. Gerade darin, daß das Genießen rein geistig war und dennoch fast völlig im Diesseits blieb, lag aber die große Gefahr für die Kirche.

Die Reaktion auf diese im letzten tief unchristliche, ja antichristliche Bewegung der Geister, die noch die ganze Renaissance durchzitterte, blieb nicht aus. Sie wurde getragen zunächst von den Vertretern der sich teils aristotelisch teils anti-aristotelisch gebärdenden, aber nach den ersten großen Leistungen sich immer mehr festfahrenden scholastischen Philosophie. Wirksamer einzulenken als diese wußten gerade die erbittersten Gegner der scholastischen "Greisenknaben, die noch am Reiten auf dem Steckenpferd Vergnügen finden,"[19] nämlich die Humanisten und als deren erster Petrarca. Es ist nicht bloß dies, daß Petrarca, angewidert von dem falschen Heidnisch-Getue der unbedeutenden und banal gewordenen Spätaverroisten seiner Tage sich

---

[16] Vgl. die Liste der *errores condemnati* von 1277 bei Denifle, *Chartul. Univers. Paris.*, I, 544ff; Mandonnet, *Siger de Brabant*[2] (Louvain, 1911), II, 3ff.

[17] Ed. M. Grabmann in: *Archives d'histoire doctrinale et littéraire du moyen âge*, VI (1931), 297–307.

[18] *Eth. Nicom.*, 1169 b, IX, 9.

[19] H. W. Eppelsheimer, *Petrarca* (Bonn, 1926), 57.

energisch gegen diese absetzte und als alter Mann, der viele seiner Ideale, ja das Kunstwerk seines sorgsam durchformten Lebens durch platte Materialisten verfratzt und ge-
fährdet sah, schließlich erklärte: "Je mehr ich gegen den Glauben Christi reden höre,
desto mehr liebe ich Christus und desto unerschütterlicher wird mein Glauben."[20] Sein
Kampf gegen die Averroisten erfolgte von einer ganz anderen Grundhaltung her.

Petrarca mochte in seiner Art des Denkens vielleicht heidnischer gewesen sein als die
Averroisten, wenn man darunter das wirklich sichere Fußen auch in eine außerchristliche
Welt verstehen will, aber er war keineswegs unchristlich oder gar antichristlich wie jene.
Davor bewahrte ihn neben Vielem — Innerem wie Äußerem — schon seine stoische
Lebens- und Moralphilosophie, deren Übereinstimmung mit der christlichen Lehre
nachzuweisen, sie im Geiste Ciceros und Senecas zu erneuern und sie mit dem eines
Hieronymus und Augustin zu verbinden er Zeit seines Lebens bemüht war.[21]Wenn er
meint, in Cicero "nicht einen heidnischen Philosophen, sondern einen christlichen
Apostel zu hören," wenn er gelegentlich erklärt, Cicero mehr als den katholischen
Zeugen glauben zu müssen und wenn er bedauert, Cicero nicht einen Katholiken
nennen zu dürfen,[22] so fließen hier und eigentlich überall in seinem Werk christlicher
Glauben und stoische Lehre leicht wie Wasser und Wein ineinander, wie das in spätantik-frühchristlicher Zeit beinah üblich war. Hatte es wirklich Zeiten gegeben, in denen
Petrarca dem Christentum gleichgültig, obwohl niemals feindlich gegenüberstand, so
hat ihn die stoische Lehre, in der er überall eine Bestätigung nicht christlicher Dogmatik,
wohl aber christlicher Lebensweisheit vorfand, stets wieder zurückgeführt, und wie in
der Divina Commedia Statius zu Vergil, so hätte Petrarca in leichter Abwandlung wohl
oft genug zu Cicero sagen dürfen:

"Durch dich ward ich ein Weiser, Christ durch dich..."

und hätte sich dabei nur in der Gesellschaft des Augustin der Confessiones befunden, der
seine eigene Bekehrung Ciceros "Hortensius" zuschreibt.[23]

Denn hierin liegt das Entscheidende: daß Petrarca gegen Aristoteles, den Abgott sowohl der Averroisten wie des "verrückten heulenden Scholastikerpöbels,"[24] nicht christliche Lehrsätze gestellt hat, sondern die stoische Lehre, die in ihm wieder ganz lebendig
geworden war, daß er das lichtere Bild des aristotelischen Weisen der nikomachischen
Ethik zwar durch das müdere, ja düstere des stoischen Weisen ersetzt hat, aber dadurch
gerade echte Antike oder echtes Heidentum — wenn auch gewiß nicht Hellenentum —
wirklich in seine eigene Gegenwart einschmelzen konnte. Cicero und Augustin waren
zu vereinigen. Eine stoisch-christliche Einheit war in vergangener Zeit schon hundertfach vorgelebt und für Petrarca selbst daher auch lebensmäßig darstellbar, während
Aristoteles' und Augustins Lehren nur buchmäßig in den Summen der Scholastiker unter

[20] In der Altersschrift gegen die Averroisten: *De sui
ipsius et multorum ignorantia*, ed. L. M. Capelli (Paris, 1906),
S. 44, übers. von H. Hefele (Jena, 1925), S. 152.
[21] Über Petrarca und sein Verhältnis zur stoischen
Lehre ein guter Abriß bei Eppelsheimer, 65ff.

[22] *De... ignorantia*, S. 45 und 52; Hefele, 153, 159; *Ep.
Fam.*, 10, 5 (II, S. 97f).
[23] *Conf.*, 3, 4. Th. Zielinski, *Cicero im Wandel der Jahrhunderte*[2] (Leipzig, 1908), S. 144.
[24] *Insanum et clamosum scolasticorum vulgus: De...
ignorantia*, 72.

Verfälschung oder Entgiftung des Griechen ausgleichbar blieben. Tatsächlich ist der seit dem Ende des dreizehnten Jahrhunderts drohende Abfall des weltlichen aufgeklärten Gelehrtentums ins Un- oder Antichristliche — besser vielleicht als durch die scholastischen Gegenargumente — durch Petrarcas stoischen Humanismus aufgefangen und wieder ins Christliche zurückgebogen worden — nachwirkend durch den ganzen ciceronianischen Humanismus hindurch bis zu den Mustersätzen im lateinischen Übungsbuch.

Dennoch ist nicht zu verkennen, daß auch Petrarca zu den Miterben jener weit ausstrahlenden aufklärerischen Geistesbewegung des Averroismus gehörte. Gegnerschaft hebt Verwandtschaft nicht auf: Petrarca ist nicht der Erste gewesen und nicht der Letzte, der, was er am meisten bekämpfte, doch zutiefst in sich trug. Er kannte Abaelards Briefe, er besaß sie sogar.[25] In seiner Schrift "Vom einsamen Leben," in der er sein eigenes Einsiedlerdasein verteidigt und heidnische wie christliche Eremiten-Vorgänger aufzählt, erwähnt Petrarca auch Abaelards Klausner-Akademie in der Einöde bei Troyes und nennt ihn einen Mann von angeblich fragwürdiger Rechtgläubigkeit, "aber wahrscheinlich von nicht geringem Ingenium."[26] Trotzdem ist es nicht einfache Abhängigkeit sowenig wie bloßer Zufall, daß Petrarcas Briefsammlung "An die Freunde" mit einer Selbstbiographie, dem "Brief an die Nachwelt," beginnt wie Abaelards Briefwechsel mit der autobiographischen "Geschichte seines Unglücks"; daß er mit gleicher Heftigkeit wie Abaelard und gleichem Sarkasmus, ja zuweilen mit den gleichen, Cicero entlehnten Worten[27] gegen die Ehe von Gelehrten wettert; daß er wie Abaelard die Einsamkeit preist und daß er in seiner "Vaucluse" wie jener im "Parakleten" ein Leben gelehrter Zurückgezogenheit führte. Was beiden gemein ist und sie über alle philosophischen Gegensätze hinweg verbindet, das ist das Wichtignehmen des eigenen Ich — keimhaft nur als ein Kult der eigenen gottverwandten Vernunft bei Abaelard, voll entwickelt als Kult nicht nur der Vernunft sondern der gesamten eigenen Persönlichkeit, des "Menschen" bei Petrarca. Das Bindeglied zwischen beiden aber wird man bei den lateinischen Averroisten des dreizehnten Jahrhunderts zu suchen haben und in ihrer schrankenlosen Aufhöhung des Philosophen als eines der seltenen Träger der überpersönlichen Weltvernunft. Trotz aller Schmähungen, die Petrarca gegen die Averroisten schleudert: seine dem Dienst und Kult des eigenen Menschen geweihte Lebensführung wäre kaum ohne jenen vorangegangenen Kult des Philosophen, wie ihn ein Boethius von Dacien etwa vertrat, denkbar gewesen. Wenn je einer das *summum bonum* in der *vita philosophi* gesucht und es schließlich in der eigenen Philosophen-, Gelehrten-, Dichterpersönlichkeit zu finden gehofft hat, so war es Petrarca. Daß ihm dies nicht vollständig glückte, weil er die Himmel nicht preisgab, ist eine Frage für sich. Aber auch der Sinn seines wissenschaftlichen Trachtens neigte sich zu Zeiten fast ganz dem Ziel der eigenen Glückseligkeit und Selbstvollendung zu, und wenn er in späten Jahren sich rechtfertigend und sich gegen die Averroisten abgrenzend erklärt: "Aus den Wissenschaften suchte ich,

---

[25] H. Schmelzer, *Petrarcas Verhältnis zur vorausgehenden christlichen Philosophie des Abendlandes* (Bonn, 1911), 13, der die positive Beziehung zu den Averroisten jedoch nicht berührt.

[26] *De vita solitaria*, 2, 7, 1; *Opera* (Basel, 1581), S. 278.
[27] Abaelard, ed. Cousin, I, S. 13; Petrarca, *Ep. sen.*, 14, 4; *De remediis*, 2, 18.

solange ich sie besonnen trieb, nichts als die Mittel um gut zu sein,"[28] so ist — ganz abgesehen von der Einräumung eines zu Zeiten doch andersgearteten Wissenschaftszieles
— auch das Gut-Sein noch nicht unmittelbar eins mit dem christlichen Ziel des jen-
seitigen Heils, sondern zunächst eher mit jener stoisch begriffenen Tugend, die lernbar
ist und erwerbbar durch Wissen. Zwar bezweifelt Petrarca in diesen späten Jahren, daß
— wie Aristoteles und andere versprächen — die Wissenschaft an Stelle von Gott
wirklich zum Guten führen könnte.[29] Aber wenn er in einer der vielen Stunden des
Zweifels die letzte Vollendung auch des Weisen in eine andere Welt verlegt, so preist er
den Himmel doch vor allem deshalb, weil in ihm der Gelehrte "im Vollbesitz seiner Vernunft aufhört, sterblich zu sein."[30]

Aber trotz mancher Fäden, die von Petrarca zu den Averroisten herüberwebten: in
ihm, in seiner christlich-stoischen Ethik, ja Mystik bleibt doch die eigentliche Gegenkraft
gegen die Aristotelesjünger scholastischer wie averroistischer Prägung verkörpert, bis die
Platoniker von Florenz ihn ablösten und sein Amt übernahmen. Denn schlummernd
noch im *somnium Scipionis* stand mit Petrarca in Wahrheit schon Platon gegen Aristoteles
auf. In einem Zeitalter, das fasziniert war von der aristotelischen Lehre: der Mensch sei
von Natur ein ζῷον πολιτικόν konnte Petrarca den Ausspruch tun: "Die Natur unsere
Führerin hat uns zu Einsamen gemacht."[31] Was konnte schärfer die völlig andere Lebens-
haltung kennzeichnen als dieses Wort! Es ist — Petrarca beruft sich gern darauf — die
"vornehmere Seele," die hier als Protest gegen das aristotelische Gemeinschaftstier
ein stoisches *odi profanum* spricht, die im Bewußtsein ihres besonderen Adels die Menschen-
gemeinschaft ablehnt, an einer erwünschten Gemeinschaft auf höherer Stufe aber ver-
zweifelt[32] und sich darum, vornehm und einsam, von dem immer geschäftigen Haufen
trennt. Hier ist eine Hybris im antiken Sinn wirksam, deren Vermeidung den großen
hellenischen Weisen gebot, sich nicht den Göttern gleich von den Menschen zu sondern
... eine Hybris, im Gewande der stoischen Verachtung des ungebildeten Vulgus, seltsam gepaart mit christlicher Weltverachtung, die in Petrarca durchaus auch Wesen
hatte. So wird es zugleich Flucht vor der Welt, deren Lockungen er nur schwer
widersteht, und Flucht vor der plebejischen Menge,[33] mit der ihn nichts verbindet, wenn
Petrarca, jung noch, die tatsächliche Einsamkeit der weltentrückten Klause aufsucht.
Der Gegensatz zwischen gebildeten und ungebildeten Ständen, denjenigen von Klerus
und Laien der früheren Jahrhunderte vertretend, war durch Petrarca plötzlich sichtbar geworden.[34] Nur für den Gebildeten, ja nur für den Gelehrten kam ein *sibi et litteris
vacare* überhaupt in Betracht, jenes "Sich und den Wissenschaften leben," wie die von

---

[28] *De ... ignorantia*, 28, Hefele, 138.

[29] Ebda.

[30] *De contemptu mundi*, in *Opp.*, 337, Hefele, 32, Eppelsheimer, 74.

[31] *Natura dux nostra nos solitarios fecit: Fam.*, 9, 14 (II,
S. 54). Über Petrarcas Weltflucht: Koerting, *Petrarcas
Leben und Werke* (Leipzig, 1878), S. 578ff., im Anschluß an
die Besprechung des Traktats "De vita solitaria";
weiteres Material bei Eugen Wolf, *Petrarca* (Leipzig,

1926), 47ff; gute Bemerkungen im Anschluß an Cicero
bei Zielinski, a. a. O., 166f, 246ff.

[32] *Vita solit.*, 1, 1, 3; *Opp.*, 227: ... *iucundam ociosamque
frequentiam solitudini meste ac sollicite preferre non metuam*.

[33] *Vita solit.*, 1, 4; 8; *Opp.*, 239; Zielinski 246f.

[34] Vgl. etwa den bekannten Brief an Boccaccio über
Dante: *Ep. Fam.*, 21, 15; die Tendenz setzt schon mit den
Troubadours ein und ihrer Antithese von *cortois* und
vilain, vgl. Wechssler, *D. Kulturproblem des Minnesangs*
(Halle, 1909), I, 31f, 52ff.

Cicero überkommene Formel lautete,[35] die ja nichts anderes umschrieb als ein gelehrtes *otium cum dignitate* in würdiger Zurückgezogenheit und anmutsvoller Umgebung — seit Petrarca der Traum aller Humanisten.

Allein, vollständig fügte sich das Leben in der Einsamkeit Petrarcas Idealbild des stoisch-christlichen Weisen, wie er selbst es gezeichnet, dennoch nicht ein.[36] Er konnte zwar mit Scipio sagen: "Nie bin ich weniger allein, als wenn ich allein bin."[37] Aber sein Wunschbild geht doch dahin, nicht nur in seiner Klause, sondern auch mitten im Lärm der Welt der einsame Einzelne zu bleiben und unberührt von dem "Gewühl des sich drängenden und stoßenden Pöbels"[38] sein inneres Gleichgewicht und sein äußeres Profil zu bewahren. "Wenn du alle Leidenschaft in dir ertötet, wenn du dich ganz der Tugend hingegeben hast, dann wirst du frei sein, bedürfnislos und unabhängig, in Wahrheit ein Mächtiger in lückenlosem Glück." So spricht in der traumhaften "Selbstbeichte" Augustin zu Petrarca und wiederholt an anderer Stelle: "So wirst du dann einmal am sicheren trockenen Ufer stehen und anderer Menschen Schiffbruch betrachten und das jammervolle Klagen der Ertrinkenden ruhigen Herzens hören. Und neben dem Mitleid, das dieses traurige Schauspiel in dir erregen mag, wirst du eine tiefe Freude empfinden über dein festbegründetes sicheres Glück, das du aus so vielen Gefahren dir errettet hast."[39] Es ist ein stoischer Augustin, der hier spricht, für den die *vanitas vanitatum* nicht eigentlich im Erdenleben überhaupt liegt, sondern zunächst im törichten Treiben der unwissenden Anderen, und der nicht in dem sicheren Schoße der anderen Welt das "festbegründete sichere Glück" sucht, sondern zunächst in dem Wissen und in der Tugend. Es ist auch weniger eine christliche Askese als die stoische Askese um der Tugend willen, die wiederum nicht zu trennen ist von Bildung und Wissen und bedingt wird durch die Abtötung der Leidenschaften: nur der Sieg der Vernunft über die Affekte kann die Tugend, kann jene Glückseligkeit und die ruhige freie Heiterkeit der Seele verbürgen, die allein dem Weisen beschieden ist und die ihm schließlich nach langer Abhärtung auch im Lärm der Städte die unerschütterbare Ruhe verleiht.

Nicht ob Petrarca so war, geht hier an, sondern daß diesem Wunschbild des antiken Weisen sein Sehnen galt. Wenn er als ein Dreiunddreißigjähriger (1337) die Stadt flieht und sich mit seinen Büchern nach Vaucluse, jenem idyllischen Fleck am Alpenauslauf, am Quell der Sorgue, am Rande fruchtbarer Triften zurückzieht, um hier durch sechzehn Jahre, obwohl mit oft langen Unterbrechungen, zu weilen, so ist ihm diese Weltflucht einmal das Mittel, sich selbst zu finden und ein stoischer Weiser zu werden. Aber es ist ihm zugleich Selbstzweck, weil er in dieser äußeren Umgebung seinem Wunschbild, nach welchem er sein Leben zu formen trachtete, auch wirklich am meisten zu entsprechen vermag. Es ist der Gelehrte, nicht etwa der Büßer und Heilige, der um des Otium willen und aus Liebe zur Wissenschaft die ländliche Stille sucht, die dem denkenden Verstande nötig ist.[40] Es spricht der Dichter aus ihm mit dem Wort des Horaz:

[35] Zielinski, a. O., 248.
[36] Wolf, *Petrarca*, 56, hat das richtig erkannt.
[37] *Vita solit.*, 2, 10, 9; *Opp.*, 292. Wolf, a. a. O., 61.
[38] *De contemptu*, in *Opp.*, 350; Hefele, 70.

[39] Eppelsheimer, 68f; *De contemptu*, in *Opp.*, 345, 351f; Hefele, 55, 74.
[40] *De . . . ignorantia*, 35; Hefele, 144.

Silva placet musis, urbs est inimica poetis....[41] Es spricht die Sehnsucht nach der beseelten Landschaft und der süßen Idylle mit blauem Himmel, Bergen, Bäumen, Blumen, Bach, nicht etwa nach der rauhen Einsamkeit, in welche einst die Wüstenväter entflohen, um den Leib zu kasteien.[42] Es spricht das Verlangen nach der zeitlosen und raumentrückten Heiterkeit der Seele, jener γαλήνη τῆς ψυχῆς über die Seneca, dem er Briefe schreibt, ein eignes Büchlein verfaßt hat. Es lockt die Freiheit, die ihm die *vita solitaria* beschert, die Freiheit von den Menschen, die er verachtet, von den Freunden, die er benötigt, denen er gern schreibt, deren Anwesenheit er aber nie lange erträgt, von der Liebe, die stört, weil sie "uns Gott und uns selbst vergessen läßt."[43] Es ist die schlechthin adlige Lebensform, die Adam, dem ersten Menschen und Urbild allen Adels, beschieden war, ehe Gott Eva schuf.[44] Es ist das Leben, das frei ist von materieller Not, aber auch von materieller Belastung, eine "fröhliche Armut,"[45] die durch Welten getrennt ist von dem mönchischen Armutsideal, das sein Zeitalter bewegte. Es ist das bekömmliche Leben, das den Leib nicht durch städtische Völlerei überlastet noch durch mönchische Askese schwächt: der *solitarius* freut sich seines "wohlschmeckenden Frühmahls" und die leichte einfache Kost dient nur dazu, sein Wohlbefinden zu erhöhen[46] und die rechte Stimmung zur Gelehrtenarbeit aufkommen zu lassen. Es ist das geistig und künstlerisch fruchtbare Leben, das mit den Großen des Altertums ungestört Zwiesprache zu halten gestattet und das Elend der Gegenwart vergessen läßt.[47] Und als das Wichtigste: das einsame Leben bringt dem *solitarius* den vollkommenen Einklang mit sich selbst. Es ist das Sichselbst-leben, Sichselbstfinden, Sichselbstentdecken, das "eine Art himmlischer Seligkeit" auslöst[48] und das Petrarca erstmals auf dem Gipfel des Mont Ventoux zum Erlebnis geworden war.

So wird die humanistische *vita solitaria* zu jenem egozentrischen *sibi soli vacare*, wie es Poggio nennt:[49] in Muße nur seinem eigenen Ich, der eignen Weiterbildung, der eignen Erbauung zu leben und doch zugleich in die Welt zu wirken durch die Werke, welche die Arbeitsklause des Humanisten verlassen. Die Säkularisation des Mönchgedankens, von Abaelard eingeleitet, ist hier vollzogen, aber der weltlich-geistige Bezirk hier so aufgeweitet, daß in ihm, fern von bloß planem Rationalismus, auch die Seele wieder ins Schwingen geriet und die Zelle Raum bot, den ganzen Menschen zu fassen. Das Mönchskleid war für ihn nicht mehr nötig: es war durch Petrarca wieder zum Philosophenmantel geworden, nicht bloß zum Talar des Gelehrten.

Dabei war Petrarca eine Sehnsucht auch nach dem Kloster gewiß nicht fremd. In das Wesen des Klosterlebens hat er sich oftmals hineinzudenken versucht, so etwa damals, als er für seinen Bruder, Mönch der Kartause Montrieux, die kleine Schrift "Über die Muße der Mönche" verfaßte. Er preist das Leben in klösterlicher Stille, in der das *vacate et videte* des Psalmisten sich verwirklicht, und er kann, wenn er mit dieser gott-

---

[41] *Vita solit.*, 2, 7, 2; *Opp.*, 279; der gleiche Vers auch: *De contemptu*, in *Opp.*, 350.

[42] Vgl. Körting, a. a. O., 581f.

[43] *De contemptu*, in *Opp.*, 358, Hefele, 92.

[44] *Vita solit.*, 2, 2, 1; *Opp.*, 253.

[45] Wolf, a. a. O., 53.

[46] *Vita solit.*, 1, 2, 1; *Opp.*, 227: *cibis pastus amenissimis.*

[47] *Vita solit.*, 1, 4, 8; *Opp.*, 240: *colloqui cum omnibus qui fuerunt gloriosi viri.*

[48] *Vita solit.*, 1, 4, 6–7; *Opp.*, 237.

[49] A. v. Martin, *Soziologie der Renaissance* (Stuttgart, 1932), S. 77.

erfüllten Einsamkeit die in der eignen Klause vergleicht, wohl einen Augenblick seufzend bedauern, daß er selbst "nur aus Liebe zur Wissenschaft die Stille suche."[50] Aber gerade als er in den Jahren tiefster Niedergeschlagenheit einmal den merkwürdigen Plan faßte, sich mit einigen humanistischen Freunden gemeinsam in ein entlegenes stilles Landhaus zurückzuziehen, wo man neben religiösen Übungen den humanistischen Studien und schönen Gesprächen leben wollte, war das als Idee nur wieder das vollkommene säkulare Gegenbild zur Gemeinschaft der Mönche: ein "humanistisches Kloster," das nur einem geistig verfeinerten Dasein dienen sollte.[51] Doch dieser Plan kam niemals zur Ausführung. Petrarca wurde nicht der Begründer eines humanistischen Konventikels. Was er als Humanist an die Nachwelt gab, war das Bild des gelehrten Klausners, der von seinen Büchern umgeben sich selbst und einem vornehm-einsamen durchgeistigten und schönen *otium cum dignitate* lebte.

Man hat die Ansicht ausgesprochen, daß dieses selbstsüchtige gelehrte Klausnertum sich in das "organisch gedachte Gemeinschaftsganze" des Mittelalters nicht mehr einordnen ließ, innerhalb dessen auch dem Anachoretentum als Stand eine ganz bestimmte Aufgabe zufiel.[52] Das ist so nicht richtig. Der Organismus des Mittelalters ist niemals ständisch "durchrationalisiert" gewesen, und ein wirklich lebendiges Gemeinschaftsganzes, das ein Glaube zusammenhielt, mußte schon so vielschichtig sein, daß es für jede Lebensform Raum hatte und jede Lebensform, auch die neu auftauchende, mit einem allgültigen Bild zu verbinden und über sich selbst hinauszuheben wußte. In den Tagen Petrarcas setzte ein besonderer Kult des Heiligen Hieronymus ein. Petrarca selbst hat einige lateinische Verse zu Ehren des Heiligen hinterlassen. Um 1330 schrieb Johannes Andreae, ein Freund Petrarcas, ein kleines Werk, den "Hieronymianus," zum Preise des Heiligen. Es fand zumal in Deutschland überraschend große Verbreitung, nachdem es von Johann von Neumarkt, Karls IV. Kanzler, dessen literarische Beziehungen zu Petrarca bekannt sind, ins Deutsche übersetzt worden war.[53] Um die gleiche Zeit nimmt eine Augustiner-Einsiedlerkongregation, deren Mitglieder sich "Hieronymiten" nannten, im besonderen den Kult dieses Heiligen auf, und es gehörten so vornehme und gebildete Klöster wie San Yuste und Escorial zu dieser Kongregation. Und "Hieronymianer" nannten sich auch die "Brüder vom gemeinsamen Leben" zu Deventer, aus deren Reihen schließlich auch ein Erasmus hervorgehen sollte.[54]

Der Heilige Hieronymus war seit der Mitte des vierzehnten Jahrhunderts zum Schutzpatron der Humanisten geworden. Und wer hätte sich auch besser hierfür geeignet als dieser leidenschaftliche Verteidiger Ciceros, dessen Zweifel, ob er Christ oder Ciceronianer sei, sich auch bei Petrarca noch widerspiegeln![55] Was für Dante Vergil, für

---

[50] *Vita solit.*, 1, 4, 8; *Opp.*, 239. Daß Petrarca sehr ernsthaft erwogen hat, in ein Kloster zu gehen, wird man E. Walser, *Ges. Studien zur Geistesgeschichte der Renaissance* (Basel, 1932), S. 52f zugeben müssen.

[51] *Fam.*, 8, 4 u. 5; Körting, a. O., 244f.

[52] So A. v. Martin, a. a. O., 76ff.

[53] Auf den humanististischen Hieronymuskult hat zuerst Burdach aufmerksam gemacht: *Aus Petrarcas*

deutschem Schülerkreis (—*Vom Mittelalter zur Reformation*, IV; Berlin, 1929), S. 32f. Die Materialien bei Joseph Klapper, "Aus der Frühzeit des Humanismus," in: *Festschrift f. Max Koch* (Breslau, 1926), 255ff., der auch den Hieronymianus mit der deutschen Übersetzung ediert hat: Burdach, *Vom Mittelalter zur Reformation*, VI, 2.

[54] Heimbucher, a. a. O., I, 592ff; II, 552ff.

[55] *De... ignorantia*, 77f, Hefele, 180.

Friedrich II. Augustus war: das eigne Gegenbild im unerreichbaren Altertum, das wurde für die gelehrten christlichen Humanisten Hieronymus, der sprachkundige Übersetzer, der Meister des lateinischen Stils, der gelehrte Anachoret. "Hieronymus im Gehäus" wurde das rechtfertigende Sinnbild gelehrten Klausnertums, und oftmals vergißt man auf den ihn darstellenden Bildern[56] den Heiligen-Eremiten und sieht nur noch den feinen Gelehrten, der sich nicht mehr bloß von Beeren und wildem Honig ernährt — so auf manchem Bild der Renaissance, wo der Kardinalshut eher für die Weltlichkeit seines Besitzers bürgt, wo der Totenkopf eher als gelehrtes Requisit denn als memento mori erscheint und wo die Klause beispielhaft wird für den bücherreichen Arbeitsraum eines vornehmen Gelehrten des Quattrocento, über dessen ungestörter Arbeitsruhe auch kein gewaltiger Löwe mehr zu wachen brauchte: es genügte statt seiner ein winziger wachsamer Spitz. Und vielleicht rief ihn sein Herr "Cicero" oder "Seneca."

[56] Für den Einfluß der Humanisten auf die Maler vgl. die Bemerkungen des Johannes Andreae in seinem "Hieronymianus": *Dictavi formam qua nunc in cathedra sedens (sc. Hieronymus) pingitur, cum capello ... deposito et leone mansueto; sic in locis diversis ipsius multiplicando picturas.* Klapper, in: *Festschrift M. Koch*, S. 261, vgl. 265.

THE SOVEREIGNTY OF THE ARTIST

A NOTE ON LEGAL MAXIMS
AND RENAISSANCE THEORIES OF ART

THAT THE WRITINGS of medieval jurists—glossators and commentators of Roman and canon law—might have been in any respect relevant to the development of Renaissance theories of art has rarely been taken into consideration. There is, however, an almost *a priori* reflection which would render such a hypothesis less improbable than might appear at first sight: the fact that in the thirteenth and fourteenth centuries the intelligentsia was represented, at least in Italy, largely by learned jurisprudents, and that therefore poets and humanists—occasionally even an artist, Alberti—not infrequently started their careers by studying law. Moreover, the general humanistic climate of Italy was certainly prepared by the jurists of the thirteenth century who, after all, trained their wits and demonstrated them by commenting upon a classical text—the Roman body of civil law—which in its entirety had been handed down from antiquity and was, as Petrarch understandingly put it, an *autoritas Romane antiquitatis plena*.[1] Finally, those scholars, many of whom were poets themselves, were also the men who first applied other classical authors to practical life and read the texts not only as *belles lettres* for edification but also as sources for the purpose of extracting from them such principles as might prove useful for expounding the law.[2] At any rate, an antiquity which was sys-

Reprinted, with permission, from *De Artibus Opuscula XL: Essays in Honor of Erwin Panofsky*, ed. Millard Meiss (New York, 1961), 267–279. The original has this prefatory note:

For valuable information in matters of medieval law I am greatly indebted to the kindness of Professors Stephan Kuttner and Gaines Post, while for various suggestions in other fields my thanks go to Dr. Robert L. Benson, to Professor and Mrs. Enrico de'Negri, and to Professor Erwin Panofsky.

[1] Petrarch, "Epistola ad posteros," in Francesco Petrarca, *Prose*, ed. G. Martellotti, P. G. Ricci, et al. (Milan and Naples, 1955), 10, states that he was far from disliking "legum autoritas, que absque dubio magna est et romane antiquitatis plena, qua delector." Cf. Domenico Maffei, *Gli inizi dell'umanesimo giuridico* (Milan, 1956), 36, who in his first chapter, 33–78, ably discusses the invectives against the jurists on the part of the humanists. Petrarch himself studied law apparently under the guidance of Oldradus de Ponte (?) and Joannes Andreae; see, for the letters to Joannes Andreae, *Epistolae de rebus familiaribus*, V, 7–9, and perhaps also the very Petrarchesquely unpleasant ones, IV, 15–16, ed. Giuseppe Fracassetti (Florence, 1859), I, 273–282, 237–247; according to Savigny, *Geschichte des römischen Rechts im Mittelalter* (Heidelberg, 1834), VI, 112, the last two letters were not addressed to Joannes Andreae at all. Petrarch was also in correspondence with Lucas de Penna, a highly educated South-Italian jurist; cf. W. Ullmann, *The Medieval Idea of Law as Represented by Lucas de Penna* (London, 1946), 33, n. 20, and Maffei, *op. cit.*, 95ff. He had some veneration also for Cynus of Pistoia (Savigny, VI, 85), and the jurist Guglielmo da Pastrengo was his close friend.

[2] Albericus de Rosate (d. 1354), *In Digestum novum*, prooem., n. 20 (Venice, 1585, f. 3r), says unambiguously: *Allegat etiam haec scientia poetas.* See also on *Dig.*, 1, 8, 6, 5 (f. 63), where Albericus defends (against Accursius and the *Glossa ordinaria* on the Roman Corpus) the thesis that when the law is deficient and a poetic allegation might clarify the cause, "authoritates poetarum et philosophorum ... possint in causis allegari" He himself actually alleged Dante quite frequently, both the *De*

tematically applied to daily life and even enforced by the authority of the law made its first appearance within the circles of jurisprudents.

It is not intended here to discuss the easily demonstrable influence which individual laws of the Roman Corpus exercised on the artistic development of Italian cities. It is, for example, noteworthy that the laws on city planning issued by the Emperor Zeno in 474, and confirmed by Justinian in 531, found their way into the statute books of almost all Italian communes as early as the second half of the thirteenth century and occasional-ly, for instance in Pisa, even by the middle of the twelfth (1164).[3] Or we may recall that the laws concerning statues, images, and the decoration of public squares, which are found in considerable numbers in the law books of Justinian, had some effect in so far as they promoted the concept of a profane art, which was *ars publica*, in juxtaposition with a sacred art, which was *ars ecclesiastica*.[4] Nor should we forget that the idea of an equilibrium of *arma et leges*, to which Justinian referred in the proems to the *Institutes* and the *Code*, was transformed by Renaissance artists into the related ideal of *arma et litterae* and was reflected by emblematic art as well as by literary disputes, e.g., between *Militia et Jurisprudentia* or *Ars et Mars*.[5] What shall be ventured here is merely to demonstrate that certain current views of later theoreticians were foreshadowed by the writings of the jurists, and that there existed, to say the least, some strong analogies between the poetico-artistic theories of the Renaissance on the one hand and the professional doctrines of medieval jurists on the other.

There was, in the first place, a whole cluster of interrelated problems which vexed the Renaissance artists and poets and to which their attention was drawn over and over again. Was art supposed to imitate nature, or should it surpass nature and proceed beyond imitation to new invention? Was there fiction involved, and how did fiction refer to truth? What was the relationship between art and inspiration, *ars* and *ingenium*— a problem nonexistent as long as an art was a craft? The answers, of course, were never uniform, and they were contradictory even within the work of the same author.[6] Those

Monarchia and the *Divina Commedia*; cf. Bruno Nardi (*Nel mondo di Dante* [Rome, 1944], 163–173—reprinted from *Studi danteschi*, XXVI [1942]), who has collected some of these references to Dante as a legal authority. Lucas de Penna, *In Tres Libros*, prooem. (Lyon, 1544, fol. IVa), makes a similar statement concerning the legal references to poets, and adds: "Ego in illorum sententiam facillime cedo qui non credunt sine lectione auctorum posse hominem fieri literatum." As Albericus cited Dante, so would Lucas de Penna cite Petrarch; see on *Cod.*, 10, 18, 1 (f. 26va), for an allegation of *Famil.*, XII, 2, and Ullmann, *Lucas de Penna*, 33, n. 20, for other references.

[3] *Cod.*, 8, 10, 12–13. On these and other related laws, cf. Moritz Voigt, "Die römischen Baugesetze," *Sitz.Ber. Sächs. Gesellschaft der Wissenschaften zu Leipzig*, LV (1903), 175–198, esp. 190ff; for the revival and reinforcement of those laws, see Wolfgang Braunfels, *Mittelalterliche Stadtbaukunst in der Toskana* (Berlin, 1953), 88, 111 (Pisa), 114. See also H. F. Schmid, "Das Weiterleben und die Wiederbelebung antiker Institutionen im mittelalterlichen Städtewesen," *Annali di Storia del Diritto*, I (1957), 85–135.

[4] E. H. Kantorowicz, "Glosses on the State Portrait,"

Paper (not yet published) read at the Annual Meeting of the College Art Association, Pittsburgh, Pa., January 26, 1956. Cf. Karl Borinski, *Die Antike in Poetik und Kunsttheorie* (Leipzig, 1914), I, 84, n. 1, and p. 269 for other instances of legal influence.

[5] E. H. Kantorowicz, "On Transformations of Apolline Ethics," *Charites: Studien zur Altertumswissenschaft*, ed. Konrad Schauenburg (Bonn, 1957), 265–274. Jacobus a Bruck (see *ibid.*, 274, n. 45), author of *Emblemata politica* (Strasbourg and Cologne, 1618), published also a mirror of princes bearing the emblematic title *Ars et Mars* (Strasbourg, 1616); cf. Borinski, *op. cit.*, I, 191, and his study "Ein Brandenburgischer Regentenspiegel und das Fürstenideal vor dem grossen Kriege," *Studien zur vergleichenden Literaturgeschichte*, V (1905), 196–225, 323–329. See also Heinrich Fichtenau, *Arenga* (Graz and Cologne, 1957), 199 (cf. 26ff), for the change from *leges et arma* to *arma et litterae*.

[6] Cf. Rensselaer W. Lee, "*Ut pictura poesis*: The Humanistic Theory of Painting," *Art Bulletin*, XXII (1940), 197–269, esp. 204f, for the inconsistencies within the theories.

various opinions shall not occupy us here; also, the struggle about the supremacy of poetry over painting or *vice versa*, and of painting over sculpture or *vice versa*, may be left aside at this time.[7] On the other hand, the group of notions such as *ars, imitatio, natura, inventio, fictio, veritas* and divine inspiration is important because it is associated with problems which can be traced back without difficulty to the medieval jurisprudents.

"Art imitates Nature" was, of course, an Aristotelian maxim. It became generally known after the *Physics* had been translated, some time before 1200, and the likewise relevant *Poetics*, around 1250. There were, however, other literary channels accessible to the Middle Ages through which knowledge of these doctrines could have been transmitted in a more indirect fashion.[8] One of those channels, which was quite independent of the normal literary currents, was Roman law. While harking back to early Roman jurists of the first and second centuries, Justinian's *Institutes* and *Digest* reproduced, and medieval jurists therefore began to interpret, the essence of the Aristotelian maxim.[9] To be sure, in the legal jargon the famous principle did not refer to visual arts or artistic vocation at all, but referred to art only in a very special sense, far removed from painting and sculpture. It was quoted for a rather prosaic and sober purpose, that is, to clarify a certain point of the law of adoption. "It is the opinion that a younger person cannot adopt an older one; for adoption *imitates nature*, and it would be monstrous if the son were older than the father."[10] That is to say, Jurisprudence, commonly defined as an art (*ius est ars boni et aequi*),[11] "imitated nature" just as every other art was supposed to do, and imitated it, in the case of adoption, by means of an artistic fiction: though blood relationship did not necessarily exist, an older person was yet entitled to recognize a younger one legally as his son, and a younger one an older one as his father. "Therefore," writes Baldus enlarging on Bartolus, "*fiction imitates nature*, and for that reason fiction can take place only where *truth* may have its place."[12] Baldus derived his thesis from Roman law exclusively. But an author of the Trecento, such as Baldus, could hardly avoid drifting into the sphere of Aristotelian influence as well, nor would he have tried to avoid it; and thus it happened that Baldus opined on another occasion, though still in connection with the law of adoption, that "*art imitates nature* as far as it can," and then added: "Notice that fiction imitates the *idea of nature* and its style (*naturae rationem atque stylum*)."[13]

Fiction, in that whole context, had not the slightest derogatory meaning. It was as little derogatory as Petrarch's definition of the "office of the poet," which was said to

---

[7] See below, notes 63ff, and, in general, E. Garin, *La disputa delle arti nel Quattrocento* (Florence, 1948).

[8] *Physics*, II, 2, 194a21, is of course decisive, and in the *Poetics* it is the general problem of *mimesis* and *poiesis* which is relevant. The *Poetics*, however, though translated in the thirteenth century by Hermann the German, became really effective in the high Renaissance only; see Lee, *op. cit.*, 201, n. 23. Horace and Macrobius were influential; cf. Ernst Robert Curtius, *Europäische Literatur und lateinisches Mittelalter* (Berne, 1948), 442ff for Macrobius, and 524f for the long history of Dante's *di natura buona scimia*; see also H. W. Janson, *Apes and Ape Lore in the Middle Ages and the Renaissance* (London, 1952), 287ff.

[9] The relevant law is *Dig.*, 1, 7, 16; but more explicit is *Inst.*, 1, 11, 4 (see next note).

[10] *Inst.*, 1, 11, 4: "Minorem natu non posse maiorem adoptare placet: adoptio enim naturam imitatur et pro monstro est, ut maior sit filius quam pater."

[11] *Dig.*, 1, 1, 1, a passage naturally discussed hundreds of times. A late jurist, Joannes Oinotomus, on *Inst.*, 1, 11, 4 (Venice, 1643, p. 45), says *expressis verbis*: "Adoptio enim ceu ars imitatur naturam."

[12] Baldus, on *Dig.*, 17, 2, 3, n. 2 (Venice, 1586, f. 120v): "Fictio ergo imitatur naturam. Ergo fictio habet locum, ubi potest habere locum veritas." Bartolus, on the same law (ed. Venice, 1567, f. 139).

[13] Baldus, on *Dig.*, 1, 7, 16 (f. 38v): "Ars naturam imitatur inquantum potest," with the *additio*: "Nota quod fictio naturae rationem atque stylum imitatur."

"disclose and glorify the truth of things woven, as it were, into a decorous cloud of fiction."[14] Fiction was rather something artfully "created" by the art of the jurist; it was an achievement to his credit because fiction made manifest certain legal consequences, which had been hidden before or which by nature did not exist. For by fiction the jurist could create (so to speak, from nothing) a legal person, a *persona ficta*—a corporation, for example—and endow it with a truth and a life of its own; or he could interpret an existing body, such as the *corpus mysticum* of the Church, in the sense of a fictitious person, and gain a heuristic element by means of which he might arrive at new insights into administration, property rights, and other conditions. In that sense fiction was a lie as little as poetry was a lie, the latter a current assumption deriving from classical antiquity against which Petrarch struggled with all his authority.[15] Therefore Aquinas could say that fiction, far from being a lie, might on the contrary be a *figura veritatis*, because, ran his argument, otherwise all that had been said by wise and holy men or even by the Lord Himself would be held to be mendacious.[16] On the other hand, the imitation of nature was thought to be praiseworthy in itself. Consequently, a jurist of the early fourteenth century, Oldradus de Ponte, came to defend alchemy because he concluded: "Since art imitates nature, alchemists do not seem to commit a sin."[17]

A more serious aspect and a deeper layer of the problem was struck by Cynus of Pistoia, Dante's friend and himself a poet. For Cynus insisted that, in general, "civil [i.e., legal] acts have to imitate nature," just as he held that "law (*ius*) imitates nature."[18] We arrive therewith at a very broad problem: that of the legislator as an artist, because he was one who *ex officio* imitated nature. The major premise, of course, must be sought in the assumption, shared by everyone in the Middle Ages, that there existed an independent Law of Nature. On that basis, a political author such as Aegidius Romanus could build up, in his *De regimine principum*, almost a theory of royal imitation of nature, a subject touched upon already by Thomas Aquinas.[19] To him the act of legislating appeared as an art imitating nature because it imitated the law of nature. The art of the legislator,

---

[14] The definition is that of the *Privilegium* which Petrarch received at his Capitoline coronation (1341). For the corrected text, see Konrad Burdach, *Vom Mittel-alter zur Reformation*, II, part 1: *Rienzo und die geistige Wandlung seiner Zeit* (Berlin, 1913–1928), 509, n. 2: "Ignorant autem poetae officium ... in hoc esse: veritatem rei, sub amoenis coloribus absconditam et decora velut figmentorum umbra contectam, altisonis celebratam carminibus et dulcis eloquii suavitate respergat." In his *Oration*, which he delivered on the Capitol, Petrarch repeated almost these very words (*sub velamine figmentorum*) and gave as his source Macrobius (*sub poetici nube figmenti*); cf. E. H. Wilkins, "The Coronation of Petrarch," *Speculum*, XVIII (1943), 175; see also his *Studies in the Life and Works of Petrarch* (Cambridge, Mass., 1955), 306f, for an English translation of the not easily accessible text. That the *Privilegium* was inspired by Petrarch can no longer be doubted; see below, n. 60.

[15] The whole second section of his *Oration* is devoted to the subject of truth in poetry; see Wilkins, *Studies*, 306f. For the classical conception of the mendacious character of poetry, see Borinski, *Poetik und Kunsttheorie*, I, 1ff; also E. R. Curtius, *Europäische Literatur*, pp. 211, n. 1, 222f, 401.

[16] *Summa theologica*, III, q. 55, art. 4, ad 1, quoting Augustine, *De quaestionibus Evangelistarum*, II, c. 51 (Migne, *PL*, XXXV, col. 1362.)

[17] Oldradus de Ponte, *Consilia*, LXXIV, n. 1 (Venice, 1571, f. 29r); cf. XCIV, n. 8 (f. 36rb): "Sic in natura videmus, quam ars imitatur, ut insti. de adopt. § minorem."

[18] Cynus, on *Cod.* 7, 37, 3, n. 5 (Frankfurt, 1578, f. 446ra): "Civiles actus naturam habeant imitari." Also, on *Cod.*, 2, 3, 10, n. 5 (f. 51r): "Ius naturam imitatur," a passage repeated verbatim by Angelus de Ubaldis, on *Dig.*, 1, 7, 16 (Venice, 1580, f. 17v).

[19] Aegidius Romanus, *De regimine principum*, III, 2, cap. 24, (Rome, 1556, f. 307): "Ius enim positivum per artem et industriam hominum adinventum *praesupponit ius naturale*, sicut ea quae sunt artis praesupponunt quae sunt naturae." On the work of Aegidius, see the brief and clear analysis by Wilhelm Berges, *Die Fürstenspiegel des hohen und späten Mittelalters* (Stuttgart, 1938), 211–228; also p. 32 for Aquinas, *De regimine principum*, I, c. 12 ("Ea quae sunt secundum artem, imitantur ea, que sunt secundum naturam").

however, though determined by the general natural law, has to "adinvent" the *particulare* of the positive law ("Ius positivum . . . est per industriam hominum adinventum")[20]—that is, the particular application of the general law of nature to a limited space and a limited time—yet in such a fashion that the *particulare* still reflected the *generale* of the law of nature. In other words, the legislator does both more and less than "imitate nature" because he "adinvents." Nevertheless, the general rule of *ars imitatrix naturae* remains valid also for Aegidius Romanus, because the legislator's work should reflect in its proportions the totality of nature.[21] It was plausible that the legislator, commonly idealized as the "animate law," by his act of re-creating nature (so to speak) within his limited orbit, showed some resemblance to the Divine Creator when creating the totality of nature. He was therefore, as the jurists and political theoreticians asserted time and time again, *sicut deus in terris*.[22]

It is well known that according to the artistic theories of the high Renaissance the *ingenium*—artist or poet—was not uncommonly recognized as a simile of the creating God, since the artist himself was considered a "creator." Ernst Robert Curtius, who devoted the last paragraph of his learned book on medieval European literature to this problem, came to the conclusion that the concept of the *poeta creator* did not antedate the eighteenth century, when it began to make its appearance sporadically, and he quoted as an example Goethe's reflections at Strasbourg in 1775. This is, however, a date which is far too late. Cristoforo Landini in the fifteenth century styled the poet Dante at least a *procreator* like to God.[23] The *creator* metaphor was even more common with artists. Professor Panofsky called attention to statements of Dürer, which he carefully analyzed, in which Dürer explained that the artist, whom he likened to God, had the power to "create," that is, create "in his heart" something that had never been in anyone's mind before.[24] This is certainly diametrically opposed to "imitation," because Dürer's *dictum* expresses the consciousness of a non-imitating, therefore original or creative, power in the heart of the artist. Panofsky, of course, was well aware of the fact that in the later Cinquecento the *creator* metaphor was quite often applied to artists, and that the preceding generations had come very close to similar concepts.[25] They should, however,

---

[20] *Loc. cit.*; see also above. n. 19, where the sentence preceding the one quoted stresses once more the "adinvention" (f. 306v): "[ius positivum] quia semper quae sunt per artem hominum adinventa, fundantur in his quae tradita sunt a natura."

[21] *Ibid.*, III, 2, cap. 8 (f. 278r): "Si rex . . . vult . . . scire desiderata quod sit eius officium, diligenter considerare debet in naturalibus rebus. Nam si natura tota administratur per ipsum Deum, qui est princeps summus et rex regum, a quo rectissime regitur universa tota natura: quare a regimine quod videmus in naturalibus, derivari debet regimen, quod trahendum est in arte de regimine regum; *est enim ars imitatrix naturae*."

[22] There is hardly one civilian who would fail to interpret the position of the *princeps* in similar terms; cf. Kantorowicz, *The King's Two Bodies* (Princeton, 1957), 92, n. 16, for the sources; cf. Otto von Gierke, *Das deutsche Genossenschaftsrecht* (Berlin, 1881), III, 562f, nos. 119–122; also Fichtenau, *Arenga* (above, n. 5), 150, n. 8. Porphyry,

Vita Plotini, c. 3, mentions a (lost) tractate by Origen having the title: "The King the Paramount Creator" (ὅτι μόνος ποιητὴς ὁ βασιλεύς).

[23] Curtius, *Europäische Literatur*, 401ff. For Cristoforo Landini, cf. Edgar Zilsel, *Die Entstehung des Geniebegriffes* (Tübingen, 1926), 281, n. 151.

[24] Erwin Panofsky, *Albrecht Dürer* (3rd ed., Princeton, 1948), I, 279ff; see also his "Artist, Scientist, Genius: Notes on the Renaissance-Dämmerung," *Metropolitan Museum of Art: The Renaissance, A Symposium, February 8–10, 1952*, (New York, 1953), 90.

[25] Panofsky, "Artist, Scientist, Genius," 90, mentions, e.g., the Annotator to Leonardo da Vinci of ca. 1550, who makes *creatore* synonymous with Leonardo's *signore e Dio;* cf. Zilsel (*op. cit.*, 282), who mentions the interesting passage from Francesco de Hollanda, *Vier Gespräche über die Malerei geführt zu Rom 1538* (Quellenschriften für Kunstgeschichte, new series, IX; Vienna, 1899), 116 (= f. 144v).

not be confused with the etymon *poesis*, *poeta*, deriving from Greek ποιεῖν and only by mistake occasionally translated by "create." This was not the meaning the medieval authorities gave to *poeta* and *poesis*, and it may suffice here to refer to Dante, who in a famous passage of *De vulgari eloquentia* interpreted *poesis* as *fictio rhetorica musicaque composita*, thereby vaguely following Huguccio of Pisa's *Magnae derivationes*. This, and not "creator," was also the meaning which Petrarch and Boccaccio as well attributed to *poeta*, and E. R. Curtius had good reasons for reminding his readers that "the poet a creator" was in fact the application not of a classical but of a Jewish-Christian metaphor.[26]

This is indisputably correct; but when one tries to find when and where this theological metaphor was originally applied, by whom and to whom, one will have to inquire in the first place into the works of the early Decretalists around and after 1200. There indeed the metaphor appears characteristically in connection with the then relatively new papal title of *Vicarius Christi* or *Vicarius Dei*, which began to spread during the twelfth century though it had been used sporadically before.[27] Through the agency of certain decretals of Pope Innocent III, who availed himself very frequently of that title, it penetrated into canon law and was consequently interpreted and glossed on by canon lawyers. Around 1220 the canonist Tancred glossed on the words *dei vicem* of an Innocentian decretal of 1198, incorporated in one of the early collections of papal decretals, the so-called *Compilatio III*, and wrote:

> In that respect [regarding the lands of the churches] he [the pope] acts as the vicegerent of God, because he is seated in the place of Jesus Christ, who is true God and true man.... Also, *he makes something out of nothing like God*.... Also, in those affairs he acts in the place of God because he has the *plenitude of power* in matters pertaining to the Church.... Also, because he can give dispensation above and against the law.... Also, because from justice he can make injustice by correcting and changing the law.... Nor is there any person who could say to him: Why dost thou act as thou dost?[28]

[26] See Alfredo Schiaffini, "'Poesis' e 'Poeta' in Dante," *Studia philologica et litteraria in honorem L. Spitzer*, ed. A. G. Hatcher and K. L. Selig (Bern, 1958), 379–389, esp. 381 (for Petrarch and Boccaccio), 384 (Huguccio of Pisa); see also Curtius. *op. cit.*, 154.

[27] For the history of his title, see the careful monograph by Michele Maccarrone, *Vicarius Christi: Storia del titolo papale* (Rome, 1952), esp. pp. 109ff., for Innocent III.

[28] The gloss of Tancred on *Compilatio III*, 1, 5, 3 (= X 1, 7, 3), mentioned by Walter Ullmann, *Medieval Papalism* (London, 1949), 52, n. 1, was rendered more completely by Gaines Post in his review of Ullmann's book in *Speculum*, XXVI (1951), 230, and by Maccarrone, *op. cit.* 120, while the full text has been published by Brian Tierney, *Foundations of the Conciliar Theory* (Cambridge, 1955), 88, n. 1, from the Cambridge, Gonville and Caius College MS 17. It deviates only insignificantly, except for one point, from the text in the Bamberg MS Can. 19, f. 124v, of which Professor Post kindly placed a copy at my disposal:

In hoc gerit vicem dei, quia sedit in loco iesu christi, qui est verus deus et verus homo, ut in constit. innocentii "firmiter credimus" [*Comp. IV.*, 1, 1, 1, = X 1, 1, 1]. *Item de nichilo facit aliquid ut deus*, arg. III. q. vi. "hec quippe" [C. III, q. 6, c. 10], et C. de rei ux.act. 1. unica in prin. [*Cod.*, 5, 13, 1–1a]. Item, in hoc gerit vicem dei quia plenitudinem potestatis habet in rebus ecclesiasticis ut. 11. q. vi "decreto" [C. II, q. 6, c. 11], infra. de usu pallii. c. ii [X 1, 8, 2]. Item, quia potest dispensare super ius et contra ius, ut infra, de concess. pre[bende et ecclesie] non vacantis. c. 1 [X 3, 8, 1]. Item, quia de iusticia potest facere iniusticiam corrigendo ius et mutando, ut in constit. domini Innocentii III. "ut debitus" [*Comp. IV*, 2, 12, 3 = X 2, 28, 59], et c. "non debet" [*Comp. IV*, 4, 3, 3 = X, 4, 14, 8]. Nec est qui dicat ei, cur ita facis [De penitencia (C. XXXIII, q. 3), D. 3, c. 21 post].

In Tierney's transcription from the Cambridge MS the words *ut Deus* in the second clause are missing, whereas they are found in the Bamberg MS as well as in Cod. Vat. Lat. 1377, which Maccarrone, *op. cit.*, 120, has reproduced (the text, unfortunately, is marred by many errors), omitting, however, the next to the last clause.

This remarkable theory concerning the pope, who *de nichilo facit aliquid ut Deus*, passed from Tancred to Bernard Botone of Parma and his *Glossa ordinaria* on the *Liber Extra* (ca. 1245), that is, on the great collection of papal decrees composed by Raymund of Peñafort and published by Pope Gregory IX in 1234. Following Tancred, the glossator said *de nullo potest aliquid facere*, repeating also most of the other arguments; but at the same time he added a few items serving to illustrate the papal plenitude of power: the pope's initiative is derived from divine judgment, and he can change the nature of things ("dicitur habere coeleste arbitrium... et ideo etiam naturam rerum immutat").[29] Shortly thereafter, Hostiensis cited the doctrine of Tancred and the *Glossa ordinaria* in his *Summa aurea* (ca. 1250–1253). While referring to Raymund of Peñafort, who in his *Summa de casibus* (ca. 1227–1234) had jotted down thirty-four cases of prerogative rights reserved to the pope exclusively, pouring them for mnemotechnic reasons into verse, Hostiensis increased their number to sixty, and produced among his *addimenta* the line "Ens non esse facit, non ens fore...."[30] That is, "He [the pope] makes something that is, not be; and makes something that is not, come into being." Hostiensis thus added to the glosses of his predecessors also the opposite and perhaps more convincing papal capability of bringing something existing to nought (*de aliquo facit nihil*), which he explained by quoting the prerogative of *mutare etiam naturam rei*.[31] *Non ens fore*, on the other hand, he explained in the traditional way: *id est, de nihilo aliquid facit*, a doctrine which he cited once more in his *Lectura*.[32] At the end of the century Gulielmus Durandus (d. 1296) quoted the doctrine in his *Speculum iuris*, repeating also the tenet concerning the papal capability of "changing the nature of things."[33]

So far these extraordinary prerogatives had been attributed to the pope alone. In the course of time, however, they ceased to represent a papal monopoly. A French jurist of the fifteenth century, Guido Papa (d. 1487), transferred the doctrine *de nihilo aliquid facit* to the secular power, to the emperor, and thereby implicitly to kings who were "emperors within their realms" and could claim the *plenitudo potestatis* with regard to their *regna*.[34] It should not remain unmentioned, however, that by an audacious somersault the doctrine was applied also to the person from whom, no less audaciously, it had been derived—to Christ. Conrad of Halberstadt, a chronographer of the middle of the fourteenth century, discussed certain effects proceeding "a Christo pontifice summo et *primo papa*... per quem *de plenitudine potestatis* omnia *facta sunt ex nichilo*."[35] By thus transferring papal

---

[29] *Glos. ord.* on X 1, 7, 3, v. "veri Dei vicem." The Gloss on the *Liber Extra* (abbreviated: X) is quoted here according to the edition of Turin, 1588. The phrase *dicitur habere coeleste arbitrium* is a quotation from *Cod.*, 1, 1, 1, 1: "... motus nostri, quem ex caelesti arbitrio sumpserimus."

[30] Hostiensis (Henricus de Segusio), *Summa aurea*, on X 1,35 [*de officio legati*, § "Quid pertinet"] (Venice, 1586, col. 319), quotes Raymundus. The passage referred to is, as Professor Stephan Kuttner kindly informed me, Raymundus, *Summa de casibus*, 3, 27 (*de differentiis officiorum*, § 2), which, however, does not contain the phrase *ex nihilo aliquid facit* or its equivalent, See, for Hostiensis, also Ullmann, *Medieval Papalism*, 51f.

[31] See n. 29 for the *Glos. ord.* ("etiam naturam rerum immutat"). For *mutare naturam rei* see perhaps Tancred (n. 28): "de iusticia potest facere iniusticiam corrigendo ius et mutando."

[32] Hostiensis, *Lectura*, on X 1, 7, 3, v. "in primo"—a reference gratefully received from Professor Kuttner.

[33] Durandus, *Speculum iuris*, Lib. I, pt. 1 [*De legato*, § "Nunc"], n. 42, (Venice, 1602, I, 50).

[34] Guido Papa, *Consilia*, LXV, n. 9 (Lyons, 1544, f. 86).

[35] K. Wenck, "Die Chronographie Konrads von Halberstadt und verwandte Quellen," *Forschungen zur deutschen Geschichte*, XX (1880), 298, *ad annum* 1353; cf. Ingeborg Schnack, *Richard von Cluny* (Berlin, 1921), 161.

authority and canonistic maxims defining papal *plenitudo potestatis* to Christ, the "first pope,"[36] everything seems to fall again into its proper place, *virtute iuris canonici*. Christ, who had been royal or imperial during the earlier Middle Ages, was papalized—also iconographically—in the late medieval centuries, when in their turn the secular powers appropriated to themselves numerous papal prerogatives.

The question might be raised whether the canon lawyers depended upon some extralegal sources. The answer would be that this is unlikely. Peter the Lombard, it is true, advanced the hypothesis that just as man could forgive sins, so man could also be said to create; but he made it perfectly clear that the forgiving of sins was a human ministry, that in fact the Lord operated *cum servo et in servo*, and that man could make something from existing matter only, but could not create *ex nihilo*. And Aquinas bluntly denied that the creations of nature and art were really creative acts, holding with St. Augustine that none but God was a creator, because even new forms introduced by nature and art were potentially "concreated" with the *materia*.[37] All this shows merely that the question of artistic "creation" was alive, but that the answers to it were in the negative. The problem of the sources of the jurists finds a much simpler and more straightforward solution. For the source of the Decretalists was clearly the *Decretum Gratiani*, that is, a passage from St. Ambrose's *De mysteriis*, in which Ambrose discussed the Lord's Words of Institution which effected the consecration of the elements or, in the language of the twelfth and later centuries, effected the transubstantiation. "The words of Christ, who could make something out of nothing, can they not change things that are into something that they were not before? For it is no less [an achievement] to give to things new natures than to change them."[38] We have to recall that the Decretalists were glossing on the words *veri Dei vicem*. Therefore what was valid for Christ was claimed to be valid also for the *vicarius Christi*. The logic was straightforward and massive, and the frequent allegation of the Ambrosian passage by later commentators shows how remote legal thinking was from unwarranted diffidence.

What was the meaning of that surprising claim *de nihilo facit [papa] aliquid sicut Deus?* Tancred, the canonist who to our knowledge coined the phrase, gave a brief explanation. The source of the claim is the *vicariatus Dei* or *Christi* by which the pope has the *plenitudo potestatis*.[39] What the pope could do by his plenitude of power, which Tancred still

[36] For the important problem of *Christus primus papa*, see Schnack (*op. cit.*, 152ff), who assumes, probably correctly, that this designation does not antedate the twelfth century.

[37] Petrus Lombardus, *Sententiae*, IV, 5, 3, also II, 1, 3 (Migne, *PL*, CXCII, cols. 852, 651). Thomas Aquinas, *Summa theologica*, I, q. xlv, art. 8, 1, and *conclusio*. See R. H. Bainton, "Man, God, and the Church in the Age of the Renaissance," *Metropolitan Museum of Art: The Renaissance, A Symposium* (New York, 1953), 53, 62a, where attention is called to these passages, from whose interpretation, however, I deviate.

[38] *De consecratione*, D. 2, c. 69: "Sermo igitur Christi, qui potuit *ex nichilo facere quod non erat*, non potest ea, quae sunt, in id mutare, quod non erant? Non enim minus est dare, quam *mutare, novas naturas rebus*." The

passage was referred to by Bernard of Parma in *Glos. ord.* on X 1, 7, 3, and by others. There is no doubt that the legal arguments and the combination of "making something out of nothing" and "changing the nature of things" were inspired by that passage. *Vice versa*, the *Glos. ord.* on the *Decretum* (by Johannes Teutonicus, ca. 1215), *De cons.*, D. 2, c. 69, v. "minus," promptly brings the allegation to *Cod.*, 5, 13, 1–1a (below, n. 42), the paramount evidence for *de nihilo facere aliquid* ever since Tancred.

[39] The papal *plenitudo potestatis* as a hierocratic password is likewise of a relatively recent date; according to Tierney, *Conciliar Theory*, 141ff, it came into general usage in the works of the Decretists around 1200 only; a similar date is suggested by Friedrich Kempf, S. J., *Papsttum und Kaisertum bei Innozenz III.* (Rome, 1954), 296ff.; and

restricted correctly to the government of the Church, was to give dispensation above and against the law, provided that his action did not violate faith and divine or natural law (for example, he could not dissolve a consummated marriage),[40] and he could create new law, thereby making injustice what had hitherto been justice. The allegations of Tancred to the *Decretum Gratiani* and Justinian's *Code*, repeated by all his successors, indicated what *de nihilo facere* meant in the language of the jurists. A number of Breton bishops had been deposed (for good canonical reasons) by the Bishop of Dol-de-Bretagne who, however, was not the competent judge (in this case, the Archbishop of Tours). Moreover, the deposed bishops had been replaced by other bishops, whose election was invalid since their predecessors, not having been deposed by the competent judge, *de iure* still held their offices. The pope ordered a new trial before the Archbishop of Tours, but without either reinstating the deposed bishops or demoting the newly elected ones: *ex nihilo* (out of a procedurally invalid removal from office) *facit aliquid* (he recognized an invalid election). "A judgment which was none, he [the pope] makes to be one," says the ordinary Gloss.[41] Similar is the content of the allegation to the *Code*: for the purpose of reclaiming a dowry, a lawsuit of stipulation was granted, even though a stipulation had never been made—hence a *creatio ex nihilo*.[42] The *Glossa ordinaria* on the *Liber Extra* seemed to presuppose that the meaning would be self-explanatory, and offered no further commentary; but a marginal gloss was later added by the Roman correctors of the *Decretales*, in which they complained that *vix aliquid explicat [glossa] propriis verbis*, and therefore pointed out: "To make something out of nothing is to found new law (*est ius novum condere*)," that is, to legislate.[43] Hostiensis gave no further explanation either, but repeated from the ordinary Gloss the words saying that the pope could also change the nature of things, a sentence to which the marginal gloss remarked that it referred to positive law only, since the pope could not override divine or natural law.[44] This, in his turn, Durandus illustrated by referring also, though only indirectly, to the *Dictatus papae* of Gregory VII: "He can make an illegitimate legitimate, and can make a monk a canon, *et huiusmodi*."[45] Guido Papa finally explained: "He [the emperor] can [legally]

G. B. Ladner, "The Concepts of 'Ecclesia' and 'Christianitas' and their Relation to the Idea of 'Plenitudo potestatis' from Gregory VII to Boniface VIII," in *Sacerdozio e Regno da Gregorio VII a Bonifacio VIII* (Rome, 1954), 63ff, demonstrates convincingly how the concept of *plenitudo potestatis* was developed, not before the twelfth century, from that of full legatine powers. See also Alfred Hof, "*Plenitudo potestatis* und *Imitatio imperii* zur Zeit Innocenz' III," *Zs. f. Kirch. Gesch.*, LXVI (1954–55), 39–71.

[40] Tierney, *op. cit.*, 89, n. 5, also brings out in full relief the hypertrophies and exaggerations of Innocent IV's hierocratic views on this point.

[41] The allegation is C. III, q. 6, c. 10; the analogy is slightly clarified (as Professor Kuttner pointed out to me) by the *Casus* in the *Glos. ord.* to the *Decretum*, which in its turn leads Bernard of Parma, *Glos. ord.* on X 1, 7, 3, v. "veri Dei vicem," to explain: "et sententiam que nulla est, facit aliquam."

[42] *Cod.*, 5, 13, 1–1a. The principle involved is discussed by Andreas of Isernia, *In usus feudorum*, on *Feud.* II, 40

["De capitulis Corradi"], n. 29 (Naples, 1571, fol. 202va), but without mentioning the maxim *de nihilo etc.* See above, n. 38.

[43] The marginal gloss added to gl. "veri Dei vicem" on X 1, 7, 3, stresses throughout the legislating capacity: "nam de nihilo aliquid facere est ius novum condere; et de iniusticia iusticiam [*sic*; cf. above, n. 31: de iusticia iniusticiam] intellige per constitutionem iuris; et immutare substantiam rerum accipi debet in his que sunt iuris positivi." The liturgical connection (indicated in n. 38) has been ignored.

[44] Hostiensis, *loc. cit.* (above, n. 30): "de aliquo facit nihil, mutando etiam naturam rei."

[45] Durandus, *loc. cit.* (above, n. 33): "De aliquo facit nihil mutando etiam rei naturam. ... Immutat ergo substantialem rei naturam, puta faciendo de illegitimo legitimum: ut extra. qui fili sint leg. per venerabilem [X 4, 17, 13], et de monacho canonicum: ut 74 dis. quorundam [D. 74, c. 6]. Et de monacho non monachum et de capaci non capacem et huiusmodi. ... De nihilo aliquid facit...." Cf. *Dictatus papae*, § 7: "Quod illi soli

vivify a dead person and give dispensation beyond the law."[46] In other words, the papal-imperial, and probably also royal, power of "making something out of nothing" was restricted to certain technicalities of the law as well as to legislation at large.

While this simple and prosaic explanation of a seemingly bewildering claim may be disappointing at first sight and appear to lead us nowhere, the concept at issue is yet interesting enough. The ideal legislator as visualized by the jurists not only became an imitator of nature by applying the law of nature to the particular circumstances of his realm, but he was also the only person who could make new laws according to the necessities of a changing time and thereby "make something out of nothing." This, of course, was an anxiously guarded prerogative of the sovereign. In the *Dictatus papae* Pope Gregory VII monopolized for the Roman pontiff exclusively the right *pro temporis necessitate novas leges condere*,[47] whereas the most efficient pupil of the popes, the Emperor Frederick II, proclaimed in his *Liber augustalis* that it was a principal duty of the *dignitas imperialis excellentiae* to produce new laws as time and circumstances demanded ("iuxta novorum temporum qualitatem de nostro gremio nova iura producimus").[48] Moreover, the legislator, when handling his art, the *ars aequi et boni*, was able to produce something new because he was divinely inspired *ex officio*. This clue was borrowed from Roman law in which Justinian claimed to take his motive power *ex caelesti arbitrio*.[49] Divine inspiration, of course, was appropriated to himself by Frederick II in his *Liber augustalis*, in which he repeatedly cited the words of Justinian,[50] and as a matter of routine it was attributed to kings and sovereigns who had become emperor-like within their territories.[51] Above all, however, the divine inspiration in accordance with the law of Justinian was arrogated to himself by the pope,[52] the *verus imperator*, who was the vice-gerent not only of Christ the High Priest, but also of Christ the King; and it was in the papal vicariate of the *royal* Christ that an early canonist, Silvester Hispanus, found the reason why attributes and privileges of the emperor could be passed freely to the pope.[53] This transfer of claims from one dignitary to another seems to have been also an important ingredient of that

licet ... de canonica abbatiam facere et e contra...." *Das Register Gregors VII.*, ed. Erich Caspar (Berlin, 1920), 203 (*Reg.*, II, 55a). The problem concerning the change of the nature of a monk was discussed quite frequently. Tancred (see Tierney, *op. cit.*, 90, n. 5) denies that the papal *plenitudo potestatis* may allow a monk to own property, "sed de monacho potest facere non monachum." Innocent IV, however, claimed that poverty and celibacy of the monk were matters of positive law only and therefore the pope had dispensatory authority; he states quite cynically: "Monachus autem nihil est quam solitarius tristis [C. 16, q. 1, c. 8] ... ex hoc patet quod papa potest dispensare cum monacho quod habet proprium vel coniugem."

[46] Guido Papa, *loc. cit.* (above, n. 34): "dicitur [imperator] quoad temporalia deus in terris. Potest enim de nihilo aliquid facere et mortuum vivificare et super ius dispensare...."

[47] *Dictatus papae*, § 7 (above, n. 45). Cf. *Cod.*, 1, 14, 12, 3: "leges condere soli imperatori concessum est...."

[48] *Liber augustalis*, I, 38, *Constitutionum Regni Siciliarum libri III*, (Naples, 1773, p. 85). To this passage the later commentator Matthaeus de Afflictis, *In utriusque Siciliae ... Constitutiones* (Venice, 1562), I, f. 155rb, remarks: "Non autem ex hoc dicitur quod ius est variable: sic etiam Deus mutavit multa ex temporum dispositione," with allegation of X 4, 14, 8: "quoniam ipse Deus ex his, quae in veteri testamento statuerat, nonnulla mutavit in novo," a canon of Innocent III, issued at the Lateran Council of 1215 (c. 50).

[49] See above, n. 29. For the illumination and divine inspiration of the ruler see the remarks of Fichtenau, *Arenga*, 77, n. 70. The inspiration attributed to the prince by the Civilians is similar to, but not quite identical with, the earlier medieval illumination by the Holy Spirit; see my *The King's Two Bodies*, 114ff.

[50] *Liber augustalis*, I, 6 and 22 (pp. 17, 54).

[51] See, e.g., Matthaeus de Afflictis (above, n. 48), on I, 6, n. 6 (f. 49v): "quod rex huius regni [Siciliae] habet arbitrium puniendi delicta a summo Deo omnipotenti, subaudi mediante eius vicario."

[52] *Glos. ord.* on X 1, 7, 3, v. "veri Dei vicem": "unde dicitur habere caeleste arbitrium." See above, n. 29.

[53] Maccarrone, *Vicarius Christi*, 119.

mysterious power *immutandi rerum naturam*: for the *Glossa ordinaria* to the Decretals defined this power as the ability "of applying the substance of one thing to another thing (*substantialia unius rei applicando alii*)."[54]

In fact, that procedure of transferring something from one orbit to another formed, we may say, the essence of the art of the jurists, who themselves called this technique *aequiparatio*, the action of placing on equal terms two or more subjects which at first appeared to have nothing to do with each other. For example, the Church, a city, and a maniac were technically on equal terms as "minors" because none of them could handle his, or its, own affairs, and therefore all three were in need of a guardian.[55] This method of "equiparation," however, which was not restricted to jurisprudence, can help us to understand in what respects the theories of the jurists might appear to have been relevant to the later artistic theories. The legislator takes his impulses from divine inspiration, and he creates certain judgments and technicalities out of nothing, but he does all that *ex officio*, just as he imitates nature likewise by virtue of his office and not as an individual poetic or artistic genius. The equiparation, however, of poet and emperor or king—that is, of the poet and the highest office representing sovereignty—began as early as Dante. When Dante sadly praised Apollo's laurel, of which in his days "so rarely frond was gathered for the triumph of either a Caesar or a poet (*per trionfare o Cesare o poeta*)," he actually "equiparated" Caesar and poet by means of a *tertium*, the crown of laurel,[56] transforming a line of Statius: "The twin laurels of poet and warrior flourish in rivalry."[57] In other words, by means of the "Peneian frond" Caesar and poet appeared to Dante potentially on one level, since only "the highest political and the highest intellectual principates" could be decorated at all with the laurel.[58] The coronation of Petrarch in 1341 made this equiparation manifest. Wrapped in the royal purple of King Robert of Naples, which had been given to him for that purpose (*regia vestis circumfusa me tegebat*),[59] Petrarch received the crown of laurel on the Roman Capitol and thereby demonstrated to the world of learning and art universally to what extent indeed king and poet moved *pari passu*. Moreover, in the diploma or *Privilegium* which the Roman senator handed over to Petrarch at the coronation ceremony and which was, to say the least, inspired by Petrarch himself,[60] we find the notion *officium poetae*, a notion repeated several times by Petrarch and defined as the disclosure of truth woven into a decorous cloud of fiction.[61] Here then poetical art itself was presented as an "office," the *officium poetae*. Finally, there occurs, thrice repeated in the *Privilegium* and eight times repeated in Petrarch's *Oratio*, the combination of "Caesars and poets," to which Petrarch in other writings referred at least six times, expressing the idea that the glory of Caesars and of poets justified the award of the wreath of laurel because the eternal verdure was earned *tam bello quam*

---

[54] *Glos. ord.* on X 1, 7, 3: "et ideo etiam naturam rerum immutat, substantialia unius rei applicando alii, argumen. C. communia de leg. 1. 2 [*Cod.*, 6, 43, 2]."

[55] *Dig.*, 4, 6, 22, 2: "Quod edictum etiam ad furiosos et infantes et civitates pertinere Labeo ait." The Church eventually was treated as a *universitas* or a *civitas*; see my *The King's Two Bodies*, 374f.

[56] *Parad.*, I, 28ff.

[57] Statius, *Achilleid*, I, 15f: "... cui geminae florent vatumque ducumque / Certatim laurus." Cf. E. H. Wilkins, "Coronation of Petrarch," 161ff, 176.

[58] Burdach, *Vom Mittelalter zur Reformation*, II, pt. 1, p. 505.

[59] Wilkins, "Coronation of Petrarch," 182.

[60] Cf. Burdach, *op. cit.*, 508f; Wilkins, *op. cit.*, 187.

[61] Burdach, *op. cit.*, 509, n. 2; see above, n. 14.

ingenio, "by both war and ingenium."[62] Clearly expressed on that occasion also was the related idea that immortality was won by both great exploits and the poet's song.[63] It was quite obviously at this point, or even with Dante's equiparation of Caesars and poets, that the ideal of *arma et litterae* began to supersede that of *arma et leges*, familiar to Justinian and current in the circles of jurists.[64]

With Petrarch's Capitoline coronation ceremony the equiparation of prince and poet ceased to be a mere metaphor: its quasi reality had been demonstrated *ad oculos*, if in a slightly theatrical and stage-like fashion. Nor did the equiparation stop at this point. On the basis of fame, or its fickleness, already Dante had treated painters and poets on equal terms.[65] And Petrarch, in good classical fashion, styled Homer a painter, *primo pittor delle memorie antiche*.[66] It was finally Horace's *Ars poetica* which extended the new and quasi-sovereign status of the poet to the painter; for the Horatian metaphor *ut pictura poesis*, or rather its inversion *ut poesis pictura*, became the passkey which eventually opened the latches to the doors of every art—first to that of the painter, then to the arts of the sculptor and the architect as well. They all became liberal artists, divinely inspired like the poet, while their crafts appeared no less "philosophical" or even "prophetical" than poetry itself.[67] It was a cascading of capacities, beginning from the abilities and prerogatives conceded *ex officio* to the incumbent of the sovereign office of legislator, spiritual or secular, to the individual and purely human abilities and prerogatives which the poet, and eventually the artist at large, enjoyed *ex ingenio*.

If the general line drawn here and leading from the legislator and his *plenitudo potestatis* to the poet and further to the artist, be recognized as valid at all, there might be yet another item worth mentioning. The many-sidedness or all-sidedness of the artist as *uomo universale*, so characteristic of the Renaissance, will correctly be traced back to Vitruvius, who demanded that the architect be literate, able to draw, educated in geometry, optics, arithmetic, that he know history, philosophy, music, and that he have some knowledge of medicine, jurisprudence, and astrology.[68] The same list replacing only jurisprudence by perspective (*prospectiva*), was considered essential by Ghiberti for the painter and the sculptor: "Conviene che 'llo scultore etiamdio el pictore sia amaestrato in tutte queste arti liberali."[69] But quite independently of Vitruvius, the jurists

[62] Wilkins, *op. cit.*, 176, 179; see p. 187 for the *Oratio* and the *Privilegium*, which both use the phrase *tam bello quam ingenio*; also pp. 176, 186.

[63] Burdach, *op. cit.*, 508.

[64] See above, n. 5.

[65] *Purg.*, XI, 79ff: the miniaturists Oderisi and Franco Bolognese, the painters Cimabue and Giotto, and the poets Guittone d'Arezzo and Guido Cavalcanti represent three pairs of artists symbolizing the vanity of fame, the fame of the earlier one being always eclipsed by that of the later one—an early parallelism of miniaturist, painter, and poet to which Professor Panofsky called my attention.

[66] *Trionfo della Fama*, III, 15; Borinski, *Poetik und Kunsttheorie*, I, 184.

[67] Borinski, *op. cit.*, I, 183ff; Rensselaer W. Lee, "Ut pictura poesis," 199ff and n. 14, reproducing the famous passage from Cennini, who coupled painting and poetry on grounds of imaginative freedom. See also Lorenzo Valla, who in *Elegantiae*, praefatio (Basel, 1571, p. 11), called the fine arts *illae artes, quae proxime ad liberales accedunt*, a passage which Professor Panofsky kindly recalled to my memory.

[68] Zilsel, *Geniebegriff*, 260ff, sounds a very necessary warning against overestimating the ideal of the *uomo universale* in the Renaissance; see also Bainton (above, n. 37), 53. The ideal of Vitruvius, *De architectura*, I, 1, however, had a lasting influence on Renaissance theories of art.

[69] Ghiberti, *I Commentarii*, ed. Julius von Schlosser (Berlin, 1912), I, 4; cf. 12f; Ghiberti himself (I, p. 16 = I, c. 18) says about Lysippus: "Questo Lisyppo fu doctissimo in tutta l'arte et universale." And the same polymathy was expected in the sixteenth century by

demanded the same kind of universalism for their trade: "Legal science," wrote Albericus de Rosate in the fourteenth century, "is commendable because it is more universal than other sciences; for other branches of knowledge deal with something particular; that one, however, deals with almost all sciences and especially with the liberal ones." And he enumerates grammar, dialectic, logic, rhetoric, arithmetic, geometry, mathematics, music, astrology, moral philosophy, medicine, and literature, showing in each case why this or that art was relevant to jurisprudence.[70] We notice that the ideal of mastering a universal complex of disciplines was something belonging to the encyclopedic ideal of the thirteenth century which, by transference, was then applied also to the artists—thus interiorizing, as it were, the universalism of the two universal powers. Or when Petrarch, in connection with the poetical examination preceding his coronation, wrote about "rex Siculus... quem e cunctis mortalibus, equiore animo, ingenii iudicem pati possum," did he not imply that, with the exception of his royal friend ("illum summum et regem et philosophum Robertum"), no mortal could judge Petrarch's *ingenium*?[71] And should we not think of that maxim encompassing the very essence of sovereignty, that privilege claimed by the pope (and soon also by the royal power), to wit, that the sovereign could judge all, but be judged by none?[72] Dante had certainly usurped the sovereign power of judging all men, just as Petrarch could not suffer to be judged by any mortal save his royal friend. Here the Pauline device (1 Cor. 2, 15), "Spiritualis autem iudicat omnia et ipse a nemine iudicatur," monopolized by the Holy See (*Sancta sedes iudicat omnia*) and forming later on a prerogative of the incumbent of the sovereign office at large, has reverted again to its original meaning: the spiritual man in general, the true *pneumatikos*, who was filled with the Spirit, could be judged by none because he was sovereign as a vessel of the Spirit. The Spirit (*pneuma*), it is true, was secularized when the *ingenium* claimed to be above and beyond judgment; but the inspiration from on high was there none the less. Again, we notice that a legal prerogative due to the sovereign *ex officio* has been passed on to the true Renaissance sovereigns, the artists and poets, who ruled *ex ingenio*.[73] And we may remember how, in the fifth circle of Dante s *Purgatory*, a pope

Francesco de Hollanda, *Vier Gespräche*, p. LXXX: the painter is required to know the Latin authors, the Greek ones at least in translation, natural philosophy, theology (including knowledge of the Bible and hagiography), history, poetics, music, cosmography, astronomy, mathematics, physiognomics, and anatomy.

[70] Albericus de Rosate, *In Dig. novum*, prooem., nos. 16ff, (fols. 2v–3r), begins by "equiparating" jurisprudence with theology: "Nec dicat quis me hanc legalem scientiam ultra debitum sublimare, eam aequiparando sacrae scripturae.... Iuris prudentia est divinarum et humanarum rerum notitia [*Dig.*, 1, 1, 10, 2; *Inst.*, 1, 1, 1], non ergo incongrue assimilatur scripturae divinae. Ex his etiam commendabilis est haec legalis scientia, quia universalior est aliis scientiis. Aliae enim scientiae de aliquo particulari tractant; haec autem quasi de omnibus scientiis et maxime liberalibus tractat." He then demonstrates why all the disciplines are needed for, and how they come into the compass of, jurisprudence, which thus emerges as a secularized theology.

[71] *Ep. famil.*, IV, 4, ed. Fracassetti, I, 211, and "Epistola ad posteros," in *Prose*, ed. Martellotti, p. 14; cf. Wilkins, "Coronation of Petrarch," 180f.

[72] For the weird history of that axiomatic notion, see Albert Michael Koeniger, "Prima sedes a nemine iudicatur," *Beiträge zur Geschichte des christlichen Altertums und der byzantinischen Literatur: Festgabe für Albert Ehrhard*, (Bonn and Leipzig, 1922), 273–300; for Boniface VIII, who quoted the maxim in his bull *Unam sanctam* (cf. *Extravagantes commun.*, I, 8, 1), see Burdach, *op. cit.*, 538ff; and for the transfer of the maxim to the royal power, see my article "Mysteries of State," *Harvard Theological Review*, XLVIII (1955), 75f.

[73] It should be mentioned, however, that in a letter to Barbatus of Sulmona (*Ep. variae*, XXII, ed. Fracassetti [Florence, 1865], III, 353ff, esp. 359) Petrarch scornfully refused to be called metaphorically king of poets: "Ingenue quidem regis poetarum appellationem respuo. Ubi enim regnum hoc exerceam quaeso? Quos mihi statuis regni fines?... Ubi sedere, quove ire iubes, ut sim vatum rex, nisi forte in solitudinem meam transalpinam, atque ad fontem Sorgiae me restringis?"

(Hadrian V) and a king (Hugh Capet) had to continue their penitence among the weeping souls, whereas the soul of a poet, Statius, was released and set free while the earth trembled.[74]

No one aware of the late medieval development of political theories will be surprised to find an analogous development within the field of artistic theories. The supreme human authority no longer was vested in the officer alone, be he emperor, king, or pope. It was vested in man as well or, as Dante would have said with Aristotle, in the *optimus homo* adorned "with mitre and with crown."[75] To be Man, in the emphatic sense of the word, had come to be an *officium*, not only for the Neo-Platonists or for Campanella,[76] but already for Dante. And through the agency of Petrarch the *officium poetae* had become a well articulated notion. Every *officium*, however, in order to assert itself, demanded or was in need of some kind of quasi-theological justification and exaltation. This arrogation of a *plenitudo potestatis* was true of the offices of the spiritual and secular powers, and it became true for the offices of poet and, by transference, of painter and artist at large. It may therefore not have been amiss to raise the question here to what extent and in what respects the artistic theology of the Renaissance followed certain trails first marked out by the political theology of medieval jurists.

---

[74] *Purg.* XIX–XXI. Professor Enrico de' Negri kindly called my attention to these interrelations between pope, king, and poet; see also his study "Tema e iconografia del Purgatorio," *Romanic Review*, XLIX (1958), 97f.

[75] *De Monarchia*, III, 12; *Purg.*, XXVII, 142; Kantorowicz, *King's Two Bodies*, 456ff, 460, 493.

[76] Cf. Lilo Ebel, *Die italienische Kultur und der Geist der Tragödie* (Freiburg, 1948), 174ff. T. Campanella, *Del senso delle cose e della magia*, II, c. 25, ed. Antonio Bruers (Bari, 1925), 125, calls man *luogotenente della prima causa*, that is, a vicar of God, though not by virtue of a high office.

THE ESTE PORTRAIT BY ROGER VAN DER WEYDEN

AMONGST THE GREAT PRINCES of Renaissance Italy many have greater claims on fame than Lionello d'Este. His life was not distinguished by great exploits or picturesque events. He was no diplomat, holding the balance of Italy, nor did he, like a Federico of Urbino, combine military prowess with enlightened patronage. His memory is more personal: he had the charm of youth, of unfulfilled promise, of full participation in the thoughts of his time; and in Pisanello's portrait he has a memorial which gives these qualities a vigorous and lasting reality. The forceful, passionate mouth, the oddly shaped head have little claim to beauty, but their distinction is the more evident for their ugliness, a distinction which accords with all that is known of this prince, who was so eager in his interest in all that his age held worth the knowing, who enjoyed love before a new disease poisoned its pleasures, who ruled his marquisate skilfully and peacefully, and who died at the age of forty-three. It was a moment when Italian humanism felt to the full the delight of new discoveries; Lionello exchanged letters with his teacher Guarino, and Poggio, Enea Silvio and Filelfo praised his Latin diction. Leon Battista Alberti wrote his treatises at Lionello's instigation and Theodore of Gaza came to Ferrara as his guest. If Caesar was the marquis's great hero, the polyglot St. Jerome was his favourite among the saints.

It is an unsolved question whether the vivid memory we retain of the princes of the Renaissance is due to their own genius or to that of the artists who transmitted the essence of their being to posterity. Poets and artists—as Italian doctrine then would have it—bestowed immortality upon princes. Poets and artists, therefore, claimed the gift of creating life anew, in an almost god-like manner, and, if the poets of the 15th century did not live up to their ambitions, the artists redeemed their promises. If we think of Federico of Urbino, the recollection of his life and his merits may be somewhat indistinct but we will immediately visualize either his portrait by Piero della Francesca or those painted by the latter's pupil, Justus van Ghent. The youthful Julius II appears to us as Melozzo saw him; as Popes, we see Julius II and Leo X as Raphael represented them, and Colleoni we see only with the eye of Verrocchio, in spite of the knowledge that the great condottiere and father of soldiers was much less demonic and superb than the statue would have us believe. Thus the princes of the Italian Renaissance seem to lead a double life in their after-days: one of their own and one that the artists bestowed upon them, and the image that dominates our mind is the more powerful the nearer the Renaissance is to its zenith, and the more the artist is swayed by his own free will and his own imagination.

Reprinted, with permission, from the *Journal of the Warburg and Courtauld Institutes*, III (1939–1940), 165–180.

This discrepancy between historical and artistic posthumous traditions, more noticeable in Central and Northern Italy than in Venice or the Southern provinces, holds good for Lionello d'Este. He lives through Pisanello's famous portrait at Bergamo, a visual statement of personality so convincing that we can form no other mental image, nor is there any reason to doubt the accuracy of the representation. Lionello took much care of outward appearances. It is said of him that, as a firm believer in the harmony of the universe, he habitually chose the colours of his clothes according to the positions of the planets and the day of the week. Something of this colour mysticism, of this cosmic conduct of life, of this endeavour to carry this stellar world into terrestrial existence, seems to have been caught by his court painter so fully that we can hardly picture the prince otherwise.[1]

There is a further reason for our seeing Lionello only as this master saw him: apart from Pisanello's painting and portrait medals of him there do not exist any other pictures or pictorial conceptions representing him. It is true that other medals are known—a very fine one was cut by Master Nicholaus[2] (pl. 35, fig. 4a)—but these, or at least the portraits they display, seem inspired by Pisanello, and the panel by the Ferrarese painter Giovanni Orioli is also completely under the same influence, though it shows none of Pisanello's concentration or intensity,[3] being nor better nor worse than a bland Roman replica of a Greek marble or bronze. A portrait by Jacopo Bellini, painted in 1441 in competition with Pisanello, has unfortunately disappeared, and Mantegna, from whom an original conception might well have been expected, may never have executed the portrait he was asked to paint. It can therefore be said that there remains but one portrait, that at Bergamo, which shows Lionello's clear-cut profile outlined against a dark background, and which reveals so much of the man's character and at the same time stimulates the imagination by its reticences and by what it seems to withhold.

Thus, when thirty years ago[4] Friedländer discovered a portrait by Roger van der Weyden which could be identified with Lionello d'Este,[5] great satisfaction was felt; indeed, it was regarded as something of a revelation (pl. 33, fig. 1). Everything seemed to fit to perfection. An interchange of relations between Ferrara and Brussels was known to have existed. Roger was said to have gone on a pilgrimage to Rome in the Holy Year 1450, Italian writers testify that pictures by his hand had been seen in Ferrara before and after this date,[6] an order for payment in connection with some work he had carried out for Lionello was found,[7] and, last but not least, the coat of arms on the reverse side of the newly discovered portrait turned out to be that of Lionello d'Este himself (pl. 36,

[1] On the intellectual and artistic life at Ferrara see: Gustave Gruyer, *L'art ferrarais à l'époque des princes d'Este,* 2 vol. (Paris, 1897); E. G. Gardner, *Dukes and poets in Ferrara* (New York, 1904); George Francis Hill, *Pisanello* (London and New York, 1905); Giulio Bertoni, *Guarino da Verona fra letterati e cortigiani a Ferrara (1429–60)* (Biblioteca dell' "Archivum Romanicum," I; Geneva, 1921).

[2] G. F. Hill, *A Corpus of Italian Medals of the Renaissance before Cellini* (London, 1930), pl. 18, no. 75; cf. pl. 17, no. 68 for a medal by Amadio da Milano.

[3] Hill, *Pisanello,* p. 152 and pl. 41; a reproduction of Orioli's panel (now in the National Gallery) in Gardner, *op. cit.,* pl. 2.

[4] Max J. Friedländer, "The Pictures of Roger van der Weyden in America," *Art in America,* IX (1920–21), 62.

[5] Roger Fry, *Burlington Magazine,* XVIII (1911), 200ff.

[6] The documents on Roger are collected by A. v. Wurzbach, *Niederländisches Künstler-Lexikon,* II (1910), 875, nos. xv and xvi

[7] A. Venturi, "I primordi del Rinascimento artistico a Ferrara," *Rivista storica Italiana,* I (1884), 608.

fig. 6).[8] There could be no doubt whatever: the portrait (now in the Friedsam Collection, Metropolitan Museum), posed in the well-known three-quarter view so characteristic of Roger, represented the famous Este. That here the activity and resolution, visible in the Pisanello portrait, were replaced by a certain sadness, by a thoughtful melancholy, was not deemed important, as being due to Roger's general conception of man. The new portrait, on the contrary, satisfied curiosity, for here at last was apparent that other conception of Lionello, and it is easy to understand the enthusiasm of the scholar who burst out with the words: "It is almost as though we were to get a glimpse of the other side of the moon."[9]

But who would trust the moon! The pleasure of discovery was soon followed by the disclosure of unpleasant disagreements. The suggestion was naturally advanced that Roger might have painted the panel at Ferrara in 1450. Yet here the first difficulty arose. Lionello had died in October, 1450, at the age of forty-three. The portrait, however, seemed to show a younger man. Moreover, Lionello succumbed to a fever, complicated by an abscess in his head; when Roger saw him he must already have been a sick man, yet the portrait reveals no physical suffering, though perhaps suffering of a different kind. Furthermore, except for a superficial similarity of features, this portrait has many differences from Pisanello's portraits of this prince; in particular the manner of wearing the hair, so typical of Lionello, is completely different in Roger's painting. The hair is no longer shaved off ears and neck and combed back in tight curls framing the head as a turban, but hangs in fringes over forehead, temples and ears. It it probable that Lionello, at the end of his life, changed the way of doing his hair? Everybody knows how important it is for a sovereign to retain, unaltered, his "historical" features, to adhere to curl and wave, to beard or moustache, and to present always the same type to his subjects. And why should he have adopted a fashion sported by the Burgundian courtiers in about 1460?[10] Friedländer had cautiously to suggest that the portrait might have been painted in the Netherlands after Lionello's death, "perhaps from a drawing made in Italy in 1450 or before."[11]

But there was also that startling name *francisque*, written on the reverse of the panel, under the coat of arms (pl. 36, fig. 6). What did it imply? Van de Put suggested an illegitimate son of Lionello, Francesco, who had spent a couple of years at the Burgundian court in the Netherlands;[12] other scholars registered the fact without drawing any conclusions from it.[13] They cannot be blamed, for the quasi-official pedigree of the Este assigns Francesco's birth to the year 1444, and this date would not have fitted in with those of Roger's life. Roger died in 1464; Francesco would then have been but twenty. But as the man of the portrait certainly is older than twenty an awkward alternative

[8] A very scholarly description by A. van de Put, *Burlington Magazine*, XVIII (1911), 235f.

[9] Fry, *op. cit.*, 200.

[10] Wilhelm Stein, "Die Bildnisse des Roger van der Weyden," *Jahrbuch der preussischen Kunstsammlungen*, IIIL (1926), 30; cf. the portrait of Jean de Gros, probably by Roger, which Friedländer, *op. cit.*, dated 1460, though redating it 1450 in his *Altniederländische Malerei*, II

("Rogier van der Weyden und der Meister von Flémalle," Berlin, 1924), 101, no. 28.

[11] *Art in America*, IX, 65; Stein, p. 15 and p. 30.

[12] Van de Put, p. 236.

[13] Friedländer, *Art in America*, IX, 65: "Unsolved remains the word 'francisque' under the coat of arms"; Stein, p. 30, however, tries to draw certain conclusions.

arose: either the portrait could not be identified with Francesco, or it could not be painted by Roger. Hence the suggestion of the portrait representing Lionello's son was put aside, especially as Roger's authorship did not meet with any question. Friedländer and other scholars admitted that the hands were painted in a less masterly way than the rest of the panel,[14] but a partial cleaning revealed that the quality of work on the fingers was finer than had been apparent, and also that a ring with a large ruby was held between the thumb and first finger of the right hand. Next, the light background, so rare in Roger's paintings, was questioned and the theory put forward that the portrait had received some final touches from the Milanese painter Zanetto Bugatto, who worked in Roger's studio between 1461 and 1463. In that case the panel might have been a posthumous portrait of Lionello, and the name *francisque* might refer to the donor, that is to say, either to Lionello's bastard son or to Bugatto's sovereign, Francesco Sforza, who might have ordered the portrait as a present for his friend Borso d'Este, the then reigning half-brother of the defunct Lionello.[15]

But these were problems of altogether minor importance and, insoluble though they were, they could not shake the universal opinion that this portrait was Roger's work and that it represented Lionello. Recently, however, Italian scholars at Ferrara have put forward a new theory.[16] The reverse of the panel bears not only the coat of arms and the name Francisque, but also, twice repeated, the initials *M E*. Proceeding from portrait-medals of Niccolò d'Este, showing the initials *N E*,[17] the Ferrarese scholars searched for some member of the Este family whose initial was *M*, and finally discovered Meliaduse d'Este, a very gifted elder half-brother of Lionello. But far from clearing the above-mentioned difficulties, this new theory only increased the perplexities. How, for instance, could Meliaduse, the elder brother, have looked so young in 1450, when the youthful appearance of Lionello had already proved a stumbling-block? Why should Lionello's heraldic emblems have been those of his brother? What, in this case, did the name Francisque on the reverse mean? Why should the initials *M E* not signify: *M*(archio) *E*(stensis), as van de Put had rightly suggested? All these questions remain unanswered. On the other hand the suggestion that the small hammer held by the so-called Meliaduse signified the opening of the Porta Santa at the beginning of the Holy Year seems contestable even on grounds of method, as it rests on a series of unproved assumptions.[18]

The identification of the portrait must certainly proceed from the indications offered by the coat of arms. The escutcheon, no doubt, refers to Lionello. It is the blazon of the Este after 1432, when Charles VII had bestowed the French Lilies upon the family. The close connection with Lionello himself is indicated by the crest, a blindfold lynx,[19] and also by the reappearance of the same heraldic beasts as supporters of the shield. The

---

[14] Friedländer, *Altniederl. Malerei*, II, 99.

[15] Stein, p. 30f.

[16] Cf. the *Catalogo della esposizione della pittura ferrarese del rinascimento* (Ferrara, 1933), p. 27, (no. 23), for which Nino Barbantini was responsible.

[17] Hill, *Pisanello*, p. 103f, pl. 27; *idem, Italian Medals*, pl. 17, nos. 73 and 74.

[18] The theory, however, has been adopted by several scholars; for example, see Hans Tietze, *Meisterwerke europäischer Malerei in Amerika* (Wien, 1935), p. 333 and pl. 126; also, Giannina Franciosi, *Gli Estensi* (Firenze, 1935), p. 44.

[19] The animal being spotted seems to be a leopard rather than a lynx; on the medals it resembles more a fat cat or a young lion which is also spotted.

usual crest of the Este is the eagle, either the head or the pinions,[20] probably in reference
to the fact that the Este, in former days, had been Vicars or Captains General of the
Holy Empire. Lionello, for some reason, made no use of this emblem, in place of which
several of his medals and coins show the blindfold lynx or a leopard seated on a square
cushion.[21] Lionello, therefore, must have added the blindfold animal as a personal
device to his coat of arms, obviously in allusion to his name.[22] The bandage over the eyes
of the feline beast, streaming and fluttering in the wind, recalls Lionello's "impresa," the
famous *vela*, a word having the double meaning of "veils" and "sail."[23] This symbolic word,
dark and ambiguous as "imprese" were wont to be, appears to have influenced the choice
of the motto: "Quae vides ne vide" (shut your eyes to what you see), which in Master
Nicholaus's medal encircles the blindfold lynx (pl. 35, fig. 4b).[24]

This device, with its cryptic allusions, does not reappear on the reverse of the Roger
portrait, where another device is found, which may perhaps be read: VOIR [?] TOUT.
This motto, conveying an exactly opposed meaning, cannot simply be a French version
of Lionello's device. However, it alludes in a like manner, though paradoxically, to the
bandaged eyes of the heraldic beast. Only a person closely related to Lionello could have
ventured to use his blazon and a similar device: for instance one of his sons, for direct
descendants certainly were authorized to use the coat of arms of their father.[25] If one of
Lionello's two sons—Niccolò, the legitimate and younger son, or Francesco, the bastard[26]
—should come into question, Francesco is the first to be thought of, as the panel displays
the French version (*francisque*) of his name. And this name, of course, is meant to be
read in combination with the initials *M E*, so that the whole inscription reads: *M(archio)
E(stensis)* or *M(arquis d')* *E(ste) Francisque*.

We shall see that Francesco, during his stay in the Netherlands, was officially styled
"Marquis" and that, furthermore, Francesco himself probably used the initials written
on the reverse of the panel.[27] The fact that Francesco d'Este was in his day a very well-
known personality was not known to the scholars studying Roger van der Weyden's
painting, and they were further misled by an erroneous pedigree of the Este family.

[20] The crest in a later period is reproduced by Litta,
Celebri famiglie Italiane (Milan, Turin, 1819ff), fasc. XXVI,
Este III. The coins of Niccolò d'Este, Lionello's father,
have usually the eagle, whilst Lionello's successor Borso
d'Este, after his elevation to the rank of a duke, displays a
two-headed eagle; cf. *Corpus Nummorum Italicorum*, vol. X,
p. 432 and tav. xxx. The head of an eagle may be found
in an early 15th century relief at Ferrara, see: *Atti e
memorie della Deputazione Ferrarese di storia patria*, XX
(1910), 45; cloth and linen, too, were frequently decorated
"con una testa ed un'ala d'aquila bianca in campo verde"
or with the Este motto *Worbas*, see: G. Pardi, "Le
suppellettile dei palazzi Estensi in Ferrara nel 1436,"
Atti e memorie della Deputazione Ferrarese di storia patria,
XIX (1908), 113.

[21] Hill, *Italian Medals*, pl. 5, no. 28; pl. 17, no. 68;
pl. 18, no. 75; also Lionello's coins, though obviously the
mezzo ducato only, show the same animal; cf. *Corp. Numm.
Ital.*, X, 425, nos. 6, 7, 15, 16 and tav. xxix, no. 34.

[22] In the Ferrarese dialect a young lion was called

liunzello, cf. Pardi, *op. cit.*, index *s.v.* The words for
leopard (*lunza*) or for lynx (*lince*) may easily have been
put into some relation with *Lionello*—*liunzello* according
to the habit of twisting and punning with words in those
days; there also may have existed a nickname of Lionello
we do not know of to-day.

[23] On this impresa see Hill, *Pisanello*, 148, also 146,
note.

[24] Hill, *Italian Medals*, pl. 18, no. 75.

[25] Lionello's son, Niccolò, at any rate, was using his
father's motto *vela*; Hill, *Pisanello*, 146; cf. van de Put,
p. 235.

[26] Ignazio Giorgi, "Frammento d'Iconografia Estense,"
Bullettino dell'Istituto Storico Italiano, no. 2 (Roma, 1887),
112, makes a Hieronimo d'Este a third son of Lionello;
but that is an error in the genealogical tablet only, as
Giorgi himself (p. 116) quotes the words: "questo
hieronimo fu fiolo al Nicolo fiolo de Leonello e fu el
primo fiolo naturale."

[27] Cf. below, n. 58.

One of the main reasons that made scholars unwilling to identify the Roger portrait with Lionello's bastard son was the date of his birth. It is true that Litta and other Italian genealogists[28] quote 1444 as the year of Francesco's birth, but this is an error. According to the principal source, a contemporaneous Ferrarese chronicle,[29] and to an iconography of the Este family, also contemporary,[30] Francesco was not born in 1444, but in that year left Ferrara and went to stay with the Duke of Burgundy.[31] Francesco must then have been a boy of at least fifteen, as it was the custom to send young princes and noblemen, when they had attained this age, to foreign courts where they received their military education.[32] Therefore, if in 1444 Francesco was at least fifteen years old, he must have been born in, or about, 1429.[33] When Roger van der Weyden died in 1464, Francesco was approximately thirty-five. It follows that Roger's portrait could easily have been painted when Francesco was thirty years old. Thus one of the difficulties is removed.

Why the genealogists should have made this mistake I do not know. However it may be worth while to sum up all the facts known about Francesco d'Este and so clarify the whole question. The sources reporting Francesco's departure from Ferrara on July 26th, 1444, are trustworthy. A Belgian chronicler relates that Francesco arrived at Liège on September 1st, that is to say, five weeks after leaving Ferrara. On the evening of this day the *jone marchi de Ferart* took a walk with his host, John of Heinsberg, Bishop of Liège, who inspected the progress of certain buildings erected while the bishop had been in Italy.[34]

For it was in John of Heinsberg's company that Francesco had travelled to Liège, and Francesco was the "jovene fis que monsangneur s'amenoit de Ferart, li queis estoit fis à marchis de Ferart."[35] The bishop, who had planned a pilgrimage to Jerusalem, but was prevented from making it by the intervention of the Turks, was evidently an old friend of Lionello d'Este. He had been to Ferrara in earlier days, when the Council of Basle had been transferred thither[36] (1438), and it is very possible that the bishop, being closely connected and related with many of the Burgundian courtiers,[37] had already arranged with Lionello at that time that, at some future date, Francesco was to be sent to the Burgundian court. At any rate, when John of Heinsberg came to Venice in 1444, he was fêted by Lionello[38] and when he returned to the Netherlands Francesco was entrusted to

[28] Litta, *op. cit.*, Fasc. XXVI, Este III, tav. XII; cf. Antonio Frizzi, *Memorie per la storia di Ferrara* (2nd ed., Ferrara, 1850), III, 25, n. 106: "nato nell 1444."

[29] *Diario Ferrarese*, ed. G. Pardi, in Muratori, *Rerum Italicarum Scriptores* (2nd ed.), XXIV, 7, p. 28: "eodem millesimo etc. (1444) a di xxvi de Luiolo, illustre signore Francesco da Este, figliolo naturale de lo illustrissimo signore messer Leonello marchexe da Este, andete a stare con il duca di Borgogna."

[30] Rome, Bibl. Naz. Centrale Vittorio Emanuele, ms. Vitt. Eman. 293; cf. Giorgi, *op. cit.*, p. 109, no. 110: "Francesco e fratello naturale di questo Nicolo de Leonello e sta in borgogna de 1444. vive 1474."

[31] See above notes 29 and 30.

[32] Lionello, born in 1407, was sent to Braccio di Montone at Florence in 1422 for this purpose.

[33] This date is suggested rightly by Gardner only, *op. cit.*, p. 66 and the genealogical tablet no. II: "born before 1430."

[34] Jean de Stavelot, *Chronique*, ed. A. Borgnet (Brussels, 1861), 540: "nuit delle Saint-Giele"; 541: "Et chi jour meismes al vesprée allat monditsaingneur l'evesque joweir tout à piet so le point des arches ... et estoit avecque lydit jone marchi de Ferart et pluseurs chevaliers...."

[35] *Ibid.*, 540; the bishop arrived with about 900 horses and men.

[36] *Ibid.*, 393.

[37] One of his attendants was the son of Simon de Lalaing; his nephew was John of Nassau-Dillenburg, Seneschal of Brabant, *ibid.*, 532; on Bishop John of Heinsberg himself see F. Henaux, *Histoire du Pays de Liège*, vol. I (Liège, 1856); Pirenne, *Histoire de Belgique* (Bruxelles, 1900ff), II: 2, 281ff.

[38] Stavelot, p. 532: "laqueile galie cheaux de Venize ly avoient presentait ... et de marchis de Ferair qui grande fieste ly at fait."

24*

him. The suggestion of a tragic embroilment with a stepmother, as a reason for his departure, is unsupported.[39]

There is not much known about the first years spent by the Italian prince at the Burgundian court. As he did not reach Brussels as early as January, 1444, Francesco's name does not figure among those of the "josnes enffans de grant maison," who on their ponies, that bore the same trappings as the chargers of the knights, rode after Charles of Charolais to welcome Philip the Good.[40] Francesco stayed only for a week with the Bishop of Liège. He left this town in the company of two German counts, the bishop's nephews, and under their guidance may have had his first military experience, for the party seized the little town of Herbesthal.[41] Some time later he joined Charles of Charolais's company. We learn that the provost of Mons, Antoine Haneron—in after-years a very skilful Burgundian diplomat—had been appointed by Philip the Good, in 1448 or before, to take in hand "le gouvernement et administracion de Franssisque, filz de monseigneur le marquis de Ferraire,"[42] then nineteen years old. But as we know that the provost of Mons, since 1441 Charles's "maistre d'école et instituteur,"[43] was still in attendance on Charles of Charolais in 1449, we may conclude that the two princes shared this Steward of the Household. And Francesco, certainly, was one of the "seigneurs nourris avec luy et de son eage,"[44] who were in his suite when, for the first time, he went to war in 1452.

During the next years the conquest of Constantinople and the enterprise of a crusade against the Turks were the main problems of the Burgundian court. We do not know if Francesco d'Este took the cross at the famous "Feast of the Pheasant" in 1454, when Philip the Good and many Burgundian and Flemish knights solemnly vowed a crusade, but we know that when Pius II summoned a council to Mantua to discuss the crusade, Francesco joined the Burgundian embassy, at the head of which stood Duke John of Cleves, whereas the former provost of Mons followed it as Duke Philip's orator.[45] On this occasion Francesco paid a visit to his family at Ferrara. He and his suite are recorded as present, when the Este received the Pope on his way through their town;[46] besides, the register of the Este library contains a notice saying that Francesco borrowed some books in 1459–60.[47]

---

[39] Pardi, in *Diario Ferrarese*, 28, suggests Lionello's marriage to have caused the removal of Francesco, son of an early and unnamed love (cf. Johannes Ferrar., *Annal. Estens.*, in Muratori [2nd ed.], XX: 2, p. 34: "ex pellice Franciscum ... relinquens"). This suggestion appears without object: the wedding took place April 25, while Francesco left Ferrara July 26 so as to join the party of John of Heinsberg at Venice. Besides, Italian princesses in those days were not very particular about the natural sons of their husbands.

[40] Olivier de la Marche, *Mémoires*, edd. H. Beaune et J. d'Arbaumont (Paris, 1883–1888), II, 51.

[41] Stavelot, p. 542; cf. p. 547 on Gerard de Blankenheim, another nephew of John of Heinsberg.

[42] Archives du Département du Nord, B 2002, f. 65ᵛ; Henri Stein, "Un diplomat Bourguignon au XVᵉ siècle, Antoine Haneron," *Bibl. de l'École des Chartes*, IIC (1937), 287, n. 2. Haneron received a certain payment for 11

months, beginning May 1, 1448, for Francesco d'Este and for the time during which either was staying with Charolais.

[43] Henri Stein, *op. cit.*, 286 and 304, no. 1; O. Cartellieri, "Über eine burgundische Gesandtschaft an den kaiserl. und päpstl. Hof im Jahre 1460," *Mitteilungen des Instituts für Österreichische Geschichtsforschung*, XXVIII (1907), 449, n. 1.

[44] De la Marche, I, 123.

[45] H. Stein, *op. cit.*, 291; Andrea Schivenoglia, *Cronaca di Mantova*, ed. Carlo d'Arco (Milan, 1857), 23f.

[46] *Diario Ferrarese, ed. cit.*, 40; Francesco must have gone to Italy earlier than the bulk of the embassy.

[47] Modena, Archivio di Stato, Este Memoriale 1457–1468; Giulio Bertoni, *La Biblioteca Estense* (Torino, 1903), 65; Francesco borrowed "una cronaca vechia, una genealogia de lo re de Franza e dui libri pizoli de l'Amorus Paradix."

It was but a brief visit to his home. The lot of younger, or of illegitimate, sons of sovereign houses, after their fathers' death, in those days was anything but happy. If they had any personality and were of active disposition they became suspect at home as possible pretenders to the throne, and, compelled by circumstances, were either driven into political machinations, rebellions and revolutions, or, taking up service with other sovereigns, looked elsewhere for a field of action. Both were to be the case with Francesco. He returned to the Netherlands and for some ten years was in charge of such diplomatic and military missions and other affairs connected with the court as it was the custom in Burgundy to entrust to young noblemen. When the Queen of England in 1463[48] came to Bruges, he was sent to meet and escort her with a suite of honour. He became one of the Duke's permanent chamberlains[49] and had to comply with the various obligations which the solemn punctilio of this very ceremonious court demanded. In 1464 he was despatched to Venice to make arrangements for the crusade, and on his return to Brussels was able to report how anxiously Venice awaited Duke Philip's help.[50] Whether or not he joined the Burgundian crusaders sent to Italy under the command of Anthony of Burgundy, the Great Bastard, is not known. In any event he was back in Italy by 1467,[51] but returned to Brussels in early spring, for he and eleven others princes and bannerets waited for the last time on Philip the Good by carrying his coffin to the memorial chapel, after this prince died at Bruges in June, 1467.[52]

Francesco now entered the service of Charles the Bold, an old friend and intimate of former days. This service began with a war against Liège and the conquest of this city in October, 1467.[53] In the following year Francesco could display his abilities in a more peaceful way, in the tilt-yard, during the almost legendary "Pas de l'Arbre d'Or." At this great tournament held at Bruges, on the occasion of the Duke's wedding with Margaret of York, the marquis was one of the twenty-six knights who were to joust in the Duke's company. Were only the results of this joust in question we might quickly pass over this tournament, for on this luckless day Francesco's charger refused to gallop along the lists.[54] But another incident arrests our attention. It was a rule of this tournament that five or six knights should unite in a team, and whenever a member of the team had his jousting day, the others, in turn, served him as companions or attendants,

---

[48] Georges Chastellain, *Œuvres*, ed. Kervyn de Lettenhove (Bruxelles, 1863–66), IV, 309.

[49] "Le Marquis de Ferrare, chambellan du Duc," is mentioned in the "Compte de Huguenin de Faletans de 1464," fol. 55; cf. De La Barre, *Mémoires pour servir à l'histoire de France et de Bourgogne* (Paris, 1729), 219.

[50] *Livre des Trahisons de France envers la Maison de Bourgogne*, ed. Baron Kervyn de Lettenhove (Bruxelles, 1873), 234, chap. clxxvii: "En l'an de grace mille IIIIᶜ et LXIIII vint de par les Vénitiens à Lille le marquis de Ferare, Francisque, pour obtenir du duc Phelippe qu'il vousist envoyer aux dis Vénitiens aucune ayde de gendarmes pour les aydier â guerroyer le Turc."

[51] He then borrowed a Lancelotto from the Este library; cf. Giulio Bertoni, *Guarino da Verona*, 179. The lending register is dated 1466 to 1469.

[52] Chastellain, V, 235.

[53] Mantua, Arch. di Stato. Gonzaga E. XI. 3, busta 567 contains a letter (dated: Ghent, January 21, 1470) by Enrico Suardo, attendant to Rodolfo Gonzaga, then at the Burgundian court, in which is reported concerning a new servant of Messer Rodolfo: "e per havere servito lo ill. miser Francesco da Este a la guerra ha la conscianza di la corte asai bene et è bon homo e si c'era asai utile."

[54] Three very detailed relations on this tournament are known, one by Messire Jean, seigneur de Haynin et de Louvegnies, *Mémoires* (= *Société des Bibliophiles Belges à Mons*, XI: 1, 1842), 113ff; a second one by Olivier de la Marche, III, 124ff; and a third one in the *Traictié des nopces de monseigneur le duc de Bourgoine et de Brabant*, pub. in De la Marche, IV, 116ff, perhaps wrongly though frequently ascribed to de la Marche; cf. O. Cartellieri, *Am Hofe der Herzöge von Burgund* (Basel, 1926), 287.

wearing on that particular day the same colours and emblems as their friend. The team Francesco belonged to was composed, almost exclusively, of members of the Luxembourg family.[55] When his turn came he entered the tilt-yard with twelve horses whose luxurious caparisons have been described as minutely as the magnificent array of his four Luxembourg companions.[56] We are told that one of his horses was covered with a blue and golden caparison—the colours of the French quarters in his coat of arms that, incidentally, he had in common with the Duke of Burgundy—*chargé de grandes lettres à sa devise, brodé d'orfavrerie blanche et dorée,*[57] and that his four friends wore coats of blue satin *broudé à lettres d'or de sa devise.* Luckily we also learn what these letters were: *a. e. m.*[58] The *e* and *m* seem to stand for *estensis marchio,*[59] and they at once remind us of the initials *M E* flanking the crest on the reverse of Roger's portrait. If this interpretation is correct, Francesco himself used the same initials *de sa devise* that appear on the reverse of the panel—a coincidence which would be of great importance for the identification of the portrait.

Italian sources supply us with news about Francesco's next years. In 1469 Rodolfo Gonzaga, a younger son of the Marquis of Mantua, arrived at the Burgundian court, then a high school of military training, and remained there for more than a year. Being a cousin of Francesco d'Este he, of course, mentions the latter's name frequently in his correspondence with his parents.[60] There followed a somewhat tragic episode when Francesco became involved in the quarrels over the succession in Ferrara. Borso, Lionello's half-brother and successor, having died in 1471, his younger brother Ercole followed him on the throne. Niccolò, Lionello's legitimate son, protested against this succession by instigating an insurrection. Francesco immediately left Burgundy for Ferrara and made his brother's claims his own. The populace at Ferrara supported Lionello's sons by shouting: "Viva la vela!" but Ercole's partisans, answering with: "Viva il diamante!" proved the stronger. Lionello's sons fought without luck; Niccolò fled to Mantua, whilst Francesco was exiled and forced to return to the Netherlands, only to find that in the meantime Charles the Bold had fully recognized Ercole's succession.[61]

[55] De la Marche, III, 182. The Luxembourgs of his team were Jacques, Sgr. de Fiennes; Antoine, Sgr. de Roussy; Jehan, Sgr. de Sottinghien; Jacques, Sgr. de Richebourg; cf. *ibid.* III, 141 (the footnote indicating Borso d'Este as this "marquis of Ferrara" is misleading), 159, 182; IV, 120, 123, 126, 131, 137, 138; Jean de Haynin, I, 127, describes very carefully the caparisons and mentions (I, 131) "le marquis de Ferrade" as *compagnon* of Jehan de Luxembourg, both of them wearing equally embroidered garments; the same appears in 1473 at Valenciennes (*ibid.*, II, 217), where the marquis is styled "frère d'armes et compagnon" of Jehan de Luxembourg; they therefore seem to have been intimate friends.

[56] See *e.g.* de la Marche, IV, 137; Jean de Haynin, I, 127.

[57] De la Marche, IV, 137; III, 182.

[58] *Ibid.*, IV, 137: "a. e. m. en brodure d'or."

[59] Since the three letters were placed on the garments of his friends, they may possibly mean: *a(mici) e(stensis) m(archionis).* Or the letter *a* may allude to the name of a lady which, according to custom, was kept secret. Cf.

Cartellieri, *op. cit.,* 138. The same usage being observed in the 16th century may be seen from Mme. de La Fayette, *La princesse de Clèves* (Paris, 1935), p. 120: "...pour mêler dans leurs chiffres ou dans leurs devises quelque chose de galant qui eût rapport aux personnes qu'ils aimaient."

[60] Mantua, Arch. di Stato. Gonzaga E.X.3 busta 2100; Hague, October 20, 1469, a letter of Rodolfo Gonzaga to his mother: "al medico, il quale mi venne a vedere forse tredi per una pocha di fredore, mi consiglia miser Francesco da Este, gli dia el drapo per uno zupone." — Gonzaga. Copiale 64; December 30, 1469: a letter of the Marquis of Mantua sent to his son by the messenger of Francesco d'Este. See also above, note 53. Lionello's first wife was Margarita Gonzaga.

[61] *Diario Ferrarese,* ed. cit., 74 (Sept. 15).—In December, 1471, a Burgundian embassy arrived at Ferrara to felicitate Ercole d'Este; *ibid.* 78. In 1473 (March 2) a Burgundian ambassador arrived at Ferrara and Modena in order to consign soldiers for Charles the Bold; cf. Jacopino de' Bianchi, *Cronaca Modenese* (Parma, 1861), I,

So Francisco d'Este, having definitely lost his home, had to resume his former duties at the Burgundian court. He is again mentioned as a chamberlain, but soon after also as having military charges: first as Captain of Westerloo,[62] then as the Governor and Captain of Le Quesnoy.[63] In 1473 he accompanied the Duke to Valenciennes, where a chapter of the Golden Fleece was held, followed by a tournament in which Francesco took part, having once more Jehan de Luxembourg as a companion-in-arms.[64] After that he was again despatched to Italy. At the chapter of Valenciennes the King of Naples had been appointed a Knight of the Golden Fleece, and Francesco, though himself not a knight of the Order, was designated to follow the Great Bastard to Naples and to present the ensigns to King Ferrante.[65] This embassy took place in the following year. Francesco, however, either stayed for a considerable time at Naples or returned there for a second time with the Great Bastard; it is reported that in the spring of 1475 both of them passed through Milan on their way to the South and that, in this town, they joined a party of Burgundian ambassadors accredited to various Italian courts, being occupied with the enlistment of Italian troops for the Burgundian army.[66] Francesco remained in correspondence with the court of Naples[67] after his duties had recalled him to the North; in October, 1475, he is again registered as a Captain of Westerloo.[68]

This is the last time his name is mentioned, and nothing is known about this later days. Perhaps he was killed in one of the many luckless battles the Duke had to fight in the last year of his life, though it is improbable that this fact should not have been noted somewhere. But it must not be forgotten that, when in 1477 Charles's empire broke up, many of the former Burgundian courtiers were left to their fate and dispersed over all parts of the world. Francesco, then a man of almost fifty, possibly entered the service of some other prince, but it may also be that he married and spent the rest of his life at some countryseat. We know nothing about it, nor do we know when or where he died.

All this, admittedly, is not very satisfactory. He led a courtier's life, a life not devoid of honours, and though perhaps it was not very brilliant, there were some bright rays—but also many disappointments. Yet the mere fact of knowing that he served the Burgundian Dukes for more than thirty years and spent most of his life in the Netherlands seems sufficient for our particular purpose, that is to say, for the solution of the problem concerning the Este portrait by Roger van der Weyden.

4. In the same year, November 26, Charles the Bold received, at Thionville near Metz, the ambassadors of Rome, Venice, Naples and Ferrara; cf. Calmet, *Histoire de Lorraine*, V (Nancy, 1752), 210, cap. xlvii; H. Vander Linden, *Itinéraires de Charles, Duc de Bourgogne, Marguérite de York et Marie de Bourgogne* (Bruxelles, 1936), 57.

[62] M. Bruchet, *Répertoire numérique*. Série B. Chambre des comptes de Lille. Fasc. II (Lille, 1921), *s.v.* Este, François; cf. Fasc. I, no. 17711.

[63] Bruchet, *op. cit.*, Fasc. I, nos. 11391, 11392 (Oct. 1, 1473, to Sept. 30, 1474).

[64] Jean de Haynin, II, 214f; cf. Reiffenberg, *Histoire de l'Ordre de la Toison d'or* (Brussels, 1830), 87f.

[65] F. de Gingins La Sarra, *Dépêches des ambassadeurs milanais sur les campagnes de Charles-le-Hardi, duc de Bourgogne, de 1474 à 1477* (Paris-Genève, 1858), I, xvii.

[66] *Ibid.*, I, 106ff, no. xxxiii (April 25, 1475). The chronological details of this embassy to Naples are not quite clear, cf. P. M. Perret, *Histoire des relations de la France avec Venise* (Paris, 1896), II, 41, n. 2.

[67] Naples, Archivio di Stato. Curie Summarie vol. XII, fol. 50. Among the letters of Alfonso, Duke of Calabria, there is a short notice, dated November 5, 1475: "Fuit scriptum sequentibus de bono statu, videlicet: Illustri et magnifico viro Francisco Hestensi, affini nostro carissimo." Other recipients of similar letters of the same date were Philippe de Croy, Guido de Humbercourt (both of them Burgundian courtiers), and Francesco Bertini, Bishop of Capoccio, Neapolitan ambassador to the Burgundian court.

[68] Bruchet, *op. cit.*, Fasc. I, no. 17717.

There is no longer a valid reason for hesitating to give the much discussed portrait, at last, its proper name: Francesco d'Este. That the son should have borne the coat of arms of his father is entirely customary, and that Francesco should have chosen a motto similar to that of his father seems plausible also. The non-appearance of a bar sinister, or of some other "brisure," in the escutcheon is of no importance whatever, least of all in the Casa Este, since Lionello, himself of illegitimate birth, omitted this heraldic sign in his personal coat of arms. Moreover, our conjecture that the Burgundian courtier, Francesco d'Este, was the object of Roger's portrait would at once solve all the outstanding problems. It explains the French form of the name "Francisque," the French device "Voir [?] tout," and it also explains the later addition of a French inscription: "non plus Courcelles."[69] It further explains why the man represented wears his hair in the Burgundian fashion of 1460 and why some of the features suggest those of Lionello, without any convincing likeness as a whole. Finally, if it was a common practice of French or Burgundian painters to inscribe, on the reverse of their portraits, the name of the person represented, they certainly did not do so in the case of the donor or of the man who had commissioned the artist.

All links seem to fit almost to perfection. But, apart from this indirect evidence, there is more direct proof. The Este Iconography in the Vittorio Emanuele Library in Rome[70] contains medaillions of all members of the Este family, from 1214 to 1476 (the manuscript must therefore have been brought to conclusion in, or soon after, 1476).[71] Among these medallions is one representing Francesco d'Este (pl. 34, fig. 2). It is a profile likeness that shows him in Burgundian costume and with a cone-shaped cap. His hair covers forehead, ears and neck with untidy fringes; the long aquiline nose, the protruding lower lip, the upright collar, the golden chain encircling his neck: all these details correspond completely with the Roger portrait, and it would be interesting to know what portrait served as model for the master of the manuscript. A comparison of the two pictures clears away the last possible doubts: Roger's panel must represent Lionello's son and not Lionello himself. As to Lionello's own appearance we must content ourselves, once more, with one single portrait, that painted by Pisanello.

This new evidence makes it necessary, above all, to re-date Roger's portrait. There is no longer any reason for assuming that the portrait was painted in 1450 at Ferrara, during Roger's alleged visit to Lionello's residence. This assumption, now, seems quite pointless. The portrait, evidently, was executed at Brussels, and since it represents Fran-

[69] This inscription being a later addition does not deserve too serious a consideration. I may mention, however, that the conjecture of van de Put, *op. cit.*, p. 235, that the portrait was brought to Belgium from Italy in 1471 and then came into the possession of the Courcelles, only provides half the truth. For the portrait had never left the Flemish-Burgundian provinces. The meaning of the inscription remains obscure. The Courcelles were a very well-known Burgundian family; Jean, Sgr. de Courcelles et de S. Lyebant, was counsellor and chamberlain to the King of France and the Duke of Burgundy in about 1418; his son Philippe, Sgr. de Bousselanges, de Poullans et d'Auvillars, was bailiff of Dijon under Philip

the Good and Charles the Bold; he was ducal counsellor and chamberlain, too. I was not able to find out any relations between the Courcelles and Francesco or any other member of the Este family. It may be that Francesco was married to a Courcelles, or that the panel came into the possession of the Courcelles after the breakdown of the Burgundian empire and Francesco's disappearance from our horizon. Yet it is well worth noting the fact that the panel obviously remained with the Burgundian court society within which it originated.

[70] Ms. Vitt. Eman. 293; see above, note 30.

[71] On the dating see Giorgi, *op. cit.*, 89.

Fig. 1. New York, Metropolitan Museum: Roger van der Weyden, Portrait of Francesco d'Este.

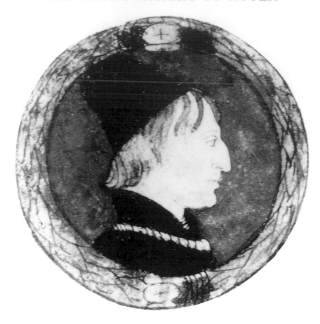

Fig. 2. Rome, Bibl. Vitt. Emanuele, MS Vitt. Eman. 293:
Portrait of Francesco d'Este (enlarged).

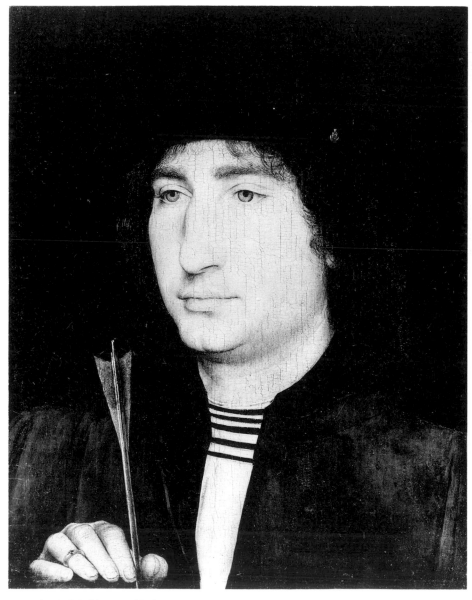

Fig. 3. Washington, National Gallery: Memlinc, "Man with the Arrow," probably
Portrait of Francesco d'Este.

Fig. 4 a-b. Medal, obverse and reverse: Lionello d'Este, by Master Nicholaus.

Fig. 5. Heidelberg, Universitätsbibl., MS Pal. germ. 848, fol. 11ᵛ: Triumph of
Duke Henry of Breslau in a tournament (reduced).

Pl. 36   THE ESTE PORTRAIT BY ROGER

Fig. 6. Reverse of Pl. 33, Fig. 1 (Roger's portrait of Francesco d'Este) : Coat of Arms.

cesco at the age of about thirty, the date must be approximately 1460. This makes it one of the later works of the Flemish master and offers ample scope for the speculation whether or not one of Roger's pupils, Memlinc or Bugatto, gave some finishing touches to it or was responsible for the light background, so unusual in Roger's work.

There remains a word to be said about the attribute, the little hammer in Francesco's hand. This hammer never seems to appear in Italian portraits of princes,[72] and evidently belongs to the Franco-German or Burgundian world of chivalry, where we may regard the hammer as being the attribute of holders of posts of honour. Other personalities of high rank have been represented with this insigne. The 14th century Heidelberg manuscript of Minnesingers contains a miniature depicting the triumph of Duke Henry of Breslau in a tournament: one valet holds the duke's helmet, a second the lance, a third the "coeffe" and also a small hammer of exactly the same shape as that visible in the Este portrait (pl. 35, fig 5.).[73] Then again in a Geneva manuscript "Réponses de Pierre le Fruitier, dit Salmon," dated 1412, John of France, Duke of Berry, holds in his left hand a similar little hammer.[74] And in another painting by Roger van der Weyden, the famous miniature in the Chronicle of Hainaut, Philip the Good has in his right hand a very fine little hammer, the head of which evidently is made of silver.[75] Finally, in yet another 15th-century manuscript, the Chronicle of the Kingdom of Jerusalem, Count Witasse of Boulogne, father of Geoffrey of Bouillon, seems to hold in his right hand a hammer[76] similar to that of Philip the Good.

There can be no doubt that the hammer with the long and slender helve was the attribute of certain dignitaries (probably military or knightly), for only princes and personalities of high rank are represented with this insigne. In fact, this assumption finds a confirmation through Froissart, who, when he reports how Olivier de Cliçon (made *Connétable de France* in 1380) was deprived of his office, adds that Olivier was ordered "que il renvoiast le martel c'est-à-entendre l'office de la connestablie de France." Froissart then explains how Philip of Artois became Constable "quoyque messire Olivier de Clichon n'y eust point renonchié, ne renvoié le martel de connestablie."[77] Nothing is known about Francesco's holding a similar office, but, since he was Captain and Governor of Westerloo and Le Quesnoy, he easily may have held some provincial High-Constableship entitling him to carry the hammer, which may, after all, have been the insigne of any military command or princely rank. But there also exists another possibility, namely, that the hammer had some connection with tournaments. It may have been used for the scoring of jousts, or for the opening ceremonies. For Olivier de la Marche reports that at the "Pas de l'Arbre d'Or" the knight, demanding admission to

[72] Arnold Goffin, "A propos du voyage de Roger de la Pasture (van der Weyden) en Italie," *Mélanges Hulin de Loo* (Bruxelles-Paris, 1931), 197ff, mentions the so-called "Fille de l'orfèvre" in the Collection Melzi d'Eril at Milan, a woman holding a little hammer in her right hand. The artist, however, seems not to be known (Bartolommeo Veneto?).

[73] Heidelberg, Universitätsbibliothek cod. pal. germ. 848, f. 11ᵛ and the facsimile edition of this manuscript.

[74] Geneva, Bibl. de Genève, Ms. franç. 165, fol. 4;

Henri Martin, *La miniature française du XIIIᵉ au XVᵉ siècle* (Paris-Bruxelles, 1923), pl. 90, fig. cxvii, and p. 102.

[75] Brussels, Bibl. Royale Ms. franç. 9242–3, fol. 1; cf. P. Post, "Die Darbringungsminiatur der Hennegau-chronik," *Jahrbuch für Kunstwissenschaft*, I (1923), 171ff.

[76] Vienna, Nationalbibliothek, Ms. franç. 2533 (156); cf. O. Smital, *Die Chronik des Kreuzfahrer-Königreichs Jerusalem* (München, 1924).

[77] Froissart, *Œuvres*, XV, ed. Brussels, 1871, pp. 97, 102.

the tilt-yard, "hurta trois fois d'ung marteau doré à ladicte porte."[78] The same author also tells that the victor of the day received a gold ring,[79] and that at the tournament held in honour of Philip the Good's wedding the prizes consisted of rubies, diamonds, golden chains and buckles.[80] Thus the hammer and the ring with the ruby in the marquis's hands may allude either to some office or to some victory at the tournament.

Signs of Francesco d'Este's presence at the Burgundian court seem to be traceable also in other pictures. Pursuing a suggestion made by Stein,[81] I should first of all like to draw attention to another of Roger's paintings. He apparently had the young Este in his mind when working at his "Adoration," now at Frankfort. The youngest of the three Kings, a youth rather of Italian than of Flemish type and bearing, shows what Francesco may have looked like in his twenties. On the other hand, Memlinc's "Man with the Arrow,"in the Mellon Collection, Washington (pl. 34, fig. 3), seems to prove that Italians in mature age are apt to grow stout, particularly when they enjoy the excellent cuisine of Brussels. The portrait must represent, as the insignia indicate, a distinguished Burgundian courtier. For the arrow was the attribute of the leader of a tournament (at least in Burgundian circles) who, to start or to end the tilts, flung the arrow into the tilt-yard. The chronicle of Jean le Fèvre, seigneur de St. Rémy, King-of-arms of the Golden Fleece, informs us that Philip the Good at a tournament made use of this missile.[82] Le Fèvre himself has been depicted by Roger van der Weyden with an arrow in his hand,[83] and so is the courtier talking to the Duke of Berry in the miniature of the Geneva manuscript.[84] Charles the Bold, too, in a manuscript at the British Museum, is represented with an arrow.[85] Finally, there is a portrait by Roger of a Knight of the Golden Fleece, probably the famous Jacques de Lalaing,[86] also with an arrow in his hand. Hence the "Man with the Arrow" by Memlinc must have been a Burgundian courtier, and, as he certainly is of a very Italian appearance, we may well ask if this is not another portrait of Francesco d'Este. Moreover the features bear a great likeness to those of the Roger portrait, although they seem coarser, somewhat puffy, and of less nobility and tenseness, differences that may be ascribed both to the advancing age of the sitter and to the fact that the painter was not as good an artist and was more bourgeois in character. This Memlinc painting may well be considered to be another portrait of Francesco, here approximately forty years old. That would mean that it was painted in about 1468–9, which is the usual date given to it.

---

[78] De la Marche, III, 126; cf. 124 and IV, 116.

[79] De la Marche, III, 140: "et paya ledit Charles une verge d'or pour ce qu'il avoit le moins rompu"; cf. pp. 132, 177, 180, 181, 191. The meaning of *verge* is usually "rod," but in the 15th century it was used just as frequently in the sense of "ring." In this sense it is taken also by Cartellieri, *Am Hofe der Herzöge von Burgund*, 135, 140.

[80] Reiffenberg, *Toison d'Or*, xx.

[81] *Op. cit.*, 30f. The young king of the "Adoration" reappears in the Flemish triptych of the Melbourne Gallery; cf. *Burlington Magazine*, XL (1922), 163ff.

[82] Jean le Fèvre, *Chronique*, ed. F. Morand (Paris, 1881), II, 318f., cap. cxci: "Le duc tenoit une flesche en sa main; sy demanda aux gardes (c'est à entendre aux

preneurs) s'ilz congnoissoient bien le signe; et ilz dirent que oil." Then follows the description of how the two knights were fighting. "Quant ilz se furent, une espasse, combatus de leurs haches, et fait l'un l'autre tourner et despasser . . . le duc gecta sa flesche en bas, et dist: 'Hola! Hola!' Adont, les preneurs les prindrent subz en ce point. Les conducteurs vindrent devers le duc, en disant qu'ilz les avoient prins subz, plustost que les patries n'eussent voulu." The passage is quoted by Stein, *op. cit.*, 22, n. 5.

[83] Antwerp, Museum.

[84] See above, note 74.

[85] London, Brit. Mus., MS. Harley 6199, f. 69; cf. Comte Paul Durrieu, *La miniature flamande* (Brussels, 1921), pl. lviii.

[86] Brussels, Museum; cf. Stein, p. 32ff.

There is one more question to discuss. If Roger van der Weyden painted the Este panel neither at Ferrara nor in the year 1450, had he at any time been at Ferrara, and, what is more, did he really ever go to Italy? Since the Este portrait can no longer be regarded as proving that Roger worked in Italy, a most important piece of evidence for his presence in the South has been destroyed. The so-called Sforza Madonna ceased a long time ago to be valid proof of Roger's visit to Milan. The "Pietà" of the Uffizi Gallery does not testify to his having been to Florence. The Madonna Medici proves nothing whatever, for the two sainted Doctors, Cosmas and Damianus, certainly do not represent Cosimo and Piero de'Medici, but two well-known Burgundian courtiers.[87] The picture, as Destrée pointed out,[88] should rather be called the "Madonna of the Physicians" than the Medici Madonna. The paintings seen by Cyriac of Ancona and Bartolommeo Facio at Ferrara do not demonstrate Roger's presence in this town, but only the fact that Roger worked in Brussels for Lionello d'Este—a fact many times recorded by the Ferrarese exchequer in the accounts preserved in the archives of Modena.

These records of the ducal *camera* are in fact not favourable for the purpose of confirming the theory of Roger's journey to Italy. An entry in the *registro dei Memoriali dell' anno 1450*, dated December 31, 1450, and countersigned with the letter *M*, testifies that Paolo Pozio, merchant of Bruges, agent and partner in the trading firm Filippo Ambrogio and Company at Ferrara, had paid twenty ducats to "Maestro Ruziero depintore in bruza per parte de certe depinture," which the latter had executed for the late Signore Lionello.[89] Another order of payment, concerning two panels painted at Brussels, is dated 1451.[90] The existence of a third, similar document has so far been overlooked. It is dated August 15, 1450, and reports the payment of twenty ducats to the "excellent and famous painter Master Roger" for some "altar-pieces," and as a part-payment for several other pictures Roger had painted for Lionello.[91] This new document clearly demonstrates that Roger cannot have been in Italy during the month of August, 1450. Moreover, it states that by August 15th the payment had already been made at Bruges by Paolo Pozio. Lionello's order of payment to Paolo Pozio must have taken about four weeks to reach the latter, and another four weeks must have elapsed before Paolo Pozio's confirmation arrived at the Ferrarese *camera*. The conclusion is that Roger

---

[87] Pierre de Beffremont and Jean le Fèvre de St. Rémy; they appear together in the fragment of an "Adoration" by Roger (Coll. Schloss, Paris) and in his Bladelin altar; cf. Stein, 19ff. Their appearance as a couple was so impressive that they seem also to have been in the mind of the artist, who designed the Alexander tapestries at the Palazzo Doria; cf. A. Warburg, *Gesammelte Schriften*, I (Leipzig, 1932), 243ff.

[88] Destrée, *Roger de la Pasture van der Weyden*, I (Paris and Brussels, 1930), 73.

[89] Venturi, in *Rivista storica Italiana*, I (1884), 608; A. v. Wurzbach, *Niederländisches Künstlerlexikon*, II, 874, no. 91.

[90] Stein, p. 15.

[91] Modena, Arch. di Stato. Camera Marchionale Estense. Mandati. Registro dei Mandati dell'anno 1450, no. 10:

L. Marchio—Mandato Ill.mi ac excelsi domini nostri Leonelli marchionis estensis, etc. vos factores generales ipsius dari faciatis Paulo de Podio et pro eo Filippo Ambrosii et sociis mercatoribus in Ferraria ducatos viginti auri quos dictus Paulus solvit nomine prefati ill.mi domini nostri in Bruges excelenti et claro pictori Mᵒ Rogerio pro aris (sic!) et pro parte solutionis nonnullarum picturarum quas ipse facere habuit praefato domino nostro. Et de ipsa pecunie solutione faciatis eas scripturas per quas dinosci possit qua causa et cui pecunia sit exoluta.

Philippus Bendidius scripsit XV augusti 1450
—Habuit mandatum.

I am much indebted to Dr. Helene Wieruszowski and to Signor Alfredo Braghiroli at Modena for their kindness in providing me with a copy of this document, hitherto unpublished as far as I know.

cannot possibly have been in Italy after June 15, 1450. The length of time Roger spent in Italy, consequently, cannot have been more than a few weeks—at most a few months—in the spring of 1450, for it is not probable that he crossed the Alps in January or February. Further we may ask: is it likely that Lionello should have chosen the complicated manner of payment through Filippo Ambrogio of Ferrara and Paolo Pozio of Bruges if the renowned and excellent painter, only a few weeks before, had been at the court of Ferrara? Is it not more plausible to assume that Lionello, whose generosity was well known, would have presented a gift to his famous guest when Roger took his leave? And does the document not testify, *ex silentio*, by omitting to mention the Flemish celebrity's presence and by merely stating about the pictures: "quas ipse [Rogerius] facere habuit praefato domino nostro," that Roger, personally, was altogether unknown to the court and had never been to Ferrara? Entries in mediaeval registers may be "short and impersonal," yet the addition of some phrase such as "quando stabat cum eo" (or something similar), would have been no more than consistent with the general customs had Roger really been at Ferrara only a short time before.

Of all the testimonials concerning Roger's journey to Italy there is left but one, and that is an artist's very vague anecdote reported by Bartolommeo Facio in the biography of Gentile da Fabriano:[92] "De hoc viro [Gentile] ferunt, quum Rogerius Gallicus insignis pictor, de quo post dicemus, jubilaei anno in ipsum Joannis Baptistae templum accessisset, admiratione operis captum Auctore requisito cum multa laude cumulatum ceteris Italicis pictoribus anteposuisse." Facio himself almost admits that this is a legend. It is a typical example of those anecdotes told in the streets and in taverns frequented by artists—the intention of which was to exalt the name of one renowned master by coupling it with that of another still more famous artist. At any rate, it is a most interesting argument for the fame Roger enjoyed in Italy in about 1456 (the year in which, probably, Gentile's biography was written), but the anecdote as such, unless supported by other documents, has no absolute historical value. And of other documents there are none.

It has always been thought remarkable that Roger's work shows no signs whatever of the influence either of Gentile, whom he is said to have admired, or of other Italian painters, as, for instance, Benozzo Gozzoli or Pisanello or Fra Angelico,[93] whose pictures, had Roger been in Italy, would certainly have been known to him. But that is not to be wondered at if Roger's visit to Italy never took place.

---

[92] Wurzbach, *op. cit.*, II, 875, no XVI.

[93] Even Domien Roggen, "Roger van der Weyden en Italie," *Revue Archéologique*, v⁰ sér., XIX (1924), 88–94, who tried to find such influences, was not in a position to give any evidence.

MYSTERIES OF STATE

AN ABSOLUTIST CONCEPT AND ITS LATE MEDIAEVAL ORIGINS

M<small>YSTERIES OF STATE</small> as a concept of Absolutism has its mediaeval background. It is a late offshoot of that spiritual-secular hybridism which, as a result of the infinite cross-relations between Church and State, may be found in every century of the Middle Ages and has deservedly attracted the attention of historians for many years. After A. Alföldi's fundamental studies on ceremonial and insignia of Roman emperors,[1] Theodor Klauser discussed more recently the origin of the episcopal insignia and rights of honor, and showed very clearly how, in and after the age of Constantine the Great, various privileges of vestment and rank of the highest officers of the Late Empire were passed on to the bishops of the victorious Church.[2] At about the same time, Percy Ernst Schramm published his compendious article on the mutual exchange of rights of honor between *sacerdotium* and *regnum*, in which he demonstrated how the *imitatio imperii* on the part of the spiritual power was balanced by an *imitatio sacerdotii* on the part of the secular power.[3] Schramm carried his study only to the threshold of the Hohenstaufen period, and he was right to stop where he did. For the mutual borrowings of which he speaks — insignia, titles, symbols, privileges, and prerogatives—affected in the earlier Middle Ages chiefly the ruling individuals, both spiritual and secular, the crown-wearing pontiff and the mitre-wearing emperor, until finally the *sacerdotium* had an imperial appearance, and the *regnum* a clerical touch. By the beginning of the thirteenth century at the latest, a certain state of saturation was reached, when both the spiritual and secular dignitaries were rigged with all the essential attributes of their offices.

The borrowings between the two orbits, however, did not then come to an end. Only the objectives changed, as the center of gravity shifted, so to speak, from the ruling personages of the Middle Ages to the ruled collectives of early modern times, to the new national states and other political communities. That is to say, the field of exchanges between Church and State, and of mutual influences, was expanded from individual dignitaries

---

Reprinted, with permission, from *The Harvard Theological Review*, XLVIII (1955), 65–91. The original has this prefatory note:

This paper was read at the joint session of the American Catholic Historical Association and the American Historical Association, on December 28, 1953, in Chicago. The title has been slightly modified; the content remains practically unchanged.

[1] Andreas Alföldi, "Die Ausgestaltung des monarchischen Zeremoniells am römischen Kaiserhofe," and "Insignien und Tracht der römischen Kaiser," *Römische Mitteilungen*, XLIX (1934), 1–118; L (1935), 1–171.

[2] Theodor Klauser, *Der Ursprung der bischöflichen Insignien und Ehrenrechte* (Bonner akademische Reden, I; Krefeld, 1949).

[3] P. E. Schramm, "Sacerdotium und Regnum im Austausch ihrer Vorrechte," *Studi Gregoriani*, II (1947), 403–457.

to compact communities. Therewith sociological problems began to shape ecclesiological problems and, vice versa, ecclesiology, sociology. Under the pope as *princeps* and *verus imperator* the hierarchical apparatus of the Roman Church—notwithstanding some important features of Constitutionalism[4]—showed a tendency to become the perfect prototype of an absolute and rational monarchy on a mystical basis, whereas simultaneously the state showed increasingly a tendency to become a quasi-Church and, in other respects, a mystical monarchy on a rational basis. It is here in these waters—brackish waters, if you prefer—that the new state mysticism found its breeding and dwelling place.

The basic problem may be approached most easily by posing a simple question: How, by what channels and by what techniques, were the spiritual *arcana ecclesiae* transferred to the state so as to produce the new secular *arcana imperii* of absolutism? The answer to this question is given by the sources on which we have to rely; for without neglecting either narratives or arts, ceremonial or liturgy, it may yet be said that our main evidence is legal. It is mainly by our legal sources that the new ways of exchange between the spiritual and the secular become evident. After all, the Canonists used and applied Roman Law; the Civilians used and applied Canon Law; and both Laws were used also by Common Law jurists.[5] Moreover, both Laws were influenced by scholastic method and thought, as well as by Aristotelian philosophy; finally, the jurists of all branches of Law applied freely, and without scruples or inhibitions, theological metaphors and similes when expounding their points of view in glosses and legal opinions. Under the impact of those exchanges between canon and civilian glossators and commentators—all but non-existent in the earlier Middle Ages—something came into being which then was called "Mysteries of State," and which today in a more generalizing sense is often termed "Political Theology."[6] Felicitous as ever, Maitland once remarked that eventually "the nation stepped into the shoes of the Prince."[7] While fully agreeing, I yet feel that we should add: "Not before the Prince himself had stepped into the pontifical shoes of Pope and Bishop."

In fact, "Pontificalism" was perhaps the outstanding feature of the new monarchies, and few princes—not even Louis XIV—were so genuinely pontifical as King James I of England. In a little juristic dictionary, published in 1607 and called *The Interpreter*, an able civilian, Dr. John Cowell, advanced certain political theories with which normally James I would not have disagreed: that the king is ever of full age; that he is not taken to be subject to death, but is a corporation in himself that liveth forever; that the king is above the laws; and that he admits legislation by the estates only by his benignity or by

[4] See Brian Tierney, "The Canonists and the Mediaeval State," *Review of Politics*, XV (1953), 378–388.

[5] This has been pointed out repeatedly by Gaines Post; see especially his study on "A Romano-Canonical Maxim, *Quod omnes tangit*, in Bracton," *Traditio*, IV (1946), 197–251, and his paper read before the Riccobono Seminar on "The Theory of Public Law and the State in the Thirteenth Century," *Seminar*, VI (1948), 42–59; also his latest study on "The Two Laws and the

Statute of York," *Speculum*, XXIX (1954), 417–432.

[6] The expression, much discussed in Germany in the early 1930s, has become more popular in this country, unless I am mistaken, through a study by George LaPiana, "Political Theology," *The Interpretation of History* (Princeton, 1943).

[7] F. W. Maitland, "Moral Personality and Legal Personality," in his *Selected Essays* (Cambridge, 1936), 230.

reason of his coronation oath.[8] Since *The Interpreter* roused the indignation of the Commons, on whom the king depended for a subsidy, the king himself was compelled to take exception to Dr. Cowell's words. And thus an irate king descended upon a poor scholar who had meant to please his sovereign lord. James I complained, in a proclamation of 1610, that nothing "is now unsearched into," neither the "very highest mysteries of the Godhead," nor "the deepest mysteries that belong to the persons or state of King and Princes, who are Gods on earth," and that incompetent men "will freely wade by their writings in the deepest mysteries of monarchy and politick government."[9] On other occasions, James I spoke of "my Prerogative or mystery of State," of the "mysterie of the King's power," and of "the mysticall reverence, that belongs unto them that sit in the Throne of God,"[10] or ordered the speaker of the House of Commons "to acquaint that house with our pleasure that none therein shall presume to meddle [—"to meddle" was a favorite expression of absolutism—] with anything concerning our government or mysteries of State."[11]

It would not be easy to decide quickly and accurately whence this notion of Mysteries of State derived. It might, of course, have been a translation of Tacitus' *arcana imperii temptari*, "to make trial of the innermost of the empire"—and Tacitus may well have been known to scholarly James I. However, Mysteries of State has perhaps more a Christian than a Tacitean flavor, although the word *arcana* served to designate both the pagan and the Christian *mysteria*.[12] There is, however, reason to think not of the Roman historian but rather of Roman Law, of a law of the Emperors Gratian, Valentinian, and Theodosius who, in 395, addressed themselves to the *praefectus Urbi* Symmachus when they said it was "sacrilege" to dispute the Prince's judgment and selection of officials.[13] "Sacrilege," to be sure, is a strong word which borders on the "zone of silence" reserved

[8] For the case of Dr. John Cowell, see Charles H. McIlwain, *The Political Works of James I* (Cambridge, Mass., 1918), pp. lxxxviiff, and, more recently, Stanley B. Chrimes, "Dr. John Cowell," *EHR*, LXIV (1949), 461–487, who prints in the Appendix the relevant passages from Cowell's *Interpreter or Book Containing the Signification of Words*, first published in Cambridge, 1607. Cowell quotes many French authors, and it may have been derived from one of those sources that he points at the king's "benignity" (s.v. "Parliament"). His contemporary Charles Loyseau, for example, when discussing the validity of the provincial *Coutumiers* and the legislative power of the provincial assemblies, says also that "sa [the king's] bonté permette au peuple des Provinces coustumières de choisir certaines Coustumes, selon lesquelles il désire vivre." Loyseau's *Traité des Seigneuries* was first printed in 1608; but Loyseau was probably not the first to use the phrase; see William Farr Church, *Constitutional Thought in Sixteenth-Century France* (Harvard Hist. Stud., XLVII; Cambridge, 1941), 325, n. 57.

[9] See Thomas P. Taswell-Langmead, *English Constitutional History*, 8th ed. by Coleman Philippson (London, 1919), 488, note (y), where the better part of the proclamation is printed; cf. Chrimes, *op. cit.*, 472f. See also *Parliamentary Debates in 1610*, ed. by S. R. Gardiner (Camden Society, 81; London, 1862), 22ff.

[10] McIlwain, *Polit. Works*, 332f, for King James' Speech in the Star Chamber, in 1616. It should be noted, however, that the king says also: "For though the Common Law be a mystery and skill best knowen vnto your selues ..." Here the word "mystery" certainly has the meaning of handicraft or trade—in the sense of "arts and mysteries," which perhaps would allow the suggestion that "mysteries of state" are the handicraft or trade of kings.

[11] See *Parliamentary History of England* (London, 1806), I, 1326f where the "mystery" is the Spanish marriage of Prince Charles; see also McIlwain, *Constitutionalism Ancient and Modern* (rev. ed., Ithaca, N.Y., 1947), 112, cf. 125. To "meddle" turns up time and time again; it is the equivalent of Latin *se intromittere*; see, e.g., Matthaeus de Afflictis (below, n. 22), I, fol. 45, on *Liber aug.*, I, 4: "Ut nullus se intromittat de factis et consiliis regis."

[12] Tacitus, *Annales*, II, 36. The expression, of course, was known; see, e.g., *Parliamentary Debates in 1610*, p. 52, where the Lords are said to "sitt neerer the sterne of government, and therefore are made acquainted first with those things that are *Arcana imperii etc.*" For the interrelations between *arcana* and *mysteria*, see Othmar Perler, Art. "Arkandisziplin," *Reallexikon für Antike und Christentum*, I (1950), 667–676, with full literature.

[13] *Codex Theodos.*, 1, 6, 9 = *C.* 9, 29, 2: "Disputari de principali iudicio non oportet: sacrilegii enim instar est dubitare, an is dignus sit, quem elegerit imperator."

for *mysteria* and *arcana*, for actions in church and in court.[14] However, this ancient law, inserted by Justinian in his *Code*, was prominent in the legislation of Roger II of Sicily as well as of Frederick II[15] and was repeated, in a slightly attenuated form, also by Bracton.[16] Nor did it fail to impress James I, who in 1616, very fittingly in a Star Chamber speech, clearly referred to it when he said: "That which concernes the mysterie of the Kings power, is not lawful to be disputed." He warned his audience "to keep in their own bounds, because it was not lawful to dispute the absolute Prerogative of the Crown. ... It is Athiesme and blasphemie to dispute what God can doe.... So, it is presumption and high contempt in a Subiect, to dispute what a King can do... ."[17] The references to the law of the three Roman emperors are evident. Needless to say this law had passed, long before, also into Canon Law where it was applied to the pope.[18]

---

[14] For the connections between *arcana-mysteria* and *silentium*, see Odo Casel, *De philosophorum graecorum silentio mystico* (Religionsgeschichtliche Versuche und Vorarbeiten, XVI: 2; Giessen, 1919). The *silentium* belonged also to the court ritual of the Roman emperors; see Alföldi, "Zeremoniell" (above, n. 1), 38f; O. Treitinger, *Die oströmische Kaiser- und Reichsidee nach ihrer Gestaltung im höfischen Zeremoniell* (Jena, 1938), 52f; and, for its representation in early Christian art, the important remarks of André Grabar, "Une fresque visigothique et l'iconographie du silence," *Cahiers archéologiques*, I (1945), 126ff. The *silentium*, however, was just as strictly imposed by Frederick II on the parties appearing in the law courts; see *Liber augustalis*, I, 32: "Cultus iustitiae silentium reputatur." The words derive from Isaiah 32, 17; but the law itself is framed on Gratian's *Decretum*, II, C. V, qu. 4, c. 3, ed. Emil Friedberg, *Corpus iuris canonici* (Leipzig, 1879), I, 548f, a passage taken from the acts of the 11th Council of Toledo (675 A.D.), which had passed through various canonical collections, including that of Pseudo-Isidorus, before it was received by Gratian and, probably through him, by Frederick II. For his law in the *Liber augustalis*, see *Constitutionum regni Siciliarum libri tres* (Sumptibus Antonii Cervonii, Naples, 1773), 82. I am quoting the law book of Frederick II throughout according to this edition (abbreviated *Liber aug.* [with book and title], ed. Cervone [with page]) because it contains the glosses of Marinus de Caramanico and Andreas of Isernia; the edition of C. Carcani (Naples, 1786), though in some respects superior because it contains also the Greek text, lacks the gloss; and the "chronological" edition of J. L. A. Huillard-Bréholles, *Historia diplomatica Friderici Secundi* (Paris, 1852–1861), IV, 1ff, though it may have some better readings, is practically useless for the legal historian because it breaks up the unity of books and titles.

[15] See the so-called Vatican Assizes, I, 17 (published probably in 1140, at Ariano in Apulia), ed. Francesco Brandileone, *Il diritto Romano nelle leggi Normanne e Sveve del regno di Sicilia* (Turin, 1884), 103. The text matches that of the *Codex* (above, n. 13), but after the word *iudicio* there is added: *consiliis, institutionibus, factis*. The same text is repeated by Frederick II, *Liber aug.*, I, 4, ed. Cervone, 15.

[16] Bracton, *De legibus et consuetudinibus Angliae*, fol. 34, ed. by G. E. Woodbine (New Haven, 1915–1942), II, 109: "De cartis vero regiis et factis regum non debent nec

possunt iustitiarii nec privatae personae disputare, nec etiam, si in illis dubitatio oriatur, possunt eam interpretari." It is difficult to follow the arguments on this passage advanced by Fritz Schulz, "Bracton on Kingship," *EHR*, LX (1945), 173, admirable though his discussion is in so many other respects. Schulz claims that "here the words *et factis regum* must be interpolated." These words, however, are well attested in this connection by the two Sicilian Law Codes (above, n. 15); there is no reason to assume an interpolation, but much reason to wonder where the *de factis* came from. Schulz claims also that the plural *regum* instead of *regis* "is conspicuous." I do not think so: the plural slipped in because *C.* 9, 29, 2, which Schulz did not take into consideration, has the heading "Idem AAA. (= Augusti) ad Symmachum praefectum Urbi," for the law was issued by the three emperors Gratian, Valentinian, and Theodosius; and the plural first slipped not into Bracton's treatise but into *Liber aug.*, I, 4, the title of which reads: "Ut nullus se intromittat (see above, n. 11) *de factis* seu consiliis *regum*"—a significant slip because the Byzantine plurality of emperors influenced the South-Italian scriptoria and chanceries not at all rarely; see G. B. Ladner, "The 'Portraits' of Emperors in Southern Italian *Exultet* Rolls and the Liturgical Commemoration of the Emperor," *Speculum*, XVII (1942), 189ff, who convincingly interprets those plurals in South-Italian liturgical texts. How to explain the similarity of Bracton's wording with that of the Sicilian law-book is a different matter; but when Bracton wrote his treatise (probably between 1250 and 1259), England was "swamped" by Sicilians; see E. Kantorowicz, "Petrus de Vinea in England," *Mitteilungen des Österreichischen Instituts für Geschichtsforschung*, LI (1937–38), esp. 74ff, 81ff.

[17] McIlwain, *Political Works of James I*, 333f; see also *Parliamentary Debates in 1610*, p. 23, § 3.

[18] The law of the three emperors penetrated also Canon Law; see the gloss on *Decretum*, II, C.XVII, qu. 4, c. 4. And, as Professor Gaines Post kindly pointed out to me, the law was transferred also to the pope; see Hostiensis, *Summa aurea* (Venice, 1586), col. 1610, De crimine sacrilegii, n. 2: "Similiter de iudicio summi Pontificis disputare non licet." See also Oldradus de Ponte, *Consilia*, LXII, n. 1 (Lyon, 1550, fol. 21rb): "De potestate vestra dubitare sacrilegium esset. arg. C. de cri. sacri. l. II (*C.* 9, 29, 2)."

"Mysteries of State," then, derived obviously from that orbit which the jurists of the twelfth and thirteenth centuries—Placentinus, Azo, and others—termed *religio iuris*, "Religion of Law,"[19] and what in the surroundings of Frederick II was termed sometimes *mysterium Iustitiae*.[20] It is true, the emperor himself in his Sicilian Constitutions mentioned only the *ministerium Iustitiae*, or rather the *sacratissimum ministerium Iustitiae*, which he entrusted to his officials.[21] But the two words—*ministerium* and *mysterium*—were almost interchangeable since early Christian times, and they were perpetually confused in mediaeval times: a later glossator of the Sicilian Constitutions, Matthaeus de Afflictis, when glossing Frederick's law, still found it necessary to point out in many words the difference between *ministerium* and *mysterium*.[22] There seems, therefore, little doubt that it was from the stratum of the "Mysteries of Justice"—"Justice" standing in that period for "Government" or "State"—that James I's concept of Mysteries of State arose. And it was from the same stratum that the Pontificalism of absolute kings originated.

The royal "Pontificalism," then, seems to be resting in the legally settled belief that government is a *mysterium* administered alone by the king-highpriest and his indisputable officers, and that all actions committed in the name of those "Mysteries of State" are valid *ipso facto* or *ex opere operato*, regardless even of the personal worthiness of the king and his henchmen.

Whence does this pontifical attitude, unknown in the earlier Middle Ages, derive? To be sure, the "king-priest," the *rex et sacerdos*, was an early mediaeval ideal of many facets,[23]

[19] The *religio iuris* is usually discussed by the glossators in connection with Justinian's Institutes, Prooem.: "... et fiat [princeps Romanus] tam iuris religiosissimus quam victis hostibus triumphator." Cf. Placentinus, *Summa Institutionum*, ed. H. Fitting, *Juristische Schriften des früheren Mittelalters* (Halle, 1876), 222, 21; Azo, *Summa Institutionum*, ed. F. W. Maitland, *Select Passages from the Works of Bracton and Azo* (Selden Society, VIII; London, 1895), 6. The Glossa ordinaria (gl. on "religiosissimus") parallels, like Azo and others did before, the notions *iuris religio* and *triumphus*. See also Andreas of Isernia, on *Liber aug.*, I, 99, ed. Cervone, 168: "Iustitia habet multas partes inter quas est religio et sacramentum ... Nam sacramentum est religio: unde dicitur iurisiurandi religio." *Iurisiurandi religio* remained a technical term of Jurisprudence, and it is significant that a 16th-century French jurist, when referring to Philo, "De specialibus legibus, II: De iureiurando religioneque," quoted Philo, "Liber de iurisiurandi religione"; see Pierre Grégoire, *De Republica*, VI, c. 3, n. 2 (Lyon, 1609, p. 137, in marg.)

[20] Petrus de Vinea, *Epistolae*, III, 69, ed. by Simon Schard (Basel, 1566, p. 512): "vendere precio iusticiae mysterium," a school letter distorting the imperial laws. Venal justice, of course, compared with simony; see Philip of Leyden (below, n. 67), Casus LX, n. 33, p. 253f; Lucas de Penna, on *C*. 12, 45, 1, n. 61, p. 915: "gravius crimen est vendere iustitiam quam praebendam; legimus enim Christum esse iustitiam [see *Decretum*, C. XI, q. 3, c. 84, ed. Friedberg, I, 666], non legitur autem esse praebendam."

[21] *Liber aug.*, I, 63, ed. Cervone, 124.

[22] For the interchangeable use of *ministerium* and *mysterium*, see F. Blatt, "Ministerium-Mysterium,"

Archivum latinitatis medii aevi, IV (1923), 80f; one might add E. Diehl, *Inscriptiones latinae christianae veteres* (Berlin, 1924), I, 4, No. 14 ("ministeriis adque mysteriis religiose celebrandis"); also *The Book of Armagh*, ed. by John Gwynn (Dublin, 1913), p. ccxxi (quotation of Romans 11, 25). Matthaeus de Afflictis, *In utriusque Siciliae ... Constitutiones* (Venice, 1562, I, fol. 216ra), on *Liber aug.*, I, 63 [60], nos. 4–5, finds the chief difference between the two notions finally in the fact that "mysterium non potest fieri in privatis domibus ..., sed ministerium iustitiae potest fieri etiam in privatis domibus," a somewhat disappointing result of a promising effort. See also A. Souter, *A Glossary of Later Latin* (Oxford, 1949), s.v. "ministerium."

[23] There is a considerable lack of clarity with regard to the *rex et sacerdos* ideal. Without trying to solve a complicated problem in a footnote, a few remarks may not be out of order. In the early Christian centuries, the *rex et sacerdos* ideal had nothing to do with consecrations: it was chiefly a survival of the imperial title *Pontifex Maximus*, though also an adaptation of that title to Christian thought by way of the biblical model of Melchizedek. The introduction of royal anointments in the 7th and 8th centuries produced the liturgical note: the new coronation anointing of Old-Testament pattern was fused with the baptismal anointing of New-Testament pattern "ut intelligat baptizatus regale ac sacerdotale ministerium accepisse" (see, among a score of similar phrasings, Amalar of Trier's response to the questionnaire of Charlemagne on baptism, *PL*, XCIX, 898D): the king, like the neo-baptized, was *rex et sacerdos*, though in a special sense, and his priesthood was esoteric only, and not clerical. After the introduction of head-anointings at

though always inseparable from the Christ-centered kingship of that age; or, if you prefer, from the liturgical kingship linked to the altar, which finally gave way to a legalistic kingship by divine right. This legalism began in the twelfth century when the king's quasi-sacerdotal character no longer was legitimized exclusively as an effluence of unction and altar, but as an effluence of the gravity of Roman Law which styled judges and lawyers *sacerdotes iustitiae*, "Priests of Justice."[24] The ancient solemnity of liturgical language mingled strangely with the new solemnity of the legist's idiom when Roger II, in the Preface to his Sicilian Assizes of (probably) 1140, called his collection of new laws an oblation to God. *Dignum et necessarium est*, "It is meet and necessary"—with these words the Preface opened to explain the purpose of the collection, and continued:

> *In qua oblatione*—By this oblation [of new laws] the royal office presumes for itself a certain privilege of priesthood, wherefore some wise man and jurisprudent called the law interpreters "Priests of Law."[25]

With the last quoted words King Roger referred to the opening paragraph of Justinian's *Digest* which naturally attracted the attention of the mediaeval jurists. Accursius (died ca. 1258), in the *Glossa ordinaria* on *D.* 1, 1, 1, drew a clear parallel between the priests of the Church and those of the Law:

> Just as the priests minister and confection things holy, so do *we*, since the laws are most sacred.... And just as the priest, when imposing penitence, renders to each one what is his right, so do *we* when we judge.[26]

An imperial judge at Florence around 1238, John of Viterbo, inferred from the *Codex* that "the judge is hallowed by the presence of God" and that "in all legal causes the judge is said, nay, believed to be God with regard to men," whereby the fact that the judge administers a *sacramentum*, the oath, and had a copy of Holy Scriptures on his table, served—or was pressed to fit—the purpose of a para-religious exaltation of the jurist-priest.[27] So great a jurist as William Durand, the *Speculator*, writing at the end of

the bishops' consecration, the king's coronation was strongly assimilated to the ordination of a bishop: the royal office was "clericalized" and the ruler considered *non omnino laicus*. Roman and Canon Laws finally produced a new, neither esoteric nor liturgico-clerical, but legalistic-clerical interpretation of the old *rex et sacerdos* ideal, though without inactivating the earlier layers completely.

[24] *Digest*, 1, 1, 1: "(Ulpianus) Cuius merito quis nos sacerdotes appellet: iustitiam namque colimus..." Who he (*quis*) was that called the judges and jurists priests is not said; see, however, Aulus Gellius, *Noctes Atticae*, XIV, 4: "... iudicem, qui Iustitiae antistes est"; also Quintilian, *Inst. orat.*, XI, 1, 69: "iuris antistes" See further the inscription *CIL*, VI, 2250: *sacerdos iustitiae*, with Mommsen's quotation of *D.* 1, 1, 1; also Symmachus, *Ep.* X, 3, 13, *MGH, Auct. ant.*, VI, 282, 28, addressing the emperors *Iustitiae sacerdotes*. For the passage itself, see Ulrich von Lübtow, "De iustitia et iure," *Zeitschrift der Savigny-Stiftung für Rechtsgeschichte*, rom. Abt., LXVI (1948), 458ff, esp. 524, 559ff, 563.

[25] Brandileone, *Diritto Romano* (above, n. 15), 94f: "In qua oblatione regni officium quoddam sibi sacerdotii vendicat privilegium; unde quidam sapiens legisque peritus iuris interpretes iuris sacerdotes appellat." Compare *Dignum et necessarium est* with the Preface of the Mass: *Vere dignum et iustum est*; and the relative junction *In qua oblatione* with *Quam oblationem* before the Consecration. Neither the similarities nor the slight variations are meaningless: one wanted the assonance with the Mass, but refrained as yet from profanation.

[26] *Glossa ordinaria*, on *D.* 1, 1, 1, gl. 'sacerdotes': "quia ut sacerdotes sacra ministrant et conficiunt, ita et nos, cum leges sunt sanctissimae... Ut ius suum cuique tribuit sacerdos in danda poenitentia, sic et nos in iudicando." A long commentary on the subject is found in Guillaume Budé, *Annotationes in XXIIII Pandectarum libros* (Lyon, 1551), 28ff.

[27] John of Viterbo, *De regimine civitatum*, c. 25, ed. Gaetano Salvemini, in *Bibliotheca iuridica medii aevi* (Bologna, 1901), III, 226: "... nam iudex alias sacerdos dicitur quia sacra dat ...; et alias dicitur: 'Iudex dei presentia consecratur' ...; dicitur etiam, immo creditur, esse deus in omnibus pro hominibus ..." The places referred to are *D.* 1, 1, 1; *C.* 3, 1, 14; *C.* 2, 59, 2, 8.

the thirteenth century, quoted the glossators to the effect "that the emperor ranked as a presbyter according to the passage where it is said [*D.* 1, 1, 1]: 'Deservedly we, the judges, are called priests'."[28] And he referred to both Roman Law and Gratian's *Decretum*, as he added: "The emperor is called also pontiff."[29] It is most significant that here a positive effort was made to prove the king's non-laical, and even pontifical, character within the Church, not as a result of his anointment with the holy balm but as a result of Ulpian's comparison of judges with priests. At any rate, kingship was about to be severed from the altar space, and the ancient ideal of priest-kingship after the model of Melchizedek and of Christ was gradually replaced by a new regal pontificalism after the model of Ulpian or even Justinian himself.

That the Mysteries of State were inseparable from the sphere of law and jurisdiction demands no further comment. The claim to universal jurisdiction which Barbarossa (advised, as the story goes, by the four Doctors of Bologna) put up on the basis of Feudal and Roman Laws, was a failure. It was not a failure when the same claim was made by the Roman Pontiff on the basis of 1 Corinthians 2, 15: "The spiritual man judges all, but himself is judged by none." We are well acquainted with the history of that maxim, and know how the "Man endowed with the Holy Spirit," the *pneumatikós* of the Apostle, finally was replaced by the incumbent of an office, the bishop, and was identified in particular with the Bishop of Rome; and how, after passing through the *Dictatus papae* of Gregory VII and the bull *Unam sanctam* of Boniface VIII, the papal maxim claiming universal jurisdiction under certain circumstances was established for all times to come: *Sancta Sedes omnes iudicat, sed a nemine iudicatur.*[30]

Far less well known is the later, secular, history of that maxim. Baldus, the great legal authority of the fourteenth century, remarked that the emperor was also called *Rex, quia alios regit et a nemine regitur*, "Ruler, because he rules others and is ruled by none."[31] Matthaeus de Afflictis, the Sicilian glossator at the beginning of the sixteenth century, declared: "The emperor commands the others, but he is commanded by none."[32] De Afflictis, of course, did not quote or twist St. Paul; he quoted Baldus, who in his turn hardly thought of the Epistle to the Corinthians, but of the canonist maxim: *Sancta Sedes*

---

[28] Guillelmus Durandus, *Rationale divinorum officiorum*, II, 8, 6 (Lyon, 1565, fol. 55ᵛ): "Quidam etiam dicunt... [D. 1, 8, 9, 3] quod [imperator] fit presbyter iuxta illud: 'Cuius merito quis nos sacerdotes appellat'."

[29] Durandus, *loc. cit.*: "Imperator etiam pontifex dictus est." Cf. *Rationale*, II, 11: "Unde et Romani Imperatores pontifices dicebantur." This is simply the customary quotation from Gratian, *Decretum*, I, Dist. XXI, c. 1, § 8, ed. Friedberg, I, 68. The passage in the Decretum is taken from Isidore of Seville, *Etym.*, VII, 12. The civilians rarely failed to allege that place of the Decretum when they came to discuss the pontifical and sacerdotal qualities of the Prince in connection with Justinian, *Instit.* 2, 1, 8 ("per pontifices deo consecrata sunt"), or with *D.* 1, 8, 9, 1 ("cum princeps eum [locum sacrum] dedicavit"). Later Budé, *op. cit.* (above, n. 26), 30, blames Accursius—and, for that matter, the whole old school of glossators—*quod ad nostros pontifices retulit*; that is, for having equated the ancient *pontifex* with the modern Christian bishop. This does honor to Budé's strongly developed historical understanding. By that time, however, the damage was done and the king had become "pontifical."

[30] See Albert Michael Koeniger, "Prima sedes a nemine iudicatur," *Beiträge zur Geschichte des christlichen Altertums und der byzantinischen Literatur: Festgabe Albert Ehrhard* (Bonn und Leipzig, 1922), 273–300; see, for Boniface VIII, also Konrad Burdach, *Rienzo und die geistige Wandlung seiner Zeit* (Vom Mittelalter zur Reformation, II, 1; Berlin, 1913–28), 538ff. See the angry 16th-century diatribe against the papal maxim by Pierre de Belloy, *Moyens d'abus, entreprises et nullitez du rescrit et bulle du Pape Sixte Vᵉ* (Paris, 1586), 61ff.

[31] Baldus, on *Digest*, Prooem., n. 23 (Venice, 1586, I, fol. 2ᵛ).

[32] Matthaeus de Afflictis, *In Sicil. Const.*, praeludia, qu. XXI, n. 3, fol. 18: "quia imperator aliis imperat, sed sibi a nemine imperatur, ut dicit Baldus in prin.ff. veteris. in ii. col." (see above, n. 31).

omnes iudicat. The same was probably true when James I declared that God had the power "to judge all and to be judged by none," not without adding, though, that "Kings are justly called Gods,[33] for that they exercise a manner or resemblance of Divine Power on earth."[34] Nor did Salmasius, an absolutist of a good vintage, think of the Apostolic Letter when, in his "Regal Defense of Charles I of England," first printed in 1649, he said plainly and simply: "He is a king in the proper sense of the word, who judges all and is judged by none."[35] Salmasius clearly twisted nothing but the papal theory by transferring its essence to the secular state. Literally, the absolute Prince had stepped into the shoes of the Roman Pontiff: he, the Prince, now became the super-man, that *homo spiritualis* whom Boniface VIII so powerfully had tried to monopolize to the exclusion of all others for the Roman Pontiff.[36]

The "Mysteries of State" were practically always bound to the legal sphere. On the accession of Henry II of France, in 1547, there was introduced into the French Coronation Order a rubric before and after the bestowal of the ring, saying that by this ring "the king solemnly married his realm"—*le roy espousa solemnellement le royaume*.[37] This was not just a metaphor introduced for its handsomeness, as perhaps occasionally in an address of James I,[38] but for its agreement with the fundamental law of the realm and with

[33] For the kings as "gods" (*dii*), see my paper "Deus per naturam, Deus per gratiam," *Harvard Theological Review*, XLV (1952), 253–277, where I have indicated (e.g., 274, n. 72) the connections with absolutist theories, though without penetrating the matter and without recognizing to what extent that notion was actually pivotal in the theories of English and French absolutists. See, e.g., above, n. 9.

[34] James I's Speech to the Lords and Commons, March 21, 1609; see McIlwain, *Political Works*, 307f.

[35] Salmasius, *Defensio regia pro Carolo I.*, c. VI (Paris, 1650 [*ed. prin.*, 1649], 169): "Rex a nemine iudicari potest nisi a Deo"; and 170: "...illum proprium [regem esse], qui iudicat de omnibus et a nemine iudicatur."

[36] See Burdach, *Rienzo* (above, n. 30), 211f, 269f, and *passim* (Index, s.v. "Übermensch"), on the idea of the "superman" and its connection with the *homo spiritualis*. The genealogy of "superman" is, however, very complicated, though a connection with St. Paul and the Epistle to the Corinthians cannot easily be denied. See Gregory the Great, *Moralia*, XVIII, c. 54 (§ 92), on Job 27, 20–21; *PL*, LXXVI, 95A. Gregory comments on 1 Cor. 2, 10, and says about St. Paul: "More suo [Paulus] 'homines' vocans omnes humana sapientes, quia qui divina sapiunt, videlicet *supra homines* sunt. Videbimus igitur Deum, si per coelestem conversationem *suprahomines* esse mereamur." The notion of *suprahomines* thus coincides largely with that of *dii* (*see* above, n. 33). See Charles Norris Cochrane, *Christianity and Classical Culture* (Oxford, 1940), 113, n. 1; J. Maritain, *Theonas, Conversations of a Sage* (London and New York, 1933), 189; see also R. Reitzenstein, *Die hellenistischen Mysterienreligionen* (3rd ed., Berlin, 1927), 368ff, for St. Paul and further Karl Holl, *Luther* (Tübingen, 1932), 222, 533. There is, however, yet another strand. Nikephoras Gregoras, writing in the 14th century, still styles the Byzantine emperor "divine and man above men" (θεῖος καὶ ὑπὲρ ἀνθρώπων ἄνθρωπος); cf. Rodolphe Guilland, "Le droit divin à Byzance," *Eos*, XLII (1947), 153. This strand, of course, leads to the very broad problem of the *theios anēr*, which cannot be broached here. Cf. L. Bieler, ΘΕΙΟΣ ANHP: *Das Bild des "göttlichen Menschen" in Spätantike und Frühchristentum* (Vienna, 1935).

[37] Th. Godefroy, *Le ceremonial de France* (Paris, 1619), 348, for the coronation of 1547, and, p. 661, for the more detailed rubrics of 1594: 'ANNEAU ROYAL: Parce qu'au jour du Sacre le Roy espousa solemnellement son Royaume, et fut comme par le doux, gracieux, et amiable lien de marriage inseparablement uny avec ses subjects, pour mutuellement s'entr[e]aimer ainsi que sont les espoux, luy fut par le dit Evesque de Chartres presenté un anneau, pour marque de ceste reciproque conjonction." The rubric after the ceremony says that the same bishop "mit le dit anneau, duquel le Roy espousoit son Royaume, au quatriesme doigt de sa main dextre, dont procede certaine veine attouchant au coeur." See, for the last remark concerning the ring finger, Gratian, *Decretum*, II, C.XXX, qu. 5, c. 7, ed. Friedberg, I, 1106. In his edict of 1607, concerning the reunion to the Crown of his private patrimony of Navarre, Henry IV quite obviously alludes to those rubrics, when he says about his predecessor kings that "ils ont contracté avec leur couronne une espèce de mariage communément appellé saint et politique"; cf. *Recueil général des anciens lois françaises*, ed. by Isambert, Taillandier et Decrusy, XV (Paris, 1829), 328, No. 191; see also Hartung (below, n. 40), 33f; and, for the *sponsus* metaphor in general, Burdach, *Rienzo*, 41–61.

[38] See, e.g., King James I's Speech to his First Parliament, in 1603; *Parliamentary History*, I, 930: "'What God hath conjoined then, let no man separate.' I am the husband, and all the whole island is my lawful wife; I am the head, and it is my body; I am the shepherd, and it is my flock."

contemporary legal concepts. In 1538, a French lawyer, Charles de Grassaille, advanced in his book "On the Regalian Rights of France" the theory that "a marriage both moral and politic" (*matrimonium morale et politicum*) was contracted between the king and his *respublica*.[39] Grassaille as well as other sixteenth-century lawyers—René Choppin, in 1572,[40] or François Hotman, in 1586[41]— declared that the king's power over the domain and the fisc was only that which a husband had over the dowry of his wife: "The domain is the dowry inseparable from the public state."[42] René Choppin actually went so far as to say that the king "is the mystical spouse of the *respublica*" (*Rex reipublicae mysticus coniunx*).[43] This has been looked upon occasionally as a "new theory."[44] In fact, however, those French lawyers, especially Grassaille, quoted verbatim from the Commentaries on the last three books of Justinian's *Codex* by a South-Italian jurist, Lucas de Penna (born ca. 1320), whose work was widely studied and six times reprinted in sixteenth-century France.[45] The passage from Lucas de Penna quoted by Grassaille contains a whole political theory *in nuce*, based on Ephesians 5, the apostolic Lesson of the matrimonial Mass, and since it leads to other relevant problems we may use Lucas de Penna's arguments as stepping stones for further discussion.[46]

Lucas de Penna commented on *Codex*, 11, 58, 7, on the Occupation of Desert Land— excepting, however, lands belonging to the fisc and the patrimony of the Prince. It is actually the fisc which he wishes to discuss, and quite skilfully he starts with a quotation from Lucan who styled Cato *urbi pater urbique maritus*, "father to the city and the city's husband."[47] From this metaphor he makes his way to the subject in which two hundred years later the French lawyers were interested, as he argues:

[39] Charles de Grassaille, *Regalium Franciae libri duo*, I, ius xx (Paris, 1545, p. 217): "Rex dicitur maritus reipublicae... Et dicitur esse matrimonium morale et politicum: sicut inter ecclesiam et Praelatum matrimonium spirituale contrahitur... Et sicut vir est caput uxoris, uxor vero corpus viri..., ita Rex est caput reipublicae et respublica eius corpus." See above, n. 38, and below, nos, 48, 56.

[40] René Choppin, *De Domanio Franciae*, Lib. II, tit. 1, n. 2 (Paris, 1605, p. 203): "Sicuti enim Lege Julia, dos est a marito inalienabilis: ita Regium Coronae patrimonium, individua Reipublicae dos"; also Lib. III, tit. 5, n. 6 (*ed. cit.*, p. 449): "Rex, curator Reipublicae ac mysticus... ipsius coniunx." See, for the French version, Choppin, *Les oeuvres* (Paris, 1635), II, 117 and 259. See also the very useful study of Fritz Hartung, *Die Krone als Symbol der monarchischen Herrschaft im ausgehenden Mittelalter* (Abhandlungen der Preussischen Akademie, 1940, Nr. 13; Berlin, 1941), 33f.

[41] François Hotman, *Francogallia*, c. IX, *in prin.*, of the 1586 edition (but not in any of the earlier editions, 1573ff); cf. André Lemaire, *Les lois fondamentales de la monarchie française* (Paris, 1907), 93, n. 2, for the editions (also 99, n. 2), and, p. 100, for the marriage metaphor, used also by Pierre Grégoire, *De Republica*, IX, 1, 11 (Lyon, 1609 [first published in 1578], p. 267A): the Prince as *sponsus reipublicae* and the fisc as the *dos pro oneribus danda*.

[42] See Filippo E. Vassalli, "Concetto e natura del fisco," *Studi Senesi*, XXV (1908), 198, nos. 3–4, and 201,

for the metaphor. The problem of inalienability of the fisc or demesne in France is one of the leading subjects in the excellent study of William F. Church, *Constitutional Thought in Sixteenth-Century France* (above, n. 8).

[43] Above, n. 40; also Church, *op. cit.*, 82.

[44] See Hartung, *Krone als Symbol*, 33.

[45] See Walter Ullmann, *The Medieval Idea of Law as Represented by Lucas de Penna* (London, 1946), 14, n. 2, for the editions. Ullmann reasonably restricts himself to a "few obvious examples" of French jurists who referred to Lucas de Penna (Tiraqueau, Jean de Montaigne, Pierre Rebuffi, Bodin); their number, however, is legion. Grassaille copies verbatim and actually cites Lucas' commentary on *C*. 11, 58, 7, in the passage quoted above (n. 39).

[46] Lucas de Penna, *Commentaria in Tres Libros Codicis*, on *C*. 11, 58, 7, n. 8ff (Lyons, 1582, p. 563f), a place which Ullmann does not seem to have discussed, though (p. 176, n. 1) he quotes another marriage metaphor of Lucas. See below, n. 49, for the biblical and ritual background.

[47] "Item princeps si verum dicere vel agnoscere volumus, ... est maritus reipublicae iuxta illud Lucani ... [*Pharsalia*, II, 388]." The history of the Roman title *pater* (*parens*) *patriae* has been admirably discussed by A. Alföldi, "Die Geburt der kaiserlichen Bildsymbolik: 3. Parens patriae," *Museum Helveticum*, IX (1952), 204–243, and X (1953), 103–124. The title *urbi maritus* is not quite rare either, since it is found in Priscian, Servius, and others, as every well commented edition of Lucan may show.

There is contracted a moral and political marriage between the Prince and the *respublica*.

Also, just as there is contracted a spiritual and divine marriage between a church and its prelate, so is there contracted a temporal and terrestrial marriage between the Prince and the State.

Also, just as the church is in the prelate and the prelate in the church . . ., so is the Prince in the *respublica*, and the *respublica* in the Prince.[48]

Here some of the roots of royal "Pontificalism" are laid bare. Lucas availed himself of the very old metaphor of the mystical marriage of the bishop to his see to interpret the relations between Prince and state[49]—a metaphor widely and generally discussed two generations before, when Pope Celestine V by his abdication of 1294 actually "divorced" himself from the universal Church to which he was married.[50]

In addition, Lucas de Penna cited verbatim a passage from Gratian's *Decretum*: "The Bishop is in the Church, and the Church in the Bishop."[51] Those words, hailing from a famous letter of St. Cyprian, have always been taken as a cornerstone of the doctrine of the "monarchic episcopate."[52] When transferred to the secular sphere—already by Andreas of Isernia, glossing the Sicilian Constitutions shortly after 1300, then by Lucas

[48] Lucas de Penna, *loc. cit.*: ". . . inter principem et rempublicam matrimonium morale contrahitur et politicum. Item, sicut inter ecclesiam et praelatum matrimonium spirituale contrahiter et divinum . . ., ita inter principem et rempublicam matrimonium temporale contrahitur et terrenum; et sicut ecclesia est in praelato et praelatus in ecclesia . . ., ita princeps in republica et respublica in principe." Lucas de Penna may have been guided by Andreas of Isernia, a Neapolitan like himself, who on I *feud.*, 3 ("Qui successores teneantur"), n. 16, *In usus feudorum* (Naples, 1571, 21ᵛ), wrote: "Est princeps in republica sicut caput, et respublica in eo sicut in capite, ut dicitur de praelato in ecclesia, et ecclesia in praelato" (see also below, n. 53).

[49] The basis is, of course, Ephes. 5, 25 ("sicut et Christus dilexit ecclesiam"), which is also basic for the nuptial mass; the early Christian marriage rings, therefore, displayed in the bezel the marriage of Christ to the Church; see O. M. Dalton, *Catalogue of Early Christian Antiquities and Objects from the Christian East . . . of the British Museum* (London, 1901), 130 and 131; a particularly beautiful specimen is in the Dumbarton Oaks Research Library and Collection, Washington, D. C. The marriage of a bishop to his see is a very common image to which, e.g., Pope Clement II, who refused to divorce himself from his bishopric Bamberg, alluded in most telling words; see Clement II, *Ep.*, VIII, *PL*, CXLII, 588B; and, above all, the decretal X, 1, 7, 2 (Innocent III), ed. Friedberg, II, 97.

[50] The argument was used especially on the part of the French legists in the trial against the memory of Pope Boniface VIII; cf. P. Dupuy, *Histoire du différend d'entre le Pape Boniface VIII et Philippe le Bel* (Paris, 1655), 453ff, and *passim*; Burdach, *Rienzo*, 52f.

[51] Gratian, *Decretum*, II, C. VII, qu. 1, c. 7, ed. Friedberg, I, 568f.

[52] Cyprian, *Ep.*, 66, c. 8, ed. W. Hartel (*CSEL*, III: 2, 1871), II, 733, 5. It would be rewarding to investigate the history of Cyprian's image of reciprocity. See, e.g., Athanasius, *Oratio III contra Arianos*, c. 5, *PG*, XXVI, 332A, quoted by G. Ladner, "The Concept of the Image in the Greek Fathers," *Dumbarton Oaks Papers*, VII (1953), 8, n. 31 ("The image might well say: 'I [the image] and the emperor are one, I am in him and he is in me'"). Or, for a much later period, Petrus Damiani, *Disceptatio synodalis*, in *MGH*, *Libelli de lite*, I, 93, 36f: "ut . . . rex in Romano pontifice et Romanus pontifex inveniatur in rege" (a place to which Professor Theodor E. Mommsen kindly called my attention). The ultimate source, of course, is in all those cases John 14, 10, whose own model is difficult to determine. See, however, Eduard Norden, *Agnostos Theos* (Berlin, 1923), 305; Wilfred L. Knox, *Some Hellenistic Elements in Primitive Christianity* (Schweich Lectures, 1942; London, 1944), 78, n. 3, believes that the Johannine saying "goes back to the pantheistic tradition of Stoicism influenced perhaps by the religion of Egypt," and quotes (p. 73, n. 2, at the very end of the note) as "the nearest parallel to the Johannine language" a phrase found several times in the magical papyri: σὺ γὰρ εἶ ἐγὼ καὶ ἐγὼ σύ; see K. Preisendanz, *Papyri graecae magicae* (Leipzig and Berlin, 1931), II, 47 (P. VIII, 37ff, 49ff) and 123 (P. XIII, 795, with some literature in the footnote). The parallel, however, does not contain the word *in* (ἐν), which in fact reflects two different "spaces" and which is essential for the development from John 14, 10, to St. Cyprian and thence to the corporational doctrines of early modern times. See also next note.

de Penna and Matthaeus de Afflictis[53]—the words of St. Cyprian fitted no less neatly as a cornerstone of the "pontifical monarchy": "The Prince is in the *respublica*, and the *respublica* is in the Prince." A certain corporational twist came into the secular version of that maxim,[54] certainly through Lucas de Penna as will be shown presently. The English crown jurists under Queen Elizabeth, however, twisted that twist when they pointed out that "the king in his body politic is incorporated with his subjects, and they with him," and when Sir Francis Bacon rendered an even more condensed formula, coined by his predecessors and defining the king as "a body corporate in a body natural, and a body natural in a body corporate" (*corpus corporatum in corpore naturali, et corpus naturale in corpore corporato*).[55] No doubt, St. Cyprian's coinage had been changed, but the die and the die-sinker are still recognizable.

This corporational aspect, though with a different emphasis, was brought into the picture by Lucas de Penna at the latest. While continuing his political exegesis of Ephesians 5, he applied to the Prince the versicle: "The man is the head of the wife, and the wife the body of the man," and logically concluded: "After the same fashion, the Prince is the head of the realm, and the realm the body of the Prince."[56] The corporational tenet, however, was formulated even more succinctly, when he continued:

> And just as men are joined together spiritually in the spiritual body, the head of which is Christ. . ., so are men joined together morally and politically in the *respublica*, which is a body the head of which is the Prince."[57]

Here we envisage that portentous equation, which became customary around the middle ol the thirteenth century: the *corpus reipublicae mysticum*, headed by the Prince, compared with the *corpus ecclesiae mysticum*, headed by Christ.[58] While ignoring here the very obvious parallelism of the ecclesiastical and the secular "mystical bodies," which has been discussed in another connection, it is pertinent to indicate the importance of Aristotle's doctrine of human society (or the state) as an entity having both moral and political ends. For it was, in the last analysis, a concept based on Aristotle that the jurists

[53] Andreas of Isernia, *Prooemium super Constitutionibus*, ed. Cervone (above, n. 14), p. xxvi, while discussing the fisc ("fiscus et respublica Romanorum idem sunt"), concludes: "Rex ergo et respublica regni sui idem sunt . . ., qui est in regno sicut caput, respublica in eo sicut in capite." The basis is clearly John 10, 30, and 14, 10 (as in the case of Athanasius, quoted above, n. 52), but the juristic allegation quoted by Andreas is the place of the *Decretum* (above, n. 51). Matthaeus de Afflictis, on *Const.*, II, 3, n. 62, fol. 11^v, refers to Lucas de Penna: "Princeps est in republica et respublica in principe."

[54] The corporational interpretation of that passage in a mystical sense was certainly very old within the Church, though it was not juristically rationalized before the 12th or 13th century. For Lucas de Penna, see below, nos. 56f.

[55] Edmund Plowden, *Commentaries or Reports* (London, 1816), 233a (Willion v. Berkley), one of a score of similar utterances; see Bacon, "Post-nati," in *Works of Sir Francis Bacon*, ed. by Spedding and Heath (London, 1892), VII, 667, who actually quotes Plowden, *Reports*, 213 (Case of the Duchy of Lancaster).

[56] Lucas de Penna, *loc. cit.*: ". . . item, sicut vir est caput uxoris, uxor vero corpus viri . . ., ita princeps caput reipublicae, et respublica eius corpus." The quotation is Ephes. 5, 23 and 28; that is, it belongs to that apostolic writing which (above, n. 49) predominantly referred to both marriage rites and corporational doctrines in their early setting. See also next note, and above, n. 38, for James I, who quoted those passages.

[57] "Item, sicut membra coniunguntur in humano corpore carnaliter, et homines spirituali corpori spiritualiter coniunguntur cui corpori Christus est caput . . ., sic moraliter et politice homines coniunguntur reipublicae quae corpus est, cuius caput est princeps."

[58] See my "Pro patria mori," *AHR*, LVI (1951), 486f, 490f, for additional examples. See also Huguccio of Pisa (d. 1210), who sets over against the body of Christ that of the Devil (". . . ita infideles sunt unum corpus, cuius caput est diabolus"); cf. Onory, *Fonti canonistische* (below, n. 84), 175, n. 2, who adds similar places.

employed when, time and again, they pointed out that the state was a *corpus morale et politicum*, which indeed could be set over against the *corpus mysticum et spirituale* of the Church with the same ease with which Dante assembled the terrestrial paradise and the celestial paradise on one denominator as the two goals of mankind.[59]

Lucas de Penna, by his *quid pro quo* method, thus arrives at an "equiparation" not only of Prince and bishop, but also of Prince and Christ. And he made the comparison with Christ poignantly clear when he added:

> Just as Christ joined to himself an alien-born, the Church of Gentiles, as his spouse..., so has the Prince joined to himself the state as his *sponsa*, which is not his ...[60]

Thus, the venerable image of *sponsus* and *sponsa*, Christ and his Church, was transferred from the spiritual to the secular and adapted to the jurist's need for defining the relations between Prince and State. We now understand how the French jurist happened to style the king the *mysticus coniunx* of France. The Prince not only donned the episcopal shoes, but also became—like the bishops' celestial prototype—both the head of a mystical body and its groom.

With this canonistic mysticism there was fused the institutionalism of Roman Law. Lucas de Penna's true purpose, when enlarging on those marriage metaphors, was to illustrate the peculiarities of the fisc. He interpreted the fisc as the dowry of the *respublica*, and maintained that the husband was entitled only to use, but not to alienate, the property of his wife. He further paralleled the vows exchanged by groom and bride at their marriage to the oaths taken by kings at their coronation and by bishops at their ordination, by which both promised not to alienate property belonging to the fisc and to the church respectively.[61]

Tempting though it would be to demonstrate how indeed the king's non-alienation promise at his coronation derived from and was related to the episcopal oath (and in the

---

[59] For the connection of *morale* ("ethical" in the Aristotelean sense) and *politicum* it will suffice here to quote Thomas Aquinas' Prooemium, c. 6, of his *Expositio in libros Politicorum Aristotelis*, ed. by Raymundus M. Spiazzi (Turin and Rome, 1951), p. 2: "... et huiusmodi quae ad *moralem scientiam* pertinent: manifestum est *politicam scientiam* ... contineri ... sub activis [scientiis] quae sunt *scientiae morales*." The expression *corpus politicum et mysticum* is found frequently in England and France as a predication of the state; see, e.g., S. B. Chrimes, *English Constitutional Ideas in the Fifteenth Century* (Cambridge, 1936), 180, 185, ("the mistik or politike body"); for France, Church, *Constitutional Thought*, 29, n. 20; 34, n. 36; 278, n. 16 ("le corps politique et mystique"). See also above, n. 37 ("saint et politique").

[60] Lucas de Penna, *loc. cit.*: "Amplius, sicut Christus alienigenam, id est, gentilem ecclesiam sibi copulavit uxorem, 35.q.l. § hac itaque, sic et princeps rempublicam, quae quantum ad dominium sua non est, cum ad principatum assumitur, sponsam sibi coniungit ..." The reference is to Gratian's *Decretum*, II, C.XXXV, q. 1, § 1 (Gratian's commentary on Augustine, *De civitate Dei*, XV, c. 16), ed. Friedberg, I, 1263.

[61] Lucas de Penna, *op. cit.*: "Nam aequiparantur quantum ad hoc etiam iuramentum super his praestitum de alienatione facta ⟨non⟩ revocando episcopus et rex. Ita et principi alienatio rerum fiscalium, quae in patrimonio imperii et reipublicae sunt et separate consistunt a privato patrimonio suo, iuste noscitur interdicta." There follows the comparison of the fisc with the *dos* which the *respublica* entrusts to the Prince at her marriage. See above, n. 41. Naturally, the *patrimonium Petri* figures as the *dos* of the papal *sponsa*, Rome; see, e.g., Oldradus de Ponte, *Consilia*, LXXXV, n. 1 (Lyon, 1550, fol. 28ᵛ), who admonishes the pope "ut sanctitas vestra revertatur ad sponsam ... et reparet suum patrimonium et suam dotem, quae multipliciter est collapsa." The doctrine finally traveled its full circular course in the 17th century, when the Roman pontiff appeared as the *maritus* of a *respublica temporalis* (the States of the Church) *iure principatus* and *ex sola ratione dominii publici*, though as a bishop he was also married to the Roman Church (*tanquam vir Ecclesiae*); De Luca, *Theatrum I de feudis*, disc. 61, n. 6, quoted by Vassalli, "Fisco," 209 (above, n. 42).

first place to the non-alienation oath of the English kings in the thirteenth century),[62] we may pass over that vexed question and turn, so to speak, to the *mysteria fisci* which Lucas de Penna, seemingly in some absurd mood, had linked to the mystic marriage of Christ and the Church. *Christus* and *fiscus*, however, were not as far apart for the mediaeval lawyers as they would be to us.[63]

In 1441, in a lawsuit tried before the Court of the Exchequer, John Paston, then a Justice of the Court of Common Pleas and well known to us as the compiler of the Paston Letters, dropped quite casually a strange remark: "What is not snatched by *Christus*, is snatched by the *Fiscus*" (*Quod non capit Christus, capit fiscus*).[64] Professor Plucknett, the learned interpreter of that lawsuit, took that sentence apparently as a *bon mot* of Paston's which he quoted because he rightly considered it "too good to be lost." But Paston's remark would not have been lost anyway. In his collection of emblems, first published in 1522, the great Italian jurist and humanist Andrea Alciati presented an emblem carrying the motto *Quod non capit Christus, rapit fiscus*.[65] And from Alciati's authoritative and incredibly influential book, the motto wandered into scores of highly respectable collections of emblems, devices, and proverbs of which the Renaissance was so fond.[66] Nor was the *bon mot* a coinage by Paston. A century before him the Flemish Civilian, Philip of Leyden, had remarked: "We compare the patrimonial possessions of Christ and the Fisc" (*Bona patrimonialia Christi et fisci comparantur*).[67] Similar remarks are found in Baldus' works; and even in the thirteenth century Bracton singled out the *res nullius*, "the things belonging to no individual," as property "only of God and the Fisc."[68]

The source of all those lawyers was Gratian's *Decretum*, the chapter on tithes: *Hoc tollit fiscus, quod non accipit Christus*, "What is not received by Christus, is exacted by the Fiscus."[69] Gratian borrowed the passage from a pseudo-Augustinian sermon. However, the genuine St. Augustine likewise talks about the *fiscus* of Christ[70]—metaphors whose importance should not be minimized, because in the course of the Poverty Struggle in the

[62] See my study on "Inalienability: A Note on Canonical Practice and the English Coronation Oath in the Thirteenth Century," *Speculum*, XXIX (1954), 488–502.

[63] Without then knowing either the origin or later history of that comparison, I have briefly discussed the problem in "Christus-Fiscus," *Synopsis: Festgabe für Alfred Weber* (Heidelberg, 1949), 225–235.

[64] T. F. T. Plucknett, "The Lancastrian Constitution," *Tudor Studies Presented to A. F. Pollard* (London, 1924), 168, n. 10.

[65] Andrea Alciati, *Emblemata* (Lyon, 1551; first edition 1522), p. 158, No. CXLVII. The motto is not found in the *editio princeps* of 1522, but in that of 1531; see Henry Green, *Andrea Alciati and the Books of Emblems* (London, 1872), 324, who indicates (p. viii) that in the wake of Alciati's publication some thirteen hundred authors published more than 3000 Emblem Books, while Alciati's original was translated into all European languages. I am indebted to Mrs. Caterina Olschki for having called my attention to the Alciati emblem.

[66] See, e.g., K. F. W. Wander, *Deutsches Sprichwörterlexikon* (Leipzig, 1867), I, 538, Nos. 54, 56, 57; V, 1102, No. 95, cf. Nos. 103, 104; Johannes Georgius Seyboldus,

Selectiora Adagia latino-germanica (Nürnberg, 1683), 306; G. Strafforello, *La sapienza del mondo ovvero dizionario universale dei proverbi di tutti popoli* (Turin, 1883) II, 86, s.v. "Fisco."

[67] Philippus de Leyden, *De cura rei publicae et sorte principantis*, I, 9, ed. by R. Fruin and P. C. Molhuysen (The Hague, 1915), 13.

[68] The phrase "fiscus et ecclesia aequiparantur" is found time and time again; cf. Baldus, on *C.* 10, 1, 3, n. 2 (Venice, 1586, fol. 236r). Especially in connection with Justinian's *Novel* 7, 2, those equiparations would be found; e.g., Bartolus, *Super Authenticis* (Venice, 1567, fol. 13v). Matthaeus de Afflictis quotes the proverb at least twice; see *In Constit. Sicil.*, praeludia, qu. XV, n. 3 (*ed. cit.*, fol. 14v), and on *Const.*, I, 7 ('de decimis'—*ed. cit.*, fol. 53v). Bracton, fol. 14, ed. Woodbine, II, 57f: "... sed tantum in bonis Dei vel bonis fisci."

[69] *Decretum*, II, C.XVI, qu. 7, c. 8, ed. Friedberg, I, 802. The passage was taken from [Pseudo-]Augustinus, *Sermones suppositii*, 86, 3, *PL*, XXXIX, col. 1912.

[70] Augustine, *Enarrationes in Psalmos*, CXLVI, 17, *PL*, XXXVII, col. 1911. The whole passage is quoted and interpreted, e.g., by Lucas de Penna, *op. cit.*, on *C.* 10, 1, 1, n. 7 (*ed. cit.*, p. 5).

times of Pope John XXII those and similar passages served to prove that Christ, since he had a *fiscus*, owned property.[71]

The antithetical juxtaposition of *Christus* and *Fiscus* may sound like blasphemy to moderns, since the magnitudes do not seem comparable. Mediaeval jurists obviously thought and felt differently. To them, *Christus* meant simply the Church, and the comparison hinged upon the inalienability of both ecclesiastical and fiscal property, of property belonging to either one of the two "dead hands," the Church or the fisc. What *ecclesia* and *fiscus* had in common was perpetuity: in legal language, the "fisc never dies," *fiscus nunquam moritur*.[72] It is immortal like the *Dignitas*, the Dignity of Prince or king, pope or bishop, which "never dies" even though the mortal incumbent may die. Nor did time run against the fisc, any more than it ran against the king—the king as King, the king in his *Dignitas*.[73]

In the last analysis, the "equiparation" of Church and fisc goes back to ancient Roman times when things belonging to the *templa* — since the fourth century gradually replaced by *ecclesiae*—were legally on equal footing with things belonging to the sacred demesne of the emperor.[74] Accordingly, Bracton called those fiscal things also *res quasi sacrae*,[75] and Lucas de Penna talked occasionally about *fiscus sanctissimus*, "the most holy Fisc"[76]—though perhaps we, today, find it easier to understand Baldus who called the fisc, owing to its immortality, "the soul of the state" (*fiscus reipublicae anima*).[77]

---

[71] The decisive passages are *Decretum*, II, C.XII, q. 1, c.12 ("Quare habuit [Christus] loculos cui angeli ministrabant, nisi quia ecclesia ipsius loculos habitura erat?") and c. 17 ("Habebat Dominus loculos, a fidelibus oblata conservans..."); both passages are taken from Augustine, *In Johannem*, 12, 6 ("loculos habens"), and they are referred to by Pope John XXII in his decretals against the Spirituals; cf. *Extravagantes Ioannis XXII*, tit. XIV, c. 5, ed. Friedberg, II, 1230ff, esp. 1233. The word *loculus*, meaning "purse," then could be taken to mean "fisc"; see Matthaeus de Afflictis, *op. cit.*, prael., nos. 7–9, who elaborates on the question whether or not Christ had a fisc in the proper sense of the word. The whole problem will be discussed separately.

[72] Baldus, *Consilia*, I, 271, n. 3 (Venice, 1575, fol. 81ᵛ): "respublica et fiscus sint quid eternum et perpetuum quantum ad essentiam, licet dispositiones saepe mutentur: fiscus enim nunquam moritur."

[73] The principle *Nullum tempus currit contra regem* was commonly acknowledged in the thirteenth century at the latest; see, e.g., Bracton, fols. 14, 56, 103, ed. Woodbine, II, 58, 167, 293, and *passim*.

[74] See Justinian's *Institutes*, 2, 1, 7; also *D*. 1, 8, 1, and *C*. 7, 38, 2. As late as the fifth century do we find that *ius publicum* and *ius templorum* are treated on equal footing; see Arthur Steinwenter, "Über einige Bedeutungen von *ius* in den nachklassischen Quellen," *Iura*, IV (1953), 138f, who shows also that terminologically *ius ecclesiae* simply took the place of *ius templorum*, although with the edict of Licinius, of 313 (at least in the form transmitted by Lactantius, *De mortibus persecutorum*, 48), the new notion of *corpus Christianorum* was connected with Church property; cf. Arnold Ehrhardt, "Das *corpus Christi* und die Korporationen im spätrömischen Recht," *Zeitschrift der Savigny-*

Stiftung für Rechtsgeschichte, rom. Abt., LXXI (1953), 299ff, and LXXII (1954).

[75] Bracton, fol. 14, ed. Woodbine, II, 57f; cf. fol. 407, Woodbine, III, 266, and *passim*.

[76] Lucas de Penna, on *C*. 10, 1, n. 2 (Lyon, 1582, p. 5), with reference to *C*. 7, 37, 2: *sacratissimus fiscus* and *sacratissimum aerarium*. Those expressions are found also, time and time again, in the works of the French jurists of the sixteenth century, though not without an intention to claim imperial rights for the king; e.g., Choppin (above, n. 40), II, tit. 1, n. 2, p. 203: "Sacrum enim existimatur, ut Imperiale, sic Regale Patrimonium, quod ideo a re privata ipsorum Principum separari solet." This is one of the numerous adaptations of imperial prerogatives to royal claims in the wake of the *rex imperator in regno suo* theory (see below, n. 84).

[77] Baldus, *Consilia*, I, 271, n. 2 (*ed. cit.*, fol. 81ᵛ): "Et, ut ita loquar, est [fiscus] ipsius Reipublicae anima et sustentamentum." This does not prevent him, of course, from saying on another occasion correctly: "Fiscus per se est quoddam corpus inanimatum"; see *Consilia*, I, 363, n. 2, (*ed. cit.*, fol. 118ʳ). Popular also was the comparison with the stomach (Lucas de Penna, on *C*. 11, 58, 7, n. 10 [*ed. cit.*, p. 564]) which is found as early as Corippus, *In laudem Iustini*, II, 249f. (*MGH, Auctores antiquissimi*, III, 2, p. 133): "... cognoscite fiscum / Ventris habere locum, per quem omnia membra cibantur," which in its turn goes back to the parable of Menenius Agrippa which itself has a long history; see Wilhelm Nestle, "Die Fabel des Menenius Agrippa," *Klio*, XXI (1926–27), 358f, also in his *Griechische Studien* (Stuttgart, 1948), 502ff; Friedrich Gombel, *Die Fabel 'Vom Magen den Gliedern' in der Weltliteratur* (Beih. z. Zeitschr. f. roman. Philol., LXXX; Halle, 1934).

Moreover, to the fisc the lawyers attributed ubiquity and omnipresence: *Fiscus ubique praesens* declared Accursius (ca. 1230) in a gloss[78] often repeated, especially by the glossators of the Sicilian Constitutions,[79] an ubiquity which made "usucaption of land due to absence of the owner" impossible.[80] As so often, it was Baldus who drew from that mysterious ubiquity and omnipresence of the fisc a straightforward conclusion: *Fiscus est ubique et sic in hoc Deo similis*, "The Fisc is omnipresent, and in that, therefore, it is similar to God."[81]

We should not be mistaken: this language does not betray, or rather does not yet betray, an effort to "deify" the fisc and the State; but it does betray an effort to explain by means of theological terms the nature of the fisc, its perpetuity or, to quote Baldus, the fact that it is *quid eternum et perpetuum quantum ad essentiam*, "something eternal and perpetual with regard to its essence."[82] The reverse side of the application of theological language to secular institutions was, on the one hand, that the fisc and the state machinery eventually *did* become godlike, whereas, on the other hand, God and Christ were demoted to mere symbols of legal fiction in order to expound the ubiquity and eternity of the fictitious person called Fisc.

It was always this *lingua mezzo-teologica* customary with the jurists which elevated the secular state into the sphere of "mystery." This is true also of that strange personification, the "Dignity which does not die." For with regard to the immortal *Dignitas* we find again the same juxtaposition: "The king [said Baldus] is under no obligation to man, though he is obligated to God and his Dignity which is perpetual."[83] It was always a problem of *time*, of perpetuity, which made the Deity comparable to the Fisc or to the Dignity or to the "King Body politic."

The speculations about the immortal Dignity as well as the application of that notion ran through many phases: from abbot to bishop and pope, from pope to emperor, and from the emperor to "kings not recognizing a superior."[84] Eventually one said that the *regia Dignitas* "never dies,"[85] or that the *regia Maiestas* "never dies,"[86] or one confronted (like Baldus) the *persona personalis* of the mortal dignitary with his *persona idealis*,

---

[78] *Glossa ordinaria*, on *C.* 7, 37, 1, v. 'Continuum.'

[79] Marinus de Caramanico, on *Liber aug.*, III, 39, ed. Cervone (above, n. 14), p. 399a: "... et sic non loquitur de fisco qui semper est praesens." See also Matthaeus de Afflictis, on the same law, n. 3 (*ed. cit.*, vol. II, fol. 186): "... nec requiritur probare de praesentia fisci, quia fiscus semper est praesens."

[80] See, e.g., Justinian, *Instit.* 2, 6, rubr.: "... inter *praesentes* decennio, inter *absentes* viginti annis usucapiantur." Presence or absence of the owner makes legally some difference, but the fisc is legally always present.

[81] Baldus, on *C.* 7, 37, 1 (*ed. cit.*, fol. 37ʳ). We should not forget that the Church also has ubiquity; Marcus Antonius Peregrinus, *De iure fisci libri octo* (Venice, 1611), I, 2, n. 22: "... quia sicut Romana Ecclesia ubique est, sic fiscum Ecclesiae Romanae ubique existere oportet." See, on the emperor's ubiquity, my paper "Invocatio nominis imperatoris," *Bollettino del Centro di studi filologici e linguistici siciliani*, III (1955).

[82] See above, n. 72.

[83] Baldus, on X, 2, 24, 33, n. 5 (*In Decretalium volumen commentaria* [Venice, 1580], fol. 261ᵛ): "Unde imperator ... non obligatur homini, sed Deo et dignitati suae, quae perpetua est."

[84] The basis is a decretal of Alexander III: X, 1, 29, 14, ed. Friedberg, II, 162; see for the development of the theory, O. von Gierke, *Das deutsche Genossenschaftsrecht* (Berlin, 1881), III, 271, n. 73. For the secular dignitaries, see Baldus, *Consilia*, III, 159, n. 3 (*ed. cit.*, fol. 45ᵛ); and, *ibid.*, n. 4, for perpetuity of the regal dignity if the king *non cognoscit superiorem*. For the origins of the doctrine of kings not recognizing a superior, see the excellent study of the late Sergio Mochi Onory, *Fonti canonistiche dell'idea moderna dello stato* (Pubblicazioni dell'università cattolica del Sacro Cuore, N. s., XXXVIII; Milan, 1951).

[85] Matthaeus de Afflictis, on *Liber aug.*, II, 35, n. 23 (*ed. cit.*, vol. II, fol. 77): "Quae dignitas regia nunquam moritur."

[86] Baldus, on X, 1, 2, 7, n. 78 (*In Decretales, ed. cit.*, fol. 18): "Nam regia maiestas non moritur."

the Dignity which never dies,[87] so that finally the French king could claim to have two guardian angels, one by reason of his individual person, and another by reason of his Dignity.[88] And perforce one arrived one day, though not apparently before the sixteenth century, at the lapidary formula: *Le roy ne meurt jamais*, "The King never dies," although English jurists of that period still were careful to say: "The king, *as King*, never dies."[89]

Other jurists compared the *Dignitas* with a more classical symbol of immortality and resurrection, the legendary bird Phoenix.[90] The comparison was not badly chosen: there was always only one Phoenix alive at a time; every new Phoenix was "identical" with his predecessor and would be "identical" with his successor; moreover, in the case of this bird—somewhat similar to the angels—species and individual coincided. "The whole kind is preserved in the individual," as Baldus put it, so that every Phoenix was at once the whole existing "Phoenix-kind." Hence, being mortal as individual and immortal as species, the Phoenix probably could claim, if he claimed at all, to be a prototype of the "Corporation sole."[91]

In the speculations about the *Dignitas* theological metaphors were effective too, and even the christological substratum is often quite unmistakable. St. Thomas Aquinas, by combining Aristotelean doctrines about the *organon*, or *instrumentum*, with a theological tenet of Byzantine origin which he came to know through John of Damascus, had expanded upon his doctrine according to which the *humanitas Christi* was the *instrumentum divinitatis* and therewith the instrument of the *principalis causa efficiens* which was God.[92]

This doctrine, too, wandered to the lawyers and was applied to their political theories. They equated the *Dignitas* "which does not die" with the *Divinitas*, and the mortal body natural of the dignitary with the *humanitas*; and on that basis Baldus could write:

> Here we recognize the Dignity as the *principalis* and the person as the *instrumentalis*. Hence, the fundament of an action is the *Dignitas* herself which is perpetual.[93]

---

[87] Baldus, *Consilia*, III, 217, n. 3, fol. 63ᵛ: ". . . [persona] personalis quae est anima in substantia hominis, et non persona idealis quae est dignitas."

[88] Grassaille, *Regalium Franciae libri duo*, I, ius xx (Paris, 1545, p. 210): "Item, Rex Franciae duos habet bonos angelos custodes: unum ratione suae privatae personae, alterum ratione dignitatis regalis."

[89] The slogan turns up quite frequently in the arguments of English jurists in the middle of the 16th century; see, e.g., Plowden, *Reports*, 233a: "for as to this Body [his body politic] the King never dies." In France, it is certainly found by the end of the century, though it should not be confused with the funerary cries *Le roi est mort! Vive le roi!* which have a quite different and non-juristic origin.

[90] The comparison, to my knowledge, is first found in the *Glossa ordinaria* of Bernard of Parma on the Gregorian Decretals; see gl. "substitutum," on X, 1, 29, 14. See further Johannes Andreae, *In Decretalium libros Novella* (Venice, 1612, fol. 206ᵛ–207), on X, 1, 29, 14, nos. 30–31, gl. "Phenix"; Baldus, on the same decretal, n. 3 (*In Decretal., ed. cit.*, fol. 107), who draws philosophically the right conclusion: "Est autem avis unica singularissima, in qua totum genus servatur in individuo." The comparison is

far more striking than can be intimated here; see Jean Hubaux and Maxime Leroy, *Le mythe du Phénix* (Liège and Paris, 1939), and the important remarks on that study by A.-J. Festugière, "Le symbole du Phénix et le mysticisme hermétique," *Monuments Piot*, XXXVIII (1941), 147–151, with which one should compare Jean de Terre Rouge, *Tractatus de iure futuri successoris legitimi in regiis hereditatibus*, esp. I, art. 2, in the appendix of F. Hotman, *Consilia* (Geneva, 1586), 35ff.

[91] Maitland, *Selected Essays*, 73–127, and *passim*.

[92] The subject has been treated very thoroughly by Theophil Tschipke, *Die Menschheit Christi als Heilsorgan der Gottheit unter besonderer Berücksichtigung der Lehre des Heiligen Thomas von Aquino* (Freiburger Theologische Studien, LV; Freiburg, 1940); see also M. Grabmann, "Die Lehre des Erzbischofs und Augustinertheologen Jakob von Viterbo († 1307/8) vom Episkopat und Primat und ihre Beziehung zum Heiligen Thomas von Aquino," *Episcopus: Studien über das Bischofsamt . . . Kardinal von Faulhaber . . . dargebracht* (Regensburg, 1949), 190, n. 10, for further literature.

[93] Baldus, *Consilia*, III, 121, n. 6 (*ed. cit.*, fol. 34): "Ibi attendimus dignitatem tanquam principalem et personam tanquam instrumentalem. Unde fundamentum actus est

Or, when discussing the two persons concurring in the Prince, he writes:

> And the king's [individual] person is the *organum et instrumentum* of that other person which is intellectual and public. And that *persona intellectualis et publica* is the one, which *principaliter* causes the actions.[94]

We now understand the method and may understand also whence derives that ecclesiological substratum which so often is perceptible in the speeches and pleadings of English Crown jurists in late Tudor times. We immediately recognize the ecclesiological doctrine of the *corpus mysticum* when, for example, one of the judges opined that suicide was a crime not only against God and Nature, but also against the king, "because he, being the Head, has lost one of his mystical Members."[95] The same, though perhaps less obvious, is true for the terminology of the English jurists whenever they argued about the king as an individual and the king as King, and then usually talked about the king's "two *bodies*," while slipping only rarely and saying instead "two *persons*"—after all, they were not Nestorians, and Sir Edward Coke as well as others cautiously pointed out that though the king has "two bodies" he "hath but one person."[96] We may actually hark far back, to the twelfth century when the Church first emerged as the *corpus mysticum*,[97] and to teachers such as Simon of Tournai or Gregory of Bergamo, to find some—later often repeated—theological formulations of the following pattern:

> Two are the bodies of Christ: the human material body which he assumed from the Virgin, and the spiritual collegiate body, the college of the Church.[98]

> One body of Christ which is he himself, and another body of which he is the head.[99]

And with those and many similar definitions of the bodies individual and collective of Christ we then may compare the legal distinctions of the Tudor judges who pointed out, time and time again, that

---

ipsa dignitas quae est perpetua." In the same paragraph he also makes the distinction "quod persona sit causa immediata, dignitas autem sit causa remota," whereby we should recall that God is often said to act (e.g. at elections) as the *causa remota*.

[94] Baldus, *Consilia*, III, 159, n. 6 (*ed.cit.*, fol. 45ᵛ): "... loco duarum personarum Rex fungitur... Et persona regis est organum et instrumentum illius personae intellectualis et publicae. Et illa persona intellectualis et publica est illa, quae principaliter fundat actus: quia magis attenditur actus, seu virtus principalis, quam virtus organica." Compare, e.g., Aquinas, *Summa theologiae*, IIIa, qu. LXII, a. 5, resp.: "Principalis autem causa efficiens gratiae est ipse Deus, ad quem comparatur humanitas Christi sicut instrumentum coniunctum"; or IIIa, qu. VII, a. 1, ad 3: "Quod humanitas Christi est instrumentum divinitis ... tanquam instrumentum animatum anima rationali." The transition to the juristic application of this doctrine may perhaps be found in Aquinas himself when he writes (IIIa, qu. VIII, a. 2): "In quantum vero anima est motor corporis, corpus instrumentaliter servit animae."

[95] Plowden, *Reports*, 261; Maitland, *Selected Essays*, 110, n. 2.

[96] Coke, in Calvin's Case (*Reports*, VII, 10a), distinguishes theologically, or even christologically, when he says that the king, though he has "two bodies" (and "two capacities"), has "but one person." Maitland, *op. cit.*, 110, n. 4.

[97] See, in addition to Lubac (next note), G. B. Ladner, "Aspects of Mediaeval Thought on Church and State," *Review of Politics*, IX (1947), 403ff, esp. 414f.

[98] Simon of Tournai, quoted by Henri de Lubac, *Corpus mysticum* (Paris, 1949), 122, n. 29: "Duo sunt corpora Christi: Unum materiale, quod sumpsit de virgine, et spirituale collegium, collegium ecclesiasticum." See also, *ibid.*, n. 30.

[99] Gregory of Bergamo, *De veritate corporis Christi*, c. 18, ed. H. Hurter, *Sanctorum patrum opuscula selecta* (Innsbruck, 1879), XXXIX, 75f: "Aliud esse novimus Christi corpus, quod videlicet ipse est, aliud corpus, cuius ipse caput est." Cf. Lubac, *op. cit.*, 185 (with n. 155), also 123f, and *passim*, for many more examples of the *duplex corpus Christi*.

the King has two Bodies, the one whereof is a Body natural ... and in this he is subject to Passions and Death as other Men are; and the other is a Body politic and the Members thereof are the subjects, and he and they together compose the corporation, and he is incorporated with them and they with him, and he is the Head, and they are the Members; and this Body is *not* subject to Passions and Death, for as to this Body the King never dies.[100]

It is from these strata of thought, I believe, that the absolutist concept "Mysteries of State" took its origin and that, when finally the Nation stepped into the pontifical shoes of the Prince, the modern ABSOLUTE STATE, even without a Prince, was enabled to make claims like a Church.

[100] Plowden, *Reports*, 233a, quoted also by Sir William Blackstone, *Commentaries on the Laws of England*, I, 249.

ON TRANSFORMATIONS OF APOLLINE ETHICS

In a recent paper—profound, solid, and unusually stimulating—Professor Rudolf Pfeiffer has discussed "The Image of the Delian Apollo and Apolline Ethics."[1] The distinguished editor of the Oxford Callimachus has placed in the center of his learned article a poem of Callimachus' *Aitia* which unfortunately has been preserved only fragmentarily in the scraps of Oxyrhynchus papyri.[2] The poem presents itself as a dialogue between an unknown person visiting the sacred island of Delos and the archaic cult-statue of the Delian Apollo.[3] The visitor ("perhaps a pilgrim or a merchant or an 'antiquarian'," or—why not?—an ambassador) puts a number of questions squarely to Apollo; and the god answers patiently. The first questions serve the purpose of identification. Apollo assures the questioner that he is "the Delian" and corroborates his answer by a formula which only a god can use—"Yea, by myself."[4] He further vouches for the material, or at least the surface appearance, of his cult-statue—"Yea, golden"— and, when asked "Art thou actually unclad?" he truthfully answers: "... [only] a belt covers me in the middle [i. e. around the waist]." Then the interrogator comes forth with a more essential question: "Why dost thou hold, O Cynthius, the bow in thy left hand, but in thy right hand the comely Graces?" The answer—fragmentarily transmitted, though not beyond repair—is: "... in order to punish fools for their insolence [I have the bow; but] to the good people I stretch out [my hand with the Graces. I carry the bow in the left hand, because I am] slower to chastise mortals [; but carry in the right hand the Graces, as I am] always disposed to distribute pleasant things." The god then added, in a not quite obvious connection, a word on μετάνοια, man's change of mind or repentance, saying: "... in order that it may be possible to repent of something." Finally, Apollo dismisses the visitor with the words ἀγαθὸν βασιλεῖ, "blessing to the king." Who that king was we do not know. Were the questions to the Delian posed in the name, or on the part, of a king? Are the words about repentance in any way connected with the king? We just do not know.

Taking the poem of Callimachus as his starting point, Pfeiffer was led to the discussion of two main topics, one archaeological, and the other "ethical." On the basis of the descriptive sections of the poem, and supported by a couple of Athenian coins, an

---

Reprinted, with permission, from *CHARITES: Studien zur Altertumswissenschaft* [Festschrift Ernst Langlotz], ed. Konrad Schauenburg (Bonn, 1957), 265–274.

[1] *Journal of the Warburg and Courtauld Institutes*, XV (1952), 20–32.

[2] Callimachus, *Aetia*, fr. 114 (Pfeiffer, 127f.)

[3] I follow Pfeiffer's translation, "Delian Apollo," 26f.

[4] Pfeiffer very interestingly indicates the parallel in Hebr. 6, 13: (Jehovah) ὤμοσεν καθ'ἑαυτοῦ. Cf. Gen. 22, 16.

intaglio (pl. 37, fig. 1), a vase painting, and a few quotations from texts, Pfeiffer succeeded in reconstructing convincingly the cult-image of the Delian Apollo: naked, except for the belt; in his right hand, the Graces (on later reproductions usually carried on a stand); and in his left, the weapon.[5] Moreover, Pfeiffer succeeded in shedding light on the ethics which the god could claim to display visibly: willing to reward rather than to punish, the Delian held out the Graces, keeping the terrible bow in reserve, perhaps for those not willing to repent and come to a change of mind—indeed an important message which shows among other things that certain fundamentals of human nature such as repentance were not a monopoly of Christian ethics.[6] Proceeding from the safe basis of his text and of the new insights which it offered, Pfeiffer was able to outline in rapid strokes the continuity of the Delian artistic formula in mediaeval and Renaissance art. He showed that—probably under the influence of Macrobius[7]—an Apollo carrying in one hand the three Graces and, in the other, his bow reappears in a tenth-century manuscript as well as in a relief of Agostino di Duccio in the Malatesta Temple at Rimini (pl. 39, fig. 5).[8] Moreover, Pfeiffer could trace the survival of Apolline ethics—"although with a big question-mark"—to Jonathan Swift, who, in one of his chapters on the Lilliputians, mentioned "The image of Justice... with a bag of gold open in her right hand, and a sword sheathed in her left to show she was more disposed to reward than to punish." Indeed, that disposition of Justice reflects the disposition of the Delian Apollo. Cautiously Pfeiffer advanced the suggestion that Swift perhaps "came across the passage in Macrobius about Apollo and adapted it to the image of justice."[9] While there is no reason for rejecting the hypothesis that Swift read and made use of Macrobius, the chief problem should be sought in a totally different sphere: how could it occur that Swift adapted "Apolline" ethics to "Justice"? Or, how could it happen that Apollo was, as it were, transformed into Justice?

About this transformation of Apolline ethics a few remarks[10] will be ventured here only to remind Ernst Langlotz, the loyal friend and companion of many years in Heidelberg and Frankfurt, of what he, who likes to roam through mediaeval art, would know anyhow: that even in his own field the student of Classics may profit from the knowledge of mediaeval *de*formations and *trans*formations of antique subjects, and that, vice versa, the mediaevalist would lose one half of his *raison d'être* without the permanent stimulus coming to him from his friends in Classics.

* * *

It was not the intention of Pfeiffer to investigate the full history of Apolline ethics. He, therefore, had no reason to consider a passage in the 15th Oration of Themistius.

---

[5] Pfeiffer, "Delian Apollo," pls. 4, a–b, d–e, and 7 a.

[6] *Ibid.*, 30ff.

[7] Macrobius, *Sat.*, I, 17, 12–13; see below, n. 24.

[8] Pfeiffer, pls. 7 b, 5 c.

[9] *Ibid.*, 29.

[10] The history of these transformations could have been broadened and deepened considerably. The space allotted to contributors, however, permitted no more than a sweeping outline of the problem. Moreover, this essay, unfortunately, had to be written very hastily. This may excuse also the use of the English language for which clerical help was available. My thanks go, as so often, to Professor and Mrs. Erwin Panofsky, to whom I owe practically all the references to the Emblem Books, and photographs of them, not to mention numerous suggestions, and to Professor Harold Cherniss, who patiently read the manuscript.

The passage, however, may serve here likewise (just as the poem of Callimachus served Pfeiffer) as the starting point for a rapid discussion of two subjects, one archaeological and the other ethical.

In the 15th Oration, Themistius addresses himself to the Emperor Theodosius.[11] The date is 381, three years after the terrific Roman defeat at Adrianople. Themistius knew how to appreciate the value of military prowess and its importance for an emperor. He knew also, however,—for this was taught in every school of rhetoric—that prowess alone did not make a true emperor, and thus Themistius came to deal with a topic frequently discussed in the schools: What is the most royal of all virtues? The virtue he is aiming at, of course, is Justice, though he admits that military valour and skill are at times equally important; but the one does not exclude the other. In a later section of his address, Themistius refers to Homer who had praised Agamemnon for being κατ'ἄμφω εὐδόκιμος, "glorious with regard to both": βασιλεύς τ'ἀγαθός, κρατερός τ'αἰχμητής, "a good king and a staunch warrior."[12] Homer, claims Themistius, could not easily have talked about "both" qualities, even if he linked them together, were there not a difference between the art of kingship and the art of warfare. A similar ἀμφότερον, however, and a similar jugate oneness of contrasts was, after all, the distinguishing mark of Apollo.

> As long as it is not the time to summon the phalanx and the hordes of soldiers and hasten to help against the wicked Scythians; and while Terror and Fear are at rest for the moment, and it is not yet fitting to sing in honor of Ares, let the Muses bring forth their chorus for the emperor, taking with them for their dance their leader Apollo. That god in fact is both archer and leader of the Muses, and he has a double equipment for both peace and war; and both are necessary for an emperor. The emperor needs the missiles for his enemies, and for his subjects he needs the lyre, with which he puts them in order and renders them harmonious and makes them ready for the struggle. . . .[13]

Thus, Apollo becomes the emperor's model. The passage, however, is interesting for several reasons, even though it seems to contain nothing but commonplaces. Apollo as archer and Musagetes is as old as the couple of attributes, bow and lyre. Themistius does not maintain that the god carries his διπλῆ σκευή at the same time, as does the Delian Apollo—that is, the bow in one hand and the lyre in the other. Nor is that distribution of symbols claimed, for example, by Themistius' contemporary Servius when he explains that the offended Apollo sends the pestilence, *quod etiam Homerus ostendit, cum eum armatum inducit sagittis. . .; contra, si citharam teneat, mitis est. . . .*[14] What Servius suggests is almost

---

[11] Themistius, *Or.* XV, 184ff (Dindorf, 227f.)

[12] *Ibid.*, 187 c (Dindorf, 229).

[13] . . . καὶ γὰρ ἐκεῖνος ὁ θεὸς τοξοφόρος τε ἄμα καὶ μουσηγέτης, καὶ διπλῆ αὐτῷ ἡ σκευή, πρὸς εἰρήνην τε καὶ πολέμους, καὶ ἀμφότερα βασιλεῖ ἐπιτήδειος. δεῖται γὰρ βασιλεὺς τῶν βελῶν μὲν πρὸς τοὺς πολεμίους, τῆς κιθάρας δὲ πρὸς τοὺς ὑπηκόους, ᾗ ἁρμόσει αὐτοὺς καὶ συμφώνους ἀπεργάσεται καὶ παρασκευάσει ἑτοίμους πρὸς τὸν ἀγῶνα . . . *Or.* XV, 185 c (Dindorf, 228). The English translation is that of Professor Glanville Downey,

who is preparing for Dumbarton Oaks the new edition (with translation) of Themistius. I am very much obliged to Professor Downey for allowing me to see his manuscript and reproduce his English version.

[14] Servius, *ad Verg. Aen.*, 3, 138 (Thilo, I, 368). Jean Seznec, *The Survival of the Pagan Gods*, Engl. trsl. by Barbara F. Sessions (New York, 1953), 178, is liable to be misunderstood if he quotes Servius as the source of the *Libellus* (see below, n. 16).

the contrary: if the god is offended, he uses his arrows, and if he is mild and gentle, he lays his weapon aside and plays on the lute. It is true, Themistius is perhaps less explicit than Servius; after all, he wants to demonstrate the oneness of the arts of kingship and warriorship, and when he talks about the "double equipment" needed by the god and by the emperor, he at least comes close to suggesting that the god carried both arrows and lyre simultaneously. Nevertheless, he does not say so, and we may wonder whether any ancient author maintained that Apollo carried the "double equipment" at the same time. At any rate, in classical art—certainly in monumental art—there does not seem to exist a single representation showing the god with both the bow and the lyre, though there are innumerable representations extant showing Apollo either as *toxophoros* or as *kitharistes*. This is not surprising: the bow would have hampered the lute-playing god, and the lute his shooting of arrows.

It is, then, all the more surprising that in the late Middle Ages we find Apollo suddenly represented with the weapon in his right hand and the lyre in his left.[15] These representations (pl. 37, fig. 3; pl. 38, fig. 4; pl. 39, fig. 5) are all late, usually fifteenth century; and they could not very well have been earlier because the precise text describing Apollo unambiguously in that attitude—*In dextra vero manu habebat sagittas, arcum et pharetram. In sinistra autem cytharam tenebat*—was written only around 1400.[16] The mediaeval mythographers and authorities—Fulgentius, Isidore, Hrabanus, Remigius of Auxerre, and the so-called *Mythographus I* and *II*—do not seem to have that phrasing.[17] Also, the highly influential *Mythographus III*, often identified with Alexander Neckham (d. 1217), follows almost verbatim his predecessors when he enumerates the *insignia Apollinis* testifying to the god's presence in heaven, on earth, and in hell: the lyre, to demonstrate the image of celestial harmony; the gryphon, or the quadriga, to show him as a terrestrial deity; and the arrows, to indicate the infernal and damaging god.[18] Upon *Mythographus III* a great number of scholars relied, including Petrarch. In the Third Book of his *Africa*, Petrarch gives a thorough description—indeed an *Ecphrasis*—of the images of ancient gods.[19] Devoting to Apollo a passage of 18 hexameters, he mentions that the lyre, as seen with the

---

[15] Erwin Panofsky, *Hercules am Scheidewege* (Studien der Bibliothek Warburg, XVIII; Leipzig-Berlin, 1930), pls. VI, VII, VIII; Liebeschütz (see next note), pl. XVII; Seznec, 177, fig. 68; see also Fritz Saxl and Hans Meier, *Verzeichnis astrologischer und mythologischer illustrierter Handschriften des lateinischen Mittelalters* (London, 1953), III, 115, 396.

[16] *De deorum imaginibus libellus*, c. IV, ed. Hans Liebeschütz, *Fulgentius Metaforalis* (Stud. d. Bibl. Warburg, IV; Leipzig-Berlin, 1926), 118; for the date, see p. 43. We owe to Liebeschütz the disentanglement of the highly complicated mythographical problems of the later Middle Ages.

[17] For Remigius of Auxerre's glosses on Martianus Capella, see Liebeschütz, 15, n. 26, and 44f, where Apollo is said to carry his "star" (the sun) in his left hand. For the mythographers, see the edition of G. H. Bode, *Scriptores rerum mythicarum latini tres* (Celle, 1834).

[18] *Mythographus III*, 8, 16, 309 (Bode, 31ff): "Inde etiam tria insignia circa eius simulacrum videmus: lyram, quae

nobis harmoniae caelestis imaginem monstrat; gryphen, qui eum etiam terrenum numen ostendit; sagittas, quibus infernus et noxius deus indicatur." *Mythogr. III* follows verbatim *Mythogr. II*, c. 18 (Bode, 80) who, however, has *quadrigam* instead of *gryphen*.

[19] Petrarch, *Africa*, III, 165–168, ed. N. Festa (Florence, 1926), 58:

> Necnon et citharae species angusta canore
> Icta videbatur sonitum perducere ad aures;
> Et pharetra atque arcus volucresque in
>   terga sagittae,
> Cirreoque ingens Phiton resupinus in antro.

Cf. Liebeschütz, 41f, and, especially, Panofsky, *Hercules*, 11ff, who, felicitously, calls Petrarch's excursus on the images of gods *Ecphrasis* as opposed to the customary mediaeval descriptions. I am very grateful to Professor Harold Cherniss for calling my attention to the fact that *terga* here has the meaning of "monsters" as in *Aeneid*, VI, 422.

god's image, seemed to bring music to our ears, while quiver and bow, and his arrows winged against monsters, reminded him of the Python slain in the cave of Cirrha. Petrarch does not say explicitly that the god was bearing both insignia at the same time, but he might have suggested it; for his friend Bersuire, who confesses that he owed his knowledge to Petrarch, describes, in his mythographic prologue to a Book of the *Ovide moralisé*, the god as carrying "in one hand" arrows, bow and quiver, and "in the other" the lyre.[20] It is relevant only peripherally that in his moral evaluation Bersuire comes to the result that every just man, especially a prelate, may be recognized in Apollo, because the just man would imitate the *Sol Iustitiae*, using the lyre for the praise of God; but he needs also to be armed with bow and arrows; and it was in Bersuire's system only a logical and consistent thought when he drew the conclusion *quod Apollo... est sol iustitie christus qui semper fuit iuvenis*, who used the lyre to console others, and used the arrow of the Cross to prostrate Lucifer.[21] Luther, later on, argued vehemently against the corrupt monks "who turned Apollo into Christ."[22] Bersuire, at any rate, said in so many words that the god carried both instruments in his hands; but it was only the author of the illustrated *Libellus de imaginibus* of ca. 1400 who finally placed the bow in Apollo's right hand and the lyre in his left. Accordingly, the Muses received their place to his left, whereas the Python cringes to his right (pl. 37, fig. 3).[23]

What happened was probably a fusion of the customary enumeration of insignia, as offered by the mediaeval mythographers, with the passage in Macrobius: *Apollinis simulacra manu dextera Gratias gestant, arcum cum sagittis sinistra.*[24] That is, while the idea of placing in Apollo's hands two different attributes was borrowed from Macrobius, the conventional attributes of bow and lyre were retained.[25] That such a fusion was possible is strikingly demonstrated by the relief in the Malatesta Temple (pl. 39, fig. 5), where Apollo holds the bow in his left hand, but carries in his right hand the lute from the neck of which the three Graces emerge together with the laurel.[26] Less convincing, perhaps, is the Apollo from the Paris *Echecs amoureux* of the fifteenth century, where the god with bow and lyre is seen enthroned while at his right side three bellied Graces are dancing around a laurel tree (pl. 38, fig. 4).[27] However that may be, at the bottom of the late-mediaeval representations of Apollo there is still effective, for all the distortions and

---

[20] See, for Petrus Berchorius (Pierre Bersuire), Liebe-schütz, 41f, n. 60; his Commentary on Ovid was later printed under the name of Thomas Walleys. I could avail myself of a copy in the Princeton University Library: Thomas Walleys, *Metamorphosis Ovidiana* (Paris, François Regnault, 1515/16), see fol. VIᴿ: "Iste [Apollo] igitur pingebatur in forma iuvenis: nunc in puerili facie, nunc in senili: nunc in capite diversimode apparens. Iste super caput portabat tripodium aureum. In una vero manu portabat sagittas, arcum et pharetram. In altera autem cytharam..."

[21] *Ibid.*, fol. VIᵛB: "Per istum Apollinem possumus intelligere quemlibet virum iustum et maxime prelatum quia revera imago Solis dicitur in quantum solem iusticie pro viribus imitatur ... Citharam divine laudis habere debet. Arcu, pharetra et sagitta iusticie debet esse armatus." *Ibid.*, fol. VIIᵛD: "Vel dic quod apollo qui est

sol iustitie christus qui semper fuit iuvenis... Citharam habuit alios consolando: arcum et sagittas alios arguendo: phitonem i.e. Luciferum, sagitta crucis prostravit..."

[22] Luther, *Enarratio in Genesim*, 30, 9; *Werke*, XLIII (Weimar, 1912), 668, quoted after Seznec, 96, n. 56.

[23] See, for the drawing, Liebeschütz, *Fulgentius*, pl. XVII (Vat. Reg. Lat. 1290, fol. 1ᵛ); Seznec, 177, fig. 68.

[24] *Sat.*, I, 17, 13, with the moralising addition "quod ad noxam sit pigrior et salutem manus promptior largiatur."

[25] The attributes, however, have changed hands, since the bow, in all the late mediaeval miniatures, is in the right hand. Bersuire, in fact, mentions bow and arrows first (above, n. 20), which may have prompted the author of the *Libellus*, by mentioning the right hand first, to equip this hand with the bow, and the left with the lyre.

[26] Seznec, 133, fig. 47.

[27] Panofsky, *Hercules*, pl. VIII, fig. 15.

errors, the formula characteristic of the Delian God and the Apolline ethics — whereby it appears as a matter of minor importance that the plate or stand carrying the three Graces has been replaced by the lyre of the Musagetes.

*   *   *

The Graces, of course, are not present in Themistius' oration either, for the rhetor introduces Apollo as the lyre-bearing god of the Muses and also as the bow-bearer. In this double function the god then became the emperor's model (pl. 37, fig. 3). After all, the emperor too needs the double equipment for times of war and of peace—"the missiles for his enemies, and for his subjects the lyre, with which he puts them in order and renders them harmonious." To assimilate the emperor to Apollo as νέος Ἥλιος or *Sol invictus* was, of course, the most common topic of imperial cults, arts, and rhetoric, though it may have been less common to equip him dialectically with the heterogeneous instruments. The Delian model, however, exercised its influence also on the imperial self-representation. Caligula, as Philo reports, transformed himself on some occasion into Apollo, "the Graces in his right hand, since it is fitting to hold out good things willingly..., but keeping the bow and arrows in the left hand, since it is fitting to hold back retribution."[28] Hence, owing to the Delian ethics, an emperor equipped with both the distributive and retributive insignia of Apollo was not something quite unheard of—even though, as in the case of Themistius, the lyre replaced the Graces.

At this juncture, however, another consideration becomes momentous. The influence, direct or indirect, of Themistius upon the jurists of the age of Justinian is a fairly well established fact. For one thing, Themistius, *Oratio XIX*, is clearly echoed by Justinian's *Novella*, 105, 2, 4, the famous passage about the emperor as the νόμος ἔμψυχος sent down by God from heaven to earth,[29] and Themistius' influence in general on Byzantine political theory has been noticed by a great number of scholars.[30] Themistius' *Oratio XV*, we recall, was devoted to the most royal of virtues: Justice. It is not surprising, then, that the author of the Prologue to Justinian's *Institutes* had in his head some echoes of Themistius' philosophic Oration on Justice[31] when he composed the famous sentences of his philosophic Prologue, saying:

> The Imperial Majesty must needs be not only decorated with arms, but also armed with laws that it be able to govern rightly in either time, in war and in peace, and that the Roman Prince may come off as victor not only in hostile battles, but also by the paths of law may expel the iniquities of slanderers, and become the most religious observer of law as well as the one triumphant over conquered foes.[32]

---

[28] Philo, *Legatio ad Caium*, 95, VI, 173, (Cohn-Wendland, 6ff): εἰς δὲ Ἀπόλλωνα μετεμορφοῦτο καὶ μετεσκευάζετο, ...τόξον δὲ τῇ εὐωνύμῳ καὶ βέλη κρατῶν χειρί, χάριτας δὲ τῇ δεξίᾳ προτείνων κτλ.

[29] See Pietro de Francisci, *Arcana Imperii* (Milan, 1948), III:2, 208; also Artur Steinwenter, "ΝΟΜΟΣ ΕΜΨΥΧΟΣ, Zur Geschichte einer politischen Theorie," *Anzeiger der Wiener Akademie*, LXXXIII (1946), 260.

[30] See my remarks in *Varia Variorum: Festgabe für Karl Reinhardt* (Münster-Cologne, 1952), 186, nos. 16f.

[31] Themistius, of course, was not the creator of that kind of legal philosophy, and the jurists may have drawn from other sources as well, e.g. from the political writings of the Neo-Pythagoreans (see below, n. 34). There are a few parallels, however (see n. 33), which would suggest the influence of Themistius.

[32] *Inst.*, prooem: "Imperatoriam maiestatem non solum armis decoratam, sed etiam legibus oportet esse armatam, ut utrumque tempus et bellorum et pacis recte possit gubernari et princeps Romanus victor existat non

The echoes from Themistius' oration are few, but they are quite significant.[33] No less significant, however, are the transformations. The reference to "both times"—war and peace—remains unchanged; so does, substantially, that to "arms." The lyre, however, by which the state is rendered harmonious and thereby attuned to the universe, has been replaced by the "laws" with which the majesty is armed. That, all by itself, is not wanting in sound logic, for the laws were often praised—especially by Themistius' "Neo-Pythagorean" sources—as the means of harmonizing the state, attuning the subjects to the king, and producing the ὁμόνοια, the concord of the citizens, without which every state is doomed.[34] That this most noble function of the law was always present to Justinian's mind cannot be denied. In the Prologue of the *Institutes*, however, the law has chiefly the retributive function to punish, "to expel the iniquities of slanderers"—even though the emperor's ideal of self-representation was still to become through his legislation *iuris religiosissimus*. At any rate, bow and lyre of Apollo corresponded with "arms and laws" of the emperor.

Justinian's *Institutes* were meant to be a textbook for those to whom the unwieldy volumes of the *Pandects* and the *Code* were not readily accessible. As a textbook, however, the *Institutes* were studied over the centuries by myriads of students and glossed by scores of jurists. When, at the turn from the eleventh to the twelfth century, there emerged a scientific jurisprudence bent upon Roman Law, the Prologue of the *Institutes* naturally was interpreted over and over again. It would not be rewarding here to inspect the individual glosses written on that passage. About 1230, however, Accursius composed the *Glossa ordinaria*, the standard gloss of the Roman *Corpus iuris civilis*, by which the work of the preceding generations of glossators was summed up. Not infrequently the glossators discussed their texts in the form of question and answer, and the Accursian Gloss on the Prologue of the *Institutes* may have been accomodated to a tradition of respectable age when its author commented on the various *Casus* of the Prologue in the form of a dialogue between a young man and the Emperor Justinian.[35] This is the gist of the dialogue on the first passage:

> A young man, pressing in upon the Emperor Justinian with questions, said: "Lord Emperor, I wonder very much, and all others wonder too: Thou art a soldier and every emperor is a soldier, for according to the *Digest* [29, 1, 1, rubr.], the emperor calls the other soldiers 'fellow-soldiers' [*commilitones*]. Since thou art a soldier, thou must attend to arms, and not to laws. And yet thou actest to the contrary, for thine attention is directed only to laws. Thou hast given orders to compile the *Code* . . . and the *Digest* . . . and to compose . . . the *Institutes* . . . . Wilt

solum in hostilibus proeliis, sed etiam per legitimos tramites calumniantium iniquitates expellens, et fiat tam iuris religiosissimus quam victis hostibus triumphator."

[33] Imperatoriam maiestatem...
  oportet...
  ut utrumque tempus et bellorum
  et pacis...
  δεῖται γὰρ βασιλεὺς τῶν βελῶν...
  τῆς κιθάρας...

διπλῆ αὐτῷ ἡ σκευή, πρὸς εἰρήνην
τε καὶ πολέμους...

[34] See, for the Neo-Pythagoreans, Louis Delatte, *Les Traités de la Royauté d'Ecphante, Diotogène et Sthénidas* (Liège and Paris, 1942), 226f, 270f, not to mention a number of other recent studies.

[35] See, e.g., *La glossa di Casamari alle Istituzioni di Giustiniano*, ed. Alberto Alberti (Milan, 1937), p. 3, and Introd., p. xif, for the date, presumably 11th century.

thou tell me therefore why thou dost all that, and why thou attendest to laws only, and not to arms, since thou art a soldier.... ." Thereupon the emperor, indicating that there are two times, that is, a time of war and a time of peace, answered graciously and said: "My Son, this is how I answer your question. It befits every emperor to be ready for those two times, that is, for arms and for laws. And the reason is this: because if the emperor is prepared for those two times, he can govern rightly in either, that of war and that of peace. Namely, the time of war he will govern by means of arms and the use of arms; and therewith he will become a conqueror and victor triumphant. The time of peace, however, he will govern by means of law and the use of law. And thus he will punish the evil doings of the culprits; and by that he will become a man most religious *(religiosissimus)* and most holy *(sanctissimus)* when he punishes the evil doings; because it is a very religious work and very holy to punish evil doings or evil doers."[36]

The journey is long from the ethics of the pagan god to the ethics of the Christian emperor. While there was little difference between Apollo holding out the Graces and Apollo reproducing with his lyre the harmony of the universe, and while the difference is still tolerable between the god with the lyre and the Prince who by means of the law attunes the state to the harmony of the cosmos, the gap between the ideal of Themistius and that of the Gloss is almost beyond measurement. Justice, the source of concord and harmony amongst the citizens, and in Roman legal philosophy a distributive power *(suum cuique tribuere)*, has been debased to the rank of a purely retributive fury. No longer is there the dialectical tension between lyre and bow, law and sword. What remains is the grimace of something that once was noble; and what looms is another variety of the doctrine of the Two Swords—one sword for the Prince's enemies without, and the other for his enemies within—so to say: a choice between war and inquisition.

* * *

The Renaissance had a different understanding of the historical as well as the human and ethical backgrounds of Justinian's Prologue. Alciati's historical school of jurisprudence had its drawbacks, to be sure, because it stopped the almost naive and unprejudiced application of Roman Law to existing conditions and thereby dried out a still trickling antique current of life. It was Alciati's great achievement, however, to have recognized that Roman Law had to be understood not from mediaeval conditions but from its own Roman surroundings and from classical sources at large. The jurists influenced by the new historical jurisprudence were not content with hunting up the juridical parallels, but tried to understand the Justinian Law by exploring the intellectual world from which it originated. They noticed, for example, that the phrase *utrumque tempus, bellorum et pacis,* may have been stimulated by Aristotle's *Politics,* where it is said that the βίος πολιτικός is divided into the activities of war and of peace; they

---

[36] The passage is too long to be reproduced here. It is found in every glossed edition of the *Institutes.* I used the edition of the *Corpus iuris civilis,* Venice, 1584, vol. IV, col. 2. Actually, the whole Prologue (the *Casus*) is glossed in the form of a dialogue.

paralleled that statement with the dialectical definition according to which all life is divided into two parts, absence of leisure and leisure, war and peace;[37] nor did they miss the fact that a majesty *armis decorata, legibus armata* reflected the supreme model of all dialectically conceived rulership: Plato demanding in the *Republic*, through the mouth of Socrates, that kings philosophize and philosophers rule so that there may concur in one man both civil power and philosophy.[38]

From this vantage ground the Prologue of the *Institutes* appeared in a new perspective, and the Renaissance emblem books—inseparable from the name of Alciati anyhow— gave the visual recording of a changing mood. It is true, Justinian's formula itself was used as an emblem: LEGIBUS ET ARMIS shows a Prince standing on a cross-bearing globe with a sword in his right hand and in his left a lawbook covered with Hebrew script (pl. 40, fig. 7).[39] Justinian's formula, almost verbatim, lay also behind the *impresa* allegedly used by the Emperor Frederick III: an iron-clad arm holding a sword over an open book with the motto HIC REGIT, ILLE TUETUR (pl. 40, fig. 6).[40] That the open book likewise was meant to be the lawbook is not only self-evident, but is also confirmed by a later repetition in an English emblem work: a sword protecting the slabs of the Ten Commandments (pl. 40, fig. 8), while the motto LEX REGIT ET ARMA TUENTUR is rendered by the doggerel:

> *The* Law *is given to direct;*
> *The* Sword, *to punish and protect.*[41]

The respectful veneration for Justinian in the Middle Ages, however, gave way to the enthusiastic cult and worship of Julius Caesar in the Renaissance—and therewith the open book assumed a totally different meaning. In the emblem works of Claude Paradin and Gabriel Symeoni, of the mid-sixteenth century, an *impresa* is found having the lapidary motto EX UTROQUE CAESAR (pl. 37, fig. 2). An emperor in the attire of a Roman general stands on a globe lacking the cross; in his right hand he holds the naked sword; in his left hand he brandishes a book, upon which his eyes are fixed. *Arma et Leges* we should be inclined to interpret. We would be very wrong.

> By this apophthegm EX UTROQUE CAESAR it is signified that by these two, that is, Arms and *Letters*, Julius Caesar ... was made the lord of the whole world.[42]

---

[37] See, e.g., Franciscus Hotomanus (Hotman), *In quatuor libros Institutionum* (Venice, 1569), 3f. He quotes Aristotle, *Polit.*, I, 1254 b, 31f, and VII, 1333 a, 30ff. For jurisprudence conquered by humanism, see Domenico Maffei, *Gli inizi dell'umanesimo giuridico* (Milan, 1956).

[38] Hotman justifies his allegation of the Platonic ideal, by saying: "Iustinianus enim principatum cum amore sapientiae, quae in decenti legum descriptione vel maxime cernitur, coniungit ... Perspicuum est, leges, quae ad publicas actiones pertinent, veram et summam philosophiam continere." Jurisprudence, of course, was considered throughout the Middle Ages as a section of moral philosophy. The Renaissance produced also tractates on the subject "Arms and Laws"; see, e.g., Flavio Biondo's tractate *Borsus sive De militia et iurisprudentia*, ed. B. Nogara, *Scritti inediti e rari di Biondo Flavio* (Rome, 1927), 130ff.

[39] George Wither, *A Collection of Emblems Ancient and Moderne* (London, 1635), Book III, 29, p. 163.

[40] Silvestro Petrasanta, *De Symbolis Heroicis* (Antwerp, Plantin: 1634), No. 224: "Fridericus III. brachium armatum, cum districto gladio, supra codicem apertum, pro Symbolo elegit ..." See, for some of the emblems quoted here, Dora and Erwin Panofsky, *Pandora's Box: The Changing Aspects of a Mythical Symbol* (Bollingen Series, LII; New York, 1955), 40f.

[41] Wither, *Collection of Emblems*, Book I, 3, p. 3.

[42] Claudii Paradini ... et D. Gabrielis Symeonis, *Symbola Heroica* (Antwerp, 1583), p. 284. The first edition of Claude Paradin's work is Lyon, 1551, and of Gabriello Symeoni's, Lyon, 1559. The works were fused in the edition quoted above; but the design seems to be the invention of Symeoni; see Symeoni, *Le Imprese Heroiche et Morali* (1574), p. 183, where he narrates the origin of the

We still hear the faint echo of the *Institutes*, still see a figure which might illustrate Justinian's Prologue. But what the inscription blazons out is the gospel of the Renaissance, the dialectical oneness of Sword and Letters, of Sword and Arts, as the doggerel interpretation of EX UTROQUE CAESAR has it:

> *A* Princes *most ennobling Parts,*
> *Are Skill in* Armes, *and Love to* Arts.[43]

Gone is the spectre of the Gloss visualizing the Prince equipped with two swords, that of war and that of justice. Instead—slowly developing since the thirteenth century and ruling without challenge since the fifteenth—the Renaissance ideal of the Prince governing by sword and *letters*, or *art*, becomes the lodestar of humanistic dreams and princely ambitions, the Renaissance variety of Plato's philosopher-king. In fact, Raffael's so-called "Dream of the Knight" in the London National Gallery shows that EX UTROQUE CAESAR was the essence, the personification, of *Virtus*.[44] The Law, legitimately, demands also a sword; letters and arts, however, must do without sword. EX UTROQUE CAESAR, therefore, implies that a dialectical tension has been restored by which the Renaissance ideal becomes at least comparable again with Apolline ethics.

It is easy enough now to recognize how it could have happened that an archaic Delian Apollo was transformed not into a Greek Δικαιοσύνη but into a Roman-Christian Justice, and that finally the essence of Apolline ethics was "adapted to the image of Justice." There is in the *Political Emblems* of Jacobus a Bruck an *impresa* with the motto NEC PRECE NEC PRECIO (pl. 40, fig. 9).[45] Two right hands are seen: one hand holds a money bag, the other a sword. The indispensable *Carmen* ends:

> *Nec Prece nec Precio* tribuatur summa potestas.
> Iustitiae sanctus nam violatur honos.

The motto, of course, symbolizes among other things the unswerving attitude of the Prince, and it has nothing to do with the oneness of the *Iustitia distributiva* and the *Iustitia retributiva* which apparently Jonathan Swift described. It may have been a "political emblem" of that pattern, however, that Swift had in mind, or made up, when he visualized Justice having "a bag of gold open in her right hand and a sword sheathed in her left." To the rather shallow and unrefined dialectic of this rewarding and punishing Justice he then applied the far too good and hardly fitting words of Macrobius—"to show that she is more disposed to reward than to punish." But, after a long round-about way, we do understand that even a trivial Justice could be haunted by "Apolline ethics."

---

impresa invented by him. The explanation matches verbatim that of Paradin: ". . . EX UTROQUE CAESAR, volendo significare, che per mezzo delle lettere e dell' armi acquistò Giuliò Cesare l'Imperio e l'Dominio di tutta la terra."

[43] Wither, *Collection of Emblems*, Book I, 32, p. 32.

[44] See, on this painting, the brilliant interpretation by Panofsky, *Hercules*, 37ff. His identification of the Knight with the younger Scipio Africanus (76ff) as well as the interdependence of the "Dream" with the Chantilly "Graces" (142ff) is now strongly supported by the Apolline ethics. The younger Scipio was the prototype of the

republican philosopher-warrior, and we now know why book and sword are linked to the Graces.

[45] Jacobus a Bruck, *Emblemata politica* (Strasbourg and Cologne, 1618) p. 141, no. XXXVI. For the motto, see *C.* 1, 3, 30 (31), 4: "Non pretio, sed precibus ordinetur antistes." That maxim, however, was twisted by the jurists. See, e.g., Cynus of Pistoia, on *C.* 9, 26, n. 2 (Frankfurt, 1578, fol. 558[ra]): "et isto casu nec precio nec precibus hoc sibi facere licet"; also Cynus, on *D.* 1, 14, n. 11, (*ibid.*, fol. 13[vb]): "quod princeps nec gratia nec pretio impartiretur honores."

Fig. 1. Intaglio: Delian Apollo
(enlarged).

Fig. 2. Paradin, *Symbole Heroica*
(1583), p. 284.

Fig. 3. Bibl. Vaticana, *Libellus de imaginibus* (MS Reg. Lat. 1290), fol. 1ᵛ: Apollo (reduced).

Pl. 38   ON TRANSFORMATIONS OF APOLLINE ETHICS

Fig. 4. Paris, Bibl. Nat., *Echecs amoureux* (MS fr. 143), fol. 39: Apollo and The Three Graces (reduced).

Fig. 5. Rimini, Malatesta Temple, relief: Apollo.

Pl. 40   ON TRANSFORMATIONS OF APOLLINE ETHICS

Fig. 6. Petrasanta, *De Symbolis Heroiis* (1634), p. 224.

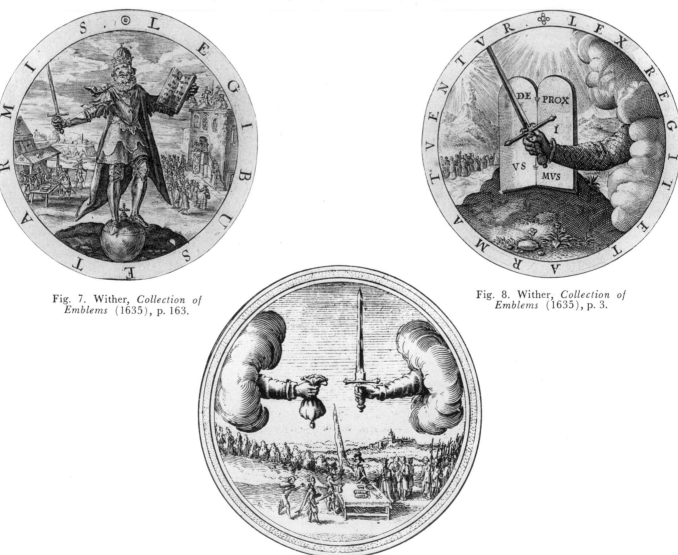

Fig. 7. Wither, *Collection of Emblems* (1635), p. 163.

Fig. 8. Wither, *Collection of Emblems* (1635), p. 3.

Fig. 9. Jacobus a Bruck, *Emblemata politica* (1618), p. 141.

INDEXED LIST OF ILLUSTRATIONS

The figure numbers assigned to the illustrations in the original publication of the various essays have been preserved, except for "The Este Portrait by Roger van der Weyden" and "On Transformations of Apolline Ethics." The original figure numbers of those two essays are appended to the appropriate entries below.

The locations of objects, if given, have been brought up to date.

The page references below (in small type, following the capital-letter title of each figure) tell where separate citations of the figures may be found on the pages of this volume, in the text and in the footnotes.

Where photographic acknowledgements are given below, they supersede any contrary acknowledgements that may be found in the text (*i.e.*, original acknowledgements in the text were not removed even though new photos were used). On the other hand, where photographic acknowledgements are lacking below, the photos either came from Prof. Kantorowicz's own collection or were copied from a source mentioned in the text of the essay.

The sizes of illustrations are remarked upon in the Preface.

* * *

Frontispiece: ERNST H. KANTOROWICZ. Photo by Trude Fleischmann, New York.

GODS IN UNIFORM

GODS IN UNIFORM

THE KING'S ADVENT

THE KING'S ADVENT

THE CAROLINGIAN KING IN THE BIBLE OF SAN PAOLO

THE ARCHER IN THE RUTHWELL CROSS

Plate 24, *following page 88.*

Fig. 1. Ruthwell Cross, uppermost section: ARCHER (pp. 95–99 *passim*, esp. p. 95, n. 4).

Fig. 2. London, Brit. Mus. Cotton MS Claudius B. IV, fol. 36ᵛ: ISHMAEL WITH HAGAR AND HIS EGYPTIAN WIFE (p. 97). Photo: courtesy of British Museum.

THE QUINITY OF WINCHESTER

Plate 25, *following page 112.*

Fig. 1. London, Brit. Mus., Offices of New Minster, Winchester (Cotton MS Titus D. XXVII, fol. 75ᵛ): OFFICIUM TRINITATIS (pp. 100–120 *passim*). Photo: courtesy of British Museum.

Fig. 2. Utrecht Psalter, fol. 64ᵛ: PSALM 109 (pp. 101n, 103, 111). Photo: courtesy of Kunsthistorisch Instituut, Utrecht.

Fig. 3. Cambridge, Trinity College, Canterbury Psalter (MS R. 17–1), fol. 199ᵛ: PSALM 109 (pp. 101n, 103, 111). Photo: courtesy of Trinity College Library.

Fig. 4. London, Maidstone Mus., Offices of Westminster, MS, fol. 32ᵛ: PSALM 109 (pp. 101, 101n, 104, 111). Photo: courtesy Courtauld Institute, London.

Plate 26, *following page 112.*

Fig. 5. London, Brit. Mus., Luttrell Psalter (Add. MS 42130), fol. 203: PSALM 109 (pp. 101, 101n, 104, 104n). Photo: courtesy of British Museum.

Fig. 6. Stuttgart Psalter, fol. 127ᵛ: PSALM 109 (pp. 101, 101n, 104, 104n). Photo: courtesy of Princeton University, Dept. of Art and Archaeology.

Fig. 7. London, Brit. Mus., seal of Godwin (Ivory, 11th Cent.): PSALM 109 (pp. 100n, 101, 101n, 104, 111n).

Fig. 8. Paris, Bibl. Nat., Book of Hours (MS lat. 757), fol. 222ᵛ: TRINITY (pp. 106, 106n, 118, 118n). Photo: courtesy of Bibliothèque Nationale.

Plate 27, *following page 112.*

Fig. 9. Oxford, Bodleian, Ormesby Psalter (MS Douce 366), fol. 147ᵛ: PSALM 109 (pp. 101, 101n, 104, 111). Photo: courtesy of University Press, Oxford.

Fig. 10. Winchester Cathedral Library, Winchester Bible: PSALM 109 (pp. 100n, 101, 101n, 104, 104n, 106, 106n, 111). Photo: courtesy of Victoria and Albert Museum, London.

Fig. 11. Washington, D.C., National Gallery, Rosenwald Collection: CHRIST IN ABRAHAM'S BOSOM (pp. 100n, 119). Photo: courtesy Dr. Erwin Rosenthal.

Plate 28, *following page 112.*

Fig. 12. Paris, Bibl. Nat., Book of Hours of Jean sans Peur (MS lat. n.a. 3055), fol. 159ᵛ: TRINITY WITH MARY (pp. 102, 120 *Ed. note*). Photo: courtesy of Bibliothèque Nationale.

Fig. 13. Utrecht Psalter, fol. 89ᵛ: GLORIA IN EXCELSIS (pp. 109, 110). Photo: courtesy of Kunsthistorisch Instituut, Utrecht.

Fig. 14. *Idem*, fol. 90: CREDO (*loc. cit.*). Photo: *idem.*

Fig. 15. Cambridge, Trinity College, Canterbury Psalter (MS R. 17–1), fol. 278ᵛ: GLORIA IN EXCELSIS (pp. 109, 110). Photo: courtesy of Trinity College Library.

Fig. 16. *Idem*, fol. 279: CREDO (*loc. cit.*). Photo: *idem.*

THE QUINITY OF WINCHESTER

INDEX

Abelard: 311, 340–342, 343, 346, 349.

Abingdon, Edmund, archb. of Canterbury: 143.

Acclamations: 41n16 (*Novus Constantinus*), 60 (doors of S. Sabina), 84 (to Prince), 329 (epiphany of emperors); pl. 19, fig. 43.

Accursius (author of *Glossa Ordinaria* to *Corp. Iuris Civilis*): 154, 158, 352n2, 386, 387n29, 395, 405.

Accursius, Francis: 148, 220, 221n37.

Achaemenid kings: 332.

Achilles (apocalyptic writing): 68n128.

Acta Joannis: 34n55, 35n63.

Acts of the Persian Martyrs: 132n56.

Adam: 2 (throne-sharer of God), 168, 267 (ruler new Adam), 270 (*idem*), 285n6 (Fred. II new Adam), 286 (Fall), 349 (before Eve).

Adam of Stratton: 179.

Adelard of Bath: 342n13.

Adoption: 123 (by anointing), 132 (via baptism).

Advent, *Adventus, entrée* (see also Epiphany): 25n3 (*occursus* & *Hypapante—q.v.*), 37–75 *pari passu* (The "King's Advent"), 38 (of the soul), 39n9 (Hellenistic, Early Christian), 42 (Exarch of Ravenna), 42n20 (Julius II), 43f (Hellenistic, Roman), 44n28 (of relics), *ibid.* (pre-Christian), *ibid.* (Popes Stephen II and Zacharias), 48n47 (distinguished from Triumph), 49 (Gnostic—cf. pl. 15, fig. 26), 50 (and Adoration of Magi), 51 (of Cardinal Legate—cf. pl. 16, fig. 29), 51n64a (Middle Ages and Renaissance), 52ff ("Eschatological"), 53n73 (in liturgical year), 55 (triumphal arches), 57 (Syrian—cf. pl. 16, fig. 31), 58 (Etruscan), 58n89 ("realistic"—"symbolical" or "historical"—"eschatological"), 60 (Porphyry the charioteer—cf. pl. 18, fig. 42), 72ff (Russian rite), 74n144 (distinguished from Triumph), 276–283 *passim* (antique and mediaeval), 277 (*entrée joyeuse*).

Advent of Christ: 45n34 (compared with Emperor's), 49–51 (into Jerusalem—cf. pl. 14, figs. 22–25), 56–57 and 58–71 *passim* (eschatological *adventus* of *Kyrios*—cf. pl. 16, fig. 30 & pl. 19, fig. 44), 60ff (Santa Sabina doors—cf. pl. 19, figs. 40–41), 69 (as *Kyrios*, as King of Glory), 74n144.

Advent of ruler: 38, 39n10 (Emp. Charles IV & son—cf. pl. 20, fig. 46), 41 (Solomon; Frederick II), 42nn20–21 (Burgundian, French, English, Imperial), 45 (Augustus, Constantine), 45n34 (Christ & Emperor), 46–48 & 55 (Roman Imperial coins—cf. pl. 13), 48–49 (Galerius—cf. pl. 14, fig. 21), 50–51 (Justinian II—cf. pl. 15, fig. 28), 51 (Solomon—cf. pl. 15, fig. 27), 57 (Imperial, on Palm Sunday), 63–64 (Christ and King), 72ff (Russian Tsar), 101n7 (mediaeval king), 278 (Frederick II).

Aegidius Romanus: 355n19, 356nn20–21.

Aegidius de Tebaldis: 224n49.

Aelfric: 97.

Aeneas: 309.